ESSAYS ON ISLAMIC PIETY AND MYSTICISM

ISLAMIC HISTORY AND CIVILIZATION

STUDIES AND TEXTS

EDITED BY

ULRICH HAARMANN

AND

WADAD KADI

VOLUME 30

ESSAYS ON ISLAMIC PIETY AND MYSTICISM

BY

FRITZ MEIER

TRANSLATED BY

JOHN O'KANE

WITH EDITORIAL ASSISTANCE OF

BERND RADTKE

TUTA SUB AEGIDE PALLAS · 1683 ·

BRILL
LEIDEN · BOSTON · KÖLN
1999

This book is printed on acid-free paper.

Library of Congress Cataloging-in-Publication Data

Meier, Fritz, 1912-
[Bausteine. English]
Essays on Islamic piety and mysticism / Fritz Meier ; translated by John O'Kane with editorial assistance of Bernd Radtke.
p. cm. — (Islamic history and civilization : v. 30)
"... selection of articles which, with a single exception, had all been collected and published in Bausteine ..."—Pref.
Includes bibliographical references and index.
ISBN 9004108653 (alk. paper)
1. Islam—History. 2. Sufism—History. I Title. II. Series.
BP25.M4513 1999
297—dc21 99-31636
CIP

Die Deutsche Bibliothek – CIP-Einheitsaufnahme

Meier, Fritz:
Essays on Islamic piety and mysticism / Fritz Meier. Transl. by John O'Kane with ed. assistance of Bernd Radtke. - Leiden ; Boston; Köln : Brill, 1999
(Islamic history and civilization ; Vol. 30)
ISBN 90-04-10865-3

ISSN 0929-2403
ISBN 90 04 10865 3

PRINTED IN THE NETHERLANDS

TABLE OF CONTENTS

Indices

PREFACE

Habent sua fata libelli. When, through a series of convoluted circumstances, Bernd Radtke came to take up employment in Norway's northern latitudes at the University of Bergen in the spring of 1989, he was pleased to find himself in scholarly surroundings which proved to be lively and stimulating beyond his expectations. As it turned out, his departmental colleagues were energetically engaged in a variety of research projects to do with the more recent history of Sufism. At the same time they maintained a serious interest in 'classical' and 'post-classical' developments in older Sufism as well, which up until then had been Radtke's major area of study.

On the basis of numerous conversations with Seán O'Fahey in Bergen, it soon became clear to Radtke that one particular shortcoming presently affecting the study of Islamic mysticism is a widespread lack of knowledge of the contribution to research on Sufism published in German. The process of globalization, so it seems, has brought with it the tendency for English to marginalize or replace completely scholarly work done in other languages in the field of Islamic studies. The result is that we now face a situation where one cannot assume that a major work published in German will be read internationally, even by those specialists whose field the work specifically deals with.

It was the merit of Seán O'Fahey to have first suggested to Radtke the idea of having a selection of Fritz Meier's best articles translated into English and thereby to make available to an international readership a part at least of the life's work of a man whom many consider the most important scholar of the twentieth century in the field of Sufism. When Radtke put this proposal before Meier who had been his teacher in Basle, Meier responded very positively.

Similarly, the publishing house Brill immediately expressed its willingness to undertake publication of the projected book. The one problem remaining was how to find a suitable translator and financial support for the work involved. It was only in 1996, seven years later, that a translator and the necessary funding materialized. In the end, the greater part of the funding was to come from a generous donation from a private source. As for the translator, when Radtke took up a teaching position in the Netherlands in 1992, he made the acquaintance of John O'Kane in Amsterdam and entered into a fruitful routine of scholarly cooperation with him. Radtke's enthusiasm convinced O'Kane to take up the challenge of translating a rather large and demanding selection of articles. Fritz Meier who had for a long time been in scholarly contact with O'Kane was pleased by this choice. Likewise, Meier agreed with Radtke's selection of articles which, with a single exception, had all been collected and published in *Bausteine* on the occasion of Meier's eightieth birthday. A full bibliography of Meier's publications is given toward the beginning of this volume.

John O'Kane began the translation at the beginning of 1997 and was finished by the spring of 1998. He was able to discuss difficulties in the text with Radtke during this period and Meier too was consulted whenever necessary. Meier eventually went through the whole translation himself with his usual meticulousness and offered numerous comments and suggestions. He completed his review by the end of May 1998 and formally gave his approval to the translation and title for the volume, and was very warm in his praise of O'Kane's work. — Sadly, a fews days later, on June 10th, the night of his eighty-sixth birthday, Meier suddenly and unexpectedly passed away. He was not to see the actual publication of his work in English. Nevertheless, we can say that the complete translation in its present form had his full approval.

The translation is entirely the work of John O'Kane. Bernd Radtke's contribution, in addition to many sessions of helpful consultation, has been to append supplementary bibliographical information at the end of some of the articles. This appears in square brackets and follows Meier's recommendation to update his own bibliography where desirable. Likewise, Radtke has compiled the indices and been responsible for producing a camera-ready copy of the text for Brill.

With Meier's approval we have adopted the transliteration system employed by the *International Journal of Middle East Studies* (*IJMES*), though not with regard to the vocalization of Persian vowels. As for the format of Meier's extensive footnotes, some degree of harmonization has been attempted but in view of the fact that the essays were written over a forty-year timespan, it was judged acceptable to retain certain differences of style wherever this would not lead to any misunderstanding on the reader's part. Persian as well as Arabic texts which accompany the essays have been reproduced by scanning Meier's original publications. We are endebted to Safeen Ghafour for his technical assistance with this procedure, and we also wish to thank Knut S. Vikør for his help in the final stages of indexing. Likewise we are grateful to Gudrun Schubert for her friendly support and cooperation.

In addition to acknowledging the generous financial support we received from private sources who have wished to remain anonymous, we wish to extend our thanks to the following institutions which also contributed to funding the present translation: The Deutsche Morgenländische Gesellschaft (DMG), Het Oosters Instituut (Leiden), the Fondation Max van Berchem (Geneva), and the publishing house Brill.

We would also like to thank Ulrich Haarmann for having accepted this work in the series *Islamic History and Civilization*.

Bernd Radtke and John O'Kane

LIST OF PUBLICATIONS
BY FRITZ MEIER

1. BOOKS

— *Vom Wesen der islamischen Mystik*, (originally Meier's inaugural lecture upon becoming a Privatdozent), Basle, 1943.

— *Die Vita des Scheich Abū Isḥāq al-Kāzarūnī, in der persischen Bearbeitung von Maḥmūd b. ʿUṯmān.* Herausgegeben und eingeleitet. Bibliotheca Islamica 14, Leipzig, 1948 (diss.).

— *Die Fawāʾiḥ al-ǧamāl wa-fawātiḥ al-ǧalāl des Naǧm ad-dīn al-Kubrā. Eine Darstellung mystischer Erfahrungen im Islam aus der Zeit um 1200 n. Chr. Herausgegeben und erläutert.* Akademie der Wissenschaften und der Literatur (Mainz). Veröffentlichungen der Orientalischen Kommission, Bd 9, Wiesbaden, 1957.

— *Die schöne Mahsatī. Ein Beitrag zur Geschichte des persischen Vierzeilers*, Bd 1. Akademie der Wissenschaften und der Literatur. Veröffentlichungen der Orientalischen Kommission, Bd 15, Wiesbaden, 1963.

— *Abū Saʿīd-i Abū l-Ḫayr (357-440/967-1049). Wirklichkeit und legende.* Acta Iranica 11, Leiden, 1976.

— *Bahāʾ-i Walad. Grundzüge seines lebens und seiner mystik.* Acta Iranica 27, Leiden, 1989.

— *Bausteine. Ausgewählte Aufsätze zur Islamwissenschaft.* I-III, herausgegeben von Erika Glassen und Gudrun Schubert. Beiruter Texte und Studien 53a-c, Istanbul-Stuttgart, 1992.

— *Zwei Abhandlungen über die Naqšbandiyya.* Beiruter Texte und Studien 58, Istanbul-Stuttgart, 1994.

— *Essays on Islamic Piety and Mysticism*, translated by John O'Kane, organized and edited by Bernd Radtke, Leiden, 1999.

— *Abū Saʿīd-i Abū'l-Khayr*, Persian translation by Afagh Bayburdī, Teheran, 1999, Iran University Press.

— *Bahāʾ-i Walad*, Persian translation (forthcoming).

2. ESSAYS

(An asterisk at the beginning indicates that the essay has been translated in this volume)

— 'Stambuler Handschriften dreier persischer Mystiker: ᶜAin al-quḍāt al-Hamaḏānī, Naǧm ad-dīn al-Kubrā, Naǧm ad-dīn ad-Dāja', in: *Der Islam* 24, 1937, pp. 1-39.
— 'Zur Biographie Ahmad-i Ǧāms und zur Quellenkunde von Ǧāmī's *Nafaḥātu'l-uns*', in: *Zeitschrift der Deutschen Morgenländischen Gesellschaft (ZDMG)* 97, 1943, pp. 47-67; *Bausteine*, I, pp. 157-177.
— 'Das Mysterium der Kaᶜba. Symbol und Wirklichkeit in der islamischen Mystik', in: *Eranos-Jahrbuch* 12, 1944, Zurich, 1945, pp. 187-214.
— 'The Mystery of the Kaᶜba: Symbol and Reality in Islamic Mysticism', in: Bollingen Series 30, 2: *The Mysteries. Papers from the Eranos-Yearbooks*, pp. 149-68.
— 'Der Geistmensch bei dem persischen Dichter ᶜAṭṭār', in: *Eranos-Jahrbuch* 13, 1945, Zurich, 1946, pp. 283-353.
— 'The Spiritual Man in the Persian Poet ᶜAṭṭār', in: Bollingen Series 30, 4: *Spiritual Disciplines. Papers from the Eranos Yearbooks*, pp. 267-304.
— 'Das Problem der Natur im esoterischen Monismus des Islams', in: *Eranos-Jahrbuch* 14, 1946, Zurich, 1947, pp. 149-227.
— 'The Problem of Nature in the Esoteric Monism of Islam', in: Bollingen Series 30, 1: *Spirit and Nature. Papers from the Eranos Yearbooks*, pp. 149-203.
— 'Die Welt der Urbilder bei Ali Hamadani († 1385)', in: *Eranos-Jahrbuch* 18, (Festschrift für C.G. Jung), 1950, pp. 115-72.
— 'Turandot in Persien', in: *ZDMG* 95, 1951, pp. 1-27.
— 'Nachtrag zu Turandot', in: *ZDMG* 95, 1951, pp. 415-21.
— 'Die Schriften des ᶜAzīz-i Nasafī', in: *Wiener Zeitschrift für die Kunde des Morgenlandes* 52, 1953, pp. 125-82; *Bausteine*, I, pp. 178-235.
— 'Der Name der Yazīdīs', in: *Westöstliche Abhandlungen, Rudolf Tschudi zum siebzigsten Geburtstag überreicht von Freunden und Schülern*, Wiesbaden, 1954, pp. 244-57; *Bausteine*, II, pp. 635-48.
— *'Der Derwischtanz. Versuch eines Überblicks', in: *Asiatische Studien* 8, 1954, 107-36; *Bausteine*, I, pp. 23-52.
— 'Die Wandlung des Menschen im mystischen Islam', in: *Eranos-Jahrbuch* 23, 1954, Zurich, 1955, pp. 99-139.
— 'Methods of Approach', in: *Unity and Variety in Muslim Civil-*

ization, ed. G.E. von Grunebaum, Chicago 1955, pp. 38-44.
— Aḥmad-i Djām, in: *EI*^{2}, I, pp. 291-93.
— ʿAlāʾ al-Dawla al-Simnānī, in: *EI*^{2}. I, pp. 357-58.
— Bakkāʾ, in: *EI*^{2}, I, 988-90
— Bishr al-Ḥāfī, in: *EI*^{2}, I, pp. 1282-184.
— *'Ein Knigge für Sufi's', in: *Rivista degli Studi Orientali* 32 (*Scritti in onore di Giuseppe Furlani*), 1957, pp. 485-524; *Bausteine*, I, pp. 53-92.
— 'Sufik und Kulturzerfall', in: *Klassizismus und Kulturverfall*. Vorträge. Herausgegeben von G.E. von Grunebaum, Frankfurt am Main, 1960, pp. 114-80; *Bausteine*, I, pp. 94-130.
— 'Soufisme et déclin culturel', in: *Classicisme et déclin culturel dans l'histoire de l'Islam*. Actes du symposium international d'histoire de la civilisation musulmane (Bordeaux, 25-29 Juin 1956), organisé par R. Brunschvig et G.E. von Grunebaum, Paris, 1957, pp. 217-24; *Bausteine*, I, pp. 94-130.
— 'Zwei islamische Lehrerzählungen bei Tolstoj', in: *Asiatische Studien* 11, 1958, pp. 143-58; *Bausteine*, II, pp. 971-86.
— 'Orientalistik', in: *Lehre und Forschung an der Universität Basel zur Zeit der Feier ihres fünfhundertjährigen Bestehens*, Basle, 1960, pp. 212-17.
— 'Rudolf Tschudi † (1884-1960)', in: *Der Islam* 38, 1962, pp. 138-41; *Bausteine*, I, pp. 3-6.
— *'Qušayrīs *Tartīb as-sulūk*', in: *Oriens* 16, 1963, pp. 1-39; *Bausteine*, I, pp. 236-75.
— 'A Difficult Quatrain of Mahsatī's', in: *Mélanges d'orientalisme offerts à Henri Massé*, Tehran, 1963, pp. 269-81.
— 'Nachbemerkungen zu *Mahsatī*, Band 1', in: *Oriens* 17, 1964, pp. 264-67.
— 'Quelques aspects de l'inspiration par les démons en Islam', in: *Le rêve et les sociétés humaines*, Paris, 1967, pp. 418-25.
— 'Some aspects of inspiration by demons in Islam', in: *The Dream and Human Societies*, Los Angeles, 1966, pp. 421-29; *Bausteine*, II, pp. 987-995.
— 'Algunos aspectos de la inspiración por los demonios en el Islam', in: *Los sueños y las sociedades humanas*, Buenos Aires 1964, pp. 307-18.
— 'Drei moderne Texte zum persischen "Wettreden"', übersetzt von Fritz Meier. Mit Anmerkungen von Richard Gramlich, in: *ZDMG* 114, 1964, pp. 289-327; *Bausteine*, I, pp. 497-535.
— *'Ein wichtiger handschriftenfund zur sufik', in: *Oriens* 20, 1967, pp. 60-106; *Bausteine*, I, pp. 276-323.

— 'Das Volk der Riemenbeinler', in: *Festschrift für Wilhelm Eilers*, Wiesbaden, 1967, pp. 341-67; *Bausteine*, I, pp. 536-63.
— 'The Ultimate Origin and the Hereafter in Islam', in: *Islam and the Cultural Divergence. Studies in Honor of Gustave E. Grunebaum*, ed. Girdhari L. Tikku, Urbana-Chicago-London, 1971, pp. 96-112.
— *'Ḫurāsān und das ende der klassischen ṣūfik', in: *Atti del convegno internazionale sul tema: La Persia nel Medioevo (Roma, 31 marzo - 5 aprile 1970)*, Accademia Nazionale dei Lincei, Rome, 1971, pp. 545-70; *Bausteine*, I, pp. 131-56.
— 'Hellmut Ritter †', in: *Der Islam* 48, 1972, pp. 193-205; *Bausteine*, I, pp. 7-19.
— 'Korrektur zum nachruf auf Hellmut Ritter in *Der Islam* 48, 1972', in: *Der Islam* 49, 1972, p. 124.
— *'Ein profetenwort gegen die totenbeweinung', in: *Der Islam* 50, 1973, pp. 207-29; *Bausteine*, II, pp. 649-71.
— 'Orientalische belege für das motiv "nur einmal zuschlagen"', in: *Mélanges d'lslamologie. Volume dédié à la mémoire d'Armand Abel*, Leiden, 1974, pp. 207-23; *Bausteine*, I, pp. 564-80.
— 'Zum 700. Todestag Mawlānās, des Vaters der tanzenden Derwische', in: *Asiatische Studien* 28, 1974, pp. 54-64.
— 'Der mystische Weg', in: *Welt des Islam, Geschichte und Kultur im Zeichen des Propheten*. Herausgeber Bernard Lewis, Braunschweig, 1976, pp. 117-40.
— 'The mystic path', in: *The world of Islam. Faith, people, culture*, ed. Bernard Lewis, London, 1976, pp. 117-40.
— 'Nachlese zu *Abū Saᶜīd-i Abū l-Ḫayr*, Acta Iranica 11', in: Acta Iranica 12, 1977, pp. 419-20.
— 'Niẓāmī und die mythologie des hahns', in: *Colloquio sul poeta persiano Niẓāmī e la leggenda iranica di Alessandro Magno (Roma, 25-26 marzo 1975)*, Accademia Nazionale dei Lincei, Fondazione Leone Caetani, Rome, 1977, pp. 55-115; *Bausteine*, II, pp. 996-1056.
— *'Ein briefwechsel zwischen Šaraf ud-dīn-i Balḫī und Mağd ud-dīn-i Baġdādī', in: *Mélanges offerts à Henry Corbin*, Tehran, 1977, pp. 321-66; *Bausteine*, I, pp. 324-69.
— *'Die ṣumādiyya, ein zweigorden der qādiriyya in Damaskus', in: *Die islamische Welt zwischen Mittelalter und Neuzeit. Festschrift für Hans Robert Roemer zum 65. Geburtstag*, herausgegeben von Ulrich Haarmann und Peter Bachmann. Beiruter Texte und Studien 22, Beirut, 1979, pp. 445-70; *Bausteine*, I, pp. 370-95.
— 'Ein arabischer "bet-ruf"', in: *Asiatische Studien* 33, 1979, pp. 153-98; *Bausteine*, I, pp. 581-631.

— *'Das sauberste über die vorbestimmung. Ein stück Ibn Taymiyya', in: *Saeculum* 32, 1981, pp. 74-89; *Bausteine*, II, 696-711.
— 'Verbesserungen zu "Ein arabischer bet-ruf", in *Asiatische Studien* 33, 2, 1979, 153-198', in: *Asiatische Studien* 35, 1981, pp. 67-68.
— 'Aussprachefragen des älteren neupersisch', in: *Oriens* 27-28, 1981, pp. 70-176; *Bausteine*, II, pp. 1057-1164.
— 'Der prediger auf der kanzel (*minbar*). Mit einem beitrag von Dorothea Duda', in: *Studien zur Geschichte und Kultur des Vorderen Orients, Festschrift für Bertold Spuler zum siebzigsten Geburtstag*, herausgegeben von Hans R. Roemer und Albrecht Noth, Leiden, 1981, pp. 225-48; *Bausteine*, II, pp. 672-95.
— 'Über die Eigenart der älteren persischen Dichtung', in: *Iranzamin*, 1. Jahrgang, Ausgabe Nr. 5/6, November 1981-März 1982, pp. 53-64.
— *'Almoraviden und marabute', in: *Die Welt des Islams* 21, 1983, pp. 80-163; *Bausteine*, II, pp. 712-96.
— *'Tahir aṣ-Ṣadafīs vergessene schrift über westliche heilige des 6./12. jahrhunderts', in: *Der Islam* 61, 1984, pp. 14-90; *Bausteine*, I, pp. 396-473.
— 'Zweite "Rettung des Cardanus"', in: *Studi in onore di Francesco Gabrieli nel suo ottantesimo compleanno.* A cura di Renato Traini. Rome, 1984, pp. 503-17; *Bausteine*, II, 1165-79.
— 'Dämonen, Dämonologie', F. Islam, in: *Lexikon des Mittelalters* (Artemis), III, 1985, pp. 483-84.
— *'Eine auferstehung Mohammeds bei Suyūṭī', in: *Der Islam* 62, 1985, pp. 20-58; *Bausteine*, II, pp. 796-836.
— *'Die segenssprechung über Mohammed im bittgebet und in der bitte', in: *ZDMG* 136, 1986, pp. 364-401; *Bausteine*, II, pp. 837-75.
— 'Der unbekannte schriftsteller al-Muwaffaq al-Ḫāṣī', in: *Der Islam* 66, 1989, pp. 311-30; *Bausteine*, I, pp. 474-93.
— *'Zum vorrang des glaubens und des guten denkens vor dem wahrheitseifer bei den muslimen', in: *Oriens* 32, 1990, pp. 1-49; *Bausteine*, II, pp. 876-925.
— 'Anfänge arabischer Logopädie', in: *Festgabe für Hans-Rudolf Singer. Zum 65. Geburtstag am 6. April 1990 überreicht von seinen Freunden und Kollegen*, herausgegeben von Martin Forstner, Frankfurt am Main, 1991, I, pp. 89-104; *Bausteine*, II, pp. 1180-95.
— 'Über die umstrittene Pflicht des Muslims, bei nichtmuslimischer Besetzung seines Landes auszuwandern', in: *Der Islam* 68, 1991, pp. 65-86; *Bausteine*, II, pp. 946-68.

— 'Kundgebungen an und hinter der front zwischen muslimen und christen', in: *Yād-nāma, in memoria di Alessandro Bausani*, Rome, 1991, I, pp. 305-25; *Bausteine*, II, pp. 926-46.
— 'Der "Urknall" eine Idee des Abu Bakr ar-Rāzī', in: *Oriens* 33, 1992, pp. 1-21.
— *'Kehrreim und *maḥyā*', in: *Festschrift für Ewald Wagner zum 65. Geburtstag*, Beiruter Texte und Studien 54, Beirut-Stuttgart, 1994, II, pp. 462-89.
— 'Meister und Schüler im Orden der Naqšbandiyya', in: *Sitzungsberichte der Heidelberger Akademie der Wissenschaften. Phil.-hist. Kl.*, Jahrgang 1995, Bericht 2, Heidelberg, 1995, pp.1-25.

3. BOOK REVIEWS

— Al-Gazzālī, Abū Ḥāmid Muḥammad: *Naṣīḥatu'l-mulūk*. Herausgeg. v. Ğalāl-i Humā'ī, Tehran, 1315-17, in: *ZDMG* 93, 1939, pp. 395-408.
— Abu'l-ᶜIlā ᶜAfīfī: *Al-Malāmatiyya wa'ṣ-ṣūfiyya wa-ahl al-futuwwa*, Cairo, 1945., in: *Oriens* 1, 1948, pp. 373-76.
— *Macallat kulliyyat al-ādāb, Cāmiᶜat Fārūq al-awwal, Farouq I University, Bulletin of the Faculty of Arts*, 1-3, 1943-1946, in: *Oriens* 3, 1950, pp. 329-30.
— A.J. Arberry: *Immortal Rose. An Anthology of Persian Lyrics*, London, 1948, in: *Artibus Asiae* 13, 1950, pp. 229-30.
— M. Moin: *L'Influence du Mazdéisme dans la Littérature Persane*, Tehran, 1948, in: *Artibus Asiae* 13, 1950, pp. 230-32.
— Abû Yaᶜqûb Sejestânî: *Kashf al-Maḥjûb (Le Dévoilement des choses cachées), Traité ismaélien du IVe siècle de l'Hégire.* Texte persan publié avec une introduction par Henry Corbin. Bibliothèque Iranienne 1, Tehran-Paris 1949, in: *Artibus Asiae* 13, 1950, pp. 232-34.
— Gholām Hosein Dārāb: *Persian Composition*, London, 1948, in: *Asiatische Studien* 4, 1950, pp. 141-42.
— P.J. de Menasce O.P.: *Arabische Philosophie. Bibliographische Einführungen in das Studium der Philosophie*, hrsg. von I. M. Bochenski, Heft 6, Bern, 1948, in: *Asiatische Studien* 4, 1950, pp. 143-44.
— Autoreferat über Mohammed im *Jahresbericht des Psychologischen Clubs Zürich*, 1951-52, pp. 35-37.
— Alfred Siggel: *Arabisch-deutsches Wörterbuch aus den drei Naturreichen, die in arabischen alchemistischen Handschriften vorkommen, nebst Anhang: Verzeichnis chemischer Geräte*,

Akademie-Verlag, Berlin, 1950, in: *Erasmus* 4, 1951, pp. 513-14.
— Našwān bin Sa^c^īd al-Ḥimjarī: *Šams al-^c^ulūm*, hrsg. von K.V. Zetterstéen, Teil I, Heft 1, Leiden, 1951, in: *Artibus Asiae* 16, 1953, pp. 147-48.
— M. ^c^Abdul Mu^c^īd Khān: *The Kitāb al-Tashbīhāt of Ibn Abī ^c^Aun*, edited with Introduction, Notes and Indexes, E.J.W. Gibb Memorial Series, New Series 16, London, 1950, in: *Artibus Asiae* 16, 1953, pp. 148-54.
— Karl Jahn: *Histoire Universelle de Rašīd al-Dīn Faḍl Allāh Abul-Khair. I. Histoire des Francs.* Texte persan avec introduction et annotation. Orientalia Rheno-Traiectana, edd. J. Gonda et H.W. Obbink. Volumen quintum, Leiden, 1951, in: *Artibus Asiae* 16, 1953, pp. 154-56.
— *Macallat kulliyyat al-ādāb, bi'l-Cāmi^c^a al-miṣriyya, Bulletin of the Faculty of Arts of the University of Egypt*, 1-14, 1933-1952, in: *Oriens* 7, 1954, pp. 184-91.
— Nāṣir-e Khosraw, *Kitâb-e Jâmi^c^ al-Ḥikmatain. Le livre réunissant les deux sagesses ou Harmonie de la philosophie grecque et de la théosophie ismaélienne.* Texte persan édité avec une double étude préliminaire en francais et en persan par Henry Corbin et Moh. Mo^c^in. Bibliothèque Iranienne 3, Tehran-Paris, 1953, in: *Oriens* 8, 1955, pp. 191-94.
— A.K.S. Lambton: *Persian Grammar*, London, 1953. *Persian Vocabulary*, London, 1954, in: *Bibliotheca Orientalis* 12, 1955, pp. 201-03.
— Hellmut Ritter: *Das meer der seele. Mensch, welt und Gott in den geschichten des Farīduddīn ^c^Aṭṭār*, Leiden, 1955, in: *Oriens* 9, 1956, pp. 319-31.
— Alfred Siggel: *Decknamen in der arabischen alchemistischen Literatur*, Akademie-Verlag, Berlin, 1951, in: *Erasmus* 10, 1957, pp. 676-77.
— Abû Bakr Sirâj Ed-Dîn: *The Book of Certainty*, London 1952, in: *Der Islam* 32, 1957, pp. 112-13.
— Richard J. McCarthy, S.J.: *The Theology of al-Ash^c^arī. The Arabic texts of al-Ash^c^arī's Kitāb al-Luma^c^ and Risālat Istiḥsān al-Khawḍ fī ^c^ilm al-Kalām, with briefly annotated translation and Appendices containing material pertinent to the study of al-Ash^c^arī*, Beirut, 1953, in: *Der Islam* 32, 1957, pp. 109-11.
— Scheikh Ibrahim (Johann Ludwig Burckhardt): *Briefe an Eltern und Geschwister*. Hrsg. von Carl Burckhardt-Sarasin und Hansrudolf Schwabe-Burckhardt, Basle, 1956, in: *Der Islam* 33, 1958, pp. 359-60.

— Ernst Bannerth: *Das Buch der vierzig Stufen von ᶜAbd al-Karīm al-Ǧīlī.* Nach einer Bagdader Handschrift hrsg., übersetzt und mit Erläuterungen versehen. Österreichische Akademie der Wiss. Phil.-hist. Kl. Sitzungsberichte, 230. Band, 3. Abhandlung, Vienna, 1956, in: *ZDMG* 113, 1963, p. 279.
— Hocein Mansûr Hallâj: *Dîwân.* Traduit et présenté par Louis Massignon. (Documents spirituels 10), Paris, Cahiers du Sud 1955,, in: *Oriens* 16, 1963, p. 374.
— Ignace-Abdo Khalifé, S.J.: *ᶜAbd ar-Rahman ibn M. ibn Ḫaldun, Šifāʾ-us-sāʾil litahzīb-il-masāʾil. Apaisement à qui cherche comment clarifier les problèmes. Edition, Introduction et Vocabulaire technique*, Beirut, 1959, in: *Der Islam* 38, 1963, p. 300.
— Arthur Joseph Arberry: *A Sufi Martyr. The Apologia of ᶜAin al-Quḍāt al-Hamadhānī.* Translated with Introduction and Notes, London, 1969, in: *Der Islam* 49, 1972, pp. 132-36.
— Franz Rosenthal: *The Herb. Hashish versus Medieval Muslim Society*, Leiden, 1971, in: *Oriens* 25-26, 1976, pp. 294-96.
— Mohammad Ebn E Monawwar: *Les étapes mystiques du shaykh Abu Sa'īd. Mystères de la connaissance de l'Unique (Asrar al Tawhid fi Maqâmât e al shaykh Abu Sa'id).* Traduction du persan et notes par Mohammad Achena, Desclée de Brouwer, Unesco, 1974, in: *Der Islam* 53, 1977, pp. 294-96.
— Richard Gramlich: *Ahmad Ghazzali, Gedanken über die Liebe*, übersetzt und erläutert. Akademie der Wissenschaften und der Literatur (Mainz), Abh. d. geistes- und sozialwissenschaftl. Kl. Jahrgang 1976, Nr. 2, Wiesbaden, 1976, in: *Der Islam* 54, 1977, pp. 330-31.
— Etan Kohlberg: *Jawāmiᶜ Ādāb al-Ṣūfiyya and ᶜUyūb al- Nafs wa-Mudāwātuhā by Abū ᶜAbd al-Raḥmān al-Sulamī (d. 412 H.).* Edited with an introduction. The Max Schloessinger Memorial Series. Texts 1, Jerusalem, 1976, in: *Der Islam* 55, 1978, pp. 104-05.
— Gerhard Böwering: *The Mystical Vision of Existence in Classical Islam.* Studien zur Sprache, Geschichte und Kultur des islamischen Orients. Beihefte zur Zeitschrift *Der Islam*, N.F. Bd 9, Berlin-New York, 1980, in: *Welt des Islams* 21, 1980, pp. 249-51.
— Richard Gramlich: *Die schiitischen Derwischorden Persiens.* Erster Teil: *Die Affiliationen*, Wiesbaden, 1965. AKM 36, 1. Zweiter Teil: *Glaube und Lehre*, Wiesbaden, 1976. AKM 36, 2, in: *Oriens* 27-28, 1981, pp. 565-70.
— Wilhelm Eilers: *Deutsch-Persisches Wörterbuch*, Wiesbaden, 1959 ff., Bd 1, in: *Bibliotheca Orientalis* 38, 1981, pp. 180-84.

— Richard Gramlich: *Die Wunder der Freunde Gottes. Theologien und Erscheinungsformen des islamischen Heiligenwunders.* Freiburger Islamstudien, hrsg. von Hans Robert Roemer. Band XI, Wiesbaden, 1987, in: *Der Islam* 65, 1988, pp. 262-300.
— Asbaghi, Asya: *Die semantische Entwicklung arabischer Wörter im Persischen*, Wiesbaden-Stuttgart, 1987, in: *Orientalistische Literaturzeitung* 84, 1989, 6, pp. 707-09.
— Meier, Fritz: *Bahāʾ-i Walad. Grundzüge seines Lebens und seiner Mystik*, Leiden, 1989, in: *ZDMG* 141, 1991, pp. 187-93, containing the most important corrections.
— Bernd Radtke: *Adab al-mulūk. Ein Handbuch zur islamischen Mystik aus dem 4./10. Jahrhundert*, BTS 37, Beirut-Stuttgart, 1991, in: *Die Welt des Orients* 24, 1993, pp. 185-87.
— Bernd Radtke: *Drei Schriften des Theosophen von Tirmiḏ.* Erster Teil: Die arabischen Texte, Beirut-Stuttgart, 1992, in: *Die Welt des Orients* 24, 1993, pp. 187-89.
— J.G.J. ter Haar: *Follower and Heir of the Prophet: Shaykh Aḥmad Sirhindī (1564-1624) as Mystic*, Leiden, 1992, in: *Der Islam* 72, 1995, pp. 372-74.

4. NEWSPAPER ARTICLES

— 'Am Grabe des Hafis', *Neue Zürcher Zeitung*, 19 June, 1938.
— 'Vom Orientalen', *Neue Zürcher Zeitung*, 19 September, 1939.
— 'Midas im Orient', *Neue Zürcher Zeitung*, 6 March, 1940.
— 'Omar der Zeltmacher', *Neue Zürcher Zeitung*, 17 and 19 May, 1944.
— 'Wie der Wein entdeckt ward. Ein persisches Märchen', *Neue Zürcher Zeitung*, 17 October, 1940.
— 'Erinnerung an Isfahan im Herzen Persiens', *Volksstimme* (Sissach), 18 October, 1941, with two continuations.
— 'Prof. Dr. Rudolf Tschudi 60jährig', *Basler Nachrichten*, 2 May, 1944.
— 'Der erste arabische Philosoph', *Basler Nachrichten*, 13 July, 1949.
— 'Zum Rücktritt von Prof. Dr. Rudolf Tschudi', *Basler Nachrichten*, 30 September, 1949.
— 'Professor Dr. Alfred Bloch', *Basler Nachrichten*, 25/26 April, 1953.
— 'Ein Querschnitt durch das islamische Denken. Rudolf Jockel, *Islamische Geisteswelt von Mohammed bis zur Gegenwart*, Darmstadt und Genf 1954', *Basler Nachrichten*, 29 October, 1954.

— 'Ein grossartiges Geschenk an die Universitätsbibliothek. Professor Rudolf Tschudis Handschriftensammlung', *Basler Nachrichten*, 14 October, 1961.
— 'Der theutzsche Protz mit den Muskeln aus Majuskeln', *Basler Nachrichten*, 4 February, 1972.
— 'Frohe aussicht. Erfahrungen mit der kleinschreibung', *National-Zeitung*, 25 May, 1974.
— '1400 Jahre Islam', *Basler Zeitung*, 21 November, 1979.

5. COMMEMORATIVE VOLUMES

— *Weströstliche Abhandlungen. Rudolf Tschudi zum siebzigsten Geburtstag überreicht von Freunden und Schülern.* Herausgegeben von Fritz Meier, Wiesbaden, 1954.
— *Islamwissenschaftliche Abhandlungen. Fritz Meier zum sechzigsten Geburtstag.* Herausgegeben von Richard Gramlich, Wiesbaden, 1974.

INTRODUCTION

Fritz Meier (1912-1998) was born in the distinguished old Swiss university city of Basle and grew up in the nearby village of Gelterkinden. Apart from a stint of teaching in Alexandria and numerous visits to Turkey and the Middle East, throughout his adult life Basle remained his home. In the 1930s he studied directly under the Swiss orientalist Rudolf Tschudi (1884-1960) and at this time also met Hellmut Ritter[1] who was by then living and working in Istanbul, and came under his shaping influence. The obituaries Meier wrote on both these scholars, which are reprinted in *Bausteine*, besides sketching their intellectual development and contribution to oriental studies, give an interesting indication of Meier's own scholarly orientation during his formative years. In several of his writings Meier thanks Ritter for having suggested a particular study project and drawn his attention to primary source materials — for example the manuscript which formed the basis of Meier's text edition of the *Firdaws al-murshidiyya* which was to be his doctoral dissertation.

During his long and productive lifetime Meier's academic interests revolved around two principal areas of research: Persian poetry and Sufism, the latter in both its Arabic and its Persian manifestations. Besides the two volumes of his selected articles referred to in the Preface, he published six sizeable books, five of which deal with major themes and personalities of Sufism. Already in his dissertation, *Die Vita des Scheich Abū Isḥāq al-Kāzarūnī*,[2] Meier displays his striking originality and personal talents. His edition of the Persian text is a very competent application of philological methods. In his introduction, written in a lucid, intelligent German, he offers a model analysis of the Persian text as well as other medieval sources which throw light on the authorship and manner of the work's composition. Most

---

1 Ritter's writings are listed by E.A. Gruber in *Oriens* 18-19 (1965-66), pp. 5-32. Perhaps his most ambitious and best known work is *Das meer der seele. Mensch, welt und Gott in den geschichten des Farīduddīn ʿAṭṭār*, Leiden, 1955.

2 *Die Vita des Scheich Abū Isḥāq al-Kāzarūnī*, Leipzig, 1948, is a critical edition of the *Firdaws al-murshidiyya*, Maḥmūd b. ʿUthmān's Persian reworking of a lost late-11th-century Arabic original. This Persian version of the life of Kāzarūnī (d. 1035) was composed in 1327.

impressive is the way Meier describes Kāzarūnī's pattern of life in the context of different currents of Sufi thought, his stance *vis-à-vis* dogmatic issues, and what is known of the early history of the Sufi order he founded. The precision and sureness of his observations set a high intellectual standard. It is interesting to note that Meier was only twenty-four years old when he presented his dissertation to the University of Basle.[3]

Between his work on Kāzarūnī and the publication of his second monograph, *Die Fawā'iḥ al-ğamāl* of Najm al-Dīn al-Kubrā, twenty years elapsed, during which time Meier was chiefly occupied with Persian poetry. The result of this period is his book on the Persian poetess Mahsatī which appeared in 1963.[4] This work delves into what is known about the origin and early development of the quatrain in Persian. Meier collects 279 poems (257 quatrains) attributed by different sources to Mahsatī, translates them and offers a detailed philological commentary on the text. — As for the *Fawā'iḥ*,[5] like the *vita* of Kāzarūnī, it consists of an edition of the text, in this case in Arabic, and an introduction. Here, however, the introduction is 252 pages and offers an extensive treatment of the subject. Indeed, the book has remained the authoritative work on Kubrā and his teachings, as well as on his Sufi order, the Kubrawiyya. Meier's introduction shows that in addition to being knowledgeable on relevant Islamic literature, he is familiar with a wide range of disciplines that lie further afield: Classical Antiquity, the Christian West, and in particular the methods and perspectives of Jungian psychoanalysis.

Meier's next monograph was devoted to the Sufi master from Mayhana, Shaykh Abū Saᶜīd-i Abū'l-Khayr (967-1049),[6] who had already been studied by the earlier renowned scholars,

---

3 Meier presented his dissertation to the University of Basle in 1936, though due to various technical problems and delays it was not finally published in book form until 1948.

4 *Die schöne Mahsatī. Ein Beitrag zur Geschichte des persischen Vierzeilers*, Wiesbaden, 1963. This work is a revised form of Meier's *Habilitationschrift* presented to the University of Basle in 1941. See Jan Rypka's enthusiastic review in *Oriens* XVII (1964), pp. 259-63.

5 *Die Fawā'iḥ al-ğamāl wa-fawātiḥ al-ğalāl des Nağm ad-dīn al-Kubrā*, Wiesbaden, 1957.

6 *Abū Saᶜīd-i Abū l-Ḫayr, Wirklichkeit und Legende*, Leiden, 1976.

Reynold Nicholson[7] and Hellmut Ritter.[8] This work, which Meier himself referred to as a bible of Sufism, is a discursive presentation of the subject, without a text edition.[9] The distinctive characteristics of Shaykh Abū Saᶜīd: his conversion to the Sufi path, early ascetic feats, his notorious antinomian behavior, overriding cheerfulness, etc., are carefully analyzed and compared with the currents of thought and religious attitudes of his predecessors and contemporaries. Around the person of Abū Saᶜīd a wide spectrum of subsidiary subjects are dealt with concerning customs, social practices and the historical development of ideas in Sufism.[10] One should read the book in small doses, focusing on separate subsections at a time that are often excellent, self-contained excursions on fundamental aspects of Sufism.

Another of Meier's books is devoted to Bahāʾ-i Walad (d. 1231), the father of Mawlānā Jalāl al-Dīn-i Rūmī, and appeared in 1989.[11] Here on the basis of Bahāʾ's diaries, the *Maᶜārif*, large parts of which are skilfully translated into German, Meier sketches the portrait of what in many respects represents a quite unique form of mysticism. Bahāʾ never refers to himself as a Sufi, and though he was a contemporary of Najm al-Dīn-i Kubrā, Bahāʾ is not directly influenced by the latter's thought. Meier's book is also an essential work for the further study of the

---

7 *Abū Saᶜīd ibn Abi'l-Khayr*, in: *Studies in Islamic Mysticism*, Cambridge, 1921, reprinted 1967, pp. 1-76.

8 In *EI*2, s.v. Abū Saᶜīd Faḍl Allāh b. Abī l-Khayr.

9 The primary source for the life of Abū Saᶜīd is the *Asrār al-tawḥīd fī maqāmāt al-shaykh Abī Saᶜīd* compiled by Muḥammad b. Munawwar. In his references Meier cites the two text editions that existed at the time he was writing, that of V. Zhukovski (1899) and Dh. Ṣafā (1953). A third improved edition was published in 1987 by Shafīᶜī-Kadkanī which forms the basis of the English translation by John O'Kane, *The Secrets of God's Mystical Oneness*, Costa Mesa-New York, 1992.

10 For instance, one might single out for special attention: Chapter 1 which presents a sweeping sketch of the diversity of spiritual approaches adopted by different Sufi personalities; Chapter 9 on Yaḥyā b. Muᶜādh al-Rāzī, an early example of the cheerful Sufi in whom hope predominates; Chapter 13 dealing with Sufi forms of association and hospices or convents; Chapter 20 on the marabout family; and Chapter 21 on the theme of 'cheerfulness' in later Sufi orders.

11 *Bahāʾ-i Walad. Grundzüge seines Lebens und seiner Mystik*, Leiden, 1989. See Meier's own review in *Zeitschrift des Deutschen Morgenländischen Gesellschaft* 141 (1991), pp. 187-93.

celebrated son, Jalāl al-Dīn-i Rūmī, on the basis of whose teachings the Mawlawiyya Sufi order was founded.

The last of Meier's larger studies deals with two topics in connection with the Naqshbandiyya: *rābiṭa* and *taṣarruf*.[12] Meier examines the methods developed by the Naqshbandiyya to create a bond (*rābiṭa*) of love and devotion between the Sufi master and the novice. The novice, for example, learns a technique for inwardly vizualizing the shaykh's face in order to achieve *fanāʾ* 'self-annihilation', first in the spiritual master and then ultimately in God. The faculty of *taṣarruf* in a shaykh refers to the virtually magic power which he is capable of exercising simply through mental concentration. He can change his appearance, thwart someone's path, induce sickness in his enemies and even cause their death. In this study Meier draws on his broad knowledge of all periods of Sufism as well as relevant Naqshbandī sources from earliest times (14th century) up to the present.

It is not easy to describe adequately the salient features of Meier's scholarly approach. Generally, he succeeds in achieving a high degree of analytical clarity. His German can be very precise, nuanced and sophisticated, in extreme cases almost eccentric in its precision. He does not duck difficulties. On the contrary, when searching for definitions or classifying phenomena with different meanings in different contexts, he tends to present a survey of gradated shades of meaning (see his treatment of *dhikr* in 'The Dervish Dance'). He is capable of disentangling thorny theological ideas and following up their religious implications as in the case of Ibn Taymiyya's complicated position on predestination. Similarly, he can trace the development of a major religious concept or institution such as the *shaykh al-tarbiya* in Nayshābūr on the basis of an original analysis of contemporary sources (see 'Khurāsān and the End of Classical Sufism'). In his long essay on the Almoravids, he brings to bear his specialist knowledge of mystics and holy men as social mediators and ideologists to offer his own synthetic interpretation of the origins of a major movement of military expansion. In his essay on Suyūṭī's explanations about Muḥammad's whereabouts and activities after death, Meier displays his talent for surveying and organizing sets of ideas and their variations over time. In all these cases the greater part of his work consists of original research. For this purpose he makes use of an exceptional variety of Arabic and Persian primary sources,

---

12 *Zwei Abhandlungen über die Naqšbandiyya*, Istanbul-Wiesbaden, 1994.

including historical writings, hagiography, medieval technical manuals on Sufism, inscriptions, biographical dictionaries, poetry and theological works. Throughout he employs a philological method which lets the textual source speak for itself by appropriate quotation and accurate translation.

As for Meier's students who have gone on to do distinguished work in the field of oriental studies, they are numerous. One may mention Rudolf Mach,[13] Benedikt Reinert,[14] Hermann Landolt[15] (who also studied with Henry Corbin), Karl Teufel,[16] Hartwig Cordt,[17] Edward Badeen[18] and Gudrun Schubert.[19] Likewise, Bernd Radtke, the editor and organizer of the present translation of selected articles was also a student and close friend of Meier. Over the years he has written on al-Ḥakīm al-Tirmidhī. Most recently, together with myself, he has published an English translation of Tirmidhī's chief work, the *Sīrat al-awliyā'*, along with the latter's autobiography, under the title *The Concept of Sainthood in Early Islamic Mysticism*.[20] He has also written numerous articles to do with Sufism in the eighteenth century which, among other things, challenge received notions about 'Neo-Sufism'.[21]

---

13 Rudolf Mach, *Der Zaddik in Talmud und Midrasch*, Leiden, 1957. A study dealing with concepts about the holy man in Judaism and Islam.

14 Benedikt Reinert, *Die Lehre vom* tawakkul *in der klassischen Sufik*, Berlin, 1968.

15 Hermann Landolt, *Le révélateur des mystères*, Paris, 1986. This is a text edition of a work by the Kubrawī shaykh Isfarāyinī, accompanied by a partial translation and commentary.

16 Karl Teufel, *Eine Lebensbeschreibung des Scheichs ᶜAlī-i Hamadānī*, Leiden, 1962.

17 Hartwig Cordt, *Die sitzungen des ᶜAlāʾ ad-dawla as-Simnānī*, Zurich, 1977. This is Cordt's dissertation which is a study of the *Chihil majlis*, a Persian work about the Kubrawī ᶜAlāʾ al-Dawla-i Simnānī.

18 Edward Badeen, *Auszüge aus ᶜAmmār al-Bidlīsīs Bahǧat aṭ-ṭāʾifa und Ṣawm al-qalb*, Basle, 1978. This is a study of Najm al-Dīn-i Kubrā's teacher, ᶜAmmār al-Bidlīsī.

19 Gudrun Schubert, *Annäherungen. Der mystisch-philosophische Briefwechsel zwischen Ṣadr ud-Dīn-i Qōnawī und Naṣīr ud-Dīn-i Ṭūsī*, Beirut-Stuttgart, 1995.

20 Bernd Radtke and John O'Kane, *The Concept of Sainthood in Early Islamic Mysticism*, London, 1996. Radtke has also published a German version of the same in volume 35b of the Bibliotheca Islamica: *Drei Schriften des Theosophen von Tirmiḏī*. Zweiter Teil, Beirut-Stuttgart, 1996.

21 For a fuller bibliography on Radtke see his pioneering article 'Sufism in the Eighteenth Century: An Attempt at a Provisional Appraisal', in *Die Welt des Islams* XXXVI, 1996, pp. 326-64.

The most prolific of Meier's former students, however, is without a doubt Richard Gramlich. Gramlich's first work of importance was a three-volume study of the Sufi orders of Persia in modern times.[22] This fundamental work, which has not received the attention it deserves outside the German-speaking world, is something of a general reference book on Sufism, especially the second volume which gives a detailed description of the teachings of the various orders. Gramlich then set out to translate the primary medieval handbooks of classical Sufism. He began with the *ᶜAwārif al-maᶜārif* of Abū Ḥafṣ al-Suhrawardī.[23] This was followed by the last part of Ghazālī's *Iḥyāʾ ᶜulūm al-dīn*,[24] the *Risāla* of Qushayrī,[25] the *Lumaᶜ* of Sarrāj,[26] and finally, in four volumes, the *Qūt al-qulūb* of Abū Ṭālib al-Makkī.[27] Except for the *ᶜAwārif al-maᶜārif*, the translations are all accompanied by a critical apparatus, as well as a commentary which chiefly notes textual parallels and additional examples. Whoever wishes to work on Sufism today can hardly do so without these tools provided by Gramlich. His most recent publication is a two-volume study which focuses on the early Sufi masters,[28] including portraits of Abū Bakr al-Shiblī and Abū Bakr al-Wāsiṭī, among others. Besides numerous smaller studies,[29] one must mention another large-scale work, *Die Wunder der Freunde Gottes*, in which both theory and practice of the miracles of saints are dealt with.[30]

---

22 *Die schiitischen Derwischorden Persiens*, Wiesbaden, 1965-1981.

23 *Die Gaben der Erkenntnisse des ᶜUmar as-Suhrawardī*, Wiesbaden, 1978.

24 *Muḥammad al-Ghazzālīs Lehre von den Stufen der Gottesliebe*, Wiesbaden, 1984.

25 *Das Sendschreiben al-Qušayrīs über das Sufitum*, Wiesbaden, 1989.

26 *Schlaglichter über das Sufitum*, Stuttgart, 1990.

27 *Die Nahrung der Herzen*, Wiesbaden, 1992-95.

28 *Alte Vorbilder des Sufitums*, Wiesbaden, Erster Teil: Scheiche des Westens, 1995; Zweiter Teil: Scheiche des Ostens, 1996.

29 For instance: *Ahmad Ghazzali. Gedanken über die Liebe*, Wiesbaden, 1976; 'Faḫr ad-dīn ar-Rāzīs Kommentar zu Sure 18, 9-12', in: *Asiatische Studien* XXXIII (1979), pp. 99-152; 'Muḥammad al-Ġazzālīs kleine islamische Fundamentaldogmatik', in: *Saeculum* XXXI (1980), pp. 380-98; 'Der Urvertrag in der Koranauslegung (zu Sure 7, 172-173)', in: *Der Islam* 60 (1983), pp. 205-30; 'Abū Sulaymān ad-Dārānī', in: *Oriens* 33 (1992), pp. 22-85; *Die Lebensweise der Könige. Adab al-mulūk. Ein Handbuch zur islamischen Mystik*, Stuttgart, 1993.

30 *Die Wunder der Freunde Gottes*, Wiesbaden, 1987.

For several decades before his death Meier was esteemed by many to be the most accomplished scholar in the German-speaking world who dealt with Islamic Persian and Sufism in its Persian and Arabic manifestations. The number of productive academics working in the field of Sufism who were his students stands as a testimony to his capacity to inspire others and transmit high standards of scholarship. Yet the fact that he wrote in German and that his writings possess a characteristic compactness which makes it difficult for the hasty reader to assess them adequately, accounts perhaps for Meier's work having had less influence than it might have had. Today his philological approach may seem old-fashioned to some, whereas for Meier philology was a fundamental hermeneutic tool for transposing ideas, experiences and sensibilities from one culture to another. By contrast, he had reservations regarding some more recent sociological and economic methodologies which neglect linguistic competence and familiarity with primary sources, but elaborate an understanding on the basis of a broader abstract cultural-anthropological theory.

In what follows I would like to offer a minimal outline of the essays translated in this volume. I stress the word 'minimal' because Meier's normal working method is to present a showcase of evidence from primary sources and to accompany this with wide-ranging comparisons and nuanced interpretation. And although each essay focuses on a precise subject or traces a particular development, Meier frequently adds remarks and judgements which go further afield, especially on matters to do with Sufism. This makes it difficult to paraphrase his work without betraying its special distinctive qualities. My purpose has not been to attempt to evaluate the significance of Meier's contribution to Oriental studies — a task which is beyond my competence — but simply to give the reader a rough idea of what subjects are dealt with in each essay.

'The Dervish Dance: An Attempt at an Overview': This essay is divided into five sections and traces the relationship between *dhikr* and *samāᶜ*. Section 1) considers the Islamic theological concept of God's absolute transcendence, in connection with the Sufi view that man can attain higher perception of God. Performing *dhikr* on spiritual retreat by repeating the formula *lā ilāha illa'llāh* constitutes recollection of God or a means of experiencing spiritual essences. But Sufis recognize the need for God's help to advance beyond themselves.

2) By way of following the Koranic injunction 'to recollect God' at all times, Sufis place *dhikr* at the center of their communal exercises. *Dhikr al-waqt* or *dhikr al-awqāt* is a group performance of *dhikr* after ritual prayer. This is to be distinguished from *dhikr al-ḥaḍra* 'assembly-*dhikr*' which only occurs from time to time and on a larger scale. Modern forms of the latter can involve intense body movements, the goal being to induce a form of dislocation of consciousness or ecstasy.

3) A second kind of ecstasy, not actively induced, was conceived of as being triggered by something outside a person: by a beautiful face, a word or a line of poetry. Music could also have this effect. Examples of suddenly triggered ecstatic states are discussed. Christian parallels are considered, but a fundamental difference between the Christians and the Sufis was that the latter would assemble communally to induce such states. Some rules regarding the dance which accompanied *samāᶜ* are discussed, as well as anticipatory mimicking of ecstatic states (*tawājud*) and the practice of casting off items of clothing in ecstasy. Differences between *dhikr* and *samāᶜ* are considered: in *dhikr* a person invokes his own forces, in *samāᶜ* he waits; in the one he speaks, in the other he listens; *dhikr* is an indispensable part of the Sufi curriculum and work routine, *samāᶜ* is almost always a concession (*rukhṣa*) performed in the context of entertainment and was combatted by many as a malignant growth on Sufism. Both could induce ecstatic states.

4) Whereas dance had originally been an expression of ecstasy, Meier describes two cases in which dance served as a form of *tawājud* to induce ecstasy: the Mawlawīs, founded in the 13th century by Jalāl al-Dīn-i Rūmī, and the ᶜĪsawīs of North Africa and Egypt, founded in the 16th century.

5) Meier sketches a process which led to the combination of *dhikr* and *samāᶜ*, and gives examples of particular hybrids which resulted. In closing, he describes in detail the separate segments of the combined performance of *dhikr* and *samāᶜ* by the Ḍayfīs which he witnessed himself in Alexandria in 1948. Other Sufi brotherhoods which regularly employed this form of combination are mentioned.

'A Book of Etiquette for Sufis': The main section of this essay presents a close paraphrase of the contents of the *Ādāb al-*

murīdīn, a small handbook for Sufis about correct behavior, written in Persian sometime after 1184 by Najm al-Dīn-i Kubrā. In his sizeable introduction, however, Meier first reviews the bewildering plethora of meanings which had developed around the word *adab*/pl. *ādāb*. In the context of Sufism the term signifies the specific customs, practices and correct mode of behavior of a Sufi. In much the same way that *regulae*, *constitutiones* and *consuetudines* eventually dominated life within the Christian monastic orders, the whole of Sufism came to be conceived of as regulated by *ādāb*. Meier considers the stages of this development and previous Sufi works which dealt with the subject of *ādāb*.

Sulamī's earlier work *Ādāb al-ṣuḥba wa-ḥusn al-ᶜishra*, for instance, derives its *ādāb* governing social behavior from the *sunna* of the Prophet and is intended for all Muslims, whereas Kubrā takes for granted a long-established Sufi tradition and addresses himself exclusively to Sufis. On the other hand, Abū'l-Najīb al-Suhrawardī's *Ādāb al-murīdīn* in Arabic is a comprehensive presentation of Sufism from the viewpoint of *ādāb*, while Kubrā's smaller work focuses on the restricted area of social intercourse and duties regarding decency, i.e. on the outward, not the inward, rules of behavior. Typical in this respect is Kubrā's attention to the symbolic meaning of the special clothing worn by Sufis.

Kubrā's book is divided into seven chapters: 1) On Wearing the Patched Frock (*khirqa*), 2) On Sitting and Rising, 3) On Entering a Convent, 4) On Eating, 5) How One Behaves When Invited for Dinner, 6) On Listening to Music (*samāᶜ shinīdan*), 7) On Correct Behavior (*ādāb*) When Travelling. Meier provides extensive notes with meticulous explanations and comparisons.

'Qushayrī's *Tartīb al-sulūk*': Meier refers to Ibn ᶜAbbād al-Rundī's observation in the 14th century that a shift from the *shaykh al-taᶜlīm* 'the lecture-giving shaykh' to the *shaykh al-tarbiya* 'the shaykh in charge of training' took place sometime between the end of the 10th and the beginning of the 11th century. This important transformation is the subject of Meier's later essay 'Khurasan and the End of Classical Sufism'. Qushayrī belongs to the period when this shift had set in and a shaykh demands absolute obedience from the novice and initiates him by 'implanting' the formula for recollecting God (*dhikr*). *Dhikr* is one of the most important means a mystic possesses for eliminating decisions of the 'self' and drawing closer to God. Associated with spiritual training in the new era is discussion of the occult phenomena which a novice experiences when performing *dhikr* in spiritual retreat.

Qushayrī's work *The Gradation of Travelling on the Path to God* is a short monograph which provides our earliest evidence of a Sufi shaykh's explanations to do with the rules and effects of *dhikr*, as well as the pitfalls the novice must seek to avoid. Particular postures or techniques to be adopted in performing *dhikr* are not mentioned. Meier discusses some contradictions in the work, as well as problems concerning its authorship and manner of composition, and concludes that the text may have been compiled by a student on the basis of Qushayrī's oral teachings.

Meier then paraphrases the contents of the work, which he has divided into 9 sections, and comments on its salient features. Recollection of God moves from the tongue to the heart and then into the so-called 'secret'. The student must forget all things, including himself and his recollection of God. Above all, the psychic phenomena he experiences must not distract him. He sees himself grow and expand, he suffers convulsions, he hears strange voices and experiences an extraordinary sweet taste. He believes he can hear ants when they walk. He yearns to be able to sleep.

The mystic's relation to his 'secret' is described. He must avoid falling into the state of *jam*ᶜ *al-jam*ᶜ 'the union of union' which overwhelmed Ḥallāj and Bisṭāmī. The devil has strategies for intervening. Mystic states, like a bird, only descend on a human being who remains motionless like a dead person. Qushayrī concludes with some examples of his own psychic difficulties and how he overcame them with the help of a friend. When his recollection of God finally moved into his 'secret', the experience was so intense he was reduced to skin and bones in the course of one day.

After a detailed paraphrase and commentary Meier provides an edition of the Arabic text, followed by a translation.

'An Important Manuscript Find for Sufism': Here Meier describes and analyzes the contents of an Arabic collective manuscript, no. 87 belonging to the Khānaqāh-i Aḥmadī in Shīrāz. It was first briefly described by Īraj-i Afshār in 1965. Eight of the thirteen texts contained in the MS are unique. These include important verses by Ḥallāj not found in Massignon's *Dīwān al-Ḥallāj* and five new works by Abū Manṣūr Ma^cmar al-Iṣfahānī, a contemporary and fellow townsman of Abū Nu^caym al-Iṣfahānī, about whom relatively little was otherwise known.

The most significant text of the collective MS is an anonymous work entitled *Adab al-mulūk* which has since been edited by Bernd Radtke and tranlated into German by Richard Gramlich. This is a compact but comprehensive handbook of Sufism from the 10th or 11th century, offering a parallel with Kalābādhī's *Ta^carruf* and Sarrāj's *Luma^c*. Meier discusses the book's value for the study of Sufism, its contents and possible authorship.

Then there is a short collection of Sufi maxims, poems and stories, attributed to Sulamī. This is followed by ninety-four sayings by or about Shāfi^cī with relevance for Sufism, which Sulamī collected. Meier translates this text and considers other collections of Shāfi^cī's sayings and his ambiguous attitude toward Sufism. In Shāfi^cī's day Sufism was still at an early stage of development (prior to so-called classical Sufism). Expanding on his comments on Shāfi^cī, Meier proceeds to give a sweeping interpretive overview of Sufism's subsequent development which concludes with special emphasis on the value of Sulamī as a source and an appeal for a critical edition of Sulamī's Koran commentary.

'Khurāsān and the End of Classical Sufism': Meier begins by specifying some important features of Sufism which have changed over the centuries. He then sets out to investigate the transformation of the *shaykh al-ta^clīm* 'the lecture-giving shaykh' into the *shaykh al-tarbiya*, the Sufi master who becomes closely involved in training a disciple to be a spiritual adept. Meier notes that it was Ibn ^cAbbād al-Rundī (d. 1390) who first pointed out this transformation and located its occurrence in the 11th century. A comparison of an early Sufi textbook like Sarrāj's *Luma^c* with the *^cAwārif al-ma^cārif* of Abū Ḥafṣ ^cUmar al-Suhrawardī (d. 1234) clearly reveals that a shift in this direction did take place.

Firstly, evidence from the 9th and 10th centuries regarding the *shaykh al-ta^clīm* is reviewed. Although training is already attested in the 10th century in Sarrāj's *Luma^c*, as well as in the *Asrār al-Tawḥīd* (the life of shaykh Abū Sa^cīd b. Abī'l-Khayr; 967-1049), by the 11th century it had acquired a new status. Aspects of training were by then dealt with in theoretical discussions and regulations in Sufi systems. The gap in status between the shaykh and the novice widened. The pact between the shaykh and the novice imposed absolute obedience on the latter, and the novitiate became an initiation, not into a Sufi order — orders only developed later — but into a particular *silsila* or 'spiritual family tree'. Sufi shaykhs claimed to be the heirs to the Prophet. Further concepts which played a role in augmenting the authority of the shaykh are considered.

Thanks to surviving evidence, we are in a position to observe the transformation of the Sufi shaykh in Nayshābūr from the 9th to the 11th century. Meier proceeds to give a detailed analysis of the shift in attitude towards *tarbiya* among the following series of important Nayshābūrī shaykhs: Abū Ḥafṣ al-Ḥaddād al-Nayshābūrī (d. circa 880), Abū ʿUthmān al-Ḥīrī (d. 910), Abū ʿAlī al-Thaqafī (d. 940), Abū Sahl al-Ṣuʿlūkī (d. 980), Sulamī (d. 1021), and finally Abū ʿAlī al-Daqqāq (d. 1015) and Qushayrī (d. 1072).

Developments in Nayshābūr reflect a more widespread trend, though Nayshābūr played a leading role in shaping that trend. The influential writings of Sulamī and Qushayrī guaranteed the future authority of the Nayshābūrī model. Our limited knowledge of the Malāmatiyya movement and the *ahl al-futuwwa* is also discussed in relation to Sufism. Qushayrī is the pivotal figure in the transition from classical Sufism with the predominace of the *shaykh al-taʿlīm* to the post-classical period and the *shaykh al-tarbiya*. Meier closes with some remarks on the general significance of this change and the later dissemination of ideas about the *shaykh al-tarbiya*.

'A Saying of the Prophet against Mourning the Dead': Muḥammad forbade lamenting over the dead but it was difficult to suppress this deep-rooted pre-Islamic custom. There is a difference between lamenting (*niyāḥa/nawḥ*) and weeping (*bukāʾ*). Canonical *ḥadīth*s express contradictory attitudes towards weeping. In this essay Meier examines the problems of interpretation which arose concerning variants of the *ḥadīth*: 'The dead atones for the weeping of his relatives over him.' Many took this to mean that the dead is punished for the weeping of his relatives, but in Islam one cannot be held responsible for the sins of others.

ʿĀʾisha rejected the *ḥadīth*'s authenticity. Ibn Qutayba's explanation in its defense is described. Or does the *ḥadīth* only refer to someone who has ordered lamentation on his own behalf? But in our context the verb *yuʿadhdhibu bi-* ('atones for' or 'is punished for') can also mean 'is tormented by' or 'suffers because of' his relatives' weeping. Muḥammad b. Jarīr al-Ṭabarī

(d. 923) understood the *ḥadīth* this way, i.e. *ᶜadhāb* is taken to mean 'pain' rather than 'punishment'.

A Zoroastrian myth maintains that the deceased must cross over a river and that this may be made difficult by the tears of the living which cause the river to swell. Meier translates pertinent sections from two Neo-Persian versifications of the Zoroastrian *Ardā-Wirāz-nāmag*: one by Zartusht-i Bahrām-i Pazhdū in the 13th century, the other being an anonymous version written in 1532. He then considers evidence on prohibiting lamentation from Mandaean and Coptic sources. The question is raised as to whether the idea of the dead being tormented by weeping was adopted in Islam from the Iranians, as with the case of the *Chinwat*-Bridge.

In conclusion Meier reviews an array of beliefs about the effect of tears on the dead from other peoples around the world. His examples are taken from such wide-ranging contexts as Graeco-Roman antiquity, German folklore, Sanskrit literature and Eskimo myths.

'An Exchange of Letters between Sharaf al-Dīn-i Balkhī and Majd al-Dīn-i Baghdādī': Whereas nothing is known about Balkhī, shaykh Majd al-Dīn-i Baghdādī (d. 1219) was a disciple of Najm al-Dīn-i Kubrā (d. 1221). Meier notes that only in Sufism's post-classical period, i.e. after Qushayrī (d. 1072), did letters form part of a novice's training by providing interpretations of dreams and visions. The latter had come to be taken seriously as a source for understanding the novice's inner state. For instance, the *Manāqib-i Awḥad al-Dīn-i Kirmānī* (d. 1238) portrays the master every morning discussing the nocturnal experiences of the novice. Kubrā attached great importance to visionary experience. Meier refers to Kubrā's advice by letter to Sayf al-Dīn-i Bākharzī (d. 1260 or 1261), as well as the letters between ᶜAlāᵓ al-Dawla-i Simnānī and his teacher Nūr al-Dīn-i Kasirqī (d. 1317).

Meier proceeds to give a close paraphrase of Balkhī's letter to Baghdādī. The visions Balkhī has had involve demon spirits (*jinn*) who pose a dilemma concerning saying 'There is no god but God' while one's ego still remains. Balkhī witnesses terrifying animals and a hugh snake burst forth from a smoking well shaft. Later he perceives beautiful forms and sounds, and a state of rapture comes over him. Many details of what he sees suggest allegorical meanings. In a final vision an old wise man appears who gives spiritual advice to Baghdādī as well as Balkhī.

Meier next paraphrases Baghdādī's reply. Here all the main features of Balkhī's visions are meticulously interpreted and accompanied by spiritual advice. For instance, the old man of the final vision is identified as probably being the demon shaykh ᶜAbd al-Raḥmān who was a close disciple of the Prophet. The well shaft represents the heart, the connecting tract between the material and the supernatural world. While the senses prevail, the heart is filled with reprehensible qualities. These are the animals Balkhī saw, etc. And Baghdādī comments on the correct way to perform the all-important Sufi practice of *dhikr*, which involves reciting the formula 'There is no god but God'. In closing Baghdādī recommends attaching oneself to human teachers instead of demons, since demons have no experience of the barriers separating man from God.

Meier follows these paraphrases with his own interesting comments on all the points dealt with in the letters, e.g. earlier views about the dilemma associated with the *tahlīl*, numerous other occasions when demons have taught human beings, and the theme of a person being absent from the recollection of God while recollecting God. Finally, Meier provides an edition of the Persian text.

'The Ṣumādiyya: A Branch Order of the Qādiriyya in Damascus': This essay is divided into three sections. In section 1) Meier examines the extant historical evidence relating to the Ṣumādiyya, a suborder of the Qādiriyya, which was founded in the Syrian village of Ṣumād but moved its headquarters to Damascus by the end of the 15th century. The Ṣumādī family claims descent from a direct disciple of ᶜAbd al-Qādir al-Jīlānī (d. 1166), as well as from a daughter of Jīlānī. Meier presents what is known from Arabic sources about the family's role in society and politics, particularly their relations with other prominent families in Damascus and the Ottoman government. While describing the successive heads of the Ṣumādī family, Meier makes numerous illuminating comments about the decentralized organization and different family branches of the Qādiriyya order. By around 1800 the family begins to disintegrate, in part due to internal splits over leadership. At the end of section 1) a detailed genealogical family tree is provided.

Section 2) discusses the prominence accorded to drum playing in the Ṣumādiyya's *dhikr-* and *samā*ᶜ-performances. According to legend a particular drum possessed by the family had been beaten at the capture of Acre from the Crusaders. Meier considers the chronological problems raised by the legend and which capture of Acre may have been intended (1187 or 1291). Miracles associated with the famous drum are described. The legend of the drum is also discussed in terms of hagiographical strategies found in other sources. The Ṣumādiyya regularly beat drums at night in the Umayyad Mosque in Damascus. There were opponents and supporters of religious uses of drumming.

Section 3) considers the positive spiritual effects of drum playing. Drums instill awe and respect (*muhība*), a sense of gravity and intimacy (*waqār* and *uns*) and inspire the desire to set out on the inner path of 'greater holy war'. The Kāzarūniyya's military music is a form of music associated with a royal residence and has nothing to do with *dhikr-* or *samā*ᶜ-performances. The courtly orchestra attached to the tomb of Imam ᶜAlī Riḍā (d. 818) in Mashhad consists of trumpets accompanied by drums and plays in honor of the Imam and by way of invoking blessings on him. Of these three different kinds of military music only that of the Ṣumādiyya is intended to induce ecstasy.

'The Cleanest about Predestination: A Bit of Ibn Taymiyya': This essay falls into three sections. Section 1), by way of introduction, characterizes Ibn Taymiyya's 'fundamentalist' thought. The Prophet Muḥammad is dead and until the Resurrection cannot intervene on our behalf with God, and certainly 'saints', whether living or dead, have no such power. We cannot know God through our own efforts. Everything we need to know about religion and how to live is contained in the Koran and the *sunna*. Nor is there a path to God through philosophical speculation, or through self-purification and self-abnegation. And exaggerated religious devotions are not required.

Section 2) elaborates these points with relation to the Sufis. Sufis give too much importance to experience and exceptional states: visions, dreams, inspirations, etc. But these are never as binding as the Koran and the *sunna*. Ibn Taymiyya views contemporary miracles as charlatanism or of satanic origin. In addition, the Sufis tend to be indifferent to the commands and prohibitions of religion, maintaining that whatever happens is the will of God. For instance Ibn ᶜAṭāʾallāh al-Sikandarī, a spokesman at that time for the Shādhiliyya in Egypt, emphasized contentment (*riḍā*) above love and advocated dropping all planning (*isqāṭ al-tadbīr*). The Sufi approach, in this respect, is one-sided. God has two wills. The one is designated as *kawnī* 'existential' and determines everything that happens. The other is *dīnī* 'religious' and refers to what should and should not be done. This is an old distinction previously described as *irāda* (God's will) and *amr* (His command). Sufis overemphasize predestination or God's existential will. It is especially reprehensible to argue against the divine commands by invoking predestination.

Section 3), the central part of the essay, is a detailed exposition of Ibn Taymiyya's nuanced and consistent thought about man's dilemma and man's duties in view of God's two forms of will. Man has no way of dealing with predestination but must render obedience and do battle in the field of divine commands and prohibitions. Meier translates an excerpt from Ibn Taymiyya's *Marātib al-irāda* which clarifies the different categories and subtle workings of God's will.

'Almoravids and Marabouts': This is the largest and most densely documented of the essays here presented, and consists of four sections. Section 1), subtitled '*Ribāṭ* and *murābaṭa*', examines the Islamic institution of the frontier guard who, on a voluntary basis, detaches himself from his tribe and family to man a fort (*ribāṭ*) against infidel invaders. Besides performing a purely military activity, those who undertake *murābaṭa* (the *ṣāliḥūn* and *murābiṭūn*) also engage in religious devotions and cultivate a sense of piety.

Section 2) '*Murābiṭ* and marabout' considers how the later meaning of marabout, 'holy man', evolved out of the meaning of *murābiṭ* as a frontier guard. This development was peculiar to North Africa and Spain, whereas *ribāṭ* in the East came exclusively to mean a civilian hospice for lodging. In the Arabic vernacular in the west *murābiṭ* comes to signify a man of piety who acts as a mediator in disputes or between the common people and the government. His family and descendants retain a sanctified status in the community and up to modern times have often played a decisive role in dynastic politics.

In section 3) '*Al-murābiṭūn* and the Almoravids', early Arabic historians who deal with the beginnings of the Almoravid movement of the 11th century are examined in light of the different meanings of *murābaṭa* in an attempt to make better sense of the unresolved contradictions in the sources. The interpretations of leading European and Moroccan historians (Huici, Norris, Levtzion, Labbadie, etc.) are weighed against the historical evidence and religious significance of the term *murābiṭ*. In this context *murābiṭ* designates a particular people, i.e. a group of Berber tribes (at the head of which stands the Lamtūna) who were originally adherents and then fighting 'comrades' of Ibn Yāsīn. In summing up, the full range of differences between a *murābiṭ* as a holy man and an Almoravid are reviewed.

Finally, section 4) 'Those who veil their mouth...' treats the subject of the origins and function of wearing a veil over the mouth, which was a distinctive custom of the Almoravids — so much so that their 12th-century rivals the Almohads strongly condemned the practice. A range of studies by European ethnographers is considered, as well as various ideas about the veil found in early Arabic historical and geographical literature.

'Ṭāhir al-Ṣafadī's Forgotten Work on Western Saints of the 6th/12th Century': This essay begins by reviewing the early Arab-ic sources describing pious Muslims and miracle-workers in the west of North Africa and the Iberian Peninsula, the earliest of which date from the 13th century. But there is a 12th-century work on this subject, composed sometime before the death of Abū Yaᶜazzā (1177) which has hitherto been neglected. Meier then proceeds to give a paraphrase of the accounts about saints, ascetics and religious scholars found in *Al-sirr al-maṣūn* by Ṭāhir al-Ṣadafī. This is a sizeable fragment preserved in al-Bārizī's *Tawthīq ᶜurā'l-īmān fī tafḍīl ḥabīb al-raḥmān*. Ṣadafī's book might rightly be described as a 'hagiographical journal' (*kunnāsh/kunnāsha*). It covers Spain, Morocco, Egypt and the Ḥijāz, though with a preponderance of persons from the west. All the individuals described are contemporaries of Ṣadafī whom he met personally or heard about. Except for Abū Yaᶜazzā and ᶜAbd al-Malik b. Masarra, the persons described are not famous saints or men of learning. These are naive, credulous reports, edifying fantasies which stress the miraculous. For all their intellectual modesty, however, they enrich our knowledge of hagiographical motifs and acquaint us with persons of the 12th century unknown from other sources.

The work falls into five sections. Section 1) describes theologians (*ᶜulamāᵓ*), jurists (*fuqahāᵓ*) and Friends of God (*awliyāᵓ*) whom Ṣadafī met in the Maghreb (Morocco and Spain); section 2) deals with pious worshippers of God (*ᶜubbād*) and ascetics (*zuhhād*) in the same region; section 3) with the same category of people he had not met but only heard about; section 4) with theologians, ascetics and men of education (*fuḍalāʾ*) he met or heard about in Egypt; and section 5) describes persons he encountered in the Ḥijāz. Meier's accompanying notes are copious and provide the reader with interesting comparisons and a wide range of pertinent bibilographical references.

'A Resurrection of Muḥammad in Suyūṭī': Meier begins by reviewing early ideas about Muḥammad's status and whereabouts after death. More popular views, in distinction to those later held by Ibn Taymiyya and the Wahhābīs, claimed that Muḥammad had died and his corpse was in Medina but that he is alive in his grave and, as in the case of the other prophets, his spirit (*rūḥ*) is free to move about and participate in the world. Evidence from tombstone inscriptions is referred to and parallels with Jesus (who in the Muslim view did not die but was translated to heaven) are taken into account. Likewise, ideas about the Prophet's ubiquity and multilocatio on the part of Friends of God are considered.

The main focus of the essay, however, is the concept of Muḥammad's continued life after death which is sketched in two works by Suyūṭī (1445-1505): the *Inbāh al-adhkiyāʾ fī ḥayāt al-anbiyāʾ* and the *Tanwīr al-ḥalak fī imkān ruʾyat al-nabī wa'l-malak*. Suyūṭī's view combines the incorruptibility of the Prophet's body and his body's revival by his surviving spirit. Hence the Prophet lives on in flesh and blood after death. He moves about feely and travels wherever he wishes on earth and in the supernatural realm (*malakūt*). He looks as he did in life but is only visible to those whom God has given special grace.

Ibn ᶜArabī held that seeing Muḥammad after the latter's death made one a Companion of the Prophet. This attitude was shared by the two founders of Sufi orders, Aḥmad al-Tijānī (d. 1815) and Muḥammad al-Sanūsī (d. 1859). Tijānī, for instance, claimed to have met the Prophet and been initiated by him and thus to have become a Companion himself. Other later figures who were influenced by Suyūṭī are discussed: Muḥammad al-Fīlālī, al-Ḥājj ᶜUmar Tal (founder of a Tijānī state on the upper Niger), etc. The Salafī-Wahhābī view, based on sound *ḥadīths*, accepts that the Prophet lives on in his grave — but only in his grave. He does not move about in the world.

'Invoking Blessings on Muḥammad in Prayers of Supplication and When Making Requests': This essay presents a broad spectrum of uses of the *taṣliya* 'invoking blessings on Muḥammad' and speculates as to their origin and meaning. It is divided into four sections:

1) In prayers of supplication (*duʿāʾ*), repeated at the beginning, middle and end, or sometimes only at the beginning: *Ḥadīth*s and other pious sayings supporting this use are cited. Ibn Taymiyya approved of the *taṣliya* in preference to formulas of conjuration. Evidence from inscriptions on wood and stone are reviewed. Uses of the *taṣliya* to overcome adversity are noted. Repeating the *taṣliya* hundreds of times is meant to 'coerce heaven', and great benefits are to be had by reciting the *taṣliya* without any specific request. Hence it is recommended to read through Jazūlī's *Dalāʾil al-khayrāt* (a collection of different forms of *taṣliyāt*) forty times in forty days. One will also benefit from dedicating to the Prophet all the reward for saying the *taṣliya*.

2) Against the plague: Meier examines a work by Aḥmad b. Abī Ḥajala (d. 1375) who argues in favor of using the *taṣliya* for protection against the plague. This author mentions all the cases of plague he knew about in the Islamic world before the plague of 1364 and describes the religious measures taken against the black death in 1348 which he witnessed himself in Damascus. Maqrīzī's supplementary evidence about plague is discussed, as well as a work by Baylūnī (d. 1632-33) which gives different remedies against plague including the *taṣliya*. But the *taṣliya* was not universally adopted as a measure against plague as Ibn Abī Ḥajala had wanted. It remained in the background only to be used occasionally in emergencies.

3) When making a request: Early on the *taṣliya* was used when requesting something from a human being. It functioned as a form of conjuration. The person addressed is called upon to invoke blessings on the Prophet. Oldest known examples are considered, for instance the clever way the poet Abū Dulāma used the *taṣliya* in a request he made to the caliph al-Mahdī (d. 785).

4) As an order to be silent: The *taṣliya* can still be used today in an attempt to settle a dispute but as a practice it goes very far back. It is referred to in early juridical discussions in connection with blasphemy, e.g. by Saḥnūn (d. 854). Recent and old examples are examined. In closing, Meier considers possible explanations for the origin of the *taṣliya* of appeasement, as well as the

taṣliya used before making a declaration or an intimate communication.

'The Priority of Faith or Thinking Well of Others over a Concern for Truth among Muslims': The intellectual and practical implications of the complex of ideas associated with *ḥusn al-ẓann* and *iʿtiqād* are investigated in a rich variety of contexts. One is impressed by the diversity of situations in which this fundamental Islamic concept turns up. Meier's wide-ranging familiarity with primary source materials permits him to pursue his subject in eight separate areas: 1) thinking well of God, 2) of the Prophet Muḥammad, 3) of ᶜAlids and descendants of the Prophet's Companions, 4) of deeply-rooted religious practices and customs, 5) of religious authorities, 6) of one's Sufi instructor, 7) Muslims' thinking well of one another, and 8) favorable or unfavorable thought as a magic power.

The *ḥadīth qudsī*: 'I (God) am as My bondsman thinks of Me' has been variously interpreted in Islam to explain the virtue and benefits of having trust in God, as well as the kinds of power resulting from firm belief. Meier provides concrete examples of how *ḥusn al-ẓann* requires Muslims to show repect for God, the Prophet, ᶜAlids, holy men and their alleged graves, Sufi shaykhs, and fellow Muslims. The way faith can heighten the efficacy of supplicatory prayer, even among non-Muslims, is also considered. Finally, four categories of magical power are examined in connection with thinking well or badly about a person. These include the psychic powers of the Friend of God, i.e. his *himma* 'effective power', *taṣarruf* 'power of disposal' and *naẓar* 'gaze', as well as *tawājud* 'anticipatory mimicking' of rapture as a means of inducing real states of ecstasy.

'Poetic Refrain and *Maḥyā*': This essay opens with a description of the panegyrical poems in praise of the Prophet which form the conclusion to the large work by Aḥmad al-Maqqarī al-Tilimsānī (d. 1631): *Nafḥ al-ṭīb min ghusn al-Andalus al-ratīb wa-dhikr wazīrihā Lisān al-Dīn b. al-Khaṭīb*. Meier analyzes the strophic structure and rhyme schemes of the poems and in particular their use of the *taṣliya*, i.e. invoking blessings on the Prophet. He conjectures that this voluminous appendix of Maqqarī's serves as one long *taṣliya* by way of concluding his book. Meier then asks whether poems with a *taṣliya* refrain might have been used in what later came to be known as a *maḥyā*-performance, i.e. communal recitation of blessings on the Prophet. The importance of the *Dalāʾil al-khayrāt* of Muḥammad b. Sulaymān al-Jazūlī (d. 1465), a very popular collection of *taṣliya* formulas, is discussed, as well as the later, more elaborate collection by Ibn ᶜAẓẓūm (d. 1553), the *Tanbīh al-anam.*

But it was Nūr al-Dīn ᶜAlī al-Shūnī (d. 1537-38) who created the *maḥyā* for invoking blessings on the Prophet and in 1492 established its performance in Cairo in al-Azhar. His student Shaᶜrānī notes in 1542 that Shūnī's *maḥyā* had spread to Alexandria, Upper-Egypt, the Ḥijāz, Syria, North Africa and Senegal. In 1563-64 ᶜAbd al-Qādir al-ᶜĀtikī performed what was now formally designated *laylat al-maḥyā* in the Umayyad Mosque in Damascus. Further developments in gatherings for communal reciting of *taṣliyāt* are considered and the relationship of the Shūnī-type *maḥyā* and the Sufi *ḥaḍra* is examined. The former gives emphasis to large numbers of repetition to induce God to be good to the Prophet. In conclusion Meier speculates on whether poems with *taṣliya* refrains such as those cited by Maqqarī might have been used in a *maḥyā*-performance.

THE DERVISH DANCE: AN ATTEMPT AT AN OVERVIEW

The study presented here had its origin in more extensive research on the phenomenology of the so-called 'listening to music' (*samāᶜ*) in earlier Islamic mysticism and is nothing other than an attempt to venture beyond the confines of that narrower subject and to reconnoitre the wider domain to which the 'listening to music' of earlier Islamic mystics belongs. But whereas the picture of the earlier *samāᶜ* reveals itself with some degree of certainty on the basis of numerous texts that are already accessible, a thick fog extends over the wider landscape and obscures the historical connections and development of the phenomena. Pertinent information is lacking in the sources, and no preliminary research has been done. Only here and there in rather isolated cases does a breach open up allowing a curious gaze to catch a partial glimpse of the interesting terrain. But even these glimpses are at times illusory forms or too unclear to permit us to make any certain pronouncements. In these circumstances it goes without saying that the arrangement of the materials attempted in what follows is to a large extent hypothetical. But there will be others who come and take up the thread again.

It is also self-evident that an essay of a limited number of pages which is meant to adopt a generally comprehensible form cannot give all the details and aim at completeness even in the area of what is presently known. Footnotes and bibliographical references have been confined to the bare essentials.

(1)

Islamic theology saw it as one of its chief tasks to purify from all anthropomorphic and sensual accretions the concept of one God which Muḥammad taught. A particularly decisive phase in this development has always been considered the rationalistic theology of the Muᶜtazilites, the actual creators of Islamic scholasticism. They went so far as to deny God those anthropomorphic features which the Koran attributes to Him and this they did by making use of the clever expedient of alternative interpretation. They explained the mention of God's hands which occurs in the Koran as a figurative way of expressing God's 'beneficence',[1] explained the mention of His eyes as the equivalent of His 'knowledge', His face they understood as God's essence, and where it says in the Koran that God sits on the Throne, they interpreted this sitting (*istawā*) as an act of taking possession (*istawlā*). Moreover, the Ash^{c}arites, the adversaries of the Mu^{c}tazila and the future Ecclesia triumphans of Islam, did not abrogate this development but, on the contrary, went so far as to raise divinity above all forms of representation. The Ash^{c}arites in fact viewed alternative interpretations as the coarsest attempts to impute anthropomorphic attributes to God. Consequently, they replaced the attempted Mu^{c}tazilite interpretations based on human reason with the full old terms which the Koran — the Word of God — used to describe God, but they explained that they neither knew nor were able to know in what way or manner these terms were to be understood. 'God has hands', they affirmed, 'but we do not know how. He has eyes but we do not know how. He sits on the Throne but we do not know how.' Thus it was conceded that God had indeed described Himself in this or that form and that man could rely on this description, but the possibility of bringing God into connection with human conception on the basis of this description or of attaining further knowledge about Him was denied. These discussions went on during the 8th, 9th and 10th centuries AD.

Islamic mysticism, which developed during the same period and in the same intellectual centers, chiefly in Mesopotamia, acknowledges the fundamental idea of theological dogma: God is indescribable, He transcends the world and is the opposite to everything that has actual existence. But here it introduces a significant qualification. Orthodoxy formulates the doctrine of God's transcendence in absolute terms and without any concessions, but in so doing exclusively has in mind a human being whose mental capacities go no further than the operation of the intellect and faith. Mysticism does not recognize this limitation as definitive but is of the view that man can cross these upward boundaries and thereby remove the dividing line which appears to separate him from God and, as it were, to relegate him wholly to nature and the realm of becoming. The new knowledge which arises for man beyond the intellect is no longer a knowledge based on thought, although it has to do with mental contents, but is a kind of higher perception, whether it be a form of vision, reception of inspired insights or an experience. The organs involved, i.e. the

1 According to an Arabic usage in which hand (*yad*) signifies 'favor' (*ni^{c}ma*). For an example see Julius Wellhausen, *Muhammed in Medina*, Berlin, 1882, p. 21.

heart, the spirit, 'the secret', etc., are believed to be of immaterial substance.

The development of these higher organs was the result of an inner schooling which is in part traceable all the way back to the mysteries of antiquity. The Sufi, as the Islamic mystic is called (after *ṣūf* 'wool', the haircloth shirt he wears), was required to undergo practices of an ascetic character which aimed at directing his psychic energy inwards and undoing his ties to the world of external appearances. The central focus and the high point of all these exercises was spiritual retreat during which the mystic withdrew from all external impressions and, inwardly as well, by means of concentration on a formula, sought to eliminate preoccupation with anything other than the idea of God. In Sufism this so-called 'recollection of God' (*dhikr Allāh* or just *dhikr*) consisted in unbroken concentration of the mind on the first phrase of the Islamic profession of faith 'There is no god but God' (*lā ilāha illā'llāh*)[2] which one pronounced to oneself out loud, or simply on the name 'God' (*Allāh*) or the representative pronoun 'He' (*huwa*).[3] The formula *lā ilāha illā'llāh* was considered especially suitable not only because it was the first part of the profession of faith but also because it expressed both the negative and the positive operation which the mystic had to accomplish in himself during the concentration. For, as the mystic would say, the carnal soul along with its band of mercenaries, passion, sensual pleasure and Satan, to begin with has complete sway over man's heart and demands absolute despotic power. By calling to mind the negation 'There is no god', man now intends to oppose the claims to dominion of this pseudo-god — high-handed egotism with its henchmen — and to eliminate its effects from his interior. By polarizing the attention on the affirmative clause 'but God', the person performing the exercise then acknowledges the one true God whose fighting forces are the human heart, knowledge, the Koran, imitation

---

2 Naturally, the exercise like so much else is traced back to a command of the Prophet. Cf. Aḥmad b. Muḥammad al-Qushāshī, *Al-simṭ al-majīd*, Hyderabad, 1327, p. 144: ʿAlī asked Muḥammad to show him the shortest, easiest and best way to God, whereupon Muḥammad recommended continuous recollection of God in spiritual seclusion.

3 This and other formulas are mentioned in Clément Huart, *Les saints des derviches tourneurs*, I, *Bibliothèque de l'École des Hautes Études*, sciences religieuses, vol. 32, 1918, p. 224. Whereas the Mawlawīs preferred *Allāh Allāh*, the Kubrawīs for example chose *lā ilāha illā'llāh*. Cf. ʿAbdallāh ibn-i Muḥammad-i Asadī, known as Najm al-Dīn Dāya, *Mirṣād al-ʿibād*, Tehran 1312/1352, p. 149; as well as the founder of the order Najm al-Dīn al-Kubrā.

of the Prophet and divine inspiration.[4] Continuously engaging the consciousness with no other content than God who in fact transcends the powers of conception, i.e. by concentrating on an inconceivable object but one worthy of striving after, was meant to empty the consciousness of all images and in that very way indirectly cause it to be receptive to the supernatural.

A text from the year 1223 gives us a description of the way and manner that the mystic performed the recollection of God in spiritual retreat. The novice sat with his legs folded under him, facing in the direction of Mecca (symbolic of turning toward God). He placed his hands on his thighs, closed his eyes and with inner commitment pronounced clearly and forcefully the words *lā ilāha illā'llāh* — but not out loud. While undertaking this, he strove as if to draw the negative *lā ilāha* 'There is no god' upward from his navel and to press the positive *illā'llāh* 'but God' downward from above into his heart, and did so in such a way that the effect and power of the mental visualization expanded from the heart into all his limbs.[5] An anonymous Arabic work from the years between 1512 and 1520 offers a more detailed description: If one wants to recollect God, one must perform a major ritual ablution, repent of all one's sins, purify one's clothing and sit in spiritual retreat with one's legs folded under one, facing toward the Kaᶜba, with hands on one's knees, the eyes closed, beginning the recollection by way of reverence, begging help from God, one's shaykh (master) and the shaykh of one's shaykh all the way back to the Apostle of God (Muḥammad, from whom the tradition of mystical knowledge and capacity was derived), while with lowered head one causes the *lā* to emerge from below the navel, then raises the head and says *ilāha*, at the same time inclining the head to the right, and then says *illā*, holding the head upright, and says *Allāh*, lowering the head to the left with a strong thrust (i.e. inner pressure) on the heart so that the effect of it goes out through all the limbs, with a gentle voice... but without causing the heart and tongue to be detached from the recollection of God, reflecting on the content of the recollection until this embraces all the limbs and settles within

---

4 Najm al-Dīn al-Kubrā (d. 1221), *Risāla ilā'l-hā'im al-khā'if*, MS Aya Sofya 2052, 64a-b. Dāya, *Mirṣād*, p. 149, compares the formula to the well-known Persian drink *sirkanjubīn* composed of vinegar (*sirka*) and honey (*anjubīn*) which was thought to eliminate the gall-like substance of forgetfulness of God. Others have compared the formula to a metallic polisher used to purify the mirror of the heart.

5 Dāya, *Mirṣād*, p. 151.

them.[6] — Thus recollecting God in spiritual retreat was accompanied with a regular movement of the head or the upper body.

Spiritual retreat as a rule lasted forty days. During this period the Sufi was required to be constantly in a state of ritual purity, he must only succumb to sleep after trying in vain to ward it off, and should limit his food intake to bread and salt.[7] The consequences of the ascetic exercise were a series of abnormal states like hallucinations in which the Sufi perceived the recollection of God as an independent visual or auditory entity outside himself, or other phenomena of an immaterial kind which he no longer interpreted as mere illusions and reminiscences from the world of the senses but as images of spiritual essences or as those essences themselves. The names for them were provided by religion. Similarly, God Himself could appear to him in images, although God stood by Himself behind all phenomena and by definition did not tolerate duality or multiplicity. Thus it was also necessary to penetrate the veil presented by these interior phenomena, and once again this was to be tackled through concentrating on the formula 'There is no god but God'.[8] The goal was to remove the opposition between the subject and the object of striving, the state concerning which Plotinus says: οὐδ' ἔτι δύο ἀλλὰ ἓν ἄμφω and an experience no longer of perception but of being or non-being: καὶ οὗτος (i.e. who or what appears) οὔ κατ' ὄψιν φανεὶς ἀλλὰ τὴν ψυχὴν ἐμπλήσας τοῦ θεωμένου (*Enneads* VI 7: 35).

One would be wrong in reproaching Sufism for wanting to force a path to God by means of this striving. The Sufis never believed in the possibility of self-redemption against the will of God. On the contrary, they were fully aware, and were frequently explicit in this regard, that the success of their undertaking and every single step along the way was only possible through God's grace and with His help, that in fact even their intention had only arisen because God had willed it.[9] None the less, one can say that the means they em-

---

6 Anonymous, *Tuḥfat al-sālikīn*, MS Fatih (Istanbul) 3567, 6b-7a. The work is otherwise largely plagiarized from Dāya's *Mirṣād*. — Along with the above-cited examples there are other forms of recollection of God which cannot be discussed here where it is only a question of presenting the bare fundamentals.

7 See Maḥmūd-i Kāshānī (d. 1335), *Miṣbāḥ al-hidāya*, Tehran, 1323, p. 166. This text is a reworking of Abū Ḥafṣ Suhrawardī's *ʿAwārif al-maʿārif*.

8 See the precise treatment of this subject in Najm al-Dīn al-Kubrā, *Fawāʾiḥ al-jamāl* (in the press).

9 Cf. also Julian Obermann: *Der philosophische und religiöse Subjektivismus Ghazalis*, Vienna-Leipzig, 1921, p. 175.

ployed demanded the commitment of their full power. They hoped, through their own exertion, to go beyond themselves.

(2)

The Sufis attempted to live in accordance with the Koranic injunction to recollect God morning and evening, i.e. at all times or at least as much as possible, among other things by placing the recollection of God at the center of their communal exercises.[10] Thus it happen that they remained together after the obligatory ritual prayers in order to repeat the formulas of recollecting God in a group.[11] In more recent times this form of the *dhikr* even acquired a special name. It is called *dhikr* of the hours (*dhikr al-waqt* or *dhikr al-awqāt*) because it is connected with the hours of the prayers. One distinguishes from this a third *dhikr* which, like the second, is also performed in a group, not every day however but only from time to time and on a larger scale. This is the so-called 'assembly-*dhikr*' (*dhikr al-ḥaḍra*).[12] Whether this distinction was already made in earlier times and when it arose is unknown to me. But we are informed that already in the 9th century at communally organized performances of the recollection of God powerful inner agitations were experienced which led to loud cries,[13] nor is there any doubt that

10 Ignaz Goldziher, *WZKM* 13, 1899. Muḥammad al-Ghazzālī: *Iḥyā' ᶜulūm al-dīn*, Cairo, 1348, I, p. 266 (*kitāb al-adhkār, bāb* 1, *faḍīlat majālis al-dhikr*). Dāya: *Mirṣād*, p. 146, l. 6 from bot. (*majālis-i dhikr*). Ibn ᶜAṭā'allāh al-Sikandarī (d. 1309): *Miftāḥ al-falāḥ*, Cairo, 1332, pp. 8, 13. Ibn Qayyim al-Jawziyya (d. 1350): *Al-wābil al-ṣayyib min al-kalim al-ṭayyib*, Cairo, 1373, p. 95. Qushāshī: *Simṭ*, p. 15, penult. line.

11 F. Meier: *Die Vita des Scheich Abū Isḥāq al-Kāzarūnī*, Bibliotheca Islamica 14, 1948, Introduction, p. 66. Aḥmad al-Ghazzālī: *Bawāriq al-ilmāᶜ*, in James Robson: *Tracts on Listening to Music*, Oriental Translation Fund, New Series 34, London, 1938, p. 105/167.

12 The only reports at my disposal are contradictory. Depont et Coppolani: *Les confréries religieuses musulmanes*, Algiers, 1897, p. 88, distinguish between 1) *dhikr al-waqt* = recollection of God in conjunction with the ritual prayers, 2) *dhikr al-jalāla* = recollection of God in spiritual seclusion, and 3) *dhikr al-ḥaḍra* = recollection of God in an assembly under the leadership of a master. On the other hand, Louis Petit: *Les confréries musulmanes*, Paris, 1899, p. 49, writes: 'Presque tous les ordres font une distinction entre le dikr quotidien ou dikr des heures (Dikr al-Aoukat), et le dikr solennel (Dikr el-Djellala), réservé aux cérémonies du culte, à celles du vendredi surtout.' According to this explanation, the *dhikr al-jalāla* in Petit would be identical with the *dhikr al-ḥaḍra* in Depont et Coppolani.

13 Abū Naṣr al-Sarrāj: *Al-lumaᶜ fī'l-taṣawwuf*, ed. R.A. Nicholson, Gibb Memorial Series 22, 1914, p. 285, l. 14.

these were indications of the kind of inner states characteristic of the phenomena we will be discussing in section (3) of this work. Here it may simply be noted that the movements in the modern forms of 'assembly-*dhikr*' are far more intense than those which served, and still serve, to focus the concentration in spiritual retreat. The participants no longer remain seated but raise themselves on their knees, in fact stand up and even move their feet. Moreover, in one and the same session a whole series of formulas can be recited in a more or a less orderly sequence. The goal in this case is not, as one might assume at least with regard to the '*dhikr* of the hours', a mere deepening and prolongation of worship, but to effect directly a dislocation of consciousness. This is certainly never achieved by all the participants and if someone succumbs to 'a state', the recitation of the whole group proceeds without him.

There are modern brotherhoods such as the Sanūsīs[14] who, besides the recollection in spiritual retreat, practice the *dhikr* of hours, and others, for example the Sammānīs in Cairo,[15] who in addition also practice the 'assembly-*dhikr*'. Particularly remarkable are the Raḥmānīs in Algeria. While reciting their formulas *Allāh* or *ḥayy*, they inhale and exhale using a strange breathing technique with heavy emphasis on the consonant *h* and making a sound that resembles sawing.[16]

(3)

Besides this there were also ecstatic states which were not brought about by means of concentration on the *dhikr*-formulas, nor by means of an active appeal to one's will, but which were caused by an

14 Louis Rinn: *Marabouts et khouan*, Algiers, 1884, pp. 503 f. = Depont et Coppolani, pp. 553 f.

15 Paul Kahle, *Der Islam* 6, 1916, pp. 167-69. According to J. Spencer Trimingham: *Islam in the Sudan*, Oxford University Press, 1949, p. 226, the Sammānīs are a branch of the Khalwatīs; according to Louis Massignon in his article 'ṭarīḳa' in *EI*, IV, they are a branch of the Shādhilīs. Paul Kahle, *Der Islam* 6, 1916, p. 154, agrees with Massignon. Louis Rinn: *Marabouts et khouan*, Algiers, 1884, p. 296, writes about the Khalwatīs that they are also familiar with a communal *dhikr* during which only one person pronounces the formulas. In the Sudan the Baytīs (a branch of the Shādhilīs), the Idrīsīs and the Tijānīs are said to practice pure *dhikr*; Trimignham, pp. 224, 230, 239.

16 W. Haas: 'Ein Dhikr der Rahmanija', *Der neue Orient* 1, 1917, pp. 210-13. Louis Massignon: 'L'idée de l'esprit dans l'Islam', *Eranos-Jahrbuch* 13, 1945, pp. 278 f. (also *JA* 234, 1943-45, pp. 437 f.).

impression from outside transmitted through the sense perceptions. We may call these passive, although some degree of being drawn along is also involved in the first case, and the case we will be discussing now also entails some active effort. The impression from outside, which is decisive in our second case, most often appears to have performed the function of a mnemonic trigger. The beautiful form of a human being, for example, could remind the mystic of the supernatural apparition of an angel or a prophet. According to Muḥammad al-Ghazzālī (d. 1111), the latter, if they revealed themselves to a visionary, frequently assumed the appearance of a well-formed human being. Thus beautiful human beings of flesh and blood could, for their part, evoke a 'supernatural' experience. In this case, higher experiences of the mystic were presupposed. But the beautiful individual could simply be perceived as a symbol for the beauty of God, who, as one heterodox doctrine in fact maintained, would one day reveal Himself as a fourteen-year-old boy. However, the mnemonic trigger could even be a word or a verse. The mystic felt reminded of his own inner situation or his relationship to God or, generally, some truth to do with the religious life.

Establishing connections of this sort was not difficult for the mystic, given the radicalism of his stance in life. He had placed his whole life under the perspective of his searching. There were rule books containing important regulations which dictated how one should behave when eating and drinking, pronouncing greetings and travelling, as well as the correct etiquette of dress. The Koran was interpreted with regard to one's own striving as a text denoting events in the psyche, and one read the book of nature, the signs of the time and poetry in a corresponding manner. Everywhere one found images, similes, allusions relevant to one's own situation. Indeed, as Muḥammad al-Ghazzālī says: 'The person whose heart is overwhelmed by something hears only this in everything he hears and sees only this in everything he sees. Whoever knows not the fire of love, whether it be real or vain love (i.e. religious or sensual love), cannot understand this.'[17]

The result of an impression which in this way touched delicate chords in the interior of the pious person was an emotional experience: sadness, joy, fear, hope, etc. Above all, a sense of nostalgic longing, a consciousness of not, or not yet, possessing something frequently appears to be triggered. The emotion could be still further intensified through aesthetic beauty in a case where the impression

---

17 *Kīmiyāy-i saʿādat*, Lucknow, 1333, p. 224.

was made by a visible object, through the expressive power of a verbal formulation in a case where it was a question of a verse or suchlike, or through the accompanying music where the arousal sprang from a song that was sung. Indeed, music just by itself could arouse feelings or intensify feelings that already existed.

The decisive point was reached when the disruption was so strong and the emotion so intense that the mystic lost self-control. In such a case, the Sufis speak of rapture or ecstasy (*wajd* or *ḥāl/ḥāla*). A consequence of this can be weeping, or letting out shouts or certain kinds of movement. But the mystic can also lose contact with his body to a greater or a lesser extent. He is then only capable of directing it imperfectly or not at all and only partially still receives impressions from outside. This is manifested, for example, by the fact that he becomes physically insensitive, makes inarticulate sounds, moves his limbs and body involuntarily, or cannot move at all, and turns pale. Occult phenomena can be associated with this situation, if one is to believe the tradition. A man in such a state stuck a lit candle in his eyes and suffered no injury. The informant claims to have seen a light or fire emanate from the eyes of the enraptured person and combat the flame of the candle.[18] Another individual took hold of glowing coals in his hands and was not burned.[19] Other people in this state are meant to have defied the laws of gravitational force and specific gravity by rising into the air[20] and walking on water.[21] One person ate nothing for twenty-four days and went on sweating all the while, though it was cold and he was only wearing a shirt.[22] Even being struck in the face with a sword is not supposed to have caused any pain.[23] In certain orders like the Rifāᶜīs, the Ḥaydarīs and the ᶜĪsawīs, for example, these phenomena were exploited as spectacles and to this day continue to be exploited as such.[24]

As for the inner state of the enraptured person, we learn very little. This is the case in part because the Sufis consider the experience to

---

18 Abū Ḥafṣ al-Suhrawardī: *ᶜAwārif al-maᶜārif*, Cairo, 1939, p. 133 (Chpt. 22).

19 Daylamī: *Vita des Ibn-i Khafīf*, MS Köprülü (Istanbul) 1589, 399a.

20 Suhrawardī: *ᶜAwārif*, p. 133. *Vita des Kāzarūnī*, ed. F. Meier, p. 494, ll. 14 ff. Max Horten, *Beiträge zur Kenntnis des Orients*, XII, 1915, p. 92. Jāmī: *Nafaḥāt*, ed. Nassau Lees, p. 490, l. 16.

21 *ᶜAwārif*, p. 133.

22 Sarrāj: *Lumaᶜ*, p. 307, ll. 4-7.

23 *Lumaᶜ*, p. 306, ll. 5-12.

24 Ibn Baṭṭūṭa: *Voyages*, ed. Defrémery and Sanguinetti, II, pp. 5-7. Edward W. Lane: *The Manners and Customs of the Modern Egyptians*, Chpt. 25.

be indescribable. Thus the earliest theorist on ecstasy, Ibn al-Aᶜrābī (d. 952-53), indicates that silence in the matter is the greatest eloquence.[25] And yet it is generally maintained that ecstasy achieved in this manner can also lead to inner vision, as in the case of the *dhikr* we discussed in sections (1) and (2). Frequently, however, the enraptured person falls into a swoon, i.e. loses consciousness, and not uncommonly, according to reports, ecstasy leads to death.

The following are some examples. When Aḥmad ibn Muqātil al-ᶜAkkī was once performing the prayers with Shiblī during a night of Ramaḍān (in the 10th century) and the prayer leader recited surah 17/86: 'If We so wished, We would remove what We have revealed to you', Shiblī cried out loud, his spirit took flight and his companion observed how his complexion turned sallow and he began shaking. Meanwhile, Shiblī went on repeating the words: 'Only loved ones are addressed like this.'[26] — When one time Junayd was speaking about love in the presence of his uncle and teacher Sarī al-Saqaṭī (9th century), the latter fell down as if lifeless and was 'absent'. Then his face turned red like a rose (*tawarrada*) so that it resembled the disk of the moon. Junayd relates: 'We could no longer gaze at him, he had become so beautiful, and we had to cover his face.'[27] — Another time two mystics who were out taking a stroll noticed a man on the roof of a house by the Tigris and heard a girl singing to him:

'Every day you are different. It would be seemlier were you not this way.
A love shown to you by me would be a martyr's sacrifice.'

Kulla yawmin tatalawwan, ghayru hādhā bika ajmal.
Fī sabīli'llāhi wuddun kāna minnī laka yubdhal.

Below the house stood a young Sufi in a patched frock with a leather bowl. He asked the girl to repeat the verses. She did so and the Sufi said: 'This refers to my own fickleness with relation to God.' He then let out a cry, gave praise to God and while the two men out for a stroll were watching, he fell down dead.[28] — Abū Ḥulmān al-Ṣūfī heard a street pedlar cry out: *Yā saᶜtarā barrī!* 'Wild thyme!' He fell

25 *Lumaᶜ* of Sarrāj, p. 313, ll. 6 ff.

26 *Lumaᶜ*, p. 282, ll. 17 ff. Qushayrī's *Risāla*, Cairo, 1346, pp. 155 f.

27 *Lumaᶜ*, p. 307, ll. 10-14.

28 *Lumaᶜ*, p. 286.

unconscious. When he was asked about what had happened, he replied that he had understood the cry as: *Isᶜa tarā birrī* (Exert yourself and you will experience my love).[29] A similar story is told about Rōzbihān-i Baqlī (d. 1210). In Shiraz he heard a greengrocer cry out: *ᶜĀshiq-i tara!* 'Lover of vegetables'. He understood the man's words as colloquial Arabic *ᶜāshiq tarā* (As a lover you will see) and he fell to the ground unconscious.[30] The Persian poet ᶜAṭṭār (12th to 13th century) in his *Ilāhīnāma* (ed. H. Ritter, p. 196, l. 17, to p. 197, l. 7) tells of the early Sufi Ibn-i Adham that one time he saw two men in the street bargaining. The buyer only wanted to pay one grain. The merchant finally shouted at him:

'I will not sell it for one grain, I will not sell it!'

Ba-yak jaw īn bi-nadham īn bi-nadham.

Ibn-i Adham threw up his hands like a bird flapping its wings — as the poet would have it — one minute losing consciousness, the next recovering himself. A passer-by asked the holy man what had happened. The Sufi replied: 'When he said *īn bi-nadham*, I thought he might have said Ibn-i Adham' (i.e. Ibn-i Adham is worth one grain). In a similar vein is the anecdote about Shiblī who once heard a merchant cry out: *Al-khiyār ᶜashara bi-dāniq!* 'Cucumbers, ten for one obole!' At that he is said to have let out a shout and remarked: 'If ten *khiyār* are only worth one obole, how do things stand with the *shirār* (the wicked)?'[31] In Arabic the word *khiyār*, besides meaning cucumbers, can also mean good people.

If one compares the circumstances in which these ecstatic states occurred, and the phenomena that accompanied them, with the materials on Christian ecstasy collected by Antoine Imbert-Gourbeyre in his book *La stigmatisation, l'extase divine et les miracles de*

---

29 *Lumaᶜ*, p. 289, ll. 7 ff. Later modified and expanded; Ibn ᶜAṭāʾallāh al-Sikandarī: *Laṭāʾif al-minan*, Cairo, n.d. (Maktaba ᶜAllāmiyya), pp. 93-94. On the word *saᶜtar* = satureia see Jean-Jacques Hess: 'Über das präfigierte und infigierte ᶜain im Arabischen', *Zeitschrift für Semitistik* 2, 1924, p. 221.

30 Ḥusayn-i Bāyqarā: *Majālis al-ᶜushshāq*, 17th *majlis*. Should one perhaps read *ᶜāshiqān-i tara* — *ᶜāshiqan tarā*? Another example of this kind occurs in Cl. Huart: *Les saints des derviches tourneurs*, I, p. 290 (*tilkü — dil kū*).

31 ᶜAbd al-Karīm al-Qushayrī's *Risāla*, Cairo, 1346, p. 157 (*bāb fī'l-samāᶜ*). Kāshānī: *Miṣbāḥ*, p. 193. Cf. also the examples in Ibn ᶜArabī: *Muḥāḍarat al-abrār*, Cairo, 1305, I, pp. 205 f.

Lourdes and more recently by Herbert Thurston in *The Physical Phenomena of Mysticism*, one is obliged to admit that from the psychological and the physical point of view the same events are taking place in both religious contexts. Gertrud Salandri experienced ecstasy while contemplating plants, flowers, fruits, and the sky, the sun, the stars, etc. St Magdalena of Pazzi reacted the same way to flowers and plants. Salvator of Horta experienced ecstasy by contemplating a pomegranate that had been cut open. Others reacted to the sight of blood which reminded them of the blood shed by Christ. Joseph of Copertino was overcome with ecstasy by contemplating the picture of a saint, as was Blasius of Caltanisetta in the presence of beautiful women, who immediately reminded him of the Virgin Mary.[32] Or it was enough to hear a name such as Jesus, Mary, Paradise, angel, St Francis, etc., a phrase such as *Verbum caro factum est*, a hymn such as *Jesu dulcis memoria*, *Veni creator spiritus*, a sermon,[33] a conversation or a prayer, the sound of a bell or an organ. Therese Neumann only had to recall certain of her own visionary experiences in order to turn pale and assume the condition of a corpse. When she recited the Our Father, she never got further than 'Give us this day our daily bread', remarking 'By the third or fourth request it already takes hold of me'.[34] She would enter into what the theologians call her ecstasy of love. It was thought possible she would one day die under the effect of such an emotion.

When entering an ecstatic state, the Christian mystic as well can shake, moan and let out shouts.[35] A distinction is made between mobile and immobile ecstasy.[36] In the mobile kind the person experiencing ecstasy walks, gesticulates, speaks, sings, moans, sheds tears or remains motionless for some moments.[37] In a state of immobile ecstasy the limbs are more or less rigid as with a corpse. The individual in question closes his eyes and turns pale or opens wide his eyes and through his facial expression gives some inkling of what is occurring inside him. Also characteristic in this case is the external insensitivity of the ecstatic person. He neither reacts to physical contacts, nor to influences from the other senses, except perhaps

---

32 Imbert-Gourbeyre, pp. 242 f.

33 Ibid., pp. 241 f.

34 Helmut Fahsel: *Therese Neumann von Konnersreuth*, Basle, 1949, p. 24.

35 Imbert-Gourbeyre, pp. 245-47.

36 Ibid., p. 240.

37 Ibid., pp. 277 f.

through the ear.[38] Fire is unable to burn him or water to make him wet. Levitation, which was frequently reported, caused a particular sensation: the person experiencing ecstasy would be raised into the air and remain in this floating state for some time.

However, between the Christian and the Islamic experiences of ecstasy there was the fundamental difference that even in early times the Sufis no longer left the means of stimulation entirely to chance, but often consciously provided them. Of course, St Francis of Assisi also contemplated nature, the sun, the birds, Ignatius Loyola gazed at the flowers and the star-filled heavens, in order to cause themselves to be swept away by a higher experience.[39] What to some extent corresponds to this in Islam is the fact that Aḥmad al-Ghazzālī, the brother of the above-mentioned Muḥammad al-Ghazzālī, at one time alternately contemplated a beautiful youth and a rose in order to achieve a divine experience.[40] On the other hand, the forms of stimulation characteristic of Islamic ecstasy were sought after by the Sufis on occasions when they would assemble communally.

Polemical writings against Sufism have left us the information that the central focus of these occasions was at times a beautiful youth. One such text from the 12th century reports: 'They often decorate him with jewelry, bright clothing and bright braid trimming believing that they can achieve an increase in their faith by gazing upon him, meditating on this and drawing inferences about the Creator on the basis of (the beauty of) His creation.'[41] None the less, practices of this kind were the exception, indeed most Sufis rejected the use of such means because the danger of slipping to a lower sexual level was too great. Instead they recommended, or they allowed, 'listening' as a more mental activity, which is why the technical designation of these communal occasions for inducing ecstasy came to be *samāᶜ* 'listening'.

This designation corresponds to the designation of a profane social gathering, an evening of musical entertainment, and the Sufi *samāᶜ* was nothing other than an appropriation of this profane activity. What one listened to were songs which a singer performed and which could be accompanied with musical instruments. We know

---

38 Ibid., pp. 248 ff., 234.

39 Joseph Maréchal, S.J.: *Études sur la psychologie des mystiques*, Paris, 1924, I, p. 209.

40 Ibn al-Jawzī: *Talbīs Iblīs*, Cairo, 1928, p. 267.

41 Ibid., p. 268.

that itinerant musicians, for instance, were hired for this purpose.[42] Sufi theorists define precisely which instruments are allowed, what the qualities of the singer should be and what kind of songs are not suitable for a mystical *samāʿ*. These rules were considered to be necessary, on the one hand, in order to set apart the Sufi *samāʿ* from its profane counterpart and, on the other hand, to keep it in agreement with the religious legal prescriptions. But in practice the rules were so different from one another and so often transgressed that in this short overview we will have to confine ourself to the fundamental observation that by and large everything in these performances functioned in symbolic terms. The performed musical pieces were mostly love songs which were intended in a purely earthly sense by the poet. It was the task of the Sufi to reinterpret them, and Muḥammad al-Ghazzālī (d. 1111) in his chief work *The Revivification of the Theological Sciences* (*Iḥyāʾ ʿulūm al-dīn*) already gives some idea of how reinterpretation of this kind could be carried out. The black locks of the beloved's temples about which the poet sings could be understood, for example, as the darkness of unbelief, their opposite, the shining cheeks, as the light of faith. Union with the beloved could be taken as an image for reaching God, separation from the beloved as an image for damnation, the observer who disturbs the lover's tryst as an image for the worldly ties which hinder any duration of intimacy with God.[43] In his Persian summary of the above-mentioned work, *The Elixir of Happiness* (*Kīmiyāy-i saʿādat*), Ghazzālī presents a quatrain and fragments of other quatrains which he analyzes according to this principle.[44] In the wake of these suggestions a series of small treatises and word lists on the symbolism of wine and love poetry were composed at a later date, mainly on Persian soil and with reference to Persian vocabu-

---

42 Daylamī: *Vita des Ibn-i Khafīf*, 402b. Muḥammad ibn-i Munawwar: *Asrār al-tawḥīd fī maqāmāt al-shaykh Abī Saʿīd*, ed. Dhabīḥallāh Ṣafā, Tehran, 1953, pp. 103 f./ed. Muḥammad Riḍā Shafīʿī-i Kadkanī, Tehran, 1366, p. 95 f./trans. by John O'Kane, *The Secrets of God's Mystical Oneness*, Persian Heritage Series no. 38, Costa Mesa (Calif.)-New York, 1992, p. 179 f. Abū'l-Najīb al-Suhrawardī: *Ādāb al-murīdīn*, MS Köprülü 702, 61b, tells of non-Sufis who can be employed to perform the songs, and moreover distinguishes between hired (*ajīr*) and voluntary (*mutabarriʿ*) performers; the latter could come from Sufi circles.

43 *Iḥyāʾ*, 8th Book of Part IV on *ʿādāt*, Cairo, 1348, II, pp. 236 ff. Translated by Duncan B. MacDonald: 'Ghazzālī on Listening to Music', *JRAS* 1901-1902. The above passage in *Iḥyāʾ*, II, p. 249.

44 *Kīmiyā*, p. 223.

lary.[45] Then not only were the great lyric poets of Persia such as Ḥāfiẓ, for example, reinterpreted mystically along the lines of these writings, but the Sufis themselves also produced poems which on the surface appear to be profane, but which, from the outset, were based on an interpretatio mystica. However, Muḥammad al-Ghazzālī stresses that one and the same poem can be interpreted differently by every mystic, in accordance with his personal association of ideas. According to Ghazzālī: 'His particular understanding does not have to agree with the poet's intention and the sense the latter gave to the words.'[46] What matters is that something in the poem 'coincides with the mystic's situation so that like steel it strikes sparks from the flints in his heart' and thus causes the fire which one calls ecstasy.[47]

Just as with the comprehension of the performed song, in these artificial, domesticated forms of listening to music the emotion as well is steered down particular paths. The most frequent movements by means of which ecstasy was induced and fostered were those of dance. In this regard one may translate the term *samāᶜ* simply as dervish dance (dervish is a Persian designation for mystic). However, the way it arises shows from the beginning that in this case we are clearly not dealing with a regulated circle dance. First of all, theorists expressly state that one should suppress any form of movement as long as possible and only give oneself over to it if one can no longer fend off the dominance of the emotion. Thus the dance was an expression and a consequence of a loss of self. Secondly, the moment in time and the intensity of such a disempowerment of self were different in each individual so that one person would be moved earlier, another later; one more deeply, another more lightly. The result was people would stand up and sit down in a disorderly fashion, or go off in different directions. In the 9th century a shaykh from Baghdad compared the Sufis during a *samāᶜ* to a herd of sheep into which wolves had made their way.[48] And yet, several concessions led to a certain degree of leveling out. Firstly, it was allowed to make artificial movements (*tawājud*) as long as one was not shamming a

---

45 I will only mention Yaḥyā ibn-i Sayf al-Dīn-i Bākharzī (circa 1300), MS Aya Sofya 4792, 628a-633b; ᶜAlī-i Hamadānī (d. 1385), MS Velieddin (Istanbul) 1799, 139b-140a. Cf. E.H. Palmer: *Oriental Mysticism*, Second Edition by A.J. Arberry, London, 1938, pp. 69-81. Muḥsin-i Fayḍ-i Kāshānī (d. 1680): *Risāla-i mishwāq*, in Arberry: *Sufism*, London, 1950, pp. 113 f.

46 *Iḥyāʾ*, II, pp. 249, 254, 255.

47 *Iḥyāʾ*, II, p. 254.

48 *Lumaᶜ*, p. 288, ll. 14-15. Qushayrī, p. 156, l. 3 from bot.

false state but was attempting by this means to enter into genuine ecstaty. Secondly, there was the rule of joining in based on solidarity (*muwāfaqa*). This meant that if someone of higher rank experienced genuine ecstasy, the others should go along with it, out of politeness and in order not to disturb him. Thirdly, when an authoritative person was present, one was always obliged to give him precedence, i.e. not to allow oneself to be swept away in any movements as long as that respected individual had not been swept away, nor to remain in a state of ecstasy longer than he did. Moreover, the earliest texts already make it clear that the dance often consisted of rotating around one's own axis and also often involved an ongoing motion along the circumference of a circle.

The dance could be accompanied by inarticulate sounds. In Persian texts I have met with the expressive exclamations *ᶜāw ᶜūy*[49] and *kakh kukh*.[50] Not infrequently the person experiencing ecstasy lost his turban, or he threw off an item of clothing or tore it up. According to the Sufi viewpoint, by throwing off a piece of clothing or tearing it, one forfeited one's right of ownership over the item, which led to discussion of the question of whom it then belonged to. In the treatment of this question considerations of the conventions of warfare come into play. The person who entered ecstasy was viewed as someone who had been fatally wounded and the apparel was allotted to the singer because the arms of a casualty belong to the victor,[51] or the decision was delegated to the shaykh who was present, just as the distribution of war booty came under the jurisdiction of the military leader.[52] That the singer acquired the cast-off clothing was strictly speaking a custom that originated in the area of profane entertainment. It was already a custom among ancient Arabian carousers to give items of clothing to the female singers as a reward.[53] Even the Prophet himself had once thrown his mantle over

---

49 Aḥmad-i Jām (d. 1141): *Miftāḥ al-najāt*, MS Aya Sofya 1728, 69a.

50 Ibid. and Asadī: *Lughat-i Furs*, ed. ᶜAbbās Iqbāl, Tehran, 1319, p. 84. From this must be distinguished the Arabic command to children to leave something alone: *kikh kikh*; Zamakhsharī: *Al-fāʾiq*, Cairo, 1947, II, pp. 370, 398 f.

51 Hujwīrī: *Kashf al-maḥjūb*, ed. Zhukovski, Leningrad, 1926, p. 544, ll. 9-12. Nicholson's translation (Gibb Memorial Series 17), 2nd edition 1936, p. 418. *ᶜAwārif*, p. 146. Kāshānī, p. 199.

52 Hujwīrī, p. 544, ll. 12-15. Trans. by Nicholson, p. 418.

53 Georg Jacob: *Altarabisches Beduinenleben*², Berlin, 1897, p. 103. Clothing was often bestowed upon Western musicians as well; Wilhelm Hertz: *Spielmannsbuch*², Stuttgart, 1900, pp. 12 f.

the shoulders of a poet as a reward.[54] In the Islamic period similar behavior was current during musical performances at the court and in taverns. The situation was somewhat different regarding torn items of clothing. After the performance these were cut into smaller pieces by the shaykh and distributed among the participants. The purpose of distributing them was to convey to those present the *baraka*, the blessing, which was inherent in such a piece of clothing. As Abū Ḥafṣ al-Suhrawardī (d. 1235) states: 'Ecstasy is an effect of God's grace, and tearing a piece of clothing (in a state of rapture) is, for its part, an effect of ecstasy. Thus the piece of clothing carries with it a trace of a divine action.'[55] The Sufis made use of the scraps of cloth by sewing them on their clothing and their prayer-rugs.

The *samāᶜ*, as sketched here, differs quite sharply in more than one respect from the *dhikr*, the recollection of God, as we have described it in sections (1) and (2). In the *dhikr* the person exerting himself invokes his own forces, whereas in the *samāᶜ* he waits for an inducement to experience to arrive from outside; in the one he speaks, in the other he listens. The *dhikr*, the recollection of God, is not only allowed at any time of day or night, but actually forms an indispensable component of the Sufi curriculum and work routine, especially as a formula of concentration in spiritual retreat. The *samāᶜ*, by contrast, was almost always only a concession (*rukhṣa*), was frequently performed within the framework of entertainment, but by many Sufis was virtually considered a malignant growth on the body of Sufi community life and combatted as such. On the other hand, certain convergences also come to light such as the liberation of the body common to both exercises, and the ecstatic emotions one observes in both the *dhikr*- and the *samāᶜ*-gatherings.

---

54 Kaᶜb ibn Zuhayr for his poem *Bānat Suᶜād*. But this gesture can be understood differently: 'Such an action was the customary practice in pagan times to bestow unlimited protection against all and everyone upon the person upon (sic) it was bestowed'; F. Krenkow in Tadeusz Kowalski: *Le dîwân de Kaᶜb ibn Zuhair*, Cracow, 1950, p. VII. Other examples of this protective ceremony are given by Julius Wellhausen in *Archiv für Religionswissenschaft* 7, 1904, pp. 40-41. Likewise, to cover with a mantle also signifies seizing and laying claim to something, Wellhausen: *Muhammed in Medina*, pp. 229-30.

55 *ᶜAwārif*, p. 145. Not in Kāshānī. Similarly, one conceived the effect of investing a Sufi with a patched frock as transference of sacred power from the donator to the receiver; Qushāshī: *Simṭ*, pp. 95, 115.

(4)

Despite the numerous attacks which it was exposed to even within Sufi circles, the *samāʿ*, listening to music, has weathered the passage of time and even managed to survive, if in adapted forms, down to our own day and age. I will only mention two of these adapted forms, both of which are characterized by a new evaluation of the *dance*. We have seen that hearing and, in some circumstances, gazing on a beautiful person, for example the singer himself, were used as means to induce ecstasy. Moreover, in many cases the artificial movement of the body (*tawājud*) was allowed as well. But dancing was exclusively meant to be the result and the expression of experiencing ecstasy.

In the environment of the Mawlawī order, which was founded in Anatolia in the 13th century by Mawlānā Jalāl al-Dīn-i Rūmī, the dance developed into an obligatory means of inducing ecstasy, i.e. in the series of preparations before an experience it occupied the position of *tawājud*, which naturally entailed a change in its character. Among the Mawlawīs it turned into a well-rehearsed circle dance. The participants, who had sat down in a circle and at a certain moment in the performance stand up, dance in an ordered circle while continuously rotating about themselves and with their arms and head held in prescribed positions. When the dance begins and ends is defined by the music. Here ecstasy is no longer the cause but the goal of the dance. Actually, the Mawlawīs themselves often conceive of their circle dance as the ritual enactment of cosmic events, as a symbol for truths of their world view, such as for example the self-unfolding of the primeval One into the world or the circle dance of the planets around their Prime Mover. But the practical purpose of the dance is to induce ecstasy.[56] The form in which the dance is still performed today is meant to go back to the beginnings of the order and to have originated with Sulṭān Walad, the son and successor of the founder, after whom part of the performance is named and who, as head of the order from 1284 to 1312, gave it a thoroughly organized form.[57] The Turks designate the Mawlawīs, because of their dance concerts and in contrast to all other orders, as the *semâ'î dervişler*,

---

56 Hellmut Ritter: 'Der Reigen der "tanzenden Derwische"', *Zeitschrift für vergleichende Musikwissenschaft* 1, 1933, pp. 28-40.

57 Hellmut Ritter: 'Philologika XI', *Der Islam* 26, 1940, pp. 125-27. The part of the dance which bears Walad's name is the *devre-i velediyye*.

'Sufis who practice listening to music',[58] and European observers have given them the name 'dancing dervishes'.

But the ᶜĪsawīs of North Africa and Egypt (founded in the 16th century by Muḥammad b. ᶜĪsā) are also dancing dervishes in the sense that ecstasy is meant to be induced by dancing. To the sound of their own peculiar tambourines and a small kettledrum they perform wild, irregular leaps, strange gestures and rotations and from time to time shout out 'God' and 'God is our Lord' in order to work themselves up into a state in which they can place glowing coals in their mouth, etc.[59]

It is quite possible that in both the above-mentioned variants foreign influences have played a role.

(5)

Up to this point in our presentation we have treated the recollection of God (*dhikr*) and listening to music (*samāᶜ*) as two separate sets of practices in Sufism. However, there are also types of dervish dancing, if we may now use this expression in a more vague, generalized sense, in which *both elements are joined together*. In such cases one must distinguish between two lines. The first of these represents a type in which *dhikr*, the recollection of God, is either included in, or preliminary and subordinated to, the *samāᶜ*, listening to music.

From Aḥmad al-Ghazzālī, who died in 1123, we know that *samāᶜ*-performances frequently took place after ritual prayer. But between the two activities, Koranic or *dhikr*-recitations could still be inserted, in the manner that these were practiced in Sufi circles. The *samāᶜ*, listening to music, was begun once these supplementary devotional exercises were over. We are not told why but may surmise that the times after an obligatory religious activity such as ritual prayer, when the Sufis were still gathered together, offered the best opportunity for further group practices. From what Aḥmad says it is

---

58 A communication from Professor Hellmut Ritter, Frankfurt am Main.

59 Lane: *Manners and Customs*, Chpt. 25. Rinn: *Marabouts*, p. 329, does not speak of dancing but only of invocations to God which were accompanied by drums and became increasingly faster. The result of the exercises was physical insensitivity, hallucinations, etc. According to Henry Lansdell: *Russisch-Central-Asien*, German edition by H. von Wobeser, Leipzig, 1885, III, pp. 789 f., the Qalandars (sic) are or were also dancers. Rinn, p. 394, says the Ḥanṣalīs as well dance (and sing). Depont et Coppolani, p. 160, speak of a 'valse frénétique à laquelle ils (viz. the ᶜAmmārīs) se livrent', while flutes and tambourines are played. According to Depont et Coppolani, p. 159, the Saᶜdīs (a branch of the Rifāᶜīs) also dance.

also perfectly clear that the recollection of God or the Koranic recitation formed the conclusion to the ritual prayers and not an introduction to listening to music.[60] At that time these elements were still separate from one another.

The situation changes in the 13th century. In a Persian treatise by Yaḥyā ibn-i Sayf al-Dīn-i Bākharzī, or more precisely an excerpt from it, several reports are found about the author's grandfather, the mystic Sayf al-Dīn-i Bākharzī, who died in the year 1260 and is buried in Bukhara. In one of these reports we learn that on a particular occasion they performed the *samāᶜ* in Sayf al-Dīn's presence but no one managed to achieve 'an experience' (*dhawq*). Then Sayf al-Dīn ordered a communal *dhikr*-exercise (*ḥalqa-i dhikr*) and said: 'Recite the recollection of God so that the turbidity of the moment (or the turbidity which hinders contact with God, the 'Nu' of Meister Eckhart — *kudūrat-i waqt*) be transformed into purity.'[61]

Here as well listening to music and recollection of God are still two separate exercises. A session of listening to music is interrupted in order to interpolate an exercise of recollecting God. Beyond that the combination is not yet a regular arrangement in its own right but is only intended for a performance in which ecstasy has not made an appearance. But in this way the foundation was laid: concentration on the *dhikr*-formula was placed in the service of listening to music. Bākharzī himself gives the explanation for this. He ascribes to the recollection of God the power to remove psychic obstacles which block the experience of ecstasy during the *samāᶜ*.

The next stage in this process of combining the *samāᶜ* and the *dhikr* was that the recollection of God was prefixed to the *samāᶜ* as a preliminary part of the program in order to clear the way. This stage appears to have been reached by the Rifāᶜīs of the 14th century concerning whom the Arab world-traveller Ibn Baṭṭūṭa has left us an eye-witness account from Wāsiṭ in Mesopotamia.[62]

A modern form of this combination would appear to be the *ḥadra* (religious gathering) of the ᶜAmmārīs in Morocco, if in fact 'the few formulas' which the assembled brethren at first recite are actually

---

60 *Bawāriq al-ilmāᶜ* in James Robson, p. 105/167.

61 *Muntakhab min al-risāla* <*allatī*> *ṣannafahā al-shaykh Yaḥyā*, etc., MS Aya Sofya 4729, 630a, ll. 7-9: *Pēsh-i shaykh Sayf al-Dīn-i Bākharzī... rōzē samāᶜ kardand. Hēch dhawqē pēdhā na-shudh. Shaykh ḥalqa-i dhikrē bunyādh kard u-guft: Dhikr gōyēdh tā kudūrat-i waqt ba-ṣafā mubaddal gardadh!*

62 *Voyages*, II, p. 5. The translation given there 'ils se mirent à chanter les louanges de Dieu' would be better translated as 'ils se mirent à réciter le *dhikr*'.

dhikr-formulas. Following the communal recitation, a flute and a kind of tambourine are played, the sounds of which gradually cause the participants who are seated in a circle to work themselves into the sought after ecstasy and to perform a kind of dance, as well as to be able to have needles stuck into their body.[63]

The *second* combination which will be considered here represents a type in which the *dhikr* is not, as above, incorporated in and subordinated to, the *samāᶜ*, but the relationship is in fact reversed. Thus this hybrid form rightly bears the name *dhikr*, and not *samāᶜ*. Clear evidence of this form comes to us from the 16th century, having been brought to light by Fuad Köprülü (the present Secretary of State of Turkey), and concerns the Turkish order of the Yesevis. In a description of their gatherings it is stated: 'Afterwards everyone sits down and then, with awe and reverence, they engage in the recollection of God (*dhikr*) until midnight. In between, the spiritual songs of the Yesevi shaykhs known as "wisdom" (*ḥikmet*) are performed with a sorrowful voice and gripping emotion in order to arouse the dervishes and cause them to heat up.'[64] Consequently, it is no longer the *dhikr*, the recollection of God, which is meant to arouse the mystics so that, as in the case of Bākharzī, they have an experience during the *samāᶜ*, listening to music, but the other way round: the *samāᶜ* is meant to make it possible for them to have an experience during the *dhikr*.

In the modern forms of this type, which one may frequently observe, the parts of the performance when the participants listen to a song in silence represent, as one would expect, no more than rest

---

63 W. Haas: 'Eine Ordensübung der Ammaria', *Der neue Orient* 2, 1918, pp. 253-56. Cf. Depont et Coppolani, p. 160.

64 Köprülüzâde Mehmed Fuʾâd: *İlk mutasavvıflar*, Istanbul, 1918, p. 118. This information comes from Ḥazīnī under Murad III (16th century) and should not automatically be transferred to the founder of the order (11th century) as Theodor Menzel does (*Mitteilungen für Orientalische Sprachen Berlin* 28, 1925, p. 95). For our purposes there is nothing to be had from Köprülüzâde's 'Influence du chamanisme turco-mongol sur les ordres mystiques musulmans' (*Mémoires de l'Institut de Turcologie de l'Université de Stamboul*, N.S. 1, 1929). One should be expressly warned against the view that the dervish dance comes from shamanistic Turks or was at least introduced into Sufism through their influence. Naturally there is also no question of a direct connection with the dance of the Bacchanals, the priests of Cybele or of Baal, although morphological similarities may exist. And equally false is the assumption of M.M. Moreno (in *Annali Lateranensi* 10, 1946, p. 109) that listening to music originates with Christians who converted to Islam; that the attitude of many Sufis to listening to music recalls similar problems among Christians is another matter.

periods and interludes. The real activity is the *dhikr*, the communal recollection of God. However, the parts involving *samāᶜ* and *dhikr* do not necessarily have to alternate with one another in a temporal sequence but they can occur simultaneously, in which case the continuous repetition of the *dhikr*-formula by the participants forms the accompaniment, the grounding, the *basso ostinato* or a kind of refrain to the song being performed.

In this combination the *samāᶜ* has lost the dance. It now only involves listening. On the other hand, the *dhikr* has maintained and intensified the movements with which it had already been accompanied earlier when practiced in spiritual retirement. In this combination in which the *dhikr* forms the accompaniment to the rendition of the song, one may view the movements (just as one may view the circle dance among the Mawlawīs and the leaping among the ᶜĪsawīs) as a new form of *tawājud* — the artificial movement to induce or to relieve ecstasy. The movements differ depending on which of the *dhikr*-formulas one concentrates on, and it is common for these formulas to alternate not only from one order to another but within one and the same performance so that the exercise can be broken down into separate sections, scenes or segments.

The Ḍayfīs[65] of Alexandria, who gather together every Sunday and Wednesday in a small mosque of the Mazarita quarter, customarily begin with the formula *lā ilāha illā'llāh*. I visited them on April 21st, 1948, at 10 in the evening and found them seated in two rows facing one another. At the upper end, between the two rows, sat a singer who was also the leader, and sitting beside him was a boy. The participants recited the formula with a sluggish rhythm, from time to time urged on by the leader who would clap his hands, and they alternately leaned their body to the right and to the left. After many repetitions the leader quickened the pace and then finally ordered a halt by drawing out the length of the final syllable *-lāh*. This was one section, which consisted of pure *dhikr*.

There then followed a song performed by the leader, slow and very elegiac, at times very expressive. He leaned alternately to the right and to the left, faltered, broke off and then began once again. The participants sat still and listened. This was pure *samāᶜ*.

Then in chorus everyone intoned a new formula: *Huwa'llāh huwa'llāh* (or *Huwa'llāhu Allāh*?) 'He is God, He is God' with a shift in accent, the first time with two stresses — i.e. on the first and

65 A branch of the Khalwatiyya; Paul Kahle in: *Der Islam* 6, 1916, p. 155; Louis Massignon in *EI* s.v. ṭarīḳa (s.n. khalwatīya).

the last syllable (*húwa'lláh*), the second time with stress only on the middle syllable (*huwá'llāh*). When putting the stress on *hú*, they flung their body to the right, when stressing the syllable *-láh*, their body was in a vertical position, and when stressing the *-ál*, they flung their body to the left. While the participants recited the formula and moved mechanically to the right and the left, the singer and the boy at his side sang an enchanting melody during the short breaks which occurred each time between completing the individual formulas. During this exercise, which went on for quite a long time, the tempo was also increased toward the end, and the movements became wild. I heard shouts. This segment represented a mixture of *samā*^{c} and *dhikr*.

Then there followed a solo performance by the singer. The participants sat listening and the mosque attendant fumigated the premises with incense from a brazier. This was pure *samā*^{c}.

Then once again everyone joined in. The singer sang a song (*samā*^{c}), and the participants repeated in chorus the single word *Allāh Allāh...*, rhythmically rocking their upper body back and forth while in a seated position (*dhikr*). After a while they intensified their voice and the pace, and raised themselves from the seated position onto their knees. Finally, they stood up completely, all the while moving their upper body to the right and to the left, and steadily becoming wilder. This was *dhikr* together with *samā*^{c}.

The next part once again consisted of pure *samā*^{c} — a solo performance by the lead singer. In the meantime another singer had arrived. Likewise, new participants had turned up.

Afterwards there was yet another section combining *samā*^{c} and *dhikr*. By now the *dhikr*-formula of the chorus had been reduced to the bare consonant *h*, the ultimate abbreviation of *Allāh* or *huwa* 'He'. The participants were in a standing position and, with each *h* that they uttered with a rasping breath, they turned their torso in a jerky fashion to the right and to the left, swinging their arms. At the same time the boy sang a beautiful song in a fine child's voice, while the lead singer clapped his hands with the rhythm of an anapest (⏑⏑–), turning first to the right and then to the left, with the main beat coming each time on the *h* of the participants. Toward the end the tempo accelerated. I left the gathering before the conclusion of the performance.

Similar combinations of *dhikr* with *samā*ᶜ are confirmed for the Shādhilīs in Alexandria,[66] but are also attested for many other orders, indeed for the majority of them,[67] including the Jahrīs in Samarqand[68] and the present-day Rifāᶜīs.[69] The common characteristic of these exercises is the subordination or the total absence of musical instruments and the prominent use made of the human voice, in particular the monotone manner of crying out the *dhikr*-formula. For this reason, not unjustly, European observers have dubbed them 'the howling dervishes', a term which is sometimes reserved for the Rifāᶜīs,[70] but sometimes also applied to the other representatives of the *dhikr-samā*ᶜ combination just described, or at least to one portion of them.[71] Moreover, the brotherhoods which only practice communal *dhikr* without mixing in *samā*ᶜ elements — we touched on them in section (2) — can also be rightly classified under the label of howling dervishes. However, the simple dichotomy of the whole of Sufism into howling and dancing dervishes is not feasible because of the various forms of combination and overlapping that exist. In this regard, I might add that I have completely left aside certain phenomena which could also have been taken into account but which, from the outset, would have disrupted our ordering (I have in mind, for example, flagellation as it is

---

66 Visited by myself in the Mosque Abū'l-ᶜAbbās al-Mursī of Alexandria at midday Friday, April the 2nd, 1948.

67 Lane: *Manners*, Chpt. 25. Idem: *Arabian Society in the Middle Ages*, London, 1883, pp. 72-77 (written 1837, one year after *Manners*). Cf. also the Darqāwa in Fez according to the memories of a Moroccan in Émile Dermenghem: *L'éloge du vin (al Khamriya)*, Paris, 1931, p. 64, ftn. 1. Rinn accords with this: *Marabouts et khouan*, Algiers, 1884, p. 247 (but p. 233 'dancing'). Similarly the Qādirīs and ᶜArūsīs in Depont et Coppolani: *Les confréries religieuses musulmanes*, Algiers, 1897, pp. 157 f., 342-45, as well as the Mirghanīs, Qādirīs, Ismāᶜīlīs, and ᶜAzmīs in the Sudan; J. Spencer Trimingham: *Islam in the Sudan*, pp. 215 ff., 222, 236, 240.

68 Henry Lansdell: *Russisch-Central-Asien nebst Kuldscha, Buchara, Chiwa und Merw*, German edition by H. von Wobeser, Leipzig, 1885, III, pp. 787 f.

69 D'Ohsson: *Tableau général de l'Empire Othoman*, IV, Paris, 1791, pp. 641 ff. John P. Brown: *The Dervishes; or, Oriental Spiritualism*, London, 1868, pp. 219 ff. Additional material (but for our purposes insufficiently recorded) in Richard Reusch: *Der Islam in Ost-Afrika mit besonderer Berücksichtigung der muhammedanischen Geheim-Orden*, Leipzig, 1930, pp. 128 ff. Von Maltzan: *Drei Jahre im Nordwesten von Afrika*2, Leipzig, 1868, IV, pp. 276 ff. (cited in Édouard Montet: *Études orientales et religieuses*, Genève-Paris, 1917, pp. 142 ff.).

70 John Brown, pp. 113 ff.

71 Lane: *Manners*, Chpt. 24 (= Everyman's Library No. 315, p. 461, ftn. 1).

practiced in some brotherhoods). Instead, we would like to note as the general results of our survey that the following larger communal exercises are practiced by the Sufis:

1. a pure form of *dhikr* (the recollection of God within the large framework of a communal performance);
2. the *samāᶜ* (listening to music, and dance);
3. hybrid forms combining *dhikr* and *samāᶜ*, including:
    a) cases in which the *dhikr* is subordinated to *samāᶜ*, and
    b) cases in which the *samāᶜ* is subordinated to *dhikr*.

In this enumeration *dhikr* in spiritual retirement is not included. It forms the common denominator in all Sufism, even if today there are orders and groups of people who consider it to be a privilege reserved for the élite.[72]

This, in broad outline, is the picture which in my view the relationship between recollection of God and listening to music presents in Islam. Given the contemporary limits of scholarly research, these contours are probably far too sharply drawn. I have already given an indication of the desiderata: there has not been a collection and assessment of all the historical traditions concerning *dhikr* and *samāᶜ*, and similarly there is a serious lack of precise information about the pertinent exercises as practiced in contemporary Sufi circles. And here everything depends on completeness and accuracy. Each phenomenon can be decisive for classification, and the ordering principles themselves can only be deduced from the data. But precisely because not enough has yet been done in this area, I felt obliged to draw the lines as sharply as possible in order to make evident the problems and to indicate the direction one might take to progress beyond the collections compiled to date which to some extent lack a clear orientation.

A further question which must be left for the future has to do with assessing the course of historical development. In this area it will be advisable to group together only what properly belongs together, i.e. the development of the recollection of God as practiced in spiritual retirement should not be lumped together with the communal recollection of God, and the degeneration on the part of the *samāᶜ*

72 R.P. Louis Petit: *Les confréries musulmanes*, Paris, 1899, p. 46: 'Pour eux (viz. les Khelouatiya)... elle (viz. la Kheloua) est de rigueur, au lieu d'être réservée, comme dans les autres ordres, à un petit nombre de sujets d'élites.' Trimingham, *Islam in the Sudan*, p. 212: 'the Sûdânî is content to leave contemplative methods to more mystically minded races.' D'Ohsson: *Tableau général*, IV, p. 658 ff.

should not be transposed to the whole of Sufism without qualification. Naturally, a precise investigation of the complete spiritual world of a modern Sufi, from his external practices to the innermost secrets of his thought and belief, would be extemely worthwile. It will not do, however, simply to compare a sample of this kind from a random present-day Sufi with the statements of a spiritual master in the Middle Ages. It is only appropriate to compare leading figures with leading figures and average individuals with other average individuals. In reflecting on the difficulties which stand in the way of any such undertakings, one is happy to take refuge in the convenient, if time-worn, maxim to the effect that the task of academic learning is to describe the existence of a phenomenon, not to define its ultimate value.

ADDITIONS OF THE AUTHOR

[P. 29, ftn. 15: The Sammāniyya is actually a branch of the Khalwatiyya; cf. S. O'Fahey et alii, Arabic Literature in Africa (HdO, Section One, XIII), Leiden, 1994, pp. 91-121; something about the founder Muḥammad b. ᶜAbd al-Karīm al-Sammān can be found in B. Radtke, 'Sufism in the 18th Century. An Attempt at a Provisional Appraisal', *Die Welt des Islams* 36, pp. 331 f., 355.]

P. 42, l. 5: The combination of *samāᶜ* with a preceding *dhikr* goes back even further. The Mālikite scholar Abū Bakr al-Ṭurṭūshī (d. 520-25/1126-31) already criticized Sufi ceremonies which began with a great amount of recollection of God and appeals to Muḥammad or invocations of blessings upon him, continued with songs with a quick beat and dancing by ecstatic individuals leading to unconsciousness, and came to a close with a meal. Ibn al-Ḥājj: *Al-mudkhal*, Cairo, 1929, III, pp. 99-100.

P. 42, l. 8: Sayf al-Dīn was the grandfather of Yaḥyā Bākharzī.

P. 43, ll. 8-9: The *samāᶜ* combined in this way with *dhikr* reached the Aïr Massif in the Sahara between the 15th and 16th centuries. H.T. Norris: *Ṣūfī Mystics of the Niger Desert. Sīdī Maḥmūd and the Hermits of Aïr*, Oxford, 1990, pp. 84-86, 163-64.

For more information on listening to music by Sufis see my *Abū Saᶜīd-i Abū l-Ḫayr (357-440/967-1049). Wirklichkeit und legende*, Acta Iranica 11, 1976, pp. 210-66.

A BOOK OF ETIQUETTE FOR SUFIS

In Arabic there is a whole series of words for 'custom': *sunna*, *ʿāda*, *ʿurf*, *daʾb*, *rasm*, *qāʿida*, etc. All of them have other terminological meanings as well. *Sunna*, as is well-known, means legal convention and in particular designates the contents of statutes which are traced back to rulings of the Prophet Muḥammad and which have been set down in the *ḥadīth*; their opposite are *bidaʿ*, the plural of *bidʿa* 'innovation'. In addition, within the five juridical categories *sunna* also designates that which, though not commanded, is none the less 'advisable, recommended', in opposition to which as a counter-concept stands *makrūh*, the 'reprehensible'. *ʿĀda*, the most general and frequent word for custom, can designate good and bad as well as legally and religiously indifferent practices, but especially refers to 'common law' rooted in local traditions which runs parallel to and often comes into conflict with canon law based on the revelation and the statutes of the Prophet, i.e. the *sharīʿa*; in Indonesia in the form of Adat it even designates the law in general and contains the *sharīʿa*, religious law, as only one component within itself. In scholasticism *ʿāda*, as God's 'habit of creation', occupies a key position in the battle against the natural-scientific concept of cause and effect. *ʿUrf* frequently designates usage in speech but often also means the unwritten law of reasons of state.[1] *Daʾb* among the Turkmens (like *ʿāda*) means binding convention.[2]

The word *adab* is derived from *daʾb* by 'Gelenkmetaplasmus'.[3] Karl Vollers has proposed this derivation: *Katalog der islamischen... Hss. der Universitäts-Bibliothek zu Leipzig*, Leipzig, 1906, p. 180, ftn. 1.[4] He postulates for *daʾb* an original plural **adʾāb* which, according to the pattern *abʾār* > *ābār*, became *ādāb* and from which, according to the pattern *āthār-athar*, at a secondary stage the singular *adab* was then derived. This, it must be added, appropriated the

---

1 *Encyclopaedia of Islam*, s.vv.

2 But perhaps Hermann Vámbéry, *Reise in Mittelasien*, Leipzig, 1865, p. 250, is correct when he derives '*deb*' from *edeb*.

3 Jakob Egli, *Heteroklisie im Griechischen mit besonderer Berücksichtigung der Fälle von Gelenkheteroklisie*, dissertation Zurich, 1954. The pattern is sing. δάκρυ – pl. δάκρυα (Gelenk) – sing. δάκρυον (Neubildung).

4 Carl Brockelmann, *GAL Suppl.*, I, p. 39, ftn. 1.

plural *ādāb* so that a new plural, *adʾub*, had to be formed for *daʾb*. Carlo Alfonso Nallino in his *Letteratura araba dagli inizi all'epoca della dinastia umayyade* (= *Raccolta di scritti*, VI, Rome, 1948, pp. 1-17) accepts the appealing etymology of Vollers and defines the basic meaning of *adab* as 'authoritative custom', considering the word to be a synonym of *sunna* which likewise originally meant nothing other than the habits of life of a community in the more narrow or broader sense which have been inherited, are desirable and indeed ought necessarily to be striven after. From there he has the meaning of *adab* diverge in three directions into further starting positions. The three new meanings are: (inwardly) morality and decency, (outwardly) customary practice and good behavior, and in the third position a certain education also in matters of knowledge and judgement. These three meanings, according to Nallino, then branch out once again. From the first meaning, 'moral attitude', emerges 'moral training' and, going still a step further, on the one hand training animals, and on the other moral teachings. From the second meaning, 'customary practice', the concept narrows in the one direction to the exemplary behavior of the Prophet, and in the other to general rules of behavior, and then further to duty, and thirdly, again directly out of customary practice, to politeness and good manners, from which is then derived elegance in every respect. The third basic meaning, 'education with regard to knowledge', is the starting point for *adab* as the designation for a whole series of fields of learning, from which today, however, only the arts, i.e. the humanities, are still referred to this way, and for technical knowledge which is required by a particular profession or class. All this is followed by Nallino in its historical development and in conclusion is schematically represented in a table. Francesco Gabrieli gives a summary of it together with his own additions in the new edition of the *EI*, s.v. adab. This is not the place to examine the proposals critically,[5] none the less one must warn against the misconception that the individual meanings Nallino gives, mostly on the basis of book titles, can al-

---

5 Above all Persian influence on the semantic development, which Nallino, p. 9, ftn. 1, briefly touches upon, should be investigated and the idea of H.S. Nyberg (*Hilfsbuch des Pehlevi*, glossary p. 70, cited in Brockelmann, *loc. cit.*) that the meaning of Pahlavi *frahang* may have played a role in the process should be examined more thoroughly. Similarly, with regard to *ādāb* as moral teachings the influence of Persian *andarz*-writings should be taken into account: on the latter see Arthur Christensen, *L'Iran sous les Sassanides*, Copenhagen, 1936, pp. 426 ff.; Henri Massé, *Le Livre de Gerchâsp*, Paris, 1951, II, p. XIX. Regarding the *adīb* see Franz Rosenthal, 'Al-Kindī als Literat', in *Orientalia* 11, 1942, pp. 439 ff.

ways be divided up according to authors; rather one and the same author can also use the word in several meanings. Further, it can also happen, as will have to be explained below in the concrete case of our more narrow subject, that the boundaries between individual meanings of the concept become unsure or even disappear completely.

Of the three families of meaning that Nallino puts forward for *adab*, we are only in fact concerned with the middle one *per se*, i.e. *adab* as customary practice and good behavior. But this concept overflows on the one side into the social-ethical and thus into the moral sphere which Nallino rightly attributes to the first family, morality, and on the other side into the sphere of learning and education, i.e. the third family. The first situation occurs as soon as certain forms of behavior come to be considered an expression of an inner attitude and emphasis is given to the necessity for bringing one's exterior into line with one's interior and one's interior into line with one's exterior. The second situation occurs as soon as a moral attitude and along with this perhaps also social-aesthetic behavior are more or less professional goals, as was the case, for example, with all *homines religiosi*, from their left to their right flank, from the Sufis to the 'wise men' (*ḥukamāʾ*). To begin with, of course, there is a far-reaching difference between the *adab* which Ibn Qutayba demands of a *kātib* and the *ādāb* which Ibn ʿAbd Rabbih reports concerning the *ḥukamāʾ* and *ʿulamāʾ*: the *adab al-kātib* is the professional education, the knowledge of the language which a secretary must possess, whereas the *ādāb al-ḥukamāʾ wa'l-ʿulamāʾ* are simply their way of behaving toward their fellow-man. But precisely this also belongs to the sphere of their philosophy and to that extent forms at least a part of their professional knowledge. It is the same with the *ādāb al-ṣūfiyya* or *murīdīn*; here as well the *ādāb* belong to the goals of their profession, especially when one considers that along with the *ādāb al-ẓāhir* they also recognize *ādāb al-bāṭin*. Furthermore, already in the *ḥadīth* the actual boundaries of the *adab* or *ādāb* are quite blurred, in fact one finds together under this concept very dissimilar recommendations of the Prophet: rules regarding piety, the forms of consideration and friendliness owed one's fellowman, i.e. commands to honor one's mother and father as well as a guest, to show understanding to children, to be generous, to maintain reserve when cursed or praised, to put on a friendly face towards particular people despite one's inner opposition, to give evasive answers in order to avoid unpleasantness, to say bless you when someone sneezes, and the issue about the permissibility of poetry, along with many other things. Additional questions along the same line and about which one would expect information, for example concerning clothing, food, behavior on journeys, etc., are not dealt with here but often receive attention in their own 'books' or are accommodated in other works.[6] One has the impression that *adab* in the *ḥadīth* in part represents a blanket term for a series of rules of behavior which for some reason have not yet been fitted in somewhere else. Moreover, if one adds to this the fact that *adab* can also mean quite generally the exemplary behavior of the Prophet, as Nallino notes, and that pious people and in particular special religious communities endeavor to model all their *ādāb* on the example of the Prophet and to trace these back to him, their moral principles, rules of conduct, professional knowledge and the authoritative behavior of the Prophet become interlinked or ordered one behind the other. This is to a great extent the case in Sufism which in fact conceives of the Prophet as 'the epitome of all comportment' (*majmaᶜ al-ādāb*) and declares: 'All *ādāb* are to be learned from him'.[7] Muḥammad al-Ghazzālī (d. 505/1111) appears to have been the first to have dared to accept certain Sufi practices as 'innovations' and to defend their acceptance by distinguishing two kinds of innovation: those which violate a sacred commandment and therefore must be rejected, and others which do not contravene any injunction of religious law. In this regard he mentions the generally established custom of standing up when someone enters the room but which Muḥammad had not known, and he wishes hereby to offer a justification for certain contested practices in the Sufi form of listening to music. At the same time he expressly takes into account the *ᶜāda* of individual regions.[8] This idea is picked up by Abū Ḥafṣ ᶜUmar al-Suhrawardī (d. 632/1234)[9] and then extensively worked out by his Persian adapter ᶜIzz al-Dīn Maḥmūd-i Kāshānī (d. 735/1335). Kāshānī explicitly states that the Sufis' wearing the patched frock (*khirqa*), the establishment of convents (*khānaqāh*), their listening to

---

6 Bukhārī, Book 78; Muslim, 38; Abū Dāwūd, 40; Tirmidhī, 41; Ibn Māja, 33. In Nasāʾī there is a book (49) entitled *Ādāb al-quḍāh*.

7 Abū Ḥafṣ ᶜUmar al-Suhrawardī, *ᶜAwārif al-maᶜārif*, Chpt. 32, in the margin of Ghazzālī's *Iḥyāʾ ᶜulūm al-dīn*, Cairo, 1348, III, p. 107.

8 *Iḥyāʾ ᶜulūm al-dīn*, Cairo, 1348, II, p. 268. D.B. MacDonald, 'Ghazzālī on Listening to Music', in *JRAS*, 1902, p. 11. According to a *ḥadīth*, the Prophet was familiar with the Persian custom of rising to one's feet as a form of politeness; Samᶜānī, *Adab al-imlāʾ*, ed. Max Weisweiler, Leiden, 1952, p. 35, ll. 3-4.

9 *ᶜAwārif* at the end of Chpt. 22; ibid., II, pp. 209-10.

music (*samāʿ*), the forty-day withdrawal in seclusion (*chilla*), etc., are innovations and assigns them to a special chapter on 'praiseworthy customs' (*mustaḥsanāt*). By these he means undertakings which the Sufis have created through their own further reflection but which all serve just as good a purpose as for instance writing books and the cultivation of theological and juridical learning, which also had not yet existed in the time of Muḥammad but are none the less justifiable. The referred to undertakings of the Sufis, however, served to purify the human interior and to prepare for illumination by means of certainty.[10]

The question immediately arises as to whether the concept of individual effort (*ijtihād*) in thinking up these practices exhaustively explains their origin, or whether one should rather think in terms of borrowings from Christianity. We are also reminded of morphologically similar relationships in Christianity. There as well the orders attempted to follow as closely as possible the example of the founder of the religion and to a certain extent considered themselves to be the most advanced, and yet, or precisely for that reason, developed their own rules for living and proper behavior which distinguished them from other Christians and from one another as well. The rule of the Benedictines which surpassed all others in the West even expressly leaves room for adaptations in altered circumstances so that, in the course of time and according to local variation, the so-called *consuetudines* of individual monasteries were able to develop.[11]

Just as the whole life in the monastic orders fundamentally came to be subjected to *regulae*, *constitutiones* and *consuetudines*, so the whole of Sufism came to be under *ādāb*. Thus we find works such as the *Jawāmiʿ ādāb al-murīdīn* by Sulamī (d. 412/1021)[12] and the *Ādāb al-murīdīn*[13] by Abū'l-Najīb al-Suhrawardī (d. 563/1168), in which all of Sufism is subordinated to the concept of *ādāb*, and other works such as the *Iḥyāʾ ʿulūm al-dīn* by Ghazzālī and the *ʿAwārif al-maʿārif* by Abū Ḥafṣ al-Suhrawardī, in which the *ādāb* at least to some extent pervade the entire repertoire of subjects. Sarrāj (d. 378/988) undertook to restrict *ādāb* to rules which a Sufi should observe when performing ritual ablutions, during the ritual prayers, in

10 ʿIzz al-Dīn Maḥmūd-i Kāshānī, *Miṣbāḥ al-hidāya wa-miftāḥ al-kifāya*, ed. Jalāl al-Dīn Humāʾī, Tehran, 1323, pp. 146 f.

11 Bruno Albers, *Consuetudines monasticae*, Stuttgart-Vienna-Montecassino, 1900 ff.

12 *GAL*², I, p. 218, no. 4. Not edited.

13 Ibid., I, p. 563. Not edited. I have used a photocopy of MS Köprülü 702.

almsgiving, when fasting, on the pilgrimage, when dealing with his peers, in discussions, when eating, when listening to music, regarding dress, when on a journey, etc.[14] Hujwīrī (d. 5th/11th century) restricts them even more narrowly to the rules regarding association among themselves, including journeying, eating, speaking and remaining silent, marriage and celibacy.[15] Ghazzālī puts this and other chapters in the 'book' on *ᶜādāt* (*consuetudines*).[16] Kāshānī follows Abū Ḥafṣ al-Suhrawardī but diverges from him as well.[17] Moreover, Sarrāj,[18] Qushayrī,[19] and Abū Ḥafṣ,[20] among others, have separate sections on the concept *adab*. In addition, Sufi writings also present monographs on the *ādāb* concerning individual activities and departments of life. The one work of this kind which has been made accessible to date is the *Ādāb al-ṣuḥba wa-ḥusn al-ᶜishra* of Sulamī which has as its subject the association of Sufis with one another and with their fellow-men, and chiefly focuses on the attitude to be maintained in such relations.[21] The editor, M.J. Kister, draws attention in his introduction to some of Sulamī's predecessors whose names have been preserved in the *Fihrist* of Ibn al-Nadīm,[22] but none of whose works has come down to us. Other sources on the same subject, likewise mentioned by Kister, are enumerated by Hujwīrī;[23] these as well appear to be lost. Only a *Kitāb al-ikhwān* by Ibn Abī'l-Dunyā (d. 281/894) seems to have survived.[24] Another specialized subject was dealt with by Sulamī in his book *Ādāb al-*

---

14 *The Kitáb al-lumaᶜ fi'l-taṣawwuf...*, ed... by Reynold Alleyne Nicholson, in E.J.W. Gibb Memorial Series 22, 1914, pp. 141 ff.

15 *Kashf al-maḥjūb*, ed. Valentin Zhukovski, Leningrad, 1926, pp. 432 ff. English translation by R.A. Nicholson, in Gibb Memorial Series 17, New Edition, 1936, pp. 334 ff.

16 *Iḥyāʾ*, II.

17 *Miṣbāḥ al-hidāya*, pp. 203 ff.

18 *Lumaᶜ*, pp. 141 ff.

19 *Al-risāla*, Cairo, 1346, pp. 128 ff.

20 *ᶜAwārif*, Chpt. 31, in *Iḥyāʾ*, III, pp. 96 ff.

21 *Kitāb ādāb al-ṣuḥba* by Abū ᶜAbd al-Raḥmān al-Sulamī, ed. by M.J. Kister in *Oriental Notes and Studies published by the Israel Oriental Society* 6, Jerusalem, 1954.

22 *Al-fihrist*, ed. Gustav Flügel, p. 184, l. 5 (Yaḥyā b. Muᶜādh al-Rāzī, *Kitāb al-murīdīn*), p. 185, l. 3 (Burjulānī, *Kitāb al-ṣuḥba*), p. 185, l. 25 (ᶜAlī b. Muḥ. al-Miṣrī, *Kitāb al-mutaḥābbīn*).

23 Zhukovski, p. 439; Nicholson, p. 338.

24 Kister in the Arabic introduction, p. 15. Kātib Čelebī in Wiener: *Der Islam* 4, p. 414, no. 3. Not listed in Brockelmann.

faqr wa-sharā'iṭuhū,[25] and the title of a treatise by Ibn Abī'l-Dunyā *Al-ṣabr wa-adab al-lisān* has been handed down.[26] The *Ādāb al-nufūs* of Muḥāsibī[27] (d. 243/857) and the *Adab al-nafs* of Ḥakīm al-Tirmidhī[28] (d. 285/898) are exclusively devoted to training the soul. What was contained in the *Jāmiᶜ al-ṣaghīr fī'l-adab* of a certain ᶜAlī b. Muḥammad al-Miṣrī (d. 338/949-50) and is listed in the *Fihrist*[29] eludes our knowledge.

Here I would like to introduce to the reader the *Ādāb al-murīdīn* of Najm al-Dīn-i Kubrā, a mystic and mystical author from Khwārazm who died in the year 618/1221 while fighting against the Mongols when they invaded his native city.[30] As far as I can see this is the third work to bear this name: the first originates with al-Ḥakīm al-Tirmidhī[31] and does not seem to be preserved, the second is the above-mentioned *Ādāb al-murīdīn* of Abū'l-Najīb al-Suhrawardī. But whereas the treatise of Suhrawardī has been conceived as a comprehensive presentation of Sufism from the viewpoint of *ādāb*, Kubrā's work only treats the small area of forms of social intercourse and duties regarding decency. Kubrā here offers somewhat less than Sarrāj and somewhat more than Hujwīrī, both of whom had also fitted into their textbooks sections on rules of decency. He focuses more strongly than they, and also more strongly than Sulamī in his *Ādāb al-ṣuḥba*, on the purely outward rules of behavior and for the inward rules refers one to the *Manāzil al-sābiqīn* (correction of *sā'irīn*) by ᶜAbdallāh al-Anṣārī al-Harawī (d. 481/1088). This last point is significant in two respects. Firstly, it shows us that Kubrā is conscious of the narrowness of the field he is treating, and secondly, it emerges from this with considerable certainty that we are dealing

---

25 *GAL*², I, p. 219, no. 9.

26 *Fihrist*, p. 185, l. 15.

27 *GAL*, I, p. 214. Available to me in a photocopy of MS Carullah (Istanbul) 1101, 59a-103b.

28 *GAL S*, I, p. 357. Edited by A.J. Arberry and ᶜAlī Ḥasan ᶜAbd al-Qādir (together with Tirmidhī's *Kitāb al-riyāḍa*), Cairo, 1947.

29 *Fihrist*, p. 185, l. 27.

30 A detailed critical biography of Kubrā is found in the introduction to my text edition: *Die Fawā'iḥ al-ǧamāl wa-fawātiḥ al-ǧalāl des Naǧm ad-dīn al-Kubrā*, Wiesbaden, 1957, so that it is not necessary to give further information here. For the MSS see my 'Stambuler Hss. dreier persischer Mystiker', in *Der Islam* 24, 1937, pp. 23-25. *GAL Suppl.*, I, p. 787, no. 14.

31 Hujwīrī, *Kashf al-maḥjūb*, ed. Zhukovski, p. 439, l. 8; trans. Nicholson, p. 338. Louis Massignon, *Essai sur les origines du lexique technique de la mystique musulmane*², Paris, 1954, p. 288.

with an early work of Kubrā, in fact the first of his writings. In all the other works that we still know from Kubrā, with the exception perhaps of his Koran commentary which is, however, a posthumous work, Kubrā treats precisely those inner *ādāb*, even if he does not call them by that name, and he would certainly have referred to his own writings and not to Anṣārī, if they had already existed at the time of his composing the *Ādāb*. The *terminus a quo* appears to be around the year 580/1184, when his Sufi training should have come to an end and he would have returned to his home city of Khwārazm.[32] Moreover, in distinction to Suhrawardī's work, the text of Kubrā is composed in Persian. In addition, an examination of both works shows that Kubrā is in no way particularly dependent on Suhrawardī. This is all the more remarkable since Kubrā and Suhrawardī not only share the same (Shāfiᶜite) *madhhab* and the same Shīᶜite tendencies but Kubrā's Sufi affiliation goes back to Abū'l-Najīb al-Suhrawardī through a single link only, that of ᶜAmmār al-Bidlīsī.[33] Most likely he is here and there dependent on Hujwīrī (5th/11th century) as some obvious similarities suggest. Yet we possess no compelling proof, and furthermore the *Qābūsnāma*, ed. Levy, p. 144, ll. 9-10 (ed. Nafīsī, p. 183, ll. 22 ff.), trans. by Levy: *Mirror*, pp. 246-47, mentions a few other works on the same subject that (aside from Qushayrī) seem not to have survived, but by which Kubrā could perhaps just as well have been influenced. Basically one can say the same thing about Kubrā's dependence as about Sulamī's *Ādāb al-ṣuḥba*. Both draw upon an already existing Sufi tradition. Neither extends over the boundaries into areas beyond the domain of Islam. Where foreign elements such as the Hellenistic elements of the Arabic Bryson tradition[34] can be established, the encroachments should be estimated at an earlier time. Kister has rightly stressed that even forged *ḥadīth*s should not be attributed to Sulamī's account.[35] But Sulamī's treatise still retains a scientific appearance; the propositions concerning social intercourse with colleagues and fellow-men are still individually derived from the alleged *sunna* of the Prophet and in this way are presented as being nothing less than universally binding and not just for Sufis. Kubrā's presentation, on the other hand, takes for granted an already firmly

32 F. Meier: *Fawāʾiḥ al-ǧamāl*, Introduction, p. 40.

33 Ibid., p. 19.

34 Martin Plessner, *Der οἰκονομικός des Neupythagoreers «Bryson» und sein Einfluss auf die islamische Wissenschaft*, in Orient und Antike 5, Heidelberg, 1928.

35 Kister, *Ādāb al-ṣuḥba*, English introduction, p. 4.

established Sufi tradition which is distinct from common practice in several respects but which carries its justification within itself as an expression of a Sufism whose goals have long been uncontested. This is perhaps most clearly visible in his prescriptions to do with dress. Here what matters is no longer the example of the Prophet — the question is brushed aside by a brief general reference to the preference of prophets for a woolen garment — but solely and exclusively the applicability of a symbolic correspondence between the appearance of the garment and the inner, mystical state of the person wearing it. The legitimacy for wearing this or that color lies purely in this reference system, and already in the introduction Kubrā is clumsy enough to mix up the bases of this symbolism. On the one hand, he stresses that the effect proceeds from the exterior to the interior but he cites sentences like 'The exterior is a sign of the interior' which originally could only have meant that the exterior is a mirror of the interior, i.e. priority belongs to the interior. To be sure he acknowledges in Chapter 1 that the interior should and can adhere to the symbolic meaning of the Arabic words for wool, patched frock, etc., but then he maintains this or that inner spiritual state or level in the mystic is a prerequisite for wearing this or that color. Finally, in enumerating the various utensils and parts of clothing in the second half of Chapter 1 he ends up with what is in the main a neutrality that allows both interpretations; for a sentence like 'The border at the neck of the patched frock is the sword belt of the profession of God's oneness', etc., can be understood as a challenge to strive in one's interior to eliminate all the pseudo-gods but also as a statement that the edging ought only to be worn if one has proven oneself as a soldier in battle against the pseudo-gods. Curiously, at this point Kubrā also vacillates once again, this time in the tenses, as soon as he describes more fully in a relative clause the action which is to be carried out. He says for example 'The hem of the patched frock is the cover which I spread over my colleagues (*pōsham*)', i.e. I do not make public their offenses but seek to overlook them and to make them as invisible as possible for others as well, with the verb in the present tense, whereas 'The cap... is the crown of reverence which I have placed upon my head (*bar sar nihādham*) and (the sign that) I have cast (*biyafgandam*) from myself arrogance and pride', i.e. with the verb in the past tense. In the unsureness of thought which is expressed in formulations such as these, I would see a further argument that the *Ādāb al-murīdīn* of Kubrā is a work of his early years.

As for the symbolism itself which Kubrā employs, one moment it is based on an interpretation of letters of the alphabet (e.g. *ṣūf*), another moment on word-play (e.g. *dastār-dastūr*), then on metaphorical language (e.g. 'To wash with the soap of remorse... to cleanse the page of the heart — white), and then again on similes (e.g. 'The border at the neck — sword belt of the profession of God's oneness').[36] One will have doubts about the practical application of Kubrā's clothing prescriptions based on this system, especially as correspondence of the exterior with the interior is hardly likely to have been something one could confirm or verify. But by way of replying to this, we do at least possess one example to show that Kubrā's recommendations, as much as they may only appear to exist on paper, could correspond with absolute precision to real practice; for Kubrā was not the first person to bring clothing into a symbolic relation with a human being's interior. If Kubrā prescribes that one can or should wear black when one is able to announce the death of the concupiscent soul, similarly ᶜAṭṭār transmits a story in which a Sufi completely dressed in black once explained before Ibn-i Khafīf (d. 371/982) that his clothing was an indication that his earlier gods, the concupiscent soul and lust, had died. When Ibn-i Khafīf had him put out of the convent and brought back in again forty times and the stranger did not utter a single word of indignation, the shaykh kissed him on the head and admitted that he had the right to wear black.[37] Moreover, one should bear in mind that with his numerous prescriptions about clothing Kubrā did not wish to provide a close-meshed net of laws but on the contrary took account of the great freedom that prevailed and acknowledged it. It is never intended that one individual should go through wearing the entire gamut of colors — which in any case would contradict the frequently cited Sufi command to own no more than one or two garments — or that by means of the color he wears he should display the rank he momentarily holds on the ladder to becoming the perfect Sufi; for that the explanations given cut across one another too often and also any hierarchical arrangement is in fact entirely lacking. All that is important for Kubrā is the relationship which the mystic is

---

36 Cf. the chapter on 'Things which if given as a gift elegant people take to be a bad omen and which they dislike because of their ugly name' in the *Muwashshā* of Washshāʾ, ed. Brünnow, pp. 132 ff.; ed. Aḥmad Muṣṭafā, Cairo, 1953, pp. 172 ff.

37 *Tadhkirat al-awliyāʾ*, ed. R.A. Nicholson, London-Leiden, 1905-07, II, p. 129, ll. 14-23. F. Meier: 'Die Wandlung des Menschen im mystischen Islam', in *Eranos-Jahrbuch* 23, 1954, p. 130.

supposed to create between exterior and interior. He should be able to confer a sense on his exterior and give adequate expression to his interior. But to be sure the individual proceeds in this with as much freedom and personal variation as the Sufi participant at musical performances (*samā*ᶜ); there as well instructions are given as to how a connection can be created between the content of what were frequently profane songs and the mystic's striving, but the individual was basically free — as long as he could create a connection.[38] Similarly, the symbolism not only of the clothing's colors but of the separate items and parts of the clothing, which is filled in in the second half of Chapter 1, had also existed before Kubrā. Perhaps he indicates this himself if the sentence 'The shaykhs have (also) said' not only goes with the Arabic saying that follows but with the whole enumeration that comes after it — which unfortunately cannot be determined with certainty. In any case, Hujwīrī provides a series of such symbolic representations (*ishārāt*) and even maintains that the 'ordinary' Sufis give far too much weight to these matters, though he admits he has written a book about it himself and also refers to a treatise on the same subject by Maᶜmar-i Iṣfahānī. The proper way to view the list of interpretations that Kubrā gives, i.e. that they are not at all meant to be taken as dogma, is made quite clear by a comparison with Hujwīrī. That is to say, to begin with, Hujwīrī gives a series based on the wealth of possible or actually current symbolic interpretations of the collar, sleeves, gore (gusset), belt, hem and trimming, which he presents as the best, but then surpasses these and replaces them with a second series which he considers 'better still' or 'more beautiful'.[39] Thus, surely, Kubrā's list in the second half of Chapter 1 is also only one possibility which he himself could replace at any time with another. As is known, in later dervish communities such symbolic representations concerning details of dress became partially fixed; there, for example, the twelve gussets signify the twelve Imams, the two earrings Ḥasan and Ḥusayn, the four parts of certain headgear renunciation of the world, renunciation of Paradise, renunciation of all hypocrisy and exclusive devotion to God, etc.[40]

---

38 F. Meier: ibid., p. 136, and 'The Dervish Dance, pp. 35 ff.

39 *Kashf al-maḥjūb*, Zhukovski, p. 62 penult. line to p. 63, l. 10; Nicholson, p. 56. Cf. also the profusion in Jean Aubin, *Matériaux pour la biographie de Shah Niᶜmatullah Wali Kermani*, in Bibliothèque Iranienne 7, Paris-Tehran, 1956, p. 290.

40 John Brown, *The Dervishes or Oriental Spiritualism*, London, 1868, pp. 113 f., 147 f.; Hermann Vámbéry, *Sittenbilder aus dem Morgenlande*, Berlin, 1876, pp. 176 ff.; Georg Jacob, 'Die Bektaschijje in ihrem Verhältnis zu verwandten Erscheinungen', in *Abh. d. K.*

And so their clothing is built up on symbolism like this. Medieval Europe was also familiar with this kind of symbolic representations of clothing.[41]

It is curious that Kubrā's predilection for symbolism actually only comes into full force in Chapter 1 on clothing. Here it assumes a prominent position so forcefully that the convincing practical reasons such as Abū'l-Najīb Suhrawardī cites for wearing the *muraqqaᶜa* (small cost, not so easily torn, long-lasting, corresponds to a Sufi's humility, resists wearing out, protects against heat and cold, is not coveted by robbers, is a good means against [inner] corruption and pride)[42] are completely left out of consideration. Instead, in later chapters precisely the practical reasons (even if not nearly so appropriate and realistic as in Muḥammad al-Ghazzālī, and as one might wish) are placed in the foreground. Only in the final chapter does symbolism appear again where the Sufi seeking accommodation is instructed to turn his staff against himself as a sign that he is waging war against himself. In this respect especially the chapter on listening to music could have offered a rich field for symbolism, in fact in a double sense: not only in connection with the reinterpretation generally required by Sufism of the love songs performed during the *samāᶜ* but also with regard to the musical instruments employed. Before Kubrā this field had been worked by Ghazzālī's brother Aḥmad, in fact entirely in the same vein as Kubrā's symbolic representations of clothing: for him the round tambourine was a symbol (*ishāra*) for the circle of all things in existence, the skin stretched over it a symbol for absolute being, the beat of the hand against the skin a symbol for the impulses which come forth from the innermost depths to the surface of being and cause the essences to take on appearance, the five bells on the tambourine signified for him *nubuwwa*, *walāya*, *risāla*, *khilāfa*, *imāma*,[43] etc., etc. In Kubrā

Bayer. Akademie der Wiss., 1. Kl., 24. Bd., 3. Abt., 1909, p. 40; John Kingsley Birge, *The Bektashi Order of Dervishes*, London, 1937, p. 232.

41 Reinhold Köhler, *Kleinere Schriften*, Berlin, 1900, II, pp. 122-25.

42 *Ādāb al-murīdīn*, MS Köprülü 702, 6b: *wa-yakhtārūna lubsa'l-muraqqaᶜāti li-maᶜānin, minhā annahā aqallu maʾūnatan wa-aqallu takharruqan wa-abqā ᶜalā ṣāḥibihā wa-aqrabu ilā'l-tawāḍuᶜi wa-aṣbaru ᶜalā'l-kaddi wa-tadfaᶜu'l-ḥarra wa'l-qurra wa-lā maṭmaᶜa fīhā li-ahli'l-sharri wa-tamnaᶜu'l-fasāda wa'l-kibr*.

43 Aḥmad al-Ghazzālī, *Bawāriq al-ilmāᶜ*, in James Robson, *Tracts on Listening to Music*, in Oriental Translation Fund, N.S., 34, London, 1938, pp. 98/157 f. (edition and translation partly incorrect).

only the interpretation of tearing one's clothing during the *samāᶜ* as a gesture of renouncing and casting off everything that is not God recalls this symbolism — which, however, is found in Chapter 1; Aḥmad al-Ghazzālī interpreted in similar fashion not the tearing of one's clothing (which he doesn't mention) but taking off one's clothes.[44] That Kubrā does not go further into this rewarding subject which is suitable to his nature I take to be one of the many indications that Kubrā wrote the compendium under consideration hastily and had not studied any sources for this purpose. This is also suggested by the fact that he nowhere cites the names of authoritative transmitters, quite apart from the unshapely disproportionate size of Chapter 1, which gives to the whole the look of a hydrocephalic or a tadpole.

As for the remaining rules put forward by Kubrā, one may quite generally assume that at least Kubrā himself followed them; for a teacher who publishes a textbook on behavior, trains his students in accordance with it and is himself constantly under their scrutiny, will scarcely be able to allow himself to offend against it. Indeed, this is perhaps what is especially valuable in the small book, that it presents before our eyes Kubrā in his outward behavior, in the ordinary details of life, in association with his fellow-men, and thus effectively adds to the picture of him we acquire from other books on his ideas and his inner experiences. We must imagine Kubrā actually going through the streets with lowered head and eating in a seat on the left-hand side. That he was in numerous ways indebted to a traditional ideal goes without saying, and the extent to which this is the case should at least be indicated by a few selected footnotes without any claim to completeness.[45] On the other hand, one should not en-

---

44 Ibid., pp. 100/160, ll. 1-2.

45 From the abundance of comparative material I have made the following selection: *Sufi sources*: Sarrāj (d. 378/958): *Al-lumaᶜ fī'l-taṣawwuf*, ed. R.A. Nicholson. Maḥmūd b. ᶜUthmān, *Firdaws al-murshidiyya*, ed. F. Meier in Bibliotheca Islamica 14, Leipzig, 1948, on Abū Isḥāq-i Kāzarūnī (d. 426/1035). Muḥammad b. al-Munawwar, *Asrār al-tawḥīd fī maqāmāt al-shaykh Abī Saᶜīd*, ed. Zhukovski, Petersburg, 1899/reprint Tehran 1313/ed. Dhabīḥallāh Ṣafā, Tehran, 1332/ed. Muḥammad Riḍā Shafīᶜī-i Kadkanī, Tehran 1366/trans. by John O'Kane, *The Secrets of God's Mystical Oneness*, Persian Heritage Series no. 38, Costa Mesa (Calif.)-New York, 1992, on Abū Saᶜīd b. Abī'l-Khayr (d. 440/1049). Kāyūs b. Iskandar b. Qābūs b. Wushmgīr, *Qābūsnāma* (written 475/1082), with a section on Sufism in Chpt. 44, ed. Saᶜīd Nafīsī, Tehran, 1313/ed. Reuben Levy, in Gibb Memorial Series, New Series 18, 1951/trans. by Reuben Levy, *A Mirror for Princes*, London, 1951. Regarding a newly discovered old MS see Richard N. Frye in *Serta Cantabrigiensia*, Wiesbaden, 1954, pp. 7-21, and

tertain any exaggerated ideas about the area of validity of his rules. How little acceptance, for instance, his recommendations on permissible instruments for listening to music may have found even among his direct students is shown by Najm al-Dīn-i Dāya who takes for granted the use of the flute, whereas Kubrā expressly advised against it (see ftn. 173 below). Even with regard to more important rules, namely those which concerned mystic training in the more narrow sense, soon after Kubrā decisive changes came into effect; for example, Kubrā's spiritual great-grandson, Nūr al-Dīn ᶜAbd al-Raḥmān al-Isfarāʾinī al-Kasirqī (d. 717/1317), the teacher of ᶜAlāʾ al-Dawla al-Simnānī (d. 736/1336), already taught a *dhikr*-procedure which diverged completely from that of Kubrā.[46]

The greatest caution is called for in attempting to use this document for a analysis of historical development. Since Sufism, as noted, is rooted within Islam and in the Prophet revers the same model as other Muslims, the boundary between Sufi and non-Sufi

---

JAOS 75, 1955, pp. 24 ff. ᶜAbdallāh-i Anṣārī-i Harawī (d. 481/1088), *Rasāʾil*, ed. Sulṭānḥusayn Tābanda Gunābādī, Tehran, 1319. Hujwīrī (5th/11th century), *Kashf al-maḥjūb*, ed. Zhukovski, Leningrad, 1926/trans. by R.A. Nicholson in Gibb Memorial Series 17, New Edition 1936. Muḥammad al-Ghazzālī (d. 505/1111), *Iḥyāʾ ᶜulūm al-dīn*, Cairo, 1348. Aḥmad al-Ghazzālī (d. 517/1123), *Bawāriq al-ilmāᶜ*, ed. James Robson, *Tracts on Listening to Music*, in Oriental Translation Fund, New Series 34, 1938. Ḥamīd al-Dīn ᶜUmar-i Balkhī (d. 559/1164), *Maqāmāt-i Ḥamīdī*, ed. ᶜAlī Aṣghar Ṣamīm Hamadānī, Tabriz, 1312, *maqāma* 8 on *ādāb al-safar* and 12 on *taṣawwuf*. Abū'l-Najīb ᶜAbd al-Qāhir al-Suhrawardī (d. 563/1168), *Ādāb al-murīdīn*, MS Köprülü (Istanbul) 702. ᶜAṭṭār (d. perhaps 627/1229-30), *Tadhkirat al-awliyāʾ*, ed. R.A. Nicholson. Abū Ḥafṣ ᶜUmar al-Suhrawardī (d. 632/1234), *ᶜAwārif al-maᶜārif*, in the margin of Ghazzālī's *Iḥyāʾ*. Najm al-Dīn-i Dāya (d. 654/1256), *Mirṣād al-ᶜibād min al-mabdaʾ ilā'l-maᶜād*, Tehran, 1312/52. Ibn al-Ḥājj, *Al-mudkhal* (written 732/1331-32), Cairo, 1929 (in part 3). ᶜAbd al-Raḥmān-i Jāmī (d. 898/1492), *Subḥat al-abrār*, Tehran, 1313. Pseudo-ᶜAṭṭār (date unknown), *Irshād-i bayān*, Tehran, 1315/55. *Profane sources*: Bryson, *Kitāb Barūsūn fī tadbīr al-rajul li-manzilihī*, in Plessner, *Der οἰκονομικός des Neupythagoreers «Bryson»*, Heidelberg, 1928. Muḥammad b. Maḥmūd al-Shahrazūrī (7th/13th century), *Al-shajara al-ilāhiyya fī ᶜulūm al-ḥaqāʾiq al-ilāhiyya*, in Plessner, pp. 262-73. Naṣīr al-Dīn-i Ṭūsī (d. 672/1274), *Akhlāq-i Nāṣirī*, in Plessner, pp. 59-104. Jalāl al-Dīn-i Dawwānī, *Akhlāq-i Jalālī* (written before 882/1477), Lucknow, 1898. Ḥusayn-i Kāshifī, *Akhlāq-i Muḥsinī* (written 907/1501-02), Bombay, 1304. *Shīᶜite sources*: *Tarjuma-i Makārim al-akhlāq*, anonymous Persian translation of the Arabic work *Makārim al-akhlāq* by Ḥasan al-Ṭabarsī (d. circa 550/1155), identical with MS Bankipore 14, no. 1218; private MS. — Additional works will be cited in the appropriate place.

46 *Fawāʾiḥ al-ğamāl*, Intro., pp. 246 f. and *EI*² s.v. ᶜAlāʾ al-Dawla al-Simnānī.

customary practices is necessarily unclear and in Muḥammad al-Ghazzālī, who wished to fuse together mysticism and orthodoxy, it has been wholly eliminated; for instance even his statements on the proper way to listen to music are not intended for a particular group but for all Muslims in general; he wished to educate Muslims as such to be Sufis, and this was actually the goal of all Sufis. Their claim was to represent the true Islam, and their certificate of authorization (*ijāza*) read 'for guiding people to God'. Moreover, the concept of good behavior involved views and feelings which were not found on one side only, but bound together both camps, indeed could extend further to bind together people of very different lines of thought; the behavior of the saintly fools and the Malāmatīs is another story. Consequently, one must be on guard not to postulate oppositions that do not exist. Then Kubrā's vade-mecum is not exhaustive regarding the material, and this in two respects: firstly, not all subjects are dealt with which could be brought in line with matters discussed in the seven chapters (missing, for example, is the behavior of the novice in sleep, when on spiritual retreat, when sick, in connection with earning money, etc.), and secondly, among the subjects dealt with by no means are all the problems that arise and all imaginable cases taken into consideration. But from this it becomes clear that it is impossible simply to conclude, because of a lack of mention in Kubrā, that a particular object or a particular problem did not exist, and then on the basis of comparisons with other sources to determine developments in Sufism. On the contrary, one will have to supplement Kubrā with regard to details by consulting other sources and only confer on him validity as an *argumentum e silentio* where other sources are silent as well. But it will be difficult to reach sure judgements, and in particular one would do well not to be hasty in extending the judgements beyond the radius of those authors on the basis of whom they were reached; Sufism is very multilayered and despite numerous common features cannot be made to conform to one pattern. How narrowly one must set its boundaries in the present case is shown for instance by the following examples:

How is it that Kubrā in his list of the colors of clothing omits to mention green, although in his mysticism and in Islam in general it plays no small role and was looked upon favorably by Muḥammad himself? Did Sufis not wear green? This would be a false conclusion; for we know from many examples that mystics could also wear green clothes[47] and that later individual orders even made

---

47 See here p. 71, ftn. 77 (Abū Saʿīd b. Abī'l-Khayr) and elsewhere.

green the distinctive color of their order.[48] One should also not conclude because of the absence of the shirt in the enumeration of items of clothing that Kubrā and his followers did not wear shirts, any more than because of the absence of the needle among the necessary utensils that the needle was unknown to him or was unimportant. Other texts mention these. Further, if Kubrā only enumerates the tambourine, bells and the *bēsha* under musical instruments, this does not mean that at that time other instruments were not played in Khwārazm or in Kubrā's surroundings, and did not pose a problem for the Sufi *samāᶜ*. On the other hand, one may perhaps construe the absence of yellow and red in the colors of clothing as an *argumentum e silentio* that Kubrā and his dervishes did not wear these colors, for in fact Muḥammad had forbidden them[49] and according to other sources these were the colors of 'effeminate men and catamites'[50] as well as of prostitutes.[51] But this conclusion is anything but certain, as for example in the previous century the followers of Aḥmad al-Badawī in Egypt wore red turbans,[52] and yellow ones are attested as well.[53] Conversely, in view of the color symbolism presented by Kubrā one can say with considerable certainty that he was unfamiliar with a difference in the color of clothing between individual schools and orders as is frequently attested at a later date. Similarly, one may interpret the absence of the axe, fleece and begging bowl as evidence

---

48 Engelbert Kaempfer, *Am Hofe des persischen Grosskönigs (1684-85). Das erste Buch der Amoenitates exoticae.* Eingeleitet und in deutscher Bearbeitung herausgegeben v. Walther Hinz, Leipzig, 1940, p. 111: the Qādirīs. John P. Brown, *The Dervishes or Oriental Spiritualism*, pp. 56 f., 113.

49 *Concordance et indices de la tradition musulmane*, s.v. *ḥumra*; Aḥmad b. Ḥanbal, *Al-musnad*, ed. Aḥmad Muḥammad Shākir, Cairo, 1946 ff., no. 829. But *Concordance*, s.v. *ḥulla*, and Ṭabarsī, *bāb* 6, *faṣl* 4 (private MS, 28b): red horse blanket.

50 *Maqāmāt-i Ḥamīdī*, p. 101 (*mukhannathān wa-muʾannathān-i ᶜālam ṣūrat-i zard wa-surkh bar gōsh wa-gardan bar-bastand ki al-ṣufra wa'l-ḥumra aᶜjab*, i.e. yellow and red objects on the ears and neck).

51 Pseudo-Nāṣir-i Khusraw, *Saᶜādatnāma*, in *Dīwān-i qaṣāʾid wa-muqaṭṭaᶜāt-i Ḥakīm Nāṣir-i Khusraw*... ed. Naṣrallāh Taqawī, Tehran, 1304-06, p. 559, l. 11, where *qaḥba* is read as a variant for *takhta* (Kaviani edition, in the supplement to the *Safarnāma*, p. 17, l. 1, *takhta*). Cf. the recommendations of Washshāʾ in G.E. von Grunebaum, *Kritik und Dichtkunst*, Wiesbaden, 1955, p. 69.

52 Edward William Lane, *Manners and Customs of the Modern Egyptians*, 1836 ff., Chpt. 10, in the edition Everyman's Library no. 315, 1954, p. 249. Quoted in Brown, *Dervishes*, p. 246.

53 Brown, *Dervishes*, pp. 55 f.

that these objects were not yet the emblems of a dervish for Kubrā; for other sources of his time as well do not make any mention of them.

No critical edition of the treatise yet exists, nor can one be provided here since I do not have at my disposal all the necessary relevant manuscripts. I only possess a photocopy of the quite good MS Aya Sofya (Istanbul), no. 4792, 738*a*-741*b* copied in Shiraz in the year 816/1413-14, to which my attention was directed at the time by a note from Prof. H. Ritter and on the basis of which Ritter's *Ilāhīnāma* has since then been published.[54] The handwriting is small but clear for a practiced reader. *K* and *g*, *j* and *c h* are not distinguished from one another, nor are *p* and *b* other than in exceptional cases; Persian *d* after vowels is everywhere *dh*. It is doubtful that Kubrā still said *dh* in view of the remarks of his contemporary Shams-i Qays concerning the then advanced stage of hardening of the sound in Ghazna, Balkh and Transoxania.[55] None the less, I follow my MS of Shiraz whether it be a southern way of writing or a 'historical orthography' of Kubrā that it presents. A certain degree of unclarity is created by the copyist consistently employing an inclusive method of dotting which writes together diacritical dots of two adjacent letters if they stand on the same level (either above or below) and give the sum of at least three dots. On the basis of this MS, I will now give as close a paraphrase of the text as possible with comparative and explanatory notes.

THE RULES FOR NOVICES (*ĀDĀB AL-MURĪDĪN*)

The Sufis (*ahl-i taṣawwuf*) have rules of behavior (*ādāb*) to do with sitting and rising, sleeping and dressing oneself, eating and drinking, parties they go to, comportment at home and on journeys and when listening to music (*samāᶜ*). Whoever dons the patched frock (*khirqa*) and sets out on the path of the dervishes must know these rules and take them by the hand (*ba-dast gīradh*) so that his exterior adopts this behavior (*adab*) and, through the blessings of the exterior, the

54 *Ilāhī-Nāme. Die Gespräche des Königs mit seinen sechs Söhnen. Eine mystische Dichtung von Farīdaddīn ᶜAṭṭār*, in Bibl. Islamica 12, 1940, Introduction, p. 8.

55 Shams-i Qays, *Al-muᶜjam fī maᶜāyīr ashᶜār al-ᶜAjam*, ed. Muḥammad Qazwīnī, in Gibb Memorial Series 10, 1909, p. 192/ed. Muḥammad Ramaḍānī, Tehran, 1314, p. 166. Muḥammad Qazwīnī, *The Taʾríkh-i-Jahán-gushá of ᶜAláʾu 'd-dín ᶜAtá Malik-i-Juwayní*, in Gibb Mem. Ser. 16, 1912, Part 1, Introduction, pp. LXVII f. Theodor Nöldeke, *Das iranische Nationalepos*[2], Berlin-Leipzig, 1920, p. 103, ftn. 5.

interior as well becomes genuinely Sufi. Whoever wishes to have a sound interior must have a pleasing exterior; an Arabic saying states: 'Whoever is endowed with a pleasing exterior also has a sound interior.'[56] One must adorn the exterior with forms of decency (*ādāb*) so that the interior becomes illuminated with divine experience (*ḥaqīqat*); (Arabic) 'the exterior is the signboard (*ᶜunwān*) of the interior.'[57] The exterior affects the interior, and the interior receives knowledge from the exterior. ᶜAbdallāh-i Anṣārī said: 'Smoke gives proof of fire, as the exterior gives proof of the interior and the student gives proof of the teacher.'[58]

CHAPTER 1. ON WEARING THE PATCHED FROCK (*KHIRQA*).

Whoever becomes a novice and wishes to put on the patched frock (*khirqa*) must receive it from a master (*pīr*) who possesses religious law (*sharīᶜat*), mystical work (*ṭarīqat*) and divine experience (*ḥaqīqat*), and who knows the basic precepts of religion and religious law, the rules (*ādāb*) of mystical work and the secrets of divine experience so that he can explain for the novice difficulties in the religious law, visions (*wāqiᶜa*) in mystical work and secrets in divine experience.[59] The novice must receive the patched frock from

---

56 Originally this sentence surely meant that one could recognize a good interior from a good exterior, and not as Kubrā uses it, that by teaching a person to maintain a good exterior one is preparing him for education of the interior. But Abū Saᶜīd al-Kharrāz (d. 286/899): Everything internal which is contradicted by something external is invalid; *ᶜAwārif*, I, p. 279.

57 The same holds true for this sentence as for the previous one. It is often cited in the following somewhat longer form: *Ḥusnu'l-adabi (fī)'l-ẓāhir ᶜunwānu ḥusni'l-adabi (fī)'l-bāṭin*; Abū'l-Najīb, 15b; *ᶜAwārif*, III, p. 285. Further variants in *Mudkhal*, III, p. 166; Sulamī, *Ādāb al-ṣuḥba*, ed. Kister, p. 86.

58 I have not found the saying in the *Rasāʾil-i Khwāja ᶜAbdallāh-i Anṣārī*, ed. Gunābādī, Tehran, 1319; the collection contains the following treatises of Anṣārī: *Dil u-jān*, *Kanz al-sālikīn*, *Wāridāt*, *Qalandarnāma*, *Haft ḥiṣār*, *Maḥabbatnāma*, *Maqūlāt*, *Ilāhīnāma*. Nor is it to be found in the *Manāzil al-sāʾirīn*, Cairo, 1908. ᶜAbd al-Raḥmān al-Sulamī, *Jawāmiᶜ ādāb al-ṣūfiyya*, MS Berlin (Ahlwardt) no. 3081, 64b: It is also one of their *ādāb* that they strive so that their being (*ḥāl*) corresponds to their dress. Muḥammad b. ᶜAlī al-Kattānī said (however) in Mecca to those dressed in patched frocks: 'My brothers, by God if this clothing of yours corresponds to your interior, then you betray a wish that the people know your interior, and if it contradicts your interior, then you shall perish' (i.e. a dilemma).

59 Knowledge is not valued in equally high terms by all Sufis with regard to the religious prescriptions, but is very generally assumed. Kubrā here even requires a certain learning or at least a central understanding, as Ghazzālī for instance had sought and found. The notion of

a master at the time when he (the novice?) knows that he can orientate himself in accordance with it (*bar ān istiqāmat tuwānadh kard*) and can endure the pains and hardship, the vita purgativa and the ascetic exercises of a mystic;[60] for whoever once sets out on this path but then turns back is an apostate of mysticism, and an apostate of mysticism is worse than an apostate of the religious law; for the apostate of religious law (*murtadd-i sharīᶜat*) can put things right again by uttering just one saying (the profession of faith), whereas the apostate of mysticism (*murtadd-i ṭarīqat*) even with the help of all men and spirits cannot put things right again (*bāz sar-i kār nayāyadh*); for whoever has once perpetrated a betrayal (*khiyānat*), no one places his trust in him any longer.[61] The great have said on this matter (Arabic): 'To recover the state (*ḥāl*, MS *ḥiyāl* or something similar) after it has disappeared is impossible' (*ṭalab al-ḥāl baᶜd al-zawāl muḥāl*). Before he puts on the patched frock, he must take off his ordinary clothes and throw them away.

The best clothing that wearers of the patched frock can put on is a woolen garment (*pashmīn*). Even Adam and Eve had worn clothing like that. After they had fallen from Paradise onto the earth, Gabriel brought them a sheep which they sheared. Eve spun and Adam wove. After them Moses, Jesus, John the Baptist and Muḥammad also wore wool (*ṣūf*).[62] The name *ṣūfī* comes from *ṣūf*.

---

wāqiᶜa oscillates between dream and vision and is here used for both. The teacher must be able to interpret visual phenomena for the student. They give him information about the inner state in particular but also even about the hereafter. Despite the gamut of detailed differences which have been postulated about the various kinds of inner phenomena, in practice dream and vision have almost the same value for the Sufi. By divine experience, as I would here like to translate *ḥaqīqat*, one should understand the experience of God's reality. In the *Risāla fī'l-sulūk* Kubrā compares the *sharīᶜa* with a ship, the *ṭarīqa* with an ocean and the *ḥaqīqa* with a pearl; see *Fawāʾiḥ*, Intro., p. 49.

60 The rule that one must wait until the suitable moment to invest someone with a frock presupposes a period of probation; this is discussed in *Fawāʾiḥ*, Intro., pp. 35 f.

61 Why one only speaks of a breach of faith with regard to a mystical apostate and what special offence is meant here is not clear to me, unless this is because in undergoing mystical *tawba* one enters an explicit bond with the teacher, which with an ordinary Muslim would only be the case if he converted to Islam from another religion. Cf. also the threat in Daylamī, *Sīrat-i Ibn-i Khafīf*, ed. A. Schimmel, Ankara, 1955, *bāb* 9, *faṣl* 2.

62 That the prophets loved to wear wool is already stated in *ḥadīths*; al-Ḥākim al-Nayshābūrī (d. 405/1014), *Al-mustadrak ᶜalā'l-Ṣaḥīḥayn*, Hyderabad, 1341, IV, pp. 187 f. Ibid. and in *Concordance*, III, pp. 443 f., one also finds *ḥadīths* about *ṣūf* worn by the Prophet

A person dressed in *ṣūf* must attempt to do justice to the demands which the word *ṣūf* expresses (*dādh-i ān az khwadh ṭalab bāyadh kard*). *Ṣūf* is comprised of the three letters *ṣwf*. With regard to the *ṣ* one is to demand of oneself *ṣidq* (sincerity), *ṣafā* (purity), *ṣabr* (steadfastness), *ṣalāḥ* (righteousness) and *ṣiyānat* (chastity), with regard to the *w wafā* (fidelity), *waqār* (gravity) and *wajd* (being moved inwardly), and with regard to the *f faraḥ* (joy), *farāghat* (freedom from cares) and *farmānburdārī* (obedience).[63]

As a wearer of the patched frock (*muraqqa*ᶜ)[64] one should foster within oneself the endeavor to sew back together every torn connection with God. With regard to the *m* of *muraqqa*ᶜ one should demand of oneself *ma*ᶜ*rifat* (higher cognition), *maḥabbat* (love), *madhallat* (humility), *mujāhadat* (spiritual battle), with regard to the *r riyāḍat* (ascetic exercises), *riḍā* (contentment), *riqqat* (sensitivity), with regard to the *q qanā*ᶜ*at* (frugality), *qabūl* (acceptance by God), *quwwat* (power), and with regard to the ᶜ ᶜ*ishq* (love), ᶜ*uluww-i himmat* (high aspiration) and ᶜ*ahd-i durust* (keeping one's word).

What color should the patched frock (*khirqa*) be?

If one has overcome the concupiscent soul (*nafs*), killed it with the sword of the vita purgativa, and one now sits mourning the soul's

---

Muḥammad; likewise in A.J. Wensinck, *Handbook of Early Muhammadan Tradition*, 46b. Ṭabarsī, *Tarjuma-i Makārim al-akhlāq*, *bāb* 6, *faṣl* 4 (my private MS, 28a, 29a, 29b-30a); among the latter the question of Abū Dharr al-Ghifārī as to whether someone can free himself from arrogance, and the answer of the Prophet: Yes, if he wears a woolen garment, rides a donkey (instead of a horse), milks his sheep with his own hands and associates with the broken and the needy. On Adam and Eve as the first who wore wool, wove it and spun it, and on Moses as a wearer of a woolen garment see Maḥmūd b. ᶜUthmān, *Firdaws al-murshidiyya*, ed. F. Meier, p. 283.

63 The interpretation *ṣ* = *ṣabr*, *w* = *wafā*, *f* = *fanā* and *ṣalāḥiyyat*, *waqār* + *wafā*, *faqr* + *fāqa* are also found in the Sufi pastiche *Mūsh u-ghurba* by Bahāᵓ al-Dīn-i ᶜĀmilī (d. 1030/1621), Cairo (sic), 1346, p. 174. Playing with letters of the words ᶜ*ilm* and *zuhd* in ᶜAṭṭār, *Tadhkirat al-awliyā*ᵓ, II, p. 89, ll. 3-4; p. 106, ll. 15-17; with *bukhl* in Sulamī, *Ṭabaqāt al-ṣūfiyya*, Cairo, 1953, p. 246, ll. 13-14. Treating words this way is frequent. J.K. Birge, *The Bektashi Order*, pp. 105, 208.

64 *Muraqqa*ᶜ alternates with *muraqqa*ᶜ*a*. Abū'l-Najīb al-Suhrawardī, *Ādāb al-murīdīn*, 48a ff. recommends old clothing which is as modest and unassuming as possible without any special distinguishing feature and only allows the *muraqqa*ᶜ*a* with special authorization (*rukhṣa*, 76b). Mentioned in ᶜ*Awārif al-ma*ᶜ*ārif*, Chpt. 12 at the end (II, p. 51), as being of the old school. Junayd had advocated it.

demise, then one should wear black (*siyāh*) and dark blue (or a dark color, *kabūdh*).[65]

If one has repented of offering resistance (to God, *mukhālafat*), if one has washed one's interior with the soap of remorse (*inābat*) and cleared the page of one's heart of the inscription (or the pictures, *naqsh*) of foreign (i.e. non-divine) elements (*aghyār*) and the lust of the concupiscent soul, then one should wear white (739a).[66]

---

65 On black see further below. That the Sufis especially liked to wear blue is well-attested: Hujwīrī, Zhukovski, p. 59, ll. 7 ff./Nicholson, p. 53. They are often referred to as 'wearers of blue robes'. Anṣārī, *Rasāʾil*, p. 68 (= *Kanz al-sālikīn*, Chpt. 3). *Asrār al-tawḥīd*, Zhukovski, p. 234, l. 12; p. 359, ll. 2-3/Tehran, 1313, pp. 147, 228/Ṣafā, Tehran, 1332, pp. 194, 286/Shafīʿī-i Kadkanī, Tehran, 1366, pp. 189, 273/trans. O'Kane, Costa Mesa (Calif.)-New York, 1992, pp. 282, 413. *Maqāmāt-i Ḥamīdī, maqāma* 12: *kabūdpōsh*. ʿAṭṭār, *Asrārnāma*, MS of Prof. R. Tschudi, Basle, 114a: *pīrōzakhirqa*. Saʿdī, *Gulistān*, Chpt. 8, ed. Furūghī, Tehran, 1316, p. 198, l. 2 (= trans. by Karl Heinrich Graf, reprint Munich, 1920, p. 286): *azraqpīrahan*. For this reason in the *Asrārnāma* 104b, conversely, the sky is called 'the wearer of the patched frock of Muḥammad's convent'. Hujwīrī, *op. cit.*, and Abū Ḥafṣ, *ʿAwārif*, Chpt. 12 at the end (II, p. 50), report that the shaykhs preferred blue for practical reasons because blue did not become dirty so quickly. Geo Widengren, 'Harlekintracht und Mönchskutte, Clownhut und Derwischmütze', in *Orientalia Suecana* 2, 1953, pp. 52 ff. The 'and' between black and blue in our text probably means the same as 'or'. Black as well as blue were both colors of mourning; *Muwashshā*, ed. Brünnow, p. 126, l. 25/Cairo, 1953, p. 164, l. 5: *azraq* and *ḥidād* clothing of widows (on the latter see Abū Ḥayyān al-Tawḥīdī: *Al-baṣāʾir wa'l-dhakhāʾir*, Cairo, 1953, p. 43). Black for example at the death of Maḥmūd of Ghazna; Farrukhī, *Dīwān*, Tehran, 1311, p. 92, l. 8 (= Tarzi and Ateş, *Farsça grameri*, Istanbul, 1942, I, p. 160, l. 7). Rūdakī, ed. Saʿīd Nafīsī, Tehran, 1319, 1024, p. 387. Niẓāmī, *Haft paykar*, the story in the black dome. *Sikāhan* 'black' in Niẓāmi, *Sharafnāma*, ed. Dastgirdī, Tehran, 1316, p. 117, l. 9. Al-Aʿshā in Goldziher, *WZKM* 16, 1902, p. 322, ftn. 4. O. Spies, 'Esman und Zeidschan', in *Anthropos* 20, p. 1009 (as well as 1031...); idem: 'Türk. Volksbücher', in *Form und Geist* 12, Leipzig, 1929, p. 107. Hellmut Ritter: *Das meer der seele*, Leiden, 1955, p. 26. With regard to Maḥmūd's death Farrukhī is contradicted by *Tārīkh-i Bayhaqī*, ed. Saʿīd Nafīsī, I, p. 14, ll. 13 ff., which reports on white mourning clothes; for white as a color of mourning among the Andalusians see Ignaz Goldziher, *Abh. z. arab. Philologie*, II, p. XLV. Blue as a color of mourning in Hujwīrī, *op. cit.*; ʿAṭṭār, *Manṭiq al-ṭayr*, litho., Lahore, n.d., p. 46 below (*kabūd*), (*nīlī*); Ritter: *Meer der seele*, pp. 24, 25, 88, 427, 514 f.; Fakhr-i Gurgānī: *Wīs u-Rāmīn*, ed. Mujtabā Mīnuwī, Tehran, 1314, p. 40, l. 14; p. 239, l. 5; Jāmī, *Nafaḥāt*, p. 55; Niẓāmī, *Sharafnāma*, p. 116, l. 2 (*nīl*); *Farsça grameri*, I, p. 140, l. 8 (*nīl*); Paul Kahle, 'Die Totenklage im heutigen Ägypten', in *Εὐχαριστήριον Gunkel*, I, pp. 347, 355, ftn. 3.

66 White wool is frequently attested in Daylamī's *Sīrat-i Ibn-i Khafīf*.

If by means of one's effective power (or high aspiration, *himmat*[67]) one has traversed the sublunar world, entered the translunar realm and attained the level of a man of high rank (*ṣāḥib maqām*) and courtier (*muqarrab*) in the heaven of effective power, then one should wear (light) blue (*azraq*).[68]

If one has had a share in all the mystical stations (virtues, *maqāmāt*) and also received a gleam (*lumᶜa*) from the light of the mystical states (emotional experiences, *ḥālāt*), then one should wear something multi-colored (*mulammaᶜ*).[69]

If one has stamped on one's exterior and interior the seal of trustworthiness (*amānat*) and religiosity (*diyānat*) and made one's heart into a treasure chamber of divine secrets, then one should add (*bar-nihadh*) a trimming (*farāwēz*)[70] to one's robe.

If one is seated on the throne (*takht*) of love and in the chair (*sarīr*) of knowledge and agreement with God, then one should sew on (*bar-dōzadh*) a hem (*kursī*[71]).

---

67 Abū'l-Najīb, *Ādāb*, 16b: *Himma* is what drives you out of your self (or: out of your carnal soul) to seek noble things. The worth of every man is his *himma* (*al-himmatu mā yabᶜathuka min nafsika ᶜalā ṭalabi'l-maᶜālī wa-qīmatu kulli'mriʾin himmatuhū*). For the important role and special meaning of *himma* as 'effective power' see *Fawāʾiḥ*, Intro., pp. 227 ff.

68 *Azraq* elsewhere has the same meaning as *kabūdh*. But since *kabūdh* was already mentioned and then designated a dark color, perhaps *azraq* should here be understood as a lighter blue. But maybe there was also another symbolic connection implied as well (blue — sky).

69 Play on words: *lumᶜa-mulammaᶜ*. In *Maqāmāt-i Ḥamīdī*, *maqāma* 12, p. 100, the Sufi who wears blue is contrasted with the worldly man dressed in multi-colored clothes (*mulammaᶜ-pōsh*). Adam, while still in Paradise, is said to have received a multi-colored patched frock (*khirqa-i mulawwan*) from Gabriel. But when he then washed it on Ceylon after being driven out of Paradise, it came out dark-blue (*nīlī*). According to *ᶜAwārif*, Chpt. 12 at the end (II, p. 51), bright colors (*mulawwan*) are preferred by some people for the same reason as blue, i.e. because bright colors are not so delicate and the Sufis, being preoccupied with their inner state, do not have time to give special care to their clothing.

70 Here the point of comparison is between 'to stamp' and 'to add'. *Farāwēz* = *sijāf*. Also mentioned in Hujwīrī, ed. Zhukovski, p. 63/trans. Nicholson, p. 56, where *farāwēz* symbolizes honesty (*ikhlāṣ*). On a Sufi garment in *Asrār al-tawḥīd*, ed. Zhukovski, p. 275, l. 7/Tehran, 1313, p. 174/Ṣafā, Tehran, 1332, p. 227/Shafīᶜī-i Kadkanī, Tehran, 1366, p. 212/trans. O'Kane, 1992, Costa Mesa (Calif.)-New York, p. 324.

71 Association of *takht*, *sarīr* and *kursī* in which *kursī* should not be understood in the usual sense of 'throne' or 'footstool' but as 'hem'. This meaning is not given in dictionaries, however. I follow the suggestion of Colonel Ranking which Nicholson adopted; Hujwīrī, *Kashf*, ed. Zhukovski, p. 63, ll. 4 and 7 variants/trans. Nicholson, p. 56. R. Dozy, *Suppl. aux*

If one has clad oneself in the armor of opposition to the concupiscent soul and Satan and donned the helmet of battle against lust, then one should put on (*bar-nihadh*) a collar (*qabb*).[72]

If one has avoided the false flattery of the concupiscent soul and entered the battle against the concupiscent soul, then one should put on coarse material (*khashin*).[73]

If one has worn oneself down and wounded oneself through a thousand blows of spiritual combat, drunken a thousand cups (*sharbat*[74]) of poison[75] and tortured (correct *biyāzīdha* to *biyāzārīdha*) one's nature (*nihādh*) with the needle of despair (*nākāmī*), then one should wear a 'thousand-needle robe' (*hazārmēkhī*).[76]

If one has rent the robe of one's existence and brought one's being to non-being, then one should wear a *lapācha* (cloak).[77]

---

dictionnaires arabes, s.v., has the following remark: 'Les Mauresques donnent le nom de *kursī* à de petites pièces d'argent ou d'or, qu'elles ont dans leurs colliers, à cause de la figure de ces ornements.'

72 Is also mentioned by Hujwīrī, ed. Zhukovski, p. 63, l. 5/trans. Nicholson, p. 56, but there it symbolizes steadfastness and patience (*ṣabr*).

73 The struggle against the *nafs* is represented symbolically in Hujwīrī by the belt (*kamar*). In *Fawā'iḥ*, Intro., p. 126, ftn. 6, I have given a more detailed explanation of why *khishan* should not be read as 'dark-blue' and that Nicholson is mistaken when he translates it thus in *Kashf al-maḥjūb*, p. 69 (ed. Zhukovski, p. 77, l. 11). It is a question of the Arabic word *khashin* or *khashan* 'rough, hard', the opposite of which is *nā'im* or *layyin* 'soft, smooth' (= Pers. *narm*). This is perfectly clear from *'Awārif*, Chpt. 12 (II, pp. 45 f.), and Ibn 'Aṭā'allāh al-Sikandarī, *Laṭā'if al-minan*, Chpt. 8, Cairo ('Allāmiyya), p. 113; *jāma-i narm* also in Nāṣir-i Khusraw, *Zād al-musāfirīn*, Berlin (Kaviani), p. 241, ll. 10 ff.; *khashindār* in Khāqānī: *Tuḥfat al-'Irāqayn*, Tehran, 1333, p. 200, l. 2. The Persian equivalent would be *durusht*.

74 The meaning 'cup' for *sharbat* is clear from *Nawrōznāma*, ed. Mujtabā Mīnuwī, Tehran, 1933, p. 69.

75 One expects a further qualifying word after 'poison', for instance *zahr-i zajr* or *zahr-i riyāḍat*.

76 *Dalq-i hazārmēkh* in Khāqānī: *Tuḥfat al-'Irāqayn*, p. 200, l. 4.

77 The symbolism is not clear to me. Perhaps Kubrā reads a *pārcha* into *lapācha*, or *lapācha* corresponds to Arabic *'abā'*, a cloak without sleeves which is open in front, i.e. looks as if it has been torn in two parts. The MS has *lapācha* pointed with *p*. Abū Sa'īd b. Abī'l-Khayr once gave someone a *labācha* of green wool as a present; *Asrār al-tawḥīd*, ed. Zhukovski, p. 174, l. 1/1313, p. 109, last line/Ṣafā, 1332, p. 145, last line/Shafī'ī-i Kadkanī, Tehran, 1366, p. 134, l. 14/trans. O'Kane, Costa Mesa (Calif.)-New York, 1992, p. 227, l. 36. Ni'matallāh (d. 834/1431) wore a *labācha* of lambskin; Aubin, *Matériaux*, p. 304, l. 9.

If one has fettered the concupiscent soul with the fetters of command and prohibition, and placed oneself in the chains of the religious law, then one should add (*bar-nihadh*) some geometric figures (*ashkāl*).[78]

If one has donned the mantle (*ridā*) of fidelity and honored the contracts of religious law and mystical work, then one should wear a mantle (*ridā*) over one's clothes.

If people at large no longer need to fear harm from one (*jumla-i khalāʾiq azō ēman gashta and*), then one should put on a turban (*dastār*).[79]

If one has tossed behind oneself everything which is not God, then one should toss the end of the turban (*shākh-i dastār*) to the back.[80]

If one has the goal before one and what one sought has been granted to one, then one should toss the end of the turban to the front.

If one has behind one the unpleasantness of associating with people (*āzār-i khalq bigudhāshta*) and if one has become weak (*zār*) and thin (*nizār*) through ascetic exercises, then one should wind around oneself (*pēchadh*) a wrap (here *īzār* instead of *izār*[81]).

If one has renounced one's qualities (*az ṣifāt-i khwadh nēst shudha*) and attained the world of being (*hastī*), then one should place a Lām-Alif wrap (*izār-i lām-alif*)[82] over one's head.

If one has become fettered by religious doctrine, an intimate (*maḥram*) of mystical work, and tried and proven in divine experience (*mujarrab*), then one should wear socks (*jawrab*).[83]

If one has preserved one's foot from the dirt of natural disposition and set it down in the world of cleanliness, then one should put on shoes (*pāchīla*).

---

78 A play on words: *shikāl* 'fetters' and *ashkāl* 'figures'.

79 The symbolism is not clear to me.

80 The two possibilites of letting the end of the turban fall either behind or in front are considered, acknowledged and given symbolic meaning in Aḥmad al-Qushāshī, *Al-simṭ al-majīd* (written 1069/1659), Hyderabad, 1327, p. 103. Since the Prophet was accustomed to toss it to the back, this is regarded as best.

81 As in Dozy, *Dictionnaire détaillée des noms des vêtements chez les Arabes*, Amsterdam, 1845, p. 32; ibid., the different meanings of the word.

82 In *izār-i lām-alif* a clear allusion to *lā*. Cf. Brown, *Dervishes*, p. 113: 'Their (i.e. the Rifāʿiyya) belt is called Alif-lamend.'

83 A play on words: *mujarrab-jawrab*.

If one has freed one's eye and tongue from the temptation of Satan (*nang-i Shayṭān*) and become worthy of seeing God, then one should wrap a handkerchief (*rōymāla*)[84] around one's neck.

In brief, the exterior and interior of a Sufi must be aligned with one another (*bar jādda-i istiqāmat*) and in tune with one another (*muwāfiq-i yakdīgar*). Whatever Sufis do outwardly must possess in their interior a spiritual reality (*ḥaqīqat*).

Furthermore, the shaykhs have said:[85]

*Muraqqa*ᶜ means *marra wa-waqa*ᶜ*a*, i.e. he went and he fell; for whoever runs away from the *muraqqa*ᶜ falls in such a way that he never again stands up.

The border at the neck (*zih*) of the *muraqqa*ᶜ is the sword belt of the profession of God's oneness (*tawḥīd*) which one has placed around one's neck.

The bosom (*jēb*) of the *muraqqa*ᶜ is a place of secrets and a sanctuary for people, i.e. I keep to myself whatever someone confides in me and whoever seeks refuge with me, I offer it to him.

The sleeve (*āstīn*) of the *muraqqa*ᶜ is the weapon which I brandish before the enemy[86]

The skirt (*dāman*) of the *muraqqa*ᶜ is the cover which I spread over the brethren.[87]

The cap (*kulāh*, omit: of the *muraqqa*ᶜ) is the crown of respect (*karāmat*)[88] which I have donned, and (the sign that) I have cast from myself arrogance and pride.

The belt (*miyānband*) is the belt of service which I have put on.[89]

The carpet (*waṭā, wiṭā*)[90] is the kelim of compassion which I have unfolded to show compassion and sympathy to everyone.

---

84 Apparently the association of the words eye, tongue, seeing and the word *rōymāla* which actually means 'face-wiper'.

85 I assume the whole of the following enumeration is the content of what the shaykhs have said, though I cannot find examples for the list in primary sources.

86 Allusion to the arms (of the body) which one uses in a fight, or the weapons carried in one's hands (the sleeves usually extend over the fingertips, but on a march, as noted in Chpt. 7, they are pulled up). One also deals out slaps for instance with long sleeves. The enemy referred to is the interior one.

87 The cover of leniency and forgiveness.

88 Respect toward one's fellow-man.

89 Keenness to serve one's fellow-man.

90 *Waṭā* must mean rug, as is clear from the predicate noun kelim. I do not understand why Reuben Levy, *A Mirror for Princes*, p. 251, l. 1 (his text edition, p. 146, l. 11) translates it as 'shoes'; the word is not found in Saᶜīd Nafīsī's edition of the *Qābūsnāma*, p. 186, ll. 2-3.

The turban (*dastār*) is the plumb-line of trustworthiness (*dastūr-i amānat*)[91] in the sense that no one need fear any harm from me.

The prayer-rug (*sajjāda*) is the rug of proximity to God (*qurb*) which I have spread out and upon which I have placed the foot of service.[92]

The staff (*ʿaṣā*) is the fortification of benefit (*takyagāh-i manfaʿat*) and what repulses harm.[93]

The leather bowl (*rakwa*) is the spring of purity and the drinking place of temperance.

The sack[94] is the treasure chamber of secrets (739b) and the chest of knowledge.

Footwear (*pāyafzār*) is the means for setting out on that journey to God, for going forward in obedience and especially for fleeing what is not God.[95]

The balance... (*tarāzūy-i namāna* or *tumāna*?)[96] is the measuring instrument for weighing friend and foe.

Tearing the *khirqa* (when listening to music)[97] signifies: everything which is a foreign element (i.e. not God, *aghyār*) I have broken in two and cast aside.

Khirqa itself means: I attribute every fault in a brother to myself so as not to see his fault.[98]

So whatever the Sufi does he must demand from his interior that it prove to be true and thereby that he is not a liar but honest, not a hypocrite but in agreement with himself, not a shammer but upright,

91 A play on words (*tajnīs-i nāqiṣ*): *dastār* - *dastūr*.

92 Service unto God.

93 The staff symbolizes the will of the dervish to be of use in the religious sense to himself and to others, and to ward off harm. A.J. Wensinck in *Oriental Studies presented to E.G. Browne*, p. 499.

94 The MS has *kyf*. I conjecture *kīsa* on the basis of Chpt. 3. Perhaps *kayfdān* 'box' would also be possible, or something similar. It is no doubt a question of a bag in which the Sufi's slippers are kept. But cf. *ktf Qābūsnāma*, ed. Nafīsī, p. 186, l. 4 (?); not in Reuben Levy.

95 The means (*ālat*) could be the *himma* which is often described as a riding animal of the Sufi, and about which it is also said that it extends just as far as the footsteps of the Sufi.

96 Not understandable to me.

97 On tearing garments during the *samāʿ* see provisionally my article 'The Dervish Dance, pp. 83 f.

98 In disputes looking for the fault within oneself.

not an asserter of empty claims (*muddaʿī*) but a representative of the truth (*muḥaqqiq*).[99]

CHAPTER 2. ON SITTING AND RISING.

One should sit with propriety (*adab*) and respect (*ḥurmat*). On the prayer-rug one is to take up a position facing Mecca. One should lay down (*biyafganadh*) one's left leg and lift up (*bar-dāradh*) one's right leg.[100] Kneeling (*ba-du zānū*) is permitted. One should not expose the legs.[101] The hands should be placed one on top of the other and withdrawn into the sleeves. One must never keep them under one's robe and never expose them up to the forearm (*sāʿid*).[102] At gatherings one should not stretch out one's legs,[103] nor should one blow one's nose (*bīnī nadamadh*)[104] or spit (*āb-i dahān nayafganadh*).[105] If one must cough or sneeze, one should place one's hand with the sleeve before one's mouth; in so doing one should make as little noise as possible. Nor should one continually scratch oneself and continually run one's fingers through one's hair and over one's face,[106] but sit occupied in thought (*ba-tafakkur*) and with respect (*ḥurmat*). When sitting on the prayer-rug, one must observe its rights, that is to say: one should immerse oneself in the recollection of God (*dhikr-i khudhāy*), ask oneself whether the acts of obedience one has to show are also accepted by God, reflect on

---

99 In Sarrāj, *Lumaʿ*, p. 144, ll. 4-5, *ṣādiq-kādhib* and *muḥaqqiq-muddaʿī* are also contrasted.

100 *Iḥyāʾ*, II, pp. 3-4: The Prophet, when eating, kneeled or sat on his left foot, while he kept his right foot upright. Similarly, *ʿAwārif*, Chpt. 42 (III, p. 268); *Lumaʿ*, p. 201, l. 9; *Qābūsnāma*, ed. Levy, p. 147, 3/ed. Nafīsī, p. 186, l. 17/trans. Levy, p. 252, forbid sitting on the prayer-rug with one's legs crossed. Yet *Lumaʿ*, p. 201. ll. 5-6, presupposes this form of sitting on the prayer-rug as well. *Muwashshā*, B(rünnow), p. 146, l. 22/Cairo, 1953, p. 193, l. 6, forbids squatting.

101 Shahrazūrī, Chpt. 4, Sect. 3, § 2. *Akhlāq-i Nāṣirī*, in Plessner, p. 91.

102 Bryson, §135. Shahrazūrī, Chpt. 4, Sect. 3, § 2.

103 *Lumaʿ*, p. 201, l. 7. *Muwashshā*, B, p. 146, l. 18/Cairo, p. 193, l. 2. *Akhlāq-i Nāṣirī*, in P(lessner), p. 90, where however kneeling is only recommended before rulers, teachers, one's father and similarly high-ranking persons. *Qābūsnāma*, L, p. 147, ll. 7-8/N, p. 186, l. 22/trans. p. 252; Pseudo-Nāṣir-i Khusraw: *Saʿādatnāma*, in *Dīwān*, p. 552, l. 6/Kaviani, p. 10, l. 1, forbid one to place one's foot on another person's rug, i.e. that one stretch out one's leg that far.

104 Bryson, § 135. Shahrazūrī, Chpt. 4, Sect. 3, § 2. *Akhlāq-i Nāṣirī*, P(lessner), p. 90.

105 Ibid.

106 Ibid. (without Bryson); *Muwashshā*, B, p. 146, ll. 18-19/Cairo, p. 193, l. 2.

which act of obedience is likely to be most pleasing to God and then also take that one by the hand (*ba-dast gīradh*). One should not speak a lot but only when absolutely necessary,[107] in doing so not employ gestures,[108] not be loud and refrain from any unsuitable movements (*ḥarakāt-i khārij*).[109]

When standing up, one should lift oneself on the right leg, place the right leg forward and put on one's right shoe (*kafsh*) first.[110] One always places the left foot outside first.[111] Never set a bare foot on the floor.[112]

When walking, one should not bear oneself proudly (*nakharāmadh*)[113] and not swing one's arms. One should neither look to the right nor to the left, neither ahead nor behind, but keep

---

107 Literally: 'One should not speak a lot, except out of necessity.' But that is not the meaning. Speaking only a little: *Qābūsnāma*, L, p. 147, l. 5/N, p. 186, l. 20/trans. p. 252; *Akhlāq-i Nāṣirī*, P, pp. 87, 89; *Al-adab al-wajīz li'l-walad al-ṣaghīr*, allegedly by Ibn al-Muqaffaᶜ, trans. by Naṣīr al-Dīn-i Ṭūsī, ed. ᶜAbd al-Raḥīm Khalkhālī, Tehran, 1312, p. 11 and frequently. Bryson, § 146; Shahrazūrī, Chpt. 4, Sect. 2, § 1.

108 Shahrazūrī, Chpt. 4, Sect. 2, § 2; one should not make signs with one's hands, eyes and brows while speaking, unless the situation demands it.

109 *Ḥarakat-i khārij* also in Rāwandī, *Rāḥat al-ṣudūr*, ed. M. Iqbāl, in Gibb Memorial Series, New Series 2, 1921, p. 282, l. 18.

110 One puts on the right shoe first and takes off the left one first so that the right foot remains covered the longest; Bukhārī, 77, 39 (following the numeration of *Concordance*), among others (see *Handbook of Early Muhammadan Tradition*, p. 213b). Samᶜānī: *Adab al-imlā'*, ed. Max Weisweiler, Leiden, 1952, pp. 122 f. Hujwīrī, Zh(ukovski), p. 451, ll. 14-16/N(icholson), p. 346. *Qābūsnāma*, N, p. 186, l. 6 (the other way around in the edition of Levy, p. 146, l. 15/trans., p. 251: one removes the right shoe first and puts on the left shoe first). Abū'l-Najīb, 46a below. *ᶜAwārif*, Chpt. 16 (II, pp. 114, 124). Ṭabarsī, *bāb* 6, *faṣl* 8 (30b).

111 Something appears to be wrong with Kubrā's text; it reads: *wa-ba-pāy-i chap bērūn kunadh*, but *ba* should probably be dropped. The sense seems to me to be clear from ᶜAbd al-Khāliq-i Ghujduwānī, *Risāla-i Ṣāḥibiyya*, ed. Nafīsī, in *Farhang-i Īrānzamīn* 1, 1332, p. 88: When he (Yūsuf-i Hamadānī) entered, he entered with the right foot, and when he went out, he went out with the left foot. Ibid., p. 91: In the mosque he first put his right foot in the shoe (*kafsh*) and guarded the heel (*pāshna-rā nigāh dāshtandē*). Then he covered his left foot (cf. the previous ftn.).

112 That one should not go out without shoes on is required by Bryson, § 139.

113 Shahrazūrī, IV, p. 3, l. 1. *Akhlāq-i Nāṣirī*, P, p. 89. *Akhlāq-i Jalālī*, p. 217.

one's head lowered.[114] While underway one should not speak and not recite the Koran out loud but only silently in one's heart. One should only go to the bazaar[115] if it is absolutely necessary. On the way one should not stand still[116] anywhere and not sit down anywhere. Disreputable and dirty places must be avoided. One should also not walk in haste,[117] unless one is afraid of missing the congregation (*jamāᶜat*). Only on visits to the sick or accompanying the dead or when on the way to the Friday prayers and other ritual prayers may one walk slowly or quickly; in any such case for every step ten credits are written down for one (in Paradise).[118]

CHAPTER 3. ON ENTERING A CONVENT.

When one comes to a convent (*khānaqāh*) for the first time, one extends one's right foot and stamps in front of the door on the ground (*bar dar-i khānaqāh pāy bar zamīn zanadh*). Upon entering one does not utter a greeting for the moment,[119] but brings forth the sack (*kīsa*) and slippers (*kafsh*) and places them before oneself (*dar pēsh nihadh*).[120] Then one first removes one's left shoe (*pāyafzār*) (740a)

---

114 Hujwīrī, Zh, p. 456, l. 5/N, p. 350: one should not gaze about but look straight ahead. Shahrazūrī, IV, p. 3, l. 1: one should not gaze about but should also not keep one's head lowered.

115 *Qābūsnāma*, L, p. 147, l. 1/N, p. 186, l. 15/trans. p. 251, last line.

116 Hujwīrī, Zh, p. 456, l. 14/N, p. 350.

117 Bryson, § 139. Shahrazūrī, IV, p. 3, l. 1. Hujwīrī, Zh, p. 456, l. 15/N, p. 350. However, these texts also require one not to walk slowly because this is a sign of pride (and laziness). *Qābūsnāma*, L, p. 147, l. 8/N, p. 146, last line/trans. p. 252. *Akhlāq-i Jalālī*, p. 217, follows Bryson and Shahrazūrī in that it interprets a slow pace of walking as a sign of laziness and attributes a stately walk (*kharāmīdan*) to pride. Cf. Muḥammad Bāqir-i Majlisī in H. Massé, *JA* 232, 1940-41, p. 64.

118 Cf. the recommendation to teachers and students to walk at a moderate pace, and the exceptional permission given to students to walk quickly in Samᶜānī, *Adab al-imlā'*, pp. 33, 113 ff.

119 Mentioned, but then rejected, by Ibn Ḥājj, *Al-mudkhal*, III, p. 186.

120 Whereas in the previous chapter by *kafsh* travelling shoes were understood, here it is a question of house shoes; I translate as 'slippers'. The whole following procedure is described in greater detail by Abū Ḥafṣ al-Suhrawardī, *ᶜAwārif*, Chpt. 16 (II, p. 119). According to him and as is clear from our context, the Sufi when travelling takes with him in a bag a second pair of shoes, his slippers. This bag in *ᶜAwārif*, II, p. 113, is called a 'slipper bag' (*kharīṭat al-madās*), which imposes on the text of Kubrā the otherwise obvious amendment *kīsa-i kafsh* for *kīsa wa-kafsh*. Before setting out the Sufi packs his slippers in the bag (an act just as regulated

and places one's left foot on top of the slipper (*ba-rōy-i kafsh nihadh*) but does not put it on. Then one removes one's right shoe. After that one first puts one's right foot in the slipper. Then one goes to the lavatory (*mutawaḍḍā*), undertakes the ritual ablution (*wuḍū*), comes back and performs a prayer involving two sets of movements (*rakʿa*).[121] Only then does one present the greeting to those present and ask after their condition. This for two reasons (*du maʿnē-rā*): firstly, it is reprehensible (*karāhiyat*) to give a greeting without a preceding ritual ablution; for *salām* (greeting, well-being, he who confers well-being) is a name of God,[122] and politeness (*adab*) enjoins upon representatives of higher knowledge only to pronounce the names of their Lord in a state of ritual purity. The Prophet was once not in a state of ritual ablution when one of his followers came in and greeted him. The Prophet quickly ran his hands over the walls, undertook the substitute ritual ablution with sand and only then returned the greeting. 'If I am not in a state of ritual ablution', he said, 'then do not greet me; for you will hear no greeting in return!' The other reason is that the Sufis are mostly immersed in the recollection of God and in meditation, and would therefore be disturbed by a sudden greeting. If one first undertakes the ritual ab-

---

as the unpacking here) and with his left hand pulls the bag through his wide left sleeve and slings it over his shoulder inside his garment. On his arrival somewhere he brings it forth again in the same way; and therefore in Kubrā 'he brings it forth' (*bērūn āradh*). In this chapter Kubrā distinguishes precisely between the two pairs of shoes, and *kafsh* (the pair of house shoes) corresponds to Arabic *madās* (from *dws*) and *pāyafzār* (the pair of travelling shoes) to Arabic *khuff*. Possibly in Hujwīrī, Zh, p. 450, l. 5/N, p. 345, where *kafsh* or *naʿlayn* are mentioned as shoes the Sufi takes with him on journeys, it is also a question of the second pair, the house shoes, and this is perhaps confirmed by the sentence, p. 450, ll. 7-8/p. 345, ll. 9 and 8 from bot.: 'One must put on the *kafsh* in a state of ritual purity before coming onto the prayer-rug.' However, at ibid., p. 456, l. 12/p. 350, *kafsh* or *naʿlayn* certainly means the travelling shoes, as is the case with Kubrā in the previous chapter.

121 Hujwīrī, Zh, p. 451, ll. 16-17/N, pp. 346-47 (not correctly translated as 'perform two bowings of the head by way of salutation in prayer'). Abū'l-Najīb 46b. *ʿAwārif*, Chpt. 16 (II, p. 119). *Qābūsnāma*, L, p. 146, l. 17/N, p. 186, l. 8/trans., p. 251, requires that the Sufi ask permission before the prayer of two *rakʿas*. The *ḥadīth*-teacher prays two *rakʿas* before sitting down; Samʿānī, *Adab al-imlāʾ*, p. 35, l. 12 (with a *ḥadīth*).

122 Hence the name ʿAbd al-Salām. *Dār al-salām*, for instance, is also conceived of this way; *Firdaws al-murshidiyya*, p. 279, ll. 11-12.

lution and comes back, they are ready to return one's greeting and to respond to one's inquiry after their condition.[123]

CHAPTER 4. ON EATING.

Before eating one must wash one's hands.[124] While eating one sits on one's left leg.[125] The bowl (*kāsa*) is not to be placed on top of the flat-bread.[126] One begins the meal with the formula 'In the name of God' and ends it with 'Praise be to God'.[127] The meal is initiated and concluded with salt.[128] The bread is broken up and soaked

---

123 *ᶜAwārif*, Chpt. 16 (II, pp. 121 ff.), with the *ḥadīth* and the same two reasons. Abū Saᶜīd b. Abī'l-Khayr once refused to return the greeting of someone who came in and greeted him while he was eating, explaining that *salām* is a name of God and he ought not to pronounce it with an 'unclean mouth' (*dahān-i ālūda*); *Asrār al-tawḥīd*, Zh(ukovski), p. 356, ll. 8 ff./(Tehran) 1313, p. 226, ll. 11 ff./(Tehran) 1332, p. 284, ll. 15 ff./(Tehran) 1366, p, 271, ll. 20 ff./trans., (Costa Mesa-New York), 1992, p. 411, ll. 18 ff. According to the *Qābūsnāma*, L, p. 146, ll. 17-18/N, p. 186, l. 8/trans., p. 251, the Sufi can greet people each time he comes and goes, or he can also refrain from doing so. According to Hujwīrī, Zh, p. 451, l. 14/N, p. 346, one must give the greeting before removing one's shoes. L. Massignon, 'Die Auferstehung in der mohammedanischen Welt', in *Eranos-Jahrbuch*, 1939, p. 13, last line: A person entering does not give a greeting to Abū'l-ᶜAbbās al-Mursī in order not to disturb him in his trance. Ubshayhī: *Al-mustaṭraf*, Cairo, 1935, II, p. 278, l. 1/trans. by G. Rat, II, p. 737, requires one not to greet a king if the latter is sick in order to spare him the effort of returning the greeting. According to Shīᶜite orthodoxy (M. Bāqir-i Majlisī), there are three kinds of persons one should not greet: those accompanying a funeral procession, those engaged in performing prayers, and those who are in the bath (*JA* 232, 1940-41, p. 75). — A quite interesting custom is reported by Ibn al-Ḥājj: *Al-mudkhal*, III, p. 187. In the case of some Sufis, when a newcomer sat down in front of the convent, one or more of the residents would come forth, insult him and break the water jug he carried with him, in order to assess his character on the basis of his reaction.

124 Aḥmad b. Ḥanbal in Wensinck, *Handbook*, p. 92. Ṭabarsī, *bāb* 7, *faṣl* 3 (35a). *Iḥyāʾ*, II, p. 3. Shahrazūrī, IV, p. 4, l. 1. *Risāla-i Ṣāḥibiyya*, in *Farhang-i Īrānzamīn* 1, 1332, p. 87.

125 Abū'l-Najīb, 51b. *Iḥyāʾ*, II, p. 4. One should not sit on the right leg; Tawḥīdī, *Baṣāʾir*, p. 237.

126 *Iḥyāʾ*, II, p. 5.

127 Wensinck, *Handbook*, p. 80. Ṭabarsī, *bāb* 7, *faṣl* 3 (31a-35a). Hujwīrī, Zh, p. 454, ll. 13-14/N, pp. 348-49. *Iḥyāʾ*, II, p. 4. Abū'l-Najīb, 51b. *ᶜAwārif*, Chpt. 42 (III, pp. 258 f.). *Risāla-i Ṣāḥibiyya*, p. 91. *Akhlāq-i Jalālī* in Plessner, p. 111.

128 Hujwīrī, Zh, p. 454, ll.4-5/N, p. 348. *Iḥyāʾ*, II, pp. 4, 17. *ᶜAwārif*, Chpt. 43 (III, p. 265). *Risāla-i Ṣāḥibiyya*, p. 87. Ṭabarsī, *bāb* 7, *faṣl* 3 (34b). Ṭabarsī, ibid., at the end of a meal requires vinegar which, however, one has already taken at the beginning after salt. Salt has the

(*tharīd kunadh*).[129] From one's bowl[130] one may not put anything back again.[131] One takes small bites[132] and chews well.[133] Before

---

effect of repulsing demons and in the East and in the Mediterranean area since ancient times has been a food which symbolizes the bond of friendship. Alfred von Kremer has written a study on the subject: *Studien zur vergleichenden Culturgeschichte, vorzüglich nach arabischen Quellen*, in Sitzungsberichte der philos.-hist. Classe der kais. Akademie der Wiss. 120, Vienna, 1890, pp. 17-34. Similarly, see C.-F. Volney, *Voyage en Syrie et en Egypte*², Paris, 1787, I, p. 377. J.G. Worbs, *Geschichte und Beschreibung des Landes der Drusen*, Görlitz, 1799, p. 22. E.W. Lane, *Arabian Society in the Middle Ages*, London, 1883, p. 144. M. Grünbaum, *Neue Beiträge zur semitischen Sagenkunde*, Leiden, 1893, p. 134 (from the Haggada). S. Fraenkel, 'Das Schutzrecht der Araber', in the *Nöldeke-Festschrift*, I, 1906, p. 294. Johs. Pedersen, 'Der Eid bei den Semiten', in *Studien zur Geschichte u. Kultur des islam. Orients*, Beiheft 3 zu *Der Islam*, 1914, p. 25. Bernhard Heller, 'Die Bedeutung des arab. ᶜAntar-Romans', in *Form und Geist* 21, Leipzig, 1931, p. 35. The Shuᶜūbīs made fun of the ancient Arabs' custom of eating salt after concluding treaties; Jāḥiẓ: *Al-bayān wa'l-tabyīn*, Cairo, 1927, III, p. 3/Cairo, 1949, III, p. 7, l. 3. O. Rescher, 'Studien über den Inhalt von 1001 Nacht', in *Der Islam* 9, 1919, pp. 60 f. Nikita Elisséef, *Thèmes et motifs des 1001 Nuits*, Beirut, 1949, p. 148. Ritter, *Meer der seele*, p. 316. C. de Landberg-K.V. Zettersteen, *Glossaire daṯînois*, III, p. 2715, s.v. *milḥ*. *Mumālaḥa* = *synalizesthai* = *metalabein halōn*; O. Cullmann, 'Die neuentdeckten Qumrāntexte', in Beiheft 21 zu *ZNTW* (Festschrift für R. Bultmann), p. 46. Bread and salt were sacramental elements among the Jewish Christians; Bousset, *Hauptprobleme der Gnosis*, pp. 227 f. Franz Joseph Dölger, *Antike und Christentum*, V, 1936, Heft 1, pp. 56 f. In Sufism bread and salt were sometimes the nourishment of those on spiritual retreat; Kāshānī, *Miṣbāḥ al-hidāya*, p. 166. To the Goethe quotation in von Kremer, p. 20, one may add Mörike (*Mozart auf der Reise nach Prag*): 'Ich würde unbedingt zu diesem Stück (der Salzbüchse) raten: das edle Salz, so viel ich weiss, ist ein Symbol der Häuslichkeit und Gastlichkeit, wozu wir alle guten Wünsche für Sie legen wollen.' Further material and writings in *Handwörterbuch des deutschen Aberglaubens*, s.v. Salz.

129 The Prophet is meant to have liked sopped bread (*tharīd*); Abu'l-Najīb, 79a. But *Muwashshā*, B, p. 130, l. 2/Cairo, 1953, p. 168, l. 3, says that the *ẓurafā᾽* did not eat *tharīd*.

130 'From *one's* bowl' (*kāsa-i khwadh*). According to a tradition, the custom of placing before every Sufi a bowl of his own was introduced by Abū Saᶜīd b. Abī'l-Khayr (d. 440/1049). When he was reminded of the saying of the Prophet 'The greater the number of hands in one bowl, the greater the blessing' and of the practice of the Prophet's Companions to eat from a single bowl, he replied: At that time one ate altruistically, as surah 59/9 shows: 'They let the others go before them, even if they are enduring poverty'; but today one eats like a plunderer (*ba-ghārat*) and would gladly eat the share of one's neighbor as well. Since Muḥammad has forbidden this and in order to hold back the dervishes from doing it, we give each person his own bowl. Iqbāl b. Sābiq-i Sīstānī, *Chihil majlis*, MS Browne (Cambridge) D

swallowing a mouthful, one does not take another bite.[134] One does not blow on the food.[135] But hot food should not be served to oneself or to a guest. A saying of the Prophet states (Arabic): 'Let the food cool off; for there is no blessing in what is hot (or in hot foods)' (*barridū'l-ṭaᶜām fa'inna'l-ḥārra lā barakata fīhi*).[136] One should let it cool off (*āsūdha shawadh*)[137] so one's hand and mouth are not burned. The toothpick (*khilāl*) is not to be used during the meal[138] and nothing that one has taken into the mouth is to be spit out again.[139] Before one has finished eating, one is not to wipe one's hands on the napkin (*dastār-i khwān*; Arabic *mandīl*).[140] Bread and

---

8, 14a-b/MS Browne D 21, 93b. None the less, Yūsuf-i Hamadānī is still said to have eaten with the believers from *one* vessel; *Risāla-i Ṣāḥibiyya*, p. 87.

131 *Muwashshā*, B, p. 130, l. 17/Cairo, 1953, p. 168, last line: *lā yaḍaᶜūna luqmatan*.

132 Bryson, § 118. Shahrazūrī, IV, p. 4, l. 1. Hujwīrī, Zh, p. 454, l. 12/N, p. 348. *Muwashshā*, B, p. 129, penult. line/Cairo, 1953, p. 167, last line. *Iḥyā'*, II, p. 4. Abū'l-Najīb, 51b. Ṭabarsī, *bāb* 7, *faṣl* 3 (34a, last line). *Akhlāq-i Nāṣirī* in Plessner, p. 92.

133 Hujwīrī, ibid. *Iḥyā'*, II, pp. 4, 18. Abū'l-Najīb, ibid. Ṭabarsī, ibid.

134 *Iḥyā'*, II, p. 4. That one should not eat quickly is also otherwise recommended. A person who monopolizes something for himself with his left hand while continuing to eat with his right hand was called in Arabic *jurdabān* or *jardabān* (probably from Pers. *girdabān*); Tawḥīdī, *Baṣā'ir*, p. 47.

135 *Iḥyā'*, II, p. 5. *ᶜAwārif*, Chpt. 43 (III, p. 271). For *ḥadīth*s see Wensinck, *Handbook*, p. 81a.

136 Not in the 'Six Books'.

137 *Ḥadīth* in Dārimī; see *Handbook*, p. 81a.

138 *Muwashshā*, B, p. 130, l. 21/Cairo, 1953, p. 169. l. 8. Shahrazūrī, IV, p. 4, l. 4. *Akhlāq-i Nāṣirī*, P, p. 93.

139 *Akhlāq-i Jalālī*, p. 219. Shahrazūrī, IV, p. 4, l. 3.

140 *Iḥyā'*, II, p. 5. Cf. Samᶜānī, *Adab al-imlā'*, p. 84, l. 2, addressing a *ḥadīth* student who has come too late: 'Slave, give him the napkin (*mandīl*)!' Only allowed at the end and after the fingers have been licked; *Iḥyā'*, II, p. 6. On the contrary, licking the fingers is generally recommended in the religious descriptions (*Iḥyā'*, ibid.; Abū'l-Najīb, 51b; *ᶜAwārif*, Chpt. 43[III, p. 270]; Ṭabarsī, *bāb* 7, *faṣl* 3 [34a]). For *ḥadīth*s see *Handbook*, 80b. In the *Muwashshā*, B, p. 130, l. 9/Cairo, p. 168, l. 11, and in the Bryson tradition (Bryson, § 119; Shahrazūrī, IV, p. 4, l. 1; *Akhlāq-i Nāṣirī*, P, p. 92) licking the fingers is forbidden but cleaning oneself with the napkin is perceived as proper (*tamandala*); *Muwashshā*, B, p. 130, l. 24/Cairo, p. 169, l. 11. *Akhlāq-i Jalālī*, p. 219, disapproves of licking the fingers during a meal but allows it at the end. Two traditions confront one another in Islam, the bedouin-Arab (cf. Alois Musil, *Arabia Petraea*, III, p. 156) which Muḥammad represented, and the Hellenistic tradition. The former ordered licking the fingers and the latter forbade it.

meat are not to be cut with the knife.[141] One should clean one's bowl.[142] One should not reach for the salt with a soiled hand.[143] During the meal if possible no water should be drunk[144] for two reasons (*du maᶜnē-rā*): firstly, it is harmful from a medical standpoint and secondly, it is unsavory (*karāhiyat*) for the others if someone places his soiled mouth on the (common) water jug. One should also not look at how the others eat.[145] Further, one should eat whatever is placed before one.[146] One's hand is not to be extended in the bowl (*dar kāsa bar-nayāradh*).[147] There is to be no talking at the table.[148] One is not to stop eating before the group has finished.[149] If while undertaking a supererogatory fast one finds oneself in a com-

---

141 *Iḥyā*ᵓ, II, p. 5. *ᶜAwārif*, Chpt. 43 (III, p. 272). One also forbade the spoon (*milᶜaqa*); Tawḥīdī, *Baṣāᵓir*, pp. 66-67: 'We (God) have given them hands with which they should eat.'

142 *ᶜAwārif*, Chpt. 43 (III, p. 271). Ghazzālī (*Iḥyā*ᵓ, II, p. 6) and Abū'l-Najīb, 51b, even recommend licking the bowl (according to an alleged *ḥadīth*).

143 One should not make the bread and salt damp with a soiled hand; Shahrazūrī, P, IV, p. 4, l. 2; *Akhlāq-i Nāṣirī*, P, p. 92; *Akhlāq-i Jalālī*, p. 219. One should not make damp what is in front of one; *Baṣāᵓir*, p. 237.

144 Bryson, § 127. Shahrazūrī, IV, p. 1, l. 8. *Akhlāq-i Nāṣirī*, P, p. 81. Hujwīrī, Zh, p. 454, ll. 10-11/N, p. 348. *Iḥyā*ᵓ, II, p. 5.

145 Bryson, § 119. Shahrazūrī, IV, p. 4, l. 2. *Akhlāq-i Nāṣirī*, P, p. 92. Hujwīrī, Zh, p. 454, l. 10/N, p. 348. *Iḥya*ᵓ, II, p. 7. Abū'l-Najīb, 52a. Ṭabarsī, *bāb* 7, *faṣl* 3 (34a).

146 Bryson, § 118. Shahrazūrī, IV, p. 4, l. 3. *Akhlāq-i Nāṣirī*, p. 92. *Akhlāq-i Jalālī*, p. 219. Iḥyāᵓ, II, p. 4. Ṭabarsī, *bāb* 7, *faṣl* 3 (34a, 36a)

147 Probably what is meant is: one should not extend one's hand in the bowl if one is not eating.

148 Similarly, one should not talk a lot while eating according to the *Muwashshā*, B, p. 139, l. 20/Cairo, p. 169, l. 7; *Baṣāᵓir*, p. 237. On this point Kubrā differs from *Iḥyā*ᵓ, II, p. 6, Abu'l-Najīb, 51b, and *ᶜAwārif*, Chpt. 43 (III, p. 272), which expressly condemn silence during the meal and represent it as a Persian-Mazdaean custom. This latter assertion is confirmed by a series of additional Islamic testimonies which M. Moin, *L'influence du mazdéisme dans la littérature persane*, Tehran, 1948, (Publications de l'Université de Téhéran, no. 9), pp. 254 ff., has collected, and is corroborated by the Mazdaean text M 55, 1*d* 10 in the Library of Munich (Christian Bartholomae, *Die Zendhss...*, Munich, 1915, pp. 140 f.). Hujwīrī, Zh, p. 454, l. 3/N, p. 348, also recommends speaking.

149 *Qābūsnāma*, L, p. 147, 5 lines from bot./N, p. 187, l. 12/trans., p. 253. Ṭabarsī, *bāb* 7, *faṣl* 3 (36a). *Iḥyā*ᵓ, II, p. 7. Abū'l-Najīb, 52a. *ᶜAwārif*, Chpt. 43 (III, p. 272). Shahrazūrī, IV, p. 4, l. 4. *Akhlāq-i Nāṣirī*, P, p. 92. According to *Akhlāq-i Jalālī*, pp. 219 f., the guest should stop before his host or in any case at the same time as the other guests. As host, one must encourage the guests to keep eating when they stop (Plessner, p. 111, is incorrect).

pany, one must then break this fast; for joining in with the group (*muwāfaqat-i jamāʿat*) has priority.[150]

After the meal has been concluded, one uses the toothpick[151] and washes one's hands.[152] While washing one's hands, one sits with one's legs folded under one and lets the water run out of one's mouth into the wash-basin (*ṭasht*) in such a way that no one can see it.[153] No saliva is to be spit into the wash-basin. One cleans one's nose and mouth with one's own cloth (*izār*).[154] It is reprehensible (*makrūh*) to clean the hands (sic) in common with a single cloth. Once one's hands have been washed, they belong back inside the sleeves.

CHAPTER 5. HOW ONE BEHAVES WHEN INVITED FOR DINNER.

One must accept invitations for dinner unless there will be illicit things present, as for example flutes (*mazāmīr*) or wall-paintings (*ṣūrat ki bar dēwār buvadh*) or if one knows that forbidden foods will be served.[155] In such cases one may refuse. In the house where one has been invited one is to sit in the place assigned to one by the

---

150 *Qābūsnāma*, L, p. 147, penult. line/N, p. 187, l. 15/trans., p. 253. *Iḥyā'*, II, p. 13. Cf. Junayd, in *Lumaʿ*, p. 165, ll. 12-14; ʿAṭṭār, *Tadhkira*, II, p. 10. ll. 14-16; *ʿAwārif*, Chpt. 40 (III, p. 230). Joining in out of solidarity otherwise also plays a great role in Sufism, for example in listening to music.

151 For *ḥadīths* see *Handbook*, 230a and *Concordance*, s.vv. *khilāl* and *miswāk*. Ṭabarsī, *bāb* 7, *faṣl* 3 (35b). *Iḥyā'*, II, p. 6. *ʿAwārif*, Chpt. 43 (III, p. 275). *Muwashshā*, B, pp. 140 ff./Cairo, 1953, pp. 184 ff. Abū Saʿīd b. Abī'l-Khayr still used the toothpick in advanced old age when he only had a single tooth left, in view of a promise in a *ḥadīth*; *Asrār al-tawḥīd*, Zh, p. 146, ll. 4-20/1313, pp. 92-93/1332, p. 124/1366, p. 114/trans., 1992, pp. 202-03.

152 For *ḥadīths* see *Handbook*, p. 92a. Hujwīrī, Zh, p. 454, l. 14/N, p. 349. *Iḥyā'*, II, p. 6. *ʿAwārif*, Chpt. 43 (III, p. 275). Ṭabarsī, *bāb* 7, *faṣl* 3 (35b). *Muwashshā*, B, p. 130, l. 24/Cairo, p. 169, l. 11. Shahrazūrī, IV, p. 4, l. 5. *Akhlāq-i Nāṣirī*, P, p. 93. *Akhlāq-i Jalālī*, p. 220.

153 Raising oneself to a crouching position after having been seated on one's left side is not mentioned in the other sources. Hiding from view the water discharged from one's mouth into the basin is also ordered by Shahrazūrī, IV, p. 4, l. 5, *Akhlāq-i Nāṣirī*, P, p. 93, and *Akhlāq-i Jalālī*, p. 220. What one has to spit out, one should spit out, according to Shahrazūrī, facing to one side (*yarmīhi khārijan*). On the other hand, *āb-i dahān* 'water of the mouth' means saliva (here Chpt. 2; Jāmī: *Tuḥfat al-aḥrār*, ed. Forbes Falconer, London, 1848, verse 1495); nor should one spit saliva into the basin (*Iḥyā'*, II, p. 7: *an lā yabzuqa fīhi*).

154 Tawḥīdī, *Baṣā'ir*, p. 237: One does not blow one's nose with the *mandīl al-sharāb*.

155 *Iḥyā'*, II, p. 13.

host.[156] One may eat as much as one likes but only accepts a guest-gift (*zalla*)[157] if the host insists on it and one knows that this is not a mere formality (*takalluf*) on his part. After the meal one should not begin to converse and not remain seated if one is not invited to do so by the host. One should not gaze about everywhere in the host's house and not ask: 'Where does this spread (*farsh*) come from? What kind of an ornament (*pērāya*)[158] is that?' The host should treat the guest well but should not make a big fuss, and simply place before him what he has.[159] He should honor the guest,[160] but should not force him to eat or to sit down.[161] He should only offer him what is licit and observe the greatest cleanliness regarding the foods. He should not say: 'I bought this for such-and-such a price', and impose admiration and gratitude on the guest (*minnat bar mihmān nanihadh*).[162] He should also not bring his children before the guest for the latter to be friendly to them and kiss them; because not everyone likes children. If one invites a person for dinner, one should not then go and invite a big company without asking the guest; because not everyone has the strength to put up with the effort this requires. The host may be certain that when the guest leaves the house, he takes away with him all their offenses (i.e. probably the offenses of the host's family) and leaves behind a blessing for him in the house; a saying of the Prophet states (Arabic): 'When the guest arrives, he brings with him whatever sustenance has been allotted to him, and when he sets out again on his journey, he takes away with him the offenses of the people he has stayed with.'[163] In addition, he

---

156 *Akhlāq-i Nāṣirī*, P, p. 90, and *Akhlāq-i Jalālī*, pp. 217-18, with sophistic explanations.

157 Hujwīrī too advised that whether one does or does not eat, one should not force oneself out of politeness (*takalluf*), and in the same breath he goes on to say that only a married man should accept a guest-gift (*zalla*) and then only from someone who is like-minded. It would be better not to bestow any guest-gifts at all. Hujwīrī, Zh, p. 455, ll. 9-13. Nicholson's translation on p. 349 (condone a fault, etc.) is wrong. The general restraint when eating which Bryson, § 116 ff., and others (Hujwīrī, etc.) commend is not mentioned by Kubrā.

158 According to Steingass, it can also mean cradle, vessel, plate of gold or silver.

159 This translation is clear from the parallels in *Iḥyāʾ*, II, p. 10; Abū'l-Najīb, 42b f. and 54b; *ʿAwārif*, Chpt. 43 (III, p. 278), also disapproves of *takalluf*.

160 For *ḥadīth*s see *Concordance*, III, p. 528a, quoted in *Iḥyāʾ*, II, pp. 16-17.

161 *Iḥyāʾ*, II, p. 7, l. 1: at most invite someone to eat three times.

162 *Iḥyāʾ*, II, p. 13 above: the person extending the invitation should in no way whatsoever pride himself on his invitation (*lā yataqalladu... minnatan*). Maktabī (circa 900/1500): *Kalimāt-i ʿaliyya-i gharrā*, Tehran, 1935, pp. 51 ff.

may be certain that he will not one day be held to account for food which he is not able to serve.

CHAPTER 6. ON LISTENING TO MUSIC (*SAMĀ*ᶜ *SHINĪDHAN*).

For listening to music three things are required: time (*zamān*), place (*makān*) and brethren (*ikhwān*).[164] The place must be spacious and inaccessible to the view of strangers.[165] One must know when it is the right time for listening to music. Outwardly the night[166] appears to be the most suited; because then the other people don't notice anything, and furthermore at that time the real mystics (*ṣāḥib ḥāl*) distinguish themselves from the simple talkers (*ṣāḥib qāl*); for the real mystic values listening to music above sleep. Similarly, at night the auditory connection of the heart with the supernatural takes place more easily.[167] In the end, however, the right time is when the 'moment' (the time of experiential contact with God, *waqt*) arrives, whether it be during the day or at night. The brethren must be in

---

163 *Al-ḍayfu idhā nazala* (probably *ᶜalā* or *bi-qawmin* should be added) *nazala bi-rizqihī wa-idhā 'rtaḥala 'rtaḥala bi-dhunūbihim* (read thus instead of *bi-dunūbihī*). A somewhat different form of this inauthentic *ḥadīth* is found in Ibn al-Daybaᶜ: *Tamyīz al-ṭayyib min al-khabīth fīmā yadūr ᶜalā alsinat al-nās min al-ḥadīth*, Cairo, 1324, p. 15: *Idhā dakhala 'l-ḍayfu ᶜalā qawmin dakhala bi-rizqihī wa-idhā kharaja kharaja bi-maghfirati dhunūbihim*.

164 A well-known saying of Junayd; *Lumaᶜ*, p. 186, l. 6 and p. 272, l. 5; *Iḥyāʾ*, II, p. 265; Aḥmad al-Ghazzālī, *Bawāriq al-ilmāᶜ*, ed. and trans. by James Robson, pp. 72-74/123-26; Pseudo-ᶜAṭṭār, *Irshād-i bayān*, p. 75, and frequently (in the *Mudkhal*, III, p. 96, changed to *makān*, *imkān* [instead of *zamān*], *ikhwān*).

165 Hujwīrī, Zh, p. 545, l. 2/N, p. 419. *Mudkhal*, III, p. 96 (Junayd).

166 Nocturnal *samāᶜ*-performances of the Sufis are frequently attested and like nocturnal profane entertainments are perfectly natural. The nighttime rest of some peaceful townspeople was disturbed by this; one example in place of many: *Asrār al-tawḥīd*, Zh, p. 287, ll. 6 ff./1313, p. 182/1332, p. 236/1366, p. 221/trans. 1992, p. 336. Those who love God, like all lovers, *cannot* sleep at night; Anṣārī, *Rasāʾil*, p. 48, ll. 3-4. Encouragement to place the *samāᶜ* above sleep in Jāmī, *Subḥat al-abrār*, *ᶜiqd* 34, litho., Tehran, 1313, p. 187.

167 Avicenna, *Miᶜrājnāma*, Rasht, 1312/1352, p. 20: 'At night people are more open (*fārightar*) because the distractions of the body and the hindrances of the sense organs disappear'; i.e. more open to perceiving higher reality. The idea that man is granted higher knowledge in dreams as well because the external senses are suspended is a commonplace of Sufism. Anṣārī, *Rasāʾil*, p. 43: 'in the night a living being's heart strives toward God'.

harmonious agreement (*yaksān bāshand*).[168] No one of alien disposition (*nā-jins*) should be present; otherwise the listening to music will not take (*dar-nagīradh*). Keeping company as equals with those of alien disposition (*nā-jinsān*) is the non plus ultra of all troubles (*warāy-i hama ᶜadhābhā*). The great have said: 'Three things are a danger (*āfat*) for the Sufi: to sit with those who have a different outlook (*aḍdād*), to associate with youths (*aḥdāth*), and to comply with the wishes of women (*muwāfaqat-i zanān*).[169] One time listening to music did not take effect with Junayd (*dar-namēgirift*). He had a search carried out everywhere for someone of alien disposition until in the end they found out that the slipper of a Sufi had been replaced by that of a layman (741a) (*yak pāykafsh-i ṣūfīyē bā az ān-i ᶜāmmiyē badal shudha*). In addition, the singer (*qawwāl*) should not be an adolescent (*amrad*);[170] because adolescents are as (dangerous as) girls (*bā dukhtarān barābarand*). One should not listen to their musical performance because this is dangerous and arouses suspicions. It is stated in a saying of the Prophet (Arabic): 'Do not sit together with the sons of kings; for they arouse (?) the same sensual lusts (*shahwa*) as women'[171] (*lā tujālisū abnāʾa'l-mulūk fa'inna lahum shahwatan ka-shahwati'l-nisāʾ*)! Tambourines (*daf*) with bells (*jalājil*) are forbidden.[172] Regarding the permissibility of the in-

---

168 *Iḥyāʾ*, II, p. 265; Abū'l-Najīb, 9a; *ᶜAwārif*, Chpt. 25 (II, p. 253); Pseudo-ᶜAṭṭār, *Irshād-i bayān*, p. 76, and frequently.

169 Objective genetive like *muwāfaqat-i jamāᶜat* in Chpt. 4.

170 Hujwīrī, Zh, p. 542, ll. 13-18/N, pp. 416 f. *ᶜAwārif*, Chpt. 22 (II, p. 196) and 23 (II, p. 220). ᶜAlāʾ al-Dawla-i Simnānī, *Mā lā budd fī'l-dīn*, MS Esad Ef. (Istanbul) 1431, in *faṣl* 6. *Mudkhal*, III, pp. 96, 114 ff., 121, and frequently. Muḥammad al-Ghazzālī was not so strict in this respect, and it is reported by his brother Aḥmad that he did in fact practice gazing at youths (see *Asiatische Studien*, 1954, p. 121); but this is not confirmed in his *Bawāriq al-ilmāᶜ*. Rōzbihān-i Baqlī (d. 606/1209) even ordered that the singer during the *samāᶜ* be good-looking (Jāmī, *Nafaḥāt al-uns*, ed. Nassau Lees, p. 288). An enthusiastic friend of such beauty was also Abū Saᶜīd b. Abī'l-Khayr.

171 Variants in Hellmut Ritter, *Das meer der seele*, p. 428.

172 The tambourine was generally regarded as permissible in the Sufi *samāᶜ*. Out of all possible instruments Sarrāj only allows the tambourine. Abū Ḥafṣ al-Suhrawardī, *ᶜAwārif*, Chpt. 22 (II, p. 187), is the only person who thinks it is better to renounce the tambourine as well. Aḥmad al-Ghazzālī, *Bawāriq al-ilmāᶜ*, pp. 96/154 and 98/157, expressly allows tambourines with and without bells (*ṣunūj*, *jalājil*). The bells are also mentioned by Jāmī: *Subḥat al-abrār*, *ᶜiqd* 34, p. 185. In present-day Egypt the tambourine without bells is called *ṭār*, and the one with bells *riqq*; Kahle: 'Die Totenklage im heutigen Ägypten', in *Εὐχαριστήριον Gunkel*, Göttingen, 1923, I, p. 350, ftn. 1.

strument *bēsha* (or *pēsha*)[173] there are differences of opinion. For the sake of piety it is more advisable to renounce it.

The Sufis' listening to music is abandonment of the spirit (or of life, *fidāy-i jān*). So do not practice listening to music artificially and do not force anything[174] (*pas samā*ᶜ*-rā takalluf ma-kun wa-pēshbāz ma-shaw*)! But if ecstasy (*wajd*) occurs, do not just sit there as if nothing had happened! Be aware of your 'moment' (*waqt*) with God! Should the impulse (*wārid*) enter into you (*dar tu furōdh āyadh*), keep still, if a master (*pīr*) is present,[175] as long as possible! But if the impulse is too strong and it moves you, do not remain seated artificially (*ba-takalluf*)! If it wears off, do not continue to

---

173 *Burhān-i qāṭi*ᶜ, ed. Moh. Moin, s.v. *bīsha*: '...It is also a musical instrument made from a reed which shepherds play. Others say: an instrument similar to the harp (*chang*). Still others say: similar to the fiddle (*rabāb*).' Ibid., s.v. *pīsha*: '...A kind of reed flute which shepherds play also called *tūtak*.' With the over hasty remark of the editor: 'Probably should be read as *naysha* (from *nay* + *cha*), as Dihkhudā informs me.' The *b* (or *p*) is assured on the basis of our text. For the *bīsha-i musta* we have the Arabic equivalent *mustaq*; J. Robson: *Ancient Arabian Musical Instruments*, in *Collection of Oriental Writers on Music*, IV, 1938, p. 15, ftn. 4; H.G. Farmer in A.U. Pope's *Survey of Persian Art*, III, p. 2788, ftn. 9 (mouth-organ). *Bīsha* itself Farmer, ibid., p. 2797, understands as 'the small flute' and in his book *Turkish Instruments of Music in the Seventeenth Century*, in *Coll. of Oriental Writers on Music*, III, 1937, p. 19, he writes: 'According to the Turkish writer on music, Aḥmad Ughlū Shukrallāh (fifteenth century), the *nay* was called the *pīsha*. This work, however, would appear to be merely a resumé of a Persian treatise on music entitled the *Kanz al-tuḥaf*.' In the case of *bēsha* we are in all probablility dealing with an approximate synonym for *nay* and an equivalent or variety of the Arabic *shabbāba* 'reed flute' which Abū Ḥafṣ: ᶜ*Awārif*, Chpt. 22 (II, p. 187), likewise mentions together with the tambourine. Abū Ḥafṣ admits that regarding both instruments the Shāfiᶜites exhibit a certain degree of tolerance, but he advises rejecting them both. Aḥmad al-Ghazzālī, *Bawāriq al-ilmā*ᶜ, p. 96/154, also places the tambourine and the Persian flute (*qaṣab fārisī*) together but he derives their permissibility from the fact that they are not forbidden in the Koran or the *ḥadīth*. Similarly, Kubrā's student Dāya, in *Mirṣād al-*ᶜ*ibād*, p. 206, takes the usage of the *daf* and *nay* for granted. *Mudkhal*, III, p. 94, mentions the difference of opinion over the permissibility of the *shabbāba*.

174 Hujwīrī, Zh, p. 545, l. 3/N, p. 419. *Iḥyā*ʾ, II, pp. 265 f. (3rd *adab*). Abū'l-Najīb, 56b, 57a. Dāya, *Mirṣād*, p. 206. Very frequent.

175 Cf. Abū Bakr al-Kattānī in ᶜ*Awārif*, Chpt. 25 (II, p. 239). Abū Muḥammad al-Jurayrī (d. 311/923 or 314/926) under this prohibition even developed his own psychic technique: if during the *samā*ᶜ a person of respect (*muḥtasham*) was present, he could store up the inner movement, so to speak, and only after the end of the performance, when he was alone, did he then give free rein to it; the *Risāla* of Qushayrī, Cairo, 1346, p. 34. Hujwīrī, Zh, p. 545, l. 2/N, p. 419, considers the presence of a master to be absolutely necessary.

move artificially![176] Because through every slip (*zalla*) the 'moment' escapes and you cannot get it back again. When moving, do not ask anyone for assistance (*yārī*, what is meant is joining in in solidarity)! But if someone asks you for assistance, comply with his wish![177]

In short, one must remain in agreement with the prescriptions of religious law, if a mystical life and supernatural revelations are to be achieved. Every listening to music which contradicts these principles brings with it danger, suspicion, sin, harm to religion...

CHAPTER 7. ON CORRECT BEHAVIOR (*ADAB*) WHEN TRAVELLING.[178]

The Sufi goes on journeys for three reasons: for pilgrimages (*ziyārat*),[179] for ascetic discipline (*riyāḍat*),[180] and in order to visit shaykhs (*dīdhār-i mashāyikh*). Every other kind of journey is for him a cause of blame (*tāwān*). On a journey it is necessary to be accompanied by a companion of similar attitude, similar manner, similar motive and similar striving (*rafīq-i hamdam-i hamdard-i*

---

176 Hujwīrī, Zh, p. 545, ll. 3-10/N, p. 419, and frequently.

177 Hujwīrī, Zh, p. 545, ll. 10-11/N, p. 419: help (*musāʿadat*) should not be expected from anyone but if it is offered, it should not be turned down. *Iḥyāʾ*, II, p. 268 (5th *adab*): joining in when someone enters a real state of ecstasy. Abū'l-Najīb, 57a: artificial movements, etc., are allowed by way of supporting someone who is really in a state of ecstasy (*musāʿada li-ṣādiq*), but it is still better not to do so.

178 In *ʿAwārif*, Chpt. 17 (II, p. 115), with regard to following rules about travel a distinction is made between Sufis from Khurasan and Persian ʿIrāq on the one hand, and Sufis from Mesopotamia, Syria and the West on the other; the former, it is said, tended to overvalue and overemphasize the rules, the latter did not take them seriously.

179 By *ziyāra Iḥyāʾ*, II, p. 218, understands visiting Mecca, Medina, Jerusalem, the frontier cites (*thughūr*), saints and scholars or their graves. But obviously in Kubrā only pilgrimages and visits to graves are meant, otherwise there would not then follow as point 3 'visiting shaykhs', under which naturally the masters of theological sciences can also be understood. One notes the absence of visits to family members. This division is quite unclear and once again seems to me to be a sign of a beginner, especially when one also takes account of the abrupt sentence which immediately follows. In its formulation the passage could be directly influenced by Hujwīrī, Zh, p. 450, ll. 2-4/N, p. 345, where although possible journeys are more fully listed, at the end it is likewise stated: Otherwise travel is a cause of blame. Hujwīrī, for his part, could be dependent on the still clearer and more complete explanations of Sarrāj, *Lumaʿ*, p. 190, ll. 5-6.

180 Ascetic discipline is also mentioned as a purpose of travel in Abū'l-Najīb, 45a, 63a, and in *ʿAwārif*, Chpt. 16 (II, p. 83).

hamirādat),[181] a partner of the same type (*hamjins*), and to have shed all ties which cause a hindrance. Furthermore, one does not travel without a staff (*ʿaṣā*) and a ewer (*ibrīq*),[182] the staff being held in the right hand and the ewer in the left hand.[183] When one arrives before a convent, one should turn the point (*sinān*) of the staff against oneself as a sign that one is waging war against oneself. At home and when travelling one must always have the following things with oneself: a toothpick (*miswāk*), comb (*shāna*), scissors (*miqrāḍ*) and a small case of collyrium (*surmadān*).[184] One should continually be in a state of minor ablution[185] because (Arabic) 'the

---

181 Asadī, *Andarznāma*, Tehran, 1306, p. 63 (from *Garshāspnāma*). *Qābūsnāma*, L, p. 146, l. 13/N, p. 186, l. 4/trans., p. 251. *Iḥyāʾ*, II, p. 223. *Maqāmāt-i Ḥamīdī*, *maqāma* 8, pp. 65 ff. *ʿAwārif*, Chpt. 17 (II, p. 106). Ṭabarsī, *bāb* 9, *faṣl* 4 (59a). 'Ibn al-Muqaffaʿ': *Al-adab al-wajīz*, trans. by Naṣīr al-Dīn-i Ṭūsī, Tehran, 1312, p. 42. *Rāḥat al-insān* in Ch. Schefer's *Chrestomathie persane*, I, p. 218. Frequent.

182 Both of these are occasionally taken from the traveller in a friendly way when he enters the convent; *Firdaws al-murshidiyya*, p. 359, ll. 7-8. When he is departing, they can be carried after him to a spot in front the convent; *ʿAwārif*, Chpt. 17 (II, p. 114); or for someone who has left too quickly, they can be brought to him afterwards; *Asrār al-tawḥīd*, Zh, p. 105, ll. 10-11/1313, p. 66, ll. 21-22/1332, p. 91, l. 11/1366, p. 82, l. 20/trans., 1992, p. 164, l. 5.

183 *Mudkhal*, III, p. 186.

184 Ibrāhīm al-Khawwāṣ (d. 291/904) is said to have carried the following utensils with him at all times: leather bowl (*rakwa*), string, needle and thread, scissors; *Iḥyāʾ*, II, p. 227, *ʿAwārif*, Chpt. 17 (II, p. 111). The Prophet on journeys: mirror, water-jug, scissors, toothpick, small case for collyrium, comb; *Iḥyāʾ*, II, p. 226, *ʿAwārif*, II, p. 112. Hujwīrī, Zh, p. 450, ll. 4-9/N, p. 345, requires a patched frock, prayer-rug, staff, leather bowl, string and a pair of shoes or sandals, while additionally allowed are a comb, needle, nailfile, and a small collyrium case. In the *Qābūsnāma*, L, p. 146, ll. 11-12/N, p. 186, ll. 2-3/trans., pp. 250-51, one finds enumerated: staff, jug, trousers (*miʾzar*), rug, prayer-rug, hat, comb, toothpick, needle, nail-scissors. According to an account in the *Asrār al-tawḥīd*, Zh, p. 80, ll. 14 ff./1313, p. 52 above/1332, p. 74/1366, p. 66/trans. 1992, pp. 143-44, in the 5th/11th century the Sufi wore a patched frock, in his hands carried a staff and jug, on his shoulders a prayer-rug and handkerchief (*rō-sutura*, probably = *rōymāla*, here Chpt. 1) with the toothpick, on his head a hat and on his feet shoes. According to Abū'l-Najīb, 47a-b, only the leather bowl (*rakwa*) or the jug (*kūz*) are necessary, of which the first is better, but recommendable are the staff, needle, thread, scissors, razor (*mūsā*) 'and suchlike'. Maḥmūd-i Shabistarī, *Gulshan-i rāz*, Basle MS M III 45, 183a, l. 14, lists: the staff, leather bowl, rosary (rejected by *Mudkhal*, III, pp. 205, 210) and toothpick. String is required in order to hang up one's washed clothes to dry and to fetch water from a well. The jug or leather bowl or ewer are used in performing ritual ablutions.

185 *Lumaʿ*, p. 145, l. 7; Hujwīrī, Zh, p. 450, l. 1/N, p. 345.

ritual ablution is the weapon of the believer'. If one has the strength, one should travel by foot since this is more meritorious.[186] One should be wearing a belt[187] and have one's sleeves rolled up (*bar-māladh*) so that one is more agile (*chābuktar*).[188] If one reaches the top of a hill or the bottom of a valley, one should pronounce the formula 'God is great!'[189] Along one's way one should not beg and only stay over night in mosques if no other possibility offers itself.

These are the outward rules of decent behavior (or: the rules of decent behavior of the exterior, *ādāb-i ẓāhir*) for novices. The beginner must follow them if he wishes to become worthy of the world of (divine) love. The interior (*bāṭin*) has other rules (*ādāb*) with innumerable entrances (*abwāb*), halting stations (*maqāmāt*) and stages (*manāzil*). At the beginning there is ascetic discipline and spiritual combat. But whoever wishes to learn those other rules, let him read the *Manāzil al-sābiqīn* (thus instead of *sāʾirīn*) of ᶜAbdallāh-i (741b) Anṣārī. Verily, only the person who walks in accordance therewith awakes from the sleep of (religious) indifference; because Sufism is a walking, seeing, working and tasting, not mere talking, listening, knowing and doing nothing. Work not talk constitutes action. Merely knowing of water does not quench one's thirst; one must drink it.

ADDITIONS OF THE AUTHOR

Three years later an edition of the text we treated was published by Serge de Laugier de Beaurecueil, O.P., under the title 'Un opuscule de Khwaja ᶜAbdallah Anṣari concernant les bienséances des soufis' in *BIFAO* 59, 1960, pp. 203-39. His edition was based solely on the

---

186 Abū'l-Najīb, 45b, with *ḥadīths* on the advantage of making the pilgrimage to Mecca on foot. On how to treat a riding animal if one is used, see *Iḥyāʾ*, II, p. 226.

187 *ᶜAwārif*, Chpt. 17 (II, p. 113).

188 *ᶜAwārif*, Chpt. 18 (II, p. 120 f.), with consideration and recognition of deviations. Cf. *Mudkhal*, III, p. 185.

189 Julius Wellhausen, *Reste arabischen Heidentums*², Berlin, 1897, p. 151: 'As often as the region changed, it was Muḥammad's practice on his campaigns to intone a takbīr in order to ward off the demons.' For *ḥadīths* see *Handbook*, p. 225a. *Iḥyāʾ*, II, pp. 225 ff. *ᶜAwārif*, Chpt. 18 (II, pp. 116 f.). Doubtlessly, this behavior is based on the ancient belief that divinities (*beᶜālīm*) reside on 'elevated places' and in the hollows of valleys, a belief to which S.I. Curtiss devotes his study *Ursemitische Religion im Volksleben des heutigen Orients*, German edition, Leipzig, 1903. These divinities are recognized in Islam as *jinn* but are subordinate to God.

MS Şehit Ali Paşa 1393, and the authorship was attributed to ᶜAbdallāh-i Anṣārī (d. 481/1089). Since de Beaurecueil was at the time engaged in looking after orphans in Afghanistan, it is understandable that he was not familiar with my preliminary study. In 1345/1966 Īraj-i Afshār published in Tehran the second volume of the *Awrād al-aḥbāb wa fuṣūṣ al-ādāb* of Abū'l-Mafākhir Yaḥyā Bākharzī (d. 736/1336) in which a major part of the prescriptions comes from our work, the *Ādāb al-murīdīn* of Najm al-Dīn-i Kubrā (d. 618/1221). Textual passages in Kubrā can be checked against the many borrowings found in Bākharzī. The work is only attributed to Anṣārī in the MS Şehit Ali Paşa 1393 which de Beaurecueil used. In 1363/1984 it was once again published in Tehran by Masᶜūd-i Qāsimī under the title *Ādāb al-ṣūfiyya* of Kubrā, on the basis of the MS Şehit Ali Paşa and five additional MSS.

[P. 53, ftn. 12: Sulamī's *Jawāmiᶜ ādāb al-ṣūfiyya* has been edited by E. Kohlberg, Jerusalem, 1976, and reprinted by N. Pourjavady in *Majmūᶜa-i āthār-i Abū ᶜAbd al-Raḥmān al-Sulamī*, Tehran, 1369, I, pp. 337 ff.]

[P. 53, ftn. 13: The book was edited by M. Milson, Jerusalem, 1977, and partly translated in: *A Sufi Rule for Novices, Kitāb Ādāb al-murīdīn of Abū al-Najīb al-Suhrawardī*, An abridged translation and introduction by Menahem Milson, Cambridge, Mass., 1975. — Parts of this work, as F. Soberoj has shown, go back to Ibn Khafīf's *Kitāb al-iqtiṣād*; see F. Soberoj, *Ibn Ḫafīf aš-Šīrāzī und seine Schrift zur Novizenerziehung 'Kitāb al-Iqtiṣād'*, BTS 57, Beirut-Stuttgart, 1998, p. 384.]

[P. 55, ftn. 26: On Ibn Abī'l-Dunyā's *Kitāb al-ṣabr* cf. R. Weipert and S. Weninger, 'Die erhaltenen Werke des Ibn Abī'd-Dunyā', *ZDMG* 146, 1996, p. 447, no. 45; two MSS are extant but the book still remains unedited.]

[P. 55, ftn. 28: Ḥakīm Tirmidhī died most probably around 300/910; cf. B. Radtke, *Al-Ḥakīm at-Tirmiḏī. Ein islamischer Theosoph des 3./9. Jahrhunderts*, Freiburg, 1980, pp. 16-38.]

[P. 55, ftn. 31: By the work *Ādāb al-murīdīn* is meant the same text which B. Radtke has edited as *Jawāb al-masāʾil allatī saʾlahū ahl Sarakhs ᶜanhā* in *Drei Schriften des Theosophen von Tirmiḏ*, Beirut-Stuttgart, 1992, I, pp. 135-67, and translated in II, Beirut-Stuttgart, 1996, pp. 175-208.]

[P. 59: On the book by Maᶜmar al-Iṣfahānī cf. in this volume 'An Important Manuscript Find', p. 166.]

P. 61, ftn. 45, ll. 11-12: The recently discovered old manuscript of the *Qābūsnāma* is a forgery.

P. 74, ftn. 94: The correct reading *kinf* (Arabic) 'knapsack' is given by Bākharzī: *Awrād al-aḥbāb*, II, p. 33, last line, and by Beaurecueil, p. 233, 8/p. 218 i. But *kīf* 'bag' also appears to be possible.

P. 74, l. 15: Bākharzī has: The balance is ritual prayer (*namāz*) because ritual prayer is the measuring instrument with which one weighs friend and foe (*Awrād*, II, p. 34, l. 3). Similarly, de Beaurecueil, p. 233, ll. 11-12/p. 218, 71, with the addition: It is also the touchstone of the heart and the needle of the balance of the innermost secret. This at least confirms the reading.

QUSHAYRĪ'S *TARTĪB AL-SULŪK*

For Hellmut Ritter on his seventieth birthday

In earlier Islamic mysticism the relationship between teacher and student appears to have been similar to that among the traditionists and in other branches of learning. One attached oneself to a teacher in order to learn something about the self-training one had to undertake, and the deeper meaning of sacred traditions and technical terms. The standard expression for this form of contact was *ṣuḥba*. The student was the *ṣāḥib* and the teacher the *maṣḥūb*. Thus it is said about Shaqīq al-Balkhī (d. 174/790), for instance, that he attached himself (*ṣaḥiba*) to Ibrāhīm b. Adham and learned (*akhadha*) the mystic path from him.[1] In this regard, as in the other sciences, e.g. among the traditionists, one did not necessarily confine oneself to a single teacher. Abū Yazīd al-Bisṭāmī (d. probably 261/874) is supposed to have visited 113 masters in Syria alone before one ordered him to return home because he was now fully trained (*kār-i tu tamām shud*).[2] Junayd (d. 297/910) claims to have served 200 masters but adds that only 7 of them were suitable as models (ᶜAṭṭār, *Tadhkira,* II, p. 8, ll. 19-20). It is said of Ibrāhīm b. Adham (d. 161/778 or 166/782-3) that he associated with Sufyān al-Thawrī and Fuḍayl b. ᶜIyāḍ in Mecca (Sulamī, *Ṭabaqāt*, p. 13, ll. 6-7), although it should also be noted that he is supposed to have previously lived in solitude for many years near Nayshābūr (ᶜAṭṭār, *Tadhkira*, I, p. 87, ll. 24 ff.). Aḥmad b. Abī'l-Ḥawārī (d. 230/845) 'was with' (*ṣaḥiba*) Abū Sulaymān al-Dārānī, Sufyān b. ᶜUyayna, Marwān b. Muᶜāwiya al-Fazārī, Maḍāʾ b. ᶜĪsā, Bishr b. al-Sarī, Abū ᶜAbdallāh al-Nibājī (Sulamī, *Ṭabaqāt*, p. 88, ll. 4-6). For further examples the reader may consult the Sufi handbooks.

Later this becomes different. The student enters into a stronger bond with the teacher, he undergoes with him a course of treatment so to speak, subordinates himself to his supervision and submits to his drill. The instruction which the student previously received more

---

1 Sulamī: *Ṭabaqāt al-ṣūfiyya*, ed. Johannes Pedersen, Leiden, 1960, p. 54, ll. 6-7.

2 ᶜAṭṭār: *Tadhkirat al-awliyāʾ*, ed. R.A. Nicholson, London-Leiden, 1905-06, I, p. 136, l. 15.

in a verbal form, whether alone or as a guest in the gathering convened by the shaykh (*ḥalqa, majlis*), is transformed into a spiritual training which he is meant to implement under the supervision of the teacher. The shaykh becomes a master of spiritual exercises and also has the power to apply punishment. At the same time the free fluctuation of the young mystic from one shaykh to another disappears. One is, of course, free in choosing a teacher, often considers at length whom to attach oneself to, and even undertakes long journeys to find the right person, but once the choice has been made one should no longer leave the person other than at his order — a principle which, needless to say, was frequently violated (cf. my remarks on Najm al-Dīn al-Kubrā, *Fawā'iḥ al-ǧamāl*, Wiesbaden, 1957, Introduction, pp. 18-19). This teacher-student relationship as well is called *ṣuḥba*. At the end of the training the student receives a graduation certificate which in turn authorizes him to take on students. This *ijāza* (often associated with external insignia like the patched frock, a banner, a ring, etc.) did not refer to the transmission of a particular doctrine but more generally to mystical maturity. This did not stop the trained individual from subsequently joining still other shaykhs from whom, as an accredited person, he now received further instruction in the old style and not infrequently obtained new tokens of honor or literary *ijāzāt* — a continuation of the old *ṣuḥba* and likewise known under this name. We cannot here enter into further problems to do with this topic.

The described shift in the relationship between teacher and student in the history of Sufism was worked out for the first time, as it seems, by Ibn ᶜAbbād al-Rundī (d. 792/1390) who coined two terms in this connection which we can adopt. He distinguished between two types of shaykhs, a *shaykh taᶜlīm* and a *shaykh taᶜlīm wa-tarbiya*, or more briefly *shaykh tarbiya*.[3] The *shaykh al-taᶜlīm*, 'the master of instruction', he locates in old times and says that formerly the teacher had not yet isolated himself (*infirād*) and the students still

---

3 *Fatwā Abī ᶜAbdallāh Muḥammad b. Ibrāhīm b. ᶜAbbād al-Rundī*, in the supplement to Ibn Khaldūn: *Shifā' al-sā'il li-tahdhīb al-masā'il*, ed. Muḥammad b. Tāwīt al-Ṭanjī, Istanbul, 1958, pp. 113 ff. Ibn ᶜArabī (*Al-futūḥāt al-makkiyya*, Chpt. 181, conclusion) distinguishes *tarbiya* from mere *ṣuḥba*, i.e. actual training from merely associating with shaykhs, just as before him Abū Saᶜīd b. Abī'l-Khayr (*Asrār al-tawḥīd*, ed. Dhabīḥallāh Ṣafā, Tehran, 1332, pp. 42 f./ed. Muḥammad Riḍā Shafīᶜī-i Kadkanī, Tehran, 1366, p. 38/trans. by John O'Kane, *The Secrets of God's Mystical Oneness*, Persian Heritage Series no. 38, Costa Mesa (Calif.)-New York, 1992, p. 107) distinguished the *shaykh-i muṭlaq* from the *pīr-i ṣuḥbat* (reference from Richard Gramlich, S.J.).

'endeavored to acquire learning and to improve their interior by social intercourse (*ṣuḥba*) and brotherly attachment (*mu'ākhāh*), received rich benefit through mutual encounters and visits, felt the effect of this in their interior and therefore travelled about in the world to meet (as many as possible) Friends of God and men of learning' (*Fatwā*, pp. 115-16). Later the *shaykh al-taᶜlīm* then became separated from the *shaykh al-tarbiya*, 'the master of training'. The latter had his students withdraw in spiritual retreat, kept them occupied with the formula of recollecting God (*dhikr*) which he had 'implanted' in them, ordered them to diminish their food, speech and sleep, etc., and in this way drilled them under his supervision until they became perfected (*kāmil*) and could now themselves be models for others (*Fatwā*, p. 115 above). According to this account, we are meant to distinguish a period of 'instruction' (*taᶜlīm*) and a period of 'training' (*tarbiya*). The second path, 'training', leads more surely to the goal in Rundī's view (*Fatwā*, p. 114) but is not the only possibility in Sufism for attaining a good end, though a shaykh is almost indispensable.

Where does the boundary between the two periods lie? Rundī lets it be understood that he locates the boundary approximately in the 4th/10th century, because for the *shuyūkh al-taᶜlīm* he refers to the works of a Muḥāsibī (d. 243/857), an Abū Ṭālib al-Makkī (d. 386/996) 'and others' in whom no trace of a *shaykh tarbiya* is to be found. Thus the period of the *shuyūkh al-taᶜlīm* would be the classical era of Sufism, before circa 400/1000, and for Rundī, an author of the 8th/14th century, would extend right to the middle of what was then the Islamic past. We may accept this but should not fall into the error of wishing to establish a sharp, impassable and absolute boundary. This reservation is unavoidable simply because of the nature of the matter. Sufi 'instruction' in practice always was, and still is, chiefly 'training' in as much as it does not in the first instance aim to transmit learning but pursues psychagogic goals and seeks to bring about a change in one's consciousness and attitude toward life. Due to the close bond which resulted between student and teacher, there will certainly not have been a lack of transference on the part of the student, and the zeal which such a student may have displayed must often almost automatically have obliged the shaykh to feel fatherly sympathy and a greater sense of responsibility and at the same time to adopt a stricter and more supervised treatment which is in fact characteristic of *tarbiya*. Everything will have been different from case to case, from person to person, and from one place to another, so that one can scarcely speak of a fixed boundary between *taᶜlīm* and *tarbiya*. Although we do not know how life was regulated in the old cenobitical associations, communal spiritual exercises and supervised pious devotions must have already been present to some extent. In the gatherings which were presided over by a shaykh, mostly discussion took place but already early on communal sessions of recollecting God (*dhikr*) and listening to music (*samāᶜ*) were held during which it was wholly natural that the young mystic in his spiritual activity came under the supervision of the shaykh. Conversely, in the second period, the era of the *shuyūkh al-tarbiya*, we constantly hear of loners who either on their own initiative or by means of all manner of varying instruction made their way into Sufism and thus in terms of their type really belonged to the earlier period. Generally speaking, however, one can say that, from the 4th/10th century on, *tarbiya* in Rundī's sense emerges into the foreground and impresses its stamp on the times that follow. A Sufi of the 4th/10th century in whom the trend of the new era manifests itself is Abū Sahl al-Ṣuᶜlūkī (d. 364/980), who requires absolute obedience from the novice and no longer even allows him the question 'why?',[4] just as later theory demands.

From among the compilers of Sufi textbooks of the 4th/10th and 5th/11th centuries, the celebrated Abū'l-Qāsim ᶜAbd al-Karīm b. Hawāzin al-Qushayrī (d. 465/1074) is also situated in the second period, the era of the *shuyūkh al-tarbiya*. In his spiritual last will and testament to his novices (*waṣiyya li'l-murīdīn*) in the appendix to his *Risāla* he mentions a trial period which the candidate must go through before the shaykh can accept him, emphasizes that the candidate must bear willingly the measures of atonement which the shaykh imposes on him for certain offenses, mentions a particular inner attitude which he is obliged to adopt before the shaykh, speaks about the formula for recollecting God (*dhikr*) which the shaykh 'implants' (*talqīn*) in him, about withdrawal in seclusion (*khalwa*) which he orders him to undertake, about the necessity of obeying the shaykh unreservedly and not concealing from him the least thoughts and impulses within the soul, and forbids him to leave the locality of his novitiate of his own accord or to undertake journeys prematurely. Indeed there are young brethren, Qushayrī writes, who especially

4 Subkī: *Ṭabaqāt al-shāfiᶜiyya al-kubrā*, Cairo, 1324, II, p. 163. Ignaz Goldziher: *Vorlesungen über den Islam*², Heidelberg, 1925, p. 339. Not Sahl b. ᶜAbdallāh al-Tustarī, as Louis Massignon: *Essai sur les origines du lexique technique de la mystique musulmane*², Paris, 1954, p. 60, might lead one to assume. Tustarī only employs the image to describe the relation of the *mutawwakil* to God.

profit from journeying but they are lay brethren whose Sufism is limited to serving the real mystics and for whom pilgrimages and visits to shaykhs with the purpose of greeting them are the highest achievement in Sufism they can attain.[5] That Qushayrī nowhere contrasts these guidelines with earlier usage which he considered to be incorrect naturally accords with the tendency not to present current practices as innovations, and yet there is no reason whatsoever to consider the recommendations as creations of Qushayrī. Rather one should assume that these are forms of behavior which had already proven themselves, i.e. that the period of the *shuyūkh al-tarbiya* had already begun before him.[6]

A striking feature of the new era is likewise the endeavor to transfer the occult phenomena associated with the spiritual training which the novice or mystic undergoes, to the realm of discussion and description. Of course this is connected with the fact that the shaykh now also follows the novice more closely in spiritual retreat and claims supervision over the least detail of his inner development, as well as with the progress of Sufism itself which has refined its observations and is now beginning to extend to things which lie outside the purely moral-religious state of mind of the mystic. In this regard also Qushayrī appears to be one of our first crown witnesses, not in his *Risāla*, however, but in a much shorter monograph which in the manuscripts bears the title *Tartīb al-sulūk fī ṭarīq Allāh* (*GAL*[2], I, p. 556; *GAL S*, I, p. 772), *Gradation in Travelling on the Path to God.* In this work, concerning which we do not know whether it was composed before or after the *Risāla* (437/1045), Qushayrī describes the psychic effects of one of the most important means a mystic possesses for approaching what he calls God and for eliminating his I-decisions — the effects of the recollection of God (*dhikr*). Recollecting God is an exercise during which, by concentrating on a brief formula whose content is the idea of God and which he repeats loudly or softly in an unbroken sequence, the mystic envisages the goal of his striving and seeks to steer thought, feeling and will (inasmuch as any will is still recognized) wholly in this direction. It is likewise the 'weapon of the believer' with which he wards off the

---

5 *Risāla*, Cairo, 1346, pp. 180 ff., translated by Richard Hartmann: *al-Ḳuschairîs Darstellung des Ṣûfîtums*, in Türkische Bibliothek 18, Berlin, 1914, pp. 176 ff. (in need of correction with regard to some details).

6 Of course this need not hinder Qushayrī from designating the instruction given to the novice by the shaykh as *taᶜlīm*, as for example in section 1 of our tract; the terminology only first originates with Rundī.

intrusion of other thoughts in his consciousness. As Qushayrī explains in the above-mentioned spiritual last will and testament to the novices at the end of the *Risāla,* in the period of the *shuyūkh al-tarbiya* the novice should have the formula for recollecting God 'implanted' in him by the shaykh, i.e. the shaykh must recite the appropriate formula before him in a particular way and in so doing initiate him into the exercise. Ibn ᶜAṭāᵓallāh al-Sikandarī[7] and Qushāshī correctly distinguish two forms: an 'unlimited' (*muṭlaq*) recollection of God which is meant to accompany the mystic everywhere and with which, quite generally, he maintains an anti-natural attitude to life, devotes himself to God; and a 'limited' one (*muqayyad*) which he practices at special times, with full concentration and in a particular posture and technique.[8] The latter once again occurs in two forms — and this already in the period of the *shuyūkh al-taᶜlīm*: in isolation (*khalwa*) and in communal gatherings (*ḥalqa*, *majlis*, etc.). In both forms of 'limited' recollection of God, the one practiced alone and the other in a group, the man of piety abandons the terrain of mere positional warfare and attempts to make territorial gains in mystic experience. Qushayrī does not distinguish these different forms either in his *Risāla* or in the *Tartīb al-sulūk.* In the *Tartīb al-sulūk* it is only said that the shaykh recites the relevant formula to the novice at a given time and orders him to carry on repeating this formula and never to stop, after which there then follows the description of its effects. The differences really appear to be blurred since accounts in the final two sections of the *Tartīb* show that the practice of the recollection of God extended over a whole timespan during which the novice sometimes sat withdrawn in seclusion and other times moved about freely. It accords with this that Qushayrī also gives no indication about a particular posture which the mystic was supposed to adopt during the recitation or about a particular technique he was meant to use. The only thing he informs us about is a trick which he performed himself under the guidance of a friend and which made it possible for him to transfer the heart's recollection of God into the so-called 'secret'. It deserves to be emphasized that the formula 'God, God, God', which constitutes the *dhikr* with Qushayrī, coincides with that of Abū Ḥāmid al-Ghazzālī.[9] More common was 'there is no god but God'.

---

7 *Miftāḥ al-falāḥ*, Cairo, 1332, p. 3 (reference from Richard Gramlich).

8 Aḥmad b. Muḥammad al-Qushāshī: *Al-simṭ al-majīd*, Hyderabad, 1327, pp. 146 f. F. Meier, in Kubrā: *Fawāᵓiḥ*, Introduction, p. 202.

9 Hellmut Ritter: *Al Ghasali, Das Elixir der Glückseligkeit*, Jena, 1923, p. 38.

It is not my intention here to write a history of the recollection of God. One may find some observations on the solitary *dhikr* in my introduction to the *Fawāʾiḥ al-ğamāl wa-fawātiḥ al-ğalāl des Nağm ad-dīn al-Kubrā*, Wiesbaden, 1957, pp. 200 ff., 247 f., and in my article entitled 'Schriften des ᶜAzīz-i Nasafī', in *WZKM* 52, 1953, pp. 164 f., as well as other information in Louis Gardet's article dhikr in the new *EI*. The history of the communal *dhikr* still remains to be written; something may be found about it in my article 'The Dervish Dance', pp. 23 ff. and in Gardet. Listening to music (*samāᶜ*) must be strictly separated from recollecting God (*dhikr*), although occasionally it also appears in connection with the communal *dhikr* ('The Dervish Dance', pp. 41 ff.). Here I wish to confine myself to presenting a first critical edition and translation of Qushayrī's monograph *Tartīb al-sulūk*.

The attribution of the treatise to Qushayrī raises some doubts. Firstly, it does not figure anywhere in the list of his works which Subkī (*Ṭabaqāt*, III, pp. 246 f.) drew up. Next, two names are mentioned in the last section which until now were not known from Qushayrī's biography and more especially from his Sufi development, and which are difficult to fit in: Abū'l-Fawāris and Abū'l-Ḥasan. Furthermore, a statement in the first section of the *Tartīb* contradicts an opinion in the *Risāla*: in the *Tartīb* the tiro is obliged not to eat anything before being accepted even if the other Sufis do so, whereas in the *Risāla* the novice is to break his fast if he finds himself among a group of Sufis who are eating.

In the face of these objections one may perhaps reply the following: the title of this treatise does not occur anywhere in the text but only as a heading in the manuscripts and could therefore have originated with a copyist. But the book as such also seems to have remained completely unknown even in Sufi circles. Najm al-Dīn al-Kubrā (d. 618/1221), who would have had reason to cite the work, makes no mention of it and likewise appears to be uninfluenced by its content in his own writings about the recollection of God (*Fawāʾiḥ*, Introduction, p. 204). Ibn ᶜAṭāʾallāh al-Sikandarī (d. 709/1309) even maintains in his own monograph about recollecting God, *Miftāḥ al-falāḥ*, Cairo 1332, p. 2, that he knows of no one who has given a complete and adequate explanation of recollecting God; here it would have been natural at least to mention a monograph on the subject such as the *Tartīb*, even if it did not attain the size of the *Miftāḥ*. But then the oldest preserved manuscripts of our book belong to the same time, the 8th/14th century, and in the year 1069/1658-59 Ṣafī al-Dīn Aḥmad b. Muḥammad al-Qushāshī mentions it by name and includes it almost completely in his work *Al-simṭ al-majīd fī shaʾn al-bayᶜa wa'l-dhikr wa-talqīnihī wa-salāsil ahl al-tawḥīd* (Hyderabad, 1327, pp. 18-24). He designates the treatise (p. 18, l. 2) as *Risālat al-dhikr.* Moreover, there are other works of Qushayrī which are not found in Subkī's list (*GAL*^{2}, I, pp. 556 f.; *GAL S*, I, p. 772). The problem of the two names Abū'l-Fawāris and Abū'l-Ḥasan is doubly tricky. Firstly, it is unclear in what way the two names are connected with one another. To begin with, the wording of the text leads one to believe that these are two separate persons but one then has the impression they are both the same person. Two *kunya*s for a single person does occur, for example in the case of Kubrā who is usually designated as Abū'l-Jannāb but can also be called Abū ᶜAbdallāh (*Fawāʾiḥ*, Introduction, pp. 9 f.), and in the case of Abū'l-Qāsim al-Qaṣrī whose *kunya* is sometimes given as Abū Bakr and sometimes as Abū ᶜAbdallāh (Jāmī, *Nafaḥāt,* s.n. Abū'l-Qāsim al-Qaṣrī). On the other hand, the way in which Abū'l-Fawāris and Abū'l-Ḥasan alternate in the text is impossible for a double *kunya*. Therefore in one place, against all manuscript readings, I find myself forced to substitute Abū'l-Fawāris for Abū'l-Ḥasan and to assume that two persons are being referred to. Who these two persons are, however, I was unable to ascertain. All that is clear is that at the time the two narrated events took place Abū'l-Ḥasan was more advanced on the Sufi path than Qushayrī because the latter let himself be guided by him. Qushayrī's actual teacher does not appear to have been either one of the two, otherwise they would have borne a title. Most probably they were two of his Sufi comrades. But where should they be fitted into Qushayrī's life? On the basis of the tradition that Qushayrī 'learned the path of Sufism from master Abū ᶜAlī al-Daqqāq' (Ibn ᶜAsākir, *Tabyīn kadhib al-muftarī*, Damascus, 1347, p. 274, l. 13; Subkī, *Ṭabaqāt*, III, p. 245, ll. 19-20), Daqqāq is regarded as Qushayrī's shaykh and this also comes to light in the *Risāla*, but Qushayrī later associated with other Sufis as well and here the tradition becomes entangled in contradictions and obscurities. Ibn ᶜAsākir (d. 571/1176) maintains that after Daqqāq's death Qushayrī entered into contact with Sulamī (Ibn ᶜAsākir, *Tabyīn*, p. 273, ll. 10-11; Subkī, *Ṭabaqāt*, III, p. 245, ll. 1-2) but then that Sulamī and Daqqāq died in the same year (412/1021)! And Yāfiᶜī (d. 763/1367), who otherwise follows the report of Ibn ᶜAsākir in Ibn Khallikān's version, maintains instead that after Daqqāq's death Qushayrī had 'travelled the path of the *vita purgativa* and the elimination of self' (*Mirʾāt al-janān*, Hyderabad, 1337, III, p. 91) but it is not clear whether in so doing he was continuing an activity he had already begun earlier or whether he now underwent a proper Sufi training for the first time. The latter is not to be totally excluded as it is only said previously that he visited Daqqāq's gatherings (*majlis*), sought after mysticism,[10] was accepted by Daqqāq, then had his attention directed to the study of theology and complied with this suggestion.[11] However this may be, the incompatibility of these reports forbids us to draw conclusions about the point in time when the two mysterious figures played a role for Qushayrī, or to deny any connection between them and Qushayrī. Finally, as far as the contradiction in the doctrine about behavior when fasting, it seems that a reconciliation is not impossible. In the *Risāla* the novice is instructed not to contradict other Sufis outwardly but to stick to his own position inwardly and 'to remain with God'; if they invite him to eat, he should have a few bites but not give free rein to his appetite (p. 183, ll. 22-23; Hartmann, p. 192). Thus, there as well the order is not given to eat with the group but to make a gesture of solidarity so as not to offend anyone like a moral censor or to appear to get on one's high horse.

More conspicuous than these deviations are the agreements. We have already emphasized that no difference is made either in the *Tartīb* or in the *Risāla* between 'unlimited' and 'limited' recollection of God, and recollecting God in a group is not mentioned at all. Moreover, in both books Qushayrī passes on directly from acceptance of the novice by the shaykh to reception of the recollection of God, and from the novice, *mutatis mutandis*, demands the same preparations and the same commitments: knowledge and observance of the religious prescriptions, permanent ritual purity, a preference for poverty over wealth, shame over honor, God over everything else, and continuous and exclusive recollection of God. In both books he warns against extra devotional practices and against preoccupation with the secondary mystical phenomena of the recollection of God. That he treats all these things more fully in the *Risāla* and only refers slightly to the effects of recollecting God, whereas conversely in the *Tartīb* he merely glides over the rules of a general kind rapidly and by way of introduction, and instead handles the stages and consequences of recollecting God in detail, is to be explained by the different purpose of the two books.

---

10 That is no doubt the sense of the words: 'He travelled the path of *irāda*.'

11 *Mirʾāt al-janān*, III, p. 91, following Ibn ʿAsākir: *Tabyīn*, p. 272, ll. 15-17; Ibn Khallikān: *Wafayāt al-aʿyān*, Cairo, 1948-49, no. 367. And also Subkī: *Ṭabaqāt*, III, p. 244, ll. 16-18.

A further difficulty, however, is presented by the linguistic peculiarities which distinguish the *Tartīb* from the *Risāla*. Among these are the uncultivated style of the *Tartīb*, the unusual meaning of certain words, e.g. *masʾala* in the sense of 'difficulty, situation', the confusion of *marra* and *rubbamā*, the use of the imperfect to designate a single event in the sense of 'I could for instance...',[12] grammatical peculiarities such as leaving out pronominal suffixes (*āthara* instead of *ātharahā*) and agreement in gender of the object-predicate with the reflexive *nafs* (*wajadtu nafsī nāʾimatan mustalqiyatan* instead of *nāʾiman mustalqiyan*), and then the presence of a smattering of Persian words (*dah yāzdah*, *dah-u nīm*, *khudhāy*).

Against some of this one could argue that, as the evidence of the manuscripts shows, the transmission early on suffered corruptions and not everything offered by the archetype — which remains to be inferred — necessarily stems from Qushayrī. But in addition, in the case of the *Tartīb* one is confronted with a special form of writing which should not be placed on the same level with the *Risāla*. As the absence of an introduction referring to God and the Prophet indicates and as a few sentences announcing direct discourse in section 5 and from section 7 on show quite clearly, the *Tartīb* is not an actual book of Qushayrī but a transcription of his words, a recording of what Qushayrī had explained orally, whether during instruction or on some other occasion. From this it follows that there are two explanations for the stylistic and grammatical deviations of the *Tartīb* from the *Risāla*: firstly, in the *Tartīb* we are dealing with the spoken language and, secondly, the student who is unknown to us and who undertook to write down Qushayrī's words can have introduced elements of his own language into the text. Apparently both factors have played a role in shaping the text before us. However, in order to form a final judgement on this question and the question of authenticity, the other writings of Qushayrī besides the *Risāla* would have to be consulted, all of which unfortunately remain unedited.

The *Tartīb* breaks down into 'sections' just like the portion of the *Risāla* which was compared with it above. I have numbered them from 1 to 9. Section 1, after an introduction, describes how the student by concentrating on the recollection of God first forgets all things, then himself and eventually the recollection of God as well. He leaves his bodily senses behind him, perceives by means of the inner senses of the heart and also expresses himself with the tongue

---

12 If our understanding of the passage in section 8 of our tract is correct.

of the heart. He now recites the recollection of God with this tongue, often even in various languages that are unknown to him, and also hears nature recollecting God. After a certain time his consciousness succeeds at making a breakthrough to another level, the level of the so-called 'secret' (*sirr*). In so doing, he loses completely his own power to decide both concerning recollecting God and concerning his psychic states, and he becomes a plaything of what Sufism designates as God and what the mystic here perceives as an ocean. Section 2 begins again with the recollection of God with the tongue, which when done properly 'retreats' to the heart and there multiplies into those strange ways of naming God which are mentioned in section 1. But the breakthrough to the so-called 'secret' only succeeds if one holds a firm course and does not allow oneself to be distracted by the unusual figures of speech used for naming God in the heart. Indeed, being distracted not only hinders progress but even results in one coming out of the state one has attained and then only still having knowledge of it. In this case, moreover, knowledge flows into one in immense abundance, but the attention one pays to it pushes one further down to a mere knowledge that one possesses this knowledge. Qushayrī calls this second, mirrored knowledge 'understanding' (*fahm*). If in the end one still contemplates this understanding, by then one finds oneself in a state of indifference to mystical striving. Section 3 once again begins at the beginning and traces a third longitudinal line through the development: after continual recollection of God with the tongue and the heart's gazing at God, the person practicing the exercise enters a state in which he sees himself grow and expand beyond everything. But a 'power'[13] from above, from God, pushes him back. Once more he grows and becomes still bigger than before but a 'power', stronger than the first time, pushes him back again. This game repeats itself and intensifies until finally a last power completely stills the person practicing the exercise and now pushes his recollection of God into his heart. Section 4 deals with the movements and convulsions which to a lesser degree recollecting God with the tongue had already occasioned in the limbs of the reciter and recollecting God in the heart then provoked more intensely, and which finally turned into strange voices and words. All the bodily parts of a human being join in, except for the tongue which (here recollecting God in the heart is meant) remains silent. If he gives his attention to these voices, his mystical progress will likewise be hindered. The subject of section 5 is about

---

13 This has to do with the fear-instilling side of God. See *Fawāʾiḥ*, Intro., p. 80.

extraordinary experiences of taste. During recollection of God in the heart, it can appear to the mystic that an infinitely sweet drink is welling up from the roots of his teeth. The pleasure from this is so great that he thinks he is about to die and in some cases in order to diminish the experience he runs away from spiritual retreat and seeks the company of people. At this point his senses are so sharp he believes he can hear ants when they walk. His greatest wish is to be able to sleep but it is precisely this that he cannot do in this state, even if the state continues for years. Section 6 is devoted to an experience which the mystic has at the level of the 'secret'. Now from time to time he hears words addressed to him from God and a reply from his 'secret'; but only when the words are friendly does the 'secret' dare to reply. If God's words are hard and stern (it is a question of the two sides 'gentleness' and 'sternness' in the nature or in the attributes of God[14]), then the 'secret' remains silent. If he hears God's address and the reply without having anything to do with this himself, he must then distinguish himself from the subject of this speech, otherwise he will fall into the state of the 'union of union' (*jam*ᶜ *al-jam*ᶜ), i.e. the state in which the famous words were spoken 'I am God' (Ḥallāj) and 'praise be to me' (Bisṭāmī). Section 7 deals with random thoughts which occur during the recollection of God or in its wake. Whether one should accept these inspirations or reject them depends on their conformity with the religious law. Moreover, an idea which is unobjectionable from the viewpoint of religious law can also come from the devil; for example, awareness of the mystical state one has reached — which Qushayrī continually fought against — comes from the devil. Thoughts like this must additionally be tested in terms of the feeling that they leave behind. The pre-condition for this is that one possesses a valid standard of judgement, i.e. one must first be in a valid mystic state and in a valid feeling, then one can recognize the reprehensibleness of a new thought by the contrast in feeling that it provokes. This is also true of the beautiful music which one hears at this time for instance and which can accompany thoughts that come from God as well as those from the devil; here as well feeling must decide. In section 8 the success of the exercises comes under discussion. Mystic states descend like a bird only on a human being who remains motionless like a dead person. Therefore the beginner must lie perfectly still in the physical sense and should not allow anything to distract him from his basic orientation, not even observation of the successes that are oc-

---

14 See previous footnote.

curring, as Qushayrī emphasizes once again. To begin with keeping to the course is difficult, but then it becomes second nature and a necessity for a person. Qushayrī recounts that it was often difficult for him during recollection of God to rise in order to eat or to perform the ritual prayers, because he was afraid of losing the recollection of God. For the same reason he also sought to avoid sleep and one time he positioned himself on a rock that jutted out over a precipice so as not to fall asleep. In this case a miracle took place: he did succumb to sleep but without falling down. Another time in a mosque at night he vainly attempted to fight off sleep and then — once more a miracle — when he woke up he found himself in a house where he had previously wanted to go. In other words, he experienced somnambulary states. Finally, in section 9 it is emphasized that at first the greater the effort one makes, the further away success remains but that success then comes when one becomes weak and begins to lose heart. Another instance of the independent laws of mystic states which he experienced with his senses: at a certain point in the beginning of recollecting God he had acquired such sharp eyesight that he saw before him all things in creation, but when the recollection of God entered his 'secret', his vision once again receded to its normal degree of acuity. And he experienced a case of pure sympathetic contact with a friend: while the latter was asleep beside him, he thought to himself how nice it would be to have some butter. His friend then called out in a dream: 'Throw away the butter!' In conclusion Qushayrī reports how from recollection of God with the heart he reached recollection of God in the 'secret'. When recollecting God with the heart had become strong in him, a friend took him along into the countryside, sat him on a rock and had him say *khudhāy* (Persian for 'God') with his mouth closed. Qushayrī did this, his mouth became full, and the recollection of God shifted from his heart into his 'secret'. But he could not get any further than the first consonant *kh* so that the recollection of God became a 'protracted recollection of God'. Qushayrī lost consciousness and did not recover until after sunset. He lost so much weight within one day that he was reduced to skin and bones. Later the effects wore off but he remained weakened for a whole year. In any case, from that time on he heard the word *khudhāy* emanating from his 'secret'.

Qushayrī's explanations are the first of their kind in Islamic mysticism and for that reason alone deserve the full attention of all those who are concerned with the inner experiences of the Sufis in the period of the *shuyūkh al-tarbiya*. The *Fawāʾiḥ al-jamāl* of Kubrā and to a lesser extent some of the statements of Yaḥyā al-Suhrawardī in his *Ḥikmat al-ishrāq* represent a further milestone in this area. For more about this and other related subjects I refer the reader to my introduction to the *Fawā'iḥ* of Kubrā (p. 242).

The following edition of the *Tartīb al-sulūk* is based on three manuscripts and the printed edition of Qushāshī's *Simṭ al-majīd*:

A = Aya Sofya 2910, 140a-147b (in my pagination). Hellmut Ritter: 'Philologika XIII', in *Oriens* 3, 1950, p. 50, no. 101, refers to the passage as: fol. 142-148. Dated 706/1306. Quite pleasant, clear *naskhī*. Ligatures, omitted pointing. Described in: *Der Islam* 24, 1937, p. 9.

V = Vatican 573, 70a-76b. Undated, from the 8th/14th century. Strong, clear *naskhī*. Several omissions due to homoioteleuta. Incorrect pointing. Described by Giorgio Levi Della Vida: 'Elenco dei manoscritti arabi islamici della Biblioteca Vaticana', in: *Studi e testi* 67, Vatican, 1935, p. 63, no. 573.

B = Berlin 3262, 79b-82b. Undated, circa 1000/1592. Compact, clear *naskhī*. Described by Wilhelm Ahlwardt: *Verzeichniss der arabischen Handschriften der königlichen Bibliothek zu Berlin*, Berlin, 1887 ff., no. 3262 (= Spr. 851)

Q = Ṣafī al-Dīn Aḥmad b. Muḥammad b. ᶜAbd al-Nabī al-Anṣārī al-Madanī al-Dajjānī (from Dajjāna near Jerusalem) al-shahīr bi'l-Qushāshī: *Al-simṭ al-majīd fī sha'n al-bayᶜa wa'l-dhikr wa-talqīnihī wa-salāsil ahl al-tawḥīd* (composed 1069/1658-59; *GAL*2, II, p. 514; *GAL S*, II, p. 535), Hyderabad, 1327, pp. 18-24. Contains only sections 2-9.

The manuscripts below were not used:

U = Ulu Cami (Bursa), tasavvuf 13, 111b-115b. Undated. Cursory *naskhī-taᶜlīq*. Described by Hellmut Ritter: 'Philologika XIII', in *Oriens* 3, 1950, p. 50, no. 101/p. 66, no. 153.
N = Nafız Paşa 745, *GAL*2, I, p. 556.

The three MSS and Qushāshī are not dependent on one another directly or indirectly but go back to original versions of the text which are unknown to us. How these originals were related to one another is unclear and does not appear to be important for restoring the text because each of the four textual witnesses consulted offers good and bad readings, is one time connected with one of its brothers and another time with a different one, and occasionally is alone in presenting the decisive reading. Generally speaking, A is the best MS and V is the worst. But no one of them could serve as the basis for the edition, and it would not be possible to manage without conjectural interventions. The apparatus criticus does not display the whole manuscript tradition, since trivial points, corrected misunderstandings and glaring impossibilities have been left out. On the other hand, wherever variants are noted, the whole manuscript tradition is always taken account of, even if it presents something impossible. Lemmata without a manuscript reference are conjectures of the editor.

بسم الله الرحمن الرحيم

(١)

قال الأستاذ أبو القاسم عبد الكريم بن هوازن القشيرى رضى الله عنه : يجب ان يكون العبد مجرّدا عن الدنيا لا يملك شيئًا ويكون عالمًا بما يلزمه من فرائض الحق سبحانه وتعالى توحيدًا له وشريعةً عليه ثم يكون أبدًا على الطهارة فى نفسه وأثوابــه ثم يتَلْمذ من بين الناس لمن سلك طريق الله تعالى وتجرّد له فلا يكون مشتغلاً بشىء سوى الحق حتى ينفعه تعليمه اياه فإن تلمذ لمن سلك طريق الله سبحانه كان اقوى واسرع سلوكًا وان تلمذ لمن لم يَثِق بعلمه بطريق الله سبحانــه فقد يُعجِّب ويصل مرّةً ولكن بعد حين ، لا يكون بتلك السرعة لانه لا تُعينه همّة استاذه فيكون كالولد عن فحلٍ سَوء والاول كالولد عن فحل نجيب ويشترط الاستاذ على المريد ان يختار الفقر على الغنَى والذلّ على العزّ والله على غيره ويشترط ان لا يأكل وإن أكل الفقراء ولا يقول ما لا يعنيه وإن قاله الفقراء ولا يؤثر الراحة وان آثر اولئك الذين يراهم معه فى الرباط ثم بعد ان قبِل هذه الشرائط يقول له الاستاذ: قبِلتُك لأُوصّلك الى

(١) الرحيم ABV : + وبه العون B + ربّ يسّر وسهّل A + وصلى الله على ... محمد V (٢) ابو القاسم (ابو القسم V) ... القشيرى BV : ليس فى A | رضى الله عنه AB : رحمه الله V (٣) مجردا عن AB : معجردا من V | ويكون VA : ثم يكون B (٤) وتعالى AB : ليس فى V | واثوابه AB : بياض فى V (٥) تعالى AB : سبحانه V | له VB : لله A بتصحيح الناسخ (٦) سبحانه VA : تعالى B (٧) سبحانه VB : ليس فى A | فقد يعجّب A : يعجب B فقد سحب V (٨) لا تعينه B : لا نفسه A تُغنيه V (٩) ويشترط AB : ويشرط V (١٠-١١) ولا يقول AB : وان لا يقول V (١١) ولا يؤثر الراحة B : ولا يؤثر الرحا A وان لا يؤثر الراحة V | آثر : اثر VAB ولعل الصواب آثرها

طريق الله تعالى بقدر ما تعرف إنّى لا أبخل عليك بقدر ما عرفتُه. ثم يعرّفه ويوصيه ان لا يسمع من الاستاذ ويرى جميع احواله من الله تعالى ويرى التوفيق منه ويقول له: قل الله الله الله ثم يوصيه ان يواظب على قول هذا الذكر ولا يشهد غيره ولا يفكر فى غيره وإن أشغله عن هذا الذكر امر من الامور يطرح ذلك الامر وإن كان موت والديه ولا يفعل شيئًا من الطاعات الا الفرائض والسنن وركعتى الضُحَى وبعد كل وضوء ركعتين فأمّا ما سواه من النوافل وقراءة القرآن فلا ويشتغل بهذا الذكر الى ان يغيب بالذكر عن جميع الأشياء بتوفيق الله تعالى لقوّة ارادته ثم يغيب بالذكر عن نفسه ثم يغيب بالذكر عن الذكر يردّد مدّةً طويلة بين غيبته عن الذكر بالذكر وبين حضور الذكر فمرّةً يغيب عن الذكر ومرّةً يحضر الذكر ثم لا يزال يرتقى فى كل غيبة وحضور الى رتبة أخرى ثم يَرِد ورود آخر عليه أعلى من هذا فيفنى العبد عن الذكر وعن هذه الاحوال فاذا رُدّ العبد الى حال البقاء بعد هذه الغيبة يُسلَب عنه لسانُه وسمعُه وبصره الا شهادةَ القلب ولا يمكنه ان يقول باللسان ويقولُ بالقلب نطقًا لا علمًا ومشاهدةً بل كما كان ينطق بلسانه قبله يذكر بقلبه حتى يرد ورود آخر عليه بعد مدّة ما شاء الله أعلى من ذلك من حيث الهيبة فيبدو على العبد من الهيبة ورود يظنّ انه قريب من الحق فيفنى العبد فيه ثم يُردَّد بين الفناء والبقاء وكل مرّة يُرَدّ الى البقاء تزداد عبارات قلبه حتى ينتهى الى أذكار يجدها من قلبه مرةً بألسنة مختلفة

---

(١) تعالى VB: ليس فى A | انى A: لى B ليس فى V | عرفته B: عرفسه (؟) A عرفنيه V (٢) لا AB: ليس فى V | من الله AB: مع الله V | تعالى VB: ليس فى A (٣) ولا يشهد VB: والا يشهد A | ولا يفكر فى غيره B: والا يفكر فى غيره A سقط فى V (٤) اشغله AB: شغله V (٥) ولا يفعل VA: لا يفعل B (٦) ويشتغل V: يشتغل A ويغتسل B (٦-٧) الى ان يغيب بالذكر VA: سقط فى B (٧) عن جمع الاشياء بتوفيق الله تعالى لقوة ارادته ثم يغيب بالذكر B: عن جميع الاشياء بتوفيق الله لقوة ارادته ثم يغيب بالذكر A سقط فى V (٨) يردّد VA: يردّده B (٨-٩) حضور الذكر VA: حضور القلب B (٩) يحضر الذكر A: يحضر للذكر VB (١٠) يرد ... من هذا AB: ترد ورود أُخَر عليه اعلى من هذه V (١١) فاذا VA: وإذا B (١٢) القلب . . ويقولُ AB: سقط فى V (١٣) كان AB: ليس فى V | قبله A: قلبه V ليس فى B ولعل عدمه صحيح (١٤) العبد AB: القلب V (١٥) يُردّد B: يتردد VA (١٦) ينتهى كذا بالياء المنقوطة B | من قلبه مرة B: مرة قلبه A من قلبه V

وعباراتٍ لم يسمعها قبله ولا خطرت بباله قبله يجد ذلك، كله فى قلبه حتى يتوهم ان جملة الكون تذكر الله تعالى بعبارات مختلفة أحيانا ويصير بحيث لا يميّز بين ذكره الذى يبدو من قلبه وذكر الكون من غلبات الذكر عليه فيسمع جميع هذه الاذكار ثم بعده يَرِد ورودٌ آخر بحيث، لو ذاق هذا الورود غيرُ من سلك هذه الطريقة على سبيل الوهلة لمات من هيبة الله تعالى حتى يفنى هذا العبد ولا يبقى منه شىء ثم يُردَ الى حال البقاء فيُسلَب عنه احوال القلب من الشهادة وغيرها فيبدو له سرّ الغيب فلم يبق للعبد شىء وليس الا الله فهو كالبحر يبدو فتصير الأنهار بحكمه فلا يكون لغير الله حُكم ولا يكون للعبد بعد هذا حركة وقبل هذا كان يتحرك بورود يرد عليه فالآن إن تحرك البحر الذى بدا له تحرك العبد وان سكن سكن العبد وانما يسمع ويبصر ويشهد بما بدا له ليس بعد هذه الحالة لبشريّته سلطان لا للذكر ولا للاحوال انما سلطان هذا للبارئ وهو الله تعالى ثم فى خلال هذه الاحوال قبل وصوله الى هذا المقام الذى هو النهاية كان يرى جملة الكون بنور كان له حتى لم يَخْفَ من الكون عليه شىء فكان يرى جميع الكون من السماء والأرض رؤية عيان ولكن بقلبه وكان لا يرى فى هذا الوقت بعين رأسه شيئًا ولكن لم تكن هذه رؤيةَ علمٍ بل لو تحرّك فى الكون ذرّةٌ ونملةٌ لرَأَى

---

(١) كله V: سه AB (٢) الكون VA: الكونين B | تعالى VB: ليس فى A | يميّز V: يمز AD (٥) لمات B: له يات A مات V | تعالى B: سبحانه A ليس فى V (٦) حال VB: حالة A | من الشهادة AB: بين الشهاده V | له سر AB: السر سر V (٧) فلا VB: ولا A (٩-١٠) وانما يسمع A: وانما يسمع العبد B فانما يسمع V (١٠) لبشريته: لبشرية B لبس به A لبشريه V (١٠-١١) لا للذكر ولا للاحوال A: ولا للذكر ولا للاحوال B ولا الذكر بعد الاحوال V (١١) انما ... للبارى AB: وانما السلطان هذا البارى تعالى V | تعالى VB: ليس فى A (١٢) النهاية VB: نهاية A | الكون V: الكوين B الكون بهن (كذا) A (١٣) من الكون عليه AB: عليه من الكون V | فكان AB: وكان V (١٤) بعين رأسه شيئا V: بعين لانّه شىء A بعين رأسه شيئًا الا به شىء B (١٥) لرأى V: رى B ليس فى A

(٢)

فصل

اذا تحقق الذاكر فى ذكر اللسان رجع ذكر لسانه الى ذكر القلب فاذا ذكر القلب يرد عليه فى الذكر احوال يجد من نفسه بل يسمع من قلبه لله سبحانه أسماء وأذكارًا لم يسمعها قط ولا قرأها فى كتاب بعبارات مختلفة وألسنة متباينة لم يسمعها مَلَكٌ ولا آدمى فان لازم همته ولم يلتفت ولم يلاحظ هذه الواردات نال المزيد والزيادة الى ان ينتهى الى ذكر السرّ وان التفت الى ما يجرى عليه من هذه الاحوال ولاحظ هذه التسميات وهذه الاذكار ونظر اليها واشتغل بها فقد أساء الادب فيعاقَب فى الوقت وعقوبته انقطاع المزيد عنه ثم يعاقب ثانيًا إن صبر عليه بان يُرَدّ الى حال العلم بهذه الاحوال وتَرِد عليه علوم حتى يظنّ انه فُتح عليه علوم الاولين والآخرين فان لاحظ الى ما يرد عليه من العلوم فهو سوء ادب ويستحق العقوبة وعقوبته فى هذه الحالة ان يُرَدّ الى حال الفهم. والفرق بين حال الفهم والعلم ان العلم وجود يرد على قلبه من حيث العلم والفهم نظر الى ذلك العلم كأنّ الفهم عِلمٌ بأنه كان له علم بتلك المسائل. فان نظر الى الفهم فقد أساء أدبه وعقوبتُه ان يُرَدّ الى حال الغفلة

(٣)

فصل

اذا ذكر العبد بلسانه فتقوى همّتُه فى الذكر حتى يذكره باللسان مواظبًا عليه

---

(٢) الذاكر QV: للذاكر A الذكر B | رجع AB: دفع V وقع Q رفع فى هامش B | القلب فاذا QAB: قلبه فاذا V (٣) يجد VAB: يجدها Q | سبحانه VAB تعالى Q (٥) المزيد VAB: المراد Q (٧) التسميات VAB: المسميات Q | الادب AB: ادبه Q ادبه V (٨) صبر VAD: اصرّ Q ولعله الصواب (٩) فتح VAB: قد فتح Q (١٠) الى ما VAB: ما Q | ويستحق VB: ومستحق A فيستحق Q (١١) حال الفهم والعلم AB: حال العلم والفهم V حال العلم وحال الفهم Q (١٢) على قلبه AB: عليه V على القلب Q | نظر ... له علم QVA: سقط «له» فى V فان نظر الى ذلك العلم كان الفهم علمه بان له علمه B (١٣) نظر QAB: نظر العبد V | حال QAB: تلك V (١٥) فتقوى: فيقوى A فيقوى VB نقوى Q | باللسان QAB: بلسانه V | مواظبا QV: مواظب A مواظب B

حريصًا وراغبًا فيه حتى لا يبقى منه جزء الا راغبًا في ذكر اللسان فاذا ذكر بلسانه ونظر بقلبه الى الله تعالى تَرِد عليه احوال يتوهم العبد أنه يربو ويعظم حتى كأنه يصير اكبر من كل شيء ثم يَرِد عليه من الحق قهر من خوف يبدهه به فيمنع العبد من ان يعظم ويذهب فيصطلمه ثم يعيده فاذا اعاده عاد العبد الى حالة اقوى من الاولى فيعظم حتى كأنه اعلى من الاول ثم يرد عليه قهر اعظم من الاول فلا يزال مردَّدًا بين هذه الاحوال في الزيادة يرتقي في كل نَفَس وفي كل ساعة حتى يرد عليه قهر عظيم بعد ان اتى عليه سنون في ذكر اللسان نفسه فاذا اعاده بعد هذا الفناء ينقطع عنه ذكر اللسان فلا يجد العبد من نفسه شيئًا لا من السمع ولا من البصر الا شيئًا ضعيفًا ثم يصير ذكره الى القلب فيسمع من قلبه ذكر القلب حتى يتمنى ان يكون في مفازة لأن عنده ان الناس يسمعون بآذانهم ذكره الذي في قلبه ولا يعلم ان احدًا غيره ليس يسمع ذلك الذكر

(٤)

فصل

وابتداء الذكر في الجوارح ان يجد حركة في جوارحه حتى لا يبقى عليه جزء من

---

(١) جزء ... ذكر اللسان AB: جزءًا ... ذلك اللسان V جزء الا كان راغبًا في ذكر اللسان Q (٢) ونظر ... احوال Q وكذالك V ولكن بدون « تعالى »: نظر بقلبه الى ان يردّ (كذا) عليه احوال B نظر بقلبه(؟) الى ان مردّ (كذا) عليه احوالا (كذا) A | يربو AB: يزيد V وهامش B يزيد ويربو Q | ويعظم QAB: او يعظم V | يصير AB: ليس في QV (٣) خوف VAB: الخوف Q | يبدهه QV: يدهشه A يبلو B (٤) يعظم ويذهب AB: يذهب ويعظم QV | فيصطلمه QV: فيصطلبه A فيصطليه D | عاد QVA: اعاد D (٥) فيعظم حتى كانه اعلى من الاول VAB: سقط في Q | فلا AB: ولا QV (٦) مردّدا VAB: متردداً Q | وفي كل VB: وكل QA (٧) سنون VAB: سنون كثيرة Q | ذكر QAV: ذلك B | هذا الفناء QA: هذه الفناء B هذا V (٨) فلا يجد QAB: ولا يحكم V (٩) ذكره QVB: ذلك A (١٠) مفازة QB: مغارة A، لا يمكنني قراءة الكلمة في V (١١) ليس QAB: لا V | الذكر VAB: ليس في Q (١٢) وابتداء QV: فابتداء A ابتداء B | ان VAB: انه Q

لحمه وعظمه الا ويجد فيه حركة واختلاجًا ثم تقوى تلك الحركات وتلك الاختلاجات حتى تصير أصواتًا وكلامًا حتى يسمع العبد من جميع جوارحه واجزائه أصواتًا الا من لسانه فان اللسان لا ينطق فى هذه الاحوال والعبد ملازم لهمّته لانه يتيقن انـه لو لاحظ وطلب علم هذه الاذكار بقى فيها فهو لا ينظر اليها حتى يرقى عنها الى غيرها وهذا بعد ان وقع الذكر على القلب فأمّا فى حال ذكر اللسان فيكون هذه الحركات والاختلاجات للجوارح ولكن لا بهذه القوة

(٥)

فصل

فى احوال ذكر القلب يظهر على العبد شىء يجد الحلاوة فى فيه وحلقـه حتى يقوم له ذلك مقام طعامه وشرابه ويجد منبع ذلك الشراب من اصول أسنانه وهو احلى من العسل وتبقى أسنانه بعضها على بعض حتى يشقّ عليه ان يفتح فاه فيجد هذا الشراب فى فيه على هذا الوصف. وفى حال هذا الشرب يقرب العبد من الموت حتى يذوب ويكاد يموت ولا يخاف فى هذه الحالة الا من الموت حتى إنه اذا بلغ العبد الى هذه الرتبة – وهى رتبة يهرب أَلْفُ رَجُلٍ من هذه اللذّة ولا يهرب واحد منهم من الأَلَم فانّ هذه االذّة اصعب واقرب من الموت – يذوب العبد فيـه

(٢) وكلامًا حتى ... اصواتًا QAB: سقط فى V (٣) لهمته VAB: بهمته Q (٤) فيها ... يرقى QV: فيها ... يترقى B سقط فى A (٥) على VAB: الى Q | فأمّا AB: وأما QV | فيكون AB: فتكون Q مكون V (٦) لا بهذه QV: هذه القوة AB (٧-٨) فصل، فى احوال ذكر القلب A: فصل فى احوال ذكر القلب Q فى احوال ذكر القلب B فصل فى ذكر احوال القلب V (٨) شىء VAB: من آثار ذكر القلب شىء Q | الحلاوة VAB: الحلاوة له Q | وحلقه QVA: وفى حلقه B (٩) له QAB: ليس فى V | طعامه QVB: طعمه A | ويجد منبع AB: ويجد العبد V فيجد العبد منبع Q (١٠) عليه QA: ذلك عليه B دلك (كذا) V (١٠-١١) فيجد هذا QAB: فيجد ذلك V (١١) وفى QVB: فى A | الشرب VA: الشراب QB (١٢) حتى يذوب QVB: بحيث يذوب A (١٣) الى QAB: ليس فى V | وهى رتبة AB: ليس فى QV (١٤) منهم من الألم AB: من الالم V من الالف ممن ادرك هذه اللذّة بطريقة موصلة اليها بمفتاح الذكر لا من الالف الاجنبى الذى لا يستطع(!) حملها بجملته Q | يذوب VAB: ويذوب Q

كأنه يتلاشى وكأنه يموت حتى يبلغ العبد فى هذه الحالة – إن صحبتْه هذه اللذّة ولم تسقط عنه الى حال يهرب من الخلوة لانه اذا خلا ساعةً تستولى عليه هذه اللذّة حتى تقرّبه من الموت فكما أن المبتدئ يهرب من الخلق ويؤثر الخلوة فكذلك العبد اذا بلغ الى هذا المقام هرب من هذه اللذّة

قال: الاستاذ وصاحب هذه الاحوال قال: أنا أهرب من الخلوة لهذا الشأن

وفى حال هذه اللذّة تقوى معرفته ويجتدّ بصره وبصيرته حتى كأنه يسمع وقع أقدام النمل وفى البداية يتمنى ان لا ينام وفى هذه المسئلة أكثرُ همّتِه ان يجد المنام فيستريح. وعلامة صحة هذه اللذّة ان العبد لا يأخذه النوم ما دام هو فى هذه المسئلة ولو بقى سنين حتى تضعف هذه المسئلة فحينئذ يجد المنام

(٦)

فصل

لأهل النهاية مسئلة وهى انهم يرد على سرّهم مرّةً خطاب لا يشكّون انه من الحق فيكون مُخاطِبَه باللطف والمناجاة فيجيبه السرّ والعبد يسمع من السرّ الجواب ومن الحق الخطاب ومرّةً يكون بالهيبة فيسكت السرّ ثم يجد مرّةً كلاماً ذلك الكلام فى

---

(١) كأنه يتلاشى وكأنه يموت A: كأنه يتلاشى ويموت B حتى يتلاشى وكأنه يموت V حتى كأنه يتلاشى وكأنه يموت Q (١-٢) ولم ... اللذة VAD: سقط فى Q (٢) من الخلوة VA: منه من الخلوة B | اذا VB: اذا ما A (٣) تقربه VAB: يقرب Q | فكما QVB: كما A | الخلق QV: الخلوة B الحلوة A | ويؤثر الخلوة؛ ويؤثر الحلوة VA ويؤثر الجلوة B يؤثر الخلوة Q | فكذلك العبد اذا بلغ B: فكذلك اذا بلغ العبد V فاذا بلغ العبد QA (٤) هرب VAB: يهرب Q | هذه اللذة QAB: اللذة V (٥) قال الاستاذ VAB: ليس فى Q | قال VAB: يقول Q | الخلوة لهذا VA: الخلق لهذا Q الخلوة بهذا B (٦) وفى حال هذه Q: وفى هذه V فى حال هذه AB (٧) لا ينام QAB: ينام V | اكثر همته ان: اكثر همته وان A اكثر همة وان B اكبر همته ان V اكثر همه ان Q (٨) فيستريح VAB: ويستريح Q | هو VAB: ليس فى Q (١٠) فصل VAB: واعلم ان Q (١١) النهاية VAB: هذة النهاية Q | وهى QAB: وهو V | سرهم VAB: اسرارهم Q (١٢) مخاطبه VAB: مخاطبته Q (١٤) يجد QVB: يجده A

نفسه خطاب وهو جواب ليس للعبد فيه شئ — يعلم العبد بمعرفته كأنه يرى نفسه فى النوم انه ليس هو الحق ولا يشكّ ان ذلك كلام الحق فان غاب عن العبد هذه المعرفة اللطيفة ارتفع التمييز فهو جمع الجمع ولذلك قال قائلهم: أنا الحق وقال ابو يزيد: سبحانى. ما قال الا الحق بمحو الأشخاص

(٧)

فصل

العبد يعرف الخواطر ويميز بينها بأن يعرضها على العلم والأمر والنهى فان صحّ على حدّ العلم فهو صحيح وان لم يصحّ فهو باطل

ثم أُلطِفَ فى هذه المسئلة وهى أنه ربما يكون العبد على حالة شريفة يريد الشيطان ان يردّه الى حالة ادنى من تلك الحالة فيُخطِر بباله تلك فاذا عرض ذلك الخاطر على العلم والأمر والنهى يكون صحيحًا ولكن يكون من الشيطان فكيف يعرفه العبد وقلّ من يعرفه من الناس

فالجواب عنه: انما يعرف العبد أن ذلك الخاطر يُوحِش بأن يعود على العبد منه وحشة فاذا ورد على القلب ضَرَبَه فأوجعه كالطعام الذى لا يكون فيه ملح فيعلم

---

(١) ليس VAB: وليس Q | يعلم B: نعلم VA بعلم Q | بمعرفته VAB: ومعرفته Q (٢) هو VAB: هو من Q | يشكّ: يسل A شك QVB | كلام QVA: هو كلام B (٣) ارتفع التميز VAB: وارتفع التميز Q (٣-٤) ولذلك ... الا QAB: سقط فى V (٤) الا الحق A: الا بحق (كذا) B ذلك الا الحق على لسان عبده Q | بمحو VAB: لمحو Q (٦) الخواطر VAB: الخواطر التى تعرض له فى باطنه Q (٧) حد QVB: هذا A | وان QAB: فان V (٨) فى AB: من QV | وهى QB: وهو VA (٩) بباله تلك VD: بباله تلك الحالة Q بباله A (١٠) يكون صحيحا VAB: فيكون صحيحا Q (١٠-١١) فكيف ... من يعرفه من الناس QV: فيكون يعرفه العبد وقل ما يعرفه الناس AB ولعله الصواب (١٢) فالجواب VB: والجواب QA | انما VAD: انه انما Q | ان ذلك الخاطر يوحش AB: ذلك الخاطر بوحش (كذا) V ذلك الخاطر بتوحش Q | بان يعود على العبد AB: فعود (!) الى العبد V يعود عليه Q (١٣) ورد QV: اورد AB | القلب QA: العبد VB | ضربه QV: ضربة B صرفه A | فيعلم QAB: ليعلم V

بالوحشة والسماجة التى به انه ليس من الحق وأنه من الشيطان وإن كان دعا الى ما هو طاعة مثل ان يأمره بالحج مثلاً او برّ الوالدين وانما قصد الشيطان ان يرجع على العبد بردّه من الحالة العليا الى الحالة الدنيا دَهْ يازْدَه ودَهُ نِيمْ ويرتفع مراده بهذا القدر. وهذا الخاطر الذى من الشيطان انما يعلم انه من الشيطان بكونه ضدًّا لِما هو به وربما يصوّر الشيطان للعبد ان تلك الحالة اعلى من حال العبد ولكن تكون ضدًّا لما هو به العبد من حيث الاستحلاء والوحشة واذا كان الخاطر من الحق وجد الشكلية معها عليه العبد فيتّفقان كشخصين التقيا متّفقين فى الصنعة والهمّة يلتقيان ويتفقان فان كانا ضدّين فى الحرفة تزاحما كذا العبد اذا كان على خاطر من الحق فيما معه من البضاعة ورأس المال اذا ورد عليه خاطر الشيطان ميّز بينهما فيجد فى نفسه ضدّية + ... + بين الوارد من الشيطان وبين ما معه من الحق فتلك الضدّية تحكم انه من الشيطان وليس من الحق

---

(١) التى به انه ليس: التى بها انها ليست VAB انه ليس Q | الحق QAB: الحق تعالى V | وانه ... دعا: وانها ... دعا VAB وانه من الشيطان وانه خاطر غير مرضىّ وان كان عاد Q (٢) مثلاً VAB: ليس فى Q | بر الوالدين AB: برّ والديه V ببرّ الوالدين Q | قصد الشيطان VAD: قصد Q | يرجع D: يرج VA يروج Q (٣) الحالة العليا الى الحالة الدنيا VAB: الحال الاعلى الى الحال الادنى Q | ده يازده وده نيم AB: ده رده وده نم V ليفسد ما هو عليه فزيادة وده يتم Q (٣-٤) ويرتفع ... القدر A: ومن يقع مراده بهذا القدر B ويرتفع مرداه (!) عن هذا المقدار V ويرفع مراده بهذا المقدار Q (٤) انما ... الشيطان VAB: سقط فى Q | بكونه: يكون QB ان يكون V انه يكون A | به QVB: ربّه A (٥) يصور الشيطان للعبد QAB: تصور العبد V | حال العبد VAB: حالة العبد الاولى Q | ولكن تكون: ولكن يكون AB ولكن تكون (كذا) V ولكن لا تكون Q (٦) هو AB: ليس فى QV | والوحشة QVA: ليس فى B | واذا VAB: وان Q | الشكلية VAB: السكينة Q (٧) معها QVA: مما B | العبد VAB: العبد من الانقطاع الى الله تعالى فيؤيده Q | الصنعة VAB: الصفة Q | ويتفقان AB: ويتوافقان QV (٨) كذا VAB: وتنازعا كذلك Q | فيما B: هما A فلما V لما Q (٩) البضاعة QVB: الصناعة A | خاطر VAB: خاطر من Q | فى نفسه QVA: بينهما B (١٠) + ... +: الوارد عليه والشكلية A الوارد عليه اذ الشكلية B الواردة عليه او الشكلية V الوارد عليه والسكينة تميز الضدية Q ولعل الصواب: الوارد عليه والشاهد اى | فتلك الضدية VAB: فبتلك الضدية لما هو فيه Q | انه: انها QVAB (١١) وليس VAB: وليست Q

وفى هذه الخواطر والاحوال التى تَرِد على العبد يسمع العبد أصواتا أحلى ما يكون واحسن ما يكون حتى يكون كانها ألذّ واطرب واشهى من اصوات الاوتار والمزامير والبرابط وكلِّ شيء من صوت حلو حسن ثم هذا الخاطر من الشيطان يكون بهذه الحلاوة وربما يكون أتمّ حلاوة من هذا الذى من الحق فى الصورة ولكن هذا الذى من الشيطان يُلِحُّ فلا يعود إلى العبد منه أُنس فاذا لم يكن للعبد من الحق هذه الاحوال وأورد عليه الشيطان لا يشكّ انها من الله تعالى وانما يعلم انها من الشيطان للضدّية التى يجد بينها وبين ما عنده من الحق ولِما يعود اليه من الوحشة فلو لم يكن له شيء من الحق لم يعلم ان هذا من الشيطان لا من الحق ولكن اذا قوى فى الذكر فيرتقى بالتدريج الى سماع هذه الاصوات المؤنِسة فحينئذ اذا ورد من الشيطان خاطر يجد الضدّية بينه وبين ما عنده من الحق

(٨)

فصل

قال: قيل: المبتدئ مع الاحوال كالطير الوحشى فان كان فى الانسان حركة وقوة وأثر الحياة والحسّ نفر منه واستوحش ولا يقع عليه وان سكن الانسان حتى توهّم الطير الوحشى انه ميّت لا حراك فيه استأنس به ووقع عليه ولا ينفر كذلك المبتدئ

---

(١) وفى هذه: وهى هذه AB وهذه QV (٢) حتى يكون كانها VB: حتى كانها A فانها كلها Q
(٣) والبرابط AB: والبربط Q ليس فى V | شيء من QVB: ليس فى A (٣-٤) بهذه الحلاوة QV: بهذه الحالة A بهذا الحالة (!) D (٤) من هذا الذى ... ولكن هذا AB: وهذا V من الذى من الحق فى الصورة وهو Q (٥) يلح فلا A: يلوح فلا QB يلوح ولا V | انس VAB: شيء Q | فاذا QAB: فأمّا ما V (٦) واورد QB: فاورد V ووارد A | عليه QVB: عليه هذه A | تعالى AB: ليس فى V تعالى للصورة الصالحة Q (٧) يجد VAB: ليس فى Q | الحق VAB: الحق الذى هو عليه Q | الوحشة VAB: الوحشة كما سبق Q (٨) لا VAB: ام Q (٩) فيرتقى B: فيترقى VA فترقى Q | بالتدريج الى سماع QAB: فى التدريج اى V | فحينئذ AB: حينئذ QV | ورد QVA: اورد B
(١٢) قال قيل A: فان قيل V قيل B مثال Q | المبتدى QVB: المبتدئين A | كالطير QAB: كالطائر V | الوحشى VAB: الوحشى اذا جاء Q (١٣) نفر Q: نفر AV يفرّ B | توهم VAB: يتوهم Q ولعله الصواب (١٤) ولا VAB: فلا Q | كذلك QV: وكذلك B كذى A

فى الاحوال يجب ان تسكن حواسّه ولا تتحرك أنفاسه ولا يحكُّ بدنَه ولا يحرّك جزءا منه ولا يردد طرفه فى الأشياء ويكون مراعيًا لهمّته ولا يحرّك البتّة جزءا من نفسه ولا من بدنه ولا من باطنه حتى تبدو الاحوال له بعد طول المراعاة ثم يجب أن لا ينظر اليها ولا الى ما يبدو له البتة لئلا يَحجَب عنها فلا يزال فى المزيد منها ان شاء الله تعالى

قال: وهذا الطريق الذى هو طريق الله تعالى لا بدّ فيه من طول المجاهدة ومقاساة ما لا تحتمله الأسماع والقلوب من الشدائد لو حُكى لها إلاّ انه يؤثر العبد هذه المجاهدات ولكن اذا سلك سبيل الله تدخل عليه هذه المجاهدات شاء ام ابى ولو كان ذلك بتكلفه لم يصبر عليه العبد الا قليلاً ولكننى كنتُ أحيانا فى بدء المجاهدة واحوال الذكر لو الله رمى بى من السماء لكان ايسر علىّ واهون من ان اقوم للاكل واتحرك للوضوء والفرض لانه كان يغيب عنى الذكر فكان يشق علىّ التفصّى ما كنت فيه لفوات الذكر فيدخل علىّ تلك المجاهدات شئتُ ام ابيت لئلا أُرَدّ الى ما عليه الناس من احوالهم

(١) بدنه QAVB: + ويتصبر حتى يصير خلقا له Q (٢) يردد طرفه فى الأشياء V: يردد طرفه
لاسـًا (كذا) A يردّ طرفه للأشياء B يرد طرفه فى الاشياء Q (٣) ولا من بدنه ولا من باطنه
AB: ولا بدنه ولا باطنه Q ولا يامن باطنه V | الاحوال له بعد A: الاحوال به بعد B له الاحوال
مع Q سقط فى V حتى «يبدو» فى سطر ٤ | يجب B: يحب (كذا) A يجب بعد ذلك Q (٤) ولا
الى ما يبدو له البتة A: ولا الى ما لا يبدو له B <...> له البتة V والى ما لا يبدو له مطلقا
البتة Q | عنها فلا VAB: به عنها ولا Q | منها ان شاء الله تعالى AB: منها V ليس فى Q (٦) قال
VA: فصل B ليس فى Q | وهذا QAB: وهذه V | الله تعالى VAB: خصوص اهل الله Q | فيه
VAB: فيها Q | طول AB: حصول V خصوص Q (٧-٩) ومقاساه ... فى بدء المجاهدة QAD:
سقط فى V | ما AB: من Q | لا تحتمله Q: يحتمله AB | لو حكى لها الا: لو حلى لها الا B لو
حكى ما لا A ولم يحك لها اى لم تخطر فى البال لا Q (٨) هذه المجاهدات QA: هذه المجاهدة B |
شاء ام ابى Q: شيًا (!) ام انا A شيئًا او انا B (٩) بتكلفه QA: بتكليفه B | العبد الا قليلا Q:
العبد قليلاً A قليلاً B | ولكننى AB: لكن Q | بدء Q: بدوAB (١٠) الله رمى بى (او: أنه رُمِىَ بى):
اسرمى بى B اسرّ منّى بى A استرمى V ارسل بى Q | لكان QAB: كان V | علىّ VAB: ليس
فى Q | واتحرك AB: او اتحرك QV (١١) لانه كان يغيب QVA: لاننى كنت اغيّب B ولعله
الصواب | عنى Q: عن VAB | التفصى مما V: المصى مما A التقضى مما B التقضى بما Q (١٢) المجاهدات
VAB: المجاهدة Q | الى QAB: على V

قال: وكان يجرى علىّ اشياء فى حال الذكر هى عند قوم كرامات لكنها كانت عندى فى ذلك الوقت اشدّ من الزنا ولو ابتليت بالزنا لكان اهون علىّ من تلك الاشياء لانى كنت اريد ان لا انام البتة لئلا اغيب عن الذكر لحظة فكنت اقعد على حجر ناتئ من جدار ينتأ منه الحجر قدر ما أضع عليه قدمى وتحتى وادٍ وفوقى شاهق حتى لا يأخذنى النوم فكنت اذا رأيت وجدتُ نفسى نائمةً مستلقية على ذلك الحجر الصغير على الهواء من غير ان يكون تحتى شىء وربما كنت فى المسجد اريد ان ادخل الكوخة فلا ادخل لأجل المطر فأقعد فى المسجد واجهد ان لا يأخذنى النوم فاذا انتبهت وجدت نفسى فى الكوخة فكنت ارى هذه الاحوال لكن كنت أعُدّها غفلات لانى كنت اقول هو ذا يقطعنى بالنوم عن الذكر ولا يجعل لى سبيلاً الى البسط

(٩)

فصل

قال: المبتدئ فى ابتداء امره يجتهد فيتباعد عنه مقصوده من الاحوال كذا

---

(١) قال VAB: ليس فى Q | حال الذكر هى AB: حال للذكر هى V احوال الذكر Q | عند قوم QVB: عبد قرب A | كانت VAB: ليس فى Q (٢) الزنا ... بالزنا VAB: المعصية ... بالمعصية Q | علىّ QAB: ليس فى V (٣) لحظة QAB: ليس فى V | اقعد QVA: افعل B (٤) ناتئ QAB: نات من الارض V | جدار QVB: جدران A ولعل الصحيح: جبل | ينتأ منه الحجر: سا منه الحجر (كذا) V بيعا من الحجر B ملسا من الحجر A حال والحجر Q (٥) النوم QVA: النومة B | وجدت QV: ليس فى AB (٦) يكون VB: كان QA | كنت QVA: اكون B (٧) الكوخة QVB: الكوجة A | المطر BV: النظر QA | فاقعد QV: فاجهد اقعد B فاجهد قعد A | النوم VAB: النوم فيأخذنى النوم Q (٨) الكوخة Q: الكوجة AB الكوحه V | لكن VAB: ولكنى Q (٩) غفلات VAB: غفلات وعقوبات Q | لى QVB: فى A (١٠) البسط VB. البسيط A النشاط Q (١١) فصل VAB: ليس فى Q (١٢) قال المبتدئ VA (كلمة «قال» غير واضحة فى V): والمبتدئ B واعلم ان المبتدئ Q | يجتهد VAB: يجتهد Q | الاحوال VAB: الاحوال الشريفة اللازمة للذكر وفتح القلب وتنويره فلا يزال دائباً على سيره Q

أجرى الله تعالى سنّته حتى اذا عجز العبد وتوهم انه لا يجيء منه شيء حينئذ يتداركه الله تعالى بفضله فيظهر له الكشف بعد يأسه ولكنى فى الابتداء كلما ازددت جُهدًا ازداد الشيء المقصود منّى بُعدًا هكذا كانت سنّته سبحانه معى وفى الابتداء فى احوال الذكر بلغت الى موضع كنت ارى جميع المخلوقات من نفاذ البصر ثم فى الانتهاء لما ظهر الحق وبلغ الذكر السرّ عاد البصر الى مثل احوال الناس

قال: ومن خلوص الاحوال بينى وبين ابى الفوارس انى كنت ليلة من الليالى معه فأخذه النوم وكانت ليلة العيد وابو الحسن عندى فخطر ببالى: لو كان لنا سمن لصنعْنا اليوم كذا وكذا. فقال ابو الفوارس فى النوم: ألقِ هذا السمن من يدك! ايش هذا؟ يكرره ثلث مرّات فأيقظتُه من النوم وقلت: ايش تقول؟ فقال: لا شيء إلاّ انى كنت ارى فى النوم كأنّا كنّا فى موضع رفيع نَزِه وكأنّ الحق سبحانه يريد ان يظهر والهيبة وقعت على الناس وانت معنا وبيدك سمن لا تلقيه فكنت اقول لك: ألق السمن من يدك!

قال: فلما اشتدّ بى ذكر القلب قال لى ابو الحسن: اذهب الى بعض الرساتيق معى! ثم مال بى فى الطريق وأقعدنى على حجَرة فقال: طبِّق بين شفتيك وقل خذاى!

(١-٢) سنته ... تعالى فى هامش B على يد الناسخ V: سنته فى سالكى طريقه حتى اذا عجز العبد وظنّ وتوهم ان لا يجيء منه فى الطريق شيء حينئذ تداركه الله Q سقط فى A (٢) بفضله VAB: بفضله ورحمته Q | فيظهر QV: يظهر AB | يأسه VAB: اياسه Q | ولكنى AB: ولكن Q ولعله الصواب، سقط فى V | ازددت AB: ازداد Q ولعله الصواب، ازادد V (٣) منى VB: منه QA ولعله الصواب | سنته سبحانه VB: سنة الله تعالى A سنة الله Q | وفى QAB: قال وفى V (٤) ارى VAB: ابصر Q | نفاذ البصر AVB: نفوذ الابصار Q (٦) قال VA: ليس فى QB | ابى الفوارس QVA: الحسن ابى الفوارس B (٧) النوم QVA: النومة B | لصنعنا VB: لطعنا (ولعله «لطعمنا») A لضيّفنا Q (٨) الفوارس: الحسن QVAB (٩) يكرره V: تكرّره B تكريره (؟) A فكرره Q ولعله الصواب | فايقظته QAB: قال فايقظته V | وقلت AV: فقلت QB (١٠) كأنا كنا VB: كأنا QA (١٠-١١) والهيبة وقعت QA: الهيبة فوقعت B الهيه (!) وقعت V (١١) وبيدك AB: بيدك QV | لا تلقيه QBV: ليس فى A | فكنت V: وكنت Q فقلت AB (١٣) قال QA: ليس فى VB | اشتد بى QB: استدى VA (١٤) مال بى Q: قال بى B قال لى VA | الطريق QAB: بعض الطريق V | حجرة AB: حجر QV | فقال QB: ليس فى VA | بين VAB: ليس فى Q

قال فقلت واجتهدت حتى لا افتح الفم فامتلأ فى وعاد الذكر الى السرّ فمن ذلك الوقت أجد فى سرّى ان اقول خذاى فبعدما جاوز الخاء ولا يجاوزها صار ذكرًا ممتدًّا ففى الوقت أُخِذتُ عنى ففنيت فلما أُعدت كان بعد الصلاة فحملنى تلك الليلة الى تلك القرية ثم فى تلك الليلة ردّنى الى البلد واخذتُ فى النحول حتى صرتُ عِظامًا لا لحم علىّ البتة الا جلدة فى يوم واحد وليلة واحدة ثم سكن عنى ذلك والى سَنَة لم أُعَدْ الى حالتى فى قوة النفس ولم يَرِد علىّ شىء يزيد فى حالى او ينقص منه البتة

تم الكتاب

(١) حتى لا افتح QAB: لأفتح V | الوقت VAB: ليس فى Q (٢) اجد QB: اخَذَ (كذا) V اجدى (ولعل المقصود «أجِدُنى») A | اقول QVB: يقول A | خذاى QAB: خذاى V | جاوز QAB: تجاوز V | الخاء QV: الخلاء AB | يجاوزها صار Q: تجاوز صار (والمقصود «تُجَاوَز» اى الخاء) V يجاوز صار (كذا) A يجاوزها (كذا) B | ذكرا QVB: ذلك A | ففى QAB: فى V (٣) ففنيت B: ففنيت A فغبت V فغبت Q | اعدت VAB: عدت Q | تلك الليلة QVB: ذلك الليلة A (٤) فى تلك الليلة QB: فى الليلة VA (٥) جلدة VAB: جلد Q | فى يوم واحد وليلة واحدة B: فى يوم واحدة (!) وليلة واحدة A فى يوم واحد وليلة V فى يوم وليلة Q | والى AB: ولى V وبى Q (٦) فى قوة VAB: من قوة Q | حالى QB: حال AV | منه البتة V: البتة AB منه والله اعلم Q (٧) تم الكتاب B: تم الكتاب بعون الله وحسن توفيقه A تم كتاب ترتيب السلوك V ليس فى Q

TRANSLATION

In the name of God the Merciful, the Compassionate!

(1)

The master Abū'l-Qāsim ^{c}Abd al-Karīm b. Hawāzin al-Qushayrī — God be pleased with him — has said:

Man must renounce the world, should not possess anything and must know the prescriptions of God which are incumbent on him, while professing the oneness of God and acknowledging these prescriptions as the law he must obey. Then he must be permanently in a state of ritual purity with regard to his person and his clothing. Next he must choose as his teacher a person who has travelled the path of God and who has devoted himself to God completely, and should no longer occupy himself with anything except God so as to derive profit from the instruction he receives. If he has a teacher who has travelled the path of God, he will advance more forcefully and more quickly. If, on the other hand, he has a teacher about whose knowledge of the path of God he is not convinced, he may in some cases cause surprise and actually reach the goal but only after a while, certainly not with the same speed, because the effective spiritual power of his master will not help him. Such a student is like the foal of an inferior stallion, whereas a student of the first kind is comparable to the foal of a noble stallion. The master imposes it as a duty on the novice that he prefer poverty to wealth, ignominy to honor and God to all other things. He obliges him to refrain from eating even if the other Sufis eat, and to refrain from speaking about what does not concern him even if the other Sufis do so, and not to choose comfort even if those he sees alongside him in the convent do so. Once he has accepted these conditions, the master says to him: 'I hereby accept you in order to lead you to the path of God to the extent of your understanding. For my part I shall not hold back from you whatever I have understood.' Then he instructs him,[15] directs him not to listen as if to a master[16] and to consider all his states and

---

15 Following Christian usage the verb could be taken to mean: 'He hears his confession.' This phenomenon did exist in Sufism as we learn from a polemic against it in Ibn al-Ḥājj: *Al-mudkhal*, Cairo, 1929, III, p. 209, ll. 15 ff. Cf. Hartmann: *Ḳuschairi*, p. 109.

16 Perhaps *<illā> min al-ustādh* 'only to listen to the master'?

his success as coming from God. And he says to him: 'Say God, God, God!' Then he directs him to persevere continually in reciting this recollection of God, not to see anything else, and not to think about anything but this. If anything at all distracts him from this recollection of God, he should reject it, even if it is his parents' death. As for pious acts of devotion, he should only perform the obligatory religious practices and those that are recommended,[17] as well as the two *rakʿa*s of mid-morning and two *rakʿa*s after every minor ritual ablution. All supererogatory devotions and Koranic recitation beside this are to be omitted. He then occupies himself with this recollection of God until due to the strength of his will thanks to God's grace he becomes unaware of all things through recollecting God, then he becomes unaware of himself through recollecting God, and then he even becomes unaware of recollecting God through recollecting God. Now for a long time he vacillates between absence from recollecting God through recollecting God and presence in recollecting God, so that one time he is absent from recollecting God and another time he is present in recollecting God, but then with each shift from absence and presence he rises to a higher level, and finally another even higher state comes over him in which he is eliminated both from recollecting God and from these states. When the person is returned to a state of persistence after this absence, he is deprived of his speech, his hearing and his sight and only still possesses the heart's senses. It is no longer possible for him to speak with the tongue but now he speaks with the heart, and indeed with a correct speech, not one based on mere knowledge and observation. Now he recites the recollection of God with the heart as he had previously recited it with the tongue. After an indefinite amount of time once again a state comes over him, higher than this in terms of sternness. The person here experiences such a state of sternness[18] that he believes he is very close to God. The person disappears in the experience. Then he vacillates between disappearance and persistence, and every time he is returned to persistence, the utterances of his heart increase until at last he sometimes perceives forms of recollecting God from his heart in various languages and modes of expression which he had never heard before and which he had never dreamed of. He perceives all this in his heart in such a way that he often imagines all nature is recollecting God in different modes of expression, and he enters a state in which because of being over-

---

17 Th.W. Juynboll: *Handbuch des islāmischen Gesetzes*, Leiden, 1910, p. 90.

18 The side of God that inspires fear.

whelmed by recollecting God he is no longer able to distinguish between his own recollecting God which emerges from his heart, and nature's recollecting God. But he hears all these forms of recollecting God. After this another state then comes over him which is so strong that if a person who had not travelled the path of God were to experience it directly, he would die because of the sternness of God (contained in it). At this point the person disappears and nothing remains of him. Then he is returned again to the state of persistence but now he has lost all the states of his heart, i.e. its sense perceptions and everything else, and now there appears to him the 'secret of the supersensory world' (or perhaps the 'supersensory secret'). Here nothing remains of the person, only God exists and He is like an ocean, and when He appears all the rivers obey His authority.[19] Now God alone rules and the person no longer even has the power to move. Previously when a state came over him he had moved. Now the person only moves if the ocean which appears to him moves. If it remains motionless, the person also remains motionless. But he hears, sees and perceives what appears to him. After this state his human nature no longer has any power, neither over recollecting God, nor over the psychic states; power over these now only belongs to the Creator who is God. Furthermore, while in these states before he reaches this level which is the end, he sees the whole of nature with a light that he possesses so that nothing of nature is concealed from him. He sees the whole of nature, all heaven and earth, with direct vision, but by means of the heart since at this time he does not see anything with the eyes of his head. This is not, however, a question of sight based on knowledge, but if in nature a mere speck of dust or an ant were to move, he would perceive it.

(2)

If the person recollecting God recollects God correctly with the tongue, his recollection with the tongue reverts back to being recollection with the heart. Once his heart recollects God, during the recollection of God states come over him in which he perceives from his soul or rather hears from his heart names and designations of God which he had never heard before nor read in any book, in various modes of expression and different languages such as no angel and no human being has ever heard. If he perseveres in his striving without turning around and without paying attention to these

---

19 Cf. Junayd in Sarrāj: *Al-lumaᶜ fī'l-taṣawwuf*, ed. R.A. Nicholson, Gibb Memorial Series 22, 1914, p. 29, l. 8.

manifestations, he obtains more and more until he finally reaches the recollection of God of the 'secret'. But if he turns his attention to these states which come over him, pays heed to these namings and forms of recollecting God, looks at them and busies himself with them, then he offends against proper behavior (toward God) and he is immediately punished for it. His punishment consists in his being denied any further progress. If he still persists, he is punished a second time by being returned to a state of mere knowledge of these states, and then he experiences such an abundance of knowledge that he thinks all mankind's treasures of knowledge have been revealed to him. But if he pays attention to the knowledge which comes to him, again this is an offense against proper behavior, and once more he deserves to be punished. Here his punishment consists in being returned to a state of mere understanding. The difference between understanding and knowledge is that knowledge is a state of being[20] which comes over the heart as knowledge, whereas understanding is gazing at this kowledge, as if to say knowledge that one has knowledge of the matters in question. Again if he looks at understanding, he once more offends against proper behavior, and his punishment is that he is returned to the state of religious indifference.

(3)

If the person recollects God with his tongue, and his endeavor in recollecting God is strong so that he recollects God continuously and is so engaged and desirous that no part of him remains which is not desirous of recollecting God with the tongue — if someone like this recollects God with the tongue and looks at God with his heart, states then come over him such that he imagines he is growing and becoming larger until it is as if he is bigger than everything else. Then a power from God comes over him in the form of fear which He suddenly instills in him. Thereby He stops the person from becoming bigger and going further, and casts him down utterly. Then He makes him come back. Once He has caused him to come back, the person returns to a state which is stronger than the first one, and he grows until it seems to him he is bigger than the first time. Then once again a power comes over him, greater than the first time. Now he continues to vacillate between these states while growing and rising higher with every moment and every hour, until when he has spent years performing the same recollection of God with the tongue, an immense power comes over him, and when he has been brought

20 Or should one conjecture *wurūd* 'experience' instead of *wujūd*?

back after this extinction, recollecting God with the tongue ceases for him. Now the person no longer perceives anything in himself, neither with his hearing nor with his sight, except for something rather faint. Then his recollection of God enters the heart, and he hears the heart's recollection of God so clearly in his heart that he wishes he were in a desert because it seems to him that people can hear with their ears his recollection of God which is in his heart. He forgets that no one but himself can hear this recollection of God.

(4)

The recollection of God in the bodily limbs begins by someone feeling a movement in his limbs, until finally there is no part of his flesh and bones in which he does not feel a movement and a convulsion. Then these movements and convulsions become stronger until they are transformed into voices and words so that the person hears voices in all his limbs and bodily parts, except for his tongue because in these states the tongue does not speak. But here the person persists in his endeavor because it is clear to him that if he paid attention to this and sought a theoretical knowledge about these forms of recollecting God, he would remain caught in them. Thus he does not look at them so that he can ascend beyond them to something else. All this takes place after the recollection of God has become located in the heart. In the state of recollecting God with the tongue, the bodily limbs likewise experience these movements and convulsions but not with this intensity.

(5)

In the states of recollecting God with the heart, it happens that a person experiences a sweetness in his mouth and in his throat, and this comes to take the place of food and drink. The source of this drink, which is sweeter than honey, he perceives to be the roots of his teeth, while his teeth remain so tightly clenched that he has difficulty opening his mouth. He experiences the drink in his mouth in this manner. And while drinking this drink the person comes so close to death that he dissolves and almost dies. In this state he only fears death. Namely,[21] when the person reaches this level — a level whose joy a thousand men flee, not one of whom would flee from pain, because this joy is more unpleasant and is closer to death — he dissolves while partaking of this drink as if he were annihilated and as if he

---

21 *Ḥattā* also appears more or less to mean 'namely' in a passage in Kubrā's *Fawā'iḥ*, § 141, and perhaps also in our treatise, p. 113, at the beginning of l. 12.

died, yes in this state when this joy accompanies him and will not leave him, he finally reaches the point where he runs away from spiritual retreat because if he is alone even for a short while this joy so overwhelms him that it brings him close to death. Just as the beginner flees from people and prefers spiritual retreat (or: solitude), so a person who has reached this level flees from this joy.

He (= Qushayrī) said: 'My master, who experienced these states (?), declared: "For this reason I run away from spritual retreat."'

In the state of this joy a person's perception grows stronger, and his eyesight and inner vision become so sharp that he believes he hears the footsteps of ants. In the beginning one wishes not to sleep but in this situation one's highest aspiration is to fall asleep and to find peace. But the sign of the authenticity of this joy is precisely that a person cannot sleep as long as he is in this situation, even if it takes years before this situation abates. Only then can he find sleep.

(6)

Those who have progressed to the end face still another situation, namely that sometimes speech comes to their 'secret' and they have no doubt that it is from God, and the speech addresses the 'secret' with grace and intimacy and the 'secret' then replies to it. The person hears the reply from the 'secret' and the speech from God. But sometimes this speech is accompanied by sternness and the 'secret' then remains silent. Further, he sometimes hears words, words which are in themselves both speech as well as reply and with which the person has nothing to do. The person knows through his perception, as if he saw himself in a dream, that he is not himself God but has no doubt that these are words of God. If this subtle perception, however, leaves the person, then the distinction is removed and this is the 'union of union'. For this reason one person said: 'I am God', and Abū Yazīd said: 'Praise be to me!' But it was God who spoke, after the effacement of the persons.

(7)

A person recognizes random thoughts[22] and distinguishes between them by examining them on the basis of (theological) knowledge and the (religious) commands and prohibitions. If when measured by

---

22 On *khawāṭir* see *Fawā'iḥ*, Introduction, pp. 127 ff., as well as Ali Hasan Abdel-Kader: *The Life, Personality and Writings of Al-Junayd*, Arabic text pp. 58-62/English pp. 178-83 (in Gibb Memorial, New Series 22, 1962).

knowledge they prove to be without objection, then they are valid. If they prove to be not without objection, then they are empty and vain.

Then he (= Qushayrī) was politely asked: Sometimes a person is in a high inner state but Satan wishes to return him to a lower one and for this reason causes him to become conscious of this higher state. If the person examines the thought in connection with knowledge and the commands and prohibitions, it appears to be unobjectionable and yet it comes from Satan. How can a person recognize it? Only a few people are capable of doing so.[23]

The reply: A person recognizes that this thought has an unpleasant effect because an unpleasant feeling from it comes over him. When the thought occurs in the heart, it hurts it and causes it to experience unpleasantness like food which has no salt in it. Because of the unpleasantness and ugliness accompanying the thought, he knows that it is not from God but from Satan, even if it is a call to do a pious act such as, for instance, if it commands him to go on the pilgrimage to Mecca or to honor his parents. Satan has only one intention: that ten come to be eleven and ten and a half (?) for a person because of being returned from a higher to a lower state, and that the goal come to be correspondingly higher.[24] He recognizes that this thought from Satan is from Satan because it stands in contrast to the state he is in. Satan often presents the new state to the person as being higher than the existing one, but it always forms a contrast to the state the person is in with regard to sweetness and unpleasantness. If the thought comes from God, the person perceives its affinity with the state he is already in. The two get along together the way two persons who meet and agree in their work and aspiration, join together and get along with one another; but if they are opposed in their work, then that is how they will behave. Likewise if a person has a thought from God and then receives a thought from Satan, in accordance with the merchandise and capital he possesses he distinguishes between the two. He feels a contrast within himself +...+[25] between the idea com-

---

23 The variant might be translated: 'Indeed a person can recognize it, but people are rarely capable of doing so.'

24 Recent retranslation: 'Satan has only one intention: by means of returning him from a higher to a lower state to overcharge a person (as in the market place) by "ten", "eleven", (or at least) "ten and a half" points, and cause the goal to be that much higher for him.

25 For the missing words of the lacuna one can probably conjecture: 'between the idea and the already existing state, i.e...' Even simpler would be to assume a larger textual corruption and to amend it for instance as follows: *idhā warada ʿalayhi khāṭiru'l-shayṭāni, fa-*

ing from Satan and what he possesses from God, and this contrast determines that the thought is from Satan and not from God.

In all these thoughts and states which come over a person, the person hears voices of the greatest sweetness and beauty such that they seem to him more delightful, charming and enchanting than the sounds of strings, flutes, Persian lutes and everything that exists in the way of beautiful, sweet sounds. But the thought which comes from Satan can also be endowed with this delightfulness, in fact it is often even more delightful in its outward form than the thought from God. But the one which comes from Satan is more importunate and a person does not experience friendly intimacy from it. If someone does not already possess these states from God and Satan sends him thoughts, the person will not doubt that they come from God. He only recognizes that they are from Satan because of the contrast which he perceives between them and what he has from God, and because of the unpleasant feeling which comes over him. Without possessing something from God, he would not recognize that this is from Satan and not from God. But if he grows strong in recollecting God and gradually rises to the point where he hears these pleasing voices, then should a thought come to him from Satan he will perceive the contrast between it and what he possesses from God.

(8)

And he (= Qushayrī) said: It has been said: The beginner as to his states is like a wild bird (sic). As long as there is motion, force, a sign of life and perception in a person, the bird will shy away from him and be frightened and will not settle on him. But if the person grows still so that the wild bird imagines he is dead without any motion in him, it begins to trust him and it lands on him and does not shy away from him. In the same way the senses of the beginner in mystical states must grow still, his breaths should not move, he should not scratch his body, nor move any part of his body, nor direct his gaze over things, but he must adhere strictly to his aspirations without ever moving his breath,[26] or his body, or his interior; then after long concentration the states will appear to him. But then he must in no case look at these or whatever else appears to him lest

---

yajidu fī nafsihī ḍiddiyyata'l-wāridi ʿalayhi wa'l-shāhidi fa-yumayyizu bihā bayna'l-wāridi mina'l-shayṭāni wa-bayna mā maʿahū mina'l-ḥaqq.

26 Not *nafs* 'soul' because the movement of the breath has just been mentioned and *bāṭin* 'interior' follows.

they be removed from him. This way he will go on gaining more and more.

And he also said: On this path, which is the path of God, it is indispensable to undergo long spiritual combat and suffering, the hardships of which the heart and the hearing cannot even bear to be told about. And yet the person chooses these spiritual combats. Once he sets out on the path of God, however, he becomes occupied with these spiritual combats whether he wishes to or not. Were the person to attempt to do this artificially, he would only be able to persevere for a brief time. But in my case at the beginning[27] of spiritual combat and the states of the recollection of God the situation was sometimes such that if God had hurled me down from the heavens,[28] that would have been easier for me and meant less than to get up in order to eat and to move in order to perform a minor ritual ablution and the obligatory prayers. If I did the latter, recollection of God might have left me. So it was difficult for me to tear myself away from what I was engaged in because I feared I would lose the recollection of God, and those spiritual combats occupied me whether I liked it or not, lest I be returned to the states in which ordinary people find themselves.

And he also said: While I was performing the recollection of God, things happened through me which some people took to be miracles. To me, however, they appeared to be worse than fornication. The misfortune of committing fornication would have meant less to me than these things. For instance I wanted to avoid falling asleep at all so as not to lose the recollection of God for a single moment. Thus now and again[29] I positioned myself on a rock[30] which projected from a wall[31] just far enough so that I could place my feet on it, while below me was a ravine and above me was a towering cliff. In this way sleep could not come over me. Then when I looked I found myself asleep and lying on that small rock in the air with nothing

---

27 *Badʾ*, or the alternative form *badw*, both meaning 'beginning'. It is probably not a question of 'appearing' even though mention has just been made of the emergence of spiritual combat as a need and as second nature in the mystic.

28 Perhaps this could also be read: 'if I had been hurled down from the heavens'.

29 The durative-iterative tense here seems to want to endow a single event with the character of an ongoing action.

30 *Ḥajar* is the collective form because of the possibility of the action occurring several times.

31 Perhaps this should be changed to 'mountain'.

underneath me! — Or now and again[32] I was in the mosque and I wanted to go to the small hut but I did not go there because of the rain (?). So I sat down in the mosque and made an effort not to allow sleep to overcome me. When I then woke up I found myself in the hut! — I experienced these events but I considered them to be signs of religious indifference, for I said to myself: All this by means of sleep cuts me off from recollecting God and does not procure for me a path to happiness.

(9)

In addition he said: The beginner exerts himself at the beginning of his career but the states which are his goal become distant from him. This is how God has arranged His procedure. But then when the person becomes weak and imagines he will never attain anything, God helps him through His grace, and now he receives the unveiling after having despaired of it. At the beginning the more effort I made, the more what I was striving after became distant from me. This is how God's procedure was with me. At the beginning while recollecting God I reached a point where because of the keenness of my sight I saw all things in creation. Then at the final stage when God appeared and the recollection of God entered the 'secret', my sight returned to being like that of ordinary people.

And he also said: The purity of my inner bond with Abū'l-Fawāris is shown, among other things, by this: One night I was in his company and sleep came over him. It was the night of the feast (of breaking the fast). Abū'l-Ḥasan was also with me. It then occurred to me: 'If only we had some butter! Then tomorrow we could prepare this and that dish.' Just then Abū'l-Fawāris[33] said in his sleep: 'Cast this butter from your hand! What is this?' He repeated these words three times. I woke him from sleep and asked: 'What are you saying?' He replied: 'Nothing. But I saw in a dream that we were in an elevated, beautiful place and that God wished to appear. Awe came over the people. But you stood among us with butter in your hand and you would not throw it away. Then I said to you: "Cast the butter from your hand!"'

---

32 *Rubbamā*: again a single action treated as described in ftn. 28 above. But basically this depends on the uncertain reading *maṭar* 'rain'. If one were to substitute *naẓar* instead, it could then be a repeated action. *Naẓar* is perhaps the gaze which one wishes to avoid — the desire not to be seen. What the little hut means is unclear.

33 A conjecture in place of Abū'l-Ḥasan which does not make sense here.

And he also said: When recollection of God in the heart affected me ever more strongly, Abū'l-Ḥasan said to me: 'Come out into the countryside with me!' Then he took me with him on the road, sat me down on a rock and ordered: 'Press your lips together and say *khudhāy* (God)!' I obeyed him and while doing this endeavored not to open my mouth. My mouth became full and the recollection of God moved into the 'secret'. Since that time I perceive that in my 'secret' I say *khudhāy*. But after the recollection of God passed beyond the *kh* without being able to pass beyond it, it became a 'protracted recollection of God'.[34] I was immediately taken away from myself and became extinguished. When I came back to myself, it was already after the (evening) prayers. Abū'l-Ḥasan brought me back to that village. Then during the same night he conducted me back to our locality. I began to lose so much weight that after one day and night I was reduced to mere bones; there was absolutely no flesh left on me but only skin. Then this abated, but until one year[35] I did not return to my old state as far as the strength of my breath was concerned,[36] and nothing whatsoever came over me which could increase my state or lower it.[37]

ADDITIONS OF THE AUTHOR

P. 102, l. 32: By today more has been published.
P. 128, l. 18: The question has since been clarified. See 'Aussprachefragen des älteren neupersisch', *Oriens* 27-28, p. 140, ftn. 59/*Bausteine*, II, p. 1127, ftn. 59.
P. 132, ftn. 36: *Quwwat al-nafs* is correct. It means 'personal force, vital force'.

Qassim al-Samarrai: *The Theme of Ascension in Mystical Writings*, I, Baghdad, 1968, pp. 155-82, provides a new edition on the basis of the same MS sources, along with a short summary of the contents. His summary, pp. 179-82, is nothing other than an English translation of what I have written here on pp. 102-106 But he does not

---

34 What is probably meant is an endless *khkhkh* (the initial sound of *khudhāy*)

35 This means: 'for one year', not 'until a year ago'. The variant in V could be translated as: 'and now it is one year that...'

36 With some hesitation I read as *nafas*; *quwwat al-nafs* would mean 'power of soul', which seems a bit strange.

37 I wish to thank my former student, Father Richard Gramlich, S.J., Schloss Bürgeln, for having proof-read this article.

acknowledge this. His criticism of my text edition is erroneous in almost all the points he raises. He has not understood my remarks concerning methodological considerations for establishing the text.

Fīr Muḥammad Ḥasan, on the sole basis of the Aya Sofya MS, has printed his own edition in his *Al-rasāʾil al-qushayriyya*, Pakistan, n.p., n.d., pp. 64-79, and identified Abū'-Ḥasan as Abū'l-Ḥasan al-Kharaqānī, and Abū'l-Fawāris as Abū'l-Fawāris al-Ḥasan b. Aḥmad b. Muḥammad b. Fāris b. Sahl al-Bazzāz (344-421/955-1030 in Baghdad). But this remains uncertain.

More on the subject is found in my essay 'Khurāsān and the End of Classical Sufism', pp. 190 ff., ftn. 1.

Īraj-i Afshār in the Tehran journal *Yaghmā* 18, 1344/1965, pp. 251-54, has publicized and briefly described an Arabic collective manuscript belonging to the Dhahabī convent Khānaqāh-i Aḥmadī, no. 87. Tehran University Library has a microfilm of the manuscript (under the title *Adab al-mulūk*), and I have had an enlarged copy of it made for myself.

The MS is undated but was probably not copied later than the 8th/14th century. It is written in very clear, partially vocalized, large *naskhī* script, and consists of 210 numbered pages, each with 19 lines. Names which the Twelver Shīʿites find objectionable have occasionally had a line drawn through them or been scratched out. On the flyleaf, written in a later hand, is a table of contents which does not correspond exactly to the order of the treatises in the MS and runs as follows:

1) *Kitāb adab al-mulūk fī bayān ḥaqāʾiq al-taṣawwuf.*
2) *Naṣāʾiḥ al-Ḥusayn b. Manṣūr al-Ḥallāj wa-ashʿāruhū.*
3) *Kitāb nasīm al-arwāḥ li-Abī ʿAbd al-Raḥmān al-Sulamī.*
4) *Kitāb faḍl al-taṣawwuf ʿalā'l-madhāhib li'l-imām Muḥammad b. Khafīf.*
5) *Al-ikhtiyārāt min kalām Abī Manṣūr Maʿmar b. Aḥmad b. Muḥammad b. Ziyād al-Iṣfahānī.*
6) *Kitāb nahj al-khāṣṣ li-Abī Manṣūr Maʿmar b. Aḥmad al-Iṣfahānī.*
7) *Kitāb sharḥ al-adhkār li-Abī Manṣūr b. Aḥmad al-Iṣfahānī.*
8) *Sharḥ abyāt Abī ʿAbdallāh al-Murshid fī tajrīd al-tawḥīd min khafī al-shirk li-Abī Manṣūr.*
9) *Kitāb al-manāhij li-Abī Manṣūr ayḍā.*
10) *Masāʾil fī'l-taṣawwuf li-Abī Manṣūr al-Iṣfahānī ayḍā.*
11) *Kitāb sharḥ al-arbaʿīn ḥadīthan fī'l-taṣawwuf li-Abī Manṣūr al-Iṣfahānī*, with the note: *suriqa min al-bayn* 'stolen'.
12) *Riyāḍ al-uns li'l-shaykh Abī Saʿīd al-Ḥasan b. ʿAli al-Wāʿiẓ.*
13) *Nubdha min kalām akābir al-ṣūfiyya.*
14) *Risāla li-Abī ʿAbd al-Raḥmān al-Sulamī fī baʿḍ kalām al-Shāfiʿī fī'l-taṣawwuf.*

No. 11 of this list would appear to be lost. No. 4., Muḥammad b. Khafīf's *Faḍl al-taṣawwuf*, had had its place between pp. 105 and 106 of our MS, was removed as Afshār informs us, and was held by the late Muḥsin-i Ḥālī, known as ᶜImād al-fuqarāᵓ, who is said to have translated it into Persian (no such work, however, is mentioned in Khānbābā Mushār: *Fihrist-i kitābhāy-i chāpī-i fārsī*, or in Īraj-i Afshār: *Index Iranicus*). Later it was returned to the convent and presently stands alongside our MS as a separate volume. The *Faḍl al-taṣawwuf* of Ibn-i Khafīf is listed among the latter's works by Daylamī: *Sīrat-i Ibn-i Khafīf*, ed. Annemarie Schimmel, Ankara, 1955, p. 212, and by Junayd al-Shirāzī: *Shadd al-izār*, ed. Qazwīnī and Iqbāl, Tehran, 1328, p. 42. The copy of this work preserved in the Khānaqāh-i Aḥmadī appears to be the only one which has so far been found. Of Ibn-i Khafīf's *Kitāb al-iqtiṣād* one MS is found in Pertev 652 (Sezgin, *GAS*, I, p. 664), another, as Professor Rudolf Mach informs me, in Princeton.

The MS Khānaqāh-i Aḥmadī 87 today contains the following writings:

1) *Adab al-mulūk*, pp. 1-80. Note: 'Checked against the original'.
2) *Dhikr baᶜḍ anfās al-shaykh Abī'l-Mughīth al-Ḥusayn b. Manṣūr al-Ḥallāj*, pp. 80-95.
3) *Wa-hādhā kitāb Nasīm al-arwāḥ mimmā jamaᶜahū al-imām Abū ᶜAbd al-Raḥmān Muḥammad b. al-Ḥusayn b. Mūsā al-Sulamī*, pp. 95-105.
4) Unknown author, unknown title, beginning incomplete, on the *ādāb* of the Sufis, pp. 106-10.
5) Abū Manṣūr Maᶜmar b. Aḥmad al-Iṣfahānī: work without title, in two parts:
   a) *Bāb al-waṣiyya bi-lisān al-ḥikma wa-ᶜibārat al-mutaṣawwifa*, pp. 111-13.
   b) *Dhikr maᶜānī al-taṣawwuf wa-ādābihī wa-ḥaqāᵓiqihī wa-rusūmihī ᶜalā shawāhid awāᵓil ḥurūf al-muᶜjam faṣlan wa-nashdan min kalām al-shaykh Abī Manṣūr Maᶜmar b. Aḥmad al-Iṣfahānī*, pp. 113-17.
6) Abū Manṣūr Maᶜmar b. Aḥmad al-Iṣfahānī: *Nahj al-khāṣṣ*, pp. 117-29.
7) Abū Saᶜīd al-Ḥasan b. ᶜAlī al-Wāᶜiẓ: *Riyāḍ al-uns*, pp. 131-40. A fragment.
8) Sayings of Sahl b. ᶜAbdallāh al-Tustarī, Shaqīq al-Balkhī, the Prophet, Saᶜīd b. al-Musayyib, anonymous, Ibrāhīm b. al-Junayd, Mujāhid, al-Ḥasan, the Prophet, Anas b. Mālik, 'I read

in books', David, anonymous, ᶜUmar b. al-Khaṭṭāb, the Prophet, revelation to Moses, sayings of Shiblī, Thawrī, the 'scholars', the Prophet, Thawrī, pp. 140-43.

9) Abū ᶜAbd al-Raḥmān al-Sulamī: sayings of Shāfiᶜī on pious behavior, pp. 145-63. Incomplete at the end.

10) Abū Manṣūr Maᶜmar b. Aḥmad al-Iṣfahānī: *Sharḥ al-adhkār*, pp. 165-84 (title p. 164).

11) Abū Manṣūr b. Aḥmad al-Iṣfahānī: *Sharḥ abyāt li-Abī ᶜAbdallāh al-Murshid fī maᶜnā tajrīd al-tawḥīd min khafī al-shirk*, pp. 184-92.

12) Abū Manṣūr Maᶜmar b. Aḥmad al-Iṣfahānī: *Al-manāhij bi-shāhid al-sunna wa-nahj al-mutaṣawwifa*, pp. 193-210 (title p. 192).

On the basis of the literature which I have consulted, from these 12 to 13 writings (cf. 5a and 5b) no less than 8 appear to be unique and new, namely numbers 1, 3, 4, 5a, 9, 10, 11, and 12. But the remaining numbers, 2, 6, 7, and 5b, are also valuable supplements to the already existing stock of manuscripts. Only the notices of no. 8 may be left aside. In what follows the works, ordered alphabetically according to their author's name, are briefly discussed:

a) ḤALLĀJ (no. 2, pp. 80-95)

(Abū'l-Ḥasan ᶜAlī b. Aḥmad b. ᶜAlī al-Mufaḍḍiḍ al-Shirwānī, alias al-Wāᶜiẓ al-Qaṣṣāṣ al-Shirwānī:) *Dhikr baᶜḍ anfās al-shaykh Abī'l-Mughīth al-Ḥusayn b. Manṣūr al-Ḥallāj.*

Incipit: ذكر بعض أنفاس الشيخ أبي المغيث الحسين بن منصور الحلاج رحمة الله ورضوانه على روحه العزيز. بسم الله الرحمن الرحيم. قال الشبلي رحمة الله عليه: دخلت على الحسين بن منصور قدس الله روحه وهو يتكلم بكلام لم أفهمه ...

Explicit: ... وأنشد عنه رحمة الله عليه

أأنت أم أنا هذا الهين فى هين   حاشاك حاشاى من إثبات اثنين

هويــة لك فى لائيتى أبدًا   كل على الكل تلبيس بوجهين

أنيّةٌ منك فى أنيتى امتزجت   فارفع بأنك أنّيّ من البين

تم ما وجد مثبته من أنفاسه رحمة الله عليه

Louis Massignon in his first edition of the *Dīwān al-Ḥallāj* in *JA* 1931, pp. 2 ff., distinguishes between two collections. To the second collection, which is strongly tinged by legend, he gives the name *ziyārāt* because it begins with an enumeration of Shiblī's visits to Ḥallāj. In the third edition of the *Akhbār al-Ḥallāj*, Paris, 1952, Massignon undertakes a more sophisticated description of the text's history and sees in the former 'second' collection a cycle of Ḥallāj-legends which emerges for us for the first time around 500/1107 in Shirwān (Sharwān) and is said to have been edited by a certain Ibn al-Qaṣṣāṣ, or perhaps more correctly Ibn al-Mufaḍḍiḍ (pp. 93 ff.). The first name is provided by Ibn Ḥajar al-ᶜAsqalānī, *Lisān al-mīzān*, IV, p. 207, the second one by Ibn al-Ṣābūnī: *Takmilat Ikmāl al-Ikmāl*, Baghdad, 1957, pp. 316 f. Our MS presents new, hitherto unknown textual evidence for this (second) cycle, and its text, judging by a comparison with the variants given by Massignon in the *dīwān*, is closely related to MS K (= Kazan, Central Library or. 68) but also contains readings which deviate from the latter and, if Massignon's information on the individual numbers of the *dīwān* is complete, additional text. The new poems which are not mentioned by Massignon either in the *dīwān* itself or in the appended 'liste des 43 pièces exclues ici comme suspectes' (*Dīwān*, pp. 148 ff.) are the following:

Khānaqāh-i Aḥmadī 87, p. 85 (*ṭawīl*):

تأمّلْ خيالى والهلال اذا بدا   لرؤيته فى أفقه أيّنا أضوا
على أنه يزداد فى كل ساعة   نموًّا وأنّى بالهوى ذائب أفنَى

Consider: my dream figure and the crescent moon when he appears
and is visible on his horizon — which of us is brighter?
Yet he increases by the hour in growth, while I melt
with passion and I fade away.

Khānaqāh-i Aḥmadī 87, p. 88 (*kāmil*):

إنى وجدتك بالعلوم ووجدها   مَن ذا يجِدْك بلا علوم [1]تظهَرُ
إنى وجدتك بالغيوب وسرها   فأذا بك السرُّ الذى هو أبتر
إنى لأعجب من حقيقٍ عارف   بلطيفِ وُدّك كيفِ لا يتدبّر

1) MS يظهر

I found you in (or: through) the sciences and their (experiential) finding.
  Who without sciences could experience you emerge into view?
I found you in the unseen (supernatural) realm and its inmost secret
  and behold, you are the inmost secret which (in itself, i.e. without the external) is devoid of sequel.
I am amazed by one who is deserving and knows
  your subtle love but does not reflect.

Aḥmadī, p. 91 (*ṭawīl*):

[1]أصرّف فى الأشياء لا علم لى به   ولا بائنٌ عما بــه قــد أصرّفُ
ومعنى جرى لى ذاكرى عن محرّكٍ   ولبس بموهــوم بـوهم يـكيّف

1) MS vocalized اصرِّف

I am given the power of disposal over things without my knowing it,
  yet I am not separate from what continues to give me the power of disposal.
And an idea that comes to me remembers me due to one who sets in motion(?)
  and this is no fantasy object such that its nature might be de-determined by fantasy.

The 3rd hemistich is perhaps corrupt. I had no success with the possible translation 'how many a thought...'

Aḥmadī, pp. 92-93 (*mutaqārib*):

ســأجمعُ غَزْلَ الهوى كُبّةً   وأنسْجُ للناس من كل فَنْ
وأسقِى نبات الهوى أدمُعى   لأنى شربت بكأس المِحَنْ

I will wind the yarn of passion into a skein
  and weave for people something of every kind.
And I will water the plants of passion with my tears
  because I have drunk from the beaker of tribulations.

Aḥmadī, p. 93 (*munsariḥ*):

السَّمُّ من ألسُنِ الأفاعِي   أعذب من قُبلة الوداعِ
ودّعتُهم والدموع تجرى   لمّا دعا للفراق داعِ
حتى إذا ما الفراق نادى   كشفتُ فى حبكم قناعى

Poison from the tongues of vipers
is sweeter than a farewell kiss.
I bade them farewell while tears were streaming,
when the call for separation was sounded.
Only when separation sounded its cry
did I lift my veil in[1] love for you.

1) Perhaps one should read *ᶜan* and translate 'out of', or keeping *fī*, translate 'from'.

Aḥmadī, p. 93 (*basīṭ*):

يا من يطوف بباب الحِبّ من [1]شغف   [2]ويستر الحُب وَهْو الظاهر الخافى
انظرْ الى وجهه لا وجهِ صيغته   إذا تجلّى لأحبابِ [3]وآلآفِ
وقُل بلا حشمة لبّيك أنت أنا   يا من [4]محا وَصْفُه إثباتَ أوصافى

1) MS شغفى 2) MS وتترك 3) MS آلآفى 4) MS محلى

Oh you who hover about the beloved's door out of passion
and conceal love, though it is a hidden thing exposed,
look into his face, not at the surface of his outer form
when he (it) reveals himself (itself) to friends and confidants,
and say without shyness: 'At your service. You are I,
oh you whose attribute has effaced the affirmation of my attributes!'

Aḥmadī, p. 94 (*basīṭ*):

ما رُمتُ تحصيله إلا ويرهقنى   سكر [1]التطوّحِ فى بحبوحة [2]الدَهشِ
حتى إذا خرجَتْ عنى روامقُه   ألفيتُنى عارفًا والكنهُ مفترشى

1) MS النطوح 2) MS الدهشى

I never wished to catch up with him but then
the intoxication of wandering overtook me in the midst of bewilderment.
When finally everything beholding him had left me,
I found myself like a knower while the ultimate truth was my bed (or: and the ultimate truth as my bed).

Aḥmadī, p. 94 (*ṭawīl*):

سموتُ سموًّا غاب عني وجودُه وغبتُ عن الوجد الذى كان فى الوجدِ

I ascended so high that his existence disappeared from me
and I disappeared from the experience that was in this perception (finding).

Aḥmadī, p. 94 (*basīṭ*, a very weak verse)

زعمت بالفقر والفاقات تُدرِكُهُ فالفقر حَظّك [1] فاحسَرْ عن مَرامِيهِ
الفقر [2] أدنى مقام الرائضين له كالطفل يُفطَم عما كان يُلهيه

1) MS فاحسن 2) sic, instead of *adnā maqāmāt*

You thought you would reach him with poverty and neediness.
But poverty is your pleasure, withdraw from its goals!
Poverty is the lowest halting station of those practicing austerities[1] for him,
like a child that is weaned of what delights it.

1) Can also mean: of those who tame it (poverty?).

In addition, our MS contains a conflation of *Dīwān al-Ḥallāj*, ed. Massignon, M 41 and M 47. Aḥmadī, p. 93 (*ramal*):

مُزِجَت روحك فى روحى كما تُمزَج الخمرة بالمسك العَبِق
فإذا مسّك شىء مسّنى فإذا أنت أنا لا [1] نفترق

1) MS تفترق

Your spirit is mixed in my spirit,
 as one mixes wine with aromatic musk.
If something touches you, it touches me.
 Thus you are I, and we do not separate.

Finally our MS provides a much desired third textual witness for *Dīwān al-Ḥallāj*, M 48. In preparing the first edition Massignon only had at his disposal a single textual witness for this poem. In his *Recherches nouvelles sur le Diwan d'al-Hallaj et ses oeuvres*, in *Mélanges F. Köprülü*, Istanbul, 1953 (= *Opera minora* II, p. 261), he adds as a second textual witness an anonymous quotation from the MS Fatih 2560, 101a, with better readings. For this reason Massignon's translation in *Dīwān*, Paris, 1955, pp. 94 f., is different from that in the first edition *JA*, 1931. Our MS (Aḥmadī, pp. 91-92), to a great extent in agreement with Fatih, has one further verse (the last one) and, after my flawed attempts at understanding and emendation have been brought to bear, presents the poem in the following form (*basīṭ*):

نعتُ الإغاثة رمزٌ فى 1) خفا لطف   عن بارق من ومبض لاح فى 2) خَلَلِه
3) فالحال يرمُقنى 4) طورًا وأرمُقه   من شاهقٍ أجتنِي الأحوالَ من قُلَله
التيه تيهٌ 5) أتاهُ التيهُ من تُوهٍ   عن فيض بحرٍ 6) توى التتويه من بَلَله
فالكل يشهَدنى كلاًّ وأشهَدُه   7) تأبَى الحقيقةُ إلاّ الشخصَ من طَلَله
8) أفنى الإغاثة حتى صرتُ أشهَدُها   + ربا + يَضِجّ إلى 9) مُبرِيه من عِلَله

1) *khafan laṭafun* (*laṭafun* an adjective modifying *ramz*). Other readings considered: *khafan laṭafin, khafā luṭfin. Laṭufa ʿan* 'to be too fine for' in *Lisān al-ʿArab*, s.v. *lṭf*; cf. Ḥallāj in Sulamī's *tafsīr* on surah 6/103 (Massignon: *Essai*, in the appendix of *Textes hallagiens*). Operations involving *barq al-luṭf* (Ibn Qayyim al-Jawziyya: *Madārij al-sālikīn*, I, p. 249) and *ḥafī al-luṭf* (Ibn Jubayr: *Riḥla*, p. 312, last line) did not prove successful.

2) MS خلَله

3) MS فيالحال. *Ḥāll* instead of *ḥāl* is likely in view of *ramaqa*.

4) *Ṭūr*, as Massignon proposes, is difficult to construe grammatically and in terms of content, despite *Tīh* in verse 3. *Ṭawran* also occurs in Ibn Qudāma al-Maqdisī: *Tawwābūn*, Damascus, 1961, p. 243, l. 12.

5) MS اتاه possibly meant as a question: *a-tāha*).

6) Either *tawā al-tatwīhi* 'destruction of causing to be lost' or *tawī* (for *tawiya*) *al-tatwīhu* 'causing to be lost has been destroyed', but perhaps it should be emended: *tarā al-tatwīha* 'you see causing to be lost'.
7) MS تاب
8) *Ufnī* for *ufniya*, but very unsure because of the corrupt text that follows.
9) MS مبدبه

The qualifier 'help' is a secret sign in something hidden, too fine
(even) for a flash that shines in its midst.
The immanent One looks at me time and again and I look at him
from a height from whose peaks I pluck spiritual states.[1]
Conceit is a desolate Tīh into which being lost entered because of a blinding
before the effusion of a stream, due to whose moisture the destruction of being made lost took place.[2]
The whole is present with me wholly and I with it.
Reality only wants the person without its phenomenal form.
Help came to disappear so that (or: until) I began to witness it like
a... who goes to him who cures him of illnesses.

What Ḥallāj really wrote and meant remains unclear for the time being. I would surmise the following meaning: the special activity[3] of God designated as 'help' is hidden behind an impenetrable veil (since it can be a 'ruse' of God). None the less, from the pedestal of an exchange of glances with the immanent God one can experience mystic states. The conceit of acting on one's own authority, as an opposite pole, arises from a blindness before the superabundance of divine action, in the stream of which one stands. Awareness of this could protect one from that error or, according to the textual conjecture, be no less confusing. But one can only experience embeddedness in God if one looks behind the façade of one's corporeality. 'Help' may be included in the package of God's action but it remains hidden so that one must ask for it (?).

Any new edition of the *dīwān* of Ḥallāj would have to be based on a thorough comparison with our MS. Our purpose here has only been

---

1 Cf. for instance *Diwān al-Ḥallāj*, M 12.

2 According to the conjecture: due to its moisture you would (no less) consider (or: experience) being made lost as correct .

3 According to *Lumaᶜ*, p. 315, l. 15 ff., qualification (*naᶜt*) is a special activity and mode of action of God.

to indicate the importance of the MS and its place in the corpus Hallajianum.

b) ABŪ SAᶜĪD AL-ḤASAN B. ᶜALĪ AL-WĀᶜIẒ (no. 7, pp. 131-40)

Riyāḍ al-uns. Mutilated. Only the beginning survives.

Incipit: الحمد لله الذى لم يزل واحدًا حكيمًا ... قال الأستاذ أبو سعيد الحسن ابن على الواعظ: إنى لمّا رأيتُ رغبة أهل زماننا هذا فى علم التذكير صادقة جمعتُ بعون الله كتبًا بأنواعه ناطقة ... وسمّيتُهُ كتاب رياض الأنس اقتداء بسيد الجن والإنس فى تسمية مجالس الذكر رياضًا ...

Explicit: ... فمن وجد المولى لم يضرّ ما فاته من الدنيا والعقبي ...

Only contains 1) *rawḍat al-uns li'l-ᶜārifīn* (132) with ten characteristics, and 2) *rawḍat al-uns li'l-muḥibbīn* (137) with ten characteristics. Complete MSS in *GAL S,* II, p. 143. According to Rieu: *Supplement to the Catalogue of the Arabic MSS. in the British Museum*, no. 236, the author wrote before 766/1365 because a MS in Munich bears this date. Persian sentences and verses are found in the Arabic text.

c) ABŪ MANṢŪR MAᶜMAR B. AḤMAD B. MUḤAMMAD B. ZIYĀD AL-IṢFAHĀNĪ (d. 418/1027)

Concerning him see ᶜAbdallāh-i Anṣārī: *Ṭabaqāt al-ṣūfiyya*, ed. Ḥabībī, Kabul, 1340, pp. 536 f.; ᶜAbd al-Raḥmān-i Jāmī: *Nafaḥāt al-uns*, s.n.; Muḥammad al-Dhahabī: *Al-ᶜibar fī khabar man ghabar*, s.a. 418, Kuwait, 1961, III, p. 129; ᶜAbdallāh al-Yāfiᶜī: *Mirʾāt al-janān*, s.a. 418, Hyderabad, 1337-38, III, p. 33; ᶜAbd al-Ḥayy b. al-ᶜImād: *Shadharāt al-dhahab*, s.a. 418, Cairo, 1350-51, III, p. 2; Ghulām Sarwar-i Lāhawrī: *Khazīnat al-aṣfiyāʾ*, Naval Kishore, 1280-81, II, p. 217.

Maᶜmar has otherwise remained unknown. Even Ibn al-Jawzī, who in his *Ṣifat al-ṣafwa* wished to fill in the gaps left by Abū Nuᶜaym: *Ḥilyat al-awliyāʾ*, has forgotten him. Jullābī-i Hujwīrī: *Kashf al-maḥjūb*, ed. Zhukovski, p. 62/trans. Nicholson, p. 56, mentions by him — he calls him Abū Maᶜmar-i Iṣfahānī — a book on the Sufi symbolism of clothing. Anṣārī: *Ṭabaqāt,* pp. 536 f., lists three works by Maᶜmar: *Nahj al-khāṣṣ*, *Arbaᶜīn-i ṣūfiyān* and *Kitāb-i ghurbat*, and quotes the following sentence from the *K. ghurbat*: *wajadnā aṣḥāb al-ghāyāt fī hādhā al-amr furādan* 'We have only met single cases of people who have advanced to the end in this matter.' Of these three works mentioned by name the first one is found in our MS pp. 117-29, the second, identical with *Sharḥ al-arbaᶜīn ḥadīthan fī'l-taṣawwuf* in the table of contents, was once in our MS but was stolen, the third, *Ghurbat*, has not been found anywhere up to now. As the sentence quoted by Anṣārī suggests, *Ghurbat* was also written in Arabic and should therefore have borne the title *Kitāb al-ghurba* or something similar.

Up to now two writings of Maᶜmar have been discovered: *Nahj al-khāṣṣ*, MS Saray III. Ahmet 1416/2, dated 862/1457-58 (*GAL S*, I, p. 770), and a *risāla* without title (or *Dhikr maᶜānī al-taṣawwuf*, etc., here c) 1b), MS *Chester Beatty Library, Arabic Mss.*, III, no. 3682, 84b-86a (*GAS*, I, p. 676). Both are also found in our MS. The work *Nahj al-khāṣṣ* has been edited and discussed by Serge de Laugier de Beaurecueil in the *Mélanges Taha Husain*, Cairo, 1962, pp. 45-76, on the basis of the Istanbul MS. He also refers to it in his article 'L'aspiration (*raghba*) rectification de l'espérance selon ᶜAbdallāh Anṣārī et ses commentateurs', in *MIDEO* 7, 1962-63, p. 6, and in his monograph *Khwādja ᶜAbdullāh Anṣārī, mystique hanbalite*, Beirut, 1965, p. 52, ftn. 9. To him belongs the merit of having brought Maᶜmar out of the darkness of oblivion into the light. Our MS contains, in addition to the two known works of Maᶜmar, five new ones: 1a, 3, 4, 5, and 6 of the works which will be discussed in this section. In two of these the author presents more detailed information about himself.

According to *Sharḥ al-adhkār*, p. 166 in our MS, Maᶜmar heard a *ḥadīth* from Abū ᶜAbdallāh al-Ḥusayn b. ᶜAlī b. Aḥmad al-Aswārī. The latter died in Isfahan in 381/982 (Abū Nuᶜaym: *Tārīkh Iṣbahān*, ed. Dedering, I, p. 285, l. 5).

In the *Manāhij*, in our MS p. 198, he lists some of the *tābiᶜūn* whom he revered: Saᶜīd b. al-Musayyib, ᶜAlqama, al-Aswad, al-Qāsim b. Muḥammad, Sālim, ᶜAṭāʾ, Mujāhid, Ṭāwūs, Qatāda, al-Shaᶜbī, ᶜUmar b. ᶜAbd al-ᶜAzīz, al-Ḥasan al-Baṣrī, Muḥammad b. Sīrīn, then from the following generation: Ayyūb al-Sikhtiyānī, Yūnus b. ᶜUbayd, Sulaymān al-Taymī, Ibn ᶜAwn, then Sufyān al-Thawrī, Mālik b. Anas, al-Zuhrī, al-Awzāᶜī, Shuᶜba, then Yaḥyā b. Saᶜīd, Ḥammād b. Zayd, ᶜAbdallāh b. al-Mubārak, al-Fuḍayl b. ᶜIyāḍ, Sufyān b. ᶜUyayna, then Shāfiᶜī, ᶜAbd al-Raḥmān b. Mahdī, Wakīᶜ, Ibn Numayr, Abū Nuᶜaym, al-Ḥasan b. Rabīᶜ, then Aḥmad b.

Ḥanbal, Isḥāq b. Rāhawayh (Rāhūya), Abū Zurᶜa al-Rāzī, Abū Masᶜūd al-Rāzī, Abū Ḥātim and 'people like them from Syria, the Ḥijāz, Egypt, Khurāsān, Isfahan and Medina', such as Muḥammad b. ᶜĀṣim, ᶜAbdallāh b. Muḥammad b. al-Nuᶜmān, Muḥammad b. al-Nuᶜmān, al-Nuᶜmān b. ᶜAbd al-Salām, 'then those whom we met and from whom we have written down learning, *ḥadīth* and the *sunna*, such as Abū Isḥāq Ibrāhīm b. Muḥammad b. Ḥamza, Abū'l-Qāsim al-Ṭabarānī, Abū Muḥammad ᶜAbdallāh b. Muḥammad b. Jaᶜfar b. Ḥayyān Abū'l-Shaykh and the traditionists who were their contemporaries, then the desired goal of the age Abū ᶜAbdallāh Muḥammad b. Isḥāq b. Yaḥyā b. Manda al-Ḥāfiẓ — God have mercy on them'. Ibrāhīm b. Muḥammad b. Ḥamza al-Iṣfahānī died in 353/964 or 359/970 (Dhahabī: *Tadhkirat al-ḥuffāẓ*, Hyderabad, 1955-58, III, p. 910; Abū Nuᶜaym: *Tārīkh Iṣbahān*, I, p. 199), Ṭabarānī 360/971 (*GAL S*, I, p. 279; *GAS*, I, p. 195; *Tārīkh Iṣbahān*, I, p. 335; Dhahabī: *Ḥuffāẓ*, III, p. 915), Abū'l-Shaykh 369/979 (*Tārīkh Iṣbahān*, II, p. 90; *Ḥuffāẓ*, III, pp. 945-47), Ibn Manda 395/1005 (*GAL S*, I, p. 281; *GAS*, I, p. 214; *Tārīkh Iṣbahān*, II, p. 306; *Ḥuffāẓ*, III, pp. 1031-36).

In the *Manāhij*, p. 208 in our MS, after he has presented his Sufism as in conformity with the Koran and *sunna*, Maᶜmar writes: 'This is my doctrine regarding the *sunna* and tradition. I adopted it (*-hā* is wrong) from all the forefathers of the people of external science and of the imams, and my imam in all this is Abū ᶜAbdallāh Aḥmad b. Ḥanbal. As for my direction in Sufism, it is continual recollection of God mornings and evenings, striving after God by singling out pure *tawḥīd* and by unadulterated love of Him, and my imams in Sufism are Abū ᶜAbdallāh Muḥammad b. Yūsuf al-Bannāʾ, Abū'l-Ḥasan ᶜAlī b. Sahl and their Iṣfahānī disciples, then Abū'l-Qāsim al-Junayd b. Muḥammad and Abū Saᶜīd al-Kharrāz.' In addition, he mentions Khawwāṣ, Nūrī, their disciples in Baghdad, Ḥīrī, Abū Ḥafṣ al-Naysābūrī, Tustarī, Dhū'l-Nūn, Ibn al-Jallāʾ, Dārānī, Aḥmad b. Abī'l-Ḥawārī, all of whom are meant to have written books about the *sunan* and to have been against *kalām*, *qiyās*, dispute and everything which fosters the formation of sects. 'The direction of the *sunna* in conjunction with Sufism we have adopted (learnt) from Abū ᶜAbdallāh Muḥammad b. Yūsuf al-Bannāʾ[4] al-Ṣūfī in the *Kitāb al-sunna*, transmitted by Abū ᶜAbdallāh al-Ṣāliḥānī, Aḥmad b. Jaᶜfar b.

4 *Ḥilya*, X, pp. 402-04. *Tārīkh Iṣbahān*, II, pp. 220-21. Anṣārī: *Ṭabaqāt*, ed. Ḥabībī, pp. 110-11. Ibn al-Jawzī: *Ṣifat al-ṣafwa*, IV, p. 65.

Hāniᵓ Abū Jaᶜfar and Abū ᶜAbd al-Raḥmān al-Wadhankābādhī — God have mercy on them.'

Maᶜmar cannot have met Bannāᵓ in person since Bannāᵓ had already died in 286/899; he was a great-grandfather of Abū Nuᶜaym al-Iṣbahānī.[5] Abū Jaᶜfar Aḥmad is mentioned by Abū Nuᶜaym: *Tārīkh Iṣbahān*, I, p. 142 (also *Ḥilya*, X, p. 405) as a Sufi whom his father had known. Concerning Ṣāliḥānī and Wadhankābādhī, I have not been able to determine anything; a whole series of Ṣāliḥānīs and Wadhankābādhīs exists (Ṣāliḥān is a neighborhood and Wadhankābādh a village of Isfahan) but none of them fits the context. This much is clear: Maᶜmar belongs to the Ḥanbalite school of Bannāᵓ in Isfahan. He was a fellow townsman and contemporary of Abū Nuᶜaym al-Iṣbahānī who was himself also close to the Ḥanbalites (*Ḥuffāẓ*, III, p. 1095, l. 9).

In our MS Khānaqāh-i Aḥmadī 87 the following works of Maᶜmar are found:

1) a. *Bāb al-waṣiyya* (nr 5a, s. 111-113)

Incipit: قال الشيخ أبو منصور معمر بن أحمد الإصفهانى رحمة الله عليه: الشره
والحرص يمنعان عن الورع ... باب الوصية بلسان الحكمة وعبارة المتصوفة: فأوصيك
بحفظ الله جل جلاله ومراقبته جل جلاله فى خلواتك ...

Explicit: ... وإن فاتكم وجوده فلا يفوتنكم بجهوده

1) b. *Dhikr maᶜānī al-taṣawwuf wa-ādābihī wa-ḥaqāᵓiqihī wa-rusūmihī ᶜalā shawāhid awāᵓil ḥurūf al-muᶜjam* (no. 5b, pp. 113-17)

Incipit: ذكر معانى التصوف وآدابه وحقائقه ورسومه على شواهد حروف المعجم
فصلاً ونشدًا من كلام الشيخ أبى منصور معمر بن أحمد الإصفهانى رحمة الله عليه

5 Cf. *Tārīkh Iṣbahān*, I, p. 133, l. 23.

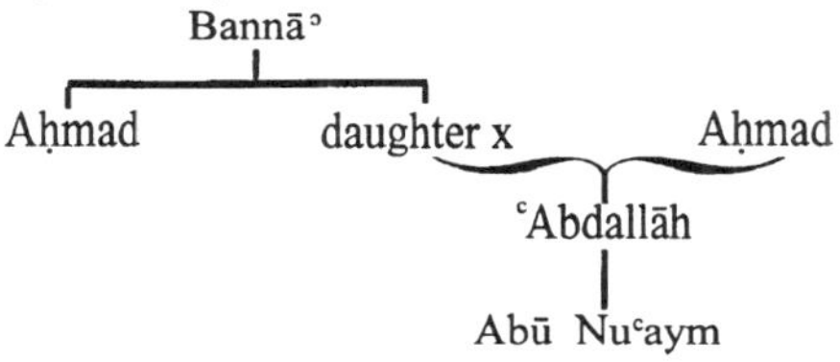

ورفع فى الملأ الأعلى ذكره. بسم الله الرحمن الرحيم. الحمد لله وحده والصلوة على النبي محمد وآله. قال الشيخ أبو منصور معمر بن أحمد صان الله قدره: التصوف ظاهر حلى المتصوفة ولبس الصوف شاهده معموما ...

Explicit: ...

يحيى التصوفُ بالتوحيد واجدَه   إنّ التصوف حال فيه ما فيه

فهذه القصيدة تصف أحوال المتصوفة الصوفية وهى مرتّبة على شاهد أوائل حروف المعجم. جعلنا الله برحمته من المتصوفة الصادقين والصوفية الخالصين إنه خير المنعمين وصلواته على محمد خاتم النبيين وعلى آله أجمعين وسلم تسليمًا كثيرًا

This work presents definitions of *taṣawwuf* in two parts: firstly, prose sentences which all begin with '*taṣawwuf* is...' and whose predicate nouns are arranged according to the order of the Arabic alphabet, i.e. *al-taṣawwuf Ifrād al-ḥaqq ta^{c}ālā ^{c}an asbāb al-khalq*, then *wa'l-taṣawwuf Baqā$^{\circ}$ al-ḥaqq wa-fanā$^{\circ}$ ^{c}an ru$^{\circ}$yat al-khalq*, etc., up to *al-taṣawwuf Yumn al-sa^{c}āda bi-ṣidq al-shahāda*. The second part consists of an acrostic whose initial letters reproduce the sequence of the Arabic alphabet (*basīṭ* meter). A predecessor of Ma^{c}mar was Ibrāhīm b. al-Muwallad al-Raqqī who collected together more than a hundred definitions (Sarrāj: *Luma^{c}*, p. 27, l. 9).

A second MS is found in *Chester Beatty Library, Arabic Mss.*, III, no. 3682, 84b-85b[6] (*GAS*, I, pp. 675 f.).

2) *Nahj al-khāṣṣ* (no. 6, pp. 117-29)

Incipit: ... الحمد لله الذى دعا الخلق الى نفسه بالآيات البينات ... وبعد فقد نظرنا فى أحوال السائرين الى الله ...

Explicit: ... وفى كل لحظة لهم آفة وتحت كل لحة عاهة الحذر منها بإخفاء الحذر عنها وللحذر مصادر وأحكام يعرفها العارف البالغ فى مشهد المعرفة. جعلنا الله عز وجل بمنه منهم ولا حجبنا عنهم وأقامنا على حرمة تذكارهم بحقيقة الطلب والافتقار إليه. إنه قريب مجيب.

It contains 40 chapters: 1) *bāb al-tawba* 2) *bāb al-irāda* 3) *ṣidq* 4) *ikhlāṣ* 5) *muḥāsaba* 6) *wara^{c}* 7) *zuhd* 8) *tawakkul* 9) *faqr* 10) *ṣabr* 11) *riḍā* 12) *khawf* 13) *rajā$^{\circ}$* 14) *mu^{c}āmala* 15) *ri^{c}āya* 16) *adab* 17)

---

6 I am gratefully obliged to the Chester Beatty Library for having provided me with a photocopy.

riyāḍa 18) *futūḥ* 19) *raghba* 20) *rahba* 21) *ḥaqīqa* 22) *maḥabba* 23) *shawq* 24) *samāᶜ* 25) *wajd* 26) *ḥaraka* 27) *sukūn* 28) *ṭumaʾnīna* 29) *mushāhada* 30) *murāqaba* 31) *mukāshafa* 32) *sirr* 33) *yaqīn* 34) *maᶜrifa* 35) *taṣawwuf* 36) *ghayra* 37) *makr* 38) *ghurba* 39) *wurūd* 40) *himma.*

Each *bāb* is arranged according to the pattern: *tawba* has three stations (*maqāmāt*), and each of these stations is subject to an evil (*āfa*). For example, no. 16: proper behavior (*adab*) exists at three stations: proper behavior in the religious law, proper behavior in service and proper behavior in God. Proper behavior in religious law is to abide by the prescriptions of knowledge (theology) with correct resolve to render service. Proper behavior in service is to break free from attachments and to eliminate side-glances. Proper behavior in God is agreement with God through cognition. The evil associated with proper behavior in religious law is interest in collecting (emended) knowledge while neglecting to apply it. The evil associated with proper behavior in service is paying attention to attachments which divert the heart and cause distraction (emended). The evil associated with proper behavior in God is dwelling with the carnal soul and being pleased with the passions.

This relentless method which for the most part does not do justice to the subject but imposes deeper insights upon it by a principle of division and playing with numbers reminds one, as de Beaurecueil rightly felt, of the *Manāzil al-sāʾirīn* of the Ḥanbalite mystic from Herat, ᶜAbdallāh-i Anṣārī (d. 481/1089). Anṣārī, as he says himself (*Ṭabaqāt,* p. 536), was familiar with the work and could have taken the structure of his *Manāzil* from it (de Beaurecueil in *Mélanges Taha Husain*, pp. 71-66, sic). In the appearance of *raghba* already in Anṣārī's *Ṣad maydān*, de Beaurecueil is tempted to see an influence of Maᶜmar's *Nahj al-khāṣṣ* (*MIDEO* 7, 1962-63, p. 18). Anṣārī claims that he composed his *Manāzil* at the request of Sufis and intended it to be an easily understandable booklet — Maᶜmar does not mention any such immediate cause. Despite the occasional surprising insights contained in this form of catechetics, the reader feels he is on the sterile soil of verbal play and wonders whether this droning series of monotonous wise sayings actually furthered the real concerns of Sufism. It seems that no commentary to the work was ever written.

A second MS, dated 862/1457-58, is found in Istanbul, Topkapı Saray, III. Ahmet 1416/2; as mentioned, it was edited by Serge de Laugier de Beaurecueil in *Mélanges Taha Husain*, Cairo, 1962, pp.

45-76, under the title 'La voie du privilégié, petit traité d'Abū Manṣūr Maᶜmar al-Iṣfahānī'. It is the only work of Maᶜmar's which until now has been made accessible to the public.

3) *Sharḥ al-adhkār* (no. 10, pp. 164/165-84)

Incipit (165): بسم الله الرحمن الرحيم وبه نستعين. الحمد لله العزيز الغفور الحميد الشكور المعبود المذكور ... قال الله عز وجل: وما خلقت الجن والإنس إلا ليعبدون. فالعبادة والذكر أحوال أولياء الله ... (166) قال الشيخ أبو منصور معمر ابن أحمد رضى الله منه: ولقد نظرت فى الطاعات والعبادات والأحوال والمقامات فأذا الطاعات والعبادات كلها شواهدها بالذكر (sic) والأحوال والمقامات كلها شواهدها التذكار ...

Explicit: ... وإذا كان الذاكر لله عز وجل فى ظاهر الشعر محمودًا استثنى من سائر الشعراء فكيف المستخرج من كل الكلام دقائق الإشارات والحكمة بالذكر بحقائق التوحيد. جعلنا الله برحمته من العارفين به الفهمين (sic) عنه السامعين به (sic). إنه قريب مجيب ...

It contains ten chapters: 1) *bāb al-ṣalāh fī maᶜnā al-dhikr* 2) *bāb al-ṣiyām fī maᶜnā al-dhikr* 3) *bāb al-zakāh wa'l-birr wa'l-ṣadaqāt fī maᶜnā al-dhikr* 4) *bāb al-ḥajj fī maᶜnā al-dhikr* 5) *bāb al-jihād fī maᶜnā al-dhikr* 6) *bāb al-tawba fī maᶜnā al-dhikr* 7) *bāb ḥaqīqat dhikr al-sirr* 8) *bāb ḥaqīqat al-irāda bi-tajrīd al-sirr wa-tajdīd* (sic) *al-dhikr* 9) *bāb tajrīd al-maḥabba bi-shāhid tajrīd al-dhikr* 10) *bāb tajrīd al-ishāra fī khafī al-dhikr.*

Religious duties are considered from the viewpoint that they are forms of recollection of God or contain recollection of God. Various kinds of deeper recollection of God are described such as the readiness of the pious man who is wholly oriented toward God to think of God even when there is only the remotest possible connection and the faintest suggestion for doing so, and among other things an attempt is made to fit the *samāᶜ* into the *dhikr* and to subordinate it to the *dhikr*. Of interest is the differentiated, sevenfold *dhikr* in Chapter 9: recollection of God's knowledge which preceded all things, of the pen, of the creation of Adam, of the primoridal covenant with God, of the preservation of one's own being through all past generations until one's birth, of Muḥammad and of the Koran (later ᶜAlī and the Imams were added among the Shīᶜite Niᶜmatallāhīs). Nowhere is there mention of the institution of recollecting God while in spiritual seclusion, although precisely the goal of eliminating self-will by recollection of God, as described in Chapter 8, would scarcely be attainable without drastic action. Nothing is said about the kind of performance and there are no occult observations regarding recollection of God. The work remains within the framework of classical discussions predating Qushayrī. This is the oldest preserved monograph on *dhikr*.

4) *Sharḥ abyāt li-Abī ᶜAbdallāh al-Murshid fī maᶜnā tajrīd al-tawḥīd min khafī shirk al-nafs* (no. 11, pp. 184-92)

Incipit: قال الشيخ أبو منصور معمر بن أحمد قدس الله روحه: سألنى بعض إخوانى عن (sic) شرح أبيات لأبى عبد الله المرشدى (sic) رحمه الله وهى هذه

أأنت أم أنا هذا الهَيْنُ [1] فى الْهَينِ   حاشاك [2] حاشاك من إثبات [3] إثنينِ
أأطلبُ الأين ذاتى [4] منك حيث أرى   فقد تَقرّر ذاتى حيث لا أينِ
بل أين أطلُبُ منك الأين من نظرى   فى ناظر القلب أم فى ناظر العينِ
هوية لك فى لائيّتى أبدًا   كلٌّ على الكل تشبيهٌ [5] لوجهينِ
بينى وبينك أنّىٌّ [6] يزاحمنا   [7] فارفع بأنّك أنّيّى من البينِ

قال الشيخ: المعنى فى ذلك إفراد الحق سبحانه بالوحدانية والفردانية والربوبية بالتفصيل من شاهد الخلق وصفات البشرية والإنسانية وشاهد إشراك النفس وذلك الشرك الخفى ...

1) When repeated on p. 190, *li'l-hayni* instead of *fī'l-hayni*.

2) When repeated on p. 190, *ḥāshāya*.

3) Read with a *hamzat al-qaṭᶜ*.

4) When the verse is repeated in the commentary on p. 185, reversed: *haythu minka*; likewise on p. 190.

5) When repeated on p. 190, *bi-wajhayni*.

6) The commentary on p. 187 and the repetition of the poem on p. 190 require this reading; pp. 184 and 187 have *yuzāḥimunī*.

7) Thus on p. 187, where the verse is repeated in the commentary, and on p. 190; p. 184 *fadfaᶜ*.

Explicit:

صح الإشارة فيما قلتُ يا عينى   حاشاك حاشاك من إثبات إثنين

This is a new and at the same time the oldest commentary on the well-known verses of Ḥallāj (*Dīwān*, ed. Massignon, M55/*Akhbār al-Ḥallāj,* no. 50) with new variants. In *Dhikr baʿḍ anfās al-Ḥallāj* (here sub a, in our MS p. 95) the same poem, as in the parallel transmissions (Massignon: *Dīwān*, M55), forms the conclusion and consists of only three verses which are cited above on p. 137 as *explicit*. In the commentary some of the new readings are confirmed: thus *aʾaṭlubu* and *taqarrara* in verse 2. The verses in the version of our MS may be translated as follows:

Are you or am I this well-off one[7] in comfort?
  Far from you, far from you be affirmation of two!
Should I seek the 'where'? But my being is from you whither I look.
  So my being has settled where there is no 'where'.
Then where should I seek from you the 'where' for my sight.
  In that which sees in the heart or in that which sees in the eye?
You have an existence eternally in my non-existence;
  a whole upon the whole would be a comparison of two faces (or: towards two sides).
Between me and you is an existence which presses us.
  Take away my existence through your existence!

Maʿmar criticizes the indeterminateness of 'existence' (*huwiyya*) in the 4th verse and, moreover, demands in place of 'existence' (or however one translates *huwiyya*) the will or the realities or the forms of evidence of God because only they are eternally in human non-existence. In addition he criticizes the insinuation in the 5th verse that God could be pressed by something; it would be better to say: 'an existence which presses me' (*yuzāḥimunī)* instead of 'presses us'. He concludes with the remark that the verses are correct in their sense but in their form they do not completely correspond with pure *tawḥīd* (p. 187). He then adds several variations on the poem which he has composed himself. Then he repeats a second time the poem he has been commenting on (p. 190) and follows it with an ampli-

---

7 Cf. Marzūqī's commentary to the *Ḥamāsa* of Abū Tammām, Cairo, 1953, IV, 1594, ll. 1-2, on *hayn*. In Suhrawardī: *ʿAwārif*, Chpt. 30, *hayn* means 'friendly, modest'.

fication of his own authorship which consists of 23 verses in the same meter and the same rhyme (the last verse is in the cited *explicit*).

The question arises: How has it come about that Ma^cmar attributes the poem to a certain Abū ^cAbdallāh al-Murshid or al-Murshidī? In this regard it should be noted that the reading Murshidī cannot be correct because *murshidī* means a member of the order of Abū Isḥāq Ibrāhīm b. Shahriyār al-Kāzarūnī who only died in 426/1035 and so in the time of Ma^cmar could not already have had followers known for such poems, quite apart from the fact that the extreme *tawḥīd* of our poem does not suit Kāzarūnī. The reading Murshidī is easily explained as a mistake of the copyist of our MS who was no doubt familiar with the Murshidīs. But to my knowledge the existence of an Abū ^cAbdallāh al-Murshid is not known either. Murshid without the article does appear as a personal name: the father of Usāma b. Munqidh bore the name (Munqidh is an earlier ancestor of Usāma), and Sha^crānī: *Al-ṭabaqāt al-kubrā*, Cairo, 1355, II, p. 133, mentions a certain al-shaykh Murshid who died a short time after 940/1533. But Murshid bears the article in Ma^cmar and there is no such Sufi before Ma^cmar's time. The solution to the puzzle is simple: We have here a code name for Ḥallāj. This is all the more likely if Ḥallāj, as the testimony of his son Ḥamd maintains, was originally known in Fārs by the name of Abū ^cAbdallāh al-Zāhid (*Tārīkh Baghdād*, VIII, p. 113, l. 9/Massignon: *Passion*, I, p. 3) and only later, after 293/905, bore the *kunya* Abū'l-Mughīth (*Passion*, I, p. 11). Massignon: *Passion*, I, pp. 331 ff., has described for us the difficulties against which the reputation of this martyr had to struggle to establish itself. Abū Nu^caym al-Iṣbahānī did not include him in his *Ḥilya* and thereby indicates that Ḥallāj in the theology of Isfahan, which was otherwise receptive to Sufism, had been rejected or was at least a controversial subject. The attitude of the school of ^cAlī b. Sahl al-Iṣbahānī (d. 307/919-20),[8] to which Ma^cmar belonged, will have been determined by the unpleasant row between Ḥallāj and ^cAlī b. Sahl (*Passion*, I, p. 96; *Akhbār al-Ḥallāj*, no. 18; Daylamī: *Sīrat-i Ibn-i Khafīf*, pp. 98 f.). Ma^cmar otherwise does not mention Ḥallāj in any of his writings that have come down to us and avoids him in the enumeration of shaykhs whom he held to be authoritative (here pp. 146 f.). Thus the existing commentary gives us an informative insight into the circumstances of Sufism in Isfahan in the 4th/10th century and especially its uncertainty and reserve *vis-à-vis* Ḥallāj.

---

8 His grave is today located within the area of a Khāksār convent.

5) *Al-manāhij bi-shāhid al-sunna wa-nahj al-mutaṣawwifa* (no. 12, pp. 192/193-210)

First part

Incipit (193): بسم الله الرحمن الرحيم. الحمد لله الواحد السميع الصمد البديع المتعال (sic) الرفيع العزيز المنيع وصلى الله على محمد الشفيع وعلى آله وسلم. وبعد فقد اقترب الزمان وفسد الأوان وحقق البرهان ومات أكثر العلماء والأولياء والحكماء والعارفين بالله والنجباء وغرب الإسلام وأهله والسنة وأهلها ... قال أبو منصور معمر بن أحمد بن زياد رحمه الله: ولما رأيت غربة السنة وكثرة الحوادث واتباع الأهواء أحببت أن أوصى أصحابي وسائر المسلمين بوصيّة من السنة وموعظة من الحكمة وأجمع ما كان عليه أهل الحديث والأثر وأهل المعرفة والتصوف من السلف المتقدمين والبقية من المتأخرين وأقول ...

Explicit (199-200): ... ونحن بحمد الله ومنّه من المقتدين بهم المتحلين لمذهبهم القائلين بفضلهم والله تعالى يجمع بيننا وبينهم فى الدارين فالسنة طريقنا وأهل الأثر أئمتنا فأحيانا الله عليها وأماتنا عليها برحمته. إنه قريب مجيب. تم كتاب المناهج بشاهد السنة ونهج المتصوفة ومِن هاهنا يحتاج اليه العلماء

An emotional complaint about the decline of piety and a presentation of orthodox doctrine, against *kalām*, *qiyās*, *naẓar*, *raʾy*, in favor of the uncreatedness of the Koran and even of its sounds, etc., in favor of absolute predestination, acknowledging Koranic anthropomorphism regarding God but without specifying 'how', acknowledging the Orthodox Caliphs and the ten personalities to whom Muḥammad promised Paradise. Enumeration of the great spiritual leaders whom the author follows. Nowhere in this first part is there mention of Sufis, apart from the fact that Fuḍayl b. ʿIyāḍ is among the enumerated models and that Bannāʾ bears the surname *al-ṣūfī*. The title, however, requires that they be discussed and therefore the following two parts still belong to the book.

Part two
Incipit (p. 200)

باب مسائل (sic) المحدثة الواقعة فى عصرنا. قال معمر بن
أحمد: فأول ذلك مسئلة الشهادة وغيرها من المحدثات ...

There then follow *bāb mas'alat al-istithnā' fī al-ru'ya*, (p. 201) *bāb mas'alat ḥadīth al-farā'iḍ...*, *bāb mas'alat al-ʿadam wa'l-wujūd*, *bāb mas'alat ṣalāt al-jamāʿa*, *bāb mas'alat al-īmān* which contains the following passage (p. 202): ...والاختيار

فى مسئلة الإيمان السكوت عنه على مذهب أحمد بن حنبل رضى الله عنه. قال معمر
بن أحمد: فهذه جملة المسائل المحدثة فى عصرنا قد شرحتُها وبينتُها وأظهرتُ مذهبى
فيها وعلى ذلك إجماع أهل العلم من أهل السنة والعارفين المتصوفة ... فمن خالفنى
فى شىء من ذلك ... فأرى مباينته وهجرانه ... فلا جمع الله بيننا وبين من خالف
الكتاب والسنة فى الدارين وأقامنا برحمته على منهاج الكتاب والسنة وطريق السلف
والأئمة من أهل العلم والمعرفة والحكماء والمتصوفة رحمة الله عليهم أجمعين. قال معمر بن
أحمد: فرحم الله امرءا نظر الى حكم زمانه فكان حذرا وإلى فساد أوانه فكان
وجلاً واعتمد على الصالحين وإن قلّوا وعلى الورعين وإن غرُبوا لأنهم أهل حقيقة
سنة المختار من العالَمين محمد صلى الله عليه وسلم وكان عاضًّا على السنة بالنواجذ كما
أمره رسول الله صلى الله عليه وسلم فقد غرُب الإسلام وأهله (203) وغربت السنة
وأهلها وغرب الصالحون والزهاد والورعون والمريدون والطالبون لطريق خاصة الله
عز وجل وأوليائه وأهل محبته ...

Maʿmar then distinguishes two paths to God: the path of the believers who make an effort by serving and on the basis of theological knowledge, and the path of the lovers of God who with their whole heart strive solely after God. The first path, the 'path of the hereafter', is only still travelled by a few people, some solitary persons (*bi-shāhid al-ghurba*) and loners (*wa-ḥukm al-waḥda*). The second, the 'path of God', is no longer travelled by anyone at all.

Explicit:

... على أنه لا يخلو الأرض من قائم لله بحجّته

Part three
Incipit (p. 203):

قال معمر بن أحمد: فأوصى نفسى وإخوانى من المسلمين بتقوى
الله ...

Exhortation to piety and to joining the righteous, warnings against worldliness, exhortations to fear of God and to other religious virtues, warnings against false Sufis. The author distinguishes between *ṣiddīq* and *mutaṣawwif*. A *ṣiddīq* is someone who maintains no false pretences in his external behavior but is honest. Such a person, however, is still not necessarily a Sufi. Someone is not a *mutaṣawwif* until he is always aware in his thoughts that God is the only agent behind his actions. (In other systems, for example in al-Ḥakīm al-Tirmidhī, the *ṣiddīq* is a high ranking Sufi). Then Ma^{c}mar distinguishes in Sufism between an 'occurring' (*wāqi^{c}*) element and an 'expectant' (*mutawaqqi^{c}*) element. What 'occurs' is a gift from God, the one given a gift is sought after by God, he has an easy time of being obedient, he first finds and only later works. The 'expectant' element is the work, one works first and only later finds. This theory (p. 206 f.), which unfortunately is not clearly harmonized with the theory of the one agent behind actions, is an early form of the later theory of the *majdhūb* and the *sālik*. The enumeration of the Sufi masters who are a model for Ma^{c}mar (here pp. 146 f.) follows next (pp. 208-09). Ma^{c}mar demands that Sufism strictly conform to orthodox theology and he rejects any alleged manifestations of God in the heart (pp. 209-10). On p. 210 he quotes from Junayd: 'Take this science only from people who write down *ḥadīth* and have mastered the principles (*uṣūl*), because our sciences are intertwined with the *ḥadīth* of the Messenger of God', and he continues: 'Whoever cannot distinguish between inspiration (*ilhām*), stray fancy (*hājis*), internal speech (*lamma*) and devilish temptation (*waswasa*) in knowledge, in experience, in description and in direct perception — it is forbidden for him to speak about the sciences of the *mutaṣawwifa*, about the realities of wisdom and the sciences of secrets. Such a person can at any time violate the *sunna* and in so doing think he is speaking about knowledge of perception without noticing (that he is on the wrong track). If God unites for a person the sciences of the external together with their implementation, the sciences of religious action together with their application, and the sciences of Sufism and spiritual states (sic), if this person then renounces the world and chooses poverty and is scrupulous in religion, if knowledge describes him before he describes knowledge, and the spiritual state speaks about him before he speaks about the spiritual state — then he is called a knower of God. Such a person, however, is as scarce as red sulphur, and only rarely do you find someone like this in our time, but the earth is never without someone who constitutes an argument for God.'

Explicit (210): فإنا بفضلهم قائلين (sic) وبمحبتهم ناطقين وبقولهم مؤمنين وبعزيز لمحجتهم منتحلين وبجملة ما هم عليه مقتدين. لا فرق الله بيننا وبينهم ولا حرّمنا نواالهم. إنه خير المنعمين ومجيب المضطرين ودليل المتحيرين وأرحم الراحمين. تم كتاب المنهاج (sic) بشاهد السنة ونهج المتصوفة والمسائل والوصية.

Judging by the doxology on p. 198 for the deceased, among whom Ibn Manda is also mentioned, the work must have been written after the latter's death in 395/1005. The frequent appearance of *gharuba* and the reiterated complaint that true men of piety are only rarely still to be found raises the question as to whether our book is not identical with the missing *Kitāb al-ghurba*, from which Anṣārī quotes a similar-sounding complaint. But the book does not contain the sentence of Anṣārī, at least not in our MS.

The purpose of the work is first of all to summon the Sufis to conform to Ḥanbalite orthodoxy, and secondly to declare publicly that true Sufism is an orthodox movement. Thus it combines the two tendencies of classical Sufism and the textbooks produced at the close of that period: the elimination of heresies and the presentation of Sufism as orthodox, indeed as the crown of orthodoxy. Formulated as a 'profession of faith', it stands together with the 'profession of faith' of Ibn-i Khafīf and is therefore one of the oldest examples of these public Sufi professions.

Ibn Taymiyya (d. 728/1328) read the work and quotes a few sentences from its beginning in *Al-ʿaqīda al-ḥamawiyya al-kubrā* (in *Majmūʿat al-rasāʾil al-kubrā*, I, p. 441) under the name of Maʿmar, 'the shaykh of the Sufis around 400 AH', but without mentioning the title of the work.

About Sufism in Isfahan in the 3rd/9th and 4th/10th centuries not much is known to us. From Abū Nuᶜaym's *Tārīkh Iṣbahān* a list of over 30 names emerges, whose bearers were Sufis from Isfahan. In the main, however, he only reports on such Sufis as possessed a foundation in theological learning and were regarded as pious. On the other hand, particular statements of Maᶜmar which are militant against heresy seem to indicate that wilder forms of Sufism also occurred there.

6) (*Masāʾil fī'l-taṣawwuf*) (no. 4, pp. 106-10)

Incipit: وأداء حقوقهم فى جميع الأسباب وموافقة مرادهم كموافقة الأحباب. وإشارات المتصوفة فى الصحبة إلى ثلاث: تعريف الألفة السابقة قبل الإجابة ... باب أدب المجالسة: وأدب (sic) المتصوفة فى المجالسة ثلاثة: القصد إليها لطلب الفائدة والاغماض عن حشو ما يجرى فى المجالسة والتواضع للجليس لحق المجالسة. وحقائق المتصوفة فى المجالسة ثلاث: فتح أبواب المذاكرات واقتضاء الوجد لتجديـــد الواردات وأخذ الشواهد فى تصريف المحاورات. وإشارات المتصوفة فى المجالسة الى ثلاث: إلى اجتماع الأسرار بشاهد الذكر والتذكار و إلى مطالعة الأرواح بخفى الأذكار وإلى قول النبى صلى الله عليه وسلم: يد الله على الجماعة. وفى ذلك الإشارة إلى شاهد الجمع الفرد ...

Explicit: باب أدب السفر: وآداب المتصوفة فى السفر ثلاثة ... وإشارات المتصوفة فى السفر إلى ثلاث: إلى رفع المنازل والوطن لحق التجريد وإلى حقيقة الغربة فى شاهد التوحيد وإلى وجود روح اليقين فى ساحة التفريد. تمت بحمد الله تعالى.

In mutilated condition without the author's name and without a title because the beginning is incomplete. The title which I have placed in brackets is given in the table of contents on the flyleaf of the collective MS, and there the work is also attributed to Maᶜmar. The title does not fit but the attribution is undoubtedly correct. The same style as in the *Nahj al-khāṣṣ*, numerous parallel statements are found in other works of Maᶜmar.

In our fragment the following chapters are found, each one with a few lines and always subdivided into three *ādāb*, three *ḥaqāʾiq* and three *ishārāt*: *bāb adab al-ṣuḥba* (beginning incomplete), *bāb adab al-mujālasa*, *bāb adab al-julūs ᶜalā'l-waḥda*, *bāb adab al-muʾākala*, *bāb adab al-akl ʿalā'l-waḥda, bāb adab al-mudhākara, bāb al-dhikr ʿalā'l-infirād, bāb adab al-muʾākhāh, bāb adab al-badhl, bāb adab al-khidma, bāb adab al-khulq, bāb adab al-faqr, bāb adab al-khalwa, bāb adab al-safar.*

A vade-mecum dealing with good behavior and the meaning of certain actions and attitudes of the Sufis.

d) ANONYMOUS (no. 1, pp. 1-80)

Adab al-mulūk

Incipit (1): بسم الله ... الحمد لله الذى أخلص أهل الخالصة للدار وأطلعهم
على حقائق الأسرار ... (6) ثم وانى جمعت فهمى ومددت بطرفى (sic) وميزت بعلمى
وفهمى واجتهدت فى استنباطى وقاسيت بعقلى وقابلت الكتاب والسنة على مبلغ علمى
فلم أر أقوامًا أمسك بالسنة ظاهرًا وباطنًا ... من العصابة المرتسمة باسم التصوف ...
(7) ثم لما رأيت سائر اهل المذهب من اهل العلوم والفقهاء وأصحاب الحديث وأهل
القرآن والآداب قد سُئلوا عن أقاويلهم ... فاحتج كل واحد منهم على أصله ...
فرأيت العصابة المرتسمة بالتصوف منتقصين مذمومين جاهلين عند أهل النظر وأكثر
الناس لما لم يظهر فيهم من أحوالهم ... رسمت كتابي هذا فبينت (hs. فبنيت) فيه
اصول القوم ورسومهم وأحكامهم وحقائقهم ورعايتهم وإشاراتهم وجميع أسبابهم الموافقة
لسنة نبيهم (sic) صلى الله عليه وسلم وترجمْتُه بأدب الملوك لأن الصوفية زهدوا عن
(sic) جميع أسباب الدنيا فصاروا ملوكًا واستراحوا وطابت قلوبهم ونفوسهم وكيف
لا يستحقوا (sic) اسم الملوكية وليس لهم همة غير الله ...

Explicit (79): ... فسيكون شفيعًا لأهل الكذب والله عز وجل ولىّ الإحسان
وذو الطول والامتنان. جعلنا الله عز وجل من أهل خالصته (80) الذين اختارهم فى
الأزل وأقامهم على خالص السبيل وعصمنا من افتراء الزور وهواجس النفوس
ومساوى الأمور. إنه قريب مجيب. الحمد لله رب العالمين وصلواته على نبيه محمد
وآله أجمعين وحسبُنا الله وحده ونعم الوكيل. تم الكتاب بعون الله وحسن توفيقه.

Marginal note at the end: 'Collated with the original.'

In a long introduction the author describes the nature of jurists, traditionists, Koran readers, Koran commentators, and philologists, and criticizes them because, with few exceptions, they only cultivate an exterior of science, only satisfy their need for admiration, but in eating, drinking, etc., they contravene what they recount and do not act in accordance with what they preach. With them are contrasted the Sufis, who live in conformity with the divine commands, put themselves in conformity with God's will instinctively as well, and thereby find peace (pp. 1-14). The work contains the following chapters:

1) *Bāb mā buniya ᶜalayhi al-taṣawwuf* (p. 14): *faqr* is meant.

2) *Bāb ḥaqāʾiq al-ṣūfiyya* (p. 17): *zuhd* is meant.

3) *Bāb rusūm al-ṣūfiyya* (p. 20): what is meant is combatting the *nafs* whose *hashāsha* and *ishtihāʾ* (p. 21) recall the para-etymology of *shahwa* in al-Ḥakīm al-Tirmidhī and would not have been brought into play without this predecessor. The *nafs* is from the earth, the spirit from the *malakūt* whither it strives to return.

4) *Bāb ishārāt al-ṣūfiyya* (p. 23): *irāda* is discussed. This is basically oriented toward God as the unique goal. Reward in the hereafter is not sought, but only God Himself. Everything besides God is prison, even Paradise.

5) *Bāb libās al-ṣūfiyya* (p. 26): wool, with interesting viewpoints according to which this clothing can be worn by Sufis: in imitation of the prophets and ascetics, to toughen up the body, and to avoid pride and an attractive appearance, as an expression of inner sorrow.

6) *Bāb zīnat al-ṣūfiyya* (p. 28): on the *muraqqaᶜa*. One wears it for lack of anything else and in order to abase oneself. Allusions to inner states can be connected with the colors of the patches: black, dark blue (*kuḥlī*) and sky-blue (*azraq*) mean sorrowfulness, black moreover, as the color of rulers (*salāṭīn*) and Friday preachers, means power.

7) *Bāb daᶜwā al-ṣūfiyya* (p. 30): the condition of being a foreigner (*ghurba*) from the viewpoint of a short-term right to hospitality on this earth, of Sufi wandering through different countries, of withdrawal from men at large.

8) *Bāb taᶜabbud al-ṣūfiyya* (p. 32): to stand by God in one's innermost interior and to know that one is observed there by Him; what matters is not the external but the internal intensity of piety. That is why Sufis often adopt different paths: some travel about, others live as hermits in the mountains or in caves, still others remain in their family and among men at large, as if they were envoys (*sufarāʾ*) of God to the people. In the Sufism around Junayd in

Baghdad all this was represented: Ibrāhīm al-Bannā' lived in seclusion, Abū Ḥamza al-Baghdādī in deserts, Nūrī in ruins, others in the mountains, Junayd himself and many others whose names are enumerated lived among the people.

9) *Bāb ʿulūm al-ṣūfiyya* (p. 36): 'knowledge of the interior' which our author does not equate with introspection and psychagogy, like Abū Ṭālib al-Makkī among others, but with inspired higher knowledge.

10) *Bāb khuṣūṣiyyat al-ṣūfiyya* (p. 39): trust in God (*tawakkul*).

11) *Bāb ḥirfat al-ṣūfiyya* (p. 43): though not forbidden, a trade is none the less likely to be harmful, because as a practitioner of a trade one cannot devote oneself completely to God. There are two possibilities to obtain one's necessary nourishment: either one entrusts the whole matter to God or one begs. The latter can make one dependent on an inner command of God which one awaits.

12) *Bāb aḥkām al-ṣūfiyya* (p. 46): steadfastness (*ṣabr*).

13) *Bāb akhlāq al-ṣūfiyya* (p. 48): good-naturedness and friendliness.

14) *Bāb sakhā' al-ṣūfiyya* (p. 50): generosity.

15) *Bāb muwāfaqat al-ṣūfiyya wa-mu'ālafatihim* (p. 52): brotherly love and goodwill toward one another. The characteristic of belonging together common to those who come together here below has been stamped on their spirits during pre-existence; here the spirits recognize one another again. Alongside brotherliness among co-religionists, which is of a general nature, there is a special brotherliness — one which is established through brotherhood; this is produced by effort, but at the same time predestined.

16) *Bāb maʿrūf al-ṣūfiyya* (p. 54): urging one's fellow-man to do good and preventing him from doing wrong.

17) *Bāb muḥāwarāt al-ṣūfiyya* (p. 54): the Sufis talk about the God-forsakenness of innovators in order to support the *sunna* and to help the right religious attitude attain success; they do not allow themselves to be prevented from this by any considerations.

18) *Bāb munāqarat al-ṣūfiyya wa-munāẓaratihim* (p. 57): discussion of the inner attitudes, experiences and achievements among Sufis. The dominant element in the individual behavior of a Sufi can always be different. In one Sufi it is love, in another desire, in a third hope, and in a fourth fear, etc.

19) *Bāb ikhtiyār al-ṣūfiyya* (p. 58): the outer side of 'choice' for Sufis is humility, the inner side is giving up choice. Chiefly humility and self-abasement are treated.

20) *Bāb isqāṭ al-ṣūfiyya* (p. 59): sincerity, ceasing to pay heed to people and renunciation of any self-will. Against a thirst for fame and ambitiousness.

21) *Bāb siyāḥat al-ṣūfiyya* (p. 62): various aspects of Sufi journeying: for refreshment, for the acquisition of knowledge, as a way of working off passion for the eternal dwelling place (i.e. a phenomenon of movement, like dance during the *samāᶜ* performances).

22) *Bāb awṭān al-ṣūfiyya* (p. 64): the home towns of the Sufis in the world are the mosques. Reference to Jesus and the 'people of the mosque-porch' in old Medina. The Sufis for the most part build no houses. When they are in need of relaxation, they go out into the open air.

23) *Bāb julūs al-ṣūfiyya* (p. 65): the Sufis sit in a circle. The Prophet is already supposed to have ordered this during a Koran recitation.

24) *Bāb akl al-ṣūfiyya* (p. 66): eating only out of necessity, little and decent food, allowing others to go ahead of oneself during meals. Some eat under regular restrictions, others only in extreme need, still others only by accident, i.e. due to 'the supernatural'.

25) *Bāb ijābat al-daᶜwa li'l-ṣūfiyya* (p. 67): invitation to banquets.

26) *Bāb inbisāṭ al-ṣūfiyya* (p.68): cheerful and friendly behavior, for the sake of one's fellow-man: openhandedness, openness of the countenance, liveliness of the bodily limbs.

27) *Bāb samāᶜ al-ṣūfiyya* (p. 69): the Sufis stand out from all other Muslims through the practice of listening to music; it is one of the foundations of Sufism. There are Sufis who listen by means of the Lord, others by means of their spiritual state, and still others by means of their learning. In addition, there is a *samāᶜ* of the heart, a *samāᶜ* of the spirit, and a *samāᶜ* of the carnal soul. The author is brief in his treatment of this subject and refers to a separate work he has written on the *samāᶜ*.

28) *Bāb wajd al-ṣūfiyya* (p. 73): ecstasy or being inwardly moved is defined as the coming together of the supernatural with the supernatural which is experienced in the innermost interior (*sirr*) and cannot be described. Nevertheless, lengthy explanations follow, as well as description of the movements of a person in ecstasy.

Conclusion (p. 75): the work is first and foremost intended as a handbook for understanding the most general manifestations of Sufism. In addition, however, some more profound matters are discussed so that the reader realizes that Sufism in this respect as well strictly adheres to the Koran and the *sunna*. Whereas only a few specialized terms are enumerated and one is then referred to the discipline of the arcane, the orthodoxy of Sufism is emphasized that much more and all unorthodox behavior is described as non-Sufi. Moreover, there is the fact that God speaks to his chosen ones by means of inspiration. This is an important difference from the representatives of jurisprudence, the science of *ḥadīth*, Koranic commentary and literature because the latter learn from books, whereas the Sufis, inasmuch as they have fulfilled the ascetic prerequisites, learn from inspired knowledge. This is a gift which must then be followed by 'acquisition' (i.e. work and assimilation). Whoever cannot distinguish between inspiration (*ilhām*), a stray fancy (*hājis*), internal speech (*lamma*) and devilish temptation (*waswasa*) (i.e. does not recognize behind his thoughts the inspirers God, the carnal soul, an angel and the devil) — such a person is not a Sufi. Real Sufis, the great, scholars and knowers of God are in fact as rare as red sulphur. God chooses them and protects them, they see by means of Him for Him, speak by means of Him for Him, and disappear from themselves by means of Him for Him, etc.

This anonymous work, not to be confused with the newly discovered *Ādāb al-mulūk* of Aḥmad b. al-Ṭayyib al-Sarakhsī which Mujtabā Mīnuwī reported on at the orientalist congress in Ann Arbor (Īraj-i Afshār in *Rāhnimāy-i kitāb* 10, no. 3, 1967, p. 220, l. 3 from bot.), is without a doubt the most important piece in our collection. It amounts to nothing less than a hitherto unknown short comprehensive presentation of Sufism from the 4th/10th or 5th/11th century, i.e. *mutatis mutandis* a small parallel work to Kalābādhī's *Taᶜarruf*, Sarrāj's *Lumaᶜ*, etc. Sarrāj, just like al-Ḥakīm al-Tirmidhī, contrasts Sufism with the two sciences of *ḥadīth* studies and jurisprudence as well as with the science of the Koran and dialectic dogmatics (*Lumaᶜ*, p. 106, l. 18). Abū Ṭālib al-Makkī enumerates nine sciences, four well-known old ones: the science of faith, the Koran, *ḥadīth*s, principles of law, and five new ones: grammar, metrics, juridical syllogistics and dispute, speculative dogmatics and *ḥadīth* criticism (*Qūt*, II, p. 47); and these he contrasts with Sufism. Tawḥīdī views knowledge of the Koran, of the *ḥadīth*, and syllogistics as only prerequisites for jurisprudence, also takes into account the mathematical and natural scientific disciplines as well as medicine, and comes to an overall total of ten sciences, to which he adds Sufism as the eleventh (*Risāla fī'l-ᶜulūm*, ed. Marc Bergé in *BEO* 16, pp. 241 ff.). Our anonymous author attacks the jurists, traditionists, Koran readers, Koranic commentators and philologists, and reproaches them for being stuck in their teaching and study, and for seeking reputation and money with their learning instead of reflecting on the meaning of the sacred tradition they have cultivated and drawing the consequences from it for their behavior. Like Sarrāj and Makkī, he places Sufism as the moral-psychagogical hermeneutics of the Koran and the *ḥadīth* alongside and above the interpretative goals of the other sciences and then in individual chapters treats the mode of thought and behavior which emerges from Sufi interpretation of the sacred tradition. The first question is: when was the book written?

In reply one may say the following: Sarrāj, Kalābādhī, Makkī, Sulamī and Abū Nuᶜaym are nowhere mentioned, not to speak of Qushayrī, Jullābī and Anṣārī. Furthermore, sayings of early Sufis are found in our anonymous author which otherwise appear not to have been transmitted or not to have been transmitted in the same form (one will only be able to say something certain on this subject once the other works have been indexed and compared with precision). A list of Sufis in Chapter 8 provides a *terminus a quo* for the composition of the work. Of the Sufis enumerated there the last to die were Abū Bakr (Muḥammad b. Aḥmad b. Muḥammad) al-Miṣrī, namely in 345/957,[9] and Abū Bakr (Muḥammad b. Dāwūd) al-Dīnawarī (al-Duqqī), namely in 359/970 or 360/970-71.[10] I am unable to identify Abū Sulaymān al-Maghribī. They were all dead at the time of the book's composition since they receive the common doxology: *raḍiya'llāhu ᶜanhum, aẓhara'llāhu ᶜazza wa-jalla kullahum li'l-ḥujjati ᶜalā'l-khalq*, as well as the remark: 'they were all gathered before God', etc. Of the direct transmitters cited by our author, Abū Bakr b. Ḥaṣṣān remains unclear to me — he reported (*ḥaddathanā*, p. 7) to the author a *ḥadīth* on the authority of a certain Ibrāhīm (b. Shaybān? or al-Khawwāṣ?). Somewhat clearer is a passage on p. 19: 'It is recounted about Abū ᶜAbdallāh al-Maghribī that for thirty years he only ate grass from the ground and drank water from springs. And Ibn Shaybān Abū Isḥāq reported to me (*akhbaranī*): I remained at his (i.e. Abū ᶜAbdallāh al-Maghribī's) grave for three years. After three years, one time I fell asleep at his grave and beheld him in a dream. I asked him for something, he granted my request and ordered me to return to my home. Thus I returned to Qirmīsīn with his permission. Abū Bakr al-Ṭarasūsī informed me of this (*akhbaranī bi-dhālika*): Ibrāhīm b. Shaybān reported it to us from Abū ᶜAbdallāh (i.e. al-Maghribī).' The last sentence subsequently, as it seems, gives the more precise chain of

9 Subkī: *Ṭabaqāt al-Shāfiᶜiyya*, Cairo, 1324, II, pp. 112-15.

10 R.A. Nicholson's Introduction to Sarrāj: *Lumaᶜ*, p. XVI.

transmitters for the preceding story. Ibrāhīm b. Shaybān al-Qirmīsīnī died in 337/948-49 or 339/950-51. As for Ṭarasūsī, this is a personality whose name is sometimes presented as Abū Bakr Aḥmad b. Muḥammad, sometimes as ᶜAlī b. Aḥmad b. Muḥammad al-Ṭarasūsī, and who died in 374/984-85.[11] Thus the author cannot have written before around 360/971 (the date of Duqqī's death), but must already have reached the age of manhood before 374/984-85 (the date of Ṭarasūsī's death). Whether he wrote already before or only after 374/984-85 remains uncertain.

That he stood relatively close to high-classical mysticism is perhaps indicated by the sentences introducing quotations: 'It was recounted to me from Junayd or Ibn ᶜAṭāᵓ' (pp. 72, 76). Less can be made of the sentence: 'One of our companions (*aṣḥābinā*) said: I saw Abū Saᶜīd al-Kharrāz perform the prayers in the mosque' (p. 38), because by these companions one should perhaps simply understand the Sufis. The absence of a chapter on the shaykh also seems to be high-classical. The same point leads one to conjecture that the work was not composed in Nayshābūr where this problem was the subject of keen discussion.

Since our text the *Adab al-mulūk* occurs in a collective MS along with several works by Abū Manṣūr Maᶜmar b. Aḥmad al-Iṣfahānī (d. 418/1027), the second question will be: is the author of the *Adab al-mulūk* perhaps Maᶜmar? There are some indications which speak in favor of this assumption and others against it.

Pro:

1) A certain similarity in terminology in the case of unusual designations:

mulūkiyya (pp. 7 f.), as in the *Waṣiyya* of Maᶜmar (our MS p. 112, l. 3) and in his *taṣawwuf*-definitions (p. 115, ll. 1, 4), as well as in *Sharḥ al-adhkār* (pp. 173 f.).

ghurba (pp. 30, 62, 64, 79), as in Maᶜmar's *Nahj al-khāṣṣ* (our MS p. 128), *Masāᵓil* (p. 110) and *Manāhij* (pp. 193, 202 f.).

tajrīd al-tawḥīd, many times.

badhl in the sense of *sakhāᵓ* (pp. 50 ff.), as in *Masāᵓil* (p. 108), *Waṣiyya* (pp. 111 f.) and *Sharḥ al-adhkār* (pp. 169 f.).[12]

bi-shāhid or something similar, frequently.

---

11 *Lumaᶜ*, p. 170, l. 14, Nicholson's Introduction, p. XXI. Anṣārī: *Ṭabaqāt*, ed. Ḥabībī, pp. 486 f. Jāmī: *Nafaḥāt*, s.n.

12 Also *ᶜAwārif*, Chpt. 30, quoted in Ibn al-Karbalāᵓī (10th/16th century): *Rawḍāt al-jinān*, Tehran, 1965, p. 294.

2) Similar statements:

Samāᶜ can take place by means of God, a spiritual state (*ḥāl*) and knowledge (*ᶜilm*), likewise *Nahj al-khāṣṣ* (p. 124). In Qushayrī: *Risāla, bāb al-samāᶜ*, one time by means of nature (*ṭabᶜ*), a spiritual state and God (likewise *Lumaᶜ*, p. 278, ll. 10 ff.); another time, by means of the moment (*waqt*), a spiritual state and God.

wajd is defined as the coming together of the supernatural with the supernatural (p. 73, l. 7), word for word the same as *Nahj al-khāṣṣ* (p.129).

Spiritual affinity (*ulfa*) is predisposed (*sābiqa*) and cannot be acquired (p. 52), as in *Masāʾil* (p. 106, l. 2; p. 108, l. 16).

Brotherliness (*ukhuwwa*) exists in a general (*maᶜmūma*) and in a special (*makhṣūṣa*) form (p. 53). In the *Nahj al-khāṣṣ* (pp. 123 f.) there corresponds to this a general (*maᶜmūma*) and a special (*makhṣūṣa*) love (*maḥabba*), to which is then added a love of God. General brotherliness and general love are explained the same way: it is a question of brotherliness or love in the faith.

The ways to God are more numerous than the stars in heaven (p. 57), as in *Nahj al-khāṣṣ* (p. 129).

Ideas are divided into inspiration (from God, *ilhām*), a stray fancy (from the carnal soul, *hājis*), internal speech (from an angel, *lamma*), and temptation (from the devil, *waswasa*) (p. 78), as in *Manāhij* (p. 210). This division already occurs in Kalābādhī and then appears again in Qushayrī and Abū Ḥafṣ al-Suhrawardī (Meier: *Die Fawāʾiḥ al-ǧamāl... des... Kubrā*, Intro., p. 128), but communication from an angel is nowhere simply described by the term *lamma* without some addition.

The knowledge of the Sufi is a divine gift (*mawhiba*) which must be followed by 'acquisition', individual action (p. 78). With somewhat different words it is also said in *Manāhij* (p. 207) about the *murād* (= the later *majdhūb*) that in contrast to the *murīd* (= the later *sālik*) he first finds and then seeks. Significant meaning (*maᶜnā*) is allotted to the *murād* as a gift (*mawhiba*).

In favor of a closer connection of the anonymous author with Maᶜmar it could also be added that Jullābī knows of a book by Maᶜmar which describes the symbolic meanings of the patched frock. In *Adab al-mulūk*, p. 29, one finds interpretations of this kind for the colors black, dark blue and sky-blue; the author thus thought along similar lines as Maᶜmar. He could be considered capable of writing a book on the subject.

Contra:

Against the two authors being identical is the fact that they use a different designation for the Sufis. In the *Adab al-mulūk* one always finds *ṣūfiyya* or variations like *al-mawsūmūn bi'l-taṣawwuf, al-murtasimūn bi'l-taṣawwuf*, etc. In the writings of Maᶜmar *ṣūfiyya* never occurs but one encounters throughout *mutaṣawwifa*, or occasionally *ahl al-taṣawwuf*, with exceptions in *Dhikr maᶜānī al-taṣawwuf* (no. 5b, pp. 113, 117) where the *ṣūfī* is described as the interior of the *mutaṣawwif* (variant Chester Beatty: of the *taṣawwuf*) and the combinations *al-mutaṣawwifa al-ṣūfiyya* and *al-mutaṣawwifa... wa'l-ṣūfiyya...* occur, and with the exception of the epithet of Bannāʾ as *al-Ṣūfī* (*Manāhij*, pp. 198, 209). The Persian title *Arbaᶜīn-i ṣūfiyān*, which Anṣārī mentions, has no significance for the work of Maᶜmar which has been lost from our MS (see here p. 145).

According to *Lumaᶜ*, p. 48, l. 8, ᶜAlī b. Sahl al-Iṣfahānī, in whose tradition Maᶜmar locates himself, is supposed to have said: 'It is (may it be) forbidden for me to associate with someone who describes our companions as *fuqarāʾ* because they are the richest of God's creatures.' Since the author of the *Adab al-mulūk* uses the expression *fuqarāʾ* 'the poor' for the Sufis without hesitation, it would be natural to think of him as separate from the tradition of ᶜAlī b. Sahl and to dismiss the possibility of the anonymous author being identical with Maᶜmar. It is true that Maᶜmar uses the term 'poverty' (*faqr*) and devotes a *bāb* to the subject in *Nahj al-khāṣṣ*, p. 120, but he never refers to his *mutaṣawwifa* as *fuqarāʾ*. Only at the end of the *Manāhij* (p. 209) could this result be overturned if one assumes a textual corruption. The text reads: *...wa-ilā waqtinā wa-ᶜasrinā kāna mashāyikhu'l-taṣawwufi wa'l-aʾimmatu minhum, wa'l-abdālu wa'l-zuhhādu wa'l-qurrāʾu wa'l-ṣāliḥūna muqtadīna (sic) bi'l-aʾimmati mubāyinīna li-ahli'l-bidᶜati*, etc., where instead of *qurrāʾ* one would have expected *fuqarāʾ*, all the more so since a few lines later one reads: 'And the true act in the *sunna* (delete *maᶜa*) is renunciation (*zuhd*) of the world in conformity with the Messenger of God, his choice of poverty (*faqr*) and wretchedness (*maskana*)', etc. The text of the MS contains several corruptions at this point.[13]

Neither the arguments for nor those against the identity of the two authors are compelling. The former could also be explained as due to mutual dependence or possibly dependence on common traditions

---

13 Ibn Taymiyya: *Al-ṣūfiyya wa'l-fuqarāʾ*, Cairo, 1348, p. 25: Some, among them Abū Ḥafṣ al-Suhrawardī, prefer the designation *ṣūfī*, whereas others, indeed the majority, prefer the designation *faqīr*.

(for *ghurba* cf., for example, Junayd in Jullābī: *Kashf al-maḥjūb*, *bāb al-taṣawwuf*, trans. Nicholson, p. 39), the latter as due to a change in the author. But the assumption of a change is very unlikely, and the weight of the arguments against is perhaps heavier, especially if one adds this point as well: all the authentic works of Ma^{c}mar in our MS bear the name of the author, in some cases even several times. Why should the *Adab al-mulūk* also not bear the author's name if it was by Ma^{c}mar? Furthermore, although the works of Ma^{c}mar coincide with the *Adab al-mulūk* in rejecting everything unorthodox and in constantly summoning the reader to the Koran and *sunna*, Ma^{c}mar is (or seems to me) rather stiff, lifeless, schematizing, harsh and quick to suspect heresy. On the other hand, the *Adab al-mulūk* when compared with Tirmidhī, Sarrāj, Makkī and others, appears rather schematic and unoriginal, whereas compared with Ma^{c}mar it is more 'mystical', more distinctive, warmer and wholly lacking the Ḥanbalite tinge.

Is it a work of Ibn-i Khafīf? This would be possible chronologically because Ibn-i Khafīf died in 371/982; and it would fit that the author of the *Adab al-mulūk* (p. 73) refers to a work by himself on the *samā^c*, because Ibn-i Khafīf wrote a *Kitāb al-samā^c* (Daylamī: *Sīrat*, p. 213, l. 3). But our work bears the clear title *Adab al-mulūk*, and nothing is known of any such book by Ibn-i Khafīf. Daylamī: *Sīrat-i Ibn-i Khafīf*, pp. 212 f., and Junayd al-Shirāzī: *Shadd al-izār*, Tehran, 1328, pp. 42 f., present a list of Ibn-i Khafīf's works with a total of 30 titles. Each of the two enumerates 27 titles but each mentions three which the other lacks so that the two sources combined provide 30 titles. Among these an *Adab al-mulūk* does not occur.

Is it a work of Sulamī? For him as well this would be chronologically possible, and he as well wrote a book on the *samā^c* (Jullābī: *Kashf al-maḥjūb*, ed. Zhukovski, p. 523, last line/trans. Nicholson, p. 401, *GAS*, I, p. 674, no. 23). But in Sulamī's case too there are no grounds whatsoever to believe he wrote an *Adab al-mulūk*. The unlikelihood that the work was written in Nayshābūr points to the same conclusion.

And regarding both of them the same question arises: why should the author's name be missing, whereas it apparently occurred in the *Faḍl al-taṣawwuf* of Ibn-i Khafīf which has been removed (see here p. 136) and is still present in the writings of Sulamī which will be discussed next.

e) ABŪ ᶜABD AL-RAḤMĀN MUḤAMMAD B. AL-ḤUSAYN AL-SULAMĪ (d. 412/1021)

1) *Nasīm al-arwāḥ* (no. 3, pp. 95-105).

Incipit: وهذا كتاب نسيم الأرواح مما جمعه الإمام أبو عبد الرحمن محمد بن الحسين بن موسى السلمى ... بسم الله الرحمن الرحيم. صفة العارفين: أسعدهم الله بإخلاص طاعته ونعّمهم بوجوه حقائق وحدانيته ...

Explicit: ... وإذا غبتُ عنهم لا يغتابونى فعرفتُه فإذا هو خالد الكاتب رضى الله عنه وعن المشايخ أجمعين.

The first sentence is not fully clear. Is *Nasīm al-arwāḥ* a collection by Sulamī or a piece compiled from collections by Sulamī. If the latter is the case: did Sulamī himself put together this partial collection, or was it put together by someone else? Whatever the answer, the work before us does not appear to be in a final form. It is either a preliminary sketch or a fragment or a record of ideas and the fruits of reading, something unfinished without a beginning and without a proper end. The title *Nasīm al-arwāḥ* gives no idea of the contents nor finds a justification anywhere in the text, but otherwise 'refreshing breezes for the spirit' are mentioned on other occasions as well (Maᶜmar: *Dhikr maᶜānī al-taṣawwuf*, our MS p. 116, l. 6; Daylamī: *Sīrat-i Ibn-i Khafīf*, p. 265, last line). A chain of transmitters on p. 102 could even raise doubts about the attribution to Sulamī: 'I heard Jaᶜfar b. Muḥammad al-Abharī say: I heard Abū ᶜAlī Aḥmad b. Muḥammad b. Mazdīn al-Nihāwandī, known as al-Qūmasān (sic), say: I heard Ibrāhīm b. Shaybān say: I heard Abū ᶜAbdallāh al-Maghribī say.' In place of Qūmasān the *nisba* Qūmasānī should be substituted which is mentioned by Suyūṭī: *Lubb al-lubāb* and was, for instance, borne by a certain Muḥammad b. ᶜUthmān b. Zayrak who died in 471/1078-79 (Dhahabī: *ᶜIbar*, III, p. 277/ᶜAbd al-Ḥayy: *Shadharāt*, III, p. 341). I have not been able to trace either our Abharī or our Qūmasānī/Nihāwandī, yet it is not this that could make one suspicious but that Sulamī here needs three intermediary links to reach back to Abū ᶜAbdallāh al-Maghribī (d. 299/911-12); in the *Ṭabaqāt* there are always only one or two. None the less, there are other cases in which Sulamī enumerates chains of intermediary transmitters of similarly varying length going back to one and the same speaker. In our case only identification of the two dubious transmitters (Abharī and Qūmasānī) will be able to provide anything conclusive.

The work opens with an impressive description of the knowers of God as God's chosen ones: God has made them into what they are. There then follow some pithy sayings on love of God, as well as maxims and poems of early Sufis, including (p. 97) *Dīwān al-Ḥallāj*, M57, in Ibn Yazdāniyār's version (*Rawḍat al-murīdīn*, Massignon: *Passion*, II, bibliographie no. 228/*GAL S*, II, p. 1006, no. 99) in the form in which Massignon has published the verses in the *Dīwān*, M57, p. 92, ftn. 3, but in our MS attributed to Bisṭāmī, not to Ḥallāj. Then comes the attitude of Sufis to language during the *samā*ᶜ and in the middle of this (p. 99) there is a *bāb uṣūl al-mashāyikh fi'l-samā*ᶜ with additional, partially known dicta of early Sufis. The story of Junayd's encounter with a hermit on Mt. Sinai and the latter's claim to have read in the Gospels that the *samā*ᶜ is only right for a certain group in Islam (p. 100), also occurs in somewhat different words in the anonymous author: *Adab al-mulūk* (our MS, p. 72). At the end once again words about knowledge (of God) and love. In the photocopy I have before me p. 104 directly follows p. 102. This is clearly because of mistaken pagination as nothing in the text appears to be missing.

2) (*Risāla fī kalām al-Shāfiᶜī fi'l-taṣawwuf*) (no. 9, pp. 145-63)

Incipit: بسم الله الرحمن الرحيم. قال الشيخ أبو بكر محمد بن الحسن رحمة الله عليه قال سمعت الشيخ الفقيه أبا الحسن على بن محمد بن أحمد قال سمعت الشيخ الأوحد أبا الحسين على بن الحسين بن على قال سمعت أبا عبد الرحمن محمد بن الحسين بن موسى السلمى رحمة الله عليه يقول الحمد لله أولاً وآخرا وصلى الله على سيدنا محمد النبي وآله وسلم كثيرًا. سألنى بعض إخوانى: هل تعرف للإمام أبى عبد الله محمد بن إدريس الشافعى رضى الله عنه شيئًا من الكلام فى نصيحة المجاهدات وآداب المعاملات واستقامة الأحوال؟ فقلت: نعم كان الشافعى رضى الله عنه صحب الصوفية وتكلم على طريقتهم وأخبر عن شمائلهم وآدابهم مما أبينه فى هذا الكتاب

عنه بأسانيد صحيحة وما يدلّ على أنه عارف برسومهم وآدابهم واستخرتُ الله تعالى فى جمع فصول وحكايات عنه تدلّ على ذلك والله المعين عليه بفضله وسعة رحمته.

فمن ذلك مـا سمعتُ أبا العباس محمد بن يعقوب يقول سمعت الربيع بن سليمان يقول: (a) دخلتُ على الشافعى وهو مريض (مرفض .hs يرفض يعنى يبكى rand) فسألنى عن أصحابنا فقلت إنهم يتكلمون فقال الشافعى: ما ناظرتُ أحدًا قط على الغلبة وبودّى أن جميع الخلق تعلموا هذا الكتاب يعنى كتبه ولا يُنسَب الىَّ منه شىء. (b) قال هذا الكلام يوم الأحد ومات يوم الخميس وانصرفنا من جنازته ليلة الجمعة ورأينا هلال شعبان سنة أربع ومائتين ...

Explicit:

وما أكثر الإخوان حين تعدّهم ولكنهم فى النائبـات قليـل

أخبرنى ابو بكر بن عبد الله بن شاذان قال سمعت جعفر بن محمد الأخلاطى

(breaks off)

The title only occurs in the table of contents on the flyleaf of the collective MS. The work is incomplete; the end is missing.

This writing was unknown until now. It deals with sayings of Shāfiᶜī which coincide with concerns of Sufism. The individual statements bear chains of transmission which in most cases go back to Shāfiᶜī. The direct transmitters from whom Sulamī received the reports for his book are in part already known as sources he used in other of his writings and in part can be verified in biographical dictionaries. Some of them still remain to be identified. In what follows I give a list of all these persons and in each case add in parenthesis where one can find them without, however, aiming at completeness. Biographical details of some of them can be looked up in the introduction and in the footnotes of Sharība's edition of the *Ṭabaqāt al-ṣūfiyya*, Cairo, 1953. By 'Pedersen' is meant the introduction to Pedersen's edition of the *Ṭabaqāt,* Leiden, 1960, where all the direct transmitters of the *Ṭabaqāt* are collected together. *Ṣuḥba* refers to Kister's edition of Sulamī's *Ādāb al-ṣuḥba wa-ḥusn al-ᶜishra*, Jerusalem, 1954. Ḍabbī refers to Muḥammad b. ᶜAbdallāh al-Ḍabbī: *Tārīkh-i Nayshābūr talkhīṣ Aḥmad b. Muḥammad b. al-Khalīfa al-Naysābūrī*, Tehran, 1339. *ᶜIbar* is Dhahabī: *Al-ᶜibar fī khabar man ghabar*, Kuwait, 1960-63. *Ḥuffāẓ* is Dhahabī: *Tadhkirat al-ḥuffāẓ*, Hyderabad, 1955-58. *Shadharāt* is ᶜAbd al-Ḥayy b. al-ᶜImād: *Shadharāt al-dhahab*, Cairo, 1350-51. Subkī is Subkī:

Ṭabaqāt al-Shāfi^ciyya, Cairo, 1324. Sam^cānī is Sam^cānī: *Al-ansāb*, Hyderabad, 1962 ff.

^cAbdallāh b. al-Ḥusayn al-Bustī (perhaps Bushtī should be read: from Busht, a district near Nayshābūr)
^cAbdallāh b. al-Ḥusayn al-Salāmī (or Sallāmī)
^cAbdallāh b. Ibrāhīm b. Ja^cfar al-Bazzār al-Zaydī (*^cIbar*, II, p. 359; *Shadharāt*, III, p. 76)
^cAbdallāh b. Muḥammad b. ^cAbdallāh al-Thallāj, in Baghdad (*^cIbar*, III, p. 34; *Shadharāt*, III, p. 122)
^cAbdallāh b. Muḥammad b. ^cAlī b. Ziyād (*^cIbar*, II, p. 342; *Shadharāt*, III, p. 56)
^cAbdallāh b. Mūsā al-Sal(l)āmī (Pedersen, p. 77, no.18)
^cAbdallāh b. Sa^cīd b. ^cAbd al-Raḥmān al-Bustī, in Hamadān[14]
^cAbd al-Raḥmān b. ^cAbdallāh al-Dhubyānī
^cAbd al-Raḥmān b. Abī Bakr al-Jurjānī
Abū ^cAmr b. Maṭar (Pedersen, p. 86, no. 112; *Ṣuḥba*, p. 42)
(Aḥmad b. Muḥammad) b. Miqsam al-Muqri^ɔ, Abū'l-Ḥasan, in Baghdad (Pedersen, p. 78, no. 35)
Aḥmad b. Muḥammad b. Rumayḥ (Pedersen, p. 78, no. 37)
^cAlī b. ^cAbdallāh (perhaps Pedersen, p. 79, no. 43)
^cAlī b. Abī ^cAmr al-Balkhī
^cAlī b. Aḥmad b. Ibrāhīm (*Ṣuḥba*, p. 45)
^cAlī b. Jandal al-Qazwīnī (Ḍabbī, p. 95, last line: ^cAlī b. Ḥabdhal al-Qazwīnī)
^cAlī b. Muḥammad b. Ja^cfar al-Bukhārī al-Adīb
^cAlī b. Muḥammad b. ^cUmar al-Faqīh, in Ray (*^cIbar*, III, p. 64; *Shadharāt*, III, p. 149)
^cAlī b. Sa^cīd b. ^cUthmān (perhaps Pedersen, p. 80, no. 54; hardly *Tārīkh Baghdād*, XI, p. 431, which does not fit chronologically)
^cAlī b. ^cUmar al-Ḥāfiẓ (al-Dāraquṭnī) (Pedersen, p. 80, no. 55)
^cAyyāsh b. al-Ḥasan (*Tārīkh Baghdād*, XII, pp. 279 f.)
al-Ḥasan b. Rashīq al-Miṣrī (Pedersen, p. 81, no. 65)
Ḥassān b. Muḥammad al-Faqīh, Abū'l-Walīd (*^cIbar*, II, p. 281; *Shadharāt*, II, p. 380)
al-Ḥusayn (?)
al-Ḥusayn b. Aḥmad b. Ja^cfar al-Rāzī, Abū ^cAbdallāh (Pedersen, p. 81, no. 68)

---

14 Possibly identical with ^cAbdallāh b. Sa^cīd al-Adīb al-Bushtī, from whom Abū ^cAbdallāh Muḥammad al-Ḥakīm al-Naysābūrī (d. 405/1014) transmitted (Sam^cānī: *Ansāb*, Hyderabad, 1963, II, p. 246, ll. 4-6).

al-Ḥusayn b. Aḥmad b. Mūsā (Pedersen, p. 81, no. 69)
al-Ḥusayn b. Yaḥyā (Pedersen, p. 82, no. 73)
Manṣūr b. ᶜAbdallāh al-Iṣbahānī (Pedersen, p. 82, no. 82)
Manṣūr b. ᶜAbdallāh al-Ushnānī al-Harawī (perhaps Pedersen, p. 82, no. 81; *ᶜIbar*, III, p. 76; *Shadharāt*, III, p. 162, none of which have the *nisba* Ushnānī)
Muḥammad b. al-ᶜAbbās al-ᶜUṣmī (Pedersen, p. 83, no. 84; *Ḥuffāẓ*, p. 1006)
Muḥammad b. ᶜAbd al-Aᶜlā al-Faqīh, Abū Bakr
Muḥammad b. ᶜAbd al-ᶜAzīz al-Zaghūrī, Abū ᶜAlī (Samᶜānī, VI, p. 306)
Muḥammad b. ᶜAbdallāh
Muḥammad b. ᶜAbdallāh b. Muḥammad b. Zakariyyā (Pedersen, p. 84, no. 89; *ᶜIbar*, III, p. 41; *Ḥuffāẓ*, p. 1013; *Shadharāt*, III, p. 129)
Muḥammad b. ᶜAbdallāh b. Shādhān, Abū Bakr (Pedersen, p. 83, no. 86)
Muḥammad b. Aḥmad al-Faqīh, Abū Sahl
Muḥammad b. Aḥmad b. ᶜAbd al-Aᶜlā al-Maghribī
Muḥammad b. Aḥmad b. Muḥammad b. Sahl (*Ṭabaqāt al-ṣūfiyya*, ed. Pedersen, p. 25, penult. line: as indirect transmitter)
Muḥammad b. ᶜAlī al-Ḥāfiẓ al-Isfarāᵓinī, Abū ᶜAlī (*Ḥuffāẓ*, p. 1002)
Muḥammad b. ᶜAlī b. Ṭalḥa al-Marwazī (or Marūdī or Marwarrūdhī, unclear, Abū Naṣr
Muḥammad b. Jaᶜfar b. Muḥammad b. Maṭar (*ᶜIbar*, II, pp. 316 f.; *Shadharāt*, III, p. 31)
Muḥammad b. Muḥammad b. Yaᶜqūb (*ᶜIbar*, II, p. 349; *Shadharāt*, III, p. 67)
Muḥammad b. al-Qāsim b. ᶜAbd al-Raḥmān al-ᶜAtakī, Abū Manṣūr
Muḥammad b. Sulaymān, Abū Sahl (Pedersen, p. 87, no. 119)
Muḥammad b. Ṭāhir al-Wazīrī (*Ṣuḥba*, pp. 26, 40, 44, 46, 58, 66)
Muḥammad b. Yaᶜqūb, Abū'l-ᶜAbbās (Pedersen, p. 87, no. 121)
Nāṣir b. Muḥammad al-Anṣārī (perhaps *Tārīkh Baghdād*, XIII, p. 438; Nāṣir b. Muḥammad al-Baghdādī, who heard Shiblī lecture)
Naṣr b. Muḥammad b. Aḥmad b. Yaᶜqūb (Pedersen, p. 87, no. 126)
al-Qāsim b. Muḥammad b. al-Ḥasan al-Miṣrī, in Mecca
Ṭāhir b. ᶜAbdallāh al-Baghdādī (Subkī, II, p. 228)

The transmitters at the other end of the chain of transmission, the eye- and earwitnesses of Shāfiᶜī, are for the most part the otherwise well-known students of Shāfiᶜī: his son Muḥammad (Subkī, I, p. 225), ᶜAbdallāh b. ᶜAbd al-Ḥakam (*Shadharāt*, II, p. 34), Abū Thawr (Subkī, I, p. 227), Muzanī (I, p. 239), al-Ḥasan b. Muḥammad al-Zaᶜfarānī (I, p. 250), al-Ḥusayn al-Karābīsī (I, p. 251), Ḥarmala b. Yaḥyā (I, p. 257), al-Rabīᶜ b. Sulaymān (I, p. 259), al-Faḍl b. al-Rabīᶜ (I, p. 268), Buwayṭī (I, p. 275), Yūnus b. ᶜAbd al-Aᶜlā (I, p. 279), Muḥammad b. Ismāᶜīl al-Bukhārī (II, p. 2), Ibn ᶜAqīl (II, p. 19), Muḥammad b. Salām al-Jumaḥī (*Shadharāt*, II, p. 71), Ḥumaydī (*ᶜIbar*, I, p. 377; *Shadharāt,* II, p. 45), Sulaymān b. Dāwūd al-Mahdī (perhaps Subkī, I, p. 263; *Tārīkh Baghdād*, IX, p. 31). In addition to these there are also Aḥmad b. Muḥammad b. ᶜAbd al-Karīm al-Baṣrī, Ayyūb b. Sulaymān, Ḥusayn b. Zayd, Ḥusayn al-ᶜIyāḍī, Maᶜmar b. Shabīb, Muḥammad b. Aḥmad (?) and ᶜUmāra b. Zayd. A few lines are not traced all the way back to Shāfiᶜī.

Our fragment contains 94 reports from and about Shāfiᶜī (not numbered in the MS):

(p. 145) 1) a. I have never disputed with someone in order to win but I would like everything that I have written to enter into the heads of people without it being attributed to me. b. This was said on a Sunday. Shāfiᶜī died on the following Thursday. We left his funeral on Thursday night and beheld the new moon of Shaᶜbān, 204 A.H.

2) The worst sinner against himself is a person who submits (p. 146) to someone who does not honor him, and shows interest in the love of someone who in no way profits him. Variant: + praises someone whom he does not know.

3) Whoever is dominated by an intense love of the world, enthusiasm to serve its representatives clings to him, and whoever is <not> satisfied (?) with modest needs?, humility (?) disappears from him.

4) ᶜAbdallāh b. ᶜAbd al-Ḥakam said to Shāfiᶜī: If you wish to reside in the place, i.e. Egypt, you have to be able to show the authorities that you have food for a year and a gathering. Shāfiᶜī replied: Whoever is not honored out of fear of God has no honor. I was born in Ghazza and grew up in the Ḥijāz. There we did not have food for one night and yet we did not spend the night in hunger.

5) Why do you always carry a walking-stick although you are not weak? Shāfiᶜī: In order to remember that I am on a journey, namely in the here and now.

6) Whoever learns the Koran, his worth increases. Whoever looks into *fiqh*, his estimation rises. Whoever writes down *ḥadīth*, his argument becomes strong. Whoever looks into philology, his spirit becomes refined. Whoever takes a look at arithmetic, his power of judgement is improved. Whoever does not protect his soul, his knowledge is of no use to him.

7) Surah 2/155: 'And We will try you with something of fear and hunger.' Shāfiʿī: fear of the Enemy, hunger during Ramaḍān. 'With loss of money': expenditure of money. 'And souls': illnesses. 'And fruits': alms. 'And congratulate the steadfast': for the alms that they give. (p. 147)

8) The most useful savings are fear of God, the most harmful are insolence.

9) Knowledge is not what is stored in the memory but what is of use.

10) Associating with someone who is not afraid of disgrace is disgrace on the Day of Judgement.

11) Mubarrad: God bless Shāfiʿī because he was the best poet, the best man of letters and the best knower of the Koran. One of my companions informed me: ʿAbd al-Raḥmān b. Mahdī lost a son. Shāfiʿī then wrote to him: My brother, comfort yourself as you would comfort others, and consider ugly in your behavior what you consider ugly in the behavior of others. Know the most painful misfortune is loss of a joy and not receiving a reward, especially when the two are joined together... Snatch your share of happiness, my brother, when it comes close to you, before you have to seek it and it is removed from you. God give you perseverance in suffering and cause a reward for perseverance to come to you and to us! And he wrote to him: two verses follow.

12) Striving after the superfluities of the here and now is a punishment which God has in store for the adherents of *tawḥīd*.

13) This knowledge of ours is not attainable by means of money and ambition, but only by means of self-abasement, restrictions, enthusiasm in serving the learned and humility. (p. 148)

14) Shāfiʿī, while under way from Ṣanʿāʾ to Mecca with 10,000 dinars, gives away all the money to suppliants who visit him at a halting station before Mecca.

15) Oh Rabīʿ, do not speak about what is not your concern, for when you speak thus, the words dominate you and not the other way round.

16) I fear that the person who seeks knowledge without an intention will acquire none of it.

17) The sign of a *ṣiddīq* is that he is a friend (*ṣadīq*) to the friend of a friend.

18) No joy is equal to being with like-minded persons (*ikhwān*), nor any grief equal to separation from them.

19) Whoever seeks the here and now, knowledge is recommended to him, and whoever seeks the hereafter, knowledge is recommended to him as well.

20) No one in the here and now will be perfected without four things: religiosity, trustworthiness, honorableness and composure.

21) On his deathbed (p. 149): Today I quit this world and leave my brethren, drink death's cup and come before God. I shall be confronted with my bad deeds, and by God I do not know whether my spirit will attain Paradise and I can congratulate it, or whether it will enter Hell and I must lament it. Then Shāfiʿī recited: five verses follow.

22) I have found a home in poverty in such a way that I will never experience fear of it.

23) What most adorns those with knowledge is poverty with modest needs, and satisfaction with both.

24) The poverty of those with knowledge is voluntary poverty; the poverty of the foolish is imposed poverty.

25) Oh Abū Mūsā, I have been reduced to rags three times, and you have seen me eat fish and dates because I couldn't find anything else.

26) (p. 150) Shāfiʿī's exhortations before Hārūn al-Rashīd.

27) Shāfiʿī: I heard my father say: I associated with the Sufis for ten years but I only learned these two sentences from them: The moment is a sword, and the best form of protection is for you to be in ecstasy.

28) Khaḍir gives Khawwāṣ information about Shāfiʿī, to the effect that: he is one of the *awtād*. (p. 151) Aḥmad b. Ḥanbal is a *ṣiddīq*. And there will never again be someone like Bishr b. al-Ḥārith. Khawwāṣ attained this encounter with Khaḍir because of his piety towards his mother.

29) Shāfiʿī hears a female singer and reproaches someone who is with him for being insensitive because the latter finds no pleasure in her singing.

30) Songs of camel drivers, homesick songs and embellishment of the voice when singing poems are permitted, but not descriptions of physical beauty.

31) Whoever does not allow himself to become excited (*ṭarab*) is neither intelligent nor noble.

32) A letter of Shāfiʿī: Hearts are cornfields of the tongues. Sow the noble word! Even if everything does not flourish, some of it will grow.

33) (p. 152) Three verses of Shāfiʿī.

34) Humility belongs to the good character of the noble; pride belongs to the stigmas of the ignoble.

35) The worthy man does not see his worth, the man of virtue does not see his virtue.

36) Oh Rabīʿ, be concerned with asceticism! Asceticism suits the ascetic better than jewelry suits the full-bosomed maid.

37) I have found a home in poverty in such a way that I will never experience fear of it (= no. 22).

38) Poverty is the adornment of men.

39) Since I found no path to the satisfaction of a scholar (? of the world?), I was obliged to use what was true in my eyes.

40) If the active *fuqahāʾ* are not the friends of God, then God has no friend.

41) (p. 153) The intelligent person is someone whose intelligence restrains (*ʿaqala*) him from everything blameworthy.

42) A sermon for the general public, advice for the like-minded (*ikhwān*) and reminding (*tadhkira*) for the special people — these are a duty which God has pre-

scribed for the intelligent among the believers so that the *sunna* does not perish and the prescriptions are not despised.

43) The best of this world and the world to come lies in five things: in the disappearance of the ego (*nafs*), in ceasing to cause others harm, in earning (also: doing) only what is permitted, in fear of God and in relying on God in all situations.

44) The jewels of the believer lie in three things: in concealing poverty so that people think you are rich. In concealing anger so that people think you are content. In concealing calamity so that people think you are a person of good fortune.

45) Whoever wishes to be judged in a friendly manner, let him think well of people.

46) Manly virtue is holding back the bodily limbs from what in no way concerns them.

47) A poem by Shāfiʿī against worldly splendor, consisting of three verses.

48) (p. 154) The Sufi is no Sufi as long as he does not possess four characteristics: he must be a lazybones, a late sleeper, a glutton and a chatterbox.[15]

49) Only a sincere man recognizes hypocrisy.

50) Generosity and nobility cover up errors as long as innovation (heresy) is not also involved.

51) A man is there where he sets himself down. Whoever is weak toward himself is lost in the end.

52) When love is a beauty (sic), it is a test. When it is ugliness, it is abandonment by God.

53) Two verses: do not accuse God of anything.

54) What does comme il faut (?) mean? Shāfiʿī: To stand by the truth the way it is.

55) Directing people is more difficult than directing animals.

56) Whoever is honest to a brother in brotherliness accepts his shortcomings, fills in his gaps and forgives him his mistakes.

57) (p. 155) Manly virtue rests on four pillars: kindness, generosity, humility and piety (*nusuk*).

58) Whoever listens with his ear becomes a narrator. Whoever listens with his heart becomes a summoner. Whoever preaches by his own action is an upright guide.

59) Whoever treats you lovingly binds you. Whoever treats you unfairly lets you go free.

---

[15] On the other hand, cf. Sulamī: *Jawāmiʿ ādāb al-ṣūfiyya*, MS Berlin, Ahlwardt no. 3081, 65a, ll. 9-10: Junayd: Our foundation consists of three things: We eat only out of necessity, sleep only when overcome and speak only when forced to. Sleeping only when overcome is also found in Kubrā: *Risāla ilā'l-hāʾim/Risālat al-sāʾir*, no. 9, ed. Molé: *Traités mineurs de Nağm al-Dīn Kubrā*, in *Annales islamologiques* 4, Cairo, 1963, pp. 36-56 (accordingly, Kubrā: *Fawāʾiḥ*, Introduction, pp. 48-49, should be corrected to *al-nawm ʿan ghalaba*).

60) God created you free. Be as He created you!

61) Adornment of knowledge is scrupulosity and patience (*ḥilm*).

62) Knowledge is handsome (?) only by means of three things: fear of God, conformity with the *sunna* and supervision (*ḥisba*).

63) Questioned by a man who wanted to bequeath something to the most intelligent of his countrymen, Shāfiʿī replied: He should give it to the most ascetic of them because no one is intelligent who loves what God hates, i.e. the world.

64) Never say: the Messenger, but always: the Messenger of God, out of respect.

65) During a religious festival I (Shāfiʿī) had no money to give away. My family said: You have made it a practice to bestow something on certain people. You should take out a loan. I borrowed 90 dinars, set aside 20 for my own expenses and distributed the rest. But then when another Qurayshī complained to me about the need he was in, (p. 156) I let him take everything I still had. Thereupon an envoy from the Barmekid Jaʿfar b. Yaḥyā appeared and took me to the latter's house where I informed him of my situation. In fact he had heard a voice at night which ordered him to fetch me. At first I received 500 dinars from the vizier and in the end 2,000 dinars.

66) Shāfiʿī recited the Koran every Ramaḍān sixty times while performing the ritual prayers.

67) Shāfiʿī divided the night into three parts: one for writing, one for praying and one for sleep.

68) A verse on *junūn*.

69) Shāfiʿī learns of a person's death and goes to the man's son to offer him his condolences, although the place is very far away. Four verses by Shāfiʿī.

70) (p. 157) I have never lied, otherwise I would not have received what I am famous for. I have never sworn an oath by God, neither a true nor a false one.[16]

71) Freedom is nobility and fear of God. When these two things are united in a person, he is free.

72) Whoever adorns himself with what is false dishonors his innermost interior.

73) Four verses by Shāfiʿī on the transitoriness of the world and against false hopes.

74) Live in the company of noble men and then you will live nobly! Do not live with the ignoble, for then you will be regarded as ignoble!

75) Shāfiʿī was accustomed to pray during one third of the night and never to recite more than 50 Koranic verses. He never (p. 158) came upon a verse which mentioned God's mercy without begging God to show mercy on himself and all the believers. Whenever he met a verse about punishment, he sought refuge with God

---

16 Cf. Sulamī: *Jawāmiʿ ādāb al-ṣūfiyya*, 65a, ll. 4-5: Sahl b. ʿAbdallāh (al-Tustarī): It is characteristic of the honest that they do not swear by God, either when telling the truth or when lying...

and begged deliverance for himself and all the believers. Hope and fear appear to have been united in him.

76) In discussions it was all the same to me (Shāfiʿī) whether what was true was spoken by me or by my partner.

77) Shāfiʿī gave a beggar a dinar, which was all he had at the time. His friends said: A dirham would also have served the purpose. Shāfiʿī: I feel ashamed if I give less than I am able.

78) God created flies in order to humiliate kings with them. A fly is not worried about all the weapons in royal palaces.

79) Dispute over theological knowledge hardens men's hearts and creates resentment.

80) God praised His Prophet, raised up his word, taught him and educated him. (p. 159) He spoke to him: Trust in someone living who will not die. The people are in various circumstances: they trust in themselves, in their money, in some authority, in a gift on the part of human beings. Everyone relies on someone living who will die, or on something which will pass away. God lifted His Prophet above this and ordered him to trust in someone living who will not die. Yesterday I fathomed two Koranic verses (*istinbāṭ*) which exempt me from seeking the world: surah 10/3: 'He directs the affair. There is no intercessor except with His permission.' Suchlike is found many times in the Koran... The intercessors are all powerless if God does not give permission for it. And surah 11/3: 'And ask your Lord for forgiveness, then turn to Him in repentance, and He will give you a good usufruct up to a fixed term.' God promises everyone who repents and asks for forgiveness, usufruct until death. It says there as well (surah 11/3): 'And He will show His favor to everyone who is blessed.' In the hereafter. We are not really repentant as one should be but God recognizes in us love of those who repent, and so He gives us in the here and now a good usufruct.

81) Speech is wakefulness of the intelligence; silence is sleep of the intelligence. Pay attention to how you look after the intelligence when it sleeps and when it is awake.

82) When Shāfiʿī transmitted *ḥadīth*s, he recited them like surahs of the Koran.

83) During a severe illness he said: Oh God, if this is Your pleasure, increase it even further! When Idrīs al-Khawlānī was informed of this, he had him told: We do not wish to live any longer if you are in misfortune (?). Shāfiʿī had him given the reply: Beseech God on my behalf! (p. 160)

84) For sixteen years the only food I had was butter (*rakhf*) and dates, of which I ate just enough so that my body could continue to exist. I did so because I wished to learn knowledge and *fiqh*. I left it to God, and God granted this to me. (Unclear: did he leave the hunger or did he turn his body over to God? The former would agree with the change in the life of Abū Saʿīd b. Abī'l-Khayr, *Asrār al-tawḥīd*, ed. Muḥammad Riḍā Shafīʿī-i Kadkanī, Tehran, 1366, pp. 34 f./ed. Dhabīḥallāh Ṣafā, Tehran, 1332, pp. 37 f./trans. by John O'Kane, *The Secrets of God's Mystical One-*

ness, Persian Heritage Series no. 38, Costa Mesa [Calif.]-New York, 1992, pp. 101 f.)

85) The ornament of those with knowledge is fear of God, their jewelry is kindness, and their beauty nobility of the soul.

86) The source of works is contentment with God. Scrupulosity is the pillar of religion. Hunger is the marrow of the worship of God. The secure fortress is being careful in speech.

87) The believer is of noble spirit. He will not let himself be deflected from his religion, though he lets himself be cheated of money; for he prefers the hereafter to the here and now, and generosity to avarice — sustaining a broken heart and many cares which he alone suffers. Should he acquire something, he then distributes it. Should he lose something, he does not search for it.

88) Those with knowledge cannot make any greater mistake than to long for something which God would have them renounce, and to renounce something which God would have them long for.

89) Two verses by Shāfiʿī:

Grief is a favor and the Decision is all-powerful.
Whatever is inscribed on the Tablet will happen.
Wait for reinvigoration and its intermediary causes,
abandoning hope, as best you can, in reinvigoration!

90) Shāfiʿī in the presence of a dying man: Oh God, by Your lack of need of him and by his need of You, forgive him!

91) (p. 161) Ibn ʿAbd al-Ḥakam: We were sitting one day discussing the ascetics and the worshippers of God and their eloquence which has been transmitted to us, until we came to Dhū'l-Nūn. ʿUmar b. Nubāta entered and asked: What are you disputing about? We answered: We were talking about the ascetics and the worshippers of God and their eloquence which has been transmitted to us. He remarked: By God, I never saw anyone more eloquent and more scrupulous than Shāfiʿī. — One day he and I and al-Ḥārith b. Labīd went to Ṣafā. Al-Ḥārith, the slave of Ṣāliḥ al-Murrī, opened surah 77/38 and recited: 'This is the day of decision; we have joined you together with the ancients', etc. At that I saw how Shāfiʿī wriggled, then wept bitterly and finally could do nothing but recite: I take refuge with You from the speech of liars and the turning away of those who are indifferent. My God, to You the hearts of the knowers (of God) submit and to You bow down the powers of comprehension of those filled with longing. My God, give unto me through Your generosity, elevate me through Your (forgiving) concealment, forgive me my cursing through the nobility of Your face, oh most Merciful of all who are merciful! — I journeyed to him in ʿIrāq to hear him lecture. While I was sitting on the riverbank to perform a minor ritual ablution, a man walked past me and said: Young man, perform your ablution well! God bestow blessings on you! I followed on his tracks. He turned around and asked me: Young man, do you have a request? I replied: Teach me something; perhaps it will be useful for me. He: Know that whoever is honest before God will be

saved. Whoever is concerned for his religion will be spared from destruction. Whoever renounces the world, his eyes will be cooled when he experiences God's reward on the final day. Should I not tell you still more? I said yes. He continued: Renounce the here and now, and strive for the hereafter, be honest before God in all things and then you will be saved on that final day. It was Shāfiᶜī. I heard these words from him.

92) When there was discussion in Shāfiᶜī's presence about the heart's understanding (*fahm al-qalb*), he said: Whoever wants God (p. 162) to open or to illuminate his heart, let him stop talking about things that do not concern him, let him give up sins, avoid acts of disobedience and be secretive about what goes on between him and God. If he acts like this, God will reveal to him a form of knowledge which will distract him from everything else, even during death, because he will be so preoccupied.

93) Shāfiᶜī is summoned at night to the court by Hārūn al-Rashīd and given money because of his family connection with him through the Quraysh. Shāfiᶜī, when coming before the caliph, recites in secret a prayer for protection used by Muḥammad. The text of the prayer is given (p. 163). Al-Faḍl b. Rabīᶜ, who accompanies him, learns it and recites it whenever he goes before someone whose unpredictability frightens him.

94) Six verses by Shāfiᶜī about protecting the soul, perseverance and other subjects.

The text breaks off.

Independently of Sulamī and shortly after him, Abū Nuᶜaym al-Iṣbahānī in his *Ḥilyat al-awliyā*ʾ, IX, pp. 63-161, likewise compiled a long series of sayings of Shāfiᶜī. From these Ibn al-Jawzī (d. 597/1200) then made a few selections and also added some materials to them in his *Ṣifat al-ṣafwa*, Hyderabad, 1355, II, pp. 140-47, which is a new reworking and a supplement to the *Ḥilya*. In this connection Sulamī was not used either by Abū Nuᶜaym or by Ibn al-Jawzī. From Abū Nuᶜaym's collection only 13 or 14 dicta correspond to sayings in our Sulamī fragment and, with the exception of two of them, they all have different chains of transmission. From the supplementary material in Ibn al-Jawzī one saying corresponds with a report of Sulamī's but likewise bears a different *isnād* and comes from a work of a certain Muḥammad b. Ṭāhir al-Naysābūrī. A comparative list looks as follows:

Sulamī	Abū Nu^c^aym: *Ḥilya*	Ibn al-Jawzī: *Ṣifa*
no. 1a	IX, p. 118	II, p. 142
no. 1b	IX, p. 68	II, p. 147
Sulamī	Abū Nu^c^aym: *Ḥilya*	Ibn al-Jawzī: *Ṣifa*
no. 6	IX, p. 123 (also *Tārīkh Baghdād*, VII, p. 276, ll. 12-13)	II, p. 144
no. 8	IX, p. 123 (same *isnād* as Sulamī)	
no. 9	IX, p. 123 (same *isnād*)	
no. 13	IX, pp. 119 f.	
no. 21		II, p. 146
no. 25	IX, p. 133	
no. 36	IX, p. 130	
no. 50	IX, p. 134	
no. 66	IX, p. 134	II, p. 145
no. 67	IX, p. 134	II, p. 144
no. 70	IX, pp. 128 and 134 f.	
no. 76	IX, p. 118	II, p. 142

This work of Sulamī along with his *Arba^c^īn ḥadīthan fī'l-taṣawwuf*, parts of his *Kitāb al-ṣuḥba*, as well as Abū Nu^c^aym's *Ḥilya*, Makkī's *Qūt al-qulūb*, etc., are attempts to demonstrate the presence of a body of Sufi thought among early authorities who otherwise had nothing at all to do with Sufism. Ibn al-Jawzī: *Ṣifat al-ṣafwa*, I, p. 4, criticizes Abū Nu^c^aym for this and cites as a justification for his criticism the two anti-Sufi sayings: 'Sufism is founded on laziness' (*Ḥilya*, IX, p. 137, l. 1), and : 'If an intelligent man became a Sufi, he would be made dumb before noon' (*Ḥilya*, IX, p. 142, ll. 2-3). Sulamī is truth-loving enough to include such sayings of Shāfi^c^ī as well: nos. 27 and 48. How can one explain the contradiction that Shāfi^c^ī rejected Sufism but at the same time expressed Sufi thoughts?

Ibn al-Jawzī disposes of the contradiction by accepting the ascetic thoughts but not the Sufi ones. With regard to the difference between asceticism and Sufism, he refers one to his *Talbīs Iblīs*. There (Cairo, 1928, pp. 160 ff.) he recognizes asceticism as the foundation of Sufism but he adds that at times the Sufis so exaggerated asceticism that due to hunger they experienced absurd fantasies, that they developed a pseudo-science out of their inner experiences and devalued so-called external, theological knowledge, moreover they arranged music and dance performances, etc. The correctness of this description is not to be disputed but the negative light Ibn al-Jawzī places it in is unacceptable in view of the facts. This can be explained by Ibn al-Jawzī's endeavor to attack so-called innovations. Already before him Abū Ḥāmid al-Ghazzālī: *Iḥyā' ʿulūm al-dīn*, II, Chpt. *kitāb ādāb al-samāʿ* (toward the end, in *al-adab al-khāmis*) had defended Sufi innovations which were in line with the intentions of divine and prophetic legislation. After him this was repeated by Abū Ḥafṣ ʿUmar al-Suhrawardī (d. 632/1234) in his *ʿAwārif* (end of Chpt. 22) and rather impressively by the latter's Persian adapter Maḥmūd-i Kāshānī (d. 735/1335): *Miṣbāḥ al-hidāya*, Tehran, 1323, pp. 146 ff., 160, 179, but also by Shāṭibī (d. 790/1388): *Iʿtiṣām*, I, p. 171. However, if one takes in without bias the sayings of Shāfiʿī presented by Sulamī, it becomes clear that the assertion that Shāfiʿī only expressed and accepted ascetic and not Sufi thoughts is incorrect because Shāfiʿī in sayings nos. 29, 30 and 31, the first of which is also cited by Qushayrī: *Risāla*, s.v. *samāʿ* as a statement of Shāfiʿī's, displayed complete sympathy for music and the excitement caused by it, and also made several statements recommending surveillance and direction of the soul in the Sufi sense well-known to us. Therefore the contradiction in Shāfiʿī still remains.

It can probably be explained by the fact that Shāfiʿī (d. 204/820) was not yet acquainted with what the Sufis later called 'the science of the interior', which is based on careful examination of, and adaptation to, tradition. What had up to then been achieved (Makkī mentions Ḥudhayfa b. al-Yamān and Ḥasan al-Baṣrī) were at best beginnings. Even Shāfiʿī's younger contemporary Dhū'l-Nūn, whom Shāfiʿī's students acknowledged in their discussion (no. 91), appears to have done little in this direction, and Muḥāsibī (d. 243/857) was still to come. Whether Shāfiʿī would not have rejected him as Aḥmad b. Ḥanbal did, is of course a debatable matter. Certainly his criticisms that the Sufis are lazybones, late sleepers, gluttons and chatterboxes (no. 48), that Sufism means being made dumb, etc., would not have been appropriate for the serious and stern demands of Muḥāsibī. Indeed, Muḥāsibī should even be seen to a certain extent as an ally of Shāfiʿī: he vehemently attacks all false piety, rejects alleged inner experiences of light, takes a stand against any forms of visionary fantasy (of love and self-surrender) and closely binds religious inwardness to the Koran and *sunna*. The Sufism which Shāfiʿī is prejudiced against is obviously the broad mystical movement of the common folk which was little burdened with theological knowledge, supported by numerous ignorant people and out of which the great masters of the 3rd/9th and 4th/10th centuries still had to forge so-called classical Sufism. The commitment of these great masters aimed at chiselling out a mysticism which was in harmony with the requirements of the Koran and *sunna*. Many odd features, many failed extremisms were retained in the process, were even cherished and glorified, and for the sake of causing astonishment were brought forth in pointed stories as a sign of exemplary radicalism, but what was unusable was eliminated and relegated to the chapters of the 'errors' of the Sufis — above all the visionary element. In this way Sufism preserved its classical character until the 4th/10th century. Meanwhile, through a kind of meditative incubation, through the *interpretatio ab intra*, the sacred tradition was 'fathomed' (*istinbāṭ*) and mysticism was adapted to the sacred tradition, i.e. a movement of convergence took place. This science, known as the 'science of the interior' (*ᶜilm al-bāṭin*), the 'doctrine of works' (*fiqh al-aᶜmāl*) or the 'science of hearts', is contrasted, at times vehemently, with the mere 'science of the exterior', to which the Koran readers, traditionists, jurists and dogmatists had devoted themselves. It is, as I have said (p. 163 f.), a moral-psychagogical hermeneutics of the sacred tradition which had not yet existed, separate from the mere cultivation of this tradtion but connected with dogmatics and non-ẓāhirite, non-Ḥanbalite jurisprudence through its sympathy for extrapolations (*mustanbaṭāt*). It was then the task of post-classical Sufism to proceed to integrate visions as well, in some cases even to incorporate pre- and non-Islamic mystical traditions, theosophies, and cosmologies, as Yaḥyā al-Suhrawardī (d. 587/1191) attempted most conspicuously. The latter could virtually be described as 'romantic'. However, the 'classicizing' Sufism of someone like Ibn ᶜAṭāᵓallāh al-Sikandarī, Ibn ᶜAbbād al-Rundī, etc., adheres once more to the classical model and goes on to measure this yet again against the Koran and *sunna*.

Ḥallāj is a special case: he did take part in the endeavors of the classical mystics 'to align' man with God by subordination to the commands and by ordering the soul in such a way that man does what God advises and is content with what God sends him. He also adopted the same priorities: following the commands is an external matter which is also an obligation for the naïve believer, whereas the real concern of Sufism is a training which makes one willing to offer no resistance to destiny and enables one to receive signs from God and to act in accordance with them. Like the classical mystics, Ḥallāj linked achieving this state of instrumentality with the elimination of self-will, with the substitution of divine attributes for human ones, or however one may describe this in specific terms. Like his contemporaries, he advocated the extreme *tawḥīd*: looking upon God as the only goal before one and as the only agent behind one. But Ḥallāj forfeits his claim to be regarded as one of the classical mystics by the fact that he continually shatters the clear form which the latter gave to their views, time and again pursues new provocative lines of thought and formulates them heretically, because for him God is so absolutely ungraspable and irrational that every attempt to define His relation to man, as soon as one leaves His actual message in the Koran, appears to him to be doomed to mere glossolalia and vertiginous antinomian positions. In this respect, with contempt for sobriety he often let himself go and in so doing was carried away by an undeniable pull to the left: he pressed man so tightly in the vice of God's immediate nearness that religious practices and even Sufi 'states' came to be excluded, and he located God so close under everyone's skin that the world was reduced to a scarcely existing epiphenomenon, separated from God only by its 'createdness'. In his wilder utterances he only still strove after the experience of this presence, while in his wildest ones, if they are authentic, he even sought release from this tormenting unification of duality in death.

If Sulamī was one of the few to acknowledge him and kept his *dīwān* in his library (Qushayrī: *Risāla*, *bāb al-firāsa*), it is not only because Naṣrābādhī, one of his sources of transmission and an authority in Nayshābūr, was an admirer of Ḥallāj (Massignon: *Akhbār*³ pp. 72-76), but also because Sulamī, for all the caution he exercised and with all the preferences he had, was still able to allow differences to exist. His *tafsīr* is criticized for containing foolish things (Dhahabī: *Ḥuffāẓ*, III, p. 1046;[17] ᶜAbd al-Ḥayy: *Shadharāt*, III, p. 197), although nothing in it comes from himself but only consists of explanations from others. He wrote a friendly book about the Malāmatiyya, although judging by the selection of sayings found in his *tafsīr* as well as other things he was an advocate of the doctrine of absolute surrender in God, i.e. he appears to have been rather on the side of al-Ḥakīm al-Tirmidhī than of Abū ᶜUthmān al-Ḥīrī.[18]

---

17 In this connection one should bear in mind that Dhahabī was an outspoken opponent of the Ashᶜarites and the Sufis so that Subkī (*Ṭabaqāt*, I, p. 190) virtually felt obliged to be ashamed of him (quoted with additional information in ᶜAbd al-Ḥayy al-Laknawī: *Iqāmat al-ḥujja ᶜalā ann al-ikthār fī'l-taᶜabbud laysa bi-bidᶜa*, Baghdad, 1966, pp. 106 f.).

18 Cf. Tirmidhī's letter to Ḥīrī in MS Ismail Saib I 1571, 61a-62a (Othman Yahya: *L'œuvre de Tirmiḏī*, no. 75, in *Mélanges Louis Massignon*, Paris, 1957, p. 455; Sezgin, *GAS*, I, p. 655, no. 5).

This is the 'objective' school of Nayshābūr which Sharība in the introduction to his edition of Sulamī's *Ṭabaqāt*, pp. 48-49, opposes to the Baghdad school of Junayd. The opposition is correct to the extent that Junayd cooperated actively and decisively in the formation of classical Sufism, i.e. intervened with a definite objective; by contrast, Sulamī (but not the other shaykhs of Nayshābūr!) was a compiler with an all-round interest who recorded the available testimony. His work dealing with Shāfiᶜī demonstrates this anew. Ibn Taymiyya formulates the following judgement: 'Sulamī possessed so much good, so much asceticism, religion and Sufism that he was compelled to gather together everything he found of the works of the shaykhs and the traditions which was consistent with his beliefs. For this reason, one finds in his books correct traditions and statements which fully promote religion, as well as spurious traditions and statements which must be rejected because they only cause harm to the uninformed. There were those who refrained from judging his tradition, indeed when Bayhaqī quoted from him, he used to say: Sulamī has informed us from the source of his tradition.'[19] I believe that in our case one may in fact assume the opposite, that the non-Sufi orthodox eliminated whatever was not consistent with their beliefs from the statements of the heads of their schools, and that consequently in Sulamī the fuller tradition, at least partially — inasmuch as it corresponded with Sulami's concerns — is available.

Beyond this, however, Sulamī still had his special reasons for examining and documenting in particular Shāfiᶜī's attitude toward Sufism: he was a Shāfiᶜite himself and in Nayshābūr at that time the Shāfiᶜite school of jurisprudence, on the whole, chiefly had ties with Sufism.[20] Thus for him and his environment the problem was natural and current, just as an interest in the question of the Malāmatiyya in Nayshābūr generally and for him in particular, given his kinship with Ibn Nujayd, was not surprising and must have imposed itself almost automatically on a scholar like him who strove to record and understand the religious movements of his time and surroundings.

Ceterum censeo commentarium Sulamii de Corano esse edendum. The Koran commentary of Sulamī is one of the most important and comprehensive collections in classical Sufism!

---

19 Muḥammad b. Muḥ. al-Manbijī: *Kitāb al-samāᶜ wa'l-raqṣ*, in Ibn Taymiyya's *Majmūᶜat al-rasāʾil al-kubrā*, Cairo, 1323, II, p. 305.

20 Richard Williams Bulliet: *The Social History of Nishapur in the Eleventh Century*, Harvard University, 1967, pp. 67-68 (thesis). A MS was kindly made available to me by Professor Annemarie Schimmel.

ADDITIONS OF THE AUTHOR

P. 135: In the original German version of this article, the MS Khānaqāh-i Aḥmadī under discussion is referred to as no. 83. The correct classification is no. 87.

P. 135: The work *Sharḥ al-arba^{c}īn ḥadīthan* by Ma^{c}mar al-Iṣfahānī listed as no. 11 in the table of contents of MS Khānaqāh-i Aḥmadī 87 but reported as stolen from the MS is preserved in an 8th /14th- or 9th/15th-century manuscript in the possession of an unnamed private party. However, only 38 of the 40 chapters of the work remain. This information is based on the statement of Muḥammad Taqī-i Dānishpazhūh in the journal *Āyanda* 16, 1369/1990, pp. 700-04 where the headings of the 38 chapters are enumerated.

[P. 136, l. 14: The *Kitāb al-iqtiṣād* has been edited and translated by Florian Soberoj; cf. F. Soberoj, *Ibn Ḫafīf aš-Šīrāzī und seine Schrift zur Novizenerziehung 'Kitāb al-Iqtiṣād'*, BTS 57, Beirut-Stuttgart, 1998.]

Pp. 144-159: On Abū Manṣūr Ma^{c}mar b. Aḥmad al-Iṣfahānī now see Naṣrallāh-i Pūrjawādī: *Abū Manṣūr-i Iṣfahānī: ṣūfī-i ḥanbalī*, in *Ma^{c}ārif* 6, 1368/1989, pp. 3-80. Idem: *Du athar-i kūtāh az Abū Manṣūr-i Iṣfahānī: Kitāb al-minhāj... wa-Dhikr ma^{c}ānī al-taṣawwuf* in *Ma^{c}ārif* 6, 1368/1990, pp. 235-83.

P. 152, ftn. 7: Richard Gramlich, *Die Gaben der Erkenntnisse des ^{c}Umar as-Suhrawardī*, Wiesbaden, 1978, p. 225, translated 'lenksam'. The poem in question from the *Ḥamāsa* is by the poet ^{c}Arandas. Friedrich Rückert, *Ḥamāsa oder die älteste arabischen Volkslieder*, Stuttgart, 1846, no. 684, translated 'mild'. Marzūqī requires 'ruhig und würdig'.

Pp. 154-158: No. 5 apparently consists of three separate works or fragments of Ma^{c}mar: *Al-manāhij bi-shāhid al-sunna*, *Al-masāʾil al-muḥdatha* and *Al-manāhij*. They have since been published (along with other works) and discussed by Naṣrallāh-i Pūrjawādī in the journal *Ma^{c}ārif* 6, 1989-90, pp. 235-83, and 7, 1990-91, pp. 243-65. On MS Khānaqāh-i Aḥmadī 87, pp. 111-13, see also Pūrjawādī, 'Guzīdaʾī az sukhanān-i Abū Manṣūr-i Iṣfahānī', in *Ma^{c}ārif* 8, 1991, pp. 131-40; and on Aḥmadī 87, pp. 106-10, idem, 'Ādāb al-mutaṣawwifa wa-ḥaqāʾiquhā wa-ishārātuhā az Abū Manṣūr-i Iṣfahānī, in *Ma^{c}ārif* 9, 1992, pp. 249-82 (the whole text edited on the basis of two MSS).

[P. 159: *Adab al-mulūk* has been edited by Bernd Radtke, *Adab al-mulūk. Ein Handbuch zur islamischen Mystik aus dem 4./10. Jahr-*

hundert, Beirut-Stuttgart, 1991, and translated into German by R. Gramlich, *Die Lebensweise der Könige. ADAB AL-MULŪK. Ein Handbuch zur islamischen Mystik*, AKM, L, 3, Stuttgart, 1993.]

[P. 160, l. 14: In this connection see *Drei Schriften*, II, p. 160 and ftn. 9/B. Radtke & J. O'Kane, *The Concept of Sainthood in Early Islamic Mysticism*, London, 1996, p. 219.]

[P. 164, l. 7: On the author and dating of the *Adab al-mulūk* see now Radtke, *Adab al-mulūk*, Einleitung, pp. 3-20; Gramlich, *Lebensweise*, Einleitung, pp. 5 f.; there are also important remarks on the subject in Hermann Landolt, *JAOS* 114, 1994, pp. 457-59.]

P. 164, l. 21: Abū Sulaymān al-Maghribī was a contemporary of Abū'l-Khayr al-Tīnātī al-Aqṭa^{c} (d. 346/957). ^{c}Abdallāh-i Anṣārī: *Ṭabaqāt al-ṣūfiyya*, ed. ^{c}Abd al-Ḥayy-i Ḥabībī, Kabul, 1341, pp. 441-42/Jāmī: *Nafaḥāt al-uns*, ed. Tawḥīdīpūr, Tehran, 1336, pp. 229-30.

[P. 164, l. 4 from bot.: *Adab al-mulūk*, ed. Radtke, p. 27/Gramlich, *Lebensweise*, pp. 62 f; cf. also 'Book of Etiquette', p. 59.]

P. 169, l. 23: Sam^{c}ānī: *Al-muntakhab*, MS Topkapı Sarayı (Ahmet III) 2953, 151b/Berlin Mss. sim. or. 80, 151b, mentions a descendant of this Aḥmad, namely Abū Ṭāhir ^{c}Abd al-Salām b. Ismā^{c}īl b. Muḥammad b. ^{c}Uthmān b. Aḥmad b. Muḥammad b. ^{c}Alī b. Mazdīn al-Qūmasānī al-Hamadhānī (477-540/1084-1145). Idem, 278b, last line, mentions a relative Abū'l-Faḍl Muḥammad b. ^{c}Uthmān b. Mazdīn al-Qūmasānī.

P. 170, l. 13: The story of Junayd and the hermit on Mt. Sinai is also found in the supplement to a MS of ^{c}Aṭṭār's *Tadhkirat al-awliyā$^{\circ}$*, ed. R.A. Nicholson, London-Leiden, 1905-07, II, English introduction, p. 59. The *Nasīm al-arwāḥ* is cited as a source but the wording of the reference is corrupt.

[P. 185, ftn. 18: this letter has been edited and translated by Bernd Radtke: *Drei Schriften*, I, pp. 190-92/II, pp. 230-31; cf. also 'Khurāsān', p. 205.]

KHURĀSĀN AND THE END OF CLASSICAL SUFISM

Sufism from its first beginnings in the 8th century AD up until today has preserved many of its traits, none the less some of them have also changed. If we compare Sufism of the 9th with Sufism of the 14th century, the following differences strike one at first glance. In the 9th century the language of Sufism, with the exception of a few surviving fragments, is naturally Arabic, as is the case with all the written products of Islamic intellectual history at that time — in the 14th century other languages are in use, especially Persian. In the 9th century Sufism is not yet associated with the generally recognized religious disciplines — in the 14th century that association has been established. In the 9th century Sufism is somewhat suspect in the eyes of government authorities — in the 14th century for the most part it enjoys special favor from the government. In the 9th century, as far as its organization is concerned, Sufism is left entirely to its own devices, being based on individual personalities — in the 14th century it is chiefly organized through orders and dynamic family initiatives, and frequently receives the support of patrons and the government. Those occupying its leadership posts are in part appointed by men of worldly power. Conversely, in some localities what was originally merely a latent opposition between Sufism and government has developed into direct political confrontation. In the 9th century Sufism displays almost no interest at all in philosophical-metaphysical questions — in the 14th century such an interest is manifest on all fronts. In the 9th century classic Sufi figures suppress as much as possible the visionary element — in the 14th century this element forms an acknowledged component of a Sufi's spiritual life. In the 9th century the Sufi shaykh, as in the case of a scholar of a branch of theological studies, is a teacher of Sufi forms of wisdom, and a person studying under him is a student — in the 14th century the shaykh is essentially in charge of a group of pupils whom he attempts to transform into spiritual adepts.

These are only some of the differences. The phenomena of a given period are naturally related to one another through numerous interconnections. But this does not mean that all these changes necessarily took place simultaneously. Nor should one assume that individual changes occurred overnight or that they can be dated with precision. And it would be false to maintain that any shift or transformation was always of an absolute nature. On the contrary, much that is old continues to be current alongside the new. Caution is to be recommended in face of the temptation to make specific external events responsible for long-term transformations. Demonstrably false is the seemingly handy idea that the Mongol invasion in the 13th century brought about these processes or accelerated their development. Change had already set in at an earlier date in all the examples referred to above.

I wish to deal here with the last mentioned phenomenon, the transformation of the lecture-giving shaykh into a shaykh who like a schoolmaster closely monitors the progress of his students. This transformation was first noted by Ibn ᶜAbbād al-Rundī,[1] a Moroccan

---

1 Paul Nwyia, *Ibn ᶜAbbâd de Ronda (1333-1390), Lettres de direction spirituelle* (al-Rasāʾil al-Ṣughrā), Beirut, 1958, pp. 106-15, 125-38. Muḥammad b. Tāwīt al-Ṭanjī, *Shifāʾ al-sāʾil li-tahdhīb al-masāʾil*, Istanbul, 1957-58, pp. 111-27. Aḥmad b. ᶜAjība (d. 1809) incorrectly ascribes the distinction to Abū'l-ᶜAbbās al-Mursī (d. probably 1287) (J.-L. Michon, *Arabica* 16, 1969, pp. 119 f.). I had already drawn attention to Rundī's view in my article 'Qushayrī's *Tartīb al-sulūk*', pp. 94-96.

Regarding Qushayrī's *Tartīb* I would here like to make the following remarks: The work has been published once again in the collective volume *Al-rasāʾil al-qushayriyya*, ed. Fīr Muḥammad Ḥasan, al-maᶜhad al-markazī li'l-abḥāth al-islāmiyya, n.p. and n.d., Pakistan, pp. 64-80, and then also by Qassim al-Samarrai, *The Theme of the Ascension in Mystical Writings*, Baghdad, 1968, I, pp. 155-77. The Pakistani edition, p. 69, ftn. 1 and 2, believes it can identify the enigmatic Abū'l-Fawāris (Qushayrī's *Tartīb al-sulūk*,, 99-100) as Abū'l-Fawāris al-Ḥasan b. Aḥmad b. Muḥammad b. Fāris b. Sahl al-Bazzāz (344-421/955-1030 in Baghdad) and the no less enigmatic Abū'l-Ḥasan as Kharaqānī (d. 428/1033). Since Qushayrī is supposed to have met Kharaqānī (*Kashf al-maḥjūb*, ed. Zhukovski, p. 205, ll. 5-7/trans. Nicholson, p. 163), the second identification is not necessarily impossible. But nothing has been proven, and the problem becomes still more complicated in view of an important reference which I received in a letter of November 17th, 1964, from Ch. Abdul Aziz, Karachi, namely that Persian extracts from the *Tartīb* — from *faṣl*s 1, 5, 8 and 9 in my edition — occur in ᶜAṭṭār's *Tadhkirat al-awliyāʾ*, II, p. 307, ll. 4-24 and p. 308, l. 25, to p. 309, l. 11, and are there attributed to Abū ᶜUthmān al-Maghribī (d. 373/983 in Nayshābūr) instead of Qushayrī. The extracts also include the story involving Abū'l-Fawāris (*Tadhkira*: Abū'l-Fāris, with variants). This question is not dealt with in J. Pedersen, 'Le Tunisien Abū ᶜUṯmān al-Maġribī et le ṣūfisme occidental', in *Études d'Orientalisme dédiées à la mémoire de Lévi-Provençal*, Paris, 1962, pp. 705-16, and still remains to be explained.

Neither the Pakistani edition of the *Tartīb* nor that of Sammarai gives me cause to change my text, except possibly in three places: 'Qushayrī's *Tartīb al-sulūk*' p. 117, l. 2, *ḥattā takūna* is perhaps a better reading than *ḥattā yakūna*; p. 117, l. 12, *mathalu'l-mubtadiʾi* perhaps better than *qīla: al-mubtadiʾu*; and p. 117, l. 13, *yatawahhama* perhaps better than *tawahhama*.

Sufi who died in 1390. He designates the older type of shaykh as *shaykh al-ta^clīm*, 'master of instruction', and the later type as *shaykh al-tarbiya*, 'master of training', or also *shaykh al-tarbiya wa'l-ta^clīm*, 'master of instruction and training'. By this he means that the second type does not simply lose the function of an academic teacher but takes on a double function, that of trainer as well as instructor. Rundī does not conceal the fact that he virtually equates the master of instruction with an ambulatory textbook. Actually, he puts it the

---

Mathalu is not found in any of the manuscripts but Qushāshī has *mithālu*. *Mathalu* can easily become corrupted to *qīla*. But this is not certain. *Yatawahhama* may well be transmitted in V but cannot be clearly made out in my photocopy. As for the Persian expression *dah-yāzdah u dah-nīm*, however, I still have no explanation. In the meantime I have come across *dah-yāzdah* in a sentence of Shams al-Dīn Muḥammad-i Daqā'iq-i Marwazī, *Rāḥat al-arwāḥ fī surūr al-mifrāḥ* (*Bakhtyārnāma*), Tehran, 1345, p. 172: 'Through these connections it became clear to her that what happened had reached the ears of the king and he had heard the circumstances of the matter *ba-dah-yāzdah*.' This would perhaps incline one to opt for a meaning like 'completely'. The corresponding clause in my translation in 'Qushayrī's *Tartīb al-sulūk*', p. 128, presents a different meaning; see my last attempt to translate the expression ['Qushayrī's *Tartīb*', p. 128 of this book]. In addition, I would like to drop ftn. 30 on p. 130 of the translation, to translate 'vitality' instead of 'strength' on p. 132, l. 17, and to drop the accompanying ftn. 36 (read *quwwat al-nafs*).

As for my apparatus criticus to the text of the *Tartīb*, I must concede to Sammarai a few trivial corrections but at the same time observe that he is culpable of many mistakes which I cannot enter into here. His repeated remark that I did not fully note all the variants is superfluous in view of my explicit statement ('*Tartīb*', pp. 106 f.) that I consciously wished to forgo presenting the complete textual transmission. In Sammarai's own edition the following textual errors should be corrected: p. 158, l. 22, *fa-ammā mā siwāhu*. P. 159, l. 10, *qablahū* (*qalbuhū* is impossible in the context). P. 159, l. 21, *laysa* (without *wa-*) *ba^cda hādhihi'l-ḥālati li-bashariyyatihī sulṭānun*. P. 159, l. 22, *sulṭānu hādhā*. P. 160, l. 6, *wa-adhkāran*. P. 160, l. 16, *yaridu ^calā qalbihī... naẓarun* (not *fa-in naẓara*). P. 160, l. 18, *adabahū* (not *al-adaba*). P. 161, l. 4, *al-lisāni nafsihī fa-idhā*. P. 161, l. 14, *ṭalaba* (not *ṭālaba*). P. 161, l. 22, *ḥāli hādhā'l-shurbi*. P. 161, l. 23, *ḥattā innahū idhā*. P. 162, l. 5, *hādhihi'l-ladhdhatu*. P. 162, l. 6, *idhā balagha*. P. 162, l. 10, *an lā yanāma* (the *lā* is necessary). P. 162, l. 5, *mukhāṭibahū* (perhaps better than *mukhāṭabatan*). P. 162, l. 17, *yajidu marratan kalāman*. P. 162, l. 20, *irtafa^ca* (without *wa-*). P. 162, l. 21, *mā qāla* (without *dhālika*, which only occurs in Zarrūq). P. 163, l. 2, *ulṭifa fī* (see Dozy). P. 163, l. 7, *ḍarabahū*. P. 163, l. 19, is not satisfactory. P. 164, l. 9, *fa-in* (not *fa-idhā*). P. 164, ll. 14-15, *juz'an*. P. 164, l. 18, drop *faṣl*. P. 165, l. 1, *al-tafaṣṣī* (my translation gives the meaning). P. 165, ll. 14-15, *ḥajar...* (the passage remains uncertain). P. 166, ll. 8-10, *khudhāy* (*dh* is required in view of the linguistic history of Persian). P. 166, ll. 9-10, *ajidu fī sirrī an aqūl*.

other way round: if a person reads a Sufi textbook, for practical purposes it amounts to the same thing as listening to a shaykh of instruction. As Rundī would have it, men of intelligence among those seeking God do not need any further help, and since in the earlier epoch, according to the well-known notion of 'the good old time', men of intelligence were the general rule, in those days only the *shaykh al-taᶜlīm* had existed. Those keen to learn acquired the necessary knowledge by means of visits and long periods of residence (*ṣuḥba*) with such masters. Of course, the surer way, which later became the standard practice, was to undergo training by a *shaykh al-tarbiya*, a form of training in which psychagogical guidance occupies the central position since basically no one is free from obstacles arising from the ego. Rundī appears to have located the change-over somewhere in the 11th century AD, as he remarks that Muḥāsibī (d. 857), Abū Ṭālib al-Makkī (d. 996) 'and others' did not yet make any reference to *tarbiya* in the sense he has in mind.

Comparison of a 10th-century Sufi textbook such as the *Lumaᶜ* of Sarrāj with a Sufi textbook from around 1200 such as the *ᶜAwārif al-maᶜārif* of ᶜUmar al-Suhrawardī immediately reveals that a shift in this direction and over this period of time has taken place. But one is suspicious of the assertion that the earlier Ṣūfiyya did not yet have need of training and therefore did not engage in it. This is a matter which requires further investigation, and to that end it must first be made clear what we mean by Sufi *taᶜlīm* and Sufi *tarbiya* — to retain these two expressions of Rundī. Then we can go on to address the question of what the sources say concerning the change-over.

The first question, that having to do with the difference between instruction and training, may be answered in the following manner:

Instruction means that a shaykh imparts information about Sufi wisdom in a conversation or in a lecture. This might involve a single student, or a whole circle of students might gather around the shaykh; whether in the shaykh's house, in a mosque, in a convent, or in some other location. Instruction could be given on more or less random occasions or in meetings organized on a regular basis. The instruction is considered a necessity and should be eagerly sought and highly valued by the students. The words of shaykhs concerning Sufism have more or less as high a value as the doctrines of jurists with regard to canonical legislation, and can diverge from one master to another in a similar way. Their oral and written transmission guaranteed a certain continuity and resulted in a constant increase of Sufi knowledge and materials for teaching.

The shaykh is seen as an experienced person who has attained the goal of mystical striving and knowledge. Tīnātī (d. after 951) insists on this and states: 'The authority of a shaykh is only merited by one who has completed self-purification. Anyone who still has something left to do is a novice, and a novice cannot take charge of another novice.'[2] The novice must imitate the shaykh's example. Abū ᶜAbdallāh al-Sijzī (10th century) remarks: 'What is most useful for the novice is keeping company (*ṣuḥba*) with the righteous, imitation of their actions, moral qualities and virtues, visiting the graves of the Friends of God, and performing service on behalf of the companions and comrades.'[3] Yaḥyā b. Muᶜādh al-Rāzī (d. 872) explains: 'A person who doesn't learn anything from a shaykh's actions will not learn anything from his words.'[4]

A shaykh enjoys and deserves veneration. Mamshād al-Dīnawarī (d. 911)[5] and Ibrāhīm b. Shaybān al-Qirmīsīnī (d. around 950)[6] demand that shaykhs be accorded reverence. Abū ᶜAlī al-Thaqafī (d. 940) requires the same, otherwise a person will receive nothing from them.[7] A shaykh who on his deathbed was urged to recite the profession of faith replied: 'Do not behave with impudence' (*bē-ḥurmatī ma-kun*).[8]

---

2 Muṣṭafā al-ᶜArūsī: *Natāʾij al-afkār al-qudsiyya fī bayān maᶜānī sharḥ al-Risāla al-qushayriyya li-shaykh al-islām Zakariyyā al-Anṣārī*, Būlāq, 1290, I, p. 193 (from Munāwī).

3 Abū ᶜAbd al-Raḥmān al-Sulamī: *Ṭabaqāt al-ṣūfiyya*, ed. Nūr al-Dīn Shurayba, Cairo, 1953, p. 255, ll. 3-5/ Johannes Pedersen: *Abū ᶜAbd al-Raḥmān Muḥammad b. al-Ḥusain b. Muḥammad b. Mūsā al-Sulamī: Kitāb ṭabaqāt al-ṣūfiyya*, texte arabe avec une introduction et un index, Leiden, 1960, p. 252, ll. 7-9.

4 ᶜAbd al-Wahhāb al-Shaᶜrānī: *Al-ṭabaqāt al-kubrā*, Cairo, 1355, sub Abū Zakariyyā Yaḥyā b. Muᶜādh, I, p. 69. Reminds one of Sulamī, *Ṭabaqāt*, Cairo, p. 113, ll. 15-16/Leiden, p. 104, ll. 5-6 (variant). Shaᶜrānī: *Al-anwār al-qudsiyya fī maᶜrifat qawāᶜid al-ṣūfiyya*, Cairo, 1962, I, p. 201, attributes the statement to Abū Bakr al-Warrāq.

5 Sulamī, *Ṭabaqāt*, Cairo, p. 318, ll. 5-7/Leiden, p. 320, ll. 3-5. ᶜAbd al-Raḥmān-i Jāmī: *Nafaḥāt al-uns min ḥaḍarāt al-quds*, ed. Mahdī-i Tawḥīdīpūr, Tehran, 1337, sub Mamshād al-Dīnawarī, p. 94. In the Sulamī editions the name, perhaps correctly, is vocalized Mumshād.

6 Sulamī, *Ṭabaqāt*, Cairo, p. 405, ll. 15-16/Leiden, p. 320, ll. 9-10. ᶜAbdallāh-i Harawī-i Anṣārī: *Ṭabaqāt al-ṣūfiyya*, ed. ᶜAbd al-Ḥayy-i Ḥabībī, Kabul, 1341, p. 404. Jāmī, *Nafaḥāt*, sub Ibrāhīm b. Shaybān, p. 216.

7 Sulamī, *Ṭabaqāt*, Cairo, p. 363, ll. 12-13/Leiden, p. 372, ll. 10-11. Anṣārī, *Ṭabaqāt*, p. 381. Jāmī, *Nafaḥāt*, sub Abū ᶜAlī al-Thaqafī, p. 203. And quite frequent elsewhere.

8 Abū'l-Qāsim ᶜAbd al-Karīm b. Hawāzin al-Qushayrī: *Al-risāla al-qushayriyya*, Cairo (many printings), *bāb aḥwālihim ᶜinda'l-khurūj min al-dunyā*. Persian sentence in Ara-

One must not offend a shaykh's feelings. Otherwise, one may experience something like what happened to the man from Hamadān who took leave of Ja^cfar al-Khuldī (d. 959) in order to consume a roast chicken: a dog snatched the chicken from him.[9] And one should not allow anything derogatory to be said about one's shaykh. Anṣārī (d. 1089) had a bad opinion of Ibn-i Sam^cūn (d. 997) because the latter had insulted Ḥuṣrī, an indirect shaykh of Anṣārī. Whoever, according to Anṣārī, tolerates that sort of behavior is worse than a dog.[10]

Before undertaking personal initiatives or journeys one must ask permission from one's shaykh. Kāzarūnī (d. 1035) insists on this,[11] Ibn-i Khafīf (d. 982) often notes violations of this rule among his students,[12] and Ḥuṣrī (d. 982) in Baghdad sends home several novices who had set out from Herat on the pilgrimage to Mecca without permission from their shaykh.[13]

Every occasion that offers itself to visit a shaykh must be taken. ^cAlī b. Bundār is asked in Damascus by Ibn al-Jallā^ɔ (d. 918-19) where he has spent the three days he had already been in the city. ^cAlī b. Bundār replies he has written down *ḥadīth* at Ibn Jawṣā's dictation. Ibn al-Jallā^ɔ scolds him, saying: 'So what is merely recommendable (*sunna*) held you back from what is a duty (*farīḍa*).' Anṣārī comments: 'Visiting *pīr*s is one of the duties of these people because by visiting *pīr*s they learn things which they could not learn anywhere else.'[14] When Abū'l-Ḥusayn al-Darrāj (d. 932) comes to

bic context. In the case of Shaykh Aḥmad b. Naṣr it is a question of the Sufi of the same name from Nasā who is mentioned in Anṣārī: *Ṭabaqāt*, p. 308, last line, and in *Nafaḥāt*, sub Aḥmad-i Naṣr, p. 289.

9 Qushayrī, *Risāla, bāb ḥifẓ qulūb al-mashāyikh.*

10 Anṣārī, *Ṭabaqāt*, p. 449. Jāmī, *Nafaḥāt*, sub Abū'l-Ḥusayn b. Sam^cūn, p. 233.

11 Maḥmūd b. ^cUthmān: *Firdaws al-murshidiyya fī asrār al-ṣamadiyya*, ed. F. Meier as *Die Vita des Scheich Abū Isḥāq al-Kāzarūnī in der persischen Bearbeitung von Maḥmūd b. ^cUṯmān*, Bibliotheca Islamica 14, Leipzig, 1948, p. 341, ll. 18-23; p. 346, l. 16, to p. 347, l. 5/ed. Īraj-i Afshār, Tehran, 1333, p. 313, ll. 9-14; p. 317, l. 14, to p. 318, l. 2.

12 Abū'l-Ḥasan al-Daylamī: *Sīrat-i Abū ^cAbdullāh* (sic) *ibn al-Khafīf al-Shīrāzī*, ed. Annemarie Schimmel Tarı, Ankara, 1955, p. 157. Anṣārī, *Ṭabaqāt*, p. 436 (abridged).

13 Anṣārī, *Ṭabaqāt*, p. 450. *Nafaḥāt*, sub Abū Naṣr-i Khabbāz, pp. 233-34. ^cAbdallāh al-Ḥusaynī al-ma^crūf bi-Aṣīl al-Dīn-i Wā^ciẓ-i Harawī: *Maqṣad al-iqbāl-i sulṭāniyya*, in Fikrī-i Saljūqī: *Risāla-i mazārāt-i Hirāt*, Kabul, 1967, p. 23.

14 Sulamī, *Ṭabaqāt*, Cairo, p. 502, ll. 3-6/Leiden, p. 534, ll. 9-12. Anṣārī, *Ṭabaqāt*, p. 249. *Nafaḥāt*, sub ^cAlī b. Bundār, pp. 115-16. Sha^crānī: *Ṭabaqāt*, sub ^cAlī b. Bundār, I, p. 107.

Ray to see Yūsuf b. al-Ḥusayn al-Rāzī (d. 916-17), the latter asks him what the purpose of his journey is. He replies: 'To visit you.' Rāzī asks: 'If on the way here you were offered a house or a girl, would that have hindered you from visiting me?' Darrāj answers: 'I don't know. In any case, God did not send me such a temptation.'[15]

Already in the 9th century visits of this kind were also undertaken in the hope of having a shaykh invoke God on one's behalf, and after a shaykh's death one acquired blessings by making a pilgrimage to his grave. For example, Bisṭāmī's grave was such a goal for pilgrims.[16]

Separate schools of thought also took form. Bazzāz (9th cent.) studied with Sarī and Bishr al-Ḥāfī, but he followed Musūḥī.[17] Khuldī (d. 959) had spent time with Nūrī, Ruwaym, Samnūn, Junayd and others, but he was renowned for his schooling under Junayd.[18] Duqqī (d. 970) as well had associated with a full array of shaykhs but he followed Ibn al-Jallāᵓ.[19] The expression Sulamī frequently uses to describe this is *intamā ilā* in distinction merely to *ṣaḥiba.* Anṣārī translates the first as *nisbat kardan ba* or *bā*, the second as *ṣuḥbat kardan.*

Training in Sufism cannot be sharply separated from teaching since Sufism as such was to a great extent training, and instruction on Sufism naturally had to address questions of training. In the literature the concepts teaching and training are therefore often randomly interchanged, and it would be futile to hope to clarify the difference by a rigorous investigation of these words. None the less, it is possible to distinguish training as something special and separate from teaching, and conceived thus in contrast to teaching, training means the direct intervention of the shaykh in the student's behavior by means of instructions, the application of which he

---

15 Reynold A. Nicholson: *The Kitáb al-Lumaᶜ fi'l-Taṣawwuf of Abú Naṣr ᶜAbdalláh b. ᶜAlí al-Sarráj al-Ṭúsí*, edited for the First Time... Gibb Memorial Series 22, Leiden-London, 1914, p. 291, ll. 10-14. Qushayrī: *Risāla, bāb al-samāᶜ*. Anṣārī, *Ṭabaqāt*, p. 360. *Nafaḥāt*, sub Abū'l-Ḥusayn-i Darrāj, p. 174.

16 *Lumaᶜ*, p. 391, ll. 17-19.

17 Sulamī, *Ṭabaqāt*, Cairo, p. 295, ll. 2-5/Leiden, p. 294, ll. 4-6. Anṣārī, *Ṭabaqāt*, p. 127.

18 Sulamī, *Ṭabaqāt*, Cairo, p. 434, ll. 2-4/Leiden, p. 454, ll. 3-6. Anṣārī, *Ṭabaqāt*, p. 419. *Nafaḥāt*, sub Jaᶜfar b. Muḥammad al-Khuldī, p. 223.

19 Sulamī, *Ṭabaqāt*, Cairo, p. 448, ll. 3-4/Leiden, p. 469, ll. 4-5. Anṣārī, *Ṭabaqāt*, p. 425. *Nafaḥāt*, sub Abū Bakr al-Duqqī, p. 188.

supervises, and the eventual outcome of which he then awaits and criticizes.

Sarrāj (d. 988) insists on a training of this kind. He considers it indispensable that the novice, if he is to avoid the tortuous paths of self-deception, submit to a master of discipline (*muʾaddib*) who will train him (*yarūḍu*) and give him a bitter draft to drink,[20] as well as correctly regulate the kind and the amount of ascetic practices he undertakes.[21] Around the year 1000 AD in Āmul (Ṭabaristān) shaykh Abū'l-ᶜAbbās-i Qaṣṣāb directed a convent with several cells for Ṣūfiyya and nights was on the look-out that none of them prayed too much.[22] Abū Saᶜīd b. Abī'l-Khayr (d. 1049) there subjected himself to Abū'l-ᶜAbbās' spiritual direction for one year. Sarrāj defines the beginner expressly as someone who must make a habit of the rules and listen obediently to a person who is familiar with his situation as a beginner and will watch over him from the beginning to the end.[23] 'The end' seems to mean completion of a period of probation or an introductory course. But also in the presence of shaykhs one meets in foreign places or otherwise, one must forget everything one believes one knows and follow their advice.[24] Assuming one knows better may entail punishment. An unnamed shaykh arrives in a place and orders an unnamed novice there to engage in begging. The novice does not obey him but later on, due to circumstances, he is forced to take up begging 'in punishment for his disobedience'.[25] Bisṭāmī (d. probably 874) is reported to have actually elevated odedience to the shaykh above religious duties. As he would have it, a student assigned a task by his master must not be hampered from carrying it out even by the call to prayer.[26] Later, in the 12th century, Ibn Ṭāhir

---

20 *Lumaᶜ*, p. 410, l. 15.

21 *Lumaᶜ*, p. 417, l. 13.

22 Muḥammad b. al-Munawwar: *Asrār al-tawḥīd fī maqāmāt al-shaykh Abī Saᶜīd*, ed. Dhabīḥallāh-i Ṣafā, Tehran, 1333, p. 50/Muḥammad Riḍā Shafīᶜī-i Kadkanī, Tehran, 1366, pp. 44-45/trans. by John O'Kane, *The Secrets of God's Mystical Oneness*, Persian Heritage Series no. 38, Costa Mesa (Calif.)-New York, 1992, p. 117. *Ḥālāt u sukhanān-i shaykh Abū Saᶜīd*, written by a descendant of Abū Saᶜīd's in the 6th/12th century, ed. Īraj-i Afshār, Tehran, 1331, p. 15.

23 *Lumaᶜ*, p. 341, ll. 17-19.

24 *Lumaᶜ*, p. 416, ll. 12-13. Daylamī, *Sīrat-i Ibn-i Khafīf*, p. 18.

25 *Lumaᶜ*, p. 191, ll. 15-21.

26 Sahlajī: *Al-nūr min kalimāt Abī Ṭayfūr, naṣṣ ghayr manshūr... yunsabu ilā'l-Sahlajī*, in ᶜAbd al-Raḥmān Badawī: *Shaṭaḥāt al-ṣūfiyya*, Cairo, 1949, Part 1, p. 144.

al-Maqdisī formulated the saying: 'Service (to the shaykh) is better than worship.'[27]

As this small selection of testimonies demonstrates, there can be no doubt that *tarbiya* had existed in the older times which Rundī claims exclusively for *ta^c^līm*. None the less, retaining Rundī's terminology is justified because it does contain a correct observation, and is simple. But we must be clear in what sense his observation is correct. Briefly put, it is correct in recognizing that from the 11th century on training gains a new status in Sufism. During the classical period, the tendency is to speak more of self-training, while the formation of the student by the master remains somewhat marginal. As the development and diversification of Sufism proceeds during the 11th century, a point is reached when the problem of the novice's training also becomes the focus of greater attention. What had been worked out over time on a practical level, now emerges into the light of theoretical discussion and comes to be included among the subjects that had previously been dealt with in the Sufi systems of regulations.

In order to justify and facilitate training greater emphasis is now accorded to the difference between master and disciple, and the distance between both, with regard to the position they occupy *vis-à-vis* one another, is increased. The rank of shaykh entails priestly traits and autocratic authority. The novice, on the other hand, is demoted to being a poor sinner and a slave devoid of will. The figure of the shaykh is extended, that of the novice suppressed. At the same time, the two are more closely bound to one another. Each can scarcely be what he is without the other. For both parties this can lead to inner tensions. The shaykh is required to fulfill two tasks, that of being a saint with regard to his knowledge and his essence, and that of guiding step by step the novice or novices — for usually a whole group is involved — and slowly leading them to himself across the great gulf that separates the status of novice and master. He maintains the claim to have reached the goal himself, and likewise undertakes full responsibility to bring the novice to the same or almost the same point. The novice is bound by two duties, that of presenting in childlike trust all his psychic impulses and most secret thoughts to the shaykh, and that of obeying unquestioningly the measures imposed by the shaykh and acknowledging him as having unlimited authority and being the ultimate judge in all matters. And yet the peaceful

---

27 Louis Massignon: *Essai sur les origines du lexique technique de la mystique musulmane*, nouvelle édition revue et considérablement augmentée, Paris, 1954, pp. 116-17.

conciliation of potential conflicts and opposing tendencies that such a relationship naturally entails had already been achieved in a parallel in a non-Sufi area of life: in the relationship between physician and patient. Thus, it comes as no surprise that the *shaykh al-tarbiya* is often compared to the physician and the novice to the patient who seeks healing. The comparison was all the more natural since it was precisely during this critical period, i.e. the 10th century, that the terms 'medicine of the soul' (*al-ṭibb al-rūḥānī*) and 'physician of the soul' were being discussed in philosophy in the struggle for a philosophical life (*sīra falsafiyya*). Abū Bakr al-Rāzī (d. 925) recommends to the person interested in philosophy that he oblige one of his friends to criticize all his failings ruthlessly,[28] and the fact that Bayhaqī (d. 1077) takes up these ideas in his *Tārīkh*[29] testifies to the wide dissemination of this conception. Even the subject of children's education was dealt with by medical philosophy of the 10th century.[30] Philosophy saw its ideal in the man of virtue who had overcome his nature and soul, and had refined the divine element of his understanding to such a degree of purity that he could grasp the highest concepts, whereas Islamic mysticism, which at first was not familiar with the idea of 'the divine spark' in man, saw its ideal in the spiritual master who had aligned his consciousness so purely with God that he could serve as God's spokesman. The high regard demanded by Sufism *vis-à-vis* so lofty and unassailable an authority was at times associated by the defenders of non-mystical theology and the prevailing political order with Shīᶜite, in particular with Ismāᶜīlī, extreme reverence for imams.[31] Indeed, this was one of the

---

28 *Abi Bakr Mohammadi filii Zachariae Raghensis (Razis) opera philosophica fragmentaque quae supersunt collegit et edidit Paulus Kraus, pars prior*, Cahirae, 1939, pp. 33-35. Translation by A.J. Arberry, *The Spiritual Physick of Rhazes*, London, 1960, pp. 36-37. Compare Abū Ḥayyān al-Tawḥīdī: *Al-imtāᶜ wa'l-muʾānasa*, ed. Aḥmad Amīn and Aḥmad al-Zayn, Cairo, 1939-44, II, p. 126: Ḥātim al-Aṣamm: 'If you see an error in your brother and keep it a secret from him, you betray him. If you tell it to someone else, you slander him. If you say it to his face, you offend him. You must simply allude to it, mention it to him in passing, weave it into a sentence.'

29 Abū'l-Faḍl Muḥammad b. Ḥusayn-i Bayhaqī: *Tārīkh-i Bayhaqī*, ed. Dr. Ghanī and Dr. Fayyāḍ, Tehran, 1324, pp. 104-06/ed. Saᶜīd-i Nafīsī, Tehran, 1319-32, I, pp. 109-12.

30 Ibn al-Jazzār al-Qayrawānī, *Siyāsat al-ṣibyān wa-tadbīruhum*, Tunis, 1968, pp. 134-38. For a work about the correct behavior of schoolteachers see G. Lecomte, 'Le livre des règles de conduite des maîtres d'école par Ibn Saḥnūn', in *REI* 21, 1953, pp. 77-105.

31 *Baḥr al-fawāʾid — dāʾirat al-maᶜārif shāmil-i kalām u taṣawwuf u fiqh u siyāsat* (from the 12th century), ed. Muḥammad Taqī-i Dānishpazhūh, Tehran, 1345/1966, p. 357.

charges to which ᶜAyn al-Quḍāt fell victim in 1131.[32] Cross-ties with the *shīᶜa* are possible, but not in the sense of a shared historical origin. What one is faced with here are the natural results of two separately proceeding developments.

By no means did all beginning Sufis allow themselves to be taken in hand in accordance with the provisions of the new guidelines of *tarbiya*, nor did all the shaykhs, at least not all to the same extent, seem up to fulfilling the prescribed double task of taking care of the novices in every possible way and at the same time ascending or occupying the highest peak of knowledge. An anonymous non-Sufi author from Aleppo whose time of activity is unknown to me, writes: 'There are three fathers — one begot you, one raised (trained) you and one gave you instruction.'[33] Clearly three different persons. Anṣārī (d. 1089) admits that he penetrated more deeply into Sufism through a single word of Kharaqānī than through the instruction of all other shaykhs he had known, and yet it was his practice to send his own students to Muḥammad al-Qaṣṣāb al-Āmulī in Dāmghān and not to Kharaqānī.[34] Anṣārī himself had learned the rules and prescriptions (*ādāb u rusūm*) with shaykh ᶜAmmū (d. 1049-50 in Herat). The latter had been his *pīr-i irshād*, his pedagogue. He had acquired his nickname *ᶜammū* in the sense of headmaster (*sālār*) from his master Abū'l-ᶜAbbās al-Nihāwandī who had recommended to the Sufis that they recognize him as their leader.[35] This might lead one to conclude that training tasks could be delegated, as is fre-

---

32 '*Shakwā-l-ġarīb*... de ᶜAyn al-quḍāt al-Hamadānī († 525-1131)', éditée et traduite, avec introduction et notes, par Mohammed ben Abd el-Jalil, in *JA* 216, 1930, pp. 35 ff., 210 ff./ᶜAfīf ᶜUsayrān: *Muṣannafāt-i ᶜAyn al-Quḍāt-i Hamadānī*, Tehran, 1962, concluding part, Introduction, pp. 11 ff.; text, pp. 10 ff./Arberry, *A Sufi Martyr*, London, 1969, Introduction, p. 16; translation, pp. 34 ff.

33 Aḥmad Shalabī, *Taʾrīkh al-tarbiya al-islāmiyya*, Beirut, 1954, p. 300. The anonymous work bears the title *Minhāj al-mutaᶜallim* and is available in manuscript form in codex 1221 of al-Maktaba al-ᶜuthmāniyya in Aleppo.

34 A.J. Arberry: 'Jāmī's Biography of Anṣārī' in *The Islamic Quarterly* 7, 1963, pp. 65-66/*Maqāmāt-i shaykh al-islām... ᶜAbdallāh-i Anṣārī-i Harawī*, ed. Fikrī-i Saljūqī, Kabul, 1343, pp. 14-17. Anṣārī, *Ṭabaqāt*, p. 309. *Nafaḥāt*, sub Muḥammad-i Qaṣṣāb-i Āmulī, p. 297. S. de Laugier de Beaurecueil, *Khwādja ᶜAbdullāh Anṣārī*, Beirut, 1965, p. 67.

35 *Maqāmāt-i shaykh al-islām*, ed. Arberry, p. 71/ed. Saljūqī, pp. 28-29. *Nafaḥāt*, sub Shaykh ᶜAmmū, p. 344. The incomprehensible **farshād* should be amended to *irshād*. De Beaurecueil, *Khwādja ᶜAbdullāh Anṣārī*, p. 36, ftn. 3. *Nafaḥāt*, sub Abū'l-ᶜAbbās-i Nihāwandī, p. 147.

quently documented at a later date.[36] In any case, in all the examples just mentioned the trainer and the teacher of wisdom are separate persons, and so the path has been demarcated along which, from now on, the old contrast between simply being a student and actually adhering to a particular school will be played out: once the Sufi has completed his training, he is a free man and can then go on to experience a decisive spiritual turning point with another shaykh whom he has come to know later by means of a book, or in some other way. However, prior to this he must or at least he ought to have gone through the fundamental schooling, i.e. training, with a shaykh. It goes without saying that, should the master die before the novice has completed his training, the novice will seek another trainer and then regard the latter as the actual shaykh who formally trained him. This was the case with Abū Sa^cīd b. Abī'l-Khayr who had first sought instruction from Abū'l-Faḍl-i Sarakhsī and then after the latter's death had attached himself to Abū'l-^cAbbās-i Qaṣṣāb.[37]

In theory the new form of training can be described as follows:

The shaykh, by means of a pact, binds the novice to practice unquestioning obedience, to carry out every order and to reveal all his secret thoughts and inner states without exception while at the same time keeping them secret and in general observing silence *vis-à-vis* a third party. The shaykh is not to pass over any mistake on the part of the novice and can assign him whatever punishments he wishes. The novice is to do only what the shaykh orders him; he is not to attempt additional religious practices on his own initiative or undertake journeys of any kind as he sees fit. Of central importance is withdrawal in seclusion (*khalwa*), during which the novice must repeat to him-

---

36 For example Jāmī, *Nafaḥāt*, sub Abū ᶜAlī-i Fārmadī, pp. 369-70: Kurrakānī (Gurgānī) had Fārmadī hold an assembly and entrusted his son to him. F. Meier: *Die Fawāʾiḥ al-ǧamāl wa-fawātiḥ al-ǧalāl des Najm ad-dīn al-Kubrā. Eine Darstellung mystischer Erfahrungen im Islam aus der Zeit um 1200 n. Chr.*, Akad. Wiss. Lit. Mainz, Veröffentlichungen der Orientalischen Kommission 9, Wiesbaden, 1957, Introduction, p. 41: Yūsuf al-Hamadānī appointed Saᶜīd as *lālā*, i.e. as director and supervisor over his disciples. Hellmut Ritter, 'Philologika XI', *Der Islam* 26, 1940, pp. 124-25: Mawlānā transferred his students to the guidance of Ṣalāḥ al-Dīn-i Zarkūb.

37 *Asrār al-tawḥīd*, ed. Ṣafā, pp. 42-43/ed. Shafīᶜī-i Kadkanī, p. 38/trans. by O'Kane, p. 107. *Ḥālāt u sukhanān-i shaykh Abū Saᶜīd*, pp. 13-16. In the same way Aḥmad-i Yasawī after the death of his first teacher Bāb Arslān switched over to Yūsuf-i Hamadānī; ᶜAlī b. Ḥusayn-i Wāᶜiẓ-i Kāshifī: *Rashaḥāt ᶜayn al-ḥayāt*, litho., Lucknow, 1905, p. 8; M. Molé, 'Autour du Daré Mansour: L'apprentissage mystique de Bahāʾ al-Dīn Naqshband', in *REI* 27, 1959, p. 42.

self a formula that the shaykh has previously given him for recollecting God (*dhikr*) — such as the first part of the profession of faith 'There is no god but God!' — so that he will totally focus his attention on the object of this recollection.[38] These exercises had already existed for a long time but now they become regulated and described with precision as a component of the training. From the 13th century on we are informed in greater detail about the posture and the manner of enunciation which the novice is to adopt during *dhikr*-recitations.[39] Since the 11th century a new literature dealing with visionary experiences and mystical states during or out of *khalwa* began to develop, while from the 13th century onwards correspondence between students and teachers has come down to us.[40] Usually at the start of the novitiate, though it may also occur at the end, the beginner has a patched frock conferred on him.[41] This form of clothing is an old phenomenon in Sufism, but now conferring the frock on the novice becomes a formal rite of passage. From the 12th century on, cropping the hair is also attested as part of the rite.[42] As is clear, the

---

38 More details in *Fawā'iḥ*, Introduction, pp. 200 ff; Gardet in *EI*² s.v. dhikr.

39 F. Meier, 'Schriften des ᶜAzīz-i Nasafī', in *WZKM* 52, 1953, pp. 164-66; *Bausteine*, I, pp. 217-19. Nasafī, *Kashf al-ḥaqā'iq*, Tehran, 1965, pp. 134-35. Nasafī, *Kitāb al-insān al-kāmil*, ed. Molé, Tehran-Paris, 1962, pp. 106-07.

40 Cf. *Fawā'iḥ*, Introduction, p. 42 (Bākharzī and Kubrā) and MS Köprülü 1589, 410a-412a (Sharaf al-Dīn-i Balkhī and Majd al-Dīn-i Baghdādī), etc.

41 *Fawā'iḥ*, Introduction, pp. 35 f. Supplementary information from this same period (circa 1200) in Abū Jaᶜfar Muḥammad b. Abī Zayd al-Kātib, '*Sharā'iṭ-i murīdī*', in *Farhang-i Īrānzamīn* 14 (1345), pp. 325-26.

42 Ibn al-Jawzī, *Al-muntaẓam fī ta'rīkh al-mulūk wa'l-umam*, Hyderabad, 1357-61, X, p. 69, l. 13 (year 531/1137). Anonymous, *Manāqib-i Awḥad al-Dīn-i Kirmānī*, ed. Furūzānfar, Tehran, 1969, Introduction, pp. 41-42. Ibn-i Bībī, *Mukhtaṣar-i Saljūqnāma*, ed. M. Th. Houtsma: *Recueil de textes relatifs à l'histoire des Seldjoucides*, IV: *Histoire des Seldjoucides d'Asie Mineure d'après l'Abrégé du Seldjouknāmeh d'Ibn Bībī*, Leiden, 1902, p. 96, l. 11/trans. by H.W. Duda, *Die Seltschukengeschichte des Ibn Bibi*, Copenhagen, 1959, p. 103, especially ftn. b. (year 617-18/1220-21). Ibn Khallikān, *Wafayāt al-aᶜyān wa-anbā' abnā' al-zamān*, ed. Muḥammad Muḥyī al-Dīn ᶜAbd al-Ḥamīd, Cairo, 1948, no. 468 (ᶜUmar al-Suhrawardī). *Firdaws al-murshidiyya*, Bibliotheca Islamica 14, Introduction, p. 65, and in the text p. 453, l. 12; p. 470, l. 8; p. 472, l. 7; p. 487, l. 19/Tehran, p. 413, l. 11; p. 427, l. 18; p. 429, l. 18; p. 443, l. 12. ᶜIzz al-Dīn Maḥmūd b. ᶜAlī-i Kāshānī, *Miṣbāḥ al-hidāya wa-miftāḥ al-kifāya*, ed. Jalāl al-Dīn-i Humā'ī, Tehran, 1323, p. 149. Ibn Baṭṭūṭa, *Riḥla*, ed. and trans. by Defrémery and Sanguinetti, Paris, 1843 ff., II, p. 28/trans. H.A.R. Gibb, Cambridge, 1956 ff., II, p. 286. For general information on further literature and the whole complex of cutting the

novitiate has become an initiation. To avoid misunderstandings it should be noted that this is not acceptance into an order but an initiation into Sufism in general. The orders are not under discussion here. However, from the 10th century on receiving a patched frock does mean acceptance into a spiritual family tree (*silsila*, *shajara-i irādat*, etc.). Perhaps another warning is in place: when a Sufi has a patched frock conferred on him, this is not equivalent to his being designated as the shaykh's successor in the sense of replacing the latter as the head of an order.

During the period of training the shaykh stands between the novice and God. In the 9th century Sahl b. ᶜAbdallāh al-Tustarī had described the lowest level of trust in God as coming before God the way a dead man lies on a plank before a corpsewasher.[43] At the beginning of the 12th century two direct students of Ghazzālī, ᶜAyn al-Quḍāh and a certain ᶜAbd al-Karīm al-Rāzī, for the first time so far as I can see, applied this image to the novice's relation to the shaykh, and ᶜAbd al-Karīm explained that the difference between teaching the law and teaching Sufism was that the former required opposition, whereas the latter forbade it.[44] Ghazzālī himself, speaking more modestly, had employed the image of a blind man who must entrust himself to a guide on the bank of a river.[45] But from this time on the literature frequently repeats that before the shaykh the novice must be *perinde ac cadaver*. Qushayrī demands what amounts to the same in the 11th century, and one finds it even earlier. The Ṣūfiyya had long since applied to themselves the saying of the Prophet that the religious scholars are the heirs of the prophets. They had left the supervision of traditional learning to the actual religious scholars, the theologians, and understood their own claim as heirs differently, namely, they followed the Prophet's way of life and as recipients of divine knowledge like him, they constituted a new form of messengers from God known as *sufarāʾ* in distinction from the prophetic

---

hair see Joseph Henninger, 'Zur Frage des Haaropfers bei den Semiten', in *Die Wiener Schule der Völkerkunde*, Festschrift zum 25jährigen Bestand 1929-1954, pp. 349-68.

43 Qushayrī, *Risāla*, *bāb al-tawakkul*. Benedikt Reinert, *Die Lehre vom* tawakkul *in der klassischen Sufik*, Berlin, 1968, p. 96 below, b) 1.

44 Letter in ᶜAfīf ᶜUsayrān, *Muṣannafāt-i ᶜAyn al-Quḍāt-i Hamadānī*, Tehran, 1962, I, Part 3 (*Shakwā*), Introduction, p. 12. Subkī, *Ṭabaqāt al-shāfiᶜiyya al-kubrā*, Cairo, 1324, IV, p. 258. Ignaz Goldziher, *Vorlesungen über den Islam*², Heidelberg, 1925, p. 339, ftn. 78.

45 *Iḥyāʾ ᶜulūm al-dīn*, Part 3: *ᶜajāʾib al-qalb*, *bayān shurūṭ al-irāda*, Cairo, 1348, III, p. 65.

apostles, the *rusul*.[46] Abū Saᶜīd b. Abī'l-Khayr (d. 1049) is reported to have said to his followers: 'Our (meaning: my) superiority (as shaykh) over you (as novices) is that you speak to us but we speak to Him, you listen to us but we listen to Him, and you are with us but we are with Him.'[47] Similarly, there is the Tradition: 'The shaykh is to his people what the prophet is to his community.' In the later period the shaykh is often compared to Khaḍir, who knew more than Moses and forbade the latter to raise any objections,[48] or he is described as 'the authorized agent of inspiration' with reference to Gabriel,[49] or is even dubbed 'the lower lord' (*al-rabb al-adnā*) in distinction to 'the higher Lord' (God).[50] He is a 'reminder' of God and His Messenger,[51] becomes God's representative on earth,[52] honoring him is honoring God,[53] his command is God's command.[54] Qushayrī, Anṣārī and ᶜAyn al-Quḍāh do warn against viewing the shaykh as infallible[55] but the idea that God speaks through the

---

46 Anonymous (10th century): *Adab al-mulūk*, MS Khānaqāh-i Aḥmadī 87 (Shiraz), *bāb taᶜabbud al-ṣūfiyya* (p. 34), *bāb khuṣūṣiyyat al-ṣūfiyya* (pp. 41-42); see 'An Important Manuscript Find for Sufism', pp. 160 f.; *Adab al-mulūk*, ed. Radtke, pp. 30-34; 36-39.

47 *Asrār al-tawḥīd*, ed. Ṣafā, p. 306/Shafīᶜī-i Kadkanī, p. 294/trans. by O'Kane, p. 447. In *The Tadhkiratu'l-Awliyá ("Memoirs of the Saints") of... Farídu'ddín ᶜAṭṭár*, ed.... by Reynold A. Nicholson..., with a Critical Introduction by Mírzá Muḥammad b. ᶜAbdu'l-Wahháb Qazwíní, London-Leiden, 1905-07, II, p. 184, ll. 17-20, attributed to his teacher Abū'l-ᶜAbbās-i Qaṣṣāb.

48 Three examples from among many: Qushayrī, *Risāla*, *bāb ḥifẓ qulūb al-mashāyikh*, at the beginning. Ghazzālī, *Kīmiyāy-i saᶜādat*, 3rd *rukn* (*muhlikāt*), 1st *aṣl*, *sharāʾiṭ-i murīd*. Abū Ḥafṣ ᶜUmar al-Suhrawardī: *ᶜAwārif al-maᶜārif*, Chpt. 51 (*ādāb al-murīd*), in the margin of Ghazzālī: *Iḥyāʾ ᶜulūm al-dīn*, in many Cairene editions. Also published separately, Cairo, 1939, and Beirut, 1960.

49 *ᶜAwārif*, Chpt. 51: The shaykh is the authorized agent of inspiration (*amīn al-ilhām*) for the novices, as Gabriel is the authorized agent of revelation (*amīn al-waḥy*).

50 *Miṣbāḥ al-hidāya*, p. 218.

51 *ᶜAwārif*, Chpt. 51: *tadhkira min allāh wa-rasūlihī*.

52 Muḥyī al-Dīn Abū ᶜAbdallāh Muḥammad... Ibn ᶜArabī, *Al-futūḥāt al-makkiyya*, Būlāq, 1293, Chpt. 181. Muḥammad b. Muṭahhar b. Shaykh al-Islām Aḥmad-i Jām, *Ḥadīqat al-ḥaqīqa* (written 1244), Tehran, 1964, pp. 12-13.

53 *Futūḥāt*, Chpt. 181.

54 ᶜAyn al-Quḍāt: *Tamhīdāt*, in *Muṣannafāt-i ᶜAyn al-Quḍāt-i Hamadānī*, Tehran, 1341/1962, I, Part 3, p. 35, ll. 7-8.

55 Qushayrī, *Risāla*, *bāb al-waṣiyya li'l-murīdīn*/commentary Zakariyyā al-Anṣārī, *Natāʾij*, IV, p. 218/trans. by Richard Hartmann, *Al-Ḳuschairîs Darstellung des Ṣûfîtums*, in

shaykh often enough led to this warning being ignored, and in itself such an idea was a theoretical justification for doing so.

We now come to the question: How, when and where did the transition from the *shaykh al-taᶜlīm* to the *shaykh al-tarbiya* take place? The answer I am in a position to give is as follows. The transition is observable as a slow process of change from the 9th into the 11th century in one particular place. That place is Nayshābūr in Khurāsān. My witnesses, arranged in chronological order, are the following:

Abū Ḥafṣ al-Naysābūrī (alias al-Ḥaddād, d. circa 880), whose importance for Khurāsān Abū Ṭālib al-Makkī compared to that of Junayd's for Baghdad,[56] on one occasion came to Baghdad with his disciples. Junayd said to him: 'You have imposed the discipline (*adab*) of sultans on your students' (i.e. drilled them the way sultans drill their soldiers). Abū Ḥafṣ replied: 'Good discipline outwardly is the best sign of good discipline inwardly.'[57] — Another time he said: 'Sufism consists of nothing but rules of behavior (*ādāb*).'[58] — When he was asked: 'How have you attained your spiritual states?', he replied: 'By adopting what my shaykhs (plural!) commended to me without experiencing any doubts or raising any objections.'[59] — One of his followers, who performed lowly tasks among his disciples, he would not allow to utter a single word, though the person in question had spent large sums of money on his behalf and had even incurred heavy debts.[60] — When Abū Ḥafṣ dismissed the young Abū ᶜUthmān al-Ḥīrī who was to become his student in the future, the lat-

---

Türkische Bibliothek 18, Berlin, 1914, p. 195. Anṣārī, *Ṭabaqāt*, pp. 462-63. ᶜAyn al-Quḍāt, *Tamhīdāt*, p. 31, ll. 4-5.

56 *Qūt al-qulūb*, Cairo, 1351, II, p. 31, ll. 2-3 (*bāb waṣf al-ᶜilm*). Josef van Ess, *Die Erkenntnislehre des ᶜAḍudaddīn al-Īcī*, Akademie Wiss. Mainz, Veröff. d. Orientalischen Kommission 22, 1966, p. 224, rightfully doubts that our mystic is identical with the Shīᶜite dogmatist Abū Ḥafṣ al-Ḥaddād. That these are two different persons is also suggested by ᶜAlī b. Muḥammad al-Daylamī, *ᶜAṭf al-alif*, ed. J.C. Vadet, Cairo, Institut Français d'Archéologie Orientale, 1962, p. 13, no. 44, and p. 80, no. 283, where an Abū Ḥafṣ al-Ḥaddād is not included among the Sufis but among the *mutakallimūn*.

57 Qushayrī, *Risāla*, *bāb al-adab*/commentary of Zakariyyā al-Anṣārī, IV, p. 18. ᶜAṭṭār, *Tadhkira*, I, p. 326, ll. 20-25.

58 Sulamī, *Ṭabaqāt*, Cairo, p. 119, l. 13/Leiden, p. 110, ll. 2-3. ᶜAṭṭār, *Tadhkira*, I, p. 331, l. 6. The thought is widely disseminated and interpreted numerous ways.

59 Sulamī, *Jawāmiᶜ ādāb al-ṣūfiyya*, MS Berlin, Ahlwardt no. 3081, 64b.

60 *Lumaᶜ*, p. 177, ll. 10-14. Qushayrī: *Risāla*, *bāb al-ṣuḥba*. ᶜAṭṭār, *Tadhkira*, I, 327, ll. 9-15.

ter keeping his face on the shaykh walked backwards out the door, dug himself into the ground outside and waited for the shaykh's permission to come out of the hole.[61]

Abū ᶜUthmān al-Ḥīrī al-Naysābūrī (d. 910) is described by Sulamī and Jullābī as the man through whom Sufism became great in Nayshābūr.[62] His profile perhaps becomes most clearly visible against the background of criticism which al-Ḥakīm al-Tirmidhī and Abū Bakr al-Wāsiṭī (alias Ibn al-Farghānī, d. after 932 in Marw) levelled against him. Tirmidhī, in a letter, reproached him for devoting all his attention to the soul's faults instead of to God; that way the heart would never emerge from darkness into the light of certainty.[63] And Wāsiṭī learned in Nayshābūr from Ḥīrī's followers that he had ordered them to perform acts of worship most meticulously but to see in them only what could still be further improved. Wāsiṭī described this as dualism and regretted that Ḥīrī had not directed their gaze unto God alone.[64] The earliest specialist on the faults of the soul whom we know of in greater detail was Muḥāsibī (d. 857). He was active in Baghdad and was no Sufi. Outside Nayshābūr as well Sufis had often spoken and written about faults and spiritual exercises, for example Tustarī in Tustar,[65] Abū Bakr al-Warrāq in Balkh,[66] Jūzjānī[67] and many others including Ḥīrī's critics. But it is

---

61 Qushayrī, *Risāla*, sub Abū ᶜUthmān Saᶜīd al-Ḥīrī. ᶜAṭṭār, *Tadhkira*, II, p. 57, ll. 11-16.

62 Sulamī, *Ṭabaqāt*, Cairo, p. 170, ll. 6-7/Leiden, p. 159, l. 7. Abū'l-Ḥasan ᶜAlī... al-Jullābī al-Hujwīrī: *Kashf al-maḥjūb*, ed. Valentin Zhukovski, Leningrad, 1926 (reprint Tehran, 1336), p. 168, ll. 15-16/Reynold A. Nicholson: *The Kashf al-Maḥjúb. The Oldest Persian Treatise on Ṣúfism...* translated from the Text of the Lahore Edition..., Gibb Memorial Series 17, New Edition, London, 1936, p. 134: 'in Nayshābūr and Khurāsān'. ᶜAṭṭār, *Tadhkira*, II, p. 56, l. 1: 'in Khurāsān'.

63 *Masʾala*, MS İsmail Saib I (Ankara) 1571, 61a-62a. Catalogued in Othman Yahya, 'L'œuvre de Tirmiḏī', in *Mélanges Louis Massignon*, Damascus-Paris, 1957, p. 455, no. 75.

64 Qushayrī, *Risāla*, *bāb tafsīr alfāẓ*, sub *maqām*/commentary of Zakariyyā al-Anṣārī, II, pp. 28-29. Anṣārī, *Ṭabaqāt*, p. 364. *Nafaḥāt*, sub Abū Bakr al-Wāsiṭī, p. 178. ᶜAṭṭār, *Tadhkira*, II, p. 268, ll. 4-7. ᶜAyn al-Quḍāt, '*Shakwā*', in *JA*, 1930, pp. 58 and 247/Tehran, 1962, concluding part, p. 33, ll. 7-9/translated by A.J. Arberry, *A Sufi Martyr*, p. 61. Instead of Wāsiṭī, Abū Bakr al-Qaḥṭabī is also cited as proffering this criticism; Abū Bakr Muḥammad b. Isḥāq al-Bukhārī al-Kalābādhī: *Al-taᶜarruf li-madhhab ahl al-taṣawwuf*, ed. A.J. Arberry, Cairo, 1933, Chpt. 42, and Anṣārī, *Ṭabaqāt*, p. 364.

65 Sulamī, *Ṭabaqāt*, Cairo, p. 206, l. 4/Leiden, p. 199, l. 5.

66 Sulamī, *Ṭabaqāt*, Cairo, p. 221, l. 6/Leiden, p. 216, ll. 5-6.

67 Sulamī, *Ṭabaqāt*, Cairo, p. 246, l. 3/Leiden, p. 242, l. 4 (variant).

striking that Ḥīrī is reproached for being afflicted with a certain fixation, and that it was then Ḥīrī's students in Nayshābūr who especially cultivated this branch of Sufi training: Abū'l-Ḥusayn al-Warrāq (d. before 932) quite explicitly in the manner (*ᶜalā sanan*) of Ḥīrī,[68] and Abū ᶜAlī al-Thaqafī (d. 940).[69] An admirer of Ḥīrī who had visited many great masters confesses that he had never seen any better knower of 'the way to God' than Ḥīrī.[70]

What Sulamī and Jullābī maintained about Ḥīrī, Qushayrī maintained about the latter's student Abū ᶜAlī al-Thaqafī (d. 940):

---

68 Sulamī, *Ṭabaqāt*, Cairo, p. 299, l. 3/Leiden, p. 298, l. 4. Cf. also Anṣārī, *Ṭabaqāt*, p. 359. Jāmī, *Nafaḥāt*, sub Abū'l-Ḥusayn (amended) al-Warrāq, pp. 173-74.

69 Sulamī, *Ṭabaqāt*, Cairo, p. 361, l. 8/Leiden, p. 370, ll. 8-9. Anṣārī, *Ṭabaqāt*, p. 381. Jāmī, *Nafaḥāt*, sub Abū ᶜAlī al-Thaqafī, p. 203.

70 Sulamī, *Ṭabaqāt*, Cairo, p. 170, ll. 8-10/Leiden, p. 159, ll. 8-11. In ᶜAṭṭār, *Tadhkira*, II, p. 55, l. 24, abbreviated to 'knower of God'. — Not applicable here is the remark Ḥīrī is meant to have addressed to his student Abū ᶜAmr b. Nujayd: 'Do not rely on the friendship of those who do not love you, unless you are faultless (*maᶜṣūm*)!' Thus in *Lumaᶜ*, p. 208, ll. 14-15. In Qushayrī, *Risāla*, *bāb al-tawba*, and also in an interpretive elaboration in ᶜAṭṭār, *Tadhkira*, II, p. 58, ll. 10-17, the remark appears in a repentance story: Ibn Nujayd, to begin with, visited an assembly of Ḥīrī and the latter's words brought about his repentance. But then a certain lack of enthusiasm set in which caused Ibn Nujayd to avoid his teacher. When they met by chance, Ibn Nujayd wanted to turn away but Ḥīrī followed him and said when he caught up with him: 'My dear son, do not keep company with people who do not love you, unless you are faultless! I can be of use to you in this situation.' Ibn Nujayd is said to have then taken up his mystic striving or his novitiate once again. In this version Ḥīrī intimates that he can make his student flawless — if he does not simply mean: I am your true friend; so you do not have to be afraid of me, but I am offering you protection. Abū Ḥayyān al-Tawḥīdī, *Al-ṣadāqa wa'l-ṣadīq*, Damascus, 1964, p. 35, cites the remark in the exact wording of the *Lumaᶜ*, but attributes it to Abū Ḥafṣ al-Naysābūrī. In this case the story goes: Abū Ḥafṣ disapproved of something in his student Abū ᶜUthmān al-Ḥīrī. The latter was utterly at a loss and would gladly have crept under the earth's surface to avoid coming before his sight. Abū Ḥafṣ noticed this and then said to him: 'Abū ᶜUthmān, do not rely on the friendship of those who do not love you, unless you are faultless!' Ḥīrī calmed down and became normal again. Probably here as well is meant: Turning to others besides friends is only advisable if one offers no target to those who wish one harm, and here too, though it is not explicitly stated, the teacher seems to be ready to help the student advance in this direction. The Persian translation of Qushayrī renders the Arabic original incorrectly: 'Do not keep company with anyone who considers you faultless (?).' Perhaps the word *dōst* has dropped out and it should be read: 'who only loves you as someone faultless' (p. 139, l. 16) — which could be brought into full agreement with the Arabic wording. But obscurities and contradictions in the transmission make it impossible to come to an unambiguous assessment and sure conclusion.

through him Sufism became well-known in Nayshābūr.[71] The necessity of submitting to a master, which had been proclaimed all along and would occasionally be less emphasized later, Thaqafī formulated with special keenness and for the first time put forward the demand for a 'training' and not simply a course of study. Though a person collected all the sciences and paid visits (*ṣaḥiba*) to a whole throng of different people, he would only become a man if he underwent spiritual training with a shaykh, an authority, a well-intentioned taskmaster (*muʾaddib*). Any person who has not been disciplined by someone who gives him orders and prohibitions and shows him the faults in his works and the absurdities of his ego, will not later be fit himself to be taken as a model for the ordering of religious actions.[72] This does not yet mean that the trainer must be a single person, and certain reports, which are unclear of course with regard to detail, appear to indicate that at this time changing one's teacher was not at all frowned upon in Nayshābūr. Murtaᶜish of Nayshābūr (d. 940) studied with Abū Ḥafṣ and Ḥīrī but then met Junayd and remained with him. Zajjājī of Nayshābūr (d. 959) was a student of Ḥīrī, Junayd, Nūrī, Ruwaym, and Ibrāhīm al-Khawwāṣ. Al-Rāzī al-Shaᶜrānī of Nayshābūr (d. 964) studied with several eminent shaykhs but especially with Ḥīrī and was greatly esteemed by the latter.[73] Abū Sahl al-Ṣuᶜlūkī of Nayshābūr (d. 980) was a student with Shiblī, Murtaᶜish and Thaqafī.[74] But these reports are unclear in so far as they do not specify with whom each of these individuals underwent his fundamental training, if one may already speak of such at this time.

Moreoever, there then appears for the first time in Nayshābūr the demand to obey the shaykh so unhesitatingly that one does not even

---

71 Qushayrī, *Risāla*, sub Abū ᶜAlī Muḥammad b. ᶜAbd al-Wahhāb al-Thaqafī.

72 Sulamī, *Ṭabaqāt*, Cairo, p. 365, ll. 8-11/Leiden, p. 373, l. 10, to p. 374, l. 3. Qushayrī, *Risāla*, sub Abū ᶜAlī al-Thaqafī. ᶜAyn al-Quḍāt: '*Shakwā*', in *JA*, 1930, pp. 47 and 226/Tehran, 1962, concluding part, p. 22, l. 17, to p. 23, l. 1/Arberry, *A Sufi Martyr*, p. 48. ᶜAṭṭār, *Tadhkira*, II, p. 282, ll. 13-16. The statement is wrongly attributed by Aḥmad b. ᶜAjība (d. 1809) to Ibrāhīm b. Shaybān al-Qirmīsīnī (J.-L. Michon in *Arabica* 16, 1969, p. 119).

73 Sulamī, *Ṭabaqāt*, under the individual names. Abū Ḥafṣ himself had several shaykhs (see ftn. 59 above). Ḥīrī is said to have been instructed and guided first by Yaḥyā b. Muᶜādh al-Rāzī, then by Shāh Shujāᶜ al-Kirmānī and finally by Abū Ḥafṣ (*Kashf al-maḥjūb*, ed. Zhukovski, pp. 167-68/trans. Nicholson, pp. 132-34).

74 Anṣārī, *Ṭabaqāt*, p. 498. I do not fully understand the report that Thaqafī was forced to speak only to himself and not to people, and therefore did not receive the blessing of his words (Sulamī, *Ṭabaqāt*, Cairo, p. 369, ll. 6-7/Leiden, p. 378, ll. 8-10).

ask the reason behind an order. Thaqafī's highly educated Nayshābūrī student Abū Sahl Muḥammad al-Ṣuᶜlūkī (d. 980) formulated the proposition: 'Whoever asks his spiritual master why shall never amount to anything.'[75] Sulamī (d. 1021), who was Ṣuᶜlūkī's student and also from Nayshābūr, put forward the rule that everything the shaykh orders must be undertaken whether one understands the sense of the order or not.[76] And Ṣuᶜlūkī's son, Sahl (d. 1014), twists the proposition 'the student's relation to the teacher is like that of a son to his father' in such a way that he maintains: 'Disobedience to one's parents can be eradicated through penance, whereas disobedience to one's spiritual master is absolutely ineradicable.'[77] Abū ᶜAlī al-Daqqāq (d. 1015) and his student Qushayrī (d. 1072) continue the strict practices in Nayshābūr. Qushayrī, however, does not wish to go as far as Sahl al-Ṣuᶜlūkī. Daqqāq cites the proposition: 'The beginning of heresy is acting in disobedience.'[78] And to this Qushayrī adds the comment: 'Which means whoever acts in disobedience to his shaykh (or: contradicts him) ends up leaving his path (*ṭarīqa*) and the bond between them both is broken, even if they both remain together in the same convent. Whoever becomes the student of a shaykh (*ṣaḥiba*) and then in his heart opposes him has broken the pact of association (*ṣuḥba*) and should do penance, although the shaykhs have said: "For disobedience to one's spiritual master there is no penance."'[79] Qushayrī herewith places his report about his lifelong respect for Daqqāq in its correct light. Daqqāq would only enter the gathering of his teacher Naṣrābādī after performing a major ritual ablution. Nor would Qushayrī ever visit Daqqāq other than after having performed a major ritual ablution, and in a state of fasting. He relates: 'I often went to the door of his school [80] and then turned back because I was too shy to go before him. But if I did pluck up the courage, when I arrived in the middle of the school a kind of numbing of the senses would come over me

---

75 Sulamī, *Jawāmiᶜ ādāb al-ṣūfiyya*, MS Berlin, Ahlwardt, no. 3081, 64b. Qushayrī, *Risāla*, *bāb ḥifẓ qulūb al-mashāyikh*. Subkī, *Ṭabaqāt al-shāfiᶜiyya al-kubrā*, II, p. 163. Goldziher, *Vorlesungen*², p. 339, ftn. 78.

76 Sulamī, *Jawāmiᶜ*, 64b.

77 Anṣārī, *Ṭabaqāt*, p. 499. In Subkī, *Ṭabaqāt*, II, p. 163, this is attributed to his father Abū Sahl and presented as a report from Sulamī.

78 An anonymous variant in *Lumaᶜ*, p. 177, ll. 5-6.

79 Qushayrī, *Risāla*, *bāb ḥifẓ qulūb al-mashāyikh*.

80 The Persian translation retains the word *madrasa*. Often *madrasa* is a synonym for *khānaqāh*, but it also often means a school of theologians different from a convent of Sufis.

so that if someone had stuck me with a needle I would probably not have felt a thing. If I then sat down because of a vision I had had, I did not first need to put a question to him. The moment I sat down, he started to explain my vision. I often experienced this with him and often I wondered to myself whether if in my time God sent another Messenger to mankind I would feel more shy before him than I felt before this spiritual master. I could not imagine that that would be possible. And as long as I frequented his gathering and was with him after having established more intimate ties with him, I cannot remember that any contrariness ever occurred in my heart or in my mind — up until he departed from this world.'[81]

One also finds in Qushayrī the rule that the novice should receive his training from a single shaykh. This is implied in the recommendation to the novices in the form of a last testament with which Qushayrī brought his *Risāla* to a close in 1046, since the training which he describes there is carried out by one and the same spiritual master. Moreover, he says explicitly that the novice may not leave the place of his novitiate and may not undertake travels before 'the Sufi path has accepted him and he has brought his heart to God' — and in another passage: 'until such time as permission is given'.[82] Here it is clear that Qushayrī has in mind a definite final conclusion of the novitiate, and at the same time the possibility is allowed that, should certain circumstances require it, the shaykh can release the novice in advance and pass him on to another spiritual master. This corresponds to later practice[83] and Qushayrī himself had previously acted this way: he allowed his student Abū ᶜAlī-i Fārmadhī, before the latter completed his novitiate, to move and attach himself to Abū'l-Qāsim-i Kurrakānī (Gurgānī).[84]

Herewith is the line of the Sufi shaykh in Nayshābūr traced to the fullest development of the *tarbiya*-type in the 11th century. It is devoid of gaps, and so firmly knit a skein of reports on the same subject is, as far as I am aware, unknown elsewhere. Of course, this should not lead us to the mistaken assumption that such a development only took place in Nayshābūr. Against that view is the simple

---

81 Qushayrī, *Risāla*, *bāb al-ṣuḥba*. Later ᶜUmar al-Suhrawardī experienced similar inhibitions before his shaykh (*ᶜAwārif al-maᶜārif*, Chpt. 51, *fī ādāb al-murīd maᶜa'l-shaykh*).

82 *Risāla*, sub *al-waṣiyya li'l-murīdīn*/commentary of Zakariyyā al-Anṣārī, IV, pp. 215 and 217/translated by Richard Hartmann, *Al-Ḳuschairîs Darstellung des Ṣûfîtums*, in Türkische Bibliothek 18, Berlin, 1914, pp. 190 and 194.

83 Further details in *Fawāᵓiḥ*, Introduction, pp. 18-19.

84 Jāmī, *Nafaḥāt*, sub Abū ᶜAlī-i Fārmadhī, p. 369.

observation that our principle sources originate in Nayshābūr and consequently other geographical areas may easily have slipped into the darkness. We do not know what was recorded in the *Kitāb al-murīdīn* of Yaḥyā b. Muᶜādh,[85] *al-Jāmiᶜ al-ṣaghīr fī'l-ādāb* of Dhū'l-Nūn,[86] the *Kitāb al-ṣuḥba* of Burjulānī,[87] the *Ṣifāt al-murīdīn* of Ibn al-Farajī (d. after 903 in Ramla),[88] and in similar works of Junayd, Aḥmad b. Khiḍrawayh, al-Ḥakīm al-Tirmidhī, Abū'l-Qāsim al-Ḥakīm, Abū Bakr al-Warrāq, and Tustarī.[89] It is also difficult to say whether the recommendations of Sarrāj mentioned earlier do not indicate backgrounds which at least resembled the conditions in Nayshābūr but which should be located elsewhere. In favor of such a conclusion are the diverse points of contact that exist between association with a shaykh and association with companions, particularly travel companions. Both forms of *ṣuḥba* display certain features in common, and it may well be that they exerted mutual influence on one another even if it is impossible for us to determine the origin of any particular feature. During journeys undertaken by a group of comrades, one person often held command and he could impose a strict regime.[90] There is a rule that states: 'Any companion to whom you say: "Get up, we're off!" and who asks you whereto, is no companion.'[91] An unknown Sufi wanted to separate from another Sufi after having been together with him for a long time. The latter only wished that the former associate with someone who surpassed him, i.e. the one being left, but then quickly withdrew this initial obligingness, reminding him of the inviolability of the first association.[92] The classification of shaykhs as a category of messengers from God, though already attested in the 10th century, is by no means docu-

---

85 Ibn al-Nadīm, *Al-fihrist*, ed. Gustav Flügel, Leipzig, 1871, I, p. 184, l. 5.

86 *Fihrist*, I, p. 185, ll. 26-27.

87 *Fihrist*, I, p. 185, l. 2.

88 Abū Nuᶜaym Aḥmad b. ᶜAbdallāh al-Iṣbahānī, *Ḥilyat al-awliyā'*, Cairo, 1932-38, X, p. 287, l. 3 from bot. Mentioned by the editor of the *Ṭabaqāt* of Sulamī, Cairo, p. 146, l. 22, and by the editor of the *Ṭabaqāt* of Anṣārī, p. 247, ftn. 1; in both cases in the singular, *Ṣifat al-murīdīn*. Samᶜānī's article on Ibn al-Farajī in *Al-ansāb*, facsimile, Gibb Memorial Series 20, 1913, p. 422a-b, does not mention the work.

89 *Kashf al-maḥjūb*, ed. Zhukovski, p. 439, ll. 6-9/trans. by Nicholson, p. 338. Jullābī cites three books with their titles. He has possibly made some mistakes in this connection.

90 *Lumaᶜ*, pp. 177-79. Qushayrī, *Risāla*, *bāb aḥkāmihim fī'l-safar*.

91 *Lumaᶜ*, p. 176, l. 20, to p. 177, l. 1. Qushayrī, *Risāla*, *bāb aḥkāmihim fī'l-safar*.

92 Qushayrī, *Risāla*, *bāb al-ṣuḥba*.

mented as being of Nayshābūrī origin.[93] Abū Bakr al-Warrāq (9th cent.), who was active in Balkh, deserves special attention as an early representative of the strict conception of *tarbiya.* He was known as a taskmaster of the Friends of God (*muʾaddib al-awliyāʾ*).[94] The books which he wrote about spiritual exercises and rules of behavior have been lost, but some of his dicta have survived and give a clear idea of what this taskmaster was like. For instance: 'A novice who is not able to get by for a week without food and drink because of the glance of his shaykh is not honest... Oh you novices, be concerned with service to the shaykhs for they are like a (sic) hunter who drives the novices away from the jaws of the devils... If your shaykh orders spiritual retreat, listen to him and do not demand proof for this!'[95] 'The origin of man is water and earth. In one man water is dominant, and you must apply discipline to him gently, otherwise he will be intimidated and not reach the goal. In another man earth is dominant, and you must give him a kick and deal with him harshly so that he may turn out suitable for something.'[96] Abū Bakr al-Warrāq forbade his students to travel and said: 'The key to all blessings is to remain steadfast in the place of your novitiate until your novitiate is accomplished.'[97] If these dicta or even just the last one which is the best attested of them are true, then already by the 9th century in Balkh, if only in the case of this one shaykh, the stage was reached which appears to have first been reached in the 11th century in Nayshābūr. Despotic discipline could also be applied in non-Sufi areas of learning. The priestly law teacher Mālik (d. 795) held sway like a prince in his gatherings in Medina. The members of the audience sat so motionlessly, it was as if they had birds perched on their heads.[98] Shāfiʿī only dared to turn the pages very gently in front of him,[99] and again Shāfiʿī's student,

---

93 'An Important Manuscript Find', p. 160 ff.

94 *Kashf al-maḥjūb*, ed. Zhukovski, p. 179, l. 5/trans. by Nicholson, p. 142. ʿAṭṭār, *Tadhkira*, II, p. 103, l. 2.

95 Shaʿrānī, *Al-anwār al-qudsiyya fī maʿrifat qawāʿid al-ṣūfiyya*, Cairo, 1962, I, p. 201.

96 ʿAṭṭār, *Tadhkira*, II, p. 105, l. 22, to p. 106, l. 1.

97 Qushayrī, *Risāla*, sub Abū Bakr Muḥammad b. ʿUmar al-Warrāq al-Tirmidhī. ʿAṭṭār, *Tadhkira*, II, p. 103, ll. 5-7.

98 Qāḍī ʿIyāḍ, *Tartīb al-madārik wa-taqrīb al-masālik li-maʿrifat aʿlām madhhab Mālik*, Beirut, 1968, I, pp. 153-66.

99 Ibn Jamāʿa, *Tadhkirat al-sāmiʿ wa'l-mutakallim fī adab al-ʿālim wa'l-mutaʿallim*, Hyderabad, 1353, p. 88.

Rabīᶜ, out of fear of Shāfiᶜī would never drink water in his presence.[100] As for the proposal to employ intermediary transmitters of his word amidst the increased number of his students, Mālik dismissed this with a reference to surah 49/2: 'Oh you who believe, do not raise up your voice before Him as you do among yourselves.'[101] This is the same Koranic passage which at a later date ᶜUmar al-Suhrawardī quoted with regard to the correct behavior of novices towards their shaykh.[102] Mālik demanded this respect on behalf of the sacred activity of transmitting prophetic sayings and the memory of Muḥammad who had become the *genius loci* of Medina, whereas Suhrawardī demanded it on behalf of the pontifical figure of the shaykh as mediator of divine wisdom.

A few traditions which at first glance appear to be evidence of a strict application of Sufi training outside Nayshābūr, on closer examination prove to be inventions. For example there is the story of Abū Sulaymān al-Dārānī (d. 830 in Syria) and his student Aḥmad b. Abī'l-Ḥawārī. The agreement existed between the two of them that Aḥmad would not disobey his spiritual master no matter what the latter ordered him. One day Aḥmad disturbed his teacher during a teaching session with the announcement: 'The oven is heated up. What are your orders?' Not receiving an answer, he repeated the question two more times. At that, Dārānī became angry and said: 'Get inside it!' Aḥmad followed his orders, and when later on Dārānī remembered him and had someone look for him, Aḥmad was still sitting in the oven but not a single hair on him had been burnt.[103] Now to begin with, no one is likely to take this story in a literal sense. Secondly, what the account describes is expressly a special agreement that Aḥmad had concluded with this shaykh. What we're dealing with here is therefore an exceptional case. Thirdly, this is a story which appears anonymously among the *isrāʾīliyyāt* of the Prophet.[104] Fourthly, variants of it are told about Muḥammad-i

---

100 Ibid. And cf. Aḥmad Shalabī, *Taʾrīkh al-tarbiya al-islāmiyya*, Beirut, 1954, p. 300.

101 Qāḍī ᶜIyāḍ, *Tartīb al-madārik*, I, p. 162.

102 *ᶜAwārif al-maᶜārif*, Chpt. 51.

103 Qushayrī, *Risāla, bāb al-irāda. Nafaḥāt*, sub Aḥmad b. Abī'l-Ḥawārī, p. 65.

104 Abū Zayd ᶜAbd al-Raḥmān b. Muḥammad al-Anṣārī al-Usaydī al-Dabbāgh and Abū'l-Qāsim b. ᶜĪsā b. Nājī al-Tanūkhī, *Maᶜālim al-īmān fī maᶜrifat ahl al-Qayrawān*, Cairo, 1968, I, p. 101.

ᶜAbdallāh-i Gāzur[105] and about Abū Ḥāmid(-i) Dūstān of Marw.[106] Fifthly, these variants do not illustrate obedience to one's teacher but in the case of Dūstān loyalty to a friend, and in the case of Gāzur the absence of feelings of loneliness among the Friends of God. What we have here is a *Wanderlegende*. — Also unhistorical is the story about Kāzarūnī (d. 1035) who orders an aspirant to beat up a certain old man. Twice the youth recoils from the act and on the second occasion he even receives hospitality from the pious old man. The third time he does strike him and then runs back to Kāzarūnī. The old man follows after him and excuses himself for all the unpleasantness he has caused the youth.[107] The situation is absurd, and the inventor wanted to set forth three lessons at once: that of blind obedience to the shaykh, as required of the young man; that of cheerfully putting up with all forms of discomfort arising from one's fellow-man; and that of at first seeking all faults within oneself, as the old man demonstrates. — The third case is the assertion of Kubrā (d. 1221) that the attachment of the heart to the shaykh and instruction by the shaykh concerning visionary experiences belonged to 'the eight requirements of the path of Junayd'.[108] Such a requirement is not attested in the surviving fragments of Junayd's writings. This is the same kind of anachronistic falsification as the later statement that Junayd could never hear more than twelve visions of his students without becoming bored.[109] — Also adjusted to the views of a later period appears to be the report of how Sulamī underwent schooling with Abū Sahl al-Ṣuᶜlūkī, which a certain Murād al-Dawsī al-Shādhilī in the 17th century has presented us with.[110]

One may perhaps sum up the relevant facts in the following manner. The *shaykh al-tarbiya* was by no means the exclusive creation of Nayshābūr but developed over time in various localities from the 9th century onwards. However, in Nayshābūr from the 9th to the 11th century there appeared an uninterrupted sequence of shaykhs who

---

105 Anṣārī, *Ṭabaqāt*, pp. 512-13.

106 *Asrār al-tawḥīd*, ed. Ṣafā, p. 272/ed. Shafīᶜī-i Kadkanī, p. 259/trans. by O'Kane, p. 390. Jāmī, *Nafaḥāt*, sub Abū Ḥāmid(-i) Dūstān, pp. 281-82.

107 *Firdaws al-murshidiyya*, p. 340, l. 19, to p. 341, l. 17/Tehran, p. 312, l. 14, to p. 313, l. 8.

108 *Fawāʾiḥ*, § 6.

109 Erika Glassen, *Die frühen Safawiden nach Qāżī Aḥmad Qumī*, dissertation Freiburg im Breisgau, 1968, p. 36.

110 M.J. Kister, *Kitāb ādāb al-ṣuḥba by Abū ᶜAbd ar-Raḥmān as-Sulamī*, Jerusalem, 1954, Arabic introduction, p. 4.

directed the greatest attentions to the strict training of their students. In so doing they were certainly reflecting a more widespread trend but at the same time they participated in shaping and furthering the development. When in the 10th and 11th centuries compilers and theoreticians such as Sulamī and Qushayrī set about their work, the problems concerning the Sufi shaykh, in particular the status he had attained in Nayshābūr, found expression in their writings. The importance which these writings came to possess then assured leading authority for the Nayshābūrī model.

It is only natural to pose the question: Why especially should Nayshābūr have come to cultivate this rigorous style of Sufi education? Nayshābūr was, from the 9th into the 11th century, something like a cultural capital of Iran, and the Iranians were renowned for their aristocratic despotism, their statesmanship, their conception of order, their formalities and protocol, and their talent for organization.[111] As for the inhabitants of the province of Khurāsān in particular, they had the reputation of being good soldiers with sturdy physiques, strong shoulders and skulls, beards and mustaches and terrifying voices,[112] in short a kind of 'Prussians', and likewise of being proud and heavyhanded. Mesopotamian and Khurāsānian were opposites. 'Khurāsānian speech'[113] is uncultivated speech. Abū Ḥafṣ al-Naysābūrī when in Baghdad extended an invitation to speak to those gathered around him, with the *captatio benevolentiae*: 'Come on now, you've got the talent for it!'[114] He was once asked why people in Nayshābūr didn't discuss as in Baghdad and elsewhere. He referred to the tradition of reticence among the shaykhs of Nayshābūr.[115] Junayd allotted the tongue to Mesopotamia and truthfulness to Khurāsān.[116] The pious Khurāsānian philosopher ᶜĀmirī did not feel comfortable in Baghdad in 975. People were hostile to

111 Jāḥiẓ, *Al-akhbār*, in Pellat, *JA* 255, 1967, I, pp. 65-105. Masᶜūdī, *Akhbār al-zamān*, Cairo, 1938, p. 78 (*dhikr mamlakat al-furs*). ᶜĀmirī, *Al-iᶜlām bi-manāqib al-islām*, Cairo, 1967, p. 174. Abū Ḥayyān al-Tawḥīdī, *Al-imtāᶜ wa'l-muᵓānasa*, Cairo, 1939, I, pp. 74 and 212. Thaᶜālibī, *Thimār al-qulūb*, Cairo, 1965, no. 310. And frequently.

112 Ibn Qutayba, *ᶜUyūn al-akhbār*, Cairo, 1925, I, p. 205, ll. 2-4.

113 Tawḥīdī, *Al-ṣadāqa wa'l-ṣadīq*, Damascus, 1964, p. 67.

114 Sulamī, *Ṭabaqāt*, Cairo, p. 117, l. 15, to p. 118, l, 1/Leiden, p. 108, l. 3.

115 Sulamī, *Risālat al-malāmatiyya*, in Abū'l-ᶜIlā ᶜAfīfī, *Al-malāmatiyya wa'l-ṣūfiyya wa-ahl al-futuwwa*, Cairo, 1945, p. 112, § 21.

116 Yāfiᶜī, *Al-irshād wa'l-taṭrīz fī faḍl dhikr allāh taᶜālā wa-tilāwat kitābihī'l-ᶜazīz*, Cairo, 1378, p. 111.

him and did not appreciate him.[117] After his return home, he admitted that the best would be a mixture between the solidity of Khurāsān and the elegance of Mesopotamia, for then both forms of onesidedness, the Khurāsānian stiffness and the Mesopotamian frivolity, would be eliminated.[118] But Khurāsān is a large region, and if the alleged characterization is accepted as accurate for the whole province, then the other cities in Khurāsān ought to have possessed the same or similar pre-conditions. In that case, then, the enumerated character traits on their own would not be adequate as an explanation, even if it could be proved that they existed in a united and more intense form in Nayshābūr. The same may be said regarding the formation of factions and the factional passions that Maqdisī emphasized, and which tore Nayshābūr apart in the 10th century.[119] After all, this factional strife took place elsewhere in Khurāsān and in many other areas as well.

Two striking phenomena in this period in Nayshābūr, the movement of the Malāmatiyya and the movement of the *ahl al-futuwwa*, are of such a nature as to enlarge our question and to shift it further afield rather than to answer it. The Malāmatiyya were Sufis who followed, or at one time had followed, the tendency which Tirmidhī and Wāsiṭī criticized in Ḥīrī. The Malāmatiyya travelled this road to the end, felt that the only correct method for eliminating the ego before God was to pursue it into its ultimate hiding places, and in whatever they achieved always to see only its mocking grimace. This spellbound fixation of their gaze on an ego that must be destroyed at all costs led them to destroy whatever forms took on appearance whether inwardly or outwardly, and even to abandon the name of Sufi and Sufi dress. One might well imagine that these relentless attempts to annihilate complacency and personal identity could not be carried out securely without someone who acted as a pace-setter and a taskmaster. And this would appear to be confirmed by Sulamī's *Risālat al-malāmatiyya*, for it frequently treats of the guidance which the Malāmatī had to submit himself to. On closer examination, how-

---

117 Abū Ḥayyān al-Tawḥīdī, *Al-muqābasāt*, ed. Ḥasan Sandūbī, Cairo, 1929, no. 90 (p. 307).

118 *Muntakhab Ṣiwān al-ḥikma*, in Miskawayh, *Al-ḥikma al-khālida, Jāwīdān khirad*, ed. ʿAbd al-Raḥmān Badawī, Cairo, 1952, p. 348.

119 *Descriptio imperii Moslemici auctore Al-Mokaddasi*, ed. M.J. De Goeje, in Bibliotheca geographorum Arabicorum 3, Leiden, 1877, p. 336. Claude Cahen, 'Mouvements populaires et autonomisme urbain dans l'Asie musulmane du Moyen Âge', in *Arabica* 6, 1959, pp. 27 ff. C.E. Bosworth, *The Ghaznavids*, Edinburgh, 1963, pp. 163-71.

ever, the treatise proves to be an extremely onesided defense of the Malāmatiyya which blurs the boundaries between *malāma* and non-*malāma*, and does not shrink from appropriating even such figures as Yaḥyā b. Muᶜādh al-Rāzī, Wāsiṭī and others for the Malāmatiyya.[120] Only towards the end of the treatise does the fog lift when Muḥammad b. Aḥmad al-Farrāᵓ (d. 980-81) declares: 'The Malāmatiyya had nothing prescribed that had to be learned and nothing written that had to be written down, but they had only one shaykh by the name of Ḥamdūn al-Qaṣṣār (d. 884-85).'[121] Accordingly, classifying Abū Ḥafṣ al-Naysābūrī and Abū ᶜUthmān al-Ḥīrī in the Malāmatiyya movement, as Sulamī does, is automatically corrected. It is not as Sulamī writes that the oldest representatives of *malāma* had trodden three separate paths: Abū Ḥafṣ had made his novices undertake works and spiritual struggle, and held up good actions as examples for them; Ḥamdūn had diminished the importance of religious practices in the eyes of his novices and constantly pointed to the deficiencies of such acts; and Ḥīrī had chosen a middle road, namely to have the novices undertake good works but then to make them conscious of the worthlessness of these.[122] On the contrary, Abū Ḥafṣ and Ḥīrī both stand outside the *malāma*, even though like most, indeed all, Sufis they frowned upon and forbade taking pride in works, receiving attention and displaying achievements. Sulamī's presentation in his *Risālat al-malāmatiyya* does, however, provide new evidence that Abū Ḥafṣ and Ḥīrī had pursued the energetic training of their novices. Furtherover, one might add that the Malāmatiyya also existed in Mesopotamia, only there they were known as 'the wise madmen' (*ᶜuqalāᵓ al-majānīn*).[123] As late as

120 ᶜAfīfī, *Malāmatiyya*, pp. 33-34. That Sulamī is not wholly objective in his description of the Malāmatiyya's current of thought is also rightly noted by ᶜAbd al-Ḥusayn-i Zarrīnkūb, *Arzish-i mīrāth-i ṣūfiyya*, Tehran, 1344, p. 109 below.

121 ᶜAfīfī, *Malāmatiyya*, p. 119.

122 ᶜAfīfī, p. 103.

123 Abū Ṭālib al-Makkī, *Qūt al-qulūb*, Cairo, 1351, III, p. 108, l. 3. Whether the views of the Malāmatiyya were brought from Nayshābūr to ᶜIrāq, as Anṣārī, *Ṭabaqāt*, p. 103 (*Nafaḥāt*, sub Ḥamdūn-i Qaṣṣār, p. 60) appears to assume, is very doubtful. Then Ibn Zīrī (probably should be read thus; Qushayrī, *Risāla*, *bāb al-samāᶜ*; Arberry, *A Sufi Martyr*, p. 77; additional passages in Anṣārī, *Ṭabaqāt*, p. 379, ftn. 1), a companion of Junayd, must have been under influence from Nayshābūr (see the stories in Daylamī, *Sīra*, pp. 105-07). The beginnings of *malāma* appear everywhere but the name *malāma* only emerged in Nayshābūr or in Khurāsān, and perhaps Ḥamdūn, the great proponent of this trend in Nayshābūr, created the

1200 they were still not called Malāmatiyya in Mesopotamia.[124] As for the *ahl al-futuwwa*, all they had in common with the Ṣūfiyya and the Malāmatiyya was a high estimation of the concept of *futuwwa*, 'the chivalrous qualities of manhood'. Around this concept like a grail, they organized different forms of societies and associations, whose range of activities embraced the aristocratic pursuit of hunting, economic and social interests, and even included living the life of irregular troops or bandits. There were persons who moved on from *futuwwa*-associations to Sufism and others who may well have combined the two together. Testimonies of their sense of self-sacrifice and their steadfastness have been preserved but we learn nothing of life in their associations at this time. Perhaps their discipline presented a certain parallel with the attitude which Sufism demanded of its students, but from this vague possibility to draw the conclusion that in some way the one association passed on its tint to the other would be rash. So in this case as well, reservation is also due since the *futuwwa*-associations were by no means the exclusive property of Nayshābūr. They existed everywhere.

Thus, for the present nothing should be added to what has already been said: Nayshābūr, as far as the development of the Sufi novitiate is concerned, represents a major bridge for the transition from the classical period with its *shaykh al-taᶜlīm* to the post-classical period with its *shaykh al-tarbiya*. Qushayrī in the 11th century closes the old and opens the new period. The authorities of the post-classical era such as Muḥammad al-Ghazzālī around 1100 and ᶜUmar al-Suhrawardī around 1200 — and naturally a whole series of others — go on to consolidate the fundamental principles laid down by Qushayrī. In the 16th century the Egyptian Shaᶜrānī provides a new detailed collection of materials.[125] Through the worldwide spread of the works of Qushayrī, Ghazzālī and Suhrawardī, through the numerous reworkings of their intellectual legacy, through the requirements of the increasingly more influential life of the orders, and through many other circumstances, these views on the master-disciple relationship are disseminated to the borders of the Islamic world. In the 18th century, in India the Naqshbandī poet Ghiyāthī

---

name. In Khurāsān what was understood by *malāma* was concealment and camouflage of one's own piety (*talbīs al-ḥāl*). The subject is too complicated to be entered into here.

124 *ᶜAwārif al-maᶜārif*, Chpt. 8.

125 *Anwār al-qudsiyya fī maᶜrifat qawāᶜid al-ṣūfiyya*, Cairo, 1962, I.

sings a hymn of praise to the sanctified shaykh,[126] in Morocco Dabbāgh and his biographer comment on a versification of Suhrawardī's chapters on the shaykh, which were written in the 13th century and at a later time were recommended for learning by heart.[127] And likewise Aḥmad b. ᶜAjība (d. 1809) repeats the doctrines of unreserved surrender to the shaykh, and indeed 'the shaykh who gives training' as he emphasizes[128] — doctrines which had long since become common property. Even non-Sufi rules of study come into the zone of influence of Sufi *tarbiya*: the Shāfiᶜī jurist Ibn Jamāᶜa (d. 1333) transposes principles of Sufi instruction — he cites Ghazzālī — to theological-juridical education.[129] In the process, contrary to Ibn Jamāᶜa's intentions the periodization emerged into view that Rundī would adopt a little later for both types of shaykh. This was so because the testimonies from earlier times that Ibn Jamāᶜa presents for *tarbiya* do not in fact support such a conclusion.

At the same time the old style continues, as does even the self-study of Sufism. The question whether one could not also get by without a shaykh is answered emphatically in the negative by Muḥammad b. al-Munawwar[130] in the 12th, and likewise by Dāya[131] in the 13th century. Rundī in the 14th century denied it as well theoretically but in practical terms affirmed it, for if one equates a textbook with the *shaykh al-taᶜlīm,* then of course shaykhs could die out

---

126 *Dīwān-i Ghiyāthī*, litho., Peshawar, n.d., pp. 87-90. This Ghiyāth al-Dīn lived in the time of a great-grandson of Ṣibghatallāh b. Maᶜṣūm (d. 1122/1710) and extolled a Mujaddidī family line from Sirhind.

127 Aḥmad b. al-Mubārak al-Sijilmāsī al-Lamaṭī *Al-ibrīz*, Cairo, n.d., pp. 236-54 (*al-bāb al-sādis fī dhikr shaykh al-tarbiya*...). More detailed information on the author of the commented upon *qaṣīda* in *rāʾ*, ibid., p. 253: The poem is by Tāj al-Dīn Abū'l-ᶜAbbās Aḥmad b. Muḥammad b. Aḥmad b. Muḥammad b. Aḥmad b. Khalaf al-Qurashī al-Taymī al-Bakrī al-Ṣiddīqī al-Sharīshī who was born in Salā in 581/1185 and grew up in Marrakesh, and then resided in Fayyūm where he died in 641/1243. His versification bears the title *Anwār al-sarāʾir wa-sarāʾir al-anwār* and is listed in *GAL S*, I, p. 802, 25a, and Sarkīs, *Muᶜjam al-maṭbūᶜāt*, II, p. 1122.

128 J.-L. Michon, 'L'autobiographie (Fahrasa) du soufi marocain Aḥmad Ibn ᶜAǧība (1747-1809)', in *Arabica* 16, 1969, pp. 118-27 [pp. 91-100].

129 *Tadhkirat al-sāmiᶜ wa'l-mutakallim*, Hyderabad, 1353, pp. 85-112.

130 *Asrār al-tawḥīd*, Ṣafā, pp. 52-53/Shafīᶜī-i Kadkanī, pp. 46-47/trans. O'Kane, pp. 119-20.

131 Abū Bakr ᶜAbdallāh b. Muḥammad b. Shāhāwar al-Asadī al-maᶜrūf bi-shaykh Najm al-Dīn-i Rāzī, *Mirṣād al-ᶜibād min al-mabdaʾ ilā'l-maᶜād*, Tehran, 1312/1352, pp. 126 ff. (*bāb* 3, *faṣl* 9).

without Sufi training having to come to an end. Ibn Khaldūn (d. 1405) answers the question in the affirmative but denies it for the part of psychic guidance involving the interpretation of visionary experiences and the bringing about of an artificial death.[132] Finally, it is reported that Zarrūq (d. 1493) considered training in the traditional sense to be superceded and called for a return to the Koran and the *sunna*. This, according to Dabbāgh, because in Zarrūq's time shaykhs who demanded obedience had only led people into error.[133] The view of Ibn Ṭufayl (d. 1185-86) that man, by himself, is capable of pressing forward to the highest levels of knowledge without any guidance, has never, as far as I am aware, led to a proposal among Sufis to do away with the role of the shaykh.

We cannot pursue these questions further here. Likewise, the problem of the necessary pre-conditions for the Sufi shaykh, teachings on other subtypes of the shaykh, on the different forms of conferring a patched frock, and much else that belongs to the history of the shaykh, lie outside the scope of the present study. Here I have only set out to examine Rundī's thesis regarding the *shaykh al-taᶜlīm* and the *shaykh al-tarbiya*, and to show that in Nayshābūr, a chief center of Sufism, the transition from the one to the other from the 9th into the 11th century can be clearly recognized and described.

ADDITIONS

[P. 205, l. 9: On this letter see 'An Important Manuscript Find', p. 188]

[P. 210, l. 7: On Ḥakīm Tirmidhī's *Ādāb al-murīdīn* cf. 'Book of Etiquette', p. 91]

---

132 Ibn Khaldūn, *Shifāʾ al-sāʾil li-tahdhīb al-masāʾil*, ed. Muḥammad b. Tāwīt al-Ṭanjī, Istanbul, 1957, pp. 70 ff.; p. 80, l. 25.

133 Aḥmad b. al-Mubārak al-Sijilmāsī, *Al-ibrīz*, Cairo, n.d., pp. 207-08 (*al-bāb al-khāmis fī dhikr al-tashāyukh*...).

A SAYING OF THE PROPHET AGAINST MOURNING THE DEAD

Muḥammad forbade lamenting the dead. This prohibition is understandable in light of the effort to sever all ties with invisible beings other than God and to direct all good feelings to God. Moreover, Islam in fact traced the origin of idolatry back to the practice of honoring the dead.[1] But additional motives may well have played their part, for instance the ideal of surrendering oneself to the will of God[2] and the desire to bring the burial of the dead into line with the style of the other Islamic rites which, aside from an old part of the pilgrimage practices, are all characterized by a solemn dignity. Muḥammad also forbade poems of lamentation (*marāthī*, sing. *marthiya*).[3] These prohibitions were doubtlessly directed against existing pre-Islamic customs. And due to the tenacity of the latter they failed! Even of the women who swore to Muḥammad never to hold lamentations for the dead again, only five are said to have remained faithful to their commitment.[4] Muḥammad himself became the subject of poems of lamentation after his death. Both the composition of poetry of lamentation and holding lamentations for the dead are known to have continued to the present day. Even men of piety from the first century of Islam make use of arguments based on the practice of lamenting the dead. ᶜUmar b. Dharr asked his father Dharr b. ᶜAbdallāh (d. 80/699): 'How is it that you cause people to weep when you speak, whereas someone else is not capable of doing so?' His father replied: 'My son, the female mourner who has lost her own child is not the same as a female mourner who has been hired.'[5]

Lamentation of the dead (*niyāḥa, nawḥ*), however, is not necessarily identical with weeping (*bukāʾ*). Lamenting the dead is an institutionalized phenomenon and can also be practiced or accompanied by

---

1 Ibn al-Kalbī: *Al-aṣnām*, ed. Aḥmad Zakī Bāshā, Cairo, 1924, pp. 50 ff./Rosa Klinke-Rosenberger: *Das Götzenbuch*, Leipzig, 1941, German translation pp. 56 ff./Nabih Amin Faris: *The Book of Idols*, Princeton, 1952, pp. 43 ff.

2 Cf. Kulaynī: *Al-kāfī, kitāb al-janāʾiz*, Tehran, 1377, III, pp. 222-26.

3 Ibn Māja, *janāʾiz* 53, no. 1592. A.J. Wensinck: *A Handbook of Early Muhammadan Tradition*, Leiden, 1927, p. 52b s.v. *dead*.

4 Irene Grütter: 'Arabische Bestattungsbräuche in frühislamischer Zeit', in *Der Islam* 31, 1954, p. 123. Muslim: *Ṣaḥīḥ, janāʾiz* 10, no. 31.

5 Ibn Qutayba: *ᶜUyūn al-akhbār*, Cairo, 1925-30, II, p. 298, ll. 4-5.

people who in reality are not mourning. For this reason Muḥammad forbade 'assistance' by other women during mourning with the words: 'In Islam there is no seconding someone' (*lā isʿāda fī'l-islām*).[6] Furthermore, lamenting the dead is something noisy and can be accompanied by shouting, scratching the face, breast-beating and tearing out the hair, apart from other gestures of mourning such as throwing one's headgear on the ground, rending one's clothing, and so on. 'To us do not belong those who strike their cheeks, rend the upper part of their clothing and emit cries like in the old pagan times.'[7] By contrast, weeping springs from an intense inner compulsion and the degree of its loudness can also be muffled. The question then arises: does Islam also forbid weeping over the dead?

The answers one finds in the *ḥadīth* are contradictory, understandably so since on the one hand it was clear that weeping was of no use, whereas on the other hand the emotions of the sorely tried relatives ought not to be wholly suppressed.

A saying of the Prophet which is poorly attested numerically (*gharīb*) declares frankly: 'Weeping without lamenting the dead (*niyāḥa*) is permissible.'[8] Another saying which defends weeping gives different circumstances under which it was uttered. One time it was on the occasion when Usāma b. Zayd cried out at the death of Ibrāhīm, the son of the Prophet,[9] another time when women gathered together and wept at the death of an unspecified member of the Prophet's family,[10] a third time when an unnamed woman wept at another funeral,[11] a fourth time when the Prophet himself wept at someone's death.[12] In any case the Prophet is meant to have declared

---

6 Nasāʾī: *Sunan*, Cairo, 1930 ff., IV, p. 16. Ignaz Goldziher: 'Bemerkungen zur arabischen Trauerpoesie', in *WZKM* 16, 1902, p. 321/*Gesammelte Schriften*, IV, p. 375.

7 Bukhārī: *Ṣaḥīḥ*, *janāʾiz* 34. Ibn Māja, *janāʾiz* 52, no. 1584. Kulaynī: *Kāfī*, *janāʾiz*, *bāb al-ṣabr*, Tehran, 1377, III, pp. 222 ff. Here and in what follows I usually only give a selection of passages from the *ḥadīth*-literature. Abū Nuʿaym al-Iṣbahānī: *Ḥilyat al-awliyāʾ*, Cairo, 1932-38, V, p. 39, ll. 2-3.

8 *Ḥilyat al-awliyāʾ*, IV, p. 344, l. 3 from bot. The second Fāṭimid, Qāʾim, 'permit-ted' the mourning of his father ʿUbaydallāh (ʿAbdallāh) al-Mahdī in 322/934 and grieved for him during his whole life; the third and the fourth, Manṣūr and Muʿizz, suppressed the sadness at the death of their respective predecessors for the sake of forbearance (*ṣabr*). Al-Qāḍī al-Nuʿmān: *Risālat iftitāḥ al-daʿwa*, Beirut, 1970, pp. 270 and 279.

9 *Ḥilya*, VI, p. 256 lower half.

10 Nasāʾī, IV, p. 19.

11 Ibn Māja, *janāʾiz* 63, no. 1587.

12 Bukhārī, *janāʾiz* 44.

that the eye's shedding tears and the sorrow of the heart or the soul are compatible with his teaching. He is also supposed to have represented his weeping as an expression of the mercifulness with which he was endowed as a human being.[13]

Other *ḥadīth*s forbid weeping. When Muḥammad heard the screaming of the women in the house of the moribund ᶜAbdallāh b. Thābit, and Ibn ᶜAtīk wanted to make them be silent, he said: 'Leave them! But once his life is over, none of them should weep anymore.'[14] This means: before the arrival of death it is permissible for the relatives to weep, but not any longer after death. Apparently in this way the virtue of submission to God's will was meant to be promoted.[15] Another time Muḥammad limited weeping to one day after the advent of death.[16] After the Battle of Uḥud (in the year 3/624) he made it forbidden for women ever to weep over their dead in the future.[17]

The subject of our investigation will be a peculiar formulation of the prohibition which is transmitted in several variants in the canonical 'six books' of the *sunna*. The statement in the main goes as follows: 'The dead atones for the weeping of his relatives over him.' 'The dead atones for a part of the weeping of his relatives over him.' 'The dead atones for the weeping of the living.' 'The dead atones for the content of the lamentation held over him.' 'The person who is bewailed makes atonement for it.'[18] The statement has caused difficulties for Islamic theologians and Orientalists both with regard to its language and content.

An initial difficulty is the ambiguity of the Arabic expression *yuᶜadhdhabu bi-* which for the time being I have on purpose translated neutrally as 'to atone for'.

---

13 Ibn Māja, *janāʾiz* 53, no. 1588. Muslim, *janāʾiz* 4, no. 11. Cf. M. Wolff: *Muhammedanische Eschatologie*, Leipzig, 1872, Arabic pp. 30-31/German pp. 52-53.

14 Nasāʾī, IV, p. 13 below.

15 Cf. Kulaynī: *Kāfī*, *janāʾiz*, III, pp. 222-26. Ignaz Goldziher: *Muhammedanische Studien*, Halle, 1889, I, pp. 251-52.

16 Wensinck: *Handbook*, p. 155b s.v. *mourning*.

17 Ibn Māja, *janāʾiz* 53, no. 1591.

18 *Concordance et indices de la tradition musulmane*, Leiden, 1936-69, s.v. *yuᶜadhdhabu*. Ibn Saᶜd: *Kitāb al-ṭabaqāt al-kabīr*, Leiden, 1904-18, III, 1, p. 148, ll. 23 f.; p. 251, ll. 15 f.; p. 263, ll. 9 f.; p. 263, ll. 19 ff. Irene Grütter: 'Arabische Bestattungsbräuche', in *Der Islam* 31, 1954, p. 160. James Robson: *Mishkat Al-Masabih, English Translation with Explanatory Notes*, Lahore, 1963, I, pp. 360-68. ᶜAbd al-ᶜAẓīm b. ᶜAbd al-Qawī al-Mundhirī: *Al-targhīb wa'l-tarhīb min al-ḥadīth al-sharīf*, Beirut, 1968, IV, pp. 348-54.

The word can mean 'to be punished for something', as for example in a *ḥadīth* where a man is referred to who 'was punished in his grave for his action' (*yu*ᶜ*adhdhabu fī qabrihī bi-*ᶜ*amalihī*).[19] Already ᶜĀ᾿isha, the spouse of the Prophet, attributed this interpretation to the saying of the Prophet we are concerned with. She protested against its wording and maintained that the Prophet had meant it the other way round, namely: 'The dead will be punished for his fault and his sin (*yu*ᶜ*adhdhabu bi-khaṭī᾿atihī aw bi-dhanbihī*) and for this reason his relatives are already weeping over him now.'[20] When ᶜUmar I was fatally wounded in Medina and Ṣuhayb began to weep, ᶜUmar forbade him to do so and mentioned the *ḥadīth*. When this reached the ears of ᶜĀ᾿isha, she accorded the same interpretation to the saying as ᶜUmar but rejected it as being inauthentic in this form and referred to the firm guarantee of God in surah 6/164: 'And no one shall be made to bear another's burden.'[21] That is to say, nobody will be punished for the action of someone else. The interpretation of ᶜĀ᾿isha has maintained itself among theologians as one along with other possible interpretations and has also been accepted since Majd al-Dīn b. Athīr (d. 606/1210)[22] and Fakhr al-Dīn al-Rāzī (d. 606 /1210)[23] in the large Arabic dictionaries *Lisān al-*ᶜ*arab* of Ibn Manẓūr (d. 711/1311) and *Tāj al-*ᶜ*Arūs* of Zabīdī (d. 1205-1791) s.v. ᶜ*adhdhaba*. Edward William Lane included it in his *Arabic-English Lexicon* s.v. ᶜ*adhdhaba* where he translates: 'Verily the dead will be punished for his family's weeping for him.' It then made its way to Ignaz Goldziher who translates it in his studies as: 'Der Todte wird bestraft für manches Wehklagen der Hinterbliebenen.'[24] 'Fürwahr, der Tote wird (im Grabe) gepeinigt wegen der Wehklage seiner Angehörigen.'[25] 'Dass der Verstorbene wegen des Weinens der Hinterbliebenen bestraft würde.'[26] O. Houdas and W. Marçais in the

---

19 *Concordance* s.v. *yu*ᶜ*adhdhabu*.

20 Muslim: *Ṣaḥīḥ, janā᾿iz* 9, no. 26.

21 Nasā᾿ī, IV, pp. 18-19.

22 Majd al-Dīn Abū'l-Saᶜādat al-Mubārak b. Muḥammad al-Jazarī Ibn al-Athīr: *Al-nihāya fī gharīb al-ḥadīth*, s.v. ᶜ*adhdhaba*, Cairo, 1963, III, pp. 195-96.

23 Ignaz Goldziher: 'Aus der Theologie des Fachr al-dīn al-Rāzī', in *Der Islam* 3, 1912, p. 243/*Gesammelte Schriften*, V, p. 267.

24 *Muhammedanische Studien*, I, p. 253.

25 'Bemerkungen zur arabischen Trauerpoesie', in *WZKM* 16, 1902, p. 327, ftn. 1/*Gesammelte Schriften*, IV, p. 381, ftn. 1.

26 'Aus der Theologie des Fachr al-dīn al-Rāzī', p. 243/*Gesammelte Schriften*, V, p. 267.

*ḥadīth*s of Bukhārī also translate it as 'être châtié pour' or 'à cause de' or 'en raison de'.[27] Ragnar Eklund does the same: 'The dead are punished because the living mourn for them',[28] and so does James Robson: 'The dead is punished because of his family's weeping for him.'[29] An obviously subsequent variant of the saying intended to give support to this conception. It goes: 'Whoever has lamentation devoted to him will be punished for these plaintive words on Judgement Day.'[30] The addition 'on Judgement Day' is meant to direct attention to the notion of 'punishment'. On the other hand, since Islam also recognizes the idea of being punished already in the grave, this interpretation is equally possible in the case of the frequently transmitted old addition 'in his grave'.

Goldziher considered the corrections which ᶜĀᵓisha made to the wording to be an invention of later theologians who wished to accommodate the custom of mourning for the dead within Islam.[31] In fact ᶜĀᵓisha's criticism touches on a sore point of this interpretation because the question is immediately raised as to why the dead is punished for the weeping of the bereaved relatives. In order to clear up this second difficulty the theologians have devised a few expedients. Ibn Qutayba (d. 276/889) rejected ᶜĀᵓisha's criticism of the authenticity of the *ḥadīth* and also disapproved of combining the *ḥadīth* with surah 6/164: 'And no one shall be made to bear another's burden.' This Koranic verse is aimed against the practice of blood revenge by the ancient Arabs. Then he considers two possibilities for saving the *ḥadīth*, and not necessarily in the sense of an either-or but rather of a mutual fulfillment or two coordinated moves in chess. For example the threat of punishment for weeping, so he reflects, may only be directed against the unbelievers because one time the Prophet, when walking past the grave of a Jew, had said: 'He will be punished, and his relatives are mourning him.' Ibn Qutayba does not work the idea out clearly enough so that one can decide with certainty what he means. Does he mean the relatives were extolling the deceased for Jewish virtues which, according to

---

27 O. Houdas-W. Marçais: *El-Bokhâri. Les traditions islamiques, traduites de l'arabe avec notes et index*, Paris, 1903-14, I, pp. 416 and 417.

28 Ragnar Eklund: *Life between Death and Resurrection according to Islam*, dissertation Uppsala, 1941, p. 4.

29 Robson: *Mishkat Al-Masabih*, I, pp. 361 and 364.

30 Nawawī: *Riyāḍ al-ṣāliḥīn*, Cairo, 1970, pp. 862-63. Robson: *Mishkat*, I, pp. 363-64.

31 'Bemerkungen zur arabischen Trauerpoesie', p. 327, ftn. 1/*Gesammelte Schriften*, IV, p. 381, ftn. 1.

Islam, would inevitably lead him to certain destruction? Or does he mean: while the deceased is heading for sure suffering in Hell or is already experiencing it, his relatives are still weeping over him unsuspectingly? Or: because such is actually the case, they are weeping over him? But according to Ibn Qutayba the *ḥadīth* can also apply to the believers. Then, as he says, one should have in mind a punishment and catastrophe that effects everyone such as already befell mankind during the Flood and such as threatens to befall mankind again in surah 8/25: 'Make yourselves ready for an affliction which in no way will only strike the wrongdoers among you!'[32] The Ḥanafite scholar Abū'l-Layth al-Samarqandī (4th/10th century) recalls that in Muḥammad's time it was a custom among the Arabs to command the relatives to lament before a person's actual death. This custom is here tacitly taken for granted. But once the prohibition had been decreed in Islam, anyone who still ordered lamentation to be carried out for himself was punishable. This explanation has been adopted by the big Arabic dictionaries and by Lane as well. Similarly, the most recent editor of Nawawī's *Riyāḍ al-ṣāliḥīn*, Dr. al-Ḥusaynī ᶜAbd al-Majīd Hāshim, repeats this explanation.[33] But Samarqandī indicates still a second possible explanation. He recalls the above-mentioned statement that Muḥammad is supposed to have made when he walked past the grave of a Jew, and explains the formulation 'The dead atones for the weeping of his relatives over him' as going back to a false interpretation of that statement by the transmitter. In support of this view he refers to ᶜĀᵓisha who did not recognize the *ḥadīth* as authentic in this form.[34] The story involving the Jew, which Ibn Qutayba and Samarqandī recount, is in fact found in the *ḥadīth*-collections, however there it is not a Jew but a Jewess.[35] The same two possibilities given by Samarqandī are also mentioned by the Twelver-Shīᶜite al-Sayyid al-Sharīf al-Murtaḍā ᶜAlam al-Hudā (d. 436/1044) in his work *Tanzīh al-anbiyāᵓ*, Najaf, 1250, pp. 124-125. He also reflects on a third possibility, i.e. the idea we have already considered in our questions about Ibn Qutayba that during mourning and lamentation deeds of the deceased were often extolled which are sins in the eyes of God and for which the de-

---

32 Ibn Qutayba: *Taᵓwīl mukhtalif al-ḥadīth*, Cairo, 1966, p. 248, last line, to p. 250.

33 Nawawī: *Riyāḍ al-ṣāliḥīn*, Cairo, 1970, p. 862.

34 Abū'l-Layth Naṣr b. Muḥammad al-Samarqandī: *Bustān al-ᶜārifīn*, Chpt. 75, Istanbul, n.d., pp. 135-36.

35 Bukhārī, *janāᵓiz* 33; Muslim, *janāᵓiz* 27. Nasāᵓī, IV, pp. 17-18. Robson: *Mishkat*, I, p. 364.

ceased will have to atone. This, it would seem, is the conception that underlies the variant of the *ḥadīth* which is worded: 'The dead atones for the content of the lamentations held over him.' And fitting rather well with this is a further variant in which the prohibition against weeping, or the danger of punishment for the one mourned, is associated with certain exclamations emitted during lamentation. It is not a question in this case of sins evoked as glorious deeds during the wailing but simply of exaggerated titles which could imply a degree of competition with God on the part of the deceased. This variant goes: 'The dead atones for the weeping of the living when they say: "Oh the strong arm! Oh the provider of clothes! Oh the helper! Oh the mountain!" And suchlike.'[36] Khalīl b. Aybak al-Ṣafadī (d. 764 /1363) cites Ibn ᶜArabī (d. 638/1240) and mentions that most people followed the first interpretation, i.e. they assumed the deceased had previously ordered the lamentation, and then considered his punishment for it to be a logical consequence. With the same logical consistency a person who had not asked for lamentation at his death was not punished (here one especially has in mind children). According to others, however, a person who has neglected expressly to forbid lamentation on his behalf is also punishable. Still others, so Ṣafadī continues, supported the third possible explanation, that is to say: they attacked the enumeration of so-called deeds of glory which in reality were sins and for which the deceased would be punished. [37] The commentator on Bukhārī, Damāmīnī (d. 827/1424), maintains that the threat of punishment is in fact aimed at a person who has generally encouraged his family to practice the custom of lamenting the dead at funerals and not simply at someone who has ordered such a practice for the occasion of his own death — which passage is

---

36 Ibn Māja, *janāʾiz* 54, no. 1594. Finer distinctions in ftn. 2 to Kulaynī: *Kāfī*, III, p. 223.

37 *Tashnīf al-samᶜ fī'nsikāb al-damᶜ*, Cairo, 1321, pp. 31-32. The exhumed corpse of the Zangids' vizier who died in Mawṣil in 559/1164, Jamāl al-Dīn Muḥammad b. ᶜAlī b. Abī Manṣūr al-Jawād al-Iṣfahānī, which was taken along on a pilgrimage to Mecca and ᶜArafāt and from there was carried to Medina to be buried near the Prophet, was accompanied by a paid man who everywhere publicly declared the merits of the deceased and also recited verses in his praise (Ibn Khallikān: *Wafayāt al-aᶜyān*, no. 675). In some particulars Ibn Khallikān's report contradicts the description of Samhūdī (9th/15th century, in Ferdinand Wüstenfeld: *Geschichte der Stadt Medina*, in Abh. Kgl. Ges. Wiss. Göttingen 9, 1860, p. 102). In Egypt lamenting the dead while enumerating the virtues of the deceased is called *ᶜadīd* and the female lamenter *muᶜaddida*; Paul Kahle: 'Die Totenklage im heutigen Ägypten', in *Ευχαριστήριον, Hermann Gunkel zum 60. Geburtstage*, Göttingen, 1923, p. 349.

quoted in the Bukhārī commentator, Qasṭallānī (d. 923/1517), who presents some of the enumerated attempts at interpretation and otherwise remains firmly convinced that the difficulties can be overcome by means of this approach.[38]

As we said, ᶜĀᵓisha bridged the gap between practice in life and the theory of this *ḥadīth* by declaring that the formulation of the *ḥadīth* had been falsified and by claiming that the threat of punishment (if any punishment is really still intended in her view) is only aimed at non-Muslims.[39] She referred to the story involving the Jewess[40] and in addition she could offer the statement of the Prophet: 'God increases the punishment (*ᶜadhāb*) of the unbeliever by means of the weeping or by means of a part of the weeping of his relatives over him.'[41] However, perhaps what is here intended by this punishment, which is intensified for the unbeliever by means of the weeping of the relatives, is the second meaning of the word which we will now discuss. It is worth noting that in this statement it is no longer a question of punishment for the weeping but of an intensification of punishment by means of the weeping.

Damīrī (d. 808/1405) classifies the *ḥadīth* on punishment of the dead for the weeping of his relatives among statements by means of which the Prophet did not wish to issue commands and prohibitions and to create a basic law, and founds this view on the neutralizing modification by ᶜĀᵓisha who would only accept it as valid in the form: 'They weep, and she (the Jewess) is punished for the weeping of her people over her' (sic),[42] if here as well the first given meaning 'punishment for' and not another meaning is still intended.

The verb *yuᶜadhdhabu bi-* can in fact be understood in another sense, the second meaning which we will refer to here. It can also mean 'to be tormented or tortured by means of something, to suffer by means of something or under something', in accordance with the example 'only the Master of the fire may torture with fire' (*yuᶜadhdhibu bi'l-nār*).[43] It appears that the *ḥadīth* was also under-

---

38 *Irshād al-sārī li-sharḥ Ṣaḥīḥ al-Bukhārī*, Būlāq, 1293, II, pp. 483-89 (*GAS*, I, p. 123, no. 29). On Damāmīnī see *GAS*, I, p. 120, no. 12.

39 Bukhārī, *janāᵓiz* 33. Ibn Saᶜd: *Ṭabaqāt*, III, 1, p. 263, l. 22. Grütter in *Der Islam* 31, 1954, p. 160.

40 Bukhārī, *janāᵓiz* 33. Ibn Māja, *janāᵓiz* 53, no. 1595. Nasāᵓī, IV, pp. 17-18. Robson: *Mishkat*, I, p. 364.

41 Nasāᵓī, IV, pp. 18-19. Muslim, *janāᵓiz* 9, no. 22.

42 Damīrī: *Ḥayāt al-ḥayawān*, s.v. *faras*, Cairo, 1356, II, p. 213 below.

43 Abū Dāwūd: *Sunan*, *adab* 164, Cairo, 1948-50, VIII, p. 115, no. 5107.

stood this way quite early on. In the case of ᶜĀʾisha this remains uncertain. But when ᶜImrān b. Ḥuṣayn recited the saying of the Prophet 'The dead atones for (or by means of) the lamentation of his relatives over him', a man asked: 'Do you really mean that someone who dies in Khurasan and whose relatives here lament over him could atone for (or by means of) the lamentations of his relatives?' ᶜImrān replied: 'The Apostle of God speaks the truth, and you (with your doubt) lie.'[44] The question of the doubter only makes sense if it takes for granted the idea that the lamentation itself affects the deceased, reaches him, and when large distances are involved, has difficulty in reaching him or is incapable of reaching him at all. Thus according to this conception it is the lamentation itself which torments the person who is mourned.

Through Ṣafadī we learn that Muḥammad b. Jarīr al-Ṭabarī (d. 310/923) understood the *ḥadīth* this way. Ṭabarī was of the opinion that the saying meant that the deceased is tormented by the weeping of his relatives and experiences pity for them (*yariqqu lahum*). Qāḍī ᶜIyāḍ (d. 544/1149) is supposed to have agreed with him.[45] To Ibn Ḥajar al-ᶜAsqalānī (d. 852/1449) we owe the information that Ṭabarī, as one would expect, had expressed this view in his work on Traditions *Tahdhīb al-āthār*. ᶜAsqalānī also presents the doctrine of Ṭabarī more clearly: the weeping which causes pain to the deceased is the forbidden lamentation, and the torment of the deceased consists of his suffering under the sin which his relatives committed by lamenting the dead.[46] Al-Murtaḍā ᶜAlam al-Hudā mentions this possible interpretation as well and says, just as Ṣafadī reports on Ṭabarī, that the deceased experiences pain (*taʾallama*) by means of the weeping of relatives and that *ᶜadhāb* is not the same as *ᶜiqāb* 'punishment' but is used more often in the sense of 'pain' (*alam*) and 'injury' (*ḍarar*) which does not presuppose any earlier offense on the part of the person suffering the pain. But he adds to this still another possibility, that 'the deceased' (*mayyit*) might refer to someone who is not yet dead but is in the process of dying. This person might hear those standing around him and be tormented by their weeping.[47] Muḥammad al-Ghazzālī (d. 505/1111) shares the first of these two

44 Nasāʾī, IV, p. 17.

45 *Tashnīf al-samᶜ*, p. 32.

46 Ibn Ḥajar al-ᶜAsqalānī: *Talkhīs al-ḥabīr fī takhrīj aḥādīth al-Rāfiᶜī al-kabīr*, Cairo-Medina, 1964, II, p. 140, no. 805.

47 Al-Sayyid al-Sharīf al-Murtaḍā ᶜAlam al-Hudā Abū'l-Qāsim ᶜAlī b. al-Ḥusayn al-Mūsawī al-Baghdādī: *Tanzīh al-anbiyāʾ*, Najaf, 1250, p. 125.

conceptions. He writes: 'Ṣāliḥ al-Muzanī (d. 152/769) asked a theologian why ritual prayer was forbidden at graves. The theologian used as an argument the saying of the Prophet: "Do not perform ritual prayers at graves because that means pain (*ḥasra*) without end."[48] Someone has recounted: "One day I set out with the intention of performing the ritual prayer at the graves. The heat had already become intense and oppressive. Then I saw at the grave of my father a man who resembled him. I fell down in fear. Then I heard him say: 'It would seem the earth has grown too narrow for you so that for some time now you have been coming to disturb us with your ritual prayer.'" In the *Ṣaḥīḥ* it says: "The Apostle of God came across an orphaned child who was weeping at his father's grave. The Prophet, full of pity, wept with him but then said: 'The dead is tormented by the weeping of the living over him.'" The meaning is: This makes him sad and causes him pain. Like many other dead, a dead man appeared in a dream and in answer to the question how he was he replied: "Not good, because a certain man and a certain woman weep too much over me", even if the dualistic heretics (*zanādiqa*) deny this.'[49] In this case the Ḥanbalite reformer Ibn Taymiyya (d. 728 /1328) is in agreement with the Ashᶜarite Ghazzālī and the Imāmite al-Murtaḍā ᶜAlam al-Hudā. He recalls the *ḥadīth*: 'If God wished to punish the inhabitants of his heaven and his earth, He would punish them without thereby doing them any injustice. And if He wished to have mercy on them, His mercy toward them would always be bigger (better) than their works' and he explains: 'If the punishment were to take place, it would happen because they deserved it, not because there was no guilt.' According to Ibn Taymiyya, punishing an innocent person would also constitute injustice on God's part which he here denies.[50] Some people, so says Ibn Taymiyya, believed that the atonement of a dead person for the weeping of his relatives contradicts surah 6/164: 'And no one shall be made to bear another's burden.' But this could not be the case because only the person lamenting will be punished for it. By constrast, what is actually meant is that the dead experiences pain through what the lamenting person does. After all the living too can experience pain through things which are not under his control. Indeed, *ᶜadhāb* has a

48 Lucien Gautier: *Ad-Dourra al-Fâkhira, La perle préciseuse de Ghazâlî*, Leipzig, 1877, Arabic pp. 30-31/French p. 26.

49 Not clear.

50 Ibn Taymiyya: *Fī sharḥ ḥadīth Abī Dharr*, in *Majmūᶜat al-rasāʾil al-munīriyya*, Cairo, 1346, reprint, Part 3, p. 209 below.

more general meaning than *ᶜiqāb*. The Prophet, for example, has said: 'Travel is a piece of torment (*ᶜadhāb*).'[51] The Ḥanbalite Muḥammad b. Muḥammad al-Manbijī sides with Ibn Taymiyya: the dead experiences pain because of the forbidden behavior of his relatives.[52] This interpretation of the matter finds expression in the west as noted by Lucien Gautier and Irene Grütter. Gautier translates: 'Les morts sont punis par les larmes que les vivants répandent sur eux',[53] Irene Grütter: 'The dead is tormented by the weeping of his people over him.'[54]

Then which of the two interpretations is the correct one: punishment or torment? The Arabic feeling for language has allowed both. None the less, the second is certainly the original and the least forced within the context of comparative investigation. Of course, it can only be the original on condition that belief had existed in a mutual influence of the living on the dead and of the dead on the living, whether in pre-Islamic or Islamic times, or in both periods, because only within the framework of this notion is there room for the idea that something which the living does can benefit or harm the dead or the other way round. This condition is fulfilled in both periods. I refer the reader to the cited passages from al-Murtaḍā ᶜAlam al-Hudā, Ghazzālī and Ibn Taymiyya, to the chapters on burying the dead and visiting graves in theological works where it is even maintained that the dead visited their relatives from time to time or that in their graves they perceived the visits of the latter, to the rich literature on dream encounters and other meetings with the dead, and to modern scholarly writings dealing with questions of death and the cult of the dead in and before the Islamic era. Goldziher, in unintentional contradiction to his conclusions, had already drawn attention to the context of comparative investigation. With regard to his translation: 'The dead is punished for many a lamentation of the relatives', he makes the quite inappropriate comment: 'This view is in full agreement with the popular religious idea frequently attested in fundamentally different circles that one ought not to mourn the dead very much and that tears which fall on him torment him like fire, that in this way his peace is disturbed, and so on.'[55] The word 'torment' in

---

51 Ibn Taymiyya, ibid., p. 209 above.

52 *Taṣliyat ahl al-maṣāʾib* (written 777/1375), edition based on autograph, Cairo, 1929, pp. 45-52.

53 *Ad-Dourra al-Fâkhira*, French p. 26.

54 Irene Grütter: 'Arabische Bestattungsbräuche in frühislamischer Zeit', p. 160.

55 *Muhammedanische Studien*, I, p. 253, ftn. 3.

this sentence does not accord with 'punished' in Goldziher's translation but does fit with the 'torment' of our second interpretation. Because of the same semantic contradiction in the Arabic text itself I would even like to consider the combination in which a certain *ḥadīth* has been transmitted as inauthentic. According to the *ḥadīth*, while in the house of a moribund person the Prophet said: 'God does not punish (*yuᶜadhdhibu*) for the tears of the eye or for the sorrow of the heart but for this — and he pointed to the tongue — or God shows mercy (i.e. does not punish when He wishes to let mercy prevail). The dead suffers (*yuᶜadhdhabu*) because of the mourning of his relatives.'[56] The two sentences reveal a certain incongrurity in terms of their formulation, as well as because of the introduction of 'the dead' in the second sentence. Moreover, *yuᶜadhdhibu* in the first sentence must be translated as 'punish' because of the antithesis with 'shows mercy', whereas *yuᶜadhdhabu* in the second sentence, for the reasons cited, must be translated as 'tormented'. It is difficult to say who in the first sentence is punished by God, the sad surviving relatives or the deceased. Similarly, the tongue in the first sentence — not the tears and not the sorrow — fits badly with the 'mourning' in the second sentence. Yet by mourning ritual lamentation for the dead could be meant which is equally or primarily undertaken with the tongue — as in the following *ḥadīth*: 'Umm Salama reported: "When Abū Salama (viz. my husband) died, I said: 'A stranger and in a foreign land (i.e. he died as a Meccan in Medina)! But I wish to mourn him in such a way that people will speak of it.' I had already prepared myself to mourn him when a woman from al-Ṣaᶜīd appeared for the purpose of seconding me. But the Apostle of God stood in her way and said twice: 'Will you lead Satan back into a house from which God has driven him?' I gave up the thought of mourning and did not do it."'[57]

In Iran 'weeping and lamentation' (*shēwan ud mōyag*) on the occasion of deaths was likewise combatted by the Zoroastrian religion.[58] In this connection the idea that the deceased is detrimentally

---

56 Bukhārī, *janāʾiz* 45. Robson: *Mishkat*, I, pp. 360-61.

57 Muslim, *janāʾiz* 10. Mundhirī: *Targhīb*, IV, pp. 351-52, no. 15.

58 Geo Widengren: *Die Religionen Irans*, Stuttgart, 1965, p. 193. Traditional ritual lamentations for the dead is another matter completely. Bīrūnī: *Chronologie orientalischer Völker*, ed. C. Eduard Sachau, Leipzig, 1878, p. 235, ll. 10-11: '*Khshwm*, at the end of this month the Sogdians weep over their old dead, lament them, cut their own faces, and put out food and drink for these dead as do the Persians on Farwardajān.' Narshakhī-Qubāwī: *Tārīkh-i Bukhārā*, ed. Mudarris-i Raḍawī, Tehran, 1317-18, p. 20: 'The inhabitants of Bukhārā have

affected by the weeping of the living is represented by the myth of a river across which the dead must swim. This river is the river of tears which the surviving relatives shed. The more they weep, the harder the crossing becomes for the dead person. The myth appears in the Zoroastrian apocalypse *Ardā-Wirāz-nāmag*. The priest Ardā Wīrāz, on his journey of reconnaissance through the beyond, is led to a river by his two heavenly companions Srōsh and Ādur, and in the river he sees a crowd of departed souls. Some are incapable of crossing over, others only manage to do so with great effort, others have no difficulty. The two angels explain to the apocalyptic voyager that the river is the tears which the surviving relatives shed when weeping and lamenting over the deceased. The illicit tears cause the river to swell. Some cannot get across because their people have wept too much, whereas others can do so easily because their people have wept very little.[59] The inconsistencies in this picture are obvious. If the innumerable tears cause the river to become more powerful, all the souls would necessarily have difficulty in getting to the other side, unless the souls made the attempt to cross over the water individually and at intervals after one another. It also seems to be unclear whether the river is composed from all tears or only from the excessive ones. A modern critic points out that if one accepts this idea, it means the dead has to cope with making a crossing twice: once over the Chinwat-Bridge and once here. Moreover, he would here have to suffer for an offense which others, his surviving relatives, are guilty of committing — i.e. the same objection that ᶜĀ᾿isha raised against the alleged *ḥadīth*.[60] But the motif as such, the obstruction of the departed soul from reaching its goal by the weeping of the living is unambiguous. Later Zoroastrian writings have adopted the idea of the river of tears. In the *Ṣad dar*, which is composed in Persian, the relatives of the deceased are warned against excessive weeping 'because

---

strange songs about the killing of Siyāwush which the musicians call "the avenging of Siyāwush" (*kīn-i Siyāwush*, see Fritz Wolff: *Glossar zu Firdosis Schahname*, s.v. Siyāvuš 3). *Tārīkh-i Bukhārā*, p. 28: 'The inhabitants of Bukhārā have songs of lamentation over the killing of Siyāwush, as these are known in all regions. The musicians have made songs out of them which they perform. The singers call these the "weeping of the Magi".' — The Shīᶜites display an equivalent in their rites of mourning on behalf of Ḥusayn and others.

59 *Ardā-Wirāz-nāmag*, p. 16, ll. 7-10. Friedrich Spiegel: *Die traditionelle Literatur der Parsen*, Vienna, 1860, p. 126. Jal Dastur Cursetji Pavry: *The Zoroastrian Doctrine of a Future Life*², New York, 1929, p. 97.

60 Pavry: *Zoroastrian Doctrine*, p. 96, ftn. 137.

every tear flows into the river before the Chinwat-Bridge, the soul of the departed then remains behind at that point and the crossing-over becomes difficult for it'.[61] The theme is treated in detail in two Neo-Persian versifications of the *Ardā-Wirāz-nāmag*. One of these versifications stems from Zartusht-i Bahrām-i Pazhdū, the author of the *Zarātushtnāma*, being thus from the 7th/13th century, and is composed in *hazaj* meter.[62] In this work it says:

Wīrāf[63] the pious speaks thus:
After I had beheld everything in the sky,
become familiar with all things to the last detail
and had understood these rewards,
Sarūsh and Urdībihisht took hold of me
by the hand and led me back from Paradise.
When I had walked some way with them,
I reached there the shore of a river (*rūd*),
a black, gloomy and foul-smelling river.
Many poor souls had been thrown into it.
Every drop of water in it was like a drop of pitch
(...one hemistich)
like pitch and ink (*anqās*), so black,
as dismal as mud, as rotten as a carcass.
Much water like this was in the river
which was deeper than the length of a lance.
I was astonished at this gloomy locality,
at the gloom of the river and the pitch-black water,
at the water composed like this in so deep a river,

---

61 Pavry: *Zoroastrian Doctrine*, p. 108.

62 Dastur Kaikhusru Dastur Jamaspji Jamasp Asa: *Arda Viraf Nameh. The Original Pahlavi Text, With an Introduction, Notes, Gujarati translation, an (sic) Persian version of Zartosht Behram*, Bombay, 1902. I wish to acknowledge my gratitude to my colleague Jes P. Asmussen of Copenhagen for a photocopy of the Persian text. The author Zardusht-i Bahrām mentions himself in the rhyme of the Persian text on p. 19, l. 7. For *āsīm* 'great master' the *Farhang-i jihāngīrī* bases itself on one of the verses translated in what follows, and names the author Zartusht-i Bahrām (Vullers: *Lexicon Persico-Latinum*, II, 1535, voces zend-pazendicae). The poem is often so nonsensical and clumsy that one is inclined to assume the presence of interpolations. Our passage is found on pp. 19-20 of the Persian text. I have not restored the *majhūl*-vowels and the post-vocalic *dh*.

63 In these Neo-Persian texts always Ardāy Wīrāf. A discussion of the name in Jehangir C. Tavadia: *Die mittelpersische Sprache und Literatur der Zarathustrier*, Leipzig, 1956, pp. 116-20.

black as pitch and dismal, cold as snow.
Then I saw in the water souls
like people who are caught in a whirling eddy.
They were in this distress and hard, dire torment,[64]
having become incapable and wretched.
They were helpless in the whirlpool,
sorrowful in the whirling eddy
...(two hemistiches)
They called out to others for help.
But no helper afforded help to anyone.
In their distress and wretchedness they raised up
lamentations, wailing, cries for help and moaning.
Constantly they said: 'Pardon us!
Forgive us for the sake of God!'
When I beheld this river, the heavy effort,
this fear, this terror and the great anxiety
and how these souls sought for help,
when I saw this, I was greatly moved to pity.
So deep a river before Hell,
such black and icy-cold water —
the souls raised cries of pain and woe,
let resound lamentation in their torment and grief.
I remained helpless and paralyzed before it,
before the gloomy valley and the dismal water.
I asked the great master[65] accompanying me:
'What sort of people are these, in this terror?
Why do they have to labor so much?
Why is the water here so gloomy?'
Sarūsh answered me: 'This pitch-black river
has flowed together from the eyes of people.
If people shed tears over a dead person,
these tear-drops then turn into such a river, behold!
All the water which flows from their eyes
comes and settles in this river.
If in taking leave (?) they weep behind a dead person,
everything unites here in (or with) the river (?).[66]

---

64 I read *ranj-i ṣaᶜb u dushwār* instead of *ranj u ṣaᶜb-i dushwār*.

65 This is how the *Farhang-i jihāngīrī* gives this verse, in Vullers, II, p. 1535. Instead of *āshīm* one should read *āsīm*.

66 I conjecture: *chu giryand az pas-i murda ba-padrūd/ badīnjā jumla gird āyad badān rūd*. The printed edition has... *babad rūz... badān rūz*.

The more they wail and lament for someone,
the more they weep for him,
so much more difficult is his crossing-over
and so much greater is his torment.
The people you see drown in the river
can no longer get out onto the embankment.[67]
They seek help...
...(one hemistich)
The more their fathers and mothers in the world
lament over them there,
the greater becomes the pain (*ᶜadhāb*) of his (sic) soul,
the greater becomes the distress here in the water.[68]
Wīrāf, say to the people:
If you have feelings for the people,[69]
if you wish them not to suffer torment and hardship,
if you don't want to be sorry for your own action,
if you don't want to make the whirlpool worse for them,
then do not shed water from your eyes behind them!
Do not talk a lot of nonsense[70] after their demise
but chant a ritual murmuring (*bāẓh*),
do something meritorious (*muzd*) and good (*kirfa*) behind these souls
there and recite from the *Avesta*,
so that these here are granted peace
and they are not distressed by you!
To raise a lament for a dead person
entails a slope and inclination to the devil's path.
When one weeps, screams and moans,
one is on the path to the devil's goal and[71] command.
The women performing lamentations resemble devils,
have strayed far from the path of the World Ruler.
If you do not wish to be like devils,
take refuge with God in resoluteness,
so that no pain (*ᶜadhāb*) comes over the soul
and it doesn't drown in such water as this!
With a hundred warnings, more warnings and more warnings still:

---

67 In the printed edition *barq*. What is probably meant is *bargh*.

68 Probably *gardad* should be read instead of *gudhārad*.

69 Read *dārīd* instead of *dārī*.

70 Read *namī-khāyīd* instead of *namī-khwāhīd*.

71 Probably *kāma u farmān* should be read instead of *kāma-i farmān*.

remove weeping from your eyes[72] and mourning from your heart!'

The other versification is from the year 902 'of the old reckoning', i.e. 1532 AD, anonymous and composed in the *mutaqārib* meter.[73] The passage that interests us runs:

Once again Ardāy Wīrāf[74] spoke, saying:
I set out for Hell, my heart full of distress.
There I beheld a place like black oil,
in the said place gloomy water which had become bad.
Its depths measured nine lances.
Throughout its (complete) breadth I saw souls.
These souls were submerged in the whirlpool.
They came into difficulties and were helpless.
The confused mass raised a cry in lamentation,
that someone possibly might offer them protection.
But no one paid them any heed.
They remained helplessly submerged, in a miserable state.
Again and again they raised cries
with lamentations which penetrated beyond the sphere,
like someone a scorpion has stung
who cries out and throws himself to the ground.
Many calmly strode across,
but many remained behind in wretched helplessness.
When I saw this place full of terror and dreadfulness,
my heart broke in two at the pitiful lamenting.
Then I asked the angel (*amshāsfand*):
'What sort of people are these who are all moaning like this?
Why are they all in difficulty, submerged in the water,
helpless? Give reply!'
The heavenly Sarūsh and Urdībihisht replied:
'You see here the gloomy and ugly water.
It is the water people weep from their eyes
on behalf of the dead. Know!
This accumulates and the people end up in woeful misery
just as you see, end up in distress on that account.
Know that the more someone is mourned,

---

72 For metrical reasons *zi-chashmān* should be read instead of *zi-chashm*.

73 Christian Bartholomae: *Die Zendhandschriften der k. Hof- und Staatsbibliothek in München*, Munich, 1915, *45: Manuscript M 20, 8, 65b-85b. Our passage 76b, ll. 709-34.

74 See ftn. 63 above.

the more he sinks in this way.
No one comes to help him.
Here he remains (?)[75] like a bird in a cage.
Those whose people moaned and lamented
suffer this agony (*ᶜadhāb*), oh noble man.[76]
Father (and) mother bring this agony (*ᶜadhāb*) on their child
when they weep and are apprehensive.[77]
So then, Ardāy Wīrāf, tell the people
they should not cause this bad harm (?),[78]
should not[79] shed tears (*āb*) and raise up lamentations.
But verily (*zinhār*) say this to the creatures of the world!
To pray after the dead
nourishes their souls in the beyond (?).[80]
If one weeps, then they remain in agony (*ᶜadhāb*)
until the resurrection and[81] the reckoning.
Perform the rite (*yazish*) (for) everyone who died,[82]
because he will not return and has taken with him what he sowed!
Bring to the fire Warahrām (= Bahrām) aromatic
sandalwood and some aloeswood as well!'
They repeated many times: 'Tell this
to the people and to the noble-minded king!'

The Mandaeans also forbade lamenting the dead.[83] In the Mandaean view 'streams of water', a water boundary, separate the light-world from the terrestrial world,[84] and the soul of the deceased is led across

---

75 MS *darīnjā waṭan* (?).

76 Clumsily expressed: *Har ān qawm kū shīwan u nāla kard/ ᶜadhābash chunīn ast ay rād mard.*

77 Uncertain.

78 I tentatively read *nayārand īn bad ziyān* instead of *nayārand īn bar zamān.*

79 Read *narīzand* instead of *birīzand.*

80 Very dubious text: *Pas az murdagān yasht sāzīdanish(?)/ ba-mīnū rawān z-ū kunad parwarish.*

81 I read *rastakhīz u ḥisāb* instead of *rastakhīz az ḥisāb.*

82 *Bisāzīd har kas yazish chūnki murd.*

83 Mark Lidzbarski: *Ginza. Der Schatz oder Das Grosse Buch der Mandäer*, Göttingen-Leipzig, 1925, index s.v. Totenklage. E.S. Drower: *The Mandaeans of Iraq and Iran*, Oxford, 1937, p. 180. Kurt Rudolph: 'Die Religion der Mandäer', in *Die Religionen Altsyriens, Altarabiens und der Mandäer*, Stuttgart, 1970, p. 439.

84 *Ginza*, p. 67, ftn. 2. Rudolph, p. 428.

these streams of water by a helper.[85] But similarly whoever weeps over the dead will, as a punishment, either be 'placed in streams of water, when they are full'[86] or barred from the beyond by seas and rivers[87] — a punishment, it should be noted, for the persons weeping, not for those being mourned. By full streams of water his own tears could possibly be meant in which he drowns or almost drowns and which he has to gulp down, or otherwise streams through which he can no longer properly advance or go forward at all. But the Mandaeans have also adopted from the Zoroastrians the idea of the river of tears which the person who is mourned must cross over. According to Lady Drower, the present-day Mandaeans say: 'Tears become a river which the soul of the departed must ford, and torn hair forms entanglements about his feet.'[88]

Among the Copts Shenute of Atripe (5th century AD) censured mourning over believing Christians who have died and advised instead weeping on behalf of the godless.[89] This is scarcely aimed against actual Coptic lamentations for the dead but simply wishes to assert that the godless are far more lamentable than the dead. But the laws of Cyril II of Alexandria forbade women to blacken their faces and to hire female mourners.[90]

Among the Armenians the Armenian Church Father Johannes Mandakuni in the 5th century forbade lamentation over the dead which involved wild gestures and weeping, and called it a Satanic and pagan practice.[91]

Thus in the above-mentioned religious communities mourning the dead was and still is considered improper but nowhere, not even among the Mandaeans,[92] has it ever come to be abolished. In Islam it is common practice and an established institution at the graves of prominent and the highest-ranking individuals and during religious

---

85 *Ginza*, index s.v. Wasserbäche.

86 *Ginza*, p. 21, ll. 8-9.

87 *Ginza*, p. 37, ll. 3-4.

88 *The Mandaeans*, p. 180.

89 Maria Cramer: 'Die Totenklage bei den Kopten', in *Sb. Ak. Wiss. Wien Phil.-Hist. Kl.* 219, 2. Abhandlung, 1941, pp. 77-78.

90 A.S. Tritton: 'Muslim Funeral Customs', in *BSOAS* 9, 1937, p. 660. Paul Kahle: 'Die Totenklage im heutigen Ägypten', in *Εὐχαριστήριον Hermann Gunkel zum 60. Geburtstage*, Göttingen, 1923, p. 352, in 1908 met a female mourner in Luxor who performed exactly the same way for both Copts and Muslims.

91 Maria Cramer: 'Totenklage', pp. 78-79.

92 Drower: *Mandaeans*, pp. 180-81.

holidays of mourning, especially among the Shīᶜites. This custom can easily be defended and justified by a reinterpretation. One only has to conceive of the weeping over the great dead or even over deceased family members as an expression of remorse and regret for one's own offenses toward the deceased, for one's inadequate love of him, as tearful supplication, etc, and so this lamentation is covered up and now belongs to the category of pious weeping.[93]

The question arises: is the alleged statement of Muḥammad concerning the torment of the dead through the weeping of his surviving relatives an echo of the Iranian idea of the river of tears which hinders the departed soul in its crossing-over? In the end it seems reasonable to postulate a connecting line from the Iranian myth to the Arabic saying if only in view of the fact that the Zoroastrian idea of the Chinwat-Bridge has been adopted into Islam. In addition there are the similar considerations that have been formulated on both sides concerning the parallel. Duplicating a motif (in this case the hindrance of a dead person during his journey through the beyond) is a well-known phenomenon, especially in connection with Islamic ideas about the hereafter. One may recall the diverse and rather incompatible elements from which the Islamic image of the Last Judgement is composed, any single one of which would be sufficient by itself since they all mean the same thing: the book of deeds under the right or the left arm, the interrogation, the scales, the fall from the Bridge of Paradise as a sign of divine judgement by ordeal, etc. But that tears can form streams and through streams pools, lakes and seas can be created is a simple hyperbole which may easily occur everywhere. It is frequently attested in Islam with regard to pious weeping and equally so with regard to mourning the dead. The Persian poet Kisāʾī (4th/10th century) addresses a dead person thus:

> All Marw became like the Flood from the water of eyes
> and in this water your coffin was like Noah's ark.[94]

In an Arabic description of a funeral at any period the words might appear: 'The bier of the deceased swam in a flood of tears.'[95] Yet the specific image of a body of water or a river which forms a barrier across the path of a departed soul is not evoked in our *ḥadīth*. The

93 Cf. *EI*² s.v. *bakkāʾ*.

94 ᶜAwfī: *Lubāb al-albāb*, ed. E.G. Browne, London-Leiden, 1903-06, II, p. 34, ll. 17-18/ed. Saᶜīd-i Nafīsī, Tehran, 1335, p. 271, l. 4.

95 *Sabaḥa naᶜsh al-faqīd bi-sayl min al-dumūᶜ*.

torment which the tears cause the deceased is rather a form of suffering, be it suffering on behalf of the relatives as in Ṭabarī's view,[96] or a pain such as a sting, a lash or from fire. In the case of the Muslims in Lebanon the belief is actually attested that tears which are shed over a dead person burn him in the hereafter like fiery flames.[97] Moreover, an Islamic description of Hell states that the tears of surviving relatives are collected in horns and are proffered to the dead to drink. This is meant to be the boiling water (*ḥamīm*) which, according to surah 88/5, the dead are given to drink in Hell.[98] Here the torment consists in the mourned person having to swallow the burning and bitter tears. An explanation which is supposed to go back to the Prophet and which likewise connects the tears of the surviving relatives with the 'boiling water' of the Koran goes as follows: 'When ᶜAbdallāh b. Abū Bakr died, Abū Bakr came forth and said: "I ask your forgiveness for these (lamenting women); they are still too close to the old paganism. For indeed, I have heard the Apostle of God say: 'The dead will be sprinkled with boiling (or the boiling) water (*yunḍaḥu ᶜalayhi'l-ḥamīm*) through the weeping of the living over him.'"'[99] Thus in this case the tears are boiling water which falls on the skin of the dead person and scalds his skin. The last two reports reveal an attempt to harmonize the statement about tormenting the dead by means of tears with the words of the Koran. On the other hand, the statement can also possibly be a saying from the ordinary people which Muḥammad took up or which was attributed to him. The way is open for other interpretations as well. For example the torment of the dead could also be the wailing which disturbs his peace or the drenching of his shroud which is the result of incessant tears. However this may be — our *ḥadīth* remains outwardly separated from the Zoroastrian-Iranian tradition and only has in common with it the basic idea that the tears do some kind of harm to the deceased.

There is nothing strange about the fact that the Arabic saying is independent from the Iranian conception if one takes into account that similar views about the effect of tears on the dead are found among other peoples. In Europe such views have found striking expression

---

96 *Tashnīf al-samᶜ*, p. 32 (p. 229 above)

97 Béchara Chémali: 'Mœurs et usages au Liban', in *Anthropos* 4, 1909, p. 43: 'Les musulmans portent leur mort sur les épaules sans aucune autre manifestation, et prétendent que les larmes versées sur le défunt sont comme des flammes qui le brûlent dans l'autre monde.'

98 Jonas Meyer: *Die Hölle im Islam*, dissertation Basle, 1901, p. 51.

99 Ibn Ḥajar al-ᶜAsqalānī: *Talkhīṣ al-ḥabīr*, II, p. 140, no. 805.

in numerous variations on the fairy tale 'Das Totenhemdchen' or 'Tränenkrüglein': a mother weeps so incessantly over her lost child that the child finally shows her its skirt which has become completely soaked in the tears, or a pitcher filled with her tears which it must drag around, and the child asks her to stop her weeping. The rich material, which goes back to the 13th century AD, has been collected together in Johannes Bolte and Georg Polívka's *Anmerkungen zu den Kinder- u. Hausmärchen der Brüder Grimm*, Leipzig, 1915, II, pp. 485-490, regarding fairy-tale no. 109 'Das Totenhemdchen', and in Hanns Bächtold-Stäubli's *Handwörterbuch des deutschen Aberglaubens*, Berlin-Leipzig, VIII, pp. 1107-09, s.v. 'Tränenkrüglein'. Lutz Mackensen's *Handwörterbuch des deutschen Märchens*, Berlin-Leipzig, 1930-33, I, p. 84b, s.v. 'Antike Motive' essentially repeats Bolte-Polívka.[100] In addition, one finds a long series of sayings in European literature which convey almost the same meaning as our *ḥadīth* but which sometimes impart more precise information on the subject. In Lucian, Protesilaus complains to the ruler of the shades: 'The love of my spouse causes me no small amount of suffering', and a dead boy reproaches his father with: 'Why do you go on moaning, unfortunate man, and causing me so much worry?' In Propertius, a departed wife calls out to her grieving husband: 'Stop troubling my grave with tears, Paulus!' In Hans Sachs, the murdered Lorenzo urges his beloved: 'Darumb so weyn nit mehr nach mir, du mehrest mir dadurch mein Leyden.' (Therefore don't weep for me any more, in doing so you increase my suffering.) In an East-Prussian legend a deceased inn-keeper asks her husband to punish her children because their weeping and lamentation allow her no rest in the quiet earth. In a Danish ballad a dead man says to his still living wife that his coffin is always full of rose petals when she enjoys herself and is always full of running blood when she worries.[101] In Scotland the belief was prevalent that excessive weeping and lamentation disturbed the deceased's peace in the grave, and in a Scottish tale a dead man scolds his wife with the words: 'My peace is disturbed by your unnecessary lamentation,

100 See also Lutz Röhrich: 'Das Verzeichnis der deutschen Totensagen', in *Fabula* 9, 1967, p. 279. — In Persia in earlier times there were bottles with a long curved neck intended for tears. One filled them with the tears one shed for Ḥusayn and hoped that by displaying such bottles one would be admitted to Paradise. Bess Allen Donaldson: *The Wild Rue. A Study of Muhammadan Magic and Folklore in Iran*, London, 1938, p. 178.

101 Bolte-Polívka, II, pp. 488-90.

your tears scald me in my shroud.'[102] In an Irish story a girl who had wept over a brother she believed was dead says: 'Every day I whimpered over the little creature until my mother told me that each drop I let fall for the poor little boy made a hole in him. Then I gave up the weeping.'[103] Adolf Wuttke in *Der deutsche Volksaberglaube der Gegenwart*, 3rd revised edition by Elard Hugo Meyer, Berlin, 1900, § 728, summarizes with regard to the German area: 'One should not shed any tears on a corpse or a shroud, otherwise one disturbs the peace of the deceased (generally); tears burn him like fire (Bavaria, Bohemia), or the person weeping soon dies (East Prussia, Posen, Mecklenburg, Bavaria, Franconia, Erzgebirge) because his tears end up inside the grave and prepare his own wasting away. On the whole one should not weep for a dead person or mourn him very much as it disturbs his peace (generally...), and he is therefore obliged to reappear (Thüringen). As many tears as someone sheds over a dead person, he pours that many drops of oil on him in purgatory (Bohemia). Especially numerous are the legends in which dead children reappear before their mother with a jar of tears in their hand and ask her to stop mourning!'[104] But the motif is spread far beyond the confines of Europe. The river of tears is found among the Japanese[105] and among the Eskimos of the Bering Straits.[106] In India, according to the Brahmanic view, mourning over the dead is not only meaningless but even a sin and in addition causes harm to the deceased. The law book of Yājñavalkya orders that one is to carry out the sacrifice for the dead but not to weep because the deceased must drink the tears. In Kālidāsa's Raghuvaṃśa (circa 5th century AD), the epic about

---

102 Felix Liebrecht: *Des Gervasius von Tilbury Otia imperialia*, Hanover, 1856, p. 198 above.

103 Liebrecht: *Gervasius*, p. 197 below.

104 Referred to in Bolte-Polívka, II, p. 488, ftn. 1 (along with other literature). Wuttke is cited in Julius Lippert: *Christenthum, Volksglaube und Volksbrauch*, Berlin, 1882, p. 409. Goldziher refers to Lippert: *Muhammedanische Studien*, I, p. 253, ftn. 3.

105 Bolte-Polívka, II, p. 488.

106 Stith Thompson: *Motif-Index of Folk Literature*, Copenhagen, 1955 ff., under F 162.2.12: 'River in underworld from tears of living'. Not in this category is the dream of the great weeper Sayyār al-Nibājī: He beheld Paradise and therein was a stream which flowed over pearls and precious stones, with tents and maidens on its banks. The maidens were intended for those who prayed during the night like Nibājī (*Ḥilyat al-awliyā'*, X, p. 166). The stream was not the tears of Nibājī but Kawthar, which is clear from a similar description in Qasṭallānī: *Al-mawāhib al-laduniyya fī'l-minaḥ al-muḥammadiyya* (with the commentary of Zurqānī), Cairo, 1325-29, VI, p. 91.

Raghu's tribe, it says: 'For the constant weeping of the relatives burns the deceased — so it is taught.'[107] The Papuans relate that dead persons return and ask the surviving relatives not to weep over them any more, otherwise they cannot find their way to the dead.[108] The Tlinkit Indians maintain that the path leading to the realm of the shades becomes sodden through tears.[109] This is a whole sample chart of possible concrete forms of the basic idea. Naturally borrowings are conceivable in this area and perhaps even demonstrable but not across the whole range of parallels.

For the time being it appears futile to seek a historical link for our saying of the Prophet about the torment of the dead through the tears of the surviving relatives. We must be content with having removed the saying from its isolation and having located it within the world of parallels. The motif is that of Stith Thompson: *Motif-Index of Folk Literature*, Copenhagen, 1955 ff., recorded under C 762.2. *Tabu: too much weeping for the dead* .

---

107 Heinrich Lüders: 'Die Jātakas und die Epik', in *ZDMG* 58, 1904, pp. 706-07. Bolte-Polívka, II, pp. 489-90.

108 *Handwörterbuch des deutschen Aberglaubens* s.v. Tränenkrüglein, VIII, pp. 1107-09.

109 *Handwb. d. deutsch. Abergl.* s.v. weinen, IX, pp. 329-31.

AN EXCHANGE OF LETTERS BETWEEN SHARAF AL-DĪN-I BALKHĪ AND MAJD AL-DĪN-I BAGHDĀDĪ

Originally the contribution I had planned for this Festschrift bore the title 'Ein seltsamer brückenschlag von Harât nach Almeria' (An Unusual Connecting Link between Herat and Almeria) and intended to demonstrate the direct dependence of the *Maḥāsin al-majālis* of Ibn al-ᶜArīf (d. 536/1141) on the *ᶜIlal al-maqāmāt* of ᶜAbdallāh al-Anṣārī (d. 481/1089). In the meantime there appeared in *REI* 39, 1971, pp. 321-33, Bruno Halff's article 'Le *Maḥâsin al-maǧâlis* d'Ibn al-ᶜArīf et l'œuvre du soufi hanbalite al-Anṣârî' in which that demonstration is carried out and an attempt is even made to improve the text of Anṣārī's *ᶜIlal* on the basis of Ibn al-ᶜArīf's *Maḥāsin*. Bruno Halff has tactfully avoided the term plagiarism, although Ibn al-ᶜArīf in the *Maḥāsin* has obviously copied the *ᶜIlal* of Anṣārī. As Alfred Bel has shown in a somewhat different case, i.e. the plundering of Ibn Abī Zarᶜ's *Rawḍ al-qirṭās* by the history writer of Fez, Jaznāʾī (both from the 8th/14th century), and as has been noted elsewhere as well, in the Islamic Middle Ages apparently different attitudes prevailed regarding the legitimate use of another person's literary productions. Carl Brockelmann, *GAL S*, II, p. 339, also describes Ibn Abī Zarᶜ's *Rawḍ al-qirṭās* as 'in the main a plagiarism from the *Bayān al-mughrib* of Ibn ᶜIdhārī al-Marrākushī'. Many authors appropriated the intellectual property of others without making the slightest mention of it and thereby have left behind a rich field for philological criminologists to work on. Paul Kraus has convicted the pious Ibn al-Jawzī (d. 597/1201) of such a theft from the *Kitāb al-ṭibb al-rūḥānī* by the philosopher Abū Bakr al-Rāzī (d. 313/925), and I have drawn attention to an example of plagiarism which, for a pious cause, was perpetrated on Najm al-Dīn-i Dāya's *Mirṣād al-ᶜibād*.[1] Conversely, matters stand the other way round in the case of the attractive book *Miṣbāḥ al-hidāya* by Maḥmūd-i Kāshānī (d. 735/1335). This work claims to be a Persian translation of the *ᶜAwārif al-maᶜārif* of ᶜUmar al-Suhrawardī (d. 632/1234) with some

1 Alfred Bel: *Zahrat al-âs*, in Publications de la Faculté des Lettres d'Alger 59, 1923, pp. 11-12. Paulus Kraus: *Abi Bakr Mohammadi filii Zachariae Raghensis (Razis) opera philosophica*, I, Cairo, 1939, p. 3. Fritz Meier: *Die Fawāʾiḥ al-ǧamāl wa-fawātiḥ al-ǧalāl des Naǧm ad-dīn al-Kubrā*, Wiesbaden, 1957, Introduction, p. 245.

additions, whereas it is in fact an adaptation which goes far afield of the original text.

But neither Bruno Halff nor I are the first to have recognized the relationship of the *Maḥāsin* to the *ʿIlal*. Ibn Taymiyya (d. 728/1328) had already observed the connections. He writes in his work *Al-tuḥfa al-ʿirāqiyya fī'l-aʿmāl al-qalbiyya* (in *Majmūʿat al-rasāʾil al-munīriyya*, II, last treatise, pp. 24-25): 'Whoever believes that trust in God belongs to the stations of the generality of travellers on the mystic path errs greatly, even if he is so eminent a shaykh as the author of the *ʿIlal al-maqāmāt* (= Anṣārī). It was from him that the author of the *Maḥāsin al-majālis* (= Ibn al-ʿArīf) took this and displayed the weakness of his line of argumentation.' If the final sentence is to be accepted as correct, it must mean: Ibn al-ʿArīf caused the weakness of Anṣārī's argumentation to become all the more clear — because Ibn al-ʿArīf did not criticize Anṣārī but only extended his explanations further. But perhaps Ibn Taymiyya has quoted from memory and then, as occurs with him elsewhere, he may have slightly distorted matters.

In any case I will use this opportunity to carry out another earlier intention, namely to publish an exchange of letters between Sharaf al-Dīn Muḥammad-i Balkhī and his shaykh Majd al-Dīn Sharaf b. al-Muʾayyad-i Baghdādī (556/1161 to allegedly 616/1219) from the 8th/14th-century collective manuscript Köprülü (Istanbul) 1589, 409b-412a (added page numbering on a photocopy of Hellmut Ritter's).[2] We know nothing about Balkhī. With regard to Baghdādī see *Fawāʾiḥ*, Introduction, pp. 40-41 (with further bibliography), Saʿīd-i Nafīsī in his new edition of ʿAwfī's *Lubāb al-albāb*, Tehran, 1335, pp. 634-37 (with further bibliography), and Muḥammad Taqī-i Dānishpazhūh: 'Khirqa-i hazārmīkhī' in *Collected Papers on Islamic Philosophy and Mysticism*, ed. M. Mohaghegh & H. Landolt, Tehran, 1971, Persian part, pp. 149-78. Baghdādī's *Risāla dar safar* has been edited ibid., pp. 179-90, by Karāmat Raʿnā Ḥusaynī. The information given by ʿAlāʾ al-Dawla-i Simnānī (d. 736/1336) in Iqbāl-i Sīstānī's *Chihil majlis*, nos. 34 and 38, was adopted by Jāmī in his *Nafaḥāt al-uns*. Baghdādī was of a delicate constitution and came from a high-ranking wealthy family of Baghdādak near Khwārazm. His brother, or one of his brothers, Bahāʾ al-Dīn Muḥammad b. al-Muʾayyad-i Baghdādī was a secretary of the Khwārazmshāh Takash and composed the famous collection of letters *Al-tawassul ilā'l-tarassul*. His mother was a doctor and he was a

2 *Fawāʾiḥ*, Introduction, p. 244.

doctor himself. According to another tradition his father and his brother, perhaps identical with the above-mentioned Bahāʾ al-Dīn, were also doctors (Dānishpazhūh, p. 165). Baghdādī donated 200,000 dinars every year for the provisions of the convent which the Khwārazmshāh had built for him (Dānishpazhūh, p. 165). As a mystic he was the disciple of Najm al-Dīn-i Kubrā (d. 618/1221). The poet ᶜAṭṭār and ᶜAwfī knew him personally. Besides the *Risāla dar safar*, a license to teach for ᶜAlī-i Lālā (circa 560-642/1165-1244) as well as two letters to ᶜAlī-i Lālā have been published (Dānishpazhūh, pp. 165-174). In the latter Baghdādī defends his secret marriage with a lady of high social position who had first called on him to have him invoke God on her behalf. This is clearly the affair which eventually led to his being killed. According to one tradition (in Nafīsī), the lady was called Laylē. Ḥamdallāh-i Mustawfī-i Qazwīnī: *Tārīkh-i guzīda*, in Gibb Memorial Series 14, I, p. 788, Jāmī: *Nafaḥāt al-uns*, s.v. Majd al-Dīn-i Baghdādī, and others maintain that the woman was the mother of the Khwārazmshāh. Against this view Wilhelm Barthold: *Turkestan down to the Mongol Invasion*, in Gibb Memorial, New Series 5, 1928, pp. 376-77, already drew attention to the old age of this princess. The love story ought also to have increased the doubts which were voiced for other reasons about dating the death of Baghdādī in the year 616/1219 since by then Baghdādī too would have been of advanced age.[3]

Correspondence between master and disciple goes back to the classical period of Sufism,[4] but only in the post-classical period, i.e. after Qushayrī, can letters form part of a novice's training and contain explanations about visionary experiences of the disciples, because in the meantime one had learned to take seriously the visionary experiences and dreams of novices as symptoms of their inner state and to make use of them in the training process. It was now completely natural for the novices no longer only to ask the shaykh about true contentment, correct trust in God, the nature of the concupiscent soul, etc., but about the meaning of their dreams and visions as well. How much this 'visualism' was practiced and fostered comes out for instance in the *Manāqib-i Awḥad al-Dīn-i Kirmānī* (d. 635/1238) where the success of the efforts of the master and the capacity of the disciple are especially revealed in the sudden inner 'opening' during

---

3 I have not been able to consult the article of Zaryāb-i Khuwayyī: 'Dāstān-i kushta shudan-i Majd al-Dīn-i Baghdādī', in the journal *Yaghmā* 7, 1333, pp. 544-48.

4 Sarrāj: *Al-lumaᶜ fī'l-taṣawwuf*, ed. R.A. Nicholson, in Gibb Memorial Series 22, 1914, p. 238, l. 3.

spiritual retreat, and the master every morning visits the cells of his novices in order to discuss with them their nocturnal inner experiences.

Najm al-Dīn al-Kubrā (d. 618/1221), Baghdādī's teacher in Khwārazm, attached great importance to visionary experience in himself and his disciples. An unoriginal and for long stretches even rather boring disiciple of Kubrā, Ṣadr al-Dīn Abū'l-Mu$^{\circ}$ayyad al-Muwaffaq b. Muḥammad b. al-Ḥasan al-Khāṣī, amply exploited Kubrā in his treatise *Al-salwa fī sharā$^{\circ}$iṭ al-khalwa* and reports the following vision from his first spiritual retreat when with him: 'He saw a small ant that wanted to go to Mecca. A bigger ant advised it to hide in the feathers of a dove and thus to fly with the dove to Mecca, because left to its own devices it would not be able to manage. This the ant did and reached the Ka^{c}ba.' Kubrā interprets the vision in terms of the indispensability of the shaykh. Khāṣī is the little ant and he, Kubrā, is the dove. Kubrā as a teacher will bring him to the Ka^{c}ba of togetherness with God (*wuṣla*).[5] From Kubrā's school several exchanges of letters between teachers and students concerning visions and auditory experiences have been preserved. Kubrā himself gave advice by letter to his student Sayf al-Dīn al-Bākharzī (585-658/1189-1260 or 659/1261[6]). A part of it has come

---

5 *GAL S*, I, p. 773. MS Saray Ahmed III, which is available to me in a photocopy, does not bear the number 1614 but rather 1416. It is unpaginated. The story is found in the second chapter. The author did not write before Aḥmad al-Ghazzālī but was a direct student of Kubrā's. He cites verses of Sanā$^{\circ}$ī in Persian and mentions a fallen (*shahīd*) teacher named ^{c}Alā$^{\circ}$ al-Dīn Ṣadr al-ḥisba al-ma^{c}rūf bi'l-Khayyāṭī as well as a generous man named Sahl b. Sa^{c}d al-Sā^{c}idī. The name of the author himself is not wholly clear to me. After the personal name given in the incipit the word *wālidī* follows. This could mean 'my father' and signify that the book has been transmitted by his son. But it is also possible that this is part of the author's name so that the name has the unusual compound form al-Khāṣ(ṣ)ī-Wālidī. The man appears to have written after Kubrā's death since the eulogy 'God is pleased with him!' occurs after the latter's name. The author reports *in extenso* the story of Kubrā's temptation, to the effect that while Kubrā was on spiritual retreat the devil wished to lure him to *ḥadīth* studies and urged him to write a book entitled *Ḥiyal al-marīd ^{c}alā'l-murīd*, and indeed the story is the same version that Kubrā relates in his *Risāla ilā'l-hā$^{\circ}$im* (*Fawā$^{\circ}$iḥ*, Introduction, pp. 30-31, 280/M. Molé: 'Traités mineurs de Nağm al-dīn Kubrā', in *Annales Islamologiques* 4, Cairo, 1963, pp. 33-34).

6 I must reject the charge of Īraj-i Afshār which appears in his edition of Yaḥyā Bākharzī's *Awrād al-aḥbāb*, Tehran, 1345, p. 7, ftn. 4, that in *Fawā$^{\circ}$iḥ*, p. 42, I have given the date of Sayf al-Dīn-i Bākharzī's death as 645 AH.

down to us in the MS Leiden 2252.[7] Bākharzī had undergone a course of training with Kubrā before the correspondence and then, on Kubrā's instructions, withdrew in seclusion in his homeland and requested by letter an explanation of his visions and dreams. He began this withdrawal in seclusion on a Thursday, the 24th of Ramaḍān. The years in question are 605/1209, 608/1212 and 613/1217. Hermann Landolt has published from ᶜAlāᵓ al-Dawla-i Simnānī's *Rasāᵓil al-nūr fī shamāᵓil ahl al-surūr* the letters exchanged between Simnānī and his teacher Nūr al-Dīn ᶜAbd al-Raḥmān-i Kasirqī-i Isfarāyinī (d. 717/1317).[8] At first lacking a shaykh, Simnānī had prepared himself with the help of the book *Qūt al-qulūb* by Abū Ṭālib al-Makkī (d. 386/996), then learned a special, very effective form of recollecting God from one of Kasirqī's students. Finally in 686/1287 he set out on the road for Baghdād where Kasirqī lived but in Hamadān was stopped from travelling any further by government authorities. Thus, for the time being, Simnānī could only communicate in two other ways with Kasirqī: through supernatural mental contact, for which his disposition and the exercises he undertook appear to have qualified him, and through correspondence. Both continued even after he had reached Baghdād in 688/1289 and made the personal acquaintance of his teacher. He later acknowledges gratitude to the beneficial compulsion for having had the opportunity to strengthen his inner tie with the shaykh[9] but still asks the shaykh for a letter confirming an inwardly communicated directive.[10] This possibility had not been available to another, older seeker, Muḥammad(-i) Abū'l-Mukhtār-i Nawbandajānī. In 620/1223 in Kāzarūn he was admitted into the Kāzarūnī order by the then leader of the convent located there. However, as it appears, he did not receive instruction from the latter but his training was based on visionary apparitions of the spirit-being of the order's patron, Abū

7 *GAL S*, I, p. 810. P. Voorhoeve: *Handlist of Arabic Manuscripts*, Leiden, 1957, p. 397: *Waqāᵓiᶜ al-khalwa*.

8 Hermann Landolt: *Correspondance spirituelle échangée entre Nuroddin Esfarayeni (ob. 717/1317) et son disciple ᶜAlaoddin Semnani (ob. 736/1336)*, in Bibliothèque Iranienne 21, Tehran-Paris, 1972. Letters of Ḥasan-i Bulghārī (d. 698/1289-90) to Simnānī are mentioned in *Chihil majlis*, no. 39.

9 Landolt: *Correspondance*, Introduction, p. 19.

10 Landolt, Persian text p. 81, ll. 3-6.

Isḥāq-i Kāzarūnī,[11] who had already died in 426/1035 and with whom, of course, it was no longer possible to correspond.

We do not have any detailed knowledge about Sharaf al-Dīn-i Balkhī's situation in life. But the fact that Majd al-Dīn-i Baghdādī describes him as a brother and a great man would appear to indicate that we are dealing with a mature person and a familiar friend or with an influential lord, rather than with one of Baghdādī's simple novices. In addition, on the basis of a passage in the explanation of the third vision (see § 13 below) one could surmise that Balkhī was undergoing training with different shaykhs at the same time. On the other hand, 'the spirits of the shaykhs' mentioned there could equally be the living as well as the deceased forefathers of his Sufi affiliation, the representatives of Sufism in general, or (according to § 24) the spirits of demons. Baghdādī specifically instructs Balkhī to seek advice from humans and to give up being taught by demons.

THE CONTENT OF BALKHĪ'S LETTER

Balkhī describes to his shaykh Baghdādī the following visions:

§ 3: He beheld demon spirits who maintained that as long as one could pronounce the profession of faith 'there is no god but God', it would not be valid, and a shaykh whom they had studied with in Alexandria explained that a human being, by exerting himself mystically, could only fully achieve the negative part of the sentence, i.e. 'there is no god', the positive part 'but God' lies beyond what is attainable.

---

11 *Firdaws al-murshidiyya*, ed. Fritz Meier in Bibliotheca Islamica 14, 1948, *bāb* 36, pp. 453 ff./Tehran, 1954, pp. 413 ff. ᶜAṭṭār: *Tadhkirat al-awliyāʾ*, ed. R. A. Nicholson, London-Leiden, 1905, I, p. 24, ll. 7-12, explains an Uwaysī as a man of piety who has no need of a shaykh but becomes trained directly in a supernatural manner through the prophecy of Muḥammad. Jāmī: *Nafaḥāt al-uns*, s.v. Farīd al-Dīn-i ᶜAṭṭār (ed. Tawḥīdīpūr, Tehran, 1336, p. 599), describes ᶜAṭṭār on the basis of a particular tradition as an Uwaysī and adds a report of Mawlānā that Ḥallāj's light revealed itself to ᶜAṭṭār and trained him. Whether these two cases belong to the same category I am not in a position to say. On the other hand, someone who received instruction not from the deceased Prophet but from a deceased shaykh can in fact also be designated an Uwaysī. Thus Dārā-Shikōh (d. 1069/1659): *Sakīnat al-awliyāʾ*, ed. Tārā Chand and Nāʾīnī, Tehran, 1965, pp. 54 and 173-74, took himself to be an Uwaysī of Miyānjīw (d. 1045/1635) because the latter even after his death had given him instruction in a supernatural manner regarding visions. Accordingly, Nawbandajānī, who claimed to have received instruction in the same way from Kāzarūnī, can also be described as an Uwaysī (of this second kind).

§ 4: Balkhī entered a desert and here beheld a smoking well shaft out of which animals burst forth, killed other creatures, went back into the well, and then alternately turned into human beings and animals. A giant snake, which likewise emerged from the well, swallowed them all and then spewed them all forth in increased numbers. At the bidding of a higher power, Balkhī, despite his great fear, wanted to catch the snake but it disappeared along with all the other animals.

§ 5: During the optional mid-morning prayer in spiritual retreat, it became so dark for Balkhī that not only external objects but even imaginative images in his interior were extinguished for him. In the light of a star, however, beautiful forms became visible to him. The number of the stars increased to seven. But they were extinguished once again through the rising of the moon in whose light many beautiful forms once more appeared and vanished again. Then marvelous voices and sounds were heard which praised God, and a fragrance diffused itself. An irrepressible state of rapture came over Balkhī. He continually heard the sentence 'there is no god but God'. Then an earthquake took place with thunder and lightning. The heavenly bodies were extinguished. In a new floodlight it seemed to Balkhī that his body melted away and multiplicity merged into oneness. A form revealed itself and then disappeared again. Balkhī experienced an ineffable joy. The sobering up which followed, the awakening from the vision, transferred him into a state of flat emptiness and weariness with life.

§ 6: Three days later in spiritual retreat he continuously beheld cities and buildings, and heard the most diverse languages. This then ceased and in the morning he perceived a magnificent, peaceful convent in shining brightness and a flower-filled meadow, in the meadow an old man of awesome appearance, encircled by other old men who sat there in dignity and directed questions to him. Baghdādī (to whom the letter is addressed) came before the group with his brother and two other dervishes. The old man in the middle said: 'Whoever utters the sentence "there is no god but God" while his ego still remains with him is a polytheist.' Fear and terror gripped the company. The old man added: 'Not a single seeker of God for the last hundred years has known the path to God, not a single person for the last two hundred years has really fulfilled the conditions of travelling the path, and no prophet and no righteous man has reached the level of the Prophet Muḥammad.' Baghdādī was overcome with ecstasy and swooned. The old man continued: 'Whoever performs the recollection of God correctly, to him the whole of existence submits itself. But whoever then turns to it sinks in the eyes of God.' The old man gripped Baghdādī (Balkhī's shaykh) by the hands: they glowed brightly but their palms were black. The old man ordered him to wash them. The old man allowed Baghdādī to ask any question he wished. Baghdādī asked: 'What is the path to God and politeness on this path and before God?' The old man replied: 'The path to God consists in knowing God. Politeness on this path is to proceed straight ahead and not to swerve... As far as politeness before God is concerned, it consists in watching over your innermost secret and your heart with the light of knowledge while you are continually absent from yourself and your characteristics are extinguished under the onslaughts of divine power.' The old man forbade listening to anything merely to pass the time, gave Baghdādī a small inscribed silver tablet, tied a white face cloth (*rōy-sutur*) around his hips and went on to say: 'Pay heed to the religious law! Speak only the true and hear only the true, then you will be led to the path of the true!' He instructed Baghdādī's brother and the two dervishes to undertake spiritual exercises to weaken the carnal soul and to strengthen the heart. Balkhī (the visionary and author of this letter) wished (in the vision) to receive advice of this kind as well. Then the old man waved to him and said: 'Whoever travels a path without being familiar with it goes astray. See that you take it upon yourself to follow the command, to adhere to the sacred tradition, to fast and to remain silent continually, to punish your carnal soul in all situations and to withdraw from men at large so that you become worthy to travel the path! God cause you to watch over your states and moments, and to keep an eye on your carnal soul!' The company rose to their feet, and Balkhī followed after the men to ask them who they and the old man were. But they disappeared and the convent and the meadow disappeared along with them. Balkhī saw that he was in the mosque again and felt overwhelmed by the old sorrow.

The Content of Baghdādī's Answer

Baghdādī's answer to this letter first of all contains an interpretation of the words of the demon spirits.

§ 10: That the sentence 'there is no god but God' presents a dilemma is confirmed by Baghdādī, for it can only be made a reality if the I-ness of a human being has ceased to exist as a second divinity. But then, firstly, the need to declare a negation of every other god ceases and, secondly, only then is the sentence really true. Baghdādī reveals in passing that he nevertheless conferred upon the novices precisely this formula in its entirety, i.e. with the negative as well as the affirmative part, because they were still in need of their own annihilation, and he considered the repetition of the solitary word 'God' (*allāh*) to be inappropriate. The criticism of the demon spirits is also justified inasmuch as the knowledge of God connected with recollection could in the absolute sense only contain God Himself, man must therefore first become God or God's mouthpiece before he could recollect God with all the implications of this word.

§ 11: Likewise, Baghdādī confirms the statement that the mystic journey remains confined to negating a second divinity alongside God, and he adds that then a passive process of being attracted sets in and travelling no longer takes place. After finiteness one then comes to experience the infinite, after travelling 'to God' one experiences travelling 'in God'. One is transformed from a seeker to that which is sought.

§ 12: Baghdādī explains Balkhī's second vision as follows: in the desert of existence stands the well shaft of the heart, the connecting tract between the material and the supernatural world. But as long as orientation toward the world of the senses prevails in man, his heart is filled with reprehensible qualities. These are the animals which Balkhī saw come forth from the well shaft. The shapes transformed themselves according to the transformation of those qualities in Balkhī. The big snake is the endeavor to reach God. It swallowed up the creatures of bad qualities. But after becoming exhausted it had to spew them forth again. The whole appeared as animals because of the effect of the power of imagination which is accustomed to represent supersensory phenomena in a disguise borrowed from the exterior world. It can happen, moreover, that this tool which is neutral in itself effects an unsuitable veiling of psychic contents. That is the same as when someone is not able to express himself adequately or gives unsuitable interpretations to visions and dreams.

§ 13: The darkness in the third vision is interpreted by Baghdādī as confinement within the world of the senses. But to perceive this confinement as darkness presupposes, according to Baghdādī, an inner capacity of sight and a certain devotion to God. Both these traits owe their existence to a supernatural light which enters into man's heart. This does not happen due to man's will but subsequently evokes in him an active willing by means of which the darkness can then also be penetrated. Once again the lights which the mystic then sees represent his own qualities. A star is inward composure, a moon signifies that the light of the heart has already penetrated into the limbs of the mystic. These were the same lights which, according to surah 6/75 ff., Abraham beheld. In Balkhī's case, however, the perceived lights represent the spirits of the shaykhs in whose care and training Balkhī presently finds himself. Due to their spiritual effect, Balkhī had acquired the capacity for inner sensory perceptions, i.e. his capacity to hear things praise God, which all things do according to surah 17/44, his capacity to experience inner fragrances, his capacity to perceive forms consisting in light. The moon which later rose for him was the light of the Prophet Muḥammad. The Prophet actually drew his light from God as the moon draws its light from the sun, and illuminated and continues to illuminate the members of his community with it. Balkhī's sense of hearing followed this tendency and then only heard the formula of the profession of God's oneness. But human, all-too-human qualities came to be mixed in and a battle, perceptible through thunder and lightning, broke out, the inner holy war, the *vita purgativa*. The light in which everything was finally engulfed can signify, according to Baghdādī, that the light penetrated into Balkhī's 'experience' (*dhawq*), or that God revealed Himself to him completely. This is nothing altogether different but only takes place once a mystic reaches perfection. Balkhī has not yet reached this stage, he is still dominated by knowledge and reason. Thus, what he has experienced up to now has been a revelation of the lights of God's aspect of friendliness.

§ 14: Into the question which Balkhī asked himself, namely what is the meaning of this vision, Baghdādī — assuming something has not dropped out of the text — reads the question as to whether the perceived heavenly bodies could not also be the stars and the moon in the sky and answers it in the affirmative because the walls of the mosque in which Balkhī was sitting during the vision did not necessarily present a hindrance to this seer. The lights of mystical vision could one time be the inner light-nature of the mystic himself, another time the spirits of angels, prophets or demons, and a third time the external heavenly luminaries themselves. In the case under scrutiny, however, they were the spirits of the shaykhs and prophets.

§ 15: Further discussion could take place later when Baghdādī and Balkhī had occasion to meet.

§ 16: The old man of the fourth vision was according to Baghdādī — but this is not certain — probably an important demon shaykh, perhaps ᶜAbd al-Raḥmān, a disciple of the Prophet.

§ 17: The statement of this old man 'whoever says "there is no god but God" while his ego still remains with him is a polytheist' agrees with the words of the demon spirits already explained in the first vision (§ 3 and 10). But one need not become disconcerted because of the contents. The profession is important in all circumstances firstly for the real polytheists who must renounce polytheism. The mystic who has renounced external polytheism must also combat internal polytheism with the same profession. Only once the Sovereign of divine reality has entered his heart will any further negation of the other deities be superfluous.

§ 18: 'Not a single seeker of God for the last hundred years has known the path to God, not a single person for the last two hundred years has really fulfilled the conditions of travelling the path.' To this it should be said: no one has ever actually become God, but there have always been earnest mystic travellers. It is true that this earnestness becomes more rare with the passage of time but God always has servants who devote themselves to mystic striving with all their strength and, moreover, He has ordered matters so that what was only conferred on the early forefathers after long effort can be attained in a shorter period by contemporary individuals. And even if nowadays no one has wholly fulfilled the conditions, none the less God's grace has helped many to achieve success, namely by means of an 'attraction' (cf. § 11).

§ 19: 'No prophet and no righteous man has reached the level of the Prophet Muḥammad.' Until one reaches the limits of humanity, mystical striving is the same among prophets and saints. But beyond this boundary the mystic is someone who is passively drawn along (cf. § 11). However, it fell to Muḥammad to be chosen in a special way so that he experienced the most perfect attraction and now all earlier and later persons are no more than parasites on his perfection.

§ 20: 'Whoever performs the recollection of God correctly, to him the whole of existence submits itself. But whoever then turns to it sinks in the eyes of God.' This is true whether one connects the 'it' to the recollection of God or to existence. Characteristic of correct recollection of God is that one becomes fully absorbed in it and sees the object of recollecting God before one's eyes. To the extent that only God still exercises control in this state of absorption, one has control over the whole world since everything in fact belongs to God and obeys Him. However, should one not turn to the object of recollecting God but to recollection itself, then one returns to the peripheral surface. And should one actually turn to existence, then one sinks from the lordliness (of God) down to the servitude (of man).

§ 21: The black palms which Balkhī discovered as belonging to his teacher and master, Baghdādī modestly interprets as a mild reproach since in Baghdādī's opinion his shortcomings would occasion more blackness than this. Baghdādī had also reproached his own teacher

Kubrā for four reprehensible actions. Kubrā had been pleased that only four were made known to Baghdādī.

§ 22: 'The path to God consists in knowing God.' The aim now is the path 'in God' and no longer simply the path 'to God'.

According to Baghdādī, everything else that Balkhī was told in this vision is to be understood literally.

§ 23: 'Whoever travels a path without being familiar with it goes astray.' This statement of the old man calls upon Balkhī to acquire for himself a solid foundation of faith and on that basis to go on gathering increased theoretical knowledge for mystic activity.

§ 24: In conclusion Baghdādī describes Balkhī's visions as the result of his contact with spirits who, though they have all sorts of desirable things to offer, will never lead a person to the goal. He praises the visionary capacity which Balkhī has attained but regrets that this success belongs to the demons. Balkhī should attach himself to human teachers because only they possess experience about the barriers which separate man from God. The demons, who do not have to break through the same kind of separating wall, only know about these obstacles from hearsay.

SOME REMARKS

On § 10: That in these visions the first part of the profession of faith 'there is no god but God' continually recurs should not be surprising since this is the formula of the recollection of God which someone who has withdrawn in spiritual seclusion repeats to himself uninterruptedly. Other ways in which the formula also manifests itself to the person on spiritual retreat are described by Qusharyī (d. 465/1074): *Tartīb al-sulūk* (see pp. 93-133) and by Kubrā: *Fawāʾiḥ* (see Introduction, pp. 200 ff.). The explanation Baghdādī gives of the statement that one can no longer pronounce the formula if it has actually been realized is this: although the words 'there is no god but God' are only true once one has lost one's ego, none the less it is precisely then that one can no longer say something of this kind in the third person because one no longer exists and consequently no longer has anything to negate. Shiblī (d. 334/946) often emphasized the impossibility of a genuine mystical profession of God's oneness (the *Lumaʿ* of Sarrāj, p. 30, ll. 4-8; p. 32, ll. 15-18).[12] Wāsiṭī (d. after 320/932), on the basis of the same viewpoint, considered someone

12 Ed. R.A. Nicholson in Gibb Memorial Series 22, 1914.

who recollected God as a swindler.[13] Ibn ᶜAṭāᵓ (d. 309/922) demanded forgetting the profession of God's oneness (*Lumaᶜ*, p. 35, ll. 6-7) and wanted becoming one with God in place of professing God's oneness. Abū Yazīd al-Bisṭāmī (d. perhaps 261/875), for a similar reason, is supposed to have renounced uttering the words 'there is no god but God' (Sahlagī, p. 80) and after thirty years to have given up the recollection of God (ibid., p. 80 below).[14] One time in Bisṭāmī's view the so-called 'greatest name' (of God) consists in pronouncing the words 'there is no god but God' without the person any longer being present, another time exactly the reverse, while the person (naturally with his heart) is present (ibid., p. 84 below; cf. p. 112), because Bisṭāmī would not tolerate the name 'God' to be spoken in indifference (ibid., p. 89) and wished to understand the 'much recollection of God' demanded in surah 33/41 not in terms of numbers but in the sense of an intense degree of spiritual presence (*Tadhkirat al-awliyāᵓ*, I, p. 166, last line). Kubrā in *Fawāᵓiḥ* § 79 wrote that God alone is the absolute knower. According to Bisṭāmī, the person who knows God cannot speak any more at all (Sahlagī, p. 129).

The shaykh in Alexandria whom the demons said they had become acquainted with can also have been a demon himself or equally can have been a human being. To list all the occasions on which demons are meant to have visited a human teacher would fill several pages. Both the Prophet and the Shīᶜite Imams were and are regarded as having been teachers of demons as well as humans. Sometimes these demons remain invisible in the institutions of learning that they frequent, sometimes they appear as snakes or as strange, unkempt gaunt figures. Demons studied the rules of Koranic recitation with Ḥasan al-Masīlī (d. 580/1185) in Bijāya.[15] Others loved the beautiful voice of a man of piety or even died upon hearing a pious man recite the Koran.[16] A demon studied jurisprudence with Ibn al-Hirmil (d.

---

13 A.J. Arberry: *Pages from the Kitâb al-Lumaᶜ of Abû Naṣr al-Sarrâj*, London, 1947, Arabic text p. 12, ll. 19 ff., with interpretations of Sarrāj. The saying in question also circulated under the name of Ibn ᶜAṭāᵓ.

14 ᶜAbd al-Raḥmān Badawī: *Shaṭaḥāt al-ṣūfiyya*, I, Cairo, 1949. ᶜAṭṭār: *Tadhkirat al-awliyāᵓ*, I, p. 159, ll. 12-13.

15 Abū'l-ᶜAbbās Aḥmad b. ᶜAbdallāh al-Ghubrīnī : *ᶜUnwān al-dirāya fī-man ᶜurifa min al-ᶜulamāᵓ fī'l-miᵓa al-sābiᶜa bi-Bijāya*, Beirut, 1969, p. 34.

16 Tādilī: *Tashawwuf*, Rabat, 1958, p. 267 f. *Lumaᶜ*, p. 282, ll. 14-17. Jullābī (Hujwīrī): *Kashf al-maḥjūb*, ed. Zhukovski, p. 513, ll. 1-3/trans. Nicholson, p. 395.

6th/12th century).[17] Muḥammad b. ᶜAbdallāh b. ᶜUlātha al-Ḥarrānī (d. 163/779-80)[18] and ᶜAlī b. al-Ḥusayn b. Muḥammad al-Khilaᶜī (d. 448/1056) were regarded as 'judges of the *jinn*',[19] ᶜUmar b. Muḥammad al-Nasafī (d. 537/1142)[20] and Ṣāᵓin al-Dīn Ḥusayn b. Muḥammad b. Salmān (d. 664/1265-66) as 'expert expounders of law for spirits and human beings'.[21] Certain Sufis held the view that if a shaykh who was speaking before an assembly suddenly fell silent, the reason could be the presence of an unworthy demon because the assemblies of Sufis were never free of the presence of some demons.[22] When one time Abū ᶜAlī al-Daqqāq (d. 405/1015) was about to return from Marw to Nayshābūr, he dreamed that a number of demons who attended his assemblies needed him to stay on longer in Marw.[23] A mystic who lived about two generations after Ghazzālī (d. 505/1111) was called 'teacher of the demons and human beings'.[24] Demons were supposed to have been novices of Mawlānā Rūmī (d. 672/1273).[25] The patron saint of Tunis, Muḥriz (d. 413/1022), was master over humans and demons, just as was Bisṭāmī[26] and many others. A standard epithet of ᶜAbd al-Qādir al-Jīlānī (d. 561/1166) is 'pole of humans and spirits' (*ghawth al-thaqalayn*). Shaᶜrānī (d. 973/1565) claims to have answered in a se-

---

17 Ignaz Goldziher: *Die Richtungen der islamischen Koranauslegung*, Leiden, 1920, p. 53/Khazrajī: *Al-ᶜuqūd al-luᵓluᵓiyya*, ed. Asal, in Gibb Memorial Series 3, 1908-1913, IV, p. 172 below.

18 *Taᵓrīkh Baghdād*, V, p. 389, ll. 21 ff.

19 Damīrī: *Ḥayāt al-ḥayawān* s.v. *jinn*, Cairo, 1356, I, p. 214, last line. Ibn al-Zayyāt: *Al-kawākib al-sayyāra fī tartīb al-ziyāra*, Cairo, n.d., pp. 46 and 164.

20 Aṣīl al-Dīn: 'Maqṣad al-iqbāl-i sulṭāniyya', in Fikrī-i Saljūqī: *Mazārāt-i Hirāt*, Kabul, n.d., I, p. 90, l. 1.

21 Junayd-i Shīrāzī: *Shadd al-izār*, ed. Muḥammad-i Qazwīnī and ᶜAbbās-i Iqbāl, Tehran, 1328, p. 176.

22 Qushayrī, *Risāla*, Chpt. *ṣamt*.

23 Qushayrī: *Risāla*, Chpt. *ṣamt*/Ibn al-Jawzī: *Ṣifat al-ṣafwa*, Hyderabad, 1355-56, IV, p. 405/ᶜAṭṭār: *Tadhkirat al-awliyāᵓ*, II, p. 189, ll. 12-15.

24 Jean Aubin: *Matériaux pour la biographie de Shah Niᶜmatullah Wali Kermani*, in Bibliothèque Iranienne 7, Tehran-Paris, 1956, p. 58, l. 3 and p. 294, l. 18. Another saint who is supposed to have given instruction to demons and clergy is found in René Basset: *Nouveaux contes berbères*, Paris, 1897, no. 97.

25 Aflākī: *Manāqib al-ᶜārifīn*, ed. Tahsin Yazıcı, Ankara, 1959-61, I, p. 93, l. 7.

26 Hady Roger Idris: *Manâqib d'Abû Isḥâq Al-Jabanyânî... et Manâqib de Muḥriz B. Ḫalaf...*, in Publications de la Faculté des Lettres et Sciences Humaines d'Alger 31, Paris, 1959, p. 158 and 172. Sahlagī, p. 111, ll. 11-12.

parate book some seventy questions posed by *jinn* about the profession of God's oneness.[27]

Conversely, that human beings could receive instructions and inspiration from demons is well-known, in particular among the poets. The incomprehensibly rapid transmission of news is likewise often attributed to the *jinn*. Other legends report that a demon or a band of demons kidnap a boy and instruct him or have him instructed in the sciences.[28] It is more rare that demons appear who as Sufi shaykhs

---

27 *Laṭā'if al-minan*, cited in Zakī Mubārak: *Al-taṣawwuf al-islāmī*², Cairo, 1954, I, p. 347.

28 Instruct him: cf. the well-known legend of Sayyid Muḥammad-i Ḥāfiẓ, an ancestor of Ṣafī al-Dīn-i Ardabīlī, from Tawakkulī: *Ṣafwat al-ṣafā* (written around 759/1358, later reworked from a Shīᶜite viewpoint), in Zeki Velidi Togan: 'Sur l'origine des Safavides', in *Mélanges Louis Massignon*, III, Damascus, 1958, p. 350: Muḥammad-i Ḥāfiẓ had the following destiny: When he was seven years old he disappeared. As much as they searched for him, no one could find any trace of him. Finally a mourning ceremony (read *ᶜazāy*) was held for him in the usual way and all hope of finding him was abandoned. But when seven more years had passed, they suddenly saw Muḥammad standing at the door of the house. He had on an *ᶜattābī*-robe and the kind of cap which was worn those days and was wrapped round with a white band, and had a Koran hung around his neck. When the people beheld him, they were astonished and greatly pleased that he had reappeared. Finally they asked him about the cause of his disappearance. He explained: 'The *jinn* had kidnapped me. During the past seven years they taught me the Koran and instructed me in the prescribed religious duties and statutes.' Afterwards he possessed perfection with regard to fear of God, piety, conscientious abstemiousness and conformity to the law, and he continuously fulfilled the requirements of religion until he passed over to the mercy of God. — Another somewhat different version is found in the anonymous *ᶜĀlamārāy-i ṣafawī* (written 1086/1675), ed. Yadallāh-i Shukrī, Tehran, 1971, pp. 5-7: The king of the demons was searching for his disappeared son and came upon the beautiful Muḥammad-i Ḥāfiẓ who was seven years old and resembled his son. He carried off the boy and regularly had the boy recite the Koran for him. He assigned a teacher to him and had him instructed in all the sciences known to the demons. After seven years the king of the demons saw the boy's father and heard him praying for the boy's return. This aroused his pity and he allowed the kidnapped boy to return home. — The story is also found in Iskandar Bayk-i Turkamān: *Tārīkh-i ᶜālamārāy-i ᶜabbāsī*, Tehran, 1334, I, p. 10, and elsewhere. — Similarly, there is a legend about the saint of Qandahār Sayyid Ḥusayn-i Zanjīrpā (9th/15th century) in the *Tārīkh-i Maᶜṣūmī* (written around 1009/1600), ed. U.M. Daudpota, Poona, 1938, p. 135. But here the demons are only the transporters who convey the child to different human educators at the command of his uncle Bābā Ḥasan-i Abdāl. It is striking that Zanjīrpā is also seven years old at the time of his kidnapping and returns after seven years. — A legend about the origin of the Bon religion in Tibet exhibits the same scheme. The founder of this religion, when he was thirteen years old, is supposed to have been kidnapped by a demon and to

teach human beings. But that belief in this possibility did exist is attested in a story found in Ibn al-Jawzī (d. 597/1201): *Ṣifat al-ṣafwa*, Hyderabad, 1355-56, IV, p. 405. According to the story, many generations ago a certain Ṣāliḥ b. ᶜAbd al-Karīm felt the desire to meet a shaykh of the *jinn* one time and to converse with him. He consequently met a female demon who dictated something to him. Najm al-Dīn-i Dāya: *Mirṣād al-ᶜibād, faṣl* 18, Tehran 1312, p. 175, l. 3, (completed 620/1223) mentions the ability of the mystic to see the spirits of demons. Muḥammad-i ᶜAwfī: *Jawāmiᶜ al-ḥikāyāt, bāb* 11, (completed after 628/1231) recounts an older Arabic story in which demons argue about whether the human or demon scholars are better, and then on the basis of a test come to the conclusion that the human scholars are superior to the demons.[29]

The special significance of the visions of Balkhī, in my opinion, lies not least in the fact that wise demon spirits appear in them.

If during the recollection of God Balkhī recited the formula 'there is no god but God' and his teacher Baghdādī expressly prefers this formula to the single word 'God', in so doing both align themselves with the majority of Sufis and with Kubrā (*Fawāʾiḥ*, Introduction, p. 201). Baghdādī also recommends this formula in his Arabic work *Tuḥfat al-barara*, Chpt. 5 (unedited), moreover with the addition 'by God' (*wa'llāh*), and refers to others such as Abū'l-Najīb al-Suhrawardī (d. 563/1168) and Abū Yaᶜqūb Yūsuf b. Ayyūb al-Hamadānī (d. 535/1140-41 or later) who left out 'by God'. Dāya: *Mirṣād, faṣl* 12, pp. 148-50, ᶜAzīz-i Nasafī: *Kashf al-ḥaqāʾiq*,

---

have been dragged through all the different regions of Tibet for thirteen years until he was once again released by his master. Thanks to his long association with the spirits, he was then able to give information about the location and the effective power of the demons, and about the sacrifices, prayers and rites by means of which one should deal with them. Helmut Hoffmann: *Quellen zur Geschichte der tibetischen Bon-Religion,* in Abh. d. Akad. d. Wiss. u. Lit., Geistes-und Sozialwissenschaftliche Klasse 4, Mainz-Wiesbaden, 1950, pp. 197 f., sees the occurrence in connection with the psychic journey undertaken by those who are in the process of becoming shamans. Perhaps knowledge of our Persian parallels is not wholly without significance for the correct assessment of the motif. — Being kidnapped by demons frequently occurs in Arabic and Persian stories and is attested very early on. In René Basset's *Contes populaires berbères*, Paris, 1887, no. 31, a kidnapped boy is given instruction by a demon. This is not the place to enter into the subject more fully.

29 Muḥammad Niẓām al-Dīn: Introduction to the *Jawâmiᶜu'l-Ḥikâyât*, in Gibb Memorial, New Series 8, London, 1929, p. 162, serial no. 587/Muḥammad-i Ramaḍānī: *Pānzdah bāb-i Jawāmiᶜ al-ḥikāyāt*, facsimile, Tehran, 1335, pp. 14-15.

Tehran, 1965, pp. 135-36,[30] Kasirqī and Simnānī[31] and many others were equally in favor of 'there is no god but God'. Qushayrī: '*Tartīb al-sulūk*', see p. 109, ll. 3/p. 123, l. 1-2, and Muḥammad al-Ghazzālī: *Kīmiyāy-i saᶜādat, rukn* 3, *aṣl* 1, Tehran, 1333, p. 450, l. 3 from bottom, adhered to repeating the word 'God' (*allāh*).

On § 11: Baghdādī's account does not coincide absolutely with the conceptions of other Sufis but agrees generally with the explanations he gives in his *Tuḥfat al-barara*, Chpt. 3, and his *Risāla dar safar* (in *Collected Papers*, pp. 188 f.). The common basic feature of all three descriptions is that the dividing line between effort (*kōshish*) and being passively drawn, 'attraction' (*kashish*), between desiring and being the object of desire, lies at the point where the mystic enters the world of divinity and the infinite. Others have more thoroughly mixed together effort and attraction or posited them as opposites alongside one another, not behind one another (*Fawāʾiḥ*, Introduction, pp. 94-96; 'An Important Manuscript Find', p. 166, even derived man's desire from a divine desire for man.

The journey 'to God' and the journey 'in God' are expressions which frequently appear from the time of Baghdādī onward. ᶜAṭṭār: *Tadhkirat al-awliyāʾ*, ed. R.A. Nicholson, II, p. 223, ll. 18-19, includes the saying of Bisṭāmī: 'I am neither settled nor journeying, but journey as one who is settled in the oneness (or uniqueness) of God.' Perhaps behind this stand Bisṭāmī's words: 'My companion is settled and not journeying, and I am settled with him (*maᶜahū*) and do not journey' (Sahlagī, p. 124). Kubrā: *Fawāʾiḥ* § 60, promises the mystic that once he has acquired increased purity 'he will journey in the purity of God, in the final stages of the journey, an infinite purity', and describes in his *Uṣūl al-ᶜashara* the shortest of the numerous paths 'to God'.[32] Maḥmūd-i Kāshānī: *Miṣbāḥ al-hidāya*, ed. Jalāl al-Dīn-i Humāʾī, Tehran (1323), pp. 426 and 430, designates the self-extinction of the mystic as the end of the journey 'to God' and the existential association with God as the journey 'in God', which is not yet found in the text he took as his model, Suhrawardī's *ᶜAwārif al-maᶜārif.* ᶜAzīz-i Nasafī (end of 7th/13th century) frequently makes

---

30 Cf. F. Meier: 'Die Schriften des ᶜAzîz-i Nasafî', in *WZKM* 52, 1953, pp. 164-65/*Bausteine,* I, p. 218-219. Similarly, the student of Kubrā, Ṣadr al-Dīn Abū'l-Muʾayyad al-Muwaffaq b. Muḥammad al-Khāṣī: *Al-salwa fī sharāʾiṭ al-khalwa* (see ftn. 5 above), prefers 'there is no god but God' and mentions others who chose 'God, God'.

31 Landolt: *Correspondance*, Persian text p. 23, ll. 6-10.

32 *Fawāʾiḥ*, Introduction, pp. 48 and 93. M. Molé: 'Traités mineurs', pp. 15-22.

use of the antithesis: *Maqṣad-i aqṣā*, pp. 130-32, 148,[33] *Kashf al-ḥaqāʾiq*, p. 124, *Tanzīl al-arwāḥ*, MS Sehid Ali Paşa 1363, 92b, *Kitāb al-insān al-kāmil*, index s.v. *sayr*, p. 571,[34] as does the Naqshbandī Ṣāḥibzāda (13th/19th century): *Risāla-i murādān*, in Molé: 'Naqshbandiyyāt', in *Farhang-i Īrānzamīn* 6, 1337, p. 310 f. The anonymous plagiarist of Dāya, *Tuḥfat al-sālikīn* (10th/16th century), MS Fatih (Istanbul) 2567, 4b-5a, distinguishes journeys 'to', 'with' and 'in God'.[35] More can be found in Maᶜṣūmᶜalīshāh (d. 1344/1926): *Ṭarāʾiq al-ḥaqāʾiq*, litho., Tehran 1318-19, I, p. 76 f.,[36] and elsewhere.

On § 12: Well shaft, desert and animals, the latter as representations of a human being's moral qualities, are well-known elements from Kubrā's mysticism (*Fawāʾiḥ*, Introduction, pp. 89, 116 f., 160, 209). Smoking shafts and animals, as well as deserts and water, already appear in the allegorical usage of Sanāʾī (d. 535/1140-41 or 545/1150-51?), especially in his *Sayr al-ᶜibād ilā'l-maᶜād*, verses 159 ff., in *Mathnawīhāy-i Ḥakīm-i Sanāʾī*, ed. Mudarris-i Raḍawī, Tehran, 1348, pp. 191 ff. The snake as effort to reach God is new and also falls outside the framework of the interpretations given by Baghdādī in his *Tuḥfat al-barara*, Chpt. 3 (unedited). On the other hand, it is found frequently enough in fairy tales as the animal of wisdom and knowledge, and if a person eats it, his sight can even be opened to the seven heavens (René Basset: *Nouveaux contes berbères* no. 95 and ftn. 174 [not 175], Paris, 1897). Baghdādī also discusses in his *Tuḥfat al-barara*, Chpt. 6, transposing what is perceived in visions, or the psychic or metaphysical contents underlying the perception, into forms from the sensorial world by means of human imagination which is bound to the world of the senses. For earlier and later theories on this subject and on its opposite, 'direct' inner perception, see *Fawāʾiḥ*, Introduction, pp. 102 ff., 243 ff.

On § 13: That recognition of the inner darkness in which man lives actually presupposes a certain dissociation from this darkness is

---

33 In the collective lithograph (Tehran, 1355) which begins with *Sharḥ-i Ashiᶜᶜat al-lamaᶜāt-i mawlānā Jāmī*. In E.H. Palmer: *Oriental Mysticism*, ed. A.J. Arberry, London, 1938, pp. 4-7, which contains a summary, the antithesis between the ideas does not emerge.

34 *ᶜAzizoddin Nasafi, Le Livre de l'Homme Parfait*, ed. Marijan Molé, in Bibliothèque Iranienne 11, Tehran-Paris, 1962.

35 *Fawāʾiḥ*, Introduction, p. 245.

36 Most of these references I owe to my friend Richard Gramlich (Basle and Freiburg im Breisgau). Cf. also Sulṭān Walad: *Waladnāma*, ed. Humāʾī, Tehran, 1315, pp. 237-38 and 359. Aflākī, p. 70.

stated in Kubrā: *Fawā'iḥ* § 2. Kubrā is also familiar with the doctrine of the Prophet's light which on the one hand originates from the light of (God's) immense power, and on the other hand emits the light of the saints and believers (*Fawā'iḥ*, Introduction, p. 116). However, the idea of Muḥammad-light as the (second) source of all light (after the first divine light) is older still. On this subject see Tor Andrae: *Die person Muhammeds in lehre und glauben seiner gemeinde*, in Archives d'Études Orientales 16, Stockholm, 1918, pp. 319 ff., A.E. Affifi: *The Mystical Philosophy of Muḥyid Dîn-Ibnu ʿArabî*, Cambridge, 1939, p. 92; idem: *Fuṣūṣ al-ḥikam li'l-shaykh al-akbar Muḥyī al-Dīn b. ʿArabī*, Cairo, 1946, pp. 319 ff., Zakī Mubārak: *Al-taṣawwuf al-islāmī*, Cairo, 1954, I, pp. 266 ff. That visionary powers of perception can overcome time and space outwardly as well, traverse wide distances, penetrate walls and otherwise know no external barriers is an old belief and represented in many Sufi handbooks in the chapter on miracles (e.g. Jullābī: *Kashf al-maḥjūb*, translated by R.A. Nicholson, in Gibb Memorial Series 17, 1911 and reprint, pp. 218 ff.). Thus, the visionary, even in an enclosed space, must be able to perceive the external heavenly bodies. The metaphorical significance which Baghdādī attributes to the heavenly bodies in Balkhī's vision finds its parallel in Joseph's dream of the eleven stars, the sun and the moon in surah 12/4 which symbolize Joseph's brothers and his father and mother (cf. Dāya: *Mirṣād*, *faṣl* 16, p. 165), and later in Simnānī as well who claims to have beheld Bisṭāmī as the planet Jupiter and Majd al-Dīn-i Baghdādī as the sun (*Chihil majlis*, no. 39). The lights of God's friendliness in which, according to Baghdādī, the vision of Balkhī ended should perhaps be contrasted with the shattering lightning of the revelation of God's sublimity (the oppositional pair *jamāl-jalāl*) which Baghdādī mentions in his *Risāla dar safar*, p. 188.

On § 16: ᶜAbd al-Rahmān is the name of a *jinnī* who is supposed to have accepted Islam from Muḥammad. Jaᶜfar-i Badakhshī (beginning of 9th/15th century): *Khulāṣat al-manāqib* (*vita* of ᶜAlī-i Hamadānī[37]), MS Berlin Pertsch no. 6, 8, 121a/MS Oxford Ethé 1264, 87a, reports that in his time ᶜAbd al-Raḥmān was still alive. In the Safavid period as well ᶜAbd al-Raḥmān was invoked: MS no. 866 in the Mishkāt catalogue (Tehran) III, 2, p. 968. This could be the same demon who in East Turkestan was summoned as a helper under the name ᶜAbd al-Raḥmān Khān by means of conjurations

---

37 Johann Karl Teufel: *Eine Lebensbeschreibung des Scheichs ʿAlî Hamadânî*, Leiden, 1962, pp. 1-8. Some of the information about the *jinn* on p. 113 needs partial correction.

(Karl Menges: 'Volkskundliche Texte aus Ost-Türkistan', in *Sb. preuss. Ak. Berlin*, Philo.-histo. Kl. 1933, pp. 1254-57). Perhaps he is also identical with the ᶜAbd al-Raḥmān who is mentioned there in a conjuration of the Jewish spirits as one of their possible fathers because he may well have adhered to the Jewish religion before his conversion (ibid., pp. 1266-67).

A scene similar to that depicted in this vision of Balkhī occurs in a series of apparently fictive visions which were collected in Seville by a certain Abū Muḥammad ᶜAbdallāh b. al-Ustādh al-Mawrūrī and taken over by Ibn ᶜArabī: *Muḥāḍarat al-abrār*, Cairo, 1305, I, p. 145. But the shaykh whom the novice sees there in the midst of others is as elsewhere (I, pp. 62, 79, 94, 98, 125, 128, 137, etc.) no demon but Abū Madyan (d. 594/1197).

On § 17: Cf. my remarks on § 10.

On § 18: Alongside the widespread notion of 'the good old times' there also existed in later Sufism the idea that it was becoming increasingly easier to travel the mystic path. Simnānī (d. 736/1336) distinctly represented this perspective which was comforting to the epigones. He saw in the continued increase in the number of shaykhs a concomitant increase in wisdom and a refinement in the understanding of things. He even pointed to the parallel situation among the prophets: Muḥammad is greater than Adam ('Sufik und Kulturzerfall', in *Klassizismus und Kulturverfall*, Frankfurt am Main, 1960, p. 148/*Classicisme et déclin culturel dans l'histoire de l'Islam*, Paris, 1957, p. 220, from *Chihil majlis*, no. 19; Hermann Landolt: *Correspondance spirituelle*, p. 113, ll. 5-6). Put differently, Shiblī (d. 334/946) by way of one-upmanship had already maintained that he had reached a more developed stage than Bisṭāmī, the latter could learn something 'from our novices' (*Lumaᶜ*, p. 397, ll. 7 ff.). The South Arabian mystic ᶜAbdallāh b. Aḥmad Bā Kathīr al-Ḥaḍramī al-Makkī (d. 925/1519) felt himself to be so strong because of what his teacher ᶜAbdallāh al-ᶜAydarūs had 'filled' him with (*malaʾanī*) that on his own he believed he was a match for all the shaykhs in Qushayrī's *Risāla* (ᶜAbd al-Qādir al-ᶜAydarūsī: *Taʾrīkh al-nūr al-sāfir*, Baghdad, 1934, p. 125). Majd al-Dīn-i Baghdādī could not praise highly enough the capacity of shaykhs to help novices advance over great distances in a short time (Dāya: *Mirṣād, faṣl* 9, *wajh* 8, p. 131, ll. 7-12).

On § 19: Islamic mysticism, being ever in danger of trespassing on the reserve of prophecy because of its claim to higher insights and closer contact with God, since the classical period has always placed great importance in the permanent competitive lead of Muḥammad over all members of his community and over all human beings in general.

On § 20: Equally conventional is the view that a person performing the recollection of God must in the end lose himself entirely in the object of his recollection. Dhū'l-Nūn al-Miṣrī (d. 245/859) is already supposed to have required 'the absence of the person recollecting God from the recollection of God' (Qushayrī: *Risāla*, Chpt. *dhikr*), and Shiblī the forgetting of the recollection of God and everything else besides God (*Lumaᶜ*, p. 220, ll. 4-6). The school of Sahl b. ᶜAbdallāh al-Tustarī (d. perhaps 283/896) also knew the demand not to become engaged with the recollection of God but with its object (*Lumaᶜ*, p. 394, l. 12). Qushayrī: '*Tartīb al-sulūk*', p. 109/p. 123, actually classifies a state of absence from the recollection of God as being on a beginner's level. Kubrā: *Fawāʾiḥ* § 51, de-scribes the third level of the mystic's immersion as 'absence of the person recollecting God from the recollection of God in the object of the recollection of God' and also mentions in § 52 the possibility of a gradual relapse outwardly, whereas earlier Qushayrī had dealt with it somewhat differently: '*Tartīb*', p. 112/p. 125. Conversely, Bisṭāmī speaks of a strange relapse inwardly caused by exhaustion, as if the outward aspect were the more laborious one: 'Whoever loves God is occupied worshipping Him by kneeling and bowing. If he is no longer able to do so, he refreshes himself by recollecting God with his tongue and by praising (God out loud). If he is no longer able to do this either, he then refreshes himself by recollecting God in his heart', etc. (Sahlagī, p. 141; cf. *Miṣbāḥ al-hidāya*, p. 323).

Similarly, regarding the first sentence 'Whoever performs the recollection of God correctly, to him the whole of existence submits itself', there are earlier analogous sayings, such as for example: 'Whoever honestly renounces the world, the world follows him against its will' (Qushayrī: *Risāla*, Chpt. *zuhd*). It is frequently stated that whoever obeys God, everything obeys him. Saqaṭī declares: 'Whoever fears God, all things fear him' (Sulamī: *Ṭabaqāt*, Cairo, p. 53, l. 7/Pedersen, p. 46, ll. 3-4; Kalābādhī: *Taᶜarruf*, ed. Arberry, Chpt. 40, p. 96, l. 5, trans. Arberry, p. 89). Bisṭāmī taught that a person who relates to God in such a way that his will coincides with the will of God — all things follow him (Sahlagī, p. 75).

On § 21: Modestly admitting that one's actual shortcomings far exceed the amount which has been exposed to view has long been a virtue of a shaykh conscious of his sins. Abū ᶜUthmān al-Ḥīrī (d. 298/910) one time had a bucket of ashes strewn over him by mistake.

He calmed down his angry students by commenting that what he really deserved was fire (Qushayrī: *Risāla*, Chpt. *khuluq*/*Tadhkirat al-awliyā*ʾ, II, p. 58, ll. 7-10).

On § 22: Cf. my remarks on § 11.

On § 6: The small inscribed silver tablet which in Balkhī's vision the demon shaykh gave to Baghdādī and which Baghdādī leaves unmentioned and unexplained in his written reply, reminds one of the silver tablet which the vassals of the Qarā Khiṭāy regularly received as a sign of submission (Wittfogel and Fêng Chia-shêng: *History of Chinese Society Liao*, Philadelphia, 1969, p. 666). Ibn al-Athīr: *Kāmil*, ed. Tornberg, year 536, Beirut, 1967, XI, p. 84, writes: 'The kings who submitted to them all girded themselves with something like a silver tablet (*lawḥ fiḍḍa*). This was the sign of those who were obedient to them.' Related to this seems to be the Mongol *pāyza* which, conversely, was understood as a sign of the authority and command of the great khan, conferred upon the bearer (Bertold Spuler: *Die Mongolen in Iran*1, Leipzig, 1939, pp. 292 f.; M. Quatremère: *Histoire des Mongols de la Perse*, Paris, 1836, I, pp. 177-79, ftn. 43). Barthold: *Turkestan down to the Mongol Invasion*, p. 339, ll. 1-2, describes the Khwārazmshāhs as vassals of the Qarā Khiṭāy. The context within which the silver tablet appears in Balkhī's vision fully justifies the assumption that it is a sign of an investiture, authorization and affiliation by the demon shaykh. Or is it a talisman?

On § 24: It deserves to be emphasized that Baghdādī considers demon shaykhs as unsuitable for training human novices because they have not been obliged to overcome the same barriers and hindrances as human beings. In this way he transfers to the demons a principle which Kubrā had proposed for those among the Sufis who were 'drawn upwards'. Kubrā demanded that the trainer of novices should himself have 'travelled' the path which they had to travel and should have become acquainted with the difficulties of the mystic path through his own experience, i.e. he should not simply have been transported beyond all obstacles by means of a rapture (*Fawāʾiḥ*, Introduction, pp. 95 f.; Molé: 'Traités mineurs', p. 35, ll. 14-22). Al-Muwaffaq b. Muḥammad al-Khāṣī: *Al-salwa fi sharāʾiṭ al-khalwa*, and others repeat this. Baghdādī, whose view of 'journeying' (*sayr* = *sulūk* 'travelling') and 'being attracted' (*jadhba*) was somewhat different (treated at length in *Tuḥfat al-barara*, Chpts. 3 and 4, *Risāla dar safar*, and here § 11), none the less adopts Kubrā's line of thought in order to exclude the demons from training novices. Of course, one should not conclude from this that Baghdādī believed that demons as such, i.e. by their very nature, were 'drawn upwards'.

Despite all their differences, Kubrā and his students have numerous characteristics in common. It is through them that one can appreciate Kubrā's significance and recognize the reason why his name stands at the head of a school.

ON THE TEXT

I have made a literal translation of the Persian text for my own use but I will not venture to publish it here because its basis, a single manuscript, still leaves much to be desired. It seems more advisable to me to wait until further manuscripts become known. Similarly, the text which follows makes no claim to be a final, unassailable edition but simply wishes to contribute to enlarging our knowledge of the mysticism of Kubrā's school and in particular, by presenting complementary manuscript material, to help create a more solid basis for understanding the correspondence under scrutiny. The manuscript at my disposal, Köprülü (Istanbul) 1589, 409b-412a, from the 8th/14th century, has post-vocalic *d* in Persian words pointed as *dh*. On the basis of Shams-i Qays: *Al-mu^{c}jam fī ma^{c}āyīr ash^{c}ār al-^{c}ajam*, ed. Muḥammad-i Qazwīnī, in Gibb Memorial Series 10, 1909, p. 192/revised by Mudarris-i Raḍawī, Tehran, 1338, p. 221, we know that around 600/1200 specifically in Ghaznī, Balkh and Transoxania the post-vocalic *dh* had already hardened to *d*. Our correspondents who lived in that period should thus have said *d*. None the less, I have kept the historical spelling of our manuscript which may also have been that of the original. On the other hand, contrary to the manuscript I have added the helpful distinction between *g* and *k*, *j* and *ch*, and *b* and *p*. The technical editorial signs which I have used are those of classical philology. < > means: not in the original but inserted by me. { } means: in the original but rejected by me. [ ] means: missing in the original due to damage and amended by me (on the basis of conjecture). + + means: corrupted. The division and numbering of the sections, as well as the punctuation and Koranic references, have been added by me. The apparatus criticus is presented in the form of footnotes to facilitate the work of the typesetter.

Addition of the author to ftn. 5: on Khāṣī see 'Der unbekannte schriftsteller al-Muwaffaq al-Ḫāṣī', *Der Islam* 66, 1989; *Bausteine*, I, pp. 474-93.

(۴۰۹ب) رسالهٔ شیخ شرف‌الدین بلخی الی مجدالدین بغدادی

(۴۱۰ آ) سلام علی من ان‌قضیت حقوقه + منت‌علی‌جدی[۱] + الیه مسلما

(۱) اصناف الطاف ربانی و خلاصهٔ سمادت دوجهانی بروزگار مبارک فضل گستر کرم‌پرور امام الهدی حجة الحق مرشد الخلق مجد الملة و الدین عماد الاسلام و المسلمین مقتدی الشریعة و الطریقة مد الله ظله متصل باذ و آثار انوار غیبی و تایید عالم قدسی بر دل مطهر و جان مقدس و سر مصفاء آن بزرگ دین متواتر و متوالی و. حق جل‌وعلا در کل الاحوال قاضی دواعی و مقاصد دینی و مطلوبات اخروی بحصول موصول.

(۲) کمترین مستفیدان و مخلصترین خدمتگاران آن حضرت محمد بلغی ارشده الله الی درك السعادة الابدیة از خلوص نیت و صدق عقیدت خدمت و دعا و تحیت و ثنا بجناب رفیع و حضرت عالی می‌رساند و بحکم حدیث نبوی علیه الصلوة و السلام که ان من العلم کهیئة المکنون لا یعلمه الا العلماء بالله و بحکم اجازت سادات طریق رضوان الله علیهم اجمعین که اذا اشکل علیکم شیء من کلام هذه الطائفة علیکم بالبحث منهم لانهم أمناء الله علی عباده و قلوبهم خزائن الله فی الارض از سر عجز و طریق استفادت قصه درد دل و وقایع بر رای مبارك که همیشه بصواب مقرون باذ عرضه می‌دارد، توقع است بکمال کرم و حسن رعایت و شفقت آن بزرگ دین که اصناف خلایق را شامل است بحکم استماع کلام الملهوف صدقة بسمع رضا اصغا فرمایذ و دامن عفو و تجاوز برین جرأت و سوء ادب پوشانند باطل و حقی که بطریق واردات[۲] و لوایح روی نموده است بتحقیق بیان‌شافی که از

۱. شاید «من علی بجذبی» خواندنی باشد.
۲. در نسخهٔ اصلی: وارادت.

آثار عیان وافی و آنچه لایق بر حوصلهٔ فهم قاصر این ضعیف باشد کشف الغطاء آن دریغ ندارذ تا بثواب جزیل و ثناء جمیل مضاف گردذ و دار معاد را مدخر ماند، و الله ولی التوفیق وعلیه‌التکلان.

(۳) چنان نموذ این ضعیف را + بعد از ظهور ارواح جن و کلام ۳ + ایشان و سؤالات ایشان که ما معنی قولك لا اله الا الله؟ و الله لوصح قولك لا اله الا الله ما استطعت ان تقول لا اله الا الله، ثم قالوا: کان لنا شیخ[۴] من الشیوخ فی الاسکندریة و هو یقول: سلوك جملة السالکین فی لااله لیس لاحد ان یتجاوز عنه و یخرج منه و ما دخل احد من السالکین فی الا الله لانه لیس للحدث مدخل فی القدم فاذا تم السلوك فی لا اله و هو النفی انتفی النافی[۵] و السالك فبعد هذا من یسلك الطریق؟

(۴) ازین جنس سوالات و کلمات رانده‌اند با ایـن ضعیف، و بعد از آن چنان نموذ این ضعیف که بزمینی رسیذی صحراء لاعوج‌فیها ولاانثناء. آوازهائـی صعب و هائل می‌شنیذی و کس را نمی‌دیذ، ناگاه چاهی عظیم وسیع بعیذ القعر پدیذ آمذی و دخانی عظیم کدر و بخاری عظیم ظلمانی از آن چاه بر می‌آمذ و انواع حیوانات و صنوف سباع چون[۶] ذئاب و خنازیر و قرده و کلاب و حیات و عقارب ازین چاه برمی‌آمذند و در خلقان دگر می‌افتاذند و بعضی خلقانرا از هم برمی‌دریذند و باز در چاه می‌رفتند و هم در حال از صورت سبعی و بهیمگی می‌بگشتند و چون صورت انسان[۷] می‌شذند و در طرفةالعین صورت خلع می‌کردند و صورتی دیگر می‌گرفتند، و ناگاه ثعبانی عظیم با طول و عرض آن[۸] که نمی‌دانم چند بوذه است ازین چـاه برآمذ و این جمله صور مختلف را بدهان فروبرد، باز از تن جمله را با اضعاف مضاعفه آن دهان برآورد، خوفی عظیم برین ضعیف مستولی شذ، ذکر از دهان و زبان این ضعیف منقطع گشت، از جانب قبلی آواز می‌شنیذم که خذها[۹] و لاتخف (قرآن ۲۰، ۲۱)، دست فرا کردم کـه دنبال او را بگیرم، ناپدیذ گشت و آن صور مختلف ناپدیذ شذند و آن اصوات ناچیز گشت و دیگر بار حاسهٔ بصر این ضعیف مدرك ورائی سقف و جدرانات گشت، یك شبانروز در هول و سیاست آن نموذه بماندم وندانستم که آن تمثیلات و تصویرات چه بوذ خارج من بوذ یا صفات نفس و قوای[۱۰] داخل من بوذ که بر سبیل تصویر و تمثیل ظاهر گشت یا قوة وهمـی و خیالـی

۳. در نسخهٔ اصلی: بعد از ظهور ارواح حس و کلام. شاید یا «بعداز ظهر» خواندنی‌باشد یا واو «و کلام» بطلان کشیدنی.
۴. در نسخهٔ اصلی: شیخا
۴. در نسخهٔ اصلی: فهو.
۵. در نسخهٔ اصلی: لناقی (کذا) کلمه «انتفی» هم واضح نیست.
۶. در نسخهٔ اصلی: حنس (کذا).
۷. در نسخهٔ اصلی: اسان (کذا).
۸. کذا در نسخهٔ اصلی
۹. در نسخهٔ اصلی: خذ.
۱۰. در نسخهٔ اصلی: قولی

بوذ، بفضل و کرم بیان فرمایذ.

(۵) دیگر در نماز چاشت در خلوت اندك اندك غبش و ظلمت ظاهر شذن گرفت، زیادت می‌شد تا بکلی مصورات و محسوسات از نظر این ضعیف ساقط گشت، در میان آن ظلمت یك کوکب ظاهر گشت، بر در جهت فوق بوذ یا بر در جهت تحت که این ضعیف خوذ جهت ادراك نمی‌کرد، و وقت وقت اشراقی و ضوئی از آن کوکب برمی‌خاست و در آن ضوء و اشراق بسیار صور نورانی ظاهر می‌گشت که {از}[11] غایت حسن و جمال ایشان این ضعیف را تحیر می‌آورد و از غایت لطف چنان می‌نموذ که گوئی نه از قبیل اجسام‌اند، بعد از آن کواکبی دیگر ظاهر شذند تا بهفت کوکب رسیذ عظمت هر یك + ازین (...) کوکب + در ظهور نور ماه محو گشت و صذ هزار صور نورانی در نور ماه پدیذ می‌آمذ و هم در نور و ضوء ماه ناپدیذ می‌شد و آوازهای عظیم خوش[12] و حزین. و تسبیحـــات و تهلیلات ظاهر شذن گرفت و بوهای خوش که هرگز در عالم هیچ مشك و عنبر بذان نمانذ همه عالم بگرفت. بر مثال بیخوذی سکری درین ضعیف پدیذ آمذن گرفت و طربی[13] که وصف آن نتوانم کرذ بر من ظاهر گشت چنانك گوئی آثار ‹و› رسومات بشری و جسمانی از من برخاست، بجمله این کلمه می‌شنوذم که لا اله الا الله، ناگاه زلازلی عظیم پدیذ آمذ و آوازی چون رعد بل‌که عظیم‌تر برخاست و بروقی عظیم و صواعـــق جستن گرفت و ماه و کواکب ناپدیذ شذند و ظلمت حاوی و محیط گشت، و بعد از آن ناگاه نوری دیگر باره عظیم ظاهر شذن گرفت چنانك در مبادی ظهور آن نور نورماه وکواکب ناچیزشذ ونیز نظر این ضعیف قابل‌آن نور نتوانست‌بوذ و ارتعاشی عظیم برین ضعیف افتاذ و آنچه تعلق جسمی و بدنی بوذ چنان نموذ این ضعیف را که همچو آب می‌روذ و این ضعیف از خوذ آگاهی می‌یافت محض ادراك و ادراك‌کلی چنانك گوئی واسطهٔ جسمانی نیست چنانك غیریت[14] و اثنینیت و تعدد و یکی[15] و آخریت و اولیت ساقط شذ، یکی حقیقت محض می‌نموذ که بخوذ ظاهر و موجود و متجلی بوذ، در تجلی و ظهور نور او صورتی ظاهر می‌کشت و هم در قوت و سلطنت تجلی آن نور ناچیز می‌شد تابحدی که آن نور و اشراق اعظم چنان متجلی (۴۱۰ ب) گشت که از آن ادراك کلی و آگاهی محض که از عین معنیء مجرد بوذ {و} حقیقت این ضعیف می‌خاست و می‌نبوذ[16] و در ضوء‹ وّ › اشراق آن نور ناچیز و ناپدیذ گشت و این بر مثال غرقی[17] می‌نموذ، اینجا این ضعیف را بهیچ‌وجه معلوم

۱۱. یا «از» یا «ایشان» زائد است.
۱۲. در اصل: خوش عظیم.
۱۳. در اصل: وطوبی.
۱۴. در اصل: غیرت.
۱۵. کذا، غیر مناسب بنظر می‌آید.
۱۶. در نسخهٔ اصلی: نمود.
۱۷. در اصل: عرومی (کذا).

و مفهوم نمی‌شوذ که چه ظاهر کشت، این‌قدر اکاهی دارذ که در آن حالت مغلوب گشتن و منطمس شذن از آن آگاهی و ادراك ذوقی و لذتی و راحتی ⟨یافتم⟩[۱۸] که بهیچ نوع از آن و از کیفیت آن این ضعیف را امکان عبارت نیست و این ضعیف خوذ نمی‌داند که من من[۱۹] بوذم یا نه بوذم یا در نموذ آن بوذ[۲۰] و آن آگاهی چه بوذ یا چه دیذم، بعد از آن شعوری و آگاهی پدیذ آمذن گرفت همچنانك از غشیان افاقت باشذ یا مصروعی را عقل باز آیذ، ضعفی و ارتعاشی بر اعضای این ضعیف غالب بوذ و خیال آن نموذها در اندرون راسخ، ملالت و سآمت تمام این ضعیف را از خوذ و از خلق و از ذکر کفتن و از نماز کردن پدیذ آمذ و قبضی بر دل مستولی گشت چنانك بمرگ و مفارقت ازین عالم مشتاق شذم و هر لحظه خاطری درمی‌آمذ که خوذ را در چاهی افکن[۲۱] یا چیزی بر خوذ زن[۲۲] همگی اندرون مستغرق تفکر کردن در آن نموذها گشت که آیا چه بوذ و آن چه ذوق داشت[۲۳].

(۶) بعد ازین حالت بسه[۲۴] روز چنان گشت حال این ضعیف: اگر نشسته بوذی و اگر بوضو ساختن می‌رفتی و اگر در نماز بوذی شهرهایی عظیم و دیههای[۲۵] بزرگ معمور و بازارهاء آراسته و مشاهد و مزارها در نظر این ضعیف می‌آمذ و ازیشان حکایتها می‌شنیذ که جنس[۲۶] آن بلاد و مردم + نکرنده[۲۷] + بوذ، بعضی عربیت می‌گفتند و بعضی ترکی و بعضی رومی و بعضی فارسی و هم در حال از نظر این ضعیف غائب می‌گشت، تا چاشتگاهی نشسته بوذ و ذکر می‌گفت، روشنائی ظاهر گشت و بقعهٔ عظیم منور با روح و راحت در نظر آمذ که این ضعیف درین عالم مثل آن ندیذه بوذ و روضهٔ عظیم با نزهت و ریاحین، نوری عظیم وضوئی تمام ساطع می‌گشت وپیری‌عظیم نورانی و باهیبت، عمامهٔ سپیذ {دیذ} برسروردائی از برد یمنی بر دوش کرفته و در میان آن روضه نشسته بوذ و جماعتی پیران نورانی با وقار و با ادب و حرمت در خدمت او نشسته و جماعتی جوانان برپای ایستاذه و آن جماعت پیران ازو سوالها می‌کردند {و} به عبارتی و اصطلاحی که این ضعیف از هیچ کس نشنیذه بود و نه نیز در کتبها دیذه و آن پیر[۲۸] بعضی را جواب میداذ و بعضی را منع می‌کرد. ناگاه آن[۲۹] بزرگ دین درآمذ

۱۸. یا ⟨یافت⟩ یا کلمه‌ای بدین معنی.
۱۹. شاید زائد باشد یا «می» خواندنی باشد.
۲۰. شاید «نور» خواندنی باشد.
۲۱. در اصل: افکند (کذا).
۲۲. در اصل: زند.
۲۳. از جواب مجدالدین بغدادی غیر ممکن بنظر نمی‌آید که اینجا چیزی افتاده باشد.
۲۴. در نسخهٔ اصلی «سه» نیز می‌شود خواند.
۲۵. کذا.
۲۶. کذا. آیا «جن» باید خواند؟
۲۷. این کلمه قابل تشخیص نیست.
۲۸. در نسخهٔ اصلی: «مر» یا «مر»
۲۹. در نسخهٔ اصلی: این.

و براذر آن[۳۰] عزیز و بزرگ و دو درویش[۳۱] دیگر، یکی آن درویش نسائی[۳۲] بوذ که در خدمت شماست و آثار رشد و صلاح در وی ظاهر است و در میان آن جماعت که بر پای ایستاده بوذند بایستاذ، چون نظر بران بزرگ افتاذ گفت: من قال لااله‌الاالله مع بقاء نفسه فهو مشرك بالله. سهمی‌تمام و هیبتی‌عظیم برشما وآن جماعت افتاذ و این ضعیف متحیر و عاجز مانده که آیا این چه بقعه است و این شحص کیست و آن جماعت چه قوم‌اند؟ شما را از سهم و هیبت این کلمه تغیری عظیم پدیذ آمذ و بکائی عظیم ظاهر گشت، آنکه آن پیر کفت: ما عرف احد[۳۳] من‌الطالبین طریق‌الحق من مائة سنة و ماسلکه احد علی شرط‌السلوك من مائتی سنة و ما دخل احد من الانبیاء و الصدیقین فی حضرة سیدی[۳۴] و شیخی امام المرسلین علیه الصلوة و السلام. شما را از استماع این کلام وجدی پیدا گشت و از پای دزافتاذی[۳۵]، بعد از آن پیر گفت: من تحقق بالذکر سخر له‌الکون ومن‌التفت الیه سقط عن عین[۳۶] الحق، و دست شما بگرفت و هر دو ساعد (و) دست شما چون نور اشراق می‌زذ الا بطنی[۳۷] کفیك فانهما[۳۸] اسودان فصافحك الشیخ الکبیر وامرك بغسلهما[۳۹] (فقال): فانظر[۴۰] بنور بصیرتك و عیون[۴۱] علمك أی حرکة و عمل و خاطر و سوء ادب فی‌حضور[۴۲] الحق صدر عنك حتی ظهر من تلك الحرارة، أثرالسواد علی باطن الکف فتدارك و استغفر لذلك. آنگاه آن پیر گفت: سل عنی ماشئت[۴۳]. شما از وی پرسیذیت: ما طریق الحق و ما أدب الطریق و ما أدب‌الحضرة؟ جواب داذ که طریق الحق معرفته و أدب الطریق الاستقامة بلامیل[۴۴] أما سمعت قوله تعالی لمحمد: بعثت علی طریق مثل حدالسیف لوزغت[۴۵] عنه هلکت؟ و أما أدب الحضرة، اینجا اهی عظیم از سینه برآورد و آنگاه گفت: مراقبة سرك[۴۶] و قلبك

۳۰. قراءت «برادران» هم ممکن است.
۳۱. در اصل: در و درویشی.
۳۲. در اصل فسائی هم می‌شود خواند.
۳۳. در نسخهٔ اصلی: واحد.
۳۴. در نسخهٔ اصلی: الحرزة ...وی ...یدی
۳۵. کذا.
۳۶. در اصل: غمر (کذا).
۳۷. در اصل: بطن.
۳۸. در اصل: فانها.
۳۹. در اصل: بغسلها.
۲۰. شاید «انظر» خواندنی باشد.
۴۱. در نسخهٔ اصلی: غموض.
۴۲. در نسخهٔ اصلی: طهور (کذا).
۴۳. جمله‌بندی فارسی بجای «سلنیَ عما شئت».
۴۴. در نسخهٔ اصلی: ملاسل (کذا).
۴۵. در نسخهٔ اصلی: رغب.
۴۶. در اصل مراقبة شرك (کذا) و الاصح بالعربیة «فمراقبة سرك»

بنورالمعرفة مع دوام غيبتك عنك و انطماس أوصافك[۴۷] تحت بوادر[۴۸] سلطنة الحضرة. آنگاه هر دو انگشت سبابه در گوش شما نهاذ و گفت: فاحذر من استماع اللهو انالله لاينظر الى قلب لاهى[۴۹] ثم قرأ هذه الآية: و لاتكونوا كالذين قالوا سمعنا و هم لايسمعون (قرآن ۸، ۲۱)، و لوحى سيمين مرقوم و مكتوب بشما داذ و روى ستره سپيذ بر ميان شما بست و گفت: احفظ الشريعة لاتقل الاالحق و لاتسمع الاالحق فانك لتهدى الى سبيل الحق، و روى ببراذر شما و آن دو درويش كرد و گفت: عليكم بمكابدة تذوب[۵۰] الجسم و تضعف النفس و تقوى القلب و فى[۵۱] القلب تظهر عجائب الملكوت. و اين ضعيف با خوذ مى‌گفت: يا ليت با من كلمهٔ بگفتى يا مرا وصيتى كردى يا راهى نموذى. در حال درين ضعيف نگريست و اشارت كرد كه بيا، اين ضعيف نزديك او رفت، دست راست اين ضعيف بگرفت و مصافحه كرد و گفت: من سلك طريقا بغير معرفة الطريق[۵۲] فقد ضل، عليك باتباع الامر والتمسك بالسنة و مداومة الصوم و الصمت و مؤاخذة[۵۳] النفس فى كل حال والانقطاع عن الناس حتى تصير اهلا لسلوك الطريق[۵۴]، جعلك الله تعالى مراقبا على[۵۵] احوالك و أوقاتك و حارساً على نفسك. بعد ازين نفعنا الله و اياك، آن جمع برخاست و از آن بقعه بيرون آمذ، اين ضعيف بر عقب ايشان روان شذ تا از جمع بپرسذ كه آن پير كيست و شما كيستيت؟ گامى چند برگرفتند و همه ناپديذ شذند و آن بقعه و روضه ناپديذ گشت و اين ضعيف دگرباره در و ديوار مسجد مى‌ديذم و همان قبض و اندوه بر من مستولى گشت.

جواب

(۷) الحمدلله رب العالمين و الصلوة على محمد و آله.

(۸) سلام حق سبحانه و تعالى و سلام فرشتگان و انبيا صلوات الله و سلامه عليهم اجمعين (۴۱۱ آ) و سلام بندهٔ خذاى مجد بغداذى برآن براذر دينى و دوست عزيز و سالك صادق و روندهٔ محقق و طالب مجد خواجه امام عالم عامل عارف شرف الدين افتخار المحققين حجة الله على المسترشدين باذ. دل عزيزش بانوار معارف منور باذ و روح پاكش بتجلى صفات ربوبيت متحلى[۵۶].

۴۷. در اصل: اوهافك.

۴۸. در اصل: بوارد (كذا).

۴۹. كذا.

۵۰. در اصل: بذوب (كذا).

۵۱. شايد «ففى» خواندنى باشد.

۵۲. در اصل: بعين المعرفة الطريق.

۵۳ در اصل: و مواجده.

۵۴. در اصل: للسلوك طريق.

۵۵. كذا. بر حسب قواعد نحوى عربى زائد است.

۵۶. در نسخهٔ اصلى: متجلى.

(۹) نوشتهٔ عزیز آن برادر دینی و یار حقیقی بذین ضعیف رسیذ و بورود و وصول آن انواع راحات و مسرات روی نموذ و بر مکاشفاتی که روی نموذه است و گشایشی که اتفاق افتاذه شکرها گزارده آمذ، فوایدی که در قلم آورده بوذ باندازهٔ فهم و نموذ خوذ جواب نوشته شذ، امیذ بفضل حق سبحانه آنست که بر وفق صواب باشذ و از حظوظ بشری پاك، و الله الموفق و المستعان.

واقعهٔ اول

(۱۰) لوصح قولك لااله‌الاالله ما استطعت أن تقول لااله‌الاالله‌کلامیست درست و حقیقت زیرا که صحت قول لااله‌الاالله مبنی است بر نفی بشریت و تا صفات بشریت باقیست گوینده درین گفت صادق نیست چه توحید منافی انانیت و اینانیت است، پس این کلمه آن وقت روی نمایذ که چون تصرف سلطان حقیقت قائم مقام صفات بشریت گرذذ معنی[۵۷] بی‌یسمع و بی‌یبصر وبی‌ینطق تجلی‌کنذ ‹ و › حقیقت لمن الملك و جواب لله الواحد القهار (قرآن ۱۶،۴۰) کشف افتذ، و ازین است که ضعیف سالکانرا ذکر لااله‌الاالله اختیار می‌کنذ و این ذکر را بر ذکر الله ترجیح می‌نهذ زیراکه تا مرد سالك است محتاج بنفی استو تا صفات وعین[۵۷*] منتفی‌نگشت هنوز احتیاج ثابت است و تا احتیاج هست کلمه بر کار است، چون سلطان حقیقت ولایت در تصرف گیرذ هم حاجتمندی بنفی برخیزذ و هم ظهور کلمهٔ لااله‌الاالله بر وی صادق بوذ، و هم ازینجاست سر قول آن بزرگ که فرموذه است من احب أن یذکرالرب فینبغی[۵۸] أن یکون الرب و من لم‌یکن ربا صرفا حقا لم‌یذکر الرب و لایکون منه‌الذکر، و لیس لله ذاکر بوجه زیراکه ذاکر چیزی عارف نتواند بوذ تا بواسطهٔ ذکر تمییز بحق توانذ کرد میان آن چیز و میان غیر او و چون معرفت علی‌الکمال جز حق عز و علا را نتواند بوذ جز حق کس ذاکر نتواند بوذ.

(۱۱) و اما آن قول که کان لنا شیخ[۵۹] فی الاسکندریة یقول: سلوك جملة السالکین فی لااله و مادخل أحد من السالکین فی الاالله، کلامی درست و قولی صحیح است زیراکه عالم کوشش که ولایت سلوك است باطول و عرض صفات‌بشریت برابر است و تمامت آن سلوك لااله است، چون بساحل دریاء بشریت رسیذ کوشش وسلوك منقطع گشت و جذبه روی نموذ، تا اکنون سفر در لااله بوذ، اینجا قرار سفر در الاالله است، آن طریق الی‌الله بوذ و این طریق فی‌الله، آن متناهی این نامتناهی، تا اینجا رونده است بخوذ، ازینجا رونده است بحق، تا اکنون مرید بوذ، پس ازین مراد شذ. پس معنی قول او که مادخل أحد من‌السالکین فی الاالله مع بقاء وجوده، درست است.

---

۵۷. در نسخهٔ اصلی: بعمی (کذا).
۵۷*. ایا «غیر» باید نوشت؟
۵۸. کذا با فاء.
۵۹. در نسخهٔ اصلی: شیخا.

واقعهٔ دوم

(۱۲) ظهور صحرا و پیداگشتن چاه تاآخر واقعه. ازوقایع راه‌آن‌صحرا صحرای وجود است و آن‌چاه چاه دل و راهی از عالم شهادت بعالم غیب و تا درین صورتست هنوز غلبهٔ حس و خیال غالب است، و ازین سبب است که صور حیوانات از وی بیرون می‌آمذ که آن صورصور ⟨صفات⟩ ذمیمه است، اما آنك صور خلع میکردند و بصورتی دیگر می‌شذ دلیلیست قاطع بر آنك آن صور صفاتست که بحسب تغییر صفات تغییر صور حاصل می‌شذ، و اما آن ثعبان که ظاهر شذ طلب حق است که خیال اورا در آن‌صورت بیان کرد، چون داعیهٔ طلب اندرون پیدا شوذ جملگی صفات ذمیمه را بخورذ، و باز آنرا از دهان برآوردن دلیل فتوری که پیدا شوذ، و اما آن خطاب که خذها و لاتخف (قرآن ۲۰، ۲۱) خطابی حق است چه همچنانك ثعبان موسی علیه‌السلام آلتی بود تا دفع سحر باطل حقیقت‌نمای بذان‌کنند[۶۰] این داعیه نیز حقیقی است که بظهور او صفات مجازی بشری حقیقت‌نمای بدو دفع شوذ پس حقیقت این نموذ نموذ صفاتست با تصرف خیال زیراکه خیال به‌نسبت با آن معانی همچون عبارتست به‌نسبت با معانی که بنطق خواهند آورد، چنانکه عبارت پوشانند[۶۱] از جهت[۶۲] تفهیم اسماع همچنین خیال این معانی را[۶۳] بصور پوشانند از جهت ادراك دیذهٔ حس باطن، پس خیال فی جمیع الاحوال مذموم نیست بل‌که آلت کار است، مذموم آن وقتست که معنی را صورتی مناسب نپوشانند همچنانك عبارت آلت تفهیم است و از وی گزیرنه اما گاه بود که گوینده و بیان‌کننده بعبارتی مطابق‌تر و بفهم نزدیك‌تر بیان تواند کرد گاه بوذ که بنطقی[۶۴] یا بلفظی مضاد[۶۵] درافتد که از خلاصه معنی دور[۶۶] بوذ، و ازین سبب[۶۷] است که ⟨آن⟩ در بعضی کلمات انغلاقی بوذ و دربعضی آسانی چنانك معبر در خوابها گاه‌بوذ که تأویلی بیان‌کند که صورت از معنی نیك دور افتاذه بوذ و گاه بوذ که تاویلی بیان کنذ[۶۸] که صورت بمعنی نزدیك بوذ.

واقعهٔ سوم

(۱۳) و آن ظهور ظلمت است، اما در اثناء آن طلوع کوکب و ماه، آدمی بسبب مباشرت احوال دنیوی در مین ظلمت است. اما او را از آن ظلمت آگاهی

---

۶۰. در نسخهٔ اصلی: کسد (کذا).
۶۱. بمعنی: چنانکه عبارت آن معانی را باصوات پوشاند.
۶۲. در نسخهٔ اصلی: از حیر. تصحیح «از بهر» هم رواست.
۶۳. در نسخهٔ اصلی: معنی را.
۶۴. در نسخهٔ اصلی: بلطفی (کذا).
۶۵. در نسخهٔ اصلی: محاد. یمکن درست باشد چه حادهٔای عاداه.
۶۶. در نسخهٔ اصلی: درو.
۶۷. در اصل سر یا سر (کذا).
۶۸. در اصل: نزدیك‌اند یا «نزدیك آیذ».

نه زیرا که بینائی ندارذ، چون بینائی پیذا آمذ و توجه اندرون بحق پدیذ شذ عین ظلمت که درمیان آنست و از آن بی‌خبر بوذ مشاهده کنذ و آن بینائی و توجه فرع نوریست غیبی که بدل بنده رسذ، چون این نور در دل پیذا گشت و توجه حاصل‌آمذ بی‌اختیار در صورت اختیار لازم آیذ[۶۹] و آن قطع حجاب ظلمت است و چون قطع حجاب اتفاق افتذ مشاهدهٔ انوار حاصل آیذ و اکر آن خرق[۷۰] بر وفق جمعیت بوذنور در صورت ستاره بیند، چون از آن درگذشت و آن نور دل زیادت شذ [...][۷۱] دل انجامذ[۷۲] و نور او بدیگر اعضا سرایت تواند کرد و فیضان ظاهر گردانید آن‌ساعت در صورت ماه بیند و مراتب مشاهدهاء ابراهیم (۴۱۱ ب) صلوات الله علیه این است، و اما واقعهٔ آن بزرگ و براذر دینی اگرچه ظلمت ازین قبیل است اماکواکب ازین قبیل نیست بل‌که کواکب ارواح مشایخ است که آن براذر در نظر و تربیت ایشان است که چون در تاریکی و ظلمت ⟨و⟩ انسانیت و وجود مستغرق شذست آن ارواح‌خاصیت تربیت دراظهار خوذ ظاهرگردانیذه‌اند تاآن بزرگ بواسطهٔ نورایشان فرا خاصیتها معانی که در عالم دل است توانست‌دیذ وآن حقائق معانی غیب‌است و چون دل بذان نوربینائی یافت حواس حقیقی دل خاصیت ادراك خوذ ظاهر گردانیذ، آنچه نصیبهٔ سمع است تهلیل و تسبیح و تحمید است که می‌شنوذ[۷۳] چه هیچ موجود نیست نه در عالم غیب نه در عالم شهادت که علی‌الحقیقه ذاکر حق نیست[۷۴] وان من شیء الا یسبح بحمده (قرآن ۱۷، ۴۴) و آنچه نصیبه شم اندرونست بویهاء خوش است که می‌شنوذ و آنچه نصیبهٔ بصر است صور نورانیست که می‌دیذ، بعد از آن ماهی که طلوع‌کرده است و آن کواکب در غلبهٔ اشعهٔ شعاع انوار او متلاشی شذه‌اند نور پیغمبر بوذ صلوات‌الله علیه که بحقیقت همچنانك ماه نور ازآفتاب اکتساب‌کند و بدیگر موجودات رساند جوهر نبوت نیز از عالم الوهیت که واسطه است[۷۵] بسبب صفای اندرون و شایستگی قبول آن در[۷۶] فیضان آن انوار استفادت کند و بامت رساند ملی اختلاف استمدادهم، پس چون این اتصال حاصل شذست و در پرتو نور نظر بر عالم توحید افتاذه سمع حقیقی که زندگی از آن عالم گیرذ و مرده‌دلان عالم بشریت از آن محجوب‌اند لو کنا نسمع او نعقل ما کنا من اصحاب السعیر (قرآن ۶۷، ۱۰) خاصیت خوذ در ادراك ظاهر گردانیذه است تا سماع[۷۷] موقوف بر کلمهٔ

۶۹. کذا.

۷۰. در اصل: حرف (؟).

۷۱. به‌سبب پاره‌گی نسخهٔ اصلی یك کلمهٔ بسیار کوتاه افتاده است.

۷۲. کذا.

۷۳. در نسخهٔ اصلی: می‌شوذ.

۷۴. در نسخهٔ اصلی: ذاکر بحق حق است. اگر این روایت درست باشد باید پیش از این چیزی از قلم افتاده باشد.

۷۵. «ایست» هم میتوان خواند.

۷۶. کذا.

۷۷. در اصل: باسماع (کذا).

توحید و مخصوص بقول لا اله الا الله شذست، بعد از آن غلبات صفات بشریت و تأثیرات تصرفات که از لوازم راه است و حقیقت جهاد درین واقعست[۷۸] پیدا گشته است و در آن منازعت و محاکمت[۷۸*] احساس آواز رعد و رؤیت صوائق وبروق[۷۹] حاصل‌آمذه وچون این غلبات + عصیب[۸۰] + آن اتصالات بوذه‌است لابد بوذکه‌ظلمت حاوی و محیط گردذ، بعد ازین عنایت ازلی ‹که› قهر و انهزام وساوس و هواجس شیطانی و نفسانی جز بذو حاصل نشوذ روی نموذه است و بواسطهٔ دل صفا یافته عکس بر جملهٔ اعضا انداخته و آن نور که در غلبات او تلاشی[۸۱] صفات بشریت و تعدد و اثنینیت حاصل آمذه است کمال او آنك بذوق پیوندذ یا[۸۱*] کمال تجلی اثبات توان‌کرد، اگرچه این‌نیز از آن قبیل است اما درین مقام حاکم بروی علم است و عقل و آن کمال نیافته است که ذوق معرفت از آن بیان کنذ و آن ذوق که نتیجهٔ وی لذت است ازین قبیل نیست و چون این‌صفت حاصل بوذه‌است دلیل آنست که این تجلی از عالم انوار جمال بوذه است که کمند دل دوستان شوذ و تشویق[۸۲] و ترغیب ازو پیذا گردذ.

اما سؤالاتی که درین واقعه فرموذه است

(۱۴) اول آنك آن کواکب و قمر تواند بوذ که همین کواکب و قمر ظاهری باشذ اگر چه این از آن جمله نیست؟ و بیان آنك تواند، حجاب جسمانی جز دیدهٔ ظاهر را حجاب نتواند کرد تا اگر مردی در خانه بوذ سقف و در و دیوار حجاب دیدهٔ ظاهر بوذ ازمحسوسات خارجی،اما حجاب روح نتوانندشذ، پس چون آن دیذه گشاذه شوذ بالای[۸۳] محسوسات افتذ و سقف و دیوار حجاب نشوذ و قرب و بعد و مسافت بنسبت باوی یکی باشذ، فی‌الجمله این کواکب و شموس و اقمار که در نظر روندکان آید گاه بوذکه مراتب نورانیت بوذ زیادت و نقصان و تلوین و تمکین گاه بوذ که ارواح ملائکه و انبیا و ارواح جن بوذ گاه بوذ که همین کواکب و آسمان[۸۴] ظاهر باشذ. اما درین مشاهده تغییر و تبدیل و پیذا گشتن کوکبی و ناپدیذ گشتن دیگری نبوذ چه این مشاهده تعبیه چنان بوذ که آن ساعت در ظاهر حاصل بوذه باشذ، پس واقعهٔ آن[۸۵] دوست عزیز ازین اقسام آنست که در قلم آورده آمذ[۸۶]، و الله اعلم.

---

۷۸. در نسخهٔ اصلی: وقعست. آیا مراد مصنف «دفعست» بوده؟
۷۸* آیا «معاکست» باید خواند؟
۷۹. در اصل: وبوق.
۸۰. احتمالا «بمعیت» باید خواند.
۸۱. در اصل: ملاشی (کذا).
۸۱* آیا «تا» باید خواند؟ در اصل: یا.
۸۲. در اصل: تسویف.
۸۳. این کلمه مشکوك بنظر میرسد. شاید «بنای» یا «بلای» خواندنی باشد.
۸۴. شاید «کواکب آسمان» درست باشد.
۸۵. در نسخهٔ اصلی: این.
۸۶. رجوع شود به فصل ۱۳.

(۱۵) اما بیان اختلاف احوال وحی و ادراك سید صلوات الله علیه مبنی بر مقدمه باقی گذاشت که ایـراد موجب تطویل شوذ و درین واقعه آن براذر بـذان محتاج نیست، بعد ازین ان شاءالله چون اتفاق ملاقات باشذ مشافهة تقریر افتذ و بردالیقین پیذا گردذ.

اما واقعهٔ چهارم

(۱۶) و آن دیذن پیر است و آن بزرگ که در غایت ‹نورانیت› ظاهر شذست و اتفاق جمعیت و مکالمت ‹و› سؤالات و جوابات. موافق ظن این ضعیف آنـست والعلم عند الله که بزرگی از بزرگان مشایخ جن بوذه است و بحسب غلبهٔ ظن چنان فراز می‌آیذ[۸۷] که شیخ عبدالرحمن بوذه است که از مستفیدان و مریدان حضرت سید اولین وآخرین صلوات الله علیه بوذه است، فی الجمله کلماتـی که فـرموذه است همه پرفایده[۸۸] است و در تحت هر یك مبلغها اسرار طریقت و حقیقت.

(۱۷) اما قوله من قال لا اله الا الله مع بقاء نفسه فهو مشرك بالله، درست است و همان ذوق سخن اول دارذ که از طائفهٔ جنیان حکایت فرموذه است و بتقریر آن بحسب وقت اشارت کرده آمذ، اما ازین گفت نبایذ که هیچ را خاطر مشوش شوذ، زیرا که محتاج این کلمه از راه ظاهر مشرك[۸۹] است تا دفع این شرك و ازالت آن کنذ، چون شرك ظاهر بایمان بدل گشت و تسلیم و استسلام حاصل آمـذ این ساعت شرك خفی در باطن ظاهر شذن گیرذ، صدق طلب ره‌رو بشمشیر ذکر هرچه قدم در حیز هستی نهذ سرش بردارذ، پس این‌کلمه جز در دفع و قهر و نفی صفات که اثبات هر یك از آن غیر[۸۹*] شرك بود بکار نشود[۹۰]، چون نفی و محو آن اتفاق افتذ[۹۱] و سلطان حقیقت در چهار بالش دل متمکن گشت و استوای او بر عرش دل پیذا شذ همه اللـه است لا اله را گُنج نه و بـذو احتیاج نـه چنانك در ابتدا بیان افتاذه است[۹۲].

(۱۸) اما قول[۹۳] ما عرف احد من الطالبین طریق الحق من مائة سنة و مـا سلکه احد بشرط السلوك من مائتی سنة، درین کلام تفصیل درازست، اگر از سلوك آن خواهذ که استحقاق ربوبیت است ‹ از› دور آدم تا انقراض عالم هیچ کس را بقوت بشریت این سلوك راست نیامذ. اما شرط سلوك سلوك خاص اگر این سالك

۸۷. «آمذ» هم میشود خواند.
۸۸. در اصل برجاده (کذا).
۸۹. در نسخهٔ اصلی: مشمرك (کذا)
۸۹.* آیا «عین» باید خواند؟
۹۰. در نسخهٔ اصلی: مبشود.
۹۱. کذا.
۹۲. رجوع شود به فصل ۱۰
۹۳. کذا.

خواهد شك نیست كه در آن قرن سالكان مجدّ بوده‌اند، روزگار بر می‌آید و عهد روزگار سید صلوات الله علیه امتداد می‌پذیرد، طلب این جدیت[۹۲*] كمتر می‌شود، این نصیب عموم است، اما از راه خصوص حق را سبحانه در همه قرن بندگـانند كـه آباذانی عالم بواسطهٔ ایشانست و در عشق این جدیت و طلب آن حضرت جان بر میان بسته‌اند و بتوفیق حق عز و علا كمند جذبات او بی‌اختیار در صورت اختیار راه حق بفرق سر [...] (۴۱۲ آ) عنایت آفریذگار سبحانه و تعالی در حق ضعفاء آخر الزمان بواسطهٔ محبت بی‌علت آن اقتضا فرموذست كه آنچه متقدمانرا بمبلغها مجاهده و سالها ریاضت روی نمودی این بیچارگان را چون قدم در راه نهند و سعادت صحبت مقتدائی مساعدت كند باندك روزگاری پیدا می‌آید، پس ‹آنكس‌كه› هیچ كس بشرط سلوك نكرده است[۹۴] زیرا كه آن در قوت بشری نیاید، اما چون عنایت بوذ بی‌واسطهٔ تكلف ‹ا› و بغیر مجاهده، نه تكسل و تن‌آسانی، بیك جـذبه عالمـها مبور[۹۵] افتذ.

(۱۹) اما قول [۹۶] ما دخل احد من الانبیاء و الصدیقین فی حضرة سیدی و شیخی امام المرسلین علیه الصلوة و السلام صدر [۹۷] عن كمال العرفان، سلوك راه تا نهایت صفات بشریت مشترك است میان انبیا و اولیا، چون بساحل دریا رسیذی از آنجا فراز كشتی در غرقاب لجهٔ هویت افتذ، تا اینجا ملاحان جد و اجتهاد و اكتساب‌دواعی‌آن‌كشتی را بواسطهٔ خله و رسن كشیذن رانند، لاجرم منازل‌ومراحل معلوم بوذ، بعد ازین باذ عنایت و جذبات در شراع بندگی افتذ و در لجهٔ هویت اندازذ، پس در آن قرب هر سالكی را بحسب عنایت و قوت رونده بساطی است كه غیر او پای بران نتوانند نهاذ و كمال براه اصطفا جـز محبوب ازل و ابـد را صلوات الله و سلامه علیه ظاهر نشذ، ذكر[۹۸] هركه بوذ تبع و طفیل راه او بوذ كه لوكان موسی حیا ما وسعه الا اتباعی و آدم و من دونه تحت لوائی.

(۲۰) و اما من تحقق بالذكر سخر له الكون و من التفت الیه سقط عن عین الحق، حین تحقیق است و هاء الیه را هم بذكر باز می‌توان برد و هم بكون و هر دو از یكدیگر خوبتر است، و تحقق[۹۹] بذكر چیست؟ مغلوب غلبات او گشتن، متصرف تصرفات او آمذن، از ذكر انسی بذكر قدسی رسیذن، در ذكر مذكور را مشاهده كردن. چون ذاكر این مقام یافت كون مسخر اوست زیرا كه تصرف او تصرف حـق است، هرچه قدم در حیز حدوث نهاذ همه مسخر و منقاد او آمذ، و التفات بذكر از

۹۲*. آیا بجای جدیت اینجا و دوسطر بعد «حدیث» باید خواند؟
۹۴. شاید «بشرط ‹سلوك› سلوك نكرده است» خواندنی باشد
۹۵. در اصل: عبوت.
۹۶. كذا.
۹۷. كذا. در عربی «فصدر» اسم است
۹۸. در اصل: ذكر.
۹۹. در نسخهٔ اصلی: تحقیق.

لب بقشر آمذن است و التفات بکون از استعلاء خداوندی و ذروهٔ محترمی با حضیض عبودیت و خادمی نشستن، ان الله یحب معالی الامور و یبغض سفسافها.

بیت[100]

آفرینش نثار فرق تو اند ومچهن چون خسان ز راه نثار

(۲۱) و اما سواد کفی هذا الضعیف، تعجب ازین نیست، از آنست که با این حالت و اختلاط جائی دیگر چون سپید دید.

بیت[101]

در هر نفسی ترا هزاران رنگست وز رنج غم تو هر دو عالم تنگست
ای بی‌خبران چه جای نام و ننگست باریست گران و بارگیری لنگست

وقتی این ضعیف با شیخ خوذ متع الله المسلمین بطول بقائه می‌گفت که امروز اشارتی آمذ که بر شیخ چهار مذموم رفته است، فرموذ که محابائی عظیم از جهت نگاه داشت تو کرده‌اند که از چهار بیش بتو نرسانیذه‌اند، این ضعیف نیز بذین واقعه مبتهج و مستبشر شذ که با این که ازو در وجود می‌آیذ بر سیاهی کف دست اقتصار افتاذ.

(۲۲) وشك نیست‌که‌درین + نزدیك‌درکتابت چیزی‌که‌ازآن‌استغنائی[102]دینی + الا این‌کلمه که طریق الحق معرفته زیرا که طریق دواست طریق الی الله و طریق فی الله، این جواب که طریق الحق معرفته اشارت بطریق فی الله است نه بطریق الی الله، باقی اشارت که فرموذه است ظاهر است و محتاج تاویلی نه و حمل او بر ظاهر واجب.

(۲۳) و اما در وصیتی که آن براذر دینی و دوست عزیز کرده است که (من سلك) طریقا بغیر معرفة الطریق فقد ضل، اشارتی بوجوب زیادتی بحثی درین باب با مباشرت و ملازمت این معاملت بنابر وقوفی تمام و یقینی کامل بوذ، درین باب تاملی تمام واجب می‌بایذ داشت و از حق سبحانه و تعالی استمداد طلبید و صحبت یاری خواست، باقی وصیت آداب کار است، هذا باب.

(۲۴) ازین وقائع معلوم شذ که غلبات مکاشفات از چه نوع است، و درین باب چون باز[103] این ضعیف مشاورتی کرد از برای براذری و مسلمانی و رعایت حقوق طریقت واجبست کلمة الحق در میان نهاذن و باقی بحسن رای و صدق طلب آن براذر دینی باز گذاشتن، این وقائع مبنی بر مخالطه و مکاشفهٔ ارواح است و این

---

۱۰۰. خفیف.
۱۰۱. رباعی.
۱۰۲. «استغنائی» هم میشود خواند.
۱۰۳. کذا.

طریق + معضی + بانواع‌کرامات وخرق عادات باشد، هرچه ازین شیوه آرزوکند در اثناء این روی نماید، اما بذان کمال که مطلوب سالکان صادق و بندگان مخلص است نرسانند + سهرح[۱۰۴] از دوست وامانی + چه زشت آن نقش وچه‌زیبا، حسن‌استعداد و قبول کمال حاصل دارذ بحمدالله دیده را بینائی حاصل آمده است، دریغ بوذ که بتصرف جماعتی دیگر باز افتذ، آن بزرگان اگر چه هر یك در دین عالمی باشد اما طریق استفادت برمقتضی سنت‌الهی جزاز مثل نتوانند بوذ، و سرقل‌انما انابشرمثلکم اینست (قرآن ۱۸، ۱۱۰) هرگاه {که} ملائکه مقرب را با کمال درجهٔ ایشان این ولایت نیست زیرا که ایشان محجوب این حجاب نیستند، پس طریق رفع این حجاب اکر دانند از راه علم[۱۰۵] دانند نه از راه واقعه (و)معرفت و ذوق، درین چند حرف از راه اشارت رموز بسیار است و متیقنم بصفاء اندرون و خاطر روشن آن برادردینی که چون تامل فرماید بانداك سعی بسر هر سری برسذ انشاءالله تعالی، حق سبحانه و تعالی امداد توفیق ارزانی داراذ و در هیچ حال او را و ما را بخوذ و هیچ‌کس باز نگذارذ بحق محمد و آله اجمعین و اصحابه و التابعین لهم باحسان الی یوم الدین.

---

۱۰۴. واضح نیست.

۱۰۵. در نسخهٔ اصلی: عالم.

THE ṢUMĀDIYYA: A BRANCH ORDER OF THE QĀDIRIYYA IN DAMASCUS

(1)

After the death of the great preacher, mystic and Ḥanbalite scholar ᶜAbd al-Qādir al-Jīlānī in 561/1166, not all his sons remained in Baghdad. One emigrated to Egypt, another to Damascus, another to Sinjār and another still to Wāsiṭ. These offshoots as well as the family members who remained in Baghdad branched out, in part changed their places of residence and settled in other new homes. Noteworthy in this respect is the Syrian city of Ḥamāh. On two occasions the shift of family members to Egypt was intensified: in 836/1433 from Sinjār in conjunction with sultan Barsbay's retreat from Āmid which he had besieged in war against an Aq-Qoyunlu, and in 914/1508-09 from Baghdad after Shāh Ismāᶜīl had conquered the city and destroyed the tomb-convent of ᶜAbd al-Qādir. Then after the Ottoman conquest of Baghdad, but before 950/1543, Süleyman the Magnificent rebuilt the convent, and members of the family returned to Baghdad. In many places individual descendants of ᶜAbd al-Qādir came to occupy high offices and eminent positions, several were famous for their public kitchen (*simāṭ*), while some are simply designated as shaykhs of the *sāda qādiriyya* of their domicile and other localities. But no one actually held an official position of authority over a part or the whole of the Qādirī order, not even a member of the family in Baghdad, although from time to time certificates of appointment were obtained there. The tomb-convent of their forebear in Baghdad naturally enjoyed a reputation of special sanctity and was frequently visited by people of the order.[1]

From these *sāda qādiriyya*, i.e. the marabout family of ᶜAbd al-Qādir, one should distinguish the Qādirī shaykhs who, though not among his descendants, conferred Qādirī patched frocks (*al-khirqa al-qādiriyya*) and accepted new adherents into the order just as the latter did. Their affiliation was perhaps already distant from the *sāda*-family under ᶜAbd al-Qādir and via disciples and disciples of disciples, or only under descendants of ᶜAbd al-Qādir and then via

---

1 Muḥammad b. Yaḥyā al-Tādifī: *Qalāʾid al-jawāhir* (written 950/1543), Cairo, 1356, pp. 42-56. D.S. Margoliouth *EI* (both editions) Ḳādirīya/Ḳādiriyya.

their disciples and disciples of disciples. Naturally, there must have been a tie with ᶜAbd al-Qādir, but connecting links to his children — a subordination to the *sāda* — no longer existed among the disciples of disciples. The Qādirī shaykhs may well have paid a certain respect to the *sāda* because of the blue blood that flowed in the latters' veins, but they acted independently.

Just as one or another of the *sāda* developed his own profile and went his own way, so too this or that Qādirī shaykh who was not counted a member of the aristocratic saintly family set out in a particular direction and, given favorable circumstances, created a particular power for himself. In so doing, he did not have to break with the overarching umbrella organization of the 'grands Cadiriens'.[2] It is a special case and an exception that in the Algerian war of liberation from 1832 onwards a newcomer from this family had homage paid to himself in opposition to the revolutionary Qādirī, ᶜAbd al-Qādir.[3] For the upstart it was rather the umbrella organization that constituted the nation which he readily prided himself on, and his smaller group of associates only acquired an appendage to their name which not infrequently was left aside for the sake of brevity. Similar events occurred in other large orders as well. Suborders also emerged in the Khalwatiyya,[4] in the Naqshbandiyya[5] and in the

2 Garcin de Tassy: *L'islamisme d'après le Coran, l'enseignement doctrinal et la pratique*, Paris, 1874, p. 306.

3 Muḥammad b. ᶜAbd al-Qādir: *Tuḥfat al-zāʾir fī tārīkh al-Jazāʾir wa'l-amīr ᶜAbd al-Qādir*, 2nd edition of Mamdūḥ Ḥaqqī, Beirut, 1964, pp. 228-91. B.G. Martin: *Muslim Brotherhoods in 19th-Century Africa*, Cambridge University Press, 1976, pp. 63-64. At the moment I have no detailed information at my disposal concerning the *shaykh al-sajjāda al-qādiriyya* al-Sayyid Muḥammad Efendi al-Azharī, the *muftī* of Ḥamāh, and other descendants of ᶜAbd al-Qādir al-Jīlānī in Ḥamāh who at a later date (1278/1861-62) offered the Algerian hero a friendly reception; *Tuḥfat al-zāʾir*, p. 668. After ᶜAbd al-Qādir's death in 1300/1883 the *shaykh al-sajjāda al-qādiriyya* of Baghdad, al-Sayyid Salmān Efendi transmitted his condolences to ᶜAbd al-Qādir's relatives in Damascus; ibid., p. 864. Emir ᶜAbd al-Qādir's grandfather Muṣṭafā (d. 1212/1797-98), between two pilgrimages, had the Qādirī patched frock conferred on him by Jīlānī's descendant in Baghdad, ᶜAbd al-Raḥmān b. ᶜAlī (ibid., p. 929), as did ᶜAbd al-Qādir's father Muḥyī al-Dīn by Sayyid Maḥmūd in Baghdad (ibid., p. 932). But both had already previously been introduced to Sufism.

4 Hans Joachim Kissling: 'Aus der Geschichte des Chalvetijje-Ordens', in *ZDMG* 103, 1953, pp. 233-89. B.G. Martin: 'A Short History of the Khalwati Order of Dervishes', in Nikki R. Keddie: *Scholars, Saints, and Sufis*, University of California Press, 1972, pp. 275-305. Some further information in H.T. Norris: *The Tuaregs*, Warminster Wilts., 1975.

Shādhiliyya.[6] Several of these shoots flourished and then died, others have survived up to today. The last branch of the Shādhiliyya, the Ḥāmidiyya Shādhiliyya in Egypt, received its official accreditation through the Bakrī shaykh in 1906.[7]

The shaykhs we have just considered, who established their independence in part or completely, display an understandable tendency to retain the leadership of their association within their family, i.e. to choose their successor from among their own family members. This can be a brother, son, or son-in-law. In India and Pakistan, where the shaykhdom immediately creates a new, small marabout family, succession to the deceased head of the family and association is transferred to the eldest son in a festive ceremony, the so-called 'turban winding' (*dastārbandī*).[8] In Damascus, on the other hand, the Qādirī shaykh Aḥmad b. Sulaymān al-Dimashqī al-Ḥanafī in 1005/1596-97 designated a certain Muḥammad al-Marzanātī al-Ṣāliḥī as his succes-

---

5 Hamid Algar: 'The Naqshbandī Order: A Preliminary Survey of its History and Significance', in *Studia Islamica* 44, 1976, pp. 123-52.

6 Louis Rinn: *Marabouts et Khouan*, Algiers, 1884, pp. 265-82. Josef van Ess: 'Libanesische Miszellen 6: Die Yašruṭīya', in *Die Welt des Islams* 16, 1975, pp. 1-103.

7 F. De Jong: *Ṭuruq and Ṭuruq-Linked Institutions in Nineteenth Century Egypt*, Leiden, 1978, p. 176. A different date is given, namely 1926, by Michael Gilsenan: *Saint and Sufi in Modern Egypt*, Oxford, 1973, p. 36. Al-Ḥasan b. al-Ḥājj Muḥammad al-Kawhan (Kūhan) al-Fāsī al-Shādhilī: *Ṭabaqāt al-shādhiliyya al-kubrā al-musammāh Jāmiʿ al-karāmāt al-ʿaliyya*, Cairo, 1347/1928-29, p. 247 below. — On the orders and their branches see J. Spencer Trimingham: *The Sufi Orders in Islam*, Oxford, 1971. Richard Gramlich: *Die schiitischen Derwischorden Persiens*, Abh. K. M. 36, Part 1, 1965; Part 2, 1976. — Because of the monarchical structure of Shīʿite dervish orders, independence movements are bound to lead to a break. In the Safavid period the Safavid order was already monarchically oriented on the direct descendants of the shahs. In the appointment certificates of local group leaders, who were basically meant to propagate the Shīʿite intellectual heritage and love of the Shīʿite Imams, a *ṭughrā* was placed in the margin which listed the predecessors of the ruling shah all the way back to the predynastic time of Ṣafī al-Dīn al-Ardabīlī. These certificates were drawn up and sealed by the spiritual representative (*khalīfat al-khulafāʾ*) of the shah. The petitioner joined an organization consisting of various branches but which culminated in the shah and in which only affiliation with these highest leaders was of importance and was even manifested at all. Cf. Klaus Röhrborn: 'Staatskanzlei und Absolutismus im safawidischen Persien', in *ZDMG* 127, 1977, pp. 325-32.

8 Garcin de Tassy: *L'islamisme*, p. 313. The celebration is described in detail in Muḥammad Ḥusayn-i Tasbīḥī: 'Rasm-i qul u dastārbandī dar Pākistān', in *Hunar u mardum* 171, 2535/1977, pp. 28-39.

sor, and his son ᶜAbd al-Qādir only succeeded in obtaining the leadership after violent clashes.[9] His branch seems never to have borne a particular name and is therefore not mentioned in any list either.

The situation is different with the Ṣumādiyya, which likewise belonged to the Qādiriyya and likewise was based in Damascus. The gentilicium Ṣumādī is derived from the place name Ṣumād. The village Ṣumād lies to the south-east of Buṣrā in Syria and appears on all the maps I have seen with an *a* in the first syllable: Ṣamād. None the less, Muḥibbī: *Khulāṣat al-athar fī aᶜyān al-qarn al-ḥādī ᶜashar*, Cairo, 1284, I, p. 49, and following him, Murādī: *Silk al-durar fī aᶜyān al-qarn al-thānī ᶜashar*, Būlāq, 1291-1301, I, p. 174, both of them Syrians, require Ṣumād with *u*. The vocalization no doubt fluctuated on account of the emphatic *ṣ*.[10]

In this village around 800/1400 lived a certain *Ṣāliḥ* b. ᶜĪsā b. Muḥammad b. ᶜĪsā b. Dāwūd b. Sālim. We are informed of this by Ibn Ḥajar al-ᶜAsqalānī: *Inbāʾ al-ghumr bi-anbāʾ al-ᶜumr*, ed. Ḥasan Ḥabashī, Cairo, 1969-72, III, p. 287, no. 11, and by Sakhāwī: *Al-ḍawʾ al-lāmiᶜ li-ahl al-qarn al-tāsiᶜ*, Cairo, 1353-55, III, p. 314, no. 1202. Muḥibbī, I, p. 48, and IV, p. 430, gives the family line in the form Ṣāliḥ b. Khamīs b. Muḥammad b. ᶜĪsā b. Dāwūd b. Muslim, and Muslim is also mentioned as the earliest ancestor by Ibn al-Ḥanbalī: *Durr al-ḥabab fī tārīkh aᶜyān Ḥalab*, ed. Fākhūrī and ᶜAbbāra, Damascus, 1972-74, II, 1, p. 168, last line. This Sālim or Muslim, or even Musallam, is supposed to have been the disciple of ᶜAbd al-Qādir al-Jīlānī (d. 561/1166). In Ṣumād a convent (*zāwiya*) had been built for the ancestors of Ṣāliḥ. Thus, even in their time they had been active in the village as Sufis. But Ṣāliḥ was the first to emerge with a larger group of followers. He owned grainfields and livestock, and would offer hospitality to travellers. One can imagine that his convent served for teaching, as well as for accommodation. Ṣāliḥ died in 825/1422 at the age of about seventy. Precisely the claim that Sālim/Muslim had been a direct disciple of ᶜAbd al-Qādir al-Jīlānī — whether this is true or false — underlines the fact that the branch in Ṣumād felt itself to be quite independent and had no need of connecting links to ᶜAbd al-Qādir's descendants in Baghdad. The vertical connection they claimed going back to ᶜAbd al-Qādir was something greater.

---

9 Muḥibbī, II, pp. 435-36.

10 My *Abū Saᶜīd-i Abū l-Ḫayr*, Acta Iranica 11, 1976, p. 440, ftn. 8, can be corrected accordingly. Trimingham: *Sufi Orders*, p. 273, lists the order in the form Ṣamādiyya. Louis Massignon *EI* Ṭariḳa does not mention it.

As if to tie this knot even more tightly, Ibn al-Ḥanbalī, II, 1, p. 169, ll. 1-2, maintains that the son of Sālim/Muslim, i.e. Dāwūd, the second oldest person in the lineage, had married the daughter of ᶜAbd al-Qādir. A quite old source, the *Tuffāḥ al-arwāḥ* of Kamāl al-Dīn Muḥammad b. Abī'l-Ḥasan ᶜAlī b. ᶜAbd al-Raḥmān (b.) al-Sarrāj al-Rifāᶜī al-Qurashī al-Dimashqī al-Shāfiᶜī from the first half of the 8th/14th century, ascribes all sorts of miracles to him[11] and also recounts one about Dāwūd's otherwise unknown daughter Ruqayya,[12] but does not provide us with any dates.

Of the descendants of Ṣāliḥ, the hospitable owner of the convent in Ṣumād, his direct son Aḥmad is known to us from the genealogical table of the younger generations, as well as Aḥmad's son ᶜĪsā and ᶜĪsā's son ᶜAlī, at least by their names. Dates pertaining to their lives are lacking. But we do know that ᶜAlī was already living in Damascus where he maintained friendly contact with Muḥammad b. Muḥammad b. Aḥmad (862-935/1458-1529),[13] the grandfather of Najm al-Dīn al-Ghazzī.[14] Thus ᶜAlī's family line — indeed he may have been the first of them to do so — had moved from Ṣumād into the city by the 9th/15th century, perhaps without completely giving up their native village.

One is on firmer ground with ᶜAlī's son *Khalīl* (b. ᶜAlī b. ᶜĪsā b. Aḥmad b. Ṣāliḥ) about whom it is recorded that he took part in a gathering of high judicial and religious dignitaries in 885/1480 in the Umayyad Mosque of Damascus.[15] The men had come together to replace the functionaries holding the post of marshal of the ᶜAlid nobility and the position of superintendant of the market.[16] Khalīl too belonged to the more narrow circle of acquaintances of Najm al-Dīn al-Ghazzī's grandfather.[17] The year of his death remains in the dark.

---

11 Nabhānī: *Jāmiᶜ karāmāt al-awliyā'*, Cairo, 1329, II, pp. 7-8. The gentilicium Baṭrāwī should probably be corrected to Buṣrāwī. Baṭrā is a village located on the Dimyāṭ branch of the Nile (*Ḍaw' lāmiᶜ*, XI, p. 191, and the maps).

12 Nabhānī, II, p. 14.

13 Najm al-Dīn al-Ghazzī: *Al-kawākib al-sā'ira bi-aᶜyān al-mi'a al-ᶜāshira*, ed. Jabbūr, Beirut, 1945 ff., II, pp. 3-6.

14 Ghazzī, II, p. 32, ll. 12-13.

15 Ibn Ṭūlūn: *Mufākahat al-khillān* (sic) *fī ḥawādith al-zamān*, ed. Muḥammad Muṣṭafā, Cairo, 1962-64, I, p. 25, l. 19.

16 A certain Khalīl Ibn Qadīm al-Ṣumādī was still alive in Damascus after 910/1504; Ghazzī, I, p. 62, l. 5. This is no doubt a different person.

17 Ghazzī, II, p. 32, ll. 12-13.

The family emerges into the full light of history with Khalīl's son *Muḥammad* b. Khalīl b. ᶜAlī b. ᶜĪsā b. Aḥmad b. Ṣāliḥ b. ᶜĪsā b. Muḥammad b. ᶜĪsā b. Dāwūd b. Sālim/Muslim, Shams al-Dīn al-Ṣumādī al-Dimashqī al-Shāfiᶜī al-Qādirī who is now designated as the shaykh of *al-ṭāʾifa al-ṣumādiyya*. This makes it clear that a real suborder of the Qādiriyya has been christened with its own distinctive surname, which even replaces the overarching name of the Qādiriyya. The historian Ibn Ṭūlūn (d. 953/1546) is supposed to have portrayed Muḥammad al-Ṣumādī with a red turban (*ᶜimāma*) and a red cummerbund (*shadd*). In the later 10th/16th century the turban worn by the Ṣumādiyya was white. Muḥammad every year recited a *mawlid* (of the Prophet Muḥammad), invited the nobles, scholars and men of piety of Damascus to be present, and entertained them with a magnificent meal.[18] Birthday celebrations on behalf of Muḥammad, to which the pious invited people, can be traced back to the 6th/12th century.[19] Ghazzī's father, Badr al-Dīn Muḥammad (d. 984/1577), went on maintaining with him the traditional friendship between the two families.[20]

---

18 Ghazzī, II, p. 31, ll. 14-26.

19 The pious Muᶜīn al-Dawla ᶜUmar b. Muḥammad al-Mallāʾ lived in Mawṣil in the 6th/12th century under the Zangid Nūr al-Dīn Maḥmūd (d. 569/1174). The ruler of Mawṣil and the other local notables came to his banquet; Ibn Qāḍī Shuhba: *Al-kawākib al-durriyya fī'l-sīra al-nūriyya*, Beirut, 1971, p. 36 (N. Siouffi: *Notes historiques et explicatives sur les inscriptions de la ville de Mossoul* [Arabic], Baghdad, 1953-56, pp. 158-59, ftn. 1), and Muḥammad Amīn al-ᶜUmarī: *Manhal al-awliyāʾ*, Mawṣil, 1967-68, II, p. 141, ftn. 2. Both have been edited by Saᶜīd al-Dīwajī and give further bibliographical information. — Near Cairo in the 7th/13th century Muḥammad b. Aḥmad b. Manẓūr b. ᶜAbdallāh (597-676/1201-77), who looked after an association of *fuqarāʾ*, every year invited people to a banquet on the Prophet's birthday; Yūnīnī: *Dhayl Mirʾāt al-zamān*, Hyderabad, 1954-61, III, pp. 280-81. — In Ceuta in the 7th/13th century Abū'l-ᶜAbbās al-ᶜAzafī held birthday celebrations for the Prophet. His son Abū'l-Qāsim Muḥammad became ruler of the city in 647/1250; see Maqqarī: *Azhār al-riyāḍ fī akhbār ᶜIyāḍ*, ed. Saqqā-Ibyārī-Shalabī, Cairo, 1939-43, I, p. 39; II, pp. 374-76. — In Ceuta and Guadix in the 7th/13th century Abū Marwān ᶜAbd al-Mālik al-Yuḥānisī (d. 667/1268-69) also gave birthday banquets of this kind; for Ceuta *El-Maqṣad* (*Vies des saints du Rîf*) *de ᶜAbd el-Ḥaqq el-Bâdisî*, traduction annotée de G.S. Colin, in Archives Marocaines 26, Paris, 1926, p. 90 and ftn. 288; for Guadix Aḥmad al-Qashtālī: *Tuḥfat al-mughtarib bi-bilād al-maghrib*, ed. Fernando de la Granja, in Rev. Instit. Egipcio de Estudios Islámicos 17, Madrid, 1972-73, pp. 76-78. — The birthday feasts of the Prophet carried out on the highest level (by Kökbüri, the Zayyānids, Marīnids, etc.) will not be discussed here.

20 Ghazzī, II, p. 32, l. 12.

Muḥammad b. Khalīl could not avoid involvement with the authorities. In 917/1511, after his father had departed this life, he escorted with his 'Ṣumādī drums' Muḥammad b. Sāᶜid, the son of the often menacing and recalcitrant Arab ruler of Barr, Ḥawrān and ᶜAjlūn, to Damascus where the latter wished to declare his loyalty to the Mamluk governor.[21] He appears to have been officially commissioned to escort him in this manner. After the change-over of power from the Mamluks to the Ottomans in 922/1516, Muḥammad b. Khalīl quickly secured the goodwill of the Turks. He travelled to Turkey and obtained from sultan Selim I (918-26/1512-20) the village Katībat Raᵓs al-Māᵓ, and then in Aleppo from Süleyman I (926-74/1520-66) the village Kanākir by Damascus — Kanākir with the arrangement that every year the village paid him 80 sacks of wheat, 40 of which went to his convent (*zāwiya*) and its inhabitants and visitors, while the other 40 were for him and his descendants.[22] This convent, which he is said to have founded himself,[23] was located in the suburban quarter al-Shāghūr.[24] Muḥammad b. Khalīl died in 948/1541 and left behind eighteen children, sons as well as daughters.[25]

His successor was his son Shams al-Dīn Abū Muslim *Muḥammad* b. Muḥammad (911-94/1505-86), he as well a respected shaykh famous for his higher supernatural gifts and his effective amulets, he as well a friend of the house of Ghazzī, esteemed by Najm al-Dīn's father, Badr al-Dīn Muḥammad, and readily visited both by the ruling authorities in Damascus and functionaries from abroad. Like Ghazzī's father, he also had the courage not to sign a certificate of good conduct on behalf of the not particularly popular Ottoman governor Muṣṭafā Bāshā, for the simple reason that he did not know him sufficiently, and this may in part be why Muṣṭafā Bāshā after his return to Turkey felt moved to describe these two persons as the only real men in Damascus. Abū Muslim Muḥammad knew a lot about the history of his forefathers and maintained that his ancestor Sālim/Muslim traced his genealogy back to the Koranic scholar and

21 Ibn Ṭūlūn: *Iᶜlām al-warā bi-man wulliya nāᵓiban min al-atrāk bi-Dimashq al-Shām al-kubrā*, ed. Muḥammad Aḥmad Duhmān, Damascus, 1964, p. 197, ll. 5-8; *Mufākahat al-khillān*, I, p. 355, ll. 7-10.

22 Ghazzī, II, p. 31, ll. 21-24; III, p. 19, l. 24, to p. 20, l. 3.

23 Muḥammad Kurd ᶜAlī: *Khiṭaṭ al-Shām*, Beirut, 1969-72, VI, p. 140. The year 1053/1643 does not fit for Muḥammad b. Khalīl al-Ṣumādī; it is too late.

24 Ghazzī, II, p. 31, l. 24.

25 Ghazzī, II, p. 32, ll. 17-18.

traditionist Saᶜīd b. Jubayr b. Hishām al-Asadī al-Wālibī[26] whom Ḥajjāj had executed in 95/714.[27] Abū Muslim Muḥammad is therefore also presented as al-Saᶜīdī al-Jubayrī.[28] In Jerusalem he met the Egyptian Muḥammad b. ᶜAlī al-Bakrī al-Ṣiddīqī, who accorded him the greatest respect and then died in 994/1586, the same year as he did.[29]

It is all the more astonishing that precisely in the days of Abū Muslim, namely in 985/1577, it should emerge that his family on his father's side was of ᶜAlid origin. The document which proved this was supposed to have been in the possession of an aunt in Nābulus without anyone having known about it. After the aunt's death the members of the family had their ᶜAlid descent certified by a *qāḍī* in Damascus, placed the green badge of their *sayyid* status on their head, and some wore green turbans.[30] In Ghazzī's time (d. 1061/1651) green was the color of their usual headgear.[31] Ghazzī attempts to clear away the contradiction between the two statements about their origin by locating their descent from Saᶜīd b. Jubayr on the mother's side, i.e. he traces the old Sālim/Muslim back to Saᶜīd through the female line. In any case he sees this as a solution.[32] Muḥibbī (d. 1111/1699) I, p. 50, l. 1, follows him without reserve and mentions in I, p. 49 below, that shortly before, in 982/1574-75, the Banū'l-Dasūqī (in Damascus)[33] had also been able to establish ᶜAlid descent.[34] One is of course justified in relating these genealogical corrections to the larger context of the mounting wave of veneration for the ᶜAlids in the 10th/16th century, which washed

---

26 Ibn al-Ḥanbalī, II, 1, p. 169, l. 3. Ghazzī, III, p. 19, l. 19.

27 Ibn Ḥajar al-ᶜAsqalānī: *Tahdhīb al-Tahdhīb*, Hyderabad, 1325-27, IV, pp. 11-13. ᶜAbd al-Ḥayy b. al-ᶜImād: *Shadharāt al-dhahab*, Cairo, 1350-51, I, pp. 108-10.

28 Ibn al-Ḥanbalī, II, 1, p. 168, l. 8.

29 On Abū Muslim Muḥammad al-Ṣumādī see Ghazzī, III, pp. 16-20. On Bakrī see Ghazzī, III, pp. 67-72.

30 Muḥibbī, I, p. 49 below. Murādī, I, p. 174 below.

31 Ghazzī, II, p. 31, l. 20.

32 Ghazzī, III, p. 19, ll. 21-23.

33 A descendant of Ibrāhīm b. Muḥammad al-Dasūqī (d. 919/1513); Ghazzī, I, p. 101.

34 From al-Shams Muḥammad b. Ṣalāḥ al-Dīn Dāwūd al-Dāwūdī al-Maqdisī al-Dimashqī al-Shāfiᶜī (942-1006/1535-1598); Muḥibbī, IV, p. 151 below. There were ᶜAlids who kept their lineage secret out of fear and for reasons of security, for example the great-grandson of Ḥusayn in Kūfa; Abū'l-Faraj al-Iṣfahānī: *Maqātil al-ṭālibiyyīn*, ed. Cairo (Ṣaqr), 1949, p. 410. Others did so out of modesty, for example Yūnīnī's father; Yūnīnī: *Dhayl*, II, pp. 56-57.

over a large part of the Islamic world and included ᶜAlid sherifism in the farthest west and the ᶜAlidization of the Safavids in Persia. But for the time being it cannot be proven that the Ṣumādī family falsified their genealogy in the 10th/16th century. It is striking that Ibn al-Ḥanbalī, who in II, 1, p. 169, ll. 1-2, reports the marriage of Dāwūd b. Sālim/Muslim to ᶜAbd al-Qādir's daughter, does not make any allusion to the Ṣumādīs' ᶜAlid descent, although ᶜAbd al-Qādir al-Jīlānī is regarded as a descendant of ᶜAlī. Did the Ṣumādīs not consider themselves to be descendants of this daughter of ᶜAbd al-Qādir but of a different wife of Dāwūd? Ibn al-Ḥanbalī died in 971/1563, i.e. before the document from Nābulus had turned up.

When Abū Muslim Muḥammad passed away in 994/1586 in Damascus, his burial was delayed until his son *Muslim* arrived from Biqāᶜ where he resided. Najm al-Dīn al-Ghazzī knew Muslim and during a bout of fever had beheld the Prophet in a dream — on the latter's left the shaykh Muḥammad, on the left next to him his son Muslim and on Muslim's left the 'subordinate leaders' (*nuqabāʾ*) of the Ṣumādiyya — which even then had been a prediction of Muslim's succession. Muslim occupied his father's position and died in 1015/1606 after making a trip to Jerusalem in the last year of his life.[35]

He was followed by his son *ᶜĪsā* b. Muslim (969-1021/1562-1613) who during his father's lifetime had led a rather extravagant life of pleasure but is now supposed to have filled the office of the *mashyakha* most excellently.[36] He possessed influence with the people but also enjoyed the favor of the Ottoman provincial government which he served diligently. He took sides against the cravings for independence and power on the part of the local petty rulers, the Druse Fakhr al-Dīn and the Kurd ᶜAlī b. Jānbūlādh, and in 1016/1606 appeared among their prosecutors before the Ottoman grand vizier Murād Bāshā in Aleppo.[37] Later, in 1020/1611,[38] the Ottoman governor of Damascus, Aḥmad Bāshā al-Ḥāfiẓ, sent him to this same Murād Bāshā in Diyarbakr to help him with billeting his troops during his campaign against Shāh ᶜAbbās.[39]

---

35 Muḥibbī, IV, p. 363. Nabhānī, I, p. 186 below, to p. 187 above.

36 Muḥibbī, III, p. 244.

37 Muḥibbī, III, pp. 244 and 439. Ferdinand Wüstenfeld: 'Fachr ed-dîn der Drusenfürst und seine Zeitgenossen', *Abh. kgl. Ges. Wiss. Göttingen* 33 (1886), p. 122. Cf. Muḥibbī, IV, p. 357. Salibi *EI*² Fakhr al-Dīn.

38 Muḥibbī, IV, pp. 357-58.

39 Muḥibbī, III, p. 244. Wüstenfeld: 'Fachr ed-dîn', p. 73.

After ᶜĪsā his brother *Ibrāhīm* b. Muslim al-Qādirī al-Shāfiᶜī al-Ṣumādī al-Ḥawrānī al-Dimashqī took over the leadership of the association. Moreover, he still had the permit for teaching his *ṭarīqa* from his father Muslim. He built up the convent handsomely within the Bāb al-Shāghūr in Damascus, travelled once to Turkey and in 1046/1637 to Mecca, and once to Aleppo with other shaykhs of Damascus,[40] and was among the escorts of Najm al-Dīn al-Ghazzī when the latter like his father journeyed for the last time to Jerusalem shortly before his death in 1061/1651.[41] He lived from 998/1590 to 1073/1662-63 and left behind four sons, each of whom, as he had wished for in a prayer, adhered to a different one of the four Sunnī schools of jurisprudence: Muslim to the Mālikites, ᶜAbdallāh to the Ḥanbalites, Mūsā to the Shāfiᶜites (traditionally the family's school) and Muḥammad to the Ḥanafites.[42]

The Shāfiᶜite *Mūsā* followed his father as leader. He had received a special document from him in 1070/1659-60 which had been signed by several scholars of the city of Damascus, including Muḥibbī's father Faḍlallāh (1031-82/1621-71). He died in 1081/1670 and was buried in the cemetery of the Bāb al-Ṣaghīr.[43]

His prayer-rug (*sajjāda*) was occupied after him by his son *ᶜAbd al-Qādir* b. Mūsā al-Shāfiᶜī. In the ancestral convent he held the recollection of God as practiced by his predecessors, and only left the house on Fridays, on the two holidays, for funerals and for official receptions. His death occurred in the year 1114/1703. His grave is located at the Bāb al-Ṣaghīr near Bilāl al-Ḥabashī.[44]

As his successor he had appointed his little son whose name is not mentioned. Those with authority, however, put in charge ᶜAbd al-Qādir's elderly brother *Ṣāliḥ* b. Mūsā.[45] The dates of this Ṣāliḥ are unknown.

So much for the heads of the family enterprise up to the time after 1114/1703. However, the family had separate branches, and Muḥibbī, I, p. 49, finds it important to distinguish a certain Ibrāhīm b. Aḥmad b. Dāwūd b. Muslim b. Muḥammad al-Ṣumādī al-Wāᶜiẓ al-Shāfiᶜī, prayer leader in the enclosure (*maqṣūra*) of the Umayyad Mosque and an effective preacher, from the above-mentioned

40 Muḥibbī, IV, p. 198.

41 Muḥibbī, IV, p. 200, l. 6.

42 Muḥibbī, I, pp. 48-49. Wüstenfeld: 'Fachr ed-dîn', p. 73. Nabhānī, I, pp. 249-50.

43 Muḥibbī, IV, pp. 430-31.

44 Murādī, III, p. 60.

45 Murādī, III, p. 60.

Ibrāhīm b. Muslim (d. 1073/1662-63). Since this other Ibrāhīm al-Wāᶜiẓ was the student of Shams al-Dīn Muḥammad b. Muḥammad al-Ḥamawī al-Dimashqī al-Maydānī al-Shāfiᶜī who died in 1033/1624,[46] he can scarcely be a great-grandson of the Muslim b. Muḥammad of our principal family line. Muslim died in 1015/1606 and Ibrāhīm al-Wāᶜiẓ in 1054/1644. Perhaps his great-great-grandfather Muḥammad is the great-grandfather of Ibrāhīm b. Muslim, i.e. the Muḥammad b. Khalīl (d. 948/1541) whom we have already treated.

Ibrāhīm al-Wāᶜiẓ's son ᶜAbd al-Razzāq or ᶜAbd al-Rāziq (d. 1112/1700-01) inherited his father's talent for deeply moving people with his words and developed this ability in such a way that he was invited everywhere as a witty conversationalist. He was a close friend of the military commander of Damascus, Muḥammad Aghā b. Sulaymān al-Tarjumān. ᶜAbd al-Razzāq's mother Zulaykhā was the daughter of a certain Muḥammad b. Muḥammad b. Aḥmad al-Marzanātī al-Ṣāliḥī al-Ḥanbalī (d. 1014/1605-06),[47] and the sister of a certain ᶜAbd al-Ḥaqq b. Muḥammad b. Muḥammad b. Aḥmad al-Marzanātī (991-1070/1583-1660).[48] Moreover, according to reports, the family tree of these Marzanātīs was rooted in no less a personage than Ibrāhīm b. Adham who died in 'Syria' in 161-62/777-79. Muḥammad b. Muḥammad al-Marzanātī had belonged to the Qādirī order but in 1005/1597 when his shaykh Aḥmad b. Sulaymān al-Qādirī died, he made a vain attempt to become his successor and thus to take over his family enterprise.[49] However, his grandson ᶜAbd al-Razzāq, thanks to that grandmother, inherited the income from an endowment of 'sultan Ibrāhīm b. Adham' in Jabala where the latter's grave is located. ᶜAbd al-Razzāq had a brother and two sons, Muḥammad and ᶜAlī. ᶜAlī concocted and adored dirty jokes, associated with the son of Muḥammad Aghā who was also named ᶜAlī, and died in Turkey.

Muḥammad (with the epithet ᶜAzrāʾīl), the son of ᶜAbd al-Razzāq, had for his part a son *Aḥmad* (b. Muḥammad b. ᶜAbd al-Razzāq b. Ibrāhīm al-Wāᶜiẓ) al-Ṣumādī al-Ḥanafī. This Aḥmad was born in 1107/1696 and inherited the income of the endowment of 'sultan Ibrāhīm b. Adham'. In order to avoid undergoing the same unpleasant experiences that his father Muḥammad had been forced to

46 Muḥibbī, IV, p. 173, ll. 4-5.

47 Murādī, I, pp. 173-74. Muḥibbī, IV, pp. 158-59.

48 Muḥibbī, II, pp. 316-18.

49 Muḥibbī, I, pp. 207-08; II, pp. 435-36 (p. 285 above).

undergo with the governor of Ṭarābulus, he attempted to secure protection for himself at the highest level and via the grand vizier Muḥammad Rāghib Bāshā he succeeded in having the management (*tawliya*) of the endowment's property conferred on him by sultan Muṣṭafā III (1171-87/1757-73). Subsequently he accumulated great wealth. He held several offices at once, was a professor in Damascus, travelled back and forth between Jabala and Damascus, and in 1195/1781, while on one such trip, passed away in the village of Quṭayyifa when he was over ninety years old.[50]

With this powerful and many-sided man who was a shrewd tactician, the second line of the Ṣumādiyya, which perhaps split off from the first in the time of Muḥammad b. Khalīl, also came to have a say in the leadership of the order in Damascus. Aḥmad is supposed to have been active on 'the prayer-rug of the shaykhdom' (*sajjādat al-mashyakha*) in conjunction with a relative whose name is not mentioned.[51] That the name of the other partner is not mentioned indicates an earlier weakening of the first family line, while a double occupation of the highest post reveals the decline of the old unity. One may surmise, though proof for this still remains to be shown, that from about this time on, i.e. from around 1200/1800, the Ṣumādiyya as a Qādirī enterprise in Damascus begins to disintegrate. Likewise, Sadık Vicdani: *Tomar-ı turuk-ı ᶜaliyye*, Istanbul, 1338-40/1919-22, II, p. 65, with the exception of a certain Ḥasan Üsküdari who is unclear to me, can no longer list any further shaykhs.[52]

Also a member of the family of our Ṣumādīs was the man of letters and respected functionary in Ottoman service in Damascus al-Sayyid Muṣṭafā b. Ḥasan b. Muḥammad al-Ṣumādī al-Ḥanafī al-Dimashqī (d. 1137/1725),[53] whose verses Murādī sprinkles throughout many of his articles.[54] The title *sayyid* alone attests to his membership in the family. But in addition Murādī mentions ᶜAbd al-Qādir (d. 1114/1701) of the first line and Aḥmad b. Muḥammad (d. 1195/1781) of the second line, as his 'relatives'.[55] Perhaps Kamāl al-Dīn Abū'l-Ḥasan Aḥmad b. Muḥammad b. Muḥammad b. Muṣṭafā al-Ṣumādī

50 Murādī, I, pp. 173-75.

51 Murādī, I, p. 173, ll. 21-22.

52 Wherever Vicdani deviates from our list regarding the earlier shaykhs, he should be corrected.

53 Murādī, IV, pp. 179-83. *GAL*, II, p. 280.

54 For example Murādī, I, pp. 257 f.; II, pp. 10, 132, 204; III, pp. 282 f., 286.

55 Murādī, I, p. 175, ll. 1-2.

al-Jarrāḥī al-Ḥasanī al-Dimashqī, who wrote a work plagiarized from Qaramānī's *Akhbār al-duwal*,[56] is his great-grandson (?).

One is unable to show membership in our family in the case of several other Ṣumādīs. A shaykh Musallam al-Ṣumādī/Ṣamādī lies buried in Nābulus along with his son and his two daughters. Over a small window of his tomb stands the date 624/1227, and in 1923 around thirty of his descendants still lived in Nābulus.[57] A certain Yūsuf b. ᶜAbd al-Qādir b. Muḥammad b. al-ᶜAzāʾim Jamāl al-Dīn al-Ṣumādī al-Ḥawrānī al-Ḥamawī al-Shāfiᶜī resided in the Madrasa al-Bāsiṭiyya in Mecca and in 886/1461-62 attended Sakhāwī's lectures in Mecca.[58] Shams al-Dīn Muḥammad al-Ṣumādī al-Qaṭṭān (d. 939/1533) was a *khalīfa* of Muḥammad b. Khalīl al-Ṣumādī (d. 948/1541) in the Jewish quarter of Damascus, al-Qiṭṭ, where a convent (*zāwiya*) was built for him or had already been built.[59] Here mention of a branch of the order in Damascus with its own leader is instructive but we do not know whether the leader's name Ṣumādī refers to membership in the family or in the order. In Jerusalem as well there was a convent of the Ṣumādiyya.[60] A certain Mūsā al-Ṣumādī, who conferred a patched frock on ᶜAlī al-Ṭayyān al-Naḥlāwī al-Shāfiᶜī al-Dimashqī (1070-1150/1659-60-1738),[61] should perhaps be distinguished from our Mūsā b. Ibrāhīm al-Ṣumādī because the latter died in 1081/1670 when al-Ṭayyān was only ten or eleven years old. I have already referred in a footnote (16, p. 287) to the doubtfulness of fitting a certain Khalīl Ibn Qadīm al-Ṣumādī into the series and the family of our Ṣumādiyya.

---

56 *GAL*, II, p. 302.

57 J.-A. Jaussen: 'Inscriptions arabes de Naplouse', in *BIFAO* 27, 1926, p. 94, no. 5. Jaussen: *Naplouse et son district*, Paris, 1927, pp. 162-63 (where the incorrect date 623 is given).

58 *Ḍawʾ lāmiᶜ*, X, p. 322.

59 Ghazzī, II, p. 69, ll. 18-21.

60 Muḥammad Kurd ᶜAlī: *Khiṭaṭ al-Shām*, VI, p. 150.

61 Murādī, III, p. 258.

SUMMARY

1st Line:

Sālim/Muslim/Musallam
Dāwūd
ʿĪsā
Muḥammad
ʿĪsā/Khamīs
Ṣāliḥ (d. 825/1422 in Ṣumād)
Aḥmad
ʿĪsā
ʿAlī (in Damascus)
Khalīl
Muḥammad (d. 948/1541)
Muḥammad (911-94/1505-86)
Muslim/Musallam(?) (d. 1015/1606)

- ʿĪsā (died 1021/1613)
- Ibrāhīm (998-1073/1590-1662-63)
  - Mūsā (died 1081/1670)
    - ʿAbdalqādir (died 1114/1703)
    - Ṣāliḥ

2nd Line:

Muḥammad (possibly = Muḥammad b. Khalīl of the 1st line, who died in 948/1541)
Muslim/Musallam(?)
Dāwūd
Aḥmad
Ibrāhīm al-Wāʿiẓ (d. 1054/1644)
ʿAbd al-Razzāq (d. 1112/1700-01)
Muḥammad
Aḥmad (1107-95/1696-1781)

(2)

The Ṣumādiyya held gatherings which were sometimes designated 'recollection of God' (*dhikr*),[62] sometimes 'listening to music' (*samā*ᶜ),[63] sometimes 'moment' (*waqt*),[64] and sometimes more neutrally 'circle' (*ḥalqa*) or 'gathering' (*majlis*). The term *samā*ᶜ is fully appropriate given the fact that music and poetry recitals (*inshād*) did take place or could take place during the gatherings.[65] It could be that these were ceremonies in which recollection of God and song recitals alternated or accompanied one another and were blended together, as has often been described in historical sources and can still be observed today.[66]

In gatherings of this kind musical instruments were only allowed to a limited degree or were forbidden altogether. Theory and the practice of the orders part company in this respect. The tambourine is frequently mentioned and, under certain restrictions, is sometimes permitted. Only more rarely does one encounter the drum (*ṭabl*). According to a tradition of Abū Naṣr Ismāᶜīl b. Muḥammad al-Runānī al-Ṣayrafī (d. 531/1137) in Isfahan, ᶜAbdallāh b. ᶜUmar (d. circa 73/692) upon hearing a drum (*ṭabl*) placed his hands over his ears two to three times and is supposed to have previously observed the Prophet do this.[67] Ibn Qayyim al-Jawziyya (d. 751/1350) in Damascus regards the drum (*ṭabl*) as being among the instruments which are in fact forbidden and would only be declared permissible through tricks of interpretation.[68]

For the Ṣumādiyya the drum (*ṭabl*) occupies a central position, indeed it constitutes the very hallmark of the order.

Here it is first of all a question of a special drum which was preserved in the family of the Ṣumādiyya or Banū'l-Ṣumādī as a relic of their ancestor. It was a drum of brass (yellow copper, *nuḥās aṣfar*) which their ancestor Sālim or Muslim is supposed to have beaten at

[62] Ghazzī, II, p. 32, l. 1; p. 32, l. 10; III, p. 18, ll. 6-7, etc. Muḥibbī, IV, p. 363, ll. 7-10. Ibn al-Ḥanbalī, II, 1, p. 169, l. 7.

[63] Ghazzī, III, p. 17, l. 2; Muḥibbī, I, p. 50, l. 3.

[64] Ghazzī, III, p. 11, l. 18.

[65] Ghazzī, II, p. 32, l. 11.

[66] *Abū Saᶜīd-i Abū l-Ḫayr*, pp. 240-43. The first sentence of ftn. 295 should be changed.

[67] Samᶜānī: *Muntakhab*, MS Topkapı Sarayı 2953 (Berlin MS sim. or. 80/Tehran (Kitābkhāna-i markazī), 46b, ll. 1-6.

[68] Ibn Qayyim al-Jawziyya: *Madārij al-sālikīn*, Cairo, 1331-34, II, p. 31, l. 17.

the capture of Acre.[69] One has the choice of two captures of Acre: the first by Saladin in 583/1187, the second by the Mamluk al-Malik al-Ashraf in 690/1291 — both against the Crusaders. Only the first would fit if Sālim/Muslim had really been a direct disciple of ᶜAbd al-Qādir al-Jīlānī (d. 561/1166) as ᶜAsqalānī: *Inbāʾ al-ghumr*, III, p. 287, indicates more or less clearly. A review of the generations of the Ṣumādiyya shows that on the average the death dates stand 31 to 32 solar years apart. From Ṣāliḥ (d. 825/1422) back to Sālim/Muslim there are five generations which is equivalent to 165 solar years. In this way (by subtracting 165 from 1422) we arrive at 1257 as the possible date of death for Sālim/Muslim, i.e. seventy years after the first capture of Acre in 583/1187. This is not impossible since Sālim/Muslim could have been present as a young man. But then he cannot also have been a direct disciple of ᶜAbd al-Qādir who had already died in 561/1166, for in that case he would have to have lived to the exceptional age of over a hundred. But if one takes into account that the first capture of Acre in 583/1187 occurred virtually without a struggle, the likelihood that this occasion is meant decreases considerably. The drum acquires a more comprehensible and a more glorious aura if one pictures it as being in the army of the Mamluk al-Malik al-Ashraf which by storming Acre in 690/1291 dealt the final blow to the Crusades and did in fact advance against the Crusaders' last bulwark with the immense din of kettledrums loaded on 300 camels, and of the drum corps of the emirs, with the blare of *jamālī*-trumpets, the shouts of heroes, the whinnying of horses and the clash of arms.[70] The editors of Ibn al-Ḥanbalī, II, 1, p. 169, ftn. 8, situate the priceless heirloom in this context. Of course, this would mean that Sālim/Muslim could not have died before 690/1291 and could not have been the direct disciple of ᶜAbd al-Qādir al-Jīlānī.

However, Dāwūd, the son of Sālim/Muslim, is also glorified as a kind of participant in the recapture of Acre. When the fighting for

---

69 Ibn al-Ḥanbalī, II, 1, p. 169. Ghazzī, III, p. 19, ll. 20-21. Muḥibbī, I, p. 50, ll. 1-3.

70 Ibn al-Dawādārī (8th/14th century): *Al-durra al-zakiyya fī akhbār al-dawla al-turkiyya*, VIII, ed. Ulrich Haarmann, Freiburg im Breisgau, 1971, pp. 309-10. Reinhold Röhricht: *Geschichte des Königreichs Jerusalem*, Innsbruck, 1898, pp. 1015, 1018. The ear-splitting war-music which Islamic armies played when they went on the attack is also noted here and there among Christian history writers; for the battle of Rio Salado (741/1340) see *Nobiliário da Ajuda*, French translation by Robert Ricard in *Hespéris* 43, 1956, p. 16; for the Ottoman siege of Azov in 1641 see Helmut Grasshoff, Klaus Müller and Gottfried Sturm: *O Bojan, du Nachtigall der alten Zeit*, Berlin, 1965, pp. 323, 324, 334, 335.

Acre broke out, he is meant to have asked his disciples in Ṣumād for a suit of armor and then to have begun to whirl about in the *samāᶜ*. It is said that those who were present heard noise and the clash of arms, and after the performance found that the clothes of Dāwūd were torn to shreds by the blows of battle. According to another version, on that day Dāwūd straightway had his bloody hands washed by his servant and replied to the latter's astonished questioning: 'We have just captured Acre.'[71] In the first story the motif of sham fighting with long-distance effect is discernible. Abū Isḥāq-i Kāzarūnī (d. 426/1035), according to a legend, swung a club about himself on the roof in Kāzarūn and by so doing routed a Christian army which was fighting an Islamic force in Asia Minor.[72] The second story is based on the motif of stigmata received at a distance. Aḥmad-i Jām (d. 536/1141), although in the east of Persia, saw himself in the midst of the fighting during the capture of Jerusalem by the Crusaders in 492/1099, and as a result of this his feet and shoes were covered in blood which one of his novices then washed clean.[73] The chronicler moves Dāwūd as well into the proximity of ᶜAbd al-Qādir al-Jīlānī: he is supposed to have married ᶜAbd al-Qādir's daughter.[74] Thus with regard to Dāwūd too the capture of Acre in 583/1187 must also be meant, which in his case raises even more serious doubts than in the case of his father Sālim/Muslim. An earlier dating for both would perhaps hold up if one could assume gaps in the reported sequence of generations or — quite naturally — longer lifespans. An additional difficulty lies in the 'doublette' that father and son, each in his own

---

71 Nabhānī, II, p. 7 below, taken from *Tuffāḥ al-arwāḥ* of Muḥammad (b.) al-Sarrāj (8th/14th century).

72 *Firdaws al-murshidiyya = Die Vita des Scheich Abū Isḥāq al-Kāzarūnī in der persischen Bearbeitung von Maḥmūd b. ᶜUthmān*, Bibl. Isl. XIV, Persian p. 199 (Chpt. 33).

73 Sadīd al-Dīn Muḥammad-i Ghaznawī: *Maqāmāt-i Žanda-pīl*, ed. Ḥishmatallāh-i Muʾayyad, Tehran, 1960, pp. 142-43. 'Zur Biographie Aḥmad-i Ǧāms und zur Quellenkunde von Ǧāmī's *Nafaḥātu'l-uns*', in *ZDMG* 97, 1943, p. 54. In a chronologically confused legend in *Evliyā Çelebi Seyāḥatnāmesi*, Istanbul, 1314, III, p. 106, a saint from Aleppo, ᶜĀbidīn Efendi, dispatches one of his eyes to the Muslim besieger of Acre, Ṭāhir Bibars (= Ẓāhir Baybars), which is meant to have suffered a martyr's death on behalf of Acre, and throws his wooden clog in the direction of Acre which causes the city to be destroyed after a seven-year siege. ᶜAbd al-Qādir al-Jīlānī one time from within Baghdad threw both his wooden platform-shoes, fatally striking two robber chieftains who had plundered a caravan, and the grateful merchants brought the shoes back to him from the desert; Tādifī: *Qalāʾid al-jawāhir*, Cairo, 1356, pp. 68-69.

74 Ibn al-Ḥanbalī, II, 1, p. 169, ll. 1-2.

way, are meant to have participated in the capture of Acre, the father in flesh and blood, and the son as a shaman-like assistant at a distance.

The above-mentioned inconsistencies and difficulties to begin with suggest that an attempt has been made here to clarify the obscure beginnings of an ancestral history through later speculations. Two central ideas prevail throughout the attempted clarification: the endeavor to connect the ancestors in question with ᶜAbd al-Qādir and to have them play a part in deciding the outcome at Acre, both perfectly understandable forms of hagiographic propaganda — the second determined by particular historical circumstances and apparently an antiquarian object: the drum. Nevertheless, the stories about Dāwūd's long-distance participation in the capture of Acre could be older than the story of Sālim's/Muslim's drum. This would even seem probable because if it were really meant to be a question of the capture of Acre in 690/1291, the author who tells about it, Kamāl al-Dīn (b.) al-Sarrāj from the first half of the 8th/14th century, would have been almost a contemporary of Dāwūd's.

However, the chronological difficulties would be solved at a stroke and the scales would tilt unambiguously in favor of the capture of Acre in 583/1187 if one could identify our Sālim/Muslim with the shaykh *Musallam* al-Ṣumādī/Ṣamādī buried in Nābulus whose tomb bears the date 624/1227 (see p. 295 above). We do not know whether this date designates the year of his death or the year of the tomb's construction, but it would be a fixed *terminus ad quem* which would also allow us to acknowledge his personal connection with ᶜAbd al-Qādir al-Jīlānī as historically possible. Nevertheless, the later legend may have had in mind — anachronistically — Acre in 690/1291. Local tradition has in mind Nābulus (583/1187). If Musallam is the correct pronunciation of the name, then without hesitation Musallam instead of Muslim can be read in the historians, and the same is true regarding his two known descendants who bore the name Muslim. There is much to recommend this solution.

The legendary parent drum which Sālim/Muslim/Musallam is supposed to have beaten at Acre and which was kept in the family, was then heard in the above-mentioned ecstatic gatherings of the following generations and was still occasionally brought forth in the 10th/16th century.[75] Miraculous things were recounted about it: once a Mamluk governor of Damascus wished to forbid an ancestor of Muḥammad b. Khalīl al-Ṣumādī from beating the drum in the

75 Ibn al-Ḥanbalī, II, 1, p. 169, ll. 3-4. Ghazzī, III, p. 19, l. 20.

Umayyad Mosque on Friday after the ritual prayers and had it removed from the mosque, but the drum returned to the mosque of its own accord borne aloft and beaten by an invisible hand, and for a long time it moved about in the air from east to west under the vaulting until it struck against a pillar.[76] Judging by its designation as *ṭablabāz* in Ibn al-Ḥanbalī, II, 1, p. 169, l. 4, it was rather small, because the Persian prototype *ṭabl-i bāz* 'falcon drum' as well as *ṭablak-i bāz* 'little falcon drum' was customarily attached to the falconer's saddle and then beaten when the falcon was meant to fly into the air.[77] Quite another matter was the legendary drum of the Almohad ᶜAbd al-Muᵓmin b. ᶜAlī (d. 558/1163), the commander-in-chief and successor of the *mahdī* Ibn Tūmart, which had a circumference of 15 cubits and is said to have been heard at a distance of a half day's journey when it gave the signal to break camp.[78]

But by the 10th/16th century at the latest one also hears of drums in the plural (*ṭubūl*) among the Ṣumādiyya. Since drumming was characteristic of the association and the association founded branch establishments, it was inevitable that the drums would be multiplied. Moreover, with the passage of time it became necessary to handle the parent drum very carefully and it was only used on special occasions. A legend from the 8th/14th century in Kamāl al-Dīn (b.) al-Sarrāj perhaps preserves a memory of drumming being practiced in branch localities already during the lifetime of the second oldest ancestor, the problematic Dāwūd. A 'singer' (*mughannī*) whom he sent

76 Ghazzī, II, p. 32, ll. 6-9. *Shadharāt*, VIII, p. 275. Nabhānī, I, p. 181.

77 Niẓāmī: *Khusraw u Shīrīn*, ed. Waḥīd-i Dastgirdī, Tehran, 1313, p. 299, l. 2, ftn. 1. Dastgirdī: *Ganjīna-i Ganjawī*, Tehran, 1317, p. 104: *ṭablak-i bāz*. Dihkhudā: *Lughatnāma*, s.v. *ṭabl* (166b below): *ṭabl-i bāz* 'one beats this drum when the falcon is sent after waterfowl. The fowl rise into the air at the sound of the drum, and the falcon then pursues one of them', i.e. here described somewhat differently. With passages for *ṭabl-i bāz*. Also under *ṭablak*. In Egypt this little drum is called *al-bāz* for short or also *ṭablat al-musaḥḥir*, because in Ramaḍān the crier for the last meal (*saḥūr*) beats it at night; Edward W. Lane: *Manners and Customs of the Modern Egyptians*, (Everyman's Library, London, 1954, Chpt. XXV, p. 481. Maḥmūd Aḥmad al-Ḥanafī: *Ālāt al-musīqī al-shaᶜbiyya al-miṣriyya*, Folk-Lore I, Cairo, 1959, p. 36.

78 Justinard: *La Rihla du marabout de Tasaft Sidi Mohammed ben el Haj Brahim ez Zerhouni*, Paris, 1940, p. 196 (from *Al-ḥulal al-mawshiyya*, p. 126). Similarly, E. Lévi-Provençal: *Documents inédits d'histoire almohade*, Paris, 1928, I, traduction p. 129, ftn. 2. Earlier in Tīnmallal Ibn Tūmart put a particular man in charge of looking after a drum in a watchtower; *Documents*, I, Arabic p. 80/French p. 129. For more detailed information see ᶜAbbādī in *Majallat Tiṭwān*, 1960, p. 156 (cf. also p. 153).

to Buṣrā is called a 'drummer' (*ṭabbāl*).[79] No doubt he played his own drum in Buṣrā. In 917/1511 Muḥammad b. Khalīl escorted the Arab ruler to Damascus 'with Ṣumādī drums', in the plural. It was said that when one heard 'their drums' and musical recitals, the heart experienced humility.[80] The Ṣumādiyya beat 'the drums' by night in the Umayyad Mosque.[81] The relic was probably never alone, indeed from the very beginning it was probably a prima donna among other drums.

Playing drums, especially in the mosque, naturally caused offense, and the friends and enemies of the Ṣumādiyya were defined by their attitude for or against drumming. As early as 860/1456, perhaps under ᶜAlī or perhaps only under Khalīl — in any case when the Ṣumādiyya had just recently moved its seat from Ṣumād to Damascus — a certain Ibrāhīm b. ᶜAlī b. Aḥmad b. Burayd al-Dayrī al-Ḥalabī al-Qāhirī al-Dimashqī al-Shāfiᶜī al-Qādirī (816-80/1413-75), author of a biography of ᶜAbd al-Qādir al-Jīlānī, wrote a treatise against the drumming and dancing of the Ṣumādiyya which was entitled *Al-naṣīḥa li-dafᶜ al-faḍīḥa*.[82] Thus a Qādirī takes up a position against a customary practice of other Qādirīs. Somewhat later the two Shāfiᶜites Shams al-Dīn Ibn Ḥāmid al-Ṣafadī and Taqī al-Dīn Ibn Qāḍī ᶜAjlūn (d. 928/1522)[83] in a legal judgement defended the drumming of the Ṣumādiyya by putting it in the same category as the drumming of the pilgrims to Mecca and soldiers,[84] i.e. they detached it from mental association with enticements to forbidden pleasures, committing sins and drinking, and recognized it as a means to encourage man's heart on the mystic path. Ghazzālī (d. 505/1111) had already referred to the singing and drum playing of the Mecca pilgrims and soldiers to show that music can also be permissible, in fact can even be good.[85] Then the Shāfiᶜite Badr al-Dīn Muḥammad al-Ghazzī (d. 984/1577), the father of Najm al-Dīn, in a legal judge-

---

79 Nabhānī, II, p. 7 below.

80 Ghazzī, II, p. 32, l. 11.

81 Ghazzī, III, p. 17, l. 3.

82 *Ḍawᵓ lāmiᶜ*, I, p. 80, ll. 20-21. The author is found in *GAL*, II, p. 122, but the work itself is only listed in the index.

83 Ghazzī, I, p. 117, l. 25. *Shadharāt*, VIII, pp. 157-58.

84 Ghazzī, II, p. 32, l. 3; III, p. 17, ll. 4-6. Muḥibbī, I, p. 50, ll. 3-6.

85 *Iḥyāᵓ ᶜulūm al-dīn*, Cairo, 1957, II, pp. 273-74. Duncan B. MacDonald: 'Ghazzali on Listening to Music', in *JRAS* 1901, pp. 220-21.

ment also endorsed the argumentation of Shams al-Dīn and Taqī al-Dīn in favor of drumming in the mosque.[86]

When and how regularly the Ṣumādiyya held their *dhikr-* and *samā*ᶜ-performance with drums has not been transmitted. That the shaykh had the drums beaten every Friday after midday worship in the circle which would be subsequently formed in the mosque, already lies in the past for Muḥammad b. Khalīl (d. 948/1541).[87] However, one need not assume a total break with this old custom. Judging by the practices in other orders, the Ṣumādiyya could have appointed one or two fixed days or nights in the week for their gatherings. Under Abū Muslim Muḥammad (d. 994/1586) drums were played by night in the mosque; a particular day of the week is not mentioned.[88] But irregular gatherings were also held, during which there is no specific reference to drumming. Abū Muslim Muḥammad, whom we just mentioned, once performed the *dhikr* in Hebron at the grave of Abraham with Muḥammad al-Bakrī and Muḥammad b. Abī'l-Luṭf. Ibn Abī'l-Luṭf beheld the spirit-being of Abraham rise from the grave and enter the circle. Abū Muslim clasped the enraptured Ibn Abī'l-Luṭf in his arms to protect him from the danger of going mad and to bring him back to the firm ground of sobriety.[89] At least once a year Badr al-Dīn al-Ghazzī (d. 984/1577) invited to his house this same Abū Muslim Muḥammad together with the latter's group,[90] probably along with the drums.

What was the job assigned to the drums during these gatherings? From the phrasing in Ibn al-Ḥanbalī, II, 1, p. 169, l. 7, and Ghazzī, II, p. 32, l. 1, one gathers that drums were played 'for (or during) the recollection of God' (*ma*ᶜ*a al-dhikr*), 'for (or during) the intensified recollection of God' (ᶜ*inda...'shtidād al-dhikr*), and 'during the ecstatic rapture of the recollectors of God' (*hayamān al-dhākirīn*). Strictly speaking, this would mean for or in the intoxication of the communal recitation of a formula. But in Muḥibbī, I, p. 50, ll. 2-3, the drumming is described as 'during their listening to music and experiencing ecstasy' (ᶜ*inda samā*ᶜ*ihim wa-wajdihim*). The latter would be performances of songs which one listened to in order to induce a flood of emotions. Apparently the terms were interchangeable

---

86 Ghazzī, II, p. 32, ll. 3-4; III, p. 17, ll. 3-6. Muḥibbī, I, p. 50, ll. 3-4. *Shadharāt*, VIII, pp. 275, 435. Nabhānī, I, p. 181.

87 Ghazzī, II, p. 32, ll. 5-6.

88 Ghazzī, III, p. 17, ll. 2-3.

89 Ghazzī, III, p. 11, l. 16, to p. 12, l. 2.

90 Ghazzī, III, p. 17, ll. 1-2.

and both practices were combined during one and the same gathering. But it may be surmised that solo drum performances also took place. When the above-mentioned Arab prince was given a special escort in 917/1511, the 'Ṣumādī drums' were no doubt played on their own. Ibn Burayd's polemical treatise of 860/1456, according to the statement of Sakhāwī, was against 'drumming (*ṭabl*) and dancing (*raqṣ*)'. It is nowhere mentioned that any other musical instruments were played in the gatherings of the Ṣumādiyya and that these were accompanied by the drums.

(3)

It is possible that the theological attack on drum playing in the *dhikr*- and *samā*ᶜ-performances of the Ṣumādiyya in the 9th/15th century and the defense of this practice by citing drumming during the pilgrimage and in war, was what first led to inventing the legend of origin involving Sālim's/Muslim's/Musallam's drumming at the capture of Acre. The parent drum which was so cherished in the family may even be younger than its children. But this is not necessarily the case. It can also be that the need arose to attribute meaning to the wordless language of drumming. If this meaning were to be holy war, then two paths were open: to recall a holy war which had already taken place and to call people to the inward 'greater holy war'. Even for the outsider the Ṣumādiyya's gatherings aroused respect and awe (*muhība*), propagated a sense of gravity and intimacy (*waqār*, *uns*[91]), and their drumming inspired a desire to set out, a readiness to travel the inner path.[92] Thus this military music produced feelings of elation in the service of a sacred cause, as well as religious enthusiasm and religious ecstasy.

The Kāzarūniyya also made use of military music. Since 620/1223 at the latest, the association of the Kāzarūniyya has unambiguously borne the character of an order. At that time Muḥammad(-i) Abū'l-Mukhtār-i Nawbandajānī in Kāzarūn had himself accepted by the leader Khaṭīb al-Khuṭabā' Khalīfat al-Khulafā' Jamāl al-Dīn Abū Ḥāmid Aḥmad b. Muḥammad, had his hair cut and had a patched frock conferred on himself.[93] Also in the 7th/13th century, in any case before 728/1327-28 which was the date of composition of the *Firdaws al-murshidiyya*, the mother house in Kāzarūn presented it-

91 Ghazzī, II, p. 32, ll. 10-11.

92 Ghazzī, III, p. 17, ll. 5-6.

93 *Firdaws al-murshidiyya*, Chpt. 36, p. 453, ll. 5 ff.

self as a royal residence. It maintained a military band which went on playing a medley of three pieces from Thursday afternoon to Friday, first the 'piece of arrival and the war-cry' (*nawbat-i qudūm u gulbāng*), then the 'piece of border duty and the sultan' (*nawbat-i thaghrī u sulṭānī*), and then the 'piece of victory and glad tidings' (*nawbat-i fatḥ u bashārat*). As is clear from the description which follows, this was drum playing, although the middle piece consisted of a rapid, confused hammering without a regular rhythm, as when someone goes on banging a piece of wood against something. The whole was meant to recall an alleged military campaign against the Christians which involved the people of Kāzarūn under the leadership of the head of the order and in association with the 'caliph of Baghdad', and the middle piece of drum playing was to represent the Hellish nocturnal din that had been raised by the soldiers on that occasion before a city they were besieging. In accordance with their instructions, at the drum signal of the leader of the order, they began wildly banging on pewter, copper and iron vessels, and played tambourines and trumpets so as to make it impossible for the monks to pray inside the enemy city.[94] This legend of origin is certainly an invention but can have influenced the musical form and naming of the separate sections of this nocturnal music. The concert served, on the one hand, to show respect to the dead saint Abū Isḥāq-i Kāzarūnī (d. 426/1035) and his successors, and, on the other, to recall the duty of holy war which the people of Kāzarūn and the Kāzarūniyya, at least in the past, are supposed to have observed. It has nothing to do with a *dhikr*- and a *samā*ᶜ-performance. The daily drumming which took place at his tomb mornings and evenings[95] also corresponded to the practices in a royal household.

However, the foundation-legend about the Ṣumādiyya's drum playing and the foundation-legend about the Friday concert in Kāzarūn have two things in common: first of all there is the idea of the demoralizing effect on the enemy of making noise, of using noise

---

94 *Firdaws*, Chpt. 23, pp. 200-03. Glad tidings (of victory) were actually 'drummed': *ḍuribat/duqqat al-bashāʾir*; Dozy *bishāra*; Yūnīnī: *Dhayl Mirʾāt al-zamān*, Hyderabad, 1954-61, I, p. 165, l. 17; IV, p. 95, l. 1 and p. 213; Ibn al-Dawādārī, VIII, p. 282, l. 14 (a reference kindly provided by U. Haarmann). The customary drumming when breaking camp is not mentioned in *Firdaws*. Surprise attacks launched at dawn with shouting and noise to the accompaniment of percussion and wind instruments are amply attested; an example from Timbuktu occurs in O. Houdas: *Tedzkiret en-nisiān fī akhbār molouk es-Soudān*, reprint Paris, 1966, Arabic p. 121/French p. 197.

95 *Firdaws*, end of Chpt. 5, p. 37, ll. 22-23.

to strike terror into the enemy and to render him defenseless — not explicitly stated among the Ṣumādiyya but portrayed in great detail among the Kāzarūniyya. But since the scope of this subject extends from the trumpets of Jericho to the liberation of the sun from an eclipse by means of instruments of noise, it cannot be discussed here. Secondly, there is the idea of the stirring effect of music on the people and animals within their own ranks — not explicitly stated among the Kāzarūniyya but attested among the Ṣumādiyya for their gatherings. Similarly, this is not the place to enter upon the long march through Sufi reports about the effects of music. I will refer, if only in passing, to the affirmation of the French officer C. Trumelet that the Arab oboes and drums did in fact excite the horses, as he often had occasion to observe for himself.[96]

Related to the drum concerts of Kāzarūn, but then again different from them, is the court orchestra of Imam ᶜAlī al-Riḍā (d. 203/818) at his tomb in Mashhad. In normal times it plays twice a day, before sunrise and before sunset, on holidays an additional two or three times, in Ramaḍān before sunrise and after nightfall, but during the Shīᶜite months of mourning Muḥarram and Ṣafar and on other days of mourning not at all. The instruments in use today are five trumpets without holes (*karranā*) of one meter in length and four drums of different sizes, of which one is beaten continuously and the others in addition and alternatingly. The drumming itself only serves as accompaniment to the trumpets, whereas the trumpets have a message to deliver, they play a text so to speak. The players themselves fit this text to their trumpet blasts and bequeath it orally to their sons who succeed the fathers in the orchestra. It consists of invocations to the dead Imam. The playing is understood as a prelude to the morning and evening prayers but also as a sign of respect for the Imam Riḍā. Earlier, the inhabitants of the city could also tell from the playing that it was time for the city gates to be opened or closed.[97] Doubtlessly this music is played primarily in honor of the Imam. By contrast with the Friday concerts in Kāzarūn (which are no longer

---

96 C. Trumelet: *Les Français dans le désert*, Paris, 1886, p. 105. Similarly, the horses in the army of the Algerian freedom-fighter ᶜAbd al-Qādir, 1833 ff.; Muḥammad b. ᶜAbd al-Qādir: *Tuḥfat al-zāʾir fī tārīkh al-Jazāʾir wa'l-amīr ᶜAbd al-Qādir*, 2nd edition by Mamdūḥ Ḥaqqī, Beirut, 1964, p. 212, ll. 6-7.

97 ᶜAlī Aṣghar-i Sharīᶜatzāda: 'Naqqārakhāna-i Āstān-i quds-i raḍawī', in *Hunar u mardum* 165-66, 1976, pp. 83-88. More information on the *naqqārakhāna* is found in H.G. Farmer's article *Ṭabl Khāna* in the Supplement to the old *EI*.

performed today), it contains no reminder of war and raising the war-cry.

Thus the three groups mentioned all play military music, but in each case they use it and interpret it differently. Only the Ṣumādiyya has adopted it in their gatherings and employed it in order to induce ecstatic states. They have become famous and notorious through their drumming.*l* [98] In this respect, however, they are also far removed from ᶜAbd al-Qādir al-Jīlānī whose disciples they consider themselves to be. ᶜAbd al-Qādir had indeed also laid down rules for the *samāᶜ* but by the latter he primarily understood communal listening to Koranic recitation and he interpreted the mere desire for songs as a weakness.[99] His *majālis al-dhikr*[100] were sermons calling for repentance.

---

98 The North African older ᶜĪsāwa (or ᶜĪsawiyya), so-named after Muḥammad b. ᶜĪsā (d. circa 930/1523-24), exhibit a certain similarity with the Ṣumādiyya. At the *mawlid al-Ḥusayn* in Cairo in the years around 1213/1798 they formed two rows in the mosque when performing their *dhikr*. The one row pronounced the formulas out loud and beat time on drums (*ṭubūl*) and tambourines (*dufūf*), while the others turned about, raised and lowered themselves shoulder to shoulder and stamped on the ground in rhythm; Jabartī: *ᶜAjāᵓib al-āthār fī'l-tarājim wa'l-akhbār*, Cairo, 1322, III, p. 41; Tawfīq al-Ṭawīl: *Al-taṣawwuf fī Miṣr*, Cairo, 1946, pp. 82-83. But according to more recent descriptions, today in Morocco they also use woodwind instruments (*ghayṭa, qaṣaba*) along with drums and large tambourines; in the countryside both can be absent; René Brunel: *Essai sur la Confrérie Religieuse des Aîssâoûa au Maroc*, Paris, 1926, pp. 92-122; Émile Dermenghem: *Le culte des saints dans l'Islam maghrébin*, Paris, 1954, pp. 312-18. One may also compare the Moroccan ᶜAmmāriyya who work themselves into a trance only by listening to the music of large tambourines without bells and of flutes, without an actual *dhikr*; a few formulas are recited beforehand; Willy Haas: 'Eine Ordensübung der Ammaria', in *Der neue Orient* 2, 1917, offprint, pp. 12 ff. The ecstatic assembly of the Moroccan Ḥamādisha is also divided into *dhikr* formulas and music with drums and oboes; Vincent Crapanzano: *The Ḥamadsha. A Study in Moroccan Ethnopsychiatry*, University of California Press, 1973, pp. 185-211.

99 ᶜAbd al-Qādir al-Jīlānī: *Al-ghunya li-ṭālibī ṭarīq al-ḥaqq*, Cairo, 1331, II, p. 114, ll. 13-20; pp. 122-23. ᶜAbd al-Qādir is familiar with the momentary loss of one's reason due to an exceptionally powerful experience: the mother screams when she learns of the death of her child, and so does the mystic in ecstatic rapture during the *samāᶜ*. In order not to be drawn into forbidden areas under effects of this kind the ascetic also renounces what is permitted; *Al-fatḥ al-rabbānī wa'l-fayḍ al-raḥmānī*, Cairo, 1960, p. 255.

100 *Al-fatḥ al-rabbānī*, p. 23.

THE CLEANEST ABOUT PREDESTINATION: A BIT OF IBN TAYMIYYA

(1)

The two authoritative documents which form the foundation of Islam are the Koran and the *ḥadīth*. The Koran contains the words of God which are meant to have been transmitted to Muḥammad by the angel Gabriel. The *ḥadīth* is the collection of the words which Muḥammad is meant to have conceived and spoken on his own initiative. The Koran has been so well transmitted that one may refer to it as the fixed unchanging source of Islam. The *ḥadīth*, on the other hand, is a variable corpus and has admitted accretions so that a great deal of what it contains must be considered very doubtful, indeed spurious. At an early date a rigorous indigenous science had already excluded a substantial amount but there is still much in the varying mass of materials which, having stood the test of that criticism, would scarcely survive a more radical examination, were it possible to undertake such a procedure. Whereas for some time Islamic thought and individual motives had still been able to introduce new texts into the *ḥadīth*, this was not possible in the case of the Koran. Here later new concepts could only be read into the text through commentary and reinterpretation. Ignaz Goldziher has sketched this process[1] and shown that a great part of the movements and denominational divisions of Islam can be traced in the history of Koranic exegesis. The pious southern Iranian Abū Isḥāq-i Kāzarūnī (d. 426/1035), by way of illustrating the fact that all endeavors, even the most eccentric and most wayward, perpetually and unabashedly have recourse to the Koran, employs the simile of rain which waters all plants and nourishes the sweet as well as the sour and bitter fruits. In the same way correct and false religious views seek support in the Koran.[2] A special problem was raised by the scientific discoveries and theories of the modern West. But confirmed Muslims bridged

---

1 I. Goldziher: *Die Richtungen der islamischen Koranauslegung*, Leiden, 1920.

2 *Firdaws al-murshidiyya*, ed. F. Meier, in Bibliotheca Islamica 14, Leipzig, 1948, p. 299, l. 15, to p. 300, l. 2 (in Chpt. 27).

this gap as well by finding that all possible results of such research were already contained in the Koran.[3]

Naturally, an outsider doesn't have the right to deny to Islam particular views which a Muslim claims for his religion. But just as a Christian theologian can reject as false and unchristian certain assertions which another Christian puts forward, by the same token a Muslim religious scholar may denounce as un-Islamic a theological thesis which another Muslim defends but which is in disagreement with that scholar's conception. And yet the scholar, as well, does not apply an independent standard based on objectivity, because normally he adheres to the positions of a particular denomination, and the Islamic denominations deviate from one another with regard to the *ḥadīth* variables and their scholastic elaboration, and rest on foundations which are different in each case. A Shīʿite does not base his views on the same assumptions as a Sunnī. To this one may add the taboo of the Islamic profession of faith which affects all Muslims equally — that there is only one God and in His revelation to Muḥammad He has communicated for the last time in a universally binding way. But even when one accepts these and a few other purely natural restrictions to freedom from prejudice, there still remains a platform on the basis of which a number of very attentive thinkers, in good conscience and with holy zeal, have been able to raise the call to return 'to the sources' and thereby to the allegedly unique, all-important and irrefutable truth. Indeed, one must even say: to the 'naked' truth because it was gained, or regained, by stripping away everything which was not in the Book and had not been usage in the original Muslim community. Whatever else was still living practice in Islam, the individuals who raised this call pejoratively designated in the traditional manner as 'innovations' (*bidaʿ*), although, as they themselves were often aware, such a term is not completely accurate since part of this living practice consisted of atavisms or sprang in fact from the vital impulse of the eternal soul, while other parts had not been intended as pious devotional practices but as helpful relief actions. The attempt to conciliate these elements with Islam and assimilate them was made by those who raised the call from the other side, the theologians who set about their work not by stripping away (privative) but by annexing and integrating (annexive and insertive), or to overstate the point, by means of procedures that were innovation-friendly. A leading figure of the first

---

3 William Thomson, 'The Renascence of Islam', in *Harvard Theological Review* 30, 1937, pp. 62 f. Cf. Henri Pérès, *La Littérature Arabe et l'Islam*, p. 47 f.

party was Ibn Taymiyya (d. 728/1328), a leading figure of the second was Abū Ḥāmid al-Ghazzālī (d. 505/1111) — two of the greatest theological thinkers within Islam and indeed beyond the confines of Islam. Ghazzālī represented a theology of the half-opened door, Ibn Taymiyya was for closure, for a return to the beginning. Here we will only be focusing attention on Ibn Taymiyya.

On the extraordinary personality of Ibn Taymiyya we possess excellent and easily accessible studies, which spares us the burden of going further afield.[4] It will suffice to touch on a few chief points here. The kernel of Ibn Taymiyya's world view is formed by the conviction that the Prophet Muḥammad was the last and the only mediator of God's communication in words to mankind who still has absolute validity. This would appear to be nothing new but Ibn Taymiyya — without declaring it explicitly each time — puts stress on the past tense 'was'. Muḥammad is dead and thus today cannot mediate, either upwards or downwards, between God and man. This he had once done, downwards, as a prophet and he will do it again, upwards, as intercessor on Judgement Day after the resurrection. But he will not do so now. Therefore, it is also not possible to invoke him and to ask him for anything, not even to put in a good word with God. Even more meaningless are any such requests directed to other beings, for example saints, the so-called 'Friends of God', or angels. At the moment there are no mediators between man and God. Furthermore, all attempts to know God through one's own efforts, to draw close to Him, or somehow to partake of Him or have some share in Him, are also worthless in Ibn Taymiyya's eyes. According to Ibn Taymiyya, there are no paths to God, neither the speculative one of the philosophers or scholastics, nor the path of mystical self-purification or self-abnegation. These are at best dead ends that come to a premature halt. Nor, in Ibn Taymiyya's view, can man find the truth by seeking a deeper hidden meaning in the Islamic fundamental texts, or by conceiving of the Islamic fundamental texts as a particu-

---

4 H. Laoust *EI*[2] Ibn Taymiyya and the literature cited there, especially H. Laoust: 'La biographie d'Ibn Taimiyya d'après Ibn Kaṯīr', in *Bulletin d'Études Orientales* 9, 1942-43, pp. 115-62; H. Laoust, *Essai sur les doctrines sociales et politiques de Taḳī-d-dīn Aḥmad b. Taimīya*, in Recherches d'Archéologie, de Philologie et d'Histoire, Cairo, 1939. Alfred Morabia, 'Prodiges prophétiques et surnaturel démoniaque selon Ibn Taymiyya', in *Actes du 8me Congrès de l'Union Européenne des Arabisants et Islamisants* (Aix-en-Provence 1976, Edisud 1978), pp. 161-72. Laoust at the end of his *Essai*, pp. 633-61, gives an extensive list of primary and secondary sources relevant to the whole subject of Ibn Taymiyya and Muḥammad b. ʿAbd al-Wahhāb.

lar form of truth concocted for the ordinary people, from which one may attempt to distill the real truth by means of abstraction. For Ibn Taymiyya the religious truth is perfectly evident, and then solely and exclusively in the holy texts of the Koran and *ḥadīth*. He says, as do others also, 'Koran and *sunna*' and by *sunna* he means the authentic *ḥadīth*s which convey the correct picture of what Muḥammad did and what he refrained from doing. These texts contain everything which man needs to know about God and is capable of knowing, everything he must do and not do before God, everything he can and should know concerning the sense and the proper conduct of his life. Nor may one change anything in this model for some purpose which is allegedly advantageous and well-pleasing to God: what is only allowed may not be presented as recommended, and what is only recommended may not be presented as something which has been commanded. Where several interpretations are possible, these do not provide definitions but only examples for illustrating a fundamental statement. Arrangements which are tolerated or created for the sake of a particular interest but are not grounded in scripture, i.e. so-called 'unsupported measures of expediency' (*maṣāliḥ mursala*), are deemed superfluous along with exaggerated religious devotions which are not required by scripture. Only acts which extend religious duties, but not exaggerated acts, are allowed since Ibn Taymiyya cannot reject the Prophet's statement about works of supererogation (*ḥadīth al-nawāfil*).

(2)

Basing himself on the principle that the whole of Islam has been sketched in the Koran and the *ḥadīth*, and an example has been set by Muḥammad and the first three generations of Muḥammad's followers, Ibn Taymiyya denies that later Muslims have any right to develop a new form of piety or new personal styles of piety. Such styles, according to Ibn Taymiyya, deviate from Islam or run contrary to Islam. The question of religious style has ceased to exist, or one may say it has been answered in the sense that only the earliest form of Islam is correct. By the same token, it would seem that judgement has been passed on Sufism as well, because the Sufis, under this name, are only authentically documented, i.e. on the basis of contemporary written sources, from the beginning of the 9th century, or around 200 years after Muḥammad. Later writings also attribute the epithet Sufi retrospectively to some earlier persons who lived as far back as the first half of the 2nd/8th century. But whether they really bore this name and, if so, why, can unfortunately no longer be established. Efforts at backdating the term to the time of Muḥammad are partly based on etymological speculation and partly on the later, 4th/10th century extension of the term to include 'mysticism, spirituality' in general. Ibn Taymiyya correctly derives the designation from *ṣūf* 'wool' and maintains that the movement of the Sufis arose in Baṣra in the 2nd/8th century, without however indicating that the name too was indigenous to Baṣra: Baṣra was the bastion of pious, ascetic fear of God, Kūfa was the stronghold of juridical acumen. This explanation easily takes us back to the generation of 'the followers of the followers', i.e. to the third and last generation of the golden age, indeed, according to certain of Ibn Taymiyya's own indications, even back to the second generation. However, Ibn Taymiyya unequivocally states: 'The designation Ṣūfiyya was not known (*mashhūr*) among the three generations.' But does this mean that Sufism was in fact excluded? No, not really. Characteristic traits of classical Sufism, of 'moral Sufism' as Ibn al-Khaṭīb (d. 776/1375) put it at a later date,[5] and of post-classical Sufism as well, Ibn Taymiyya believes he recognizes already among the Companions of the Prophet and, vice versa, characteristic traits of the Prophet's Companions are found among some celebrated Sufis. He mentions with praise, besides Ḥasan al-Baṣrī who was certainly too early to be a Sufi, Ibrāhīm b. Adham, Fuḍayl b. ᶜIyāḍ, Maᶜrūf al-Karkhī, Abū Sulaymān al-Dārānī, Bishr al-Ḥāfī, ᶜAbdallāh b. al-Mubārak, Shaqīq al-Balkhī, Ḥīrī, Junayd, Sahl al-Tustarī, ᶜAmr b. ᶜUthmān al-Makkī, Abū Ṭālib al-Makkī, ᶜAbd al-Qādir al-Jīlānī, ᶜAdī b. Musāfir, Abū Madyan and others still, and he has nothing against supporting those Sufis of his own day and age who live in convents on charitable donations and deserve to do so. There is a form of Sufism, however, which goes beyond the limits, and from this he fears dangers to Islam as he understands the latter, indeed he sees that these dangers have to a large extent already set in and inflicted devastation. He warns against such Sufis because his zeal and the injunction to stand up for the good and condemn the false make it impossible for him to allow evil things to run their course and the Sufis simply to behave as they do (*taslīm al-ḥāl ilayhim*).

It should be immediately added that his call to action did not unleash a persecution of the Sufis or bring about changes in Sufism. Neither the Mamluk government in Cairo, nor its deputy authority in Damascus were inclined to reshape established society according to

---

5 *Rawḍat al-taᶜrīf bi'l-ḥubb al-sharīf*, Cairo, 1966, p. 614, l. 7.

Ibn Taymiyya's blueprint, or to set up an inquisition against the Sufis in any form whatsoever. As matters stood, it was the other way round: Ibn Taymiyya was prosecuted on several occasions and locked up because of his unflinching and consistent behavior. His theses did repeatedly give impetus to efforts to renew Islam on the basis of the old sources, and he had some able disciples, though only much later in the 12th/18th century. When Muḥammad b. ᶜAbd al-Wahhāb once again took up Ibn Taymiyya's ideas of reform and succeeded in winning over the princely family of Ibn Saᶜūd, a new situation emerged and through this association of reformist theology with political and military power a danger did arise for Sufism. But things had not gone this far during Ibn Taymiyya's lifetime. There was much that Ibn Taymiyya found fault with in Sufism. Here I only wish to single out some small amount, just so much as is necessary to clarify the relationship between his criticism of Sufism and his teaching about divine predestination. The accusations can be divided into two separate piles.[6]

a) One thing Ibn Taymiyya holds against the Sufis is their excessive valuation of experience and exceptional states. According to Ibn Taymiyya, they often place both of these above the Koran and the *sunna*. Ibn Taymiyya does not dispute the existence of religious experiences and exceptional religious states. But whatever these phenomena mean always remains on a lower level than the Koran and the *sunna*. Ibn Taymiyya does not even deny dreams or waking visions in which man may see God. But the person dreaming or having the vision does not see God directly, according to Ibn Taymiyya, but only by means of an image which depends in each case on the individual's inner disposition. In Ibn Taymiyya's view man can definitely experience revelations and inspirations but these can be erroneous and man ought never to value them so highly that he considers them to be as true and binding as the Koran and the *sunna*. The caliph Abū Bakr is better than the caliph ᶜUmar because Abū Bakr in his capacity as a *ṣiddīq* was exclusively guided by the Koran and the *sunna*, whereas ᶜUmar in his capacity as a *muḥaddath* 'one who receives supernatural speech' also listened to higher voices which can give information but may also deceive.

---

6 My primary sources are Ibn Taymiyya's treatises in the *Majmūᶜat al-rasāʾil al-kubrā*, 2 vols., Cairo, 1323, and in the *Majmūᶜat al-rasāʾil wa'l-masāʾil*, 2 vols., ed. Muḥammad Rashīd Riḍā, Cairo, 1341-49, as well as Ibn Taymiyya's *Fatāwī*, 5 vols., Cairo, 1326-29. But not exclusively. I only quote directly by way of exception and for the first two collections mentioned use Laoust's abbreviations *MRK* and *MRM*.

Overestimating the value of an exceptional state is especially dangerous when miraculous powers are involved, as for example in the case of the thaumaturgic feats (*ishārāt*) of the Rifā^ciyya. Indeed, participants as well as the onlookers easily fall into the erroneous belief that higher powers are at work here, that God has intervened. In these circumstances it is often a question of charlatanism in Ibn Taymiyya's view, and where this is not the case the devil is operating under the surface because for Ibn Taymiyya when something cannot be divine but does exist, it must originate with the devil. Thus in his view Satan enters on the stage when persons in a state of ecstasy rise into the air, dance about on the heads of others, walk on fire, foam at the mouth and scream out. For Ibn Taymiyya is as far removed from 'enlightenment' as Luther.[7] In his thinking the idolatrous Tartars are black and the Muslims white; the Rifāᶜiyya, on the other hand, are covered with black and white speckles.

According to Ibn Taymiyya, however, the means employed by the Sufis to attain such questionable, even Satanic, achievements are not only to be rejected because they lead to doubtful, in fact erroneous, results, but also because they do not belong to the acts which God or Muḥammad have established as religious worship. Ibn Taymiyya counts among correct religious practices the ritual prayers, reading the Koran, the recollection of God (*dhikr*) and prayers of supplication — in this sequence, though for Muslims who so wish or for whom it must be otherwise a different order of precedence can be agreed upon. And he also holds it to be licit at times to withdraw in seclusion (*iᶜtikāf*) in the mosque. But he disapproves of the spiritual retreat (*khalwa*) of the Sufis and rejects their argumentation based on Muḥammad's long rites of atonement in the cave of Ḥirāᵓ, because a form of behavior of the Prophet from before Islam cannot be considered valid. As for the forty days associated with spiritual retreat, they are of Jewish and Christian origin and were not admitted into Islam by Muḥammad. Ibn Taymiyya condemns the 'absolute' night vigils that were customary during Sufi spiritual retreats and condemns the 'absolute' observance of silence, as well as the practice of fasting during which the ration of food was ingeniously diminished by weighing it with wood that was in the process of drying out: the more the wood dried out and thereby decreased in weight, the less the person on retreat would eat. Recollection of God (*dhikr*) he acknowledges in the form that the early forefathers practiced, as well

7 Muḥammad Kurd ᶜAlī compared him with Luther. Laoust, *Essai* (cf. ftn. 4 above), rejects this comparison. In my opinion, despite all the differences, the comparison is inescapable.

as in the form of concentration on the profession of faith 'There is no god but God' or sentences expressing a wish and an assertion like 'Glory be to God', 'Praise be to God', 'God is great', but not by way of stammering such as 'God, God' or 'He, He' which by itself does not mean anything. It is even more wrong in his view if the Sufis justify abbreviations like this by saying they did not intend to recollect God with them but only to focus their heart, and for that purpose any means will do. The result, of course, is that Satan enters into the formulas. The correct way to empty the heart, according to Ibn Taymiyya, is to remove from it everything God would not want to be in it and to make room for pious fear of God, love for Him and trust in Him. Forms of entertainment involving music or generally 'inspired by the Muses' (*samāᶜ*) Ibn Taymiyya relegates entirely to ignominy in the profane realm and to the company of women out to have a good time at weddings with a tambourine and hand-clapping. Nowhere in the law is music and poetry prescribed as 'a path to God' and as a means to induce a pious mood, a sense of nostalgia or sadness, but they are extraneous intrusions and thus illicit. The first three generations of Islam knew nothing of this. Only by the end of the 2nd century, i.e. around 800 AD, did the religious *samāᶜ* first appear and it immediately mobilized the great theologians against it. Ibn Taymiyya mentions Shāfiᶜī (d. 204/820) who is meant to have been a witness of this practice in Baghdad. Ibn Taymiyya ought also to have referred to Mālik (d. 179/795) who even somewhat earlier received news of *samāᶜ*-performances among the Sufis in Nisibis in Northern Syria,[8] and would then have noted that the last of the three model generations could well have already known something about the *samāᶜ*. But, of course, Ibn Taymiyya only wishes to say that the exemplary forefathers themselves did not perform the *samāᶜ*. He equates this practice with 'the whistling and hand-clapping' which in surah 8/35 is expressly described as heathen. Pious emotion triggered by music and poetry he only judges permissible if it happens without being prearranged, i.e. through the accidental hearing of sounds and verses. He rejects any measures taken to provoke a reaction. Finally, Ibn Taymiyya feels obliged also to speak out against hashish and *banj* which he considers to be a commodity imported by

---

8 Qāḍī ᶜIyāḍ, *Tartīb al-madārik*, ed. Muḥammad Tāwīt al-Ṭanjī, ᶜAbd al-Qādir al-Ṣaḥrāwī, Aḥmad Barkāsh, Rabat, 1965 ff., II, pp. 53-54/ed. Aḥmad Bukayr Maḥmūd, Beirut, n.d., I, p. 180. Variants in Aḥmad b. Muḥammad al-Khallāl, *Al-ḥathth ᶜalā'l-tijāra wa'l-ṣināᶜa wa'l-ᶜamal*, Damascus, 1348, p. 24; Ibn al-Jawzī, *Talbīs Iblīs*, Cairo, 1928, p. 370 (toward the end of *bāb* 10).

the Tartars, thus of quite recent date (from the 7th/13th century), and puts it on a par with wine which is prohibited. He forbids both of them in general but remarks that at that time hashish was misused for religious purposes and dubbed 'a morsel (*luqma, luqayma*) for the recollection of God and meditation' — a not unimportant confirmation of somewhat earlier reports from the 13th century which had noted with disapproval that the Sufis made use of hashish.

Ibn Taymiyya demanded the comprehensive discontinuation of exceptional states, experiences, visions and revelations in so far as they were elevated to the level of equal or even higher sources of authority than the Koran and the *sunna*, and the discontinuation of all forms of worship (*ᶜibādāt, qurubāt*) which were not prescribed or recommended. In their place he put theological knowledge and the legally prescribed religious acts. Preferences and feelings which stand in the way of these, well-being, successes and failures, practical considerations, and inferences based on reason alone have no place in true Islam. The only valid standards for Muslim thought and action are the Koran and the *sunna*. Ibn Taymiyya is in favor of 'Apollonian' intellectual clarity and against all forms of 'Dionysian' rapture. He writes: 'Thus anyone who receives inspirations, inner communications and revelations, since he is no better than ᶜUmar, must conduct himself in such a way that he adheres to the Koran and the *sunna* and follows what the Apostle of God proclaimed and does not subordinate to his own emotional experiences what the Apostle of God proclaimed. Those who made false judgements and erred, did not do this but were content with what they had as an experience, believing that the latter released them from the duty to conform to transmitted knowledge.'[9]

---

9 *Al-furqān bayn al-ḥaqq wa'l-bāṭin*, *MRK*, I, p. 56 (I read *tarakū* instead of *wa-tarakū*). — That Ibn Taymiyya in a small commentary on ᶜAbd al-Qādir al-Jīlānī's *Futūḥ al-ghayb* always considers inspiration (*ilhām*) as better than sayings of the Prophet which are based on weak authority should not be understood any differently than when Ibn al-Marzubān (d. 309/921) prefers dogs to a good many people who have distinguished themselves through their coarseness; Muḥammad b. Khalaf Ibn al-Marzubān, *Faḍl al-kilāb ᶜalā kathīr mimman labisa'l-thiyāb*, ed. Ibrāhīm Yūsuf, Cairo, 1341/*The Superiority of Dogs over many of Those who wear Clothes by Ibn al-Marzubān*, trans. and edited by G.R. Smith and M.A.S. Abdel Haleem, Warminster, 1978. One tradition has invented a patched frock of the Qādiriyya for Ibn Taymiyya because of his interest in ᶜAbd al-Qādir and because of the instruction he received from Shams al-Dīn ᶜAbd al-Raḥmān b. Abī ᶜUmar Ibn Qudāma al-Maqdisī (d. 682/1283); on this instruction *Shadharāt al-dhahab* (year 682), V, p. 378, and Ibn Rajab: *Dhayl ᶜalā Ṭabaqāt al-ḥanābila*, ed. Muḥammad Ḥāmid al-Fiqī, Cairo, 1372, II, p. 308 (nothing about a patched

b) The other thing Ibn Taymiyya reproaches the Sufis for is not their overzealousness but rather the opposite: their lack of a sense of duty just referred to above. Ibn Taymiyya believes he detects among the Sufis an inclination towards indifference to the commands and prohibitions, indeed a tendency almost to hold the laws in contempt. They view the religious prescriptions and any infringement of them much too lightly and are happy to let things turn out however they may turn out. They consider what they do as being on the same plane as what happens to them, and they gloss this over by referring to the doctrine that only what God has predetermined comes to pass, and by invoking the virtue that one should be content with everything which God sends.

Here Ibn Taymiyya is touching on an old well-known concern of the Sufis: their endeavor not to have endeavors but to acquiesce in everything, including what is unpleasant, to be thankful, to submit to the will of God, to entrust themselves completely to God (*riḍā*, *tafwīḍ*, etc.), in the presence of God to be like a corpse on the board of the corpsewasher.[10] Old classical Sufism had already chosen this state of renouncing one's will before God as one of its highest goals, though not its very highest. But this is also a characteristic trait of the Sufism contemporary with Ibn Taymiyya, in particular of the classicizing (neo-classical) mysticism of the Shādhiliyya. Their spokesman at that time in Egypt, Ibn ᶜAṭāᵓallāh al-Sikandarī (d. 709/1310), had recently placed the old 'giving up planning' (*tark al-tadbīr*) in the form of 'dropping planning' (*isqāṭ al-tadbīr*)[11] in a central position and elevated contentment (*riḍā*) above love.[12] If the same Ibn ᶜAṭāᵓallāh in 707/1308 tripped up Ibn Taymiyya before the court in Cairo, playing on the fact that the latter had declared it forbidden to call upon Muḥammad for help and seek Muḥammad's me-

---

frock). But from this to infer membership in an order is to misunderstand the language of such artificial constructions. Such a thesis is represented by George Makdisi, 'Ibn Taymiyya: A Ṣūfī of the Qādiryya Order', in *The American Journal of Arabic Studies* 1, 1973, pp. 118-29; idem, 'L'Islam hanbalisant', in *REI* 43, 1975, pp. 57-58; on Ibn Taymiyya's acknowledgement of inspiration (*ilhām*), *American Journal*, p. 128.

10 'Khurāsān and the End of Classical Sufism', p. 202. The saying about the corpsewasher was applied to God in early times and then transferred to the shaykh.

11 Abū'l-Wafā al-Ghunaymī al-Taftāzānī: *Ibn ᶜAṭāᵓallāh al-Sikandarī wa-taṣawwufuhū*, Cairo, 1958, passim.

12 Ibid., p. 209.

diation in prayers to God,[13] this appears rather strange. After all, Ibn ᶜAṭāʾallāh himself always emphasized the direct proximity of God and consequently encouraged man to entrust himself and his affairs to God alone. But he felt Ibn Taymiyya's verdict lacked the warmth of piety and perhaps that is why, on this point, he came forth as the advocate of popular devotions. To explain the hostility between the two men it is alleged that Ibn Taymiyya had criticized Ibn ᶜAṭāʾallāh's litany formulas and his doctrine of the inner stations leading to God.[14] In fact, as we have seen, Ibn Taymiyya did attack certain *dhikr*-formulas of the Sufis. It may well be that he had Ibn ᶜAṭāʾallāh in mind, or that the latter felt himself implicated since he had actually composed a treatise on 'knowledge of the isolated name'.[15] Perhaps one may read the following sentences as an exchange of blows between them. Ibn Taymiyya writes: 'Many who turn to God and travel the mystic path behold in their travelling the perfected lordliness (*rubūbiyya*) and permanence (*qayyūmiyya*) [i.e. of God] which embraces all creation, individuals and qualities.'[16] And Ibn ᶜAṭāʾallāh writes: 'Do not listen to those who attack our people and mock them... These our people sit before God in genuine sincerity and honest loyalty, and they watch over all their breaths in His presence, have recognized His leadership over them and cast themselves down before Him as prisoners, have given up wishing to help themselves on their own, in shame before His lordliness (*rubūbiyya*) and contenting themselves with His permanence (*qayyūmiyya*)... God has afflicted our group with people [who think differently], especially with the representatives of external theo-

---

13 Ibn Kathīr: *Al-bidāya wa'l-nihāya*, Cairo, 1351-58, XIV, p. 45 below. The reading in the printed text must be incorrect. Laoust, 'Biographie' (cf. ftn. 4 above), has the correct reading without comment.

14 Laoust, 'Biographie' (cf. ftn. 4 above), p. 143, is silent about the source for the view that Ibn Taymiyya composed his treatise *Darajāt al-yaqīn* (*MRK*, II, pp. 146-51) against him and criticized his *dhikr*-formula and his doctrine of the inner stations on the path to God. According to Taftāzānī (cf. ftn. 11 above), p. 56, a source for this view is Ibn al-Alūsī al-Baghdādī's *Jalāʾ al-ᶜaynayn*. Alūsī belongs to the 13th/19th century.

15 *Al-qaṣd al-mujarrad fī maᶜrifat al-ism al-mufrad*. *GAL S*, II, p. 145. Cf. Makdisi *EI* Ibn ᶜAṭāʾallāh.

16 Letter to Naṣr al-Manbijī, *MRM*, I, pp. 164-65. Also *Aqwam mā qīl*, *MRM*, V, p. 129. *Al-irāda wa'l-amr*, *MRK*, I, p. 336.

logy.'[17] It is striking here that both men make use of the same expressions 'lordliness' and 'permanence'.

But Ibn Taymiyya does not just have it in for the Shādhiliyya, and they are scarcely one of his top priorities. He mentions by name the Qalandariyya,[18] Aḥmad al-Badawī (d. 675/1276),[19] and the Rifāᶜiyya with whom he had had skirmishes in Damascus and whose strange 'states', which Ibn Taymiyya viewed as demonic, their shaykh described as sent directly from God and defended with the saying: 'Nothing happens in the heavens or on earth without the will and wish of God.'[20] But Ibn Taymiyya focuses his attack fiercestly against the doctrine in which it seems to him the value distinctions concerning everything that exists or happens are most brazenly abolished and the question of what is right and wrong, licit and illicit, is no longer even posed: against the doctrine of the equality of all things through their existence, against the doctrine of the unity of all things in their being and the deification of this being, against the ontological monism of Ibn al-ᶜArabī (d. 638/1240) and his disciples. For Ibn Taymiyya this doctrine means nothing more and nothing less than that the Creator and creation are one and the same. By way of labelling it with a name of ill repute that had existed for centuries, he called it 'unification' (*ittiḥād*), indeed 'absolute unification' (*ittiḥād muṭlaq*), because in this case all creatures were one with God, in distinction from merely 'limited unification' (*ittiḥād muqayyad*) according to which only single chosen individuals merged with God in a unity and which Ḥallāj (d. 309/922) had taught.[21] The other well-known expression of heretical reputation, 'incarnation' (*ḥulūl*), he applies, likewise in the two forms 'absolute' and 'limited', to other arch-enemies. The most earnest of them, who exaggerate their religious practices in the sense of the first group discussed above in a) and do too much in the field of good, he designates elsewhere by the name 'those who devote themselves to God' (*mutaʾalliha*), while the most indifferent among them who rather pay too little attention to the commandments, he dubs 'scorners of the law' (*ibāḥiyya*). Yet in both these cases he judges the results and the assumptions to be the

---

17 *Laṭāʾif al-minan*, n.d., p. 130 below. Taftāzānī (cf. ftn. 11 above), pp. 56-57 (read *iktifāʾan*).

18 *MRM*, I, pp. 121-46.

19 *MRM*, I, p. 52 (not p. 56 as Laoust, *Essai* [cf. ftn. 4 above], p. 24, writes).

20 *Munāẓara*, *MRM*, I, p. 142, ll. 1-4.

21 *Tuḥfa ᶜirāqiyya*, in *Majmūᶜat al-rasāʾil al-munīriyya*, Cairo, 1343-46, reprint 1970, IV, end, p. 44, ll. 1-5.

same: a one-sided, only half-correct interpretation of the proposition that everything comes from God.[22]

Ibn Taymiyya does not doubt the correctness of this proposition *per se* because he knows that the devil was also created by God and cannot do anything except what God wants him to do. Ibn Taymiyya cannot do otherwise than acknowledge that God is at the hub of all that happens. But what upsets him about those who constantly cite this proposition but refuse to obey God is their blindness to the other half of its contents, namely that the commands of revelation also come from God! Since nothing happens which God does not will, then certainly not only the good and pleasant, but idolatry, sins, errors and all evil committed by man are also willed by God. That is one part. However, what has also been willed by God is avoidance of idolatry and sins, prevention of evil in the world, obedience to God's commandments, love of God, etc. That is the other part. The one has to do with that which happens, the other with that which a person should do and not do. One may designate both as the will of God because He wills both, each in a different way. The Sālimiyya in the 4th/10th century expressed this point by saying that God willed good acts from (*min*) human beings, the bad acts through (*bi*) them.[23] But one can also designate both as the command of God, since in fact for everything God decides upon He issues the command (surahs 2/117; 3/47): 'Be!' Ibn Taymiyya gives a whole series of other terms for this double will of God: power (*qudra*), ruling (*ḥukm*),[24] realities (*ḥaqāʾiq*), reality (*ḥaqīqa*), permission (*idhn*), decision (*qaḍāʾ*), dispatching (*baʿth*), sending (*irsāl*), effecting (*jaʿl*), words (*kalimāt*). All have two aspects, one for the area of what happens and one for the area of what should be. Except for 'reality' and 'realities', he documents both forms of usage of each of these terms with verses from the Koran, though he does this incorrectly in my opinion for the term 'will' (*irāda*) when he cites surah 6/125.[25] The adjectives which must be added to distinguish between the two trends of each of these terms are 'existential' (*kawnī*) for the will of God which causes something to happen and 'religious' (*dīnī*) for the will of God concerning what should be done or not done, more rarely 'predestined'

22 Letter to Naṣr al-Manbijī, *MRM*, p. 165.

23 I. Goldziher: 'Die dogmatische Partei der Sālimijja', in *ZDMG* 61, 1907, p. 77, ll. 35-38. F. Meier: *Abū Saʿīd-i Abū l-Ḫayr*, in Acta Iranica 11, 1976, pp. 74-75.

24 *Aqwam mā qīl*, *MRM*, V, pp. 150 and 158.

25 *Al-furqān bayn awliyāʾ al-raḥmān wa-awliyāʾ al-shayṭān*, Damascus, 1962, pp. 111, 123, 127-35.

(*qadarī*) for the first and 'commanded' (*amrī*) or 'legally prescribed' (*sharʿī*) for the second. The division of the divine will into one half for creation, to put it more generally, and into another half for what is only a command, a liking, a preference, something pleasing, is an age-old distinction in Islamic theology, and already at an early date the tendency emerged to designate the will of causation, the existential will, simply as will (*irāda*) and the religious will, the will of commands, simply as command (*amr*).[26] By way of replying to a written inquiry from Egypt in the year 714/1315 about the nature of God's power of creation and His command, Ibn Taymiyya himself composed a somewhat lengthy legal response which bears the title *The Will and the Command*.[27]

In this and other writings as well Ibn Taymiyya stresses and repeats time and again that the Sufis leaned too heavily in the direction of God's existential will and at the same time forgot about His commands or pushed them into the background — or worse yet — cast His commands to the wind and then covered this up with the thesis of God's existential will and predestination. As Muslims and Sufis they knew that the one real and highest determiner of everything that happens and is done is God. But, consciously or unconsciously, they overlooked the fact that God is also the only one who can give them commands unconditionally. For Ibn Taymiyya God is called 'Lord' (*rabb*) because He is the decisive Determiner and Creator of all things, and that explains the acknowledgement of this fact in 'the profession of His unique lordliness' (*tawḥīd al-rubūbiyya*). The Sufi who fixes his one-sided gaze on this 'existential reality' 'sees that God is the Creator and Lord of all things and does not distinguish between what God loves and finds pleasing and what He hates and disapproves of, even if the latter is something He has determined and decided Himself.' 'He beholds the kind of joining together (*jamʿ*) which all creatures have in common, those who are saved and those who are lost', 'the friends and the enemies of God, the angels close to God and the insubordinate devils. For they all have in common this joining together, that is to say this existential reality. It consists of the fact that God is their Lord, Creator and Master and there is no Lord besides Him. But he does not see the separation (*farq*) which

---

26 Some references in *Abū Saʿīd-i Abū l-Ḫayr* (cf. ftn. 23 above), pp. 74-76; Louis Gardet: *Dieu et la destinée de l'homme*, Paris, 1967, p. 121. In connection with Ibn Taymiyya cf. Daniel Gimaret: 'Théories de l'acte humain dans l'école ḥanbalite', in *BEO* 29, 1977, p. 165 (*Mélanges Henri Laoust*, I).

27 *MRK*, I, pp. 318-86.

God placed between His friends and His enemies, between believers and unbelievers, pious and impious, candidates for Paradise and candidates for Hell.'[28] 'Here many scholastics and Sufis have slipped... They affirmed His predetermination and believed that God is the Lord and Possessor of all things, that what He wills exists and what He does not will does not exist, that He is the Creator of all things — and this is good and right. But they were lacking with regard to command and prohibition, promise and threat, and went so far in this that they let themselves be seduced into heresy (*ilḥād*) and turned into a form of polytheists like those who exclaimed (surah 6/148): "Had God so wished, neither we nor our fathers would have practiced idolatry and we would not have declared anything forbidden."'[29] Ibn Taymiyya does not perceive it as a contradiction to lower this one-sided 'profession of God's unicity' (*tawḥīd*) to the level of 'polytheism' (*shirk*) because in the Koran the polytheists themselves take refuge in God's world domination and defend themselves by referring to His predestination.[30] Thus he also boldly calls it 'the polytheists' profession of God's unicity' (*tawḥīd al-mushrikīn*) and considers it more erroneous than Judaism and Christianity, and more erroneous than the other extreme, i.e. only acknowledging the divine commands and denying predestination. He explains that it is especially reprehensible for someone to make use of divine predestination to argue against obeying the divine commandments. 'Whoever affirms predetermination and uses it to argue for abolishing the commands and prohibitions is worse than the person who affirms the commands and prohibitions, and does not affirm predetermination.'[31]

So according to Ibn Taymiyya, there exists this other second one-sidedness which denies predetermination and only conceives of God as Commander and Judge. In this case God's relation to man is a looser one. Here, to the observer, man possesses the freedom to obey

---

28 *Al-hajr al-jamīl*, *MRM*, I, p. 3.

29 *Aqwam mā qīl*, *MRM*, V, pp. 127-28. *Al-irāda wa'l-amr*, *MRK*, I, pp. 334-35.

30 As opposed to determinist propaganda which conversely represents the denial of divine predestination as polytheism; Josef van Ess: *Zwischen Ḥadīṯ und Theologie. Studien zum Entstehen prädestinatianischer Überlieferung*, in Beihefte zur Zeitschrift *Der Islam*, N.F. 7, Berlin, 1975, p. 159. In this fundamental work earlier studies on the Islamic doctrine of predestination are made use of and recorded. In this connection see also the speculative insights and comparisons with Christian conceptions in Louis Gardet: *Dieu et la destinée de l'homme*, Paris, 1967.

31 *Aqwam mā qīl*, *MRM*, V, pp. 128-30. *Al-irāda wa'l-amr*, *MRK*, I, p. 335.

or not to obey. His will is not kept on a leash by God. Ibn Taymiyya calls this other position, which only recognizes God's commands and places the decision to act one way or another completely in man's hands, 'the profession of the unicity of divinity' (*tawḥīd al-ulūhiyya*), because for him 'God' in the narrower sense means the one who issues commands. He reproaches the Muᶜtazilites and the Shīᶜites for maintaining this attitude and for being blind to God's penetrating and all-embracing existential will, thus making it clear that he does not attribute any Sufi-like talents to these two groups. As far as this opinion is concerned, he is advocating what had been a conventional judgement.[32] But, of course, the relations are not so simple as would seem from Ibn Taymiyya's depiction of the counterpoles.

(3)

The correct attitude of the Muslim according to Ibn Taymiyya is full acknowledgement of both propositions, the proposition of divine predetermination that lies behind all events, and the proposition concerning the divine command which one should obey. The proposition of predetermination or the existential will of God allows the believer to be thankful in good fortune and in misfortune to recognize that God is testing him. The proposition concerning God's will expressed through His commands admonishes man to recoil from the forbidden and urges him to repentance, to action, to doing his duty.[33] To begin with one conceives of the combination of the two propositions as the joining together of two components of a whole that lie close to one another. Ibn Taymiyya actually placed the two sides opposite one another as extremes. But on the basis of this treatment, one might well come to the conclusion that one should consider God's predeterming will as His preponderant, overarching, highest will. Ibn Taymiyya certainly leaves no doubt that in all circumstances predetermination lies behind everything, has the first and the final word in all matters. But the doctrine of divine predetermination is of such subordinate significance for the practical area that Ibn Taymiyya is

---

32 The Sufi Muᶜtazilites Faḍl al-Ḥadathī, Abū ᶜImrān al-Raqāshī and Ḥusayn al-Kūfī, who supported an 'akratia' and at the very least demanded that one immediately depose a ruler who offended against religion, are not relevant for this judgement; Josef van Ess: *Frühe muᶜtazilitische Häresiographie*, Beiruter Texte und Studien 11, 1971, Arabic text of Nāshiʾ, pp. 82-83/commentary, pp. 43-44.

33 *Ibṭāl waḥdat al-wujūd*, *MRM*, I, p. 75.

concerned with and seems to him in his day and age and among the people he is addressing and those he is talking about to be such a commonplace and so obvious that he only treats it as a preparatory topic and seeks progress by means of respecting the will expressed in God's commands. The concept of predestination approximates the human inclination to follow the lusts and is dismissed as 'instinctive and natural judgement'. That as backing it can also be an incentive to acts of self-sacrifice Ibn Taymiyya did not take into consideration. But he says correctly that one should not extinguish oneself (*fanāʾ*) in 'the profession of God's unique lordliness', but one must go forward to 'the second judgement'.[34] For Ibn Taymiyya this step constitutes advancing beyond the preliminary goal toward the real goal,[35] the step out of 'the joining together' in which everything is the same way, namely as God has willed it, and into 'separation' in which good and bad are distinguished. It is the step from lower to higher, since as Ibn Taymiyya would have it: 'The polytheists are worse than the Zoroastrians.'[36]

But besides this the two propositions are different in another way. 'Predetermination is something one can only believe in; one cannot use it to argue with', writes Ibn Taymiyya.[37] One cannot dispute with God on the basis of a correct or good act — in this regard Ibn Taymiyya cites a saying of Sahl b. ᶜAbdallāh al-Tustarī (3rd/9th century)[38] — rather man must unambiguously give precedence to obedience, because what he can know or know in advance is never his ability or his destiny, whereas he is certainly familiar with the commands. These have been revealed or issued by Muḥammad and possibly explained by theologians and jurists and interpreted in their ramifications. Since by definition God's predetermination embraces everything that happens, this also includes the decisions taken by human beings, their knowledge, and their compliance with and implementation of His religious commands. Therefore, not only what happens to a person, but what he does as well, is predetermined. Thus two forms of predetermination constantly stand face to face: an objective one, predetermination of what exists or results if I inter-

34 *Al-iḥtijāj bi'l-qadar*, *MRK*, II, p. 115.

35 Ibid., p. 89.

36 *Aqwam mā qīl*, *MRM*, V, p. 128, ll. 3-4. The Islamic non-determinists were metaphorically designated as the 'Zoroastrians of this community'. On the emergence and the early history of this term Josef van Ess (cf. ftn. 30 above), pp. 137-48.

37 *Ibṭāl*, *MRM*, I, p. 89, ll. 13-14.

38 Ibid., p. 93.

vene correctly or falsely or not at all, and a subjective one, predetermination as to whether I intervene and how. Neither of these two is accessible to me or only a part of the first kind, the part which is graspable in a chain of causation or 'God's habit of creation' — though even this is not considered absolutely certain. On the other hand, the law, located on a higher level, is accessible to me though only 'if God so wills', and in it God has made known the will of His command. This I am obliged constantly to play off as the binding expression of God's will against the other one — though once again this can only be done 'if God so wills' — to seek by means of it to correct or hinder His other will, that of disobedience. In support of this Ibn Taymiyya frequently cites, though not always with precisely the same wording, the pronouncement of the Ḥanbalite Sufi ᶜAbd al-Qādir al-Jīlānī (d. 561/1166) whom he greatly esteemed: 'Many are stopped if they arrive before [God's] decision and predetermination. But for me a door has opened in this situation: I fight against what God has predetermined, with God for the sake of God. A real man is the person who fights against what is predetermined, not the person who adapts himself to it.'[39] And Ibn Taymiyya himself expresses this in the following terms: 'A human being has been commanded to fight on the path of God [i.e. for the sake of God] and to repel predetermined sins with obedience which has likewise been predetermined. For the sake of God he must combat what is forbidden and has been predetermined by means of what is commanded and has been predetermined. This is the religion of God with which He sent forth the first and the last of His prophets.'[40] His eloquent disciple Ibn Qayyim al-Jawziyya (d. 751/1350 in Damascus) repeats the golden words of ᶜAbd al-Qādir, while he describes and clarifies the view of his teacher as follows: 'A man's interests even here in this life are only fulfilled by repelling predeterminations by means of other predeterminations. How could it be otherwise for their life in the hereafter? God ordered the repulsion of a bad act, although it is due to His predetermination, by means of a good act which is also due to His predetermination. Thus hunger is due to His predetermination, and He has ordered it to be repelled by eating which is likewise due to His predetermination. Were man to surrender to hunger and die although it was in his power to repel it through the predetermination of eating, he would then die a sinner. In the same way cold, heat and thirst are due to God's predetermination. God has ordered

39 Letter to Naṣr al-Manbijī, *MRM*, I, p. 166. *Al-iḥtijāj bi'l-qadar*, *MRK*, II, p. 89.

40 *Iḥtijāj*, *MRK*, II, pp. 89-90.

them to be repelled by means of the predeterminations of their opposite. What repels, what has been repelled and repulsion are due to His predetermination.'[41] According to Ibn al-Qayyim, on the basis of this 'second judgement' man should give supremacy to 'the reality of religion' over 'existential reality'.[42] In the school of Ibn Taymiyya the divine existential will is thus demoted to the level of a common denominator concerning which man no longer has to waste many words. It sets the tone and though it must be borne in mind, one is not obliged to keep one's sight permanently fixed on it. Man does not have to deal with predetermination but he must do battle on the field of commands and obedience. Even correct behavior in the face of immutable destiny or good fortune also comes under the jurisdiction of the divine command, of God's religious will.

Since everything that exists and happens is based on God's existential will and this corresponds to God's predetermination, man's capacity to do what is right — his decision to do so, his carrying it out and his success — is determined by God. The passage cited from Ibn al-Qayyim and many similar ones found in the writings of his master Ibn Taymiyya show moreover that the secondary causes (*asbāb*), not least of which are the actions of man for which he will be punished or rewarded in the hereafter, are also provided by the Creator and should be used by man. Naturally, this as well is only possible for man if God intends it for him and wills it. Thus in view of this all-embracing predestination the question of God's justice recedes from the foreground. Nevertheless, a Muslim may only refer to God as 'just' and never as unjust because the Koran so stipulates. Where one can glimpse His justice remains mysterious. One is safest if one proceeds on the assumption of a 'higher' justice which cannot be measured with earthly standards, a justice 'without how'. It was precisely here that the Muᶜtazilites erred. Whereas they removed the sensual conceptions from the image of God, they introduced abstract human ideals, especially man's conception of justice. The principle that applies to all God's attributes also applies to God's justice: it exists but we do not know how. According to Ibn Taymiyya, all God's actions are good and beautiful, just[43] and wise.[44] Whoever, as is proper, acknowledges 'the commands' and 'predetermination' but disputes 'God's higher justice and wisdom' resembles the devil who

---

41 *Madārij al-sālikīn*, ed. Muḥammad Rashīd Riḍā, Cairo, 1331-34, I, p. 109 above.

42 Ibid., p. 137.

43 *Qāᶜida fī'l-muᶜjizāt*, *MRM*, V, p. 28.

44 *Aqwam mā qīl*, *MRM*, V, pp. 119-26, 146-47.

opposed his manner of thinking to God and, by way of taking revenge because God caused him go astray, has resolved to do the same to man by means of dissembling temptations (surah 15/39).[45]

Ibn Taymiyya has summarized the elements of his doctrine of predestination in a section of his treatise *Marātib al-irāda*, *The Divisions of God's Will*, in which he gives answers to a series of questions on the subject of the work's title. One of these questions was whether in surah 51/56: 'And I only created mankind and the *jinn* in order that they might serve Me' the conjunction 'in order that' (*li*) is meant in a consecutive or in a final sense. Ibn Taymiyya understands it in the final sense and thus must explain how something God would like does not necessarily have to happen. For this purpose he presents an outline of his doctrine of predestination which I have here translated and provided with numbers and letters:[46]

'One must know that two kinds of [divine] will (*irāda*) occur in the Koran.

1) The first kind is the existential will (*al-irāda al-kawniyya*). This is the will which necessitates the coming about of that which is wished and concerning which one says: "Whatever God wills, happens; whatever He does not will, does not happen." It is this will which is mentioned in surah 6/125: "And if God wills to guide a man, He opens his breast to Islam, and if He wills to mislead him, He makes his breast narrow and closed", and in surah 11/34: "And my counsel, when I [Noah] counsel you, shall not profit you if God wills to mislead you." In addition, it says in surah 2/253: "And if God (p. 70) had willed it, they would not have fought against one another; but God does whatsoever He desires", and in surah 18/39: "When you entered your garden, why did you not say: 'What God wills [is what I see]! There is no strength save in God'", and there are other similar passages. And it is this will which is referred to by the words "to that end" in surah 11/118-19: "But they continue to be disunited, except those on whom your Lord has shown mercy. To that end [i.e. for disunity] He created them." The earliest members of the [Muslim] community said: He created one group for disunity and one group for mercy, and since His will here as well as there[47] was of the existential kind, what was willed in that way also came about: certain people became disunited, others found mercy.

2) The second kind is the will of religion, God's will as expressed in the law (*al-irāda al-dīniyya al-sharʿiyya*). This is the will with which God loves what He has wished and finds pleasure in it, the will with which He also loves and finds pleasure in the people concerned and rewards them with what is best as in surah 2/185: "God

---

45 *Al-irāda wa'l-amr*, *MRK*, I, p. 348.

46 *Majmūʿat al-rasāʾil al-kubrā*, Cairo, 1323, II, pp. 69-71.

47 The printed text is corrupt.

wishes ease for you and does not wish hardship for you", surah 5/6: "God does not wish to place a burden on you; rather He wishes to purify you and to perfect His favor to you", and surah 4/26-28: "God wishes to make this clear to you and to guide you along the path of those who went before you, and to turn to you in mercy. God is All-knowing and All-wise. And God wishes to turn to you in mercy but those who follow their lusts wish for you to go far astray. God wishes to lighten your burdens, for man was created weak."[48] This will does not necessitate the coming about of that which is wished, unless the first kind of will is joined with it.[49]

In view of the above a fourfold division results, namely:

a) The first involves both kinds of will (i.e. 1 and 2). This is the case with pious works which actually come about since, on the one hand, God wills these with His will of religion and law, orders them, loves them and finds pleasure in them, and, on the other hand, He also wills them with His existential will so that they then come about. Without the latter this would not happen.

b) The second only involves God's will of religion. This is the case when God commands that pious works be carried out but the unbelievers and sinners do not obey this command. All such works belong to the will (p. 71) of religion. God loves them and finds pleasure in them, whether they come about or not.

c) The third involves the existential will only. This is the case with occurrences which God has predetermined and wills but which He has not ordered, i.e. actions which are merely allowed (*mubāḥāt*) and sins (*maᶜāṣī*), for He has not ordered them, finds no pleasure in them and does not love them. Indeed, He does not order any shameful actions and finds no pleasure in the unbelief of His bondsmen. But without His willing (*mashīʾa*), His power and His creation they would not have occurred and would not exist because only what God wills happens and what He does not will does not happen.

d) The fourth involves neither the first nor the second kind of divine will. This is the case with the most dissimilar actions which are merely allowed and with sins, none of which actually occurs.'

Thus in Ibn Taymiyya's doctrine of predestination obedience and disobedience to God (sin) are defined quite simply: obedience is an

---

48 Ibn Taymiyya has been misled by the idea that God *loves* these things. But since He does them directly Himself, they belong to His existential will and not to His commands which others carry out — which is what is actually meant. There appears to be no example of this usage of *irāda* in the Koran. That is why in theology there is a preference for the term 'command' (*amr*) instead of religious will. The compulsion to base oneself on the Koran in this case led to a distorted and unconvincing justification from scripture. A predilection on God's part for actions which people and spirit-beings are not involved in and which they are not even commanded to do, really has no place here at all.

49 'With it' (*bihī*) means 'with that which is wished'.

act in which the two kinds of God's will, His existential will (or predetermination) and His will expressed in the law (or His command), coincide. Disobedience is an act in which God's existential will and His will expressed in the law diverge from one another. In this view Ibn Taymiyya gives so much weight to the love of God and to His command that he also includes in disobedience what is merely allowed, because this has not been ordered and cannot be the object of God's pleasure. In this simplification the important distinction between what is merely allowed and what is directly forbidden is cancelled and remains unexplained.

If on our own initiative we transpose Ibn Taymiyya's theory onto the plane of theological cosmic history, the first event in which the convergence and divergence of both God's wills manifested themselves in this extreme form was the devil's fall through sin. The devil is not a fallen angel in Islam but a fallen 'spirit' (*jinnī*), since Islam also recognizes good spirits. Formerly, though a foreigner, the devil — not yet known as such — had been a leading member in the community of angels when God gave the latter the command to bow down before Adam. Among the angels who obeyed, God's existential will and His will as expressed in the law coincided: they bowed down. In the devil, who felt himself called upon to obey but refused, the two kinds of divine will diverged from one another: the devil did not bow down before Adam. God did not will it 'existentially', although he 'commanded' it, that is to say He willed it through His will as expressed in the law.[50] The attempt to save the devil's honor by saying that as a non-angel he was not addressed by the command founders on the Koranic passage 18/50 which expressly states that the devil 'deviated from the command of his Lord'.

The second example that one might perhaps think of turns out to be unsuitable on closer inspection. God ordered Abraham to sacrifice his son — in Islam usually Ishmael — but then God hindered him from actually carrying out the sacrifice. Abraham accepted the command and intended to obey it, i.e. he experienced within himself the convergence of God's existential will and the divine will as expressed in the law before the act came to be carried out. The gruesome exercise was then interrupted prematurely, i.e. in good time,

---

50 Awzāʿī (d. 157/774), in an anti-Qadarite context against Ghaylān al-Dimashqī, but at this early date without the intellectual panoply of Ibn Taymiyya: 'Has God commanded anything which He then prevented (*ḥāla dūnahū*) from being realized?' Answer: 'Yes. He ordered Satan to bow down before Adam but then He did not allow it to happen.' Josef van Ess: *Anfänge muslimischer Theologie*, pp. 208-09.

because, as the Koranic commentator Muqātil b. Sulaymān (d. 150/767) says, God 'ordered' Abraham to sacrifice his son but did not 'will' that he do so.[51] But one is also obliged to say that God cancelled His command.

Not without appeal is the remark that a theology which theoretically carries the power of predestination to extremes is, in practice, inclined to ignore it almost entirely. The fact that predestination is assumed everywhere leads to it becoming something so much taken for granted that one is no longer obliged to talk about it. Even the virtue of coping with it in a proper manner whenever it results in an unalterable situation belongs, as we have seen, to the area of religious commands. Only 'the second judgement', that between good and bad, counts as an act of obedience, even if it at first depends on God's grace and its success in the end lies in the stars. In this way Ibn Taymiyya almost repeats the old non-interventionist slogan with its recommendation simply to do what is ordered and to refrain from what is forbidden,[52] in fact almost switches over to the old Qadarite counter-propaganda which had always warned against people who commit sins and boldly maintain that their actions were predetermined by God.[53]

Fatalism, letting things take whatever course they take, is alien to this theology, as well as to the theology of Ibn Taymiyya's oldest opponent Ghazzālī and Islam as a whole! By contrast, the latter demand individual initiative and action. The means (*asbāb*) at one's disposal for attaining a goal must be utilized. For effecting cures medicines are available, for salvation there are pious works, even if one's ability and success has been predetermined.

Whoever understands predestination incorrectly and makes no serious effort to achieve salvation is a religious renouncer (*mufawwiḍ*). This is someone who leaves everything to God and says: 'Go ahead and act! In any case, everyone only progresses to the stage for which he was created. Whoever belongs to those who will be saved acts as is fitting for salvation. Whoever belongs to those who are lost acts as

51 Ibn Qutayba: *Ta'wīl mukhtalif al-ḥadīth*, Cairo, 1966, p. 30. The assumption that God changes his mind (*badā'*) is considered heretical and is a Jewish accusation leveled against Christians and Muslims; *Schahrastânîs Religionspartheien und Philosophen-Schulen*, trans. by Theodor Haarbrücker, Halle, 1850-51, I, p. 249; Būṣīrī, *Dīwān*, ed. Muḥammad Sayyid Kaylānī, Cairo, 1955, pp. 15-16 (in the *Hamziyya*). Būṣīrī writes Isaac (p. 16, l. 8), not Ishmael.

52 Josef van Ess (cf. ftn. 30 above), p. 155.

53 Ibid., p. 119.

is fitting for perdition. God ran His hand across Adam's back and made two piles with what He removed from him. To the one pile on the right He said: "Get ye into Paradise through My mercy!" To the other pile on the left He said: "Get ye into Hell! Ye matter not to Me." The one who is saved is already saved in his mother's womb; he who is lost is already lost in his mother's womb.'[54] According to Ibn Taymiyya and all theologians, correct behavior consists in this: everyone must strive to belong to the pile on the right because, while he does not know what has been predetermined for him, by following the divine commands he stands the chance of being on the right-hand side.

In order to progress in the here and now it is proper to put one's trust in God (*tawakkul*). But from a theological point of view there are two forms of wrong behavior: if man puts his trust in God instead of making any effort himself, and if man provokes God to act by deliberately ignoring the secondary causes, for example by deliberately travelling in the desert without provisions. Here as well the correct behavior is to combine pious virtue with action. The Prophet, as is stressed, only practiced putting trust in God as an inner state, otherwise he characterized gainful employment as the norm of behavior.[55] Whoever condemns business activities is therefore offending against the norm of behavior, and whoever rejects putting trust in God is violating faith.[56] The Prophet forbade a bedouin to let his camel run free

---

54 Ibn Qutayba (cf. ftn. 51 above), pp. 5-6. The word *muyassar* is somewhat hazy. *Lisān al-ʿarab* translates the sentence in question: 'Everyone is prepared (*muhayyaʾ*), becomes led (*maṣrūf*) and experiences ease (*musahhal*) in the direction of that for which he has been created. That is to say: a person feels unavoidably inclined toward what has been predetermined for him. This is how the determinists — and Ibn Qutayba is one of them — understood the sentence, as J. van Ess (cf. ftn. 30 above), p. 42, correctly states. On the various forms and conceptions of predestination cf. van Ess, ibid., pp. 39-47. — *Mufawwiḍ* is used by Ibn Qutayba in the well-known 'Sufi' sense for someone who surrenders himself and lets God prevail, not in the converse Qadarite sense for someone whom God has allowed to act on his own initiative; J. van Ess (cf. ftn. 50 above), pp. 119-20, and index, p. 267, *f-w-ḍ*; W. Montgomery Watt, *Free Will and Predestination in Early Islam*, London, 1948, index, p. 178, *fawwaḍa*.

55 *Al-risāla al-qushayriyya*, Cairo, 1318, p. 91, ll. 21-22 (*tawakkul*). Benedikt Reinert: *Die Lehre vom* tawakkul *in der klassischen Sufik*, in Studien zur Sprache, Geschichte und Kultur des islamischen Orients, Beihefte zur Zeitschrift *Der Islam*, N.F. 3, Berlin, 1968, p. 248. This outstanding work of Reinert's cannot be recommended strongly enough.

56 *Risāla qushayriyya* (cf. ftn. 55 above), p. 92, ll. 4-5 (*tawakkul*).

while putting his trust in God, and advised him to fetter the camel *and* to put his trust in God.[57]

Ibn Qutayba (d. 276/889) found the same wisdom, without any direct connection with God, in the Indian book of fables *Kalīla wa-Dimna*: 'The certainty of predetermination does not hinder the resolute person from protecting himself against dangers. No one should have his eye on hidden predetermination, but everyone should act with firm resolve.'[58]

However, the Koran and Muḥammad advise believers not to have the nerve to act against God's existential will either in their decisions or their opinions, but to take this great unknown factor into consideration in all their intentions and predictions and to give expression to this by uttering the fixed phrase for exceptions, 'If God so wills!' The use of this phrase has long since been extended to cover all occurrences in the present and the past, whose factuality one cannot absolutely guarantee. The commonness of this phrase along with the similar catchwords 'kismet', 'mektub', etc., that one hears with equal frequency, conveys to Oriental speech an element of belief in destiny and has certainly contributed to reinforcing the false image of Muslims as being fatalistic.[59] As far as this eastern mode of expression is concerned, it is no more than a religious veneer, which is a cover-up or a substitute for utterly simple particles and adverbs, precisely as our 'thank heavens', 'thank God' or 'in God's name'. Translated according to its real meaning, no one would be misled by this turn of phrase. In the sentence 'I will come, if God so wills' it is equivalent to a future particle. In response to 'Will you come?', the reply 'If God so wills' means: 'Yes.' 'If God so wills, nothing has

---

57 Ibid., p. 90, ll. 20-21 (*tawakkul*). Reinert (cf. ftn. 55 above), p. 223.

58 *Taʾwīl mukhtalif al-ḥadīth*, p. 30. ʿAbdallāh b. al-Muqaffaʿ: *Kalīla wa-Dimna*, ed. Ṭāhā Ḥusayn et ʿAbd al-Wahhāb ʿAzzām, Cairo, 1941, p. 241, ll. 10-12: 'Predetermination should not stop a resolute person from protecting himself against something fearsome and from seeking safety in face of a menacing danger, but he must combine belief in predetermination with the mustering of his force and resoluteness.'

59 *Itinéraire d'Anselme Adorno en Terre Sainte (1470-1471)*, Paris, 1978, p. 88: 'Item omnes suos actus et operationes referunt ad voluntatem Dei. Ideo in adversis raro desperant, nec frenetici communiter sunt. Dicunt enim ita esse voluntatem Dei.' But then the author also confirms the existence of the false belief in fatalism: 'Si in loco pestifero sunt non fugiunt quia dicunt esse volutatem Dei quod sint in loco pestifero quem fugere non debent. Si que sit voluntas ejus quod moriantur omnimode exanimentur; si vero sunt extra locum pestiferum illum fugiunt, alias essent causa sue mortis.' The avoidance of places contaminated with the plague as expressed at the end once again corresponds to the theological guideline.

happened to him' means: hopefully. 'If God so wills, he will still come' means: probably. 'If God so wills, he has already come' means: perhaps.

As for any Muslims who are characterized by fatalism — and Ibn Taymiyya criticizes such people — they can find full support for such beliefs in the words of God and the Prophet. But other words stand face to face with these sacred words and demand the opposite attitude. Ibn Taymiyya with his theory of the interaction of God's existential will and the will of His command expressed in the law wishes to show how the contradiction can be resolved and balance can be restored.

ALMORAVIDS AND MARABOUTS

1. *RIBĀṬ* AND *MURĀBAṬA*

From the time that Muḥammad became a statesman in Medina, Islam has also been a religion with regulations for a state community and for waging war against non-Muslims. Thus Islamic soldiers fulfill a religious duty, a duty viewed as being particularly meritorious because not everyone is required to perform it but only men, and then only a sufficient number of them. In addition, this duty is regarded as harder, more urgent and more worthwhile than the pilgrimage to Mecca which, of the five basic obligations of Islam, poses the most difficult demands. Succinct sayings that draw comparisons express the importance and the greatness of holy war. Abū Ḥanīfa (d. 150/767): 'A military expedition (*ghazwa*) after one has performed the prescribed pilgrimage is better than fifty additional pilgrimages.'[1] Muᶜāwiya b. Qurra (d. 13/634): 'It has been said: Every community (*umma*) has its monasticism (*rahbāniyya*). The monasticism of this (the Islamic) community is war on the path of God.'[2] The Islamic community, which from the beginning was warlike and militarily successful and was led as a state, does not look back to a tale of affliction on the part of individuals who professed the faith or forms of passionate suffering as does Christianity or the Shīᶜite opposition within Islam, but to a series of military victories, war heroes and persons who fell in battle. In Islam the place of Christian martyrologies is occupied by the history of *jihād* and *jihād*-romances. Moreover, Muslims who fell in battle had nothing 'to bear witness to'. The word *shahīd* 'blood-witness' appears to have a Christian tinge. The high value conferred on the pilgrimage and holy war creates an oppositional tension between the two: the warrior pursues the tension to the frontier, the outer limit of the circle, whereas the pilgrim is drawn by this tension to Mecca, the central point of the *dār al-islām*.

---

1 Abū'l-Faraj al-Iṣfahānī: *Maqātil al-ṭālibiyyīn*, ed. Aḥmad Ṣaqr, Cairo, 1949, p. 378, below.

2 ᶜAbdallāh b. al-Mubārak: *Kitāb al-jihād*, ed. Nazīh Ḥammād, Tunis, 1972, p. 35. Ignaz Goldziher: *Le Livre de Mohammed ibn Toumert*, Algiers, 1903, p. 383, below.

In both zones, in the middle field around the center and in the frontier area at the periphery, there are two situations for the Muslim and accordingly two forms of behavior: an acute situation and an active form of behavior, on the one hand, and a remaining still and waiting, on the other. At the holy places in the center of the Islamic world the acute situation and positive activity — to retain these expressions — is the pilgrimage (*ḥajj*, *ᶜumra*) itself, whereas the quiet permanent state is voluntary longer- or shorter-term residence in Mecca or Medina, *mujāwara* or *jiwār* 'residing in the neighborhood of the holy shrines'. At the edge of the Islamic world the acute peak is formed by armed conflict, by war (*jihād*) itself, while the quiet intermediary state consists of waiting and watching in military readiness, *murābaṭa* or *ribāṭ* 'being on guard duty or guarding the frontier'. When according to legend Salmān al-Fārisī sought after the pious Abū'l-Dardāᵓ in Damascus, he was informed that the latter was 'on guard duty, guarding the frontier in Beirut' (*murābiṭ bi-Bayrūt*).[3] Towards the end of the Mamluk period the pious still spent time in Beirut for the purpose of *murābaṭa* and *jihād*,[4] and in the Ottoman era in the 10th/16th century a Sufi collected bows and arrows in the weapons market of Damascus for the *murābiṭūn* on the coast of Beirut.[5] A pious individual who was keen to wage war reproached the Mamluk Qānṣūh al-Ghūrī for not having undertaken any action against the infidels, and at his own cost he built or repaired the tower (*burj*) in Damietta.[6] Many a person in the 2nd-3rd/8th-9th centuries died 'on guard duty' (*murābiṭan*) against the Byzantines, not due to actual combat but through illness, accident or old age while on service at the frontier. Disciples of the man of piety Maᶜrūf al-Karkhī (d. 200/815-16) are supposed to have served in a fort south of Sfax

---

3 Ṣafadī: *Al-wāfī bi'l-wafayāt*, part 15, ed. Bernd Radtke, Bibl. Isl. 6, 1979, p. 309, l. 17 to p. 310, l. 1.

4 Najm al-Dīn al-Ghazzī: *Al-kawākib al-sāᵓira bi-aᶜyān al-miᵓa al-ᶜāshira*, ed. Jabbūr, Beirut, 1945 ff., I, p. 61, l. 23 to p. 62, l. 3.

5 Ahmet Halil Güneş: *Das Kitāb ar-rauḍ al-ᶜāṭir des Ibn Aiyūb. Damaszener Biographien des 10./16. Jahrhunderts*, Berlin, 1981 (Islamkundliche Untersuchungen, Band 60), Arabic p. 56, ll. 15-16.

6 ᶜAbd al-Wahhāb al-Shaᶜrānī: *Al-ṭabaqāt al-kubrā*, Cairo, 1954, II, pp. 182-83. Ghazzī: *Kawākib sāᵓira*, I, pp. 84-85. The pious individual in question was Muḥammad al-Dayrūṭī/al-Ḍayrūṭī (d. 921/1515), a wealthy Sufi and merchant who already in his lifetime was venerated by the common people. Ghazzī writes (I, p. 84, l. 23) that he performed *murābaṭa* day and night in a tower built by himself in the border city of Damietta. He was buried in the same city in his *zāwiya*. The tower may have formed part of the latter.

in Tunisia and to have been overtaken there by death.[7] For frontier service of this kind and such cases of death praise was also allotted and a reward in heaven was promised. The activity of the *murābiṭ* 'the man on frontier duty' was the only work, it was said, that continued to grow after his death. One night of *ribāṭ/murābaṭa* surpassed a thousand nights of vigil and a thousand nights of fasting, was better than a thousand such nights of watching at the Kaᶜba or at the Prophet's grave.[8] In a Persian reworking of Aḥmad al-Sanūsī's call to fight against the Italians in the year 1330/1912 we find inserted: 'One encounter with the enemy is better than a thousand visits to the Prophet's grave. A single hour of vigilance in war is better than seventy pilgrimages to Mecca.'[9] There were voices which even elevated guard duty at the border above holy war, because protecting the life of Muslims was meant to be higher than shedding the blood of the polytheists.[10] When it came to commanding or recommending *murābaṭa*, one could refer to the last verse of surah 3: 'You who believe, be patient, vie with one another in patience (*ṣābirū*) and be steadfast (*rābiṭū*)!' And within both fields, in the center and at the outer rim of Islam, the merit of individual acts of piety is combined with giving help to others: at the frontier by protecting the community, and at the central holy places by praying for friends at home — which prayers, it is believed, have a particularly good chance of being heard.[11]

The firmest frontier against the Christian enemy — to remain in the west — was the eastern and southern coastline of the Mediterranean and, beyond the Straits of Gibraltar, along the Atlantic

---

7 ᶜAbdallāh b. Muḥammad al-Tijānī: *Riḥlat al-Tijānī*, ed. Ḥasan Ḥusnī ᶜAbd al-Wahhāb, Tunis, 1958, p. 84/cited in Muḥammad b. Muḥammad al-Andalusī al-Wazīr al-Sarrāj: *Al-ḥulal al-sundusiyya fī akhbār al-tūnisiyya*, Tunis, 1970, I, p. 341.

8 Muḥammad b. Khilfa al-Ubbī: *Ikmāl Ikmāl al-Muᶜlim*, Cairo, 1328/reprint, Beirut, V, pp. 261-62.

9 Abdul-Hadi Hairi: 'The Responses of Libyans and Iranians to Imperialism as Reflected in two Documents', *ZDMG* 130, 1980, p. 377.

10 Ibn al-Ḥājj: *Al-mudkhal*, Cairo, 1929, III, p. 19 (with additional statements of this kind). Ubbī, V, p. 262. Special sayings were invented to stress the merits of guarding the borders in Andalusia: Khālid b. ᶜĪsā al-Balawī: *Tāj al-mafriq fī taḥliyat ᶜulamāᵓ al-mashriq*, Mohammedia, n.d., II, pp. 151-53.

11 Abū Sālim al-ᶜAyyāshī: *Al-riḥla al-ᶜayyāshiyya* (Māᵓ al-mawāᵓid), litho., 1316/ reprint Rabat, 1977, I, p. 9.

southwards as far as Wādī Nūn (Nūl).[12] This enormous front against the sea, across which the enemy had to come, gradually became endowed, in varying degrees of frequency and strength, with watch-towers and forts which could contain larger or smaller garrisons or often perhaps only watchmen. Ibn Marzūq (d. 781/1379) extols the uninterrupted series of watch-towers on the long curving coastline from Safi, 'the end of the world', to Algeria during the time of the Marīnid Abū'l-Ḥasan (732-749/1331-1348, died 752/1361), and the swift pace of the fire signals which in the course of a small part of the night were supposed to have traversed a distance of two months travel.[13] But additionally, between these observation posts and forts, a kind of gathering place was established which was not so much intended for the caravans of domestic trade and longitudinal communication between the fortified points but rather for cautious intercourse with the enemy, and accordingly was surrounded by walls. Maqdisī (4th/10th century) means by this certain cities on the coast of Palestine, such as Ghazza, Ascalon, etc. He notes that in these cities people await Byzantine ships in order to redeem and to sell prisoners of war. A system of signal-towers informs the governing locality in advance, by means of fires or smoke signs, of the hostile party's arrival so that the Muslims have time to arm themselves before negotiating with them. Thus the defenders by no means permanently resided in their defenses in full force but for the most part only flocked together from the outlying area once the signals ap-

---

12 Until 1456 Cape Nun represented the southernmost point of the explored African coast. Cf. Gomes Eanes de Zurara: *Chronique de Guinée*, trans. Léon Bourdon in collaboration with Robert Ricard, MIFAN, Dakar, 1960, p. 66, ftn. 2. Nūn was interpreted by the Portuguese as a negation: no one who journeyed further ever returned. *The voyages of Cadamosto and other documents on Western Africa in the second half of the fifteenth century*, translated by G.R. Crone, The Hakluyt Society, Second Series, No. LXXX, 1937, p. 2. The wording of the German edition of Strassburg, 1534, *Die New welt, der landschaften vnnd Insulen, so bis hie her allen Altweltbeschrybern vnbekant...*, 1b: Also hat er (viz. Henry the Navigator) alle jar die Moren/ seinem furnemen noch/ angereytzt/ vnd schickt seine schiff/ bis sie komen zu dem vorgestaden/ das man nent Caput de non/ das es ein anzeygung sey/ das welche je das vorgestaden furgefaren seyen/ das die selben nit wider komen sind. Darumb haben die alte schiffleut an diesem ort allweg jhrer fart ein end gemacht.

13 Ibn Marzūq: *Al-musnad*, Chpt. 39, *faṣl* 2, in E. Lévi-Provençal, *Hespéris* 5, 1925, pp. 30-31/*Ibn Marzūq, El* Musnad: *Hechos memorables de Abū l-Ḥasan sultan de los Benimerines*, estudio, traducción, anotación, índices anotados por María J. Viguera, Madrid, 1977, p. 330.

peared.[14] In Maqdisī these gathering places are called *ribāṭāt*, sing. *ribāṭ* — a nomen loci which is connected by a common root with *ribāṭ* or *murābaṭa* as an activity 'to be on guard duty', and to begin with means something like 'tethering place for horses' and then 'station for lodging', whether for military or civilian purposes.[15] In the east the exclusively civilian meaning came to prevail, while in the west the exclusively military meaning gained the upper hand. Yet in Maqdisī's description of the sea fortifications on the Palestinian coast the military sense is retained and is even transferred from the fortification itself to all the cities. Perhaps these *ribāṭāt* referred to by Maqdisī were meant when at a later date it was said that in the *diyār miṣriyya* and the *ribāṭāt shaʾmiyya* Ibn Tūmart (d. 524/1130) had already found adherents before his appearance in the west.[16] *Ribāṭ* is also occasionally used in the west for a larger settlement. But there as well it is first of all only a fortified gathering place (camp de concentration)[17] on the Mediterranean and Atlantic coast, on the Iberian Peninsula [18] and frequently in the interior of North

---

14 Maqdisī: *Aḥsan al-taqāsīm*/Al-Mokaddasi: *Descriptio imperii Moslemici*, ed. M.J. De Goeje, BGA 3, Leiden, 1877, p. 177/trans. Gildemeister, *ZDPV* 7, 1884, pp. 170-71/trans. (dependent on the latter) Guy le Strange: *Palestine under the Moslems*, Cambridge, 1890, pp. 23-24.

15 Earlier observers took the military meaning to be the original and the civilian meaning to be a later watered down one. Henri Lammens still held this view: *Études sur le siècle des Omayyades*, Beirut, 1930, p. 247. In this regard Albrecht Noth had a clarifying effect: *Heiliger Krieg und Heiliger Kampf in Islam und Christentum*, Bonner Historische Forschungen 28, Bonn, 1966, pp. 76-83. He subdivides the term *ribāṭ* into four meanings: military base, hospice, center for a saint's cult and a kind of cloister. These coexist together. There are, however, *ribāṭ*s which lost their military character and became cloisters. Noth is aware of the distinction between *ribāṭ* as an activity and Ribāṭ as a settlement (pp. 66, 71, 77).

16 E. Lévi-Provençal: *Documents inédits d'histoire almohade*, Paris, 1928, Arabic p. 32/French p. 47/'Ibn Tūmart et ʿAbd al-Muʾmin', in *Mémorial Henri Basset*, Paris, 1928, II, p. 29. In *Documents* translated as couvents 'cloisters' which does not fit with *diyār miṣriyya*. Lévi-Provençal considers the passage to be spurious. There is often mention of *al-thughūr al-shaʾmiyya*.

17 Lévi-Provençal in *Hespéris* 5, 1925, p. 15.

18 Ibn Bashkuwāl: *Al-ṣila*, ed. ʿIzzat al-ʿAṭṭār al-Ḥusaynī, Cairo, 1955, I, p. 199, ll. 3-4. Ibn al-Abbār: *Al-ḥulla al-siyarāʾ*, ed. Ḥusayn Muʾnis, Cairo, 1963, II, pp. 202-03. Hans-Rudolf Singer: *Conquista und Reconquista im Spiegel spanisch-arabischer Ortsnamen*, in Beiträge zur Namensforschung 18, Heidelberg, 1980, p. 128. — The transition from 'fortress' to 'fortified locality' is attested for several words: *ḥiṣār* in Nāṣir-i Khusraw's *Safarnāma* chiefly means 'fortified locality', otherwise frequently 'fortress'. *Qalʿa* and *qaṣaba* in the east

Africa and Spain. In the case of some of them it is known what they looked like on the basis of archaeological finds or descriptive accounts.[19] The allegedly oldest *ribāṭ* in North Africa, which was founded 180/796 on the coast of present-day Tunisia and has a yearly festival on the 10th of Muḥarram, gave the impression of being a monastery so that the local inhabitants who still spoke Greek, Latin and Berber dubbed it Monastir, a name which was then transferred to the city as well. In connection with nearby Sūsa, instead of *ribāṭ* the term *maḥras al-ribāṭ* 'guard post for serving at the frontier' (*ribāṭ* in the infinitive sense = *murābaṭa*) was employed.[20] Sūsa possessed shipyards and was the base of operations for Asad b. Furāt's venture against Sicily in 212/827 and later as well, and thus served

---

and in the west switched meanings with one another. '*Qalᶜa* appears in the west to have especially designated the fortified city and not the citadel of a city, as in the east; on the other hand, the citadel in the west is *qaṣaba*' (which in the east means rather 'small town', bourg); Louis di Giacomo: 'Une poétesse andalouse du temps des Almohades: Ḥafṣa bint al-Ḥājj ar-Rukūnīya', *Hespéris* 34, 1947, p. 29, ftn. 52. *Qaṣr* means 'castle'; *Kitāb al-istibṣār fī ᶜajāᵓib al-amṣār*, ed. Saᶜd Zaghlūl ᶜAbd al-Ḥamīd, Alexandria, 1958, p. 189, l. 12. But in Morocco it also designates a fortified settlement. G. Spillmann: *Districts et tribus de la haute vallée du Draᶜ*, Tribus berbères II, Villes et Tribus du Maroc, Vol. IX, Paris, 1931, p. 97: 'The inhabitants of the Darᶜa valley sit in fortified settlements which are called qsar (*qaṣr*), pl. qsour (*quṣūr*). These small towns are surrounded by walls and protected by towers. They have one, two or three gates, depending on their importance. As they are they offer protection and a refuge against nomadic robber bands, on condition of course that the residents take the trouble to post a guard.' Many place names have *qaṣr* as their first component. Place names with *burj* 'tower, castle' are said to be as little known for Africa as such names with pyrgos/burgus from pre-Islamic times; A. Pellegrin: *Essai sur les noms de lieux d'Algérie et de Tunisie*, Tunis, 1949, p. 141. In Arabic historiography dealing with the Ful kingdom of Sokoto, on the other hand, the fortified village is almost always called a *ḥiṣn*; A. Brass: 'Eine neue Quelle zur Geschichte des Fulreiches Sokoto', *Der Islam* 10, 1920, p. 36, ftn. 1. In certain regions of the Anti-Atlas the word *mudaa* (moudaa < *mawḍiᶜ*) is used for the fortified village in Shilḥa; Marquis de Segonzac: *Au coeur de l'Atlas*, Paris, 1910, p. 139.

19 Ḥasan Ḥusnī ᶜAbd al-Wahhāb has written something on the subject (cf. his *Waraqāt*, Tunis, 1964-72, II, p. 27). But a corresponding title is not found in his bibliography (III, pp. 26-29).

20 Bakrī: *Al-mughrib fī dhikr bilād Ifrīqiya wa'l-maghrib/Description de l'Afrique septentrionale par Abou-Obeid-el-Bekri*, ed. and trans. by MacGuckin de Slane, 1911-13, new edition Paris, 1965, Arabic p. 35/ French p. 77.

for going on the offensive.[21] For defensive purposes, against attacks from land and from sea, and as a help and refuge for Muslims, further in the south a pious man on the same occasion and using his own resources, expanded the Qaṣr Ziyād into a *ribāṭ* which possessed its own grainfields for the inhabitants.[22] In Algerian Shirshāl (Cherchell) there were several *ribāṭāt* in which many people congregated every year.[23] On the Atlantic Ocean there was a *masjid ribāṭ* 'a mosque for being on border-guard duty'[24] on Cape Spartel, and in the 3rd/9th century, after unpleasant experiences with the Normans, the Berbers transformed the locality Aṣīlā (Arzila) further south on the Atlantic into a *ribāṭ* which was visited by replacements from all the cities, and where a large market was held three times a year[25] — thus once again a transference to the whole locality. Still further south, at the mouth of the Bu Regreg, there arose in the 3rd/9th century on the right-hand side in Salā a *ribāṭ* in which the Muslims mounted guard, and on the left-hand side of the river additional *ribāṭāt* around the ruins of old Salā (Chella). From time to time in the order of 100,000 frontier guards assembled there. The border protection (*ribāṭ*) they undertook was directed against enemies on the mainland, the Barghuwāṭa,*ribāṭ* [26] whose territory lay in

---

21 Georges Marçais: *Mélanges d'histoire et d'archéologie de l'Occident musulman*, Algiers, 1957, I, p. 27. Ḥ.Ḥ. ᶜAbd al-Wahhāb: *Waraqāt*, II, pp. 22-33.

22 Abū Bakr ᶜAbdallāh al-Mālikī: *Riyāḍ al-nufūs fī ṭabaqāt ᶜulamāʾ al-Qayrawān wa-Ifrīqiya*, etc., ed. Ḥusayn Muʾnis, Cairo, 1951, I, pp. 327-32. Albrecht Noth: *Heiliger Krieg*, p. 83.

23 Bakrī, p. 82, ll. 2-3/French p. 165. Martin Forstner: *Das Wegenetz des Zentralen Maghreb in islamischer Zeit*, Wiesbaden, 1979, p. 251.

24 Bakrī, p. 113/French p. 222.

25 Bakrī, p. 112/French p. 220. De Slane interprets *ribāṭ* here as a building, Dozy s.v. *intāba* as the infinitive (= *murābaṭa*). *Intāba* as 'alternatingly visiting' a place is attested; Muḥammad al-Mukhtār al-Sūsī: *Al-maᶜsūl*, Casablanca, 1961, II, p. 54.

26 Ibn Ḥawqal: *Ṣūrat al-arḍ*, ed. De Goeje, BGA 2, 1873, p. 56/ed. Kramers, Leiden, 1939, pp. 81-82. According to De Goeje's edition here as well the city Salā itself is the *ribāṭ* (*wa-hiya ribāṭ*). The text and translation of De Goeje's version also in *Rabat et sa région* I, Paris, 1918, p. 8 (Villes et Tribus du Maroc, Vol. III). Concerning the location H. Basset-E. Lévi-Provençal: *Chella*, Paris, 1923, pp. 6-7 (Extrait d'*Hespéris* 1922), based on De Goeje's edition of Ibn Ḥawqal and therefore inaccurate. A discussion in ᶜUthmān ᶜUthmān Ismāᶜīl: *Tārīkh Shāla al-islāmiyya*, Beirut, 1975, XLIX, pp. 89-95. Later there was a similar confusion about old and new Salā, now clarified by Robert Ricard and J. Caillé: 'Salé-le-Vieux et Salé-le-Neuf', *Hespéris* 34, 1947, pp. 441-42; Louis di Giacomo: 'Ḥafṣa bint al-Ḥājj', ibid., pp. 62-63, ftn. 158. Cf. Muḥammad Ḥajjī: *Al-zāwiya al-dilāʾiyya*, Rabat, 1964, p. 170, ftn. 14; Ken-

the south on the left-hand side of the river and who at that time adhered to their own distorted form of Islam. In the first half of the 13th/19th century, Muḥammad Bello, following the old models, still maintained such *ribāṭ*s or built new ones at the strategically important border points of his kingdom of Sokoto. They were fortresses and walled settlements.[27] These few examples suffice to show that the nomen loci *ribāṭ* designates a base for Islam which, under the influence of the similar-sounding infinitive *ribāṭ/murābaṭa* that describes the activity carried out in it, was moved to the frontier. It can be a fortress or a locality.

But a *ribāṭ* — Bakrī (d. 487/1094) already also has *rābiṭa*, pl. *rawābiṭ*, for *ribāṭ* (Arabic p. 35) — was not simply left to itself but was frequently placed under the supervision and direction of a pious individual. We do not actually know this about all *ribāṭāt* but about such leading ones as Monastir, Qaṣr Ziyād and Tīṭ n-fiṭr at Mazagan/al-Jadīda.[28] Servants were present as well.[29] Monastir had a mosque on its second storey and a shaykh resided there who regulated everything. Men of piety (*ṣāliḥūn*) and *murābiṭūn* detached themselves from family and tribe, and lived here.[30] Others visited the convent at fixed times and then returned home after several days.[31] Among these are to be included the *murābiṭāt*, i.e. women counterparts who were lodged separately.[32] However, women were usually not admitted.[33] The holy war (*jihād*) of women is the journey to Mecca, the pilgrimage.[34] Otherwise, those dedicated to religious de-

---

neth Brown: 'An urban view of Moroccan history. Salé, 1000-1800', *Hespéris Tamuda* 12, 1971-72, pp. 17-18. — One finds the readings Barghuwāṭa, Barghawāṭa and Baraghwāṭa.

27 Murray Last: *The Sokoto Caliphate*, London, 1967, pp. 74-80, and index Ribāṭ (walled frontier town).

28 Yūsuf b. Yaḥyā al-Tādilī, Ibn al-Zayyāt: *Al-tashawwuf ilā rijāl al-taṣawwuf*, ed. Adolphe Faure, Rabat, 1958, pp. 190-92. Henri Basset et Henri Terrasse: 'Le ribâṭ de Tiṭ', *Hespéris* 7, 1927, pp. 117-56.

29 Hady Roger Idris: 'Contribution à l'histoire de l'Ifriḳiya... d'après *Riyāḍ En Nufūs* de Abū Bakr El Mālikī', *REI* 9, 1935, pp. 295-96.

30 Bakrī, p. 36/French p. 78-79.

31 Ibn Ḥawqal, p. 49/ed. Kramers, p. 73.

32 Bakrī, p. 36/French p. 79.

33 Idris, p. 295.

34 Rudolph Peters: *Islam and Colonialism*, The Hague-Paris-New York, 1979, p. 16.

votions (*ᶜubbād*[35]) and *murābiṭūn* are also supposed to have visited the stations and castles (*ḥuṣūn*) between Sfax and Bizerta.[36] Similarly, in the Palestinian coastal fortress (*ḥiṣn*) and city (*madīna*) Arsūf/Ursūf (between Caesarea and Jaffa) there were on hand before the 6th/12th century 'a number of theologians (*ᶜulamā'*) and *murābiṭūn*'.[37] One could insist on the distinct meaning of these terms and wish to separate the *murābiṭūn* from the others, just as one could be tempted to distinguish between *qaṣr*, *ḥiṣn*, *maḥras* and *ribāṭ*. To do either is impossible.[38] Yāqūt contracts the combination 'theologians and *murābiṭūn*' for Arsūf to *murābiṭūn* and counts among them (following Samᶜānī) the traditionist Zakariyyā b. Nāfiᶜ al-Arsūfī (3rd/9th century). We read that Muḥammad b. Saḥnūn (d. 256/870) was once on his way to Qaṣr al-Ṭūb for worship (*ᶜibāda*) and guard duty (*ḥaras*) and while still travelling, with the help of *murābiṭūn*, i.e. a group of men from the fortress, and people from the desert, drove off Christians who had just come ashore. Ibn Saḥnūn, who only had a mule with him, swore never again to go on guard duty without a horse.[39] Even earlier his more famous father Saḥnūn (d. 240/854) had one time in Ramaḍān set out for Monastir as a *murābiṭ* with friends and teachers — just as the man of piety ᶜAbdallāh b. Saᶜīd al-ᶜĀmilī (d. 432/1040-41) did in Toledo[40] and people in Morocco around 600/1200 also did in the *ribāṭ* Shākir (Sidi-Chikèr) in Tensift[41] — and there along with his companions

35 Not *ᶜibād*, as Marçais: *Mélanges*, I, p. 32, writes. Correct in Noth: *Heiliger Krieg*, p. 80.

36 Yaᶜqūbī: *Al-buldān*, ed. De Goeje, BGA 7, Leiden, 1892, p. 350, l. 15.

37 Samᶜānī: *Ansāb*, s.v. Ursūfī. Yāqūt: *Muᶜjam al-buldān*, s.v. Arsūf. Guy le Strange: *Palestine*, p. 399.

38 Idris, pp. 297 f., under the heading Ribāṭs enumerates a series of *quṣūr*.

39 *Riyāḍ al-nufūs*, I, p. 348/Idris, p. 293.

40 Ibn Bashkuwāl, p. 261, no. 591. Albrecht Noth: 'Das *ribāṭ* der Almoraviden', in Wilhelm Hoenerbach: *Der Orient in der Forschung. Festschrift für Otto Spies*, Wiesbaden, 1967, p. 502.

41 *Tashawwuf*, p. 26. Muḥammad Ḥajjī: *Al-zāwiya al-dilā'iyya*, Rabat, 1964, p. 23. Women were also among them. A certain Munya bint Maymūn al-Dukkālī even went there on pilgrimage in the year of her death 595/1198 and is supposed to have said: this year thousands of female saints came into the *ribāṭ*; *Tashawwuf*, p. 313. The author of the *Tashawwuf*, Tādilī, visited the *ribāṭ* from Marrakesh in 603/1207 and spent Ramaḍān there until the eve of the 27th. On the return journey at night a pious old woman fell from her donkey because of a verse a singer sang, and she was dragged on the ground a long time (ibid., p. 394) before anyone noticed. The *Tashawwuf* contains much information about this sacred place.

engaged in lengthy ritual prayers. His teacher Mūsā b. Muʿāwiya al-Sumādiḥī prayed there on the 27th of Ramaḍān through the whole night.[42] The *maḥras al-ribāṭ* of Sūsa served expressly as 'accommodation for the good and the pious' (*maʾwā li'l-akhyār wa'l-ṣāliḥīn*).[43] The same is said of the *ribāṭāt* in Tripoli[44] and in Māssa on the Atlantic Ocean — Māssa which had a *mawsim* 'a yearly fair' in Bakrī's time in the 5th/11th century, and later was to become shrouded in legend.[45] In the *ribāṭ* Ūjdām a certain Abū Muḥammad Jaldāsun al-Rakūnī died in 570/1174-75; as a child he had lost both his hands by falling from a fig-tree and was thus unfit for bearing arms.[46] In the harbor of Algerian Nedroma, Marsā Māsīn, two towers were erected as well as a *ribāṭ* which people visited for the sake of al-Rakūnī's blessing and in which every theft and every sinful offense swiftly met with punishment.[47] Thus in the middle and at both ends of North Africa's long coastline the *ribāṭ* fulfilled the same two purposes: to be a castle for men who were on guard duty and ready for war, and to provide the pious shelter for their religious exercises. Men on guard duty and the pious often must have been one and the same persons.[48] Perhaps one is justified in supposing that mystical interpretations of surah 3/200, which in the east had conferred inward connotations on *murābaṭa*, had penetrated to North Africa or had actually even been thought up there. In that case the *murābiṭ* could have conceived of himself as someone who in his deepest interior remains joined to God, keeps his heart firmly in

---

42 Abū'l-ʿArab Muḥammad b. Aḥmad al-Tamīmī: *Ṭabaqāt ʿulamāʾ Ifrīqiya/Classes des savants de l'Ifriqiya par Abū l-ʿArab... et Moḥammed... al-Ḥošanī*, texte arabe publié avec une traduction française et des notes par Mohammed Ben Cheneb, Algiers, 1915-20, 2 vols., Arabic p. 107/French p. 185. Ed. ʿAlī al-Shābbī and Nuʿaym Ḥasan al-Yāfī, Tunis, 1968, p. 191.

43 Bakrī, p. 35/French p. 77.

44 Bakrī, p. 7/French p. 21.

45 *Ibn Khaldûn, The Muqaddimah*, trans. Franz Rosenthal, Bollingen Series 43, II, pp. 196-97. Vincent Monteil: 'Al-Bakrî (Cordoue 1068), Routier de l'Afrique blanche et noire du Nord-Ouest, traduction nouvelle de seize chapitres', *BIFAN* 30, sér. B., 1968, p. 97. Māssa was reinterpreted as Sijilmāsa when Abū Maḥallī, who was from Sijilmāsa, appeared as the Mahdī in Wādī'l-Sāwira in the 11th/17th century; *Sources inédites de l'histoire du Maroc*, Angleterre, II, pp. 465-74. His name Aḥmad b. ʿAbdallāh was transformed into Om Hamet (= Mḥammad) ben Abdela to bring him into conformity with the predicted Mahdī (ibid., p. 466, ftn. 2).

46 *Tashawwuf*, p. 210.

47 Bakrī, p. 80, ll. 9-12/French p. 162.

48 Noth, pp. 80-81: hendiadys.

agreement with God, instills in his spirit the capacity for vision and in his interior remains loyally attached to love and longing for God or the higher realities — to paraphrase a few remarks of Sulamī.[49] This is not provable. Just as there was a 'greater holy war', the war against oneself, and an inner pilgrimage, the mystic journey, in certain individuals external guarding of the frontier may well have been accompanied by the notion of an inward counterpart. However, we do not know this. But being on guard and praying (both together *al-murābaṭ* instead of *murābaṭa*) in the mosque, in the hinterland as well, was in old times meant to have put to flight the armies of temptations (*fitan*) which are worse than the enemies.[50] In fact, someone could feel himself to be a *murābiṭ* who, in a scarcely or only slightly Islamicized environment, remained unshaken regarding Islam and everything it demands of the faithful, because *rābaṭa al-amr* means 'to adhere strictly to a commitment (or to a command)'. Conversely, instructions concerning municipal government in Seville around 500/1100 require from the judge resolute activity and energy, because his office is a kind of holy war, *ribāṭ* and pilgrimage,[51] i.e. it demands the same zeal and commitment as these do. The main difference, however, between the inhabitants of the *ribāṭāt* and the groups of men in an ordinary fort, judging by Spanish conditions, would appear to have been that the former came together voluntarily and for a reward from God,[52] and likewise they disbanded again whenever they wished. Henry de Castries rightly emphasizes the voluntary aspect when he defines *ribāṭ* as 'a fortified camp where volunteers train themselves for holy war'.[53] Possibly, regular troops

---

49 Abū ᶜAbd al-Raḥmān Muḥammad b. al-Ḥusayn al-Sulamī: *Tafsīr al-ḥaqāʾiq*, on surah 3/200; MS Fatih 262, 30b. Different in Ibn Marzūq: *Musnad*, Chpt. 42, *faṣl* 3/trans. Viguera, p. 339.

50 Abū'l-Ḥasan ᶜAlī b. Aḥmad al-Ḥarāllī (d. 638/1241): *Al-īmān al-tāmm bi-Muḥammad ṣallā'llāhu ᶜalayhi wa-sallam* (perhaps a mistake for *ᶜalayhi al-ṣalāh wa'l-salām*), MS Berlin 1743 (Sprenger 908), 11a, ll. 1-2.

51 E. Lévi-Provençal: 'Un document sur la vie urbaine et les corps de métiers à Séville au début du XIIe siècle: Le traité d'Ibn ᶜAbdūn', *JA* 224, 1934, p. 198, ll. 13-14/Francesco Gabrieli: 'Il trattato censorio di Ibn ᶜAbdūn sul buon governo di Siviglia', *Rend. R. Acc. Lincei* VI, 11, 1935, pp. 884-85/E. Lévi-Provençal y Emilio García Gómez: *Sevilla a comienzos del siglo XII: El tratado de Ibn ᶜAbdūn*, Madrid, 1948, pp. 50-51 (§ 7).

52 E. Lévi-Provençal: *L'Espagne musulmane au Xe siècle*, Paris, 1932, pp. 138-39. Lévi-Provençal: *Histoire de l'Espagne musulmane*, Paris, 1967, III, pp. 78-80.

53 *Sources inédites*, Angleterre, III, p. 105, ftn. 1.

and volunteers could be billeted alongside each other in one and the same *ribāṭ*.[54]

The unusual mixture of warlike spirit and pious mentality and learning which prevailed in the *ribāṭ* as an installation for defense and as an activity, and was characteristic of the institution, is clearly expressed, for instance, in the person of the Spanish religious scholar ᶜAbdallāh b. Saᶜīd b. Lubbāj al-Umawī al-Shantajiyālī (d. 436/ 1045). He lived many years in Mecca and undertook *ribāṭ* numerous times in the west of Spain and what at a later time came to be Portugal. When he sat on his horse, he would voice the wish that God confer on him a martyr's death in the saddle, but then died in Córdoba after a *ribāṭ*-sojourn in the Algarve. In the places where he spent his *ribāṭ*-sojourn people learned sayings of the Prophet from him. Shantajiyālī combined the virtue of residing at the center of the Islamic world (*jiwār/mujāwara*) with the virtue of residing at the frontier (*ribāṭ/murābaṭa*). He remained almost four decades in Mecca, performed in addition to the required once-in-a-lifetime pilgrimage another 35 supererogatory pilgrimages, and on each one he included two visits to the Prophet's grave in Medina so that altogether he honored the Prophet 72 times.[55] But just as one did not limit one's residence in the center at the holy places to breathing in the local air and simply hoping for religious merit, neither did one do this at the frontier. Rather both activities to a certain extent consisted of performing devotions.

So *ribāṭ/murābaṭa* is a complex phenomenon. Armed intervention in order to protect the frontier and threaten non-Muslims forms the foreground. In the background another pious activity was always included. Besides tilling the fields, which could be required, and perhaps other activities that provided a livelihood, residence was chiefly taken up with religious devotions and cultivating a deeper sense of piety, occasionally under the guidance of teachers as well. Or, to put it another way, *ribāṭ/murābaṭa* stands in the middle, so to speak, between religious worship (*ᶜibāda*) and war (*jihād*), and therefore, in the texts, is sometimes associated with the one and sometimes with the other. It is worship pushed forward to the frontier and a form of war which is held back or withdrawn from the battlefield; it appears on one occasion as a *pars pro toto* of worship, and then again as a *pars pro toto* of war. It is a cross between the two, or similarly an

---

54 Noth, pp. 61-66.

55 Ibn Bashkuwāl, pp. 263-65, no. 597, with p. 263, ftn. 1.

overarching concept because it embraces simultaneously both worship and war.

2. *MURĀBIṬ* AND MARABOUT.

The title *murābiṭ*, a participle used as a substantive, should be considered in terms of the complexity referred to above. Just as a *mujāwir* is not a Mecca pilgrim (*ḥājj*) or a visitor to Medina (*zāʾir*), a *murābiṭ* is not primarily a warrior for the faith or a religious war hero (*mujāhid*). To begin with the *murābiṭ* only goes as far as *ribāṭ* as an activity and *ribāṭ* as a bulwark. There he leads a life which combines the two elements of piety and guarding the frontier at the edge of Islamic territory in a state between war and peace. He is a *bellator* and *orator* in one, and to a certain extent perhaps even a *laborator*. Certainly he is located at the front but in a manner of speaking in the second echelon where there is room enough for other things besides the din of arms and language of military command. Whereas *jihād* takes place in a more forward position, *ribāṭ* constitutes its quieter hinterland. In *jihād* there is no time for prayer and talk. The warrior is on the move. When a Muslim is on the move, ritual prayers can be shortened and combined, fasts can be broken. In the *ribāṭ* and during *murābiṭa*, on the contrary, there is a great amount of prayer, preaching and fasting. The *murābiṭ* resides in one fixed place and even has the time to marry.[56] Should no fortification be on hand, those committed to undertaking the defense can form the actual bulwark themselves. When towards the end of the 3rd/9th century in Eastern Algeria the Fāṭimid propagandist Abū ᶜAbdallāh al-Shīᶜī no longer felt sure of his personal safety and moved his residence, many of his adherents, leaving their tribes, attached themselves to him and settled in his immediate surroundings, 'mounting guard over Abū ᶜAbdallāh and prepared to fight for him and to protect him from those who would do him harm' (*murābiṭīn maᶜa Abī ᶜAbdallāh wa-muntaṣibīn li'l-jihād dūnahū wa-manᶜihī mimman arādahū*).[57] Here it is a question of a movement to overthrow the existing power. But otherwise, as a *murābiṭ*, one is involved in war to the extent that one accepts combat operations, indeed trains and at times even goes out looking for action. This is why the Spanish expression *rebato*, derived from

---

56 Ghazzī: *Kawākib sāʾira*, I, p. 62, l. 2.

57 Al-Qāḍī al-Nuᶜmān: *Risālat iftitāḥ al-daᶜwa*, ed. Wadād al-Qāḍī, Beirut, 1970, p. 101, ll. 12-13. Tilman Nagel is incorrect: *Frühe Ismailiya und Fatimiden im Lichte der Risālat iftitāh ad-daᶜwa*, Bonn, 1972, p. 25: 'indem sie an der Seite Abū ᶜAbdallāhs *kämpften*...'

the Arabic *ribāṭ* as an activity, means 'surprise attack'.[58] But *ribāṭ* never has this meaning in Arabic. In any case Ibn Marzūq in his work the *Musnad*, composed in 772/1371, defines *ribāṭ* as 'devoting oneself to holy war and guarding the frontier',[59] though here holy war is the larger framework within which guarding the frontier is one part. Ubbī (d. 828/1425) and Muḥammad al-Sanūsī (d. 892/1487) spend time 'guarding the frontier',[60] and al-Wazīr al-Sarrāj (d. 1149/1736-37) maintains 'unflinching watch where danger from the enemy threatens'.[61] It must be admitted that the living verb with the infinitive *ribāṭ/murābaṭa* later gives greater emphasis to guarding the frontier, whereas the participle *murābiṭ* as a title stresses piety. Both usages then diverge so far from each other that one can say: not everyone who performs *murābaṭa* bears the name *murābiṭ*, and not every *murābiṭ* performs *murābaṭa*.[62] None the less, the pious work of voluntarily guarding the frontier continued to be practiced in Morocco up until modern times. In the second half of the 9th/15th century ᶜAbdallāh al-Waryājilī only taught in Habṭ during the winter

---

58 Noth: *Heiliger Krieg*, p. 86. Noth: 'Das *ribāṭ* der Almoraviden', *Festschr. Otto Spies*, p. 502, ll. 2-5. Lévi-Provençal: *L'Espagne musulmane*, pp. 138-39. Paulo Fernando de Moraes Farias: 'The Almoravids: Some questions concerning the character of the movement during its periods of closest contact with the Western Sudan', *BIFAN* 29, sér. B, nos. 3-4, 1967, p. 816. All from J. Oliver Asín: 'Origen árabe de "rebato", "arrobda" y sus homónimos', *Bull. Real Acad. Española* 15, 1928. Additional information in Robert Ricard: 'A propos de "rebato". Note sur la tactique militaire dans les places portugaises du Maroc', *Bulletin hispanique* 35, 1933, pp. 448-53/reprinted in Ricard: *Études sur l'histoire des Portuguais au Maroc*, Acta Universitatis Conimbrigensis, 1955, pp. 345-55.

59 Ibn Marzūq, Chpt. 42, *faṣl* 3/Lévi-Provençal in *Hespéris* 5, 1925, p. 35/trans. Viguera, p. 339.

60 *Ikmāl Ikmāl al-Muᶜlim*, V, p. 261. Sanūsī in the same place in the same volume.

61 *Ḥulal sundusiyya*, I, p. 241.

62 Subsequently I have read in Jacques Berque on the 8th/14th century: *L'Intérieur du Maghreb, XVe-XIXe siècle*, Paris 1978, p. 53: 'to put oneself in the *ribāṭ*-state' always means more or less to stand one's ground against the infidels, and still several centuries later the emir ᶜAbd al-Qādir used the very same expression. Yet it is strange that from a certain time on, which for the moment we are unable to define precisely, the active participle *murābiṭ* loses this original meaning and comes to designate those 'receivers of the divine' ('capteurs de divin') who establish themselves pretty much everywhere throughout rural society. Maraboutism becomes a special group-term which corresponds with the impetus of popular mysticism and is endowed with an economic and social momentum which at first has no counterbalance in that of the sherifs. This means that the term becomes too broadly extended to preserve a sharp sociological clarity.

and spring. In the summer and fall he was on duty at the frontier.[63] In Tetuan in the 12th/18th century men still took turns replacing one another on *ribāṭ* duty and *jihād*, and then returned again to professional jobs, farming, the crafts or trade.[64] Men presented themselves for *ribāṭ* against Ceuta which at the time was held by the Spanish.[65] In so doing one became a full *murābiṭ* for the duration. In addition there was a form of permanent *murābiṭūn*: the tribes that lived at the sea coast and were obliged to maintain its defense. In exchange they were exempted from paying tax.[66] But otherwise by then the participle *murābiṭ* usually had a different meaning from 'voluntary frontier guard': for a long time it had meant 'pious person', indeed 'holy' man. In other words the two components of the old *murābaṭa* and the old *murābiṭ* had separated from one another and they now openly revealed the two faces of the earlier unity.

Murābiṭ is used much more frequently in the west than in the east. In the east it appears from about the 7th/13th century above all as a laudatory epithet of a ruler in the series *mujāhid murābiṭ muthāghir* 'warrior for the faith, frontier guardian, frontier keeper', and for the generals subordinate to the ruler in the derived form that expresses affiliation *murābiṭī*.[67] In the west, which is all that interests us here, from the later Middle Ages on it tends, as I have said, to have a somewhat different meaning than in early times. In inscriptions it is almost completely absent as a title of Spanish and North African rulers. In early times it is and remains still closely associated with protecting the frontier. If Qaṣr Ziyād, which a pious private individual expanded into a *ribāṭ*[68] in 212/827 and inhabited, was really

---

63 Muḥammad Ibn ᶜAskar al-Shafshāwanī: *Dawḥat al-nāshir li-maḥāsin man kāna bi'l-maghrib min mashāyikh al-qarn al-ᶜāshir*, ed. Muḥammad Ḥajjī, Rabat, 1976, p. 31, no. 16/trans. A. Graulle in *Archives Marocaines* 19, 1913, p. 60.

64 Muḥammad Dāwud: *Tārīkh Tiṭwān*, Tetuan, 1957-75, III, p. 161.

65 Ibid., II, p. 315.

66 *Rabat et sa région IV, Le Gharb (Les Djebala)*, Villes et Tribus du Maroc, Paris, 1918, p. 53: Comme toutes les populations établies sur le bord de la mer, et chargées de ce fait de la défense des côtes, les Baharas jouissaient de certains privilèges et étaient exemptés de toute charge et de tous impôts.

67 Examples in Max van Berchem: *Matériaux pour un Corpus inscriptionum Arabicarum*, Paris, 1903, I, and in the *Répertoire chronologique d'épigraphie arabe*, from vol. X on, quite numerous. The downgrading of subordinates by means of the form in -ī is of course only incidental. In exceptional cases subordinates as well called themselves *mujāhid murābiṭ*, etc.

68 *Riyāḍ al-nufūs*, I, p. 327.

called Qaṣr Ziyād al-Murābiṭ,[69] then the Ziyād in question must have been an early pious frontier guard. ᶜAbd al-Muᵓmin b. al-Mustanīr al-Jazarī belongs to more or less the same period. This person performed a great deal of voluntary frontier service (*ribāṭ*), knew numerous traditions which encouraged such activity (*raghāᵓib al-ribāṭ*) and one time rode through the streets on an old nag to inspire the people to engage in this service.[70] Doubtlessly, Jazarī had deserved the epithet al-Murābiṭ. But he did not bear this surname. On the other hand, 200 years later in Almería we find a judge and expounder of Islamic law Muḥammad b. Khalaf b. Saᶜīd who was known by the name Abū ᶜAbdallāh b. al-Murābiṭ and referred to himself this way on his gravestone. He died 485/1092.[71] The *murābiṭ* alluded to was either his father or an earlier ancestor. Here there is no doubt that the person had some connection with *ribāṭ* as an activity and frontier fortress.

When in the 6th-7th/12th-13th centuries under the aegis of more comprehensive state organization Islamicization in the west had progressed further and was still progressing, the need was felt for more numerous religious centers and places of spiritual guidance and instruction. In cities and rural areas pious individuals founded circles of religious devotion and hermitages which, each according to its particular circumstances, expanded into larger-scale settlements. These gathering points no longer served military purposes and were no longer called *ribāṭāt* (*rubuṭ*, *arbiṭa*), but were known as *rawābiṭ* (sing. *rābiṭa*) and then, for the most part, *zawāyā* (sing. *zāwiya*) 'corners, cells, convents'.[72] Their founders and owners were border guards against unbelief rather than against the enemy, but they were still called, at least by the common people, *murābiṭūn*, since it was customary to apply this term to persons who made a bigger sacrifice on behalf of an Islamic life. The most striking characteristic of the *murābiṭūn* who followed them was not necessarily a high degree of

---

69 Abū'l-ᶜArab, ed. Moh. Ben Cheneb, p. 112/French trans. p. 192/ed. Tunis, 1968, p. 197, penult. line.

70 Abū'l-ᶜArab, p. 11/French p. 191/Tunis p. 197. *Riyāḍ al-nufūs*, p. 205. Georges Marçais: *Mélanges*, I, p. 34.

71 Ibn Bashkuwāl, pp. 527-28, no. 1224. Ṣafadī: *Wāfī*, III, pp. 46-47. Ziriklī: *Al-aᶜlām*, Beirut, 1969-70, VI, p. 348.

72 Cf. *EI* s.v. zāwiya (Lévi-Provençal, IV, pp. 1320-21). The fortified border places of the Sokoto kingdom in the 13th/19th century, following the old examples, take their name *ribāṭ* directly from literature. They were missionary posts and military bulwarks; cf. Murray Last: *The Sokoto Caliphate*, pp. 77-80. The sources were not accessible to me.

education but the piety by means of which they won respect, indeed veneration, in their surroundings and were thus often able to confer a sacrosanct character on their settlement. They themselves wandered across the countryside without any hindrance and also transferred this protection to those accompanying them. Already in the 6th/12th century a certain Abū Ṣāliḥ ᶜAbd al-Ḥalīm al-Haskūrī in Morocco performed this escort service against robbers, and free of charge.[73] In the 19th century the Sharqāwa of Boujad performed the service for money.[74] The exception proves the rule: in 1538 a letter from Fez informs King João III of Portugal that wars had made the roads so unsafe that even the saints (santos) were no longer sure of their lives.[75] But they themselves had little to do with war, or only in the sense that, by dint of their status and relative independence as well as because of their love of peace, they were readily called upon to be mediators in the conflicts of their surroundings. In 709/1310 the Marīnid Sulaymān informed the King of Aragon Don Jaime that the Naṣrid of Granada had sent to him the *ṣāliḥūn*, *murābiṭūn* and the theologians for the purpose of concluding peace.[76] At a later date this pattern repeats with endless frequency. Just as their house was no longer a *ribāṭ*, so their activity was no longer called *ribāṭ* or *murābaṭa*, but came to be known as *murābiṭiyya* (derived from *murābiṭ*), at least according to later texts which shed particularly clear light on the new conditions. Muḥammad al-Mukhtār al-Sūsī writes that when the clan of Yaḥyā al-Ḥāḥī (d. 1035/1626) failed in its attempt to retain power in Tarudant in the south of Morocco, it retreated to a particular Tafilalt in the High-Atlas, which no doubt owed its name to the more famous Tafilalt of Sijilmāsa, in order there to devote itself once again to *murābiṭiyya*:[77] *murābiṭiyya* as the opposite to *mulk* 'rule'. And referring to the Wafqāwiyya tribe in the Anti-Atlas, he writes: 'Today it has renounced *murābiṭiyya* (acting as *murābiṭūn*) and has become submerged in the mass of ordinary

73 *Tashawwuf*, p. 341. Not yet referred to as *murābiṭ*.

74 Dale F. Eickelman: *Moroccan Islam. Tradition and Society in a Pilgrimage Center*, Austin-London, 1981, p. 44, from Charles de Foucauld: *Reconnaissance au Maroc*.

75 *Sources*, Portugal, III, p. 168.

76 *El Ouataïq*. Recueils périodiques publiés par la Direction des Archives Royales, Rabat, I, 1976, p. 307.

77 *Īlīgh qadīman wa-ḥadīthan* (posthumus), Rabat, 1966, p. 79. The transference of the name Tafilalt is conjectured by Émile Laoust: 'Contribution à une étude de toponymie du Haut Atlas', *REI* 14, 1940, p. 48, no. 570.

people (*ghimār al-ᶜawāmm*):[78] *murābiṭiyya* as the opposite of impious people. The 'old Berber word'[79] *agurram* 'pious, saintly', pl. *igurrāmen*, fem. sing. *tagurramt*, to my knowledge cannot be etymologically interpreted as 'border guardian' but is equated with *murābiṭ*[80] and not infrequently replaced by *amrābed*, pl. *imrābden*, which is derived from the latter.[81] Another word for it in Arabic is *faqīr*.[82] In an inscription from Chella, the deceased Marīnid Abū Yūsuf Yaᶜqūb (656-685/1258-1286) bears, among others, the titles *al-zāhid al-murābiṭ al-ṣāliḥ*, *al-murābiṭ* here being placed between 'ascetic' and 'man of piety'.[83] Perhaps this already contains a suggestion of the new meaning, and what is being celebrated is not so much the military dimension as the pious activities associated with his *murābaṭa*. Edmond Doutté rightly points out that Arabic literature in Morocco makes relatively sparing use of the word *murābiṭ* and he explains this as due to a reluctance on the part of educated persons in face of the anti-Islamic overtones the word had acquired in the mouth of the ordinary people, since the common folk applied it to trees, lions, storks, swallows and wagtails when these were considered to be 'holy' and 'sacrosanct'.[84] To this Haedo (Valladolid

---

78 Sūsī: *Maᶜsūl*, III, p. 105.

79 Émile Laoust: 'Pêcheurs berbères du Sous', *Hespéris* 3, 1923, p. 301.

80 Sūsī: *Maᶜsūl*, XV, p. 134, ftn. 1; XI, p. 24, l. 4 from bot. Justinard: *Les Aït Ba Amran*, in Villes et Tribus du Maroc, Vol. VIII, Tribus berbères, Tome I, Paris, 1930, p. 58, l. 5 from bot.: *Chrif d ougerram*/p. 64, l. 7: O chérif, ô marabout. 'Sentry-post, observation-post' in Berber is called *aḍāf/taḍāft*, Émile Laoust: 'Contribution à une étude de la toponymie du Haut Atlas', *REI* 13, 1939, p. 272, no. 197, 199. 'Guard-post' *agauz*, ibid., pp. 273-74, no. 206. More on Berber watch-towers is found in Edmond Doutté: *En Tribu*, Paris, 1914, pp. 314-15. For a sociological perspective on the *agurram* cf. Ernest Gellner: *Saints of the Atlas*, London, 1969, pp. 20, 74, and index.

81 Edm. Destaing: *Dictionnaire français-berbère*, Paris, 1914, p. 211. Biarnay: 'Étude sur les Betᵓtᵓioua du Vieil-Arzeu', *RAfr.* 54, 1910, p. 110, no. 8.

82 Al-ᶜAbbās b. Ibrāhīm: *Al-iᶜlām bi-man ḥalla Marrākush wa-Aghmāt min al-aᶜlām*, Rabat, 1974-77, V, p. 83, ll. 10-11.

83 Henri Basset et E. Lévi-Provençal: 'Chella, une nécropole mérinide', in *Hespéris*, 1922, p. 40/*Répertoire chronologique d'épigraphie arabe*, no. 5201. Not so clear in a later inscription from Fez, Alfred Bel: 'Inscriptions arabes de Fès', *JA* 1917, pp. 321-26/special edition Paris, 1919, pp. 19-24/*Répertoire chronologique d'épigraphie arabe*, no. 6083.

84 'Les Marabouts', *RHR* 41, 1900, p. 27. Doutté: *En Tribu*, Paris, 1914, pp. 4-6: The Moroccan prefers *faqīr*, the Algerian *murābiṭ*.

1612) even added snails.[85] The Berbers also use *agurram* precisely the same way.[86] In better circles a speaker prefers the term *sayyid*[87] for a *murābiṭ* and in written reports a pious person and a holy man are mostly referred to as *al-walī al-ṣāliḥ* or something similar, often coupled with additional expressions including *murābiṭ*. Doutté writes that in the *Nashr al-mathānī* by Muḥammad b. al-Ṭayyib al-Qādirī (d. 1187/1773) the word *murābiṭ* is only ever applied to the rebellious warrior for the faith Muḥammad b. Aḥmad al-ᶜAyyāshī (d. 1051/1641).[88] Doutté overlooks Qādirī's comment on Muḥammad al-Murābiṭ al-Dilāʾī (d. 1089/1678) whose surname he explains as due to his simple clothing, not for instance because of his piety or his service at the frontier.[89] He also overlooks the report on the unusual holy man Aḥmad b. Yaḥyā al-Bādisī (d. 1100/1688) whom the sultan scolds at the tomb of ᶜAlī b. Ḥirzihim in Fez with the following words: 'I know that you are a *murābiṭ* but you are the most badly brought up of the *murābiṭūn*.'[90] Doutté forgets the *murābiṭūn* of Fez mentioned several times in different parts of the *Nashr* who represent a special class of dignitaries along with the sherifs and religious scholars,[91] and most of all those documents in which a holy man's (*walī ṣāliḥ*) descendants, who enjoy privileges conferred by the state, frequently bear the title *murābiṭūn*. Otherwise, authors behave dif-

85 Haedo: 'Topografía e historia general de Argel', French trans., *RAfr.* 15, 1871, p. 219.

86 P. Ange Koller, O.F.M: *Essai sur l'esprit du Berbère marocain*, Freiburg, 1949, p. 322.

87 ᶜAbd al-Munᶜim Sayyid ᶜAbd al-ᶜĀl: *Muᶜjam shimāl al-Maghrib Tiṭwān wa-mā ḥawlahā*, Cairo, 1968, p. 111 (*syyid*). Confirmed by G. Kampffmeyer: 'Weitere Texte aus Fes und Tanger', *MSOS*, 2. Abt. Westasiat. Sprachen, 1913, Jg. 16, p. 53, ll. 21-22, and Muḥammad Dāwud: *Tārīkh Tiṭwān*, Tetuan, 1975, VII, p. 107: In Tetuan circles, especially among women, one uses *sayyid* for every saint (*walī ṣāliḥ*), whether living or dead, whom the people visit and whose blessing they receive. But the same occurs in the east as well, see Rabah Naffakh: 'La conception du monde chez les Beggāra', *REI* 39, 1971, pp. 136-41.

88 'Les Marabouts', *RHR* 41, 1900, pp. 27-29.

89 Muḥammad al-Qādirī: *Nashr al-mathānī*, trans. in *Archives Marocaines* 24, 1917, p. 267. Not in Norman Cigar: *Muhammad al-Qadiri's* Nashr al-mathani: *The Chronicles*, Oxford University Press, 1981 (edition and trans. of the historical parts only). Muḥammad Ḥajjī: *Al-zāwiya al-dilāʾiyya*, Rabat, 1964, p. 82. Without explaining the surname, Muḥibbī: *Khulāṣat al-athar fī aᶜyān al-qarn al-ḥādī ᶜashar*, Cairo, 1284, IV, pp. 203-04 (with his death given as 1090/1679).

90 *Arch. Maroc.* 24, 1917, p. 410.

91 A few passages are given below in ftn. 175.

ferently. Judging by the quotations in Sūsī's *Maᶜsūl*, Abū Sulaymān Dāwūd b. ᶜAlī al-Rasmūkī (d. around 1180/1767[92]) is more generous in his attribution of the title *murābiṭ* than Abū ᶜAbdallāh Muḥammad b. Aḥmad al-Ḥuḍīgī (d. 1189/1775[93]). The author of the *Tārīkh al-fattāsh* (10th/16th century), though he often speaks of 'marabouts', does not use the word at all, but substitutes for it the Mande word *mōri*.[94] Presumably, use of the word *murābiṭ* was limited by the tendency to follow the authoritative standards of literary Arabic of the east.

Thus the European marabout (from *murābiṭ*), in the sense of 'a religious person', was adopted from the vernacular Arabic of Spain and North Africa, not from literary Arabic. Indeed, the Europeans as well did not read Arabic literature but acquired their information on the spot by word of mouth. The word is already found in the Latin plural *morabiti* (id est viri religiosi) in Anselm Adorno who visited Tunis in the year 1470.[95] In 1505 Pedro de Alcalá presents the Christian who wishes to undertake missionary work among the Muslims in reconquered Spain with the three words for 'hermit, recluse' (ermitaño): *murábid* (= *murābiṭ*), *ráhib* 'monk' (= *rāhib*) and *mutebétil* 'a celibate' (= *mutabattil*), and in another place he supplies the Arabic explanation *al morabidin* for the Spanish word al (sic) fráiles which was intended for Arabic ears.[96] The Spanish his-

---

92 ᶜAbd al-Salām b. ᶜAbd al-Qādir Ibn Sūda: *Dalīl muᵓarrikh al-maghrib al-aqṣā*, Casablanca, 1950, no. 986.

93 Ibn Sūda: *Dalīl*, no. 1076; date of death no. 881

94 O. Houdas et M. Delafosse: *Tarikh el-fettach ou Chronique du chercheur*, par Mahmoûd Kâti, Paris, 1913-14, reprint 1981. An explanation of the word in ibid., French trans., p. 25, ftn. 5. More in Vincent Monteil: *L'Islam noir*, Paris, 1971, p. 94 (missing from the enumeration of African synonyms p. 137); Yves Person: 'Samori and Islam', in John Ralph Willis: *Studies in West African Islamic History*, I, London, 1979, pp. 260-63, 270; and elsewhere.

95 *Itinéraire d'Anselme Adorno en Terre Sainte (1470-1471)*, texte édité, traduit et annoté par Jacques Heers et Georgette de Groer, Paris, 1978, pp. 80-81, 146-47.

96 Robert Ricard: 'Remarques sur l'Arte et le Vocabulista de Fr. Pedro de Alcalá', in *Mémorial Henri Basset*, Paris, 1928, II, pp. 233-34. Cf. Marcelin Beaussier: *Dict. pratique arabe-français*, ed. Mohamed Ben Cheneb, 1931, 378b: *murābiṭ al-naṣārā* 'prêtre, moine, religieux'. Charles de Foucauld (d. 1917) was known among French-speakers as the marabout or the marabout des roumis; René Bazin: *Charles de Foucauld. Explorateur du Maroc*, Paris, 1921, pp. 453 ff. And in Arabic: A part of the Shaᶜāniba (Chaanba) who reside in East Algeria call the year 1959 *ᶜām al-murābiṭ* (Aam el-marabout) because a certain Père Blanc visited their camp at that time; A. Cauneille: *Les Chaanba (leur nomadisme)*, Paris (CNRS), 1968, p. 293.

torian of North Africa Mármol (1573) calls the Moorish holy man *Morabito*, pl. *Morabitos*,[97] also describes one of the seven patron saints of the city of Marrakesh as *Morabito*[98] and knows that in the literal sense the Almoravids are *Morabitos*, although they would be called *Morabitinis* (= *murābiṭīn*) by the indigenous writers.[99] In a planned treaty in Spanish between King Philip IV (1621-1665) and the Moriscos of the *qaṣaba* of Rabat, the previously mentioned rebel opponent ᶜAyyāshī is described as *morabito*.[100] According to Haedo, the Moriscos considered the Christian saints and the Apostles, especially Santiago, to be *Morabutos* and recognized them as such.[101] Written forms such as *moravito* are also found (*Sources inédites*, Espagne, I, p. 155; Angleterre, III, p. 142). In 1561 the Portuguese chronicler of Aṣīlā (Arzila), Bernardo Rodrigues, describes the marabouts as *moravatos* que são os *mais relijiosos* em sua seta[102] and also uses the form *morabete* for the singular.[103] The editor gives

---

P.A. Peyriguère, in El-Qbab 1928-59, was considered as a 'marabout des Chrétiens et des Ichqern'; Jeannine Drouin: *Un cycle oral hagiographique dans le Moyen-Atlas marocain*, Paris, 1975, p. 88, ftn. 1.

97 Luis del Mármol Carvajal: *Descripción general de Affrica*, 1573/facsimile, Madrid, 1953, I, 196b-197a, 252a, 276b, etc.

98 Ibid., I, 247a.

99 Ibid., I, 149a. In Latin chronicles in Spain (*Chronica Adefonsi Imperatoris*, ed. L. Sanchez Belda, C.S.I.S., Madrid, 1950, España Sagrada XXI, and *Chronique latine des rois de Castille*, ed. Çirot, *Bull. Hisp.* 1912, 1913) under the influence of a Biblical thought pattern the Almoravid morabitos (as well as the earlier ones elsewhere) were designated *Moabitas* (sic); Nevill Barbour: 'The significance of the word *Maurus*, with its derivatives *Moro* and *Moor*, and of other terms used by medieval writers in Latin to describe the inhabitants of Muslim Spain', in *Actas IV Congresso de Estudos árabes e islâmicos Coimbra-Lisboa*, Leiden, 1971, pp. 260-61. Cf. Bernard Richard: 'L'Islam et les musulmans chez les chroniquers castillans du milieu du Moyen Âge', *Hespéris Tamuda* 12, 1971-72, p. 122: O Jesus of Nazareth, here are the *Moabites* (sic) and the *Agareni*, your enemies as well as ours.

100 Georges S. Colin: 'Projet de traité entre les Morisques de la casba de Rabat et le roi d'Espagne, en 1631', *Hespéris* 42, 1955, pp. 17-25 (Spanish original and French translation).

101 Louis Cardaillac: *Morisques et Chrétiens*, Paris, 1977, p. 33 (Spanish quoted). Trans. in *RAfr.* 15, 1871, pp. 218-19. Cf. Robert Ricard: *Mazagan et le Maroc sous le règne du sultan Moulay Zidan (1608-1627) d'après le "Discurso" de Gonçalo Coutinho, gouverneur de Mazagan (1629)*, Paris, 1956, p. 69.

102 Bernardo Rodrigues: *Anais de Arzila. Crónica inédita do século XVI*, ed. David Lopes, Lisbon, 1915-19, II, p. 215.

103 Ibid., I. p. 380.

as further Portuguese forms *morábito* and *morábita* as well as *marabuto*[104] derived from the French marabout. Moreover, the form *morabat* also exists (*Sources*, Portugal, III, p. 216). Occasionally in its place one finds *faqueres* (pl. of *faqīr*, Portugal, II, p. 123), very frequently the more general *caciz*, *caxis*, *cassis*, its Arabic word of origin *qasīs* designating in fact a Christian priest (presbyter),[105] once translated as *Beguynos* (Portugal, II, p. 133, ftn. 2) but usually as *samtos* (II, p. 528) or *santos* (III, pp. 50, 168, 169).[106] Accordingly, the Netherlanders have *Sante* (Pays-Bas, VI, pp. 242 f.), *Santon* (VI, pp. 307, 520), *sant of prins* 'saint or prince' (p. 609), and similarly the English: *saint* (Angleterre, II, p. 269, III, pp. 35 ff., 569), *holly men, saints* (II, p. 303), *the great saintes of Suz* (II, p. 575), *Foker* (= *faqīr*) (II, p. 352), *Morabit or Sainct* (II, p. 23), *Morabitt or Saincte* (III, p. 65), *morabittes or saintes* (p. 141), *the Sainte or Marabite* (p. 267), *a Saint or Marabitt* (p. 359). John Braithwaite (1729) writes *Marabou* and *Marabout*,[107] Mungo Park (1799) sometimes uses *Maraboo*, sometimes *Marraboo*, for the Islamic 'priest',[108] James

---

104 Ibid., I, p. 380, ftn. 2.

105 Several times in the letters of Bastião de Vargas, *Sources inédites*, Portugal, III; in addition, Portugal III, p. 308, II, pp. 528, 537; cf. index alphabétique in Portugal, V, p. 209 s.v. Marabouts ('cacizes'); 1re sér., France, III, p. 21. Bernardo Rodrigues: *Anais de Arzila*, I, p. 380 (ftn. 4). Manuel Augusto Rodrigues: 'Aspectos da presença árabe no "Itinerário da Terra Santa" de Fr. Pantaleão de Aveiro', in *Actas IV Congresso de Estudos árabes e islâmicos Coimbra-Lisboa*, Leiden, 1971, pp. 402-43. The Ayyūbid al-Ṣāliḥ Ismāᶜīl only speaks of the *qusūs al-muslimīn* in order to make himself understandable to the crusaders; Subkī: *Ṭabaqāt al-shāfiᶜiyya al-kubrā*, Cairo, 1970 ff., VIII, p. 244, l. 9. My colleague Germán Colón has drawn my attention to J.P. Machado: *Dicionario etimológico da lingua portuguesa*, Lisbon[2], 1967, s.v. caciz: 'Caciz', s. Do ár. qasīs 'religioso, sacerdote'. Séc. XV: '... sendo hi presentes os outros Cacizes...' Azurara: *Crónica de D. Duarte de Meneses*, nos *Inéditos de História Portuguesa*, III, p. 160 (cap. 70). Even older, according to a friendly communication from Germán Colón, is a Catalan testimony: Francesc Eiximenis (d. 1409): *Primer libre del Crestià*, ed. Valencia, 1483, fol. e[6]v: 'Açò mateix appar per altra via, car com lo gran *cassis* lur e cap de morisma en lo spiritual que dieu que sta a Mecha...' Doutté: *En Tribu*, p. 201, ftn. 2.

106 Gonçalo Coutinho, the governor of Mazagan, also translates it this way in 1629; Robert Ricard: *Mazagan et le Maroc sous le règne du sultan Moulay Zidan (1608-1627), d'après le "Discurso" de Gonçalo Coutinho, gouverneur de Mazagan (1629)*, Paris, 1956, p. 39: marabout de grand crédit, c'est-à-dire saint dans le langage des Maures.

107 Captain Braithwaite: *The History of the Revolutions in the Empire of Morocco upon the Death of the late Emperor Muley Ishmael*, London, 1729, reprint Mnemosyne, Miami, 1969, pp. 359-65.

Grey Jackson (1809) *fakeer or maraboot* for 'the priest or saint' who resides in one of the 'Zawiat' Sanctuaries,[109] Richard Tully's sister in Tripoli (published in 1816) *Marabut*,[110] Denham (1826) *Maraboot*, pl. *Marabooteens*,[111] Clapperton (1824) *Marauboot* for a holy man in Sokoto.[112] In the French reports one reads *sancton* (*Sources*, 1re sér., France, III, pp. 358-68), *santon* (pp. 366, 429), *Sainct* (p. 679), *saint* (p. 552), *un saint ou morabito* (p. 585), *Morabito* (p. 585), *Morabit* (pp. 414, 446), *Morabite* (pp. 539 ff., 544 f., 635, 640; 2e sér., France, II, pp. 6, 42), *marabout* (1re sér., France, III, p. 333), *marabout, houme, à leur oppinion, de saincte vie* (III, p. 372), *marabout qu'ils tiennent estre de saincte vie* (p. 373). Jean Mocquet, in the German translation, writes *Santon oder Marabou*.[113] These examples from the 17th century should be sufficient.[114] For the old French forms and their black African synonyms see Vincent Monteil: *L'Islam noir*², Paris, 1971, pp. 94 and 136-37.

The European attempts to define the gist of the term marabout have followed the same line from the 15th to the 20th centuries. Accordingly, the marabouts are viri religiosi, viri sancti, einsiedler, personnages religieux, ecclésiastiques, gifted persons, holy men[115] and suchlike. When Adorno presents the morabiti as the only religiosi (i.e. 'monks') in Islam and says that they usually live as recluses outside the cities, are held to be very holy, had long, unkempt hair, slapped men with impunity and unabashedly embraced women, it is

---

108 *Travels in the interior districts of Africa: performed... in the years 1795, 1796, and 1797*, London, 1799, pp. 48 and 252.

109 *An Account of the Empire of Marocco and the District of Suse*, London, 1809, p. 39.

110 Richard Tully: *Narrative of a ten years' residence at Tripoli in Africa*, London, 1816, pp. 15, 25, 28, and 32.

111 Dixon Denham and Hugh Clapperton: *Narrative of Travels and discoveries in Northern and Central Africa, in the years 1822, 1823, and 1824*, London, 1826, I, pp. XXXVI, XXXVII, XLIX, LX, LXII; I, pp. 3, 41, 290.

112 Ibid., II, p. 97.

113 Jan (sic) Mocquet: *Wunderbare Jedoch Gründlich- und warhaffte Geschichte und Reise Begebnisse*, trans. by Johann Georg Schoch, Nuremberg, 1688, pp. 144-46.

114 I could only consult those volumes of the *Sources inédites de l'histoire du Maroc* which are still available for purchase.

115 *Itinéraire d'Anselme Adorno* pp. 80-81; 146-47. Haedo trans. *RAfr.* 15, 1871, p. 60. Jean Chaumeil: 'Histoire d'une tribu maraboutique de l'Anti-Atlas: Les Aït ᶜAbdallah ou Saᶜid', *Hespéris* 39, 1952, p. 197. Denham-Clapperton: *Travels*, I, p. XXXVI; I, p. 97.

clear he is referring to individuals known as 'those drawn unto God' (*majādhīb*). In giving this definition he is narrowing the term. Conversely, Haedo overextends its range when he depicts marabouts as including all kinds of religious functionaries, lamplighters in the mosque, muezzins, preachers, Koran reciters, corpse escorts, as well as ecstatics, conjurers, magicians and the mad.[116] All these could be marabouts but do not necessarily have to be. Mármol maintains that pilgrims who return from Mecca are looked upon as marabouts, i.e. as holy persons.[117] G. Mouette (1683), who spent eleven years (1670-81) in captivity in Morocco, attempts to resolve the contradictions found in his sources and perhaps in his observations as well. He distinguishes between the simple-minded and poor in spirit who are considered holy, and the actual *morabites* who mostly lived in forests and on mountains, led the life of a recluse, wore multi-colored patched frocks, carried pilgrim staffs and hung large rosaries around their neck.[118] He has in mind Sufis with whom, however, the *murābiṭūn* can in no way simply be equated. He compares them with the pagan philosophers (of antiquity or India?) and the Christian monks.[119] More accurately, an anonymous English report from 1609 writes that the *Fokers* or *Saints* of Morocco lived in the best localities in the countryside, offered abundant hospitality to all travellers, presented an example of a moral life, did much good by means of their generosity, helped the needy and those in difficulty, settled disputes between hostile parties and resolved would-be uprisings, and consequently they were greatly loved and venerated by the ordinary people and resided in houses whose inviolability even the king would only infringe in emergencies.[120]

In the end the word marabout provided European reporters and observers with a convenient artificial term for all holy men of this kind, even if the latter did not refer to themselves this way or were active in non-Arabic language areas. The Haussa word *maalam* (<Ar. *muᶜallim* 'teacher') and the Fulfulde words *mōrike* and *mōdibbo*

---

116 *Topografía*, French trans. *RAfr*. 15, 1871, pp. 60-69. In Portuguese *alcorão* means 'koran, minaret, mosque, the profession of faith in the call to prayer'; Robert Ricard: *Un document portugais sur la place de Mazagan au début du XVIIe siècle*, Paris, 1932, p. 40, ftn. 2.

117 Mármol: *Descripción*, I, p. 243b.

118 *Sources inédites*, 2e sér., France, II, pp. 157-58.

119 Ibid., II, p. 16.

120 *A True Historicall Discourse*, by Ro. C., London, 1609, in *Sources inédites*, Angleterre, II, pp. 400-01.

(<Ar. *mu'addib* 'educator') were translated into French as marabout to make their meaning clear to the European reader.[121] In Senegambia the defenders of Islam against the local non-Muslims (*soninke*) are called marabouts.[122] In Mauritania the Zawāyā tribes[123] are marabouts and so are the *sādāt* in Kabylia,[124] which is perfectly correct but should be taken as a warning against the false assumption that in all translations the European use of marabout stands for the Arabic *murābiṭ*. Thus in North Africa the meaning of *murābiṭ* first detached itself from the literary language and then began to lead its own life as a European borrowing. The French marabout has even wandered back to North Africa and is employed there for the sake of better communication with foreigners. [125]

The ambiguity of the word marabout is further increased by the fact that it is not only used to designate a holy man, but, understandably, the grave in which he is buried. E. Daumas and Delvoulx, fils, blame the French for this usage.[126] Indeed, it is already found in

---

121 André Salifou: *Le Damagaram ou Sultanat de Zinder au XIXe siècle*, Niamey, 1971, p. 37. Henri Gaden: *La Vie d'El Hadj Omar. Qacida en Poular* (par Mohammadou Aliou Tyam), Paris, 1935, pp. 22, 64, 173.

122 Charlotte Alison Quinn: 'Maba Diakhou and the Gambian Jihad, 1850-1890', in John Ralph Willis: *Studies in West African Islamic History*, I, London, 1979, pp. 239-40.

123 Aḥmad b. al-Amīn al-Shinqīṭī: *Al-wasīṭ fī tarājim udabā' Shinqīṭ*, Cairo, 1911, pp. 455-71. René Basset: *Mission au Sénégal*, III, Recherches historiques sur les Maures, Publ. de l'École des Lettres d'Alger 39, pp. 455-75. H.T. Norris: 'Shaykh Mā' al-ᶜAynayn al-Qalqamī in the Folk-Literature of the Spanish Sahara', *BOAS* 31, 1968, pp. 113-14. Norris: 'Znāga Islam During the Seventeenth and Eighteenth Centuries', *BSOAS* 32, 1969, pp. 496-526. Norris: *Shinqīṭī Folk Literature and Song*, Oxford, 1968, pp. 15 ff. F. de la Chapelle: 'Esquisse d'une histoire du Sahara occidental', *Hespéris* 11, 1930, p. 68. Robert Montagne: *La civilisation du désert*, Paris, 1947, pp. 249-51. John Ralph Willis in *Studies in West African Islamic History*, edited by himself, I, pp. 1 ff. Nehemia Levtzion: 'ᶜAbd Allāh b. Yāsīn and the Almoravids', in the same collective volume, I, p. 101: '"Zawāyā" or "Marabouti tribes" (to cite the French corruption)'. E. Destaing: 'Notes sur des manuscrits arabes de l'Afrique occidentale', *RAfr.* 55, 1911, pp. 231-38, 510-19.

124 An example in F. Patorni: 'Délibérations de l'année 1794 dans la Grande Kabylie', *RAfr.* 39, 1895, pp. 315-20. A legal decree in Arabic language abolishing some financial rights of women. The word *sādāt* is always translated as *marabouts*.

125 Jeannine Drouin: *Un cycle oral*, p. 207, [83]/88, ftn. 1, heard *mṛbbu/mṛabbu* among the Berbers in the Middle-Atlas. I heard something like *marâbu* in Arabic speech near Fez.

126 E. Daumas: *Mœurs et coutumes de l'Algérie*, Paris, 1858, p. 230, ftn. 1. Devoulx, fils: 'Les édifices religieux de l'ancien Alger', *RAfr.* 6, 1862, p. 377.

Mouette in 1683.[127] Moreover, Richard Tully's sister — by no means the only case — follows Mouette's usage in English in her correspondence on Tripoli (1785-1793).[128] In the French governmental registers these 'marabouts', the graves of holy men, are listed separately.[129] But in using the word like this, the Europeans were following the indigenous vernacular language. Hamed Bouderbah: 'Réflexions sur la Colonie d'Alger', *RAfr.* 57, 1913, pp. 241-42, gives advice about how the property of the 'Mrabtin' in Algiers should be administered by the French, by which he means the tomb buildings and the *zawāyā* of the deceased holy men. Thus *murābiṭūn/mrabtin* as well can mean these grave monuments. The same holds true for *sayyid/syyid/sīd*, the other designation for the marabout[130] and likewise for the grave of a holy man. A quick glance at the *Lexique français-touareg* of Cortade and Mammeri (1967) is enough to show how ingrained the word marabout in this sense has become in French. If one looks up *marabout* (p. 295), one does not find a marabout himself but only his grave: *erreouḍet, erreouḍetîn,*[131] *rawḍa* in literary Arabic, for which *qubba* (pl. *qubab*) is known to be used as a synonym and thus is also translated as *marabout*.[132]

The founders of the religious centers and pious settlements mentioned earlier on (pp. 350 f.) often achieved political importance. In particular they emerged on the scene as a spiritual power. The proper scholars of scripture, theologians and jurists, did not enjoy the support of the common people to this extent since in North Africa, as elsewhere, the miracle is the favorite child of religious faith and the people confer their affection and veneration most readily on those who provide them with help and fulfill their wishes. With the support and under the leadership of the marabouts, however, the people not only resolved their factional conflicts but also resisted the

---

127 *Sources*, 2e sér., France, II, pp. 86, 90.

128 Richard Tully: *Narrative of a ten years' residence*, pp. 92, 110, 219.

129 Michaux-Bellaire in *Archives Marocaines* 17, 1911, p. 174.

130 G. Salmon: 'Une tribu marocaine', *Arch. Maroc.* 1, 1904, pp. 244-50. G. Kampffmeyer: 'Weitere Texte aus Fes und Tanger', *MSOS*, 2. Abt., Westasiat. Sprachen, 1913, Jg. 16, p. 53, l. 19 (*ibāṭ fsīdī* 'I spent the night in the saint's tomb', *ṣibnâ ssîjid mʿámmar bírrižāl* 'we found the saint's tomb full of people').

131 Cf. the title of the work by Cauvet: 'Les marabouts. Petits monuments funéraires et votifs du Nord de l'Afrique', *RAfr.* 64, 1923, pp. 274-329, 448-522.

132 Thus the Algerian place name *Tagouba*, which is a Berberized form of the Arabic *qubba*, is translated as 'coupole, marabout'; Pellegrin: *Essai sur les noms de lieux*, p. 106.

legitimate intervention or the illegitimate intrusion of the government authorities. And even in their dealings with the highest level of government it appeared to the people that the marabout was the appropriate speaker, petitioner and legal representative. But the government itself also took account of the marabout's popular influence and even appointed him as an authority.[133] At the cost of the governor or by way of lightening the latter's responsibilities, the government transferred to him the task of looking after peace and order in his district and of actively playing a civilizing and educational role, and remunerated him for this by exempting him from compulsory labor and state taxation, and by according him the right to spend the taxes demanded from him by religion on the poor of his family and for his own undertakings, in fact even to levy such taxes on certain parts of the population and to keep the money for the same purpose. Suitable descendants or such as were successful in finally eliminating their rivals had the same rights conferred on them, whereupon the head or heads of the establishment, which was basically self-sufficient (in accordance with the manorial system),[134] designated the personnel directly, and the beneficiaries of these privileges were appointed at least according to the degree of their family connection — an arrangement which continued up until very recent times. All the members of the family as a whole remained marabouts or were raised to this status in retrospect after the discovery or promotion of such an ancestor in their family tree. Marabout families could extend themselves to become clans or tribes. These marabout tribes should not be confused with the 'marabout tribes' (mentioned earlier on p. 349) that performed military *murābaṭa* on the coast.

The beginnings of this development can be traced back to a time when the term marabout in this meaning was not current. Thus the future patron saint of Tunis Muḥriz b. Khalaf (d. 413/1022), according to the report of his grandson Abū'l-Ṭāhir al-Fārisī, is supposed to have received a document (*ẓahīr*) from the Zīrid Muᶜizz b. Bādīs which guaranteed to him the inviolability of his extensive properties and freedom from land-taxes and tithes, and, as the text expressly

---

133 Described concisely and clearly by Abdallah Laroui: *Les origines sociales et culturelles du nationalisme marocain (1830-1912)*, Paris, 1977, pp. 139-50.

134 On this economic principle, characteristic of medieval Europe in contrast to the medieval East's urban orientation, cf. Fritz Steppat: 'Die Entwicklung der ländlichen Gesellschaft. Ein Versuch vergleichender Geschichtsbetrachtung', in *Festschrift für Hans Robert Roemer zum 65. Geburtstag*, Beirut, 1979, pp. 642-56.

states, was only confirming rights which had been conferred on him earlier. Since the document is dated 417/1026 and issued to persons in the plural (*-kum*), it must not have been addressed to him but to his immediate children.[135] The first Naṣrid of Granada Muḥammad al-Ghālib-bi'llāh renewed a similar tax exemption in 645/1247 on behalf of Ibn Mahīb and his spouse in Almería. Both were permitted to spend their tithes and alms contributions themselves in the best way according to their own discretion and were likewise freed from paying all additional government taxes. Included in this concession of privilege were their descendants, their employees and their servants. Ibn Mahīb, in 635/1238, acted as intermediary in drawing up the treaty of capitulation between the previous possessor of the city and the Naṣrid ruler. He was a Friday preacher, a traditionist and an ascetic, and is the celebrated author of the *takhmīs* to the laudatory poems on Muḥammad composed by Fāzāzī (d. 627/1230), each of which consists of twenty verses, but he is still not described anywhere as a *murābiṭ*.[136] Tax privileges for real marabouts, however, are known from the time of the Marīnids (8th/14th century)[137] and later more extensively during the centuries when the Saᶜdī and Filālī sherifs rose to power. In documents pertaining to such privileges, the marabouts resemble vassals. But the ancestor of such a family could already have occupied his *zāwiya* under the Almohads in the 6th/12th century.[138] A picture of the procedure for drawing up the

---

135 Hady Roger Idris: *Manâqib d'Abû Isḥâq Al-Jabanyânî par Abû l-Qâsim al-Labîdî et Manâqib de Muḥriz B. Ḫalaf par Abû l-Ṭâhir al-Fârisî*, Paris, 1959, Arabic pp. 148-51/French 316-19. Note the cautious remarks of the scholar. But I believe that by postulating different addressees in the document as I have done, the difficulties can be resolved the simplest way.

136 Ibn al-Khaṭīb: *Al-iḥāṭa fī akhbār Gharnāṭa*, ed. ᶜInān, Cairo, 1974, II, pp. 420-21. The events are mentioned ibid., p. 419, and in Ibn ᶜIdhārī: *Al-bayān al-mughrib*, III parte, ed. Ambrosio Huici Miranda, Tetuan, 1963, pp. 335-37.

137 Ibn Marzūq: *Musnad*, Chpt. 19, *faṣl* 3 (50v)/trans. Viguera, p. 210: Abū'l-Ḥasan al-Marīnī (732-49/1331-48) saw to it, as did his predecessors and successors, that the heirs of the saints and the marabouts (santos y morabitos) were not deprived of their feudal estates (*iqṭāᶜ*) and tax exemptions (*taḥrīrāt*) which had been granted to their fathers — as happened in other times. — Abū Ḥammū Mūsā (d. 791/1389): *Wāsiṭat al-sulūk fī siyāsat al-mulūk*, Tunis, 1279, p. 164, l. 7, advises his son to be especially generous to the pious worshippers of God, to treat the scholars and the upright in a friendly way, and to confer exemption from taxes (*taḥrīrāt*) on the *murābiṭūn*.

138 Such was the case, for instance, with Abū ᶜAbdallāh Muḥammad b. ᶜAmr/ᶜUmar al-Āsrīrī in the city Āsrīr in Wādī Nūn, a member of the Lamṭa (later called Baᶜamrān, *Maᶜsūl*, II, p. 196), who lived in the 6th/12th century and is already mentioned in *Tashawwuf*, p. 345. His

official documentation in the 14th/20th century has been sketched by Paul Marty: 'Les zaouias marocaines et le Makhzen,' *REI* 3, 1929, pp. 575-600. We cannot enter into the details here.

However, if the supposed law of God came into conflict with the injustice of rulers, loyalty to the state among the marabouts could begin to waver. Then under certain conditions they took up arms, and the marabout, who earlier in times of peace had been a *murābiṭ*, became a *mujāhid*, a warrior for the faith. The reasons and pretexts for such action were grievances and transgressions against Islam, and the actual enemies were rulers thought to be guilty of these crimes, allegedly or in fact in alliance with Christian powers that threatened an Islamic region or had actually attacked or had already even occupied territory. The same thing always recurs: the marabout and the people defended Islam against the rulers who were in some way allied with the foreigners or who had not taken the initiative against them energetically enough. The question whether it was allowed to wage war without or even against the will of the ruler, was answered in various ways by the jurists. One answer only permitted warfare under the leadership of an emir, another set the sovereignty of the people above the sovereignty of the ruler when it came to defending Islam.[139] One judgement, which attempted to do justice to both parties, stated that *jihād* was illegal in a country where holy war was only a duty for a sufficient number (*farḍ kifāya*), whereas it was legal in a country where circumstances imposed holy war on every individual (*farḍ ᶜayn*), and thus a peace treaty concluded by the ruling authorities with the enemy was not binding.[140] Such uprisings only had the prospect of success in times when the government was weak. In such cases the personal goals of marabouts were not always transparent from the outset. One marabout might pursue the goal of

---

descendants were later the heads of the *zāwiya* and have documents from the Saᶜdīs and Filālīs. Every year a *mawsim* is celebrated at the tomb of Muḥammad at Āsrīr which Muḥammad al-Mukhtār al-Sūsī visited in 1379/1959-60. Sūsī: *Maᶜsūl*, XII, pp. 189-90.

139 *Nozhet-Elhâdi. Histoire de la dynastie saadienne au Maroc* (1511-1670), par Mohammed Esseghir ben Elhadj ben Abdallah Eloufrâni, texte arabe publié/traduction française par O. Houdas, Paris, 1888-89, I (Arabic), p. 265/II (French), p. 440. Ḥajjī: *Al-zāwiya al-dilāʾiyya*, pp. 144-45. Abū Fāris ᶜAbd al-ᶜAzīz b. al-Ḥasan al-Zayyātī (d. 1055/1645): *Al-jawāhir al-mukhtāra fī-mā (or mimmā) waqaftu ᶜalayhi min al-nawāzil bi-jibāl Ghumāra*, in Jacques Berque: *L'Intérieur du Maghreb*, p. 166.

140 Émile Amar: 'Consultations juridiques des faqihs au Maghreb', *Arch. Maroc.* 12, 1908, p. 220: from the *Miᶜyār* of Wansharīsī (d. 914/1508).

setting himself up as ruler, while another would be satisfied with bringing about a change.

One can already perceive such a marabout uprising in the rebellion of the *murīds* of Ibn Qasī[141] and Ibn al-Mundhir in the 6th/12th century which was directed against the regime of the Almoravids in southern Spain and Portugal, and hastened its collapse. Ibn Khaldūn (d. 808/1406) in the *Muqaddima* refers to these *murīds* as *murābiṭūn*.[142] Thus new *murābiṭūn* fought against old ones. They in turn fell victim to the subsequent Almohads. Around 700/1300 the *murābiṭ* Saᶜāda with his *murābiṭūn*, whom he programmatically called *sunniyya*, fought in Algerian Zāb against bandit gangs and against the oppression of the Ḥafṣid governor.[143] Gangs were often the cause for marabouts to take up arms. Around 900/1500 Portuguese bases on the Atlantic coast acted as a thorn in Morocco's flesh. Since the Waṭṭāsids were consuming all their energies fighting off the Christians in the harbors of the north and were obliged to abandon the south to its fate, the tribes of Sūs turned to the highly esteemed marabout Muḥammad b. al-Mubārak (d. 924/1510) in Aqqā at the southern foot of Bani. He did not become their leader himself but referred the petitioners to the two brothers Aḥmad al-Aᶜraj and Muḥammad al-Shaykh who were better armed and were allegedly descended from a sherif family. In this way a course was set for a future which has in fact persisted to this day: not simply a marabout family, but a sherif family should wield the authority of state. Marabouts supported the brothers as fighters[144] and as

---

141 Ibn al-Abbār: *Al-ḥulla al-siyarā'*, ed. Ḥusayn Mu'nis, Cairo, 1963-64, II, pp. 197-208. Alfred Bel: *Les Benou Ghânya*, Paris, 1903, pp. 5-8. Jacinto Bosch Vilá: *Historia de Marruecos: Los Almorávides*, Tetuan, 1956, pp. 287-88. A. Faure in *EI*[2] s.vv. Ibn Barradjān and Ibn Ḳasī. On Ibn Qasī's activity and mysticism from a different viewpoint see Tilman Nagel: *Staat und Glaubensgemeinschaft im Islam*, Zurich, 1981, I, pp. 266-70.

142 *Ibn Khaldûn, The Muqadimmah*, trans. Rosenthal, I, p. 323.

143 *Ibn Khaldoun: Histoire des Berbères*, trans. Le Baron de Slane, nouvelle édition Paul Casanova, Paris, 1925 and 1968, I, pp. 81-86; II, pp. 131-32. Robert Brunschvig: *La Berbérie orientale sous les Ḥafṣides*, II, Paris, 1947, pp. 334-36. Doutté: 'Marabouts', *RHR* 41, 1900, pp. 27-29. Ibn Marzūq: *Musnad*, 76v/trans. Viguera, pp. 276-77.

144 Edmond Doutté enumerates alleged tombs of such *mujāhidūn* on the Atlantic coast: *En Tribu*, Paris, 1914, pp. 312-13. Activities of marabouts in the north in the vicinity of the Mediterranean are reported in *Sources inédites*, Espagne, I, pp. 448, 456, 493-94, 532-33, 551; Angleterre, I, pp. 61-75.

diplomatic negotiators,[145] but also incurred their suspicion. After Muḥammad al-Shaykh had eliminated the say of his elder brother, he subjected the owners of the *zawāyā* to close scrutiny because he did not feel fully sure of those 'through whose door he had attained power', as the historian Wafrānī (d. 1140/1727-28) expresses it.[146] This fear proved to be well founded a few decades later in the 11th/17th century when the Saᶜdīs, having become hostile to one another in a conflict over the succession, found themselves confronted with a multi-headed hydra of marabouts of the same type. This is what an English report on the situation in 1638 means when it describes the *faquers* (saints), who had won the hearts of the oppressed common people, as presenting a dangerous threat to the sherifs' rule and considers this constellation as the result of the power relations at that time among a series of marabouts.[147] First of all, after being driven out of Fez,[148] Zaydān (Zīdān) is supposed to have found in Aqqā in 1604 a well-meaning supporter and negotiator in one of the descendants of the Muḥammad b. al-Mubārak who had helped the Saᶜdī dynasty into the saddle of power.[149] But then the surrender of Larache to the Spaniards in 1019/1610 and other

145 *Sources*, Portugal, II, pp. 535/537; III, pp. 50, 302, 427, 489; Espagne, I, p. 155. These are only a few examples.

146 *Nozhet-Elhâdi*, p. 41/French pp. 76-77. Ibn ᶜAskar: *Dawḥat al-nāshir*, p. 103/trans. Graulle, *Arch. Maroc.* 19, 1913, p. 177. A critical description of the whole procedure is found in Roger Le Tourneau: *Les débuts de la Dynastie Saᶜdienne de 1509 à 1557*, Bibliothèque de l'Institut d'Études Supérieures Islamiques d'Alger IX, Algiers, 1954. Another object of suspicion was the *zāwiya* of ᶜAbd al-Karīm al-Fallāḥ and his successor ᶜAbdallāh al-Kūsh al-Marrākushī (d. 960/1553). Muḥammad al-Shaykh had it evacuated: *Dawḥat al-nāshir*, p. 110/Graulle, *Arch. Maroc.* 19, 1913, p. 190. A third one was the *zāwiya* of ᶜAlī al-Lahabī; al-ᶜAbbās b. Ibrāhīm: *Al-iᶜlām bi-man ḥalla Marrākush wa-Aghmāt min al-aᶜlām*, Rabat, 1974-77, V, p. 74 (from *Mirʾāt al-maḥāsin* of al-ᶜArabī b. Abī'l-Maḥāsin Yūsuf al-Fāsī al-Fihrī).

147 *Sources*, Angleterre, III, p. 486.

148 *Chronique anonyme de la dynastie saᶜdienne*, ed. Georges S. Colin, Rabat, 1934, p. 82.

149 *Sources*, Angleterre, II, pp. 303, 352. Anonymous report of 1607. P. 380: Sidie Abdela Imbark (= ᶜAbdallāh b. Mubārak) finally withdrew back to Aqqā when he saw that Zaydān would not listen to advice. He died 1015/1606. An article on him is found in Justinard: *Fawaid al jamma bi isnadi ʾouloumi al oumma, Abouzid Sidi Abderrahman ben Mohammed le Jazouli, le Tamanarti, le Mghafri*, Chartres, 1953, pp. 75-77. There is a story about the marabout family in Sūsī: *Maᶜsūl*, XVIII, p. 166-91. He prefers the spelling Maḥammad b. Mubārak. There is some information in Sūsī: *Khilāl Jazūla*, Tetuan, 1379, pp. 54-55, 62-68, 75, 84.

circumstances provoked the uprising of the marabout Abū Maḥallī from Wādī'l-Sawīra, who exploited expectations regarding the Mahdī and had himself declared the new sultan in Marrakesh. Zaydān asked another marabout, Yaḥyā al-Ḥāḥī from the High-Atlas, for help. Yaḥyā did depose Abū Maḥallī in 1022/1613 but then cherished ambitions for absolute power himself. Earlier the same fear had existed concerning Yaḥyā's father, and Zaydān's father and predecessor, Aḥmad Manṣūr, had warned about him[150] without anything happening at the time. Zaydān fully approved of Yaḥyā's armed intervention but not of his bid for the crown.[151] However, Yaḥyā was forced back into his place, not by Zaydān, but by another marabout in the south, Abū Dumayᶜa (Bū Dmīᶜa, Abū Ḥassūn ᶜAlī b. Muḥammad) of Tazerwalt from the family of the holy man Aḥmad b. Mūsā (d. 971/1564). In 1039/1629-30 Abū Dumayᶜa conquered Tarudant, the former capital city of Yaḥyā, and snatched the whole south from the Saᶜdīs so that he came to have command over the extensive region from Sūs to the Niger. On the northern Atlantic coast the defense against the Spaniards was taken over by the marabout Muḥammad b. Aḥmad al-ᶜAyyāshī who soon found himself confronted with opposition from the Saᶜdīs and yet remained the only leader who did not aspire to the monarchy. But he infringed on the preserve of another marabout of the north, the powerful leader of the *zāwiya* of Dilāʾ at the foot of the Middle-Atlas, Muḥammad al-Ḥājj who sought to succeed to the Saᶜdīs. After losing a battle in 1051/1641, ᶜAyyāshī took refuge with an Arab tribe that was allied with the head of Dilāʾ and was put to death among them. When the Christians of Alexandria (sic) learned of this, they are supposed to have smiled and said: 'A *ṣānṭū* (= santo) in Morocco has been killed', which Wafrānī translates as *mujāhid* 'warrior for the faith'.s[152] The translation indicates that in Morocco one thought one knew what the Christians at that time understood by an Islamic holy man in the west, namely a marabout who waged war. Wafrānī perhaps also thought to himself that the death of a belligerent enemy rather than of a holy man was the cause for joy. But in the European

150 *Nozhet-Elhâdi*, p. 210/French p. 344.

151 *Nozhet-Elhâdi*, pp. 215-18 / French pp. 352-58.

152 *Nozhet-Elhâdi*, p. 271/French p. 451. Italian santo/santa is represented in inscriptions with *ṣnt*; *Répertoire chronologique d'épigraphie arabe*, no. 3140 (Palermo 544/1149). — Our ᶜAyyāshī, not to be confused with the famous Moroccan traveller, is missing from EI^2 and Supplément. A summary of his history is found in *Sources inédites*, 1re sér., France, III, pp. 189-98, by Henry de Castries.

documents of his time ᶜAyyāshī is the very epitome of the *Morabit or Sainct*, the *Morabito*, *Morabite*, etc. *Murābiṭ* would therefore have been the better and more accurate translation. In any case, after the fratricidal war between the Saᶜdīs and power struggles among the marabouts, it was the Filālī sherifs (from Tafilalt as their name indicates) who became masters of Morocco: they conquered the northern marabout kingdom of Dilāᵓ and the sourthern marabout kingdom of Tazerwalt. Whereas the Saᶜdī dynasty came to hold sway thanks to marabout cooperation and also fell from power through marabout opposition, the Filālīs had to create lebensraum for themselves by first destroying the marabout state formations that had arisen. Yet later as well, several other adventurers from among the marabouts came forward to engage in armed conflict with the Filālī government in an attempt to overthrow it. The most successful of them were Māᵓ al-ᶜAynayn and his son Aḥmad al-Hayba (Hība) who came forth from the Spanish Sahara, belonged to a branch of the Qādirī order and twice occupied Marrakesh, Māᵓ al-ᶜAynayn in 1910 and Hayba in 1912. They wished to drive out the Filālī sultan as well as the French but on both occasions came off worst.[153]

But usually marabouts were in fact people who did not use weapons and understood nothing about them. According to Gerhard Rohlfs, a marabout travels only with his rosary, not with a sword,[154] and the *murābiṭūn* from Kerzaz (in Algeria), who were sherifs, conducted their caravans of merchandise without weapons and were extremely peace-loving. As Rohlfs writes: 'Whereas all the peoples living in the area constantly go about armed to the teeth, they are truly fearful of even touching a rifle.'[155] The members of the marabout family of Ibrāhīm b. ᶜAlī from Tighānīmīn among the Ida w-Tanān in the western foothills of the High-Atlas, when issued with an order to pay a penalty, could not deposit a rifle as security because they had none, but paid with a sacrificial animal.[156] Muḥammad al-

153 *EI* s.v. Māᵓ al-ᶜAinain (Lévi-Provençal). A description of the movement of Māᵓ al-ᶜAynayn and Hayba by a certain Muḥammad al-Manūzī (d. 1365/1946) is found in Muḥammad al-Mukhtār al-Sūsī: *Maᶜsūl*, III, pp. 366-402. More occurs scattered throughout the *Maᶜsūl*; compactly dealt with in IV, pp. 83-305. Werner Ende has reminded me of the overall survey in B.G. Martin: *Muslim Brotherhoods in Nineteenth-Century Africa*, Cambridge University Press, 1976, pp. 125-51. Cf. ftn. 333 below.

154 *Reise durch Marokko*, Bremen, 1869, p. 204.

155 Ibid., pp. 121-22.

156 Robert Montagne: 'Organisation sociale et politique des tribus berbères indépendantes', *REI* 1, 1927, p. 236.

Mukhtār al-Sūsī (d. 1963) does not attribute any special military capacity to the tribe of the Murābiṭū ᶜAbdallāh b. Saᶜīd from Illigh, to which he himself belonged. As he notes, though they all had a rifle at home, they were looked down on by the aggressive tribes that surrounded them. The only thing which conferred on them a certain reputation was the staff and rosary they carried about with them, or the books they possessed, and their position with regard to religion. Once when the alarm was sounded the bravest of these marabouts had resolutely ventured forth, but a single young man of the Majjāṭ paralyzed them with a warlike cry and disarmed them.[157] Opposed to participation in armed skirmishes, they became set on legal prohibition in their weakness.[158] Mukhtār's father ᶜAlī al-Darqāwī (d. 1328/1911) gave fiery speeches encouraging *jihād* against the French, but was once challenged by one of his listeners to lead the way himself with his disciples. Another time he demanded of the government authorities that they force him, the *ṭalaba*, the *murābiṭūn* and the *fuqarāʾ* to take up arms and prepare themselves to defend the country.[159] The unsentimental and domineering al-Ḥusayn b. Hāshim (d. 1303/1886) from Tazerwalt, a descendant of Abū Dumayᶜa, sent in the warlike Majjāṭ in order to wring taxes out of the weak marabouts from Taghlūlū who were unable to ward off a fly.[160] Certain marabout state formations are specifically defined by the fact that the rulers ex officio make no use of military power but leave this exclusively to their subordinates.[161] The towers of the sherif-marabout city of Tamaṣlūḥt south of Marrakesh have no battlements or embrasures and the sherif does not reside in a *qaṣaba*. Religious prestige (and the protection of the English) replaces weapons, as was the case specifically in 1902.[162]

A difficult problem is presented by those marabout tribes which, as fate would have it, must live together with Arab bedouins, because their origins remain completely in the dark. That each of these tribes is descended from a particular holy man, as they are pleased to maintain, is scarcely acceptable. Whereas so small a unit as the marabout family is a part or even the nucleus of a tribe and is protected by the latter, a marabout tribe represents an independent for-

157 *Maᶜsūl*, II, p. 16.

158 *Maᶜsūl*, XII, pp. 184-85.

159 *Maᶜsūl*, XII, p. 185.

160 *Maᶜsūl*, XX, p. 218.

161 Ernest Gellner: *Saints of the Atlas*, pp. 65, 74.

162 Eugène Aubin: *Le Maroc d'aujourd'hui*, Paris, 1913, pp. 48-49.

mation among the tribes. It has no other option but to work out how to get along with them, to provide its own defense, to enter into alliances with them, to achieve dominance over them or to subordinate itself to them. On the other hand, there are grounds for assuming that a tribe actually becomes a marabout tribe due to an unfavorable balance of power, that in fact the others force it to be militarily inactive and to take on religious functions. Thus the *murābiṭūn* (*mrabṭīn*, sing. *mrābiṭ*) in the Western Desert of Egypt and in Libya are old tribes of the region which the warlike Awlād ᶜAlī accepted in their midst as protégés perhaps in the 15th or 16th century,[163] but then exercised a close control over. They were obliged to give up their warrior activity and to earn respect for themselves through their piety. If they had not been marabouts earlier, they now became so of necessity.[164] They were allowed to bear arms in self-defense[165] and to guard border points in times of real wars[166] — as if they were *murābiṭūn* in the old sense — otherwise they assumed the tasks of a priestly tribe, so to speak, as the Magi had done in ancient Iran according to Herodotus. Only in exceptional circumstances, by going over to the warriors of the counter-party[167] and providing them with special assistance,[168] could they shed their downgraded status — this is how their social position was perceived[169] — and once again become recognized as combatants (*muḥāribūn*).[170] Among them the distinction was made between those who were left in peace for the sake of their *baraka*, and others who were obliged to pay *ṣadaqa*

---

163 Rifᶜat al-Jawharī Bak: *Asrār min al-Ṣaḥrāʾ al-Gharbiyya*, Cairo, 1947, p. 226. A member of the Awlād ᶜAlī told Paul Kahle in 1912 that ᶜAqār, the forefather of the tribe whose son ᶜAlī gave his name to their descendants, went back in time 'to about 200 years ago', which would be roughly around 1700. But he contradicted himself when giving other dates so that one may doubt his statements. Paul Kahle: 'Die Aulād-ᶜAli-Beduinen der Libyschen Wüste', *Der Islam* 4, 1913, pp. 357, 359.

164 Kahle, pp. 361-62. Thus the ᶜötebī Mûhidz, who was active in Egypt, explained: ᵉmrâbit (pl. ᵉmrābtîn) among the Aulâd ᶜAlī is a kind of hermit 'who wanders around alone in the desert in order to worship God'; J.J. Hess: *Von den Beduinen des innern Arabiens*, Zurich-Leipzig, 1938, p. 153.

165 Rifᶜat, p. 236.

166 Rifᶜat, pp. 224-25.

167 Rifᶜat, pp. 229, 232.

168 Kahle, p. 365.

169 Kahle, p. 362.

170 Rifᶜat, p. 232.

'alms-tax' in order to be left alone.[171] The so-called *zawāyā* (*zwāya*) in Mauritania and what was then the Spanish Sahara present the same picture. Put simply, they were indigenous Berbers who in the course of the 8th-9th/14th-15th centuries came under the dominance of the incoming Arab Maᶜqil bedouins, the Dhawū Ḥassān. They rose up in revolt in the 11th/17th century and had to be suppressed in a thirty-year war (1644-1674).[172] At least those *zawāyā* which took part in the uprising have since then been obliged to concede the right to water from their springs to the Arab ruling class and to provide any of them on journey with a riding animal.[173] In addition, they pursue agriculture, dig wells, practice hospitality and cultivate theology.[174] Some foreign elements known as *tyāb* (= *tāʾibūn*) 'the repentant' have also attached themselves to them.[175] If the *zawāyā*, as they maintain and as is generally accepted about them,[176] are really descendants of the Almoravids of the 5th/11th century or even only continue the religious tradition of the latter, then they were already marabouts before their power to make decisions for themselves was usurped by the Dhawū Ḥassān — this possibly in distinction to the *mrabṭīn* in the Libyan desert, although they as well — rather implausibly — are also considered to be a remnant of the Almoravids, namely such of them as drifted to the east.[177] But concerning the designation *mrabṭīn* and *zawāyā*, both should mean more or less the same thing: *zawāyā* is an abbreviation of *ahl al-zawāyā*[178] and so

---

171 A. Cauneille: *Les Chaanba*, p. 189. E.E. Evans-Pritchard: *The Sanusi of Cyrenaica*, London, 1949, p. 53.

172 A critical description of the war in H.T. Norris: 'Znāga Islam During the Seventeenth and Eighteenth Centuries', *BSOAS* 32, 1969, pp. 509-22.

173 Aḥmad al-Shinqīṭī: *Al-wasīt*, p. 470. Basically a variant of the *dhabīḥa*-right which Arab and Berber nomads have assumed *vis-à-vis* many agriculturists.; Segonzac: *Au cœur de l'Atlas*, pp. 96, 259.

174 *Wasīt*, p. 457. René Basset: *Mission au Sénégal*, II, p. 475. H.T. Norris: *Saharan Myth and Saga*, Oxford, 1972, p. 205.

175 *EI* s.v. Mauretanien (de la Chapelle, III, p. 482a). H.T. Norris: *Shinqīṭī Folk Literature and Song*, Oxford, 1968, p. 20. *Saharan Myth*, pp. 190-91.

176 *EI*: Mauretanien (III, pp. 479b, 480a, 483a). Norris: *Shinqīṭī Folk Literature*, pp. 15, 20. *Saharan Myth*, pp. 215-16, with a warning against over-simplification. Willis: *Studies in West African Islamic History*, I, p. 1-13. Nehemia Levtzion: 'ᶜAbd Allāh b. Yāsīn and the Almoravids', in the same collective volume, p. 101.

177 E.E. Evans-Pritchard: *The Sanusi of Cyrenaica*, p. 66.

178 The abbreviation is also not unknown in Morocco. A set of equivalents is: Shurafāʾ: *murābiṭūn*: ᶜulamāʾ = ashrāf: *murābiṭūn*: ṭalaba = shurafāʾ: *zawāyā*: ṭalaba = ashrāf: *zawāyā*:

should not be understood as much different from *al-murābiṭūn*, i.e. 'men of piety', even with the secondary meaning of the German word *fromm* 'harmless, who does not strike a blow'. As for the equivalent to the *zawāyā* among the Tuaregs in Mauritania, they are the *ineslemen* (sing. *anislem*, derived from Islam), the 'priest caste', as H.T. Norris puts it,[179] the 'Tolba', 'peaceable tribes, whose occupation consists of religious exercises and to a limited extent theological learning', as Heinrich Barth describes them.[180]

3. *AL-MURĀBIṬŪN* AND THE ALMORAVIDS

The survey presented above makes it easier, in my opinion, to understand the Almoravids/*al-murābiṭūn* who in precisely the reverse way developed the military side of the old *murābaṭa*.

---

fuqahā'; Muḥammad al-Qādirī (d. 1187/1773): *Nashr al-mathani*, ed. Cigar, Arabic pp. 70, 71, 72, 76, 78, 84, 85/English pp. 184, 185, 186, 190, 194, 202. Similarly, a Daymānī text, *Dhāt alwāḥ wa-dusur*, combines the terms but has nothing precise to say. It states: Perhaps the *zawāyā* are called thus because they attended the remote *zāwiya* for study and worship... Perhaps they are called *ṭalaba* because they strove after knowledge. Perhaps they are called *murābiṭ* because *ribāṭ* in the sense of *murābaṭat al-ᶜaduww* 'to be stationed at the enemy frontier' is meant. But the name could also be a derivation from the famous Almoravids in the Maghreb...; Norris: 'Znāga Islam', *BSOAS* 32, 1969, p. 511, ftn. 20; *Saharan Myth*, pp. 190-91. *Zāwiya* can also designate the settlement where members of a marabout family reside outside their original *zāwiya*; *Rabat et sa région III, Les Tribus*, Villes et Tribus du Maroc V, Paris, 1920, p. 352. *Zawāyā* can then be the villages which are the benefices, i.e. endowment or feudal properties, of other real *zawāyā*; *Rabat et sa région IV, Le Gharb (Les Djebala)*, p. 50: '*Zouaia* is the name of the douars whose crops (the choice of the word *revenus* must be a mistake) the last Marīnids allotted to the *zawāyā* of the Jazūlite shaykhs(?)', who lost their privileges after the establisment of the two new agricultural taxes (*tartīb*) of 1881 and 1902. According to documents from the 11th/17th and 12th/18th centuries, *zawāyā* can be the inviolable and inalienable estates of a marabout along with the people found on those estates, the two rather strikingly joined together; Charles Féraud: 'Exploitation des forêts de la Karasta dans la Kabylie orientale sous la domination turque', *RAfr.* 12, 1868, pp. 384-86. The people only in Michaux-Bellaire et Salmon in *Arch. Maroc.* 6, 1906, p. 369: The Daᶜāf between Wād Redat and Wād Ouerer'a in the Gharb are viewed as *zawāyā* of the Beni Malek.

179 H.T. Norris: *The Tuaregs*, Warminster Wilts, 1975, p. 19. The equivalence to the *zawāyā* is not complete in all respects; Norris, p. 5; *Saharan Myth*, pp. 46, 57.

180 Heinrich Barth: *Reisen und Entdeckungen in Nord- und Central-Afrika in den Jahren 1849 bis 1855*, Gotha, 1857-58, V, p. 581.

The two valuable old reports about the beginning of the Almoravid movement are mainly in agreement but contradict one another in a few secondary points. According to the contemporary Abū ᶜUbayd al-Bakrī of Córdoba who wrote in the year 460/1068, Yaḥyā b. Ibrāhīm from the Mauritanian Berber tribe Juddāla on the Atlantic coast, being the leader of this tribe and perhaps even of a confederation of the tribes Juddāla, Lamtūna and Massūfa[181] — though this is highly uncertain — on his return trip from the pilgrimage visited the Mālikite religious scholar Abū ᶜImrān al-Fāsī (d. 430/1039) in Qayrawān probably in 428/1036-37, in any case before 430/1039.[182] Abū ᶜImrān found him to be ignorant in religion but keen to learn something. Yaḥyā complained that the only teachers who came to them were not very particular and did not even know the regulations. He asked Abū ᶜImrān to send along with him one of his students, someone whose knowledge and religion he was sure of and who would be able to establish the regulations of religious law among them. Abū ᶜImrān did not find anyone willing to do this. He then advised Yaḥyā to turn to Wajjāj b. Zallūy[183] in Malkūs who had

181 Nehemia Levtzion: 'ᶜAbd Allāh b. Yāsīn and the Almoravids', in Willis: *Studies in West African Islamic History*, I, p. 90 below, doubts the confederation although there is no way to deny its mention in Ibn Abī Zarᶜ: *Rawḍ al-qirṭās/Annales regum Mauritaniae*, ed. Tornberg, Uppsala, 1846, pp. 76-77/Latin pp. 102-04. Translations from the *Rawḍ* in Joseph M. Cuoq: *Recueil des sources arabes concernant l'Afrique occidentale du VIIIe au XVIe siècle (Bilād al-Sūdān)*, Paris, 1975, pp. 228-39, and in N. Levtzion and J.F.P. Hopkins: *Corpus of the early Arabic sources for West African history*, Cambridge, 1981, pp. 234-48.

182 Date of death also in *Rawḍ al-qirṭās*, p. 77, l. 9/Latin p. 103. H.R. Idris: 'Deux maîtres de l'école juridique kairouanaise sous les Zîrîdes (XIe siècle): Abû Bakr b. ᶜAbd al-Raḥmân et Abû ᶜImrân al-Fâsî', *AIEO* 13, 1955, p. 60. Cf. pp. 54-55. The dating of the pilgrimage to 444/1052-53 by Ibn ᶜIdhārī al-Marrākushī: *Al-bayān al-mughrib*, Tome troisième (I cite this volume elsewhere as vol. II), ed. Lévi-Provençal, Paris, 1930, p. 242, contradicts the date of death, as does the dating to 440/1048-49 by the *Ḥulal mawshiyya*, p. 9/trans. Huici, p. 26/Cuoq, p. 365/Levtzion-Hopkins, p. 311.

183 His name and father's name are Berber. One also reads Wājāj, Wagāg, Wāgāg, Wakāk, etc., Zallū, Zalwī, Zalwān, etc. Some information about him and his family in Muḥammad al-Mukhtār al-Sūsī: *Maᶜsūl*, XI, pp. 30-39; XIII, pp. 301-02, 440-42; XIV, p. 8; XVII, p. 314; *Khilāl Jazūla*, Tetuan, 1379, I, pp. 74-79. An early Almohad official in Marrakesh was named Abū Ḥafṣ ᶜUmar b. Wākāk/Wājāj; Aḥmad al-Nāṣirī al-Salāwī: *Al-istiqṣā li-akhbār duwal al-Maghrib al-aqṣā*, Rabat, 1954, II, p. 73, l. 109/trans. Colin, *Arch. Maroc.* 31, 1925, p. 214 (Wâggâg); trans. Hamet, *Arch. Maroc.* 32, 1927, p. 47 (Ouaggag). *Tashawwuf*, p. 420, records an Abū Wājjāj ᶜAffān b. Ismāᶜīl al-Maṭmāṭī (d. 604/1208) and, p. 436, a Wājjāj b. Abī ᶜAlī Manṣūr. Sūsī writes in *Maᶜsūl*, XI, p. 80: 'Wagāg is derived from Shilḥa *īgīg*

studied with him and who fulfilled all the necessary requirements. On his journey through Malkūs Yaḥyā looked up Wajjāj and the latter gave him a student to take with him named ᶜAbdallāh b. Yāsīn al-Jazūlī whose mother originally came from the Sahara.[184] — According to Qāḍī ᶜIyāḍ (d. 544/1149), the author of the second report, it was not Yaḥyā b. Ibrāhīm but a certain Jawhar b. Sakkam (emended thus[185]) who asked Wajjāj for a man who could give his people instruction about Islam. He complained to him that most of his people were still heathens (*jāhiliyya*), at best only knew the two sentences of the Islamic profession of faith but were not familiar with the religious duties. Wajjāj sent with him a pupil of his house in Sūs which he had built 'for religious learning and the good' and named *Dār al-murābiṭīn*: ᶜAbdallāh b. Yāsīn who was known 'for religious learning and the good'. There is no mention in this report of ᶜIyāḍ of an earlier visit to Abū ᶜImrān al-Fāsī in Qayrawān.[186]

Evidently, what we have here are two traditions with an opposed political tendency and different actors, because Jawhar is one of those rare Juddāla who took Islam more seriously. However, only Qāḍī ᶜIyāḍ and Ibn al-Athīr (d. 630/1233)[187] relate that Jawhar

---

"thunder" (*raᶜd*). Perhaps he acquired this epithet because of his extensive learning.' Norris: *Saharan Myth*, p. 117: 'Wajjāj/Aggāg - "thunder-rain maker"'. — Wajjāj is not an epithet but the personal name of the man. There was also the masculine name Īgīg. Ismāᶜīl Īgīg was an early disciple of Ibn Tūmart in Aghmat; Lévi-Provençal: *Documents inédits de l'histoire almohade*, French p. 113.

184 Bakrī: *Al-mughrib/Description de l'Afrique septentrionale par Abou-Obeïd-el-Bekri*, ed. and trans. by de Slane, 1911-13, new edition, Paris, 1965, Arabic pp. 164-65/French 313-14/Vincent Monteil: 'Al-Bakrî (Cordoue 1068), Routier de l'Afrique blanche et noire du Nord-Ouest, traduction nouvelle de seize chapitres, avec notes et commentaire', *BIFAN* XXX, sér. B., no. 1, 1968, pp. 59-60/Cuoq, p. 87/Levtzion-Hopkins, p. 71. According to *Rawḍ al-qirṭās*, p. 78, ll. 6-7/Latin p. 105/Cuoq, p. 232/Levtzion-Hopkins, p. 239, this meeting with Wajjāj took place in Rajab 430/April 1039. Later the home of Ibn Yāsīn was sought in Tamanart in the Anti-Atlas; Justinard: *Fawaid al jamma*, VIII, p. 16; Norris: *Saharan Myth*, p. 95.

185 Printed text *Skn*.

186 Al-Qāḍī ᶜIyāḍ: *Tartīb al-madārik wa-taqrīb al-masālik li-maᶜrifat aᶜlām madhhab Mālik*, Beirut, n.d., IV, p. 781/cited in Sūsī: *Maᶜsūl*, XI, pp. 46-47/trans. H.T. Norris: 'New Evidence on the Life of ᶜAbdallāh b. Yāsīn', *JAH* 12, 1971, pp. 255-57/Cuoq, pp. 125-26/Levtzion-Hopkins, pp. 101-03.

187 Ibn al-Athīr: *Al-kāmil fī'l-tārīkh*, Beirut, 1965-67, year 448 (IX, pp. 618-21)/trans. Cuoq, pp. 191-93/Levtzion-Hopkins, pp. 158-60. Ibn al-Athīr, who has the event take place

brought with him to the Sahara the new man from the north. In Bakrī and in Ibn ᶜIdhārī al-Marrākushī (8th/14th century)[188] he only turns up later, after Ibn Yāsīn had already begun his missionary work among the Juddāla. Jawhar criticized Ibn Yāsīn, hatched a plot against him, deprived him of his right to make decisions and have a say, tore down his house and took away from him the treasury of the community that had formed around him. Jawhar is not mentioned in Ibn Abī Zarᶜ (d. after 726/1326)[189] or in the anonymous *al-Ḥulal al-mawshiyya* (composed 783/1381-82).[190] Ibn al-Athīr, on the other hand, concentrates entirely on Jawhar and presents a novel-like description in which the two friends, Jawhar and Ibn Yāsīn, work together on the closest possible terms, at first among the Lamtūna without much success, then more sucessfully among the Juddāla, and finally, after confronting more unified resistance, agree to transfer leadership of the military struggle to the chief of the Lamtūna, Abu Bakr (sic) b. ᶜUmar. They remain, however, among the Juddāla. Ibn Yāsīn and Abū Bakr go on to achieve such an overwhelming supremacy that Jawhar then attempts to undermine it. He is brought before a court and sentenced to death. This version[191] is not historically viable, although it does agree with the other reports that a break took place between Jawhar and Ibn Yāsīn, and that, in some

only in 448/1056, does not maintain there was a meeting with Abū ᶜImrān in Qayrawān any more than Qāḍī ᶜIyāḍ does.

188 Ambrosio Huici Miranda: 'Un fragmento inédito de Ibn ᶜIḏārī sobre los Almorávides', *Hespéris Tamuda* 2, 1961, pp. 46-51/Ibn ᶜIdhārī al-Marrākushī: *Al-bayān al-mughrib fī akhbār al-Andalus wa'l-Maghrib*, ed. Iḥsān ᶜAbbās, Beirut, 1967, IV, pp. 7-15 /Cuoq, pp. 221-24/Levtzion-Hopkins, pp. 217-23. For the sake of simplicity in what follows I only cite the Arabic text in the Beirut edition of Iḥsān ᶜAbbās.

189 *Rawḍ al-qirṭās/Annales regum Mauritaniae*, ed. Tornberg, pp. 75-81/Latin trans. pp. 100-111/printed edition, Rabat, 1972, pp. 119-28.

190 *Al-ḥulal al-mawshiyya*, ed. I.S. Allouche, in Institut des Hautes Études Marocaines 1936, pp. 5-12 (not accessible to me)/trans. Ambrosio Huici Miranda: *Colección de Crónicas árabes de la Reconquista, Tomo I, "Al-Ḥulal al-Mawshiyya"*, Tetuan, 1952, pp. 22-32/Cuoq, pp. 364-67/Levtzion-Hopkins, pp. 310-13.

191 Nuwayrī (d. 732/1332): *Nihāyat al-arab*, the unprinted part, follows it; preprint with translation in 'Historia de los musulmanes de España y Africa, por En-Nuguairi. Texto árabe y traducción española, por M. Gaspar Remiro', *Revista del Centro de Estudios históricos de Granada y su Reino*, Granada, 1917-19, Spanish pp. 181-84.

way or another, this quarrel is connected with Ibn Yāsīn's drawing closer to the Lamtūna.[192]

According to Ibn ᶜIdhārī, after Jawhar's rebellion Ibn Yāsīn went over to the Lamtūna who resided to the east of the Juddāla and were commanded by Yaḥyā b. ᶜUmar, but he also returned to his teacher Wajjāj in Malkūs, or at least wrote to him as another tradition would have it. According to Bakrī, the community had previously already chosen Yaḥyā b. ᶜUmar from the Lamtūna as leader, and after the rebellion Ibn Yāsīn now travelled directly to Wajjāj in Malkūs. As both authors, Bakrī and Ibn ᶜIdhārī, relate in agreement, the *éminence grise* Wajjāj voiced the most fierce reproaches against the guilty Juddāla, explained to them that anyone who acted against his protégé placed himself outside the community (*jamāᶜa*) and, according to Bakrī, would be an outlaw. He ordered Ibn Yāsīn to return to his post. The latter obeyed and convened a bloody criminal court against his opponents as well as others who in his eyes deserved to be executed for the sake of religion. He imposed the *sunna* everywhere among those tribes and from the Lamṭa, whose life he apparently judged to be in need of expiation, he demanded one third of their possessions so they might legally dispose over of the remaining two-thirds.

Here a break is clearly recognizable between the first and the second act of Ibn Yāsīn's activity in the Sahara. It consists of a temporary retreat on the part of Ibn Yāsīn. He had in fact already been able to acquire a following in the first phase and to accumulate a communal treasury, but his strict requirements were not in accord with the modest level of power he disposed over. Likewise, connections with the Lamtūna were even then already established, but only with his second attempt, after the interruption, did Ibn Yāsīn seek the full support of the Lamtūna. In the first act he went about his work peacefully, in the second act he struck out with the sword. His recourse to Wajjāj and the latter's harsh orders issued to the Juddāla reveal two things: firstly, the existence of a pious movement whose spiritual driving force was Wajjāj and which extended deep into the Sahara and, secondly, an agreement between this movement and the chief of the Lamtūna, Yaḥyā b. ᶜUmar. The boundaries between this movement and Islam, and similarly the boundaries between Yaḥyā b.

---

192 Norris: *Saharan Myth and Saga*, p. 95, attempts to eliminate the difference between the two versions by proposing that Jawhar, as a scholar, could have accompanied the leader Yaḥyā b. Ibrāhīm on his pilgrimage and negotiated as his spokesman with Abū ᶜImrān in Qayrawān.

ᶜUmar's duties toward his tribe on the one hand and toward the movement on the other, are not clear. One sees that Ibn Yāsīn's religious community is out to acquire a political footing and to harness the existing political power for its own ends. The Lamtūna appear to offer the framework and Yaḥyā b. ᶜUmar the personal authority for this purpose. What Wajjāj understood by 'the community', from which he threatened to exclude the malicious, remains in the dark. One can take this to mean Islam or the particular movement in question. The people he was addressing probably lumped the two together. Ibn Yāsīn's retreat and preparation for the second phase of his missionary activity can be seen as his *hijra*.

Yaḥyā b. Ibrāhīm, the leader of the Juddāla, who had brought Ibn Yāsīn to the south, disappears without a trace in Bakrī and is never mentioned at all in Qāḍī ᶜIyāḍ and Ibn al-Athīr. According to Ibn ᶜIdhārī, he died before the crisis between Jawhar and Ibn Yāsīn, and one even harbors the suspicion that this disagreement could have had something to do with a dispute over succession since, to begin with, Ibn Yāsīn did in fact remain among the Juddāla and had the task of completing their Islamicization. But this remains open. The *Ḥulal mawshiyya* leaves all this out of the picture. Ibn Khaldūn (d. 808/1406) likewise situates Yaḥyā b. Ibrāhīm's death before the rupture, without however any reference to Jawhar or to a retreat or switching sides on the part of Ibn Yāsīn. According to Ibn Khaldūn, Ibn Yāsīn only ever resided among the Lamtūna and never among the Juddāla, and in his description unrest only arose among the Lamtūna, not among the Juddāla. None the less, according to Ibn Khaldūn's explanation, Ibn Yāsīn won over to his cause the two brothers Abū Bakr and Yaḥyā b. ᶜUmar, and with them carried out a withdrawal movement, his *hijra*, not to the north but southwards to the Senegal and lived there with them on an island in the river performing religious devotions.[193] They acquired numerous supporters and veneration, and when thousands of Lamtūna had joined them, Ibn Yāsīn set out with them for the north and with the weapons of his determined force conquered one tribe after another: the Lamtūna, Juddāla and Massūfa. He authorized his people to collect the tithe from the Muslims, gave them the name *al-murābiṭūn* and placed at their head the emir Yaḥyā b. ᶜUmar. Wajjāj, who, according to Ibn

193 This version of Ibn Khaldūn is followed by Georges Marçais: *La Berbérie musulmane et l'Orient au moyen âge*, Aubier Paris, 1946, p. 239, and Gustav Edmund von Grunebaum: *Der Islam*, in *Propyläen-Weltgeschichte*, V, 1963, p. 156, where however the name ᶜAlī ibn Jāsīn should be changed to ᶜAbdallāh ibn Jāsīn.

Khaldūn did not reside in Malkūs which cannot be identified with certainty but in Sijilmāsa (Tafilalt),[194] called upon the warrior host for help against the oppression of the ruling Maghrāwa, which led to the conquest and annexation of this oasis complex.[195] Thus Yaḥyā b. ᶜUmar had traversed the Sahara from its southern to its northern rim.

Ibn Abī Zarᶜ adopts a similar framework but gives Yaḥyā b. Ibrāhīm a life which extends beyond the *hijra* of Ibn Yāsīn and keeps Ibn Yāsīn as long as possible in the company of the Juddāla who were living on the coast. According to Ibn Abī Zarᶜ, the Juddāla and the Lamtūna, among whom Ibn Yāsīn was working, found his laws too strict, and Ibn Yāsīn considered the idea of changing over to the already Islamicized blacks, i.e. to push further south in order to gather forces there and at a given moment to return to the north,[196] perhaps with an army of black warriors. That is not explicitly stated, but Yaḥyā b. Ibrāhīm must have feared something of this kind, since he made him a counter-proposal to withdraw to an island in the sea, not in the south but to the west, and there to lead a life of hunting and fishing in pious isolation. At low tide the island was easily accessible by foot, at high tide by ship. Ibn Yāsīn followed the advice and, according to this account, undertook a *hijra* to the west. He went to the island along with Yaḥyā b. Ibrāhīm and seven other Juddāla, built a *rābiṭa* there and lived in it with his companions for three months. They acquired a reputation for seeking Paradise and deliverance from Hell. Sympathizers joined them. Ibn Yāsīn taught them the Koran and aroused in them a feeling for the good and God's reward. He named the approximately one thousand aristocratic Berbers who attached themselves to him *al-murābiṭūn* because they resided with him in his *rābiṭa*. In so doing — one may observe — he gave an Islamic name to the community of his like-minded followers who had renounced their tribal ties and formed an independent, religiously defined corporation. He impressed on them that the work of conversion should be carried out by force if need be. They moved

---

194 Ibn Khaldūn: *Histoire des Berbères*, trans. de Slane, II, pp. 68, 117/Levtzion-Hopkins, p. 329, ... (not translated).

195 *Histoire des Berbères*, II, pp. 67-70/Levtzion-Hopkins, pp. 328-30.

196 It has also been said: because he hoped to find a more rewarding field of activity among the more receptive blacks; A. Benachenhou: *La dynastie almoravide et son art*, Algiers, 1974, p. 18. On the earlier Islamization Bakrī, p. 172/French p. 324/Monteil, p. 68/Cuoq, p. 96/Levtzion-Hopkins, p. 77/*Kitāb al-istibṣār fī ᶜajāʾib al-amṣār*, ed. Saᶜd Zaghlūl ᶜAbd al-Ḥamīd, Alexandria, 1958, p. 217; J. Spencer Trimingham: *A History of Islam in West Africa*, Oxford University Press, 1963, p. 28.

onto the mainland and subdued the individual tribes one after the other: the Juddāla, Lamtūna, Massūfa and others. Ibn Yāsīn 'purified' each individual who did penance with a hundred lashes, taught him the Koran and instructed him about the legal prescriptions, ritual prayer, as well as the duty of giving alms and paying the tithe. He met the costs of waging war from the treasury. When Yaḥyā b. Ibrāhīm from the tribe of the Juddāla then died, he appointed as supreme commander Yaḥyā b. ᶜUmar from the tribe of the Lamtūna. In the future the emir Yaḥyā b. ᶜUmar led the military operations, while Ibn Yāsīn undertook the spiritual tasks. The latter also kept control of the judiciary office and taxation.

Unmistakably this was a question of the birth of a religious state whose highest level of leadership consisted of a duumvirate. However, as a remark in Ibn ᶜIdhārī (p. 4, l. 12) and further events show, one should not deny political tasks to the one and attribute them exclusively to the other. Ibn Yāsīn was also fully active in the political area and was even present on the military campaigns. He did not stand alongside but rather behind the emir Yaḥyā b. ᶜUmar. 'He was in reality the emir who issued commands and prohibitions.' If and as long as Wajjāj was still alive, he had the final decision in the Sahara through Ibn Yāsīn. When Wajjāj died or if he was already dead — Muḥammad al-Mukhtār al-Sūsī dates his death around 445/1053[197] — then Ibn Yāsīn was his successor and representative in the Sahara.

All those who present reports are agreed that the men of piety who set up the new state came forth from the desert as *murābiṭūn* and conquered Sijilmāsa as *murābiṭūn*. This cannot mean anything else except that they were united under the banner of *ribāṭ/murābaṭa*. They were not simply 'holy warriors' or something of that sort, but this was their *specific name*, and according to most authors[198] Ibn Yāsīn had given them this name. Concerning the reason for their being given this name there are two traditions. The one goes back to Ibn Abī Zarᶜ, that Ibn Yāsīn designated his adherents in the *rābiṭa* on the island this way. Natural-geographical observation and historical considerations have led to the conclusion that Ibn Khaldūn's island in the Senegal deserves little trust and that Ibn Yāsīn's island should rather be sought in the sea, even though 'sea' in Ibn Abī Zarᶜ can

---

197 *Maᶜsūl*, VIII, p. 130, l. 7. Pure conjecture.

198 Ibn ᶜIdhārī, IV, p. 12/Cuoq, p. 223/Levtzion-Hopkins, p. 221. *Ḥulal mawshiyya*, p. 11/Huici, p. 30/Cuoq, p. 366/Levtzion-Hopkins, p. 312. *Ibn Khaldoun: Berbères*, II, p. 69/Levtzion-Hopkins, p. 329. Ibn al-Athīr, year 448, IX, p. 620/Cuoq, p. 192/Levtzion-Hopkins, p. 160.

also mean river.[199] Moreover, on the basis of field research it has emerged that the island meant by Ibn Abī Zar^{c} which was located near the sea coast, if his report is correct, could be the island Tīdra in the Mauritanian shoal of Arguin.[200] It is not possible, however, to build a *rābiṭa* there because there is no stone and no clay on this completely flat island. On the other hand, Ibn Yāsīn was only meant to have resided there for a short period. That he would have named the people who stayed in his *rābiṭa* and listened to his sermons and lessons and followed the Islamic laws *murābiṭūn* would not be out of place in view of the reports about life in the old *ribāṭāt*.[201] Furthermore, by the *rābiṭa* in question we should perhaps not understand much more than was meant by the *rābiṭa* of the later Ibn Tūmart in Īgīlīz in 514/1120-21. According to Ibn Khaldūn (*Berbères* II, p. 168)[202] in 515/1121-22 Ibn Tūmart there built a *rābiṭa* for religious practices (*^{c}ibāda*) and in it gave instruction on his basic writings to people from different tribes. In this case it was no more than a cave which he then surrounded with a fence (Berber āsārāg)[203] for the horses,[204] and this place Īgīlīz (south-east of Tarudant) was then called 'the *ribāṭ* of the tribe Hargha'[205] in the 7th/13th century, per-

199 Paulo Fernando de Moraes Farias: 'The Almoravids: Some questions', *BIFAN* 29, sér. B, nos. 3-4, 1967, pp. 821-22. Jacinto Bosch Vilá also came out against the Senegal or the Niger: *Historia de Marruecos: Los Almorávides*, Tetuan, 1956, pp. 56-57. Of course, the Wād Nūn is also wrong, lying much too far to the north; Justinard: *Les Aït Ba Amran*, p. 78.

200 Seeking it in that location was suggested by the description which Bakrī gives of an island there; Bakrī, p. 171/French p. 323/Monteil, p. 66 (106)/Cuoq, p. 95 (§ 122)/Levtzion-Hopkins, p. 77/*Istibṣār*, pp. 214-15. It accords with the description in *Rawḍ al-qirṭās*, p. 79/Latin p. 106. Moraes Farias, pp. 829-30.

201 Henri J. Hugot: 'Mission à l'île de Tîdra', *BIFAN* 28, sér. B, 1966, pp. 555-64, 1019-23. Recapitulation in Attilio Gaudio: *Le dossier de la Mauritanie*, Paris, 1978, pp. 52-55. Moraes Farias: 'The Almoravids', *BIFAN* 29, sér. B, pp. 821-43.

202 Arabic in I. Goldziher: *Le Livre de Mohammed ibn Toumert*, Algiers, 1903, Arabic p. 57.

203 On this word Émile Laoust: 'Contribution', *REI* 13, 1939, pp. 276-77, no. 221.

204 Baydhaq in E. Lévi-Provençal: *Documents inédits d'histoire almohade*, Paris, 1928, Arabic pp. 72-73/French pp. 116-17. Ambrosio Huici Miranda: *Historia política del imperio almohade*, Tetuan, 1956, I, p. 64.

205 *Al-ansāb fī ma^{c}rifat al-aṣḥāb* in Lévi-Provençal: *Documents inédits*, Arabic p. 40/French p. 60. Ambrosio Huici Miranda: *Historia política*, I, p. 181. Map with approximate location ibid., p. 60. Not to be confused with the mountain Īgīlīz near Marrakesh; Louis di Giacomo: 'Une poétesse andalouse du temps des Almohades: Ḥafṣa bint al-Ḥājj ar-Rukūnīya',

haps because it contained still older pious premises, or perhaps only subsequently in memory of Ibn Tūmart. According to Ibn ᶜIdhārī, Ibn Tūmart lived there in not simply one but in two *rābiṭas*.[206] Thus the possibility of a *rābiṭa* on Tīdra is not to be dismissed categorically. Similarly, the accusations of untrustworthiness which have been made against Ibn Abī Zarᶜ[207] should not be transferred without further consideration to everything he has to say. However, he is admittedly a skilful narrator who makes the events fit together smoothly and loves large, simple contours. Because of this tendency he could well sacrifice accuracy. It is clear that by his *rābiṭa* he does not mean a *ribāṭ* of the old style but something similar to what Ibn Khaldūn has in mind for Ibn Tūmart, i.e. a *zāwiya* of pious seclusion, and that in his derivation of the name *murābiṭūn* from *rābiṭa* he is only following a clever idea, namely to compare the old Almoravids with the inhabitants of a *zāwiya* of his own time, the 8th/14th century. How unimportant the existence of a *rābiṭa* or a *ribāṭ* for the origin of the Almoravids' name appeared to the 8th/14th century is indicated by the retelling of the same story about the island in Ibn al-Khaṭīb in 774-776/1372-74. He also maintains that Ibn Yāsīn gave the name *murābiṭūn* to his loyal followers on the island, but for the purpose of waging war (*jihād*) against their opponents. He does not say a word about a *rābiṭa*, or about a *ribāṭ* for that matter.[208] *Murābiṭūn* is dissociated from *ribāṭ*.

This is even more clearly the case in the other tradition which Ibn ᶜIdhārī and the anonymous *Ḥulal mawshiyya* present us with. Here it is the Lamtūna who receive this honorific name. Ibn Yāsīn sends Yaḥyā b. ᶜUmar with his troops against a heathen mountain population which refuses to convert to Islam, and conquers them after battles involving heavy casualties. This was the first time Yaḥyā b.

---

in *Hespéris* 34, 1947, p. 89, ftn. 232; Jillīz in E. Lévi-Provençal: 'Notes d'histoire almohade', *Hespéris* 10, 1930, p. 66 (Arabic)/p. 85 (French). Cf. photos in Huici, pp. 68 and 144.

206 *Al-bayān al-mughrib*, III parte, ed. Ambrosio Huici Miranda, Tetuan, 1963, p. 122, ll. 3-7/trans. Huici, I, p. 48. A. Huici Miranda: *Historia política del imperio almohade*, I, p. 68.

207 Especially Ambrosio Huici Miranda: 'La salida de los Almorávides del desierto y el reinado de Yūsuf b. Tāšfīn', *Hespéris* 46, 1959, pp. 155-82. Idem: 'El *Rawḍ al-qirṭās* y los Almorávides', *Hespéris Tamuda* 1, 1960, pp. 513-41.

208 The text, which was not available to me, is translated in Norris: *Saharan Myth*, p. 97, from Ibn Khaṭīb: *Tārīkh al-maghrib al-ᶜarabī fī'l-ᶜaṣr al-wasīṭ*, vol. III of *Kitāb aᶜmāl al-aᶜlām*, ed. Aḥmad Mukhtār al-ᶜAbbādī and Muḥammad Ibrāhīm al-Kattānī, Casablanca, 1964, pp. 227-28.

ᶜUmar as emir obtained a fifth portion of the booty. Ibn Yāsīn named him *amīr al-ḥaqq* and the troops *murābiṭūn*. He encouraged them to persevere (*kāna yuṣabbiruhum*) until they were victorious.[209] The author of the *Ḥulal mawshiyya* clarifies this with the words: 'He gave them this name when he saw their staunch perseverance and their brave endurance (*shiddat ṣabrihim wa-ḥusn balāʾihim*) in battle against the polytheists.'[210]

The two accounts are completely divergent. The time, place and circumstances in each are different. The reason for their acquiring their name and the meaning attributed to the word *murābiṭ* are explained one way in one account and another way in the other account. Are the two differences irreconcilable or can they perhaps, independently of one another, both be true? The Moroccan scholar Aḥmad Mukhtār al-ᶜAbbādī (Labbadie) thinks a solution is possible and in his essay *Dirāsa ḥawl kitāb al-Ḥulal al-mawshiyya fī dhikr al-akhbār al-marrākushiyya wa-ahammiyyatihī fī tārīkh al-Murābiṭīn wa-l-Muwaḥḥidīn*[211] in the journal *Tiṭwān* 5, 1960, pp. 139-58, works out the question accordingly:

The following results from Ibn Abi Zarᶜ's presentation:

1) The designation *murābiṭūn* was given by Ibn Yāsīn to the tribe Juddāla living on the Atlantic coast. The number of those who joined his cause came to a thousand men under the leadership of their emir Yaḥyā b. Ibrāhīm al-Juddālī.

2) The word *murābiṭūn* here has the meaning 'those who remained withdrawn with Ibn Yāsīn in his *ribāṭ* on the island for the purpose of worship (*ᶜibāda*) and exclusive devotion to God'.

3) The name was applied relatively early, already at the beginning of Ibn Yāsīn's propaganda and missionary activity.

---

209 Ibn ᶜIdhārī: *Bayān*, IV, p. 12/Cuoq, p. 223/Levtzion-Hopkins, pp. 220-21.

210 *Ḥulal*, ed. Allouche, p. 11/Spanish trans. Huici Miranda, p. 30/Cuoq, p. 366/ Levtzion-Hopkins, p. 312. Noth: 'Das *ribāṭ* der Almoraviden', pp. 504-05. *Ḥusn al-balāʾ* is otherwise used for God's 'friendliness'. Lane's *Dict. balāʾ*: *balāʾ ḥasan*. Abū Dāwūd: *Sunan*, VII, p. 343, with ftn. 3. Ibn al-Khaṭīb: *Al-iḥāṭa fī akhbār Gharnāṭa*, ed. ᶜInān, Cairo, 1974, II, p. 122; p. 135: *ḥasuna balāʾuhū* 'he acquit himself well'. Ibn Athīr: *Kāmil*, year 499, X, p. 414 (*dhikr ᶜiddat ḥawādith*): *ablā balāʾan ḥasanan* 'he stood the test'.

211 Mentioned by H.T. Norris: 'New Evidence on the Life of ᶜAbdallāh b. Yāsīn', *JAH* 12, 1971, p. 261, and *Saharan Myth*, p. 102, ftn. 2. — ᶜAbbādī is well-known as the editor of Ibn al-Khaṭīb's *Nufāḍat al-jirāb*, Cairo, n.d., *Aᶜmāl al-aᶜlām*, Casablanca, 1964, etc.

From the strand of tradition found in Ibn ᶜIdhārī and the *Ḥulal,* which both possibly draw on the same source from the time of the Almoravids, perhaps Ibn al-Ṣayrafī,[212] what can be extracted is:

1) The designation *murābiṭūn* was given by Ibn Yāsīn to the tribe Lamtūna, located to the north and east of the Juddāla, and this after the Lamtūna had fought a hard battle under the leadership of their emir Yaḥyā b. ᶜUmar al-Lamtūnī against the heathens in the north (sic) of the Sahara. The number of the Lamtūna who took part amounted to more than a thousand horsemen.

2) Here the word *murābiṭūn* does *not* have the meaning 'residing in a *rābiṭa* or in a *ribāṭ*', but means 'warriors for the faith (*mujāhidūn*) who are steadfast on the path of God', without attachment to a *ribāṭ* where they would form the garrison.

3) The name was applied relatively late, only after Ibn Yāsīn had already undertaken a considerable propaganda and missionary activity.

ᶜAbbādī reflects: on the assumption that both groups of texts transmit the truth, one must inevitably conclude that Ibn Yāsīn conferred the name *murābiṭūn* on two occasions:

1) firstly at the beginning of his missionary activity to the Juddāliyyūn who responded to Ibn Yāsīn's call and lived in his *ribāṭ* (on the island) until the death of their leader Yaḥyā b. Ibrāhīm (sic).

2) then to the Lamtūniyyūn who spread his propaganda further and served his cause with bravery and perseverance until all Morocco and Spain were won (sic).

The change — according to ᶜAbbādī — was understandable. Between the two Ṣanhāja tribes there was an old rivalry for the leadership. It appears that after the death of their leader Yaḥyā b. Ibrāhīm the Juddāla wished to propose another leader from their own midst. Ibn Yāsīn was against this (sic). They then tore down (sic) his house and expelled him. Ibn Yāsīn judged the future lay with the Lamtūna because of their northern position which appeared to be suitable for an advance on Morocco (sic) but also because of their military ability. Furthermore, the Lamtūna were the most devoted to him and the most pious. This, as it seems, led to the Juddāla breaking with Ibn Yāsīn which Bakrī describes with the words: 'They opposed him and acted in defiance of him and withdrew from him to the seacoast'

---

212 Huici: *Ḥulal* (trans.), p. 11. Noth: 'Das *ribāṭ*', p. 505. Levtzion-Hopkins, pp. 217, 465. Ibn ᶜIdhārī, IV, p. 49, ll. 2-3/Ambrosio Huici Miranda: 'Un fragmento inédito de Ibn ᶜIḏārī sobre los Almorávides', *Hespéris Tamuda* 2, 1961, p. 68. ll. 1-2, gives the title of Ibn al-Ṣayrafī's work: *Taqaṣṣī* (to be read thus) *al-anbāʾ fī siyāsat al-ruʾasāʾ*.

(Bakrī, p. 167/French pp. 315-16/Monteil, p. 61, bot./Cuoq, p. 90 (§109)/Levtzion-Hopkins, p. 73), that is, to their ancestral regions. Ibn Yāsīn was now forced to draw his support only from the Lamtūna, and they took upon themselves great privations and battles involving heavy losses. And for this reason Ibn Yāsīn conferred on them the title *murābiṭūn*, i.e. because of their steadfast perseverance and their brave endurance. In the future the Lamtūna — ᶜAbbādī goes on — also bore the burden of spreading his teaching and his power. *Murābiṭūn* became synonymous with Lamtūna (*Ḥulal*, Arabic p. 152/Spanish, Huici, p. 206). In this way the leaders of the Lamtūna became the kings of this dynasty of the Almoravids.

Under the most successful of these kings, Yūsuf b. Tāshfīn (453-500/1061-1106), the Murābiṭūn/Almoravids — as ᶜAbbādī continues — directed their gaze toward Spain and therewith began a new phase in their struggle, the holy war against the Christians. Possibly — according to ᶜAbbādī — this revived the concept of *murābiṭūn* once again. This is suggested by a passage in ᶜAbd al-Wāḥid al-Marrākushī's *Muᶜjib* (ed. Dozy, p. 114, last line):[213] 'From then on he was reckoned among kings and he earned the name of ruler. He and his comrades were called *murābiṭūn*', namely after the conquest of Spain. And similarly with regard to his son ᶜAlī (*Muᶜjib,* p. 122):[214] 'After him (Yūsuf) his son ᶜAlī took over the government. Like his father he called himself Ruler of the Muslims, and his comrades were called *al-murābiṭūn*. He followed in his father's footsteps by promoting the holy war, menaced the enemy and defended the country.'

ᶜAbbādī concludes from all this, but with a degree of caution, that the real meaning of the word *murābiṭūn* only emerged after the leadership change from the Juddāla to the Lamtūna, when Ibn Yāsīn praised the Lamtūna as being brave warriors for the faith and that the old meaning of the word which Ibn Yāsīn had used earlier for his adherents in the *ribāṭ* of the country of the Juddāla (= on the island) was lost (sic) when the Juddāla withdrew from the union of his loyal supporters. ᶜAbbādī takes the original meaning of *murābaṭa* to be 'residing in a *ribāṭ*', and 'proving one's worth in holy war' to be the figurative sense.

One might wish to touch up a few details in this simple picture of ᶜAbbādī's but the conflicting reports of the sources are brought into

---

213 Translation Ambrosio Huici Miranda: *Kitāb al-muᶜŷib fī taljīṣ ajbār al-Magrib*, in his *Colección de Crónicas árabes de la Reconquista*, IV, Tetuan, 1955, p. 119.

214 Huici, ibid., p. 127.

harmony with one another. Their inherent contradictions are removed by chronologically staggering the events, they are shown to be merely apparent and are thus eliminated. That *murābaṭa* can mean 'to withdraw in a *ribāṭ* to undertake religious practices and devotions' and 'to stand one's ground bravely' is undisputed. The first meaning was long accepted usage in the 5th/11th century, and the second at any time could, and still can, be read into surah 3/200.[215] A relatively educated man like Ibn Yāsīn must have been aware of these ideas.

But despite this the question whether Ibn Yāsīn really conferred the name this way, and on two separate occasions, still remains unanswered. Huici[216] and Norris[217] have doubts about the story of the island, in fact actually reject it. Norris suspects a narrative motif. A hermit living in 'the woods', as Ibn Khaldūn depicts him,[218] is also a motif.[219] Noth, after reflecting on the central concern of the Almoravids, i.e. to lead by force of arms the heathens and lukewarm Muslims to the just path, arrived at the same scepticism about the *rābiṭa* on the island.[220] Abdallah Laroui is not willing to give up the story of the island. In his view Ibn Yāsīn's withdrawal to the island represents an intentional imitation of the *hijra* of the Prophet.[221] On the other hand, in my opinion doubts also arise about extolling bravery with the concept of *murābaṭa* because the authors of this version in fact already knew the name 'Almoravids' and could easily have come up with surah 3/200 to explain it. Levtzion maintains a degree of reserve and neutrality.[222] Obviously one has no criterion at

---

215 Pseudo-Ibn-al-Aḥmar: *Buyūtāt Fās al-kubrā*, Rabat, 1972, p. 29, ll. 2-3, establishes the connection with surah 3/200 more clearly by means of an expansion. He says Ibn Yāsīn called the people *murābiṭūn* because of 'their *ṣabr* and their *ribāṭ* (= *murābaṭa*) against them' (= the enemies). Thus with *ribāṭ* he also covers the *rābiṭū* of the Koranic verse as well.

216 'La salida', *Hespéris* 46, 1959, p. 160, ftn. 9. 'El *Rawḍ al-qirṭās* y los Almorávides', *Hespéris Tamuda* 1, 1960, pp. 518-19.

217 'New Evidence', *JAH* 12, 1971, pp. 257-62.

218 *Berbères* II, p. 69, l. 1/Levtzion-Hopkins, p. 329, l. 30. Moraes Farias, *BIFAN* 29, sér. B, 1967, p. 804.

219 Abū Ṭālib al-Makkī: *Qūt al-qulūb*, Cairo, 1932, III, p. 79/Abū Ḥāmid al-Ghazzālī: *Iḥyā' ʿulūm al-dīn*, Cairo, 1957, IV, p. 323, penult. line.

220 'Das *ribāṭ* der Almoraviden', pp. 503-10.

221 Abdallah Laroui: *L'histoire du Maghreb*, Paris, 1976, I, p. 147.

222 'ʿAbd Allāh b. Yāsīn and the Almoravids', in Willis: *Studies in West African Islamic History*, I, pp. 85, 92.

one's disposal for preferring one of the two traditions or indeed for accepting both of them.

Distancing oneself from both accounts, however, allows one to consider a third possibility. That is to trace the name *al-murābiṭūn* 'Almoravids' to Wajjāj's Dār al-murābiṭīn. We do not know exactly what one should understand by this house of the *murābiṭūn*. Ibn Abī Zar[c] considered it was a *ribāṭ*,[223] whereas Muḥammad al-Mukhtār al-Sūsī took it to be a *rābiṭa*, no different from the doubtful *rābiṭa* on the island, hence a *zāwiya* like the innumerable *zāwiya*s that existed in Islamic Africa in the Middle Ages and still exist today, i.e. a convent.[224] Nor do we know where this house of Wajjāj's was located. Attempts have been made to equate Malkūs with present-day Melkis on the Ziz in the Tafilalt, i.e. near Sijilmāsa, where Bakrī and Ibn [c]Idhārī located it.[225] Ibn Khaldūn actually transfers Wajjāj to Sijilmāsa[226] and with logical consistency writes that Wajjāj later called the Almoravids of his disciple Ibn Yāsīn to Sijilmāsa to purify Islam and drive out the ruling Maghrāwa.[227] But according to Qāḍī [c]Iyāḍ, the house was in Sūs, and today Wajjāj's grave is pointed out there in Aglu by the sea,[228] though it is said to be in other localities as well.[229] His *rābiṭa* (*ribāṭ*, Dār al-murābiṭīn) is not known in

---

223 *Rawḍ al-qirṭās*, p. 77, penult. line (read *ribāṭihī*)/Levtzion-Hopkins, p. 238.

224 The *zāwiya* of Abū Isḥāq al-Ilbīrī (d. 459/1067) in Granada which Ibn Baṭṭūṭa visited in 751/1350 was called *Rābiṭat* al-[c]Uqāb; *Voyages d'Ibn Batoutah*, ed. Defrémery et Sanguinetti, IV, p. 372/E. Lévi-Provençal: 'Le voyage d'Ibn Baṭṭūṭa dans le royaume de Grenade', in *Mélanges William Marçais*, Paris, 1950, pp. 216, 219-20. *Iḥāṭa* II, p. 155. *Rābiṭa* embraces *ribāṭ* and *zāwiya*. For *rawābiṭ* in Spain cf. the remarks of L. Torres Balbás: 'Rábitas hispanomusulmanas', in *Al-Andalus* 13, 1948, pp. 475-91. He as well draws attention to the mixed usage of the terms *ribāṭ*, *rābiṭa* and *zāwiya*.

225 Henri Terrasse: *Histoire du Maroc*, Casablanca, 1949/1975, I, p. 214. Émile Laoust: 'Contribution à une étude de la toponymie', *REI* 14, 1940, p. 36: *amĕlkīṣ* qṣār of Tafilalt. Jacinto Bosch Vilá: *Historia de Marruecos: Los Almorávides*, Tetuan, 1956, pp. 50-51; map on p. 274.

226 *Berbères*, II, p. 117.

227 *Berbères*, I, pp. 69-70/Levtzion-Hopkins, p. 330.

228 Sūsī: *Khilāl Jazūla*, I, p. 78. Moraes Farias, p. 806. Norris: 'New Evidence', *JAH* 12, 1971, p. 262. Norris: 'Muslim Sanhāja Scholars of Mauritania', in Willis: *Studies*, I, p. 149, below. Justinard: *Fawaid al jamma*, p. 114. Sidi Waggag of Aglu receives visitors especially on Sundays and Thursdays, but never women: Edward Westermarck: *Ritual and Belief in Morocco*, London, 1926, reprint New York, 1968, I, pp. 174, 196.

229 *Khilāl Jazūla*, I, pp. 78-79. *Ma[c]sūl*, XI, pp. 38-39. Justinard in *Arch. Maroc.* 29, 1933, pp. 116-17.

Aglu,[230] and his alleged descendants (his marabout family) live elsewhere. Ibn Abī Zar^{c} locates Wajjāj's residence one time in 'the countryside' and then in 'the city' Nafīs,[231] i.e. north of the High-Atlas and south-west of the later Marrakesh, which must both be a mistake, although an Almoravid fort did stand there subsequently.[232] It deserves to be stressed that the Dār al-murābiṭīn of Wajjāj in the words of Qāḍī ^{c}Iyāḍ was founded 'for religious knowledge and the good (*khayr*)', and according to Tādilī 'for those studying religious knowledge and for Koran readers'.[233] According to Ibn Abī Zar^{c}, the pious Wajjāj in his *ribāṭ* served God, taught theology there and called the people to the good.[234] Norris describes the *ribāṭ* as a 'school of meditation and indoctrination'.[235]

The name of the Almoravids has already been traced back to Wajjāj's Dār al-murābiṭīn by others. Ed. Michaux-Bellaire supported this derivation in 1928 with a general model, the model based on the geographical origin of many religious movements. The best known example of this, he says, is precisely the Almoravids who started from the Dār al-murābiṭīn in Sūs with Ibn Yāsīn — thus he follows Qāḍī ^{c}Iyāḍ — and then succeeded in bringing about the advance of Ṣanhāja tribes to the north and the founding of the Almoravid kingdom.[236] Another principle seems to me to be equally striking: the rule one may frequently observe that it is only 'the second man', in this case Ibn Yāsīn, who accomplishes the breakthrough of a movement, here that of the Dār al-murābiṭīn.[237] It is mistaken to demote Ibn Yāsīn, because he followed in Wajjāj's footsteps, to being an

---

230 *Khilāl Jazūla*, I, pp. 78-79.

231 *Rawḍ al-qirṭās*, pp. 77-78/Latin pp. 104-05/Cuoq, p. 232 (inexact)/Levtzion-Hopkins, pp. 238-39. The city was located presumably at the confluence of the Nefis and the Tensift; Doutté: *En Tribu*, p. 12.

232 Baydhaq in Lévi-Provençal: *Documents inédits d'histoire almohade*, Arabic p. 130, l. 9/French p. 220, penult. line.

233 *Tashawwuf*, ed. Faure, p. 66.

234 *Rawḍ*, p. 77, penult. line/Latin p. 104, l. 3 from bot./Levtzion-Hopkins, p. 238.

235 *Saharan Myth and Saga*, p. 95.

236 'Le Touat et les Chorfa d'Ouazzan', *Mémorial Henri Basset*, Paris, 1928, II, pp. 144-45.

237 *Abū Sa^{c}īd-i Abū l-Ḫayr*, p. 455. Cf. Abdallah Laroui: *Les origines sociales et culturelles du nationalisme marocain (1830-1912)*, Paris, 1977, p. 137: The founder of all these great *zawāyā* is a man of ardent faith, meditation and mystical teaching. In the second generation the aspect of organization and consolidation is dominant. In the third nothing new is added.

'imitator' of the latter, as Cuoq 1975 (p. 89, ftn. 2) does. In this connection we may also mention Muḥammad b. Tāwīt al-Ṭanjī who in 1960 came up with the same idea in his review of Faure's edition of the *Tashawwuf*. He writes: 'Thus the designation came about (viz. through Wajjāj's Dār al-murābiṭīn) and continued to adhere to the cause and its prominent representatives. It already included Ibn Yāsīn, the disciple. It was not first coined by Ibn Yāsīn or indeed by those who followed him, but was borrowed from Wajjāj.'[238] Paulo Fernanado de Moraes Farias then expressed the same view, independently and cogently, in *BIFAN* 29, sér. B, 1967, pp. 805-08. H.T. Norris followed him cautiously in 1971. He based himself on Qāḍī ᶜIyāḍ and considered it not impossible, though wholly uncertain, that the designation of the Almoravids simply continued the name which Wajjāj had given his disciples.[239] John Ralph Willis and Nehemia Levtzion upheld the position more firmly in 1979.[240] Levtzion recalls the Tunisian *ribāṭ*s, originally military fortifications against the Byzantine fleet in the Mediterranean, which with the strengthening of the Muslim naval forces increasingly became centers of piety and Muslim missionary activity but were always kept in military readiness. For the possibility of linking the name of the Almoravids with Wajjāj's Dār al-murābiṭīn he refers to Moraes Farias. The teaching activity of the Mālikites had contained an interaction of jurisprudence, asceticism and permanent *jihād*. To begin with, only *jihād* had been alive among the Ṣanhāja. Ibn Yāsīn was the first to bring in the other elements. He had taught the Koran, *ḥadīth* and law, then introduced demands for repentance and threats of court action and had even established punishment for past sins. He applied strict rules regarding omissions in religious practices, and this discipline was at the same time a preparation for waging holy war.[241] Thus Levtzion has already said much of what I would have said on the subject. I can take up the discussion where he left off.

The hindrance which first of all stands in the way of tracing the Almoravids back to the Dār al-murābiṭīn is the fact that Wajjāj and Ibn Yāsīn are not themselves designated as *murābiṭūn*. They are presented to us as *fuqahāʾ*. That does not, however, rule out that they

---

238 The journal *Tiṭwān* 5, 1960, p. 196.

239 'New Evidence', *JAH* 12, 1971, p. 262.

240 Willis: 'Reflections on the Diffusion of Islam in West Africa', in the work edited by himself: *Studies in West African Islamic History*, I, p. 4. Levtzion: 'ᶜAbd Allāh b. Yāsīn and the Almoravids', ibid., I, p. 85. In passing also in Jeannine Drouin: *Un cycle oral*, p. 19, ftn. 1.

241 Levtzion: 'ᶜAbd Allāh', p. 85-86.

may none the less have been *murābiṭūn*, and in the traditional sense: men of piety who were on one or more occasions at the frontier to undertake daringly the meritorious work of defending Islam. Perhaps the Dār al-murābiṭīn was nothing other than a place where former and future border guardians gathered to discuss religious and political questions and questions concerning *murābaṭa*, and to promote this kind of voluntary service. Indeed, at a later date further in the north there was an association of Mecca pilgrims (*ḥujjāj*) into which only former pilgrims were admitted,[242] and in Safi there was a society for the promotion of the pilgrimage which was founded by Abū Ṣāliḥ Muḥammad (d. 631/1234).[243] In the same way the Dār al-murābiṭīn could have been engaged in propagating *murābaṭa*.

A second difficulty is that, according to Bakrī, Ibn Yāsīn did not himself undertake *murābaṭa* in the south but only incited others to do so and to proclaim the truth and what is right.[244] Furthermore, his *murābiṭūn*, the Almoravids, whenever they converted and subjugated opponents included them in 'their' *ribāṭ* (= *murābaṭa*) after they had 'cleansed' them of their earlier sins by giving them a beating, i.e. in 'their', not 'his' *ribāṭ*, according to Bakrī's words.[245] Again that places Ibn Yāsīn outside *murābaṭa*, as Bakrī is referring to their procedure during Ibn Yāsīn's lifetime. Later no new members were any longer admitted.

Thus Wajjāj and Ibn Yāsīn, as Abdallah Laroui has rightly understood,[246] were on the Sunnī-Mālikite side more or less what the *du*ᶜ*āh* 'propagandists' on the Fāṭimid-Shīᶜite side were. Ibn Yāsīn corresponds to Abū ᶜAbdallāh al-Shīᶜī. In 200/893 Abū ᶜAbdallāh was brought to Eastern Algeria as a teacher for the Kutāma, as Ibn Yāsīn, at a later date, was brought to Mauritania for the Juddāla. Of course, from the start Abū ᶜAbdallāh worked for a revolution on behalf of someone who was not yet ruling, namely the Fāṭimid. Ibn

---

242 Ibn Qunfudh: *Uns al-faqīr wa-*ᶜ*izz al-ḥaqīr*, ed. Muḥammad al-Fāsī and Adolphe Faure, Rabat, 1965, p. 64.

243 Aḥmad b. Ibrāhīm al-Mājirī: *Al-minhāj al-wāḍiḥ fī taḥqīq karāmāt Abī Muḥammad Ṣāliḥ* (written after 698/1299), Cairo, 1933, pp. 131 ff. Muḥammad b. Aḥmad al-ᶜAbdī al-Kānūnī: *Āsafī wa-mā ilayhi*, Cairo, 1353/1934, pp. 98-101. Muḥammad al-Manūnī: *Min ḥadīth al-rakb al-maghribī*, Tetuan, 1953, pp. 7-8.

244 Bakrī, p. 164/French p. 311/Monteil, p. 59/Cuoq, p. 86/Levtzion-Hopkins, p. 70. Noth: 'Das *ribāṭ*', p. 503: 'Propagierung des rechten Glaubens'. *Da*ᶜ*wa* too is not easy to render, as Dozy already remarked in his dictionary. It can also be translated 'slogan, cause'.

245 Bakrī, p. 169/French p. 319/Monteil, p. 64/Cuoq, p. 93/Levtzion-Hopkins, p. 75.

246 Abdallah Laroui: *L'histoire du Maghreb*, I, p. 147.

Yāsīn, on the contrary, sought with the help of the ruler, first Yaḥyā b. Ibrāhīm and then Yaḥyā b. ᶜUmar, to transform the nation from above downwards. The parallel does not fully apply to the next level down as well but what is important here for us is the gradation as such. The *murābiṭūn* of Ibn Yāsīn were comparable to the *mutasharriqūn*, *muʾminūn* and *awliyāʾ* of Abū ᶜAbdallāh.[247] Ibn Yāsīn stands one grade higher than his *murābiṭūn*.

In addition, at first glance a difference is immediately obvious between the old *murābaṭa* and the new one which Ibn Yāsīn taught. *Murābaṭa* no longer means service at the frontier but is connected more closely with holy war. Consequently, de Slane and Monteil translate *ribāṭ* the first time it appears in Bakrī, when Ibn Yāsīn raises the call to *ribāṭ* and to proclaiming the truth and what is right, as 'holy war', and at its second appearance, where the *murābiṭūn* incorporate their newly acquired adherents and their defeated opponents in their *ribāṭ*, as 'sect' — obviously in connection with their name *murābiṭūn*. Noth translates the latter as 'Almoravid way of life', by which he means what he calls 'holy struggle', the more restrained form of holy war.[248] Levtzion-Hopkins have opted for 'holy war' in both passages. The activity of the Almoravids appears wholly to justify such a translation but to qualify Ibn Yāsīn and in particular Wajjāj as warriors is to say the least exaggerated. The gap between the Almoravids and the Dār al-murābiṭīn continues to exist.

And yet a continuity is undeniable. One cannot disregard that Ibn Yāsīn comes from the Dār al-murābiṭīn and creates the *murābiṭūn*. The owner of the Dār al-murābiṭīn, Wajjāj, was Ibn Yāsīn's teacher and took an active interest in his work in the Sahara. He even intervened powerfully when Ibn Yāsīn met with difficulties and, if Ibn Khaldūn's report is to be trusted,[249] is meant to have summoned Ibn Yāsīn's available Almoravid troop potential to Sijilmāsa. Seen from this point of view, it would not then be so surprising if some of what Ibn Yāsīn achieved in the Sahara had already been worked out in the

---

247 Al-Qāḍī al-Nuᶜmān: *Iftitāḥ al-daᶜwa*, pp. 93, 95, 97, etc. Tilman Nagel: *Frühe Ismailiya und Fatimiden im Lichte der Risālat iftitāḥ al-daᶜwa*, Bonn, 1972, pp. 20-25.

248 Noth: 'Das *ribāṭ*', p. 504.

249 *Berbères*, II, p. 69/Levtzion-Hopkins, p. 330. The call to return, according to Bakrī, p. 167/French p. 315/Monteil, p. 61/Cuoq, pp. 89-90/Levtzion-Hopkins, p. 73, must have been sounded in the year 446/1054. In that case Wajjāj could not already have died around 445/1053, as Sūsī conjectures (see above p. 378). Ibn ᶜIdhārī IV, p. 13/Levtzion-Hopkins, p. 222 offers the choice of 446/1054 or 448/1056. On the whole question see Levtzion: 'ᶜAbd Allāh b. Yāsīn', in Willis: *Studies*, I, p. 96.

planning bureau of the Dār al-murābiṭīn and that perhaps even the new concept of the *murābiṭ* originated there. On the other hand, as far as the concept of *murābaṭa* is concerned, perspectives which take in a still more distant background as far away as Abū ᶜImrān al-Fāsī in Qayrawān, are mistaken. One does know how much Qayrawān contributed to the spread of the Mālikite school of jurisprudence in the Iberian Peninsula, especially through the students of Saḥnūn (d. 240/854),[250] but there are no indications that Ibn Yāsīn's *murābaṭa*-undertaking in the Sahara sprang from a leader in Qayrawān. The Almoravids did not, as is maintained, break forth from the desert at the command of Abū ᶜImrān.[251] Abū ᶜImrān was dead by the time Ibn Yāsīn's movement began in the Sahara.

As for what Ibn Yāsīn understood by *ribāṭ/murābaṭa*, it emerges quite clearly in Bakrī: there Ibn Yāsīn is the man who calls those tribes of the Sahara to *ribāṭ* and to proclaiming the truth or what is right;[252] his adherents after 440/1048 implement the proclamation of truth and what is right, the struggle against injustices and the abolition of illegal taxes,[253] and incorporate in their *ribāṭ* the opponents they have defeated and then given a thorough thrashing.[254] Here one easily recognizes the oppositional pair, the proclamation of truth and what is right on the one hand, and *ribāṭ* on the other. Proclaiming the truth can only refer to speech by means of the tongue, whereas *ribāṭ* can only refer to intimidation and speech by means of arms. Thus the *murābiṭūn* assume their name on the basis of bearing arms. The role of preaching and propaganda is suppressed in their name. Only the military side of missionary activity — the counter-concept of which is the proclamation of the truth — finds expression. It is a *pars pro toto* which presents the missionary as a warrior. And that is what the Almoravids were. But Ibn Yāsīn stood above and behind them, was their teacher and ideologist.

That they used a special name is clear. They had to distinguish themselves from the others who stayed behind. This made the most sense at an early date when their circle did not yet coincide with the tribal boundaries. The dichotomy based on adherents and opponents within the tribe called for a naming of the groups. Thus the adherents

---

250 M. Talbi: 'Kairouan et le Mālikisme espagnol', in *Études d'orientalisme dédiées à la mémoire de Lévi-Provençal*, Paris, 1962, I, pp. 317-37.

251 H.R. Idris: 'Deux maîtres', *AIEO* 13, 1955, p. 55.

252 Bakrī, p. 164/French p. 311/Monteil, p. 59/Cuoq, p. 86/Levtzion-Hopkins, p. 70.

253 Bakrī, p. 164/as above.

254 Bakrī, p. 169/French p. 319/Monteil, p. 64/Cuoq, p. 93/Levtzion-Hopkins, p. 75.

of Abū ᶜAbdallāh in Eastern Algeria were designated *mutasharriqūn* and *muʾminūn* in order to separate the sheep from the goats within a single tribe and throughout the tribes. In the case of the Almoravids, according to unanimous tradition, it was Ibn Yāsīn who gave them the name.

The two versions, that of Ibn ᶜIdhārī and the *Ḥulal* on the one hand, and that of Ibn Abī Zarᶜ on the other, claim to record the moment and the occasion when this happened. As a baptism legend only Ibn Abī Zarᶜ's story of the island is suitable. The followers of Ibn Yāsīn were then meant to have banded together for the first time in the *rābiṭa* on the island. But the account ignores Ibn Yāsīn's origin from the Dār al-murābiṭīn and derives the name from a *rābiṭa* that has nothing to do with the *ribāṭ* activity for which, according to Bakrī, Ibn Yāsīn swore in his Almoravids. It is obviously a later invention which refers back to the concept of an old *ribāṭ*-house which is alien to our *murābiṭūn*. The other account praises Ibn Yāsīn's adherents for their steadfastness in battle and tacitly derives their name from the brave endurance which surah 3/200 requires of Muslim warriors.[255] This explanation is mistaken from another point of view. Again it ignores the *ribāṭ* activity Ibn Yāsīn urged his men to undertake and which in any case must primarily have given the *murābiṭūn* their name. It recalls the friends of Abū ᶜAbdallāh al-Shīᶜī who had gathered around him *murābiṭīn maᶜa Abī ᶜAbdallāh wa-muntaṣibīn li'l-jihād dūnahū wa-manᶜihī mimman arādahū* (previously p. 347). But Ibn Yāsīn did not desire *ribāṭ maᶜahū* but simply *ribāṭ,* i.e. intervention on behalf of the cause, not on behalf of his person. Therefore the words of praise Ibn Yāsīn bestowed on them in war cannot have been the cause for giving them their name but at most confirmed it, gave it a new interpretation and disclosed to his followers a new meaning contained in their name. Evidently they already bore the name. Whether this story as well is invented can no longer be determined. It may also stem from a later time when the Almoravids had proved themselves to be brave soldiers. However, the warlike note would well suit the warlike meaning which *ribāṭ/murābaṭa* had for Ibn Yāsīn.

His warlike *murābaṭa* differs from the old *murābaṭa* still further in that it is a *profession*. The old *murābiṭ* was, as we indicated in section 1, a man of piety who of his own free will and for a limited time went to the frontier. Some of them remained there for their whole

---

255 An interpretation of *rābiṭū* in surah 3/200 as the Almoravid military technique of the tightly-knit host, which Moraes Farias p. 811-19 proposes, seems to me inadvisable.

life.[256] The *murābiṭūn* of Ibn Yāsīn all perform their service during their whole life. How this actually worked is not precisely known. Perhaps they alternated with one another, were under arms for a period and then on vacation, or one group was on active service while another group was on leave. The Almohads of the 7th/13th century were divided into two parts: one group served in Marrakesh and were paid — the *jumū*ᶜ. The others remained at home and reported for duty at times of mobilization — the *ᶜumūm*.[257]

The old *murābiṭūn*, as we know them from section 1, were from diverse origins. Ibn Yāsīn's *murābiṭūn* were and continued to be members of *very particular Berber tribes*. The Lamtūna held the leadership under their supreme chief Yaḥyā b. ᶜUmar who was completely submissive to Ibn Yāsīn. To him Ibn Yāsīn delegated the military command, and the other founding tribes, the Massūfa and the Juddāla (the latter at least in the beginning), subordinated themselves to him. In this way he clarified the boundary between himself and the *murābiṭūn*. The *murābiṭūn* were left to their more or less natural chief and remained to that extent what they had always been: tribal warriors, albeit now under the banner of Islam. In order not to lose his troop leader and to keep him subservient to himself he forbade him to take part in the battles personally.[258]

Thus the *dual nature* of the government was laid out, the division into a spiritual and a worldly leadership, a well-known model which Ibn Tūmart and his troop commander ᶜAbd al-Muᵓmin also followed at a later time among the Almohads, the one holding power and the other carrying out tasks. Although Ibn Yāsīn, as a *faqīh* in the background, held the reins of power, his sole preoccupation was to take account of the interests of his armed helpers and to adapt his own concerns to conform with theirs. Already during the campaigns against Sijilmāsa and Darᶜa he attempted to kill two birds with one stone: to abolish oppression, the illegal taxes, musical instruments

256 H.R. Idris: 'Contribution', *REI* 9, 1935, p. 294.

257 ᶜAbd al-Wāḥid al-Marrākushī: *Al-muᶜjib fī talkhīṣ akhbār al-Maghrib*/R.P.A. Dozy (ed.): *The History of the Almohades... by Abdo-'l-Wáhid al-Marrékoshí*, Leiden, 1847, p. 248/Ambrosio Huici Miranda: *Colección de Crónicas árabes de la Reconquista, Volumen IV, Kitāb al-muᶜŷib fī taljīṣ ajbār al-Magrib por Abū Muḥammad ᶜAbd al-Wāḥid al-Marrākushī* (traducción española), Tetuan, 1955, pp. 280-81. *Ibn Khaldoun: Berbères*, II, pp. 258-59, ftn. 1.

258 Bakrī, pp. 166-67/French p. 315/Monteil, p. 61/Cuoq, p. 89/Levtzion-Hopkins, p. 72.

and wine shops — his own concern,[259] and to drive out the Zanāta to whom the local rulers, the Maghrāwa, belonged — the concern of his tribes. Yaḥyā b. ᶜUmar fell at the Sahara front in Jabal Lamtūna (in Mauritanian Adrar) in a heavy clash between his Lamtūna and the Juddāla who had broken away.[260] His brother Abū Bakr b. ᶜUmar became supreme commander. The good cooperation persisted and facilitated the conquest of the Atlas region. Ibn Yāsīn, according to reports, had once studied in Spain and on his return journey through Morocco had noted with displeasure the country's fragmentation into tribes that were feuding with one another. The Berbers behaved no differently from the reyes de táifas in Spain, apparently even worse. At the time Ibn Yāsīn supposedly asked a man from the Maṣāmida whether the people here didn't believe in God and Muḥammad, and the answer is meant to have been: 'They do indeed, but no one of us will tolerate that a person from another tribe stands over him.'[261] When after completing their mission in the Sahara the Almoravid troops under Yaḥyā b. ᶜUmar's brother and successor, Abū Bakr b. ᶜUmar, then had firm control over the first agricultural zones in the north of the Sahara, Sijilmāsa and Darᶜa, Ibn Yāsīn again journeyed to the north over the High-Atlas to find out whether local conditions still looked as bad as they had been earlier. He found them unchanged but was able to convince the people that a uniform regime under Islamic auspices would be more advantageous than eternal fragmentation. He proposed Abū Bakr as sovereign who was waiting in the south, and won their assent. With an agreement to this effect he set out on his return journey, and in 450/1058 Abū Bakr could begin his march northwards.[262] It is quite possible that Berber particularism at that very moment had exceeded the limits of tolerance and that the Almoravids seizure of power was perceived as a salubrious political change.

After Ibn Yāsīn's death in battle against the Barghuwāṭa in 451/1059, the spiritual office steadily lost its significance. Ibn Yāsīn's successor at the side of Abū Bakr, who carried out the war against the Barghuwāṭa to its end, was a certain Sulaymān b. ᶜAddū

---

259 *Ibn Khaldoun: Berbères*, II, pp. 70, 71/Levtzion-Hopkins, p. 330. *Rawḍ al-qirṭās*, p. 81/Latin pp. 110-11/Cuoq, p. 236/Levtzion-Hopkins, p. 243. Abolishing instruments and wine shops could also simply be a literary motif.

260 This was in 448/1056-57. Bakrī, p. 167/French p. 316/Monteil, p. 62/Cuoq, p. 90/Levtzion-Hopkins, p. 73.

261 Ibn ᶜIdhārī, IV, p. 10/Levtzion-Hopkins, p. 219.

262 Ibn ᶜIdhārī, IV, p. 15/Levtzion-Hopkins, p. 223.

but he only survived his predecessor for a short time.[263] When Abū Bakr then returned to the Sahara for good in 465/1072 and left the north to his cousin Yūsuf b. Tāshfīn, he took along with him Muḥammad b. al-Ḥasan al-Ḥaḍramī al-Murādī (d. 489/1096) and installed him as *qāḍī* in Azuggi.[264] But the emirate emerged into the foreground, consolidated the power of the founder tribes, maintained order under them and developed the dynasty. In the foremost position stood the Lamtūna, from whom the rulers originated, and for this reason the Almoravids were also called al-Lamtūniyyūn al-Murābiṭūn or simply Lamtūna. But strictly speaking from now on only members of the founder tribes were allowed to bear the name of *al-murābiṭūn* 'Almoravids'. Restricting the name to this core group must have made them appear increasingly like an aristocracy since the army became steadily bigger and more varied through the enlistment of foreign contingents. Whereas the first *murābiṭūn* of Ibn Yāsīn 'incorporated' their tribal comrades and other Berbers into their *ribāṭ/murābaṭa* (*adkhalūhu fī ribāṭihim*) after 'cleansing' them with a beating, this no longer occurred at a later time. The commander of the northern wing Yūsuf b. Tāshfīn in 464/1071-72 purchased black as well as white slaves (from Spain)[265] to strengthen his military forces. They were not counted among the *murābiṭūn*. In 470/1077-78 he obtained another large group of *murābiṭūn* from the founder tribes in the Sahara, the Lamtūna, Massūfa, Juddāla and 'others'. But otherwise whoever else presented themselves, men from the Jazūla and Lamṭa, Zanāta and Maṣmūd warriors, he kept separate and called them 'the followers' (*al-ḥasham*), not to mention the foreign mercenaries.[266] The Arabic municipal regulation of Seville from the beginning of the 6th/12th century insists that only the Ṣanhāja, Lamtūna and Lamṭa, who constituted the real Almoravids (*murābiṭūn*), were allowed to wear the regular garb of this ruling caste, the veil over the mouth,[267] and reproaches 'the followers' (*ḥasham*) and the black slaves who wear the same veil over the

---

263 *Ibn Khaldoun: Berbères*, II, pp. 71-72. Norris: 'New Evidence', *JAH* 12, 1971, p. 267.

264 Moraes Farias, p. 856. Levtzion: 'ᶜAbd Allāh b. Yāsīn', in Willis: *Studies*, I, p. 100.

265 Ibn ᶜIdhārī, IV, p. 23/Levtzion-Hopkins, p. 229.

266 *Ḥulal mawshiyya*, pp. 21-22/trans. Huici, p. 46. Bosch Vilá: *Los Almorávides*, pp. 118-20. Bosch Vilá, pp. 212, ftn. 26, takes *ḥasham* to mean a kind of troop of guards. But that does not seem correct for the beginning period.

267 Regular garb: otherwise the Berbers who were not *murābiṭūn* also wore the veil over the mouth.

mouth only to intimidate the decent city-dweller and the authorities and subject them to extortion.[268] The list of tribal names in this source is erratic and contradicts the list in the previous report about the expansion of the army by Yūsuf b. Tāshfīn.[269] But historians mention Zanāta and Maṣāmida separately when they fought on the side of the *murābiṭūn*. Thus among the Almoravids *murābiṭūn* was a designation for a *people*, for the closed society of the Berber founder tribes who wore a veil over the mouth. Similarly, at a later date the name *al-muwaḥḥidūn* 'Almohads' attached itself to the closed society of the founder tribes consisting of eight Maṣāmida tribes or parts of them. Parallel to conditions among the Almoravids, in the case of the Almohads as well one of these tribes provided the ruling house, the emir who stood above everyone else.[270]

Whether and to what extent the Almoravids again restricted the right to the name within the founder tribes is not known to us. Was one a *murābiṭ* immediately from birth? Was there an age at which one was admitted? Did military service constitute one of the requirements? Or was a member of the tribe also a *murābiṭ* if he set out on the career of a religious scholar and only fought for the cause of the Almoravids with his tongue? Many will have employed both at the same time, the sword and the tongue, for although they wore a veil over their mouth their tongue was by no means inhibited. In this regard, one should reckon in particular the 'shaykhs' (*ashyākh*, *mashyakha*) of the tribes and the Almoravids, the spokesmen of the aristocracy, who transmitted and lived according to the spiritual legacy of Ibn Yāsīn's life[271] — whom it is difficult to view as Ibn Yāsīn's purely spiritual successors distributed among the tribes. *Fuqahā'* and *ᶜulamā'* from other tribes and another origin were not

---

268 E. Lévi-Provençal: 'Un document sur la vie urbaine et les corps de métiers à Séville au début du XIIe siècle: Le traité d'Ibn ᶜAbdūn, publié avec une introduction et un glossaire', *JA* 224, 1934, pp. 200, 218/Francesco Gabrieli: 'Il trattato censorio di Ibn ᶜAbdūn sul buon governo di Siviglia', *Rendiconti della R. Academia Nazionale dei Lincei* VI, 11, 1935, pp. 886, 904-05 (Italian)/Lévi-Provençal y García Gómez: *Sevilla a comienzos del siglo XII: El tratado de Ibn ᶜAbdūn*, Madrid, 1948, pp. 54-55 (§9), pp. 98-100 (§56). If the black slaves are going to veil their mouth, then they should do so with a different kind of veil in order to keep a distinction. Norris: *Saharan Myth*, p. 43.

269 The various branches of the tribe in Norris: *Saharan Myth*, pp. 28, 38, 58, 229.

270 Marrākushī: *Muᶜjib*, pp. 246-48/trans. Huici, pp. 279-82. *Ibn Khaldoun: Berbères*, II, pp. 258-59.

271 Al-Qāḍī ᶜIyāḍ: *Tartīb al-madārik*, IV, p. 781, ll. 18-19/Cuoq, p. 125, last two lines (les anciens for *mashyakha* is not correct)/Levtzion-Hopkins, p. 102, ll. 29-31.

Almoravids, even if they made themselves very useful to the cause of the latter, as for instance the Ḥaḍramī in Azuggi or the religious scholars in Córdoba who approved the burning of Ghazzālī's *Iḥyā*ʾ.[272] Did the name also extend to the women of the Almoravid tribes? Were there *murābiṭāt*? The wives of the leading men among the Lamtūna and Massūfa are said to have increasingly set the tone and to have hastened the decline of morals.[273] But no female figure of the founder tribes appears under the designation *murābiṭa* and certainly not one related by marriage such as the beautiful and clever royal widow from Aghmat whom Abū Bakr b. ᶜUmar had married and then handed over to his cousin and deputy in the north, Yūsuf b. Tāshfīn.[274]

Nevertheless, *murābiṭūn* was nothing other than a *renaming* of the Lamtūna and the founder tribes which had joined them, originally the adherents and then the fighting 'comrades' of Ibn Yāsīn and their incorporated fellow-warriors, and finally their descendants. In this way they bore an Islamic nameplate, complied with a new idea of the state and formed its warrior caste, its warrior aristocracy, just as the original Almohads did later on. With the collapse of the Almoravids, first in 541/1147 in Marrakesh, then after a final episode in 633/1235-36 involving their Balearic branch the Banū Ghāniya in Algeria, they lost the title again. Afterwards it is more or less only the descendants of the ruling family who are still referred to as being of Almoravid origin.[275] It was perhaps different in the south, in Mauritania, where still today a few families and tribes purely as a formality trace their lineage back to the Lamtūna or at least claim to have taken part under Abū Bakr. Others in that area also consider themselves to be descendants of Abū Bakr b. ᶜUmar or Ḥaḍramīs as well.[276]

---

272 Ibn ᶜIdhārī, IV, pp. 59-60. *Ḥulal mawshiyya*, p. 85/trans. Huici, pp. 124-25.

273 Marrākushī: *Muᶜjib*, p. 128/trans. Huici, p. 135. Bosch Vilá, p. 245.

274 Levtzion: 'ᶜAbd Allāh b. Yāsīn', in Willis, pp. 97-98.

275 *Nozhet-Elhâdi*, p. 297/French p. 493. Similarly, an Abū ᶜAbdallāh Muḥammad b. Wābūr (Wāyūr) al-Murābiṭ al-Mutalaththim who was a pious man one could meet in Mecca in the 6th/12th century. He was one of the old emirs and 'descendants of the Almoravid kings' (*awlād al-mulūk al-murābiṭīn*). Ṭāhir b. Muḥammad b. Ṭāhir al-Ṣadafī (6th/12th century) in Bārizī: *Tawthīq ᶜurā'l-īmān*, MS Sprenger 127b, fol. 171b (Ahlwardt Berlin no. 2569).

276 F. de la Chapelle: 'Esquisse d'une histoire du Sahara occidental', *Hespéris* 11, 1930, p. 74. Pierre Amilhat: 'Petite chronique des Id ou Aich, héritiers guerriers des Almoravides sahariens', *REI* 11, 1937, pp. 44, 49, 50, 107. Moraes Farias, pp. 850-51. Norris: *Shinqīṭī Folk Literature and Song*, p. 15; *Saharan Myth*, pp. 110, 114-15, 215-16. Gernot Rotter: 'Die

A glance back in time teaches us that *murābiṭ* as a designation for the Almoravids contains a *semantic shift* not different in kind from *muwaḥḥid* 'one who professes God's oneness' among the Almohads — both are personal names. The Almoravids are no longer volunteers at the frontier but armed activists who pursue a campaign of Islamicization across the frontiers. The term being used is *murābiṭ* but the sense is *mujāhid*. Furthermore, these *murābiṭūn* are now not just any men of piety but the men of a particular group of Berber tribes, at the head of which stand the Lamtūna who had followed the teaching of Ibn Yāsīn. In early times, those who converted and were subdued became incorporated until the iron circle of the club was reached, but later this was no longer the case. Such exclusivity was demanded by the jealous older warriors who, after a few successes and with an eye to future ones, were not willing to give up their privilege. They themselves and the state certainly could not live without portions of the population who did not fight and did not have the same ambition. A monopolization of this kind, carried to the extreme, would naturally make the continuation of the old *murābiṭ* way of life impossible and, applied as a half measure, would result in the term having a double meaning. Thus the name for the Almoravids came to exist alongside the appelative for the free *murābiṭ*. We do not know anything precise about the fate of the participle, but the activity as such, the free *murābaṭa*, did in fact continue to exist at least to a certain extent. Ibn al-Mundhir (d. 580/1184) from Silves performed *murābata* (*rābaṭa*) in the Ribāṭ al-Rayḥāna on the seashore before he joined the opposition and the uprising of Ibn Qasī against the Almoravids.[277] Yūsuf b. Tāshfīn used the old concept to adorn his intentions of conquest with a mantle of piety. When he wished to attempt the leap from the Moroccan to the Spanish coast, he came up with the following plan: 'We request permission from the ruling ᶜAbbāsid of Seville, Muᶜtamid (461-484/1069-1091), to send across men of piety (*ṣulaḥāʾ*) from among us who wish to perform *ribāṭ/murābaṭa* there in Andalusia, to wage holy war against the enemy and to reside until their death in certain castles (*ḥuṣūn*) that neighbor on the Christians.'[278] In view of these communications one can easily imagine that the Almoravids harbored a degree of mistrust

Herkunft der arabischen Stämme (Banū Ḥassān) in Mauretanien', in *Festschrift für Bertold Spuler*, Leiden, 1981, p. 346. See p. 370 f. above.

277 Ibn al-Abbār: *Ḥulla siyarāʾ*, II, pp. 202-03; 204, ftn. 1.

278 Marrākushī: *Muᶜjib*, p. 97/trans. Huici, p. 109.

toward the free *murābiṭ*. Unsupervised places of assembly for people bearing arms aroused their suspicion. They didn't construct *ribāṭ*s as it were for the pious irregular fighters,[279] but for their standing army,[280] and stationed their garrisons in already existing one. A lampoon in Spain, which would like to see them all return to the Sahara, hopes that once again they will soon exchange 'tethering horses' (*irtibāṭ al-khayl*) with milking sheep and no longer wear a veil over their face.[281] Old *ribāṭ*s were maintained. Surrounded by the Almohads, Tāshfīn b. ᶜAli b. Tāshfīn in 539/1145 retreated to a *ribāṭ* or *rābiṭa* on a mountain near Oran and then in his hasty flight fell to his death in the dark night.[282] The *rābiṭa* at Ibn Yāsīn's grave in Kurīfalat was a sepulchral shrine.[283]

---

279 Lévi-Provençal: *L'Espagne musulmane au Xe siècle*, pp. 138-39, writes that the arrangement of the *ribāṭ* as living quarters in Spain from the time of the Almoravids on had its great period, and in *Rabat et sa région* I, Paris, 1918, p. 8 (Villes et Tribus du Maroc III), one finds the sentence: 'La pluspart des ribât du Maroc ont été crées par les Almoravides.' What are the sources for these assertions? The first *ribāṭ* which the Almohads build is supposed to have been the *ribāṭ* Tāzā in 528/1134 at the boundary between the Middle and the Extreme Maghreb; *Rawḍ at-qirṭās*, p. 122/Latin p. 164. *Istibṣār*, p. 186, gives the date as 568/1172-73. That fits with 'twenty years ago', since *Istibṣār* was composed in 587/1191. Georges Marçais: *Mélanges d'histoire et d'archéologie*, I, pp. 30-31, follows the earlier dating and comments in *EI* Tāzā: 'Explaining the fortification as a new *ribāṭ* was meant to confer on it the value of a pious work. In reality Tāzā never played the religious role of a *ribāṭ*. As in the past it was a military post intended to protect the road to Fez.'

280 Baydhaq in Lévi-Provençal: *Documents inédits*, Arabic pp. 128-31/French pp. 218-22. In addition, Āmargū is given in *Istibṣār*, p. 190, l. 14 (apart from the 'city' Tāwudā, p. 190, l. 10). Other forts (*ḥuṣūn*, etc.) which were occupied by the Almoravids are mentioned in Ibn ᶜIdhārī, for instance. The word *ḥiṣn* is not in use today in Morocco and most of these forts are now designated as *qaṣaba* or *qalᶜa*; Georges S. Colin: 'Notes de dialectologie arabe', *Hespéris* 10, 1930, p. 113. Cf. ftn. 18 above.

281 Marrākushī: *Muᶜjib*, p. 127, ll. 20-21/trans. Huici: *Kitāb al-muᶜŷib*, p. 134. I leave *allā* in the text instead of Huici's *illā*. Noth: 'Das *ribāṭ*', pp. 505-06.

282 Aḥmad al-Nāṣirī: *Istiqṣā*, II, pp. 70-73/trans. Colin, *Arch. Maroc.* 31, 1925, pp. 209-14.

283 Bakrī, p. 168/French p. 318/Monteil, p. 63 (mosquée)/Cuoq, p. 92 (*ribāṭ*)/Levtzion-Hopkins, p. 74 (hostel). Levtzion in Willis p. 87: hospice. *Istibṣār*, p. 209, l. 15, and *Rawḍ al-qirṭās*, p. 84, call the building a *masjid*. The place, about 40 km south of Rabat, was described by A. Benachenhou: 'Sîdî ᶜAbdallâh Moul l-Gâra ou ᶜAbdallâh ibn Yâsîn', *Hespéris* 33, 1946, pp. 406-13/Benachenhou: *La dynastie almoravide et son art*, Algiers, 1974, pp. 63-73. *Rabat et sa région III, Les Tribus*, pp. 134, 160-62: Qorifla (text)/Korifla (map). Gâra = *qāra* 'plateau'.

Moreover, there is a considerable difference between this Almoravid *murābiṭ* and the later marabout which was discussed earlier in section 2. The Almoravid *murābiṭ* is under state control and from the outset a warrior. The later marabout is a pastor and bearer of *baraka*. The Almoravid is a member of the warrior caste which to begin with by taking up arms wished to help the teachings of its *faqīh* to achieve success and then had to obey a deputy, its emir. The Almoravid *murābiṭ* is the creation and the instrument of a *faqīh*. The marabout is himself something like a *faqīh*, even if not necessarily an educated religious scholar. Thus the Almoravid and the marabout stand on two different levels. The earlier pre-Almoravid *murābiṭ* had still combined both *jihād* and *ʿibāda*. In the *murābiṭ* under Almoravid state control the *jihād* has predominance, indeed to such a degree that *ʿibāda* fades alongside it. The later marabout is almost exclusively a man of piety or even a saint. In other words, there is no path leading from the Almoravid to the marabout. On the contrary, the Almoravid constitutes a hindrance for such a development.

Both appear comparable perhaps in terms of the permanence and the hereditary nature of being a *murābiṭ*. The Almoravid is a *murābiṭ* for his whole lifetime from birth onwards. The marabout, as a member of a marabout family, is also characterized by both these traits. But in this respect he resembles much more the member of a Sufi shaykh family in the east. Up until the 9th/15th century the marabouts in the west, who inherited their position as a marabout, are by preference referred to as 'sons' (*awlād*) and 'grandsons' (*ḥafada, aḥfād, ḥufadāʾ*) of their holy ancestor. Usually they are also connected with his tomb or convent just like the members of a family of a Sufi saint or founder of a Sufi order.

If then the Almoravid and the later marabout stand so far apart from one another and yet both derive from the earlier *murābiṭ*, a bifurcation in development must have taken place. The Almoravid favors exclusively the *jihād*, the marabout exclusively *ʿibāda*. The Almoravid dominated what was geographically only a band in the extreme west, from Senegal to Lisbon and Saragossa, as well as the Balearic Islands,[284] and only from approximately 440/1050 to 540/1145, though somewhat later in the Balearics. East of there the *murābiṭ* was free and could develop in the other, pious direction. When the Almoravids then disappeared from the scene, the free *murābiṭ* could once again spread to the west. Even more viable, it seems to me, is the assumption that the Almoravid *murābiṭ* even in

284 Map in Moraes Farias, p. 799.

the west never completely ousted the free *murābiṭ* and the common folk never allowed themselves to be dispossessed of their image of the free *murābiṭ* by the figure of the veiled desert warrior. The common folk, as the future would show, inclined to the other side: to seek in the *murābiṭ* a pious prince of peace and miracle-worker who made visible to them an allegedly higher justice, a homo religiosus, perhaps a *faqīh* like Ibn Yāsīn but in no way a soldier from the Sahara with a veil over his mouth.

4. THOSE WHO VEIL THEIR MOUTH AND THOSE WHO HAVE HAD THEIR MOUTH VEILED

According to Bakrī (460/1068), all Berber tribes of the Sahara veiled themselves with two veils, a veil for the forehead (*niqāb*) and a veil for the mouth (*lithām*), thus leaving only the eye sockets free. The men, as he reports, only knew one another with their veil on and often could only identify a dead person with his veil on since no one ever showed himself unveiled, not even to a friend. They called other people who went about without a veil 'mouths of flies' (*afwāh al-dhibbān*).[285] This means: those without a veil, so to speak, stuck their nose in everything, did not show enough reserve in their dress, were impudent. The older Ibn Ḥawqal (wrote in 378/986 and earlier) notes that they considered the mouth to be a private part of the body (*sawʾa*) and from early childhood were accustomed to cover it up since, as they said, what came out of the mouth smelled even worse than what came out of the lower part of the body.[286] Ibn Khaldūn (d.

---

285 Bakrī, p. 170/French pp. 320-21/Monteil, pp. 64-65/Cuoq, p. 94/Levtzion-Hopkins, pp. 75-76/*Hulal*, Spanish trans. Huici, p. 22, ftn. 3.

286 Ibn Ḥawqal: *Ṣūrat al-arḍ*, ed. Kramers, p. 102 (missing from De Goeje's edition) /Cuoq, p. 75/Levtzion-Hopkins, p. 49/Monteil, p. 105. Znāga-speaking inhabitants of south-western Mauretania, who still wore the veil up until the 17th century, gave a quite similar explanation in the 15th century to the Venetian traveller Cadamosto; *The voyages of Cadamosto*, trans. Crone, The Hakluyt Society, Second Series, No. LXXX, 1937/reprint 1967, p. 19 (quoted in Norris: *Saharan Myth*, p. 70). The wording of the German edition of Strassburg, 1534, *Die New welt, der landschaften vnnd Insulen...*, 5a (chapt. 10): Diese Azenagi haben ein böse weis/ sie vmbbinden das haupt mit einer leinen binden/ vnd hencken den zipffel da von fur das angesicht/ von der stirn herab bis vber den mund/ dann si beschamen sich des munds als vbel/ als der andern scham. Sie decken den mund gleich als ein schentlich ding/ zum anzeichen/ das er (sic) allweg so ein wüster gestanck gleich als aus einem wüsten loch gehet. Darumb decken sie den mund nit auff/ sie wellen dann essen. — The agreement is very striking.

808/1406) enumerates seven of their tribes by name: the Juddāla, Lamtūna, Massūfa, Watzīla, Tārgā, Zaghāwa and Lamṭa, and reckons they all belong to the Ṣanhāja.[287] The Tārgā, as has long been surmised, are apparently the later Tuaregs (Arabic *tawāriq*, sing. *tāriqī*). The first three are the founder tribes of the Almoravids which we are familiar with. The Lamṭa are the tribe to which Wajjāj had belonged.[288] The Almoravids therefore bear the second name 'those who wear a veil over their mouth'. Ibn ᶜAbdūn from Seville (beginning of the 6th/12th century) considered this veil to be a privilege of the Almoravids and forbade others to claim this right and in so doing to behave as if they were lords. Only the Ṣanhāja, Lamtūna and Lamṭa, as he expressed it, were authorized to wear the real Almoravid veil.[289] He overlooks the fact that Ṣanhāja is a term which either includes the Lamtūna, Lamṭa and many other tribes,[290] in other words should subsume the other two names, or at most may be placed alongside the Lamṭa.[291]

Scholars have puzzled much over what veiling the face among the Tuaregs and related peoples signifies. From time to time attempts at explanation are undertaken in ethnographic studies such as in Johannes Nicolaisen's *Ecology and Culture of the Pastoral Tuareg*, Copenhagen 1963, p. 14, and again at a later date in Jeremy Keenan's *The Tuareg, People of Ahaggar*, London, 1977, pp. 127-136. On this subject I would like to make the following remarks:

The information provided by the Arabic poet Dhū'l-Rumma (d. circa 117/735-36) about wearing a veil in the desert is very old. The poet here protects himself with a veil against heat, dust and wind.[292]

---

287 *Berbères*, II, p. 64/Cuoq, p. 332/Levtzion-Hopkins, p. 327.

288 ᶜIyāḍ: *Tartīb al-madārik*, IV, p. 781/Norris, *JAH* 12, 1971, p. 25/quoted in *Maᶜsūl*, XI, p. 47. Tādilī: *Tashawwuf*, p. 66 / quoted in *Ḥulal sundusiyya*, I, pp. 1 and 274. *Rawḍ al-qirṭās*, p. 77/Latin p. 104. ᶜAbd al-Wahhāb b. Manṣūr (Benmansour): *Qabāʾil al-maghrib*, Rabat, 1968, I, p. 33a. Cuoq and Levtzion-Hopkins in the index under Waggāg.

289 Lévi-Provençal, *JA* 224, 1934, p. 218/trans. Gabrieli, *Rendi. Acc. Naz. Lincei* VI, 11, 1935, pp. 904-05/Lévi-Provençal y García Gómez, pp. 98-99 (§ 56). See p. 394 f. above.

290 *Ḥulal mawshiyya*, p. 5/trans. Huici, pp. 22-23/Norris: *Saharan Myth*, p. 38. *Ibn Khaldoun: Berbères*, II, pp. 64-65, contradicts itself in saying 'de race sanhadjienne' and 'frères des Sanhadja'. These peoples are either the one or the other. But here by 'Sanhadja' are meant other peoples of this group.

291 Norris: *Saharan Myth*, pp. 29, ftn. 3; 59; 226, ftn. 24. Ibn Yāsīn early on forced the Lamṭa, the tribe of his teacher Wajjāj, into his movement; Bakrī, p. 166/French p. 314/Monteil, p. 61/Cuoq, pp. 88-89/Levtzion-Hopkins, p. 72. See p. 375 above.

292 Björkman *EI* lithām. WKAS *talaththama* (II, p. 196a).

This agrees with the otherwise questionable statement of the historian Ibn al-Athīr (d. 630/1233) that the Lamtūna before they seized power already veiled their mouth against heat and cold, as the Arabs also did.[293] Gerhard Rohlfs views the use of the veil by the Tuaregs as a protective measure against the desert wind which constantly irritates the eyes, nose and mouth with dust.[294] Apparently used at first as necessary effective protection during heavy sandstorms, veiling then became a permanent custom.[295] He says he did not see any veiled men in Ghadames but the local men, when travelling, also veiled their mouth with the end of a turban like the Tuaregs.[296] That no veil was worn over the mouth in Ghadames, in contrast to the Berbers of the Sahara, is already documented in the 6th/12th century.[297] Gustav Nachtigal and his companions in 1869 made their way from wild Tibesti to Fezzan, 'All of them covering their mouth and nose as much as possible in order to reduce their thirst'.[298] He believes this is the purpose for wearing the veil over the mouth and likewise sees in its use a practice common to the Tubu and the Tuaregs. It is 'a precautionary measure produced (sic) by the dry desert air' which then became a custom 'of national significance'.[299] Thus according to Nachtigal more a protection against the body drying out, but according to Rohlfs rather against heat and cold. Likewise, the French officer Georges Drague (= Georges Spillmann), the Targi Ghubayd Alūjaly and Norris trace veiling among the Ṣanhāja back to the necessity of protecting oneself against sun and airborne sand.[300] A hero in the *Ḥamāsa* is celebrated as:

---

293 *Kāmil*, year 448 (IX, p. 622, penult. line).

294 *Reise durch Marokko*, Bremen, 1869, p. 192.

295 *Quer durch Afrika*, Leipzig, 1874, I, p. 260.

296 Ibid., I, p. 80. Contradictory to I, p. 120: 'Melathemin sind alle Bewohner der Grossen Sahara: Die Tuareg, die Bewohner von Rhadames, von Ain-Salah, von Rhat, auch die nomadisierenden Araber von Tuat, wogegen die Araber und Berber, welche sich nicht dauernd dort aufhalten, keinen Schleier vors Gesicht zu nehmen pflegen.' Also contradictory to Henri Duveyrier: *Les Touareg du Nord*, Paris, 1864, p. 391.

297 *Istibṣār*, p. 145.

298 *Sahârâ und Sûdân*, Berlin, 1879-1881, I, p. 369.

299 Ibid., II, p. 192.

300 Georges Drague: *Esquisse d'Histoire religieuse du Maroc*, Paris, 1951, p. 29. Norris: *Saharan Myth*, pp. 40, 68.

Ein Rauhwolf des Reisens; kommt entgegen wie Feuer ihm
der Hauch des Samûm, wird er darum nicht verschleiern
sich.[301]
(A tough wolf of travel; let the Samūm blow
like fire against him, he doesn't veil himself.)

— a form of heroism involving self-torment which, however, is also meant to have been represented religiously by Muḥammad. The Prophet, it is said, only disliked veiling the face against dust because he expected a higher divine reward for these sufferings.[302] On the other hand, ᶜAlī and his three sons Ḥasan, Ḥusayn and Muḥammad b. al-Ḥanafiyya, along with their travel group, are supposed to have marched into Baṣra wearing veils.[303] Also included in travel and combat clothing was the turban (of red silk) with which in 75/695 Ḥajjāj kept his face veiled in the mosque of Kūfa until the people had assembled before whom he wished to deliver his threatening speech. When he began to speak, he uncovered his face.[304]

Unrightly E.-F. Gautier rejects the role of the veil as protecting the respiratory tract from the desert wind but with some justification he proposes instead protection of the nose and mouth against penetration by evil spirits.[305] Yet one is obliged to ask along with Keenan: why only the men and not the more vulnerable women and children as well? But this theory cannot be wholly dismissed because demons are often conceived of as lurking behind or in the midst of swirling sands. The fact that the Targi sleeps with his veil on could also be taken as support for this view (Keenan, p. 134).

Another thesis is that people wish to make themselves unrecognizable by wearing the veil. Dozy had already cited in favor of this the idea of Edward W. Lane that a veil renders a bedouin unrecognizable to someone seeking to exact blood revenge from him,[306] and

301 Friedrich Rückert: *Hamâsa oder die ältesten arabischen Volkslieder, gesammelt von Abu Temmâm*, Stuttgart, 1846, II, p. 305 (no. 771).

302 Majd al-Dīn Ibn al-Athīr: *Al-nihāya fī gharīb al-ḥadīth wa'l-athar*, Cairo, 1963, IV, p. 231; WKAS *talaththama*.

303 Norris: *Saharan Myth*, p. 69.

304 Ṭabarī: *Annales*, II, p. 863, l. 17 to p. 864, l. 1, and the parallel sources given there. The historical context in Julius Wellhausen: *Das arabische Reich und sein Sturz*, Berlin, 1902, p. 142.

305 *Le Sahara*, Paris, 1946, p. 209.

306 R.P.A. Dozy: *Dictionnaire détaillé des noms des vêtements chez les Arabes*, Amsterdam, 1845, pp. 399-400. Cf. Norris: *Saharan Myth*, p. 69.

he showed by means of passages in the *1001 Nights* that the *lithām* also concealed one's sex. This motif appears among the earlier Lamtūna in two forms: 1) In their original homeland in Yemen, even before the time of Muḥammad, they are meant to have become his followers and suffered persecution because of this. By putting on veils they made themselves resemble women and thus were able to leave the country in small groups.[307] 2) The Lamtūna are once supposed to have set out on a plundering expedition. But their enemies outflanked them and planned to attack the camp where their women, children and old people had been left behind. On this occasion their women disguised themselves as men with veils and made themselves unrecognizable as women by closely covering their faces. When the enemy caught sight of them, they were content merely to drive off the cattle. But they fell into the snare of the men who were just then returning and now, with the women arriving from the rear, they were caught on both sides and annihilated. Subsequently, the men are supposed to have adopted this veil over the face as their regular clothing.[308] Not a very convincing aetiology since the veil for the face would already have previously been a characteristic of the men. But what is meant is the especially close-fitting veil which conceals the difference between men and women, in imitation of the brave women of the story. Indeed, the bedouin Arabs, for instance, also veiled themselves in order not to be recognizable, as in the case of a conspiracy against the Prophet.[309] A. Jaussen gives two purposes for which the bedouins covered their face with the kefīeh while journeying: 1) to conceal themselves and to pass by unnoticed, and 2) to protect themselves against the sun and dust.[310] In an urban setting it occurred that a judge ordered or advised those who had taken part in stoning a malefactor to veil their face in order to be unrecognizable (*mutanakkirīn*). And ᶜAlī did the same in two cases.[311] The other way round, the caliph Muᶜtaḍid (279-289/892-902) ordered that a

---

307 *Ḥulal mawshiyya*, pp. 8-9/trans. Huici, p. 25-26/trans. Norris: *Saharan Myth*, pp. 38-39. O. Houdas: *Tarikh es-Soudan par Abderrahman ben Abdallah ben ᶜImran ben ᶜAmir as-Saᶜdi*, Paris, 1913-14, reprint 1964, Arabic pp. 25-6/French pp. 43-44 (from *Ḥulal*).

308 Ibn al-Athīr: *Kāmil*, year 448 (IX, p. 623).

309 Aḥmad b. Ḥanbal: *Musnad*, Cairo, 1313/reprint Beirut, V, pp. 453-54. Wāqidī: *Al-maghāzī*, ed. Marsden Jones, London, 1966, III, p. 1043, l. 4/J. Wellhausen: *Muhammed in Medina*, Berlin, 1882, p. 409.

310 A. Jaussen: *Coutumes des Arabes au pays de Moab*, reprint Paris, 1948, p. 281, ftn. 2.

311 Al-Kulaynī: *Al-kāfī*, VII, Tehran, 1379, pp. 187-88 (*k. al-ḥudūd*).

few highway robbers who were to be executed have their faces concealed (*talthīm*) in order to make them unrecognizable and to pretend that he was even punishing melon thieves with the death penalty — the highway robbers were then substituted for the latter. This feigned harshness served as a deterrent.[312] That every disguise makes a person unrecognizable is not in need of supporting evidence, and precisely this is sensational among the Berbers who wore the veil over the mouth that they were only supposed to recognize one another with their veil on. When a Rweyli meets someone with a veil on, he shouts to him: 'Remove the curtain, so that I can recognize thee!'[313] According to Bakrī, for a Berber it was the other way round; to recognize someone who had fallen in battle and lost his veil, he had to cover the person's face again.

Two other contradictory statements about men wearing a veil are the following: on the one hand, the veil expresses servility and, on the other, grandeur. The common element between these two extremes could lie in the distance which one adopts toward another by veiling oneself, even when the other person is also veiled. Sukayna or Fāṭima, both daughters of Ḥusayn b. ᶜAlī, once cautioned one of her sons when he put on a veil and said that wearing a veil during the day meant servility (lowliness, disgrace, *madhalla*), whereas at night it aroused suspicion (*rība*).[314] Certain Znāga-speaking Trarza conceal their mouth with their hand when they wish to show modesty and respect.[315] Otherwise baring one's head is often a sign of humility and submissiveness. 'He regretted what he had done to our shaykh and once again sought access to him by baring his head and suchlike.'[316] 'He feared the anger of the sultan and hastened to meet with him (the shaykh) in order to clear up the matter. When this was not possible, he sat down in a corner where the shaykh was accustomed to perform his prayers, until he came. He went up to him, bareheaded, submissive (*dhalīl*), kissed his feet and begged him in

---

312 Ibn al-ᶜImrānī: *Al-inbāʾ fī taʾrīkh al-khulafāʾ*, ed. Qasim al-Samarrai, Leiden, 1973, p. 142, l. 9 and p. 145, l. 11.

313 Alois Musil: *The Manners and Customs of the Rwala Bedouins*, New York, 1928, p. 120.

314 Abū Bakr Muḥammad b. al-Walīd al-Ṭurṭūshī: *Al-ḥawādith wa'l-bidaᶜ*, ed. Muḥammad al-Ṭālibī, Tunis, 1959, p. 66.

315 Norris: *Saharan Myth*, p. 40, ftn. 4.

316 Sakhāwī: *Al-ḍawʾ al-lāmiᶜ li-ahl al-qarn al-tāsiᶜ*, Cairo, 1353-55, VII, p. 120, ll. 17-18.

clear words for pardon and forgiveness.'[317] One reads sentences like these quite often. When in Baghdad in 547/1152-53 a few *fuqahā'* of the Niẓāmiyya attacked inheritance officials who wanted to seal the legacy left by one of the residents and two of them had to be arrested, their rector Abū'l-Najīb al-Suhrawardī bared his head under the palace al-Tāj and obtained forgiveness. But when he then began to teach again without permission from the caliph, he was incarcerated. Later his head was uncovered in public and he received five strokes of the lash. Another person who was suspected of Shīᶜite inclinations likewise had his head uncovered and was flogged.[318] Inflicting humiliation on someone and self-humiliation: both find expression in uncovering the head. Uncovering the head during the official prayer for rain[319] — apparently also for the sake of self-humiliation — is a well-known practice which is by no means prescribed by Islam. Better attested is the notion of grandeur associated with wearing the veil. Here one may recall Ibn ᶜAbdūn's injunction to the so-called 'followers' (*ḥasham*) and the black slaves of the Almoravids forbidding them to wear the veil like lords and to conduct themselves arrogantly.[320] In this case, however, it is perhaps not a question of the significance of the veil in itself but as an attribute of the Almoravid ruling nation. In an edifying story from the end of the Almoravid period the veil is an emblem of the ruling nation, as well as of pride: a certain Abū Isḥāq Bārān b. Yaḥyā al-Massūfī, a prominent man who died in 570/1174-75 in Sijilmāsa, wanted to join the Sufis in Marrakesh. The shaykh ordered him to remove the veil

---

317 *Ḍaw' lāmiᶜ*, VIII, p. 130, ll. 16-18.

318 Ibn al-Jawzī: *Al-muntaẓam fī tārīkh al-mulūk wa'l-umam*, Hyderabad, 1357-60, X, pp. 147-48 (year 547). Cf. Menahem Milson: *A Sufi Rule for Novices. Kitāb Ādāb al-Murīdīn of Abū al-Najīb al-Suhrawardī*. An Abridged Translation and Introduction, Harvard University Press, 1975, pp. 14-15/*Kitāb ādāb al-murīdīn li-Abī'l-Najīb ᶜAbd al-Qāhir al-Suhrawardī*, ed. Menahem Milson, The Max Schloessinger Mermorial Series 2, Jerusalem, 1978, [5].

319 Examples in Tādilī: *Tashawwuf*, p. 117, ll. 1-2; p. 199, l. 16; Muḥammad Taqī-i Dānishpazhūh: *Rūzbihānnāma*, Tehran, 1347, p. 353, ll. 7-8. In Algeria they sing about the doll which is carried around in the rain procession that it has bared its head, or the children who come along on the pilgrimage to a saint's tomb walk bareheaded while the religious authorities march barefoot; Alfred Bel: 'Quelques rites pour obtenir la pluie en temps de sécheresse, chez les musulmans maghribins', *Recueil de mémoires et de textes publié en l'honneur du XIVe Congrès des Orientalistes*, Algiers, 1905, pp. 64-67. Rather remarkable during these rites for rain are the bareheaded children. Additional information in Westermarck: *Ritual and Belief in Morocco*, index Head, uncovering the.

320 See p. 401 above.

covering his mouth, to go to the marketplace and to come back with a flat basket (or a platter) on his head full of Jewish meat products that had not been properly prepared according to Jewish law (?).[321] When the man appeared again without the veil and with the basket on his head, the shaykh said: 'In this way you have joined those who travel the path, and pride (*kibr*) has abandoned you.'[322] This is something of a variant on the story about Abū Yazīd al-Baṣṭāmī's advice to a similar aspirant, namely to hang a sack of nuts around his neck and to promise and to give a nut to every boy who slapped him — a piece of advice which the fellow decided not to follow.[323] Given the revolutionary effect Ghazzālī exercised in the west particularly against the Almoravids, the command of the shaykh from Marrakesh could also be influenced by one of Ghazzālī's exempla in which it is related that a man who was ashamed to carry meat home from the market, hung the meat around his neck in order to abase his ego.[324] The Tuaregs attach importance to the veil: 'It is not proper for noble people to show themselves.'[325] According to A. Hanoteau an idea of honor (dignité) is connected with the custom.[326] Keenan along with others finds that among the Tuaregs the veil has to do with 'propriety' and creates or maintains 'social distance',[327] that it bolsters an individual's self-awareness and dignity, and moreover

---

321 *Ṭabaq min al-*ṭrf. Presumably this is a plural from *aṭrīf* 'impure meat of animals killed by Jews but not ritually slaughtered' (< Hebr. *ṭ^e^rēfā*), perhaps to be read as *ṭuruf*. On *aṭrīf* (= *ṭrīf*) see Dozy and E. Fagnan: *Additions aux dictionnaires arabes*. On *ṭārūf* see Fagnan and Beaussier. Reading *ṭaraf* and taking it in the sense of *shawāh* 'extremity of an animal, remnant, remains, scraps, worthless and contemptible thing' (see Lane under *ṭaraf* and *shawā*) does not work because it is in the singular, unless one takes it to be the material the *ṭabaq* is made from. Thus Norris translates it as 'a covering of rag' or 'a covering of material' (see following ftn.).

322 *Tashawwuf*, pp. 241-42/trans. H.T. Norris: 'Muslim Ṣanhāja Scholars of Mauritania', in *Studies in West African Islamic History* (ed. Willis), I, 1979, p. 151/Norris: *Saharan Myth*, p. 42.

323 Sahlagī: *Al-nūr min kalimāt Abī <Yazīd> Ṭayfūr*, in ᶜAbd al-Raḥmān Badawī: *Shaṭaḥāt al-ṣūfiyya*, I, Cairo, 1949, p. 87. Cf. also Meier: *Fawāʾiḥ al-ğamāl wa-fawātiḥ al-ğalāl des Nağm ad-dīn al-Kubrā*, Wiesbaden, 1957, Intro., pp. 45-46.

324 Ṣafadī: *Al-wāfī bi'l-wafayāt*, Bibl. Islamica VI, Part 1, p. 276, ll. 2-3.

325 E. Daumas: *Le Sahara algérien*, p. 325, quoted in Goldziher: 'Materialien', *ZDMG* 41, 1887, p. 101/*Ges. Schr.*, II, p. 262.

326 *Essai de grammaire de la langue tamachek*², Algiers, 1896, p. XVIII.

327 *The Tuaregs*, pp. 131-33, 136.

distinguishes the Tuaregs from other ethnic groups, thereby contributing to their ethnic unity.[328]

In the case of certain individuals veiling the face, beyond simply indicating the adoption of distance, can also symbolize the mystery of sanctity. The first person who veiled his face, claimed to be God incarnate and won supporters, was Hāshim b. Ḥakīm, known as al-Muqannaᶜ 'the Veiled One', in Transoxania. He was surrounded in 163/779-80 by the ᶜAbbāsid forces of order and committed suicide with all his wives.[329] He is supposed to have veiled himself, according to his friends, so as not to cause anyone's destruction by the radiant splendor of his face — according to his enemies, in order to hide the ugliness of his head from his followers. But perhaps what lies behind this is the necessity for a mask of sanctity. One thinks of the veiled representation of several holy men, in particular Muḥammad, in miniatures. Abū'l-Qāsim Yaḥyā b. Zikrawayh (d. 290/903), the Qarmaṭian propagandist was veiled.[330] Naturally, the veil has a role in the expectations concerning the Mahdī in North-West Africa where it was widespread among the Berbers of the desert. In the 8th/14th century people still travelled to the *ribāṭ* Māssa in the hope of finding there a leader of the end of time, by which they had in mind a veiled man from among the neighboring Juddāla.[331] This belief remained alive into the 14th/20th century. A historian of Sūs, Muḥammad b. Aḥmad al-Manūzī/Mānūzī (d. 1365/1946 or 1366/1947) came to Afīlāl in 1329/1911 and there at the tomb of Balqāsim al-Fīlālī (d. 10th/16th century) pronounced a prayer on behalf of the saint. He was immediately surrounded by women. When they beheld his impressive appearance, they called a man. Mānūzī had veiled his

---

328 Ibid., p. 135.

329 Narshakhī: *Tārīkh-i Bukhārā*, Pers. trans. by Qubāwī, ed. Mudarris-i Raḍawī, Tehran, 1318, pp. 87-89. Eduard Sachau: *Chronologie orientalischer Völker von Albêrûnî*, Leipzig, 1878, p. 211. *Mujmal al-tawārīkh wa'l-qiṣaṣ*, ed. Malik al-shuᶜarā'-i Bahār, Tehran, 1318, pp. 334-35. ᶜAwfī: *Jawāmiᶜ al-ḥikāyāt,* no. 1625 and 2004, following Niẓámu'ddín's *Introduction to the Jawámiᶜu'l Ḥikáyát*, Gibb Mem. New Series VIII, 1929. Ṭabarī: *Annales*, III, pp. 484, 494. Gholam Hossein Sadighi: *Les mouvements religieux iraniens au IIe et au IIIe siècle de l'hégire*, diss. Paris, 1938, pp. 163 ff. Bertold Spuler: *Iran in früh-islamischer Zeit,* Wiesbaden, 1952, p. 198 f. Richard N. Frye: *Bukhara*, Norman, 1965, pp. 22-23. Freely retold in the little collective volume of Saᶜīd-i Nafīsī: *Māh-i Nakhshab*[2], Tehran, 1334, pp. 9-29. In German verse by Friedrich Rückert: *Sieben Bücher morgenländischer Sagen und Geschichten*, Stuttgart, 1837, II, pp. 82-87 (following d'Herbelot s.v. Hakem Ben Haschem, sic).

330 Ṭabarī: *Annales*, III, p. 2225, l. 1.

331 *Ibn Khaldûn, The Muqaddimah*, trans. Rosenthal, II, pp. 196-97. Cf. ftn. 45 above.

face (*multathim*). When the man laid eyes on him, he cried out: '*Al-imām al-mahdī, al-imām al-mahdī*!' The people quickly gathered together. Mānūzī explained to them who he was and told them they should go away. But that only increased the tumult. Mānūzī left the *qubba* and set out for the *murābiṭūn* of Afīlāl, while someone continually had to ward off the people. He experienced similar behavior among the Simlāla. He was amazed by the naïvity of the people.[332] The image of the veiled religious leader had shortly before acquired new vividness through the appearance of the Mauritanian marabout Māᵓ al-ᶜAynayn (d. 1328/1910).[333] He had presented himself wearing a veil as a sign of his sanctity.[334] On the title page of his *dīwān* which was lithographed in 1322/1904 he is called 'the one who veils himself in the mouth veil of divine impenetrability and wraps himself in the mantle of divine mercifulness' (*al-mutalaththim bi-lithām al-ṣamadāniyya al-mutajalbib bi-jilbāb al-raḥmāniyya*). His son and successor Aḥmad al-Hayba (Hība) is celebrated in a eulogy as:

A king: if the veil over his mouth is lifted
he is a full moon shining on the sky's horizon.[335]

Men have veiled themselves for other reasons as well. But we only know why in a very few cases. Some did it because they were so handsome that they believed they had to protect themselves from the evil eye and from women. Among the Arabs of the Umayyad period there were Waḍḍāḥ al-Yaman, al-Muqannaᶜ al-Kindī and the Chris-

---

332 *Maᶜsūl*, III, pp. 353-54, from Mānūzī's *Tārīkh Sūs wa-rijālihī*; indeed the whole section of *Maᶜsūl*, III, pp. 241-415, is taken from the latter. On Mānūzī's work see Ibn Sūda's *Dalīl muᵓarrikh al-maghrib al-aqṣā*, Casablanca, 1960, no. 1000. That belief in the coming of the Mahdī among the Moroccan people in Māssa at the beginning of our century was still alive is attested by Doutté: *En Tribu*, pp. 4, 241.

333 Detailed description in *Maᶜsūl*, IV, pp. 83-305. Numerous references in other passages of the *Maᶜsūl* as well: II, pp. 377, 381; III, pp. 26-28, 29-34, 57, 247, 327-29, 366-402 (extract from Mānūzī); VII, p. 79; XII, pp. 79-80, 109-10, 136-44; XIII, 139-40; XIV, pp. 160-61; XIX, p. 161. The literature on Māᵓ al-ᶜAynayn and his movement is extensive. Cf. ftn. 123 and 153 above. Segonzac: *Au cœur de l'Atlas*, pp. 620-24.

334 Chapelle in *Hespéris* 11, 1930, p. 92. Norris: 'Shaykh Māᵓ al-ᶜAynayn', *BSOAS* 31, 1968, p. 115. Willis in *Studies in West African Islamic History*, I, p. 10.

335 *Maᶜsūl*, IV, p. 213.

tian Abū Zubayd al-Ṭāʾī.[336] In the Persian adventure story *Samak-i ʿAyyār* it is the fourteen-year-old son of the king.[337] In the Turkish *Book of Dede Korkut* the handsome youth Kan Turali and three others as well wear a veil.[338] The Circassian Muḥammad b. ʿIrāq (d. 933/1526), an eminent Sufi living first in Damascus and then from 924/1518 in Medina, made his young son wear a veil whenever he left the house to protect him from discomfort and temptations.[339] The Tuaregs also harbor similar anxieties and in this way justify their wearing the veil,[340] not because they think they are handsome but chiefly out of fear of the evil eye.

We have no knowledge about the reason why the Sufi Abū'l-ʿAbbās Aḥmad b. Muḥammad al-Mulaththam (d. 672/1274) in the city Qūṣ in Upper-Egypt always wore a veil covering his face.[341] He was a Ḥusaynid and originated in the 'east'. In the case of his contemporary in Lower-Egypt, Aḥmad al-Badawī (d. 675/1276), the veil seems to be more comprehensible. He had come to the east from Fez with his father in 603/1206-07 and acquired the name 'the Bedouin' (al-Badawī) because like the inhabitants of the desert he mostly veiled his face. But he was the only one in his family to do so. Thus he did not necessarily bring this item of dress with him from the west. On the other hand, it is also reported that already as a child he

---

336 Julius Wellhausen: *Reste arabischen Heidentums*, Berlin, 1897, p. 196. *Aghānī*, VI, p. 33; XV, pp. 157-58/new VI, p. 211; XVII, p. 108. Ibn Qotaiba: *Liber poesis et poetarum*, ed. De Goeje, Leiden, 1904, pp. 462-63.

337 Farāmarz b. Khudādād al-Arrajānī: *Samak-i ʿAyyār*, ed. Parwīz Nātil-i Khānlarī, Tehran, 1347, I, p. 9.

338 *Das Buch des Dede Korkut*, trans. Joachim Hein, Zurich, 1958, p. 192.

339 Shaʿrānī: *Lawāqiḥ al-anwār al-qudsiyya fī bayān al-ʿuhūd al-muḥammadiyya*, Cairo, 1961, p. 605, penult. line.

340 Keenan, pp. 130, 134. Nicolaisen, p. 14.

341 Udfuwī: *Al-ṭāliʿ al-saʿīd al-jāmiʿ asmāʾ nujabāʾ al-Ṣaʿīd*, Cairo, 1966, no. 70, pp 131-35. Subkī: *Ṭabaqāt al-shāfiʿiyya al-kubrā*, VIII, pp. 35-37. Shaʿrānī: *Al-ṭabaqāt al-kubrā*, Cairo, 1954, no. 277, I, p. 157. Jean-Claude Garcin: *Un centre musulman de la Haute-Égypte médiévale: Qūṣ*, thèse, Paris, 1976 (IFAO), pp. 167-69. Translation of Subkī in R. Gramlich in *Der Islam* 55, 1978, pp. 8-9. By way of explanation: ʿAbd al-Ghaffār, the disciple of the saint, distinguishes between a 'substitutionality' or 'badal-ship' (*badaliyya, tabaddul*), i.e. a 'self-duplication' through projecting a likeness of the person (*shibh*), and a kind of long-distance sight through removing all walls which otherwise stand in the way of vision, during which the distance remains: material unveiling (*kashf ṣūrī*).

wore two veils,[342] and these two veils remind one of the manner of veiling of certain Berbers as Bakrī describes them. Suspicious in this respect is the gentilicium of a certain ᶜAbd al-Malik b. ᶜAbd al-Ḥaqq b. Hāshim al-Ḥarbī al-Maghribī (d. 845/1441) who directed the *ribāṭ* Ḥasan b. ᶜAjlān in Mecca and always shaved his beard and mustache, and was veiled. Although ultimately he was supposed to be a Ḥasanid from Yanbūᶜ, his gentilicium Maghribī betrays a connection with Morocco.[343] No doubt wearing the veil in the case of the Koranic reciter and religious scholar Abū ᶜAbdallāh Muḥammad al-Sūdānī (d. 1308/1891) is to be traced back to his origin in Marrakesh,[344] whereas not all inhabitants of the sub-Saharan Sudan are veiled Berbers; Ibn Baṭṭūṭa's times lie far in the past when most of the residents of Timbuktu were still veiled Massūfa.[345] The head of the Kattāniyya order, Muḥammad al-Kattānī (d. 1327/1909), who was a handsome man, wore a veil most of the time but people did not dare to ask him the reason why and were content with the reassuring comment that even the Prophet had veiled himself on occasion and that great men of the past who had veiled themselves included Moses, Diḥya al-Kalbī, Abū Yaᶜazzā (d. 572/1177),[346] Aḥmad al-Badawī, Abū'l-ᶜAbbās al-Mulaththam and others as well.[347]

Why did the religious scholar Abū'l-ᶜAbbās Aḥmad b. ᶜAlī al-Manjūr (d. 995/1587) in Fez wear the veil? When Abū ᶜAlī al-Ḥusayn b. Ibrāhīm al-Khaladī/Khuldī al-Saktānī appeared with his Koranic tablet before him and remained silent, al-Manjūr, who had

---

342 ᶜAbd al-Ṣamad: *Al-jawāhir al-saniyya wa'l-karāmāt al-aḥmadiyya*, Cairo, 1305, p. 11, above; p. 24, below: Aḥmad was continually veiled with two veils (*lithāmān*) so that people saw nothing but his eyes. One person before whom he uncovered his face is supposed to have dropped down dead. — As for Badawī, he was pockmarked, had a hooked nose with moles and a scar between his eyes, in short he was ugly, i.e. had good reason to veil his face (ᶜAbd al-Ṣamad, p. 11) Wearing a veil while on the roof in Tanta was no doubt of use to him as protection against the sun. Followers interpret his wearing a veil, even his wearing two veils, as a precautionary measure to cover the spiritual light of his face, as was the case with Muqannaᶜ; Aḥmad Muḥammad Ḥajjāb: *Al-ᶜiẓa wa'l-iᶜtibār, ārā' fī ḥayāt al-sayyid al-Badawī al-dunyawiyya wa-ḥayātihī'l-barzakhiyya*, Cairo, 1386/1966, pp. 86, 134-35.

343 *Ḍaw' lāmiᶜ*, V, p. 85.

344 Ibn al-Muwaqqit: *Al-saᶜāda al-abadiyya fī'l-taᶜrīf bi-mashāhir al-ḥaḍra al-marrākushiyya*, litho., 1336/1917, II, p. 106. Al-ᶜAbbās b. Ibrāhīm: *Iᶜlām*, VII, p. 68.

345 Ibn Baṭṭūṭa, IV, p. 430. Norris: *The Tuaregs*, p. 45, below.

346 Lévi-Provençal, *EI*[2] Abū Yaᶜazzā.

347 Muḥammad al-Bāqir al-Kattānī: *Tarjamat al-shaykh Muḥammad al-Kattānī al-shahīd*, n. pl., 1962, p. 115 (cf. also p. 114).

on a veil covering his mouth, ordered him to read out loud. But the student replied: 'Only if you remove your veil (*lithām*). Haven't you heard that teaching comes forth from the mouth?'[348]

A number of Arabs of the Sahara have adopted the veil over the mouth from the Berbers.[349] That conversely the Arabs brought the veil from their original home to Africa and transmitted it to the Berbers[350] is unlikely, in particular because the Saharan veil covering the face goes back to the era before the immigration of the Arabs.[351] On the other hand, the argument that veiling was not a regular feature of dress among the Arabs would not in itself be conclusive since the fez, for example, only became widely popular outside its own homeland. As for evidence of wearing the veil among African Arabs: Muḥammad al-Mukhtār al-Sūsī visited the Jbel Bani in 1362/1943. The chief of the Ida w-Bilāl, the *qāʾid* Mḥmād ad-Dawbilālī, called Abū'n-Nuᶜaylāt, and his son Ḥusayn appeared in the dress of the local Arab camel owners who look after transportation by land, i.e. in black clothes and with a black veil covering the mouth.[352]

Some of the reasons enumerated above for veiling could be valid in explaining the custom of the veil among the Berbers. If one brings them into an ordered, rational relationship, something like the following picture emerges: the veil would have originated as protection against sun, wind, dust and cold. The men, who were constantly exposed to these effects of the weather, would consider the facial veil as a necessary accessory of their dress and see in it the outward sign of their desert way of life and their desert virtues, indeed even of their status as warriors. To give up the veil would be a contradiction

---

348 Justinard: *Fawaid al jamma*, pp. 57-58. On Manjūr see Ibn al-Qāḍī: *Jadhwat al-iqtibās*, Rabat, 1973, pp. 135-36. *Durrat al-ḥijāl*, ed. Allouche, I, pp. 84-86 (no. 186). Aḥmad Bābā: *Nayl al-ibtihāj*, in the margin of Ibn Farḥūn, pp. 95-98. *Fihris Aḥmad al-Manjūr*, ed. Muḥammad Ḥajjī, Rabat, 1976. Mohammed ben Cheneb: 'Étude sur les personnages mentionnés dans l'Idjāza du cheikh ᶜAbd el Qādir el Fāsy', *Actes du 14ᵉ Congrès des Orientalistes*, Paris, 1907, tome IV, pp. 248-49 (no. 28). Nothing about a veil in these sources.

349 Norris: *Saharan Myth*, pp. 40-41.

350 Cf. the reflections in *Saharan Myth*, pp. 68-69.

351 See p. 413 below. Bovill believed that the veil over the mouth was introduced into the Sahara between 600 and 1000 AD, i.e. only during the Islamic period, since it is not mentioned either in antiquity or by the Byzantines; E.W. Bovill: *The Golden Trade of the Moors*, London, 1968, p. 47; *Caravans of the Old Sahara*, London, 1933, p. 24; taken from F.R. Rodd, 1926.

352 *Khilāl Jazūla*, III, pp. 89-90, 92.

to their idea of manliness. An uncovered face would be indecent to the Saharan Berbers, to allow one's face to be seen would amount to self-exposure and an offense to one's sense of shame. Once they become accustomed to veiling, they would add other reasons in accordance with their way of thinking and their superstitions, among them the necessity for a decent man to conceal from the sight of others the orifices of the upper body as well as those of the lower body, and to guard them against pernicious influence. Dictated by journeys and raiding expeditions through the desert, the veiling of the men favored the unveiling or absence of the veil among the women who neither had to combat the wind and weather, nor to fight with enemies, those seeking blood revenge or peaceful cattle breeders and travellers. But we are unable to provide proof that things proceeded like this or a reason why they should only have developed this way here. Why did such a widespread practice as protecting the face while travelling in the desert in the one case, among the Berbers, turn into a regular form of male dress and in the other case, among the Arabs, not do so? Only when the answer to that is found — and it must be found on the level of historical evidence or at least on the basis of ethnological findings — can the hypothesis of initial protection against the weather be regarded as fairly secure.

A critical response to this view was already presented in 1949 by Raffaele Corso.[353] He enumerates a series of African peoples who by no means exclusively inhabit sandy regions and yet, at least among the upper classes, make use of the veil over the mouth. They wish in this way, as in fact the Tuaregs more or less say, to hinder pernicious effects from penetrating their body. This is particularly the case during the taking of nourishment when a person opens his mouth. Corso found the veil as far back as in prehistoric scratchings on stone; either directly depicted as such, or at least indicated by the fact that the people represented had no mouth, and thus he concludes that the custom in the Sahara is of extraordinarily great antiquity. Furthermore, he points to the Abyssinian custom of even covering or wrapping drinking vessels with cloths against the evil eye.[354] He could also have referred to Wadai where the pitchers with water destined for the king were wrapped with material and even the fountain the water was taken from had a cloth enclosure around it as protection against

353 'Il velo dei Tuàregh', Istituto Universitario Orientale di Napoli, *Annali*, Nuova Serie, Vol. III (Scritti in onore di Francesco Beguinot), 1949, pp. 151-66.

354 Ibid., p. 159.

the evil eye.[355] In addition, one might perhaps also mention the rule of the Tuaregs to veil themselves before strangers and their parents-in-law, especially before their mothers-in-law,[356] for a comparison with other peoples, including Africans, shows that in particular the parents-in-law, in the husband's case the mother-in-law and in the case of the wife the father-in-law, were and continue to be regarded as bearers of the evil eye.[357] In short, the broad spread of such evidence and its agreement with the reasons the Tuaregs give for their use of the veil led Corso to consider the magical apotropaic function of veiling as the starting point and to trace the accumulation of additional purposes, including physiological ones, in the opposite direction, i.e. from the superstitious to the realistic.[358] But, as is easy to see, this does not explain the peculiarity of veiling on the part of men, even if one must admit that the path from a person of quality to a man in general is a short one and the taboo concerning the mouth can have transferred from the one to the other without difficulty and women, for the time being, could have been left behind. But this is only a possibility, and the real problem, the problem of the veil as an item of male dress, remains unsolved.

Thus, we do not know what the situation was to begin with, whether it was a question of protection against the elements or defensive magic or something else. None the less, as the reasons given above show, everything is interconnected and every individual characteristic has found its proponents, among the indigenous and the oriental observers as well.[359] The contradictory standpoints are not, however, so far removed from one another and are by no means irreconcilable. What they have in common is that they conceive of the veil as a defensive and prophylactic measure, on the one hand against magic, and on the other against physical damage, both cases representing a 'hygienic' safety device and, as I mentioned above, often enough uncanny forces were also imagined as lurking behind

---

355 Richard Andree: *Ethnographische Parallelen und Vergleiche*, Stuttgart, 1878, p. 38 (from Nachtigal in *Verh. Ges. f. Erdkunde zu Berlin*, vol. II, 1875, p. 145).

356 Nicolaisen: *Ecology*, p. 14. Keenan, p. 130.

357 S. Seligmann: *Die Zauberkraft des Auges und das Berufen*, Hamburg, 1922, pp. 139-41. In the first version under the title *Der böse Blick und Verwandtes*, Berlin, 1910, I, pp. 101-04.

358 'Il velo', p. 161.

359 Corso is mistaken when on p. 157 he stresses that the Arabs have mentioned nothing about the Berbers wearing the veil as protection against the weather. He has overlooked Ibn al-Athīr. See ftn. 362 and pp. 401 f. above.

the wind and sands. In any case, for men the inclemency of nature was the more dangerous. A third standpoint would be the 'social' one: to begin with the mask (persona) which people give themselves would uphold their dignity and the dignity of others, maintain the distance between the age groups, the social classes, sexual categories, between the sexes in general — this as well being a protective device but for preserving social health and order. What in this situation was the original reason and how and in what sequence the other elements were added and complemented one another we do not know. All this is discernible to us is the final complex out of which every individual, including the natives themselves, is pleased to select a particular element in order to explain the whole.[360] Already in the 15th century certain Tuaregs admitted they didn't know anything precise about the matter and were simply following an old custom.[361]

Ibn al-Athīr (d. 630/1233), for his part, transmits the information that this facial veil of the Berbers originated among the Lamtūna and then only after they had broken forth from the desert. Judging by the context, this would only have been after the conquest of northern Morocco under Yūsuf b. Tāshfīn, perhaps at the time of the additional recruitment of 470/1077-78. He writes that previously the Lamtūna had in fact worn the veil covering the mouth but only like the Arabs against heat and cold, in a casual manner and if one wished. Afterwards, they were meant to have 'tightened' the veil (*ḍayyaqū ḥīnaʾidh lithāmahum*).[362] We do not know what this new veil looked like but it was clearly a close-fitting veil covering the mouth, as is typical for men of the Sahara. This could mean that the Tuaregs as well only subsequently took over their veil from the Al-

360 Norris: *Saharan Myth*, p. 41, considers it hopeless, in view of the custom's enormous diffusion and its many deviations in detail, to attempt to derive it from a single cause.

361 Antonio Malfante from Genoa 1447. Charles de La Roncière: 'Découverte d'une relation de voyage datée du Touat et décrivant en 1447 le bassin du Niger', Comité des travaux historiques et scientifiques, *Bulletin de la section de géographie*, tome XXXIII, 1918 (Paris, 1919), p. 8. Text ibid., pp. 24-25: 'Portant os et nasum coopertum. Vidi ex ipsis plures, et per interpretem eos interrogavi quare sic os et nasum tenerent coopertum. Respondentes dixerunt: Talem hereditatem habemus a nostris antiquis.' The same text with French translation Charles de La Roncière: *La découverte de l'Afrique au moyen âge*, Mémoires de la Société royale de géographie d'Égypte, tome V, Cairo, 1924, p. 153, with the deviation 'Vidi ex aliis hic plures'. English: *The Letter of Antoine* (sic) *Malfante*, in the volume *The voyages of Cadamosto*, trans. by Crone, The Hakluyt Society, Second Series, No. LXXX, 1937, reprint 1967, p. 87.

362 Ibn al-Athīr: *Kāmil*, year 448, IX, p. 622, l. 3 from bot./Levtzion-Hopkins, p. 161.

moravids. This contradicts what Bakrī reports that earlier the Berbers of the Sahara were already doubly veiled. However, immediately afterwards Ibn al-Athīr reports another, divergent tradition which locates the origin of the close Berberveil, which was different from that of the Arabs, back in the time when the Lamtūna still lived in the Sahara.[363] This is the story of the brave womenfolk who on the advice of the old men donned men's veils during an attack on their camp and wrapped them around themselves so tightly that one could no longer tell their sex, i.e. they covered the bottom part of their face with them so completely that one could no longer see whether there was a beard underneath or not. The good disguise was the decisive cause of the enemy's defeat and led to the men of the Lamtūna deciding to adopt the tight-fitting veil, to the glory of their women. The legend takes up the widespread motif of clever and brave women and in this form does not deserve any special trust. But in moving the time of origin back to the Sahara it may claim greater plausibility and in addition, without expressly mentioning it, also contains the possibility of an aetiology based on the ceremonial investiture of young Tuaregs with the veil covering the mouth. This in fact takes place when a young man's beard begins to grow.[364] The youthful Targi covers it up with the veil over the mouth: in order to conceal it? Or the other way round, in order to draw attention to it and to place himself among the adults? In the first case in what one might call an oppositional, in the second case a parallel imitation of the women who covered their naked chin and naked upper lip and cheeks in order to appear as men? But perhaps the preconditions for such an aetiology did not exist at that time since according to Ibn Ḥawqal in the 10th century the veil covering the mouth was worn in the Sahara starting from early childhood (see above p. 401). Thus here as well we cannot make out what the situation is. But this much it is possible to say: 1) the legend is closer to the truth than the allegedly historical report. The Almoravid custom of wearing the veil originates without a doubt in the Sahara. 2) Ibn al-Athīr considers the usual veiling of the face, as is also customary among the Arabs, to be a protective measure against heat and cold but traces back the tight-fitting veil, i.e. the typical veil of the Saharan Berbers, more precisely of the Lamtūna, in two ways to an event in the history of

---

363 *Kāmil*, year 448, IX, p. 623/Levtzion-Hopkins, p. 161. The English translation should read: 'But it is also said that' — not simply: 'It is said that'. Ibn al-Athīr does not express himself precisely enough in the whole passage.

364 Corso: 'Il velo', p. 153.

the latter, on the one hand to a tightening of the veil (as a form of uniform) after their emergence from the Sahara — which is not explained in detail: the allegedly historical report, and on the other hand, to an allegedly memorable victory which the Lamtūna, while still in their Saharan homeland, had achieved because their women had wrapped themselves in the usual veil of a man, which was already by that time in use, and tied it so tight that one could not see that they were women: the legend.

The wearing of the veil by men as practiced by the Almoravids was fiercely attacked in the 6th/12th century by their opponents and conquerors, the Almohads. Among them 'wearers of the veil over the mouth' is a term of abuse.[365] Ibn Tūmart (d. 524/1130), the architect of the uprising, did not originate from the Sahara but from the Anti-Atlas and gathered around him the Berbers of his mountainous homeland and of the High-Atlas. They did not belong to the wearers of the veil. Veiling on the part of the men and leaving the face uncovered among the women appeared illicit to him. When after his return from Mecca in 514/1120 he met the Almoravid sultan ᶜAlī b. Yūsuf b. Tāshfīn and his vizier in a mosque in Marrakesh, he spoke out harshly saying he beheld nothing but veiled slave-women.[366] He was shocked that the sultan's sister appeared unveiled in public with her female household.[367] In his writings he reproached the Almoravids for resembling women because of wearing veils and accused their women, with their uncovered faces, of behaving like men.[368] In the year 540/1146 the former Almoravid ruler of Tlemcen, Āngmār, appeared with his Massūfa before Fez to place himself at the service of the Almohad ᶜAbd al-Muᵓmin. They took off their uniform, the veil covering the mouth, and put on the dress

---

365 Though even stronger is *mujassimūn* 'those who think of God as corporeal' and enigmatically *zarājina*; *Ḥulal mawshiyya*, trans. Huici, p. 133, ftn. 1; Huici: *Historia política del imperio almohade*, I, pp. 66-67; Bosch Vilá: *Los Almorávides*, p. 223.

366 Baydhaq in Lévi-Provençal: *Documents inédits*, pp. 67-68/French p. 108.

367 Ibn al-Athīr: *Kāmil*, year 514, X, pp. 570-71. Baydhaq, French p. 109, ftn. 1. *Ibn Khaldoun: Berbères*, II, p. 167.

368 I. Goldziher: *Le Livre de Mohammed ibn Toumert*, p. 263 below/'Materialien', *ZDMG* 41, 1887, p. 102/*Ges. Schr.*, II, p. 263. Huici: *Historia política del imperio almohade*, I, p. 91. Cf. Goldziher, *Ibn Toumert*, Arabic introduction with the biographies, p. 51, l. 3, from *Rawḍ al-qirṭās*, p. 118/Latin p. 159. Goldziher, ibid., p. 259, l. 3.

of the Almohads.[369] When later in 580/1184[370] the Balearic Almoravids crossed over to Bijāya (Bougie) with the intention of reconquering North Africa, they wished to oblige the local *qāḍī* Ḥasan b. ᶜAlī al-Masīlī and others to take the oath of allegiance to them. But because they were veiled and did not show their faces, the *qāḍī* refused to take the oath on the grounds that: 'We do not pay homage to people regarding whom we cannot tell whether they are men or women.' Their Mallorcan chief uncovered his face.[371]

The Mālikite jurist from Spain Abū Bakr al-Ṭurṭūshī (d. 520-525/1126-1130) judged the veiling of the head among men somewhat more mildly but was set against according *carte blanche* in the matter. He knew that in the Maghreb in his time the Almoravids, despite adhering to the Mālikite school of jurisprudence, were veiled and he considered this to be a reprehensible innovation, even if at the moment it was an undisputed custom (*sunna*) among otherwise respectable people. He referred to Mālik who had permitted covering the face (*taqannuᶜ*) against heat and cold and 'for other pardonable reasons' but he added: 'I only like wearing the veil if there is a special reason for doing so. I know that it is not forbidden, but honorable people (*khiyār al-nās*) do not dress that way.'[372] Ibn Tūmart certainly could have been familiar with Ṭurṭūshī's writing. He is supposed to have met Ṭurṭūshī in Egypt.[373]

Given that several authors, by way of abbreviation, describe the Almoravids as 'Lamtūna wearing a veil over the mouth' or simply as 'the wearers of a veil over the mouth', the question thus arises as to whether the passive *mulaththamūn* or the active *mulaththimūn* should be read. The passive participle *mulaththam* 'one whose

---

369 E. Lévi-Provençal: 'Notes d'histoire almohade', *Hespéris* 10, 1930, p. 63 (Arabic)/p. 82 (French). Bosch Vilá, p. 275. Huici: *Historia política*, I, p. 138, ftn. 2.

370 Bel: *Benou Ghânya*, pp. 41-42. Huici: *Historia política*, I, p. 323.

371 Ghubrīnī: *ᶜUnwān al-dirāya fī-man ᶜurifa min al-ᶜulamāʾ fī'l-miʾa al-sābiᶜa bi-Bijāya*, Beirut, 1969, pp. 34-35. Aḥmad Bābā al-Tinbuktī: *Nayl al-ibtihāj*, in the margin of Ibn Farḥūn's *Al-dībāj al-mudhahhab*, Cairo, 1330, pp. 104-05.

372 Abū Bakr al-Ṭurṭūshī: *Al-ḥawādith wa'l-bidaᶜ*, ed. Muḥammad al-Ṭālibī, Tunis, 1959, p. 66. Ṭurṭūshī's formulation: 'Veiling oneself with cloth on the head is widespread in the Maghreb', etc., does not make it clear whether he means only the real Almoravids or that this garb had also been adopted there by others as well.

373 Ibn Khallikān: *Wafayāt al-aᶜyān*, ed. Iḥsān ᶜAbbās, V, p. 46, l. 8. Ṭurṭūshī had supported in writing the suggestion of the Almoravid Yūsuf b. Tāshfīn to depose the refractory Arab-Islamic rulers in Andalusia, i.e. he was aware of the conditions in the west; *Ibn Khaldoun: Berbères*, II, p. 80; Bosch Vilá: *Almorávides*, pp. 149-50.

mouth is veiled' is widely in use and is lexicographically recorded by Beaussier with the meaning 'la figure couverte avec le *liṯām*'. This would be a parallel with *muqanna*ᶜ, *mubarqa*ᶜ*a* and suchlike.[374] But next to this Beaussier also gives the second form of the active verb *laththama* in the sense of 'se voiler avec le *liṯām*', and that would require the active participle *mulaththim* for 'wearer of the veil over the mouth, one who veils his mouth' — a parallel with the well-known factional names from earlier Islamic history *musawwida* 'wearers of black', *mubayyiḍa* 'wearers of white', *muḥammira* 'wearers of red'. In Morocco the reading *mulaththimūn* was justified to me on the grounds that *mulaththamūn* would be persons who had had a veil put over their mouth by someone else. This is in agreement with H.L. Fleischer's conception as expressed in his *Kleinere Schriften*, II, pp. 1, 243. He only accepts the active participle *mulaththimūn*, and W. Björkman follows him in *EI* lithām. The active participle is supported by the infinitive *talthīm* meaning wearing a veil over the mouth, firstly by Ibn Tūmart himself: 'They make themselves similar to women by covering their face with a veil over the mouth (*talthīm*) and a veil over their forehead (*tanqīb*), and the women make themselves similar to men by leaving their face uncovered without a veil over their forehead and their mouth. It is forbidden to imitate them',[375] and then by means of a verse about the Balearic Almoravids who were defeated at Gafsa in 583/1188:[376]

What a disgrace for veiling the mouth (*yā dhallata'l-talthīmi*)
during the new attack,
if they are striving to achieve a return to power![377]

This 'absolute' infinitive is mentioned in *WKAS*, II, p. 195b. It would seem appropriate to me also to add the 'absolute', i.e. the active, participle in *WKAS,* II, p. 201a-b and similarly to place alongside

374 In this same category are people attired in other garments besides veils. Al-ᶜAbbās b. Ibrāhīm: *Al-i*ᶜ*lām bi-man ḥalla Marrākush*, V, pp. 364-65, vocalizes the epithet of Abū'l-ᶜAbbās Aḥmad b. Muḥammad al-Qaysī al-Rundī al-Musalham 'the one with the *silhām*' (d. 653/1255) passively (Marrākushī: *Al-dhayl wa'l-takmila*, VI, pp. 61-64).

375 Goldziher: 'Materialien', *ZDMG* 41, 1887, p. 67, ftn. 5; p. 102, ftn. 2/*Ges. Schr.*, II, p. 228, ftn. 5; p. 263, ftn. 2. The same text in Goldziher: *Le Livre de Mohammed ibn Toumert*, Arabic p. 263, bot., has mistakenly *talaththum* instead of *talthīm*.

376 Huici's Spanish translation of the *Bayān*, Tomo I, Tetuan, 1953, p. 140, ftn. 2. Huici: *Historia política del imperio almohade*, I, p. 338. Bel: *Benou Ghânya*, p. 84.

377 *Ibtiṣār*, p. 151.

mulaththamūn/mulaththama 'those who have had the veil put over their mouth' — I cannot really believe in the form *mulaththama* — *mulaththimūn/mulaththima* 'those who veil their mouth'.[378] The Arabic synonym is *ahl al-lithām* 'people of the veil over the mouth' and the Berber self-designation of the Tuaregs *Kel Tagelmust* 'people of the veil over the mouth'.[379]

ADDITIONS OF THE AUTHOR

P. 347, ftn. 56: On the separation of *ribāṭ* (infinitive) and warfare see Josef van Ess: *Die Gedankenwelt des Ḥāriṯ al-Muḥāsibī*, Bonn, 1961, p. 103.

P. 362, ftn. 138 and additional passages on pages 375, 390, 401: If the *nisba* is Lamaṭī as Muḥammad al-Akhḍar (Lakhdar): *Al-ḥayāh al-adabiyya fī'l-Maghrib ᶜalā ᶜahd al-dawla al-ᶜalawiyya* (1075-1311/1644-1894), Casablanca, 1977, p. 237, states, then the tribe must have been called Lamaṭa and its eponymous ancestor Lamaṭ. Thus, also correct is Jean-Claude Garcin: 'La mosquée al-Lamaṭī à Minyā', *Annales islamologiques* 13, 1977, pp. 101-11.

P. 370, l. 1: Or perhaps it is not a question of *ṣadaqa* 'alms-tax', but of *ṣadāqa* 'friendship'? We know that the individual *mrābeṭ* was regularly attached to a 'friend' (*ṣadīq*) from the ruling tribe of the Saᶜādī who supported him in conflicts with a member of the ruling

---

378 In my typescript that I sent in to the editors I had relied completely on Fleischer and rejected the passive participle. Stefan Wild's criticism has led me to adopt the present toned down formulation. — On the conjectured derivation of *lithām* from *li-tham/*li-fam 'for the mouth' see Karl Vollers: *Volkssprache und Schriftsprache im alten Arabien*, Strassburg, 1906, pp. 9-10, Theodor Nöldeke: *Neue Beiträge zur semitischen Sprachwissenschaft*, Strassburg, 1910, p. 176, ftn. 3. Le Comte de Landberg: *Glossaire daṯînois*, ed. Zettersteen, Leiden, 1942, III, p. 2615.

379 Norris: *Saharan Myth*, p. 34, ftn. 4. *Tuaregs*, p. 192. Keenan, pp. 9, 128. The Tuareg word for the veil over the mouth is given in different forms. Charles de Foucauld: *Dictionnaire touareg-français*, Imprimerie Nationale de France, 1951, I, 439-40: *taġoûlmoust*, pl. *tiġoûlmâs*. Keenan p. 128: *tagelmoust*. Norris: *Tuaregs*, p. 192: *tagilmus*. Corso p. 152: *tighelmûst*. Dierk Lange: *Le Diwān des sultans du [Kānem-] Bornū: Chronologie et histoire d'un royaume africain*, Wiesbaden, 1977, p. 109: *tigelmust*. Henri Duveyrier: *Les Touareg du Nord*, p. 406: *tiguélmoust*. Heinrich Barth: *Reisen*, I, pp. 269, 439-40, 464; II, pp. 28, 51; IV, pp. 100, ftn., 348, 511; V, pp. 163, 704: *tessil-gemist*. Norris: *Saharan Myth*, p. 40, ftn. 4, gives *agaġmuš* as the Znāga word for *lithām*, from which the Ḥassāniyya-Arabic word *kāmiz* is supposed to come.

tribe and who could also be changed. Carlo Alfonso Nallino: *Raccolta di scritti editi e inediti*, Rome, 1939-48, VI, p. 391.

P. 379, ftn. 200: Already in 1915 René Basset had surmised its location was there. *Mélanges Africains et Orientaux*, Paris, 1915, p. 199, ftn. 1.

P. 395, last line: A learned Almoravid emir (*min umarāʾ al-murābiṭīn*) was a certain Maymūn b. Yāsīn al-Ṣanhājī al-Lamtūnī who died in Seville in 530/1136 but had studied in the east; Ibn al-Abbār: *Takmilat al-Ṣila*, ed. Codera, I, p. 396, l. 6.

P. 420, ftn. 378: But Manfred Ullmann is absolutely right in reminding me that the infinitive does not permit one to conclude anything about an active or passive sense.

ṬĀHIR AL-ṢAFADĪ'S FORGOTTEN WORK ON WESTERN SAINTS OF THE 6TH/12TH CENTURY

A few specialized works have come down to us about pious Muslims and miracle-workers in the west of North Africa and the Iberian Peninsula. The oldest date from the 7th/13th century.[1] All of them deal with people from a narrow geographical area, some venturing into neighboring districts, whereas most remain limited and incomplete in their choice of persons. They are the following writings:

Ibn al-ᶜArabī (d. 638/1240): *Rūḥ al-quds fī munāṣaḥat al-nafs*,[2] composed in Mecca in 600/1203-04. In the second part of this work Ibn al-ᶜArabī describes a total of 55 Sufis whom he had personally known and who had in part even given him instruction. Printed several times. I have at my disposal the two editions by ᶜIzza Ḥuṣriyya, Maṭbaᶜat al-ᶜilm, Damascus, 1964-65 and 1970, both unsatisfactory. Spanish translation by M. Asín Palacios: *Vida de Santones Andaluces*, Madrid, 1939/reprint Madrid, 1981.

Ibn al-ᶜArabī: *Al-durra al-fākhira fī dhikr man intafaᶜtu bihī fī ṭarīq al-ākhira*,[3] already partly composed before his emigration to the east in 598/1201 but left behind in the west and restored from memory after 608/1211-12, or perhaps only after 620/1223, with abridgements and additions. Contains 26 of the 55 persons listed in the *Rūḥ al-quds* along with 16 new names, i.e. a total of 42 Sufis.

Both works have been presented in summarized form with excerpts by R.W.I. Austin: *Sufis of Andalusia. The Rūḥ al-quds and al-Durrat al-fākhirah of Ibn ᶜArabī*, London, 1971. He gives the 55 Sufis that occur in the *Rūḥ al-quds* and the *Durra fākhira* with the additional 16 new ones from the *Durra*, amounting to 71 Sufis altogether.

Ibn al-ᶜArabī only enumerates people whom he had seen himself, most of them from Spain but also others from North Africa up to Tunis. He takes delight in being able to show by his list that the old

---

1 Comprehensive prosopographical works of the 6th/12th century such as Qāḍī ᶜIyāḍ's *Tartīb al-madārik*, Ibn Bashkuwāl's *Ṣila*, Ḍabbī's *Bughyat al-multamis*, among others, naturally contain some names which likewise belong in this category.

2 Osman Yahya: *Histoire et classification de l'oeuvre d'Ibn ᶜArabī*, Damascus, 1964, no. 639. Brockelmann: *GAL*, I, p. 445, no. 56 (58); *GAL S*, I, p. 800, no. 157; confusion.

3 Osman Yahya, no. 105. *GAL*, I, pp. 445, no. 56 (58); confusion with *Rūḥ al-quds*.

Sufism is not dead (*Rūḥ*, 1970, p. 127). For us it constitutes valuable evidence about Sufi life at that time in the west.

Abū Yaᶜqūb Yūsuf b. Yaḥyā al-Tādilī, alias Ibn al-Zayyāt (d. 627/1229): *Al-tashawwuf ilā rijāl al-taṣawwuf*, composed in 617/1221, dealing with saints of Morocco, as well as Algeria and Spain, chiefly in the 6th/12th and the early 7th/13th centuries, in loose chronological order from the older to the younger, omitting all who were still living in 617/1221. Edition by Adolphe Faure, Rabat, 1958. *GAL S*, I, pp. 558-59.

The same Tādilī: *Manāqib al-shaykh Abī'l-ᶜAbbās Aḥmad al-Sabtī* (d. 601/1204-05), the life story and title to glory of the patron saint of Marrakesh. Manuscripts given in E. Levi-Provençal: *Les manuscrits arabes de Rabat*, Publications de l'Institut des Hautes-Études Marocaines, Tome VIII, Paris, 1921, no. 403; I.S. Allouche et A. Regragui: *Catalogue des Manuscrits arabes de Rabat*, Deuxième série (1921-1953), II, Rabat, 1958, no. 2204 (title *Akhbār Abī'l-ᶜAbbās al-Sabtī*), no. 2205, no. 2206. ᶜAbd al-Salām b. ᶜAbd al-Qādir Ibn Sūda: *Dalīl muʾarrikh al-maghrib al-aqṣā*, Casablanca, 1960-65, no. 867. *GAL S*, II, p. 1013, 157 (in need of correction).

Abū'l-Ḥasan ᶜAli b. Muḥammad al-Marrākushī: *Manāqib al-awliyāʾ*, extracts preserved in Bādisī: *Al-maqṣad al-sharīf,* trans. G.S. Colin (see below). Marrākushī died in Bādis where he had come between 630/1232-33 and 640/1242-43 or between 640/1242-43 and 650/1252-53, unclear because of Colin's contradictory information on p. 1, ftn. 4, and on p. 153. The book contains the miracles that Marrākushī witnessed on his journey. At the time of his death it was found underneath his pillow (Colin pp. 52-53).

Abū'l-ᶜAbbās Aḥmad b. Ibrāhīm b. Yaḥyā al-Azdī al-Qashtālī (7th/13th century): *Tuḥfat al-mughtarib bi-bilād al-maghrib li-man lahū min al-ikhwān fī karāmāt al-shaykh Abī Marwān*, dealing with the saint Abū Marwān ᶜAbd al-Malik b. Ibrāhīm b. Bishr al-Qaysī al-Yaḥānisī (d. 667/1268-69) in Guadix and Ceuta. The author was married to a cousin of Yaḥānisī. Edition by Fernando de la Granja in *Revista del Instituto Egipcio de Estudios Islámicos en Madrid* 17, 1972-73, Arabic part pp. 5-181. *GAL S*, II, p. 898, 13 (in need of correction).

Abū'l-ᶜAbbās Aḥmad b. Ibrāhīm b. Aḥmad b. ᶜAlī b. Abī Muḥammad Ṣāliḥ b. Yanṣāran al-Maghribī: *Al-minhāj al-wāḍiḥ fī taḥqīq karāmāt Abī Muḥammad Ṣāliḥ*, composed after 698/1299, deals with the saint of Safi Abū Muḥammad Ṣāliḥ (d. 631/1234). Edited Cairo, 1933. Ibn Sūda: *Dalīl*, no. 887. The first part up until p. 130 treats Sufism in general. The author was the great-grandson of the saint. On Abū Muḥammad Ṣāliḥ see Muḥammad b. Aḥmad al-ᶜAbdī al-Kānūnī: *Āsafī wa-mā ilayhi qadīman wa-ḥadīthan*, Cairo, 1353/1934, pp. 98-101; Muḥammad al-Manūnī: *Min ḥadīth al-rakb al-maghribī*, Tetuan, 1953, pp. 7-8; Ibn Qunfudh: *Uns al-faqīr wa-ᶜizz al-ḥaqīr*, ed. Muḥammad al-Fāsī and Adolphe Faure, Rabat, 1965, index Ṣāliḥ al-Haskūrī.

Abū Muḥammad ᶜAbd al-Ḥaqq b. Ismāᶜīl b. Aḥmad b. Muḥammad b. al-Khaḍir... b. Qays b. Saᶜd b. ᶜUbāda al-Bādisī al-Gharnāṭī al-Khazrajī (722/1322-23 still alive in Bādis): *Al-maqṣad al-sharīf wa'l-manzaᶜ al-laṭīf fī dhikr ṣulaḥā' al-Rīf*, composed in 711/1311-12, deals with pious miracle-workers of the Rīf, between Ceuta and Tlemcen. He mentions Abū Marwān ᶜAbd al-Malik al-Yaḥānisī/al-Waḥānisī only because he had also passed through the Rīf. '*El-Maqṣad* (Vies des saints du Rîf) de ᶜAbd al-Ḥaqq el-Bâdisî', Traduction annotée de G.S. Colin, *Archives Marocaines* 26, Paris, 1926. *GAL S*, II, p. 337.

Abū'l-ᶜAbbās Aḥmad b. Aḥmad b. ᶜAbdallāh al-Ghubrīnī (d. 714/1315 or 10 years earlier): *ᶜUnwān al-dirāya fī-man ᶜurifa min al-ᶜulamā' fī'l-mi'a al-sābiᶜa bi-Bijāya*, deals with religious scholars and men of piety who were in Bijāya (Bougie) in the 7th/13th century. Edition by ᶜĀdil Nuwayhiḍ, Beirut, 1969. *GAL*, II, p. 239; *GAL S*, II, p. 337.

Abū'l-ᶜAbbās Aḥmad al-Khaṭīb al-shahīr bi-bn Qunfudh al-Qusanṭīnī (d. 810/1407-08): *Uns al-faqīr wa-ᶜizz al-ḥaqīr*, deals with saints from western North Africa up into the 8th/14th century, often based on personal acquaintance. Edition of the Université Mohammed V, Centre Universitaire de la Recherche Scientifique, Publications de la Faculté des Lettres: Abū l-ᶜAbbās Aḥmad b. Ḥasan b. ᶜAlī b. al-Ḫaṭīb Ibn Qunfuḏ († 810=1407, 1408): *Uns al-faqīr wa ᶜizz al-ḥaqīr*. Enquête sur al vie, les maîtres et les disciples de Sīdī Bū Madian et voyages à travers le Maroc. Contribution à l'étude de l'histoire religieuse du Maroc. Texte arabe établi et publié par Mohammed El Fasi (et) Adolphe Faure, Rabat, 1965. *GAL*, II, p. 241; *GAL S*, I, p. 784; II, p. 341.

Literature of this type from further east, for instance from Tunisia,[4] we will leave aside here. It extends back to the 5th/11th century.

But now it is possible to identify and even to make accessible a still older source dealing with the furthest west and the Iberian Peninsula. It does not appear to have been preserved as an indepen-

---

4 Hady Roger Idris: *Manâqib d'Abû Isḥâq Al-Jabanyânî par Abû l-Qâsim Al-Labîdî et Manâqib de Muḥriz B. Ḫalaf par Abû l-Ṭâhir Al-Fârisî*, Paris, 1959, pp. XVII-XVIII.

dent work but is included in a larger book which was widely disseminated and has come down to us in numerous manuscripts, though it has not been edited. This more extensive work in which our source lies buried is the *Tawthīq ᶜurā'l-īmān fī tafḍīl ḥabīb al-raḥmān* of Sharaf al-Dīn Abū'l-Qāsim Hibatallāh b. Qāḍī'l-quḍāh Najm al-Dīn ᶜAbd al-Raḥīm b. Qāḍī'l-quḍāh Shams al-Dīn Ibrāhīm al-Bārizī al-Juhanī al-Ḥamawī al-Shāfiᶜī (d. 738/1338),[5] an extensive compilation of edifying reports about the Prophet but also about the miracles of saints which in the view of Bārizī (and others) are ultimately miracles of the Prophet. The manuscript of Bārizī which I have used is the two-volume Berlin MS Sprenger 127a and 127b which Tor Andrae had consulted for his work *Die person Muhammeds in lehre und glauben seiner gemeinde*, Stockholm, 1918 (ibid., p. 401). Wilhelm Ahlwardt in his *Verzeichniß der arabischen Handschriften der Königlichen Bibliothek zu Berlin*, Berlin, 1887-99, II, pp. 607-09, no. 2569, gives a detailed summary of the contents and on page 609 of his catalogue mentions for one of the last sections of the second volume (*rukn* 4) of the MS (Sprenger 127b, *146a-172b*) the heading *Min* (this is correct and not *fī* as Ahlwardt writes) *kitāb As-sirr al-maṣūn fī-mā ukrima bihī l-muḫlaṣūn*,[6] *ta'līf Ṭāhir b. Muḥammad b. Ṭāhir aṣ-Ṣadafī al-Andalusī*. This is the older source I mean, which is preserved only in the form of a long quotation in Bārizī.[7]

Ṭāhir al-Ṣadafī's *Sirr maṣūn* has remained almost completely unnoticed. It is missing from Brockelmann, Ziriklī and Kaḥḥāla as well as the Arabic reference works of such authors as Ibn al-Qāḍī, Maqqarī, etc., nor is it to be found in Muḥammad b. Jaᶜfar al-Kattānī, who in his *Salwat al-anfās*, litho., Fez, 1316, III, pp. 357-63, enumerates no less than 140 hagiographies but makes no mention of Ṣadafī. Only Kâtib Çelebi (d. 1067/1657) lists him, indeed in his *Keşf-el-zunun*, Istanbul, 1941-43, I, p. 989/ed. Flügel, III, p. 596, no. 7150, var. 7, 758, in the mutilated form *Al-sirr al-maṣūn fī-mā* krm

---

5 *GAL S*, II, p. 101. Ibn Ḥajar al-ᶜAsqalānī: *Al-durar al-kāmina fī aᶜyān al-mi'a al-thāmina*, Hyderabad, 1348-50, IV, pp. 401-02, no. 1103.

6 *Mukhliṣūn* 'sincere' would also be possible. But only *mukhlaṣūn* 'chosen' rhymes perfectly with *maṣūn*. The title could be translated: *The Well-kept Secret: On the Wonderous Grace Conferred on the Chosen*.

7 The Paris MS 1970 (Cat. de Slane), which Brockelmann lists as the only still extant European MS, like Sprenger 127a, contains only half the work, i.e. *rukn* 1 and 2. Our Ṣadafī only occurs in *rukn* 4 and is thus missing from the Paris MS.

bihī al-mukhlaṣūn, li'l-shaykh Ṭāhir... al-Ṣadafī[8] *al-mutawaffā sanat...* Perhaps Kâtib Çelebi had another manuscript of the book before him. How much Bārizī gives us of the original and how much he has left out (*min!*) we have no way of knowing. Introductory words that customarily appear at the beginning of books and a proper coda concluding the book are lacking so that in any case only a part of the work is preserved. This part would represent no more than a mere fraction of the whole if the book were taken to be composed along the lines of Ibn al-ᶜArabī's *Rūḥ al-quds*, for instance, or Bādisī's *Maqṣad.* Apparently, however, none of the biographies have been damaged.

The significance of the fragment lies in its age. It must have been written between the death of ᶜAbd al-Malik b. Masarra in 552/1157[9] and the death of Abū Yaᶜazzā in 572/1177.[10] Ṣadafī notes that ᶜAbd al-Malik b. Masarra is dead (fol. *150b-152b*) and that Abū Yaᶜazzā is still alive (fol. *164a*). One could even wish to date the work's composition precisely to 567/1171-72 because Ṣadafī learned that Abū Yaᶜazzā was exactly 125 years old. Since Abū Yaᶜazzā died in 572/1177 at the age of 130, he would have been 125 years old in 567/1171-72. But these figures are too fantastic to accept them at face value, and precise calculation with uncertain numbers leads to false conclusions. The fact that contemporary scholarship has not yet evaluated these figures for Abū Yaᶜazzā is another sign of the extent to which Ṣadafī's work has remained unknown, for old sources on Abū Yaᶜazzā are meager and are much sought after.

Ṣadafī remains silent about his home. But he resided in the Iberian Peninsula,[11] North Africa, in Egypt and in the Ḥijāz. He made the pilgrimage via Upper-Egypt (*166b*). Once someone described to him

---

8 Flügel, III, p. 596, no. 7150 has mistakenly *Ẓāhir al-Ṣūfī.*

9 Ibn Bashkuwāl: *Al-ṣila fī tārīkh aʾimmat al-Andalus wa-ᶜulamāʾihim wa-muḥaddithīhim wa-fuqahāʾihim wa-udabāʾihim*, ed. ᶜIzzat al-ᶜAṭṭār al-Ḥusaynī, Cairo, 1955, I, p. 348, no. 778. Ibn ᶜUmayra al-Ḍabbī: *Bughyat al-multamis fī tārīkh rijāl ahl al-Andalus*, ed. Codera and Ribera, Madrid, 1884/reprint Khānjī Cairo, p. 369, no. 1079. Not to be confused with the philosopher Ibn Massara (d. 319/931, *EI*[2] s.v.). Whether our Ibn Massara was really the chief judge of Córdoba as Ṣadafī states remains an open question. The above-mentioned biographers say nothing, and he is not included in Ibn Ḥasan al-Nubāhī: *Histoire des juges d'Andalousie intitulée Kitab al-markaba al-ᶜulya* (= al-marqaba al-ᶜulyā), ed. E. Lévi-Provençal, Cairo, 1948. The additional details which Ṣadafī gives, however, do not exlude the possibility that this is a new, supplementary piece of information.

10 *EI*[2] Abū Yaᶜazzā (E. Lévi-Provençal).

11 Clear from *162a-b* in the story of a siege of a city in Andalus by the Christians.

the bay of Rammāda (*jūn Rammāda*) between Alexandria and Barqa — perhaps the Gulf of Sollum[12] — as 'belonging to your administrative districts' (*min aᶜmālika, 160a*). The words do not necessarily mean that the author right then or at the time of writing his book occupied a corresponding post. But they do not exclude this either. Did Ṣadafī administer a governmental district toward the close of the Fāṭimid and the beginning of the Ayyūbid period?[13] An indication of such a possibility could be the fact that in Upper-Egyptian Qinā he was once capable of providing a pilgrim, who later turned out to be a high-ranking saint, with provisions and a riding animal (*167b-168a*). Was this in connection with an official appointment? Or did Ṣadafī on one occasion simply reside in Qinā for a longer time as a grand seigneur in a private capacity? For Ṣadafī was also in the position to give someone a new suit of clothes on command (*148b-149a*). Or had he come back to Qinā on his return journey after his own pilgrimage? For the story relates that he subsequently travelled to Alexandria. But the text can also be taken to mean that the donor of the provisions and the riding animal was actually someone else, not Ṣadafī himself.

Nor do we know where Ṣadafī composed his book. He appears to be equally far from all the places he reports on. But it is notable that he sometimes lumps Andalus and Maghreb together and sometimes distinguishes between them. To include the Iberian Peninsula in the idea of Maghreb at a time when the Almoravids and the Almohads had added large parts of Spain to their African land of origin must have seemed quite natural. This is attested for instance by ᶜAbdallāh b. Ibrāhīm al-Ḥijārī who put together a historical work on Arab Spain with the title *Al-mushib fī gharāʾib al-Maghrib* and thereby laid the foundation for the well-known more comprehensive encyclopedic work *Al-mughrib fī ḥulā'l-Maghrib* which was then completed in the 7th/13th century by another Spaniard, Ibn Saᶜīd al-

12 MacGuckin de Slane: *Description de l'Afrique septentrionale par Abou-Obeid-el-Bakri*, Algiers, 1857/2nd edition Algiers, 1910, réimpression Paris, 1965, Arabic p. 4/French p. 13, with ftn. 1 and 2. R. Dozy and M.J. De Goeje: *Description de l'Afrique et de l'Espagne par Edrîsî*, Leiden, 1866/réimpression Leiden, 1968, Arabic p. 137/French p. 164/Al-Idrīsī: *Opus geographicum*, Naples-Rome (on sale from Brill, Leiden), p. 318. Dozy-De Goeje (French p. 164, ftn. 1 and 5) identify Rammāda as 'Râs Halem (Kharaib Abī Halîma)', i.e. the bay of Rammāda with the Gulf of el-Mellah (= *al-milḥ*) on Heinrich Barth's map of the coastal lands of North Africa. On more recent maps it is called the Gulf of Sollum.

13 Cf. ftn. 159 below.

Maghribī.[14] But it must have been just as natural, if not more natural, for a man in the east to combine Andalus with Maghreb (which after all means 'the west') and to subordinate the former to the latter. It may well be, therefore, that Ṣadafī wrote his book in the east or at least from the viewpoint of the east and for the inhabitants of the east — from a universal Islamic outlook so to speak. Apparently, the lost work *Al-mughrib fī (akhbār) maḥāsin al-Maghrib* of Abū Yaḥyā al-Yasaᶜ b. ᶜĪsā b. Ḥazm al-Ghāfiqī al-Jayyānī (d. 575/1179) was written in Egypt in the 6th/12th century,[15] and similarly the widely travelled Spaniard Ibn Diḥya (d. 633/1235), with the above work in mind, entitled his anthology of Spanish poets, which he composed in Egypt, *Al-muṭrib fī ashᶜār ahl al-Maghrib*.[16] Certainly, just like these authors, Ṣadafī must also have come from Spain. Such a conclusion is inevitable given the frequent occurrence of his gentilicium in the Iberian Peninsula, his intimate acquaintance with western circumstances and also perhaps the sequence of geographic regions in his account: first the west, where he came from, and then the east, where he had gone. Yet he did not write his book in Mecca since in *172a* he speaks of carrying on correspondence with a man in Mecca.

The gentilicium Ṣadafī is connected with a Ḥimyarite tribe al-Ṣadif (with i) b. Sahl(a).[17] In the west the most famous bearer of this name is Abū ᶜAlī Ḥusayn b. Muḥammad b. Fierro b. Ḥayyān b. Sukkara al-Ṣadafī (d. 514/1120) from Saragossa, whose text of Bukhārī in the version of his nephew and student Ibn Saᶜāda (d. 565/1170) became the authoritative edition of Bukhārī in the west.[18]

---

14 *EI*2 Ibn Saᶜīd al-Maghribī (Ch. Pellat). *GAL S*, I, p. 576. In detail Ibn Saᶜīd al-Andalusī: *Al-mughrib fī ḥulā al-maghrib, juzʾ* 1, on Egypt, ed. Zakī Muḥammad Ḥasan, Shawqī Ḍayf and Sayyida Kāshif, Cairo, 1953, Zakī's Introduction.

15 Ibn al-Abbār: *Al-takmila li'l-Ṣila*, ed. Codera, II, pp. 744-45, no. 2112. Maqqarī: *Nafḥ al-ṭīb* (Analectes), ed. Dozy et alii, I, p. 713. ᶜAbd al-Salām b. ᶜAbd al-Qādir Ibn Sūda: *Dalīl muʾarrikh al-maghrib al-aqṣā*, Casablanca, 1960, p. 164, no. 608 (Al-mughrib fī tārīkh al-Maghrib).

16 *EI*2 Ibn Diḥya (F. de la Granja). *GAL*, I, pp. 310-12, *GAL S*, I, pp. 544-45.

17 Samᶜānī: *Al-ansāb*, s.v. Ṣadafī. ᶜUmar Riḍā Kaḥḥāla: *Muᶜjam qabāʾil al-ᶜarab al-qadīma wa'l-ḥadītha*, Beirut, 1968, II, p. 637b.

18 E. Lévi-Provençal: *Le 'Ṣaḥīḥ' d'al-Buḫārī. Reproduction en phototypie des manuscrits originaux de la récension occidentale dite 'Récension d'Ibn Saᶜāda'*, Vol. I, Paris, 1928. ᶜAbd al-Ḥayy al-Kattānī: *Fihris al-fahāris*, Fez, 1346-47, II, pp. 110-13, 220, 367-68. Johann Fück: 'Beiträge zur Überlieferungsgeschichte von Buḫārīs Traditionssammlung', *ZDMG* 92, 1938, p. 77. On Ṣadafī and Ibn Saᶜāda see Lévi-Provençal, pp. 17-19; Ziriklī: *Al-aᶜlām*, II, pp. 279-80 (Ibn Sukkara); VIII, p. 23 (Ibn Saᶜāda). — On the early Ṣadafiyyūn who

Our Ṣadafī did not make use of written sources for the section of his work which has come down to us, other than perhaps his own notes. He only records such miracle-workers as he met himself or who were described by someone who had known them directly or indirectly. Therefore the *Sirr maṣūn* is a book which deals exclusively with contemporaries, precisely as was later the case with Ibn al-ᶜArabī's *Rūḥ al-quds* and Bādisī's *Maqṣad.* The three authors also resemble one another in that they do not mention any dates. Only quite rarely does Ibn al-ᶜArabī make an exception in this respect. Bādisī differs from the other two in making use of a written source, ᶜAlī al-Marrākushī's *Manāqib al-awliyāʾ*. The three works cannot be considered as belonging directly to the literary genre of *fahrasa* 'lists of teachers'. They should rather be assigned to the genre *kunnāsh/kunnāsha*, pl. *kanānīsh/kunnāshāt* 'journal',[19] in particular the hagiographical journal. Bādisī restricts the scope of his descriptions to the relatively small region of the Rīf (between Ceuta and Tlemcen). Ibn al-ᶜArabī expands the scope to include Spain and Tunisia. Our Ṣadafī covers in his notices Spain, Morocco, Egypt and the Ḥijāz. He is by no means only concerned with contemporaries in the west, but rather with contemporaries in general whose miracles he has witnessed or heard about. Most such people, however, he had come to know in the west and it was about these that he was best informed. If one counts those mentioned by name, one finds almost twice as many from the west as from the east. If one also considers those who are unnamed, there are approximately a quarter more in the west than in the east. Ṣadafī's information on people from the west in the manuscript takes up somewhat more than double the space given to those from the east.

A hundred years later in 679/1280-81 at the age of 84 Ṣafī al-Dīn b. Abī'l-Manṣūr, that is Abū ᶜAbdallāh Ḥusayn b. Abī'l-Ḥasan ᶜAlī b. Abī'l-Manṣūr Ẓāfir b. Ḥusayn al-Azdī al-Anṣārī al-Khazrajī, the son of the famous Jamāl al-Dīn Abū'l-Ḥusayn ᶜAlī (d. 613/1216 in Egypt)[20] wrote a *Risāla* about the shaykhs he had met in Egypt, in

---

are buried in Cairo see Ibn al-Zayyāt: *Al-kawākib al-sayyāra fī tartīb al-ziyāra*, reprint Baghdad, n.d., pp. 102-05, and Sakhāwī: *Tuḥfat al-aḥbāb wa-bughyat al-ṭullāb fī'l-khiṭaṭ wa'l-mazārāt wa'l-tarājim wa'l-biqāᶜ al-mubārakāt*, Cairo, 1937, pp. 231-32.

19 A series of examples of such notebooks of the most varied kind in Ibn Sūda: *Dalīl muʾarrikh al-maghrib al-aqṣā*, pp. 461 ff., and index *kunnāsha*. Description of the genre *kunnāsha* ibid., pp. 461-62.

20 *GAL*, I, p. 321; *GAL S*, I, pp. 553-54.

the Maghreb, in Syria, in Iraq and in the Ḥijāz, which was widely quoted from but appears only to be available in one manuscript in Cairo.[21]

A common characteristic of the three above-mentioned authors as well as of Tādilī and Ṣafī al-Dīn is their credulity, their uncritical attitude in dealing with the subject and their unbridled interest in miracles. They are not unique in this respect. The biographical literature of Islam is otherwise generally caught up in the endeavor to mention miraculous and unbelievable occurrences. It readily recounts disruptions in the normal course of events, extraordinary occurrences, which are meant to demonstrate God's power and the fact that certain individuals are especially chosen. But our authors on the whole report only such matters and do so without the slightest shadow of a doubt. This is particularly astonishing in the case of so great a mind as Ibn al-ᶜArabī. He even trustingly accepts the story

---

21 Ibn al-Zayyāt: *Al-kawākib al-sayyāra fī tartīb al-ziyāra*, reprint Baghdad, n.d., p. 182, ll. 5 ff. Sakhāwī: *Tuḥfat al-aḥbāb wa-bughyat al-ṭullāb*, Cairo, 1937, p. 176, writes the name correctly as Abū'l-Ḥasan b. ᶜAlī b. Abī'l-Manṣūr, but gives the man's exact dates: 595-682/1199-1283. According to this source, he composed his *Risāla* in 679/1280-81. He was born in Cairo and died there as well. One of his students was Athīr al-Dīn Abū Ḥayyān Muḥammad b. Yūsuf b. ᶜAlī b. Yūsuf b. Ḥayyān al-Nafzī al-Atharī al-Gharnāṭī (d. 745/1344, *GAL*, II, pp. 109-10); Maqqarī: *Nafḥ al-ṭīb*, ed. Dozy et alii, I, p. 835, l. 12. The *Risāla* is mentioned in *GAL S*, I, p. 554, l. 4. But Ṣafī al-Dīn also wrote other works; Ibn al-Zayyāt, p. 182; Sakhāwī: *Tuḥfa*, p. 177. His great-grandson Shihāb al-Dīn Aḥmad b. Muḥammad b. ᶜAlī b. Ṣafī al-Dīn (d. 739/1338-39) directed a Sufi circle with a *dhikr* which Ṣafī al-Dīn had created; Ibn Ḥajar al-ᶜAsqalānī: *Al-durar al-kāmina*, I, pp. 281-82, no. 720; Sakhāwī: *Tuḥfa*, p. 177. — Later quotations from Ṣafī al-Dīn's *Risāla* mostly stem from Yāfiᶜī's *Rawḍ al-rayāḥīn*, Cairo, n.d. Yāfiᶜī has preserved for us in the 442nd story, pp. 271-72, the latter's autobiographical description of his conversion to Sufism. The decrease in social status which this brought with it for Ṣafī al-Dīn entailed difficulties similar to those that ᶜAlāʾ al-Dawla al-Simnānī (d. 736/1336) experienced; *EI*[2] ᶜAlāʾ al-Dawla al-Simnānī; Hermann Landolt: *Correspondance spirituelle échangée entre Nuroddin Esfarayeni (ob. 717/1317) et son disciple 'Alaoddawleh Semnani (ob. 736/1336)*, Bibliothèque Iranienne 21, Paris-Tehran, 1972; Hartwig Cordt: *Die sitzungen des ᶜAlāʾ ad-dawla as-Simnānī*, diss. Basle, Zurich, 1977. Ṣafī al-Dīn married the daughter of his shaykh Abū'l-ᶜAbbās Aḥmad al-Ḥarrār, whose date of death is not recorded anywhere. In the article on him Nabhānī: *Jāmiᶜ karāmāt al-awliyāʾ*, Cairo, 1329, I, pp. 299-300, only repeats the conversion of Ṣafī al-Dīn at his hand taken verbatim from Yāfiᶜī. Ibn al-Zayyāt, pp. 151-55, and Sakhāwī, pp. 272-74, are also silent about the year of his death. Massignon: 'La Cité des Morts', *BIFAO* 57, 1958, p. 45, l. 1, writes: circa 620 AH, and p. 54 bot.: circa 630 AH. The date of Ṣafī al-Dīn's death given in Massignon ibid., p. 57, as 683 AH should be corrected to 682 AH.

that his own servant and companion of many years standing, Ḥabashī, after death opened his eyes and smiled at the corpsewasher when the latter considered himself unworthy to wash him (Austin, p. 159).[22] Yet these naïve reports are embedded in his forceful intellectual oeuvre and consequently remain relatively insignificant. In the case of the other authors this background is lacking. The stories give the impression of being legends. But legends are edifying fantasy and in that sense the very opposite of what our accounts claim to be. As far as our stories are concerned the miraculous is only miraculous because it is the absolute truth. Due to this contradiction the effect they wish to have is not achieved among critical readers.

The pantheon of pious men who are discussed in these works only contains a few real gods. Great names of figures who subsequently exercised an influence on Sufism only occur in an appreciable number in Tādilī. In Ibn al-ᶜArabī the absence of famous personalities appears to be for pious reasons: he gratefully recalls the many ordinary people whom he had met in the west and from whom he had received encouragement and support. In Ṣadafī's series of Sufis only two names are of importance: ᶜAbd al-Malik b. Masarra (d. 552/1159) and Abū Yaᶜazzā (d. 572/1177). He presents the earliest information on both of them and, with regard to ᶜAbd al-Malik, the first definite wise sayings attributed to him at all which are supposed to have been contained in a letter (*150a-152b*). Ṣadafī himself had actually met ᶜAbd al-Malik, but not Abū Yaᶜazzā.

Ṣadafī was not uneducated. To that extent his Arabic is correct. Mistakes in the manuscript should perhaps be blamed on the copyist. Ṣadafī also knows how to use rhymed prose which he readily employs in the laudatory passages he addresses to the persons. Wherever he goes, he listens to traditionists and other theologians, and writes down wise sayings which he has the opportunity to hear. Once he was asked by a Sufi if he, the Sufi, had the right to receive alms (*155a*). Ṣadafī must therefore have given the impression or enjoyed the reputation of knowing a lot about *fiqh*. But he was anything but an inquiring mind. In everything he writes he deals only with the surface of what is before him, he doesn't go into anything more precisely, and accepts all the omissions and distortions of his memory and whatever is reported to him. Thus the actual name of the chief judge of Ceuta Ibn Yarbūᶜ slips his mind. He leaves it at that (*162b*). He appears to think that the traditionist Sufyān b. ᶜUyayna (d.

---

22 Legends of this kind are numerous. A few examples in Yāfiᶜī: *Rawḍ al-rayāḥīn*, pp. 137 f.

198/813) was a Companion of the Prophet — at least the context in which he mentions him (*171a*) would lead one to believe this. He writes concerning one of his saints that he regularly liked to recite an edifying exchange of words between the well-known Companion of the Prophet, Abū ᶜUbayda b. al-Jarrāḥ who died in the year 18/639 (*EI*² Abū ᶜUbayda b. al-Djarrāḥ) and a certain al-Ḥārith (b. Muᶜāwiya b. Zurᶜa b. Masᶜūd) al-Thaqafī who was killed in Kūfa in the year 77/696[23] — without considering that these two men never could have met, apart from the impossible formulation presented in our manuscript which, however, may possibly be the fault of the copyist or copyists. From another saint whom he did not know himself he reports a story which is supposed to have taken place between a Spanish Umayyad caliph and a pious judge, Ibn Mundhir al-Ballūṭī. The narrator did not remember the actual name of this judge (*168a*). Of course it would not have been difficult to find out the name and to supply the omission or correction in one way or another. Most probably it is not a question of a 'son' or 'descendant' of Mundhir but of Mundhir himself, i.e. the by no means obscure Mundhir b. Saᶜīd al-Ballūṭī who was the chief judge of Córdoba from 339/950 to 355/966 under ᶜAbd al-Raḥmān III and Ḥakam II.[24] It is also a pity that Ṣadafī did not feel the urge to travel himself to Tāgyā in the Middle-Atlas to meet and speak with Abū Yaᶜazzā whom he only knew about from hearsay. He could have given us the only first-hand information about him.

Ṣadafī divides the surviving portion of his *Sirr maṣūn* into five sections which he does not, however, number. In the first section he reports on the theologians (*ᶜulamāʾ*), jurists (*fuqahāʾ*) and saints (*awliyāʾ*) whom he had met in the Maghreb (*146a-155a*), in the second the pious worshippers of God (*ᶜubbād*) and ascetics (*zuhhād*) of the same region (*155a-162b*), i.e. men of piety who had not received any special theological education. In both sections people are discussed who lived in Morocco and Spain. In the third section he deals with men of piety from the same region of the west whom he

---

23 Ṭabarī: *Annales*, II, p. 958, l. 1.

24 Ibn al-Ḥasan al-Nubāhī: *Histoire des juges d'Andalousie intitulée Kitab al-markaba al-ᶜulya*, ed. E. Lévi-Provençal, Cairo, 1948, pp. 66-75. Yāqūt: *Muᶜjam al-udabāʾ*, ed. Margoliouth, Gibb Memorial Series 6, VII, pp. 178-85/new edition Beirut, n.d., XIX, pp. 174-85. Ballūṭī, already by 330/941-42, was a judge over whole frontier areas in the Iberian Peninsula; Ibn Ḥayyān al-Qurṭubī: *Al-muqtabis*, V, ed. Chalmeta, Madrid, 1979, p. 488, l. 9. Maḥmūd ᶜAlī Makkī, the editor of the first volume, prefers for the title of the latter work the passive form *Muqtabas* (Introduction, pp. 66-67).

himself had not met (*162b-164a*). In the fourth section he discusses theologians (*ᶜulamāʾ*), ascetics (*zuhhād*) and men of education (*fuḍalāʾ*) whom he had met in Egypt (*al-bilād al-miṣriyya*) or whom he had heard stories about or who had themselves told him stories (*164b-169b*). In the fifth section he mentions the people whom he had encountered in the Ḥijāz (*169b-172a*). He concludes the journal with a supplement, which by rights ought to be included in the fourth section, about Abū Muḥammad ᶜAbdallāh b. Sinān al-Rudaynī[25] whom he had visited in his mosque at the foot of Muqaṭṭam outside Fusṭāṭ (*172a-172b*).

The works we mentioned here at the opening dealing with western saints have been printed, and Ibn al-ᶜArabī and Bādisī have been translated. It does not seem proper that an earlier source, which is no worse and no better, should remain hidden once it has been discovered. A critical edition cannot be presented here. The one manuscript at my disposal, MS Sprenger 127b (Ahlwardt, no. 2569), being corrupt in many ways, is not adequate for producing a translation. In what follows I will therefore present a summary of the contents. For all the intellectual modesty that characterizes stories of the miraculous and which Ibn al-ᶜArabī and Bādisī for their part do not surpass, this small work enriches our knowledge of motifs, increases the instances of them we possess and — what seems particularly useful to me — makes us acquainted with a series of persons from the 6th/12th century who hitherto have not appeared anywhere else.

For the sake of greater clarity I will number the five sections into which this fragment of Ṣadafī is divided. The numbers given in italics in the English text and the numbers in the index refer to the folios of MS Sprenger 127b.

---

25 Rudaynī probably connected with the Upper-Egyptian locality Rudaynī (sic). *Edrîsî*, ed. Dozy and De Goeje, French part, p. 17, ftn. 2. In the cemetery Qarāfa in Cairo is buried a traditionist and Koran commentator Abū'l-Ḥasan ᶜAlī b. Marzūq al-Rudaynī who died in 540/1145-46; Ibn al-Zayyāt: *Al-kawākib al-sayyāra fī tartīb al-ziyāra*, reprint Baghdad, n.d., p. 302. The reading Rudaynī is confirmed by a saying which a debtor must pronounce at Rudaynī's grave to be freed from his debts: 'Oh God, by the connection between You and the man in this grave, Your bondsman al-Rudaynī, pay my debt (*daynī*)!' Sakhāwī: *Tuḥfat al-aḥbāb wa-bughyat al-ṭullāb fī'l-khiṭaṭ wa'l-mazārāt wa'l-tarājim wa'l-biqāᶜ al-mubārakāt*, ed. Maḥmūd Rabīᶜ and Ḥasan Qāsim, Cairo, 1937, pp. 384-85.

(*146a*) 1. THEOLOGIANS AND SAINTS (FRIENDS OF GOD) WHOM I MET IN THE MAGHREB.

Al-faqīh *Abū'l-Rabīᶜ Sulaymān b. Yaḥyā al-Jazūlī al-Maṣmūdī*[26] (? MS al-Ṣamūdī). Was a powerful and influential emir of his country. Annoyed by a fly, he thought: 'If I had a rebellious king over me and could retreat to a safe place (surah 11/80),[27] this feeble creature would be rid of me and I would be rid of it.' He resigned from his position, no longer mounted a horse and carried a sword, but dressed in complete humility in the poorest rags. He divided his year into four periods: in the summer he guarded gardens. In the winter he copied out books. In the autumn he drove a wagon. In the spring he collected fresh fodder, lived from the money he earned for it and gave away any of the money left over as alms. The kings of the Maghreb revered him and obeyed him. His mere glance was a profit to a person. He was knowledgeable about the Arabic language, jurisprudence and genealogies. He forbade his adherents (*ikhwān*) to accept alms and denied himself everything that the Prophet had forbidden. In this respect he was different from others of his kind.

When he guarded the gardens the birds would gather around him, pick grains out of his hand and position themselves at his side during ritual prayers. This was reported to me after his death by an eyewitness.

He left behind a wife who was loath to display herself, and a child who could not yet walk.

For the prayers over his corpse most of the inhabitants of the surroundings were on hand though without having been invited,[28] but rather because of a dream or an inspiration, or because someone who had had a dream told them — a miracle of his that took place after his death.

He had always encouraged his visitors to be obedient to God, to undertake fasting and to rise at night to pray.

---

26 Self-contradictory. *Jazūlī* and *Maṣmūdī* are ethnic designations and exclude one another.

27 He has in mind a fortress in the safe mountains of what was later called *bilād al-sayba*, under a king who no longer wishes to have anything to do with the central government. He transposes this to his religious situation and sees that he should avoid the worldly affairs that he is caught up in.

28 Also *Tashawwuf*, p. 241, ll. 10-11; Sharjī: *Ṭabaqāt al-khawāṣṣ*, Cairo, 1321, p. 101, ll. 8-11.

Abū ʿAbdallāh Muḥammad b. Nāhiḍ al-Lakhmī. He was an upright judge who ordered practicing justice and works of charity. When in a litigation brought before him the law turned against a friend of his, he felt the urge to dimiss the case. (*147a*) He forbade himself to do so and dispensed justice. His friend left him in anger. Thereupon Lakhmī gave up his post, took off his judge's *ṭaylasān* and adopted the dress of the *fuqarāʾ*. He gave away everything he owned and from then on lived from the fifteen or so small olive trees he possessed. From this he still managed to give alms. When these small trees were taken away from him illegally and he begged God for a replacement, he received instructions from God to collect (*ishtiyār*) wild honey (*ḍarab*). In the wall of his cell of retirement in the mountains he installed beehives (*khalāyā naḥl*), and inside them there emerged nations of bees. Out of fear of too copious a yield he prayed to God to reduce the abundance. God answered his prayer.

Whoever studied with him became well-educated in his religion. Lakhmī would repeat the questions until they sank in.

While I was with him a student complained that he didn't understand much and was falling into error. Lakhmī gave him three pills of barley — he ate only barley bread — and in addition broke off some salt and ordered him to eat only this and nothing else, until it was finished. After three days the student had a clear head and it remained clear. He grasped everything immediately, whereas the others had to repeat things.[29]

(*147b*) Some of Lakhmī's sayings: 'God loves an emir who acts in accordance with his (religious) knowledge. God hates an emir devoid of knowledge who acts without taking counsel. A just emir is more pleasing to God than a hundred worshippers of God (*ʿābid*) with knowledge.' He was always repeating the saying of the Prophet: 'The prayer of the just imam will not be rejected.'[30] He cited the well-known story about al-Ḥārith al-Thaqafī who said to Abū

---

29 Similar subject here *154b* and in *Tashawwuf*, pp. 115-16. A person suddenly acquires a permanent capacity for speaking because someone spits in his mouth: Sadīd al-Dīn Muḥammad-i Ghaznawī: *Maqāmāt-i Žanda-pīl*, ed. Muʾayyad, Tehran, 1960, pp. 52-53, and frequently.

30 The complete saying goes: 'There are three persons whose prayer is not rejected: the righteous imam, someone fasting when he breaks the fast, and the prayer of the oppressed: he raises it above the clouds, the gates of heaven open before it, and the Lord says: "By my immense power, I shall help you (oh prayer), even if perhaps only later"', *Concordance et indices de la tradition musulmane*, II, 134a, *daʿwa*; Tirmidhī, *janna* 2, and others.

ᶜUbayda b. al-Jarrāḥ,[31] the governor in Syria: 'Pray for me!' To which Abū ᶜUbayda replied: 'One should ask you for a prayer; you combine knowledge and asceticism and have increased this in your office of governor.'[32] Lakhmī called his students to monotheism and to withdrawal from the world, saying: 'Withdrawal from the world is necessary ever since corruption made its entry on the earth.' Lakhmī devoted himself to the service of his fellow-man by bringing requests before emirs and sultans. He considered this to be worship (*qurba ilā'llāh*) and a way to draw near to God (*zulfā*). He said: 'Wherever I can I perform intercession, indeed to the utmost of my ability, for surah 4/85 says: "Whoever intercedes with a good intercession receives his own share of it. And whoever intercedes with a bad intercession receives the equivalent."' He acted according to the proposition: 'A person will be held responsible for how he makes use of his reputation as well as his money. There is no difference between charity by means of one's reputation and charity by means of money, and sometimes charity by means of reputation is more effective and more godfearing because it can even lead to money and other things again.'

I was not able to take part in his funeral. Someone who had been there told me that at death's approach Lakhmī had covered himself before the people. When he was dead they then spread a veil over him and from behind this veil they heard Koranic recitation without there being anyone else present.

Abū'l-Qāsim ᶜAbd al-Raḥmān b. ᶜĪsā al-Khazrajī. Possessed considerable knowledge and, above all, had practiced extreme asceticism. He was also a master in jurisprudence. He had prayed God to keep him from hearing indecent language (*khanā, hujr*). His prayer was heard. At times one of us would adopt his gentlest voice and speak nicely. Khazrajī would answer him. Other times we would fall to arguing among ourselves in a loud, coarse fashion. Then he heard nothing. He lived by copying the Koran and the *ḥadīth*. If he observed that he had earned too much money, he became ill and could not go on copying any longer which caused his income to diminish by itself, indeed he even had to go into debt. When it had gone that far, he recovered again. But his debts did not oppress him thanks to God's favor. Sometimes he was given alms to distribute among the needy. He frequently displayed his clairvoyant under-

---

31 P. 433 above.

32 Text completed in the margin. The story cannot be correct in this form. The governor of Syria was Abū ᶜUbayda, and he was famous for his knowledge and his asceticism.

standing of people (*firāsa*). When one time a heretic (*zindīq*) appeared before him as a poor beggar although he was a rich man, just to put Khazrajī's ability to the test, he was unable to continue writing. The heretic asked him for alms. Khazrajī went to get something for him and then came back in a state of anger and chased him away. He put a curse on him, and after the man had taken a few steps a wall collapsed and crushed him to death. Those who acted unjustly feared his divine invocation and he threaten to use it against them so that several of them changed their ways.

He gave special importance to three principles and asked me if I always adhered to them: association with the pious, keeping a distance from people and speaking the truth.

I left him when he was still alive. But then news of his death reached me. One of his students told me he had heard an unknown voice in a dream recite the following two verses about his death (*ṭawīl, -addu*):

Thus the days pass and with them the old nobility.
God's will cannot be held back by His creatures.
The sun of the horizon suffers an eclipse just when it's bright
and the full moon also enters darkness and is then called back again.[33]

---

33 In the MS is written *wa-yakhsifu ʾal-badru'l-munīru*, to be read with *hamzat al-qaṭʿ* of the article of *badru*. It is vocalized as the nominative. A second hand has made it into the metrically smoother *wa-yukhsafu bi'l-badri'l-munīri* which, as G. Schoeler informs me, according to Dozy (*khasafa*) is documented in Ibn Abī Zarʿ: *Rawḍ al-qirṭās*, with the same meaning as *khasafa* 'to darken itself' (of the moon). It is difficult to decide which is the correct reading. Either could be taken as the lectio difficilior, *khusifa bi-*, on the basis of the meaning, *yakhsifu ʾal* on the basis of the use of the hamza. — At the end of the verse the passive *yurtaddu* should be read, an allusion to the religiously prescribed prayers for solar and lunar eclipses (A.J. Wensinck: *A Handbook of Early Muhammadan Tradition*, Leiden, 1927, pp. 66-67, s.v. eclipse) and to folk practices on such occasions, in particular making noise which is meant to drive away the monster of darkness; examples: Muḥibbī: *Khulāṣat al-athar fī aʿyān al-qarn al-ḥādī ʿashar*, Cairo, 1284, III, pp. 225-26; *Reisen und Gefangenschaft Hans Ulrich Kraffts*, ed. K.D. Haszler, Bibliothek des litterarischen Vereins in Stuttgart, 61, 1861, p. 227 (from the year 1577); Richard Tully: *Narrative of a ten years' residence at Tripoli in Africa*, London, 1816, p. 166 (report from 1788); Eijūb Abēla: 'Beiträge zur Kenntnis abergläubischer Gebräuche in Syrien', *ZDPV* 7, 1884, p. 95, no. 97. J.-A. Jaussen: *Naplouse et son district*, Paris, 1927, p. 174; Georg Nioradze: *Der Schamanismus bei den sibirischen Völkern*, Stuttgart, 1925, pp. 33-34; and then the rich material in Jacob Grimm: *Deutsche mythologie*[4], Berlin, 1875, I, pp. 202-03; II, 588-90; Friedrich Panzer: *Bayerische sagen und bräuche*, II, Munich,

Abū ʿAbdallāh Muḥammad b. Ḥassān al-Sharafī (? MS Sharqī[34]). Religious scholar and ascetic (*148b*). He instructed others in practicing piety. Certain kings obeyed him implicitly. A vizier reproached one of these kings for this in Sharafī's presence. Sharafī described it as justified by the Koran. The critic asked to be shown proof. Sharafī referred to surah 28/10-13, according to which the mother of Moses was at first unconsolable when she had to give away Moses as a babe but then got him back again, and likewise to Jacob who found his son Joseph again, and other similar passages in the Koran.[35] Thereupon the vizier repented and acknowledged that he, Sharafī, was

---

1855, pp. 310 ff., 330-36; Felix Liebrecht: *Des Gervasius von Tilbury Otia imperialia*, Hanover, 1856, p. 167.

34 The *nisba* only occurs this one time in our MS and is clearly Sharqī. For Sharqī there are the more distant reference points which Samʿānī, those who copied from him, and the old *EI* s.v. Sharḳī enumerate, perhaps the orient as such, and in addition some regions of Muslim Spain: *al-jazāʾir al-sharqiyya* (= Balearic Islands), *al-kuwar al-sharqiyya* (eastern interior of Muslim Spain), *al-thaghr al-sharqī* (*al-thughūr al-sharqiyya*, north-eastern borderlands of Muslim Spain), *sharq al-Andalus*. In Morocco at a later time Sharqī is above all known due to M(a)ḥammad al-Sharqī (d. 1010/1601), the saint of Boujad, his descendants and clients being the Sharqāwa; Lévi-Provençal, *EI* Sharḳāwa; Dale F. Eickelman: *Moroccan Islam*, Austin Texas, 1981. ʿAbd al-Ḥayy al-Kattānī: *Fihris al-fahāris*, Fez, 1347, II, p. 396, is annoyed by the false spelling Sharafī for the scholar Muḥammad b. al-Ṭayyib b. Muḥammad b. Mūsā al-Fāsī al-Madanī al-Shargī (Sharqī, d. 1170/1756-57; *GAL S*, II, p. 522: Sharāgī), connected with the tribes Sharāga/Sharāqa/Cheraga. Regarding these Sharāga, Aḥmad b. Khalīd al-Nāṣirī: *Al-istiqṣā li-akhbār duwal al-maghrib al-aqṣā*, Casablanca, 1954-56, VI, p. 52, writes: These Sharāqa are Arabs of the desert of Tlemcen and its surroundings. They bear this name because they live in the east of the Furthest West. The inhabitants of Tlemcen and its administrative districts call the people of the Furthest West *maghāriba*, and the inhabitants of the Furthest West call the people of Tlemcen and its administrative districts *mashāriqa*. But the common folk deform this gentilicium to Sharāqa. — I conjecture Sharafī in our passage with reference to the well-known foothills al-Sharaf/Aljarafe west of Seville; Austin: *Sufis of Andalusia*, p. 76; Muḥammad b. ʿAbd al-Munʿim al-Ḥimyarī: *Al-rawḍ al-miʿṭār fī khabar al-aqṭār*, ed. Iḥsān ʿAbbās, Beirut, 1975, pp. 339-40 (s.v. al-Sharaf); Edrîsî, ed. Dozy and De Goeje, Arabic p. 178/French p. 215.

35 This apparently means: Kings as well fare best when they are receptive to the ideals of the Koran and make knowers of the Koran their advisers. One such ideal is trust in God which a knower of the Koran would recommend to them. He would show them on the basis of the above-mentioned examples that when it comes to tests God guides those whom He has chosen to a good end. — But the text is corrupt at this point.

supported by the spirit of God.[36] Another time Sharafī said: 'The king must choose someone as a companion who has knowledge and

---

36 That God supports (*ta'yīd*) human beings with His spirit or the Holy spirit is a Koranic notion. According to surah 2/87 and 253 and surah 5/110, God supported Jesus with His spirit or with the Holy Spirit, even when he was still a speechless infant so that he could suddenly speak. The divine spirit reinforces the spiritual capabilities of human beings. God can also support the faithful in general with such a 'spirit from Himself', as surah 58/22 teaches. Sometimes the helping spirit of God is equated with Gabriel but also, among other things, with the divine Word, with a light in the heart, with the Koran or simply with assistance. Likewise, the *ḥadīth* corpus is familiar with support by the Holy Spirit and sometimes makes use of the synonym for it *iᶜāna* 'helping' or the image of presence in a human being, assistance (*maᶜa*, *maᶜiyya*), especially when the transformation of the poet Ḥassān b. Thābit from Saul to Paul, from opponent to follower, is described. Muḥammad is said to have invoked the support of the Holy Spirit for him, chiefly to intensify the effect of his defamatory verses against his heathen adversaries. The Holy Spirit is thereby meant to have taken the place of the demonic genius which inspired the heathen poets. In the unhistorical contest with words between the Muslims and a delegation of the Tamīm in Medina in the year 9/630, to begin with Muḥammad expresses the conviction that God will support his poet Ḥassān with the Holy Spirit and later, on the side of the Tamīm, it is admitted that Muḥammad must have been 'supported': Waqidī: *Al-maghāzī*, ed. Marsden Jones, London, 1966, p. 979, ll. 2 and 5; W. ᶜArafat: 'An interpretation of the different accounts of the Tamīm delegation to the Prophet in A.H. 9', *BSOAS* 17, 1955, p. 418, ftn. 4. In this connection as well it is more or less equated with Gabriel because in fact the Holy Spirit of Islam is basically Gabriel. One finds information on this in Bukhārī, *ṣalāh* 68, *adab* 91/Muslim, *faḍā'il al-ṣaḥāba* 151 (no. 2485)/*Aghānī*, IV, p. 4/new ed. (Dār al-kutub), IV, p. 137/Goldziher: *Abhandlungen zur arabischen Philologie*, I, p. 4. Bukhārī, *adab* 91/Muslim, *faḍā'il al-ṣaḥāba* 153 (no. 2486). Muslim, ibid. 157 (no. 2490)/*Aghānī*, IV, p. 7/ new ed., IV, p. 145. Abū Dāwūd, no. 4850 (VII, p. 294)/*Aghānī*, IV, p. 8/new ed., IV, p. 146. *Aghānī*, IV, p. 6/new ed., IV, p. 142. In addition, ᶜAbd al-Razzāq Ḥamīda: *Shayāṭīn al-shuᶜarā'*, Cairo, 1956, pp. 150-53. Abū Manṣūr ᶜAbd al-Malik al-Thaᶜālibī: *Khāṣṣ al-khāṣṣ*, Cairo, 1908, p. 80. On the heathen or non-pious genius see Jāḥiẓ: *Ḥawayān*, ed. Hārūn, VI, p. 205; IV, p. 370; VI, p. 225; V, p. 228. By the Holy Spirit which accompanied Ḥassān, Yūnus b. Ḥabīb (d. 182/798) wanted to understand protection (against mistakes and slips or against attacks? *ᶜiṣma*) and divine help (in life or in composing poetry and poetic effectiveness? *tawfīq*) and based this on an alleged saying of Moses which wishes every human being the support of the spirit of God; *Ḥayawān* I, p. 340. Thus he demythologized the Holy Spirit. Similarly the eighth Shīᶜite Imam al-Riḍā (d. 203/818) maintained that God supported the ᶜAlid Imams with a spirit from Himself, a holy and pure spirit, which before them had only assisted Muḥammad and was not to be confused with an angel; none the less, he still described it as a column of light; Ibn Bābawayh: *ᶜUyūn akhbār al-Riḍā*, Najaf, 1970, II, p. 200, below. In the non-demythologized conception Gabriel and the other angels were still beings who offered Muḥammad and his followers military help; Muslim, *faḍā'il al-ṣaḥāba* 157 (no. 2490/Ibn

is ascetic, for I fear: if he does not have knowledge, he will allow himself to be beguiled by the king's great prestige, and if he is not ascetic, by the king's money.' And he added: 'The companion of the king must be ever more humble the closer he becomes to the king. He should not experience any difference whether he is with the king or absent from him. Only in this way will he be preserved from arro-

---

Hishām, II, p. 829/Ḥassān b. Thābit: *Dīwān*, ed. ᶜArafat, Gibb Memorial New Series 25, 1971, no. 1, pp. 14-21. Ibn Hishām, II, p. 617/Ḥassān, no. 11, pp. 11-12. Ibn Hishām, II, p. 629/Ḥassān, no. 162, pp. 18-19. Ibn Hishām, I, pp. 528, 444, 449-50, 461, 474. Paul Arno Eichler: *Die Dschinn, Teufel und Engel im Koran*, diss. Leipzig, 1928, pp. 90-93. By way of summary the following picture emerges: 'Support' or 'assistance' by means of the Holy Spirit or Gabriel is not automatically revelation. Revelation is not subject to any human input. On the other hand, support specifically presupposes human effort and cooperation. Here the theological thesis of a divine subject behind man's actions is to be kept aside for the time being. The poet must therefore content himself with divine help and renounce revelation. However, every human being, including the poet, can receive from angels, if not actual revelations, none the less so-called 'inspirations' or 'sudden insights' which are not binding for other people — as we know in particular from Sufism; Fritz Meier: *Die Fawāʾiḥ al-ǧamāl wa-fawātiḥ al-ǧalāl des Naǧm ad-dīn al-Kubrā*, Wiesbaden, 1957, Introduction, pp. 127-34; Richard Gramlich: 'Weisungen islamischer Mystiker über das rechte Handeln', in *Mystische Erfahrung*, Freiburg i. Br., 1976, pp. 82-83. Therefore the 'support' can be more than only a guideline and a focusing of thought in the right direction. It can also consist of thoughts, even sudden insights and inspirations. Thus parallel to Gabriel as adviser (*wazīr*) to Ḥassān (*Dīwān*, no. 162, l. 19) appear the demonic helpers (*ashyāᶜ min al-jinn*) who, according to the frightened Rāᶜī, stand behind the poetic attacks of his opponent Jarīr; *Aghānī*, XX, p. 170/XXIV, p. 209. But the notion of a duality and of a genius and a human being acting in combination frequently remains preserved. In the *maqāma iblīsiyya* of Badīᶜ al-Zamān al-Hamadhānī (d. 398/1008) the devil boasts: There is no poet who has not had a helper from us (*maᶜahū muᶜīn minnā*). The poet *has* (*maᶜa*) a satan who composes (*yaqūlu maᶜahū*) with him (or in him); *Ḥayawān*, VI, p. 229, l. 3. And surprisingly the poet is then forgotten and only the genius remains: Every poet has, in the view of the Arabs, a satan who composes *through his mouth*; D.S. Margoliouth: *The Letters of Abu'l-ᶜAlā of Maᶜarrat al-Nuᶜmān*, Oxford, 1898, no. 27 (Arabic p. 66)/Mufaḍḍal b. Salama: *Al-Fākhir*, ed. Storey, Leiden, 1915, p. 4, ll. 9-11. Imam Riḍā said to the poet Diᶜbil: Oh Khuzāᶜite, the Holy Spirit spoke these two verses through your mouth: *ᶜUyūn akhbār al-Riḍā*, II, pp. 269-70. Naturally these few observations by no means exhaust the subject and the evidence in the sources. They are only meant to serve to further understanding of our Ṣadafī passage. Thus what is meant there by support through God's spirit is that Sharafī owes to divine assistance either the thought itself which he expressed, or the correct preparation and cleverness which produced it. In the treatises of the Brethren of Purity the reader is frequently addressed with the wish: 'God give you and us support with a spirit from Himself!'

gance.' One time an emir rejected Sharafī's intercession on behalf of an oppressed person. Sharafī prayed: 'Oh God, extinguish his sustenance and disfigure his external appearance!' The emir was removed from office and grew physically smaller and smaller until he fit in children's clothing. He then died being the size of a seven-year-old.

One day when I was with him and somebody begged for a garment, he ordered me to give the person one (*149a*). When he beheld the man in his new finery, he made a wish on my behalf: 'God protect you as to your person (*fī nafsika*) and grant you acceptance with Himself and see that you find the same with his bondsmen!' Thereafter everyone was in fact well-disposed toward me. One of his friends recounted to me that Sharafī once said God had promised him he would never set foot in the land of polytheism. Then it happened that Sharafī and his friend, while picking olives in one of the lands of Andalus, were attacked by Christians, put in chains and dragged away. They marched from sunrise to sunset. The friend reminded him about what he had said. Sharafī replied: 'We will not set foot in the land of polytheism.' When it became dark, thanks to God who made the iron soft, he was able to remove the chain from their neck. They both fled and, after covering in one hour the distance they had marched during a day, they reached home. Sharafī lived from operating a ship on the sea (*baḥr*). If someone who acted unjustly came aboard, the ship would lurch from side to side and would not stay upright on the water, at which point they would turn back and put the unwelcome guest ashore.

A disobedient son[37] whom he threatened to destroy with his glance retorted that he did not have the power to do so. Sharafī replied: 'Take leave of your mother, you will not be performing the Friday prayers tomorrow.' In fact the son was attacked by a robber and killed. The father washed his corpse and buried him but did not weep. When he was asked about this, he replied: 'I say with God (surah 23/28): "Praise be to God who has saved us from a nation of sinners!"'

---

37 Cf. p. 466 below. Ibn ᶜArabī: *Rūḥ al-quds*, p. 98/Austin, p. 99. From the grammarian and expert on the Koran Abū'l-Ḥasan ᶜAlī b. Ibrāhīm al-Ḥawfī (d. 430/1039) there is the saying: 'The death of a disobedient son is continual happiness'; Ibn al-Zayyāt: *Al-kawākib al-sayyāra*, p. 162, l. 23. This means: because of such a death one can always be happy over and over again. On effectively causing the death of one's own son through a curse see Sharjī, p. 154, ll. 7-12.

The latest news I had about him was that he set out on a journey. But I have no information as to whether he is still alive or is already dead.

Abū'l-ᶜAlā' Sālim b. ᶜAbd al-Qādir al-Kindī. Was to begin with a man of letters and an expert in Arabic. He was (*149b*) very popular. He travelled several times from the Maghreb to Mecca. I saw him in the Maghreb when he was already over 90 years old. But he still enjoyed good health and a cheerful state of mind and taught the Koran, *fiqh* and literature, without remuneration.

One night while praying in his house he was attacked by a robber and threatened with a sword. He shouted at him and the robber could no longer move his raised hand. Only after he had repented did he regain the use of his hand. Other villains wished to try this out but they were all obliged to retreat after suffering some outward or psychic harm. Because of this they called him 'Bundle of Thorns' (*Ḥuzmat al-shawk*),[38] and he was known by this name.

I never saw him eat anything and asked him about this. He replied: 'For fifty years I have not eaten any bread or any garnishing, but only raw and boiled vegetables'. The reason: he had bought sheep and regularly took them out to graze. At first he brought some bread and vegetables with him. After a while he made do without the bread and finally forgot about it.[39] He then did the same with garnishing and fruits. I asked him about his children. He had three and, as he informed me, had only ever had intimate contact with women three times: once for the sake of God, once for the Prophet's and once for his own sake. He explained: 'For God's sake because of surah 24/32: "Take in marriage those among you who are single and those of your male and female slaves who are honest!" For the Prophet's sake because of his saying: "Marry with one another and propagate, for I wish to be able to take pride in you, the nations!"[40] For my own sake

---

38 This refers to thorny underbrush which one carries on one's back and uses for making a fire at home. It is prickly. A parallel is fire wood, except that it is harmless if there is no snake lurking in it. Muḥammad b. ᶜAlī al-Sanūsī al-Khaṭṭābī al-Sharīf al-Ḥasanī al-Idrīsī (d. 1276/1859): *Īqāẓ al-wasnān fī'l-ᶜamal bi'l-ḥadīth wa'l-qur'ān*, Algiers, 1914, p. 69, ll. 3-4, cites: Whoever strives after knowledge without having a line of argumentation is like a nocturnal gatherer of fire wood who carries a bundle of fire wood (*ḥuzmat ḥaṭab*) in which a viper sits and suddenly bites him (or stings him, *yaldughuhū*).

39 Similarly Abū Yaᶜazzā, *Tashawwuf*, p. 197; cf. ftn. 136 below.

40 Not authentic. Ibn al-Daybaᶜ: *Tamyīz al-ṭayyib min al-khabīth fī-mā yadūr ᶜalā alsinat al-nās min al-ḥadīth*, Cairo, 1323, pp. 74-75 (variants). The Prophet on the Day of

because of the Prophet's words: "When the true-believing bondsman dies, his work ceases except in the case of three things: a charitable donation that continues, knowledge which others make use of, or an honest child who prays for his father."[41] I obtained a son each time. The first one died early and was received by God, he was of use to me because of the divine reward he earned for me. The second (*150a*) had a son and the latter in turn had twelve sons. The third was pious toward me; he stayed awake nights and each time would bestow on me half the merit for his devotions.'[42]

Judgement will be able to lead forth the greatest number of followers. In a document from 748/1349 pertaining to the marriage of the Waṭṭāsid Aḥmad b. Muḥammad with the ᶜAlid al-Ḥurra bt. ᶜAlī it says: For marriage is a goal with which one draws close to the Lord of mankind (= God), and the highest *wasīla* for propagation thanks to which the Prophet of this community will excel in number (*yukāthir*) all other communities on the Day of Judgement; in the Moroccan journal *El Ouataïq* (= *wathāʾiq*) 1, 1976, p. 349. ᶜUmar b. al-Khaṭṭāb is supposed to have said that in fact he had no need of women but that he wished with his descendants to help Muḥammad to excel numerically (*yakthur*) the other religious communities on the Day of Judgement; Ibn al-Ḥājj: *Al-mudkhal*, Cairo, 1929, II, p. 187. The recognized form of the underlying saying of the Prophet goes: 'Marry! For I wish to excel the other peoples by means of your number (or to seek to excel, *mukāthir*).'

41 *Concordance*, III, p. 291b, *ṣadaqa*; Muslim, *waṣiyya* 14, as well as other authors.

42 Ibn al-ᶜArabī's paternal uncle read the whole Koran every day and bestowed half the reward for this on a boy who had brought him to the Sufi path; Ibn al-ᶜArabī: *Rūḥ al-quds*, p. 98/Austin p. 99. Giving away the merit for religious achievements was and is common practice in Islam, in particular bestowing it on the dead, as well as on saints and even on the Prophet. The instances of this are legion. Here only an indication of some secondary source literature: Edward William Lane: *Manners and Customs of the Modern Egyptians*, 1860 text, Everyman's Library reprint 1954, pp. 515-16 (acceptance into a guild). C. Snouck Hurgronje: *Mekka*, The Hague, 1888-89, II, pp. 54, ftn. 1, 67-68, 191, 377-78. 'Mekkanische Sprichwörter,' in *Verspreide Geschriften*, V, pp. 59-60. Louis Massignon: 'Documents sur certains waqfs des Lieux saints de l'Islam', *REI* 19, 1951, pp. 90-91. Hellmut Ritter: *Das meer der seele*, Leiden, 1955/1978, pp. 317-18. W.S. Cuperus: *Al-Fātiḥa dans la pratique religieuse musulmane du Maroc*, diss. Utrecht, 1973, pp. 27, 28, 31, 32, 34, 37, 38, 39. One can also buy oneself the merit through a legacy to hired prayers and readers. This is true as well of the pilgrimage which one can bestow or pay to have performed for oneself. Performing the pilgrimage in place of, or for the benefit of, one's old father who is incapable of travel was already supposed to have been allowed by the Prophet; Bukhārī, *ḥajj* 1. Regarding the paid pilgrimage in place of someone else (pèlerinage par procuration, pilgrimage by proxy), only the following secondary source literature will be referred to here: Georg Höst: *Nachrichten von Marókos und Fes*, Copenhagen, 1781, p. 207. *Voyages d'Ali Bey en Afrique et en Asie*, Paris, 1814, I, p. 301.

Kindī said to me: 'For twenty years I have not seen any gold and any silver or touched either of them.'[43] One time people came to visit him and he had to offer them a meal. He placed a *tharīd*[44] before them which, however, they found to be faulty: the bread was not properly spiced (?)[45] and the vegetables were uncooked. He left them in irritation. But he reminded them that the Prophet would eat whatever pleased him of the food he was served and leave the rest. He said: 'If a sultan had served you this meal, you would have been delighted. But even this meal here is a gift from God. How savory it would be if it were eaten with gratitutde (*bi'l-qabūl*)!' One of the guests asked him for forgiveness.

Johann Ludwig Burckhardt: *Reisen in Arabien*, German, Weimar, 1830, p. 368. Jaffur Shureef: *Qanoon-e-Islam or The Customs of the Moosulmans of India*, trans. G.A. Herklots, London, 1832, p. 60. Snouck Hurgronje: *Mekka*, II, pp. 310-11. *The Achehnese*, Leiden, 1906, II, p. 308. G.H. Bousquet: 'Introduction à l'étude de l'Islam indonésien', *REI* 12, 1938, p. 189. Gaudefroy-Demombynes: *Le Pèlerinage à la Mekke*, Paris, 1923, pp. 312-13, 315-21. Janine et Dominique Sourdel: 'Nouveaux documents sur l'histoire religieuse et sociale de Damas au moyen âge', *REI* 32, 1964, pp. 1-25. 'À propos des documents de la Grande Mosquée de Damas conservés à Istanbul. Résultats de la seconde enquête', *REI* 33, 1965, pp. 73-85. Reports on this subject in original sources are also numerous. — Moreover, according to one tradition, parents automatically receive the reward for the good actions of their children, and this without anything being deducted from the latter in the process; Ibn al-Ḥājj: *Al-mudkhal*, Cairo, 1929, III, p. 289.

43 Hagiographical motif, see Fritz Meier: *Die Vita des Scheich Abū Isḥāq al-Kāzarūnī*, Bibliotheca Islamica 14, Leipzig, 1948, Introduction, p. 51. But it may well have occurred that individuals followed the practice, at least in the sense of an external style. A judge Yaghmūr under the Fāṭimid ᶜĀḍid (555-567/1160-1171) supposedly would not allow the exhortatory preacher 'Ibn Najība' al-Anṣārī al-Ḥanbalī to go ahead of him because he had seen him touch gold; 'and still he maintains he is a *wāᶜiẓ*!' Sakhāwī: *Tuḥfat al-aḥbāb wa-bughyat al-ṭullāb fī'l-khiṭaṭ wa'l-mazārāt wa'l-tarājim wa'l-biqāᶜ al-mubārakāt*, p. 173. The person meant is ᶜAlī b. Ibrāhīm b. Najā b. Ghanāʾim al-Anṣārī al-Dimashqī, known as Ibn Nujayya (d. 599/1203); Ibn Rajab: *Al-dhayl ᶜalā Ṭabaqāt al-ḥanābila*, III, pp. 436-40.

44 Wehr's *Dict.*: 'A dish of sopped bread, meat and broth.' In this case it must have also contained some greens (*baql*).

45 Corrupt text? In the MS it says that his children had not spiced the bread and not cooked the vegetables (and served them). The fault-finding of the guests is absent. Immediately after 'his children' is a small erasure. The fault-finding of the guests which the context requires could have fallen out through homoioteleuton or could have been in the sentence changed by the erasure.

Women who were in labor liked to be given his walking stick which he used to support himself because of his age,[46] and they would grip it tightly in their hand in order to give birth more easily.

He had given up eating honey. After a long time he felt a desire for it again. Khaḍir appeared to him in a dream, offered him a bowlful and promised to bring him honey again in the future any time he wanted. When he woke up his desire had left him.

I was not present at his death but I was informed that a prominent personality wished to recite the prayer over his corpse, though he was not worthy to do so. A gust of wind from the east whirled dust into his eyes so he could not lead the prayer. Someone else took his place.

Al-faqīh *Abū Marwān ʿAbd al-Malik b. Masarra al-Yaḥṣubī* (d. 552/1157).[47] Was at the end of his life the chief judge of Córdoba and its environs in Andalus. Was an eminent expert on *ḥadīth*. (*150b*) Also knew the *uṣūl al-dīn* and the branches of *fiqh*, the expert legal opinions and decisions. Everywhere he alighted he would listen to *ḥadīth*. I heard *ḥadīth* from him, read *ḥadīth*-books with him and received written *ḥadīth* from him for further transmission (*munāwala*).[48] The sultan of the Maghreb[49] called him and other *fuqahāʾ* from Andalus to himself. In coming before the sultan each of them was concerned to have a particularly good appearance. Only Yaḥṣubī remained in his coarse apparel and on a donkey. The notables of the kingdom who went forth to meet them had to ask which one was Yaḥṣubī. Then they escorted him with great respect to the royal court, walking alongside his stirrup and ahead of him. But he did not want this and for his part got down from his donkey. Now they mounted up again so that he would also continue to ride. And so he arrived before the sultan who honored him all the more for this and made him accept judicial offices in Andalus.

Yaḥṣubī was so modest that he personally brought the risen dough for bread to the oven when the servant was late in coming and then also brought back the baked bread by himself and would in no case allow the bread to be taken from him by people who were eager to be

46 Not simply in the past but during Kindī's lifetime.

47 See pp. 427 and 432 above.

48 I. Goldziher: *Muhammedanische Studien*, Halle, 1889-90, II, p. 189. *EI*[2] ḥadīth, IV. Étude et transmission de la Tradition, no. 4 (J. Robson).

49 Unclear who this could have been, though apparently an Almoravid. Marrakesh fell into the hands of the Almohads in 541/1147.

of service.[50] Occasionally persons seeking justice met him along the way. Then he laid the bread aside, gave a decision, picked up the bread again and left. One day a man complained about his wife who had locked him out of the house. Yaḥṣubī had himself taken to the house which was close by and knocked at the door with his stick. The woman came out and the *qāḍī* asked her why she had locked the man out of the house. (*151a*) The woman replied that the man had promised her a dress for a long time and never bought her one. The man explained that he could not afford to pay the price. Yaḥṣubī gave him a dinar: 'Buy her the dress with this!'

Yaḥṣubī was enthusiastic for war, ever determined to fight against the polytheists (i.e. the Christians). He performed voluntary service at the frontier (*ribāṭ al-khayl*). In an encounter he was attacked, fell from his horse and crawled up onto a hill but was caught. The Christians wanted to remove his armor. When he defended himself, they tried to kill him. But God hindered it. No one managed to get at him with the lance. The Muslims regained their courage again and rescued Yaḥṣubī, indeed put the enemy to flight. The Christians requested a disputation (*mufāwaḍa*)[51] with him. Their scribe, a Jew who had knowledge of Arabic, asked him what he had used to protect himself against the polytheists. He sent them in reply his treatise *Al-radd ᶜalā'l-naṣārā* (*Refutation of the Christians*) which is famous in Andalus, the Maghreb and elsewhere.[52]

He had resolved to look after the concerns of people and to provide orphan girls with what they needed to get married. One time he did this and borrowed some jewelry from a rich woman which the bride was supposed to wear on the wedding night. Among the jewelry was an expensive necklace. By chance this broke apart (*tafarraṭa*). A maid gathered the pearls together and hid them. When it was noticed that the necklace was missing, Yaḥṣubī said it would not be lost (*151b*) and he put off the owner for three days. Even by the second

---

50 Similarly *Tashawwuf*, p. 227, ll. 5-8, and p. 181, ll. 1-4.

51 Here and *165b*, l. 8: *muᶜāwaḍa* (*mudhākara*, *muʾānasa*, *muḥāḍara*). It would be a small change to substitute in both places *muᶜāraḍa*. Here, *151a*, l. 15, the *wāw* is written almost as thin as a *rāʾ* but in *165b*, l. 8, it is clearly a thick *wāw*. *Muᶜāwaḍa/taᶜāwuḍ* in the original meaning 'exchange' was perfectly normal usage in the 6th/12th century in Spain; R. García de Linares: 'Escrituras árabes pertenencientes al Archivo de Ntra. Sra. del Pilar de Zaragoza', in *Homenaje á D. Francisco Codera*, Saragossa, 1904, pp. 180-83.

52 Books with this title in *GAL*, index. Our work is not among them. Books dealing with the same subject in Kâtib Çelebi: *Keşf-el-zunun*, I, p. 838, s.v. *radd al-naṣārā*, one *li-baᶜḍ al-maghāriba* which does not necessarily have to be ours.

day the maid came to him with the intact necklace and explained she had wanted to sell the individual pearls but had not been able to do so.

Before his appointment as judge Yaḥṣubī was a jurisconsult (*faqīh mushāwar*). A man once brought him a letter from another *faqīh* which recommended him as a brave warrior. He wanted to put in a good word for him with the *qāḍī* of Córdoba so that he might be furnished with a horse and the necessary weapons for war. Yaḥṣubī accompanied the man to the judge. The latter replied: 'We will examine the matter.' Repeating this phrase, Yaḥṣubī left the house in a huff. The next morning he once again appeared with the petitioner before the judge. Just then an inhabitant of the desert arrived leading a valuable horse on a halter and inquired after the man from the judge. As he explained, he had received instructions in a dream to give the horse to so-and-so as alms for war. 'God grant you Paradise! Here is the horse I have brought you.' The man was completely equipped. Yaḥṣubī said: 'Thanks be to God, not to the *qāḍī*!'[53]

Another time he gave one of his students (or friends) as a gift a cluster of grapes that weighed almost 16 *raṭl*s. Along with it he wrote him the following note: 'Dear friend, see what God has created and how this point of junction unites everything on a single piece of wood! This is how the theologians as well diverge from one another in the branches of religious law and yet are united in a single root. Their difference of opinion is a mercy from God,[54] and their unity a divine favor and a blessing. Blame no one, refute no one and do not attach yourself to those who do what is most reprehensible![55] My dear friend, seek knowledge, the outward and the inner kind! (*152a*) My dear friend, be satisfied with as little as possible from the world, with some grapes, a flat-bread, pure water! My dear friend, I know about matters to do with flavor (? *ṭuʿūm*): what looks the best stinks the most. The world is the same: what has the most pleasures chiefly brings with it affliction; what is most wretched is the most helpful. My dear friend, do not seek after the world too much; one soon wades in it like in mud. But if there is no way around it, direct your

---

53 In this section the MS twice has Ibn Maysara instead of Ibn Masarra. On the phrase *yuḥmadu'llāhu lā yuḥmadu'l-qāḍī* cf. *158a* below.

54 Regarding the shift in meaning of *raḥma* in this frequently cited sentence from simple 'permission' to 'beneficial', see Rudi Paret: 'Innerislamischer Pluralismus', in *Festschrift für Hans Robert Roemer*, Beirut, 1979, pp. 523-29.

55 Unclear *al-akhsarīn aʿmālan*. *Al-akhsaʾīn aʿmālan* 'who do what is most shameful' would also make good sense.

steps through it and beyond; it will then be easier to cleanse yourself of it again. My dear friend, the pleasures of the world are associated with regret, by contrast the affairs of the hereafter are secure against non-existence. My dear friend, call upon God for help in order to be able to reflect on my words correctly! He opens the heart of His friends to Islam and holds them back from doing what is wrong. Ask Him on your behalf to fulfill what is His right and the right of His other bondsmen! Do not ask Him for anything besides that! My dear friend, wander throughout the world! That will dispel your pride in your home, for scarcely ever can a noble man become the leader of his own people. My dear friend, God hates persons who resemble Him in several respects: in greatness, in lordliness, in swift vengeance and in wealth. The Prophet said: "God has declared: 'Greatness is My mantle (*ridāʾ*) and lordliness is my robe. Whoever contests one of these with Me, I shall destroy.'"[56] Surah 85/12: "Surely Your Lord's assault is terrible." Surah 26/130: "And when you assault, do you assault like tyrants?" Surah 47/38: "God is the rich one, you are the poor." My dear friend, a worldly man with attractive clothes and after him a worn-out man in threadbare clothes sat down with the Prophet. The rich man gathered up his clothes in the presence of the pauper. The Prophet asked him if he was afraid of some dirt. The rich man apologized and declared that he was prepared to give the pauper half of his money. The poor man refused because he was afraid of becoming as deluded as the rich man. My dear friend, in an emergency take from the world only as much as you need, like a sick man takes medicine. Whatever comes to you without begging, accept but do not save up anything. My dear friend, if sometime you absolutely must pursue the world, do not do so with your religion but with the labor of your hands! (*152b*) Saḥnūn al-Qayrawānī (d. 240/854) said to his son: "My dear, to eat of the world by means of a tambourine and a flute (i.e. as a musician) is better than by means of religion."[57] Al-Ḥasan b. Abī'l-Ḥasan al-Baṣrī (d.

---

56 *Concordances*, IV, p. 279a, *ʿaẓama*; Abū Dāwūd, *libās* 25; Ibn Māja, *zuhd* 16, and other authors as well.

57 What is meant is acquiring material gain by religious behavior or also by religious activity, such as for instance giving instruction in the Koran, etc. Cf. *157b*, *169b*. The saying of Saḥnūn is not found in the articles on Saḥnūn and Muḥammad b. Saḥnūn in Qāḍī ʿIyāḍ: *Tartīb al-madārik wa-taqrīb al-masālik li-maʿrifat aʿlām madhhab Mālik*, Beirut, n.d., I-II, pp. 585-630; III-IV, pp. 104-18/al-Muḥammadiyya (Morocco), 1965 ff., V, pp. 45-88, 204-21. The traditionist Abū Shuʿayb ʿAbdallāh b. al-Ḥasan al-Ḥarrānī (d. 295/907-08) was regarded as a

110/728) when asked about earning money by means of religion, replied: "That is too monstrous for Ḥasan to speak about."[58] My dear friend, exercise frugality, then you will be the furthest ahead! My dear friend, make a habit of practicing forgiveness, that is most likely to assure that you will also be forgiven! My dear friend, God protect you from lusts and may He show you favor even before death, because if He shows you favor beforehand, He will be good to you afterwards as well.'[59]

Yaḥṣubī had inherited a considerable amount of wealth from his father. He gave away two-thirds of it as alms and bought himself valuable books with the remaining third. These he made copies of and then sold the originals.[60] He only kept the copies. I was not present at his death. But it was recounted to me that the leading men (*ruʾasāʾ*) of Andalus scrambled to get hold of his books. The *Sunan* of Abū Dāwūd al-Sijistānī (d. 275/889) in three parts cost 80 dinars.

Abū ᶜAlī al-Ḥasan b. Muḥammad[61] known as Ibn al-Dallāl al-Qurashī, the student of Ibn al-ᶜArīf (d. 536/1141).[62] Was a zealous traditionist. Occupied himself deeply with literature as well. Was averse to all complacency. Sought after solitude, wandered from

---

reliable transmitter but was tainted with the stigma of having received money for *ḥadīths*; Dhahabī: *Mīzān al-iᶜtidāl*, Cairo, 1963, II, p. 406, no. 4266.

58 The story is not found in the sources on Ḥasan enumerated by Ritter; *EI*² al-Ḥasan al-Baṣrī; 'Studien zur Geschichte der islamischen Frömmigkeit I', *Der Islam* 21, 1933, p. 13.

59 Like everything in these summary accounts, presented in abbreviated form and by way of extracts. The piece is written in rhymed prose. The constantly repeated address 'my dear friend' is 'my dear son' (*yā bunayya*) in the original, a form of address which is natural for a Muslim because of surah 31 where Luqmān imparts his wise lessons to his son and quite appropriately adresses him as 'my dear son'. Teachers frequently use *yā bunayya* in speech and in writing when they address a student.

60 This way of acquiring a library for oneself is not mentioned in W. Wattenbach: *Das Schriftwesen im Mittelalter*, Leipzig, 1896. The wealthy scholar ᶜAbd al-Raḥmān b. ᶜAlī Saqīn (d. 956/1549) in Fez hired educated people with beautiful handwriting to copy learned books; *Fihris Aḥmad al-Manjūr*, ed. Ḥajjī, Rabat, 1976, p. 61, l. 3 from bot.

61 MS has Abū'l-Ḥasan, without ᶜAlī. The presumably correct name is clear from the forms of address in the text that follows: *yā Ḥasan*, *yā Bā ᶜAlī*.

62 Ibn al-ᶜArīf is the well-known Andalusian mystic; Miguel Asín Palacios: *Ibn al-ᶜArīf, Maḥāsin al-Majālis*, texte arabe, traduction et commentaire, Paris, 1933; Bruno Halff: 'Le Maḥāsin al-majālis d'Ibn al-ᶜArīf et l'oeuvre du soufi hanbalite al-Anṣārī', *REI* 39, 1971, pp. 321-35.

place to place. No house remained closed to him. He said: 'I have prayed God to give me sustenance abroad and to help me find solitude. My prayer was answered.' He travelled about in the barren wastes.

I saw him once when he came back from a journey. He related to me that a well-dressed young man came to see him in a mosque on a mountain and after the evening prayer placed before him a pot containing (*153a*) a delicious pudding (*khabīṣ*). After he had eaten it, the young man said to him that it had been seaweed (*ḍarīᶜ*) from the ocean.[63] He showed him more of it in a sack[64] and added: 'Everywhere in the world God has bondsmen for whom, should they only wish so, honey would flow forth from the rocks. Be honest with God and eat what you wish! You will find it tasty (amended to *sāʾigh*).[65] God chooses from among His friends.'

Once I beheld him with bared head, sighing, weeping and moaning in the desert, and I followed him without his observing me. While shedding tears, he said: 'Ḥasan, why should you not weep and sob? Indeed, the beloved has come close by, and you have been thrust aside. The sinners have been treated with leniency, and you have been given a severe scolding. You are given admonishment but you close your ears to it and have no interest in what is with God. You refuse to be warned. This is the slaughter of one who has angered the world and God.' Since I feared he could suffer some harm, I called to him: 'Abū ᶜAlī, what is upsetting you so?' He replied: 'My sight

---

63 Saints frequently transform bad foods into delicacies. Cf. here Abū Yaᶜazzā (*164a*), salt water becomes drinkable (*165a*). *Tashawwuf*, pp. 188 below, 193 above (sea water becomes sweet), 197 below (oleander sweet), 418 (a variation on the motif). Ibn al-ᶜArabī: *Rūḥ al-quds*, p. 97/Austin, p. 97. Austin, p. 110 (from *Durra fākhira*): a brackish spring becomes sweet. Yāfiᶜī: *Rawḍ al-rayāḥīn*, p. 305 (488th story): sea water is sweet. Al-Ḥusayn b. Muḥammad al-Warthīlānī (d. 1193/1779): *Nuzhat al-anẓār fī faḍl ᶜilm al-tārīkh wa'l-akhbār al-mashhūra bi'l-Riḥla al-warthīlāniyya*, Algiers, 1908, p. 64, ll. 1-3; ll. 6-10. Muḥammad-i Ghaznawī: *Maqāmāt-i Žanda-pīl*, p. 39 (vinegar and onions turn into an unsurpassable meal). A remarkable saint from Jerusalem who died in 832/1428-29 ate dung-beetles and snakes and experienced the dung-beetles as raisins and the snakes as cucumbers; Mujīr al-Dīn al-Ḥanbalī: *Al-uns al-jalīl bi-tārīkh al-Quds wa'l-Khalīl*, Amman, 1973, II, p. 169. The left-over bitter Zamzam water from which a saint had drunk tasted like milk with honey; Yāfiᶜī: *Rawḍ al-rayāḥīn*, p. 76 (69th story).

64 *Arwānī* instead of *arānī*, for which, as one knows, *awrānī* 'he made me see' also occurs. Dozy: *Suppl. aux dictionnaires arabes*, I, p. 573 (rwy).

65 The taste of such foods depends on one's unselfish devotion to God, similar to *150a* where it depends on receiving the food with gratitude as a gift from God.

has come to coincide with a tear (?) and helplessness has become a lesson. How nice of you that you are there like myself and share in my sorrowful sobbing (?)! How close it is when one is drinking wine and yet how far still from the shadow (?)!'[66] He then left me.

On another day I saw him sleeping in a mosque of the Companions of the Prophet.[67] When he woke up, I asked him about the meaning of a saying of the Prophet and he gave me a most excellent answer. But I sensed from his words that he was hungry and asked him whether he would like something to eat. He replied: 'Do you still seek advice about something good you want to do?' I asked; 'What would you like?' He said: 'In the end I would only like a blessing and a mercy (*153b*) which would bring me close to the beloved.' I also heard in this that he wanted to eat something. Fortunately, I had with me bread, meat, honey and milk. He ate. After the meal he performed two prostrations of prayer, and I said to him: 'God have mercy on you, is there a tradition about these prostrations of prayer?' He replied: 'Not from the Prophet himself but from a man of piety, and imitation of a person who has done good is for an intelligent person all the more proper and gains for him good in this world and in the world to come.'

One of his students said to me: 'He made the pilgrimage to Mecca, and one night I heard him weeping in a corner of the sacred precinct and reciting the four verses (*rajaz, -adi*):[68]

---

66 A number of things are doubtful and not completely understandable. Perhaps the sense is this: The sight of my condition has brought me to tears, and my helplessness *vis-à-vis* my situation has taught me a warning lesson. If you look upon this with me sympathetically, you are in fact on the way to your own self-knowledge, but then only theoretically. The whole passage is rhymed. — Dialogues like this have been part of the Sufi literature of edification from time immemorial. Cf. for instance Abū Nuʿaym: *Ḥilyat al-awliyāʾ*, II, p. 89; X, p. 21 (= Friedrich Rückert: *Sieben Bücher morgenländischer Sagen und Geschichten*, Stuttgart, 1837, II, pp. 295-97, translated from Kosegarten's *Chrestomathia Arabica*, p. 60 f., from Biqāʿī's *Aswāq al-ashwāq*; also Ibn al-Jawzī: *Ṣifat al-ṣafwa*, Hyderabad, 1355-56, IV, p. 309), with Abū Sulaymān al-Dārānī. Qushayrī's *Risāla*, Cairo, 1318, p. 85 (*bāb mukhālafat al-nafs*), with Ibrāhīm al-Khawwāṣ. *Ṣifat al-ṣafwa*, IV, pp. 311-12/*Firdaws al-murshidiyya*, ed. Fritz Meier, p. 95/ʿUlaymī: *Al-manhaj al-aḥmad fī tarājim aṣḥāb al-imām Aḥmad*, Cairo, 1963-65, II, p. 34, with Abū Ṣāliḥ al-Dimashqī. Frequently in Yāfiʿī's *Rawḍ al-rayāḥīn*. — Following a saint and watching him without being noticed is also a favorite motif in the legends of saints.

67 It is not said where.

68 Acatalectic dimeter with rhyme only at the end of the complete verse. W. Wright: *A Grammar of the Arabic Language*, II, p. 362.

My lord, my lord,
    you have driven me out of my land.
You have banned slumber from my eyes.
    They have become intimate with sleeplessness.[69]
God hears whoever on the bed of exhaustion
    spends the whole night without sleeping
and dies in secrecy
    without bemoaning his passion to anyone.

He went on repeating these verses in a sad voice until morning. Then I lost sight of him' — so his student told me.

Abū ᶜAbdallāh Muḥammad b. Yaḥyā al-Maṣālī[70] (?). Was chaste and gave away everything he had, practiced firm self-control and mastered himself. He had one son who was numbered among the men of piety. He gave young boys instruction in the Koran for the reward of God. Was an expert in Koranic commentary and on problems of language in the Koran. He read Muḥāsibī[71] and trained himself this way into his old age. At the age of fifty he abandoned everything and withdrew in solitude. He only appeared among the people on Friday and holidays. He was often ill, scarcely in good health for three days in a row, was pale and emaciated.

I visited him one day and found him weeping. He complained that he had been in the such-and-such mosque the previous day and toward the time of evening prayer a young man dressed in woolen rags had appeared at the door, sounded the call to prayer, then after announcing that the prayers were about to begin, had gone on to per-

---

69 The somewhat damaged rhyming word with wrong pointing should be read as *bi'l-sahadi*.

70 Uncertain. Cf. *EI*² Ibn Maṣāl.

71 Qāḍī ᶜIyāḍ (d. 544/1149) received an *ijāza* for Muḥāsibī's *Riᶜāya* from a certain Muḥammad b. Khamīs al-Ṣūfī in Andalus; Ibn Abbār: *Takmila*, ed. Codera, I, p. 158 (no. 555). Abū Madyan (d. 594/1197) heard the *Riᶜāya* of Muḥāsibī in Fez from ᶜAlī b. al-Ḥasan Ibn Ḥirzihim (d. 559/1164; *Uns al-faqīr*, p. 14, l. 1); *Tashawwuf*, p. 319, l. 17. Abū ᶜImrān al-Mārtulī went the way of Muḥāsibī, i.e. he accepted nothing from anyone and neither begged for himself nor for others; Ibn al-ᶜArabī: *Rūḥ al-quds*, p. 90/Austin, p. 87 (for Muḥāsibī's position on the question of earning a living see my Kāzarūnī: *Firdaws al-murshidiyya*, Introduction, pp. 57-59). A certain Abū or Ibn Jaᶜdūn al-Ḥinnāwī (d. 597/1200-01) once opened the *kitāb al-maᶜrifa* of Muḥāsibī in the presence of Ibn al-ᶜArabī: *Rūḥ al-quds*, p. 110/Austin, p. 115. Perhaps what is meant is Muḥāsibī's *Mukhtaṣar al-maᶜānī* which begins with *maᶜrifa*; Sezgin: *GAS*, I, p. 642.

form the prayers. They then undertook supererogatory devotions together until the night-time prayer. After the night-time prayer the young man continued to pray in a corner and in the morning, without having eaten, was still engaged in prayer. Before morning prayer Maṣālī went outside to perform his ritual ablutions again and there he found the man sleeping with his cheek on the ground. But the man woke up before Maṣālī had time to awaken him. They performed the morning prayers together. After that the young man set about reciting the recollection of God until the sun rose. They performed the mid-morning prayers together. Then they went outside and the man offered him a torn loaf of bread he had brought with him in a sack. They consumed it together and then separated. 'I had decided to ask him to invoke God on my behalf', Maṣālī recounted. But then, in view of the impression the man had made on him, he didn't dare to do so. Subsequently, he wanted to try it again but by then the man had already set out walking across the sea to an island which lay far from the shore, and there he performed the prayers.[72] Maṣālī watched him from a distance. That he had missed obtaining the invocation and lost the man was the cause of his sorrow.[73]

Another time when he was sick, I heard him say as he kneeled during prayer: 'Oh God, protect me according to Your way of giving protection, in front of us, behind us, to the right and to the left, above us and below us, and all around us! Oh God, guard over us! You are the Guardian. Surah 13/11: "He has guardians before and after him who watch over him, beings from the logos of God." There is no strength or power except through God.' I asked him who had taught him this prayer. He replied: 'I once said to the Prophet when he ap-

---

72 Walking on water is an ever recurrent commonplace of Islamic legends, especially in connection with saints in the west. Here a few examples only from the *Tashawwuf*: pp. 38 f., 64, 93, 98, 99, 104 f., 137, 140, 192, 196, 216, 217, 251, 305, 364, 381, 436, 438. In the Gulf of Ismid in 1080/1669 there was a crossing point called 'The path of the Maghribī', because a saint from the west, who asked for a free passage across and was refused, scattered sand from within his robe into the sea and made himself a path across the water; Ibrāhīm b. ᶜAbd al-Raḥmān al-Khiyārī: *Tuḥfat al-udabāᵓ wa-salwat al-ghurabāᵓ*, n.p., n.d., I, p. 236. But this miracle is by no means limited to the west. It is commonly met with in the east as well. Already Abū Yazīd al-Basṭāmī (3rd/9th century) is supposed to have warned against overestimating the importance of this miracle and of miracles in general; Sarrāj: *Al-lumaᶜ fī'l-taṣawwuf*, ed. Nicholson, Gibb Mem. Series 22, 1914, p. 324, ll. 12-18. The numerous source references cannot be presented here. Christian legends are also familiar with this miracle; Günter: *Psychologie der Legende*, pp. 199-202. The motif is already documented in antiquity; ibid., p. 40.

73 The same type as *161a*.

peared to me in a dream: "I am afraid sometimes when I am journeying in the desert that complacency might come over me and God could allow animals to become masters over me."[74] The Prophet replied: "I have a treasure for you which Gabriel conveyed to me at God's command during the War of the Ditch. I protected myself with it on that occasion, and in the same way the inhabitants of heaven and earth have protected themselves." Then the Prophet taught me this prayer.'[75]

(*154b*) Maṣālī had a small palm orchard (*makhraf*), the fruits of which he would reap in order to obtain what he needed to live on.[76] One day he visited *Abū Yaᶜazzā*[77] who was famous for his miracles. Just then a tax-collector (*ᶜāmil*) took possession of his orchard. On his return Maṣālī had it communicated to him that he would knock out both his eyes if he did not give him back the orchard. People told the tax-collector that Maṣālī's prayers were always answered. He was gripped by fear and returned the stolen property to him.

When I left him, he was still living but I do not know what has since become of him.

Abū ᶜAbdallāh Salāma b. Daḥmān al-Kutāmī. Was a young man of virtuous nature and cheerful mien, gentle and dignified, and with an

---

74 The combination of 'complacency' (*iᶜjāb*) with 'animals' (*dawābb*) is not really satisfying. Are wild animals meant which threaten him as punishment for his complacency as an ascetic in the desert, or are they of a different kind, psychic animals which together with his complacency and because of it overwhelm him in the deserts of his soul? Legend recounts that one time ᶜAlī b. Muḥammad al-Muzayyin (d. 328/939-40), while travelling through the desert, was overcome by a similar conceit; Kalābādhī: *Al-taᶜarruf li-madhhab ahl al-taṣawwuf*, ed. Arberry, Cairo, 1933, p. 117 (chapt. 68)/trans. Arberry: *The Doctrine of the Ṣūfīs*, Cambridge, 1935, p. 155; Yāfiᶜī: *Rawḍ al-rayāḥīn*, p. 91 (95th story). The same experience befell Ibrāhīm al-Khawwāṣ (d. 291/904 or earlier); Yāfiᶜī, ibid.

75 The Prophet is meant to have frequently provided saints with helpful prayers in their dreams.

76 *Yatakaffafu bihī*, from *kafāf* 'what is sufficient for life'; the verb is not found with this meaning in the dictionary.

77 In our MS always written with *tāʾ marbūṭa* instead of *yāʾ*, perhaps to avoid the false reading *Yaᶜazzī, Yaᶜzī, Yuᶜāzzī*. In any case for this reason one preferred the spelling *Taghāza* with *tāʾ marbūṭa* for the locality *Taghāzā* (with *yāʾ*) — to avoid *Taghāzī*; this according to the journal *El Ouataïq* 1, p. 368, ftn. 1. It is not however true that from an original *Walīla* for Volubilis the false form *Walīlī* emerged, but the other way round: *Walīlī* is the original, even though *Walīla* already appears in Ṭabarī (III, p. 561, l. 5) and the early geographers, and then *Walīlā* is found in Yāqūt.

eloquent tongue. Already as a boy he had acquired judgement and as a young man he was endowed with wisdom. He related to me: 'When I was seven years old,[78] I had a dream in which the Prophet drew me to him and ran his right hand over my mouth and his left hand over my breast, while reciting surah 87/6: "We shall make you recite and you shall not forget", as well as surah 54/17: "And We have made the Koran easy to remember. But is there anyone who will take heed?" Then with his hand he gave me water to drink from a vessel. Since that dream it has been easy for me to retain dictation of a sixtieth, indeed even a thirtieth, of the Koran after it is read out three times.[79] Previously I had had difficulty. Then nights in my dreams another teacher would regularly dictate to me a portion (*mīᶜād*) from the *Muwaṭṭaʾ* of Mālik b. Anas (d. 179/795). I would always write down these portions immediately in the dream and would know them by heart in the morning. Thus I learned both by heart at the same time, the Koran during the day and the *Muwaṭṭaʾ* at night.

Kutāmī also knew by heart other things after they were repeated three times. He learned *ḥadīth*, *fiqh*, history and genealogy, all by heart. However, he only lived to be thirty. He never became angry, had no disputes with anyone and he never felt anything unpleasant about someone. This was visible in his face. (*155a*) He never complained about an illness. But when his early death was close at hand, he said: 'I know that I will only become thirty years old and that I

---

78 *ᶜInda raʾs sabᶜ sinīn* 'at the end of seven years'. A prediction of Muḥammad's death at the age of 63 was read into the passage 'God will give no one a deferment once his appointed time has come' in surah 63/11, at the 'end of 63 surahs', *raʾs thalāth wa-sittīn sūra*; Suyūṭī: *Al-iᶜmāl bi-ḥukm ᶜĪsā ᶜalayhi al-salām*, in his *Al-ḥāwī li'l-fatāwī*, Cairo, 1352/reprint 1395/1975, II, p. 160, l. 19. This *raʾs* is frequently used in speaking about the centennial renewers of Islam, as in the case of Abū Dāwūd: *Mukhtaṣar al-sunan*, *malāḥim* 1, Maṭb. al-sunna al-muḥammadiyya, 1948-50, VI, p. 163: 'God will send to this community at the end (*raʾs*) of every century (*miʾat sana*) someone who will renew its religion.' Correctly given by Dozy in the Glossaire of his *Edrîsî* (1866), pp. 303-04, and in the *Suppl. aux dictionnaires* s.v. *raʾs*, but also *fī* and (more rarely) *ᶜinda raʾs*, as well as other prepositions: *ḥawālay raʾs*, etc. Persian adopted this usage of *raʾs*: Muḥammad Ḥasan-i Shīrāzī in Samarra (d. 1312/1895) was regarded as *mujaddid-i madhhab-i jaᶜfarī dar raʾs-i qarn-i sīzdahum*. *ᶜAlā raʾs sittīn wa-arbaᶜmiʾa* means 'around 460'. This is clear from Sharjī, p. 54, ll. 8-11, where it is said about the son of someone who died in 630 that his death took place *ᶜalā raʾs al-sabᶜmiʾa*, i.e. 'at the end of 700'. Cf. Friedrich Schulthess: *ZDMG* 70, 1916, p. 412.

79 Cf. p. 436, *147a*, above.

will die in such-and-such a month and such-and-such a day.'[80] And that is what happened.

I was not present when he died but it was reported to me that the white birds which are seen at the funerals of men of piety fluttered about his bier and went with him into the grave.[81]

This is the last of the jurists (*fuqahāʾ*) and theologians (*ᶜulamāʾ*) whom I saw and from whom I have transmitted and about whom I received reports.

2. THE WORSHIPPERS OF GOD (*ᶜUBBĀD*) AND ASCETICS (*ZUHHĀD*), MIRACLE-WORKERS (*ARBĀB AL-KARĀMĀT AL-MASHHŪRA*) AND OCCUPANTS OF HIGH HALTING STATIONS (*WA'L-MAWĀQIF AL-MASHHŪDA*) WHOM I SAW IN THE MAGHREB.

Abū'l-ᶜAbbās Aḥmad b. Abī Yaᶜlā, known as *al-Gharīb* (or *al-Ghurayyib*). He suffered from leprosy (*judhām*), knew the Koran by heart and only slept after he had recited the whole of the Koran and had performed the prescribed and the voluntary ritual prayers.

Now and then we invited him to our place. He would come but he never ate with us. Then when he had finished his recitation and bedded down on his prayer-rug, we would hear him still reciting from the Koran in his sleep. When he woke up, he would start reciting the Koran from the beginning which makes it clear that he was unaware of reciting in his sleep. He once asked me whether he should accept

---

80 Foreknowledge of death is frequent; *Tashawwuf*, pp. 145, 149 f. *Rūh al-quds*, p. 98/Austin, p. 99; Yāfiᶜī: *Rawḍ*, p. 276, l. 19/Nabhānī: *Jāmiᶜ karāmāt al-awliyāʾ*, I, 300, ll. 2-3. The Jewish saint Abū Ḥaṣīra in Damanhūr is supposed to have known in advance that his day of death would be a Sunday; ᶜAbd al-Ḥamīd Ḥawwās and Ṣābir al-ᶜĀdilī: 'Mulāḥaẓāt ḥawl baᶜḍ al-ẓawāhir al-fūlklūriyya bi-muḥāfaẓat al-Buḥayra', in the journal *Al-funūn al-shaᶜbiyya* 12, 1970, 70a.

81 *Nazalat maᶜahū qabrahū*. Cannot mean: 'and settled with it (the bier) on his grave'. — Sometimes green birds are supposed to be seen; Abū Nuᶜaym: *Ḥilya*, IX, p. 363, last line. A certain Abū'l-Faḍl Muḥammad al-ᶜAṣāfirī, who was buried in the Qarāfa in Cairo, bore this epithet because small green birds had fluttered into the grave with him or because a small green bird flew into the grave with him and was found there dead or after a while came forth alive, on which occasion a voice was heard: 'We have released it', since another explanation says that ᶜAṣāfirī previously had bought little birds and set them free; the wording is: *rafrafa ilā'l-qabr, nazala ilā qabrihī, nazala fī'l-qabr*; Ibn al-Zayyāt: *Kawākib sayyāra*, p. 145/Sakhāwī: *Tuḥfat al-aḥbāb*, pp. 266-67. On this subject Massignon: 'La Cité des Morts', *BIFAO* 57, 1958, p. 55: he released little birds which children caught with bird lime in order to cut off their wings (Damietta); the birds came to his funeral.

alms. I said yes and he replied that this had also been the opinion of several *fuqahā'* he had questioned. Thus he had aleady known but wished to follow me (*taqlīd*) because I was so young and yet so far removed from avarice (*nahma*). One night we heard him cry out in his sleep 'Mercy, mercy!' It must have been a bad dream. We woke him up. He related: 'In my dream I was in Seville. People were selling pitchers (*jirār*) filled with fire and would always place some of the fire from the pitcher in the customer's hand, and the customer would swallow it. I (Gharīb) did not know what this was meant to signify until an angel with a sword in his hand descended from heaven and beheaded fifteen of the men, while the others took flight. I experienced a fright and then (*155b*) you woke me.' That was his account. Afterwards it turned out that at that time in Seville people had offered for sale boiled wine which was not intoxicating but underneath the containers they still kept a container in which they had smuggled real wine (*dakka*, Dozy). This had reached the ears of the *ḥākim* of Seville Qāḍī Abū Bakr al-Ghāfiqī.[82] He had arrested fifteen persons in the market, beheaded them and crucified them on their shops.[83] The others had fled.[84]

---

82 Perhaps this is the *wālī* of Seville Abū Bakr, whom Ibn ʿIdhārī al-Marrākushī: *Al-bayān al-mughrib*, ed. Iḥsān ʿAbbās, IV, p. 77, l. 3, refers to for the year 522/1128. Ibn Bashkuwāl: *Ṣila*, mentions two individuals named Abū Bakr al-Ghāfiqī who have no relevance for us.

83 According to surah 20/71, Pharaoh threatened to have a magician's hands and feet maimed and then to have him crucified. For people who wage war against Islam or stir up unrest, the Koran in surah 5/33 prescribes alternatively execution *or* crucifixion *or* maiming of the hands and feet *or* exile. According to a *ḥadīth*, the same punishment, although without maiming, also applies to Muslims who abandon the faith and fight against Islam (Nasāʾī, VII, pp. 101-02). This was taken over by the Islamic jurists. Otto Spies in 'Religion und Religionen', *Festschrift für Gustav Mensching*, Bonn, 1967, pp. 143-56, has written something on this subject. In practice, however, maiming, execution and crucifixion were often combined with one another. The law-breaker was sometimes executed before crucifixion, sometimes afterwards, and sometimes left to a slow death on the cross. Among the Romans crucifixion served as a means of execution, among the ancient Jews persons who were stoned to death were subsequently hung up by their hands for a short time (Ernst Haenchen: *Der Weg Jesu*, Berlin, 1968, p. 540). In Palestine at the time of Jesus only the Romans had the right to crucify someone; Eduard Lohse: *Die Geschichte des Leidens und Sterbens Jesu Christi*, Gütersloh, 1964, p. 83. In Islam there are examples enough of crucifying living persons who were then either killed on the cross or left to die. But there are at least as many examples which show that the sinner was first killed and only then nailed to the cross — in extreme cases even exhumed for the purpose of crucifixion. Where only 'crucifixion' is mentioned, it can mean 'first execution

and then crucifixion'. Thus Ibn al-Zayyāt: *Kawākib sayyāra*, p. 203, l. 16, only writes about the execution of a murderer in 533/1138-39 in Cairo: 'he was crucified'. But the parallel text in Sakhāwī: *Tuḥfat al-aḥbāb*, p. 316, l. 8, says: 'he was killed and crucified'. The purpose of such crucifixion was to dishonor the delinquent individual and to give a warning to others. It was generally believed on the Muslim side that the alleged substitute who was nailed to the cross in place of Jesus was crucified alive and died on the cross (Nuwayrī: *Al-ilmām bi'l-iᶜlām fī-mā jarat bihī al-aḥkām wa'l-umūr al-maqḍiyya fī waqᶜat al-Iskandariyya*, Hyderabad, 1968-1976, I, p. 98, l. 2; which in fact contradicts the previous sentence, p. 98, ll. 1-2) — a partial concession to the evangelical tradition. Regarding Peter and Paul, on the other hand, it is said that they were both first killed and then crucified upside-down, with their head in the lower position (Nuwayrī, III, p. 328, ll. 9-10) — a form of crucifixion which was occasionally practiced in Islam as well. Qāḍī ᶜIyāḍ (d. 544/1149), still under the Almoravids, in the Mālikite manner left it up to the judge whether to kill a blasphemer of the Prophet (with a sword) or to crucifiy him (alive) (*Shifāᵓ*, Cairo, 1977, pp. 936, 1015). The creator of the Almohad theology, Ibn Tūmart (d. 524/1130), forbade crucifying someone alive. 'If the man deserves to be killed', he said, 'then execute him and crucify him afterwards!' (Baydhaq in E. Lévi-Provençal: *Documents inédits d'histoire almohade*, Paris, 1928, Arabic p. 62/French p. 96), and numerous reports document that this was followed in practice. If it is the case that Abū Bakr al-Ghāfiqī was Abū Bakr the Almoravid governor of Seville, naturally he was not under the law of Ibn Tūmart. But that makes no difference. Our text does not mean that he had some of the fifteen beheaded and the others crucified, but: he had all fifteen first beheaded and then crucified. Here crucified often means simply hung up, exhibited. On this subject the historians of the Shīᶜites and the ᶜAlids especially have a lot to report. Already in 60/680 Muslim b. ᶜAqīl was beheaded in Kūfa, his body and his head were thrown from the roof into the street, and then his body was crucified and his head was sent to Damascus (Masᶜūdī: *Prairies d'or*, ed. Barbier de Meynard et Pavet de Courteille, V, p. 142/ed. Pellat, III, p. 256; Ṭabarī, II, pp. 267, 270). Abū'l-Sarāyā, who led a Shīᶜite revolt in Kūfa, was beheaded in 200/815; his head was 'crucified' in Baghdad on the east bank of the Tigris and his body on the west bank (Abū'l-Faraj al-Iṣfahānī: *Maqātil al-Ṭālibiyyīn*, Cairo, 1949, p. 549). Under Hārūn al-Rashīd an active supporter of the ᶜAlids named Ḥāḍir was beheaded and crucified (*Maqātil* p. 625, l. 1). The Barmakid vizier Jaᶜfar b. Yaḥyā was beheaded in 187/803 and both halves of his body were crucified at different bridges over the Tigris in Baghdad (Jahshiyārī: *Al-wuzarāᵓ wa'l-kuttāb*, Cairo, 1938, p. 234). In 333/944 Mustakfī had Abū'l-Ḥusayn al-Barīdī beheaded and had his head carried through Baghdad and his body crucified on one of the gates at the Tigris (Muḥammad b. ᶜAbd al-Malik al-Hamadhānī: *Takmilat tārīkh al-Ṭabarī*, Beirut, 1961, p. 145). An Armenian local ruler was beheaded and crucified in the 3rd/9th century in Samarra by Mutawakkil (Yaᶜqūbī: *Historiae*, II, p. 298). An agitator in Morocco who presented himself as a descendant of the Fāṭimid family was beheaded in Fez in 611/1214, and his head was sent to the Almohad Abū Yaᶜqūb Yūsuf II in Marrakesh and his body was crucified in Fez (ᶜAbd al-Wāḥid al-Marrākushī: *Al-muᶜjib fī talkhīṣ akhbār al-maghrib*, ed. Dozy, Leiden, 1847, pp. 240-41/trans.

When we once asked him after a journey what he had experienced, he recounted: 'Something so wondrous happened to me myself that I didn't even pay attention to miracles connected with other people. A travel companion often helped me with my ritual ablutions with water as well as with sand. Once in an unguarded moment when I wanted to perform an ablution at the edge of the ship, a rope of the ship knocked me into the sea. But I fell onto a rock. On my friend's giving the alarm, they drew in the sails and sounded the water around the ship with oars until they found me stuck onto the ship and pulled me up. My robe was not even wet. The rock onto which I had fallen had miraculously carried me to the ship and stuck me onto it. The captain affirmed that there had never been a rock here in the sea and that this must have been a miracle of God solely in order to rescue me.'[85]

Gharīb meditated a great deal. One day due to a particular thought the earth became too narrow for him. He rode away on his donkey without any plan and together with his donkey fell into an overgrown well. The donkey — the water in the shaft did not even reach to its knees — formed a kind of bench on which Gharīb remained seated.[86] The animal died and lay leaning against the wall in an upright position. After one day and night a man in a date basket (*maktal*) and with a lit candle lowered himself down and brought along with him a second date basket on another rope. 'He was frightened by me', Gharīb related. 'But when he heard who I was and

---

A. Huici Miranda, Colección de crónicas árabes de la reconquista, IV, *Kitāb al-muʿŷib*, Tetuan, 1955, p. 272). However, the draconian measure of the ruler of Seville in our story does not correspond to the legal punishment for flaunting the Islamic prohibition on drinking wine.

84 The fight against wine is the concern of the Muslim ruling authorities, judiciary, theologians and saints, and a favorite proof of true Islamic piety and of the loyal fulfilment of the injunction 'to command the good and to prohibit what is bad'. Abū Ibrāhīm Isḥāq b. Muḥammad al-Hazrajī (d. 581/1185) by stirring the grapes saw to it that they did not ferment in their container; *Tashawwuf*, p. 229. Ibn al-Ḥājj even forbids vinegar which to begin with is stored as wine; *Mudkhal*, IV, p. 94.

85 Another man of piety who was journeying to Mecca and was obliged to witness scenes of pederasty on the ship simply tied up his bundle and marched overboard. He didn't sink but came to stand on a firm surface ankle-deep in the water. Thereupon he happily went his way and eventually proceeded along the beach arriving in Alexandria before the ship he had left; *Tashawwuf*, pp. 104-05.

86 From this it is clear that Gharīb was not seated astride the donkey but crosswise, with both his legs on the same side.

recognized me, (*156a*) he knew that God had sent him to rescue me, for he referred me to a dead, bloated man who lay below me in the water and whom he had come to take up. It was his brother.' They lifted them both out, and Gharīb was able to ride home again on another donkey as if nothing had happened.

Another time he passed by a hamlet with a caravan. He had to go into it. The caravan waited on his account. Some people took him into a dilapidated mosque but abandoned it in flight when they noticed it was threatening to collapse. Gharīb, who was physically handicapped, was left behind. The mosque actually did fall down, but the wall Gharīb was resting against remained standing in a leaning position, and only collapsed once they had brought him out unharmed.

A friend of his had a milch cow that became ill and didn't give any milk. Gharīb replied: 'You're just saying that so as not to have to serve me any milk', and he wanted to see the cow. Gharīb was taken along, felt the cow's udder and found it was full to bursting. The owner of the cow, having felt it, ascertained the same thing much to his surprise. He milked the cow and gave the milk to his guest. That Gharīb persisted in believing his friend had lied to him, preoccupied the latter for some time.

One day an ascetic visited Gharīb and expressed a desire for fish. But Gharīb's servant found no fish in the market. Gharīb prayed: 'Oh God, bless the fish for this month!' The servant had to go to the market again and now he found fish in great abundance that had just been caught by the fishermen. There had never been so many fish available as in that month.

Gharīb had a cat that once urinated on his prayer-rug. (*156b*) Gharīb put a curse on it: 'How cheerfully your urine comes forth! May your eyes come forth the same way!' The next morning the cat only had two holes in its head instead of eyes.

Every time he recited the Koran, when he reached surah 9 (*Tawba*, 'Repentance') he would suddenly stop. He came to have an inner resistance and dislike toward it. Then in a dream someone asked him: 'You come to a halt in the Koran and you have a feeling of resistance and an aversion to it, do you?', and tugged him by the earlobe so violently that it caused him to bleed. He had to recite the surah for the person and was able to do so in the dream without interruption. When he woke up, his ear was hurt but he now felt a special love for surah 9 and whenever he read out the Koran, he could hardly wait (*lā yuṣaddiq annahū*, cf. Dozy) till he came to it and recited it by heart.

I said to him one time: 'I know you only have to ask God to give you something and He gives it to you. You probably know the greatest name of God.'[87] He replied: 'Yes, and it is: "in the name of God, the Compassionate, the Merciful". With this name I ask God for everything.'

One time in worn-out rags he came upon people in the desert who found his presence to be a blessing and asked him to invoke God on their behalf. In return they offered him a robe and expressed the hope that because of this the blessing for them would be even greater. But he fled from them and entered the city. I went to greet him. He had me buy him a soft cotton robe, put it on and said: 'Thanks to God, I have been saved from temptation.' I asked: 'From what temptation?' Gharīb: 'You will see shortly.' Two days later those people came to him when I happened to be with him, and brought him a shirt, a turban, a pair of trousers (*izār*) and a mantle (*ridā*ʾ). He could tell them he had everything. 'Bring it rather to someone who deserves it besides me!' And that was that. A few days later I learned that they had previously attacked a person and stolen these clothes from him.

A student or friend of Gharīb's was reading *fiqh* in a study circle. Gharīb sent a messenger to tell him: 'Bring a robe to your father! He is sitting among the gardens naked.' Indeed, he found him in the specified place and delivered a robe to him. He had been shipwrecked at sea, lost everything and come ashore naked. The father and son asked Gharīb how he had known this. He replied: 'Through a chance thought (*khaṭra*).'

One day he sent a student or a friend with books he had copied (*157a*) to another locality to sell them. He told him to give away the proceeds there as alms. The caravan was attacked and plundered. The robbers took away everything except the animals and things that were too heavy for them. The travel-bag containing the books weighed scarcely a third of a *qinṭār*. Everyone of the robbers was well capable of carrying two *qinṭār*s. But when they wanted to take it with them, it suddenly acquired a weight as if it contained iron and

87 Fritz Meier: *Die Fawāʾiḥ al-ǧamāl wa-fawātiḥ al-ǧalāl des Naǧm ad-dīn al-Kubrā*, Wiesbaden, 1957, Introduction, pp. 136-54. Richard Gramlich: *Die schiitischen Derwischorden Persiens. Zweiter Teil: Glaube und Lehre*, Wiesbaden, 1976, pp. 30-33. Georges C. Anawati: 'Le Nom suprême de Dieu (*Ism Allāh al-aʿẓam*)', in *Atti del Terzo Congresso di Studi Arabi e Islamici Ravello 1966*, Naples, 1967, pp. 7-58. According to Ibn Māja, *janāʾiz* 55 (II, p. 1267, no. 3855-59), Muḥammad did not designate the *basmala* in particular as the greatest name of God.

lead so that after futile efforts they let it lie. The student or friend sold the books as intended and gave away the money thus realized.

Gharīb became paralyzed and blind due to an illness. After eight months he found it tedious and had his wife bring him to the mosque where the seriously ill were accustomed to gather for prayer. She and another woman carried him there in a mat and set him down near a wall. A young man greeted him and introduced himself as Hudhayl — about whom Gharīb had already heard. To the question what had made him paralyzed and blind, Gharīb replied: 'The command of God, against which there is no resistance, and His will, against which no one can do anything.' The man spoke: 'Tell your wife she should bring me water for a minor ritual ablution!' She brought the water. The man washed himself. The used water dripped into a container. He wiped Gharīb's face and knees with it, pronounced a few incomprehensible words and disappeared. Gharīb bade his wife to take him home. He could walk and made his way home supported by her hand. And at home he asked his wife: 'Who put the books over there?' and he pointed in their direction. His wife said: 'They're not there!' He replied: 'Yes they are!' 'Then give me the book with the black binding', she said. He handed it to her. Beside herself with joy, the wife exclaimed: 'Not only can you walk but you can see as well!' He: 'Through the praise of God and the blessing (*baraka*) of the pious young man. It was Hudhayl who is famous for his miracles and the effects of his blessings (*barakāt*). Be on the look out (*157b*), he will no doubt come on Friday to visit me and to congratulate me on my recovery.' And in fact he did come. The wife asked him to invoke God on her behalf. He prayed for her and congratulated Gharīb on his cure, also prayed on his behalf and then disappeared again.

I knew Gharīb before, during and after his above-mentioned illness, but was not present at his burial. His death, however, was recounted to me.

Abū ʿAbdallāh Mālik b. ʿAlī, known as *al-Qalānisī*. An expert on the Koran. He gave Koranic instruction to boys. He was characterized by asceticism and fear of God. He spoke sparingly. He never gave instruction in his house to more than ten boys at a time and only accepted a new pupil when another one had left the school. Otherwise he made caps (*qalānis*).[88] With the income from his teaching he

---

88 Muḥammad b. Qassūm did the same work; *Rūḥ al-quds*, p. 88/Austin, p. 84. The Sufis often lived from the work of their own hands. Cf. *Die Vita des Scheich Abū Isḥāq al-*

nourished his family and with the proceeds from his caps he supported himself.[89] A pious man once performed his prescribed prayers (*ṣallā maktūbatahū*)[90] and fell asleep in a state of ritual purity. In a dream he beheld the Resurrection, the gathering of the people and a ladder from the heavens to earth, on which angels descended with fiery hooks in their hands. However, from out of the earth an angel came before them with a fiery lance that bore several prongs and asked them what they wanted. They replied: 'We want to exterminate the inhabitants of this village because they are all oppressors.' The angel retorted: 'Don't you know that Mālik al-Qalānisī lives here?' They: 'By God, it is good that you have reminded us of him. Were we to exterminate them, then we ourselves would be in danger of being exterminated by God.' The man woke up and came to Qalānisī to tell him this. I happened to be with him. Qalānisī bade him to keep his dream secret.

I was not at his funeral. But someone who was on hand told me that when they carried him to where the prayer over his corpse was to be performed, they beheld that the desert and the mountains, as far as the eye could see, were filled with people dressed in bright white clothes who prayed over him along with those present.[91]

Abū'l-ᶜAbbās Aḥmad b. ᶜUbaydallāh, known as *al-Fāʾida*. An admonitory preacher, ascetic, uttered many religious wise sayings, preached in a mosque which belonged to him,[92] was open, simple, trustworthy, unpretentious and irrefutable.

A poor man once came up to him during his sermon (*158a*): 'I have nothing to wear, the cold is affecting me badly, ask the people

---

Kāzarūnī, Introduction, p. 18, ftn. 2; Richard Gramlich: *Die schiitischen Derwischorden Persiens. Zweiter Teil: Glaube und Lehre*, pp. 436-40.

89 He perhaps adopted this division so as not 'to sell his religion for the world' (see ftn. 57 above; p. 493 *169b*, below). What he gave to his family he could consider as alms.

90 The word appears to have a singular (*WKAS*) and a plural (Dozy) meaning. Here the singular fits better, whereas at *166b*, p. 486 below, the plural is better. In the *ḥadīth* one finds the singular *ṣalāh maktūba* much more frequently than the plural *ṣalawāt maktūba* (see *Concordance*). Often one reads *al-ṣalawāt al-maktūbāt* for the plural.

91 These 'people' (*unās*) in white can have been mysterious saints as well as *jinn* or angels.

92 This is often the case: here *172a*; *Tashawwuf*, p. 167, ll. 14-15. *Die Vita des Scheich Abū Isḥāq al-Kāzarūnī*, Introduction, p. 47, last two lines. Fritz Meier: *Abū Saᶜīd-i Abū l-Ḫayr (357-440/967-1049). Wirklichkeit und legende*, Acta Iranica 11, Leiden, 1976, pp. 430-31.

to give me a garment!' It was not in accordance with his practice to take up a collection.[93] But the man persisted in his demand. Fāʾida said to someone who was present: 'Give him a garment! In return God will give you another one in Paradise.' The person addressed replied jokingly: 'Your kind normally only asks God', and was about to give him something. But then Fāʾida no longer wanted anything from him and said to the beggar he should come to see him tomorrow in his house. He brought his sermon to a close and went home. At night he rose and prayed: 'Oh God, clothe so-and-so and do not humiliate me in his eyes but show him Your omnipotence!' He had scarcely said this when someone knocked and delivered money to him, saying: 'With this buy a garment for a poor person you think is worthy!' He accepted the money and gave thanks to God. In the morning the beggar appeared before him. Fāʾida went with him to the market and bought him a fine garment. Then he told him to go to the man he had asked yesterday during the sermon to give him a garment and to say to him: 'I now have a garment thanks to God, not thanks to you.'[94] The beggar went to see the man and the latter nearly died out of regret for the heavenly reward he had lost.

One day Fāʾida came across a tax and customs inspector (*mushārif*[95]) with a customs official (*muʿāmil al-dīwān*) who had been called to account for something by the government authorities (*ʿalayhi tabiʿatun li'l-sulṭān*). He had ordered his henchmen (*aʿwān*) to remove the man's turban from his head and strangle him with it. They were just then giving him a whipping. He fell forward and was

---

93 Similar to *164b* below. Refusing to take up such a collection proves it was a practice. We have numerous reports about the subject. One may compare for instance my *Vita des Kāzarūnī*, Introduction, pp. 45-53, 70; *Abū Saʿīd*, p. 67; money for personal needs of the Sufis in R. Gramlich: *Die schiitischen Derwischorden Persiens, Zweiter Teil*, pp. 150-51. In the Christian Church there was the *karaza li-shakhṣ*; Ibn Abi Useibia, ed. August Müller, Königsberg i. Pr., 1884, I, p. 172, l. 5; August Müller: 'Über Text und Sprachgebrauch von Ibn Abî Uṣeibiʿa's Geschichte der Ärzte', *Sb. kgl. bayer. Ak. Wiss., Philosophisch-philologische Cl. 1884*, p. 966.

94 *Bi-ḥamdihī lā bi-ḥamdika*, the same as in *151b* above: *Yuḥmadu'llāhu lā yuḥmadu'l-qāḍī*, pointed thus; also possible perhaps is *bi-ḥamdi'llāhī lā bi-ḥamdi'l-qāḍī*.

95 E. Lévi-Provençal: *L'Espagne musulmane au Xème siècle*, Paris, 1932, pp. 98-99: *almojarifes*, inspecteurs des impôts et des douanes, comme les *mušrif*. G.S. Colin: 'El-Maqṣad', *Arch. Maroc.* 26, Paris, 1926, p. 185, no. 178: administrateur de la douane. Fagnan: *Additions aux dictionnaires arabes*, p. 87b. Maqrīzī: *Ittiʿāẓ al-ḥunafāʾ bi-akhbār al-aʾimma al-fāṭimiyyīn al-khulafāʾ*, ed. Jamāl al-Dīn al-Shayyāl and Muḥammad Ḥilmī Muḥ. Aḥmad, Cairo, 1967-73, III, p. 492a (index). Yāfiʿī: *Rawḍ*, p. 282, l. 15: *mushārif awqāfihā*.

dragged away on his face and beaten further. Fāʾida shouted at the inspector (*mushrif*): 'If you really feared God, you would act more friendly to this weak human being who is in your captivity and completely at your mercy.' The inspector (*mushrif*) had Fāʾida arrested, beaten and locked up. Fāʾida, who had wanted to buy something for his family to eat, was worried about them. But in a dream the Prophet appeared to him and reassured him: 'Be of good cheer, we have brought your family something for dinner, tomorrow you will be free again and you will see your enemy suffer the same treatment you have suffered today.' In the morning the cases of those who had been arrested were presented to the governnor (*wālī*), including that of Fāʾida. The governor knew Fāʾida and asked what crime he had committed. They informed him that he had reproached the inspector (*mushārif*) in connection with the helpless offender. (*158b*) The governor had them fetch Fāʾida and apologized to him. Then he had the inspector (*mushārif*) summoned, shouted at him and had him beaten and thrown in jail. Fāʾida came home and found that everything was just fine. The previous night someone had placed before the door an ample amount of flour, butter, honey and oil, and they had heard a voice say: 'Abū'l-ᶜAbbās (Fāʾida) has sent you this through me.' Fāʾida thanked (*ḥamida*) God and had before him proof of the Prophet's saying that Satan never presents himself in the shape of the Prophet.[96]

Fāʾida had seven children. One day, however, he felt that in his poverty they were too great a burden and he uttered the wish: 'God free me from you!' Thereupon they died one after the other in the space of less than one month.[97] Afterwards Fāʾida and his wife were then able to live better.

When I left him he was alive but I do not know whether he is still living now.

Abū ᶜAbdallāh Muḥammad b. ᶜUthmān al-Maghribī, known as *al-Rammād*. A dignified shaykh who continually fasted. He wove clothing. Whenever he began to do well in business, he immediately rid himself of his prosperity. Seventeen times he gave away everything he had. But he never wove on commission for others because he feared he might lose a thread of the yarn given him and for that reason fall into confusion and doubt. Instead he would buy his own yarn, first weave something for himself and then try to sell it. In

---

96 *Concordance*, VI, p. 170b, *tamaththala*.

97 P. 442 above. *Rūḥ al-quds*, p. 98/Austin, p. 99.

buying the yarn, he would weigh out the measure just barely, but when he paid for it, he would weigh out the silver amply. He owned a workshop that he sold from and where his journeymen (read *ṣunnāᶜuhū*) worked. One day a Berber came with some yarn and wanted to have him make a cloth (*thawb*) from it. Rammād replied: 'I never do that. I only weave with my own yarn.' The Berber insulted him in the coarsest way. A worker (? *ṣāḥib*) took Rammād's side but without doing anything further. The Berber picked up an instrument (*adāh*) used in weaving and threw it at him. The instrument banged against the wall, bounced back into the Berber's face and knocked out one of his eyes. He fell into a rage and once again began abusing Rammād (*159a*). Rammād said: 'Isn't the injury to your sight enough for you? God bring damage to your whole body!' The Berber grabbed hold of the worker and wanted to drag him before the governor (*wālī*). People tried to bring about a conciliation, when a loud noise was heard and everyone ran toward where it came from. The Berber let go of the worker and rushed in that direction as well. A horse had broken loose. It forced its way through the people, dealt the Berber, who was preoccupied with his eye, so disastrous a kick in the head that a piece of his head flew off and he fell down dead.

Between the evening prayer and the night-time prayer Rammād was never to be seen. No one could tell me where he was. Then one time I watched him without being observed from the mid-morning prayer onwards. He went off to a remote mosque and there performed twelve prostrations of prayer, accompanying each one with the first surah and nothing else. When he was finished, he noticed me at the entrance. We had not yet become acquainted. He asked me who I was, and then I asked him why he only recited the first surah and none of the other surahs. He replied: 'I love the easiest and the best words,[98] and after all it says in surah 11/7: "So that He might test you to see which of you would act the *best*." My dear friend, I cannot add anything to what you have seen. But do not reveal this place of mine to anyone, in fact come and spend time here yourself. It will profit you!' I retorted: 'Doesn't the law say that places do not

98 A certain Fāṭima bt. Abī'l-Muthannā in Seville at the end of the 6th/12th century got along solely with the first surah and used it for everything; *Rūḥ al-quds*, p. 126/Austin, p. 143. Not in W.S. Cuperus: *Al-Fātiḥa dans la pratique religieuse musulmane du Maroc*, diss. Utrecht, 1973.

bestow sanctity?'[99] He replied: 'They bestow sanctity as long as they are sanctified for His sake (= for the sake of God).'

Rammād related to me: 'I once saw Abū'l-ᶜAbbās al-Khaḍir on one of my journeys. He said to me: "My brother, guard against being too bold toward the Sublime, for there is no more slippery and unsafe staircase than this. If you see a man of piety, make an effort to receive his blessing (*tabarruk*) and to ask him to invoke God on your behalf! If you hear of one, hasten to visit him; that will bring you closest to God and obtain for you in the quickest way God's mercy and forgiveness. If he performs the ritual prayers somewhere, then you pray there also,[100] even if you haven't seen him there yourself, because the tracks of men of piety leave traces in the stones and rocks, and the effects of the blessing of these locations will last until the Day of the Resurrection."'

One of his friends (or followers or disciples or companions, *aṣḥāb*) recounted to me: 'I saw him early one morning going to the sea and I followed him because I said to myself (*159b*) he is surely going to a holy place to perform the ritual prayers. But he marched from the shore out into the sea, sat down on a rock, spread out his prayer-rug and mumbled something. A fish lept into his prayer-rug. He said: "This is not enough." Another one lept out of the water, and so it continued until ten fish lay on the prayer-rug. He said nothing further but three more fish lept onto it. When he gathered up the prayer-rug and turned around, he saw me and asked what brought me here. I replied: "I am simply running after you and follow you as my

99 Subsequently *aḥadan* was added so that it would have to be translated: Doesn't the law state that places do not sanctify anyone? The added *aḥadan* replaces *insānan* 'any person' in the original wording of the *Muwaṭṭaʾ*, *waṣāyā* 7; likewise according to *Concordance* s.v. *insān*, I, p. 125b, final entry. The reference to Muslim, *waṣāyā* 7, in *Concordance* s.v. *qaddasa*, V, p. 319b, should be corrected. Furthermore in the original wording it says: 'The earth does not sanctify any person', not: 'Places do not sanctify'. That no place *is* in its own right sanctified (and consequently cannot bestow sanctity on anyone) is a frequently expressed idea. It is especially evoked in connection with the Black Stone at the Kaᶜba; Nāṣir-i Khusraw: *Safarnāma*, Kaviani Berlin, 1340, p. 125, below; Batanūnī: *Al-riḥla al-ḥijāziyya*, Cairo, 1329, pp. 155-56. Nor is Medina holy in itself, literally 'ennobled', but only through the immigration and the residence of the Prophet, as Ibn al-Ḥājj: *Mudkhal*, I, pp. 256-57, emphasizes, and then especially certain localities in Medina: 'Things are ennobled through him; he is not ennobled through them.' Thus the month Rabīᶜ I is not holy in itself but only because the Prophet was born in it: *Mudkhal*, II, p. 29. Indeed, this is specifically arranged so that it does not seem as if the Prophet is venerable because of the month (ibid.).

100 Cf. the previous paragraph.

leader." He: "In any case your footsteps have been accepted, that is to say God has bestowed three more fish than usual for your sake." I thanked God (*ḥamidtu*) and said: "I will only accept them roasted." He: "I myself have not dared make such an audacious demand. But go off, they will follow after you just as you wish." Another of his followers (*aṣḥāb*) brought a wooden bowl with three roasted fish to my house. I ate them together with my family, and there was still some left over for another time.'

One of his followers related to me: 'Once I saw him in the gardens in the shade of a willow-tree. He was eating something like resin (or gum, *ṣamgh*) and while he slowly chewed, he said: "Oh God, make that which You have bestowed on us good and include us among the men of piety whom[101] You have created (?)!" When he set eyes on me, he told me to have some with him. I ate. It tasted delicious, better than everything I had eaten up till then. While we were eating, this food kept on dropping from the tree. I implored him to explain to me this extraordinary yield of a willow-tree. He said: "My dear friend, this tree is called 'the Host of the saints' (*Ḍayyāfat al-awliyāʾ*). On my travels I found beneath it a man named Muᶜallā who had vowed not to set foot in any other settlement besides Mecca and Medina. He was eating this food, invited me to join him just as I invited you and told me what I'm telling you about the tree." I praised God (*ḥamidtu*) and left the place with him', so my informant concluded. 'I did return again at a later time but found nothing of this food either on the tree or under it.'[102]

I left Rammād in the Maghreb (*160a*) when he was about to go on the pilgrimage. A person who accompanied him on the journey told me later that he reached Mecca, performed the sacred rites and also visited the grave of the Prophet in Medina. 'Then he set out to return with us. But when he reached the bay of Rammāda (*jūn Rammāda*),[103] one of your (!) districts (*min aᶜmālika*), an illness came over him which carried him off within two days. We dug him a grave and after having washed him and wrapped him in his clothes, we went off to perform our ablutions for the prayer over the corpse. But when we came back from the ablutions, we found him already

---

101 Rather unsure, somewhat overwritten text.

102 God, in a miraculous way, saw to the nourishment of a man who had vowed never to set foot in any other settlement except Mecca and Medina. Why Rammād alone is allowed to enjoy the extraordinary food from the willow-tree is not explained.

103 On *jūn Rammāda* see pp. 428 above.

laid to rest in his grave. We scattered the earth over him and continued on our way.'[104]

Abū Muḥammad ᶜAbdallāh[105] *b. Sulaymān*, known as *al-Bāghī*, referring to the place Bāghu (= Priego)[106] in Andalus. His father (Sulaymān) was a man of piety and is said to have prayed to God to make his son a pious man and in turn to bestow on him pious sons as well. His prayer was answered, and ᶜAbdallāh has three sons who, despite having much property, are meticulous in the attention they give to religion. They maintain a common cashbox (*ṣundūq*), and each of them takes from it what he needs. As far as I am aware, they have never yet worked out their accounts with one another.

One day I saw ᶜAbdallāh come down from the mountain carrying a large jug of water on his shoulder. I asked him: 'Couldn't one of your sons have seen to this?' He replied: 'Were I to betray them, they would betray me in turn. I share with them equally in the chores. This is what my father particularly asked me to do on his deathbed when he pronounced that prayer which laid the foundation for our welfare. This world and the world to come are two scales of a balance. If the one sinks downward, the other rises. Think of surah 72/16: "If they had kept to the straight path, We would have given them abundant water to drink." May God cause you to recognize the truth as truth and cause you to follow it as well! May He cause you to recognize the false as false and grant that you shun it!' Thereupon he left me.

One night he stayed in a *ribāṭ* outside the city Rūṭa (= Rota) in Andalus by the sea (by Jerez de la Frontera). At midnight a bright light shone through the windows that looked out toward the sea (160b) and filled the entire mosque. He beheld alongside himself a

---

104 The deceased can have been buried by mysterious saints (for instance the saintly hierarchy of the *abdāl*), *jinn* or angels. An example of involving angels occurs in the 2nd story in Yāfiᶜī: *Rawḍ al-rayāḥīn*, p. 31, and in the 324th story, p. 208. Those who recovered the corpse in the 31st story, ibid., p. 50, remain unknown.

105 Written over it is *Muḥammad*.

106 On this place name cf. Dozy: *Edrîsî*, French p. 251, ftn. 1. Sometimes written *Bāghuh* and in this form often read mistakenly as *Bāgha*; *Rūḥ al-quds*, p. 106; on the other hand, correctly p. 122/Austin correctly, pp. 110 and 134; Ibn al-Abbār: *Takmila*, ed. Codera, incorrect in the index, correct in the text passages. Regarding this frequently occurring mistake see my 'Aussprachefragen des älteren neupersisch', *Oriens* 27-28, 1981, p. 174. *Tashawwuf*, p. 270, l. 9 and ftn. 4, forms the gentilicium as *Bāghānī* and *Bāghī*. The place figures in Ḥimyarī's *Rawḍ miᶜṭār*, p. 122, under *Bīghū*.

figure who introduced himself as Khaḍir and asked him how he was. Bāghī said: 'Well now, where do you live? I want to visit you when I have a longing for you.' Khaḍir replied: 'I have no permanent place. Wherever I am remembered, that is where I am. I wander through the whole world, even the uninhabited parts, and visit the saints and inquire everywhere how the godfearing are doing.' He added: 'I visit you as often as God makes it possible.' Thereupon he left Bāghī, and once again it grew dark in the mosque.[107]

Bāghī: 'Khaḍir once visited me in the night on ᶜArafa[108] and spoke to me: "Yes, give my greetings to the house of God (the Kaᶜba) and to the Prophet (in Medina)!" Then he disappeared. Another time he came again and asked whether I had a wish he could fulfill. I answered: "Yes, ask God for forgiveness for me!" He retorted: "You ask God for mercy for me as well and ask Him not to punish me in Hell." I was astonished that as the topmost (*zimām*) of the Friends of God he should be in need of my prayer. He replied: "No one is as dear to God as Muḥammad, and yet we also pray for him and pronounce a blessing on his behalf. He even asked God to do this, and God as well did it for him."[109]

Bāghī related to me: 'Near my house was the shop where a weaver (*ḥāʾik*) did his work. When I would get bored with being in the house, I would sit down in front of his shop. One day I found him in deep sorrow. At first he gave no reply to my questions. Only when I said I could perhaps help him did he come round to speaking. He said: "You know the young man who works at this loom (*minwāl*) every day. He would weave thirty ells a day. That is as much as three journeymen (*ṣunnāᶜ*) normally produce. I gave him his wages every night, of which he didn't keep a single grain till the next day. Yesterday at noon I found him sitting before the loom without doing any work. But he had two fine flat-breads in front of him, the kind that are only baked in Aleppo. At my request he gave me some bread to eat as well. It became clear to me that he was one of the *ᶜāmilūn*.[110]

---

107 *Tashawwuf*, p. 339: Abū Muḥammad Yaskar (d. 598/1202) on a dark night entered the mosque of Fez and illuminated the whole space. He performed ritual prayers and when he departed the mosque became dark again. *Tashawwuf*, p. 381, penult. line: Another individual illuminated a cave.

108 From the 8th to the 9th of Dhū'l-Ḥijja.

109 Allusion to surah 33/56: 'God and His angels bless the Prophet. Oh believers, do you also bless him and greet him as is fitting!'

110 'The active', what is probably meant is persons who translate their religious knowledge into religious action and in particular act as benefactors. It occurs again in *165b*, *171a* and

After he had received his wages that evening (*161a*) and left, I had the workshop closed and I followed him without being noticed. I saw how on his way he distributed the money to the poor. When he arrived at the sea, he performed a ritual ablution,[111] looked around cautiously and then walked out onto the sea.[112] How he did this[113] I could not make out. My curiosity induced me to spend the night right there hidden by a wall from behind which I had observed him. At daybreak he appeared again and unnoticed I followed him back to my shop. Here he waited until I opened the door for him and went inside with him. Now I could no longer remain silent. When the workers (*ṣunnāʿ*) were present, I declared to him: 'I would like you again to give us some of the same bread you gave us to eat yesterday.' He darted a glance at me which almost killed me. Once more I attacked him the same way (*fa-radadtu ʿalayhi bi-an*), saying to him: 'If I told you to take me with you out on the sea the way you walked out on the sea yesterday, how would you do that?' He exclaimed: 'What are you talking about?' I described to him what I had observed yesterday, one thing after the other. He said to the other journeymen: 'Do you see now? Your master (*muʿallimukum*) is making up stories today! He must be ill.' Then he waited around a while, and at a

---

perhaps also *166a*. The meaning comes perhaps from *ʿamal* in *171b*. The basis to the term is the Koranic meaning of *ʿāmilūn* in surah 3/136; 29/58; 39/74, which R. Paret translates 'die (im Guten) tätigen'. On the grave of Ḥumayd, who died in 634/1236 and was the caretaker of Dhū'l-Nūn's grave in the Qarāfa in Cairo, is written surah 37/61: 'And for the like of this (i.e. Paradise) let the active be active!' Here 'the active' in fact means no more than 'one'. Sakhāwī: *Tuḥfat al-aḥbāb*, p. 340, editor's footnote. Sahl al-Tustarī: *Tafsīr*, Cairo, 1329, p. 53 (on surah 15/40): 'People are all dead except for the scholars. The scholars are all asleep except for the active (*ʿāmilūn*). The active are all beguiled except for the chosen. And the chosen are in great danger.'

111 Sea water is allowed for washing; Nuwayrī: *Ilmām*, II, pp. 254-55. This is important not only for cases where drinking water becomes scarce on a ship, but also for pilgrims on the Red Sea who must enter a consecrated state on the ship and in so doing undertake a major ritual ablution; cf. Saleh Soubhy: *Pèlerinage à la Mecque et à Médine*, Cairo, 1894, pp. 52-53; H. Kazem-Zadeh: 'Relation d'un Pèlerinage à la Mecque en 1910-1911', *Revue du Monde Musulman*, offprint Paris, 1912, pp. 57-58.

112 See ftn. 72 above.

113 *Kayfa dhahaba*. One would expect instead *ayna dhahaba* 'where he went', but *kayfa kāna yakūnu ʿamaluka* 'how would you do that', a few lines further down in the text, supports retaining the translation 'how'.

moment when no one was watching he disappeared. That was the reason for my sadness.'"[114]

Abū'l-Walīd Khālid b. Maᶜbad al-Shāṭibī. Died while still a young man, before he had really entered the world and been able to travel around. Born and raised in Shāṭiba (Játiva). Spoiled by his parents, when ten years old he fell in with a crowd of people who were encircling an ascetic named *ᶜAtīq al-Mallāḥ*. The latter had hidden himself from them in a ruined shop and didn't want anything to do with them. But he espied the boy, told him to come closer and kissed him between both eyes. Shāṭibī attached himself to him, and they went together to the house of his parents. (*161b*) He asked his parents to dress him in rags similar to the ones the ascetic was wearing, and to let him wander off with the ascetic. The parents did everything the youngster wanted. The ascetic warned him about the long, hard road he had before him, and told him he could only accompany him if his parents gave their permission. The parents came out of the house and handed over their son to the ascetic, or as they said, to God. The boy remained with him until he grew up.

I met him in a region of Andalus as he went along humbly and didn't dare to raise his sight to the sky. I accompanied him for a while and by my friendly words I got him to tell me why he never looked up. Shāṭibī explained: 'For twenty years now I have not looked at the sky out of shame for Him who has raised it on high without supports and has counted the number of its uncountable stars.[115] I only discern the advent of dawn when I see its light on the ground.'

He never ate anything during the daytime except on the day of breaking the fast and on the day of sacrifice.[116]

One time he came across a host of almost a hundred Christian horsemen. He cried out: 'God is great!' Then God's host appeared

---

114 As in *154a*.

115 This is also recounted about Abū Yaᶜqūb Yūsuf b. al-Shaffāf; Bādisī: *Maqṣad*, trans. Colin, p. 82.

116 If he only broke his fast on the 10th of Dhū'l-Ḥijja — and this is the meaning of the words *yawmay al-fiṭr wa'l-aḍḥā* — then in his excessive zeal he would contravene the law which disapproves of fasting on the 11th, 12th and 13th of Dhū'l-Ḥijja. Ibn Saᶜd, II, 1, p. 134, ll. 9-19; Th.W. Juynboll: *Handbuch des islāmischen Gesetzes*, Leiden-Leipzig, 1910, p. 156. Dhū'l-Nūn al-Miṣrī responded to the question as to why fasting was disapproved of (*kuriha*) on these days: 'One is a guest of God and a guest eats'; *Ḥilya*, IX, p. 379, ll. 18-19.

and defeated the enemies of God.[117] A shout from the host of God went through their midst and they scattered. The horse of the one man fell down with its rider,[118] another fell from his horse, yet another threw away his weapons, one of them dismounted, took off his breastplate and fled to a hiding place, still another lost his unit and was seized by lions and attacked by wolves and hyenas (!). Only very few escaped.

One day he suddenly came upon a man in the desert who had knocked a woman to the ground and chained her (*162a*) and intended to rape her. Shāṭibī tried to stop him from doing this. The man came at him with a sword. But the sword stuck in its sheath. He pressed the sheath against the left side of his chest and pulled on the hilt. The blade struck his neck arteries and severed them so that he fell to the ground dead.[119] Shāṭibī undid the chains from the woman and released her after this judgement by God.

One day he saw close to the coast a Christian ship with Muslim prisoners on board who had been captured in an attack on a Muslim ship. He cried out: 'Come to the shore! To the shore!' Then the wind fixed (?)[120] the sails toward the mainland and drove the ship so impetuously toward the shore that the crew cut the ropes of the sails. The ship ran aground without sails. The Muslims immediately at-

117 Read *fa-ẓahara* instead of simply *ẓahara*. By God's host is meant the angels. Help through the angels is already Koranic: surah 33/9 (referring to the War of the Ditch in the year 627), surah 9/26 (referring to the Battle of Ḥunayn in 630). But already at the Battle of Badr in 624 the Muslims are supposed to have been supported by angels; Ibn Hishām, ed. Wüstenfeld, I, p. 474; J. Wellhausen: *Muhammed in Medina*, Berlin, 1882, p. 56. Ibn ᶜAbbās maintained the thesis that the angels had really only participated in the fighting at Badr. At other battles they were only present in order to swell the numbers; Ibn Hishām I, p. 450. Later someone claims to have seen angels fighting on the side of Mukhtār; Balādhurī: *Ansāb al-ashrāf*, V, ed. Goitein, p. 234, ll. 7-12. And thereafter quite frequently. But supernatural helpers are sometimes prophets or saints or *jinn* or remain unknown. The idea can be connected and mixed up with that of 'the Furious Host' and 'the Wild Hunt'.

118 *Yataqanṭaru bihī farasuhū*. The horseman can also be the subject: *taqanṭara al-sulṭān (Lājīn) bi'l-maydān*; Zetterstéen: *Beiträge zur Geschichte der Mamlūkensultane*, Leiden, 1919, p. 44, l. 8/Ibn al-Dawādārī: *Kanz al-durar*, ed. Haarmann, VIII, p. 371, l. 8.

119 In the 296th story in Yāfiᶜī's *Rawḍ al-rayāḥīn*, p. 192, a man of criminal disposition who rents out mules suffers the same accident with a knife which would not come out of its sheath.

120 Illegible. The general shape of the writing and the number of cusps permit one to read *fa-thabbatat* 'fixed'. But the pointing, which I find incomprehensible, forbids this. 'The wind swelled the sails' would be: *fa-ᶜabbaʾat*... This is not what is written.

tacked from the land and freed the prisoners. Now the enemy ended up as captives or were massacred.

Abū ʿAbdallāh Muḥammad b. Maṭar al-Arkushī (MS Adhkushī or Azkushī[121]). I left him while he was in the prime of his life. He had never done anything that is forbidden or neglected a religious duty.

I experienced the following miracle on his part. In a particular city of Andalus someone cried out: 'You warriors on the path of God, the Resurrection has dawned, and the tongues (?)[122] of the Christians have already reached the wall of the fortress!' The people rushed for their weapons, shut the gates of the city and manned the fortifications. Then behold, the plain was swarming with the enemy. An officer, however, had already gone out through an open gate with his troop and stopped before the gate. The people on the battlements were directing him forward. Just then the Christians attacked him from behind. Among those on the fortification was also Arkushī. The Muslims cried out: 'Abū ᶜAbdallāh, don't you see the plight the Muslims are in and the victory of the Christians that is threatening? Pray to God for us!' He said a few words to himself, went up onto a tower of the fortress and waved his mantle (*ridāʾ*)[123] at the enemy (*162b*), shouting: 'Away with you! Disperse from here!' I have never seen a host break up more quickly than this one did.

A person who had made the pilgrimage with Arkushī informed me: 'Once when the caravan had encamped and there was no fire for cooking, he went to a long-extinguished fire of an earlier caravan and stuck a stick into it. The stick caught fire, gave off smoke and the people of the caravan took fire from him to prepare their food.

An emir of his locality, in the slaughtering for a big feast (*walīma*), made use of the livestock of the inhabitants as well. Our Arkushī owned an ox for ploughing. The emir took it away from him and brought it to his own stable. But the ox escaped in among the horses. His mule stepped into the place where the ox had stood and was slaughtered. The mistake was only discovered when they noticed the mule's skull among the heads of the slaughtered animals. The emir

---

121 From Arcos (de la Frontera). In Cairo around 700/1300 there was a *madrasa azkashiyya* (Ibn Abī'l-Wafāʾ: *Al-jawāhir al-muḍiyya fī ṭabaqāt al-ḥanafiyya*, Cairo, 1978, I, p. 368, l. 6) or *azkūjiyya* (*Durar kāmina*, I, p. 358, l. 3, no. 892).

122 Probably not *asinna* 'lances' instead of *alsina*.

123 One waves with a piece of clothing; *Tashawwuf*, p. 175, l. 7. A shipwrecked person on an island, *Rawḍ al-rayāḥīn*, p. 193, l. 3. With the sleeve, Ibn al-Jawzī: *Bustān al-wāʿiẓīn*, Cairo, 1934, p. 301, penult. line. Lane's *Dict.*: *thawwaba*.

returned the ox to Arkushī and asked him for forgiveness and to invoke God on his behalf. As for the feast, absolutely no one ate any of the meat because the mule is not an edible animal.[124]

I left Arkushī while he was still living. I do not know what has become of him.

3. PEOPLE FROM THE SAME COUNTRIES (WHOM I DID NOT SEE MYSELF BUT) ABOUT WHOM ONLY RELIABLE EYEWITNESSES HAVE INFORMED ME.[125]

The chief judge of Ceuta Ibn Yarbūᶜ — I have forgotten his actual name — related to me that he possessed a fertile garden which was watched over by a guardian (*ḥāris*).[126] After his death a man was presented to him who wished to take over this job. He was hired, but would always leave the garden unattended just when the fruits had become ripe. Whenever the judge went there, he never found him on hand. He called the man before him and took him to task. The guardian responded: 'I will be responsible for everything that is taken away.' The judge now engaged one of his slaves to steal fruits from the garden and bring them to him in a basket. He wanted to show the guardian that his service (*163a*) was of no worth. The slave climbed into the garden and did as he was ordered. But he couldn't climb back over the wall with the fruits. He was forced to leave them in the garden. The judge was puzzled when he learned of this and now ordered the guardian himself to bring something from the garden. The guardian found the full basket of the slave, brought it before the judge and said: 'How obliging of you! You had surely only sent the slave to save me the trouble of doing the picking.' The judge was

---

124 A.J. Wensinck: *A Handbook of Early Muhammadan Tradition*, Leiden, 1927, p. 81b (s.v. food): Mule's meat prohibited.

125 Textual corruption, perhaps *fī'l-bilād al-madhkūra* instead of *wa'l-bilād al-madhkūra*. — Out of the six saints of this third section four are nameless. The fifth one, al-Mughāwir, could have borne this name as an epithet (but not necessarily). The sixth, Abū Yaᶜazzā, is named Yalannūr b. Maymūn and is regarded as one of the great saints of Morocco.

126 Foresters, guardians of the crops, garden watchmen are met with frequently; here *146b*, *167b*. Cf. my *Vita Kāzarūnī*, Introduction, p. 35, ftn. 1. Bādisī: *Maqṣad*, trans. Colin, p. 124 (guarding a planted area against boars). *Tashawwuf*, p. 242, below (a man of piety lives from guarding gardens, crops, and other services). On p. 243 there follows a variant of the well-known story of the honest gardener which I have discussed in *Abū Saᶜīd-i Abū l-Ḫayr*, p. 104. In Yemen a raised seat with a roof, a kind of platform for watching over the fields, is or was called a *mishbāb*; Yāfiᶜī: *Rawḍ*, p. 227, l. 17 (447th story)/Sharjī, p. 44.

astonished that the guardian knew everything and appointed him guardian over the garden for life.[127] When he died, the judge had him buried alongside the garden.

I wanted to visit the grave but I found it had been washed away by the rain.

Another trustworthy man related to me: 'An ascetic always came to the locality for the Friday prayers, placed his leather water-container and his sandals at the door of the congregational mosque and went in to pray. Everyone who went past put some money in the leather container and this always came to a sizeable sum. But coming forth after his prayers, the ascetic each time would empty out the bag and even shake it against the wall so that nothing at all would remain inside.'

A man of piety recounted to me that he had had a turner (*kharrāṭ fī'l-khashab*) as a neighbor. At night one often heard how he argued with a woman, abused her and sometimes even struck her. Yet no one ever heard her cry for help. But then another time one could hear that he was affectionate with her. Yet in those cases as well one never heard an answer. People thought she must be a foreigner who was loath to betray her presence. (*163b*) One night the wife of my informant went into labor. In this emergency he decided to fetch the woman from next door. When he presented his request to the turner, the man explained that no woman had ever crossed his threshold. The neighbor would not believe it, searched the whole house but in fact did not find a woman. He then asked him how he accounted for his nightly disputes with a woman. The turner replied this woman was his concupiscent soul.[128] Then my informant knew that he had a saint before him and asked him what he should do with his wife who was having difficulties giving birth. The turner gave him some wood shavings from his lathe (*khurāṭat hādhā'l-khashab*) and said: 'Fumigate her with this!' It brought relief.

Another reliable informant recounted to me: 'A pious ascetic lived in a hamlet (*ḍayʿa*, Spanish *aldea*) outside Almería,[129] which was

---

127 Saints can hinder something undesirable by simply saying firmly that it will not happen; *Tashawwuf*, p. 252 (a female donkey no longer goes to its foal), *Maqṣad*, p. 124 (a boar leaves a cornfield in peace).

128 A loud argument with one's concupiscent soul also in *Tashawwuf*, p. 171, ll. 1-5.

129 In passing a conjecture on the linguistic derivation of this name: In Bakrī: *Description de l'Afrique septentrionale*, Arabic p. 62, l. 3 and p. 89, l. 20, the place is called *mariyyat Bajjāna* 'watch-tower of Pechina'. Dozy: *Edrîsî*, translation p. 243, ftn. 3, explains *mariyya* as 'observation-point, tower' (beffroi) and derives it from Arabic *raʾā* 'to see', likewise in his

not fortified, had no soldiers and consequently was defenseless against the Christians. It fell into their hands, and they plundered everything it contained: people, furnishings and livestock. But the ascetic hid himself in his farmhouse (*dār*) and locked the door. The Christians searched the whole place and even plundered (*intahakū*) ruined buildings. His house, however, they passed by and saw no entrance (*bāb*) to it and no drainage conduit (*sirāb*).[130] After the enemy had withdrawn, his relatives congratulated him on his deliverance. They complained to him that they had no milk anymore because the enemy had driven off their livestock. The ascetic assured them that God would bring back their livestock again.[131] In the night the people were awakened by a knocking. It was the cattle that were knocking against the door with their horns. They were let in. Not one head of cattle was missing.'

A man of piety related: 'In a place in Andalus there still lives today a famous itinerant homo religiosus (*sāʾiḥ*) by the name of al-Mughāwir,[132] who has been everywhere and travelled through

---

Suppl. aux dictionnaires arabes s.v. *rʾy*. But feminine passive participles from the first form verb are not nomina loci. Consequently, *mariyya* cannot be *marʾiyya* in this sense. But perhaps an analogy offers some additional help. *Mirʾāh* 'mirror' became *mirāʾa* in Spanish Arabic (Corriente: *A Grammatical Sketch of the Spanish Arabic Dialect Bundle*, Madrid, 1977, 5. 1. 11), *mirāya* (Dozy). Thus **marāya* could have evolved out of *marʾāh* 'lookout' and then, by means of *imāla* which is very frequent, become *mariyya*. In this conjectured development the meaning 'lookout' for *marʾāh* is not attested. Primarily it only means 'sight; a place which one looks at', not 'a place from which one has a view'. Evidence for such a development is also lacking in historical sources.

130 Rhymed prose. *Sirāb* would be the plural of *sarab* (Dozy). On the other hand, there is also the plural form *sirābāt* (Fagnan) 'sewers', as found for instance in Ibn al-Ḥājj: *Al-mudkhal*, III, p. 270, last line to p. 271, ll. 10, 12. Regarding the miracle of remaining undiscovered cf. *Maqṣad*, p. 142, no. 38. Also affected with blindness were the horsemen (not Christians) who did not see Tīlijjī in his tent; *Tashawwuf*, p. 414. Invisible predatory Arabs, *Tashawwuf*, p. 423, ll. 10-11.

131 Cf. ftn. 127 above, the negative counterpart.

132 Rare as a personal name. A Mughāwir b. Ḥakam b. Mughāwir al-Sulamī (d. 509/1115-16) in Játiva with learned descendants in Ibn Abbār's *Al-takmila li'l-Ṣila*, no. 1169. The word otherwise means 'member of a raiding party', from *ghāwara al-ʿaduwwa* 'to launch a surprise attack on the enemy' (Lane). It has gone into Castilian in the form *almogávar* and is already documented there in the 13th century (Corominas: *Diccionario etimológico*; F. Soldevila: *Els almogavers*, Barcelona, 1952, mentioned by Rachel Arié: *L'Espagne musulmane au temps des Naṣrides*, p. 52, ftn. 2). The word is also used in Portuguese. It is employed

deserts.[133] *(164a)* He divided his year between making the pilgrimage and holy war. He would leave his home at the beginning of the year to fulfill these two tasks and then returned again at the end of the year. One time when he came back home, he was confronted with the fact that an emir had appropriated his house and evicted his horses and slaves. He entered his house in his worn-out travelling clothes. The emir had him thrown out. The man of piety said: "I will charge you before the Prophet." He found lodgings with a friend and wished to go off travelling again. That night, however, many slaves with lanterns came looking for him and called him. He went with them and in his house he found the emir crying for help. His eyes had come out of his head. He handed over to him his old property again and had himself carried out.

In the Maghreb there still lives today a man by the name of *Abū Yaᶜazzā*[134] (d. 572/1177) who is famous for his miracles and his

---

for horsemen of this kind both on the Christian and Muslim side; the latter is the case for example in *Sources inédites de l'histoire du Maroc*, Portugal II, pp. 490-91. A native raiding unit in Portuguese service against the Saᶜdīs can be called *almogavaria*; *Sources*, ibid., p. 423. The *almogavares* were disbanded on the Portuguese side in the 17th century, Robert Ricard: *Un document portugais sur la place de Mazagan au début du XVIIe siècle*, Paris, 1932, pp. 56-57; 68-74. On the mercenaries from the mountains of Aragon see Lévi-Provençal, *EI*² Almogávares. — An eastern contemporary of Ṣadafī was called Mujāhid al-Dīn Abū'l-Hayjāᵓ *Ghāzī* b. al-Faḍl b. ᶜAbd al-Wahhāb al-Ḥalāwī al-Dimashqī; Sakhāwī: *Tuḥfat al-aḥbāb*, p. 201, ll. 18-19. Other *Ghāzīs* ibid., pp. 201-02.

133 Rhymed prose, literally: for whom God has made the distance near and for whose feet He has folded up (or rolled up) the deserts. But this does not refer to the miracle of shortening time and space, which Richard Gramlich discusses: 'Zur Ausdehnung der Zeit und Verwandtem', in *Festschrift für Hans Robert Roemer*, Beirut, 1979, pp. 180-92.

134 The MS always writes Abū Yaᶜazzā with *tāᵓ marbūṭa*. Cf. p. 455, ftn. 77 above. Abū Yaᶜazzā died according to other sources in 572/1177 at the age of 130. Our book must have been written five years earlier, i.e. in 567/1171-72. Ṣadafī, however, only knows Abū Yaᶜazzā's age from hearsay. Moreover the numbers 125 and 130 appear to be very approximate and exaggerated. And finally the notice on Abū Yaᶜazzā's age can predate the composition of the book by several years. Therefore one has no really firm basis for the book's time of composition. Even the statement that Abū Yaᶜazzā is still alive contains a small factor of uncertainty because the author also only knows this from hearsay, and this as well can go back to earlier information. Scepticism is appropriate in view of the character of Ṣadafī's mode of writing. I would recommend adopting the dates but with a question mark placed after them so that others do not construct castles on their foundation. Cf. the discussion on pp. 427 ff. above. — Abū Yaᶜazzā was and still is visited for the purpose of fulfilling wishes. The two

lofty halting stations. Everyone who travels there or comes from there knows him. I have never seen him but I have heard he is 125 years old and nourishes himself only with oleander leaves (*waraq al-diflā*) which are notorious for their bitterness. He is supposed to boil[135] them and eat them without salt and oil.[136] Anyone who eats

---

scholars of Fez, Muḥammad b. Mujbar al-Masārī (d. 983/1575) and Muḥammad b. Aḥmad al-ᶜAbsī (d. 963-64/1556), were the same age. Their fathers had made a pilgrimage to Abū Yaᶜazzā's grave and had each asked him for a son who would be a Koranic reciter, after which their wives immediately became pregnant; *Fihris Aḥmad al-Manjūr*, p. 69.

135 *Maṣlūq* for *maslūq* (as also in *149b*, l. 12) in accordance with a tendency of western Arabic to change *sīn* into *ṣād*. Norman Cigar: *Muhammad al-Qadiri's* Nashr al-mathani: *The Chronicles*, London, 1981, p. L, remarks correctly that in Moroccan dialects emphatic consonants are often replaced by non-emphatic ones and vice versa. Thus one reads in his Arabic text p. 83, l. 4, *ṣurra* for *surra* 'he was delighted'. In a letter of complaint from the inhabitants of Azemmur to the Portuguese king João in 1529 *kaṣara* is written for *kasara* or *kassara* 'to break' and *khaṣara* for *khassara* 'to destroy' as well as *aṣr* for *asr* 'being taken prisoner'; *Sources inédites*, Portugal II, p. 460, ll. 2 and 12, about which the editor writes on p. 463, ftn. 1, that this undoubtedly follows the contemporary local pronunciation. The name of the city Essaouira (formerly Mogador) provoked much confusion. James Grey Jackson: *An Account of the Empire of Marocco*, London, 1809, p. 108, maintains that the founder sultan Muḥammad III had given it this name in 1760 because of its beauty since it was the only city of the kingdom laid out with geometrical order. Thus he understood the name as coming from *al-ṣuwayra* 'little picture'. Similarly, Gerhard Rohlfs: *Mein erster Aufenthalt in Marokko*, Bremen, 1873, pp. 402-03, interprets the city's name as 'liebliches Bildchen', as did also Eugène Aubin: *Le Maroc d'aujourd'hui*, Paris, 1913, p. 2: 'The city architect of Mogador in 1760 was a Frenchman, Cornut of Avignon, and he laid out the streets of the city in straight lines following the French model; this earned the city the name Es-Soueira "le petit tableau"'. In fact this was and still is what is mostly said and written in Morocco, and the Berber designation of the city is *Taṣṣūrt*, the equivalent in meaning of *al-ṣuwayra* 'little picture'. But the real meaning of the name is *al-Suwayra* 'little city wall' or 'little rampart', from Arabic *sūr* 'city wall'; E. Doutté: *En Tribu*, Paris, 1914, pp. 51-53; Émile Laoust: 'Contribution à une étude de la toponymie du Haut Atlas', *REI* 13, 1939, p. 272, no. 196; Paulette Galand-Pernet: 'Notes sur les mss. à poèmes chleuhs du fonds berbère de la Bibl. Nat. de Paris', *REI* 41, 1973, p. 285, ftn. 1; Muḥammad al-Mukhtār al-Sūsī: *Al-maᶜsūl*, Casablanca, 1961 ff., XV, p. 180-81. In literature as well one often finds *ṣūr* for *sūr*, *aṣwār* for *aswār*, Cigar, p. L, Arabic text p. 81, l. 10. The 'mistake' also occurs in the east, for instance in an inscription of the Assassin fortress of Maṣyāf from the 7th/13th century: *Répertoire chronologique d'épigraphie arabe* no. 4286/van Berchem-Oppenheim: *Matériaux*, no 21; in Ibn al-Ḥājj: *Mudkhal*, IV, p. 191, l. 6, but elsewhere as well quite frequent; see K.V. Zetterstéen: *Beiträge zur Geschichte der Mamlūkensultane*, Leiden, 1919, p. 1, and in the Coptic-Arabic legend of Abū Mīnā (unedited). Our own

with him finds them as tasty as he himself does and as good as other vegetables.[137] A man from the Maghrebian city of Salā did not believe in his miracles. He went to visit him and remained with him for three days as his guest. At the end of the third day he asked permission to leave. Abū Yaᶜazzā said: 'Not until tommorow.' None the less, the man left him (*164b*), at a moment when Abū Yaᶜazzā was not paying attention to him. Immediately he sent people after him, saying: 'He will be held captive by a snake at the foot of the mountain. Take this staff with you and place it on the snake; then it will release him!' They found him encircled (?) by a snake and all his limbs enwrapped by it,[138] with his breath at an end and unable to free himself. They placed the staff on the snake and the snake detached itself from him. Brought back before Abū Yaᶜazzā, he had to admit that God endowed certain people with a higher power and made things turn out the way they wanted, in which case they were naturally acting according to God's command. He was converted to believing in his miracles.

This was the last of all the saints whom I heard about in the Maghreb and whom I saw there.[139]

---

lemma *slq* is also rendered emphatic in Lebanon; Werner Diem: *Hochsprache und Dialekt im Arabischen*, Abh. K. M. XLI, 1, Wiesbaden, 1974, p. 60: *yataṣallaq* 'he climbs'.

136 According to *Tashawwuf*, p. 197, Abū Yaᶜazzā when he was still guarding cattle for others received from the owners two flat-breads every day. He regularly gave away one of them to a Koran reciter in the mosque, and later gave the second flat-bread to a second Koran reciter who had likewise withdrawn into the mosque. From then on he contented himself with eating plants (cf. *149b* above). He also ground up the leaves of ivy or bindweed (*lablāb*) and ate them with little balls of acorn flour which he had with him. In addition people saw him cook and dry mallows (*khubbāzā*). Moreover, according to *Tashawwuf*, p. 200, l. 7, he is supposed to have eaten the buds and sprouts of oleander (*ᶜuyūn al-diflā*). This is meant to have made him capable of chasing away lions. On different kinds of *lablāb* see Ahmed Issa Bey: *Dictionnaire des noms des plantes en latin, français, anglais et arabe*, Cairo, 1930, index *lablāb*.

137 The same also in *Tashawwuf*, p. 197, last two lines: 'I came to Abū Yaᶜazzā one day when he was eating "heart" of oleander (*qulūb al-diflā*). He gave me one of them. I found it to be sweet.' On this motif cf. ftn. 63 above.

138 *Qad washshaḥathū wa'ltaffat ᶜalā sāʾir aᶜḍāʾihī*; *iltawā ᶜalā* occurs elsewhere with the same meaning.

139 The sentence refers back to the previous chapter; hence 'whom I met'.

4. THEOLOGIANS, ASCETICS AND EDUCATED PERSONS WHOM I MET IN EGYPT.

Abū Ṭālib b. Muᶜāfā. He taught the sciences in Alexandria and was well acquainted with them. He was content with the very bare necessities of life...

A reliable informant related to me: 'A governor (*wālī*) of the frontier fortress behaved very unjustly and autocratically. One day more than twenty people assembled before Ibn Muᶜāfā in a circle and each of them brought the same charge against the governor. Ibn Muᶜāfā recited a prayer that was generally said for the benefit of all Muslims, and those present concluded it with amen.[140] Shortly thereafter the inhabitants of the place stormed the house of the emir and plundered it. But he had hidden himself, and only because he was predestined to have a long life did he manage to escape.'

Another time a poor man asked him to take up a collection for him in his circle. Ibn Muᶜāfā refused because he never did this.[141] But he added: 'On the other hand, I will ask the audience for something which will none the less lead you to your goal.'[142] He extended his hands and prayed for earthly wealth for him. The people responded: 'Amen!' After that the man found a purse with money in the street (*165a*). And then he heard a crier announce: 'Whoever finds a sum of cash[143] and returns it to the owner will receive a reward!' The

---

140 A frequent form of division of labor and sharing responsibility. Sometimes the shaykh recites the prayer and those present add amen, or the other way round; the latter was the case with the prayer which is said to have caused the death of the Zoroastrian governor of Kāzarūn; *Vita des Kāzarūnī*, Introduction, p. 22 (Persian text p. 155, l. 23 to p. 156, l. 22/offprint, Tehran, 1333 and 1358, p. 144). Both examples have in common that the shaykh does not want to pray for something bad. Kāzarūnī follows this principle in that he only says amen, Ibn Muᶜāfā in that he recites a prayer for the general good. Sometimes the proceeds from this kind of prayer are shared. The one who said amen claims his share in story no. 73 in Yāfiᶜī: *Rawḍ al-rayāḥīn*, p. 81. The division of labor already occurs in the *ḥadīth*. When the Prophet prayed against certain bedouin tribes during the introduction of the 'standing prayer' (*qunūt*) in the ritual prayers, the people behind him are meant to have said amen; *Concordance*, I, p. 107, l. 3 from bot. (*wa-yuʾamminu man khalfahū*), *Mukhtaṣar sunan Abī Dāwūd*, no. 1393.

141 The same in *158a*, ftn. 93 above. A study on the important social function of pious gatherings is long overdue; *Abū Saᶜīd*, p. 347.

142 What is meant is the amen which the audience is supposed to recite.

143 *Nafaqa* here appears to be almost the same in meaning as *ṣurra*, in any case the money *and* the purse. A possible translation seems to me to be 'cash'. Occurs also in this sense

poor man who had found the money asked for a description of the purse. The crier took him along to the owner who was a high-ranking emir. The emir was able to describe the purse and correctly established what the contents were. The finder handed over the purse to him and left. The emir inquired about the circumstances of the honest man and learned that he lived from hand to mouth. He had just asked Ibn Muᶜāfā for assistance. The emir had him brought back and asked him why he hadn't claimed the reward. The poor man replied: 'I have requested my livelihood from its real provider (God) and am now waiting for the benefit He will send me.' The emir gave him the fifty dinars that were in the purse and said: 'In any case, I had intended to spend them on God's behalf. When I lost them, I was afraid they might come into the wrong hands. That's why I had people look for them. But you deserve them totally and completely.'

I left Ibn Muᶜāfā while he was still alive. But later his death was reported to me.

One day I went outside Alexandria to look at the sea. When I reached Baḥr al-silsila (?)[144] and sought refuge in the shade of a watchtower (*maḥras*) there which is built out into the sea, a shaykh came along, took a lure (*ṭuᶜm*) out from under a stone, put it in the container (?)[145] and threw it into the sea, saying: 'In the name of God, the Compassionate, the Merciful. Then he pulled it out again, and a fine fish was inside. He collected some sea grass (*ḥashīsh al-baḥr*), made fire by striking against a stone a piece of iron he had in his pocket, kindled the (wet) grass, roasted the fish, ate some of it and throwing the rest in the sea, said: 'Thanks be to God who has kept me from eating their (the people's) food!' He drank salt water from the sea and said: 'Thanks be to God who has kept me from

---

in *170a*, l. 3, where it is likewise a question of a lost purse. 'Money, cash' (without purse) in *165b*, l. 12. Clear separation of the two words in Ibn al-Zayyāt: *Kawākib*, p. 139, l. 10/ Sakhāwī: *Tuḥfa*, p. 262, l. 8: *ṣurra fīhā nafaqa*.

144 I cannot prove this. In Damietta there was a Burj al-silsila, Ibn al-Dawādārī, VII, p. 196, l. 17; in Baghdad a Darb al-silsila, Mujīr al-Dīn al-Ḥanbalī: *Al-uns al-jalīl bi-tārīkh al-Quds wa'l-Khalīl*, Amman, 1973, I, p. 301, l. 18; in Jerusalem a Qubbat al-silsila, ibid., II, pp. 18-19; and a Bāb al-silsila, ibid., II, pp. 19-21.

145 *Fī'l-ẓarf*. What could 'the container' be? The usual leather purse (*rakwa*) of the Sufi? The *fī* supports the translation 'container'. *Ṭaraf* could be a rope. Sufis usually carried with them a length of string for fetching water and hanging up their laundry to dry. *Ṭarf* can be a sharply pointed stick, perhaps even a pointed stick used for catching fish.

drinking their water!'[146] Then he lay down to sleep. He got up for the noonday prayer, washed himself and performed the prayer. I went to him and prayed with him. Then I asked him to invoke God on my behalf. He prayed for me, and after he had asked me my name, he gave me the following piece of wisdom for life: 'My dear friend, when you see a man of piety, do just what he does,[147] and never be content that a man of piety has invoked God on your behalf! Only the incapable are content with that.' Thereupon he went away.

Shaykh *Abū'l-Ḥasan ᶜAlī b. al-Muslim* (or *al-Musallam*) *al-Anṣārī*, known as *Ibn Abī Saᶜd*. A dignified, ascetic, learned and active shaykh (*165b*) who cast away the world far from himself like a burning log. In his nourishment he avoided what is forbidden and in his relations with people he trod the path of the noble.

I visited him immediately after my arrival in Fusṭāṭ and then most days of my sojourn there. I never heard him say anything indecent. Kings came to visit him and sought his blessing. They listened to his sermons and behaved in accordance with them. He was regarded as a saint. When I attended his assemblies, he was pleased to see me and he readily engaged me in intimate conversations, sometimes when the others had gone. Whenever I was sick I visited him so that he could invoke God on my behalf, and this always helped.

One day the two of us were alone conversing about the miracles of the saints and the *ᶜāmilūn*.[148] A needy person asked to come in. But Ibn Saᶜd had nothing. I wanted to give the poor person a dinar from my money. Ibn Saᶜd, however, first wanted to hear his story and said to me: 'If God sends someone else who helps him, then you deserve

---

146 P. 451, ftn. 63 above. Radicalism early on confronted men of piety with the question as to whether they ought to take part at all in the everyday dealings of men at large, and led many of them to break off contact with the world. Cf. Josef van Ess: *Die Gedankenwelt des Ḥāriṯ al-Muḥāsibī*, Bonn, 1961, pp. 101-04. The basis for this was the fear of indirectly misappropriating someone else's property and making oneself partially to blame. ᶜAbdallāh b. Muqbil al-Tamīmī, here *171a*, is expressing such scruples when he confines himself to eating only what comes from his allegedly centuries old inheritance. When Taqī al-Dīn Ḥiṣnī came to Jerusalem he only resided and ate with Muḥammad Fūlād b. ᶜAbdallāh, a doorman at the Khānaqāh Ṣalāḥiyya who is said to have made the pilgrimage sixty times and died in 844/1440. He took him to be a man of proven integrity; Mujīr al-Dīn: *Uns jalīl*, II, p. 174.

147 MS unclear: 'what he knows' or 'what he teaches'. But it should probably be read as *yaᶜmal*.

148 As in *160b*, pp. 471 f. above.

your dinar better than he does.' The beggar complained that he didn't have enough to eat and had debts. The shaykh prayed: 'Oh God, help him!', and waited. Then quite soon a high-ranking statesman came, sat down with the shaykh and conversed with him. When he got up, he whispered something to him in his ear and pointed under the prayer-rug (*muṣallā*). Ibn Saᶜd said to the petitioner: 'God has fulfilled your request.' He brought out a money purse from under the rug[149] and handed it to him. To me he said: 'God reward your helpful intention!'

One of his followers related to me: 'I met the shaykh one day in front of his door and saw that he was giving a viper water to drink from the cup of his hand. When it had drunk its fill and slithered away (*166a*), I noticed that he found it unpleasant to be surprised by me. He asked me to be silent about this.

I was not present at his burial. But a man who had always begged from him during his lifetime also visited his grave, pressed his breast to the grave, wept and complained about his need. Sleep came over him. Ibn Saᶜd appeared to him in a dream and said: 'I feel sorry for your situation but I don't have anything at the moment. Come back tomorrow!' The next day he sat down at his grave again, asked God to have mercy on the dead shaykh, and on a stone he found two dinars shining in the sun. He picked them up because he knew that this was what Ibn Saᶜd had promised him.

I also saw him in a dream after his death, in fact while I was residing at Shāfiᶜī's grave as an act of devotional piety (*mujāwara*). It seemed to me that I had entered his house as previously, a spacious house with white walls, new and well-built and finely furnished. He was sitting there and his face was like the full moon, his teeth — which he had lost earlier — were all present, he was strong-looking and not bent over. I said: 'Your house is truly spacious enough for those who pray.' He: 'Here no one prays with me anymore.' I remembered in the dream that he was dead and I asked him: 'What did you find most useful when your soul took leave and you were laid in the grave?' He: 'The declaration "There is no god but God."' I: 'Who from among the pious men you knew in life is the most pleasing to God?' He: '*Aḥmad al-Najjār* who dedicated himself completely to undertaking a pious residence (*mujāwara*) in Mecca and Medina until he died.' Thereupon I woke up. That was the last that I experienced of him.

---

149 Money (as well as other things) frequently found under the rug. Cf. *Tashawwuf*, p. 315; *Maqṣad*, p. 108.

I heard the following recounted: 'In Cairo there lived one of the *ᶜāmilūn*[150] who became seriously ill. He lost consciousness, his breathing ceased and his senses grew cold. His relatives thought he was dead, covered him up (*166b*) and made preparations for his burial. But when the corpsewasher threw water over him, be began to move and stretched his limbs. The corpsewasher fled, and his helper with the water fell unconscious. When the relatives turned up, the man who had appeared to be dead asked them what they had done with him. They asked in amazement whether he wasn't dead. He said: 'No! Put me back again in my old bed but leave the washing-table (*mughtasal*) standing there (*manṣūb*) and the grave clothes! When you were weeping over me, I saw myself in the midst of other people. The Resurrection had taken place, and the bridge to Paradise and the weighing scales had been set up. The people were standing ready to undergo the final reckoning. Figures with beautiful faces and in white clothes surrounded me and led me before a locked gate. They wished to be admitted but were turned away. Someone from inside told them: "One week later!" My escorts left me alone, I opened my eyes and beheld you. In one week, when it's Thursday again, I will really die!' The person who had appeared to die was a rich man. He had his wife, children and relatives come to him and put his affairs in order. He performed his prescribed ritual prayers (*yuṣallī maktūbatahū*)[151] and many supererogatory prayers and recited the Koran until the following Thursday. Then he undertook a major ritual ablution, changed his clothes, took leave of his people, performed ritual prayers, recited the Koran and died facing in the direction of Mecca. He was lifted onto the washing-table once again and now for the last time dressed in the grave clothes.

When I travelled to Upper-Egypt in order to go on to the Ḥijāz,[152] in the ship on the Nile there was a poor old man (*shaykh*)

---

150 See here *160b* and *165b*; ftn. 110. On the other hand, in this passage a tax-collector could also be meant as in *154b*.

151 Cf. *157b*, ftn. 90.

152 Two routes were used through Upper-Egypt. Travellers sailed up the Nile as far as Aswan and then marched from there to ᶜAydhāb on the Red Sea. Aḥmad Taymūr Bāshā: *Al-āthār al-nabawiyya*², Cairo, 1971, p. 42: 'From shortly after 450/1060 to somewhat after 660/1260 this was the route of pilgrims for the journey there and back.' But this is the way Nāṣir-i Khusraw travelled already in 441-42/1050. Or one sailed up the Nile only as far as Qūṣ and marched from there the long stretch to ᶜAydhāb. That is how Ibn Jubayr travelled in 579/1183, and so apparently did our Ṭāhir al-Ṣadafī (*166b-167a*). However, a shorter route, di-

'disheveled, covered in dust and ignored by everyone'.[153] When the passengers became too packed together, he was placed in a flat dinghy (*qayyāsa*, Dozy) alongside the ship and we travelled this way in the middle of the river (*tawassaṭnā thabaj al-baḥr*). When the wind picked up and the waves began to foam, I saw that the water was menacing to swallow up the little boat and gripped by a sudden emotion, I feared that the man could be drowned. I had him taken out of the boat. He attached himself to me more closely and I couldn't deny him my love. (*167a*) In Qūṣ we disembarked and, along with another friend of mine, we shared the same lodgings. One night rain drove us from the roof where we had been. We all went downstairs and slept in the house. But the old man slept badly, and I and my friend woke up. At midnight we heard someone call out: 'Rizqallāh, Rizqallāh!' That was the old man's name.[154] He replied: 'Yes', stood up, performed a ritual ablution and kept vigil praying until the break of day. In the morning my friend sent me to him, as I was the more prominent of the two of us (*fa-innaka adallu ᶜalayhi minnī*), to ask him who had been calling. I asked the old man. He answered: 'I don't know but he calls me every time I remain asleep when I should recite my litany.' We stayed together all the way to Mecca and until the end of the pilgrimage. I asked him in Mecca to relate to me something miraculous that had happened to him. He reported: 'I have made the pilgrimage thirteen times. This is the fourteenth time. On one journey sleep overcame me and I missed the departure of the caravan in a campsite. On the second day during which, thirsty and exhaused by the heat, I was wandering about in the desert, now in a desperate state, I came upon a milk sheep under an acacia-tree whose teats I could drink from. I then fell asleep and when I woke up the sheep was still there. It accompanied me and gave me nourishment during all the while I wandered about until I had caught up with the caravan. Then it disappeared.'

During the circumambulation of the Kaᶜba someone pointed out the same old man to me who was actually a date palm climber (*ṭallāᶜ li'l-nakhl*)[155] and said: 'I saw him climb a very high palm-tree in

---

rectly to the east, led to the port al-Quṣayr; Batanūnī: *Al-riḥla al-ḥijāziyya*, Cairo, 1329, p. 28. Perhaps Ṣadafī took this route.

153 A stock phrase from the *ḥadīth*; cf. *Tashawwuf*, p. 430, ll. 3-4.

154 The name is Muslim and Coptic.

155 They are necessary for pollinating the female palm; Julius Euting: *Tagbuch einer Reise in Inner-Arabien*, Leiden, 1896-1914, I, p. 110. Likewise for the date-picking; A. Frhr.

Rashīd (Rosetta) in such-and-such a place. At the highest point his belt (*ḥizām*) snapped and he fell (*167b*) off. But he simply brushed the dust off himself as if he had been asleep.

In Qinā in Upper-Egypt I once met a man at the Nile (*baḥr*) who was regarded as a saint (or a pious man, *ṣāliḥ*). We sat down together and I asked him about the saints he had met. He recounted: 'I had a shaykh who planted a cucumber field (*maqthaʾa*), fenced it in (*sayyaja*) and left it to itself. No one watched over it.[156] One night a group of bad companions came with animals and containers and wanted to harvest it. But the field and the fence (*siyāj*) disappeared from their sight and they couldn't find the least trace of its boundaries. In the daytime they returned and could watch how the owner harvested the cucumbers. The same thing repeated itself several nights until the owner had gathered up all the cucumbers and only the dried out roots were left.

After the Friday prayer in the congregational mosque of Qinā I and another person remained seated and waited for the afternoon prayer. The man said: 'I can tell you something miraculous about this mosque. I had heard that three *abdāl* had performed prayers together in this mosque on a certain night. I kept a look-out and behold, the three of them came and prayed and I prayed behind them. When a part (*hazīʿ*) of the night had passed, they left the mosque and went forth from the city. I followed them. But outside the city they disappeared from my sight. I wanted to return to the city but the gate was shut.[157] I had to wait outside until the gate was opened in the morning.

In the same Qinā one time a traveller who was making the pilgrimage to Mecca spent the night with me. I wanted him to stay longer with me but he declined. I offered him travel provisions and a riding animal. He refused them both. When he had departed, by means of one of my friends (*aṣḥāb*) I sent a riding animal after him for him to mount. Again he refused to accept it (*168a*), and then before my envoy's eyes he disappeared in the distance like a phantom. That was

---

von Fircks: *Ägypten 1894*, Bonn, 1895, I, p. 90, below. But perhaps *ṭallāʿ* means 'date pollinator', from *ṭalʿ* 'spadix of the palm-tree'.

156 Cf. watching over the fields in ftn. 126 above.

157 The saints, along with our informant, reached the open countryside through the locked gate or with the gate mysteriously opening: a well-known motif in legends.

eleven days before the *ḥajj*.[158] Shortly after the pilgrimage, however, I met him in Alexandria. I asked him if he had ever caught up with the pilgrims. He answered: 'I was in Mecca three days ahead of them and was in Medina just ten days ago. Doubts crept over me but later when the pilgrims arrived on their return journey from the holy cities some confirmed to me that they had seen him in Mecca, others that they had seen him in Medina.[159]

A man of piety recounted to me the following experience he heard from another pious man: 'I' — this is how he reported it to me — 'was sailing across the Red Sea to the Ḥijāz in a *jalba*.[160] Along with

---

158 I.e. eleven days before the 9th of Dhū'l-Ḥijja, when one has to have 'lingered' in ᶜArafat if one wishes rightfully to bear the title *ḥājj* and the pilgrimage is to be valid.

159 It is unclear who the narrator is in this story. Is it a report of our author or an additional account by the man whom he met in the chief mosque of Qinā? If the former is the case, conclusions could be drawn regarding the life of Ṣadafī. He would not merely have been travelling through Qinā on his way to Mecca, since the informant was in fact already back in Alexandria before the return of the pilgrims. It is possible that he was also in Qinā on his return journey from the Ḥijāz, and the fact that in the whole book he has no experiences to recount from Syria-Palestine would be in agreement with this. Indeed, pilgrims from Egypt and North Africa do not have to set foot in Syria-Palestine. It is also striking that the informant was in the position to offer someone accommodation in Qinā and provide him with provisions and a riding animal for the rest of the journey to Mecca. Surely only a resident could do this. Had Ṣadafī settled down for a while in Qinā or did he fulfill some function or perhaps hold a public office there? Must or ought one to associate this with the unclear statement in *160a* that the bay of Rammāda on the Mediterranean belonged 'to his financial districts' (p. 427 f. above)? Might he in this capacity also have had something to do with Qinā in Upper-Egypt? On the other hand, he was also not sparing of expenses in Mecca and appears there as well to have lived in a manner befitting his station. There he invited a man of piety who was passing by his lodgings (*manzil*) to come into his house (*bayt*) in order to perform two prostrations of ritual prayer inside and bless the premises (*171a*). It is not likely that he held an appointment as a functionary in Mecca. Despite these unanswered questions, one has the impression that the report is from Ṣadafī rather than from his acquaintance in Qinā, and it fits most smoothly with what else we know about Ṣadafī if we assume that he spent a period of time residing in Qinā on his return journey from Mecca. A contemporary of Abū'l-ᶜAbbās b. al-ᶜArīf (d. 536/1141) from the west claims that on a fantastical journey to Mecca he had come to Aswan by the road through ᶜAydhāb, intending then to take a ship from Alexandria to the west. But, as he states, he forced himself to strike out westwards into the desert from Aswan; Yāfiᶜī: *Rawḍ*, pp. 286-87.

160 The *jalba* was made of Indian and Yemenite wood which was bound with coconut fibers and caulked with tow from palm wood. No nails were used in its construction. The sails were from leaves of a gum-tree. The boat is described in detail by Ibn Jubayr: *Riḥla*, ed.

us there was a young man who looked completely sallow and frail, and had nothing with him either to eat or drink. He didn't eat or drink anything for eight days. In al-Yanbūᶜ some sailors went to the market. The young fellow also disembarked but he bumped into one of the seamen and the latter gave him a hard punch. At the same moment a man who was one of the *abdāl* was asleep on the ship. He awoke with a start and asked about the young man. He had dreamed that the fellow bumped into a sailor in the market and the sailor had punched him, but then the same sailor came across a bedouin and the latter had chopped off his head with a sword. In fact the sailor didn't return with the landing skiff (*sanbūq*), and the passengers who came on board again confirmed the dream of the man who was one of the *abdāl*. But we never found the frail young man anywhere again.'

A man of education (*baᶜḍ al-fuḍalāʾ*) reported to me: 'On a journey a dignified and humble shaykh rode alongside me. We became friends and also remained close to one another in the night encampment (*muᶜras, muᶜarras*).[161] One day I couldn't find him, but then discovered him praying in front of a *miḥrāb* which he had drawn on the ground, surrounded trustingly by timid wild animals, like a shepherd surrounded by his flock. I prayed with him and[162] (*168b*) then asked him to give me a wise saying. He said: "Take it as good advice to fulfill people's requests and to lighten their sorrow. Nothing is more pleasing in God's eyes than when the grief of a Muslim is eliminated. Should you acquire a position of power over Muslims, see that you make an effort to get rid of it, for on the Day of Judgement you will be held to account because of it." He continued:[163] "My father reported to me with a chain of transmitters: 'A Spanish

---

Wright and De Goeje, Gibb Memorial Series 5, 1907, pp. 70-71/trans. Gaudefroy-Demombynes, Paris, 1940-51, pp. 80-81. The landing craft *sanbūq* mentioned further down in Yāfiᶜī: *Mirʾāt al-janān*, year 748/1347, IV, p. 318, l. 17; illustration Hugh Scott: *In the High Yemen*, London, 1947, p. 189, no. 110.

161 This is not a question of the locality al-Muᶜarras (with the article) outside Medina; Fayrūzābādī: *Al-maghānim al-muṭāba fī maᶜālim Ṭāba*, ed. Ḥamad al-Jāsir, Riyadh, 1969, p. 386; Aḥmad b. ᶜAbd al-Ḥamīd al-ᶜAbbāsī: *ᶜUmdat al-akhbār fī madīnat al-Mukhtār*, ed. Muḥammad al-Ṭayyib al-Anṣārī, 5th edition of Ḥamad al-Jāsir, n.p., n.d., p. 420; Ḥarbī: *Al-manāsik wa-amākin ṭuruq al-ḥajj wa-maᶜālim al-Jazīra*, ed. Ḥamad al-Jāsir, Riyadh, 1969, p. 406, ftn. 2; Ibn al-Ḥājj: *Mudkhal*, IV, p. 239, l. 6.

162 Small lacuna. The copyist made a mistake turning the page and skipped something.

163 This is not in the text. One must assume, however, that what follows is not from the author but that the shaykh is still speaking.

Umayyad caliph divided his life into four parts in the following order. During the first part he sought to learn sciences. In the second he did building. In the third he drank wine and enjoyed music and beautiful things of the world. In the fourth he waged holy war.[164] His story is well-known. Now at the end of his life when he wanted to wage war, he summoned the pious judge Ibn al-Mundhir al-Ballūṭī[165] who is famous for his miracles and writings — I don't know his actual name, but he was the chief judge of his time — and said to him: "I am transferring to you the office of judge over all the provinces. It now goes from me to you, and it will then go from you to God!"[166] The judge replied: "That does not free you from God, because you are responsible for the subjects before God, not me. If that were the end of the matter, then the Prophet would not have said: 'For a Muslim there is no good to be had in holding command (*imra*).'[167] ᶜAlī once saw the caliph ᶜUmar running somewhere and asked: 'Where are you in such a hurry to go?' ᶜUmar: 'I'm looking for one of the camels bearing the alms-tax, which has run off.' ᶜAlī: 'But in doing this you humiliate the caliph who will come after you.' ᶜUmar: 'Do not reproach me! God would even hold me responsible for a lamb that gets lost on the bank of the Euphrates.'[168] ᶜUmar did not say God would hold the governor of that region responsible."

---

164 Dividing life into four phases recalls the ancient Indian scheme of four stages in life but has nothing to do with it historically; Helmuth Glasenapp: *Die Religionen Indiens*, Stuttgart, 1933, pp. 90-91.

165 Probably meant is Mundhir b. Saᶜīd al-Ballūṭī (d. 355/966) who was active under the caliphs al-Nāṣir ᶜAbd al-Raḥmān III and al-Ḥakam II. Cf. pp. 432 f. above.

166 This means: I hereby transfer the responsibility to you and wish to have nothing more to do with it. You will then be accountable to God, in any case not to me.

167 *Concordance*, I, p. 104b, *imra*.

168 Braulio Justel Calabozo: *La Hidāya de al-Raŷrāŷī (un Espejo de Príncipes medieval)*, edición crítica, traducción y estudio, Madrid, 1983, Arabic p. 26, ll. 1-2/Spanish p. 112, ll. 15-16. The Arabic wording there deviates from our text but agrees with that of Ghazzālī in his *Iḥyāʾ ᶜulūm al-dīn*, Cairo, n.d., II, p. 343, ll. 19-20. It can be translated: 'If a lamb were to die on the banks of the Euphrates because it was neglected (*ḍayᶜatan*), I would have to fear...' This is shown by Ghazzālī's Persian parallels in *Kīmiyāy-i saᶜādat*, Tehran, 1333-34, p. 415, and *Naṣīḥat al-mulūk*, ed. Jalāl al-Dīn-i Humāʾī, Tehran, 1351, pp. 306 and 353-54: 'If someone lets a mangy sheep run free on the banks of the Euphrates and I do not rub ointment on it' (*Naṣīḥat*, p. 306), or: 'If someone lets a mangy sheep run free on the banks of the Euphrates, without ointment on it (pp. 353-54 and *Kīmiyā*, variant), I would then fear...' The word *ḍayᶜatan* 'left to itself, not looked after' is absent from our text and was perhaps not understood by Ṣadafī or by the copyist. Calabozo's *perdido* is not correct.

The judge went on: "Oh Prince of the Believers, I will call my governors to account once every month. You call me to account twice every day! If you leave me to my own devices, God will hold you responsible for it.""'"

A truth-loving man in Cairo (*169a*) who had travelled about in the world informed me: 'In Persia I met a shaykh who fasted for fifteen days without interruption and then only partook of sugar and milk. One day he said to an envoy of the king Sanjar (MS Sinjār):[169] "Tell him the Prophet has uttered the statement: 'For every hot liver there is a heavenly reward',[170] even when it is a question of animals and creatures that have no reason and naturally all the more so in the case of Muslims and believers! (Tell him:) I saw the Prophet in a dream and complained to him: 'I continually order the king to adopt mercy and justice toward his subjects and to fulfill their needs. Yet persons without a conscience in his surroundings prompt him to do otherwise.' The Prophet replied: 'You just continue like this. God will reward you for it. If the king follows you, it will be good for him. If he does not follow you, it will be bad. These persons behave toward the king like Satan when Satan says to the people: "Do not believe!", and afterward protests his innocence. I (the Prophet) have once declared: "Whomever God has chosen to do good, to him He gives an honest vizier who reminds him when he forgets and helps him when he needs help."'"'[171] With this message the envoy went off to Sanjar. But the shaykh once again turned to me (to Ṣadafī's informant) and the others who were present with him and said: "The reason for dispatching this envoy to me was this: In the country there was a warrior for the faith whose horse an emir[172] took away, giving him another better one in return. But the warrior for the faith did not want it at all. They both demanded a judgement from me. The emir insisted on the fact that he had given him something of greater value for the

---

169 The Seljuk Sanjar was 'king', i.e. a local ruler, 490-513/1097-1119, then 'sulṭān', i.e. supreme sovereign, until 552/1157. But this finer distinction no doubt lies beyond the interest of our informat.

170 *Concordance*, V, p. 508a, *kabid*. The *ḥadīth* has different variants. A brief explanation in Ibn Māja, II, p. 1215, ftn. to no. 3686.

171 *Concordance*, VII, p. 200b, *wazīr*. Our text has *ista^cāna* 'needs help'. The *ḥadīth* has *dhakara* 'to remember' as the opposite to the preceding 'forgets'. Nasā'ī, VII, p. 159. Also in Ibn Marzūq: *El* Musnad: *Hechos memorables de Abū l-Ḥasan, sultan de los benimerines*, estudio, traducción, anotación, índices anotados por María J. Viguera, Madrid, 1977, p. 296 (Chapt. 34).

172 I.e. not Sanjar himself.

horse he took from him. The judgement I reached was that the horse must be returned to its original owner. People began to talk about the case and reproached me for involving myself in matters that were none of my business. I defended myself with the following story: Among the Israelites there were two men of piety, an old and a young worshipper of God. During a famine the old man was first to pray for rain. It didn't rain (*169b*). Next the young man prayed. Then rain fell. The old man asked himself why his prayer had not been answered. God revealed to him: 'You occupy yourself with Me for your own sake, whereas he does so for the sake of others.'"'

That is the last of the miracles which I heard about in Egypt from trustworthy informants or which I saw myself.

5. PEOPLE I MET IN THE ḤIJĀZ.

Abū Muḥammad ʿAbdallāh b. Aḥmad, known as *Ibn ʿĪṣar* (?) *al-Miṣrī*. I was his student in Mecca for a time and heard from him the traditions he had to transmit. He knew the Koran, lexicography (*lugha*) and grammar.

He reported to me: 'When I left the Maghreb to travel to Mecca, the Christians attacked our ship, took me and my family prisoners and wanted to sail to Syria. But God caused the wind to die down so that they did not move from the spot for three days.[173] They believed the fault was that they had taken me and my family prisoners. When they had put us ashore, in fact they were able to sail on. Arab bedouins brought us to Alexandria on camels.'

One of his students (or followers) related to me: 'I was once with him on a boat in the Nile which sunk with all its passengers. He couldn't swim. He recited surah 22/65: "And He holds the sky from falling down; this it shall not do except by His own will." Then a piece of wood appeared under his feet. He stood up on it in the middle of the river until another ship picked him up and brought him to the shore.'[174]

I was not on hand when he died but I heard that he passed away in Mecca and is buried there.

---

173 Cf. also *170b* below and *Maqṣad*, p. 23.

174 Here the saint cannot simply walk on the water (p. 454, ftn. 72) but needs a piece of wood to stand on, just like Gharīb needed a rock (155b). The various miracle motifs are ready to be used and are *selected* by legends just as by fairy tales and by stories about demons; one element is rejected and another is adopted.

Abū'l-ᶜAbbās Aḥmad b. Ismāᶜīl, known as *al-Fanakī al-Muqrī* (or *al-Maqrī* or *al-Maqqarī*). One of the greatest worshippers of God and ascetics, an expert on the Koran. He devoted himself entirely to teaching the Koran without remuneration[175] and to being of service to the poor.

One day while circumambulating the Kaᶜba he noticed that one of the treasurers (*?khazana*[176]) pushed aside a woman and blocked her way. He prayed: 'Oh God, see that he has enough to do with himself and leaves the woman along!' The man let out a cry (*170a*) and fell to the ground. A scorpion had stung him in the foot. He was carried from the spot and died.

A pilgrim who had lost money asked him to pray God to cause the money to be returned to him.[177] Fanakī prayed and went to the judge to report the loss. An employee there said he had received a lost item (*luqṭa*). The man who had lost the money was summoned. The details he gave were correct, and he obtained his cash once more. Fanakī thanked God that He had helped the poor man through him, and said to the gathering: 'The most splendid religious practice (*aᶜẓam al-qurubāt ilā'llāh*) is looking after the concerns of your fellow-man.' Someone asked: 'In other words not simply equal to the other acts of obedience?' Fanakī: 'No, greater. If it were equal, the men of piety of the earliest generations (*al-salaf al-ṣāliḥ*) would not have especially urged people to do it, and ᶜUmar b. al-Khaṭṭāb himself would not have acted this way. Indeed, one night when he was making his way through Medina, ᶜUmar heard some young boys weeping. He followed their voices and came to a woman who was lighting a fire under a cooking pot while her children were standing around her crying. She explained to the caliph that the children had nothing to eat but to appease them she pretended she was cooking something for them though there was only water in the pot. ᶜUmar wept and brought flour, butter, fat, dates, clothes and money from the government storehouse (*bayt māl al-muslimīn*).[178] He carried it there himself in a sack, although his client and servant Aslam wanted

---

175 Here in *152b*, *157b*.

176 The sources do not mention any officials at the Kaᶜba with the designation *khazana*. They are called *sadana* in Batanūnī: *Al-riḥla al-ḥijāziyya*, Cairo, 1329, p. 101. Batanūnī there enumerates other employees of the holy places as well, but no *khazana* although naturally there was a *khizāna* in Mecca just as in Medina. *Khadama* 'attendants' would be more general and more comprehensible.

177 In this section *nafaqa* occurs once (*170a*, l. 3), as in *165a*, ll. 1 and 8.

178 *EI*[2] Bayt al-māl.

to take it from him. He said: "I am the one who will be held to account for them on the Day of Judgement." When he arrived before the woman, he shook out the flour, butter, fat and dates, put them in the cooking pot himself, stirred them and blew on the fire. Aslam who accompanied him saw how the smoke rose up through his long beard. When the meal was ready, ᶜUmar served it with his own hand, feeding the children one mouthful at a time until they were full. Then he lay down in front of them like a lion and waited until they began playing again and laughing.'[179]

I left Fanakī while he was still alive.

Abū'l-Ḥasan ᶜAlī b. Ḥamza, known as *al-Bukhārī*. Fasting and vigils had weakened him. The signs of fear for the Last Judgement were visible in him. On holidays (*mawāsim*) he was visited by the *abdāl*. When he was once in the shade of a rock in ᶜArafa, two of them who looked as emaciated as he did came up to him, greeted him and delivered to him greetings from Abū'l-ᶜAbbās al-Khaḍir who intended to perform his 'lingering' this year in direct proximity to the valley (*baṭn*) ᶜUrana.[180] Abū'l-Ḥasan answered: 'I have never heard that he performed his "lingering" there.'

One time Abū'l-Ḥasan travelled from his locality[181] over the sea in a completely full sailing-boat[182] on the pilgrimage. The Christians

---

179 The story is in Ṭabarī I, pp. 2743-45, Ibn al-Athīr: *Kāmil*, Beirut, 1965-67, III, pp. 57-58. Somewhat changed in Muḥammad-i Ghazzālī: *Naṣīḥat al-mulūk*, ed. Jalāl al-Dīn-i Humāʾī, Tehran, 1351, pp. 115-18/Arabic trans. by Abū'l-Ḥasan ᶜAlī b. al-Mubārak b. Mawhūb: *Al-tibr al-masbūk fī naṣīḥat al-mulūk* (F. Meier *ZDMG* 93, 1939, pp. 398-402; in addition Ibn Khallikān, ed. Iḥsān ᶜAbbās, IV, p. 151), Cairo, 1968, pp. 56-57/English trans. by F.R.C. Bagley: *Ghazālī's Book of Counsel for Kings*, London, 1964, pp. 66 f. The problems discussed by Humāʾī regarding the narrator Zayd b. Aslam (in his edition pp. 115-16, ftn. 9) are resolved by the fact that the correct name is Aslam; the mistake stems from Ghazzālī.

180 The writing of the MS is unclear. It could also be ᶜArafa. However, vowels added later indicate ᶜUrana. This *wādī* near ᶜArafa also caused difficulties in the edition of Ḥarbī's *Kitāb al-manāsik*, Riyadh, 1969, pp. 509-11, as p. 510, ftn. 4, shows. — According to tradition, every year Khaḍir and Elias spend the month of fasting in Jerusalem and every year appear at the gathering of the pilgrims in ᶜArafa (*mawsim*); Mujīr al-Dīn: *Uns jalīl*, II, p. 29.

181 In any case not Bukhārā. The journey is through the Mediterranean. The 'accursed enemy' (*al-ᶜaduww al-laᶜīn*) normally refers to the Christians. Indeed, in the 6th/12th century the Christians even turned up with hostile intentions in the Red Sea; Ibn Jubayr p. 59/trans. Gaudefroy-Demombynes pp. 65-67. But this first state of insecurity in the Red Sea because of the Crusaders, long before the appearance of the Portuguese in the 16th century, only took place after the composition of our book, in the year 578/1182. Ibn al-Athīr, year 577 and 578,

attacked the ship with several vessels. All his fellow-passengers rushed to Abū'l-Ḥasan in fear: 'Look at the situation we're in!' He came up out of his cabin (*ṭārima*)[183] and saw the danger. He prayed to God. The enemy ships came to a halt and it seemed to the Christians that they were sitting on dry land. They cried out: 'You Muslims, if a priest (*qasīs*[184]) among you has prayed against us, tell him to pray now so that we come afloat again! We swear we will not do you any harm.' Abū'l-Ḥasan prayed: 'Oh God, turn them away from us!' The ships shot apart from one another as quickly as arrows, and the pilgrim ship sailed on its way unhindered.[185]

In Medina there was once a great famine and rise in prices. The attention of the inhabitants was drawn to Abū'l-Ḥasan who could pray on their behalf. Abū'l-Ḥasan replied to them that he had already prayed and God had promised to answer his prayers. Whoever wished should go to al-Yanbūᶜ where he would find deliverance for himself and his family. Some had their doubts, others followed his counsel and in al-Yanbūᶜ (*171a*) they found Egyptian and Yemenite ships with provisions. With the provisions they looked after their

---

XI, pp. 470, 490-91. Ibn al-Dawādārī VII, pp. 71-72. Jean-Claude Garcin: *Un centre musulman de la Haute-Égypte médiévale: Qūṣ*, dissertation Paris, 1974, p. 136. Joseph Henninger: 'Menschenopfer bei den Arabern', *Anthropos* 53, 1958, pp. 758-61. Additional literature in Gaudefroy-Demombynes p. 67, ftn. 1.

182 *Markab mashḥūna*. *Markab* fem., Dozy. Thus throughout the whole section. *Fulk mashḥūn* surahs 26/119, 36/41, 37/140.

183 *Ashrafa min ṭārimatihī*. In Fāṭimid Cairo the caliph, seated in or under a wooden lodge *al-Ṭārima*, inspected the troops as they marched past; Maqrīzī: *Ittiᶜāẓ al-ḥunafāʾ bi-akhbār al-aʾimma al-fāṭimiyyīn al-khulafāʾ*, ed. Shayyāl and Muḥammad Ḥilmī Muḥammad Aḥmad, Cairo, 1967-73, II, p. 14.

184 The Christians picture the Muslims as having 'priests' and refer to the latter with the Christian (originally Syriac) term *qasīs* which is also used in Ibero-Romanic for Muslim religiosi as well as marabouts; 'Almoravids and Marabouts', p. 356, ftn. 105: *caciz*, etc. The Ayyūbid al-Ṣāliḥ ᶜImād al-Dīn Ismāᶜīl uses it about Muslims to make himself understood when talking with Christians; Subkī: *Ṭabaqāt al-shāfiᶜiyya*, VIII, p. 244, l. 9.

185 A certain Abū ᶜAbdallāh Muḥammad b. Yūsuf al-Takrūrī in Būlāq was once invoked, according to legend, by a woman whose child blacks had carried off in their ship. He ordered the wind to stop blowing, which it did. But when the negroes refused to give up the child, he went to them walking across the water and fetched it. It is unclear in the story whether *baḥr* means the Nile or the sea. Ibn al-Zayyāt: *Kawākib sayyāra*, p. 129/Sakhāwī: *Tuḥfat al-aḥbāb*, p. 257.

relatives and also undertook trade. This brought about the disappearance of the famine in Medina.

One time in Mecca I walked with Abū'l-Ḥasan and some other pious men to the cemetery al-Maᶜlā[186] to visit the graves of the Companions of the Prophet. When we reached the grave of Sufyān b. ᶜUyayna (d. 198/815),[187] Abū'l-Ḥasan said to me in secret: 'This is the grave of Sufyān but the other grave I see there is the grave of a tax-collector (*makkās*). An emir from Mecca unjustly appropriated the space and had him buried there. Between the two graves these plants have grown up. Taste them!' I tasted the plants. The ones by Sufyān's grave had a sweet smell and taste, whereas the ones by the tax-collector's grave were repulsive although they looked exactly the same.

I left Abū'l-Ḥasan in Mecca while he was still alive but then heard that he had died and was buried there.

Abū Muḥammad ᶜAbdallāh b. Muqbil al-Tamīmī. One of the *abdāl* and saints, and one of the *ᶜāmilūn* and religious scholars. He attempted to conceal his real nature as much as possible and hid his piety behind frivolous talk (*ṭaysh fī kalāmihī*), a foppish manner of walking (*khaṭal fī mashyihī*) and wrong answers. In this way he wanted to find out which people really possessed piety and asceticism, and afterwards he kept company with them behaving from then on like a wise, modest, humble, calm and dignified man. Several persons recounted to me in Mecca that they had seen the Prophet in a dream and heard him say: 'Whoever wants to see one of my companions, look at ᶜAbdallāh b. Muqbil!'

One day he came by my lodgings (in Mecca). I asked him to come inside in order to bless the house and perform two prostrations of prayer. He did this and when he had completed his ritual prayers, I wanted to give him something to eat. He declined and said: 'I have never eaten anything from anyone.' I remarked: 'Why do you not

---

186 The same form in *Mudkhal* III, p. 272, l. 8; J.L. Burckhardt: *Reisen in Arabien*, Weimar, 1830, p. 188 (Mala); Richard F. Burton: *Personal Narrative of a Pilgrimage to Al-Madina and Meccah*, (in 1853), London, 1893, II, pp. 152-53 (Ma'ala); C. Snouck Hurgronje: *Mekka*, II, p. 67; etc. Otherwise *al-Maᶜlāh* (*al-Maᶜlātu*). The masculine no doubt emerged by the accent being moved forward. In the designation for the lower town of Mecca *al-Masfala* the feminine form has been kept; Oscar Löfgren: *Arabische Texte zur Kenntnis der Stadt Aden im Mittelalter*, Uppsala, 1936, I, p. 112; Snouck Hurgronje: *Mekka*, I, on the map: èl-Mèsfalah.

187 Wüstenfeld: *Die Chroniken der Stadt Mekka*, III, p. 444. The house where this traditionist lived in Mecca is also pointed out; *Chroniken* II, p. 14.

follow the *sunna* of the Prophet in this regard?' He replied: 'I am not against that but nowadays earning a living is full of corruption and all nourishment is doubtful. Food that is unobjectionable (as in your case) I leave aside because I fear on another occasion I will unwittingly end up with something illicit. I have land in Yemen which has been passed down to us by inheritance since the beginning of Islam, an inalienable pious endowment on behalf of a number of people. Until now no illegal encroachment has occurred. We till the land according to the law[188] (?) and share it fairly (*171b*). But I made the pilgrimage with my family and settled down for years as a pious resident in Mecca. Then my relatives felt a longing for their home again. I brought them back to Yemen. Yet there they missed the call to prayer of Mecca and the sight of the Kaᶜba. Already after three days we set out for Mecca again, carrying only the most essential provisions. When we arrived in Mecca our supplies were used up. I wanted to pray and ask God what would happen to me if I had to let my family go hungry. I went to perform the *circumambulatio*. In the Sūq al-layl[189] I ran into an acquaintance who had previously brought me dates for instance, dates from a palm-tree that a man of piety had planted on licitly acquired ground. He provided me with a sack of dates for five *ṣāᶜ*. Shortly after that the ships from Yemen arrived with our food.'

I left him in Mecca and have no knowledge of what has become of him.

Abū ᶜAbdallāh Muḥammad b. Wābūr[190] (?) *al-Murābiṭ al-Mutalaththim.* Belonged to the former emirs and descendants of the Almoravid kings,[191] was a rich man, highly respected but modest,

---

188 *ᶜAlā'l-shurūᶜ*. This plural should not exist. Landberg: *Glossaire daṯînois*, III, ed. Zetterstéen, Leiden, 1942, p. 2040, lists under *sharᶜ*, pl. *shurūᶜ*, a meaning *routine, custom*. That would allow us to translate: in accordance with the (old) customs. But there can easily be a mistake in our MS. — On the refusal to eat something from others, cf. ftn. 146 above.

189 Wüstenfeld: *Chroniken*, II, p. 385 (index).

190 This Berber name also appears in the form Wāyūr, *Tashawwuf*, p. 198, l. 11.

191 This mode of expression is unclear. Was Abū ᶜAbdallāh himself an emir (*min*) with real military power or was he so-called only because he was a member of an Almoravid royal family? By royal family is the house of the chief dynasty of Yūsuf b. Tāshfīn or another leading house of the core tribes Lamtūna, Massūfa, etc., meant? If he was only a descendant and a late comer of one of these houses, would one not rather expect the appellation *al-Murābiṭī* instead of *al-Murābiṭ*? The Almoravids were not usually called *al-Mutalaththimūn* but *al-Mulaththimūn* (possibly *al-Mulaththamūn*). On this subject see 'Almoravids and Marabouts',

and he never disappointed a person in need. In every emergency he always provided help most swiftly. I met him in Mecca and he treated me in the most friendly manner without our having met one another previously, simply because of his noble nature. I learned from others that he had abandoned his property and his children and had taken refuge with God and in God's holy sites. He has no other habit besides action (*ᶜamal*). He was very kind to the poor and the weak. Alms came to him from Iraq and from other regions, and he spent them here, always firstly on the needy (*172a*), and then what remained over on himself.

One time he set out with a caravan (from Mecca) to Medina to visit the grave of the Prophet. The people were afraid of the unsafe road and considered turning back. But one of them beheld a person in a dream who said: 'A caravan in which so-and-so is present has nothing to fear.' They made the journey and were never attacked.[192]

One night I saw him standing in the sacred precinct of Mecca and while weeping he repeated the following verses (*basīṭ*, *-ūbu*):

I love what he loves, and even when he's angry I find it pleasant.[193]
Everything the beloved does is lovable.

I left him in Mecca, and up to today he writes to me and I write to him.

He is the last of those whom I met in the Ḥijāz.

(Supplement:) Shaykh *Abū Muḥammad ᶜAbdallāh b. Sinān al-Rudaynī*, the great religious scholar and ascetic, an authority on the Koran and the *sunna*. In place of a love of the world he was inspired with a love for the things of God. He enjoyed the favor of kings and the respect of masters and bondsmen. Thanks to his reputation he

---

pp. 418-19. More clear is the case of Maymūn b. Yāsīn al-Ṣanhājī al-Lamtūnī (d. 530/1136 in Seville) who was also *min umarāᵓ al-murābiṭīn* and at the same time a scholar; Ibn Abbār: *Takmila*, ed. Codera, I, p. 396, l. 6.

192 For saints who act as escorts to protect caravans see Sharjī pp. 96, 141, 186. And pilgrim caravans, Sharjī pp. 14-15, 25, 45, 102, 171, 176. R.B. Serjeant: 'Ḥaram and Ḥawṭah, the Sacred Enclave in Arabia', in *Studies in Arabian History and Civilisation*, Variorum Reprints, London, 1981, III, p. 55. 'Almoravids and Marabouts', pp. 351.

193 Reading uncertain: *taᶜattubuhū*. *Taghayyubuhū* 'his staying away' seems less probable to me.

was able to turn the heart of kings toward the people and would awaken their conscience when they appeared to be forgetful, especially with regard to matters of justice and charity.

I visited him in his mosque[194] at the foot of Muqaṭṭam outside Fusṭāṭ in order to obtain through his blessing an indication of the just path and through his learning and wisdom a hint about what is right and the elimination of my doubts. He immediately admitted me to his confidence as if we had already known each other previously. I had before me a human being who was an entire world and the pupil of the eye (*insān al-ᶜayn*) of his day and age. To describe him in greater detail is utterly beyond my capacities.

(172b) With him I wish to conclude the series of saints whom I have met.

TABLE OF CONTENTS OF THE *SIRR MAṢŪN*

LIST OF THE PERSONS TREATED

194 See ftn. 92 above.

OTHER PERSONS, PEOPLES, DYNASTIES, RELIGIOUS PARTIES (AS THEY APPEAR IN THE SUMMARIES GIVEN, NOT IN THE ARABIC TEXT)

PLACE NAMES

ADDITIONS OF THE AUTHOR

P. 426, ftn. 7: From what I have heard a critical edition of the Arabic text of Ṣadafī's *Al-sirr al-maṣūn* is presently being prepared in Spain, on the basis of additional manuscripts that have been found in the meantime. [Maribel Fierro informs us thatt H. Ferhat has prepared an edition of the text and published the article '*As-sirr al-maṣūn* de Ṭāhir al-Ṣadafī: un itinéraire mystique au XIIe siècle', in *Al-Qanṭara* xvi (1995), pp. 273-288; see M. Fierro, 'Opposition to Sufism in Al-Andalus', in Frederick De Jong & Bernd Radtke (ed.): *Islamic Mysticism Contested*, Leiden, 1999, p. 194, ftn. 91.]

[P. 431, ftn. 21: The *Risāla* has been edited by Denis Gril: *La Risāla* de Ṣafī al-Dīn Ibn Abī l-Manṣūr Ibn Ẓāfir., Cairo, 1986]

P. 453, ftn. 70: The substantive of affiliation *Maṣālī* could be connected with the name of the Berber tribe *Māṣala* (sic) *b. Luwāta*; Al-Jaḳûbî: *K. al-boldân*, ed. M.J. De Goeje, Leiden, 1892, p. 342, l. 17, for which reason Gaston Wiet in his translation *Les Pays*, Publ. IFAO 1, 1937, marginal no. 342, gives *Maṣāla b. Luwāta*. In *Ibn Khaldoun*: *Histoire des Berbères*, trans. Le Baron de Slane, nouvelle édition par Paul Casanova, Paris, 1968-69, I, p. 292, one finds *Messala*; in Mohamed Talbi: *L'Émirat aghlabide*, Paris, 1966, ftn. on p. 596, *Maṣṣāla*. Al-Yaᶜqūbī in his *Historiae*, ed. M.Th. Houtsma, Leiden, 1883, I, p. 216, l. 1, speaks of the tribe *al-Maṣālīn*.

P. 483, ftn. 144: *Baḥr al-silsila* in Alexandria gets its name from Fort Silsila on a spur of the coastal strip of the eastern harbor basin. *Baḥr al-silsila* is also mentioned in Ibn ᶜAṭāʾallāh al-Sikandarī: *Laṭāʾif al-minan*, Cairo, n.d., p. 56, l. 4 from bot./Richard Gramlich: *Die Wunder der Freunde Gottes*, Wiesbaden, 1987, p. 301, below, in fact in the mouth of Abū'l-ᶜAbbās al-Mursī (d. 685/1287). Near there the latter is meant to have fished out of the water two pots of honey which were thrown into the sea for him in Tunis. Moreover, there is also a *Bāb al-silsila* on the citadel of Cairo (Ibn Iyās, index).

P. 487, ftn. 155: That *ṭallāᶜ* could have something to do with the date-tree's spadix *ṭalᶜ* is refuted by the synonym *ṣaᶜᶜād* 'one who climbs up' in Ghars al-Niᶜma Muḥammad b. Hilāl al-Ṣābiʾ: *Al-hafawāt al-nādira*, ed. Ṣāliḥ al-Ashtar, Damascus, 1967, no. 87.

A RESURRECTION OF MUḤAMMAD IN SUYŪṬĪ

When Muḥammad died in Mecca in the year 11/632, there were those among his followers who found this difficult to believe. ᶜUmar b. al-Khaṭṭāb, who in the future would become the second caliph, put forward in a speech the thesis that Muḥammad, like Moses on Mt. Sinai, had simply gone up to his Lord and would come back after forty days.[1] The brusqueness with which he offered this explanation and his political ability which was widely acknowledged at a later date could give rise to the suspicion that he had wished in this way to hush up the truth so as to nip in the bud the malicious joy of opponents and gain time to regulate the succession. Yet reports relate that he broke down in despair when he then had to admit the truth. Thus (if there is any truth at all in the matter) he appears honestly not to have been up to coping with the news of the Prophet's death[2] — the dire effect of too inflexible an imago-identification with an object which suddenly ceased to exist and at the same time perhaps also the start of the recovery of that energy for which he was then to become famous in history. The next day ᶜUmar himself admitted he had said something false and had merely *hoped* Muḥammad would continue to live.[3] The other people had also shared this hope and expected a parallel with Jesus about whom they had been taught the Islamic doctrine that Jesus had not died but had simply been translated.[4] Under the third caliph ᶜUthmān (23-35/644-656), ᶜAbdallāh b. Sabaᵓ in fact transposed this doctrine to Muḥammad and sought to

---

1 Based on surah 7/142. Here as in the Koranic passage the place name Sinai is not specified. But it is *this* absence of Moses which is meant, not his death. On the other hand, there is the Jewish legend that Moses did not actually die but disappeared in a cloud; Marcel Simon: *Recherches d'Histoire Judéo-Chrétienne*, Paris-The Hague, 1962, p. 165.

2 Ibn Hishām, ed. Wüstenfeld, pp. 1012-13. Ibn Saᶜd, II, 2, pp. 53-57. Dārimī, *muqaddima* 14, I, p. 39, and other sources. Muḥammad b. Yaᶜqūb al-Fayrūzābādī: *Al-maghānim al-muṭāba fī maᶜālim Ṭāba*, ed. Ḥamad al-Jāsir, Riyadh, 1969, pp. 187-88. *Ibn Babuje el Kummis Kitābu kamālid-dini wa tamāmin-niᵓmati fī ithbātil-ᵓraibati*, Part One, ed. and discussed by Ernst Möller, Heidelberg, 1901, p. 31.

3 Ibn Saᶜd, II, 2, p. 56, l. 25.

4 Ibn Saᶜd, II, 2, p. 57, ll. 5-9. ᶜAbd al-Qāhir al-Baghdādī: *Al-farq bayn al-firaq*, Cairo, 1948, p. 14, antepenult. and penult. line. Shahrastānī: *Al-milal wa'l-niḥal*, ed. Cureton, p. 11/trans. Th. Haarbrücker, I, p. 17, already attributes the comparison with Jesus to ᶜUmar.

promote it by reflecting rhetorically that it was strange to maintain that Jesus would return, though Muḥammad would not.[5] He then applied the same interpretation to the death of the fourth caliph ᶜAlī (40/661) and in so doing initiated the long series of beliefs about translation and expected returns among the Shīᶜa. But outside Shīᶜite circles as well individual deaths were here and there interpreted as translations. When the Tijānī shaykh and founder of a state al-Ḥājj ᶜUmar Tal died on the upper Niger in 1864, his death was denied.[6]

Abū Bakr, who on the very day of the Prophet's death became his first caliph (successor), along with others maintained a cool outlook and rejected the fable of the Prophet's translation.[7] Bedouin tribes that wanted to use the Prophet's death as an excuse to break away were reminded of God to Whom Muḥammad had called them and Who did not pass away, even if the Prophet was mortal.[8] The sober party retained the upper hand, and Muḥammad was laid to rest. The sources give an account down to the smallest detail of how everything was carried out. At a later date texts dealing with the events were produced for recitation, the *wafayāt nabawiyya*, a counterpart to the *mawālid*, the legends about Muḥammad's birth.[9]

---

5 Ṭabarī, I, p. 2942, ll. 5-9. Israel Friedlaender: 'The Heterodoxies of the Shiites according to Ibn Ḥazm', *JAOS* 29, 1908, p. 24. Theodor Nöldeke and Friedrich Schwally: *Geschichte des Qorāns*, II, 1919, pp. 81-83. Régis Blachère: *Le Coran*, traduction, Paris, 1947-50, III, p. 892, ftn. to surah 3/138.

6 Paul Marty: 'L'Islam en Mauritanie et au Sénégal', *RMM* 31, 1915-16, pp. 282-83.

7 Ibn Hishām, pp. 1012-13. Ibn Saᶜd, II, 2, pp. 53-57, etc. Dārimī, *muqaddima* 14, I, p. 39, mentions Muḥammad's uncle, al-ᶜAbbās b. ᶜAbd al-Muṭṭalib, in place of Abū Bakr.

8 Wilhelm Hoenerbach: 'Waṯīma's *Kitāb ar-Ridda* aus Ibn Ḥağar's *Iṣāba*', *Ak. Wiss. u. Lit. Mainz, Abh. d. geistes-u. sozialwissenschaftl. Kl.*, Jahrgang 1951, no. 4, pp. 253, 276, 279. My *Abū Saᶜīd-i Abū l-Ḫayr*, Acta Iranica 11, 1976, pp. 313-14.

9 Several writings are given in Wilhelm Ahlwardt: *Verzeichniss der arabischen Handschriften der Königlichen Bibliothek zu Berlin*, nos. 9614-19. From the 9th/15th century a whole series of texts of this kind are known to us, at least by name: Sakhāwī: *Al-ḍawʾ al-lāmiᶜ li-ahl al-qarn al-tāsiᶜ*, Cairo, 1353-55, VII, p. 246; VIII, p. 142. ᶜAbd al-Ḥayy al-Kattānī: *Fihris al-fahāris*, Fez, 1347, II, p. 87. Maulavi Muinuddin Nadwi: *Catalogue of the Arabic and Persian Mss in the Oriental Public Library at Bankipore*, vol. XV, no. 1015, 1. Ribera y Asín: *Manuscritos árabes y aljamiados de la biblioteca de la Junta*, Madrid, 1912, MS IX, no. 4: Traditions on the life and death of the Prophet from Ibn ᶜAbbās and Abū Bakr (MS from the first half of the 15th century in aljamía). And see the impressive chapter on Muḥammad's death in Muḥammad Rabadan's long poem about the Prophet written in Spanish in 1603, ed. by H.E.J. Stanley, *JRAS* N.S. 3, 1867, pp. 98-104: Canto a la muerte de nuestro anabi Muhamad salam. Muḥammad al-Mukhtār al-Sūsī: *Al-maᶜsūl*, Casablanca, 1960 ff., XVI, p.

For Muslims Muḥammad has since then lain buried in the earth in Medina. Jesus, by contrast, is believed by Muslims to have been translated to heaven without having suffered death, whence he will return some time before the end of the world. A Nestorian catholicus in a conversation with an Islamic scholastic at the beginning of the 3rd/9th century is meant to have laid out the positions in the following way: 'We are agreed in acknowledging the prophethood and the heavenly book of Jesus and that he is alive in heaven, but we diverge from one another regarding the mission of Muḥammad though we then do agree that (in distinction to Jesus) he is dead'[10] — where by 'alive' the catholicus can only have meant 'alive once again'. The Persian poet Khāqānī, who in his poem *Tuḥfat al-ʿIraqayn* describes the pilgrimage he made in 551/1156, feels obliged to place his Muḥammad on a higher level than Jesus, despite appearances to the contrary, i.e. though Muḥammad is at rest in the earth and Jesus resides in the fourth heaven. He effects this manoeuvre by an elegant leap of the imagination according to which Muḥammad is the dead sultan in his tomb and Jesus, the caretaker of Muḥammad's tomb, is on the roof.[11]

Islamic theology continued along the realistic course which was set by Abū Bakr, in fact emphasized, not without some complacency, that Muḥammad's tomb in Medina was the sole tomb of a prophet which had been identified with certainty, and only with reservation half accepted the tomb of Abraham in Hebron as genuine.[12] An au-

---

254, lists the opening lines of some poems on the death of the Prophet written by a certain al-Ḥanafī b. al-Hāshimī (d. 1370/1951) from the south of Morocco. For Swahili cf. Ernst Dammann: 'Die Überlieferung der islamischen Suahelidichtung', *ZDMG* 108, 1958, pp. 41 and 50-51. For Persia A. Chodzko: *Théatre persan*, Paris, 1878/Tehran, 1976, pp. 29-67: La mort du Prophète (Shīʿite passion play). For India Garcin de Tassy: *L'islamisme*, Paris, 1874, pp. 336-37. Jaffur Shurreef: *Qanoon-e-Islam*, trans. G.A. Herklots, London, 1832, pp. 233-36. Annemarie Schimmel: *Und Muhammed ist Sein Prophet*, Diederichs, 1981, p. 124.

10 Ibn Shahrāshūb: *Manāqib āl Abī Ṭālib*, Najaf, 1956, III, p. 462.

11 *Tuḥfat al-ʿIrāqayn*, ed. Yaḥyā Qarīb, Tehran, 1333, pp. 144-45.

12 Ibn Taymiyya: *Majmūʿat al-rasāʾil wa'l-masāʾil*, Cairo, 1341-49, I (Ahl al-ṣuffa wa-abāṭīl baʿḍ al-mutaṣawwifa fīhim), pp. 58-59. Idem: *Al-fatāwī al-kubrā*, Cairo, 1326-29/reprint Baghdad, IV, p. 304. Ibn al-Ḥājj: *Al-mudkhal*, Cairo, 1929, IV, p. 244. Mujīr al-Dīn al-Ḥanbalī: *Al-uns al-jalīl bi-tārīkh al-Quds wa'l-Khalīl*, Amman, 1973, II, p. 76. Ibn Mājid: *Al-fawāʾid fī uṣūl ʿilm al-baḥr wa'l-qawāʿid*, facsimile. Gabriel Ferrand: *Instructions nautiques et routiers arabes et portugais*, I, Paris, 1921-23, 69a, last line, to 69b, l. 1. Yūsuf Rāghib: 'Deux monuments fatimides au pied du Muqaṭṭam', *REI* 46, 1978, p. 92, with ftn. 1,

thentic holy tomb of Jesus in Jerusalem is, of course, unthinkable for Islam because in the Islamic view Jesus was never crucified. Carried to its full implication this realistic attitude concerning the death of the Prophet would have put the Muslims at a disadvantage *vis-à-vis* the Christians. Muslims would no longer have been able to turn to him after his death and would be directed exclusively to God Who cannot be represented in images. All they could still have done was to mourn Muḥammad, and the Shīᶜite poet Kumayt b. Zayd (d. 126 /743 or 127/744) did just that, lamenting the loss of such a man in almost gruesome words:

Could a living man redeem the dead, he would say:
I and my children wish to be compensation for those *bones*![13]

And:

I give up my soul as a ransom for those *bones* in your tomb,
a tomb filled with temperance and nobility.[14]

---

where additional bibliographical information is given. Christian polemical writings against Islam also admit that the grave of Moses is unknown; Dionysius Carthusianus: *Contra Alchoranum et sectam Machometicam libri quinque*, lib. III, art. X (Cologne, 1533, pp. 313-14)/D. *Dionysii Cartusiani opera omnia*, vol. 36, Tournay, 1908, *Contra perfidiam Mahometi*, lib. III, art. X, pp. 383-84. This is Old Testament tradition, Deut. 34/6: 'And He (the Lord) buried him in the valley, in the land Moab opposite Beth-Peor, and to this day no one has known his grave.' The Jewish-Persian poet Shāhīn (14th century) sees a wise purpose of God in this: He did not want the Israelites to present their requests in prayers there and possibly to fall into unbelief if their prayers were not answered; Wilhelm Bacher: *Zwei jüdisch-persische Dichter, Schahin und Imrani*, Strassburg, 1907-08, p. 164 (in the book of Moses). In 1534 Greffin Affagart, a pilgrim to Jerusalem, describes meeting in a square cloister-like building some Turks, 'priests of their law', who claimed that Moses was buried there. He rejects this claim on the basis of the passage in Deuteronomy; Greffin Affagart: *Relation de Terre Sainte*, ed. J. Chavanon, Paris, 1902, p. 127. In fact ordinary people located the grave of Moses in several places. But learned Muslims never acknowledged this. ᶜAlī al-Harawī (d. 611/1215) expressly states in his guide for pilgrims: *Al-ishārāt ilā maᶜrifat al-ziyārāt*, ed. and trans. by Janine Sourdel-Thomine, Damascus, 1953-57, p. 13, ll. 5-6/French p. 31, ll. 6-8, that the grave of Moses is unknown, although he mentions locations for the grave which the common folk accepted.

13 Joseph Horovitz: *Die Hāšimijjāt des Kumait*, Leiden, 1904, no. I, verse 52.

14 Horovitz: *Hāšimijjāt*, no. III, verse 58.

Around 400/1010 the question was even raised as to whether, after his death, Muḥammad was really still a prophet at all.[15] It may be that the tension evoked by the small Christian advantage to some extent contributed to the Muslims not completely accepting matters as they stood. But human nature — here one is tempted to say the *anima naturaliter christiana* — will have been much more strongly responsible for the fact that the Muslims too did not get away from the idea of a second life for their Prophet.[16] Already the respectable traditionist of Medina Saᶜīd b. al-Musayyib (d. 94/712) believed that the dead Prophet had been resurrected from the earth forty days after his burial and that twice every day his community is shown to him. Samhūdī (d. 911/1506), who reports this, has no doubts that Ibn al-Musayyib recognizes that Muḥammad has a close spiritual relationship to his tomb.[17] The deviations from the strictly realistic line which resulted from efforts such as these ran directly counter to the concepts of a reformer around 700/1300: Ibn Taymiyya (d. 728/1328) who sought to restore what he alleged had been the correct situation at the beginning. He declared resolutely that Muḥammad was dead and therefore incapable of undertaking anything or of helping in any way or even of mediating during this interim period up to the Resurrection, i.e. during the same period that, on the Christian side, Jesus had promised to be present 'until the end

15 I. Goldziher: 'Zur Geschichte der ḥanbalitischen Bewegungen', *ZDMG* 62, 1908, 13-4. Raimund Köbert: *Bayān muškil al-ḥadīṯ des Ibn Fūrak*, Analecta Orientalia 22, Rome, 1941, p. XVII. Tor Andrae: *Die person Muhammeds in lehre und glauben seiner gemeinde*, Archives d'Études Orientales 16, Stockholm, 1918, pp. 287-89. ᶜAbd al-Raḥīm b. al-Ḥasan al-Asnawī: *Ṭabaqāt al-shāfiᶜiyya*, Baghdad, 1970-71, II, p. 267 (no. 879); from which ᶜAbd al-Ḥayy b. al-ᶜImād al-Ḥanbalī: *Shadharāt al-dhahab*, III, p. 182 above. Ibn Rajab: *Al-dhayl ᶜalā Ṭabaqāt al-ḥanābila*, ed. Henri Laoust et Sāmī al-Dahhān, Damascus, 1951, I, p. 70, l. 3. Suyūṭī: *Al-rasāʾil al-tisᶜ*, Hyderabad, 1961, in which *Inbāh al-adhkiyāʾ fī ḥayāt al-anbiyāʾ*, p. 8, l. 1; ibid., p. 8, ll. 8-9 (the words of Abū Bakr al-Bayhaqī). Hibatallāh b. Najm al-Dīn Ibn al-Bārizī: *Tawthīq ᶜurā'l-īmān*, MS Sprenger 127a (Ahlwardt 2569), 179b (the words of ᶜAbd al-Qāhir al-Baghdādī). According to Suyūṭī the character of prophethood is retained by every prophet after his death; *Al-iᶜlām bi-ḥukm ᶜĪsā ᶜalayhi'l-salām*, in *Al-ḥāwī li'l-fatāwī*, Beirut, 1975, II, p. 165.

16 The following inscription is found on a 3rd/9th century gravestone from Upper-Egypt: 'Had God wished to ward off the blows and the advent of death from someone because of his high rank, He would have done so in the case of Muḥammad'; *Répertoire chronologique d'épigraphie arabe*, II, no. 518.

17 ᶜAlī b. ᶜAbdallāh al-Samhūdī: *Khulāṣat al-Wafā bi-akhbār dār al-muṣṭafā*, Medina, 1972, pp. 97-98/Cairo, 1316, p. 46.

of the world'. Ibn Taymiyya's adherents remained a minority. Other reformers of that time such as Ibn al-Ḥājj (d. 737/1336), for example, who were no less sharply critical of what in their view were objectionable religious practices, at least left the people their Prophet, and so too did the Sufis at a later date in the wake of Aḥmad b. Idrīs (d. 1253/1837) so far as they were reform-minded: they withdrew their feelings from the saints, but instead directed them all the more passionately to the Prophet.[18] In Arabia Muḥammad b. ᶜAbd al-Wahhāb (d. 1206/1792) again took up the ideas of Ibn Taymiyya and, according to malicious gossip, once described Muḥammad as a mere messenger (*ṭārish*) and raised no objection when one of his followers said in his presence: 'This walking stick of mine is better than Muḥammad because at least I can use it for something, whereas Muḥammad is dead and thus no longer of any use.'[19] But the Wahhābīs were only able to foster a complete breakthrough of Ibn Taymiyya's views in Arabia itself and then only at a later time through military and political means, thereby settling the dispute for precedence between Muḥammad's birthplace and the site of his burial in favor of his birthplace Mecca. The waves of Wahhābism have reached Somalia in the south and the coast of the Atlantic Ocean in the west but have not inundated the moderate, traditionalistic conception of Muḥammad's death anywhere in those areas.

The traditionalistic conception holds to a middle position, neither denying the death of Muḥammad nor the possibility of the Prophet continuing to live and exercising influence. One laments his demise

---

18 On the other hand, a polemical work would have it that the Ṣāliḥiyya, following the Wahhābī view, forbade the pilgrimage to the Prophet's grave; B.G. Martin: *Muslim Brotherhoods in Nineteenth-Century Africa*, Cambridge University Press, 1976, p. 199.

19 From the defensive tract of Jamīl Efendi Ṣidqī al-Zahāwī (d. 1936): *Al-fajr al-ṣādiq fī'l-radd ᶜalā munkirī'l-tawassul wa'l-karāmāt wa'l-khawāriq*, Cairo, 1323/offset Istanbul, 1980, p. 18. *Ṭārish* is also found in Abū Ḥāmid b. Marzūq: *Al-tawassul bi'l-nabī wa-jahalat al-wahhābiyyīn*, offset Istanbul, 1980, p. 106. The word occurs in Landberg: *Glossaire datînois*, ed. Zetterstéen, Leiden, 1920-42, III, p. 2202, with several references.

and, in prose and verse,[20] and especially on gravestones,[21] takes it as a consolation for one's own losses, in justification of which one can even refer to an alleged invitation to do so from the Prophet himself.[22] But in the firm conviction that he still participates in the world, one calls upon him as a witness, a protector and an avenger. On the great Moroccan seal of the sultan there presently stands as a slogan verse 135 of Būṣīrī's *Burda*, as it once stood on the seal of the Algerian freedom fighter ᶜAbd al-Qādir (1832-47), as well as in letters, written declarations of allegiance and documents:

Whoever receives help through the Apostle of God,
though lions meet him in their thicket, they will be gripped with silent terror.[23]

---

20 Ibn ᶜAbd Rabbih: *Al-ᶜiqd al-farīd*, Cairo, 1935, II, p. 397 (Ḥajjāj b. Yūsuf). Diᶜbil in Abū'l-Faraj al-Iṣfahānī: *Maqātil al-ṭālibiyyīn*, ed. Ṣaqr, Cairo, 1949, p. 570, last line/Leon Zolondek: *Diᶜbil b. ᶜAlī*, University of Kentucky Press, 1961, no. 201, l. 3. Ṣūlī: *Akhbār al-Rāḍī li'llāh wa'l-Muttaqī li'llāh*, ed. J. Heyworth Dunne, London, 1935, p. 72 (Ṣūlī). Maqqarī: *Nafḥ al-ṭīb/Analectes*, ed. Dozy et alii, II, p. 658 (Ibn al-ᶜArīf). Ibn al-Khaṭīb: *Al-katība al-kāmina fī-man laqīnāhu bi'l-Andalus min shuᶜarā' al-mi'a al-thāmina*, ed. Iḥsān ᶜAbbās, Beirut, 1963, p. 214, l. 10. And there are many others. It is strange that remembering the death of the Prophet does not lighten personal grief, but in fact induces hopelessness; in a North African dirge from the 13th/19th century it says:

If I were not bound by my parents,
I would cause the she-camel to grow thin with a long journey
to Tunis or Fez or Egypt or to the city of the best
of mankind (= Muḥammad) where I would become a pious resident.
But how should the heart raise itself above the flood of suffering
when the best of mankind of all time himself lies in the tomb.
(Sūsī: *Maᶜsūl*, V, p. 125)

When writing condolences and elegiac verses, surah 33/21 is sometimes also recalled: 'In the Apostle of God you have a good example' where, however, *uswa ḥasana* actually has nothing to do with *ta'assī* 'consolation' but alludes to the steadfastness of the Prophet. Examples in *Maᶜsūl*, XIII, p. 130; XIV, p. 78; XIX, p. 198.

21 There the death of the Prophet is mostly only described as 'the greatest misfortune', but this is meant as consolation. *Répertoire chronologique d'épigraphie arabe*, nos. 67, 86, 137, 142, 144, 145, 149, 150, 152, 155, 156, 160, 165, etc. Louis Massignon: 'La Rawda de Médine', *BIFAO* 59, 1960, pp. 260 ff. *Abū Saᶜīd-i Abū l-Ḫayr*, p. 314.

22 Dārimī, *muqaddima* 14, p. 40. Ibn Māja, *janā'iz* 55, nos. 1599-1600, I, p. 510. Ibn al-Ḥājj: *Mudkhal*, III, pp. 265-66; cf. II, p. 15.

23 C.A. Ralfs: *Die Burda. Ein Lobgedicht auf Muḥammad von al-Buṣîrî* (sic), Vienna, 1860, Arabic p. 29/German p. 16. *Dīwān al-Būṣīrī*, ed. Kaylānī, Cairo, 1955, p. 199, l. 6.

And in how many cartouches on doors and walls, especially in the Islamic west, does one find that the *barakat Muḥammad* 'Muḥammad's blessing' (which, however, is a hazy, rather elastic concept) is invoked!

Georg Höst: *Nachrichten von Marókos und Fes, im Lande selbst gesammelt, in den Jahren 1760 bis 1768*, Copenhagen, 1781, pp. 180-81. N. Lacroix: 'Notes sur les cachets et les sceaux chez les musulmans', *RAfr.* 48, 1904, pp. 211-14; 54, 1910, pp. 212-14. Aḥmad b. Khālid al-Nāṣirī: *Al-istiqṣā li-akhbār duwal al-maghrib al-aqṣā*, Casablanca, 1954-56, IX, pp. 110-11. Muḥammad Dāwud: *Tārīkh Tiṭwān*, Tetuan, 1957-76, II, p. 282; III, pp. 257, 289; IV, p. 242; VI, pp. 11, 69, 397-98; VII, pp. 33, 47. *Maᶜsūl*, XX, pp. 243, 251, 257, 261. Māᵓ al-ᶜAynayn's son, Aḥmad al-Hayba (Hība), also made use of a seal of this kind in a certificate of appointment in 1330/1912 (*Maᶜsūl*, XX, p. 190), but his brother Murabbīh Rabbuh did not do so after his seizure of power in 1337/1919 but used a different inscription which is given in *Maᶜsūl*, XX, p. 196. The verse is also found on a portico in Algiers dated to the year 1173/1759-60 (Gabriel Colin: 'Deux Inscriptions arabes du Musée de Mustapha', *RAfr.* 59, 1918, p. 134), on wood in the *al-qubba al-khaḍrāᵓ* of the *qaṣaba* of Tangiers (Georges S. Colin: 'Une nouvelle inscription arabe de Tanger', *Hespéris* 4, 1924, p. 99, ftn. 1), and on a battleaxe of unknown provenance and date owned by a blacksmith in Salā (Alexandre Delpy: 'Note sur des haches d'arme', *Hespéris* 34, 1947, p. 450). I will not give any further examples. For ᶜAbd al-Qādir see Muḥammad b. ᶜAbd al-Qādir al-Jazāᵓirī: *Tuḥfat al-zāᵓir fī tārīkh al-Jazāᵓir wa'l-amīr ᶜAbd al-Qādir*, 1964, p. 308, l. 1. The verse also appears on a pulpit given by ᶜAbd al-Qādir to the Abū Madyan Mosque in ᶜUbbād near Tlemcen; Brosselard *RAfr.* 3, 1859, p. 406. The verse is often preceded or followed by a verse which does not come from the *Burda* but which has the same rhyme and meter. It goes:

Whoever takes cover behind you, oh best of mankind in honor,
is protected by God from every avenger.

This verse, which is addressed to Muḥammad, appears to be an adaptation of an old verse by Manṣūr al-Namarī which was addressed to the caliph Hārūn al-Rashīd and has been transmitted in two versions (Abū'l-Faraj al-Iṣfahānī: *Al-aghānī*, XVII, p. 142/new edition, XIX, p. 74; and XII, p. 20/new edition, XIII, p. 147). The one which is relevant here goes:

Whoever does not take cover behind God's representative (Hārūn al-Rashīd)
receives no benefit at all from the five ritual prayers.

Goldziher mentions this verse with a variant in a different connection and without referring to Būṣīrī or our seals (*Muhammedanische Studien*, Halle, 1889-90, II, p. 55. ftn. 8). In Moroccan documents other combinations also appear: the verses 116 and 135 of the *Burda* (*El Ouataïq*, Receuils périodiques publiés par la Direction des Archives Royales, 2, 1976, p. 364) or the three verses 116, then the inauthentic 'whoever takes cover behind you...', and then 79 (*El Ouataïq* 2, 1976, pp. 353-54). Limits of space preclude a more detailed treatment of this subject.

The view is in fact widespread in Islam that at death the soul or the spirit (*rūḥ*) separates from the body and is wafted up to higher realms or, in the case of wicked individuals, is consigned to nether regions. In one version of the prayer over the dead God is called upon to cause the soul (*rūḥ*) of the deceased to rise up to heaven and to see to it that his corpse does not feel narrowly confined in the earth.[24] We cannot here go into details, nor can we deal with the interrogation and punishment which takes place in the grave. Already in some old representations of the story of Muḥammad's death, according to the actual wording it is only his soul or spirit which ascends and it is *this* which is compared with Moses.[25] Thus what is being thought of is not the physical but the spiritual absence of Moses.[26] The belief that the spirit of Muḥammad, separated from the body and raised on high, spatially unattached, lives on, while his corpse lies in Medina, will continue to have its representatives up until our day and age. The previously mentioned Algerian military commander ᶜAbd al-Qādir, who adhered to the monism of Ibn al-ᶜArabī, is convinced that generally speaking the corpses of the

---

24 Sakhāwī: *Al-qawl al-badīᶜ fī'l-ṣalāh ᶜalā'l-ḥabīb al-shafīᶜ*, Medina-Beirut, 1977, p. 205.

25 Dārimī, *muqaddima* 14, I, p. 39, ll. 9-11. Ibn Saᶜd, II, 2, p. 53, ll. 18-20.

26 By this the death of Moses cannot be meant because in fact after his death he never returned again. In the Arabic stories about the death of Moses God or the angel of death does take his soul (*rūḥ*) but this is nothing other than his life. Thus in the dream God sends to the Israelites to dispel their suspicion that Joshua murdered Moses, God simply says: 'We have taken him (Moses) up to Ourself' which means no more than 'caused him to die' (Ṭabarī, I, p. 503, l. 10). Cf. the angel of death's rather lengthy palaver with Moses about the spot on the body through which he should remove Moses' soul, in Kisāʾī: *Qiṣaṣ al-anbiyāʾ*, ed. I. Eisenberg, Leiden, 1922, p. 239 below. In Thaᶜlabī's *Qiṣaṣ al-anbiyāʾ*, Cairo, 1925, p. 156, l. 15, Joshua asks the deceased Moses in a dream: 'What was the experience of death like?' Moses replies: 'Like a sheep that is flayed alive.' In view of all this our Arabs in Medina cannot have been seduced into taking Moses' death as something other than death and persuaded themselves that Muḥammad's death was also an illusion. — Even less satisfying, it seems to me, is the recollection that in surah 7/143, upon beholding Sinai crumble before an epiphany of God, Moses then collapsed as if struck by lightning — unconscious according to standard interpretation, 'dead' as Qatāda believed (Thaᶜlabī: *Qiṣaṣ*, p. 127, l. 12), for three days (Ibn-i Khalaf al-Naysābūrī: *Qiṣaṣ al-anbiyāʾ*, ed. Ḥabīb-i Yaghmāʾī, Tehran, 1961, p. 234, ll. 7-8) or for an indeterminate time (Ṭabarī, I, p. 490, ll. 16-17). Because to compare Muḥammad's demise with this would be to demean the Prophet. On the other hand, the temporary absence of the spirit would fit here because Moses 'woke up again' (Ṭabarī, ibid.) or recovered his 'spirit' or 'vital spirit' once again (Thaᶜlabī, p. 128, ll. 1-2).

prophets, in so far as they have not simply been translated as was the case with Jesus and Enoch according to Islamic belief, rest in the earth, whereas their spirit is free.[27] In an exchange of polemical poems about Mecca and Medina from the 4th/10th century, the Meccan contributor disparages Medina with the following verses:

> Without the pilgrimage to the Prophet's grave
> you would be like the others who have set off into the desert.
> Yet the Prophet doesn't even really live there (in Medina)
> but lingers in the gardens on high.[28]

It is said that Muḥammad was given the choice as to whether to remain on earth or to go to God. He chose for the second option whereupon God raised up to Himself the Prophet's spirit.[29] A conception taken over from the Christian idea of Jesus pictures Muḥammad after his death as actually sitting on God's Throne. This view was attacked and defended.[30] A certain Muḥammad b. Musallam al-Tūnisī al-Mālikī (d. 977/1596) in Aleppo was still rebuked for making such an assertion.[31] But unfortunately, on close inspection all these reports leave the question open as to whether Muḥammad really ascended so high in the spirit only and not in the body as well, in fact in their unclear and careless form of expression they rather suggest the second situation, which would make the parallel with Jesus complete.

But Muḥammad was also accorded an ongoing life in the grave itself, first of all in the form of a coming and going of his soul. In a saying which is also recorded in the canonical collections the Prophet promises to return the greeting of anyone who greets him at his tomb because God would give him back his 'spirit' for this pur-

---

27 ᶜAbd al-Qādir al-Jazāʾirī: *Al-mawāqif fī'l-taṣawwuf wa'l-waᶜẓ wa'l-irshād*, Damascus, 1967, II, p. 702 (*tanbīh* a).

28 Ibn al-ᶜArabī: *Muḥāḍarat al-abrār wa-musāmarat al-akhyār*, Cairo, 1305, I, p. 161, ll. 18-19. Andrae: *Die person Muhammeds*, pp. 286-87.

29 Abū Nuᶜaym al-Iṣbahānī: *Dalāʾil al-nubuwwa*, Hyderabad, 1950, pp. 549-50.

30 As an interpretation of surah 17/79: 'a praiseworthy station' (*maqām maḥmūd*). Andrae, pp. 270-72. Abū'l-Futūḥ-i Rāzī: *Tafsīr*, Tehran, 1334-35, VI, p. 349. Goldziher: *Muh. Stud.*, II, p. 168.

31 Ibn al-Ḥanbalī: *Durr al-ḥabab fī tārīkh aᶜyān Ḥalab*, ed. al-Fākhūrī and ᶜAbbāra, Damascus, 1972-74, II, 1, pp. 131-33.

pose.[32] By spirit one would at first sight understand life, i.e. the corpse would come alive again for a short time. But Aḥmad al-Tijānī (d. 1230/1815) took the saying to mean that Muḥammad's spirit rushed back from the court of the heavenly Jerusalem and entered his body only in order to return the pious person's greeting and then set out again for its heavenly abode.[33]

Yet whether one accepts that the spirit returns in haste or that the body comes back to life in the grave, in both cases a particular precondition must be fulfilled: the spirit or the life force must find its earthly outer frame again, the latter cannot have disintegrated. But Medina is in fact endowed with such dry soil that corpses normally decompose in about six months and by then the graves can be used again.[34] Thus, as far as one can judge, it is scarcely possible for any physical remains of Muḥammad to be left over. On the other hand, there is another saying of the Prophet which denies this fact, and in religion it is not natural science but holy sayings and faith which determine the truth. According to the Prophet's word, God has forbidden the earth to consume the bodies of the prophets, and sometimes martyrs as well are included and sometimes even callers to prayer.[35] Animals are also meant to be barred from devouring a living prophet. The captured wolf that was supposed to have devoured

---

32 Abū Dāwūd, *manāsik* 96, and others; *Concordance et indices de la tradition musulmane*, II, p. 318 (*rūḥī*). Muḥammad al-Ghazzālī: *Iḥyāʾ ᶜulūm al-dīn*, Cairo, n.d., I, p. 312. Nawawī: *Al-adhkār al-muntakhaba min kalām sayyid al-abrār*, Beirut, 1973, p. 106. Aḥmad b. Maᶜadd al-Uqlīshī (from Ucles in Spain, d. circa 550/1155 in Qūṣ on his return from Mecca; Maqqarī, I, p. 872-73; Yāqūt: *Geograph. Dict.*, Uqlīsh, I, p. 339): *Anwār al-āthār fī faḍl al-ṣalāh ᶜalā'l-nabī al-mukhtār*, in Bārizī: *Tawthīq ᶜurā'l-īmān*, MS Sprenger 127b (Ahlwardt 2569), 199b, penult. and last line. And many other sources. The *ḥadīth* is rejected by Ibn al-Daybaᶜ: *Tamyīz al-ṭayyib min al-khabīth fī-mā yadūr ᶜalā alsinat al-nās min al-ḥadīth*, Cairo, 1324, p. 183.

33 ᶜAlī Ḥarāzim b. al-ᶜArabī Barrāda al-Maghribī al-Fāsī: *Jawāhir al-maᶜānī wa-bulūgh al-amānī fī fayḍ sayyidī Abī'l-ᶜAbbās al-Tijānī*, Beirut, 1383, II, p. 48. Taken from there, Aḥmad b. al-ᶜAyyāshī Sukayrij/Skīraj: *Kashf al-ḥijāb ᶜamman talāqā maᶜa'l-shaykh al-Tijānī min al-aṣḥāb*, n.p., 1961, p. 503.

34 M.S. Makki: *Medina, Saudi Arabia: a geographic analysis of the city and region*, Avebury, 1982, pp. 146-47.

35 Goldziher: *Muh. Stud.*, II, p. 314. Yūsuf Rāghib, *REI* 46, 1978, p. 91, ftn. 2 (with a few *ḥadīth* passages). Ismāᶜīl b. Isḥāq al-Jahḍamī al-Mālikī: *Faḍl al-ṣalāh ᶜalā'l-nabī*, ed. al-Albānī, Beirut, 1977, pp. 37-38. Ibn Taymiyya: *Fatāwī kubrā*, IV, p. 304. Suyūṭī: *Inbāh al-adhkiyāʾ*, pp. 7-8, in *Al-rasāʾil al-tisᶜ*, Hyderabad, 1961, no. 7/in *Al-ḥāwī li'l-fatāwī*, Beirut, 1975, II, p. 149. The literature is endless.

Joseph declares to his father Jacob: 'I have not devoured any son of yours. Oh prophets, your flesh and your blood are forbidden to us.'[36] In this way the spirit or the life force of the Prophet is capable of slipping back into his abandoned outer frame, and there are several reports recounting how the pious, and in particular family descendants of the Prophet, not only perceived his voice at his graveside but that the Prophet even extended his finger or his hand to them.[37]

Beyond that, however, there are further reports which make the coming and going of the Prophet's spirit entirely superfluous. These reports maintain that prophets simply live on in their graves as intact persons, just as they were wont to live in their earthly existence. In this regard one has recourse to the legendary night journey of the Prophet or to another occasion when the Prophet beheld Moses praying in his grave at 'the red dune'.[38] Frequently in connection with the

---

36 Tha^clabī: *Qiṣaṣ*, p. 73.

37 Three examples of the Prophet returning someone's greeting from the grave: Ghulām Sarwar-i Lāhawrī: *Khazīnat al-aṣfiyā'*, litho., Nawal Kishore, 1281, II, p. 36, ll. 18-19. Sha^crānī: *Al-ṭabaqāt al-kubrā*, Cairo, 1954, II, p. 147, no. 50 (Ṣadr al-Dīn al-Bakrī). Muḥibbī: *Khulāṣat al-athar fī a^cyān al-qarn al-ḥādī ^cashar*, Cairo, 1284, I, p. 373, l. 3. Cf. also Charles M. Doughty: *Travels in Arabia Deserta*, Cambridge, 1888, II, p. 160, ll. 4-9. The index finger emerging from the grave: Ibn ^cAyyād: *Al-mafākhir al-^caliyya fī'l-ma'āthir al-shādhiliyya*, Cairo, 1937, p. 26, ll. 16-17 (Abū'l-Ḥasan al-Shādhilī). The hand: Mufīd: *Al-ikhtiṣāṣ*, Tehran, 1379, p. 274, ll. 10-12; p. 275, ll. 2-4 (for ^cAlī). The Prophet extends his hand from the grave and confers a robe of honor on a preacher; *Manāqib-i Awḥad al-Dīn-i Kirmānī*, ed. Furūzānfar, Tehran, 1969, p. 210, ll. 18-21. He dressed Rōzbihān-i Baqlī (d. 606/1209) in a *durrā^ca*, placed a crown upon his head, and gave him a *ṭaylasān* and a banner, *Rūzbihānnāma*, ed. Dānishpazhūh, Tehran, 1347, pp. 177-78. The person best-known for the fact that the Prophet had extended him his hand from the grave is Aḥmad al-Rifā^cī, a Ḥasanid, i.e. a descendant of the Prophet. He arrived in Medina on the pilgrimage in 555/1160, was audibly greeted by the Prophet, and at his request the Prophet extended his right hand to him which he kissed; ^cIzz al-Dīn Aḥmad al-Ṣayyād al-Ḥusaynī al-Rifā^cī (d. 670/1271-72): *Al-ma^cārif al-muḥammadiyya fī'l-waẓā'if al-aḥmadiyya*, maṭb. Muḥammad Muṣṭafā al-bahiyya, 1305, pp. 34-35; Margoliouth *EI* Rifā^cī (III, p. 1249b). Rifā^cī bears the honorary title *ṣāḥib madd al-yad* 'the man of the extended hand'. The Qādiriyya could not countenance this and transferred the story to ^cAbd al-Qādir al-Jīlānī; ^cAbd al-Qādir al-Qādirī b. Muḥyī al-Dīn al-Irbilī: *Tafrīj al-khāṭir fī manāqib ^cAbd al-Qādir*, Alexandria, 1300, p. 31. The Indian Ādam-i Banūrī (d. 1053/1643) managed to achieve even greater honor: Muḥammad extended both his hands to him (through the automatically opening door which does not actually exist on the grave of the Prophet); Lāhawrī: *Khazīnat al-aṣfiyā'*, I, p. 632, penult. line, to p. 633, l. 8.

38 Aḥmad b. al-Ḥusayn al-Bayhaqī: *Ḥayāt al-anbiyā' fī qubūrihim*, MS Or. 2481, 2b, 3a-b, in Leiden University Library (catalogue of Voorhoeve, p. 111). Suyūṭī: *Inbāh*, pp. 3-4/in

incorruptibility of the prophets, Muḥammad is meant to have given assurance that blessings and greetings uttered on his behalf do reach him, directly in that he hears them, or indirectly through an angel who conveys them to him.[39] Here the spirit of the Prophet remains linked most intimately to his body and is at home in the grave. But if it then for some reason becomes detached from the body, this is not different from what happens in the case of a living person. In fact, according to a Shīᶜite view, on Thursday nights Muḥammad's spirit ascends to heaven along with the spirit of other deceased prophets and ᶜAlid imams, and not to be forgotten, with the spirit of the living imam, in order to circumambulate God's Throne seven times in this company, performing two *rakᶜas* of prayer before each foot of the Throne and then returning joyfully to his body on earth with new higher knowledge.[40] On the other hand, that one carried out repair work on the Prophet's grave with the utmost caution is understandable simply in view of the fear with which one approaches a dead holy personage. In this regard there was no need of speculation about the Prophet's life after death. One time in the 6th/12th century a chunk of clay from the inner wall fell into the grave area,

---

Ḥāwī, II, p. 148. Sakhāwī: *Al-qawl al-badīᶜ fī'l-ṣalāh ᶜalā'l-ḥabīb al-shafīᶜ*, Medina-Beirut, 1977, p. 168. Yūsuf Rāghib, *REI* 46, 1978, p. 91, ftn. 3.

39 Subkī: *Ṭabaqāt al-shāfiᶜiyya al-kubrā*, ed. Ṭanāḥī and Ḥulw, Cairo, 1964-76, I, p. 170. Muḥammad b. ᶜAbd al-Raḥmān al-Waṣṣābī al-Ḥubayshī: *Al-baraka fī faḍl al-saᶜy wa'l-ḥaraka*, Cairo, 1354, p. 171, l. 16/Cairo, after 1354, p. 164, ll. 2-3. Bārizī MS Sprenger 127a, 98a. Suyūṭī: *Inbāh*, p. 2, l. 14/in *Ḥāwī*, II, p. 147, penult. line. Several angels: Nasāʾī, *sahw* 46 (III, p. 43) and others; *Concordance*, III, 45a: *sayyāḥ*. Bayhaqī, 6a. One angel: Bayhaqī, 5a. Suyūṭī: *Inbāh*, p. 3, ll. 1-9/in *Ḥāwī*, II, p. 147, last line to p. 148, l. 5. In the Persian Koran commentary of Sūrābādī on surah 33/56 the angel is called Ṣalṣābīl, which should probably be amended to Ṣalṣāʾīl; partial facsimile, Tehran, 1345, p. 354, l. 5. Perhaps the name is connected with *ṣalṣala* (= *taṣliya*/*ṣalāh*): an angel for the invocation of blessings on the Prophet. He writes down people's invocations of blessings and shows them to Muḥammad. What sounds the most authentic and the oldest is a statement of ᶜAbdallāh b. Masᶜūd in which both an element of doubt and hope can be heard. It goes: 'When you invoke a blessing on the Prophet, formulate it nicely for you do not know, *perhaps* it will be brought to him; Jahḍamī: *Faḍl al-ṣalāh ᶜalā'l-nabī*, p. 59; Qāḍī ᶜIyāḍ: *Al-shifā bi-taᶜrīf ḥuqūq al-muṣṭafā*, ed. Bijāwī, Cairo, 1977, II, p. 647. In the form: 'Adorn your gatherings with an invocation of blessings on my behalf because your invocation of blessings reaches me or will be brought to me!' the *ḥadīth* is a concoction borrowed from Suyūṭī; *Al-ḥāwī li'l-fatāwī*, Beirut, 1975, I, pp. 372-73.

40 Kulīnī: *Al-uṣūl min al-Kāfī*, Tehran, 1375, I, pp. 253-54. Andrae: *Die person Muhammeds*, p. 305.

another time a cat found its way inside, and a third time a wall collapsed. In each of these cases it was a complicated procedure to repair the damage because someone had to enter the all-holy space[41] which otherwise no one dared to do. An Ayyūbid whom the emir of Medina wished to accord special distinction by opening the inner space refused this honor out of politeness towards the Prophet.[42] In the 11th/17th century a lamp fell on the grave. A carefully selected man was lowered down on a board and he removed the item.[43] In the time of the ᶜAbbāsids objects like this which had come into contact with the holy grave made their way to Baghdad as relics, for example a shattered wooden cup which was found in the grave in one of the above-mentioned earlier cases and, later, the lamp in question turned up in Constantinople. Wanton acts appeared to be punished immediately by an invisible hand. In 91/710 a Christian artisan who had the audacity to urinate on the Prophet's grave was snatched away and smashed to pieces.[44] In the 7th/13th century a person from Qūṣ in Upper-Egypt who was in charge of the renovation of the cupola over the grave violated the rules of decency by allowing the carpenters to climb around on top of it and by not preventing their hammering. Immediately afterwards, as a conspicuous coincidence connected with the episode, he fell into disfavor and was punished with a beating.[45] When between 1804 and 1813 the Wahhābīs wanted to destroy the cupola, two of the demolition workers slipped and fell to the ground, which was interpreted as a miracle of the Prophet in defense of his tomb.[46] But the idea that the Prophet continued to live in his tomb in Medina like a Pharaoh must have already been current in the 2nd/8th century, otherwise on the occasion of the collapse of the tomb's roof (unrecorded by the history writers that have come down to us) when the workers were merrily climbing up and down, Jaᶜfar al-Ṣādiq (d. 148/765) would not have admon-

---

41 Samhūdī: *Khulāṣat al-Wafā*, pp. 285-86. Ferdinand Wüstenfeld: *Geschichte der Stadt Medina*, Abh. kgl. Ges. Wiss. Göttingen IX, 1860, pp. 80-82 (following Samhūdī).

42 Yūnīnī: *Dhayl Mirʾāt al-zamān*, Hyderabad, 1954-61, I, pp. 126-27.

43 Muḥibbī: *Khulāṣat al-athar*, III, p. 69, ll. 9-15.

44 Ibn Rosteh: *Kitâb al-aᶜlâk al-nafīsa*, ed. De Goeje, BGA 7, Leiden, 1892, p. 69, ll. 8-22.

45 Udfuwī: *Al-ṭāliᶜ al-saᶜīd al-jāmiᶜ asmāʾ nujabāʾ al-Ṣaᶜīd*, Cairo, 1966, p. 89 below. Jean-Claude Garcin: *Un centre musulman de la Haute-Égypte médiévale: Qūṣ*, thèse Paris, 1976 (IFAO), p. 206.

46 Johann Ludwig Burckhardt: *Reisen in Arabien*, Weimar, 1830, pp. 509-10. Idem: *Notes on the Bedouins and Wahábys*, London, 1831, II, p. 110.

ished his adherents: 'I do not want any one of you to climb up. I am not sure that he would not see something which would take away his sight or that he would not catch a glimpse of the Prophet performing his prayers or even being together with one of his wives.'[47]

The traditions concerning Muḥammad's night journey up to heaven inevitably led to a further development. Indeed, on that occasion Muḥammad had not merely seen Moses in his grave but had met him in one of the heavens through which he travelled, and had likewise met Adam, Enoch and Abraham, each of them as well in one of the heavens — moreover it was not simply their spirit or their departed soul that he had encountered but their person in flesh and blood.[48] This meant that after their death the prophets were in no way bound to their graves but were capable of quitting their graves and travelling about everywhere in the world and even visiting the heavenly realms. This was also the inference one could draw from one of God's statements about the posthumous fate of the martyrs and from another such statement about the pious in general. According to surahs 3/169 and 40/40 both groups are immediately transferred to Paradise after their death where they indulge in the pleasures of food and drink. As Muḥammad b. Aḥmad al-Qurṭubī (d. 671/1273) and others reasoned, if this was said regarding the martyrs and the pious generally, how much more true it must be about the prophets who in fact had a higher standing and moreover were often martyrs themselves.[49] One thought seriously of according this double entitlement to Muḥammad since he had himself attributed the illness which brought about his death to the effects of a piece of poisoned meat which four years earlier he had placed in his mouth but then spit out again.[50] The result of such considerations is reflected in the statements of two scholars of the 5th/11th century, Abū Manṣūr ᶜAbd al-Qāhir al-Baghdādī (d. 429/1037) and Aḥmad b. al-Ḥusayn al-Bayhaqī (d. 458/1066), both of whom say more or less the same thing: Muḥammad came back to life again after his death. He continues to participate in his community, takes pleasure in their acts of obedience and is saddened by their sins. The blessings which are in-

---

47 Kulīnī: *Uṣūl*, I, p. 452. Andrae, p. 286.

48 Bukhārī, *ṣalāh* 1, and parallels. B. Schrieke: 'Die Himmelsreise Muhammeds', in *Der Islam* 6, 1916, p. 1-30. Horovitz *EI* Miᶜrādj.

49 Suyūṭī: *Inbāh*, pp. 5-7/in *Ḥāwī*, II, pp. 148-49. Sakhāwī: *Qawl*, pp. 168-69. For Qurṭubī's *Tadhkira bi-aḥwāl al-mawlā* see *GAL S*, I, p. 737.

50 Frants Buhl: *Das Leben Muhammeds*, German trans. by Schaeder, Leipzig, 1930, pp. 293-94.

voked on his behalf reach him. He has retained the character of a prophet. All prophets come back to life after their death and are not bound to their grave but go about freely wherever God allows them to go. As proof of this, Muḥammad saw Moses in his grave and in heaven.[51] Bayhaqī points out that Moses and other deceased prophets, on the night of Muḥammad's heavenly journey, were first translated to Jerusalem and then like Muḥammad to heaven where they were met again by Muḥammad. He closes with the words: 'That the deceased prophets at different times reside (*ḥulūl*) in different places is possible on the basis of reason as well as being attested by a statement from our Prophet who speaks the truth. All this is proof of their survival after death'[52]

In the second half of the 9th/15th century two Egyptian scholars now took up the theory again, the first of them merely on the side, whereas the second dealt with it more extensively. The first is Sakhāwī (831-902/1427-1497), known for his indispensable dictionary of persons from the 9th/15th century, *Al-ḍawʾ al-lāmiʿ li-ahl al-qarn al-tāsiʿ*, Cairo, 1353-55. He composed a treatise about invoking blessings on the Prophet after his death which appears not to be preserved,[53] and in the year 860/1456 or 861/1457 wrote a monograph about invoking blessings on Muḥammad generally, under the title *Al-qawl al-badīʿ fī'l-ṣalāh ʿalā'l-ḥabīb al-shafīʿ* which is not only preserved but has also been printed.[54] In a particular section of this work he touches on the thesis of the continued life of Muḥammad and the other prophets after their death and clarifies his thesis with *ḥadīth*s and statements of earlier writers (pp. 167-70). Sakhāwī had a high opinion of this composition of his and relates in his autobiography with pride that several of his admirers, in particular ʿAbd al-Ḥaqq al-Sanbāṭī, apparently in 884/1479, read it out loud to others at the Prophet's grave in Medina. He says this work was widely circu-

51 Bārizī: *Tawthīq*, MS Sprenger 127a, 179b-180b. Suyūṭī: *Inbāh*, pp. 7-9/in *Ḥāwī*, II, pp. 149-50. The work of Bayhaqī's from which the extract comes is entitled *Al-iʿtiqād wa'l-hidāya ilā sabīl al-rashād* (*GAL S*, I, p. 619, l. 20)

52 Bayhaqī: *Ḥayāt al-anbiyāʾ*, MS Or. 2481, 4a (Leiden). Sakhāwī: *Qawl*, p. 168, from Bayhaqī.

53 Sakhāwī: *Ḍawʾ lāmiʿ*, VIII, p. 18, l. 14.

54 Medina-Beirut, 1977. *GAL*, II, p. 35, no. 12/*GAL S*, II, p. 32, no. 12, with other printings. As the year of composition the Medina-Beirut edition, p. 265, l. 4, has the date 860. Ahlwardt in his description of the MS Berlin 3921 gives the year 861.

lated. And he adds that there were even people who, after changing the text for the worse, passed it off as their own work.[55]

The second of the two Egyptian scholars is the universally known, many-sided Suyūṭī (849-911/1445-1505) who expressed himself on the subject in two writings. The one is entitled *Inbāh al-adhkiyāʾ fī ḥayāt al-anbiyāʾ*,[56] *The Waking Up of the Intelligent: On the Life of the Prophets*. In this work one is immediately struck by the similarity of his conception and his argumentation with the presentation of Sakhāwī who was almost a generation older, and the suspicion is raised that Suyūṭī could have copied Sakhāwī's book. An answer to the question is offered by both scholars themselves. Sakhāwī in fact reproaches Suyūṭī, as has been known for a long time, for frequently having altered older writings and then claiming them as his own. Beyond that, moreover, he accuses him of having stolen (*ikhtalasa*) during his association with him, Sakhāwī, the contents for some of his writings, in particular 'the invocation of blessings on the Prophet'.[57] Suyūṭī, on the other hand, does not refer to the conflict, nor does he mention Sakhāwī but stresses that he has worked out (*istinbāṭ*) the different possible interpretations of a *ḥadīth* all by himself, interpretations which bear striking resemblances to those of Sakhāwī,[58] in fact he expressly asserts that he has not found them transmitted (*manqūl*) by anyone.[59] Thus as it stands, it is one person's word against another's.

The fierce defamatory attacks which Sakhāwī directed against Suyūṭī, not only in this affair but more generally as well, induced well-known people to take Suyūṭī's part against him.[60] It was thought that the feud — Suyūṭī did eventually defend himself against his adversary — had its origin in the natural competition between

---

55 *Ḍawʾ*, IV, p. 38, last line; VIII, pp. 27-28.

56 In *Al-rasāʾil al-tisʿ li'l-shaykh al-ʿallāma Jalāl al-Dīn ʿAbd al-Raḥmān b. Abī Bakr al-Suyūṭī*, Hyderabad, 1961, no. 7/in *Al-ḥāwī li'l-fatāwī... li-ʿālim Miṣr... al-Suyūṭī*, Beirut, 1975, II, pp. 147-55 (title: *Inbāʾ al-adhkiyāʾ bi-ḥayāt al-anbiyāʾ*). I also had at my disposal a xerox copy of the Berlin MS Ahlwardt 2534, 40a-47a (Lbg 329) entitled *Inbāh al-adhkiyāʾ li-ḥayāt al-anbiyāʾ*. One often meets with *Inbāʾ* or *Anbāʾ* in the indirect transmission, i.e. in quotations in other authors.

57 *Ḍawʾ*, IV, p. 66, ll. 20-21.

58 *Inbāh*, p. 15, l. 12/in *Ḥāwī*, II, p. 153, l. 7.

59 *Inbāh*, p. 11. ll. 16-17/in *Ḥāwī*, II, p. 151, ll. 14-15.

60 Muḥammad b. ʿAlī al-Shawkānī: *Al-badr al-ṭāliʿ bi-maḥāsin man baʿd al-qarn al-sābiʿ*, Cairo, 1348, I, pp. 332-34. ʿAbd al-Ḥayy al-Kattānī: *Fihris al-fahāris*, Fez, 1347, II, p. 338. But there were also those who defended Sakhāwī against Suyūṭī.

contemporary professional colleagues, and adopting someone else's knowledge in the field of learning was glossed over as the most normal thing in the world. But in our case it should especially be remembered that both parties were in fact obliged to use the same literature and the same sources, and they did use them and quoted from them which automatically resulted in a significant degree of common elements in their work. It would be an easy matter to demonstrate that Sakhāwī was also dependent on older religious scholars. The only question one might ask is why Suyūṭī overlooked his immediate predecessor Sakhāwī. Two possibilities exist: either Sakhāwī at a later time backdated his *Qawl badīᶜ* and is not Suyūṭī's predecessor in this respect, or Suyūṭī did not really know of Sakhāwī's work. In the second case this could be because of a deliberate choice to ignore Sakhāwī or because of an accidental lack of knowledge. For a later backdating of Sakhāwī's treatise, we have no clear evidence to go on. It appears more probable that, throughout the ongoing tension between the two men, the blame, if one can speak of such, lies with Suyūṭī. But it is no longer possible to judge whether he deliberately disregarded Sakhāwī or was simply uninformed by chance. Intentionally brushing aside a professional colleague, except in a case where one wishes to break off an irresolvable feud once and for all, would not be consistent with honest scholarship, but ignorance resulting from a situation based on such feuding would at least be comprehensible. Whereas accidental ignorance could be a sign of blameworthy carelessness, it might also be the result of preoccupation and too high a demand on one's time, and would then be understandable. And Suyūṭī was indeed a man who was absorbed in work beyond all measure. Without any proof we are not entitled to make a choice between these possibilities.

We do not want to deprive Sakhāwī of the honor of priority. But here we wish to let Suyūṭī speak because his treatment of our subject is more comprehensive.

The other of the two writings of Suyūṭī is his *Tanwīr al-ḥalak fī imkān ruʾyat al-nabī wa'l-malak*,[61] *Illumination of the Dark: On the Possibility of Seeing the Prophet and Angels.*

Each of Suyūṭī's two treatises elucidates the problem of Muḥammad's continued life from a different side. But in what follows I will only make selective use of both works, that is to say only to the extent that they provide answers to our questions, and I will only

---

61 In *Al-ḥāwī li'l-fatāwī*, II, pp. 255-69 (no. 70). I also had at my disposal a xerox copy of the Berlin MSS Ahlwardt 4277, 74b-83a (1) and 63a-74a (2).

take from the first the above-mentioned *ḥadīth* interpretation with its numerous echoes of Sakhāwī which affirms a continued life after death for the Prophet, in other words the premise on which everything else is based. The second treatise occurs in the editions under the legal judgements (*fatāwī*) and is thus quite out of place, for as far as we can see there is no evidence of an inquiry to which Suyūṭī might have been replying. From this work it is clear that Suyūṭī, following the example of his predecessors, supported a kind of counterpart to the Christian doctrine of resurrection. He propounded *a resurrection of Muhammad without an ascension*.[62] He

---

62 Given this state of affairs, it is advisable not to designate Muḥammad's nocturnal journey to Jerusalem and then upward to heaven, in brief the *mi*ᶜ*rāj*, as an 'assumption, ascent, ascension', etc. The ascension of Christ is *ṣu*ᶜ*ūd* in Arabic. We understand by 'assumption, ascension' an upward journey after death involving a permanent home-coming. Such a conception is alien to the theology and the myth concerning Muḥammad. Ali Bey, regarding the average Muslim, in fact relates: 'Every good Muslim believes that after the death and burial of the Prophet his soul was united with his body and he undertook his ascent to Paradise in body and in soul while riding on the angel Gabriel's mare named Boràk, which has the head and neck of a beautiful woman. This is not an article of faith but a Muslim who refuses to believe this would be viewed as impious and treated as such. ᶜAbdulwahhāb (= Muḥammad b. ᶜAbd al-Wahhāb), however, declared this event to be absolutely false and that the mortal remains of the Prophet, like those of all human beings, have stayed in the grave' (*Voyages d'Ali Bey en Afrique et en Asie*, Paris, 1814, II, pp. 442-43). But is the mistake perhaps not to be attributed to Ali Bey? In any case, among the Indian Muslims the common people celebrate Muḥammad's heavenly journey on the day of his death (*bārā wafāt*), on the 12th of Rabīᶜ I, which is likewise regarded as his birthday, whereas the educated and those who are particularly pious celebrate it in Rajab; Jaffur Shurreef: *Qanoon-e-Islam*, trans. Herklots, pp. 233-36, 251. Suyūṭī makes use of the heavenly journey of the Prophet to support the doctrine that Muḥammad was not only sent to mankind and the *jinn* (*al-thaqalān*), but to the angels as well, and considers it not impossible that one reason for his heavenly journey was in fact to present himself to the angels and the lovely-eyed maidens and good-looking boys of Paradise; *Tazyīn al-arāʾik fī irsāl al-nabī ilā'l-malāʾik*, in *Ḥāwī*, II, pp. 144, 145. A similar idea was contemplated by his contemporary Muḥammad Abū'l-Mawāhib (b. Aḥmad al-Tūnisī al-Qāhirī al-Mālikī) al-Shādhilī (d. 882/1477-78; *Shadharāt al-dhahab*, VII, pp. 335-36), as a passage in Shaᶜrānī's *Ṭabaqāt kubrā*, Cairo, 1952, II, p. 80, ll. 24-26, indicates. Thus Muḥammad's heavenly journey became a kind of counterpart to Christ's descent into Hell. In the one case Christ immediately after his death extends his redemption to the dead, whereas in the other case Muḥammad in the middle of his life also extends his influence among the heavenly beings. A preacher from Ghaznī, Burhān al-Dīn Abū'l-Ḥasan ᶜAlī b. al-Ḥusayn al-Ghaznawī (d. 551/1156), in Baghdad one time had the presumption to claim — Ibn al-Jawzī heard it himself — that Muḥammad was allowed to behold Paradise and Hell during the *mi*ᶜ*rāj* so he would not

combined the old conception of the incorruptibility of the body of prophets with its revival by means of the surviving spirit, but without having Muḥammad ascend to heaven like Christ. Muḥammad remains here below. But he is free to rise higher, if he wishes. Let us review the important points of the doctrine.

The first treatise, the *Inbāh*, provides the foundation by thoroughly exploiting the alleged saying of the Prophet: 'Whoever greets me (when I am in the grave), God gives me back my soul (or spirit) so that I can return his greeting.' What Suyūṭī finds strange about this statement is the idea that the soul or spirit is continually involved in entering and exiting the body. This form of ceaseless coming and going must be painful for the Prophet's body and likewise must be degrading to the Prophet because it puts him in a lower category than the martyrs who do not suffer anything of this sort. Moreover, it is in violation of the Koran which states that no one experiences more than two lives and two deaths, namely — and this is the interpretation of surah 2/28 — life before death and life after the resurrection, and death while in the male sperm before procreation and death as the end of earthly life. Suyūṭī therefore considers that *rūḥ* might have another meaning. Several possibilities occur to him: it could be the capacity of speech which is given back to the Prophet, or the inner ears or attentiveness or waking from absorption in the supernatural dimension of the world and time after death (*barzakh*), in addition refreshment (reading *rūḥ* as *rawḥ*) or mercifulness or the angel who is appointed over his grave, and other meanings as well. He favors waking from engrossment in the things of the world after death. But he also thinks of a different way of taking the verb *radda*, which

---

experience fright on the Resurrection. When God spoke to Moses, the latter's staff was changed into a snake so that he would not be afraid when he flung it down before Pharaoh; Ibn al-Jawzī: *Al-muntaẓam*, Hyderabad, 1357-59, X, p. 166 (year 551). This preacher is the same person for whom his fellow-countryman, the poet Sanāʾī, sent a rough draft of his *Ḥadīqat al-ḥaqīqa* to Baghdad, allegedly to have its theological soundness checked but also to assure that the book would not be scattered and destroyed by enemies, or for other reasons as well such as for the use and exaltation of the preacher. While this first version was in Baghdad, Sanāʾī wrote out a fair copy of what he had before him but died in the process so that the extant individual parts of the *Ḥadīqa* still had to be collected and assembled together. The job was undertaken by Raffāʾ who wrote the preface which has come down to us. Cf. Mudarris-i Raḍawī in his edition, Tehran, 1329, l-lā. More details in the recent work of J.T.P. de Bruijn: *Of Piety and Poetry. The Interaction of Religion and Literature in the Life and Works of Ḥakīm Sanāʾī of Ghazna*, Leiden, 1983, pp. 81, 120.

could have an anterior sense, as if it were preceeded by the particle *qad*. The meaning of the sentence would then be: 'Whoever greets me, God has given me back (once and forever) my spirit (or life force) so that I can return his greeting.' Suyūṭī subsequently found a confirmation for this interpretation in Bayhaqī who actually provides the *qad*.[63] In the Leiden MS Or. 2481, 5b, of Bayhaqī's *Ḥayāt al-anbiyā'* it is missing. In any case, as Suyūṭī acknowledges, a more or less permanent attachment of the spirit to the body would naturally result through the fact that in the world blessings and salvation are actually called down upon Muḥammad uninterruptedly so that he would never cease to give an answer. Suyūṭī later on discovered that Tāj al-Dīn b. al-Fākihānī (d. 731/1331) had already expressed this last thought in his treatise *Al-fajr/al-fakhr*[64] *al-munīr fī-mā fuḍḍila bihī al-bashīr al-nadhīr*.[65] Almost all these considerations with minor deviations are already to be found in Sakhāwī, even the quotation from Fākihānī which Sakhāwī, however, has not merely stuck on at the end but has correctly worked in at the very beginning. Be this as it may, Suyūṭī in the *Inbāh* defends the thesis that the Prophet lives on in flesh and blood after his death.

The second treatise, the *Tanwīr*, only towards the end speaks of the theory which interests us and then makes four particular observations (*tanbīhāt*).[66] These four points are as follows:

1) The most common perception of the deceased Prophet — and this is the subject of the second treatise — occurs, according to Suyūṭī, in the heart and is thus an interior vision. When the experience is more intense, then the exterior eye also sees him, not in the usual sense but by means of collectedness within an exceptional state (*jamᶜiyya ḥāliyya*) in a kind of state after death (*ḥāla barzakhiyya*) as a spiritual (*rūḥānī* according to one MS) or a lived emotion (*amr wijdānī*), the reality of which can only be grasped by someone who has experienced it directly (*bāsharahū*) for which a kind of raptus is necessary. We would perhaps say that this was a question of a hybrid

---

63 *Inbāh*, p. 19, ll. 8-12/in *Ḥāwī li'l-fatāwī*, II, p. 154, ll. 23-26. Taqī al-Dīn al-Subkī: *Shifā' al-saqām fī ziyārat khayr al-anām*, Beirut, 1371, pp. 51-52, mentions this possibility as well as the possibility that waking up from preoccupation with the supernatural world could also be meant.

64 In the Hyderabad edition, p. 11, ll. 17-18 one finds *fakhr*, in *Ḥāwī*, II, p. 151, l. 15 and in the MS Lbg. 329, 44a, ll. 7-8 (Ahlwardt 2534) *fajr*. The rest of the title's wording deviates from the title as transmitted elsewhere; *GAL S*, II, p. 15.

65 All to be found in *Inbāh*, pp. 8-20/in *Ḥāwī*, II, pp. 150-55.

66 *Al-ḥāwī li'l-fatāwī*, II, pp. 262-66.

phenomenon or a union between external sight and internal visionary sight. But seeing the Prophet is a special, wide-ranging topic which we cannot enter into here at length.

2) When the Prophet appears, one does not always (and not according to everyone's opinion) see the Prophet himself but often only an image (*mithāl*) of him. In this connection Suyūṭī cites Muḥammad al-Ghazzālī according to whom the deceased Prophet only displays himself to a human being in an image which may correspond to the Prophet's reality or, because of the person's inadequate purity of soul, may be distorted. Similarly, it is only in an image that God appears to man in dreams. This agrees in broad outline with what Ghazzālī presents in a somewhat lengthy discussion in his text *Al-maḍnūn bihī ᶜalā ghayr ahlihī*, which Duncan Black MacDonald has translated in his book *The Religious Attitude and Life in Islam* (Chicago 1909/new edition New York 1970, pp. 80-83) and likewise agrees with what Vincent Lagardère has translated from another text of Ghazzālī and published with the Arabic original in his article 'À propos d'un chapitre du *Nafj* (= *Nafkh*) *wa-l-taswiya* attribué à Ġazzālī' in *Cuadernos de Historia del Islam* 11 (1984), pp. 73-86. Only in the latter passages it is much clearer that by image Ghazzālī does not mean a likeness but a symbol which does not possess external common features with Muḥammad but 'signifies' Muḥammad, as for instance the sun in a dream can 'signify' the ruler and the moon his vizier. This is correctly recognized by MacDonald and Lagardère.[67] Elsewhere, moreover, Ghazzālī writes that Muḥammad can appear to an individual in a dream in an existence graspable by the senses (*wujūd ḥissī*), which in this context means in an image or likeness based on transmitted descriptions, not as a person who has left his grave.[68] Later on he must have also abandoned this position since he praises the Sufis because in a waking state they beheld the angels and the spirit — at very least the spirit! — of the prophets, heard their voices and received instruction from them.[69] Our quotation from Ghazzālī in Suyūṭī was repeated by Muḥammad Haqqī al-

---

67 The form in which the angel Gabriel revealed himself is naturally not the head of a dog (*diḥyat al-kalb*) as Lagardère thinks, but the handsome man Diḥya al-Kalbī. The treatise *Al-nafkh wa'l-taswiya* is acknowledged by Aḥmad Zarrūq (d. 899/1493): *Qawāᶜid al-taṣawwuf*, Cairo, 1968, p. 129, no. 207, as an authentic work of Ghazzālī's and listed under those of his writings which one is warned against. The same is also true of *Maḍnūn*.

68 *Fayṣal al-tafriqa bayn al-islām wa'l-zandaqa*, Cairo, 1961, pp. 176-77.

69 *Al-munqidh min al-ḍalāl*, the section on the Ṣūfiyya.

Nāzilī (d. 1301/1883-84) in his *Khazīnat al-asrār*, Beirut, n.d., p. 175.

Suyūṭī compares Ghazzālī with the Mālikite jurist and traditionist Abū Bakr b. al-ᶜArabī (d. 543/1148) who had met Ghazzālī in Baghdad. This *qāḍī*, according to Suyūṭī, had only intended to speak of a mere likeness in those cases where the manifestation of the Prophet deviated from his appearance as transmitted in literature. Otherwise the Prophet was actually still supposed to be directly visible after his death because like all prophets he had received his spirit again shortly after death and was able to leave his grave when he wished and to move about unhampered in the sublunar as well as in the translunar world (*malakūt*). Quotations from Bayhaqī's *Dalāʾil al-nubuwwa* and *Iᶜtiqād* are inserted, according to which the prophets just like the martyrs are alive in the presence of their Lord, and the statement of the writer on heresies ᶜAbd al-Qāhir al-Baghdādī which is cited in the *Inbāh* is also not left out. As in the *Inbāh* (pp. 6-7/in *Ḥāwī* p. 149), here as well Qurṭubī is once more brought into the picture to support the view that everything points to the conclusion that the deceased prophets are alive and are simply removed from our sight just like the angels. Only people upon whom God has conferred His special grace are capable of seeing them as well.

Then Suyūṭī becomes even clearer citing words from Bayhaqī which he likewise mentioned in the *Inbāh* (p. 3, ll. 10-14/in *Ḥāwī*, p. 148, ll. 5-8) and which Sakhāwī too had already introduced (*Qawl*, p. 167 below). This includes the alleged saying of Muḥammad: 'The prophets are not left in their grave longer than forty days and then they perform the ritual prayers in the presence of God until the trumpet (on the Final Day) is sounded.' And the assertion of the Medinan traditionist Saᶜīd b. al-Musayyib (d. 94/712): 'No prophet remained longer than forty days in his grave and was then taken up.'[70] Suyūṭī next goes on to say that Imām al-Ḥaramayn Abū'l-Maᶜālī ᶜAbd al-Malik al-Juwaynī (d. 478/1085) in his *Nihāyat al-maṭlab fī dirāyat al-madhhab* and Rāfiᶜī (d. 623/1226) in his commentary to the *Musnad* of Shāfiᶜī define the period of time in the grave as much shorter,

---

70 Bayhaqī: *Ḥayāt al-anbiyāʾ*, MS Leiden Or. 2481, 2b. Bayhaqī notes that the first sentence is unclear. It could mean that the prophets then pray in their grave after forty days go by or that they are translated upwards in flesh and blood (and pray there). — Suyūṭī adds other variants. The reading: 'No prophet remains longer than forty mornings until his spirit is given back to him in the grave', is rejected by Ibn al-Jawzī: *Al-mawḍūᶜāt*, Medina, 1966-68, III, p. 239, and by Shawkānī: *Al-fawāʾid al-majmūᶜa fī'l-aḥādīth al-mawḍūᶜa*, Beirut, 1392, p. 325, no. 1011. Sakhāwī (*Qawl*, pp. 167-68) also indicates doubts about it.

namely three days,[71] indeed following an alternative reading of the text no more than two days. Abū'l-Ḥasan ᶜAlī al-Zāghūnī al-Ḥanbalī (d. 527/1133)[72] holds the view that it is only half a day.

Suyūṭī then has recourse to the *tadhkira* of a certain Badr al-Dīn b. al-Ṣāḥib,[73] who stresses that Muḥammad's allusions and surah 3/169 can only be understood to mean that the Prophet after his death lives on in the so-called intermediary realm (*barzakh*). Indeed, the same rank is accorded to martyrs but only ones who are especially select because of their loyal allegiance to the Prophet, who for his part as well is to be considered a martyr.[74] If Muḥammad saw Moses praying in his grave, this proves that Moses is still alive in a physical sense. This is all the more certain because of the precise designation 'in the grave', since no one would conceive of the spirits of the prophets as imprisoned (*masjūn*) in their graves. Muḥammad is also meant to have seen the prophet Jonah in a narrow defile wearing a woollen robe and riding on a reddish-brown she-camel.[75] Moreover, Badr al-Dīn also held the view that the banqueting of the martyrs in the presence of God as described in the Koran did not exclude the possibility that they also fasted, prayed, performed the pilgrimage and fulfilled the other religious duties. Whereas the hereafter is no longer the place of work and probation (*dār al-ᶜamal*), these departed ones find themselves, although in the hereafter (*ukhrā*), none the less still in the here and now (*hādhihī'l-dunyā*). Only once the time period of the here and now has run out and is followed by the real hereafter as a place of reward (*dār al-jazāʾ*), will action cease.

---

71 Likewise, cited earlier by Sakhāwī (*Qawl*, p. 168, ll. 1-4) but with the greatest reserve and from Ghazzālī. — But in a more complete version the opposite is affirmed, namely that Muḥammad by contrast with the other prophets has not arisen from the dead at all. Ibn al-Ḥājj: *Mudkhal*, II, p. 42: 'No prophet has been buried without having arisen after three days, except me; for I have prayed God to allow me to remain among you, i.e. mankind, until the Day of Resurrection.' And this could provide the exegesis for surah 8/33: 'And God could not possibly punish them as long as you tarried among them.'

72 There is an article on him in Ibn Rajab al-Ḥanbalī: *Al-dhayl ᶜalā Ṭabaqāt al-ḥanābila*, Beirut, 1953, III, pp. 180-84.

73 He wrote before 797/1394-95 because Ibn Abī'l-Ḥijja composed a *takhmīs* in that year to rival his work; Hitti-Fāris-ᶜAbd al-Malik: *Descriptive Catalogue of the Garrett Collection of Arabic Mss. in the Princeton University Library*, Princeton, 1938, no. 97. Mentioned in *GAL*, II, p. 17, no. 23; *GAL S*, I, p. 779, no. 52.

74 See pp. 519 above.

75 The alleged saying of the Prophet only specifies that it seemed to Muḥammad as if (*kaʾannī*) he saw Jonah in that valley. That is to say a visionary form of seeing.

This is what Qāḍī ᶜIyāḍ (d. 544/1149) is supposed to have said. But if the martyrs leave their graves and make the pilgrimage to Mecca, how can this be disputed with regard to the Prophet Muḥammad? Thus Muḥammad's body must be in heaven and not buried in the earth. This is how far Badr al-Dīn goes.

On the basis of these sacred claims and the inferences drawn from them, Suyūṭī comes to the dogmatic conclusion that Muḥammad is alive in the spirit and the body, that he moves about freely and travels wherever he wishes on the earth and in the supernatural world (*malakūt*), that he still looks as he was before death, but that he eludes the external eye like the angels and is only visible to those for whom God lifts the veil by means of special grace. And the latter do not then simply see a likeness but they behold the Prophet himself.

3) To the question concerning ubiquity of the Prophet: 'How can the deceased Prophet be seen simultaneously in places which are far removed from one another?', Suyūṭī gives a rather vapid reply. A man — according to another source he was a certain Ibn Abī Jamra[76] — was said to have answered the question with a verse in which the Prophet was compared to a sun which sheds its light over all lands. He writes that supposedly Ibn ᶜAṭāʾallāh al-Sikandarī (d. 709/1309) was once seen by one of his disciples at all the holy places of the pilgrimage, yet in reality he had never left Cairo. By way of explaining this, Ibn ᶜAṭāʾallāh had said: 'The great man fills the entire world.'

4) Suyūṭī knows people who conclude from what has been said that individuals who see the Prophet today should be reckoned among the Prophet's Companions. Suyūṭī rejects this and justifies his view with the explanation: 'If someone merely sees an image of the Prophet — which does in fact happen —, a claim to being among

---

76 Shaᶜrānī: *Ṭabaqāt kubrā*, Cairo, 1954, I, pp. 160 and 203, mentions two persons named Ibn Abī Jamra, a Muḥammad b. Abī Jamra (I, p. 160) without a date and an ᶜAbdallāh b. Abī Jamra (I, p. 203) with the death date 675/1276-77. In the history of literature one finds an ᶜAbdallāh b. Saᶜd b. Saᶜīd b. Abī Jamra al-Azdī al-Andalusī (d. 695/1296 or 699/1299-1300); *GAL*, I, p. 372; *GAL S*, I, p. 635 (where he is equated with ᶜAbdallāh b. Abī Jamra from 675/1276-77); Ziriklī: *Al-aᶜlām*, IV, p. 221; Mohammed Ben Cheneb: 'Étude sur les personnages mentionnés dans l'*Idjâza* du cheikh ᶜAbd el Qâdir el Fâsy', *Actes du 14e Congrès des Orientalistes*, Paris, 1907, tome 4, no. 107. Aḥmad Bābā: *Nayl al-ibtihāj*, in the margin of Ibn Farḥūn, Cairo, 1329, p. 140. Makhlūf: *Shajarat al-nūr al-zakiyya fī ṭabaqāt al-mālikiyya*, Beirut, reprint of the edition of 1349, p. 199, no. 674. In our text the last-named ᶜAbdallāh b. Saᶜd is apparently meant whose *Bahjat al-nufūs* on this subject is occasionally cited. — The name of Ibn Abī Jamra is mentioned by Fīlālī; see pp. 541 below.

the Prophet's Companions (*ṣuḥba*) is out of the question because only someone who has really seen him in flesh and blood (*ruʾyat dhātihī al-sharīfa*) can be a Companion of the Prophet.[77] But if someone really does see the Prophet, he is still not a Companion because in addition he must have seen him in his original action in the world of the senses (*mulk*). For whoever now really sees the Prophet for the first time, long after his death, sees him, even in a waking state as indicated in 1), 2) and 3), in the transfigured intermediary realm (*malakūt*). For Suyūṭī the correctness of this limitation is easily inferred from the fact that in the future all the members of the Prophet's community will be brought before him, but they will not thereby be promoted to being Companions, precisely because this encounter will take place in the intermediary realm (*malakūt*).

Let us summarize. According to Suyūṭī, Muḥammad has died a proper human death and been buried, but after several days, or even on the same day, has been resurrected again in his body. In this way he fulfills exactly the presupposition of Jesus' incorruptibility which is mentioned in the New Testament by Peter (Acts 2:30-32) and by Paul (Acts 13:34-37). Muḥammad's resurrection is not followed by an ascension but after his death he is none the less in the position to go everywhere in his body and also to rise up to heaven which he had already done once during his lifetime on his night journey. Thus Muḥammad acquires two characteristics which otherwise are typical of the Christian Jesus: he has experienced death (which the Muslims deny to Jesus) and he remains alive among human beings until the end of the world (Mathew 28: 20).

Perhaps a few further comments on this will be appropriate.

Regarding points 2) and 4): the *malakūt* in which the prophets after their death appear to human beings is evidently neither the world of the senses nor the kingdom of heaven, but is a supernatural or intermediary world which binds the two realms together and thus a deeper sight than the eye's vision is required to perceive it. As Suyūṭī's quotations themselves indicate, it is a hereafter within the here and now, perhaps the spatial counterpart to the temporal intermediary state *barzakh* between death and resurrection. The *malakūt* appears to be so inseparably linked with the *mulk* that one scarcely dares to think of either one without the other, perhaps the world of archetypes of the here and now in contrast to the likenesses (here

---

77 *Dhāt* in these texts often does not mean the inner essence, the kernel of a matter, but the individual in his whole appearance, 'himself, herself, itself', the thing or the person in reality.

mithāl) which presuppose the concrete original in the here and now. One even ends up in doubt about whether the *malakūt* disappears with the destruction of the world or only first emerges when the real hereafter starts to set in.[78] In fact the second situation appears to be the case. But under point 4) Suyūṭī situates mankind's encounter with Muḥammad after the final resurrection before entering Paradise as still within 'the world of the intermediary realm' (p. 266, l. 1). For this reason it is also understandable that the deceased prophets and the martyrs can neither enjoy their wives who are still living, nor the women of Paradise: their wives are out of reach because the latter are still completely in the here and now, and they cannot enjoy the women of Paradise because these only arrive on the scene within Paradise and have not been created for this hybrid world. Thus sexual intercourse cannot take place across the boundaries of the intermediary world in the here and now, nor across the boundaries of the intermediary world in the hereafter. The deceased remain among themselves in the *malakūt*. Whoever dies before his wives or was never actually married cannot get married in the grave. This latter fact indicates quite clearly how closely bound the background of the *malakūt* is to earthly existence: since no earthly wife was on hand, she cannot then appear in a transfigured state. These questions concerning marriage are only answered later than Suyūṭī's time and without express reference to the concept of the *malakūt*, namely by the Shāfiᶜite Ramlī (d. 1004/1596) and the Mālikite Ujhūrī (d. 1066 /1656).[79]

The pressure of old reports even obliged Ibn Taymiyya himself to make a concession and to exercise some small degree of reserve toward his strict denial of the continued life of the prophets. For Ibn Taymiyya as well was incapable of refuting the traditions that Muḥammad had seen his predecessor Moses praying in the grave and that the traditionist Saᶜīd b. al-Musayyib had heard the call to prayer sounding forth from Muḥammad's grave during the Nights of Ḥarra in 63/683. Thus, in contradiction to the basic model of his own theory, he condescends to acknowledge a possible existence of the prophets and the pious after death, at least to some extent, but whatever action is undertaken by this category of the deceased, like that of the angels, he subordinates entirely to God's 'existential com-

78 Tahānawī's *Dictionary of the Technical Terms Used in the Sciences of the Musulmans*, ed. A. Sprenger, Bibliotheca Indica 1854-1862, II, p. 1339, *al-malakūt*, gives no information on the sense of the word required by us. A study of the subject would be useful.

79 Fīlālī: *Taḥrīrāt*, 55b-56a; on Fīlālī see pp. 541-43 below.

mand' (*al-amr al-kawnī*).[80] This means that they only do what God makes them do in robot-like fashion, because where they are now they have ceased to be under the legal obligations (*taklīf*, = *amr dīnī*) which are in force for the living, and are only subject to God's will of creation, against which they can no longer oppose any moral and legal principles.[81] For this reason Ibn Taymiyya still maintains his prohibition against seeking connections with these dead. He thus moves the dead as a whole, the prophets included, closer to God and distances them from the realm of the living by means of a wide gulf, a kind of no man's land. At a later date Muḥammad b. ᶜAbd al-Wahhāb (d. 1206/1792), his disciple, probably under pressure from the same traditions and considerations, brought himself to make a further concession. He writes: 'We believe that the Prophet in his grave lives a life characteristic of life in the intermediary realm... One cannot, however, ascribe to him a kind of life that entails rational knowledge, movement and control over behavior.'[82] Thus, to begin with, Ibn Taymiyya, from a position that denied life after death to the prophets, admitted that they did in fact continue to live but not for us, and then later the Wahhābīs made the further concession that Muḥammad was alive in his *grave*.

With regard to point 3): as far as the question about Muḥammad's ubiquity, Suyūṭī gives two different answers — more by way of suggestion than fully worked out — the first for people who are not really willing to believe that Muḥammad has mobility after his death, and the second for others who, on the contrary, would like to hold on to the belief that Muḥammad goes everywhere and can be everywhere at the same time. For the first case the comparison with the sun which shines for all people is made to serve again. According to this, Muḥammad is a light that permeates the whole world, and while remaining in the same place and position can be seen simultaneously

80 Ibn Taymiyya: *Qāᶜida jalīla fī'l-tawassul wa'l-wasīla*, Beirut, 1979, pp. 139-40, 155; *Iqtiḍā᾽ al-ṣirāṭ al-mustaqīm mukhālafat aṣḥāb al-jaḥīm*, Cairo, 1907, p. 179/Muhammad Umar Memon: *Ibn Taymiyya's Struggle against Popular Religion*. With an Annotated Translation of his *Kitāb iqtiḍā᾽ aṣ-ṣirāṭ al-mustaqīm mukhālafat aṣḥāb al-jaḥīm*, Mouton/The Hague/Paris, 1976, p. 293. The *layālī'l-Ḥarra* are of course not 'summer nights'. Cf. Samhūdī: *Khulāṣat al-Wafā*, Medina, 1972, p. 95, ll. 1-4/Cairo, 1316, p. 45, ll. 7-10.

81 *Qāᶜida jalīla*, p. 155. Regarding 'existential command' and 'command of religion' as well as other expressions for God's creation and command see 'The Cleanest on Predestination', pp. 321-334.

82 Henri Laoust: *Essai sur les doctrines sociales et politiques de Taḳī-d-dīn b. Taimīya*, Cairo, 1939, pp. 518-19.

in the most distant regions — a parallel to a 'Christ-filled' earth and a somewhat watered-down form of the light of God which, according to a panentheistic view, illuminates all things. A congenial seeker of the modern era, the Darqāwī Muḥammad b. Masᶜūd al-Ṭālibī al-Maᶜdarī al-Būnuᶜmānī (d. 1330/1912), at first a Nāṣirī, then an adherent of Māʾ al-ᶜAynayn, then a party supporter of the Nāṣirī-Darqāwī Bulkhayr al-Būshtī (later the Mahdī) and finally of the shaykh of Illigh in the Anti-Atlas, maintains that he constantly perceived as a direct experience the light of the Prophet which is in all things.[83] Others such as ᶜAbd al-ᶜAzīz al-Dabbāgh (d. 1132/1719) wish to distinguish between the person of the Prophet and his light: the latter, which is with (*maᶜa*) everyone, constitutes a kind of mirror in which the Prophet's person can become apparent so that simultaneously one individual in the east sees the Prophet with himself and another individual in the west sees him with himself, and though it is only a dream or an image, it is none the less unfalsified. Normally only someone with illuminated vision can penetrate to the Prophet himself.[84] Otherwise, the Prophet sends his likenesses or his mirror image as a substitute to those who see him in a dream. An earlier author, Aḥmad b. Ṭāhir b. Muḥammad al-Qazwīnī, whose precise name and dates have not yet been determined but who must have lived before Bārizī (d. 738/1338), also wished to answer the question why many people see the Prophet at the same time but with a dissimilar appearance. He leaves Muḥammad's integrity unimpaired and attributes the dissimilarities to the different constitution of the mirrors which are held up to the Prophet or of the lenses (we would say glasses) through which he is perceived. To a person who is true to the religious law he shows himself with a friendly mien, to the ungodly he appears in anger.[85] According to all these interpreta-

83 *Maᶜsūl*, XIII, p. 88.

84 Aḥmad b. al-Mubārak al-Lamaṭī: *Al-ibrīz min kalām sayyidī ᶜAbd al-ᶜAzīz*, Cairo, n.d., pp. 101-02/reprint, Cairo, n.d., pp. 172-73/quoted in al-Ḥājj ᶜUmar (Tal) b. Saᶜīd al-Fūtī al-Ṭūrī al-Kidiwī: *Rimāḥ ḥizb al-raḥīm ᶜalā nuḥūr ḥizb al-rajīm*, in the margin of ᶜAlī Ḥarāzim: *Jawāhir al-maᶜānī*, I, p. 203. Muḥammad b. Muḥammad al-Ṣaghīr al-Shingīṭī al-Tishītī: *Al-jaysh al-kafīl bi-akhdh al-thaʾr mimman salla ᶜalā'l-shaykh al-Tijānī sayf al-inkār*, in the margin of Sharqī's *Bughyat al-mustafīd*, Cairo, n.d., p. 87.

85 Bārizī: *Tawthīq ᶜurā'l-īmān*, MS Sprenger 127b, 58b-59a. Qazwīnī's work from which the passage comes is entitled *Sirāj al-ᶜuqūl fī minhāj al-uṣūl*. It remains unedited. The passage in that work is *bāb* 22, *faṣl* 3: *fī ruʾyat rasūl allāh ṣlm fī'l-manām*. In Bārizī the name of the author is given as Aḥmad b. Ṭāhir b. Muḥammad al-Qazwīnī. In Shaᶜrānī: *Al-yawāqīt wa'l-jawāhir fī bayān ᶜaqāʾid al-akābir*, Cairo, 1959, II, p. 3, l. 11: Abū Ṭāhir al-Qazwīnī.

Kâtib Çelebi/Ḥājjī Khalīfa, ed. Flügel, III, p. 588/Istanbul, 1941-43, II, p. 983, only calls the book *Sirāj* and promises to give the author's name. Flügel, VI, p. 217: Muḥammad b. Ṭāhir al-Qazwīnī *al-mutawaffā sanat* (the number is missing). *Keşf-el-zunun zeyli*, Istanbul, II, p. 7 below: Bahā᾿ al-Dīn Abū Muḥammad Ṭāhir b. Aḥmad b. Muḥammad al-Qazwīnī *al-mutawaffā sanat* [756]. Pertsch: *Kat. herzogl. Bibliothek Gotha*, no. 844: Abū Muḥammad Ṭāhir b. Aḥmad al-Qazwīnī (in the MS not original but added). *GAL S*, II, p. 978: Abū Ṭāhir b. Aḥmad al-Qazwīnī. This is meant to distinguish him from his alleged son. It originates with Pertsch: *Gotha*, no. 844. I do not know where the death date in brackets [756] in the *zeyil* of the *Keşf-el-zunun* comes from but it must be wrong if Qazwīnī is cited by Bārizī (d. 738/1338). Qazwīnī considers himself to be the first to interpret the various dream appearances of the Prophet the way he does, and at the same time acknowledges that one really sees the Prophet in such dreams. He cannot understand why Ghazzālī thinks one can only see the Prophet's spirit-being and not his external form as well (MS *Gotha*, 844, Chpt. 22, *faṣl* 3/Bārizī, 59b). He claims the same priority for his view that one also really sees God in dreams, although like all non-visual concepts such as faith and unbelief God naturally only presents Himself in images (*mathal, mithāl*), i.e. in translations. This is also the case with the letters and sounds of the Koran which serve as means (*wāsiṭa*) for His uncreated word (MS *Gotha*, Chpt. 22, *faṣl* 4). — At the end of his work the *Sirāj al-ᶜuqūl*, Qazwīnī several times affirms that he is the author and threatens with curses others who would adorn themselves with it or falsify it, but he does not mention his name which we would be so glad to know. To facilitate establishing his identity I will give a list of his writings which he enumerates there but which I have found no trace of anywhere else: Poems. *Sirāj al-ᶜuqūl fī minhāj al-uṣūl*. *Nūr al-ḥaqīqa wa-nawr al-ḥadīqa* (on higher knowledge). *Masālik al-baḥth ᶜan madārik al-baᶜth* (which is cited in the *Sirāj*). *Naqḍ al-taᶜlīm wa-kashf al-tawhīm*. *Yawāqīt al-ᶜulūm wa-darārī'l-nujūm* (questions from thirty sciences). *Dhikr al-khawāṣṣ fī fasr sūrat al-ikhlāṣ*. *Risālat qūt al-rūḥ*. On the *adabiyyāt*: *Ṣiwān al-adab fī lisān al-ᶜarab*. *Rafᶜ al-khayāl ᶜan ru᾿yat al-hilāl*. *Sharḥ tasbīḥat al-abdāl wa-maᶜnā'l-jamāl wa'l-jalāl*. *Al-ibāna ᶜan maᶜnā'l-iᶜāna*. *Ḥall al-ᶜayba ᶜan ḥāl al-ghayba* (sayings of shaykhs). Two *juz᾿* from the *Qūt al-qulūb*. *Al-yāqūt fī tasbīḥ al-mulk wa'l-malakūt*. *Miṣfāt al-ṣifāt wa'l-radd ᶜalā'l-nufāt*. *Sharḥ bad᾿ al-naḥw min kalām al-Tirmidhī*. *Risālat al-fatwā fī qawlihī taᶜālā 'wa-alzamahum kalimat al-taqwā'*. Commentary on various sayings and words in the sermons of ᶜAlī. *Al-manāhij fī ᶜilm al-makhārij*. *Al-masā᾿il al-mustadraka* (questions on the Koran). *Zubdat al-aqwāl fī qawlihī taᶜālā 'thumma ātaynā Mūsā'l-kitāb tamāman' al-āya*. Various *maqāmāt* in the mouth of *al-faqīh al-miṣrī*, written in Sāwa. *Al-ifāda ᶜan tarjamat al-shahāda*. A *juz᾿* on *Muqārabat al-qaḍiyya ᶜan muqāranat al-niyya*. *Khidr* (in the margin by the same hand: perhaps *ḥidhr*) *al-lithām ᶜan al-ḥarf wa'l-kalām*. *Risālat al-istibḥāth ᶜan al-aḥwāl al-thalāth*. On *ᶜarabiyya*: *Lubāb al-albāb fī marāsim al-aᶜrāb (iᶜrāb?)*. *Ghāyat al-taᶜrīf fī ᶜilm al-taṣrīf*. *Jumlat al-ḥadīth ᶜan al-tadhkīr wa'l-ta᾿nīth*. *Al-durr al-manẓūm fī'l-taᶜdiya wa'l-luzūm*. *Al-uṣūl wa'l-fuṣūl*. *Al-nukat*, fī'l-naḥw (?). *Al-lamḥa*, fī'l-naḥw (very short). *Al-shamma*, fī'l-naḥw. *Qāᶜida*, fī'l-naḥw. *Jawharat al-taṣrīf ᶜalā'l-ḥurūf*. *Al-rā᾿iqa*, fī'l-taṣrīf. *Al-fā᾿iqa*, as a commentary to it. *Risāla* on *mushājarat al-mutaᶜallim* tions Muḥammad does not have to move from his position — only Dabbāgh, in contradiction to his own theory, further concedes that Muḥammad will also go to visit someone who honestly burns with passion to see him but does not have illuminated vision (*ghayr al-maftūḥ ʿalayhi*), i.e. the keener vision to be able to perceive him. However, it would be to misunderstand the comparison of Muḥammad with the sun in the verse which Suyūṭī quotes, if one imagined the deceased Prophet as light, for Suyūṭī has emphasized clearly enough that Muḥammad appears in his body after death just as he appeared in his earthly body. Precisely for this reason the comparison with the sun is not an appropriate explanation.[86]

As for the second case, in the example of Ibn ʿAṭāʾallāh it seems to me that the end does not fit with the beginning. If the unknown man sees his shaykh Ibn ʿAṭāʾallāh at all the holy places of the pilgrimage in orderly sequence but looses sight of him between each place, this can only mean that Ibn ʿAṭāʾallāh himself one minute disappeared and the next reappeared somewhere else. This interrupted ubiquity would then presuppose the ability to traverse great distances with lightning speed (*ṭayy al-makān wa'l-zamān*), a well-known motif in the hagiographical literature:[87] the man with the large stride

---

wa'l-faqīh wa'l-adīb wa'l-mutakallim. Letters and poems to the *qāḍī* Ẓahīr al-Dīn al-Bisṭāmī. A *risāla fī nisbat al-layālī ilā'l-laʾālī* (?) to the *raʾīs* ʿImād al-Dīn b. Qāʾid in Khuwayy. Commentary on surah 1 and on 20 verses of surah 2, dictated in the Friday mosque in Qazwīn, unfinished. *Mujawwid (mujawwad?) qirāʾat Abī ʿAmr b. al-ʿAlāʾ*. *Risālat al-īmāʾ fī lafẓi'l-mā*, written in Hamadān to shaykh Abū'l-ʿAlāʾ al-Ḥāfiẓ. *Bahjat al-qurrāʾ*, on the secrets of the variant readings of the Koran. *Al-burhān ʿalā anna hādhān (?, ʿalā -ān hādhān?)*. *Al-talqīn fī muhimmāt al-dīn*, an abridged version in Persian. *Al-iktifāʾ fī ʿilm al-istīfāʾ*. Commentary to two verses of Mutanabbī. *Mukhtaṣar fī tanzīh al-ḥaqq wa-badw al-khalq*. *Al-ifāda fī tashīl al-wilāda*. *Risālat bathth al-shakwā*. *Al-risālat fī naqḍ aḥkām al-nujūm*.

86 Cf. also Ibn al-ʿArabī in Tishītī: *Al-jaysh al-kafīl*, in the margin of Sharqī's *Bughyat al-mustafīd*, p. 62. Muḥammad b. Khilfa al-Ubbī's and Muḥammad b. Muḥammad b. Yūsuf al-Sanūsī's commentaries on Muslim, Cairo, 1328/reprint Beirut, n.d., VI, p. 80, ll. 2-11. For a more extensive treatment of the problems of Muḥammad's dream appearances with many quotations including from Ubbī, see Abū Sālim al-ʿAyyāshī: *Māʾ al-mawāʾid* (*Al-riḥla al-ʿayyāshiyya*), litho., Fez, 1316/reprint Rabat, 1977, I, pp. 24-39.

87 Richard Gramlich: 'Zur Ausdehnung der Zeit und Verwandtem', in *Die islamische Welt zwischen Mittelalter und Neuzeit, Festschrift für Hans Robert Roemer zum 65. Geburtstag*, Beirut, 1979, p. 182.

(*ṣāḥib al-khaṭwa*).[88] An allegedly 'higher' species of this power would be the so-called 'whizzing off' (*taḥayyuz*) by means of which a person does not even have to take a step but can merely project himself (*taḥarraka min majlisihī*) and he is then in another place along with those in his company, if necessary.[89] But since Ibn ᶜAṭāᵓallāh was at home at the same time, what we have in his case is a form of multilocatio:[90] he himself remained in Cairo and sent out in the world his doubles (Doppelgänger) who represented him in other places — which corresponds to the likenesses of Muḥammad in Dabbāgh. Real multilocatio, however, would have been if Ibn ᶜAṭāᵓallāh had multiplied himself exactly, then drawn himself together again as a single person in any one given place and in this way also been able to transfer himself spatially. Only then could he rightly say everywhere: 'I am already here'(ick bün all hier: reference to the German fairy-tale *The Hare and the Porcupine* [see the Grimm Brothers], in which the porcupine, by means of trickery, ap-

---

88 Innumerable examples. Cf. for the moment C. Snouck Hurgronje: 'Saᶜd ès-Suwênî, ein seltsamer Walî in Ḥadhramôt,' *ZA* 26, 1912, pp. 238-39 (*Festschrift für Ignaz Goldziher*)/*Verspreide Geschriften*, V, pp. 418-19. At the end Snouck Hurgronje notes that saints of this kind are described in the literature as *ahl al-khaṭwa*, but in Ḥaḍramawt as *ahl al-daḥqa* (ahl èd-daḥgèh); *daḥqa* 'footstep, stride'. An article about the historical Suwênî, which Snouck Hurgronje did not consult or did not find, is given by ᶜAbd al-Qādir b. ᶜAbdallāh al-ᶜAydarūsī: *Tārīkh al-nūr al-sāfir ᶜan akhbār al-qarn al-ᶜāshir*, Baghdad, 1934, pp. 466-80. The full name of the saint is Saᶜd b. ᶜAlī b. ᶜAbdallāh Bāmadhḥij al-Ḥaḍramī al-Tarīmī (ibid., p. 470, ll. 9-10). He died in 857/1453 and for that reason does not figure in Sharjī's *Ṭabaqāt al-khawāṣṣ*.

89 Sharjī: *Ṭabaqāt al-khawāṣṣ ahl al-ṣidq wa'l-ikhlāṣ*, Cairo, 1321, p. 131, ll. 17-19. Another series is given by a certain Sawdī (d. shortly after 700/1300): the lowest level is flying to ᶜArafa, then the footstep, then simply wishing (*hamm, himma*); the highest is that God gathers together (*yajmaᶜu*) the earth before the saint; ibid., p. 49.

90 Gramlich: 'Ausdehnung der Zeit', pp. 185, 192. To the extent that the spirit, and not the body as well, is thought to be involved, multiplication is that much easier to grasp. The Egyptian shaykh Mufarrij al-Damāmīnī/Damāmīlī (d. 648/1250) who was famous for his miracles of this kind was once supposedly seen at the same time in ᶜArafa and at home in Damāmīn/Damāmīl. He explained: 'Real sainthood gives a person the power to show himself in numerous forms (*ṣuwar*), his spirit-being (*rūḥāniyya*) can appear in many places at the same time, and the form (*ṣūra*) is true in all these places. But the person himself is not in two places at the same time because only the spirit-forms (*al-ṣuwar al-rūḥāniyya*), not the body-forms (*jismāniyya*), are able to multiply themselves.' From Yāfiᶜī's lost work *Kifāyat al-muᶜtaqid* in Suyūṭī: *Al-khabar al-dāll ᶜalā wujūd al-quṭb wa'l-awtād wa'l-nujabāᵓ wa'l-abdāl*, in *Al-ḥāwī li'l-fatāwī*, II, pp. 254-55. Another story provides the occasion for more lengthy explanations in Udfuwī: *Al-ṭāliᶜ al-saᶜīd al-jāmiᶜ asmāᵓ nujabāᵓ al-Ṣaᶜīd*, Cairo, 1966, pp. 649-54.

pears to arrive everywhere more quickly than the hare). Ibn ᶜAṭāᵓallāh's concluding statement 'The great man fills the whole world' recalls another miracle of Islamic holy men which in Persian is designated by the technical term *ṭawāmm*: the ability of the holy man to make himself gigantic in size,[91] in this case increased to immeasurable proportions. But Ibn ᶜAṭāᵓallāh goes on to add the sentence: 'If the highest arch-holy man (*quṭb*) is invoked from inside a stone, he will reply.' Again this can only mean that he pervades the whole world, which is what induces Suyūṭī to conclude: 'Thus if the highest arch-holy man fills the whole world, the Prophet is all the more capable of doing so.' And he quotes the statement of Abū'l-ᶜAbbās al-Ṭanjī: 'Behold, heaven and earth, God's Throne and God's Footstool, are filled with the Apostle of God!'[92] In this way once again we come back to the comparison with the sun. Thus with the second example Suyūṭī also provides an explanation which falls outside the framework of his treatise. The explanation belongs in the context of the so-called 'Muḥammadan reality' (*al-ḥaqīqa al-muḥammadiyya*) which is extraneous to the present discussion.

Here it would have been easy for Suyūṭī to bring into accord with his theory a particular explanation of Muḥammad's ubiquity as well as of his various appearances at one and the same time, and Suyūṭī was in fact quite close to doing this. The explanation in question is the above-mentioned multilocatio. Indeed, Suyūṭī could have continued his reflections in the same style and only had to say: if a holy man such as Ibn ᶜAṭāᵓallāh can be seen in several places and, as in other traditions, is capable of doing various things in several places simultaneously and assuming a different appearance, why should it not be even more likely that the Prophet too could perform the same feat. After all, the devil can do this as well. Thus it should not be more difficult for Muḥammad in his body after death than for a holy man in his earthly body to multiply himself as he wishes and to appear to many individuals at the same time and to appear differently to each one of them.

Similarly, the very opposite — the absence of the Prophet — could easily be incorporated into Suyūṭī's doctrine about the Prophet's life

---

91 *Abū Saᶜīd-i Abū l-Ḫayr*, pp. 272-73. The phenomenon was also known in Southern Arabia; Sharjī: *Ṭabaqāt al-khawāṣṣ*, p. 70, l. 26.

92 Ṭanjī and one of his daughters are buried in Cairo; Sakhāwī (d. 902/1497): *Tuḥfat al-aḥbāb wa-bughyat al-ṭullāb fī'l-khiṭaṭ wa'l-mazārāt wa'l-tarājim wa'l-biqāᶜ al-mubārakāt*, Cairo, 1937, p. 158. Ibn al-Zayyāt (d. 814/1412): *Al-kawākib al-sayyāra fī tartīb al-ziyāra* (completed 804/1402), Cairo, n.d., does not have this notice.

after death. Even assuming the nearly impossible case that excavations were carried out at the Prophet's grave in Medina, as occurred for example in St Peter's in Rome, and that nothing was found in the grave, then the very theory of Suyūṭī about Muḥammad's posthumous mobility could provide arguments which would refute any embarrassing conclusions drawn by materialist religious scholars. The theory would confront them with the position that firstly the Prophet is only visible in the intermediary world, as it has been described, to certain persons and secondly that, being under no constraints, he may have left the grave and indeed could well have made use of this freedom because of the excavation work.

One cannot deny a certain degree of ingenuity to Suyūṭī's idea in view of its many-sided applicability. But Suyūṭī seems not to have recognized its full scope.

Today the concrete conception of the Prophet's ubiquity or the possibility of his ubiquity seems to be greatly limited. On the one hand, it is relegated to the realm of fable, on the other, it becomes diluted. The Wahhābīs, of course, are against it and say: the people who call upon a prophet or a saint and ask for help are often located in the most diverse places and they can number hundreds of thousands. They all believe that the person they call is immediately present in all these different places. The mere fact of calling for help constitutes unbelief and polytheism because they attribute divine characteristics to the helper which runs counter to all good sense. It is simply impossible for a single body to be in many places at the same time. Thus the Wahhābīs deny ubiquity. In response the traditionalists maintain — in any case one particular traditionalist from Iraq did so — that a correct Muslim does not at all believe in the invoked individual's personal presence in different places at the same time because that would be unbelief and impossible. Rather the conception of Muslims is that in those places where the Prophet is invoked — just to deal with his case —, God creates the (helpful) blessing (*al-baraka*) out of goodness and mercy towards the beseecher and as a token of favor on behalf of the one invoked. The Iraqi traditionalist who speaks this way thus simply transforms the disputed presence into a somewhat hazy 'blessing'. He thereby dilutes the idea of the concrete presence of the Prophet, as so many others had conceived of it, and basically denies it just as the Wahhābīs do.[93]

---

93 Jamīl Efendi Ṣidqī al-Zahāwī: *Al-fajr al-ṣādiq fī'l-radd ʿalā munkirī'l-tawassul wa'l-karāmāt wa'l-khawāriq*, Istanbul, 1980, p. 62.

A further remark regarding point 4): it is Suyūṭī's personal opinion that if someone today sees the Prophet and speaks with him, he cannot be reckoned as one of the Prophet's Companions (*ṣaḥāba*). Muḥyī al-Dīn b. al-ᶜArabī (d. 638/1240) held a different opinion. For him such people are Companions of the Prophet. The founder of the Sanūsiyya, Muḥammad b. ᶜAlī al-Sanūsī (d. 1276/1859), cites the relevant passages of the *Futūḥāt al-makkiyya* (Chpts. 313 and 318) in his work *Īqāẓ al-wasnān fī'l-ᶜamal bi'l-ḥadīth wa'l-Qur'ān* (Algiers, 1914, pp. 107-112[94]). A contemporary of Suyūṭī, Aḥmad al-Zawāwī (d. 923/1517), once said to his disciple Shaᶜrānī: 'Our *ṭarīqa* consists in repeating the invocation of blessings on the Prophet over and over again until he sits with us while we are in a waking state. Thus we may become his disciples, just as his Companions were, and we may ask him about all sorts of difficulties in the *ḥadīth*.'[95] The members of the Tijāniyya, whose founder Aḥmad al-Tijānī (d. 1230/1815) is meant to have been appointed and initiated by Muḥammad in 1196/1782,[96] prided themselves on having been designated by the Prophet himself as his Companions and believed that in the future they would be allowed to enter Paradise with the Prophet's original Companions.[97] Thus Suyūṭī's view is but one among others, and he also maintained this view in a different connection, namely with regard to the question of the status of Jesus after his return at the end of time when for a short period he will be obliged to give judgements according to Islamic law. Is he acquainted with this law? Suyūṭī assumes so because the revelations of all prophets are basically one and are contained in the revelation of Muḥammad. Jesus, who did not die according to Islamic belief, can also meet with the Prophet now and be taught by him, and this is supposedly what clairvoyants had already confirmed. But the tradition is also aware that he had already had contact with Muḥammad during the latter's lifetime, and there is nothing that bars the possibility that after his return he may learn something further from Muḥammad. But Jesus is only a Companion of the Prophet because he had already met Muḥammad several times in the years before

---

94 Printed once again in the collective volume *Al-majmūᶜa al-mukhtāra min mu'allafāt... sayyidī Muḥammad b. ᶜAlī al-Sanūsī*, Beirut, 1968.

95 Al-Ḥājj ᶜUmar: *Rimāḥ ḥizb al-raḥīm*, in the margin of ᶜAlī Ḥarāzim: *Jawāhir al-maᶜānī*, I, p. 199.

96 *Jawāhir al-maᶜānī*, I, p. 51. Jamil M. Abun-Nasr: *The Tijaniyya*, Oxford University Press, 1965, p. 19.

97 *Rimāḥ*, II, pp. 43, 48-49.

11/632. Thus in the Islamic Jesus prophethood and the status of Companion of the Prophet overlap, which otherwise can only be said of Elias (Ilyās) and according to some of al-Khaḍir as well — if indeed he had been a prophet at all.[98] Suyūṭī refers to explanations given by a certain Subkī (probably Taqī al-Dīn, d. 756/1355) and cites Dhahabī (d. 748/1348): 'Jesus, the son of Mary, is a prophet and a Companion of the Prophet because he saw Muḥammad, and he is the last of the Companions of the Prophet who will die,[99] namely after his return at the end of time when everything will perish.'

Suyūṭī's explanations are a good example of the theological mode of thinking. On the basis of what are taken to be irrefutable assertions which have thoroughly abandoned the domain of verifiability, a closed system of relationships and perspectives is devised which is immediately clear to 'the visualizing cognition' and is consistent with itself. But that is not yet enough for this to qualify as truth, for which conformity with natural observations of the real world and experiences is also required outside the basis of faith. None the less, Suyūṭī's conception was far from reaching all theologians and did not win the approval of all traditionalist scholars. A certain ᶜAbd al-Raḥmān b. Najm al-Dīn Muḥammad b. ᶜAbd al-Salām b. Aḥmad Zayn al-Dīn al-Batrūnī al-Ṭarābulusī al-Shāfiᶜī al-Ṣūfī, known as Ibn al-Gharāmī (d. 977/1569), who taught and preached in Aleppo and supported the thesis that the Prophet was alive in his grave, encountered the opposition of Muḥammad b. Musallam al-Mālikī al-Maghribī whom we have mentioned above. The latter wanted to declare him an unbeliever and only gave way when he learned that Batrūnī based himself on a work of Suyūṭī, apparently our treatise *Tanwīr al-ḥalak* — because Suyūṭī was taken to be an authority.[100]

But even later on the theologians were not unanimously on Suyūṭī's side, indeed they were probably not familiar with all his writings which is not surprising in view of his enormous produc-

---

98 An initiation of Khaḍir by the Prophet during the latter's lifetime is referred to in Muḥammad b. ᶜAlī al-Sanūsī: *Al-manhal al-rawī'l-rā'iq fī asānīd al-ᶜulūm wa-uṣūl al-ṭarā'iq*, in *Al-majmūᶜa al-mukhtāra*, Beirut, 1968, p. 49. — The limitation to two or three prophets indicates that the *ṣaḥābī* as well cannot already have died but must still partake of his physical life in order to be recognized as a Companion of the Prophet. Adam, Abraham and Moses do not fulfill this pre-condition, although they met the Prophet.

99 Suyūṭī: *Al-iᶜlām bi-ḥukm ᶜĪsā ᶜalayhi'l-salām*, in *Al-ḥāwī li'l-fatāwī*, II, p. 161.

100 Ibn al-Ḥanbalī: *Durr al-ḥabab*, I, 2, p. 770; II, 1, p. 132 (cf. p. 514 above).

tivity.[101] It is worth mentioning here the difficulties that Muḥammad b. Muḥammad al-Maghribī al-Fīlālī, who had been educated in Cairo, found himself faced with in Medina during his pilgrimage in 1155/1743 because of his view about the posthumous miracles of the Prophet. After his return to Egypt he decided to take the time to present his standpoint more clearly and comprehensively while enlisting support from the necessary sources. Thus in 1155/1743 he wrote the small treatise *Al-taḥrīrāt al-rā'iqa* which has been preserved in the Berlin MS We 1719 (Ahlwardt 2599) and merits being read. It is essentially based on Suyūṭī's *Tanwīr al-ḥalak* and presents everything important from Suyūṭī's exposition almost more clearly than Suyūṭī himself, because he treats the subject more from the viewpoint of the Prophet's continued life than his visibility. In addition to Suyūṭī's treatment, he distinguishes among the proponents of Muḥammad's small resurrection, if we may refer to it this way, between those who like Suyūṭī do not conceive of the Prophet as bound to his grave and others who, contrary to Suyūṭī, would bind the Prophet to his grave. The latter group held that the spirit of Muḥammad, and that of all prophets, was free and was capable of wandering through the translunar spheres but did not have the power to take its body with it out of the grave. So once again we have before us the Shīᶜite view as propounded by Kulīnī. These people, Fīlālī says, reject the doctrines which represent Muḥammad as rising from his grave forty days after being laid to rest, as well as the alleged sightings of the Prophet in a waking state in far-off lands. The most that these visionaries could have seen, according to those who deny the mobility of the Prophet, were likenesses (*mithāl*) of the Prophet, and not the Prophet himself, likenesses which were called forth because of their intense longing for him — unless one were to assume that a divine miracle had brought about a multiplication of Muḥammad which would be difficult to explain in detail but not inconceivable. Fīlālī calls these appearances images, shapes, forms (*ṣuwar*) which have arisen (*nasha'at*) from Muḥammad, and no doubt has in mind something like our multilocatio as a possible solution to the enigma. Another solution within the framework of the same theory of the immobility of the Prophet, he says, would be the comparison proposed by Ibn Abī Jamra — here this name is mentioned — that the Prophet is like the sun which is seen by all people. In this way one could easily sail

101 Sakhāwī: *Ḍaw'*, IV, pp. 65-70, attacks him vehemently, giving examples of his behavior.

around the rocks associated with the dilemma of having to split the one into the many (56b-57a).

Fīlālī only presents a survey. He does not decide either in favor of the mobility or the immobility of the deceased Prophet, and he concedes to the possible criticism that the *ḥadīth* foundation for all these matters is highly fragile. But he refers to the Shāfiᶜite Ramlī (d. 1004 /1596), according to whose guidelines *ḥadīths* about the circumstances of the Prophet, about his family tree for instance, his grave and suchlike, should not be judged with the same standards as *ḥadīths* containing rules of conduct for the faithful. Only the latter constitutes 'knowledge' (*ᶜilm*), whereas *ḥadīths* of the first kind constitute 'articles of faith' (*ᶜaqāʾid, iᶜtiqādāt*), and the chains of transmission of the articles of faith do not have to be tested so rigorously as to their tenability as do the commands and prohibitions (60b-61a). This principle had already been put forward by Aḥmad b. Ḥanbal (d. 241/855).[102]

Fīlālī's treatise which still remains unedited, met with the approval of two of his students whose testimonials are included in the manuscript at the beginning and the end of the work. The first testimonial (51a) comes from the Khalwatī shaykh Muḥammad al-Ḥafnāwī (d. 1181/1767),[103] the second one from his student Aḥmad al-Mallawī (also d. 1181/1767).[104]

Here it is appropriate to introduce a philological rectification. *GAL*, II, p. 366, assigns this work to Muḥammad b. Muḥammad al-Fullānī al-Kishnawī al-Sūdānī who had died in Cairo in 1154 /1741.[105] But that is too early for the author of our treatise, and Makhlūf's *Shajarat al-nūr al-zakiyya fī ṭabaqāt al-mālikiyya*, no. 1330, does not ascribe a book with this title to the Kishnawī in question. In another place (*GAL S*, II, p. 494) regarding our author Brockelmann has recourse to Kattānī's *Fihris al-fahāris*, II, p. 264, l.

102 Ibn Qayyim al-Jawziyya: *Rawḍat al-muḥibbīn wa-nuzhat al-mushtāqīn*, Cairo, 1956, introduction of the editor Aḥmad ᶜUbayd, p. *zāy*. Similar observations in Ẓāhir Shāh Miyān b. ᶜAbd al-ᶜAẓīm Miyān Madyan (?): *Ḍiyāʾ al-ṣudūr li-munkir al-tawassul bi-ahl al-qubūr* (modern, not in *GAL*), litho., pp. 36-37, printed in the appendix to Jamīl Efendi Ṣidqī al-Zahāwī: *Al-fajr al-ṣādiq fī'l-radd ᶜalā munkirī'l-tawassul*, Istanbul, 1980. Ignaz Goldziher: *Muhammedanische Studien*, Halle, 1889-90, II, pp. 153 ff.

103 Muḥammad Khalīl Efendi al-Murādī: *Silk al-durar fī aᶜyān al-qarn al-thānī ᶜashar*, Būlāq, 1291-1301, IV, pp. 49-50. J. Spencer Trimingham: *The Sufi Orders in Islam*, Oxford, 1971, p. 77.

104 Murādī, I, pp. 116-17.

105 Ziriklī, VII, pp. 293-94.

3 line from bot. (?), where, however, the entry concerns a different Fullānī, namely Ṣāliḥ b. Muḥammad b. Nūḥ al-ᶜUmarī, who died as late as 1218/1803. But he did not leave behind a book with this title either. Similarly, in our MS the author is not called Ghilālī or Ghīlālī, as *GAL*, II, p. 366, ftn. 1, indicates and as Ahlwardt repeats, but Fīlālī at 51b, l. 5, in the text and Muḥammad al-Maghribī al-Fīlālī in Ḥafnāwī's testimonial at 51a, l. 19. Thus the man or his family originally comes from Tafilalt. The correct ascription is given by Bağdatlı İsmail Paşa in his *Keşf-el-zunun zeyli*, Istanbul, 1945-47, I, p. 231. There the work is referred to as: '*Al-taḥrīrāt al-rāʾiqa wa'l-risāla al-fāʾiqa* of Muḥammad b. Muḥammad b. al-Ṭayyib al-Tāfilātī al-Maghribī, *muftī* of the Ḥanafites in Jerusalem, who died 1191/1777. Incipit: *naḥmaduka bi-jamīᶜi ṣifātika wa-asmāʾika yā ḥayyu yā qayyūm.*' This is our book exactly, except that in the MS We 1719 both in the heading as well as in the text when the authentic name of the work is given, the additional words *wa'l-risāla al-fāʾiqa* are lacking. They do not belong to the title but come from the introduction where it says: *fa-hā ana ajmaᶜu shawāridahā fī risālatin fāʾiqa wa-usammīhā bi-l-Taḥrīrāti'l-rāʾiqa,* 'Thus I gather the scattered communications (about the problem) in a superior treatise and name it *The Clear-Written Compositions*' (52a, ll. 4-5). A second error of İsmail Paşa occurs in the author's name. His real name is not Muḥammad b. Muḥammad b. al-Ṭayyib but Muḥammad b. Muḥammad al-Ṭayyib without *ibn* before al-Ṭayyib. Tāfilātī is another form for Fīlālī. Murādī, IV, pp. 102-08, presents the necessary information about him. There as well the date of his death is given as 1191/1777 (IV, p. 108, ll. 4-5) along with the statement that his two eulogists Ḥafnāwī and Mallawī were his teachers (IV, p. 105). Murādī does not mention the *Taḥrīrāt* but reports in detail about a not uninteresting religious discussion which Fīlālī had with the Christians during his captivity on Malta. Our Tāfilātī only figures in Brockelmann as the author of a commentary on Ibn ᶜArabī's *Al-dawr al-aᶜlā* (*GAL*, I, p. 447, no. 114; *GAL S*, I, p. 799, no. 118). Now that it has been established that the *Taḥrīrāt* is his work, he deserves to have his own separate entry.

To return again to Suyūṭī's later influence: about a hundred years after Fīlālī, in 1261/1845 the Torodo al-Ḥājj ᶜUmar Tal, before he founded his Tijānī state on the upper Niger, in Chapter 31 of his *Rimāḥ ḥizb al-raḥīm ᶜalā nuḥūr ḥizb al-rajīm*,[106] the chapter about the life after death and the visibility of the deceased Muḥammad,

106 In the margin of ᶜAlī Ḥarāzim: *Jawāhir al-maᶜānī*, I, pp. 204-10.

went back to Suyūṭī's *Tanwīr al-ḥalak* and copied extensive passages from it. The good theological connections, which Suyūṭī himself had already established with the Western Sudan, led to a great number of his writings penetrating to the interior of Africa.[107] Ḥājj ᶜUmar could have become acquainted with the treatise there or during his pilgrimage in the east. The Tijāniyyūn could make good use of Suyūṭī's explanations about Muḥammad's continued life after death, because Aḥmad al-Tijānī claimed to have received substantial parts of his doctrine and his instructions in a waking state from the mouth of the Prophet. Therefore, Muḥammad al-ᶜArabī (b.) al-Sāʾiḥ al-Sharqī al-ᶜUmarī al-Tijānī (d. 1309/1892) likewise draws his chief arguments in defense of this claim from Suyūṭī, whose *Tanwīr* and *Inbāh* — he calls the latter *Anbāʾ* — he mentions by name.[108]

The concept of Muḥammad's continued life after death has always had adherents and opponents. But the positions did not remain fixed. The ordinary people are counted as friends of the idea. They do not know a lot about the subject and much that they believe is contradictory. For this reason Suyūṭī had propounded his theory. An old man in a sail boat recounted to the folklorist Hans Alexander Winkler in 1934 that every day at the Prophet's grave in Medina twenty black slaves provide the pitchers of water which the Prophet needs for performing his ablutions for prayer. 'Muḥammad is alive', he affirmed, 'and he comes and prays there.' And does the Prophet arrive from Paradies? The old man was in complete agreement with this and said: 'God and His Apostle know this. He resides with God in Paradise.'[109] So Muḥammad is meant to reside in Paradise, but descends to Medina to perform his ablutions for morning prayer?

---

107 Elisabeth M. Sartain: *Jalāl al-dīn al-Suyūṭī*, Vol. I: Biography and background, Cambridge, 1975, pp. 46-52, gives information about the further dissemination of Suyūṭī's writings in the east and in the west. A long questionnaire by the Berber 'scholar' Shams al-Dīn Muḥammad b. Muḥammad b. ᶜAlī al-Lamtūnī from Takrūr was answered by Suyūṭī in a work entitled *Fatḥ al-maṭlab al-mabrūr wa-bard al-kabid al-maḥrūr fī'l-jawāb ᶜan al-asʾila al-wārida min al-Takrūr*, printed in Suyūṭī's *Al-ḥāwī li'l-fatāwī*, I, pp. 284-94. The questions are especially informative regarding the customs and the religious and social circumstances in black West Africa. At the end Suyūṭī promises to send his questionner two of his treatises, one about the shape of the heavens and earth, and another about the sequence of the letters of the Arabic alphabet. Najm al-Dīn al-Ghazzī: *Al-kawākib al-sāʾira bi-manāqib aᶜyān al-miʾa al-ᶜāshira*, Beirut, 1945 ff., I, p. 228, ll. 6-7: Most of his writings were known during his lifetime in the Ḥijāz, in Syria, Aleppo, Asia Minor, in the Maghreb, in Takrūr, India and in the Yemen.

108 *Bughyat al-mustafīd bi-sharḥ Munyat al-murīd*, Cairo, 1959, pp. 209-16, 357.

109 H.A. Winkler: *Ägyptische Volkskunde*, Stuttgart, 1936, p. 56.

Commuting like this could easily be reconciled with the conception found in the *jihād*-romances according to which the warrior who is seeking a martyr's death accepts messages to deliver to the Prophet in the hereafter.[110] Also friends of the view that Muḥammad continues to live after death are the Sufis for whom 'the world of divine omnipotence' (*ʿālam al-qudra*) in any case stands in the foreground before 'the world of God's wisdom', the normal world order. Muḥammad al-Kattānī/Kittānī, the Moroccan head of a Sufi order who is rather famous for his political anticipations, sought in vain to convince sultan ʿAbd al-Ḥafīẓ (1325-1330/1907-1912), who sympathized with the Salafiyya, that the Prophet lived on after death. He even wrote a book on the subject.[111] Johann Ludwig Burckhardt, who travelled in Arabia in 1814-1815, places the Turks of that time universally on the side of those who believe that Muḥammad is still alive and take it to be self-evident that, in view of the high rank he enjoys with God and on the basis of which men swear oaths (*bi-jāh*), he is without a doubt capable of helping where and when he pleases.[112] Their opponents, the Wahhābīs, we have already touched on twice, indeed in connection with the very question of Muḥammad's continued activity and omnipresence after death. But they knew how to distinguish between the uneducated folk who were inclined to exaggerated veneration, and the educated classes who ought to be better at recognizing the boundaries of religious veneration. In order to preclude all eventualities (*saddan li'l-dharīʿa*) they bore themselves absolutely as the advocates of Ibn Taymiyya's fundamentalist cleansing. But with regard to one point, however, they came closer to the traditionalist conception, because old attested *ḥadīth*s, which from a fundamentalist standpoint could not be refuted, commanded them to halt. This was the proposition of the incorruptibility and the continued life of the prophets at least in their graves, which their teacher Ibn ʿAbd al-Wahhāb had brought back in favor.[113] That his doctrine survived him is shown by a report on the year 1226/1811 when sultan Sulaymān of Morocco, who himself fostered Wahhābī ideas, sent his son Ibrāhīm with the pilgrims' caravan to Saʿūd, the contemporary ruler of Mecca and Medina. The

---

110 Pseudo-Wāqidī: *Futūḥ al-Shām*, Kafr al-Zaghārī, 1935, I, p. 124, l. 12; p. 137, l. 15 (the Battle of Yarmūk)

111 Muḥammad al-Bāqir al-Kattānī/Kittānī: *Tarjamat al-shaykh Muḥammad al-Kattānī/Kittānī al-shahīd*, n.p., 1962, p. 215.

112 *Notes on the Bedouins and Wahábys*, II, p. 106-07.

113 See p. 532 above.

spokesman for the delegation, Ibrāhīm al-Zaddāghī,[114] having been invited by Saᶜūd to speak frankly, stated to him: 'We have been told that you deny the continued life of Muḥammad and the other prophets in their graves.' Saᶜūd replied: 'God forbid! We say rather that he lives in his grave, just as the other prophets, and indeed he enjoys a higher life than the martyrs.'[115] But only in the grave! Theologians of a Salafī-Wahhābī persuasion in the west as well would not accept anything that had to do with Muḥammad wandering about outside of his grave. The religious scholar Muḥammad b. al-ᶜArabī al-ᶜAlawī — as distanced from enlightened thinking as Luther — in 1340/1921 imparted the following as food for thought to a Tijānī in Fez who was keen for knowledge: 'If after his death the Prophet could appear to someone and intervene in the affairs of the world, he would not have shown himself for the first time to Aḥmad al-Tijānī but would have done so much earlier on more important occasions such as during the disagreement between the Anṣār and the Muhājirūn immediately after his death, during the tense relationship between Abū Bakr and Fāṭima, in ᶜAlī's war against the coalition between Ṭalḥa, al-Zubayr and ᶜĀʾisha, and in the so-called first civil war between ᶜAlī and Muᶜāwiya.'[116]

ADDITIONS OF THE AUTHOR

P. 510 ftn. 19: The same remark about the walking stick being better (because more useful) than Muḥammad, expressed by an ordinary Wahhābī in the year 1925 in Mecca, is noted in Eldon Rutter: *The Holy Cities of Arabia*, London-New York, 1928, I, p. 272.

P. 517 ftn. 39: *Ṣalṣābīl* is also found in manuscripts of the Persian translation of ᶜAbdallāh b. ᶜUmar b. Muḥammad b. Dāwūd's *Faḍāʾil Balkh* which was composed in Arabic in 610/1214. The Arabic original appears to be lost. The Persian translation is from the year 676/1279 and was produced by a certain ᶜAbdallāh b. Muḥammad-i Ḥusaynī-i Balkhī. Charles Schefer: *Chrestomathie persane*, Paris,

114 From the Ida ou Zeddagh on the southern slopes of the High-Atlas.

115 Abū'l-ᶜAbbās Aḥmad b. Khālid al-Nāṣirī: *Al-istiqṣā li-akhbār duwal al-maghrib al-aqṣā*, Casablanca, 1954-56, VIII, pp. 121-22. Nāṣirī everywhere writes Ibn Saᶜūd instead of Saᶜūd. The delegation from Morocco is also mentioned by Burckhardt: *Notes on the Bedouins and Wahábys*, II, pp. 210-11.

116 Muḥammad Taqī al-Dīn al-Hilālī: *Al-hadiyya al-hādiya ilā'l-ṭāʾifa al-tijāniyya*, Casablanca (?), 1973, pp. 17-20.

1883, I, Persian Part, p. 75, l. 2, prints in his extract from the Persian translation *Ṣalṣāʾīl*, but in his accompanying commentary, French Part, p. 67, l. 2, he writes *Salsabyl* with *b* although his Paris MS apparently lacks the required dot. ᶜAbd al-Ḥayy-i Ḥabībī's critical edition of the Persian translation of *Faḍāʾil Balkh*, Tehran, 1350, p. 23, l. 6, likewise has *Ṣalṣāʾīl* in the text but gives *Ṣalṣābīl* as a variant from two St. Petersburg MSS. Here and in the case of a second angel of this type Ḥabībī rightly restores the form in *-ʾīl* by analogy with *Jabrāʾīl, Mīkāʾīl*, etc. The text of the *Faḍāʾil Balkh* on p. 23, l. 6, describes *Ṣalṣāʾīl* as the angel who was appointed regent over the earth (*al-malak al-muwakkal bi'l-arḍ*). The name thus has an association with *ṣalṣāl* 'clay' rather than the *taṣliya*.

INVOKING BLESSINGS ON MUḤAMMAD IN PRAYERS OF SUPPLICATION AND WHEN MAKING REQUESTS

1. IN PRAYERS OF SUPPLICATION

Islamic ritual prayer (*ṣalāh*) is either 'correctly' or 'incorrectly' performed. It is valid or invalid. It is not a question of its being 'heard' but of being 'accepted' (*maqbūla*), as one normally says. In the Christian usage of the Copts the same Arabic word (*ṣalāh*), like our *orare* and 'prayer', designates prayers in general, whether liturgical or private. *Ṣallā ᶜalā* among the Copts can mean 'to pray for someone' but also 'to consecreate' or 'to bless', as for instance in the case of water or oil.[1] The nocturnal 'prayers' (*ṣalāh*) and 'readings' (*qirāʾa*) of the Patriarch are supposed to have been a source of comfort to the Umayyad Hishām (105-125/724-743) in Damascus. He wished 'to listen' to them.[2] One 'prays' (*ṣallā*) the Gospel.[3] They reproached the Patriarch Dionysius, saying: 'You hold the mass (*tuqaddis*) apart with your companions.' He replied: 'We never cease to pray (*ṣalātanā*), neither day nor night'[4] — thus the mass and prayer are one and the same. A few lines later: 'They should say their prayers (*yuṣallū ṣalawātihim*) and read the mass (*yuqaddisū quddāsātihim*)'[5] — thus prayer and the mass are two different things. But prayers of supplication can be exclusively meant as well: 'Listen to my *ṣalāh* and hear my *duᶜāʾ*[6] — evidently a case of hendiadys. These Christian *ṣalawāt* are listened to by God as well as heard and accepted. In the Arab west, in the Iberian Peninsula, *ṣalāh* was the Arabic translation for mass. Pedro de Alcalá (1505) in his handbooks (*Vocabulista* and *Arte*) for the Christian mission among the Moriscos gives for mass: *çalá*, pl. *çalaguát* (= *ṣalāh*, pl. *ṣalawāt*),[7] and for the

---

1 Severus ibn al Muqaffaᶜ: *Alexandrinische Patriarchengeschichte*, ed. Chr. F. Seybold, Hamburg, 1912, p. 67, l. 18; p. 179, l. 10.

2 Ibid., p. 145, ll. 7-9.

3 Ibid., p. 57, l. 9.

4 Ibid., p. 29, ll. 9-10.

5 Ibid., p. 29, ll. 22-23.

6 H.A. Winkler: *Salomo und die Ḳarīna*, Stuttgart, 1931, p. 98, penult. line.

sentence 'I go to church to hear the mass': *ani namxi la gimie bex nazmáa a callá* (= *ana amshī ilā'l-jāmi^c likay asma^ca'l-ṣalāh*).[8] This Spanish equation shows perhaps better than the Coptic examples what Islamic ritual prayer involves.

Ritual prayer can be framed by invoking blessings on Muḥammad at the beginning and at the end, i.e. by the *taṣliya*,[9] as I would say for the sake of brevity (in texts mostly *al-ṣalāh ^calā'l-nabī*). The *taṣliya* in the so-called supplication of inauguration (*du^cā^o al-iftitāḥ*) before ritual prayer was only exceptionally viewed as compulsory, for example by the otherwise insignificant Ḥanbalite Abū Bakr b. Abī Majd b. Mujāhid al-Sa^cdī al-Dimashqī al-Miṣrī (d. 804/1402).[10] Another matter is the *taṣliya* at the conclusion of ritual prayer where it is pronounced at the very end in the so-called 'last' or 'second *tashahhud*' and was possibly already added by Muḥammad during the last years of his life, between 5/627 and 11/632, namely after the revelation of surah 33/56. Surah 33/56 states: 'God and His angels bless the Prophet. Oh you who believe, you too bless him and greet him in the best manner you can!'[11] The disciples of Muḥammad asked how their invocation of blessings should be worded and they then came to hear the formula which now occurs in the last *tashahhud*[12] and which, because Abraham is mentioned in it, is

---

7 Petri Hispani *de lingua Arabica libri duo*, ed. Paul de Lagarde, Göttingen, 1883, p. 312, ll. 7-9. Robert Ricard: 'Remarques sur l'*Arte* et le *Vocabulista* de Fr. Pedro de Alcalá', in *Mémorial Henri Basset*, Paris, 1928, II, p. 232.

8 Petrus Hispanus, p. 31, ll. 21-22. Ricard, p. 234.

9 In this form (form II of the verb) the roots *ṣlw* 'to pray' and *ṣly* 'to roast' look identical. Edmond Doutté believes he recognizes in this a sign that the Arabs originally also made burnt offerings; *Magie et religion dans l'Afrique du Nord*, Algiers, 1908, p. 453, ll. 1-2. — In Arabic usage the infinitive *taṣliya* is not popular for our invocation of blessings. One would think of *wa-taṣliyat jaḥīm* 'and roasting in a Hell-fire' (surah 56/94). But *ṣalāh* in our case would lead to misunderstandings.

10 Sakhāwī: *Al-ḍaw^o al-lāmi^c li-ahl al-qarn al-tāsi^c*, Cairo, 1353-55, XI, p. 67, ll. 7-8, from Maqrīzī's *^cUqūd*.

11 The Persian term *durōdh/durūd-i sharīf* 'the holy *taṣliya*' can designate this Koranic formula, as in Muḥammad Ḥusayn-i Tasbīḥī: 'Rasm-i qul u dastārbandī dar Pākistān', in *Hunar u mardum* 171 (year 2535), p. 34. But it can also designate another formula, i.e. 'Oh God, bless and greet the lord of creation Muḥammad and his family!, as in ^cIwaḍ-i Bukhārī: 'Tarjuma-i ṭālibīn wa īḍāḥ-i sālikīn', ed. M. Molé, in *Farhang-i Īrānzamīn* 8, 1339, p. 130/offprint, p. 39 (*faṣl* 3).

12 Muslim, *ṣalāh* 17, I, pp. 305-06. Bukhārī, *tafsīr* to surah 33/56.

called *ṣalāh ibrāhīmiyya*, or because of its completeness is also called *ṣalāh tāmma* 'the full *taṣliya*'.[13] Muḥammad is supposed to have designated it as an alms-tax of ritual prayer and declared that ritual prayer without it was 'unacceptable' for God.[14] The Companion of the Prophet Sahl b. Saᶜd al-Sāᶜidī claims to have heard when he was not yet 15 years old: 'Whoever does not pronounce the blessing on the Prophet has not done his ritual prayer',[15] which sounds rather strange in the 3rd person. The interpretation was that ritual prayer is not complete without *taṣliya*, or that at least once in one's lifetime one must have pronounced or pronounce the blessing on Muḥammad if one's prayer is to be valid.[16] In fact its status as a religious duty is disputed both in the Sunna and among the Shīᶜa.[17] Is the *taṣliya* in the last *tashahhud* simply recommended or is it an unalterable duty? Shāfiᶜī (d. 204/820) took it to be a duty.[18] Others were content to leave it as no more than a recommendation. The Mālikite judge Qāḍī ᶜIyāḍ (d. 544/1149), otherwise so zealous a venerator of the Prophet, was reproached for the fact that even he was in this latter camp.[19]

Here, though, the prayer of supplication (*duᶜāʾ*) will be our subject, and it does not hold the rank of a 'pillar of Islam'. Ritual purity is not required in its case. If God so wills, it may also be accepted, though one says more frequently and more in accordance with the nature of the matter 'heard' (*mujāb*). Muḥammad is supposed to have made the success of a prayer of supplication as well dependent on invoking blessings on him. His statements diverge from one an-

---

13 Shaᶜrānī: *Al-ṭabaqāt al-kubrā*, Cairo, 1954, II, p. 73 below (no. 318). Braulio Justel Calabozo: *La Hidāya de al-Rayrāŷī (un Espejo de Príncipes medieval)*, Madrid, 1983, Arabic p. 77/Spanish p. 166. — But *ṣalāh tāmma* can also be used as an appellative, with the meaning 'complete blessing'; Sakhāwī: *Al-qawl al-badīᶜ fī'l-ṣalāh ᶜalā'l-ḥabīb al-shafīᶜ*, Medina-Beirut, n.d., p. 50, l. 19.

14 Dāraquṭnī: *Sunan*, Cairo, 1966, I, p. 355.

15 Ibn Māja, *ṭahāra* 41, I, p. 140.

16 Ibn al-Qaṣṣār in Qāḍī ᶜIyāḍ: *Al-shifā bi-taᶜrīf ḥuqūq al-muṣṭafā*, Cairo, 1977, II, p. 632.

17 Ṭūsī: *Al-istibṣār fī-mā'khtulifa fīhi min al-akhbār*, Najaf, n.d., I, pp. 341-44. *Tahdhīb al-aḥkām*, Najaf, 1378-82, I, pp. 139, 159, 320; II, pp. 140, 158, 318.

18 *Kitāb al-umm*, Būlāq, 1321-26, I, p. 102. ᶜIyāḍ: *Shifā*, II, pp. 628-30. Nawawī: *Al-adhkār, al-muntakhab min kalām sayyid al-abrār*, Beirut, 1973, p. 63. Discussed by Ibn Qayyim al-Jawziyya: *Jalāʾ al-afhām fī'l-ṣalāh wa'l-salām ᶜalā khayr al-anām*, Kuwait-Beirut, 1977, pp. 185 ff.

19 Muḥibbī: *Khulāṣat al-athar fī aᶜyān al-qarn al-ḥādī ᶜashar*, Cairo, 1284, III, p. 186.

other in their details. Impressive is a particular formulation which triply connects the *taṣliya* to the prayer of supplication: 'Do not treat me like the horseman treats his water-container! Should he wish to set out, he attaches his water-carrier and fills another container with water. If he then needs ithe water to wash, he washes with it. If he needs it to drink, he drinks some of it. If not, he empties it out. Rather, place me in the middle, at the beginning and at the end of the prayer of supplication!'[20] Similar and yet different is the version: 'Whenever you ask your God for something, begin with praise of God, then in the second place pronounce the invocation of blessings on your highly lauded Prophet! Place your invocation of blessings on him at the beginning, in the middle and at the conclusion of your prayer of supplication! In your praise for him set forth his magnificent titles to glory. That way you will become a person whose supplication is heard.'[21] A third saying is content with a double interconnection, a bracketing of the supplication by means of a *taṣliya* at the beginning and at the end: 'Whoever is worried about a religious or a worldly matter, let him pronounce many blessings on me because God is loath to refuse a bondsman something if his supplication stands between two invocations of blessings on me, one at the beginning and one at the end of the request.'[22] More briefly: 'A prayer of supplication between two invocations of blessings will not be refused.'[23] Admittedly not from Muḥammad but from the Syrian man of piety Abū Sulaymān al-Dārānī (d. 215/830) comes the same form of wisdom with an explanation: 'Whoever wishes to ask God to fulfill a request should begin by invoking blessings on the Prophet,

---

20 With variants. Aḥmad b. Maᶜadd b. ᶜĪsā b. Wakīl al-Tujībī al-Uqlīshī (from Ucles in Spain, d. 550/1155 in Qūṣ on his return from Mecca; Maqqarī: *Analectes sur l'histoire et la littérature des Arabes d'Espagne*, Publ. par R. Dozy et alii, Leiden, 1855-61, I, pp. 872-73; some information in Yāqūt: *Geogr. Wörterbuch*, ed. F. Wüstenfeld, Leipzig, 1866-70, s.v. Uqlīsh, I, p. 339): *Anwār al-āthār fī faḍl al-ṣalāh ᶜalā'l-nabī al-mukhtār*, 40 *ḥadīths*, in Bārizī: *Tawthīq ᶜurā'l-īmān*, MS Sprenger 127b, 200a-b (Ahlwardt no. 2569). Ibn al-Qayyim: *Jalāʾ*, p. 212. Subkī: *Ṭabaqāt al-shāfiᶜiyya al-kubrā*, ed. Ṭanāḥī and Ḥulw, Cairo, 1964-76, I, p. 176. Sakhāwī: *Al-qawl al-badīᶜ fī'l-ṣalāh ᶜalā'l-ḥabīb al-shafīᶜ*, Medina-Beirut, n.d., pp. 221-22. Kulīnī: *Al-uṣūl min al-Kāfī*, Tehran, 1375-77, II, p. 492. Ibn al-Jawzī: *Bustān al-wāᶜiẓīn wa-riyāḍ al-sāmiᶜīn*, Cairo, 1934, p. 305. Abbreviated to 'at the beginning and at the end' in Ḥubayshī: *Al-baraka fī'l-saᶜy wa'l-ḥaraka*, Cairo, 1354, p. 172. E.W. Lane: *Arabic-English Lexicon*, London, 1863-93, *qadaḥ*.

21 Sakhāwī: *Qawl*, p. 221.

22 Ibn al-Jawzī: *Bustān al-wāᶜiẓīn*, p. 295.

23 Sakhāwī: *Qawl*, p. 223.

next put his request to God and then conclude with an invocation of blessings on behalf of the Prophet, because the request to bless the Prophet will always be accepted and God is too noble to refuse what is placed in between.'[24] And the latter may have taken this from Jaᶜfar al-Ṣādiq (d. 148/765) who had expressed it before him in almost the same words.[25] Older still, and reduced to the demand for a single *taṣliya* only, one finds this version already in a wholly similar formulation by the very early Muslim Abū'l-Dardāᵓ (d. 32/652): 'When you ask God for something, begin by invoking blessings on the Prophet because when you make two requests of God, He is too noble to grant one of them and to refuse the other.'[26] But he most likely cited this saying as the very words of the Prophet using the phrase 'invoking blessings on me', not 'on the Prophet'.[27] It can be shown that surprisingly the oldest of the three men of piety, Abū'l-Dardāᵓ, is the most probable source for the saying. There are other statements which only demand one invocation of blessings on the Prophet in a supplication, statements which are perhaps more likely to have originated from the Prophet himself. One such is: 'If one of

---

24 Ghazzālī: *Iḥyāᵓ ᶜulūm al-dīn*, Cairo, 1957, I, p. 309. Ibn al-Qayyim: *Jalāᵓ*, p. 212. Sakhāwī: *Qawl*, pp. 223 and 233, variant. Muḥammad b. Sulaymān al-Jazūlī: *Dalāᵓil al-khayrāt*, Introduction (before the *aḥzāb*). Some remarks on the subject in the commentary of Muḥammad al-Mahdī b. Aḥmad b. ᶜAlī b. Yūsuf al-Fāsī al-Qaṣrī (d. 1109/1698): *Maṭāliᶜ al-masarrāt bi-jalāᵓ Dalāᵓil al-khayrāt*, Cairo, 1970, pp. 36-38. The commentator is not listed with the correct author's name in *GAL*, II, p. 253/*GAL S*, II, p. 360. The author is Muḥammad al-Mahdī who has an article in *GAL S*, II, p. 703. The dictum of Dārānī is often quoted, as for instance by ᶜAbd al-Ṣamad al-Tihāmī Gannūn (d. 1352/1934): *Al-nasaq al-ghālī wa'l-nafas al-ᶜālī sharḥ naṣīḥat Abī'l-ᶜAbbās al-Hilālī*, Cairo, 1973, p. 590. The first part is also presented as a saying of the Prophet and transmitted in the following two forms: 'The invocation of blessings on the Prophet is never rejected' (what is meant is the request made to God to bless Muḥammad, and the good work which is contained in the invocation of blessings). 'All works can be accepted or rejected, except for the invocation of blessings on my behalf which is only accepted and never rejected'; Muḥammad Ṭāhir b. ᶜAlī al-Hindī al-Fattanī: *Tadhkirat al-mawḍūᶜāt*, Bombay, 1343, p. 89.

25 Kulīnī: *Al-uṣūl min al-Kāfī*, II, p. 494, no. 16. Expanded by adding the command also to invoke blessing on Muḥammad's family, as in many other cases as well. The saying is not found in the article on Jaᶜfar in Abū Nuᶜaym: *Ḥilyat al-awliyāᵓ*, Cairo, 1932-38, III, pp. 192-206.

26 Sakhāwī: *Qawl*, p. 233. Ibn al-Daybaᶜ: *Tamyīz al-ṭayyib min al-khabīth fī-mā yadūr ᶜalā alsinat al-nās min al-ḥadīth*, Cairo, 1324, pp. 119-20. Aḥmad b. al-Mubārak (al-Lamaṭī): *Al-ibrīz (fī manāqib sayyidī ᶜAbd al-ᶜAzīz)*, Cairo, n.d., p. 329 (in Chpt. 11).

27 *Iḥyāᵓ*, I, p. 309.

you prays for something, let him begin with praise and laudation of God, then pronounce a blessing on the Prophet and then pray for whatever he wishes.'[28] Ibn Qayyim al-Jawziyya summarizes the three possibilities:

1) Invoking blessings on the Prophet only once: after praising God and before one's actual request;

2) invoking blessings two times: at the beginning and at the end of one's prayer;

3) invoking blessings three times: at the beginning, in the middle and at the end.[29]

His teacher Ibn Taymiyya (d. 728/1328), who judged severely all later accretions of pious practice, recognizes the *taṣliya* as a legal, indeed as a prescribed prayer to God on behalf of Muḥammad and thus sees no hindrance to employing the *taṣliya* in supplication. This, as he says, is preferable to forms of conjuring God such as 'by the dignity (*jāh*) of the Prophet', for which one cannot cite any legal justification at all.[30] He would not have anything to do with the latter. This remark reveals that in a supplication the *taṣliya* had assumed the role of a conjuration. Among the many supplications with *taṣliya* which Abū Ṭālib al-Makkī (d. 386/996) sets before the reader in his collection there is still one which stands out as having a genuine formula of conjuration: 'Oh God, I beseech You by the Prophet Muḥammad, by Your friend Abraham, etc.'[31] In the life of Islamic prayer up until today both the *taṣliya* and the oath-formula have been preserved alongside one another and even in combination, although the one could replace the other and in the strictest view, as we just heard above, only the *taṣliya* is unimpeachable.

Alleged sayings of Muḥammad illustrate, by means of powerful images, the necessity of providing supplications with an invocation of blessings on his behalf. According to a Zaydite tradition, he is meant to have described the invocation of blessings as 'the pass of your prayer' (*jawāz duʿāʾikum*).[32] The Prophet, the imams and the caliphs do not accord any chance to a supplication without this pass.

---

28 Ibn al-Qayyim: *Jalāʾ*, p. 211.

29 *Jalāʾ*, p. 211.

30 Ibn Taymiyya: *Qāʿida jalīla fī'l-tawassul wa'l-wasīla*, Beirut, 1979, pp. 150-51.

31 *Qūt al-qulūb*, Cairo, 1932, I, p. 12, l. 12.

32 Yaḥyā b. al-Ḥusayn Abū Ṭālib: *Taysīr al-maṭālib fī amālī'l-imām Abī Ṭālib*, Beirut, 1975, p. 353. An alternative reading has 'protector' (*muḥriza*) instead of 'pass'; Sakhāwī: *Qawl*, p. 128, l. 4. A confusion resulting from the resemblances between *jwz* and *ḥrz* in Arabic script.

As they say, a supplication requires, as it were, a push from the *taṣliya* if it is actually to rise on high and reach heaven. Without this impulse or special credential it flutters around one's head, remains suspended between heaven and earth (*muᶜallaq*), held back (*mawqūf*), excluded from heaven (*maḥjūb*), is demoted to a cloud (*turjaᶜu ᶜalā saḥāba*), a veil or something similar (*ḥijāb*) blocks the way upward. The veil is only torn away once blessings are invoked on behalf of Muḥammad.[33]

Thus the custom of not sending a supplication on its journey without the *taṣliya* seems to have won itself a place in practice quite early on. The following are some examples chosen at random from the 1st/7th century:

Muslim b. ᶜAqīl, before his execution in Kūfa in the year 60/680, asked God for forgiveness, invoked blessings on Muḥammad, the other prophets and the angels, and beseeched God to judge between the party of the ᶜAlids and the treacherous Kufans.[34] Al-Ḥasan al-Baṣrī (d. 110/728) called on God in times of emergency and invoked blessings on Muḥammad before he presented his request.[35] In face of personal threat from the governor Ḥajjāj he prayed: 'Oh You who hear my call... by

---

33 Ismāᶜīl b. Isḥāq al-Jahḍamī: *Faḍl al-ṣalāh ᶜalā'l-nabī*, Beirut, 1977, p. 69. Kulīnī, II, pp. 491, 493. Ibn Bābawayh: *Thawāb al-aᶜmāl wa-ᶜiqāb al-aᶜmāl*, Najaf, 1972, p. 155. Uqlīshī in Bārizī: *Tawthīq ᶜurā'l-īmān*, MS Sprenger 127b, 200a-b. ᶜIyāḍ: *Shifā*, II, p. 635. Ibn al-Jawzī: *Bustān*, p. 305. Nawawī: *Adhkār*, p. 108. Muḥammad b. Mūsā b. al-Nuᶜmān (d. 683/1284; *GAL*, I, pp. 384-85): *Miṣbāḥ al-ẓalām fī'l-mustaghīthīn bi-khayr al-anām*, in Bārizī, MS Sprenger 127b, 48a. Subkī: *Ṭabaqāt*, I, p. 176. Ibn al-Qayyim: *Jalā'*, p. 212. Yāfiᶜī: *Al-irshād wa'l-taṭrīz fī faḍl dhikr allāh taᶜālā wa-tilāwat kitābihī'l-ᶜazīz*, Cairo, 1378, p. 236 (Chpt. 7). Sakhāwī: *Qawl*, pp. 222-24. Mujīr al-Dīn al-Ḥanbalī: *Al-uns* (or *ins*) *al-jalīl bi-tārīkh al-Quds wa'l-Khalīl*, Amman, 1973, I, p. 223. Muḥammad Ṣiddīq Ḥasan Khān Malik Bhōpāl: *Nuzul al-abrār bi'l-ᶜilm al-ma'thūr min al-adᶜiya wa'l-adhkār*, Constantinople, 1301, p. 166. — In an unsuccessful Shīᶜite *ḥadīth* in which there is no mention of a prayer of suppliction at the beginning, invoking blessings on the Prophet by itself is not sufficient. Invoking blessings on 'the people of his house' is also required as a pacesetter. Leaving out this addition creates seventy veils between the invocation of blessings (sic) and heaven, and God turns away the prayer of supplication (sic) of those who commit sins of omission; Ibn Bābawayh: *Thawāb al-aᶜmāl*, p. 157, last three lines.

34 Abu'l-Faraj al-Iṣfahānī: *Maqātil al-ṭālibiyyīn*, Cairo, 1949, p. 107 below. Ṭabarī: *Annales*, Leiden, 1879-1901, II, p. 267, ll. 16-18. In *Maqātil* the doxology is incorrectly set apart. 'His prophets, apostles of God and angels' belongs to the prayer, not to the doxology.

35 Ibn al-Jawzī: *Al-Ḥasan al-Baṣrī*, ed. Sandūbī, Cairo, 1931 (Rasā'il nādira), p. 41.

khy^cs, *th*, *ys*[36] and the wise Koran bless[37] Muḥammad and Muḥammad's family, the pure ones, spare me his (i.e. Ḥajjāj's) evil and the evil of every malicious person, protect me from Ḥajjāj, his party, those who share his opinions, and his soldiers... And bless, oh God, our lord Muḥammad, the Seal of the prophets, and greet him with the best of greetings!'[38] Here we have the double *taṣliya*. In moments of distress[39] Ja^cfar al-Ṣādiq (d. 148/765) is supposed to have prayed with a single *taṣliya* and a long predicate, as did Imam Riḍā (d. 203/818) in the curse he directed against the caliph Ma'mūn.[40] A quite old explanation concerning how to behave at the grave of Muḥammad in Medina, which is communicated from Ibn ^cAbd Rabbih (d. 328/940), prescribes that, after greeting the Prophet, Abū Bakr and ^cUmar, one should turn toward Mecca and first invoke blessings on the Prophet and only then pronounce one's desired supplications.[41]

Especially welcome are examples on stone or wood because in this case only rarely has a later hand falsified the original phrasing. In an inscription from the year 363/974 on wooden tablets the Būyid Twelver Shī^cite ^cAḍud al-Dawla Abū Shujā^c Fannā-Khusraw, after the *basmala*, turns to God with the request: 'Oh God, bless Muḥammad and his family, and cause my faith to reach perfection, make my right hand develop into the best right hand, let my intention develop into the best intention and my work develop into the best work! Oh God... Oh God, bless Muḥammad and his family, and save me from worries which could distract me, employ me for that which You will one day question me about, etc.'[42] On stone, innumberable grave inscriptions could be mentioned in which, after the *taṣliya*, the surviving relatives pray for mercy, not for themselves but for the deceased. The typical form is: 'Oh God, bless the Prophet and have mercy on so-and-so!' Allegedly from Syria as early as 200/815-16 one finds: '*Basmala*. Oh God, bless Muḥammad and the family of Muḥammad, as You blessed Abraham and the family of Abraham — You are

36 Cryptogramms of surahs 19, 20 and 36.

37 Read *ṣalli*.

38 Ibn al-Jawzī: *Ḥasan*, p. 42.

39 Sakhāwī: *Qawl*, p. 219 (connected with oaths 'by every name which You have given Yourself in Your Book', etc., as frequently elsewhere).

40 Ibn Bābawayh: *Akhbār al-Riḍā*, Najaf, 1970, II, pp. 170-71/Ibn Shahrāshūb: *Manāqib āl Abī Ṭālib*, Najaf, 1956, III, p. 456.

41 Ibn ^cAbd Rabbih: *Al-^ciqd al-farīd*, Cairo, 1353/1935, IV, p. 286 below/trans. by Muḥammad Shafī^c: 'A Description of the Two Sanctuaries of Islám by Ibn ^cAbd Rabbihi († 940)', in *^cAğabnāma. A Volume of Oriental Studies Presented to Edward G. Browne*, Cambridge, 1922, p. 434 below.

42 *Répertoire chronologique d'épigraphie arabe*, Cairo, 1931 ff., V, no. 1831. In the same inscription there then follows a long *taṣliya*-litany to Muḥammad and the Imams of the Twelver-Shī^cites, as is frequently attested elsewhere. Instead of *anbih* I read *intahi* by changing the *b* into *t*.

praised on high and worthy of laudation. I beseech You, oh God, forgive ʿAbd al-Wadd (?) b. Yaḥyā his sins, the old and the new, illuminate his grave, open wide for him the entrance (to Paradise) and cause his face to bloom...'[43] But only later on is this formula well attested and then in the Nile Valley where it was jealously guarded and never exported, if one is justified in following the *Répertoire chronologique d'épigraphie arabe* to this extent. There the formula appears quite frequently up into the 12th century and then sporadically in Upper-Egypt still in the 8th/14th century[44] but, aside from the Dahlak group of islands in the Red Sea,[45] it does not appear either in Jerusalem or Qayrawān, or anywhere else in the Mediterranean area. In Upper-Egypt from 279/892 one finds: '*Basmala.* Oh God, bless Muḥammad the Prophet and his family, and greet them, and have mercy on Fāṭima, the daughter of ʿAbdallāh b. Ṭāhir b. Sulaymān...'[46] From Egypt in 287/900: '*Basmala.* Oh God, bless Muḥammad and the family of Muḥammad with the best blessings and the most perfect of greetings (*taḥiyya*), and have mercy on the *umm walad* of al-Qāsim b. Muḥammad b. Hārūn, be pleased with her, forgive her...'[47] From Fusṭāṭ in 290/903: '*Basmala.* Oh God, bless Muḥammad and the family of Muḥammad with the best blessings that You have spoken on his behalf, whose rank You have honored, whose excellence You have assured and whose share in Your plentiful gifts and powerful greetings You have given him completely, and have mercy on al-Miswar b. Muḥammad b. Hārūn and forgive him...'[48] Thus, one finds everywhere the *captatio benevolentiae* of the *taṣliya* used for personal supplication.[49]

43 *Répertoire*, I, no. 114.

44 Judging by the *Répertoire*, although the whole stock of inscriptions of the period has still not been included in it. The last offshoots of the *ṣalli-wa'rḥam*-formula are XIII, no. 4923, from 689/1290 in Aswan and XV, no. 5635, from 733/1333 in Tāfa in Upper-Egypt. In XI, no. 4276 is an example from Ankara and nos. 4293 and 4294 are examples from Mosul, the latter with *wa'ghfir* and *wa-taqabbal* instead of *wa'rḥam*, all dated to the 7th/13th century. Pure *ighfir-*, *irḥam-* and *taʿaṭṭaf*-prayers without preceding *taṣliya* are from the desert of Ḥarra and from Turkish regions, but are also attested elsewhere. This is how matters originally stood and can be traced back to the 1st/7th century in Arabia; *Rép.*, I, nos. 20 and 21.

45 Giovanna Ventrone: 'Tre stele provenienti dalle Dahlak in una collezione privata romana', in *Studi in onore di Francesco Gabrieli nel suo ottantesimo compleanno*, Rome, 1984, pp. 833-35.

46 *Rép.*, II, no. 761.

47 *Rép.*, III, no. 812.

48 *Rép.*, III, no. 834.

49 Adolf Grohmann: 'Beiträge zur arabischen Epigraphik und Papyruskunde', in *Islamica* 2, 1926, pp. 223-24 (= *Rép.*, VI, no. 2142), regarding this formula refers to G. Salmon: 'Notes d'épigraphie arabe', William Wright: 'Kufic tombstones in the British Museum', and M. Lanci: 'Trattato delle sepolcrali iscrizioni'. Today one would refer to *Répertoire chronologique*, II, no. 761, and subsequent volumes of this work. Both elements from which it

Thaᶜālibī (d. 429/1038) presents to the stylists of his day and age a *taṣliya* which begins with the phrase: 'God bless Muḥammad, with whose mention supplications are best begun and with whose blessing (passive) the success of requests is best prayed for.'[50] In the far west on the Atlantic coast of Dukkāla the man of piety Ibrāhīm b. Mūsā, known as Aṣāṣāy (d. circa 615/1218), in the presence of many people pronounced the *basmala* one thousand times, the *ḥamdala* one thousand times and blessings on Muḥammad one thousand times, and then prayed one thousand times against the unjust tax-collector or governor of the region. On the same day the latter fell into disgrace.[51] A very pious man and great benefactor from Granada, Muḥammad b. Muḥammad b. ᶜAbd al-Raḥmān al-Tamīmī Ibn al-Ḥalfāwī (d. 715/1315), in every request he directed to God in his supplications following the ritual prayers, repeated the invocation of blessings on Muḥammad whom he adopted as his mediator.[52] According to a legend, Joseph hmself was rescued from the pit into which his brothers had thrown him, thanks to a prayer the angel Gabriel taught

---

is composed, the *taṣliya* and the prayer, occur separately in earlier grave inscriptions and have perhaps been brought together under the influence of the theology of prayer of supplication in the second half of the 3rd/9th century. In the limited space of an inscription, however, the profession of faith in Muḥammad and the prayer of supplication also often stand close to one another. Cf. *Rép.*, II, nos. 454, 457, 560, 603. No. 454 reads: 'There is no god but God, and Muḥammad is His bondsman and Messenger. "It is He who has sent His Messenger with guidance and the true religion to help it to victory over every other religion — even if this is contrary to the heathens" (surah 9/33). God bless him and greet him! Oh God, have mercy on him (i.e. the dead person), by Your mercifulness, and in his case let leniency prevail, by Your magnanimity!' — If in a reversed sequence the prayer for the dead comes first, then the *taṣliya* follows mostly in the 3rd person: 'God bless Muḥammad!', and usually concludes the inscription. Already on a gravestone from the year 127/745 from the environs of Aswan; William M. Randall: 'Three engraved stones from the Moritz Collection at the University of Chicago', in *The MacDonald Presentation Volume*, Princeton, 1933, pp. 328-29. Two other examples in *Rép.*, II, no. 659 (year 263/877), and *Rép.*, IV, no. 1473 (year 344/955). No. 659: 'Oh God, forgive him, pardon him and let him reach his disappeared ancestors and his pure fathers! And God bless Muḥammad, the Prophet, and the people of his great house, the pious!' — In some cases God is implored to be merciful for the sake of Muḥammad; *Rép.*, I, nos. 221 and 225. No. 221: 'Oh God, have mercy on his solitariness, brighten his desolation, strengthen his speech at the interrogation, open the gates of heaven for his soul and place him inside, by Muḥammad! God bless and greet him! ...Oh God, spare him every terror this side of Paradise, etc.' (The translation 'près de Mahomet' is incorrect).

50 Abū Manṣūr ᶜAbd al-Malik al-Thaᶜālibī: *Siḥr al-balāgha wa-sirr al-barāᶜa*, Damascus, 1350, p. 12, ll. 7-8.

51 Tādilī: *Al-tashawwuf ilā rijāl al-taṣawwuf*, ed. Adolphe Faure, Rabat, 1958, p. 437.

52 Ibn al-Khaṭīb: *Al-iḥāṭa fī tārīkh Gharnāṭa*, Cairo, 1973-76, III, p. 272.

him which went as follows: 'Oh Creator of all creation, oh Restorer of all that has been broken, etc., I beseech You: bless Muḥammad and the family of Muḥammad, and give me liberation and a way out of my situation and my confinement, grant me what I might calculate and I might not calculate.'[53] And in the form of an anonymous anecdote: A perfume seller from Karkh (Baghdad) who did many good things and was known to be reliable came to have debts and felt ashamed to appear before people. He stayed at home, began to pronounce supplications and blessings on Muḥammad and to fulfill his religious duties and then came through his difficulties with the help of the Prophet.[54] Another person who was beset by hardship complained about it to his shaykh. The shaykh beheld the Prophet in a dream. The Prophet revealed to him a means which if honestly employed would help in every case. The man should say 'praise be to God' one hundred times, 'laudation unto God' one hundred times, 'God is great' one hundred times, 'oh God, bless Muḥammad the unlettered prophet' one hundred times, 'there is no god but God, there is only He; He has no partner' one hundred times, perform twelve prostrations of prayer, next pronounce a supplication, then perform two prostrations of prayer, then recite the last fifty verses of surah 2, then perform twenty-four prostrations of prayer and thereupon pronounce the following supplication... The man did this and the distress he had been suffering from disappeared.[55] A Berber Sufi from Sūs by the name of Muḥammad b. Aḥmad (d. 1251/1835) made use of no less heavy artillery. He maintained that invoking blessings three hundred times before the supplication would guarantee that it was heard, and he reinforced this 'coercion of heaven' by saying the *taṣliya* one thousand times in four packets (300 + 200 + 300 + 200) and by pronouncing the supplication between each packet.[56] A Mauritanian Tijānī of the 13th/19th century gave a forced justification of the composition of the litany (*wird*) of the Tijānī order in which the *taṣliyāt* follow the requests for forgiveness of sins, by referring to the wisdom of the *ḥadīth* that the barrier to supplications before heaven must be removed by the invocation of blessings.[57] In reality the two compo-

53 Thaʿlabī: *Qiṣaṣ al-anbiyāʾ*, Cairo, 1325, p. 72.

54 Ibn al-Nuʿmān (d. 683/1284): *Miṣbāḥ al-ẓalām fī'l-mustaghīthīn bi-khayr al-anām fī'l-yaqaẓa wa'l-manām* (*GAL*, I, p. 385), in Bārizī: *Tawthīq ʿurā'l-īmān*, MS Sprenger 127b, 12b.

55 Ibn al-Ḥājj: *Al-mudkhal*, Cairo, 1929, IV, p. 129.

56 Muḥammad al-Mukhtār al-Sūsī: *Al-maʿsūl*, Casablanca, circa 1960, VI, p. 213.

57 ʿUbayda b. Muḥammad al-Ṣaghīr b. Anbūja al-Shinqīṭī al-Tīshītī (d. 1284/1867): *Mīzāb al-raḥma al-rabbāniyya fī'l-tarbiya bi'l-ṭarīqa al-tijāniyya* (written 1268/1850), Cairo?, 1973, p. 61. The *wird* of the Tijāniyya consists of *istighfār* 100 times, *taṣliya* 100 times and *haylala* (= *tahlīl*) 100 times. From 1196/1782 to 1200/1786 it contained the first two parts and only afterwards came to include the *haylala*; ʿAlī Ḥarāzim b. al-ʿArabī Barrāda al-Maghribī al-Fāsī: *Jawāhir al-maʿānī wa-bulūgh al-amānī*, reprint Beirut, 1383, I, p. 51. Another work of the author is referred to in Abun-Nasr: *The Tijaniyya*, Oxford University Press, 1963, p. 191

nents have nothing to do with one another or are differently joined to one another, i.e. in the reverse way, as another Tijānī says: 'The request for forgiveness should first bring about the necessary purity for invoking blessings.'[58] In more recent times: a Khalwatī in commenting on the didactic poem *Bulghat al-murīd wa-mushtahā muwaffaq saᶜīd* of Muṣṭafā al-Bakrī (d. 1162/1749) explains sophistically the praise and gratitude which the poet offers up to God at the beginning as a kind of supplication because according to surah 14/7 God rewards expressions of thanks with even more gifts,[59] and he justifies the *taṣliya* that immediately follows in the poem by saying that 'whether or not our supplications are heard depends on (*mawqūf*) our invoking blessings on our lord and master Muḥammad.' The commentary was written in 1315/1897-98.[60] Naturally, at the same time innumerable supplications without *taṣliya* were despatched to heaven and, as far as one may have trust in the traditions, were none the less heard. This fact by itself supports the view of the parliament of theologians, if I may refer to them this way, which only agreed on (*ajmaᶜa*) the desirability (*istiḥbāb*), not the necessity, of the *taṣliya* in the supplication.[61]

(Ibn Anbuj; Ibn Anbūj also within the text of the *Mīzāb*, p. 195, l. 1). ᶜUbayda is the brother of the author of *Al-jaysh al-kafīl* (Abun-Nasr, p. 195: Tashiti and *al-Jaish al-kafīl*).

58 Muḥammad al-ᶜArabī (b.) al-Sāʾiḥ al-Sharqī al-ᶜUmarī al-Tijānī (d. 1309/1892): *Bughyat al-mustafīd li-sharḥ Munyat al-murīd*, Cairo, 1959, p. 344, ll. 11-18. Alongside this I have also made use of another Cairene edition, undated and containing *Al-jaysh al-kafīl* in the margin.

59 Already Jaᶜfar al-Ṣādiq was supposed to have said about this Koranic verse: 'If God grants you a piece of good fortune and you care about its existence and continuance, then simply express a great deal of praise and thanks in return for it!' ᶜAbdallāh b. Muḥammad al-Shabrāwī: *Al-itḥāf bi-ḥubb al-ashrāf*, Cairo, 1318, p. 54. *GAL*, II, p. 281, and *GAL S*, II, p. 390, have Shubrāwī; Ziriklī: *Al-aᶜlām*, tabᶜa 2, Cairo, 1954-59, IV, p. 274, correctly Shabrāwī. Expression of gratitude is also demanded by Sakhāwī: *Ḍawʾ lāmiᶜ*, Cairo, 1353, XI, p. 209, and by ᶜAbbās b. Muḥammad b. Aḥmad Ibn al-Sayyid Riḍwān al-Madanī: *Mukhtaṣar Fatḥ rabb al-arbāb bi-mā uhmila fī Lubb al-lubāb min wājib al-ansāb*, Cairo, 1926, p. 30 (with reference to our author).

60 Sulaymān b. Yūnus b. ᶜAlī al-Juhanī al-Shāfiᶜī al-Khalwatī: *Fayḍ al-malik al-ḥamīd wa-fatḥ al-quddūs al-majīd bi-sharḥ Bulghat al-murīd wa-mushtahā muwaffaq saᶜīd*, naẓm sayyidī Muṣṭafā al-Bakrī fī ādāb al-ṣūfiyya ᶜalā'l-ṭarīqa al-khalwatiyya (in the margin: *Tuḥfat al-akhyār bi-sharḥ al-Istighfār* lahū ayḍan), Cairo, 1320. The book and author are missing from Sarkīs and Brockelmann. Muṣṭafā al-Bakrī's *Urjūza* and a different commentary on it are listed in *GAL*, II, pp. 349-50.

61 Sakhāwī: *Qawl*, p. 221.

The effect of the *taṣliya* was highly estimated. One even attributed to it a certain degree of independent efficacity, not in the sense of exercising a direct influence on things, but in the sense of a pious feat which as such is rewarded by God. In this case the request can remain unvoiced. The *taṣliya* itself is sufficient. Pointing in that direction are the alleged words of the Prophet: 'Whoever pronounces the *taṣliya* on my behalf one hundred times every day, God fulfills for him a hundred requests, seventy in the hereafter and thirty in the here and now.'[62] Another such saying is even more to the point: 'Whoever is troubled by some concern, let him pronounce many blessings on me because this unties the knots, removes care and worries, and increases one's daily sustenance.'[63] From this viewpoint the Islamic religious scholars interpret a well-known account from a *ḥadīth* differently than an outside observer might at first expect. In the *ḥadīth* it says: 'Someone said to Muḥammad that he frequently pronounced blessings on his behalf and asked him how much of it he should dedicate to him — a quarter? Muḥammad answered: "As much as you wish. The more you dedicate to me, the better it will be for you." The man increased his bid: "Half of it? Two-thirds?", and he finally said: "I will dedicate to you all the blessings I invoke." To that Muḥammad replied: "In this way you will be relieved of your cares, and your sins will be forgiven."' The usual reader who considers himself somewhat familiar with Islam will understand that what the man wished to dedicate (*jaʿala*) to the Prophet is the merit for invoking blessings, because donating to the Prophet the reward for a pious action is a practice that is attested innumerable times. But it is only in exceptional cases that the statement is actually understood this way.[64] The prevailing view is that the man introduced the

---

62 Ibn al-Qayyim: *Jalāʾ*, p. 239. Kulīnī: *Uṣūl*, II, p. 493, no. 9.

63 Ibn al-Jawzī: *Bustān*, p. 300; somewhat differently p. 304. Sakhāwī: *Qawl*, p. 219. Not in the name of Muḥammad and with deviations in Muḥammad b. Aḥmad al-shahīr bi'l-Manla in a collective volume *Al-safīna al-qādiriyya*, Tunis, 1305/reprint Tripoli-Beirut, n.d., p. 60.

64 Shaʿrānī: *Lawāqiḥ al-anwār al-qudsiyya fī bayān al-ʿuhūd al-muḥammadiyya*, Cairo, 1961, p. 285. Abū'l-Mawāhib al-Shādhilī (d. 882/1477-78) claims to have received this interpretation from Muḥammad himself in a dream; Shaʿrānī, ibid., p. 288. The interpretations in Sakhāwī's *Qawl*, p. 139, swing now one way, now another. How should one understand: 'What is meant is the *taṣliya* in reality and what is meant is the reward of the *taṣliya* or something similar to the reward for it'? — Jaʿfar al-Ṣādiq gave a not wholly satisfying explanation. Someone asked him: 'What does it mean: "I give you all my invocations of blessings"? He replied: 'The man places him (the Prophet) before each of his requests; he never asks God for anything without beginning with the Prophet and having invoked blessings

invocation of blessings on Muḥammad in place of his supplication or supplications (*makān duʿāʾihī*), substituted the invocation of blessings for his supplications, only prayed for Muḥammad and by this means or for this reason became free of all his troubles.[65] And this is also what the instruction sounds like to read through Jazūlī's *Dalāʾil al-khayrāt* forty times in forty days, this work being nothing more than a collection of *taṣliyāt*. Then one's wishes will be fulfilled and one's troubles will be removed.[66] The Shādhilī al-ʿArabī al-Darqāwī

---

on him. Only then does he ask God for any of his own needs'; Kulīnī: *Uṣūl*, II, p. 492, no. 4; p. 493, no. 12. — For practical usage an example from ʿAlī Ḥarāzim: *Jawāhir al-maʿānī*, II, pp. 167-68: Aḥmad al-Tijānī (d. 1230/1815) recommended for warding off all manner of troubles one of two things: either (firstly) saying *yā laṭīf* 1000 times after every ritual prayer or at least in the morning and the evening, or (secondly) the *ṣalāt al-fātiḥ* 100 times after every ritual prayer or at least 100 times in the morning and 100 times at night, and conferring the merit for it on the Prophet. This will have the effect that God will free one from troubles, indeed without delay, and also from debts, money difficulties and family burdens. Even better would be to perform both these exercises. Effective help is provided by frequent recollection of God and frequent invocation of blessings on Muḥammad both in this world and in the world to come.

65 Ibn Taymiyya: *Qāʿida jalīla*, pp. 43-44. Ibn al-Qayyim: *Jalāʾ*, p. 228. Sakhāwī: *Qawl*, pp. 119, 139. ʿIyāḍ: *Shifā*, p. 651, ftn. 8 (interprets: 'How much time should I use for invoking blessings on you?'). Khafājī on *Shifā*, p. 652, ftn. 2 (concludes: 'The *taṣliya* removes the necessity of still having to ask anything for oneself'). Jahḍamī, pp. 30-31. The sources disagree regarding details. Ibn al-Jawzī: *Bustān*, p. 298, clarifies the common interpretation with the following variation: 'The man asks: "Which is the best prayer of supplication?" The Prophet: "The invocation of blessings on me." — "Should I make a third of my worship into invocations of blessings on you?" — "Then you will be rightly guided." — "Two-thirds?" — "Then you will be protected." — "Should I make my whole worship into invocations of blessings on you?" — "Whoever makes his whole worship into invocations of blessings on me, God will fulfill all his wishes in this world and in the world to come."' Differently but just as clearly and in the same sense, Ibn Abī Ḥajala: *Dafʿ al-naqma fī'l-ṣalāh ʿalā nabī al-raḥma*, MS Escorial 1772, 18a: 'Ubayy' — the man's name is given here — 'had a prayer of supplication with which he asked God for all kinds of things. He asked the Prophet whether he should make a quarter of it into an invocation of blessings on him, etc., and said finally: "I dedicate to you my whole *ṣalāh*."' The author (or his source) interprets: 'This means: "I make my whole prayer of supplication (*duʿāʾ*) into an invocation of blessings on you."'

66 Al-ʿAbbās b. Ibrāhīm: *Al-iʿlām bi-man ḥalla Marrākush wa-Aghmāt min al-aʿlām*, Rabat, 1974 ff., V, pp. 53 and 98 above. Ibn al-Muwaqqit: *Al-saʿāda al-abadiyya fī'l-taʿrīf bi-mashāhīr al-ḥaḍra al-marrākushiyya*, litho., Fez, 1336/1918, II, p. 30. Muḥammad al-Mukhtār al-Sūsī: *Maʿsūl*, XIII, p. 285. Idem: *Munyat al-mutaṭalliʿīn ilā man fī'l-zāwiya al-ilighiyya min*

(d. 1239/1823) expected a similar direct success from litanies of this kind. He advised every Muslim when experiencing insurmountable difficulties in life or facing a dilemma in making a decision, unwaveringly either to perform ritual prayers, to recite the Koran and to invoke blessings on the Prophet, or to undertake studies. Then if it happens he is a good Muslim, God Himself will intervene and see that there is a happy outcome.[67] When Hāshim, the lord of Tazerwalt, laid siege to Tiznit at the beginning of the 13th/end of the 18th century, the Nāṣirī Maḥammad (sic) Wāᶜazīz (d. 1248/1833) went about in the city and pronounced blessings on the Prophet a number of times in front of every house so that God would protect everything.[68] The Aït Wäryāgher do this on a lesser scale in the Rīf. When they wish to have rain, they walk three times around the mosque of the village or a saint's tomb, slaughter a sheep or a goat and recite the *fātiḥa*. If this doesn't help, after the evening prayers in the mosque the more religious men pronounce one thousand blessings on the Prophet, during which each person counts and after every hundred places a pebble in front of himself.[69] A somewhat weakened form of the same hope in fact attributes to the *taṣliya* the chief effect but still accords a supportive directional function to the supplication. An example of this is provided by ᶜUmar b. ᶜAlī al-Fākihānī (d. 731/1331) in his *Al-fajr al-munīr*, in the person of a shaykh of his own time Mūsā al-Ḍarīr. This Mūsā happened to be in a ship at sea. The vessel was caught in a raging storm, known by the name *al-iqlābiyya*,[70] and was on the point of sinking. In a dream the Prophet ordered him, together with the other passengers, to recite a thousand times: 'Oh God, bless Muḥammad so that You thereby save us from all fears and dangers, thereby fulfill our every wish, thereby cleanse us of all wicked deeds, thereby raise us to the highest levels and thereby cause us to attain the ultimate goal of all good in life and in

---

al-fuqarā᾽ al-munqaṭiᶜīn, Tetuan, 1379, p. 51. Justinard: 'Sidi Ahmed ou Moussa', in *Arch. Maroc.* 29, 1933, p. 218.

67 *Rasā᾽il*, Fez, 1318, p. 199, ll. 8-16.

68 Sūsī: *Maᶜsūl*, XII, p. 94.

69 Edward Westermarck: *Ritual and Belief in Morocco*, London, 1926/reprint New York, 1968, II, p. 257.

70 Not in Kahane and Tietze: *The Lingua Franca in the Levant*, Urbana, 1958. *Iqlāba* is a festivity in Mecca celebrating the complete recitation of the Koran by a student; C. Snouck Hurgronje: *Mekka*, The Hague, 1888-92, II, p. 146. *Aqlaba* means 'to throw into confusion, overturn'.

death!' They followed this counsel, and after only about three hundred times God caused the wind to die down, thanks to the blessing (*baraka*) of the *taṣliya*.[71] The consecutive clause 'so that You thereby' is in Arabic an asyndetic relative clause which causes its object — literally: 'Bless Muḥammad a blessing by means of which You...' The seemingly distorted shift to God as the subject of the relative clause is an attempt to conform to a hinted at theological demand not to make anything happen through things themselves but to make everything happen only through God by means of things. But the shift in this form of the *taṣliya* is generally in use and for our ideas more or less equivalent to saying: 'a blessing which saves us'. A certain al-Ḥasan b. ᶜAlī al-Uswānī who was a *qāḍī* in Edfu and perhaps died in 723/1323 or 724/1324,[72] considered this formula, if repeated a thousand times, an infallible means in every situation.[73] It became widespread under the designation '*taṣliya* of deliverance' (*ṣalāt al-najāh*) and remained in use up until quite recent times. When Aḥmad b. Muḥammad b. Muḥammad al-Darᶜī intended to implant (*talqīn*) in the warlike Muḥammad al-Ḍawᵓ al-Bagārī al-Maghrāwī (d. 1327/1909) the name of God 'the Coercor' (*al-jabbār*) as a word for recollecting God, the Prophet told him in a dream or in a vision: 'Postpone this until we see each other again (*najtamiᶜ marra ukhrā*)! But order him to pronounce on my behalf the formula of blessings for deliverance forty times a day!'[74]

Finally, one finds in the Tijāniyya a special *taṣliya* for speeding up (*taᶜjīl*) the acceptance of a prayer. It was pronounced seven times before and seventy times after a litany. The wording of this *taṣliya* was: 'Oh God, bless handsomely and greet handsomely the lord of those who are handsome and the leader of those who are shining, Muḥammad, the Apostle of God — God bless him and greet him!'[75]

---

71 Ibn Abī Ḥajala: *Dafᶜ al-naqma fī* (sic)*'l-ṣalāh ᶜalā nabī al-raḥma*, MS Escorial 1772, 33b-34a. Sakhāwī: *Qawl*, pp. 219-20. Quoted from Ibn al-Mulaqqin (d. 804/1401) in Muḥammad al-Sayyid al-Tijānī (not in *GAL*): *Al-fawz wa'l-najāh fī'l-hijra ilā'llāh*, n.p. (Dār al-fikr), n.d., (2nd edition), p. 238.

72 Udfuwī: *Al-ṭāliᶜ al-saᶜīd al-jāmiᶜ asmāᵓ nujabāᵓ al-Ṣaᶜīd*, Cairo, 1966, p. 207. Ibn Ḥajar al-ᶜAsqalānī: *Al-durar al-kāmina fī aᶜyān al-miᵓa al-thāmina*, Hyderabad, 1348-50, II, p. 29.

73 Sakhāwī: *Qawl*, p. 220.

74 Muḥammad al-Mukhtār al-Sūsī: *Al-maᶜsūl*, XV, pp. 266-67.

75 Aḥmad b. al-Ḥājj al-ᶜAyyāshī Sukayrij/Skīraj (d. 1363/1944): *Kashf al-ḥijāb ᶜamman talāqā maᶜa'l-shaykh al-Tijānī min al-aṣḥāb*, n.p., 1961, p. 411, ll. 1-3: *ṣalātan*

2. AGAINST THE PLAGUE

If invoking blessings on Muḥammad is quite generally recommended against hardships (*shadāʾid*), the use of such invocations against distress at sea, as in the above-mentioned case in Fākihānī, is not simply a logical derivation from this. On the contrary, some form of special instruction was required, namely the dream in which the Prophet appeared. And the situation is exactly the same with regard to their usage against the plague. We have assigned this application its own separate section because we possess more detailed information on the subject: the monograph *Dafʿ al-naqma fī'l-ṣalāh ʿalā nabī al-raḥma* by Aḥmad b. Yaḥyā b. Abī Ḥajala (d. 776/1375)[76] and in an auxiliary capacity the descriptions of Maqrīzī (d. 845/1442).

Ibn Abī Ḥajala concentrates his attention on the plague of 764/1363. He makes it perfectly clear that people at the time did not automatically turn to the *taṣliya* to protect themselves against it, and he recounts in the *maqāmāt* style how the practice came about: the epidemic began in Jumādā II 764/March-April 1363 in Cairo and its environs. One month later Ibn Abī Ḥajala learned from a certain Shams al-Dīn Muḥammad b. Khaṭīb Yabrūd that a man of piety had told the latter that invoking many blessings on Muḥammad would ward off the plague. Ibn Abī Ḥajala took the hint and repeated constantly the formula: 'Oh God, bless Muḥammad and the family of Muḥammad so that You thereby protect us from terrors and dangers and thereby cleanse us of all wicked actions!' That is to say, almost the same formula as the somewhat older one against distress at sea, but shorter. Ibn Abī Ḥajala spread it about Cairo and met with especially enthusiastic approval from one of his friends as far as its usefulness against the plague was concerned, but he was asked by a *faqīh* to give a theologically valid proof for it. Ibn Abī Ḥajala admits that an explicit *ḥadīth* could not be furnished for it but he enumerates five Traditions on the basis of which the use of the *taṣliya* against the plague could be justified.[77] Sakhāwī, who had the treatise of Ibn Abī Ḥajala before him, examines these Traditions and only accepts the

---

muḥassanatan/muḥsanatan... salāman muḥassanan/muḥsanan... sayyid al-muḥassanīn/muḥsanīn wa-imām al-muḥajjalīn.

76 *GAL S*, II, p. 6, no. 10. MS Escorial 1772.

77 *Dafʿ*, 4a-5a.

validity of one of them.[78] It is more or less the same *ḥadīth* which we just became familiar with above, only that here the name of the man who is conversing with Muḥammad is mentioned: Ubayy b. Kaᶜb. When Ubayy declared himself ready to 'dedicate' to the Prophet not only a part but all his numerous invocations of blessings, the Prophet assured him: 'Then you are relieved of all your cares and your sins will be forgiven.'[79] Ibn Abī Ḥajala himself had already considered

78 *Qawl*, pp. 220-21.

79 Tirmidhī, *qiyāma* 23, IV, pp. 636-37. Jahḍamī, pp. 31-32, variant. ᶜIyāḍ: *Shifā*, II, pp. 651-52. Ibn Taymiyya: *Qāᶜida jalīla*, p. 152. Ibn al-Qayyim: *Jalāʾ*, p. 228. Bārizī, MS Sprenger 127a, 97a. Ibn al-Nuᶜmān in Bārizī, MS Sprenger 127b, 48a. Sakhāwī: *Qawl*, pp. 118-19. Shaᶜrānī: *Lawāqiḥ al-anwār al-qudsiyya*, Cairo, 1961, p. 288 and others, for example, ᶜAbd al-Ṣamad al-Tihāmī Gannūn: *Al-nasaq al-ghālī wa'l-nafas al-ᶜālī sharḥ naṣīḥat Abī'l-ᶜAbbās al-Hilālī*, Cairo, 1973, p. 24, where mention is made of bestowing 'the page of the *taṣliya*' on the Prophet and transferring the *taṣliya* to the Prophet's page. Aḥmad b. ᶜAlī al-Hashtūkī (d. 1046/1636) is talking to ᶜAbd al-Raḥmān b. Muḥammad al-Fāsī (d. 1036/1626). Here we are confronted with the question we touched upon earlier as to what one should understand by this 'dedication' of invocations of blessings. The two *ḥadīths*, the anonymous one and the one involving Ubayy b. Kaᶜb, have been transmitted in various versions but in all respects they are too similar to be severed from one another. Sometimes the wording strongly suggests bestowing the merit for the invocations of blessings, as for example: 'Should I dedicate (*jaᶜala*) to you one third of my invocations of blessings on your behalf? I pronounce many blessings on you. How much of my *ṣalāh* should I dedicate?' Or: 'Should I dedicate to you a third of my *ṣalāh* on your behalf?' In the case of all these sentences mention has previously been made of invoking blessings on Muḥammad, and something is then meant to be done on the basis of this or because of this. But properly speaking one cannot make a *ṣalāh ᶜalayka* from a *ṣalāh ᶜalayka* because the end result of a transformation should be something different from one's starting point. The other extreme, the actual change and not the 'bestowing', is suggested by other forms of wording, such as for instance: 'Should I make (*jaᶜala*) half of my *ṣalāh* into prayers of supplication for you?' Or: 'I have agreed to make one third of my *ṣalāh* into prayers of supplication for you.' Here we are clearly dealing with a transformation. Commentators, by way of explaining the *ṣalāh* presented here as a starting point, have come up with the solution that prayers of supplication (*duᶜāʾ*) are meant (Ibn Taymiyya: *Qāᶜida*, p. 44, ll. 4-5; p. 152, ll. 14-15. Albānī in Jahḍamī, p. 32, ftn. 1). The latter should be transformed into invocations of blessings on Muḥammad. One could also imagine vigils or supererogatory ritual prayers in general, in place of which invocations of blessings should be substituted. But the snag in this is the *ᶜalayka*. Invocations of blessings 'on you' could not rightly be ritual prayers, and if they were prayers of supplication for the Prophet, once again one ends up with the fatal equation 'end result = the starting point'. I would therefore like to consider whether other prophets and saints or other individuals could not have been included in the invocations of blessings on Muḥammad which form the point of

this proof to be the strongest, in fact to be scriptural proof, because 'cares' could certainly include fear of the plague.[80] He is also aware that the *ḥadīth* makes the intended effect dependent on two conditions, namely that, first of all, a person invoke many blessings on Muḥammad and, secondly, that he dedicate all these invocations of blessings, perhaps even the merit for this pious action, wholly to Muḥammad. However, Ibn Abī Ḥajala also reports that at the time in Cairo a man of piety beheld the Prophet in a dream and learned from him a supplication which contained three invocations of blessings on his behalf, one at the beginning, one in the middle and one at the end, i.e. as is prescribed in the strictest *ḥadīths*.[81] The man who had experienced the dream woke up and found it written on the palm of his hand, and the plague was mentioned in it.[82]

Ibn Abī Ḥajala several times mentions the exceptional case of Medina which according to a prediction of Muḥammad would never become subject to the plague.[83] The city is also meant to have maintained this situation in the world-wide plague of 749/1348. The epidemic did make its way into Mecca but not into Medina.[84] Ibn Abī

---

departure. In that case the person posing the question perhaps wanted to know whether he should dedicate the blessing involved in this to a greater extent or exclusively to Muḥammad, since in earlier times one was more charitable than later with invocations of blessings on others than Muḥammad. To reiterate: my question concerns the *ḥadīths* with *ṣalāh ᶜalayka* at the beginning. The *ḥadīths* are found in Sakhāwī: *Qawl*, pp. 118-20, and some on p. 139. Cf. also Kulīnī, II, p. 491, ftn. 3.

80 *Dafᶜ*, 4b, ll. 14-15.

81 Sakhāwī, pp. 221, shortened it and in fact left out the invocations of blessings at the beginning and at the end.

82 *Dafᶜ*, 56a-b.

83 *Dafᶜ*, 5a. That plague and the Antichrist will not enter Medina belongs to the old *ḥadīth*-repertory; *Concordance et indices de la tradition musulmane*, Leiden, 1936-69, IV, p. 3b, *ṭāᶜūn*. The saying is quoted by Jāḥiẓ: *Kitāb al-buldān*, ed. Ṣāliḥ Aḥmad al-ᶜAlī, in *Majallat kulliyyat al-ādāb*, Baghdad, 1970, p. 486. Muḥammad b. ᶜAbdallāh al-Zarkashī: *Iᶜlām al-sājid bi-aḥkām al-masājid*, Cairo, 1384, pp. 253-55. Muḥammad b. Muḥammad al-Ruᶜaynī al-Maghribī al-Makkī al-Khaṭṭāb (d. 954/1547) wrote two books on the subject: *Al-bishāra al-hanīʾa bi-anna'l-ṭāᶜūn lā yadkhul Makka wa'l-Madīna* and *Al-qawl al-matīn anna'l-ṭāᶜūn lā yadkhul al-balad al-amīn*, as well as a work *ᶜUmdat al-rāwīn fī aḥkām al-ṭawāᶜīn*; Aḥmad Bābā: *Nayl al-ibtihāj*, in the margin of Ibn Farḥūn: *Al-dībāj al-mudhahhab*, Cairo, 1330, p. 338.

84 *Dafᶜ*, 59b. In the year 1830-31, however, the plague raged in both cities, although only for three days in Medina. In order to justify the *ḥadīth* there were those who wished to see

Ḥajala in the last chapter (59b-76b) gives a complete list of the plague epidemics which afflicted the Islamic region until 764/1363, in chronological order with all the annual dates. For a few cases from earliest times he refers to the lists in Ibn al-Jawzī's *Mudhish* (Beirut, 1973, pp. 64-65) and Nawawī's *Adhkār* (Beirut, 1973, p. 139, *bāb al-taᶜziya*) as well as in the latter's commentary on Muslim (at the beginning).[85] But Ibn Abī Ḥajala extends the register to about 30 cases, not all of which appear to have actually been plague.[86] Two of the epidemics were universal: the plague of 449/1057[87] and that of 749/1348. The plague of 749/1348 is known to have ravaged extensive parts of Europe, and in Ibn Abī Ḥajala's opinion it caused the population of mankind to be reduced by half.[88] At that time he was in Damascus and he describes the religious measures that people undertook there in Rabīᶜ I/June in order to avert misfortune. He does not forget to note that during the standing supplication (*qunūt*) of the ritual prayer the preacher pronounced blessings on the Prophet as usual.[89] On the 13th of Rabīᶜ I a three-day fast was arranged. On the following Friday everyone, including the non-Muslims, went out into the desert and there they beseeched God with tears to end the

---

in the plague of the *ḥadīth* a particular kind of disease; H.T. Norris: *The Pilgrimage of Ahmad, Son of the Little Bird of Paradise*, Warminster, 1977, pp. 42, 46.

85 The old cases of plague come from a lost work of the historian Abū'l-Ḥasan ᶜAlī b. Muḥammad al-Madāʾinī (d. 235/850 or earlier) and from Ibn Qutayba's *Maᶜārif*, Cairo, 1960, pp. 601-02.

86 The list is continued from 761/1360 to 923/1517 in Michael W. Dols: *The Black Death in the Middle East*, Princeton, 1977, pp. 305-14. I must thank Ewald Wagner for drawing my attention to this book.

87 The author describes first of all a plague in 448/1056 as world-wide (66b, ll. 11-12). It is not once mentioned by historians, however, and later (74b, ll. 8-10) he himself refers to the odd coincidence that both great epidemics occurred in years ending in 49. The plague of 449/1057 devastated Central Asia and the north of Iran, especially Ādharbāyjān, but then penetrated southwards into Iraq. It was not as widely spread and did not cause as much damage as the plague of 749/1348. Maqrīzī: *Ittiᶜāẓ al-ḥunafāʾ bi-akhbār al-aʾimma al-fāṭimiyyīn al-khulafāʾ*, Cairo, 1967-73, II, p. 235, reports quite extensively on the year 449/1057.

88 *Dafᶜ*, 75a, ll. 4-5. Other more unfavorable estimates put the losses at 7/10ths of mankind; Marcus Joseph Müller: 'Ibnulkhatîbs Bericht über die Pest', in *Sitzungsberichte der bayer. Akademie der Wissenschaften* 2, 1863, p. 9/p. 22.

89 On *qunūt* see *EI*[2] ḳunūt. Nawawī: *Adhkār*, p. 58. A solitary early voice rejected the *qunūt* as impermissible innovation (*bidᶜa*) which was not seen to be practiced by the Prophet or by his first four successors; Nasāʾī, *taṭbīq* 32, II, pp. 203-04.

plague. Nevertheless, it still continued until the beginning of 750/ March-April 1349.

Ibn Abī Ḥajala's report on the plague of 749/1348 is supplemented by Maqrīzī.[90] He gives an even better idea of the extent of the devastation caused by the epidemic and also indicates the far-reaching economic consequences and the social changes, as well as the depopulation and shifts in ownership of property, which the catastrophe brought about.[91] His information also extends to North Africa. Ibn Khaldūn (d. 808/1406) lost his parents in Tunis at that time.[92] The black death also gripped the furthest west, and the modern historian of Southern Morocco, Muḥammad al-Mukhtār al-Sūsī (d. 1383/ 1963), who has read Ibn Khaldūn[93] and documents of his home area which are inaccessible to us, ventures the conjecture that an important political phenomenon in the Anti-Atlas, namely the dichotomy of the local Berber population into two leagues or alliances (leff; Arabic *laff/liff, niḥla*) could be connected with it. He considers it not impossible — but emphasizes that he cannot prove it — that under the pressure of Arab tribes advancing westwards Berbers of the Sahara were at that time pushed into the mountains of the Anti-Atlas where from 749/1348 the black death had heavily reduced the population. The new arrivals from the Sahara on the one hand and the long-established Berbers on the other at the time naturally formed a front against one another and consequently what had been an ethnic difference was transformed into a purely political one and has maintained itself up until recent times in the opposition between the two alliances Tāgūzūlt (Iguzūlen, etc.) and Tāḥggāt (Aogg^{u}a, etc.).[94] As early as 1365/1946 Sūsī had communicated this proposal

90 Maqrīzī: *Al-sulūk li-ma^c^rifat duwal al-mulūk*, Cairo, 1956-73, II, 3, pp. 759, 770-91.

91 Especially p. 785.

92 Robert Brunschvig: *La Berbérie orientale sous les Ḥafṣides*, Paris, 1940-47, II, p. 385. Additional information on the plague ibid., II, pp. 374-75.

93 Cf. Ibn Khaldūn: *The Muqaddimah*, trans. by Franz Rosenthal, New York, 1958 (Bollingen Series XLIII), I, p. 64.

94 *Ilighiyyāt*, Casablanca, 1377, III, pp. 166-69. Sūsī often has occasion to speak about the alliances in his work *Al-ma^c^sūl*, Casablanca, from circa 1960 onwards, III, pp. 104, 263, 288-89, 338, 339, 349-50, 356-57; IV, p. 38; VI, p. 271; XIV, pp. 111-12, 267; XVI, pp. 25-26, 171; XVIII, pp. 156-57; XIX, pp. 147-49, 250, 253, 265, 277; XX, pp. 189, 246, 247, 255-56, 268-69. More in *Khilāl Jazūla*, Tetuan, 1943-44, III, pp. 25, 72, 73, 93, 94, 96-97, 139, 154-55, 157-58, 168. *Īlīgh qadīman wa-ḥadīthan* (written 1358/1939, published posthumously, Rabat, 1966), pp. 238-40, 266-68, 279-84. From the French literature on the subject I will only cite the following: G. Salmon: 'Les institutions berbères', in *Arch. Maroc.* 1, 1904, pp. 143-45.

in a letter to a European who had asked him about it. It could have been Justinard or Robert Montagne. Montagne had himself proposed a similar thesis back in 1930 regarding the origin of the dichotomy but did not say anything about the plague in this connection. He considered the Aogg^{u}a to be the old established population and the Iguzūlen to be the immigrants.[95] A vague tradition of the Ilalen in the Anti-Atlas, who belong to the Iguzūlen, says that they immigrated to the area from the south-west under pressure from the Saharan tribes,[96] but this can be interpreted different ways, depending on whether one understands their first acquisition of land to be in earliest times or in the period of pressure referred to here. Conversely, Sūsī believes the Iguzūlen were the native population and the Aogg^{u}a were the intruders. The fact that the present-day *leff* of Iguzūlen is primarily a *leff* of mountain dwellers appears to support this view.[97] However, the twofold division of Berber society is not limited to the south of Morocco but is found throughout the whole tribal population of Morocco and Algeria, only in the north the

---

Segonzac: *Au cœur de l'Atlas*, Paris, 1910, pp. 260, 409, 453. Robert Montagne: 'L'Aghbar et les hautes-vallées du Grand-Atlas', in *Hespéris* 7 (1927), pp. 10-29. *Un magasin collectif de l'Anti-Atlas. L'agadir des Ikounka*, Paris, 1930, p. 14. 'Le développement du pouvoir des caids de Tagontaft (Grand-Atlas)', in *Mémorial Henri Basset*, Paris, 1928, II, pp. 169-84. 'La limite du Maroc et du Sahara atlantique', in *Hespéris* 11, 1930, pp. 115-16. *Les Berbères et le Makhzen dans le Sud du Maroc*, Paris, 1930, pp. 162, 182, 185-90, 199-216. 'Un épisode de la "siba" berbère au XVIIIe siècle d'après la "Rihla" de Sidi Mohammed ez-Zerhouni de Tasaft' (trans. by Justinard), in *Hespéris* 28, 1941, pp. 91-93. *La civilisation du désert*, Paris, 1947, p. 261. Justinard: 'Sidi Ahmed ou Moussa', in *Arch. Maroc.* 29, 1933, pp. 59, 64-70, 72. *Fawaid al jamma bi isnadi ʾoulouml al oumma, Abouzid Sidi Abderrahman ben Mohammed le Jazouli, le Tamanarti, le Mghafri*, trans. by Justinard, Chartres, 1953, p. 116. Émile Laoust: 'Contribution à une étude de la toponymie du Haut Atlas', in *REI* 14, 1940, p. 35, no. 515 (Iguzūlen); p. 53, no. 592 (Tauggat). Laoust writes *tagizūlt/taguzūlt* and *aogg^{u}a*. Justinard requires *ahoggoua* because the texts always write an *ḥ* (*Arch. Maroc.* 29, 1933, p. 59, ftn. 1). E. Lévi-Provençal: *Histoire de l'Espagne musulmane*, Paris, 1967, III, pp. 171-72, ftn. 1, found as the earliest passage with the technical term *laff* Ibn Bassām: *Al-dhakhīra fī maḥāsin ahl al-jazīra*, Cairo, 1942, I, 2, p. 169, l. 2, and in the same connection Ibn Idhārī: *Al-bayān al-mughrib fī akhbār mulūk al-Andalus wa'l-maghrib*, ed. Lévi-Provençal, Paris, 1930, III (= II), p. 171, l. 7, in a quotation from Ibn Ḥayyān (d. 469/1076), i.e. from the 5th/11th century.

95 *Les Berbères et le Makhzen*, p. 215.

96 Segonzac: *Au cœur de l'Atlas*, p. 556.

97 Laoust: *Contributions*, p. 35, no. 515.

league is not called *leff* but *çoff* (Arabic *ṣaff*).[98] Moreover, the dividing line often runs through the middle of tribes so that small unified groups also fall into dualities. And the two counter-parties are far from being called everywhere Iguzūlen and Aoggᵘa, but bear names which vary from place to place. Then again the division of a community into two camps is by no means confined to the Berbers. In the Gharb, 'in the middle of Berber Morocco', Arabic tribes are divided into two *çoffs* which call themselves Sufyān and Banū Mālik. Similarly, Montagne makes mention of the two parties in Lebanon the Junblāṭiyya and the Yazbakiyya, the Kalb and Qays[99] and the beginnings of related groupings among the present-day bedouins of Najd.[100] In earliest Arabic times one meets with the ᶜAdnān and the Qaḥṭān. The Kurds are formed into two confederations which were formerly called 'the right' and 'the left',[101] and the Pathans are not unified but are organized into two groups.[102] The very dichotomy indicates their shared identity; the fact of being a couple provides the basis for the whole. But all these dualisms have their historical starting points. The French theory simply locates such a starting point in the arrival of newcomers from the desert, while Sūsī adds the complementary factor of a vacuum created by the black death of 749/1348. Both views are unproven. But Jean Brignon who is receptive to the workings of cause and effect in history admits that, as a result of the black death, the middle of the 8th/14th century brought with it a change in the population structure of Morocco and mentions at any rate a flight from the countryside and a continuation of the stream of nomads from the south-west to the

---

98 E. Daumas: *Mœurs et coutumes de l'Algérie*, Paris, 1858, pp. 222-24. Péraud: 'Tebessa', in *Revue africaine* 18, 1874, p. 451. Michaux-Bellaire in *Arch. Maroc.* 17, 1911, p. 6. *Villes et Tribus du Maroc. Casablanca et les Châouia*, Paris, 1915, II, pp. 133-34. *Villes et Tribus du Maroc. Rabat et sa région III, Les Tribus*, Paris, 1920, pp. 124, 152-53. Montagne: *Les Berbères et le Makhzen*, p. 196. Idem: *La civilisation du désert*, p. 261. René Maunier: *Mélanges de sociologie nord-africaine*, Paris, 1930, p. 65, ftn. 1; pp. 79, 155, 172. And many others.

99 Montagne: *La civilisation du désert*, pp. 241-42. On Junblāṭiyya and Yazbakiyya cf. Henri Lammens: *La Syrie. Précis historique*, Beirut, 1921, II, p. 101.

100 Montagne: 'Notes sur la vie sociale et politique de l'Arabie du Nord' in *REI* 6, 1932, pp. 66-67.

101 M.M. van Bruinessen: *Agha, Shaikh and State*, dissertation Utrecht, 1978, pp. 73-76.

102 Barth: 'Segmentary opposition and the theory of game: a study of Pathan organisation', in *Journal of the Royal Anthropological Institute* 89, 1959, pp. 5-21 (cited in Bruinessen, p. 75, ftn. 47).

north-west:[103] the Andalusian scholar Ibn al-Khaṭīb (d. 776/1374) maintains that the tent-dwelling and nomadic Arabs in Ifrīqiya and elsewhere remained healthy due to the fresh air in which they lived.[104]

Ibn al-Khaṭīb is also the one who at the time gave a dig in the ribs to Islamic theology. He presented an exact description of the plague and dared to come out against religious prejudice, i.e. against a saying of the Prophet that there was no such thing as contagion.[105] He blamed the death of innumerable people on certain scholars of scripture who in their blind zeal for *ḥadīth* totally refused to recognize the dangers of contagion, and reminded them that reason demanded they reinterpret religious traditions based on hearsay which contradicted sense perceptions and appearances.[106] Although he can also not cure

103 Jean Brignon, Abdelaziz Amine et alii: *Histoire du Maroc*, Casablanca, 1967, pp. 153-54. Cf. the lines of confrontation between Berbers of the mountains and Berbers of the plain in the 18th and 19th centuries, ibid., pp. 262-67.

104 M.J. Müller: 'Ibnulkhatîbs Bericht', p. 7 below/p. 19 below.

105 Müller, ibid. *Concordance et indices de la tradition musulmane*, IV, p. 159a, *lā ʿadwā*.

106 Müller, ibid., p. 7-8/p. 20. Partial translations by Max Meyerhof in *The Legacy of Islam*, ed. Thomas Arnold and Alfred Guillaume, Oxford, 1931, p. 340. Cited by G.E. von Grunebaum: *Der Islam im Mittelalter*, Zurich, Artemis 1963, p. 425. Manfred Ullmann: *Die Medizin im Islam*, Leiden, 1970, (*Handbuch der Orientalistik*, Abt. 1, Ergbd. 6, Abschn. 1), p. 246. Ibid., pp. 242-50, gives more information about plague and contagion; cf. also Michael W. Dols: *The Black Death in the Middle East*, pp. 92-94. Ghazzālī acknowledged infection with the plague by breathing in pestilential air but did not designate this as contagion; *Iḥyāʾ*, IV, p. 283/Richard Gramlich: *Muḥammad al-Ġazzālīs Lehre von den Stufen zur Gottesliebe*, Wiesbaden, 1984, (Freiburger Islamstudien X), p. 622. Could Christian thoughts about *contagium pestis* have had an influence on Ibn al-Khaṭīb? A certain Muḥammad b. Muḥammad b. ʿAlī al-Lamtūnī from Takrūr (Senegal) wrote to Suyūṭī (d. 911/1505) in the context of a more lengthy question that the people around him firmly believed in the contagion of some illnesses. Suyūṭī wrote back: 'That is a false belief. The Prophet has said: "There is no such thing as contagion"'; Suyūṭī: *Al-ḥāwī li'l-fatāwī*, Cairo, 1352/reprint Beirut, 1975, I, pp. 288, 292. The first step to a sensible interpretation of the denial of contagion might consist in unearthing the educational purpose behind the view and explaining this in terms of the circumstances of the early period. The commentators of these *ḥadīths* have made attempts in this direction. The famous Moroccan scholar al-Ḥasan al-Yūsī (d. 1102/1691) rescued contagion by conceiving of all chains of causation as an arrangement of God's wisdom and by attributing to a wise decision (*ḥikma*) of God the miraculous deliverances and exceptions to the rule which were otherwise associated with God's omnipotence (*qudra*); Yūsī: *Al-muḥāḍarāt*, ed. Muḥammad Ḥajjī, Rabat, 1976, pp. 60, 97-100.

the plague and is obliged to limit himself to general instructions to do with prevention, he none the less rejects entering into non-medical questions. He does not recommend a religious form of prevention or treatment of the plague, indeed he says nothing at all about such methods.

Thus this is all of no significance for us. What is more pertinent is that Maqrīzī through his description of the plague of 749/1348 gives us background information which allows us to understand better and to evaluate more correctly the attempts in 764/1363 to ward off the plague by means of *taṣliya*. In fact he reports that already in 749/1348 during the great plague a man from the mountains of Asia Minor (*jibāl al-rūm*) heard the Prophet say in a dream: 'Recite 3360 times surah 71 and ask God to do away with the situation in which you are suffering!'[107] The people in Damascus had followed this advice and in addition sacrificed many cattle and sheep for the poor. The epidemic from that moment forward began to decrease. Subsequently, they had recited Bukhārī for three days and nights, and then together with the young boys at the *muṣallā* they had prayed out loud with bared head just as when performing a prayer for rain. After three days the plague abated and finally disappeared completely. But in Aleppo as well a man of piety had seen the Prophet in a dream and had been given the mission of telling people that they should do penance and recite the following prayer: 'Oh God, subdue the dreadful blows of the lion of wars by means of the favors which come from the outflow of Your heavenly kingdom so that we may cling to the hem of Your grace and protect ourselves through You Yourself against the descent of Your severity, You lord of power, of all-embracing greatness and perfect omnipotence, lord of sublimity and mercy!' The governor of Aleppo had also made the prayer known in Ḥamāh, in Syrian Tripoli and in Damascus. In Cairo they had recited Bukhārī in al-Azhar and beseeched God for help in the standing supplication (*qunūt*) of the ritual prayers.[108]

The parallel in behavior between 749/1348 and 764/1363 is obvious. The theological repertoire (Bukhārī-recitations, fasts, public prayer, alms) is not fully adequate for warding off the plague. Special orders are required from men of piety. In the year 749/1348 both pious men had received their instructions in a dream from the mouth of Muḥammad, while in 764/1363 only one of them did, the second

---

107 *Sulūk*, II, 3, p. 779 below. Similarly, Ibn Abī Ḥajala: *Dafʿ*, 75a-b, but 3363 times instead of 3360 times.

108 *Sulūk*, II, 3, pp. 780-81.

of the two. At any rate, with regard to the first one this is not specified. In the year 749/1348 neither of the two ordered the *taṣliya*, whereas in the year 764/1363 both do order the *taṣliya*, one more or less exclusively and the other three times embedded within the supplication. What emerges from this is that invoking blessings on the Prophet was not a standard measure against the plague, any more than against a disaster at sea, but was only used if a man of piety advised it, at best with the authority of an inspiration of the Prophet. Ibn Abī Ḥajala's attempt to harmonize its use against the plague with *ḥadīths* did not completely fail, to judge by Sakhāwī's criticism, but the one *ḥadīth* which is referred to for support is formulated in very general terms and does not explicitly mention the plague. In 764/1363 invoking blessings on Muḥammad was not officially ordained. It was merely propagated on a personal basis by Ibn Abī Ḥajala and his friends, and to state this at a later time had been one of the purposes of his treatise.

The fundamental theological position on the issue is to be found in the handbook *Al-ṭibb al-nabawī* by Ibn Taymiyya's student Ibn Qayyim al-Jawziyya who died in 751/1350, i.e. 13 years before the plague of 764/1363. It does contain a section on the plague, in which religious measures against it, including supplications and recitation from the Koran, are mentioned.[109] But he does not refer to the *taṣliya* which, moreover, he does not praise anywhere else either as a cure or an effective prayer against any form of evil. In this work he regards the *fātiḥa*[110] and ritual prayer[111] to be helpful against all possible suffering. Similarly, in a special treatise on invoking blessings, *Jalāʾ al-afhām*, he is silent about the plague. It is only Sakhāwī, one hundred years later, who is familiar with the *taṣliya* as a measure against the plague but exclusively from our Ibn Abī Ḥajala. The important Wahhābī Indian Muḥammad Ṣiddīq (b.) Ḥasan Khān, king of Bhōpāl (d.1307/1890), who discusses the *taṣliya* in detail within the framework of his treatise on supplications does so, however, as if he never heard of it being used against the plague.[112] Therefore, Ibn Abī Ḥajala in this respect as well turns out to be the literary father of the *taṣliya* against the plague, and this *taṣliya* appears to be like a child that never properly found its way into the world.

---

109 *Al-ṭibb al-nabawī*, Cairo, 1957, pp. 28-35.

110 Ibid., pp. 268-70.

111 Ibid., p. 163.

112 Muḥammad Ṣiddīq Ḥasan Khān Malik Bhōpāl: *Nuzul al-abrār bi'l-ʿilm al-maʾthūr min al-adʿiya wa'l-adhkār*, Constantinople, 1301, pp. 159-201.

What is the situation like among people who didn't write about invoking blessings but wrote about the plague or individual cases of the plague? Are they also unfamiliar with making use of the *taṣliya* against the plague? In the 11th/17th century a certain Muḥammad Fatḥallāh b. Maḥmūd al-Ḥalabī al-Baylūnī al-Shāfiʿī (d. 1042/1632-33) composed a small work on means of defense against the plague entitled *Khulāṣat mā taḥṣulu* (or *taḥaṣṣala* or *yuʿawwilu*) *ʿalayhi'l-sāʿūn fī adwiyat dafʿ al-wabāʾ wa'l-ṭāʿūn, Outline of What Those Who Seek Remedies against Epidemic and Plague Can Obtain* (or *Rely on*) *for Themselves.*[113] Here one finds enumerated preventive measures and remedies of a dietary, pharmacological and especially of a spiritual nature, such as prayers, conjurations and amulets. The *taṣliya* also frequently occurs, sometimes only at the beginning and the end of prayer texts, but sometimes also as a part of the actual prescriptions. In a prayer which is meant to be worn as an amulet, it says: 'Oh God, bless and greet our lord Muḥammad, his family and his Companions, confer mercies on us for a long time to come, etc.' (164a of the Berlin MS), and in another one which is meant to be hung up in the house: 'In the name of God, the Compassionate, the Merciful, God bless and greet our lord Muḥammad, his family and his Companions, praise be unto You, etc.' (168a); and it also closes with the *taṣliya* (168b). A third one 'against the plague and all evil' begins with: 'Oh God, confer blessings, greetings and benedictions on Muḥammad and the family of Muḥammad to the amount that Your knowledge contains and which Your Pen has written down' (174a). Lengthier measures are recommended for a cure: as is often the case a ram is first sacrificed with accompanying specific prayer-formulas on behalf of the afflicted person[114] and the meat is distributed, again with accompanying prayer-formulas, among the poor in exact portions. A *fātiḥa* is written in a vessel, dissolved in water and then the water is drunk. A person places his hand, or someone places it for him, on the painful spot and pronounces seven times:

---

113 *GAL*, II, p. 274; *GAL S*, II, p. 385. Shihāb al-Dīn Maḥmūd al-Khafājī: *Rayḥānat al-alibbā wa-zahrat al-ḥayāh al-dunyā*, Cairo, 1306, p. 101. Muḥibbī: *Khulāṣat al-athar*, III, pp. 254-57. Muḥibbī, p. 255, ll. 4-5, has *yuʿawwil* in the title. I made use of the MS Lbg. 1044 (Ahlwardt no. 6374) of the Staatsbibliothek Preussischer Kulturbesitz Orientalabteilung. I wish here to thank the Staatsbibliothek for its photographic service which is always quick and reliable.

114 In this connection cf. the penetrating remarks of broad scope which Edmond Doutté: *Magie et religion dans l'Afrique du Nord*, Algiers, 1908, pp. 419-540, based on the views of Hubert and Mauss.

'Oh God, bless our lord Muḥammad to the amount of all sicknesses and all remedies' or after the *fātiḥa* beseeches God by the Prophet seven times to drive away the sickness, and repeats each time the blessing and greeting on Muḥammad (179b-180a). For protection against falling ill Baylūnī recommends quite generally repeating as often as possible: 'Oh God, bless our lord Muḥammad so that thereby You untie the knots, drive away cares, open the breast and make things easy!' This is the same distorted phraseology which, for the sake of theology, confers on God the honor of remaining the subject of all action as we saw at the end of our first section and then again at the beginning of this second section. On the basis of his own experience of illness Baylūnī adds: 'As a young man I myself had "this illness". When I recited this *taṣliya*, the heat I felt disappeared. Then one time I beheld the Prophet in a dream and said this *taṣliya* in his presence. He exclaimed: "Say in the here and now and in the hereafter!" — he obviously meant say "this" — "Then (he went on to say) things will become easy." I woke up and the pains had gone. Whoever wishes to add the "this" may do so. But the original wording did not contain "this"' (171a). So says Baylūnī. Here the person suffering from the illness has been using the *taṣliya* before the dream. In the dream the Prophet simply confirms its use. As far as the kind of *taṣliya* is concerned, it stems from the tradition we are familiar with but perhaps in a combination that is due to Baylūnī although at the beginning of the chapter he generally has recourse to 'scholars' of the past. However, he mentions no names anywhere, thus not Ibn Abī Ḥajala either. In fact he may not know of him at all. The inclusion of the *taṣliya* in prayers, conjurations and amulets was an old tradition and here appears to be used by chance against the plague as well.

In 1072/1662, thirty years after Baylūnī's death, Abū Sālim al-ᶜAyyāshī (d. 1090/1679) was travelling through North Africa with the pilgrimage caravan to Alexandria. When fear of the plague which was prevalent there caused a number of pilgrims to be faced with the decision as to whether they should continue their journey or turn off to Awjila to wait, ᶜAyyāshī composed in verse a prayer to God in which he did not string together a series of *taṣliyāt* but conjured God by Muḥammad and a few high-ranking saints to save his travel companions from the worst, to protect them against the plague and to reunite them happily with their loved ones — a *qaṣīda* of 40 verses which one could rightly call a *wasīla*.[115] ᶜAyyāshī writes that he had wished to obtain God's attention 'through the mediation of the person who is most beloved to Him as mediator' (*mutawassilan ilā'llāhi bi-aḥabbi mā yutawassalu bihī ilayhi*). He begins and concludes with an invocation of blessings but this belongs to the style of supplications and the poem, not to the substance, and does not serve as a means for driving away the plague as in the case of Ibn Abī Ḥajala.[116] A few years later in 1088/1677 when the plague was raging in Tetuan, there a certain ᶜAlī Baraka and Aḥmad b. ᶜAbd al-Ḥayy al-Ḥalabī each composed a *qaṣīda*, the first consisting of 39 and the second of 59 verses.[117] The first one — the exact wording of which is known to us — contains in the appropriate place the wish that God should bless the Prophet, and also closes with a *taṣliya*, but otherwise, as in the poem by ᶜAyyāshī, conjures God by Muḥammad, his Companions, their followers, by the arch-saints, by the saints of Fez and Miknāsa, and by Abū Yaᶜazzā (d. 572/1177), to drive away the plague. The poet (Baraka) throughout achieves the feat of avoiding the use of the word *wabāʾ* for 'epidemic, plague' in the rhyme, although the poem is based on each line ending in *-āʾi*; the word does appear once in the middle of a verse.[118] One looks in vain for any allusion to a *taṣliya* being of help against the plague.

---

115 Poems with this name are found in ᶜAbd al-Qādir b. ᶜAbdallāh al-ᶜAydarūsī: *Tārīkh al-nūr al-sāfir ᶜan akhbār al-qarn al-ᶜāshir*, Baghdad, 1934, pp. 28, 33, 34, 88, 376, 419; Ibn ᶜAbd al-Malik al-Marrākushī: *Al-dhayl wa'l-takmila li-kitābay al-Mawṣūl wa'l-Ṣila*, al-sifr al-sādis, ed. Iḥsān ᶜAbbās, Beirut, 1973, p. 482, l. 1; Muḥammad al-Mukhtār al-Sūsī: *Al-maᶜsūl*, XVIII, p. 379, l. 21. Originally they were probably only poetic prayers with oaths invoking holy persons who were meant to serve as mediators (*tawassul*), but then other prayer-poems also developed. To this category belong the first two poems of Ewald Wagner's 'Arabischen Heiligenliedern aus Harar', in *ZDMG* 125, 1975, pp. 29-47, where 'bei' instead of 'zu' should be the translation throughout. And of course *bi-ḥaqq*, etc., p. 53, l. 2, and *bi-ḥurmat*, p. 59, verse 5, are also oaths. A long poem of this kind is found in Muḥammad b. ᶜAlī al-Sanūsī: *Al-salsabīl al-maᶜīn fī'l-ṭarāʾiq al-arbaᶜīn*, pp. 107-12, in *Al-majmūᶜa al-mukhtāra min muʾallafāt... Sayyidī Muḥammad b. ᶜAlī al-Sanūsī*, Beirut, 1968.

116 *Al-riḥla al-ᶜayyāshiyya Māʾ al-mawāʾid*, litho., Fez, 1316/1898/reprint Rabat, 1977, I, pp. 112-15. Under the name of Abū'l-Ḥasan al-Shādhilī (d. 656/1258) is found an apotropaic litany with the title *Ḥizb al-ikhfāʾ* which is supposed to be good against enemies and against falling ill with the plague. It as well only contains the *taṣliya* in the obligatory concluding sentence: Ibn ᶜAyyād: *Al-mafākhir al-ᶜaliyya fī'l-maʾāthir al-shādhiliyya*, Cairo, 1937, pp. 157-58.

117 Muḥammad Dāwud: *Tārīkh Tiṭwān*, Tetuan, 1957, I, pp. 257-58.

118 Ibid., I, pp. 365-66.

Aḥmad al-Tijānī (d. 1230/1815) takes the matter to its furthest extreme. Invoking blessings on Muḥammad was in fact 'the pillar of his order and the key to everything good in this world and the world to come.'[119] But when the plague broke out in Morocco, he did not in fact advise making use of the *taṣliya*, as one might have expected, but recommended none other than the prayer of the man of piety of Aleppo 'Oh God, subdue the dreadful blows of the lion of wars, etc.', which Maqrīzī mentioned for the year 749/1348 and which was known in Morocco under the designation 'prayer of the Imam al-Qalshānī'.[120] As a household blessing against the plague he recommended writing on the wall surah 10/98: 'Why did no other city besides that of Jonah's not also repent in time so as to avoid the menacing tribunal?' (as Rudi Paret correctly paraphrases it)[121] — a call to seek the blame in oneself and to repent, as is also attested elsewhere for Tijānī. To others he gave an apotropaic vaccination certificate like this in the form: '*Basmala. Taṣliya.* Oh God, this constitutes alms (*ṣadaqa*) for Your holy face as a ransom (*fidāʾ*) for the gentlemen Muḥammad b. al-ᶜArabī, Muḥammad b. al-Jalālī, al-Ḥājj Ibn al-Musqim,[122] Ibrāhīm b. al-Shaykh and their four or five bands of

---

119 Aḥmad b. al-Ḥājj al-ᶜAyyāshī Sukayrij/Skīraj (d. 1363/1944): *Kashf al-ḥijāb ᶜamman talāqā maᶜa'l-shaykh al-Tijānī min al-aṣḥāb*, n.p., 1961, p. 341, ll. 16-17. Tijānī attempted to replace the *vita purgativa* with the *taṣliya*. Muḥammad al-ᶜArabī (b.) al-Sāʾiḥ al-Sharqī al-ᶜUmarī al-Tijānī (d. 1309/1892): *Bughyat al-mustafīd li-sharḥ Munyat al-murīd*, Cairo, 1959, p. 79: 'The pole around which in our eyes progressing on the path in the *ṭarīqa muḥammadiyya* revolves is to bless and to greet the Apostle of God very much, during which one must be in the best and most perfect state while vizualizing the sense of the recited formula and listening precisely... and vizualizing in one's interior the figure of the Prophet, etc.'

120 Sukayrij, p. 414. Morocco was ravaged by a great plague in 1212/1797-98; Aḥmad b. Khālid al-Nāṣirī (al-Salāwī): *Al-istiqṣā li-akhbār duwal al-maghrib al-aqṣā*, Casablanca, 1954-56, VIII, p. 106. Octave Houdas: *Le Maroc de 1631 à 1812... de Aboulqâsem ben Ahmed Ezziâni*, Paris, 1886/reprint Amsterdam, 1969, Arabic p. 98/French p. 181. But the existence of Tijānī's *zāwiya* in Fez seems to be taken for granted and this was only first founded in 1215/1800; Sukayrij, p. 21. Abun-Nasr, p. 20. Qalshānī is a Tunisian family of scholars from the 9th/15th century. Several of its members are listed in Muḥammad b. Muḥammad al-Andalusī al-Wazīr al-Sarrāj: *Al-ḥulal al-sundusiyya fī'l-akhbār al-tūnisiyya*, Tunis, 1970, Part 4, 1346b (index s.n. Qalshānī). The prayer cannot stem from one of these Qalshānīs.

121 *Der Koran. Kommentar und Konkordanz*, Stuttgart, 1977, p. 229.

122 Perhaps *al-Masqam* should be read. *Masqam*, like *asqam*, is a Maghrebi word derived from *mustaqīm* and, like the latter, means 'straight'. *Asqam* occurs as an adjective with *ṣirāṭ* in the notorious litany-formula *Jawharat al-kamāl* of Aḥmad al-Tijānī and is explained and reproved in the polemical work against the Tijāniyya written by Muḥammad Taqī al-Dīn al-

riders against the blow of every plague and epidemic, against every death, against every illness and against the entry of the plague into the Sahara with them and by means of them. This is a ransom for all of them from everything that has been mentioned, from today until thirty years have elapsed.'[123]

These samples show that the invocation of blessings on Muḥammad did not become a customary practice for warding off the plague. The attempt by Ibn Abī Ḥajala to establish it as such did not achieve a very widespread lasting effect. The *taṣliya* remained in the background, available in emergencies. For its usage a new impetus was required on each occasion.[124]

3. WHEN MAKING A REQUEST

Early on, i.e. already by the 2nd/8th century, the close connection of the *taṣliya* with the prayer of supplication exerted an influence on

---

Hilālī: *Al-hadiyya al-hādiya ilā'l-ṭā'ifa al-tijāniyya*, n.p., 1973, pp. 110-11, but defended (against an earlier attack) by Muḥammad b. Muḥammad al-Ṣaghīr al-Shingīṭī al-Tishītī: *Al-jaysh al-kafīl bi-akhdh al-tha'r mimman salla ʿalā'l-shaykh al-Tijānī sayf al-inkār*, in the margin of Sharqī's *Bughyat al-mustafīd*, Cairo, n.d., pp. 112-16.

123 Sukayrij, pp. 459-60. In another escort-text Tijānī directs his request for protection of a caravan against the encroachment of certain men of power, not to God but to the Prophet (ibid., p. 457). If Tijānī did not himself have permission from the Prophet for an undertaking, he would in some cases make use of the tried and tested Muḥammad b. al-ʿArabī al-Damrāwī (d. 1214/1799-1800, ʿAlī Ḥarāzim: *Jawāhir al-maʿānī*, II, p. 154, l. 1; not 1204/1789-90, as one reads in Sharqī: *Bughyat al-mustafīd*, p. 255/Sukayrij, p. 99) as an intermediary (*wāsiṭa*) and then follow the advice the latter received from the Prophet. A request of this kind via Damrāwī asking the Prophet not to unleash his far more terrible wrath on people with whom he, Tijānī, was angry, and the Prophet's answer which Damrāwī wrote down, is recorded by Sukayrij, pp. 458-59. Early on Tijānī sometimes pronounced a magic 'fortification' or 'immunization' (*taḥṣīn*, pl. *taḥāṣīn*, Sukayrij, p. 442, l. 7; p. 460, l. 7) on behalf of whole groups, tribes and villages, until the Prophet forbade him to do so because Tijānī's enemies were also enjoying protection in this way (Sukayrij, p. 458).

124 The fundamental work on the plague in the Islamic east, Michael W. Dols: *The Black Death in the Middle East*, contains some of what we have said here and much more besides, but nothing regarding the *taṣliya*. The study of Jacqueline Sublet: 'La peste prise aux rêts de la jurisprudence. Le Traité d'Ibn Ḥağar al-ʿAsqalānī sur la peste', in *SI* 33, 1971, pp. 141-49, reports on the question of praying during plague epidemics and also notes that ʿAsqalānī allowed or recommended prayers, but says nothing about the *taṣliya*. Equally little in Lawrence I. Conrad: 'Arabic Plague Chronologies and Treatises', in *SI* 54, 1981, pp. 51-93.

requests which were not directed to God but to human beings. In such cases the *taṣliya* occurs only once and then at the beginning, and constitutes the conjuration so to speak. Here the person to whom the request is directed is called upon to pronounce blessings on Muḥammad, just as one calls upon God to do so in the supplication. In the background stands the idea expressed by Abū Sulaymān al-Dārānī (d. 215/830), Jaᶜfar al-Ṣādiq (d. 148/765) and Abū'l-Dardāᵓ (d. 32/652) that God is too noble only to fulfill the request to invoke blessings on the Prophet and to refuse the other personal request associated with it which has now been transferred to the human being addressed. It is as if by means of the *taṣliya* the latter has been clasped by his sword and conjured by his nobility not to close his mind to the personal request of the beseecher. This is a matter of urgent requests which are accompanied by a subliminal fear of the power of the addressee.

A good example, which is likewise the most instructive, is the story of the poet Abū Dulāma and the caliph al-Mahdī (158-169/775-785). When the caliph returned from al-Rayy to Baghdad, which will have occurred before his assumption of office, still under Manṣūr, the poet addressed these impudent verses to him:

I have sworn: if I see you again safe and sound
    in the villages of Iraq and you're well-off for cash,
then you should invoke blessings on the Prophet Muḥammad
    and fill the hem of my robe with coins!

Mahdī went along with the first part and said: 'God bless and greet the Prophet!' and then continued: 'But the money? No!' Abū Dulāma replied: 'You are too noble to separate the two and then to choose the easier one.' Thereupon the caliph had the hem of his robe filled with coins.[125] — This is precisely the justification which Dārānī, Jaᶜfar and Abū'l-Dardāᵓ give for combining the *taṣliya* and the supplication together. But here we find the combination in the

---

125 Abū'l-Faraj al-Iṣfahānī: *Al-aghānī*, Būlāq, 1285, IX, p. 130/Cairo, 1927 ff., X, p. 253. Ibn Khallikān: *Wafayāt al-aᶜyān*, Beirut, 1968-72, II, p. 325, variant. ᶜAbd al-Raḥīm b. ᶜAbd al-Raḥmān b. Aḥmad al-ᶜAbbāsī: *Maᶜāhid al-tanṣīṣ ᶜalā shawāhid al-Talkhīṣ*, Cairo, 1947-48, II, p. 221. Translated by Mohammed Ben Cheneb: *Abû Dolâma. Poète bouffon de la Cour des premiers Califes abbassides*, (Thèse) Algiers, 1922, p. 64. Mahdī is replaced by Abū Dulaf, which is chronologically impossible, in Ibn ᶜAbd Rabbih: *Al-ᶜiqd al-farīd*, Cairo, 1353/1935, I, p. 132. — Abū'l-Faraj took the story from the non-extant work of Muḥammad b. Ṣāliḥ Ibn al-Naṭṭāḥ (d. 252/866) from which he frequently quoted; Sezgin: *GAS*, I, p. 317.

context of a worldly request. The caliph or crown prince was apparently unfamiliar with this, otherwise he would certainly not have rewarded the poet so handsomely for his comment. Did this comment spring from an inspiration of the poet's? If so, by himself he would simply have invented anew the justification which Abū'l-Dardāᵓ (or Muḥammad) and Jaᶜfar al-Ṣādiq had given for the prayer of supplication — Dārānī is not concerned here as he lived at a later time. But it is equally possible that the dark-skinned poet who was pleased to display his neglect of religious duties[126] consciously borrowed it from the sphere of piety and in so doing once again allowed himself a small violation of the boundaries of modesty. In this case the most likely source to suggest itself would be the dictum of Abū'l-Dardāᵓ (or Muḥammad), since at that time sayings of Jaᶜfar al-Ṣādiq would not necessarily have reached the ears of everyone, and especially not the ears of every foreigner. The question cannot be answered with certainty. Only one thing is sure: the combination of the *taṣliya* with a profane request was already current before Abū Dulāma. This is demonstrated by an earlier story which is meant to have taken place in Medina. The story goes as follows:

In Medina there lived an aged woman who by means of her evil eye put a jinx on everything she looked at and found attractive. When in 154/771 the singer Ashᶜab was on the point of dying, he forbade his daughter to initiate a great lamentation because of his piety. The people would only curse him. He had scarcely said this when he caught sight of the old lady who was notorious for her evil eye. He covered his face with his sleeve and warned her: 'By God, if you find something still attractive about my situation, invoke blessings on the Prophet — do not kill me!' The old woman replied: 'What would I find attractive here? In fact you're at your last gasp.' Ashᶜab said: 'I know that but you had better not find it attractive that I am dying so easily, otherwise it will only become more difficult for me.' The old woman went away uttering abuse, and everyone laughed.[127] — Here of course the *taṣliya* is not meant to ward off the evil eye as is frequently the case but only to heighten the urgency of the request.

Accordingly, already in the 2nd/8th century the *taṣliya* had sunk from being a prayer of supplication to a request and then become

126 *Aghānī*, IX, p. 120/new edition, X, p. 235, ll. 8-9.

127 *Aghānī*, XVII, p. 103/new edition, XIX, pp. 178-79. Translated by Quatremère in *JA*, 1838, 1, pp. 242-43. — Abū'l-Faraj's source was Madāᵓinī (d. at the latest 235/850); concerning him see: *GAS*, I, p. 314.

petrified into a kind of oath-formula which was meant to confer emphasis on a request,[128] naturally without having lost its use on the traditional religious level. The counter-thesis that the combination could have arisen following the opposite path, from below upwards, from a request to the prayer of supplication, would break down in view of the old *ḥadīth*s which had long ago linked the *taṣliya* with the supplication. A counter-thesis that might perhaps have an easier job of it would be that not the combination itself but only its clever explanation by means of aristocratic behavior had arisen on this path from below upwards because the pious sayings of Abū'l-Dardāʾ, Jaʿfar al-Ṣādiq and Dārānī in fact rest on a very weak foundation and could themselves possibly be derived — *horribile dictu*! — from the inspiration in question of Abū Dulāma. On the other hand, his witty reply was a requirement of the anecdote and could also simply be an invention attributed to him.

4. AS AN ORDER TO BE SILENT

What still remains is the *taṣliya* used to settle a dispute. Edward William Lane reports that in his day in Egypt, i.e. 1825-1834, it was customary to conclude a more important business transaction by reciting the *fātiḥa*. If a dispute broke out between the parties, by way of establishing peace or calming the emotions one of them would usually exclaim: 'Blessing on the Prophet!' or 'Bless ye (or bless thou) the Prophet!', whereupon the disagreement would then proceed more peacefully.[129] This custom was not, nor is it today, limited to Egypt. Émile Amar, without citing Lane, writes that everyone who has travelled in an Islamic region is familiar with the words 'bless Muhammad' or 'bless the Prophet' as a means of ending arguments. The person addressed this way replies, for the most part, in a more

128 An example of oaths instead of *taṣliya*, and indeed oaths sworn on sacred concepts and on sacred objects that were brought along, in Michel Abitbol: *Tombouctou au milieu du XVIIIe siècle d'après la chronique de Mawlāy al-Qāsim B. Mawlāy Sulaymān*, Paris, 1982, Arabic pp. 15-16/French pp. 26-27: 'The *shurafāʾ*, *ṭulabāʾ* and the *qāḍī* approached with the banner of the pilgrimage and the Koran before Muṣṭafā and said: "We come to you: By God, by His Apostle, by this Koran, Bukhārī and the banners, go (*illā an tamshiya*) with us and make your peace with the pasha!"'

129 *The Manners and Customs of the Modern Egyptians*, (Everyman's Library), London, 1954, Chpt. XIII, p. 284 with ftn. 2.

gentle tone: 'God bless him and greet him.'[130] C. Snouck Hurgronje remarks in an essay about Ḥaḍramawt: 'The appeal to bless (*ṣalāh*) the Prophet, which every believer is obliged to answer with "Oh God, bless and greet him!", is one of the most used formulas for ordering someone to be silent.'[131]

As one may deduce from juridical discussions, use of the *taṣliya* to stop disputes goes far back in time. Indeed, the appeal to invoke blessings on Muḥammad in many cases did not appease a person who was incensed and thought he was in the right but, on the contrary, led him to make rash replies and to outbursts of blasphemy. Since religious disparagement, depending on the level of seriousness, could entail the death penalty, the question arose as to whether an irritated debtor who lost his composure and instead of the *taṣliya* answered: 'God bless no one who invokes blessings on the Prophet!' deserved to be put to death, whether he had indeed blasphemed against the Prophet or the angels who, according to surah 33/56, pronounce the blessing on Muḥammad. Saḥnūn (d. 240/854) and others were prepared to turn a blind eye in such a situation since the enraged individual did not in fact really have the Prophet or the angels in mind.[132]

If one pursues the same train of thought which provided us with an explanation of the *taṣliya* used for a profane request, one could consider the possibility of linking this *taṣliya* of appeasement in a dispute to the theory of descent. One could well wonder whether the appeal to the disputant was not originally composed of two parts, the *taṣliya* and the request to calm down. For psychological reasons, namely to avoid provoking the angry person further and inciting him all the more, one would then have omitted the request to calm down and the *taṣliya* would have been left on its own — according to this line of reasoning. The sense of the suppressed request would have

---

130 'Consultations juridiques des faqihs du Maghreb', in *Arch. Maroc.* 12, 1908, p. 329, ftn. 1.

131 'L'interdit séculier (rifghèh) en H'adhramôt' (1905), in *Verspreide Geschriften*, III, Bonn-Leipzig, 1923, p. 225, ftn. 1. I use my own translation where it makes no difference to retain the original.

132 ᶜIyāḍ: *Shifā*, II, pp. 979-80. Amar in *Arch. Maroc.* 12, 1908, pp. 329-30, from the *Miᶜyār* of Wansharīsī (d. 914/1508). Khalīl b. Isḥāq: *Précis de la jurisprudence musulmane*, trans. by Perron, Paris, 1844-52, V, pp. 520-21, and others. — The warning against invoking blessings on the Prophet in anger (*ghaḍab*) sprang from the consideration that in such a case there was no pre-condition for a genuinely pious wish and a *taṣliya* at such a moment would necessarily sound like a curse; Gannūn: *Al-nasaq al-ghālī*, p. 22, last line.

been transferred to the *taṣliya* by means of a 'semantic epenthesis'. Thus the *taṣliya* would have taken on the task of the request which was no longer explicitly stated, and in so doing would have sunk one level lower. In brief, what we have before us is an ellipsis for the double imperative 'bless the Prophet and stop it now!' From the point of view of the theory of descent this account works out smoothly, and one could even produce a concrete example in which the two parts that made up the original form still remain intact and joined together. In a transcription of the spoken dialect from Djidjelli (Algeria) two younger women abuse one another in angry tones. An old woman then turns up and says: 'Invoke blessings on the Prophet, my daughters, and stop this bickering!'[133]

Two things warn against being too hasty and show that one will not succeed with the theory of descent. The first consists of certain observations recorded in the Arabian Peninsula. When among the Rwala bedouins a travelling merchant lost something, he would ride through the camp and cry out: 'O ye who hear this voice, praise the Prophet! He is for you the first, ᶜAlī is the second, and Fâṭima, the Prophet's daughter, is the third. Who has seen this and that?'[134] And when in Ḥaḍramawt a nobleman wished to proscribe a settlement he would have a crier go to the locality and proclaim: 'First of all invoke blessings on him (i.e. the Prophet), secondly invoke blessings on him, thirdly invoke blessings on him! Listen carefully: A b. B says: "This locality is proscribed."'[135] Perhaps — but only perhaps — certain practices among the Berbers of southern Morocco also belong to this category. In the 7th/13th century the inhabitants of two villages in Timggidsht[136] fought over the land downhill of a spring and remained caught up in a blood feud for forty years. There then arrived on the scene two sayyids, a certain Abū Yaḥyā al-Gersīfī (d. 685/1286) and a certain Zaᶜm b. ᶜĀṣim al-Ragrāgī along with their companions in order to bring about a reconciliation and they 'bellowed' (*yajʾarān*) the invocation of blessings on the Prophet.

---

133 Philippe Marçais: *Textes arabes de Djidjelli*, Algiers, 1954 (Publications de la Faculté des Lettres d'Alger, Sér. 2, 26), p. 38/p. 39.

134 Alois Musil: *The Manners and Customs of the Rwala Bedouins*, New York, 1925, p. 454. By 'praise the Prophet!' is actually meant 'invoke blessings on the Prophet!'

135 Snouck Hurgronje: 'L'interdit séculier (rifghèh) en H'adhramôt' (1905), pp. 224-25.

136 Approximately 120 km east of Tiznit (*Maᶜsūl*, VI, p. 172). This pronunciation according to Ibn Sūda: *Dalīl muʾarrikh al-maghrib al-aqṣā*, Casablanca, 1960-65, no. 826 (p. 211), on the authority of Muḥammad al-Mukhtār al-Sūsī. Noted by the latter in *Maᶜsūl*, XV, p. 355, last line.

Both hostile parties received them in common, concluded peace and turned over the disputed land to the sayyids whose descendants still occupy it today.[137] The case is uncertain because at a later date the Nāṣiriyyūn — members and supporters of the marabout family of Maḥammad (sic) b. Nāṣir (d. 1085/1674) — drew attention to themselves upon entering a settlement by repeatedly invoking blessings out loud[138] in order to call the inhabitants together, and one time it had also been possible in this way to call forth a *qāʾid* for the purpose of hearing a complaint.[139] Another time, in 1322/1904, people 'bellowed' an invocation of blessings before a *qāʾid* who they feared was going to take unjust measures against their teacher.[140] It could be that this later custom was backdated to the time of the sayyids. We will therefore leave this example aside. None the less, another customary practice in the west appears to parallel rather closely the practices in Arabia. In Algeria a story-teller can bridge a pause in his narrative before introducing something new and decisive by a call to invoke blessings on the Prophet, and those present can even comply with this command by saying out loud 'May He (God) bless him.'[141] The pious call surely has the same purpose in Arabia and in North Africa, namely to attract people's attention and focus it on what one has to say to them. In the first case from Arabia a question is involved, in the second a declaration and in the Algerian examples a communication. It is not necessarily a matter of a request.

The second is that other formulas also serve to settle a vociferous argument, formulas which could not have developed out of the *taṣliya* in connection with a request. Even Lane's variant 'Blessing on the Prophet!', as a call to order employing a noun form, appears nowhere in prayers of supplication or in requests, and thus by the same token cannot have 'sunk down' from that context. This is even less possible in the case of another variant which we owe to the seri-

---

137 Sūsī: *Maʿsūl*, IX, p. 150.

138 *Maʿsūl*, I, p. 259, with ftn. 1, and p. 312; III, p. 46; V, p. 163. Maḥammad's son Aḥmad b. Nāṣir al-Darʿī (d. 1129/1717), for instance, is also put forward as the founder of the order; Aḥmad b. al-ʿAyyāshī Sukayrij/Skīraj (d. 1363/1944): *Kashf al-ḥijāb ʿamman talāqā maʿa'l-shaykh al-Tijānī min al-aṣḥāb*, n.p., 1961, p. 196: Aḥmad b. Nāṣir al-Darʿī = Bnāṣir. Cf. also p. 530, l. 5.

139 Sūsī: *Khilāl Jazūla*, I, p. 46.

140 *Maʿsūl*, XV, p. 274.

141 A. Dhina: 'Textes arabes du Sud-Algérois', in *Revue africaine* 84, 1940, pp. 101-02. The interpolated phrase *allāhumma ṣalli ʿalā'l-nabī*, ibid., p. 105, appears to serve a similar transitional function.

ous utterance of a certain Abū Bakr Muḥammad b. Yaḥyā — perhaps Abū Bakr Muḥammad b. Yaḥyā b. Sulaymān al-Marwazī (d. 298/910-11).[142] This person, a *faqīh* and man of letters, advised against calling out 'Recollect God!' or 'Invoke blessings on the Prophet!' to someone who was aroused in anger, precisely because of the danger that the angry man could commit a sin through a rash reaction.[143] Consequently, instead of the *taṣliya* one could also call out 'Recollect God!' which no longer has anything to do with the *taṣliya* in the prayer of supplication and in requests.

It is easy to draw the conclusion from this. The *taṣliya* of appeasement in conflicts and the *taṣliya* of announcing a declaration or an intimate communication do not stem from the prayer of supplication, or from formulating a request. Nor do they have anything to do with a *captatio benevolentiae* for a request. Rather, the *taṣliya* of appeasement means — or at least originally meant — just what it says, namely: 'You fighting-cocks, invoke blessings on the Prophet instead!'[144] If no further clarifying request follows this demand, the person addressed then replies obediently with the sentence 'God bless and greet him!' or something similar. The demand was genuinely meant. If the speaker, however, adds the request to stop fighting, the other person does not necessarily comply with the command to pronounce the *taṣliya* but at least fulfills the request — on a favorable occasion. The young women in Djidjelli did not invoke blessings on the Prophet as they were asked but they did stop their shouting in accordance with the old woman's request. If one takes the demand to pronounce the *taṣliya* as a declaration or a communication, one might also possibly pronounce it but, to judge by the examples, it can also be left out. What is more important is to prick up one's

---

142 The source of transmission who reported what follows is al-Naḥḥās (Nawawī: *Adhkār*, p. 326, l. 7). This can be none other than Abū Ja^cfar Aḥmad b. Muḥammad b. Ismā^cīl al-Naḥḥās (d. 338/950) whom Nawawī shortly before (*Adhkār*, p. 323, l. 17) quoted along with his work *Ṣinā^cat al-kuttāb*. On Naḥḥās see *GAL*, I, p. 132; *GAL S*, I, p. 201; *GAS*, VIII, p. 242. Of the various Abū Bakr Muḥammad b. Yaḥyās whom the Egyptian Naḥḥās could have met in Baghdad or from whom he could have transmitted something, al-Khaṭīb al-Baghdādī: *Tārīkh Baghdād*, Cairo, 1349, III, pp. 422-26, lists three (if we leave aside the famous Ṣūlī who also bore these names). The best-known of them is Marwazī, although he is really quite unknown.

143 Nawawī: *Adhkār*, p. 326, ll. 7-9.

144 Because of its synonymous meaning with the call to recollecting God it does not seem to me advisable to derive this *taṣliya* from the *taṣliya* which concludes a talk or a written work, i.e. as if one wanted to say to the conflicting parties: 'Now pronounce the *taṣliya* of conclusion in your conflict!' In terms of our contemporary speech: 'Stop this now!'

ears in order to receive the communication. Thus demanding the *taṣliya* in all the mentioned forms of usage has become a command for silence, whether the one addressed is meant to stop shouting or to prepare him or herself for a communication. Snouck Hurgronje appears to have recognized this common denominator. Otherwise he would scarcely have added his remark about the *taṣliya* of appeasement to his example of the *taṣliya* of a declaration.[145] On the other hand, I admit that transfers from begging a request to the command to silence, and the other way round, are conceivable. Finally, in all these cases the *taṣliya* more or less amounts to the English expression 'would you be so kind!'

That the demand to pronounce the *taṣliya* and the *taṣliya* itself in these contexts were actually meant to calm the emotions is confirmed by the somewhat different but well thought out and religiously moulded behavior of the Berber marabout whom we have already mentioned once, Muḥammad b. Aḥmad (d. 1251/1835) of the Aït Ḥusayn in Sūs. After the mid-morning prayers when people sought his advice, this man of piety regularly began reading Jazūlī's *Dalāʾil al-khayrāt*, the famous compilation of formulas of blessings on behalf of Muḥammad. He would listen to one person after the other, explain to them whatever had to be explained and pray for them. When it was time to deal with disputes, he would continue calmly reading in the *Dalāʾil* and let the parties go on talking among themselves until they were ready to listen to him. Then he would speak to them in a friendly, gentle manner until they were reconciled, and he would pray for them. He said: 'Reading the *Dalāʾil al-khayrāt* in the presence of mutually hostile persons contains a blessing (*baraka*) which drives wrath out of their heart, sows love among them and establishes peace.'[146] Here the call that commands silence and separates quarreling parties has been refined into a recitation of the formulas of blessings from a book which is reputed to be holy.

---

145 I find it difficult to judge the form of speech no. 652 in S.D.F. Goitein's *Jemenica*, Leiden, 1934/reprint 1970, p. 95: *ṣallī ʿala n-nábī al-ḥâḍür*. Goitein translates: 'Pray for the Prophet who is here!' It is used when someone suddenly changes the subject, or also in the sense of: 'Take what is there.' Thus the saying would mean: 'Invoke blessings on that Prophet who is actually alive and is present!' In this case it has nothing to do with our subject.

146 *Maʿsūl*, VI, p. 211. Here as often the title of the collection is written *Dalīl al-khīrāt*, in accordance with the pronunciation current in the country.

ADDITIONS OF THE AUTHOR

P. 571, l. 15: Today I would add to all the cases I cited the dichotomy in Persian city quarters between Ḥaydariyān (*ḥaydarī-khānahā*) and Niᶜmatiyān (*niᶜmatī-khānahā*) from the 9th/15th up into the 14th/20th century. Cf. the article of the Japanese scholar Kan (Hiroshi) Kagaya: 'Du-dastagī-i ijtimāᶜī u madhhabī dar Īrān', in *Āyanda* 15, 1368, pp. 733-39.

P. 583, l. 5: Eldon Rutter: *The Holy Cities of Arabia*, London-New York, 1928, I, p. 2. writes: '"Ask blessings on the Prophet," said he in order to stop my speaking so that he himself might have a clear field. The lower classes in Egypt make use of the Korânic injunction to "ask blessings and the salutation of peace on the Prophet" for this purpose. In the midst of an argument one will say to another, "Ask blessings on the Prophet!" and while his companion, as in duty bound, says "O God! bless him," the first man is able to vociferate his point without interruption. "O God! bless him," I said in respone to the tout's prompting.'

This form of speech is also current in Persian. Yūsuf-i Raḥmatī: *Farhang-i ᶜāmmiyāna*, Tehran, 1951, p. 98: 'Invoke blessings on the Prophet!' is said when one wishes to end a verbal dispute. Cf. my translation 'Drei moderne Texte zum persischen "Wettreden"', in *ZDMG* 114, 1964, p. 300 below: 'In order to induce complete silence a few more invocations of blessings on the Prophet and the holy family are pronounced.'

THE PRIORITY OF FAITH AND THINKING WELL OF OTHERS OVER A CONCERN FOR TRUTH AMONG MUSLIMS

'To think well of' is a very broad and unclear concept which means no more than that one thinks well or thinks good of someone or something. One can do this because of one's individual nature or with a particular purpose in mind. At the same time one can persuade oneself of something, whether in order to reassure oneself or to avoid causing pain to others, or out of principle or simply on the spur of the moment. In any case it is regarded as a virtue and not infrequently gives rise to good actions. Its reverse side is subjectivity which leaves wide scope for individual blindness and false hope, and can go as far as self-deception and distortion of one's feelings, indeed even as far as shamming false feelings. Thinking well of people or things can also spring from doubt in the correctness of an opinion previously held by oneself or others and provide the basis for an objective assessment or examination of circumstances, and conversely it can also lead to embellishing the truth or covering it up and thus give rise to incorrect ideas and distorted viewpoints. Consciously remaining silent about part of the truth can be a sign of piety but equally the expression of fear, also fear of what people will think, and can serve to maintain peace as well as to preserve one's own security. It is here that 'faith' in the sense of trust comes into the picture. However, it would be a misunderstanding if the reader were to conclude from the title of this sketch that I consider the priority of faith and thinking well of people over the search for truth to be a special characteristic of Muslims behind which other evaluative classifications have once and for all receded and even disappeared. Absolutely not! In what follows I simply wish to examine to a limited extent the attitude of certain Muslims as referred to in the title and to shed some light on the main forms of this phenomenon on the basis of a few cases and examples taken from the relevant literature. Of course the literature is full of information on the subject. I will only select a few representative samples and treat them in the following order: 1) thinking well of God, 2) thinking well of Muḥammad, 3) thinking well of ᶜAlids and Companions of the Prophet, 4) thinking well of deeply-rooted religious ideas and customs, 5) thinking well of natural and religious authorities, 6) thinking well of one's Sufi instructor, 7) people's thinking well of one another in society, and by way of an appendix 8) thinking well (and badly or wickedly) as magical power.

Thinking well of someone in Arabic is *ḥusn al-ẓann*, *iḥsān al-ẓann*, more rarely *taḥsīn al-ẓann*. In Persian one can say *gumānī nīk burdan ba-kasī*[1] 'thinking good of someone'. To express a less calculated, less voluntarily sustained, more convinced and spontaneous faith in someone or something the Arabic language disposes over *ḥusn al-iᶜtiqād*, or simply *iᶜtiqād*, and similarly one finds *iᶜtiqād* in Persian.

1. HOPE IN MERCY BEFORE JUSTICE, AND CONSOLATION THROUGH BELIEF IN HIGHER WISDOM.

The absolute 'belief in Oneness' (*tawḥīd*) which Ashᶜarite theology along with its forerunners professes, as does Sufism to a large extent, places man in a slave-like dependence on God: the actions of human beings conceal within them God's doing because without the intervention of God man's hands are tied, and every movement in this world originates with the Prime Mover. Nevertheless, voices are also to be heard which speak of a movement upwards and of a reaction of God downwards affecting the behavior and suffering of man. One such is the un-Koranic statement of God (*ḥadīth qudsī*): 'I (God) am as My bondsman thinks of Me', occasionally with additions like: 'I am with him when he remembers Me. If he remembers Me in a public gathering, then I remember him in an even better public gathering. If he draws closer to Me by one span, then I draw closer to him by the space of two outstretched arms. If he comes toward Me walking, then I come toward him running.' This version is to be found, for instance, in the book *tawḥīd* 15 of Bukhārī's *Ṣaḥīḥ*.[2] Thus God always shows Himself to man from the side that man envisages in his conception of Him, and indeed many times more actively than in that conception. The *ḥadīth* in the version cited only mentions pleasant expectations. In other variations, however, the unpleasant side as well is not forgotten: 'I am as My bondsman thinks of Me. If he thinks good, I am good. If he thinks bad (or in anger), then I am

---

1 The two ī at the end are the ī of indeterminateness, i.e. the old ē.

2 Passages in *Concordance et Indices de la Tradition musulmane*, s.v. *ẓanna*, IV, p. 87. Munāwī: *Al-itḥāfāt al-saniyya bi'l-aḥādīth al-qudsiyya*, ed. Muḥammad ᶜAfīf al-Ziᶜbī, Beirut-Ḥims, n.d., pp. 37-39. The last mentioned saying above, due to its strong anthropomorphic representation of God, is considered as unexplainable by the Ḥanbalites, but absolutely to be believed. Ibn Abī Yaᶜlā: *Ṭabaqāt al-ḥanābila*, reprint Beirut, II, p. 23.

bad (or angry).' Or: 'If he thinks good, that is what he receives. If he thinks bad, then that is what he receives.'[3] A person therefore obtains the experiences he has with God through what he thinks of Him. In whatever way the Muslims have explained it,[4] the statements advise thinking and speaking only good of God. The Egyptian Sufi ᶜAlī b. Wafāʾ (d. 807/1405) cites the *ḥadīth* in the above-mentioned short form: 'I am as My bondsman thinks of Me, and I am with (*maᶜa*) him when he thinks of Me',[5] a variant which is also found in Munāwī.[6] ᶜAlī b. Wafāʾ explains it thus: 'With whatever image you conceive of Me, from the horizon of that form I will send you its effect (*ḥukm*).'

The commentaries on the *ḥadīth*s and the monograph on *ḥusn al-ẓann bi'llāh* of Ibn Abī'l-Dunyā (d. 281/894)[7] show that the *ḥadīth qudsī* is not meant to be wise advice for life, but a guideline for a peaceful death; thus its underlying purpose is to strengthen man's hope in the face of death that he will meet with a friendly reception in the hereafter. Aḥmad-i Jām (d. 536/1141): *Rawḍat al-mudhnibīn wa-jannat al-mushtāqīn*, ed. by ᶜAlī-i Fāḍil, Tehran, 1355, p. 170, clarifies this with the following words: 'Since (God's) mercy comes before (His) wrath and (His) mercy knows no boundaries, what cause is there for hopelessness? God says: "I am as My bondsman thinks of Me. Let him think of Me what he wishes!"[8] If He wishes to punish me, and in particular because I talk about His mercy and think good of Him, I should prefer that instead of thinking bad of Him and He not punishing me (printed text, us) for it. To think good of God is very beautiful, and to think bad of Him is very ugly and reprehensible. In the *ḥadīth* it is related: "On the Day of Resurrection they bring forth a man and settle accounts with him. His record of deeds shows no obedience. The command goes out: 'Take him off to Hell!' He is surprised and says: 'Oh God, this was not the idea I had of You, that You would send me off to Hell.' The voice is heard: 'What was your idea of Me then?' He replies: 'That You would show mercy to me.' God responds: 'Make his idea come true! Whoever thinks something of Me, I will pay it out to him in full.'" And

3 Munāwī: *Itḥāfāt*, nos. 71, 73.

4 Cf. Tirmidhī: *Al-jāmiᶜ al-ṣaḥīḥ, daᶜawāt* no. 132, Cairo, 1937-65, V, p. 581.

5 Shaᶜrānī: *Al-ṭabaqāt al-kubrā al-musammāh bi-Lawāqiḥ al-anwār fī ṭabaqāt al-akhyār*, Cairo, 1954, II, p. 23, ll. 25-26.

6 *Itḥāfāt*, no. 68.

7 Ibn Abī'l-Dunyā: *Majmūᶜat al-rasāʾil*, Cairo, 1935, pp. 39-72.

8 Munāwī: *Itḥāfāt*, nos. 67, 72.

the man is conducted from the road to Hell onto the road to Paradise.'[9] Najm al-Dīn al-Kubrā (d. 618/1221) also made thinking well of God from this point of view into a rule especially for a mystic who should always assess the qualities of divine kindness (*jamāl*) as being greater than the extent of his sins.[10] That is why O. Houdas in his translation of Bukhārī employs the future tense in the *ḥadīth* cited here at the beginning: 'I will be for My worshipper whatever he will believe that I must be.'[11]

Yet this confidence does not by any means have to be limited to the end of one's life or to when one stands before the Throne of Judgement, but early on in life can strengthen the hope of Paradise in one's love of God. In any case that is what an author from the Maghreb of the 7th-8th/13th-14th centuries says who distinguished between renunciation of the world (*zuhd*) out of fear of Hell and renunciation of the world out of hope of Paradise, and he classifies the second as higher because, as he says, 'hope brings about love and love increases hope by means of thinking well about the reward on the part of the Lord'.[12] The Spanish Sufi Ibn Qasī of the 6th/12th century promised himself and his followers that thinking well of God would give them easier inward access to Him even here in this world.[13] Moreover, thinking well of God entails for the man of piety even in the here and now contentment with destiny, gratitude for what is pleasant, admiration for creation, an eye for the wisdom with which everything has been ordered and is carried out, the understanding that everything is in its proper place and that one does not simply have to bow to a higher power but ought to entrust oneself to it as well.[14] The Persian author of the 8th/14th century Najm al-Dīn

---

9 The same story is already found in Ibn Abī'l-Dunyā: *Majmuʿat al-rasāʾil*, p. 52, § 58.

10 *Ādāb al-sulūk ilā ḥadrat mālik al-mulk wa-malik al-mulūk*, in Marijan Molé: 'Traités mineurs de Najm al-Dīn al-Kubrā', in: *Extraits des Annales Islamologiques* IV, p. 68.

11 El-Bokhâri: *Les Traditions islamiques*, traduites de l'arabe avec notes et index par O. Houdas et W. Marçais, Paris, 1903-14, IV, pp. 588, 624.

12 Aḥmad b. Ibrāhīm al-Māgirī: *Al-minhāj al-wāḍiḥ fī taḥqīq karāmāt Abī Muḥammad Ṣāliḥ*, Cairo, 1933, p. 316, ll. 1-5.

13 Josef Dreher: 'L'imāmat d'Ibn Qasī à Mertola', *MIDEO* 18, 1988, p. 201.

14 On the relationship between a good opinion of God and trust in God cf. Benedikt Reinert: *Die Lehre vom* tawakkul *in der klassischen Sufik*, in Studien zur Sprache, Geschichte und Kultur des islamischen Orients, Beih.z.Zs. *Der Islam*, NF Bd 3, Berlin, 1968, pp. 44 f., 50, 123, 270. In connection with acknowledging our world as the best possible world see Eric L.

Maḥmūd b. Saᶜdallāh-i Iṣfahānī writes in his book *Manāhij al-ṭālibīn wa-masālik al-ṣādiqīn*, ed. by Māyil-i Hirawī, Tehran, 1364, pp. 149-151: 'In accordance with the statement "I am as My bondsman thinks of Me", one must practice thinking good (or having a good opinion, *ḥusn-i ẓann*), accept as sweet the bitter and sour aspects of reprehensible qualities (?), turn one's glance from the bad in hope of the good, not be afraid of the tracts of human darkness when striving after the water of life of knowledge and, without expecting to be able to cause anything oneself, to hurl oneself into the ark of trust in God. Then at the end one will perhaps have a share in (divine) friendliness and perfection, and attain a sip of the cool water of union (with God)... From the viewpoint of (metaphysical) reality in the eyes of the knowers of meaning nothing is ugly and bad, but everything in its place is pleasing and good... On the other hand, with some things the beautiful and good is evident and plain to see, whereas with others it is concealed and invisible, and not everyone can recognize their use (or sense, *fāᵓida*)... God has not created anything which does not contain some wisdom and secret in its being and appearance. It is clear and visible to those with sharp perception that if something were not the way it is, then some harm would come about in the kingdom (of the world). Therefore everything that exists is the result of the perfection of God's action and power, and a cause of something useful and necessary. To look upon this with eyes of deficiency is a sign of limited intelligence and limited knowledge on the part of an individual and his distorted way of seeing... The meaning of our remarks is: Since it is undisputed that a human being can occupy various stages and categories and endless grades, all these in their place are pleasing and good. And God has endowed man's soul with the capacity to reach the highest stage, if he makes the effort.' Bahāᵓ-i Walad (d. 628/1231), the father of Jalāl al-Dīn-i Rūmī, wished to understand by *abrār* 'men of piety', who according to surah 82/13 are 'in bliss', those people for whom pain itself was bliss thanks to their 'good faith' (*iᶜtiqād-i khūb*), who are always in bliss, who feel like they are in the garden not only when they are in the garden but when they are in the fire as well because their trust in God's promises has become their bliss and their Paradise.[15] There

---

Ormsby: *Theodicy in Islamic Thought. The Dispute over al-Ghazālī's "Best of all possible worlds"*, Princeton, 1984, pp. 43, 255-58, 264.

15 Muḥammad b. Ḥusayn-i Khaṭībī-i Balkhī mashhūr ba Bahāᵓ-i Walad: *Maᶜārif*, ed. Badīᶜ al-Zamān-i Furūzānfar, Tehran, 1333/1955, [I] p. 410, ll. 12-17.

were those who said certainty (*yaqīn*) of God is not perfected without thinking well of Him.[16]

The *ḥadīth qudsī* was referred to in answering various questions. The imaginative so-called 'renewer of the second millenium', the Naqshbandī Aḥmad al-Fārūqī al-Sirhindī (d. 1034/1624), wondered why the saint ᶜAbd al-Qādir al-Jīlānī (d. 561/1166) had performed so many miracles whereas his predecessors had not, and explained this as due to the difference in their personalities. According to him, the one group, the sober ones, never let the world of causes out of their sight, whereas the others, the intoxicated ones, lost this very connection and only saw God at work everywhere. In accordance with these different attitudes, the field of causality increased for the first group and they were able to trace the chain of causation far back. For the others, the Romantics so to speak, the Primary Cause alone immediately appeared in their eyes and they overlooked the natural interconnections. This was true of the miracle-workers themselves as well as of their public. God behaves one way with one person and differently with another, depending on their attitude, completely in accordance with the statement 'I am as My bondsman thinks of Me.'

Sirhindī's words according to the Arabic version of Muḥammad Amīn al-Kurdī al-Irbilī (d. 1332/1914): *Al-mawāhib al-sarmadiyya fī manāqib al-naqshbandiyya*, Cairo, 1329, pp. 191-94, are as follows: 'Know that sainthood (*walāya*) means passing away and remaining, and miracles (*khawāriq*) have their place here as well. But it is not the case that sainthood is more complete and perfected the more miracles one exhibits, but the miracles are fewer in number the more complete and perfected[17] sainthood is. The quantity of miracles depends on two things: the ascent (*ṣuᶜūd*) at the time of going upward (*ᶜurūj*) must be greater and the descent (*hubūṭ*) at the time of coming down (*nuzūl*) less, whatever the degree of going upward may be (have been) because the one who comes down does so into the world of causes (*asbāb*), finds things there connected with causes and perceives the action of the First Cause only in the background. The person who does not come down or does not come down to the level of causes, his sight remains fixed on the Cause of all causes and the causes themselves escape his perception. God behaves toward each person according to how the person thinks (*ẓann*). He conducts the affairs of someone who (so to speak only) perceives causes, by means of causes, and the affairs of someone who does not perceive causes, without causes. *Ḥadīth qudsī*: "I am as My bondsman thinks of Me." For a long time I asked myself why the miracles which

16 Aḥmad Ḍiyāᵓ al-Dīn al-Kumushkhānalī: *Jāmiᶜ al-uṣūl*, Cairo, 1328, p. 297, l. 10.

17 'Complete' rather in the sense of all-inclusive is meant here. Perfected and complete are scarcely ever really distinguished.

took place through ʿAbd al-Qādir had not been accomplished earlier by saints before him. Finally, God revealed the secret to me: ʿAbd al-Qādir's (mystical) ascent was higher than that of most saints, whereas on the side of his descent his coming down was only to the level of the spirit (*rūḥ*) which is still above the world of causes.'[18] Also relevant here is the story of al-Ḥasan al-Baṣrī (d. 110/728) and Ḥabīb al-ʿAjamī. Ḥasan was standing on the shore waiting for the ship. Ḥabīb then came along, saw him standing there and asked him: "What are (emended) you waiting for?" Ḥasan: "For the ship." Ḥabīb: "Who needs a ship? Don't you have certainty of faith?" Ḥasan: "And do you have no knowledge (of the necessity of using means in this world)?" At that Ḥabīb walked over the water, whereas Ḥasan waited until he could use the ship. Since Ḥasan had come down into the world of causes, in his case things proceeded by means of causes, and since Ḥabīb had not come down so far (p. 193), in his case they proceeded without causes. The advantage lies with Ḥasan because he is the one with knowledge, the one who unites knowledge of the certainty of faith with certainty of faith itself, and perceives things as they are; in the things themselves the (incalculable divine) power (*qudra*) is hidden behind divine wisdom (*ḥikma*) (which is manifested in the things). Ḥabīb al-ʿAjamī is a man of intoxication and has certainty (only) of the metaphysical agent without perceiving the participation of causes. This vision does not correspond to reality because the mediation of causes is a fact and regularly occurs. The task of mystical perfection and instruction (through the shaykh) presents a (certain) contradiction to the path of the appearance of miracles, for the greater the descent of the instructor to the level of instruction the more perfected he will be in giving instruction because a correspondence between the instructor and the one receiving instruction is indispensable and that depends precisely on the descent (of the instructor into the world of causes).

Know that the higher the ascent, the greater is the descent. Therefore, because the ascent of our Prophet was higher and further upward than the ascent of all other prophets, his descent was also greater than that of all the others and his call (to God) was thus more perfect. That is why (in distinction to all the others) he was sent to the whole world because by being the greatest descent this came to correspond to the call to all people and in his case the path of instruction (*ifāda*) was more complete. At times the instruction by intermediates on this path is also better than that of those who have ascended the highest and have not returned (to the world of causes) because the correspondence of the intermediate with the beginner is better than that of the one who has ascended the highest. The strength and the weakness of instruction depend on this descent and return, not on the height to which someone has or

---

18 This statement of Sirhindī has also been misunderstood and reproved as a disparagement of ʿAbd al-Qādir. Shāh Ghulām ʿAlī-i Dihlawī, alias ʿAbdallāh-i Dihlawī (d. 1240/1824; cf. Storey: *Persian Literature*, I, pp. 1034-35), the Indian teacher of Khālid al-Naqshbandī, defends Sirhindī in his *Makātīb-i sharīfa*, litho., n.p., 1371/reprint Istanbul, 1976, p. 50, lower half; p. 84, penult. line, to p. 85, l. 7.

has not climbed. Herein is a subtlety which consists of the following: As it is clearly not a requirement of sainthood that a saint be aware of his sainthood,[19] so it is also not a requirement that he be aware of his miracles. Often people report the most varied miracles of a saint without the saint himself being aware of them. Our shaykh (Muḥammad al-Bāqī, d. 1012/1603) said: "It is strange but people come to me from all areas and regions and one group says: 'We have seen you in Mecca', and others say: 'We have seen you in Baghdad' (in connection with the alleged multilocatio of Bāqī),[20] and they refer to schooling, knowledge and mystical states (supposedly acquired from me), whereas I have never set foot outside my house. What kind of slander is this!"' — Another Arabic translation of the original Persian text, apparently more precise, is given in Muḥammad Murād al-Qazānī al-Makkī's *Muᶜarrab al-maktūbāt*, Acre, 1317/1899, reprint n.d. Istanbul, I, pp. 187-188, part of letter no. 216.[21] A Persian rendition is to be found by his student and biographer

---

19 On this problem and relevant sources see Richard Gramlich: *Die Wunder der Freunde Gottes, Theologien und Erscheinungsformen des islamischen Heiligenwunders*, Freiburger Islamstudien, ed. by Hans Robert Roemer, vol. XI, Wiesbaden, 1987, pp. 60-71.

20 On the miracle of reduplicating oneself cf. Gramlich: *Die Wunder der Freunde Gottes*, pp. 207-12, and 'Zur Ausdehnung der Zeit und Verwandtem', in: Ulrich Haarmann and Peter Bachmann (ed.): *Die islamische Welt zwischen Mittelalter und Neuzeit. Festschr. f. Hans Robert Roemer zum 65. Geburtstag*, Beiruter Texte und Studien 22, Beirut, 1979, pp. 185-86.

21 In dividing saints into those who become lost in God and others who return in order to be active as teachers, Sirhindī follows the corresponding explanations of his two-hundred-year-earlier predecessor Muḥammad-i Pārsā (d. 822/1419) who viewed the former, i.e. the intoxicated ones, as overcome by God's majesty (*jalāl*) and the latter as blessed with God's friendliness (*jamāl*). The former, according to Pārsā, remain engulfed in the state of self-effacement, while the latter are sent back in the state of persistence (and sobriety). These Pārsā also calls 'saints of sociability' (*awliyāy-i ᶜishrat*). Muḥammad-i Pārsā: *Risāla-i qudsiyya*, ed. Malik Muḥammad-i Iqbāl, Rawalpindi, 1395/1354/1975, pp. 175-77. Naturally this is a new version of the opposition between 'travelling' (*sālik*) and 'drawn upwards' (*majdhūb*). In this regard see *Die Fawāʾiḥ al-ǧamāl wa-fawātiḥ al-ǧalāl des Naǧm ad-dīn al-Kubrā. Eine Darstellung mystischer Erfahrungen aus der Zeit um 1200 n. Chr.*, Ak. d. Wiss. u. d. Literatur, Veröffentlichungen der Orientalischen Kommission, vol. IX, Wiesbaden, 1957, Intro., p. 95. Richard Gramlich: *Die schiitischen Derwischorden Persiens. Zweiter Teil: Glaube und Lehre*. Abh. f. d. Kunde des Morgenlandes XXXVI, 2-4, pp. 189-96. But the designation 'saints of sociability' (*awliyāy-i ᶜishrat*) in Pārsā takes us back still further by a different path. Another student of Naqshband, namely Yaᶜqūb-i Charkhī (d. 851/1447), contrasts the 'saints of solitude', the *ᶜuzlatiyān*, with the saints of sociability whom he calls the *ᶜishratiyān*. Thus we acquire clear local names for both groups, and happily Charkhī also refers in this connection to the Koran commentary *ᶜAyn al-maᶜānī* by a scholar from his part of the world, Shams al-ᶜĀrifīn Muḥammad b. Ṭayfūr al-Ghaznawī al-Sajāwandī, who died in 560/1165 (Ṣafadī: *Al-wāfī bi'l-wafayāt*, Bibl. Islamica 6, III, p. 178, no. 1152; *GAL*, I, p. 408/*GAL S*, I, p. 724).

Muḥammad Hāshim-i Kishmī in *Barakāt-i aḥmadiyya* yā *Zubdat al-maqāmāt*, litho., Cawnpore 1307/1890, reprint Istanbul, 1977, pp. 259-261. Further discussion of the subject in letter no.107 of Sirhindī. The Persian original of Sirhindī's letters is not available to me. On Sirhindī see Yohanan Friedmann: *Shaykh Aḥmad Sirhindī. An Outline of His thought and a Study of His Image in the Eyes of Posterity.* McGill-Queens University Press Montreal and London, 1971.

Charkhī says that the *ᶜishratiyān* are the representatives or successors of the prophets in calling the people to God and are only recognized as such by their novices. One could describe the *ᶜuzlatiyān* as the drinking companions (*nudamā*) and the *ᶜishratiyān* as the viziers of the king. The latter outwardly appear among mankind but inwardly are with God. Thus they are the correct teachers among the Ṣūfiyya. Should an *ᶜuzlatī* commit a sin, the *quṭb* (the highest) of the *ᶜishratiyān* then tries to obtain forgiveness for him; the *quṭb* of the *ᶜuzlatiyān* cannot do this (which of course is also not to be expected of him as the highest of the intoxicated). This information is found in Charkhī's *Risāla-i abdāliyya*, ed. Muḥammad Nadhīr-i Rānjhā, Islamabad, 1978, pp. 18-24. Sirhindī (d. 1034/1624), the 'renewer of the second millennium', thinks that the general weakness of religion in his time and the lack of miracles clearly heralds the end of the world because miracles are the old means of strengthening religion. But God was increasingly withdrawing as 'true guide' (*hādī*) and appearing as 'false guide', and the result of this was that now the *awliyāy-i ᶜishrat* as well as the *awliyāy-i ᶜuzlat* scarcely performed any more miracles. Muḥammad Hāshim-i Kishmī: *Barakāt-i aḥmadiyya* yā *Zubdat al-maqāmāt*, litho. Cawnpore, 1307/1890/reprint Istanbul, 1977, p. 255, lower half. — Charkhī's comparison of the two counterparts among the saints finds its parallel in Jāmī's teacher Saᶜd al-Dīn-i Kāshgharī (d. 860/1456), who considers the king's water jug attendant to be more enviable than the chancellor because through the water jug he is more permanently, more closely and more exclusively in the company of the king than is the highest minister of state. ᶜAlī b. Ḥusayn-i Kāshifī: *Rashaḥāt ᶜayn al-ḥayāt*, ed. ᶜAlī Aṣghar-i Muᶜīniyān, Tehran, 2536/1977, pp. 216-17. Kāshgharī even attributes this advantage to the saints over the prophets. The prophets, he says, envied the saints because of this. An argument with a Naqshbandī about *ᶜuzlat* and *ᶜishrat* is found in the Kubrawī Sharīf al-Dīn Ḥusayn: *Jāddat al-ᶜāshiqīn* (written 973/1565-66); Devin DeWeese: 'The Eclipse of the Kubravīyah in Central Asia', *Iranian Studies* 21, 1988, p. 72.

In Sirhindī's view, every Naqshbandī experiences God differently in accordance with the 'subtle substance' (*laṭīfa*) activated within him. An individual can experience Him as being one (*ᶜayniyyat*) with himself in existence (*wujūd*) or see (*shuhūd*) Him as something other (*ghayriyyat*) opposite himself. In a letter Sirhindī's son Muḥammad Saᶜīd takes the word 'think' in our *ḥadīth* to mean 'see' and writes that, as the *ḥadīth* says, one is treated by God the way one sees Him on this level.[22]

2. POLITENESS TOWARD MUḤAMMAD.

Naturally in Islam Muḥammad is also entitled to a good name and to people maintaining a favorable opinion of him. In this regard Muḥammad is more seriously threatened than God because in the area of his expansion and in his immediate environment as well there are Jews and Christians who do not ackowledge Muḥammad as a prophet and yet they worship the same one God. Thus a Jew or a Christian can subscribe to the first part of the Islamic profession of faith, that there is no god but God. As for the second sentence, that Muḥammad is the Messenger of God, they will both evade it and, ever worse, protest against it.[23] The Muslims deal more mildly with the Jews and Christians. They revere Moses as well as Jesus, though they have some different ideas about them, especially about Jesus.

---

22 Muḥammad Saᶜīd b. (Aḥmad-i Fārūqī) Imām-i rabbānī Mujaddid-i alf-i thānī-i Sirhindī: *Maktūbāt-i saᶜīdiyya*, ed. ᶜAbd al-Majīd Aḥmad-i Sayfī-i Mujaddid-i Naqshbandī, litho., Lahore, 1385/1965, p. 56, ll. 19-20. Ibid., p. 66, ll. 5-6: The workshop of the knower of God is bound to seeing (*shuhūd*). In this respect there is no mutual exclusion between what one sees (*shuhūdāt*) and what one experiences inwardly (*wijdāniyyāt*). But how one is then judged and treated by God is wholly in accordance with the sentence 'I am as My bondsman thinks of Me'.

23 Christianity in principle does not dispute that within or even outside its own framework other prophets could appear after Jesus, and the Nestorian katholikos Timotheus I (d. 823 AD) between 786 and 795 AD fully acknowledged before the caliph Mahdī that Muḥammad had travelled 'the path of the prophets'. Hans Putman: *L'Église et l'Islam sous Timothée (780-823)*, Recherches publiées sous la direction de l'Institut de Lettres Orientales de Beyrouth, NS, B. Orient chrétien, tome III, Beirut, 1975, text and trans. § 158-168. None the less, the French explorer René Caillé, for example, in 1828 in Timbuktu reports that locals often pestered the English traveller, Major Laing, to force him to say the words 'There is no god but God. Muḥammad is the Messenger of God', and that Laing would only answer 'There is no god but God'. René Caillé: *Journal d'un voyage à Temboctou*, Brussels, 1830, II, p. 80.

Yet no Muslim will disparage Jesus or Mary.[24] Under the Fāṭimid Ḥākim (386-411/996-1021) it happened in Egypt that the holy books of the Jews and Christians were torn up and treated like waste paper.[25] But shortly before that in the year 972 AD when the abbot Majolus of Cluny was captured by the Saracens and a Saracen trampled his Bible under foot, some of the latter's comrades shouted at him saying one should not humiliate the great prophets like that.[26] They meant the men of God of the Old Testament such as Zacharias, and John the Baptist and Christ. In response to an inquiry, the Egyptian Mālikite Aḥmad b. Muḥammad, called Ibn Taqī (d. in the 9th/15th century), forbade the use of pages from the Bible for cleansing oneself after defecation, although its text had been falsified. He saw its holiness as being in its letters.[27] Muslim men of piety felt obliged to wage war against the philosophy of the Greeks, on the one hand, and that of the Brahmans, on the other, because they taught a view of the world based on reason without prophets. But with regard to belief in God-sent apostles, doubters, even deniers, arose among the Muslims, among them even such a man as the doctor and natural scientist Abū Bakr al-Rāzī (d. 313/925) who had been affected by Greek science.[28] Already earlier the ex-Muᶜtazilite and the notorious

---

24 Greffin Affagart: *Relation de Terre Sainte (1533-1534)*, ed. J. Chavanon, Paris, 1902, pp. 215-16: On the journey from Beirut to Damascus in 1534 the group was accompanied by a 'priest' of the Muslims who was very reasonable. Text: 'I frequently asked him what he thought about our religion but he always answered me very cautiously without saying anything bad about Christianity. He said there is only one difference between you and us, that we do not profess our faith in Muḥammad the way you do in Jesus Christ. (Namely) you readily profess that Jesus was a Messenger of God sent to bring the law of the Gospel, but we are unwilling to profess that Muḥammad was a Messenger of God sent to bring us this swinish law which you have.'

25 Silvestre de Sacy: *Exposé de la religion des Druzes*, Paris, 1838, I, p. CCCLXXIV.

26 Rodulfus Glaber: *Historiae*, lib. I, cap. IV, ed. Prou, p. 11. M. Reinaud: *Les invasions des Sarrazins*, Paris, 1836, pp. 204-05. R.W. Southern: *Western Views of Islam in the Middle Ages*, Harvard, 1962, p. 28, ftn. 25/Ger. trans. *Das Islambild des Mittelalters*, Kohlhammer, 1981, p. 76, no. 25.

27 Aḥmad Bābā al-Tinbuktī: *Nayl al-ibtihāj bi-taṭrīz al-Dībāj*, in the margin of Ibn Farḥūn: *Al-dībāj al-mudhahhab fī maᶜrifat aᶜyān ᶜulamāʾ al-madhhab*, Cairo, 1330, p. 77.

28 For a discussion of the subject cf. Abū Bakr Muḥammad b. Zakariyyāʾ al-Rāzī: *Rasāʾil falsafiyya* (Opera philosophica I), Cairo, 1939, pp. 291-316, ed. Paul Kraus. Kraus: 'Beiträge zur islamischen Ketzergeschichte. Das *kitāb az-zumurruḏ* des Ibn ar-Rāwandī', *RSO* 14, 1933-34, pp. 93-129, 335-79. Idem: *Epître de Bērūnī, contenant le répertoire des ouvrages de Muḥammad b. Zakarīyā ar-Rāzī*, Paris, 1936, p. 18, no. 138 (text?). Mahdī-i Muḥaqqiq:

arch-heretic Ibn al-Rāwandī (d. around 250/864) had attacked most fiercely and ridiculed belief in prophets and especially belief in Muḥammad. He had posed the not unjustified question as to whether the challenging power to convince of the doctrines of a Ptolemy or a Euclid proved that they were both prophets, because this was exactly what the Muslims maintained when they presented the Koran as proof of Muḥammad's prophethood.[29] The saying that Moses, Jesus and Muḥammad were the three greatest deceivers originates in Islam and was only later imputed to the Hohenstaufer Friedrich II (1212-1250) or the Hohenstaufer may have actually repeated it. The Muslims attribute it in the most succinct form to the Qarmaṭian from Laḥsā Abū Ṭāhir b. Abī Saᶜīd who carried off the Black Stone of the Kaᶜba from Mecca to Kūfa,[30] and in a more extended form to the Ismāᶜīlī and first Fāṭimid caliph ᶜUbaydallāh al-Mahdī (297-322/909-934) in Tunisia.[31] Yet Ibn al-Rāwandī is already meant to have described the alleged miracles of Abraham, Moses, Jesus and Muḥammad as a fraud (*makhārīq*).[32] The reputation of Muḥammad

---

Fīlsūf-i Ray Muḥammad b. Zakariyyāy-i Rāzī, Tehran, 1349, pp. 125-26, 160, 215, 267, 273, 275. Arthur J. Arberry: *The Spiritual Physick of Rhazes*, London, 1950, p. 9.

29 Hellmut Ritter: 'Philologika VI', *Der Islam* 19, 1931, p. 5/12-13. ᶜAbd al-Amīr al-Aᶜsam: *Tārīkh Ibn al-Rīwandī al-mulḥid*, Beirut, 1975, pp. 157-58, 196.

30 Niẓām al-Mulk: *Siyar al-mulūk* (*Siyāsatnāma*), ed. Hubert Darke, Tehran, 1962, pp. 287-88.

31 ᶜAbd al-Qāhir al-Baghdādī: *Al-farq bayn al-firaq*, ed. Muḥammad Zāhid b. al-Ḥasan al-Kawtharī, Cairo, 1948, p. 178, l. 18 to penult. line. On p. 182 Baghdādī reports that an apostate told him that the Qarmaṭians/Ismāᶜīlīs/Bāṭinites considered prophets like Noah, Abraham, Moses, Jesus, Muḥammad and others to be lawgivers and swindlers who had even used magic tricks in order to obtain power over the uneducated. — Both sources (Niẓām al-Mulk and Baghdādī) for the sentence about the three deceivers were discovered by Louis Massignon. Around 1335 AD the saying is attested in connection with Thomas Scotus who abandoned his religious order, and later in Aragon as well after 1380. Martin Grabmann: *Mittelalterliches Geistesleben*, II, 1936, p. 137. R.W. Southern: *Western Views of Islam in the Middle Ages*, p. 75, with ftn. 16/*Das Islambild des Mittelalters*, p. 53, with ftn. 16. Richard Walzer: *Al-Farabi on the Perfect State. Abū Naṣr al-Fārābī's Mabādiʾ ārāʾ ahl al-madīna al-fāḍila*, Oxford, 1985, p. 423. The saying has also been attributed to Ibn Rushd; Ernest Renan: *Averroès et l'Averroïsme*, Paris, 1852, pp. 295, 304, 428/reprint 1867, Veröffentlichungen des Institutes für Geschichte der Arabisch-Islamischen Wissenschaften, Frankfurt am Main, 1985, pp. 295, 304, 428. Cited in Léon Gauthier: *La théorie d'Ibn Rochd (Averroès) sur les rapports de la religion et de la philosophie*, Paris, 1909, pp. 2 and 4.

was somewhat undermined in India from two sides at once when the first millennium of Islam came to a close: on the one hand by the pontifical eclectic deism (*dīn-i ilāhī*) of the emperor Akbar (963-1014/1556-1605)[33] and then also by Sirhindī's speculations on prophecy and his own high saintly rank,[34] but in neither of the two cases because of thinking ill of the Prophet. Many a European, by making a careless remark or a clumsy allusion to Muḥammad open to misinterpretation, has come to experience the sensitivity of Muslims, and others in the Middle Ages had provoked them intentionally in order to suffer a martyr's death. There are laws for punishing insults to the Prophet. But we do not wish to discuss this any more than the somewhat divergent dogmatic teachings about Muḥammad, but only to mention a few questions concerning politeness toward him, with regard to which a pious Muslim can alternate between too much and too little.

Does it offend Muḥammad's honor if someone ascribes to him glorious deeds that he did not do? And what is glorious for him? In the 5th/11th century a Spanish religious scholar from Jazīrat Shuqr (Alcira on the Júcar, between Valencia and Denia) nurtured the conviction that Muḥammad had written the treaty of Hudaybiya himself, that he therefore was able to write which is no disgrace in itself but is rejected on theological grounds. But then in a dream he beheld the tomb of the Prophet in Medina which flew open and shook in an eerie manner. He repented and admitted that the Prophet had never written a single letter.[35] The idea that he was capable of reading and writing would not have excluded his possibly having copied out some of his revelations for others, and moreover contradicts Muḥammad's own statement that he was not able to write. But above all one must guard against statements which ascribe anything disadvantageous to the Prophet such as a military defeat. An imam in Cairo who committed an offense in this respect was first thrown in

---

32 Abū'l-Ḥusayn ᶜAbd al-Raḥīm b. Muḥammad b. ᶜUthmān al-Khayyāṭ al-Muᶜtazilī: *Al-intiṣār wa'l-radd ᶜalā'bn al-Rawandī al-mulḥid*, ed. and trans. by Albert N. Nader, Beirut, 1957, Arabic p. 12/French pp. 2-3/Aᶜsam: *Tārīkh Ibn al-Rīwandī*, pp. 19-20.

33 *EI*², s.v. Dīn-i Ilāhī (Aziz Ahmad). Emmy Wellesz: *Akbar's religious thought reflected in Mogul painting*, London, 1952, pp. 17-23.

34 Friedmann: *Shaykh Aḥmad Sirhindī*, pp. 61, 88-89, 96-101.

35 Ibn al-Abbār: *Al-takmila li-kitāb al-Ṣila*, ed. Codera, Madrid, 1889, I, pp. 453-54.

prison in 744/1343 and then sentenced to be flogged.[36] Does that mean, therefore, that one wished to maintain the truth regarding the Prophet? No, but to follow the traditional doctrine which was believed to be true, and to express the politeness (*adab*) which was considered necessary. Politeness toward the Prophet is a very serious matter and is just as much a duty as politeness toward God who, although He is behind everything that happens, ought not to be branded with an epithet corresponding to all the ugly and shameful things that take place. Qāḍī ᶜIyāḍ (d. 544/1149) gives instructions concerning how one should remain within the framework of politeness when describing the Prophet. One avoids ugly expressions like 'foolishness, lie, sin', one does not use the word 'ignorance' (*jahl*) if one asks rhetorically whether the Prophet did not have any knowledge before the revelations, one eschews the word 'sin' if one mentions his having committed small offenses.[37] The speaker must keep a tight rein on his tongue if he criticizes something in connection with the Prophet, even if he has no intention of belittling him. A slip of the tongue is not regarded as an excuse.[38] What is decisive is the remark made.[39] Qāḍī ᶜIyāḍ praises the forefathers for having eradicated unfavorable elements from the accounts of war and the descriptions about Muḥammad's life and for leaving out the attacks against him in their reports. The philologist and theologian Abū ᶜUbayd al-Qāsim b. Sallām (d. 224/838-839) considered the learned citation of even a half verse of a poem which abused Muḥammad as a sign of unbelief. In the old verse examples which he used for illustration in his books, he replaced the names of the reviled Muslims with other names that fit metrically so as not to be guilty of further disseminating the nasty rebukes against them and of course espe-

---

36 Maqrīzī: *Al-sulūk li-maᶜrifat duwal al-mulūk*, ed. Muḥammad Muṣṭafā Ziyāda, II, 3 (1958), p. 647, ll. 10-21.

37 Abū'l-Faḍl ᶜIyāḍ b. Mūsā al-Yaḥṣubī: *Al-shifā bi-taᶜrīf ḥuqūq al-Muṣṭafā*, ed. ᶜAlī Muḥammad al-Bajāwī, Cairo, 1977, pp. 1011-14.

38 Ibid., pp. 971-73.

39 Ghars al-Niᶜma Abū'l-Ḥasan Muḥammad b. Hilāl al-Ṣābiʾ (d. 480/1088): *Al-hafawāt al-nādira*, ed. Ṣāliḥ al-Ashtar, Damascus, 1967, is, as the title explains, a collection of 'peculiar slips' by persons for whom an unsuitable word in the presence of a ruler had unpleasant consequences, including cases in which the powerful man had a sufficient sense of humor and could laugh (for example, no. 27). However, in the eyes of their venerators God and Muḥammad understandably do not tolerate any fun, even if it is involuntary, and do not appear in such anecdotes. The author was born a Muslim. His father was a convert.

cially in order himself not to drag the honor of Muḥammad through the mud yet again.[40]

The question of the correct measure was raised for the general public for instance with regard to the formulas of blessing which it was customary to pronounce on behalf of Muḥammad, whether informally or on special occasions. Since according to tradition Muḥammad himself instituted rules about this, is one allowed to deviate from them following one's own discretion? Here piety (*ṭarīq al-birr*) toward the Prophet can exercise a moderating effect and restrain the more extreme swings of emotion on the part of the pious.[41] But others believed they could meet the requirements of piety better or at least just as well with new formulas.[42] A conflict flared up over the title *sayyid* 'lord' in the blessings pronounced on behalf of Muḥammad during acts of worship such as in the so-called 'final *tashahhud*' of the ritual prayers. Was one to say here 'Oh God, bless Muḥammad!' or 'Oh God, bless our *lord* Muḥammad!'? The Shāfiᶜite theologian ᶜIzz al-Dīn ᶜAbd al-ᶜAzīz b. ᶜAbd al-Salām (d. 660/1262) called the first form, i.e. the fundamentalist variant, 'obeying orders' (*imtithāl al-amr*), and the second form 'politeness' (*sulūk al-adab*). The Prophet had in fact only required 'Muḥammad', without 'lord'. But it was argued that one never introduced oneself as 'lord' and the Prophet had only wanted to be modest, that the forms of politeness in the course of time had also changed and grown more intricate and when referring to the Prophet one should keep abreast of the times. The Mālikite religious scholar Ubbī (d. 827-828/1423-25) approved of *mawlā* 'master' and *sayyid* 'lord', even where the two words were not transmitted by tradition,[43] and a student in Tunis who did not consider the title *sayyidunā* 'our lord' for Muḥammad in the prayers as necessary, escaped into hiding after being issued a summons to appear in court.[44] On the other hand,

---

40 *Shifā*, pp. 1002-03. It is a different matter when Ibn Khallikān omits three verses from those written by the highly esteemed poet Ṣurradurr (d. 465/1073) on behalf of the vizier Kundurī, because the latter was not pleased with them. Ibn Khallikān: *Wafayāt al-aᶜyān wa-anbāʾ abnāʾ al-zamān*, ed. Iḥsān ᶜAbbās, Beirut, 1972, p. 141, ll. 2-3.

41 Sakhāwī: *Al-qawl al-badīᶜ fī'l-ṣalāh ᶜalā'l-ḥabīb al-shafīᶜ*, Medina, 1977, p. 57.

42 Ibid., p. 59.

43 Muḥammad b. Khilfa al-Ubbī: *Ikmāl Ikmāl al-Muᶜlim*, II, p. 165 below, in *Ṣaḥīḥ Muslim* with the two commentaries Ubbī: *Ikmāl Ikmāl al-Muᶜlim*, and Muḥammad b. Muḥammad al-Sanūsī: *Mukammil Ikmāl al-Ikmāl*, reprint of the Cairo edition, Beirut, 1328.

44 Ubbī, ibid., II, pp. 165-66. Robert Brunschvig: *La Berbérie orientale sous les Ḥafṣides des origines à la fin du XVᵉ siècle*, Paris, 1940-47, II, p. 315. Wansharīsī: *Al-miᶜyār*

Maqrīzī, who in 805/1402-03 in the ᶜAmr Mosque in Cairo said 'and God bless our lord Muḥammad', was instructed by a colleague that it should only be 'Oh God, bless Muḥammad and the family of Muḥammad!' and thanked him for drawing his attention to the necessity of remaining true to the letter of tradition.[45] We cannot here pursue the long controversy over this question between those who would comply with the letter of tradition and those who were concerned with politeness. Another religious scholar in Lower-Egypt in the 10th/16th century was attacked because rather than adding the honorary title 'the best of Your creatures' for Muḥammad in the same formula, he preferred the meager original form without this title.[46] The traditionist Ibn al-Ṣalāḥ (d. 643/1245) permitted the people in his field of study, indeed encouraged them, when writing down the sayings of the Prophet not to be bound by their particular examples as regards putting in the formula of blessing but, exactly as in the case of God, to add the proper formula of their own accord whenever it was missing. Offenses against this politeness in Aḥmad b. Ḥanbal (d. 241/855) were to be excused, he said, because Aḥmad had often only pronounced the formula out loud but not written it. Others in the haste of writing had at least left a gap in order to add the formula later on.[47]

Discord also prevailed with regard to the treatment of the different prophets. Quite apart from the distinction between so-called prophets and so-called apostles of God, they do not all have an equally high status (surahs 17/55; 2/253). The most prominent from the Biblical era for a Muslim are Abraham and Moses. But although Muḥammad for a Muslim is unquestionably the highest prophet and apostle of God and is acknowledged as such in all Islamic professions of faith,[48] for the sake of politeness toward the others one should not

---

al-muᶜrib wa'l-jāmiᶜ al-mughrib ᶜan fatāwā ᶜulamāʾ Ifrīqiya wa'l-Andalus wa'l-Maghrib, ed. Muḥammad Ḥajjī, Beirut, 1982, XI, p. 81.

45 Sakhāwī: *Al-ḍawʾ al-lāmiᶜ li-ahl al-qarn al-tāsiᶜ*, Cairo, 1353-55, V, p. 164.

46 Shaᶜrānī: *Laṭāʾif al-minan wa'l-akhlāq fī bayān wujūb al-taḥadduth bi-niᶜmat allāh ᶜalā'l-iṭlāq*, Cairo, 1357, I, p. 217.

47 *Muqaddimat Ibn al-Ṣalāḥ wa-maḥāsin al-iṣṭilāḥ*, ed. ᶜĀʾisha ᶜAbd al-Raḥmān (Bint al-Shāṭiʾ), Cairo, 1974, pp. 306-09.

48 On this point see Henri Laoust: *La profession de foi d'Ibn Baṭṭa*, Damascus, 1958, French p. 112, ftn. 2. Jalāl al-Dīn-i Humāʾī: *Mawlawīnāma. Mawlawī chī mī gūyad? ᶜAqāʾid wa afkār-i Mawlānā Jalāl al-Dīn Muḥammad-i Mawlawī*, Tehran, 2536/1977, pp. 243-45.

always emphasize this. Already Muḥammad had not wanted this.[49] When mentioning a pre-Islamic prophet one often first pronounces a blessing on Muḥammad and only then on the older prophet, such as for instance: 'Abraham — God's blessing be upon our Prophet and upon him!' or something similar.

A pious individual is in a difficult dilemma if a person with some kind of leadership claims appears before the people and bases his authority on a dream in which he had beheld the Prophet. Indeed, there is a saying of Muḥammad's that specifies: 'If someone sees me in a dream, it is I; for Satan does not disguise himself in my form',[50] and moreover a Muslim should only think good of another Muslim. These sentences, which if taken at face value will render impossible any rational decision, were made use of in the first half of the 13th/19th century in sourthern Morocco by a certain Aḥmad b. Dāwūd al-Tīmlī, who gave himself the airs of a great Sufi, and it required the authority of a critical religious scholar to warn the people concerning him, as they had not dared to undertake anything against him.[51]

3. LAURELS, DESERVED OR UNDESERVED, FOR THE TWO LINEAGES OF RELIGIOUS ARISTOCRACY.

There are two groups of people intimately associated with Muḥammad who, though they stand below him in rank, enjoy, thanks to their closeness to him, special reverence, protection, consideration and indulgence. The one group consists of the ᶜAlids, especially in the narrow sense of the blood descendants of the Prophet through his daughter Fāṭima and her husband ᶜAlī b. Abī Ṭālib, i.e. the Ḥasanids and Ḥusaynids. In the Middle Ages a register of them was kept by local marshals of the aristocracy (*nuqabāʾ al-ashrāf*, sing. *naqīb*).[52] They have swollen to an incalculable multitude. The other group is the so-called 'Companions of the Prophet' (*ṣaḥāba*), Muslims who had had closer contact with Muḥammad and the last of whom, Abū'l-Ṭufayl ᶜĀmir b. Wāthila al-Kinānī, is meant to have

---

49 Muḥammad al-Mahdī b. Aḥmad al-Fāsī al-Qaṣrī (d. 1109/1698): *Maṭāliᶜ al-masarrāt bi-jalāʾ Dalāʾil al-khayrāt*, Cairo, 1970, p. 123.

50 *Concordance et Indices de la Tradition musulmane*, II, p. 200a. With a number of variants.

51 Muḥammad al-Mukhtār al-Sūsī: *Al-maᶜsūl*, Casablanca, 1960-62, VI, p. 61.

52 *EI* and *Handwörterbuch des Islam*, s.v. sharīf (C. van Arendonk).

died in the year 100/718-719 or somewhat later.[53] Naturally, their descendants have likewise attained a considerable number.

To begin with the ᶜAlids: Muḥammad had described his daughter Fāṭima as 'a piece of myself', and the Sufi Aḥmad Zarrūq (d. 899/ 1493) commented: 'The part is as inviolable (*ḥurma*) as the whole.'[54] Qāḍī ᶜIyāḍ wrote: 'Showing reverence (*tawqīr*) to the Prophet and piety (*birr*) toward him is also reverence to the people of his house and piety toward them.'[55] A certain Abū'l-ᶜAbbās Aḥmad al-Marīnī (7th/13th century) from the west repeatedly travelled to Mecca and Medina to distribute to the pious shrine residents (*mujāwirūn*) and to the poor money he had received for this purpose or obtained by begging. He left out the ᶜAlids because of their notorious indifference to Islamic law, until in a dream Fāṭima took him to task and said: 'After all your nose belongs to you even if it is affected with leprosy!' By this she meant to indicate that even the degenerate *ashrāf* were a part of her and of Muḥammad.[56] Impoverished ᶜAlids were especially dependent on private charity since they were excluded by the law from disbursements from the actual alms-tax. On the other hand, they were exempt from compulsory labor and they received state pensions. Often they were and still are favored for no other reason than that they are descendants of the Prophet. The Īl-Khān Ghāzān (d. 703/1304) who converted to the *sunna* gave preference in his religious foundations to needy ᶜAlids,[57] and the philologist Taftāzānī is supposed to have died in 792/1390 of grief after Tamerlane passed him over in favor of the ᶜAlid al-Sayyid al-Sharīf al-Jurjānī because of the latter's lineage.[58] In order to keep this blue blood pure, women in whose veins it flowed were coun-

---

53 *EI* and *Handwörterbuch des Islam*, s.v. aṣḥāb (I. Goldziher). Ibn ᶜAbd al-Barr: *Al-istīᶜāb fī maᶜrifat al-aṣḥāb*, ed. ᶜAlī Muḥammad al-Bajāwī, Cairo, n.d., II, pp. 798-99. Ibn Ḥajar al-ᶜAsqalānī: *Tahdhīb al-Tahdhīb*, Hyderabad, 1325-27, V, pp. 82-84. Idem: *Al-iṣāba fī tamyīz al-ṣaḥāba*, Cairo, 1323-25, VII, p. 110, no. 670.

54 *Concordance et Indices*, s.v. baḍᶜa, I, p. 187. Aḥmad Zarrūq: *Qawāᶜid al-taṣawwuf*, Cairo, 1388, p. 31.

55 Norman Cigar: *Muhammad al-Qadiri's* Nashr al mathani: *The chronicles*, London, 1981, Arabic p. 66/English p. 178.

56 Denis Gril: *La* Risāla *de Ṣafī al-dīn Ibn Abī l-Manṣūr Ibn Ẓāfir. Biographies des maîtres spirituels connus par un cheikh égyptien du VIIe/XIIIe siècle*, IFAO, 1986, Textes arabes et études islamiques XXV, Arabic p. 59/French pp. 152-53.

57 Ulrich Haarmann: *Geschichte der arabischen Welt*, Munich, 1987, p. 258.

58 Ṭāshkubrīzāda: *Al-shaqāʾiq al-nuᶜmāniyya fī ᶜulamāʾ al-dawla al-ᶜuthmāniyya*, Beirut, 1975, p. 29 below. *GAL S*, II, p. 301.

selled against marrying ordinary mortals,[59] and there was a tendency to regard children from such marriages as no longer being sherifs. 'Injustice perpetrated against us by them (the ᶜAlids)', said Zarrūq, 'we regard as destiny which is independent of any causation',[60] and Shaᶜrānī's teacher ᶜAlī al-Khawwāṣ (d. after 941/1534-35) repeats this in different words.[61]

Aḥmad al-Tijānī (d. 1230/1815) was entirely against people who associated with ᶜAlids only to acquire advantages by so doing, or indeed in order to cheat them.[62] Others, on the contrary, considered it an honor to be cheated by an ᶜAlid. Indeed, willingness to undertake this risk, incautiousness in associating with them, could only be construed as the best sign that one trusted them and thought well of them. In this regard it was mostly no more than a question of the authenticity of their family tree. The man of piety Abū'l-Ḥasan ᶜAlī b. Aḥmad al-Ḥarāllī (d. 638/1241, or one year earlier) in Bijāya (Bougie) did not show any discomposure when he was told that an alleged ᶜAlid whom he had accorded great respect and presented with an expensive cloak was the well-known so-and-so from Marrakesh (where Ḥarāllī was born). Ḥarāllī replied: 'We know exactly whom we have treated this way.' This means: Ḥarāllī did everything solely out of reverence for the Prophet. If the man was authentic, so much the better. In the opposite case, at least the intention (*niyya*) was achieved.[63] Therein lies the moral, according to Shaᶜrānī, ir-

---

59 *EI* and *Handwörterbuch des Islam*, sharīf. Aḥmad al-Tijānī in ᶜAlī Ḥarāzim b. al-ᶜArabī Barrāda al-Maghribī al-Fāsī: *Jawāhir al-maᶜānī wa-bulūgh al-amānī*, Cairo, 1383/reprint Beirut, I, pp. 83-84. Muḥammad Rashīd Riḍā (d. 1354/1935) defends the freedom of female ᶜAlids in this area. *Fatāwā al-imām Muḥammad Rashīd Riḍā*, ed. Ṣalāḥ al-Dīn al-Munajjid and Yūsuf Q. Khūrī, Beirut, 1970, I, no. 163, pp. 383-94.

60 Aḥmad Zarrūq: *Qawāᶜid al-taṣawwuf*, p. 31, l. 6.

61 Shaᶜrānī: *Laṭāʾif al-minan*, I, p. 219, ll. 28-32. The death date of Khawwāṣ is unclear. His student Shaᶜrānī mentions him as still being alive in 941/1534-35. Najm al-Dīn al-Ghazzī: *Al-kawākib al-sāʾira bi-manāqib aᶜyān al-miʾa al-ᶜāshira*, ed. Jibrāʾīl Sulaymān Jabbūr, Beirut, 1945 ff., II, p. 221, l. 23, and ᶜAbd al-Ḥayy b. al-ᶜImād: *Shadharāt al-dhahab fī akhbār man dhahab*, Cairo, 1350-51, VIII, pp. 233-34, gives his death as early as the year 939/1533. The correct title of Ghazzī's work is the one given above (thus in *Kawākib*, I, p. 7, ll. 3-4).

62 ᶜAlī Ḥarāzim: *Jawāhir al-maᶜānī*, I, p. 84.

63 Aḥmad b. Aḥmad b. ᶜAbdallāh al-Ghubrīnī: *ᶜUnwān al-dirāya fī-man ᶜurifa min al-ᶜulamāʾ fī'l-miʾa al-sābiᶜa bi-Bijāya*, ed. ᶜĀdil Nuwayhiḍ, Beirut, 1969, p. 147/Émile Dermenghem: 'Al-Hirrâlî', *AIEO* 7, 1948, p. 45.

respective of whether the sherif is genuine or contested.[64] Just as the Filālī of Morocco in the previous century assigned to every section of the army an ᶜAlid emir with the title 'sherif of the army' (*sharīf al-maḥalla*),[65] in the same way the Tijānī al-Ḥasan b. Aḥmad al-Kezūyī (d. 1347/1929), who gave away everything to sherifs, maintained a sherif who at times experienced exceptional spiritual states and was known among the people simply as 'the sherif'. Kezūyī defended him against critics, and against criticism of his lineage as well, and after his death had him buried with a copy of Jazūlī's *Dalāʾil al-khayrāt* so that he could continue to read it in the grave. He rejected every objection against burying the names of God contained in this book together with the corpse. A year later he had himself buried behind the sherif. 'His (Kezūyī's) politeness (*adab*) toward the descendants of the Prophet in words and deeds was indescribable.'[66] 'Behold this marvelous politeness toward the offspring of the blessed Prophet (even in his death)!'[67] Shaᶜrānī sees it as an honor that he only thinks well of the ᶜAlids and reveres them, and he enumerates some of the privileges that he ascribes to them. He writes:

'Another mercy which God has accorded me is my deep respect for the sherifs, even when people contest their lineage.[68] I consider showing them respect to be a duty which I owe to them... The least with which I can honor and respect a sherif is the reverence I display for instance to the governor of Egypt (or Cairo) or to the judge of the army... Part of the politeness due to sherifs is that one never sits on a rug or a seat or a bench if the sherif does not do so, in addition that one does not marry one of their divorced women or widows. One should also not marry a female sherif unless one is aware of the possibility of fulfilling her rights and always behaving in a way that pleases her. Otherwise, one should neither marry such a woman nor take her as a concubine, and one ought not to deny her the level of food and clothing one can afford, though she may be told: "Your ancestor, the Messenger of God, preferred this." Nor ought we to withhold from her any permitted pleasure she asks us for. We should bring her her sandals when she gets up and requires them, and should stand up when she appears, because she is a piece of the Messenger of

64 Shaᶜrānī: *Al-yawāqīt wa'l-jawāhir fī bayān ᶜaqāʾid al-akābir*, Cairo, 1959, II, p. 78, l. 6.

65 Sūsī: *Maᶜsūl*, XX, p. 19. Cf. ibid., XX, p. 40.

66 *Maᶜsūl*, XIX, p. 134.

67 *Maᶜsūl*, XIX, p. 135.

68 Differently in *Maᶜsūl*, II, p. 34, where Mālik demands the harshest punishment for false ᶜAlids.

God. It is also part of politeness that we should not look at any part of her body, either when buying or making a sale, unless it is our duty according to religious law. Thus we should not look at her foot if we are shoe sellers, and refrain from closely inspecting her shawl when she walks past, because all this would anger her ancestor if he caught us doing it. Moreover, politeness requires that we do not refuse a sherif anything he asks us for whether it be our daily food, our turban or an expensive outer garment, unless we have an excuse that the Prophet would accept, because all this (that we sacrifice in such a case) is no more than a speck of dust from the ground in comparison with the Messenger of God. We have dealt with what one's duty is toward the sherifs in the work *Al-baḥr al-mawrūd*,[69] and here in the *Laṭāʾif al-minan* we have already mentioned that we never open an assembly of recollection of God when a sherif is present without asking him to initiate it and then following him.'[70] — Cf. also *Laṭāʾif*, I, p. 111, and in more detail and with greater insistence *Laṭāʾif*, II, pp. 33-34 where Shaᶜrānī speaks of his love for the ᶜAlids.

Likewise, Shaᶜrānī gratefully prides himself on possessing the grace or virtue of paying a pilgrimage visit every year to all the graves of the family of the Prophet, which otherwise no one else does, whether out of ignorance of their location or because the people in Egypt have doubts about the authenticity of these graves. As far as Shaᶜrānī is concerned, the mere assumption (*ẓann*) is sufficient.[71] The culmination of this form of favorable thinking is reached when one transforms uncertainty into a certainty. One then loves and honors those who through this process of restyling have been drawn into the circle of acknowledged descendants of the Prophet even more than those whose family tree is uncontested! This thought as well is traceable back to Shaᶜrānī. It has appeared again in the attempt to ascribe an ᶜAlid genealogy to the founder of the Dār al-murābiṭīn, Wagāg b. Zallūy (spelt other ways as well) in Sūs in the 5th/11th century.[72] Well-known is the extreme reverence paid to the ᶜAlid

---

69 *GAL*, I, p. 337, no. 16.

70 *Laṭāʾif al-minan*, I, p. 107.

71 *Laṭāʾif*, II, p. 34, last three lines. And taken from the latter, Shabrāwī: *Al-itḥāf bi-ḥubb al-ashrāf*, Cairo, 1318, p. 33.

72 *Maᶜsūl*, II, pp. 31-32. 'Almoravids and Marabouts', p. 373. — Farīd al-Dīn-i ᶜAṭṭār makes the same kind of exaggerated demand on his readers when he places the shaykhs who maintain they were educated directly by the spirit-being of the Prophet instead of by a normal teacher, i.e. the *Uwaysiyān*, on the same level as those who had a normal teacher (*Tadhkirat al-awliyāʾ*, ed. Reynold A. Nicholson, London-Leiden, 1905, I, p. 24, ll. 7-12). Jāmī added to their number those who claimed to be educated not by the spirit-being of the Prophet but by that of a deceased shaykh (*Nafaḥāt al-uns*, ed. Tawḥīdīpūr, Tehran, 1336, pp. 20-21). On

Imams among the Shīᶜites, especially among the Sevener- and the Twelver-Shīᶜites. They are regarded as infallible. Should we speak of a chrīsma, an 'anointment', among the ᶜAlids which, despite their numbers, has enabled them to withstand becoming 'commonplace', in contrast to chárisma which can distinguish a single individual?

In earlier times the ᶜAlids were recognizable through two plaited braids. For this reason in Iraq billy-goats which had two strands of hair on their neck were called 'ᶜAlid he-goats' (sing. *tays ᶜalawī*) which an ignorant marshal of the ᶜAlid aristocracy who heard this expression in the cattle market of Baghdad took as referring to himself.[73] In Transoxania where the Ḥanafite-Māturīdite school of jurisprudence had struck deep roots, the Naqshbandī Niẓām al-Dīn-i Khāmūsh/Khāmōsh (9th/15th century) deemed himself fortunate not to live in a land where numerous ᶜAlids resided because he feared he would not be able to fulfill their high claim to honor. He knew that Abū Ḥanīfa (d. 150/767) during a teaching session had repeatedly risen to his feet and sat down again. In the courtyard children were playing, among them an ᶜAlid, and every time the ᶜAlid came within view he would stand up out of respect for him.[74] In the year 773/1371 the Mamluk Nāṣir al-Dīn Shaᶜbān in Cairo decreed that the ᶜAlids should wear green cloth on their turban.[75]

Now to turn to the others who stood in a closer relationship to Muḥammad: the Companions of the Prophet and their descendants! They as well ought to be especially respected and loved. On this subject Ḥarāllī writes:

Uwaysiyān see Richard Gramlich: *Die schiitischen Derwischorden Persiens. Zweiter Teil: Glaube und Lehre*, AKM XXXVI, pp. 235-36. Jāmī's contemporary ᶜUbaydallāh-i Aḥrār (d. 895/1490) maintains that among the ancient Israelites the people who exchanged high insights of wisdom with one another by simply being together without speaking were designated as *Burkhiyān* after a certain black slave whom God especially loved, Burkh-i Aswad from the time of Moses, and the *Uwaysiyān* were their counterpart in Islam; ᶜAlī b. Ḥusayn-i Kāshifī: *Rashaḥāt ᶜayn al-ḥayāt*, ed. ᶜAlī Aṣghar-i Muᶜīniyān, Tehran, 2536/1977, p. 103.

73 Muḥammad b. Hilāl al-Ṣābiʾ: *Al-hafawāt al-nādira*, no. 64. And a similar story from Kūfa, ibid., no. 65.

74 ᶜAlī b. Ḥusayn-i Kāshifī: *Rashaḥāt ᶜayn al-ḥayāt*, p. 467/Muḥammad Amīn al-Kurdī: *Al-mawāhib al-sarmadiyya fī manāqib al-naqshbandiyya*, Cairo, 1329, pp. 168-69.

75 *Die Chronik des Ibn Ijās*, ed. Mohamed Mostafa, Bibliotheca Islamica 5, 1 b; I, 2, pp. 107-08. Suyūṭī: *Al-ᶜajāja al-zarnabiyya fī'l-sulāla al-zaynabiyya*, in *Al-ḥāwī li'l-fatāwī*, Beirut, 1395/1975, II, pp. 33-34 (reprint 1352). Ignaz Goldziher: "ᶜAlī b. Mejmûn al-Maġribî und sein Sittenspiegel des östlichen Islam', *ZDMG* 28, 1874, p. 313.

'A sign of love for the Prophet is love for his descendants (i.e. the ᶜAlids), friendliness toward them and avoidance of criticizing (*intiqād*) them. No one who loves Muḥammad has ever criticized his descendants. A further sign of love for the Prophet, however, is love for his Companions as well, and a sign of love for his Companions is love for their descendants, especially the descendants (*awlād*) of Abū Bakr who placed Muḥammad above his own property and above himself and sacrificed his property and himself on the latter's behalf, and this he did in deeds, not just in words. And the same regarding the descendants of ᶜUmar who consumed his money and himself on behalf of the believers and the community of Muḥammad and through whom God opened up to them all the numerous cities and countries so that they could establish themselves there. And the same for the descendants of ᶜUthmān who held out steadfastly and did not seek to help himself although this possibility had existed, until finally God's decision regarding him came to pass. And the same also concerning the children and the descendants of all ten (to whom Muḥammad had promised Paradise), Zubayrids (not Zuhriyyīn), ᶜAwfids and ᶜUbaydids, the sons of Abū ᶜUbayda, as well as all the children of the Muhājirūn and Anṣār. Let the believer look upon them today just as he would have looked upon their fathers yesterday, if he had lived at the same time they did. Let him know that their seed is a pure seed and their progeny are a blessed progeny, and that when one of them is present at a gathering everyone receives his blessing (*baraka*). Let him not treat them the same as other people.[76] The Prophet said about the Anṣār (his Companions in Medina): "They fulfilled what was required of them, and what remains is the benefit they have in return."[77] In speaking thus the Prophet gives an indication of the high degree of blessing one can obtain from them, and the promise of bliss which one can receive from their glance at the end of time. The Prophet says: "People will then cry out: 'Oh would that I were an Azdite, and ah that my mother had been an Azdite!'"[78] May the believer avoid criticizing the children of

---

76 The MS has *wa-lā yusāwūhum*. I read *wa-an lā yusāwiyahum*.

77 Bukhārī, *manāqib al-anṣār* 11/trans. Houdas, III, pp. 8-9.

78 Something like this according to the MS, but the text is clearly corrupt. In Tirmidhī, *manāqib* 72/ed. Aḥmad Muḥammad Shākir and Ibrāhīm ᶜAṭwa ᶜIwaḍ, Cairo, 1937-65, V, p. 727, no. 3937: 'Oh would that my father had been an Azdite and my mother had been an Azdite!'

the Companions of the Prophet, as he avoids (he should avoid?) criticizing the descendants of the Messenger of God and the people of his house[79].'[80]

There then follows in the faulty manuscript that I have at my disposal a corrupt sentence which appears to say that these descendants of privileged family lines will not be judged by God for their actions as strictly as other people. In conclusion it is also noted that in certain regions the descendants of the Companions of the Prophet are designated as *ashrāf* (sing. *sharīf*) and the descendants of the Prophet himself (i.e. the ᶜAlids) and the people of the house as *sāda* (sing. *sayyid*).[81]

Qāḍī ᶜIyāḍ, as well as Hibatallāh al-Bārizī (d. 738/1338) when copying him, consider it to be respect and pious behavior toward the Prophet if one displays reverence (*tawqīr*) and pious behavior (*birr*) toward his Companions, acknowledges their rights and exemplariness, praises them, prays for their forgiveness, refrains from interfering in their disputes, stands up against those who have maintained a feud with them, detests any reports of historians and ignorant transmitters, false doctrine of the Shīᶜites and heretical innovators, which have attacked a single Companion of the Prophet, and strives to find for their discord the interpretation that would be most favorable for them and the best of solutions since this is what they deserve. A person should never refer to one of them slightingly but only mention their good sides, their merits, their glorious achievements and leave aside any controversial circumstances.[82] This is an unmistakable declaration of gratitude for services rendered by the Companions of the Prophet in the consolidation and spread of Islam, but at the same time represents a clear rejection of inquiry and the

---

79 Muḥammad's family including the women and relatives. A rather fluid concept; see *EI* sharīf and *EI*² ahl al-bayt. Muḥammad once defined the people of his house as consisting of the families of ᶜAlī, Jaᶜfar, ᶜAqīl and ᶜAbbās; Bārizī: *Tawthīq ᶜurā'l-īmān*, MS Sprenger 127a, 90b; W. Ahlwardt: *Verzeichniss der arabischen Handschriften der Königlichen Bibliothek zu Berlin*, I-X, Berlin, 1887-99, II, no. 2569.

80 Abū'l-Ḥasan ᶜAlī b. Ḥarāllī al-Tujībī: *Al-īmān al-tāmm bi-Muḥammad — ṣalla'llāhu ᶜalayhi wa-sallam*. The correct form probably *ᶜalayhi ('l-ṣalātu wa)'l-salām*. MS Sprenger 908, a, 36b-37a. Ahlwardt: *Verz. d. arab. Hss. Berlin*, II, no. 1743.

81 On the fluctuating terminology see Arendonk *EI*, sharīf.

82 ᶜIyāḍ: *Shifā*, pp. 611-12. Bārizī: *Tawthīq ᶜurā'l-īmān*, MS Sprenger 127a, 91b. — Cf. Sakhāwī: *Al-iᶜlān bi'l-tawbīkh li-man dhamma al-tārīkh*, Damascus, 1349, pp. 48 and 64/Franz Rosenthal: *A History of Muslim Historiography*, Leiden, 1952, pp. 265 and 288 (trans.).

publication of certain truths, a command to close one or both eyes to any unpleasantness which had occurred among them because one should only think and speak well of them. A good example of the viewpoint with which one should look at the past is provided by the case of the first Umayyad caliph Muᶜāwiya (41-60/661-680). Muᶜāwiya had indeed been wrong, according to Qushayrī (d. 465/1072), in entering the field against ᶜAlī, but he had been striving after what is right. Therefore the believers did not consider him to be a sinner (*fāsiq*) against religion but thought well of him, since he was after all a Companion of the Prophet, had written down the Koran and had done penance, and the Prophet had expressly given the order not to revile his Companions.[83] Shaᶜrānī tacitly agrees with Qushayrī when he concedes that both ᶜAlī and Muᶜāwiya had only wanted what is right although they had sought it in different ways: ᶜAlī had wanted to postpone taking revenge for ᶜUthmān's murder, whereas Muᶜāwiya wanted revenge immediately.[84] One is obliged to acknowledge that the Companions of the Prophet one and all strove after what is right and to think well of them (*wujūban li-iḥsān al-ẓann bihim*) and to love fully the ᶜAlids out of respect for their progenitor Muḥammad.[85] However, with regard to the ᶜAlids and the Companions of the Prophet Shaᶜrānī requires that the caliphs Abū Bakr, ᶜUmar and ᶜUthmān be placed before ᶜAlī, as occurred in history, but that the descendants of Fāṭima and ᶜAlī, i.e. the ᶜAlids, be placed before the descendants of Abū Bakr, not out of natural love but in order to maintain a balance as the Prophet did.[86] Thus even among the Sunnīs the ᶜAlids enjoyed a certain precedence over the descendants of 'the Companions of the Prophet'. The learned Naqshbandī Aḥmad al-Fārūqī al-Sirhindī (d. 1034/1624) represents the same opinion as Qushayrī and Shaᶜrānī. He characterizes Muᶜāwiya's political mistake against ᶜAlī as simply an error in seeking the law and what is right (*khaṭaʾ ijtihādī*) which would not brand anyone as an unbeliever.[87] This is exactly the line of thinking

83 Richard M. Frank: 'Two short dogmatic works of Abū'l-Qāsim al-Qushayrī', *MIDEO* 16, 1983, Arabic p. 73/English p. 91.

84 Shaᶜrānī: *Al-yawāqīt wa'l-jawāhir*, II, p. 77 below.

85 *Yawāqīt*, II, pp. 77-78.

86 *Laṭāʾif al-minan*, II, p. 81.

87 Aḥmad al-Fārūqī al-Sirhindī: *Muᶜarrab/Muᶜarrib al-maktūbāt*, Arabic translation by Muḥammad Murād al-Qazānī/al-Qāzānī al-Makkī, Acre, 1317/1899 (reprint Istanbul, n.d.), I, p. 230, letter no. 251. — Herewith a certain allowance is made for error. Along with mistakes which occur in efforts involving juridical research (*khaṭāy-i ijtihādī*), there are also mis-

in the modern oecumenical Association for the Rapprochement of the Islamic Denominations where the oppositions are not to be eliminated but an effort of mutual conciliation is undertaken since differences of opinion in striving for what is correct (*ikhtilāf ijtihādī*) do not necessarily have to lead to hatred and hostility.[88]

Just as the recommendation to think well of people inclined the pious to allow a dubious descendant of ᶜAlī to be regarded as an ᶜAlid rather than to drive him away, by the same token the fear of denying a Companion of the Prophet his due respect also protected dubious Companions of the Prophet from premature rejection or even from being subjected to closer examination. The mere fact that such persons were alleged to belong to this category was sufficient as an *argumentum ad verecundiam*. To take an example from the west of the Islamic world: there among the contested Companions of the Prophet were reckoned seven legendary members of the Berber tribe Ragrāga from western Morocco which, as it seems, in the 6th/12th century was pushed out of its territory north-west of the High-Atlas and partially went south to the Anti-Atlas where it became dispersed over wide areas. A well-known legend has it that the seven men from the then allegedly Christian tribe wandered eastwards to Muḥammad and then brought Islam to the west directly from its source.[89] One of them died along the way but was later exhumed and transferred to the west. Their scattered graves today still form the stations of a yearly procession of pilgrims, and if someone from the far west un-

---

takes or errors connected with mystical experiences (*khaṭāy-i kashfī*), i.e. with supernatural vision and inspirations. For this the inspired individual himself is likewise not held responsible, whereas a person who adopts this error without examining it is at fault. In the case of a legal error, on the other hand, neither the one who formulates the false legal judgement nor the person who follows it in good faith is considered at fault (Kishmī: *Barakāt al-aḥmadiyya*, p. 211, l. 16 to end of page). But in both cases one should be attentive enough not to follow a false statement (Kishmī, p. 227, ll. 9-11). Friedmann: *Sirhindī*, p. 64.

88 Muḥammad Muḥammad al-Madanī (ed.): *Daᶜwat al-taqrīb min khilāl Risālat al-islām*, Cairo, 1966, p. 289, ll. 20-21. In Arabic the association is called *Jamāᶜat/Jamᶜiyyat (dār) al-taqrīb bayn al-madhāhib al-islāmiyya*; in English, for instance, Society for Taqreeb (Rapprochement) among Muslim Schools, but other ways as well. Muḥammad Rashīd Riḍā (d. 1354/1935) is for investigating the truth in the case of Muᶜāwiya, but for maintaining peace. *Fatāwā al-imām Muḥammad Rashīd Riḍā*, ed. Munajjid and Khūrī, Beirut, 1970, II, nos. 198 and 289. Against cursing Muᶜāwiya, ibid., II, no. 166.

89 Muḥammad is said to have spoken Berber with them. With Salmān al-Fārisī he is supposed to have spoken Persian. Qalqashandī: *Ṣubḥ al-aᶜshā*, Cairo, 1963 ff., I, p. 166.

dertakes the *ḥajj* to Mecca, he will often first complete the circuit of these seven indigenous saints. To omit to do so could be interpreted as impoliteness (*sūʾ adab*) toward the Companions of the Prophet.[90] The religious scholar Abū ʿAbdallāh Muḥammad b. Saʿīd al-Marghītī (resided in Marrakesh, d. 1089/1678[91]) was perfectly familiar with the doubts regarding the legend but warned against denying the Companionship with the Prophet (*ṣuḥba*) of the seven men. He ordered that one should show them politeness and take them as examples to follow. Showing them reverence (*ḥurma*) was part of showing reverence to the Prophet. Muḥammad had left behind 124,000[92] disciples, and more than 70 biographies and a great number of collections of sayings had been compiled about him. No one knew all this material. But as Mālik had expressed it, one should leave people in 'the breadth of God's mercifulness and in the spaciousness of their religion', i.e. in their not too strictly regimented religiosity. In any case, a lack of knowledge did not justify rejection. God did not want their acceptance, which was so generally spread throughout the west, to be abolished. Aside from the famous personalities who had taken part in the pilgrimage in question, 'those who can see the dead' (*ahl al-kashf*, meaning *kashf al-qubūr*) were convinced of the authenticity of the graves. One of them had visited the seven before his pilgrimage to Mecca, in order not to behave impolitely. Another had first waited for permission from God (in a dream or in a vision) to visit them before setting out on his journey to the east. Marghītī concludes with admonition not to presume to pass judgement on things which one does not understand. 'I do not know' was for people like him (Marghītī) a form of worship. In this way a person's religion and the peace of certainty would be best preserved.[93] To this day doubts about the Companionship of the seven Ragrāga with the Prophet have not been cleared up, and the dividing line between the credulous and the incredulous by no means corresponds to that between those who are pious and those who are not. The learned source from whom we have taken the above information, Muḥammad al-Mukhtār al-Sūsī (d. 1383/1963), rejects the authenticity of the seven Ragrāga just as does the mystic ʿAbd al-ʿAzīz

---

90 *Maʿsūl*, VIII, p. 200.

91 The date of his death given in Ibn Sūda: *Dalīl muʾarrikh al-Maghrib al-aqṣā*, Casablanca, 1960, no. 430.

92 *Maʿsūl*, IV, p. 13, ll. 15-16. Ibid., IV, p. 16, l. 15, gives the figure 114, 000.

93 *Maʿsūl*, IV, pp. 12-16 (in excerpts). More information on the Ragrāga, ibid., IV, pp. 5-10; III, pp. 109-10; V, pp. 305-23; VIII, p. 200; XI, p. 290; XIV, pp. 137-38; XVII, p. 5.

al-Dabbāgh (d. 1132/1719).[94] Rather the boundary lies between those who exercise criticism and those who do not. The independent religious scholar al-Ḥasan b. Masᶜūd al-Yūsī (d. 1102/1691) cautiously manoeuvred between the two opposing views. He participated as an observer in a procession to the graves of the Ragrāga in the year 1095/1684, but did not take part in many of the practices so as not to furnish the common people with an argument on behalf of their excesses and abuses.[95] The modern historian of Safi Muḥammad b. Aḥmad al-ᶜAbdī al-Kānūnī: *Āsafī wa-mā ilayhi*, Cairo 1353/1934, pp. 22-27, acknowledges the doubts concerning the authenticity but retreats piously to the neutral position of Maghrītī.

The situation is not much better with the graves of other Companions of the Prophet in Algeria and Tunisia who do not originate from the country itself but are supposed to have migrated there from Arabia.[96] The early date of the false saying of the Prophet that a Companion who dies in a foreign land will be the leader and the light of the local people at the Resurrection[97] presupposes that the tendency to form legends about such graves had already begun toward the end of the first century of the Islamic era, and must have subsequently continued to promote this tendency.

A still more dubious group of Companions of the Prophet consists of the *jinn* who are supposed to have heard the Prophet reciting the Koran during his morning prayers in the Nakhla valley. Their number oscillates between 7, 8 and 9,[98] and when it comes to their names the matter is also not clearly worked out. But Islamic religious

---

94 Aḥmad b. al-Mubārak al-Lamaṭī: *Al-ibrīz*, Cairo (Ibn Shaqrūn), n.d., p. 118.

95 Al-Ḥasan al-Yūsī: *Al-muḥāḍarāt*, ed. Muḥammad al-Ḥajjī, Rabat, 1976, p. 44.

96 Miklos Muranyi: *Die Prophetengenossen in der frühislamischen Geschichte*, Bonn, 1973, pp. 158-64. — Graves like these are found in very many places outside Arabia.

97 Albrecht Noth: *Quellenkritische Studien zu Themen, Formen und Tendenzen frühislamischer Geschichtsüberlieferung*, I, Bonn, 1973, pp. 52-53. Muranyi, pp. 155-58. Tirmidhī, *manāqib* 59, V, p. 697, no. 3865. Al-Khaṭīb al-Baghdādī: *Tārīkh Baghdād*, Cairo, 1931, I, p. 128, ll. 1-3.

98 For example they are seven in Abū Nuᶜaym al-Iṣbahānī: *Ḥilyat al-awliyā᾽ wa-ṭabaqāt al-aṣfiyā᾽*, Cairo, 1932-38, VII, p. 395, ll. 13-14; Ibn Ḥajar al-ᶜAsqalānī: *Al-iṣāba*, III, p. 17, penult. line; in codex E in Ferdinand Wüstenfeld: *Das Leben Muhammed's nach Muhammed Ibn Ishâk bearbeitet von Abd el-Malik Ibn Hischâm*, Göttingen, 1858-60, II, p. 41 below; and in Nöldeke-Schwally: *Geschichte des Qorāns*, Leipzig, 1909, I, p. 132, ftn. 6. Eight in Nöldeke-Schwally, I, p. 133. Nine in the following: ᶜAsqalānī: *Iṣāba*, I, p. 27, no. 77; Damīrī: *Ḥayāt al-ḥayawān al-kubrā*, s.v. *jinn*, Cairo, 1356, I, p. 207, l. 5/al-Ḥākim al-Naysābūrī: *Al-mustadrak*, III, p. 519. Some sources do not mention a number.

scholarship has accepted them among the Companions of the Prophet.[99] The last of them, or next to last, is supposed to have been found as a dead snake and been carefully buried wrapped in a piece of cloth.[100] Ḥasan al-Baṣrī (d. 110/728) is meant to have been asked whether any one of these *jinn* was still alive. He referred to a 135-year-old contemporary who claimed to have himself buried the last one in the form of a snake.[101] No consideration is given to any descendants of them. Consequently at any time an invented story could make use of this motif. The Prophet did not himself see this category of his disciples, but they beheld him.

4. RESTRICTED AREAS WHERE ONLY THINKING WELL, NOT A KNOW-IT-ALL ATTITUDE, IS ALLOWED TO ENTER.

Aḥmad-i Jām (d. 536/1141) wrote: 'Thinking well of God is very good but to think that way of people is also good.'[102] This principle safeguarded many established judgements, notions and practices. It was thought necessary to condemn chroniclers and historians as having a passion for dragging out into the open whatever was bad and detrimental apparently because with their disclosures they catered to the reader's love of the sensational, perhaps also because they were too impartial toward the theologians. Qāḍī ᶜIyāḍ, and in his wake Bārizī, frown upon 'history writers' (*muʾarrikhūn*) altogether. They do not distinguish between good ones and bad ones (see earlier p. 612). Perhaps they have in mind the general denigration of the Umayyads.[103] The historian of Jerusalem and Hebron Mujīr al-Dīn al-Ḥanbalī (wrote in 900/1495, with later additions) follows the guideline of leaving aside anything that is unpleasant. He states explicitly that he has only mentioned what is praiseworthy and has not reported anything dishonorable about each personality he has devoted an article to or whose dates he records. Most chroniclers, he is

---

99 Ibn Ḥajar al-ᶜAsqalānī: *Iṣāba*, I, p. 4 below; III, p. 18, l. 1.

100 As the last, for example, in *Ḥilyat al-awliyāʾ*, II, p. 305, l. 6. As next to last, e.g., in Wüstenfeld: *Das Leben Muhammed's*, II, p. 42, ll. 3-4/Damīrī, I, p. 207, ll. 12-13.

101 *Ḥilya*, II, pp. 304-05. This would come to about the same time as indicated in Wüstenfeld, II, pp. 41-42/Damīrī, I, p. 207, ll. 9-13, according to whom the dead snake was buried by the Umayyad ᶜUmar b. ᶜAbd al-ᶜAzīz. — Regarding the *jinn* in Sunni theology cf. Ibn Taymiyya's summary *Īḍāḥ al-dalāla fī ᶜumūm al-risāla*, in *Majmūᶜat al-rasāʾil al-munīriyya*, Cairo, 1343/reprint Beirut, 1970, II, 2, no. 5, pp. 97-152.

102 *Rawḍat al-mudhnibīn*, p. 170, ll. 16-17.

103 Franz Rosenthal: *A History of Muslim Historiography*, 1952, pp. 56-57.

aware, did the very opposite. That is a mistake, however, and a disparagement of the dead.[104] Muḥammad b. Muḥammad al-Ṣaghīr al-Shingīṭī al-Tishītī (still alive after 1320/1902) refers to an alleged *ḥadīth* which condemns anyone who despises and forgets his Muslim brother, and enjoins friendship with the latter and thinking well of him, and he refers to a second *ḥadīth* which praises most highly thinking well of God and one's fellow-man and disapproves of thinking ill of God and one's fellow-man as the worst of behavior.[105] In Tishītī's eyes it is even thinking bad of someone if you describe a person who believes he has beheld the Prophet in a waking state as having misconstrued an experience of psychic rapture,[106] this being a reinforced new variant of the warning of the *ḥadīth* against excessive scepticism toward the Prophet's appearance after death which was briefly mentioned at the end of section 2. There it was a question of a dream image, whereas here his concrete presence among later generations is meant. With regard to thinking well of people unanimity did not always prevail. The important Mālikite Bāqillānī (d. 403/1013) discusses such a case: 'If someone claims that Abū Ḥanīfa considered it permissible to recite the Koran in Persian and to say the ritual prayers in Persian, one must first know where the person found this information. If he backs down and says he only claimed this because he had a favorable opinion (*ḥusn al-ẓann*) of Abū Ḥanīfa, he must be told that someone with a favorable opinion of Abū Ḥanīfa would not maintain this about him.'[107] Similarly, Muḥammad Zāhid b. al-Ḥasan al-Kawtharī (d. 1371/1952) did not allow himself to include demons and people of exceptionally old age in his chains of transmission because the blessing hoped for by means of short connecting lines to the Prophet would be undone again by this kind of fraud.[108] Ibn Ḥazm (d. 456/1064) warns against too good an estimation (*ḥusn al-ẓann*) of the discourses of false theologians.[109] On the other hand, one could relax a bit the standards of acceptance for

---

104 *Al-uns al-jalīl bi-tārīkh al-Quds wa'l-Khalīl*, Amman, 1973, II, p. 101.

105 *Al-jaysh al-kafīl bi-akhdh al-tha'r mimman salla ʿalā'l-shaykh al-Tijānī sayf al-inkār*, in the margin of Muḥammad al-ʿArabī b. al-Sāʾiḥ al-Sharqī al-ʿUmarī: *Bughyat al-mustafīd li-sharḥ Munyat al-murīd*, Cairo (Ibn Shaqrūn), n.d., p. 77.

106 Ibid., p. 61.

107 Abū Bakr al-Bāqillānī: *Nukat al-intiṣār li-naql al-qurʾān*, ed. Muḥammad Zaghlūl Salām, Alexandria, 1971, p. 339.

108 ʿAbd al-Fattāḥ Abū Ghudda in his edition of ʿAlī al-Qārī al-Harawī: *Al-maṣnūʿ fī maʿrifat al-ḥadīth al-mawḍūʿ*, Aleppo, 1969, p. 219, ftn.

109 *Al-fiṣal fī'l-milal wa'l-ahwāʾ wa'l-niḥal*, Cairo, 1321, IV, p. 207 below.

chains of transmission in the case of *ḥadīth*s whose content appeared in some way to be advantageous to a person and in the case of *ḥadīth*s about glorious deeds and good qualities (*aḥādīth al-manāqib wa'l-faḍā'il*) which did not regulate any legal questions but described individuals,[110] as well as when they had to do with undertaking pious practices at times not prescribed for them, such as fasting in Rajab.[111] According to Shaᶜrānī, it can happen that trust in the forefathers (*iḥsānan li'l-ẓann bi-salafihim*) correctly bridges a gap in the tradition before one has succeeded in providing proof scientifically. Thus it was, according to Shaᶜrānī, with regard to implanting the recollection of God in individual persons by the Prophet long before Sufism as we know it. The breakthrough to scientific acknowledgement of this (alleged) fact was first achieved by Shaykh Yūsuf al-ᶜAjamī al-Kūrānī (d.768/1367). The personal connection of al-Ḥasan al-Baṣrī (d. 110/728) to ᶜAlī (d. 40/661) and along with it the first investiture of a patched frock had supposedly been proven by Ibn Ḥajar al-ᶜAsqalānī (d. 852/1449) and Suyūṭī (d. 911/1505).[112] Thus it could be more correct to uphold the unexamined tradition shaped by numerous kinds of objectives than to criticize it. In such a case trusting faith did not stand in contradiction to the search for truth but was in fact in its service and only had precedence over it in so far as faith made it at all possible in the first place. In this sense then the whole of modernistic Koranic interpretation as well should or could certainly feel itself obliged to maintain favorable opinion toward revelation, for without long-term patience, trust and faith (instead of premature rejection) the *jinn* would never have allowed themselves to be identified as the bacilli that cause illness[113] and the possibility of Muḥammad's ascension would never have been proven by the latest successes in space travel which has ovecome the earth's

---

110 'A Resurrection of Muḥammad in Suyūṭī', p. 542. Suyūṭī in *Al-la'ālī' al-maṣnūᶜa fī'l-aḥādīth al-mawḍūᶜa*, Cairo, n.d., I, p. 461, also refers to the tolerance of Aḥmad b. Ḥanbal with regard to these *aḥādīth al-faḍā'il*.

111 M.J. Kister: '"Rajab is the Month of God..."', in *Studies in Jāhiliyya and Early Islam*, XII, p. 213.

112 Shaᶜrānī: *Al-anwār al-qudsiyya fī maᶜrifat qawāᶜid al-ṣūfiyya*, Cairo, 1962, I, pp. 27-30. Cf. Aḥmad b. Muḥammad al-Ghumārī: *ᶜAlī b. Abī Ṭālib imām al-ᶜārifīn aw Al-burhān al-jalī fī taḥqīq intisāb al-ṣūfiyya ilā ᶜAlī*, Cairo, 1970, pp. 213-21.

113 Ignaz Goldziher: *Die Richtungen der islamischen Koranauslegung*, Leiden, 1920, p. 356.

gravity.[114] In short, one must carry on maintaining an attitude of trust until the time is ripe for knowledge.

Old graves can also be the object of both forms of consideration, on the one hand of reverence and on the other, of investigation. Reverence puts trust in tradition, whereas investigation mistrusts it, can either confirm it one way or another, or can reject it one way or another. The grave of the female ancestor of certain Tuaregs, Tin Hinan 'She of the Tents', was excavated and something was actually found in it.[115] No one, however, would dare to doubt the authenticity of Muḥammad's grave in Medina, although Muslims do hold the opinion that many graves of prophets are uncertain or false.[116] The grave of the Prophet in Medina is in fact the only one which is thought to be sure. Regarding Abraham, all that is certain according to Muslim belief is that he is buried in Hebron but no one knows in which grave.[117] The Muslims say that the Franks who held Hebron 487-583/1094-1187 had arbitrarily determined which were the graves of Abraham, Isaac, Jacob, Joseph and Sarah.[118] Nevertheless, one should visit all of the local graves of prophets, saints, theologians, martyrs and men of piety. Even if there are some fake graves among them, one will still acquire the reward for a good intention

---

114 In a section dealing with the old doubt concerning the physical ascension of Muḥammad, Jalāl al-Dīn-i Humāʾī: *Mawlawīnāma*, p. 733, writes in conclusion: 'I would add that the progress of the most recent positive sciences and the astonishing experiments of space travellers in ascending to the spheres and in flying to the planets have proven the doubts of the philosophers to be untenable and removed the main object of the difficulties'. — But Humāʾī himself professes faith in a reinterpretation: in his view Muḥammad exchanged a merely 'qualitative nearness' for an 'essential nearness' to God and progressed from mere 'knowledge of certainty' to 'certainty itself' and 'its truth' (*ʿilm al-yaqīn, ʿayn al-yaqīn, ḥaqq al-yaqīn*). That is his *miʿrāj*. Ibid., pp. 735-36.

115 H.T. Norris: *Saharan Myth and Saga*, Oxford, 1972, pp. 28-29. Idem: *The Tuaregs. Their Islamic Legacy and Its Diffusion in the Sahel*, Warminster Wilts., 1975, p. 31. Jeremy Keenan: *The Tuareg*, London, 1977, pp. 20-23. Marceau Gast: 'La société traditionnelle des Kel Ahaggar', in : *Islam, Société et Communauté, Anthropologie du Maghreb*, Paris, 1981, p. 117.

116 ʿIyāḍ b. Mūsā: *Tartīb al-madārik wa-taqrīb al-masālik li-maʿrifat aʿlām madhhab Mālik*, Rabat, 1965 ff., II, p. 102/ed. Aḥmad Bukayr Maḥmūd, Beirut, 1965-68, I-II, p. 212, l. 13.

117 Ibn al-Ḥājj: *Al-mudkhal*, Cairo, 1929, IV, p. 244. Mujīr al-Dīn al-Ḥanbalī: *Al-uns al-jalīl*, II, p. 76. Yūsuf Rāghib: 'Deux monuments fatimides au pied du Muqaṭṭam', *REI* 1978, p. 92, with ftn. 1.

118 *Mudkhal*, IV, p. 245.

(*niyya jamīla*).[119] This was said of other graves as well.[120] Undertaking excavation of the Prophet's grave in Medina for the purpose of attaining scientific certainty and knowledge of other facts is out of the question because prophets, according to the majority of Islamic theologians, live on within their graves or in heaven or in Paradise, and naturally Muḥammad ought not to be disturbed. But at the same time it would be a violation of the area of tabu around the Prophet, into which only thinking well of someone and not the simple desire for knowledge ought to penetrate. The whole of Medina, in itself quite cheerful, was transformed into a holy city, less because of the numerous ᶜAlids who resided there than because of the serious head of the Medinan school of jurisprudence, Mālik (d. 179/795), such that one ought not even to criticize its soil (*turba*) although it is not of the best quality. Mālik condemned a man to corporal punishment because he had described Medina's earth as 'wretched' (*radīʾa*).[121]

---

119 *Mudkhal*, IV, p. 247.

120 Ibn al-Zayyāt: *Al-kawākib al-sayyāra fī tartīb al-ziyāra*, Baghdad, n.d., p. 141 below; p. 283, ll. 4-5/Sakhāwī: *Tuḥfat al-aḥbāb wa-bughyat al-ṭullāb fī khiṭaṭ wa'l-mazārāt wa'l-tarājim wa'l-biqāᶜ al-mubārakāt*, Cairo, 1937, p. 264, ll. 3-4; p. 374, l. 4. Dubious is a complex of walls located on the mountain to the north of Shiraz where occasionally people who turn to ᶜAlī with firm belief have their wishes fulfilled, although ᶜAlī was never in that region. This is reported by Mīrzā Furṣat-i Shīrāzī: *Āthār-i ᶜajam*, litho., Bombay, 1354, p. 480. And by way of illustrating how such localities become sanctified he relates that one time someone sat down on the grave of a non-Muslim and a passer-by asked him for the name of the grave. For fun he described it as the grave of a saint. The next day the man went there, recited the first surah of the Koran and expressed a wish. Thanks to his firm belief and his sincere intention his wish was fulfilled. Furṣat designates the locality near Shiraz as Chāh-i Murtaḍā ᶜAlī. But other more recent authors call the place Chāh-i Murtāḍ ᶜAlī, i.e. they assign it to an otherwise unknown ascetic. Ḥasan-i Imdād: *Shīrāz dar gudhashta wa ḥāl*, Shiraz, 1339, p. 195. Muḥammad Taqī-i Muṣṭafawī: *Iqlīm-i Pārs*, Tehran, 1343, p. 55. Raḥmatallāh-i Mihrāz: *Buzurgān-i Shīrāz*, Tehran, 1348, p. 4. Another story about how something like this can take place is found in A. Jaussen: *Coutumes des Arabes au pays de Moab*, Paris, 1908, p. 301: In Zerqā, not far from ᶜAmmān, a farmer buried the head of a boar that he had killed, surrounded it with stones, set up a *rujum* and said for fun: 'This is shaykh Khanzīr.' A little while later another farmer who worked his field nearby placed his implements under the protection of the alleged grave of the saint. A third farmer wanted to make use of them illegitimately. Thereupon the oxen refused to render him service, and one of them even fell down dead struck by an invisible stone. The farmer put the implements back, and fear of the *walī* Khanzīr spread throughout the region.

121 *Shifā*, p. 620. Bārizī, MS Sprenger 127a, 93a. Muḥammad b. ᶜAbdallāh al-Zarkashī: *Iᶜlām al-sājid bi-aḥkām al-masājid*, ed. Abū'l-Wafā Muṣṭafā al-Marāghī, Cairo, 1384, p. 272 below.

Moreover, he would not allow himself to ride a mount over this holy earth.[122] Subsequently, this developed into a custom, and many people would only walk about barefoot.[123] Mālik reminded the caliph Manṣūr in Muḥammad's sepulchral mosque of God's command (surah 49/2, etc.) to be quiet before the Prophet. For one should honor him just as if he were still alive.[124] Some pious individuals turned down invitations to teach *ḥadīth* in the sepulchral mosque[125] or to give a Friday sermon or any ceremonial sermon at all, out of respect for the Prophet.[126] To strut about in Medina made an unfavorable impression.[127] In order to counteract the dirtying of the city and its surroundings Ibn al-Ḥājj (d. 737/1336) thought it best to advise against pious residence (*mujāwara*) in excess of what was required for a visit to the grave.[128] Decreasing reverence associated with longer residence also spoke in favor of this.[129] Shaᶜrānī was happy that he had never let himself be seduced by a *mujāwara* in Mecca because he would not have been able to muster the necessary piety for it. He censures someone who in 953/1547 at his house in Mecca had unrestrainedly disparaged an acquaintance in Medina,[130] and is aware that being with a person too frequently diminishes the respect one has for him.[131] The circumstances at Muḥammad's grave itself and the events that have taken place there cannot be described here. In addition let it simply be mentioned that at the time of the Prophet no prayer-niche (*miḥrāb*) had yet existed in the mosque. It

---

122 ᶜIyāḍ: *Tartīb al-madārik*, Rabat, II, pp. 53, 102/Beirut, I-II, pp. 180, 212. Samhūdī: *Khulāṣat al-Wafā bi-akhbār dār al-Muṣṭafā*, Medina, 1972, p. 132.

123 Numerous references to this in primary sources.

124 *Tartīb al-madārik*, Rabat, II, p. 101/Beirut, I-II, p. 211.

125 Sakhāwī: *Ḍawʾ lāmiᶜ*, I, p. 237.

126 *Ḍawʾ*, XI, p. 89.

127 Ḥusayn Khūja b. ᶜAlī b. Sulaymān al-Ḥanafī: *Al-dhayl li-kitāb Bashāʾir ahl al-īmān fī futūḥāt āl ᶜUthmān*, Tunis, 1908, pp. 229-31.

128 *Mudkhal*, IV, pp. 239-42. Idrīs b. Baydakīn al-Turkumānī: *Al-lumaᶜ fī'l-ḥawādith wa'l-bidaᶜ*, ed. Ṣubḥī Labīb, Wiesbaden, 1986, I, p. 146, ll. 10-12. Similar misgivings about pious sojourns in Mecca occur in Quṭb al-Dīn al-Nahrawālī; *Die Chroniken der Stadt Mekka*, ed. Ferdinand Wüstenfeld, Leipzig, 1857, III, Arabic pp. 20-21/Eldon Rutter: *The Holy Cities of Arabia*, London-New York, 1928, I, pp. 191-92.

129 Raḥmatallāh b. ᶜAbdallāh al-Sindī (d. 993/1585): *Jamᶜ al-manāsik wa-nafᶜ al-nāsik*, in the margin of Aḥmad b. Muṣṭafā Ḍiyāʾ al-Dīn al-Kumushkhānalī: *Jāmiᶜ al-manāsik ᶜalā aḥsan al-masālik*, Constantinople, 1289/1872, pp. 387-88, for Mecca and Medina.

130 *Laṭāʾif al-minan*, I, pp. 189-92.

131 *Laṭāʾif*, I, pp. 106-07.

was first installed by the Umayyad ᶜUmar b. ᶜAbd al-ᶜAzīz (caliph 99-101/717-720).[132] But the direction of prayer which the Prophet adopted is regarded as 'authoritatively established' (*naṣṣ*), on the basis of a demonstration by Gabriel, i.e. as absolutely correct. It would be out of the question and superfluous to undertake any more detailed inquiry into the subject.[133] Otherwise, Muḥammad's grave in its above-ground parts, his mosque and its history were already precisely described by religious scholars in the Middle Ages.

5. FAITH BASED ON AUTHORITY.

Who should be accorded trust and granted protection from criticism was decided by a class of people who already enjoyed these benefits to a lesser degree themselves: the parents and teachers. Due to their position or their profession they are designated as the representatives of those authorities that they teach their pupils to obey. Muḥammad was already aware of this: 'Every new-born child is born into the true religion but its parents then make it into a Jew, a Christian or a polytheist.'[134] According to Muḥammad al-Ghazzālī (d. 505/1111), there is a credulity (*ḥusn al-iᶜtiqād*) in children which responds to the call of parents and teachers, being already attuned to the latter and easy to evoke, and which is sustained by a sense of trust, and other people as well can be drawn into this circle who are not their parents and their teachers. One will believe things from trusted persons of this kind that one would not accept from someone else, and one holds firmly to such beliefs only because it was these very people who put them forward. Similarly, acceptance of the profession of faith among the ordinary people also comes about without a need being felt for conclusive argumentation. Existing belief in authority (*taqlīd*) and willing faith (*ḥusn ẓannihim*) are sufficient. Ghazzālī classifies this form of acquiring someone's belief as fourth in a series of six possibilities. The best in his view would be careful logical argumentation by means of which a young person could be led step by step to knowledge of the truth of the contents of faith. He adds, however, that at most this would only succeed with one or two persons in a century, and if the world were dependent on this ap-

---

132 Samhūdī: *Khulāṣat al-Wafā*, p. 272. Samhūdī: *Wafāʾ al-Wafā bi-akhbār dār al-Muṣṭafā*, ed. Muḥammad Muḥyī al-Dīn ᶜAbd al-Ḥamīd, Beirut, 1955, I, p. 370. Jean Sauvaget: *La mosquée omeyyade de Médine*, Paris, 1947, pp. 83-84, 145-49, 154-55.

133 Zarkashī: *Iᶜlām al-sājid*, pp. 258-60. Samhūdī: *Wafāʾ al-Wafā*, I, pp. 383-84.

134 In several variants. *Concordance et Indices*, s.v. *hawwada*.

proach, there would be very few saved souls. The next best way, Ghazzālī continues, would be to adopt the argumentation of theology; the third way, to persuade people by means of easily graspable examples, as one finds masterfully employed in the Koran for instance; the fourth, the above-mentioned assertion by persons of authority whom the student, from the outset, considers to be knowledgeable; the fifth, to arouse a person's emotional willingness so that one succeeds without using words that are a hundred percent convincing; the sixth and the worst, to tell the people what they want to hear and to adapt oneself to them without enjoying their special trust (*ḥusn iᶜtiqād*). Finally, in the most general terms Ghazzālī recommends that, when implanting the faith, one make use of the ability of the young to learn and to take things in and the imitative instinct of people. But in any case firm belief is not necessarily connected with learned study and keen argumentation.[135] Shaᶜrānī, however, is of the opinion that a subsequent rational explanation is necessary to safeguard what a person first accepted by way of faith and uncritical imitation. Of course, thought alone is also not sufficient.[136] Already Ashᶜarī (d. 324/935-936) had defended supporting belief by means of reflection and argumentation, as well as theology (*kalām*).[137]

What is chiefly required for this purpose, however, are professional experts who have been adequately trained to master greater difficulties. Laymen should not involve themselves in the process with their own interpretations. Ghazzālī impresses this point on them in his last treatise *Iljām al-ᶜawāmm* which we just quoted from above. And this is also the view of his contemporary Aḥmad-i Jām (d. 536/1141). He says one should leave alone the statements open to misinterpretation (*mutashābihāt*[138]). In accordance with surah 3/7, only God Himself understands their meaning. It is better to admit one's ignorance than to fall into 'anthropomorphism' (*tashbīh*). One should be content merely to state the fact that: 'God has said' or 'the Messenger of God has said' or 'ᶜAbdallāh-i ᶜAbbās (d. 68/687-688) has reported' — the famous αὐτὸς ἔφα by which the Pythagoreans referred to Pythagoras. The simple acknowledgement of the questionable passages, whether they be words of God or of the Prophet,

---

135 *Iljām al-ᶜawāmm ᶜan ᶜilm al-kalām*, Cairo, 1351, pp. 53-56.

136 *Al-yawāqīt wa'l-jawāhir*, I, pp. 23-24.

137 Richard M. Frank: 'Al-Ashᶜarī's *Kitāb al-ḥathth ᶜalā l-baḥth*', *MIDEO* 18, 1988, pp. 83-152.

138 Recently on this subject Leah Kinberg: '*Muḥkamāt* and *mutashābihāt* (Koran 3/7): Implication of Koranic pairs of terms in Medieval exegesis', in: *Arabica* 35, 1988, pp. 143-72.

presents no danger and constitutes belief, whereas rejection amounts to unbelief.[139] According to Ghazzālī, the same silent acknowledgement and compliance is also especially appropriate in the case of commands which in themselves appear to have no meaning, such as casting stones in Minā and running back and forth between the hills of Ṣafā and Marwa in Mecca during the pilgrimage. Whereas it was easy to make immediate sense of the alms-tax as a means of supporting the poor, fasting as a means of subduing one's lust,[140] and bowing and kneeling down in the ritual prayers as a sign of humility before God, and the other ritual acts during the pilgrimage lent themselves to all kinds of profound interpretations, the uninterpretable prescriptions could only make sense as a way of imposing on people obedience to the bare command of God without any questions and against man's natural instinct.[141] Today as well, pilgrims are still offered this explanation of the purpose of these exercises in popular brochures.[142] The *locus classicus* requiring unquestioning obedience, which has equal validity for Jews, Christians and Muslims, is God's command to Abraham to sacrifice his own son. Here obviously man is called upon to outdo himself in an attempt to surmount the conflict between God's command and its senselessness, and to confer on it a sense which is not inherent in the action itself but in obedience *per se*, i.e. an enslavement whose absurdity can only be overcome by means of thinking well of the Lord who, for a good end, has ordered and arranged everything the one way it must be, and who is the sole authority before whom man must justify himself.

6. UNCRITICAL TRUST IN THE SHAYKH.

In Sufism, which endeavors to bring a pious person into a radical inward harmony with God (and from the sociological viewpoint is both a 'virtuoso' as well as a 'mass religiosity'), slave-like submis-

---

139 *Rawḍat al-mudhnibīn*, pp. 32-33.

140 Badr al-Dīn Ḥasan b. Yaḥyā... b. Muzallaq al-Anṣārī al-Dimashqī al-Shāfiᶜī (d. 965/1557-58, according to others 966/1558) believed he had a *ḥadīth* supporting this. Ibn Ayyūb: *Al-rawḍ al-ᶜāṭir fī-mā tayassara min akhbār al-qarn al-sābiᶜ ilā khitām al-qarn al-ᶜāshir*, ed. Ahmet Halil Güneş under the title *Das Kitāb ar-rauḍ al-ᶜāṭir des Ibn Aiyūb. Damaszener Biographien des 10./16. Jahrhunderts. Beschreibung und Edition*, Islamkundliche Untersuchungen, Band 60, Berlin, 1981, Arabic p. 44, ll. 7-13.

141 *Iḥyāʾ ᶜulūm al-dīn*, Cairo, 1377/1957, I, pp. 267-68.

142 Jean R. Michot: 'La signification du pèlerinage (hajj) dans trois brochures populaires égyptiennes', *MIDEO* 18, 1988, pp. 213, 228.

sion to God is learned on the practical level through a disciple's relationship with his master. The attitude which the novice must adopt in this process is compared to the lack of will on the part of a corpse in the hands of the corpsewasher, and this was also transferred to the novice's relationship with God.[143] To give only a few references in this connection: Najm al-Dīn-i Iṣfahānī (wrote 728/1328), not otherwise known, correctly summarizes the basic requirements for the novitiate when he demands that the disciple not offer any resistance to his master or refuse him anything, that he interpret everything he hears from his master or sees him do in a good sense, and if he cannot find a possible way of doing so that he seek the cause for this in his own ignorance because one does not always grasp the purpose and the sense of the matter, just as Moses too had not been able to fathom the unpleasant behavior of his guide Khaḍir (surah 18/65-82). When one reports to the shaykh the inner states, dreams and suchlike that one has experienced, one must accept his interpretations and orders with the best trust (*az sar-i ḥusn-i iᶜtiqād*) and follow them, for shaykhs are so to speak doctors (who understand what they prescribe). One must always think of what the shaykh would like, and ought not to begin anything that the shaykh would not approve of.[144] Bahā᾽ al-Dīn-i Naqshband (d. 791/1389) likewise forbade thinking anything bad about one's shaykh and only allowed absolute beginners a single question (apparently so as not to cause them to have doubts about their shaykh), but this was no longer permitted even by the time the novices were in the midway stage of the course.[145] Another author also forbids the novice to perform any

---

143 Richard Gramlich: *Die schiitischen Derwischorden Persiens. Zweiter Teil: Glaube und Lehre*, Abh. f. d. Kunde des Morgenlandes XXXVI, 2-4, Wiesbaden, 1976, pp. 243-45.

144 Najm al-Dīn Maḥmūd-i Iṣfahānī: *Manāhij al-ṭālibīn wa-masālik al-ṣādiqīn*, ed. Māyil-i Hirawī, Tehran, 1364/1405/1985, p. 164, ll. 3-17; p. 209. The author's name on the title page, Sayyid Muḥammad-i Bukhārī, is incorrect. Najm al-Dīn Maḥmūd b. Saᶜdallāh-i Iṣfahānī was a teacher of the more famous Yūsuf b. ᶜAbdallāh al-ᶜAjamī al-Kūrānī (d. 768/1367). Ibn al-Mulaqqin: *Ṭabaqāt al-awliyā᾽*, ed. Nūr al-Dīn Shurayba, Cairo, 1973, p. 492, l. 8. Shaᶜrānī: *Ṭabaqāt*, II, p. 65, no. 316.

145 Muḥammad Amīn al-Kurdī al-Irbilī: *Al-mawāhib al-sarmadiyya fī manāqib al-naqshbandiyya*, Cairo, 1329, p. 124, last two lines. Thinking well of the shaykh is still today one of the fundamental requirements of the novitiate among the Naqshbandiyya. Ḥusayn al-Dawsarī: *Al-raḥma al-hābiṭa fī dhikr ism al-dhāt wa'l-rābiṭa*, in the margin of Sirhindī's *Muᶜarrab al-maktūbāt*, I, p. 195. Praise was conferred on outsiders who thought well of a shaykh, and this was reckoned to their glory and to the glory of the shaykh. ᶜIwaḍ-i Bukhārī:

devotions of his own choice which the shaykh has not ordered him to do.[146] A third one adds that the novice should not simply copy (*iqtidā*) the behavior of the shaykh but must do precisely and exclusively what the shaykh orders him.[147] Otherwise, one could in fact also educate oneself just as well without a shaykh by following a textbook. However, there is a need for the shaykh who alone knows when the time for this or that exercise has arrived for the novice. A fourth warns novices against expecting miracles from their master (i.e. as if they wanted to put him to the test), even if this is something they do not say openly; only the unbelievers, never the believers, had put this request to the prophets.[148] Was this then an education that aimed at instilling dependence, absolute obedience? One could describe it that way, but what is intended is the elimination of self-overestimation and the acknowledgement of a higher authority who denies to a human being's normal self-preoccupation the rights which are its due. The goal is to detach the ego from its habits and to attain the readiness to perceive the voice of a higher master.[149] To begin with this master is the shaykh but he only remains master until the pupil himself can replace him. The shaykh represents God for the novice and is regarded as His mouthpiece. The shaykh's will is God's will. Certainly, the novice has complete freedom to choose his master himself and in so doing to follow his own feeling,[150] yet Sufi psychotherapy, or more correctly psychagogy, does not wait for the

---

Tarjuma-i ṭālibīn wa īḍāḥ-i sālikīn, ed. Marijan Molé, *Farhang-i Īrānzamīn* 8, 1339, p. 20, ll. 10-11, and frequently elsewhere as well.

146 Lamaṭī: *Al-ibrīz*, p. 237, last three lines. Against supererogatory pious devotions and recollecting God in the shaykh's presence without his permission cf. Sirhindī's *Muᶜarrab al-maktūbāt*, I, p. 347, ll. 10-13; letter no. 292.

147 Abū'l-Mafākhir Yaḥyā Bākharzī: *Awrād al-aḥbāb wa-fuṣūṣ al-ādāb*, ed. Īraj-i Afshār, Tehran, 1345, II, p. 77. ll. 13-14.

148 Sirhindī: *Muᶜarrab al-maktūbāt*, letter no. 292; I, pp. 347-48.

149 In a treatise without title which Īraj-i Afshār published in *Farhang-i Īrānzamīn* 14, 1345, pp. 321-37, under the heading *Sharāʾiṭ-i murīdī*, by a certain Abū Jaᶜfar Muḥammad b. Abī Zayd b. ᶜAbd al-Raḥmān, it says (pp. 324-25) that no person knows the way to God on the basis of his own absolute authority (*istibdād*), even though within himself he may be thoroughly acquainted with God as this is inherent in man's primordial nature. When one becomes attached to a shaykh, one must renounce the 'free choice of one's own reason'.

150 Muḥammad b. ᶜAbdallāh al-Khānī al-Khālidī (d. 1279/1862): *Al-bahja al-saniyya fī ādāb al-ṭarīqa al-ᶜaliyya al-khālidiyya al-naqshbandiyya*, Cairo, 1319/1901, p. 22, last line, to p. 23, l. 2.

emergence of what one nowadays calls 'transference' but prescribes it and insists on this until the novice is closely linked to the authority which the shaykh embodies. No one less than Ibn ᶜArabī (d. 638/1240) taught that revering God lay in revering the shaykh, and impiety (*ᶜuqūq*) toward God lay in impiety toward the shaykh who is a chamberlain (*ḥājib*) of God,[151] and Abū Saᶜīd-i Abī'l-Khayr said, putting it the other way round, if the novice obeys the *pīr* (= shaykh), it is as if he is obeying God.[152] This conception prevailed particularly in the post-classical period of Sufism after the 'teaching shaykh' (*shaykh al-taᶜlīm*) had been transformed into the 'shaykh of training' (*shaykh al-tarbiya*).[153] Of course, this firmly based form of psychic guidance was still embedded in the traditional world-picture, and one had not yet allowed the transcendental world in the soul to disappear. But one did not seek it by way of a flight through the spheres, but by means of an inner journey (*sulūk*) or rapturous translation (*jadhba*), whose itinerary is neither compatible with the ascension of Jesus nor with the route Muḥammad travelled on his heavenly journey, and is certainly by no means the very same as the latter. The shaykhs appeared as the priests of this transcendental world, to which and through which they wished to guide the soul of the novices along the inner path.

A Sufi shaykh who had taken on the task of leading his disciples into God's proximity should of course already have reached this position himself, i.e. should be a 'Friend of God' or 'saint', and in addition should be familiar with the difficulties of the study course and how to overcome them. But there were many who had not com-

---

151 *Al-futūḥāt al-makkiyya*, Chpt. 181, Cairo, 1293, II, p. 483, l. 11.

152 Muḥammad b. Munawwar b. Abī Saᶜd b. Abī Ṭāhir b. Abī Saᶜīd-i Mayhanī: *Asrār al-tawḥīd fī maqāmāt al-shaykh Abī Saᶜīd*, ed. Dhabīḥallāh-i Ṣafā, Tehran, 1332, p. 310, ll. 6-7/ed. Muḥammad Riḍā Shafīᶜī-i Kadkanī, Tehran, 1366, p. 297, ll. 4-5/trans. John O'Kane, *The Secrets of God's Mystical Oneness*, Persian Heritage Series no. 38, Costa Mesa (Calif.)-New York, 1992, p. 453, ll. 19-20.

153 On this transition cf. 'Khurāsān and the End of Classical Sufism', pp. 189-219. A section on the state of affairs in post-classical Sufism is found in the introduction to *Die Fawāʾiḥ al-ğamāl wa-fawātiḥ al-ğalāl des Nağm ad-dīn al-Kubrā*, pp. 93-240. Additional information in Richard Gramlich: *Die Gaben der Erkenntnisse des ᶜUmar as-Suhrawardī*, Chpts. 10, 51, 52. Idem: *Die schiitischen Derwischorden Persiens. Zweiter Teil: Glaube und Lehre*, pp. 182-251. Humāʾī: *Mawlawīnāma*, pp. 615-19. Certain heretical groups also demanded obedience to the leader without any criticism. Pseudo-Sayyid Murtaḍā b. Dāᶜī-i Ḥasan-i Rāzī: *Tabṣirat al-ᶜawāmm fī marᶜifat maqālāt al-anām*, ed. ᶜAbbās-i Iqbāl, Tehran, 1313, p. 181. The literature on venerating the shaykh and training the novice is very large.

pletely fulfilled this prerequisite. In such a case a harmony between souls (which does not have to mean sameness) was able to help an individual through much, as long as the 'transference' actually took place. Consequently, in Sufism the relationship between the disciple and the teacher is associated with a certain remnant of imponderable elements, which one can scarcely get a grasp of from outside. One will therefore attach great significance to the personal note in this association and the requirements for the relationship between the partners will not be measured according to one yardstick. What remains decisive is the mutual positive interrelationship. Two individuals accept one another, two others repel one another, and in this way a colorful picture of many varied Sufi ways of life emerges, even within one and the same school. The proper novice will naturally try to make a good impression on his shaykh so that the latter gives him a good prognosis and God then looks after its realization, because the supposition (*ẓann*) of the believer (in this case the shaykh) does not err — so writes Gēsūdarāz (d. 825/1422). Indeed, God has said: 'I am as My bondsman (here the shaykh) thinks of Me.'[154] Should a shaykh himself contravene laws, written or unwritten, and thereby tempt the novice to breach the ban on criticism, even if only in his thoughts, then the latter is obliged only to think well of the matter and to excuse the shaykh. More is to be learned from the mistakes of the shaykh than from his correct behavior — so one saying goes.[155] Sirhindī writes: 'Should it occasionally happen that a shaykh commits an offense against the law, the novices ought not to imitate him in this respect but should attempt, whenever it is possible, on the basis of benevolent trust (*bi-ḥusn al-ẓann*) to find some sense for the action and to read a good interpretation into it. If this good interpretation simply will not emerge, one should turn to God in humility and take refuge with Him in order to ward off this affliction from oneself, and one should beseech God with earnest tears to keep the shaykh from harm and to maintain his good reputation.'[156] The counter-image is that of the shaykh who, the other way round, thinks

---

154 Ṣadr al-Dīn Abū'l-Fatḥ Muḥammad-i Ḥusaynī-i Gēsūdarāz/Gīsūdirāz: *Khātima*, litho., Hyderabad, 1356, p. 75, section 113.

155 Muḥammad-i Pārsā: *Risāla-i qudsiyya*, ed. Malik Muḥammad-i Iqbāl, litho., Rawalpindi, 1395/1354/1975, p. 148, last line, to p. 149, l. 1.

156 *Muʿarrab al-maktūbāt*, letter no. 313; I, p. 383, ll. 2-5.

good of his disciples to such an extent that in their mistakes he only sees a reflection of his own mistakes.[157]

The name of the Sufis did not have the same connotation for everyone. In the view of many they were parasites and shammers. But in the eye of Shaᶜrānī who was by nature inclined to be lenient toward his fellow-man and constantly nourished this inclination with intense gratitude to God — in Shaᶜrānī's eyes the Sufis had received a bonus from the outset, similar to that of the ᶜAlids and the descendants of the Companions of the Prophet. He already praises this attitude toward them on the part of his teacher Zakariyyā al-Anṣārī (d. 926/1520) who had exercised caution in passing judgement on people reputed to be saintly, and had said: 'Beware of rejecting someone whom God has made known as a saint in your country because surely God only does this for a wise reason.' Shaᶜrānī declares: 'One of the favors God has conferred on me is this: from my earliest youth I have not been against anyone among the Sufis and always say to myself whenever I don't understand something about them: "This belongs to the knowledge that God has not given me any insight into."'[158] This is also recommended to Sufis themselves and people in general when they take offense at the ecstatic utterances (*shaṭhiyyāt, sukriyyāt*) of enraptured individuals, which in ordinary people's ears sound blasphemous toward God. But it is said that they should free themselves from their bad thoughts and wait until they understand the words better, exactly as one should leave the ambiguous words in holy scripture (*mutashābihāt*) alone and not censure them prematurely with a false judgement.[159] For example one warned against a hasty condemnation of the great mystical poet Ibn al-Fāriḍ (d. 632/1235) and wrote: 'The work of the shaykh demands a correct interpretation. In his case it is not a question of the outward wording but behind that lie other corresponding significances. Thus think favorably, do not criticize, but maintain a positive attitude (*fa-*

157 Muḥammad Hāshim-i Kishmī: *Barakāt-i aḥmadiyya* yā *Zubdat al-maqāmāt*, litho., Cawnpore, 1307/1890/reprint Istanbul, 1977, p. 22, ll. 16-19. Storey, I, pp. 988-89.

158 Quotation in Muḥammad b. Sulaymān al-Ḥanafī al-Baghdādī: *Al-ḥadīqa al-nadiyya fī ādāb al-ṭarīqa al-naqshbandiyya*, in the margin of ᶜUthmān b. Sanad al-Wāʾilī al-Najdī: *Aṣfā al-mawārid min salsāl aḥwāl al-imām Khālid*, Cairo, 1313/1895, p. 103, ll. 1-3.

159 Kishmī: *Barakāt al-aḥmadiyya*, pp. 149-53. One witness among many. The *locus classicus* is Abū Naṣr al-Sarrāj: *Al-lumaᶜ fī'l-taṣawwuf*, ed. R.A. Nicholson, E.J.W. Gibb Memorial Series XXII, Leiden-London, 1914, pp. 375-77.

aḥsin al-ẓann wa-lā tantaqid bal iᶜtaqid)!'[160] So here as well it can be that a favorable opinion does not cover up the truth but on the contrary first creates the conditions for finding it. Favorable opinion expresses itself here in a temporary pause (*tawaqquf*), in the willingness to postpone judgement. ᶜAlāᵓ al-Dawla al-Simnānī (d. 736/1336) also calls for tolerance when he seeks to enlist understanding for those Sufis who, due to an inborn penchant and from a viewpoint which in his opinion is justified, indulge in the controversial 'listening to music' (*samāᶜ*):

> 'If you have not reached this station, at least look with friendliness upon the men who are at this station and think well of them, for then you too will not be excluded from what otherwise falls from their table, because God says: "I am present when My bondsman thinks favorably, so let him think favorably!"'[161]

7. THINKING WELL OR ILL OF SOMEONE.

According to a saying attributed to ᶜUmar I, in general human relations anyone who is to some extent in the public eye should by his actual behavior take care that a bad opinion about him does not arise.[162] However, one should never simply feign integrity because hypocrisy could one day be unmasked and then not only would the good opinion one had acquired oneself among others be destroyed, but thinking well of genuine men of piety which has been strictly commanded would also suffer a setback.[163] In any case, those who are on the other side should bear in mind the words of the Prophet: 'Were a person to think well even of stones, he would obtain some benefit from them.'[164] Consolation was sought concerning the real

---

160 Ibrāhīm b. ᶜAbd al-Raḥmān al-Khiyārī al-Madanī (d. 1083/1672): *Tuḥfat al-udabaᵓ wa-salwat al-ghurabāᵓ*(= *Riḥlat al-Khiyārī*), ed. Rajāᵓ Maḥmūd al-Sāmarrāᵓī, III, Baghdad, 1980, p. 39.

161 ᶜAlāᵓ al-Dawla Simnānī: *Opera Minora*, ed. W.M. Thackston, Jr., Harvard University, 1988, p. 114 below. Changed wording of the *ḥadīth*.

162 Mājirī: *Minhāj wāḍiḥ*, pp. 271-72: *Man waqafa mawqif al-ẓann*.

163 Abū Ḥafṣ ᶜUmar al-Suhrawardī: *ᶜAwārif al-maᶜārif*, *bāb* 25, Cairo, 1939, p. 143/trans. Richard Gramlich: *Die Gaben der Erkenntnisse des ᶜUmar as-Suhrawardī*, Freiburger Islamstudien VI, Wiesbaden, 1978, p. 188. In connection with ecstatic manoeuvres of the Sufis while listening to music.

164 Ibn al-Daybaᶜ: *Tamyīz al-ṭayyib min al-khabīth fī-mā yadūr ᶜalā alsinat al-nās min al-ḥadīth*, Cairo, 1324, p. 162: *Law aḥsana aḥadukum ẓannahū*. Ibn Qayyim al-Jawziyya: *Al-manār al-munīf fī'l-ṣaḥīḥ wa'l-ḍaᶜīf*, Beirut, 1970, no. 319. An Egyptian miracle-story about

state of affairs in the saying attributed to Abū Ḥanīfa that differences of opinion in the community were a mercy (*raḥma*) from God, that is to say a concession.[165] None the less, the existence of good relations between two partners facilitates understanding and in particular assists the weaker party. One should think well of a saint whose grave one visits because God can fulfill a person's request through the saint's intercession.[166] The Naqshbandī ᶜAbdallāh Bāᶜalawī al-Ḥaddādī (d. 1132/1720) blamed the small amount of benefit one received in his day from men of piety and saints on the lack of attention and the all too weak trust one accorded them (*ḍaᶜf al-ẓann bihim*).[167] Another Naqshbandī, ᶜAbdallāh al-Dihlawī (d. 1240/1824) classed thinking well of people among the moral virtues which everyone had a duty to practice, and he described it as the ability 'because of noble-mindedness (*ba-taʾwīl-i nēk*) to consider the bad characteristics of another as good and one's own good sides as not to be assumed.'[168]

A Muslim was quite aware that having a good opinion of another also brings with it benefit for himself and that mutual goodwill results in happiness and blessings for all concerned. Muḥammad-i Pārsā (d. 822/1419) is supposed to have uttered the verses:

> Practice patience and self-contentment! Be an optimist and think well of others (*bāsh... nēkō-ẓann*)!

---

the saint Abū'l-Ḥajjāj Yūsuf al-Mughāwir (d. 619/1222) illustrates the saying. Denis Gril: *La* Risāla *de Ṣafī al-Dīn*, Arabic p. 48/French pp. 138-39. Muḥammad Rashīd Riḍā (d. 1354/1935) is annoyed that such an idolatrous saying is so popular among the Muslims. *Fatāwā al-imām Muḥammad Rashīd Riḍā*, ed. Ṣalāḥ al-Dīn al-Munajjid and Yūsuf Q. Khūrī, Beirut, 1970, I, no. 17, pp. 55-57.

165 Rudi Paret: 'Islamischer Pluralismus', in: *Die islamische Welt zwischen Mittelalter und Neuzeit. Festschrift für Hans Robert Roemer*, Beiruter Texte und Studien 22, Beirut, 1979, pp. 523-29.

166 Aḥmad Ḍiyāʾ al-Dīn al-Kumushkhānalī: *Jāmiᶜ al-uṣūl*, Cairo, 1328, p. 289, last line.

167 Dawsarī: *Al-raḥma al-hābiṭa*, in the margin of Sirhindī's *Muᶜarrab al-maktūbāt*, I, p. 195. ᶜAbdallāh Bāᶜalawī, a Ḥusaynid from Tarīm, who should be called al-Ḥaddādī, not al-Ḥaddād as he is referred to everywhere in Dawsarī. *GAL*, II, pp. 407-08/*GAL S*, II, p. 566. Sarkīs: *Muᶜjam al-maṭbūᶜāt*, I, pp. 189-90.

168 Muḥammad Amīn al-Kurdī al-Irbilī: *Mawāhib sarmadiyya*, p. 244, l. 9. The original is in Shāh Ghulām ᶜAlī-i Dihlawī (= ᶜAbdallāh-i Dihlawī): *Makātīb-i sharīfa*, litho./reprint Istanbul, 1976, p. 127, ll. 18-19.

In these four things lies the key to much joy.[169]

The indisputably successful Rashīd al-Dīn Faḍlallāh, the powerful vizier and great scholar under the Īl-Khāns in Iran, expresses this with gratitude. He writes:

'In my judgement the cause of my success, after the outflowing of God's goodness, is due to the blessing (*baraka*) and the good portent of several things. One is the blessing from my good faith (*ḥusn-i ᶜaqīdat*) and my pure thoughts regarding the Seal of the Prophets, Muḥammad the Chosen One — to him are due the best invocation of blessings and the most perfect greetings — from whose loftiness, breath after breath, one moment after another, fine substances, illuminations, meanings and truths flow into my heart and soul. As for all the success I have experienced and experience now, I am aware of it being a gift from his loftiness.[170] Then there is the blessing which has accrued from my having generally had genuine reverence (*iᶜtiqādē durust*) and unconditional trust (*ḥusn-i ẓann*) in all people but especially in theologians and the righteous, knowers and fathomers of the truth, who are the leaders in religion and models on the path of certainty, and from this company destined for felicity I have requested, outwardly and inwardly, a dispensation from their effective power. Further, there is the blessing from the faith without guile (*ᶜaqīdat-i pākīza*) and the favorable thought (*ḥusn-i ẓann*) of Mawlānā Muᶜaẓẓam,[171] model for the learned who fathom the truth, the best of contemporary

---

169 Kāshifī: *Rashaḥāt*, p. 112.

170 M. Quatremère: *Histoire des Mongols de la Perse, écrite en persan par Raschid-eldin*, Paris, 1836, I, pp. V-VIII, denies that Rashīd al-Dīn had ever been a Jew. Mujtabā Mīnuwī surmises that his father was already a Muslim (*Waqfnāma-i Rabᶜ-i rashīdī*, ed. Mujtabā Mīnuwī and Īraj-i Afshār, Tehran, 1350, p. 19). Bertold Spuler: *Die Mongolen in Iran*, Leipzig, 1939, pp. 247-49, believes Rashīd al-Dīn had originally been a Jew and then converted to Islam, as does Josef van Ess: *Der Wesir und seine Gelehrten*, AKM XLV, 4 (1981), p. 1. Additional literature on this question in these same sources (apart from Quatremère).

171 Always appears thus without *iḍāfa* in this text. — Here by pure faith and favorable thought the attitude of Mawlānā Muᶜaẓẓam toward Rashīd al-Dīn is meant because the object of favorable thought in this text is normally expressed with *dar ḥaqq-i*; but here we have the genitive which is to be understood as the genetivus subjectivus. The same is the case with the favorable thought of supportive friends which is mentioned next. But one is not sure whether the object is Rashīd al-Dīn or the friends among themselves. The subsequent *taᶜākus* (which is otherwise rarely attested) makes it clear that Rashīd al-Dīn is speaking of reciprocal good thought.

human beings, Shams al-Milla wa'l-Dīn al-Hamadānī[172] — may his good qualities long endure — because thinking favorably (*ḥusn-i ẓann*) and good faith (*ᶜaqīda-i nēkō*) exercise a powerful effect, as the heavenly *ḥadīth*[173] says: "I am as My bondsman thinks of Me; so let him think what he will!" And the Prophet — to him are due an invocation of blessings and greeting — ordered favorable thinking (*ḥusn-i ẓann*) with the words: "Think well to yourself of your brother!" And likewise he forbade ill thoughts (*isāʾat-i ẓann*): "Do not think ill of a word that escapes your brother's lips if you can find a good meaning for it!" Especially (effective is) the favorable thought of sympathetic friends and upright comrades whose pure breath and association provide the blessing of religious and worldly gains. Indeed, the reciprocity (*taᶜākus*) of souls has a powerful effect. The reason for this effect can be what we referred to earlier, namely that every soul has a specific nature (*khāṣṣiyyat*) and perfection of its own which it shares with no other soul. Thus if two souls unite with one another (*ittiḥād*) and undertake something and adopt a goal in common, as is natural their power and their perfection will be stronger in a state of association (*ijtimāᶜ*) than if each proceeded separately.'

Now there is a saying attributed to the Prophet which stands in opposition to the saying we cited of Abū Ḥanīfa and it says pretty much the opposite thing, namely that not the differences of opinion as in the case of Abū Ḥanīfa, but unity, a sense of solidarity or community, is a mercy, here however mercy not in the sense of a concession but as a special distinction, just as the saying about differences of opinion more or less came to be understood later on.[174] Here where it is a question of shared views and the unity of two or more souls, of their harmony and their concord in the same desire, Rashīd al-Dīn cites the second saying, that of the Prophet, and concludes:

'This is what is meant by the statement of the Prophet: "The community is a mercy."[175] If someone wants this to be corroborated, he only has to look at the opposite situation and vizualize the opposite to himself, i.e. the opposite of favorable thoughts, of friendship, genuine faith and concern on behalf of human beings and of

---

172 Spiritual adviser and correspondent of Rashīd al-Dīn. J. van Ess: *Der Wesir und seine Gelehrten*, index.

173 Non-Koranic word of God, *ḥadīth qudsī*.

174 Paret: 'Islamischer Pluralismus', pp. 525-26. But Paret does not explain the change in the understanding of the saying of Abū Ḥanīfa by means of this *ḥadīth*.

175 *Concordance et Indices*, s.v. *jamāᶜa*; I, p. 370.

love and friendliness toward them, namely ill thoughts, hostility, opposition and resentment, for "by means of their opposite things become clear".'[176]

Rashīd was unaware at that time that he would one day fall victim to this very form of malicious attitude and hostility, the workings of intrigue. Old opponents denounced him in 718/1318 as having intentionally brought about the demise of the Īl-Khān Öljäitū in 716/1316 by wrong medical treatment. He was executed near Tabrīz along with his young son Ibrāhīm who had assisted him, and his life's work (buildings and writings) were to a large extent destroyed.[177]

But thinking good thoughts quite generally is also a means of helping oneself when one is threatened with sinking into the marsh of one's own incapacity and peavishness. The Naqshbandī ᶜUbaydallāh-i Aḥrār (d. 895/1490) advises thinking good thoughts (*andēshahāy-i khūb*) in order to become cheerful, and maintains that only in this way had he been able to recover his strength and return to good spirits after he had collapsed under the weight of his shaykh's litter which he helped to carry, though he had been debilitated by a bout of typhus.[178] Mawlānāy-i Rūm had compared speaking well of someone with a flower garden which one lays out around one's own home and each time one looks at it one imagines oneself to be in Paradise.[179]

8. THE 'MAGIC' OF FAVORABLE AND ILL THOUGHTS

A final question which the above remarks of Rashīd al-Dīn bring to mind is whether and to what extent the strength of a person's thought and faith influences the level of its effect, independently of whether it is a matter of good, bad or malicious thought, or of proper or false hoping, fearing or desiring. Does the intensity of wishing for something make any difference as far as attaining one's goal? The theo-

---

176 Rashīd al-Dīn Faḍlallāh-i Hamadānī: *Laṭāʾif al-ḥaqāʾiq*, ed. Ghulām-Riḍā Ṭāhir, Tehran, 2537/1978, II, pp. 707-08.

177 Quatremère: *Histoire des Mongols de la Perse*, I, pp. XXXVI-XLIV. Spuler: *Die Mongolen in Iran*, pp. 120, 248. Mīnuwī-Afshār: *Waqfnāma-i Rabᶜ-i rashīdī*, p. 19. J. van Ess: *Der Wesir und seine Gelehrten*, pp. 4-5. Bernard Lewis: *The Jews in Islam*, Princeton (N.J.), 1984, p. 101.

178 *Rashaḥāt*, pp. 422-23.

179 *Fīhī mā fīhī*, ed. Furūzānfar, Tehran, 1348, p. 201/trans. Annemarie Schimmel: *Von Allem und vom Einen*, Diederichs, 1988, p. 321.

logical views of Islam as to whether religious faith (*īmān*) can increase or decrease are known to differ from one another.[180] But they only define an amount of faith in terms of the completeness or incompleteness of the elements which comprise it. Here in our case, however, the issue has to do with the density and inflexibility of a hope or conviction. The Sufis were thoroughly familiar with this question concerning the energetics of faith. For example Sahl b. ᶜAbdallāh al-Tustarī (d. 283/896), without beating around the bush, ventures to state that the religious faith of 70-year-olds becomes worse,[181] by which, of course, incompleteness is not primarily meant but a dropping off in energy and increasing weakness. Does the volume of commitment of a thought which is focused on a desired goal have an effect on success? In any case Mawlānā (d. 672/1273) connects the attainment of a goal, as do others, with the force one has expended in the effort.[182] In thought involving a desire, which is what we are concerned with here, I would distinguish two forms of commitment.

The first is the prayer of supplication. In prayer a human being turns to powers or a power and asks it to intervene. If a prayer is answered, then help comes on behalf of the suppliant and his friends, and whatever particular opponent is involved, even should it simply be a sandstorm, is thwarted. Success is therefore dependent on engaging that outside power, and thinking well of it should, in view of what we know, exercise an influence on it, if there is any truth in the fundamental assertions of the Muslims we quoted earlier. Thus the outside power, God in our context, acts under the pressure or impression of the favorable thought and the expressed wish of the person who prays. One appeals to this favorable thought when one asks a friend to pray for one (*al-duᶜāʾ bi-khayr, duᶜāy-i khayr, duᶜāy-i ba-khayr*). The person who could statistically count on his prayers being heard and a supernatural intervention on his behalf was either a prophet or a saint (= a Friend of God) — two classes of human being that God did not like to say no to but regularly helped with spectacular or at times less remarkable miracles. But the Muslims knew that the mechanism also functioned in non-Islamic communi-

---

180 *EI*2 s.v. īmān (Louis Gardet).

181 Sarrāj: *Al-lumaᶜ fī'l-taṣawwuf*, ed. Reynold Alleyne Nicholson, E.J.W. Gibb Memorial Series XXII, Leiden-London, 1914, p. 327, l. 1. Richard Gramlich: *Die Wunder der Freunde Gottes*, Freiburger Islamstudien XI, Wiesbaden, 1987, p. 439. Cf. my remarks in *Der Islam* 65, 1988, p. 299.

182 Humāʾī: *Mawlawīnāma*, pp. 550-51.

ties, in 'enemy territory' among 'the enemies of God', and they emphasized this as well when they were concerned to shed light on the power of faith or prayer. Mawlānā's father, Bahā'-i Walad (d. 628/1231), who had a lot of contact with Indian artisans in his homeland in Central Asia, learned from one of them that the gods in India were called *dev^o^* (*dēw*)[183] and were decorated with the most expensive ornaments. Everyone believed his god was real, genuine and truthful, and incapable of deceiving his worshippers. If someone had a request, he would stay before his god for 10 to 20 days without eating and not let himself be dismissed until, exhausted from the long fasting and in a state between waking and sleep, he would hear whether his wish had been fulfilled or not. If he remained at the spot despite having obtained a negative reply, in some half-waking state he would receive a slap in the face, even though the idol had no arms. Bahā sees in this the confirmation of his conception that what assists in the experience of miracles is not cleverness and philosophy (nor even adhering to Islam) but only the highest degree of faith (*nihāyat-i i^c^tiqād kardan*) in him whom one is worshipping.[184] Only rock-solid faith in the kingdom of heaven had caused the body of Muḥammad, Jesus and Enoch to lose all its physical weight thus enabling it to be translated through the air.[185] Bahā did not recognize any upper limit to the strength of faith (*īmān*).[186] A legend from the environment of the Akhīs in Asia Minor wants to show that they too could make the idols act if they only presented their wishes before them with the necessary fervor. A young man who worships a magnificent marble statue — a work of Greek sculpture is intended — and obtains everything he wishes from it, was required to respond to previous hospitality by a round of expensive invitations. When he beseeched the statue not to abandon him now, the statue broke apart

183 The Hindi or Sindhi word is written in Bahā' al-Walad just as in Abū Rayḥān al-Bīrūnī (d. 440/1048): *dyw*. *Kitāb al-Bīrūnī fī taḥqīq mā li'l-hind*, Hyderabad, 1958, pp. 68 ff. Cf. the relevant passages in Edward C. Sachau's English translation, *Alberuni's India*, London, 1910, II, p. 408 (index s.v. deva). Sachau everywhere gives the Sanskrit pronunciation of the words but in an earlier essay has also written on the later stage of language intended by Bīrūnī. 'Indo-Arabische Studien zur Aussprache und Geschichte des Indischen in der ersten Hälfte des 11. Jahrhunderts', *Abh. d. kgl. Akad. d. Wissenschaften zu Berlin*, 1888, Abh. 1, pp. 42-44. The form *dev^o^* is casus rectus sing. of the Sindhi word.

184 Bahā'-i Walad: *Ma^c^ārif*, I, pp. 317-18.

185 *Ma^c^ārif*, I, p. 318, lower section. On this subject see Ushnuhī in my remarks in *Der Islam* 65, 1988, p. 285.

186 *Ma^c^ārif*, I, p. 418, penult. line.

and revealed a heap of gold inside it. His friends who were regally entertained with the money chose him thereafter to be their representative. The legend concludes with the moral: 'If even a lifeless stone image is capable of such things, imagine then what one may expect from a man of God in whom one has firm and honest faith!'[187] What this means is that the strength of belief with which one reveres a man of God can prompt him to perform impossible actions and induce miraculous experiences. When the Spanish had conquered areas around Tetuan and the Moroccans were obliged to pay damages of 20 million reals, formal legal opinions were obtained. In the legal opinion of the then head of the sepulchral shrine of Idrīs II in Fez, issued in 1277/1860, one reads, with reference to Ibn ᶜArabī among others, that non-Muslims too can gain the upper hand if the intensity of their faith (*iᶜtiqād*) is fully perfected, even though their religion is false.[188] Under these circumstances a good understanding between a ruler and the dervishes can also provide the foundation for the welfare of both partners. The army of the pious prays for the health and victory of the prince if the latter is committed to them and to Islam. Sirhindī's son Muḥammad Saᶜīd, in a letter to Awrangzēb (1068-1118/1658-1707), indicated this as being precisely the task of the dervishes.[189] How many stories exist in which they withdrew their support from the ruler and invoked God against him!

Despite an unmistakable undertone of godlessness or at any rate of subordinating God to the power of the human soul which one can perceive in some of these statements, as long as energy goes on being generated in a prayer, God can still not have finally abdicated. As long as a human being prays, he is still not able to act directly himself, but only indirectly by means of a separate power. All the same it is always conceded that the conceptions one forms of God are allowed to be different, in fact can be false, without God becoming annoyed. For God is supreme. One recalls the legend of 'the dancer of Our Lady' who, because he could not do anything in accordance with the rules of the Church, performed a dance before the Virgin Mary until she smiled and nodded to him.[190] Differently, but at bottom not really so far removed from the latter, Bahāʾ-i Walad sees the

---

187 Aflākī: *Manāqib al-ᶜārifīn*, ed. Tahsin Yazıcı, II, revised edition, Ankara, 1976-80, I, pp. 460-62.

188 Muḥammad Dāwud (sic): *Tārīkh Tiṭwān*, Tetuan, 1957-75, V, p. 105, ll. 6-14.

189 *Maktūbāt-i saᶜīdiyya*, p. 99, ll. 14-16.

190 *Abū Saᶜīd-i Abū l-Ḫayr (357-440/967-1049). Wirklichkeit und legende*, Acta Iranica 11, Leiden, 1976, pp. 256-59.

decisive element in the purity and intensity of one's trusting devotion (*iʿtiqād*) to God, nor does it matter in what religion. Unhindered by any knowledge of the Old Testament, he maintains that Moses never attacked anyone and that God protected the Israelites without their having to wage war, whereas in the case of the Muslims harshness, prohibitions and wars occupied the foreground. Bahā sees the experience of all pleasure (*maza*) as being in faith as such (*iʿtiqād*), and believes that only in faith is the occurrence of miracles possible. God observes and 'whenever and in whatever religion, in whatever denomination and in whatever purchase or sale He finds true faith and sincerity', there He shows, 'through this window' (the intensity of faith), His delight, His divinity, His miracles of power and proofs.[191] This had already happened in the interim periods when there were no prophets, and still happens today as well in regions where people have not yet heard of prophets. God looks at the sincerity of the individual praying.[192] Whatever a person receives, he owes to his intention (*niyyat*) and not to anyone else (sic). For if someone were to go before a prophet harboring a bad intention, he would not receive anything from him. If someone were to go before a Zoroastrian without knowing he was a Zoroastrian, he might well come away with a gain. What this shows is that everything people attain they attain through themselves and likewise everything unpleasant which they suffer they must ascribe to themselves.[193]

By this Bahā is not advocating polytheism or any form of undefined monotheism. Elsewhere in no uncertain terms he declares that Muḥammad is his great model. But since he is incapable of imitating what Muḥammad has done, his emulation of Muḥammad is confined to his faith in him (*iʿtiqād*). He believes this to be typical of all those who revere a model and in particular of the student's relationship to the teacher. The teacher is therefore to have consideration for the image his followers have of him, and he should not destroy it but try to some degree to live up to their expectations. If his students believe that water and fire can do him no harm, he must not cause them to have doubts about this. Muḥammad has succeeded in transforming in the course of 600 years after the *hijra* forms of architecture and ideas of faith in regions which had earlier been inhabited by other religious communities. But God had created him, Bahā, too weak for the many required works and only demanded from him as his one

191 *Maʿārif*, I, p. 377, l. 14, to the penult. line.

192 *Maʿārif*, I, p. 380, ll. 6-10.

193 *Maʿārif*, I, p. 416, ll. 8-11.

achievement faith or respect (*iʿtiqād*) and his gaze (toward Him, *naẓar*).[194] Thus faith — in the sense of believing to be true, revering and thinking well of someone— is here a substitute for missing or insufficient capability, and precisely for that reason the necessary measure for still maintaining a connection with the model. Believing and thinking well of someone here bridge the gap between what one should and what one can do. One feels reminded of the doctrine of St Paul that faith eradicates the guilt of deficient works, and one even believes one recognizes a plausible reason for it. Another time Bahā asked himself whether he ought ever to think of calling God his beloved. He tells us he contented himself with the claim that his faith (*iʿtiqād*) in God and his certainty of God (and not God Himself) were his beloved. He beseeched God never to separate him from faith and certainty and to direct him to something else.[195] For Bahā Paradise is, so to speak, created from the stuff of faith (*iʿtiqād*),[196] and in his view all pleasure, as we have already seen (p. 639), lies in faith. Therefore he advises: 'Increase faith and certainty, then you will reach (full) pleasure!'[197]

To reiterate: the first form in which the weight of faith exercises an effect on events is prayer. It is directed toward a higher power and can cause the latter to intervene through ways and means which are not decernible to the person praying. Prayer works indirectly, by means of a higher power.

The second form in which the power of faith and hope can operate is as a direct influence on an object, without making a detour via a higher power (although according to religion nothing at all happens without that power's accord). Here a human being by himself is in possession of a supernatural power. It makes a difference whether he says: 'I can rely on God sending me a dream tonight with the Prophet in it', or simply maintains: 'If I wish, I can behold Paradise with the eyes in my head, and if I wish, I can behold Hell with all its snakes',[198] because in the second case the human being carries out what he wishes without hindrance — although this text only means to say that believing something to be true and faith are the prerequisites for someone experiencing phenomena such as these. However, when a human being enjoys the direct power to effect others at

194 *Maʿārif*, I, p. 378, l. 2, to l. 3 from bot.

195 *Maʿārif*, I, p. 173, ll. 17-19.

196 *Maʿārif*, I, 318, l. 17.

197 *Maʿārif*, I, p. 319, l. 1.

198 *Maʿārif*, [II], Tehran, 1338/1959, p. 180, ll. 2-3/I, p. 304, ll. 1-2.

will, according to the enlightened usage of our age and without making a value judgement, we speak of magical capabilities. Following the Islamic way of speaking, however, we would encounter at least four different varieties of this direct, magical power to produce an effect. We could distinguish:

1) The philosophic conception of miracles in general. According to the philosophers all miracles performed by human beings are the effects of their especially strong soul which by means of purification has drawn closer to the souls of the spheres and therefore is capable of undertaking works such as they undertake.[199] In medieval Islam one also included quite generally Brahmans and yogis among the philosophers or at any rate in their close proximity, because one was convinced that no prophets had ever appeared in India. Paul Kraus traces this view back to the heretical ideas which Ibn al-Rāwandī put in the mouth of the Brahmans.[200] ᶜAbdallāh al-Dihlawī (d. 1240/1824) is thinking of yogis when he maintains that 'effects of heat from states of the heart, supernatural revelations and miracles' also occur among non-Muslims (*kuffār*).[201] Yet Sirhindī claimed to know that prophets had definitely also appeared among the Indians but, as he says, they never had more than three followers at most.[202] But according to the Islamic philosophers all prophets and saints in any case perform their miracles due to their own perfected power, by dint of their inner strength.

2) Magic (*siḥr*) in the broadest sense of the word, about whose reality there can be no doubt, given the Koranic stories about Egyptian and Arab magicians.[203] All the practices known from tradition would be included under the term, such as conjuration and command over subordinate spirits and demons. As far as miracles are concerned, transformations, spells, healings, causing sickness and suchlike are to be found. Whether a form of magic is good or bad must be judged by the context and the character of those who practice it. Acts of magic are not in themselves necessarily distinguishable from miracles.

3) The man of piety employs his psychic powers in order to cause something to happen for another person. What is primarily involved

199 Richard Gramlich: *Die Wunder der Freunde Gottes*, pp. 96-97, 133.

200 'Beiträge zur islamischen Ketzergeschichte', *RSO* 14, p. 349.

201 *Makātīb-i sharīfa*, p. 160, ll. 1-2; p. 161, ll. 10-11. In these texts *jōgiyya* are often mentioned.

202 Kishmī: *Barakāt al-aḥmadiyya*, p. 183, ll. 15-19. Friedmann: *Sirhindī*, p. 71.

203 Gramlich: *Wunder*, pp. 127-34. *EI* siḥr (D.B. MacDonald).

is his 'effective power' (*himma*). By this one means a goal-oriented willing, mostly in the sense of promoting or supporting someone. The Naqshbandī (and 'greatest large-scale landowner in Central Asia') ᶜUbaydallāh-i Aḥrār (d. 895/1490) defines it as: 'concentrating the thoughts on a single thing in such a way that nothing else can any longer enter a person's mind', and advises that one continually test the capacity for it in oneself. He himself practiced it and tested it in Herat as a spectator at wrestling matches where he would make the one or the other wrestler win as he pleased.[204] Naturally, it can also be employed to cause damage.[205] Aḥrār makes the following comment about it:

> 'The great have said: "Just as nothing permanent can be set up against the Koran, likewise nothing permanent can be set up against the *himmat*." The *himmat* is discerning and creative at the same time (or: the *himmat* of one who discerns is a creator): the object desired does not make one wait for it. Whoever sets himself against such a *himmat* is unfailingly overwhelmed, for it has been said: "Even an unbeliever who constantly focuses his thoughts on something and directs his *himmat* to something meets with success." Faith and pious acts are not a prerequisite. Just as pure hearts exercise an influence, so bad souls also exercise an influence.' — *Rashaḥāt*, p. 518, ll. 2-7.

---

204 ᶜAlī-i Kāshifī: *Rashaḥāt ᶜayn al-ḥayāt*, pp. 516-17. The displays of power went so far among the *khwājagān* that during a gathering Amīr Kulāl (d. 772/1370) asked his student Bahāʾ al-Dīn-i Naqshband to bring about certain effects in his (Kulāl's) son who was present. He simply wished to know how far his student had now advanced. Jāmī: *Nafaḥāt*, p. 382. Here it is called *taṣarruf* 'power at one's disposal' instead of *himma* 'ability to effect'. This is the same power. With it one is able to impose one's will on another person. The Naqshbandiyya readily gave demonstrations of this art among themselves. Sometimes two individuals tested their powers like this against one another in silence and it would end in a draw (*Rashaḥāt*, p. 165), or the one would concede to the other voluntarily (*Rashaḥāt*, pp. 165, 168). But not infrequently this led to ill feelings when people became aware of the indecency and unworthiness of this demonstration of strength in the inappropriate place. A preacher could no longer speak when a powerful man in the audience covered his ears and hypnotized him (*Rashaḥāt*, p. 183 f.). — On *himma* cf. *Die Fawāʾiḥ al-ǧamāl*, index; Gramlich: *Die schiitischen Derwischorden Persiens. Zweiter Teil*, index.

205 In this category is the Persian expression *tawajjuhāt gumāshtan* which can mean 'harboring and transmitting evil thoughts'; Kishmī: *Barakāt al-aḥmadiyya*, p. 30, ll. 16-17. But *tawajjuh gumāshtan* by no means carries this bad meaning *per se*. One also frequently finds *himmat ba/bar... gumāshtan*.

'Effective power' or the 'disposal over power' (*taṣarruf*) often operates as *actio in distans*. Mere belief in the phenomenon and especially the fact that its occurrence was constantly attested, were conducive to creating an uncanny atmosphere. The *res gestae* of the Naqshbandīs, who were noted for their prowess in this area, must have spread, at least in people's minds, a whole network of incalculable powers across Central Asia. The authorities nowhere appear to have taken measures against the implied danger of an inconceivable criminality, although hagiography openly speaks of such means of power and its use by men of religion. Ultimately, if this magic is accompanied by gestures which assist or 'anticipate', or by manipulations, it then depends on the standpoint of the observer whether or not he wishes to classify it among the forms of sorcery. No Muslim will be prepared to describe the Prophet's throwing of sand (if it was not arrowshots) in the Battle of Badr as a magical practice, nor would this occur to a pious person who reads that a saint brandished his sword in the air in order to decide in favor of the Muslims a battle against unbelievers which was raging at a great distance. All the same, ready to go into action is the potent gaze, or simply 'the gaze' (*naẓar*), by which the saint or shaykh is able to effect a change of heart in others, to convert or educate people, to cause their presence or drive them away, to put animals to flight, to destroy one thing and revive another, to make lamps light and to do numerous other feats. But here as well it will depend on the viewer's standpoint and the context whether one speaks of magic or casting spells, for instance by means of 'the evil eye' of envy. The 'gaze' brings about the same result by means of physical contact as 'effective power' does through supernatural contact.[206] The Shādhilīs and others prided themselves on being able to educate their novices with 'effective power' and the 'gaze'.[207]

---

206 Gramlich: *Wunder*, pp. 173-79. Shaʿrānī: *Laṭāʾif al-minan*, II, pp. 77-78.

207 Aḥmad b. Muḥammad b. ʿAyyād: *Al-mafākhir al-ʿaliyya fī maʾāthir al-shādhiliyya*, Cairo, 1937, p. 106, l. 1. — Shaʿrānī: *Yawāqīt*, II, p. 104, ll. 3-11, considers some groups in middle North Africa (Ifrīqiya) to be especially gifted so as to be able to kill people with 'effective power', to depose them from offices and to appoint them to offices. He does not dispute the fact that non-Muslims are also capable of this but maintains they can only do so by means of professionally measured out drugs (*ʿaqāqīr*). — Among the Naqshbandiyya there is mention of their 'gift-dispensing gaze' or 'gaze of beneficence' (*naẓar al-mawhiba, naẓar-i ʿināyat*) which helps others on the right track or makes possible for them something unexpected.

4) In distinction to the above-mentioned kind of 'effective power', the Sufi focuses his will in the first instance upon himself in order to exercise a magic effect, pretends something to himself and at times to others, and acts out what he wishes to make of himself so as to become it. This has to do with the problem of the semantic ambiguity of the sixth-form Arabic verb. The meaning of *tawājada* (*wjd* VI) bifurcates in two directions: shamming the experience of rapture, and movement in 'anticipatory mimicking' of rapture. Both are a kind of lie in as far as one makes believe one is having an experience. According to theory, shamming movement is forbidden when its only purpose is to make an impression, but often permitted as anticipatory gesturing when this helps induce a real state of ecstasy or to lighten its effect.[208] Behind this lies a whole philosophy concerning the possible function of a mask, a persona, a facade, of play in the context of training, self-training or self-realization. But it applies as well to very many aspects of religion that have taken on fixed or ritual forms. In such cases what one does or says can be shallow or sincere, or at least accompanied by sincere effort. A rule of the Naqshbandīs requires that when performing the repeated inward recitation of the formula 'there is no god but God', each time or whenever the breath is exhaled one should turn to God and say the words: 'Lord, my goal is You and doing what pleases You!' This is the so-called 'return' (*bāzgasht*) to giving assurance that one only seeks Him.[209] A student of Jāmī (d. 898/1492) did not dare say the sentence because he knew he would be lying to God. Jāmī directed

---

208 A few passages which approve: Richard Hartmann: *Al-Ḳushairîs Darstellung des Ṣûfîtums*, in: Türkische Bibliothek 18, Berlin, 1914, index s.v. tawâdschud. Jullābī-i Hujwīrī: *Kashf al-maḥjūb*, ed. Zhukovski, Leningrad, 1926/reprint Tehran, 1336, p. 541, ll. 9-15/trans. R.A. Nicholson: *The Kashf al-Maḥjúb*, Gibb Memorial Series XVII, reprint London, 1936, pp. 415-16. Ghazzālī: *Iḥyā'*, II, pp. 292-93/trans. D.B. MacDonald *JRAS* 1901, p. 731. Abū'l-Najīb ᶜAbd al-Qāhir al-Suhrawardī: *Ādāb al-murīdīn*, ed. Menahem Milson, Jerusalem, 1978, §146/Abridged Translation: *A Sufi Rule for Novices*, Harvard University Press, 1975, § 146. Bākharzī: *Awrād al-aḥbāb*, II, p. 204, ll. 7-12. 'The Dervish Dance', pp. 37 f. *Abū Saᶜīd-i Abū l-Ḫayr*, p. 210. — Feigned ecstatic movements are sometimes also permitted when supportive cooperation is required. 'A Book of Etiquette for Sufis', p. 88, ftn. 177.

209 Cf. Gramlich: *Die schiitischen Derwischorden Persiens. Zweiter Teil*, p. 401. John A. Subhan: *Sufism: Its Saints and Shrines*, Lucknow, 1960, p. 192. J. Spencer Trimingham: *The Sufi orders in Islam*, Oxford, 1971, p. 203. The Persian word *bāzgasht* cannot mean 'stop, restraint'. *Rashaḥāt*, p. 47, ll. 1-3. Dihlawī: *Makātīb-i sharīfa*, p. 123, l. 12. Muḥammad Amīn al-Kurdī: *Tanwīr al-qulūb fī muᶜāmalat ᶜallām al-ghuyūb*, Cairo, 1372, p. 504, ll. 4-7. Idem: *Mawāhib sarmadiyya*, p. 315, l. 4.

him to Bahāʾ al-Dīn ʿUmar-i Jaghāraʾī and the latter reassured him with the old wise saying of ʿAlāʾ al-Dawla al-Simnānī (736/1336): 'Even if the traveller on the path does not at first find sincerity in his striving, he should none the less say: "God, You are my goal!" until eventually real sincerity results from it.'[210] This is exactly the same case as when one makes believe while striving after ecstasy during a musical function: one mimics the look of something and then also seeks to become it or, put another way, one induces in oneself a state by acting it out to oneself. But the double face of shamming and genuineness is not only exhibited by the outrageous proposal of the above reassurance but can also be exhibited in the recollection of God itself. As is well-known the recollection of God out loud is often frowned upon by the Naqshbandīs. A man of this order suspected someone of hypocrisy (*riyā*) after ascertaining that he practiced the recollection of God out loud and with bodily movements. Jāmī pointed out that on the Day of Resurrection this very recollection of God which at present is perhaps contaminated with hypocrisy will be a shining light seen from afar. For indeed, he added, the person recollecting God first pictures the words of the formula to himself, then thinks of what he says, and then also hears what he pronounces. This in turn is a stimulus to the imagination, the soul and the intelligence. To this inward circular movement there

---

210 Kāshifī: *Rashaḥāt*, pp. 44-45. Cf. Kurdī: *Mawāhib sarmadiyya*, pp. 90-91. I have only been able to find this saying of Simnānī in his treatise *Fatḥ al-mubīn li-ahl al-yaqīn* in the following form: 'When drawing out the *lā* (of the *lā ilāha*...) the novice calls to mind the shaykh: "Oh shaykh, be my witness: I am completely honest in the claim that I want nothing except God."' Simnānī: *Opera minora*, ed. Thackston, p. 123, ll. 17-19. One might perhaps combine with this a passage from Simnānī's oral communications that Amīr Iqbāl collected. According to the passage, a novice who is still not able to adhere to all the rules of spiritual retreat should not declare an absolute intention before entering on retreat but confine himself to the following moderate formulation: I now turn exclusively to God for forty days and renounce everything else in the hope that God will give me sucess in spending the rest of my live this same way. *Risāla-i iqbāliyya: Fawāʾid-i shaykh ʿAlāʾ al-Dawla-i Simnānī*, in *Opera minora*, p. 230 below/Hartwig Cordt: *Die sitzungen des ʿAlāʾ ad-dawla as-Simnānī*, diss. Basle 1971, Zurich, 1977, p. 216. This means: I undertake the firm resolution, at least during the coming forty days, only to have God before my eyes and I *hope* that I will have success in achieving this subsequently as well. That is certainly not the same as saying: I am hardly in the position to obey God completely now but I hope I will be able to do so eventually. Rather, for the time being one strives after a situation which realistically speaking can only be temporary; none the less, one's goal is to extend this to one's whole life at some later date when it becomes possible, i.e. one hopes later to be able to achieve fully what one at first can only do halfway.

corresponds the outward circular movement which he performs during his exercise by means of repetition and with his body. The visible and audible recollection of God therefore supports vizualization of the formula and realization of its contents.[211] I would even like to include here the highest mystical achievements, and see in the frequently referred to saying of Ḥallāj (d. 309/922) 'I am God' a not inappropriate symbol for the unattainable summit of mystical endeavors.[212] And precisely in order to go some way beyond himself by means of 'anticipatory mimicking' in this direction, to begin with the disciple has need of a master 'to imitate', a master whom he reveres like a demi-god.[213] It was recognized that 'blind imitation' (*taqlīd*), which was otherwise frowned upon, does not have to be empty but can pass over into genuine action and being (*taḥqīq*). ᶜAlāᵓ al-Dīn-i ᶜAṭṭār from Khwārazm (d. 802/1400 in Dih-i naw-i Chaghāniyān) guaranteed this and confessed that Naqshband had ordered him simply to imitate him blindly, and that he was still today witnessing and experiencing the effects and genuine good which resulted from it.[214] But naturally not everyone succeeded in traversing

---

211 Kāshifī: *Rashaḥāt*, p. 266, ll. 5-13. On body movements in general see *Fawāᵓiḥ*, Intro., pp. 202-03. Gramlich: *Derwischorden*, II, pp. 395-407.

212 For an orientation cf. my remarks in *Bahāᵓ-i Walad. Grundzüge seines lebens und seiner mystik*, Acta Iranica 27, 1989, pp. 337-38. They have to do with the measures adopted by the mystic in order to appropriate the (imagined) attributes of God.

213 ᶜAlāᵓ al-Dīn-i ᶜAṭṭār (d. 802/1400) said (interpretative translation): 'To attach oneself to the (*ṣūfī*) educator (*murshid*), although in reality he is not God and in the end must be dismissed, is in the beginning a means to reach the goal, and yet it is necesary to reject attaching oneself to anything other than God. One must seek one's (*ō* = *khwad*, as often) complete existence in pleasing the educator and only destroy what is not God in the right place and at the right time, because rejection in the wrong place and inopportunely is of no help.' This is in Kāshifī: *Rashaḥāt*, p. 145. Thus one is only to set aside the shaykh once one has overtaken him. In what then follows (ibid., pp. 145 ff.) ᶜAlāᵓ al-Dīn-i ᶜAṭṭār impressively depicts the interplay between student and teacher and between intense work and unpredictable attainment of self-effacement. Without intending it, he gives (p. 150) a parallel to the appropriation of God's attributes by a mystic when he comes to talk about the connection of a living person, even of a Sufi, with the spirit of someone who is dead. Here, as he says, one has no need whatsoever of a dream or memory image (*ṣuwar-i mithāliyya*) of the deceased, but must be familiar with his 'attribute' (*ṣifat*), i.e. in this case his essential characteristic trait. But this is the same situation the mystic finds himself in when he must assimilate or work himself into the attributes (*ṣifāt*) of God which he knows about through tradition.

214 *Rashaḥāt*, p. 153, ll. 1-4: 'I guarantee that everyone who enters this *ṭarīqa* in blind imitation (*taqlīd*) will without any doubt advance to authenticity (*taḥqīq*). Naqshband ordered

the path from *taqlīd* to *taḥqīq* or in traversing it at the same speed and with the same ease or effort.

These are some examples of the second, i.e. the direct form of exercising psychic-spiritual influence on other people and things, and on oneself. It takes place through an act of the will. But in addition to this there are still other direct ways of exerting an influence which emanate from a human being though they are less sought after and less focused: the aura that radiates from individual personalities whether it be engaging, repulsive or of some other kind. But it is not our intention here to enter any further into this subject.

ADDITIONS OF THE AUTHOR

P. 629, ftn. 155, the following should be added: The saying usually occurs in the unambiguous and more plausible form: 'The mistake of the master is better than what is correct on the part of the novice'; for example in Sirhindī: *Mabdaʾ u maᶜād*, reprint of litho., Istanbul, 1989, p. 75, ll. 12-13. This is also what Pārsā appears to mean.

P. 635, l. 7, Tabrīz: according to others in Abhar-i Zanjān.

P. 635, l. 19: a bout of measles instead of typhus.

P. 640, l. 18, add the following: Shams-i Tabrēzī (disappeared 645/1247-48) goes still one step further. He relates an anecdote about a wounded pilgrim led back to his caravan by a higher being which presents itself as the devil. Shams closes with the point of wisdom that one who firmly believes in the devil attains his goal and one who turns to Muḥammad without true faith perishes (*Maqālāt-i Shams-i Tabrīzī*, ed. Muḥammad ᶜAlī-i Muwaḥḥid, Tehran, 1369/1990, I, p. 264, l. 20, to p. 265, l. 11; variant, I, pp. 228 f./ed. Aḥmad-i Khwashniwīs, Tehran, 1349/1970, p. 321; variant, pp. 289 f.). Thus he has arrived at the point where religion is abolished or bypassed by faith. Either Muḥammad and the devil are equally strong or both are incapable of anything, and the one only amounts to something or becomes stronger than the other through the faith which a person places in him (which is not otherwise consistent, however, with Shams' outlook on the world).

---

me to imitate him blindly. With regard to everything in which I have imitated him and still imitate him, I truly behold (or: experience, *mushāhada*) the effect and the authenticity.'

POETIC REFRAIN AND *MAḤYĀ*

The imposing work *Nafḥ al-ṭīb min ghusn al-Andalus al-ratīb wa-dhikr wazīrihā Lisān al-Dīn b. al-Khaṭīb*, *Wafting of Aroma from the Sap-Laden Branch of Andalusia and Description of its Vizier Lisān al-Dīn b. al-Khaṭīb*, which Aḥmad b. Muḥammad al-Maqqarī al-Tilimsānī (d. 1041/1631) completed as his largest and last composition in 1038-39/1629-30, in the edition published by Dozy, Dugat, Krehl and Wright in 1855-61 only contains, as is known, the first part dealing with the geography and cultural history of Muslim Spain, but not the second part on the Naṣrid of Granada Muḥammad V's famous vizier, Lisān al-Dīn b. al-Khaṭīb (d. 776/1374), about whom the work was actually written. Not until the new edition of Iḥsān ᶜAbbās, Beirut, 1968, in eight volumes was the second part made available to us in a critical edition. This second part closes with a long appendix on panegyrical poetry for the Prophet Muḥammad, which also clearly serves the purpose of appropriately concluding the large work with praise of the Prophet. But a process of association was sparked off — by our standards in a rather round about way — by an artfully stylized spiritual last will and testament of Ibn al-Khaṭīb to his sons which reminded Maqqarī of another such last will and testament composed by a man of letters named Ibn al-Jannān on behalf of Muḥammad b. Yūsuf b. Hūd who had usurped the throne in 625/1228.[1] Abū ᶜAbdallāh Muḥammad b. al-Jannān al-Mursī, who thus comes into view, was an exceptionally short man who from behind resembled an eight-year-old child but possessed a remarkable talent for artful stylistics in the field of writing. He is meant to have died in the 50s of the 7th century/1253-1261 in Bijāya (Bougie) in Algeria.[2] What leads Maqqarī at the end of his work to the poems on the Prophet is the fact that among Ibn al-Jannān's poetry are also found poems on Muḥammad from which he immediately cites a prime example, a *mukhammasa* with a refrain which calls upon the listeners to bless the Prophet (*taṣliya*) and to greet him (*taslīm*). As everyone knows, the term for blessing the Prophet (*taṣliya*), when a human being is called upon to do so, is two-tiered: a human being does not himself bless the Prophet but asks God to

---

1 Maqqarī: *Nafḥ al-ṭīb*, VII, pp. 406-14.

2 *Nafḥ al-ṭīb*, VII, p. 431, ll. 16-17.

bless him. The words are actually *ṣallā'llāhu ᶜalayhi* 'God bless him' but when one orders a person *ṣalli ᶜalayhi* 'bless him', this means 'Say: "God bless him!"' And it is the same for the greeting, there as well the meaning is 'Say: "God greet him!"' But this is impractical. Thus when referring to a human being, we also simply say may he bless and greet Muḥammad. Now the refrain in our poem of Ibn al-Jannān runs *ṣallū ᶜalayhi wa-sallimū taslīmā* (= *taslīman*) 'bless him and greet him heartily!', which is in fact nothing other than surah 33/56. The first strophe of the poem goes as follows:

God heaped high honors upon Muḥammad,
conferred on him great privilege
and distinguished him among the apostles of God as noble,
 full of compassion for the believers, and merciful!
 Bless him and greet him heartily!

The refrain repeats throughout the 29 strophes of the poem. The number 29 is the number of the 29 Arabic letters with *lām-alif* which, however, has no further significance here. The refrain stands out from the other three hemistiches of each strophe because of its internal rhyme. Maqqarī reports that he often quoted this poem during teaching sessions (*majālis al-tadrīs*) and beforehand would always cite another poem on the Prophet from another Maghribī because the people of the Maghreb, he says, took their midday and night-time rest at the halting stations of praise for the Prophet, i.e. they refreshed themselves in this way everywhere and at all times.[3] The anonymous *mukhammasa* which he presents next has no refrain, but at the very end once again closes with the hemistich from surah 33/56 *ṣallū ᶜalayhi wa-sallimū taslīmā* 'bless him and greet him heartily!' Maqqarī designates it as a *qaṣīda milādiyya* 'a poem for the Prophet's birthday celebration' because this day is mentioned in it. But, as he declares, it is as if it had been created as an introduction to the preceding *mukhammasa* of Ibn al-Jannān.[4]

Maqqarī then confesses that upon concluding a complete reading of Qāḍī ᶜIyāḍ's *al-Shifā bi-taᶜrīf ḥuqūq al-Muṣṭafā*, *Satisfaction by Announcing the Rights of the Chosen One* (ᶜIyāḍ died 544/1149), he had composed a poem similar to Ibn al-Jannān's, and presents a *mukhammasa* consisting of only three strophes, the last of which like

3 *Nafḥ*, VII, pp. 432-38.

4 *Nafḥ*, VII, pp. 438-39.

the *mīlādiyya* ends with *ṣallū ᶜalayhi wa-sallimū taslīmā*.[5] Next he again has recourse to Ibn al-Jannān and introduces a *qaṣīda* which in several verses begins anaphorically with *ṣallū ᶜalā* 'bless (the Prophet)', throughout maintains the rhyme *-īmā*, and in the final hemistich once again concludes with the formula *ṣallū ᶜalayhi wa-sallimū taslīmā*.[6]

The *mukhammasāt* with the refrain *ṣallū ᶜalayhi wa-sallimū taslīmā* continue. Among them is one by Abū Isḥāq Ibrāhīm b. Sahl al-Isrāʾīlī al-Ishbīlī (drowned 649/1251-52),[7] one by a preacher presumably from the east and one by an unnamed poet from the west.[8]

A certain Idrīs b. Muḥammad b. Muḥammad b. Mūsā al-Anṣārī al-Qurṭubī (d. 647/1249-50) brings off the feat of making the final hemistich of each strophe of his *mukhammasa* rhyme in *-īmā* without giving in to the temptation to employ *ṣallū ᶜalayhi wa-sallimū taslīmā*. Ibn al-Jannān has devoted to it a rhymed recommendation to read it (*taqrīẓ*).[9]

Others employ the artistic device of closing the hemistiches of the strophes with the consecutive letters of the alphabet. Mālik b. ᶜAbd al-Raḥmān b. al-Murahḥal al-Mālaqī al-Sabtī (d. 699/1299-1300)[10] even regularly places the name of the letter by itself and in its full form at the beginning of the strophe, and then likewise begins the strophe with that consonant. For example:

Alifun: The most sublime (*ʾajallu*) of the prophets is a prophet (*nabīʾu*),
through whose brightness the sun of the day shines (*tuḍīʾu*)
and through him hope the good and the bad (*musīʾu*)
to receive great good from God the great (*ᶜaẓīmā*).
Bless him and greet him heartily (*taslīmā*)!

---

5 *Nafḥ*, VII, pp. 439-40.

6 *Nafḥ*, VII, pp. 440-41.

7 *Nafḥ*, III, p. 526. *GAL*, I, pp. 273-74/*GAL S*, I, p. 483.

8 *Nafḥ*, VII, pp. 441-53.

9 On these recommendations to read a particular work, which are especially striking in the west, cf. Franz Rosenthal: '"Blurbs" (*taqrīẓ*) from fourteenth-century Egypt', *Oriens* 27-28, 1981, pp. 177-96/Rosenthal: *Muslim Intellectual and Social History. A Collection of Essays*, Variorum, 1990.

10 Ibn al-Qāḍī: *Durrat al-ḥijāl fī ghurrat asmāʾ al-rijāl*, ed. I.S. Allouche, Rabat, 1936, no. 897. Bağdatlı İsmail Paşa: *Hadiyyat al-ᶜārifīn. Asmāʾ al-muʾallifīn wa-āthār al-muṣannifīn*, Istanbul, 1951-55, II, p. 1, gives the date of his death as 672/1273-74.

Bāʾun: He appeared (*badā*) on the horizon of Mecca as a star (*kawkabā*), etc.

Such *mukhammasāt* according to the letters of the alphabet with *lām-alif* contain 29 strophes.[11] The feat of employing final letters in the rhyme in alphabetical order is also achieved by Abū'l-ᶜAbbās Aḥmad b. Muḥammad b. al-ᶜAbbās al-Maghribī (lived before 707/1308) — he was older than Ibn al-ᶜAṭṭār al-Jazāʾirī[12] — in a *mukhammasa* whose first strophe reminds one of the first strophe of the *mukhammasa* of Ibn Jannān[13] mentioned at the beginning of this essay. The *mukhammasa* of our Maghribī — he is also called Ibn Jamāl al-Dīn[14] — likewise has the refrain 'bless him and greet him heartily'.[15] But it also has some strophes left over which do not maintain alphabetical rhyme[16] so that, as the editor himself remarks, one does not know whether they should actually still be counted as part of this *mukhammasa*. A certain Abū'l-ᶜAbbās Aḥmad b. al-Qāsim al-Ishbīlī, Ibn al-Qaṣīr, is represented with a *mukhammasa* of 10 strophes, in which not only the first three hemistiches but the fourth as well rhyme with one another and whose final hemistich then skips out of the series with the refrain 'bless him and greet him heartily'.[17] A *qiṭᶜa* of four verses from a certain Jamāl al-Dīn b. Jalāl al-Dīn al-Jawzī is cited by Maqqarī and goes as follows:

Muḥammad the Apostle of God surpassed the other prophets
as greater in nobility and exceeded them in high esteem.
A unique pearl in glory. Indeed, the most beautiful jewel
is always the jewel which is unique.
He predominated over the noble prophets and they all
blessed him and greeted him heartily.
God Himself blessed him out of respect.
Therefore (you too) bless him and greet him heartily![18]

---

11 *Nafḥ*, VII, pp. 453-59.

12 *Nafḥ*, VII, p. 485.

13 *Nafḥ*, VII, p. 432.

14 *Nafḥ*, VII, p. 485.

15 *Nafḥ*, VII, pp. 459-65.

16 *Nafḥ*, VII, pp. 465-67.

17 *Nafḥ*, VII, pp. 468-70.

18 *Nafḥ*, VII, p. 470.

To this Maqqarī adds *musaddasāt* with the same refrain, firstly two whose strophes, following the Arabic alphabet, bear the same consonants both at the beginning and at the end of each hemistich, while the fifth hemistich only has this consonant at the beginning and at the end has instead a rhyming word in *-īmā* which rhymes with the refrain of the 6th hemistich *ṣallū ͨalayhi wa-sallimū taslīmā*. Thus the rhymes of a strophe look like this: aaaabb, whereas the corner letters are as follows:

a - a a - a
a - a a - a
a - b ṣ - b (where b = *-īmā*)

These *musaddasāt* originate from a certain ͨAlāͻ al-Dīn Muḥammad b. ͨAfīf al-Dīn al-Ījī al-Ḥasanī al-Ṣafawī al-Zaynabī who must have lived in the 9th/15th century or around 900/1494-95 because he gave instruction to someone who died in 930/1524 and to someone else who died in 934/1527.[19] In the second *musaddasa* (VII, p. 478, l. 16), if my reading and understanding are correct, he reveals his name as Muḥammad b. Muḥammad. I read *li-Muḥammadin huwa Muṣṭafan wa-muͻammilu...* and translate as:

(honoring) a Muḥammad who is chosen and hopes[20]
for Muḥammad b. Muḥammad what the latter hopes for himself.

Maqqarī notes the artificiality (*takalluf*) of both poems but gives three reasons why he none the less accepted them in the series:

1) The author is a man of piety (*ṣāliḥ*) to whom one gladly consigns oneself and whose blessing one seeks.
2) Both poems entail praise of the Prophet.
3) The intention was to bring together everything that could be found with meter, rhyme and meaning.[21]

In addition, however, Maqqarī had wanted to oppose the assertion of a learned scholar that one could only find all this in Ibn Jannān. But

19 *Nafḥ*, VII, pp. 470-79. — Najm al-Dīn al-Ghazzī: *Al-kawākib al-sāͻira bi-manāqib aͨyān al-miͻa al-ͨāshira*, ed. Jabrāͻīl Sulaymān al-Jabbūr, Beirut, 1945 ff., I, p. 172, ll. 3-4; II, p. 191, l. 22. The correct title of the book is the one given here, as is clear from I, p. 7, ll. 3-4.

20 *Muͻammil* 'hoping for what is good' is an honorific name of Muḥammad like *muṣṭafā* 'chosen'.

21 *Nafḥ*, VII, p. 479.

the main point, he says, was praise of the Prophet and in particular pronouncing the formula for invoking blessings *ṣallū ᶜalayhi wa-sallimū taslīmā*. Maqqarī admits that he entertains the idea of writing a book on this form of poetry involving *taṣliya*, with the title *Rawḍat al-taᶜlīm fī dhikr al-ṣalāh wa'l-taslīm ᶜalā man khaṣṣahu'llāhu taᶜālā bi'l-isrāʾ wa'l-muᶜāyana wa'l-taklīm, Meadow of Instruction. On Invoking Blessings and Greetings on the One Whom God Distinguished with the Ascension, Direct Vision of Him and Speech with Him*, and he hopes still to be able to undertake the task.[22] But he does not appear to have ever carried out his plan.[23]

Maqqarī names his source for the earlier mentioned Abū'l-ᶜAbbās Aḥmad b. Muḥammad b. al-ᶜAbbās al-Maghribī, Ibn Jamāl al-Dīn — the 25th volume of the large work *Muntahā al-sūl fī madḥ al-rasūl, Everything One Could Wish about Praising the Apostle of God*, written by a certain al-Ḥasan b. ᶜAbd al-Raḥmān b. ᶜAbd al-Raḥīm b. ᶜUdhra al-Maghribī al-Anṣārī, regarding the end of whose life no date is known to me and Bağdatlı İsmail Paşa: *Keşf-el-zunun zeyli*, Istanbul, 1947, also appears to know nothing. He belongs, however, to the 7th/14th century because Ibn Jamāl al-Dīn whom he mentions was older than a certain Ibn al-ᶜAṭṭār al-Jazāʾirī, concerning whom we know that he was still alive in 707/1308.[24] In fact the pilgrim traveller Abū Sālim al-ᶜAyyāshī (d. 1090/1679) saw in Mecca the 9th volume of this *Muntahā al-sūl min* (sic) *madḥ al-rasūl* in a copy made by a certain Muḥammad b. Abī'l-Qāsim b. Aḥmad b. ᶜAbd al-Raḥmān al-Anṣārī as far back as the year 673/1274. It contained information and poems on the footprints (*aqdām*) of the Prophet and related matters, as well as a treatise on the image (*mithāl*) of the Prophet's sandal entitled *Al-laʾāliʾ al-majmūᶜa min bāhir al-niẓām wa-bāriᶜ al-kalām fī ṣifat mithāl naᶜl al-nabī — ᶜalayhi al-ṣalāh wa'l-salām, Collected Jewels of Shining Poetry and Excellent Speech on the Image of the Prophet's Sandal — Blessings and Greetings Be upon Him.* In ᶜAyyāshī's opinion Maqqarī, who had published a book about the sandal of the Prophet in poetry, would have been jubilant if he had known this rich collection of poetic out-

22 *Nafḥ*, VII, p. 480.

23 Cf. the list of Maqqarī's works in the editor's introduction to the *Nafḥ al-ṭīb*, I, pp. 12-14, where the editor has in fact forgotten to mention this plan. Under no. 24 he mentions another plan which Maqqarī likewise appears not to have carried out.

24 ᶜĀdil Nuwayhiḍ: *Muᶜjam aᶜlām al-Jazāʾir*, Beirut, 1980, p. 233, under al-ᶜAṭṭār.

pourings about the Prophet.[25] It is an error if ᶜAyyāshī thinks Maqqarī was not familiar with the gigantic work, the *Muntahā al-sūl*. Our passage proves the contrary. It can at most be a question of Maqqarī not having seen volume IX of the *Muntahā*.

For further *musaddasāt* and other poems on the Prophet, Maqqarī acknowledges his debt to a collection by the Algerian scholar and judge Abū ᶜAbdallāh Muḥammad b. Muḥammad b. ᶜAbdallāh b. Muḥammad b. Muḥammad b. Aḥmad b. Abī Bakr b. Yūsuf al-ᶜAṭṭār, called Ibn al-ᶜAṭṭār, who was from Algiers (Jazāʾir Banī Mazghanna). His collection bears three titles: *Durar al-durar, Pearls of Pearls*; *Naẓm al-durar fī madḥ sayyid al-bashar, Stringing Pearls. On Praising the Lord of Mankind*; *Al-wird al-ᶜadhb al-maᶜīn fī mawlid sayyid al-khalq ajmaᶜīn, The Watering Place with Sweet Spring Water. On the Birthday of the Lord of All Creation.* The author is not to be confused with the later Shihāb al-Dīn Aḥmad b. Muḥammad b. ᶜAli al-Dunaysarī Ibn al-ᶜAṭṭār who has also produced a work of panegyrical poems on the Prophet, with the title *ᶜUnwān al-saᶜāda, Frontispiece of Felicity*, but who only died in 794/1391-92.[26] Maqqarī warns about confusing the two and calls the younger one Mashriqī and the older one Maghribī.[27] From our western author, who was still alive in 707/1308, Maqqarī first takes a *musaddasa* whose strophes are once more ordered alphabetically with regard to their rhyming letters and have the refrain *ṣallū ᶜalayhi wa-sallimū taslīmā*. The rhyming letters follow one another in the Maghribī order. The strophes are also full of *ṣallū ᶜalā* internally.[28] There then follows a second *musaddasa* of the same Ibn al-ᶜAṭṭār al-Maghribī, once again full of *ṣallū* within the strophes but with the refrain *ṣallū ᶜalayhi bukratan wa-aṣīlā* 'bless him in the morning and in the evening!', in which the Koranic *sabbiḥūhu* 'glorify Him', referring to God, is replaced by *ṣallū ᶜalayhi* (surah 33/42) and refers to Muḥammad. It contains 19 strophes without further rhetorical padding.[29] Next there appear a few other poems which are not composed in strophes, all of them by the same Ibn al-ᶜAṭṭār al-Jazāʾirī,

---

25 Iḥsān ᶜAbbās in the introduction to *Nafḥ*, I, p. 13, no. 10. Abū Sālim al-ᶜAyyāshī's *Riḥla ᶜayyāshiyya Māʾ al-mawāʾid*, litho., Fez, 1316, reprint Muḥammad Ḥajjī, Rabat, 1977, II, p. 254 (not p. 256, as Iḥsān ᶜAbbās indicates).

26 Ibn Ḥajar al-ᶜAsqalānī: *Al-durar al-kāmina fī aᶜyān al-miʾa al-thāmina*, Hyderabad, 1348-50, I, pp. 287-89, no. 732.

27 *Nafḥ*, VII, p. 489.

28 *Nafḥ*, VII, pp. 480-84.

29 *Nafḥ*, VII, pp. 485-88.

and at the end the colophon which says that the collection was completed in Algiers on the 2nd of Shaᶜbān 696/the 26th of May 1297.[30]

Of some importance for Islamic mysticism and Arabic literary history is the fact that the Spanish-Arab mystic Ibn al-ᶜArīf (d. 536/1143) is said to have composed a book with the title *Maṭāliᶜ al-anwār wa-manābiᶜ al-asrār, Places of Ascent of Lights and Fountainheads of Secrets*, from which Maqqarī selected two poems on the Prophet and a concluding poem which consists solely of verses with anaphoric *ṣallā*.[31] After a further *qaṣīda* by a certain Abū ᶜAbdallāh Ibn ᶜImrān, each verse of which is prefixed with the name of a letter of the Maghribī alphabet (*alifun*, *bāʾun*, etc.) and then opens with a word beginning with the same letter, the whole in accordance with the number of the letters of the alphabet amounting to 29 verses and concluding with an additional 30th verse containing the *taṣliya* — as I say, after this rhetorically demanding *qaṣīda* in *-ādhi*[32] taken from Ibn al-ᶜArīf, Maqqarī once again turns to Ibn Jannān al-Andalusī with whom he had initiated this seemingly unending appendix, though he still allows himself some poems and *muqaṭṭaᶜāt* on the Prophet by others as well. He closes with the following excuse: 'These are a few *qaṣāʾid* in praise of Muḥammad. I ask God to count them toward my atonement for the frivolities and foolishness which I have committed for the sake of my own glory and in order to become known. But, by God, that was only talk and not action.[33] It was in the manner of men of letters like the *ḥāfiẓ* and *shaykh al-islām* Ibn Ḥajar (al-ᶜAsqalānī, d. 852/1449) and several others who have written on literature and made compilations.'[34]

Yet even with this he still does not stop but goes on to say: 'Thus it is not out of place if we further bolster these (poems collected here) with a few *maqṭūᶜāt* which can reinforce the performance of atonement. For someone who seeks to entrust himself to the lord of existence (Muḥammad), it is right if he does not allow the means for achieving this simply (without being used) to become lost. All the more so since the Prophet is the possessor of the praiseworthy station, of intercession and of the leadership.'[35] The poems which then

---

30 *Nafḥ*, VII, pp. 496-97.

31 *Nafḥ*, VII, pp. 497-99.

32 *Nafḥ*, VII, pp. 500-01.

33 Allusion to surah 26/226: 'They say what they do not do.' The poets are meant.

34 *Nafḥ*, VII, pp. 505-06. The earnest Ibn Ḥajar al-ᶜAsqalānī began his career as a publicist with prosody and poems. F. Rosenthal, *EI*² 'Ibn Ḥadjar al-ᶜAsḳalānī'.

35 *Nafḥ*, VII, p. 506.

follow are by Ibn al-Jannān, Abū'l-Yumn Ibn ᶜAsākir (d. 686/1287)[36] and ᶜAbd al-Raḥmān b. Yakhluftan al-Fāzāzī (d. 627/1230).[37] Only after presenting a *musaddasa* of Abū'l-Ḥajjāj Yūsuf b. Mūsā al-Muntashāqirī (Monte Sacro) from Ronda, a contemporary and correspondent of the vizier Lisān al-Dīn b. al-Khaṭīb (d. 776/1374) does Maqqarī finally come to a standstill.[38] This *musaddasa* contains 28 strophes with rhymes following the letters of the Maghribī alphabet. The strophe in *m* is missing. The one in *w* had already disappeared from the original and was replaced by Maqqarī's own versification. The verse with the refrain always stands at the head of each strophe and then repeats again at the end of the last strophe so that the hemistich *fa-ᶜalayhi'l-ṣalātu wa'l-taslīmu* regularly runs throughout the *musaddasa* and frames it at the beginning and at the end.[39]

Maqqarī's collection of panegyrical poems on the Prophet Muḥammad is naturally only one drop from an ocean but it is remarkable for its wealth of poems with refrains consisting of diverse forms of invoking blessings on Muḥammad which were in vogue in daily life and in literature. This leads one to conjecture that the whole appendix is meant to be nothing other than a long drawn-out *taṣliya* on behalf of Muḥammad with which the author wishes to conclude the book and which forms a symmetrical counterpart to the long introduction where he speaks about himself.[40] From this point of view one could indeed pursue threads in all possible directions. But I wish to direct my attention solely to the question of whether these poems also had or could have had a place in life, and in this connection to compare the *taṣliya*-poems amassed here with a social occasion during which precisely the repetition of invocations of blessings on Muḥammad stands at the center and which one im-

---

36 His date of death varies. Kutubī: *Fawāt al-Wafayāt*, ed. Iḥsān ᶜAbbās, Beirut, 1973-74, II, pp. 328-30, no. 282. Taqī al-Dīn Muḥammad b. Aḥmad al-Ḥasanī al-Fāsī al-Makkī: *Al-ᶜiqd al-thamīn fī tārīkh al-balad al-amīn*, ed. Fuᵓād Sayyid, Beirut, 1985, V, pp. 432-39, no. 1813. Yāfiᶜī: *Mirᵓāt al-janān*, year 686. Ibn Kathīr: *Al-bidāya wa'l-nihāya*, year 686. ᶜAbd al-Ḥayy b. al-ᶜImād: *Shadharāt al-dhahab*, year 686. Ziriklī: *Al-aᶜlām*, IV, p. 133.

37 Other dates for his death are also given. *GAL*, I, p. 273/*GAL S*, I, p. 482. Ziriklī, IV, p. 118.

38 On Muntashāqirī see Lisān al-Dīn b. al-Khaṭīb: *Al-katība al-kāmina fī-man laqīnāhu bi'l-Andalus min shuᶜarāᵓ al-miᵓa al-thāmina*, ed. Iḥsān ᶜAbbās, Beirut, 1963, no. 42. *Nafḥ*, VI, pp. 138-46.

39 *Nafḥ*, VII, pp. 512-17.

40 *Nafḥ*, I, pp. 1-121.

mediately recalls when one comes to hear the eternally unchanging melody of the invocation of blessings in these poems. I am referring to the so-called *maḥyā*. Under this term one first of all understands simply 'life', but then 'to be lively' and particularly in the sense of staying awake (instead of sleeping). For 'staying awake at night' it is perfectly normal in Arabic to say *iḥyāʾ al-layl* 'to keep the night lively, i.e. awake'. One could therefore entertain the idea of substituting for *maḥyā* in our sense the passive participle of the fourth-form verb in the infinitive meaning or in the meaning of a period of time during which one remained awake: *muḥyā*. But in so doing one would not get very far and would violate established usage.[41] We can more or less translate *maḥyā* as 'communal staying awake at night' and *laylat al-maḥyā*, which the night referred to here can also be called, as 'night of communal staying awake'. The adjective 'communal' belongs to the meaning at least implicitly.

Already in the 4th/10th century we hear of such a night. During the night of the 15th of Shaʿbān 327/June 7th 939 when people in Baghdad wanted to celebrate the *maḥyā*, the Ḥanbalites sought to hinder this and especially went after the musicians and pimps who had shown up. The police intervened.[42] In any case, one was supposed to pray 100 *rakaʿāt* and while doing so recite surah 112 ten times after surah 1[43] but, as the report reveals, the nocturnal gathering would regularly degenerate into indecent behavior. In Jerusalem this non-canonical celebration, as well as a similar one in Rajab, is meant to have first been introduced in 448/1056 by a certain Ibn Abī'l-Ḥamrāʾ

41 The title of an anonymous work *Muḥyā al-ṭarīqa al-damirdāshiyya* which Ernst Bannerth: 'La Khalwatiyya en Egypte. Quelques aspects de la vie d'une confrérie', *MIDEO* 8, 1964-66, p. 6, ftn. 1 and p. 73, cites, represents a false pronunciation. For a discussion see Goldziher, *WZKM* 15, 1901, p. 42. — On the other hand, Muḥyāy-i Bastakī is a Persian folk-poet from Bastak in Lāristān who lived in the 11th/17th century and was named Muḥyī al-Dīn. Aḥmad-i Ḥabībī: 'Muḥyāy-i Bastakī na Muḥyāy-i Bardkhūnī', *Āyanda* 15, 1368, pp. 542-44. Thus Muḥyā like Ṣadrā for Ṣadr al-Dīn (pronounced Ṣadr id-Dīn)

42 Abū Bakr Muḥammad b. Yaḥyā al-Ṣūlī: *Akhbār al-Rāḍī wa'l-Muttaḳī*, ed. J. Heyworth Dunne, Cairo, 1935, p. 135, ll. 15-19/trans. by Marius Canard: *Akhbâr Ar-Râdî billâh wa'l-Muttaqî billâh*, Publication de l'Institut d'Études Orientales de la Faculté des Lettres d'Alger. Tome I, Histoire d'Ar-Râdî, Algiers, 1946, pp. 205-06. Important commentary in ftns. 3, 4 and 5. Henri Laoust: *La profession de foi d'Ibn Baṭṭa*, Institut Français de Damas, Damascus, 1958, p. XL.

43 Muḥammad al-Ghazzālī: *Iḥyāʾ ʿulūm al-dīn*, Cairo, 1377/1957, I, p. 367, l. 11. Canard: *Akhbâr*, I, p. 205, ftn. 3.

from Nābulus.[44] Here it is not a question of the *taṣliya*. Rather, the ritual prayer in the night of the 15th of Shaᶜbān was called, among other things, *ṣalāt al-niṣf min shaᶜbān al-alfiyya* 'the thousandfold ritual prayer on mid-Shaᶜbān' because in the course of it surah 112/1: 'Say: "He is God, the One"' was recited a total of one thousand times (i.e. not merely ten times, as Ghazzālī says).[45] The celebration appears to be entirely orientated on God. At that time the Prophet still played a smaller role in worship. The Mālikite judge of public morals Ibn al-Ḥājj (d. 737/1338) accused particular dubious shaykhs of luring people to their cell of retirement in the cemetery on mid-Shaᶜbān night and of celebrating with them by lamplight the *laylat al-maḥyā* — here this name is mentioned — at which time tents were also set up and — what always especially angered the zealots — men and women mixed together.[46] Along the same lines the Ḥanbalite Ibn ᶜAqīl (d. 513/1119) was incensed that *maḥyā*-performances in his day were sprouting up like mushrooms: 'Before God I renounce gatherings (*jumūᶜ*) such as people in our time hold in mosques and tombs (*mashāhid*) on nights and which they call "revival" (*iḥyāʾ*). Verily, these nights are no more than a revival of their lusts...'[47] One person in honor of whom a *maḥyā* was held was the controversial shaykh Abū'l-Ḥasan ᶜAlī b. al-Ḥusayn b. Manṣūr al-Ḥarīrī from near Damascus. After his death on the afternoon of the 26th of Ramaḍān 645/1247, which was a Friday, every year on the eve of the 27th of Ramaḍān, a holy night, a *maḥyā* was carried out during which one danced until dawn to the accompaniment of flutes and tambourines so that ᶜAlāʾ al-Dīn al-Wadāᶜī (d. 716/1316) composed the verses:

Ḥarīrī has received a privilege
    which has not been conferred on anyone else:

---

44 Abū Bakr al-Ṭurṭūshī (d. 520-25/1126-31): *Al-ḥawādith wa'l-bidaᶜ*, ed. Muḥammad al-Ṭālibī (Talbi), Tunis, 1959, p. 121, with ftn. 4.

45 Ṭurṭūshī, p. 121, ftn. 4. Ibn Taymiyya: *Iqtiḍāʾ al-ṣirāṭ al-mustaqīm mukhālafat aṣḥāb al-jaḥīm*, Cairo, 1907, p. 145, l. 18/trans. by Muhammad Umar Memon: *Ibn Taimīya's Struggle against Popular Religion*, The Hague, 1976, p. 249, rejects alleged *ḥadīth*s about it.

46 Ibn al-Ḥājj: *Al-mudkhal*, Cairo, 1929, I, p. 312.

47 Yūsuf b. ᶜAbd al-Hādī (d. 909/1503): *Thimār al-maqāṣid fī dhikr al-masājid*, ed. Muḥammad Asᶜad Ṭalas, Beirut, 1975, p. 174, ll. 12-13. This *iḥyāʾ* comes very close to **muḥyā*.

on every Night of Destiny
people experience through him a revivification (*maḥyā*).[48]

With a similar double meaning, in the 8th/14th century on the eve of the 27th of Rajab, which is celebrated among the Sunnīs as 'the Night of the Heavenly Ascension' (*laylat al-miᶜrāj*) of Muḥammad, the Shīᶜites stayed awake at the grave of ᶜAlī in Najaf. At the time of the evening prayers one brought paralyzed persons to the grave, placed them on top of the grave, spent the night praying, recollecting God and gazing at the grave, and waited until the paralyzed stood up healed with the Shīᶜite profession of the faith on their tongue: 'There is no god but God, Muḥammad is the Apostle of God, ᶜAlī is the friend of God.' Ibn Baṭṭūṭa, who reports this, did not witness the event himself. But he met three lame persons who had arrived too late and were now waiting for the next *laylat al-maḥyā*.[49] Thus, here a night during which a company stayed awake in expectation of a miraculous cure through the revival of paralyzed persons at the grave of the highest Shīᶜite saint.

In the cases mentioned up till now Muḥammad is nowhere in the field of vision of the participants. However, in a whole series of *ḥadīth*s it is recommended to bless and greet the Prophet as often as possible, and from earliest times the ritual declarations and activities of Muslims have been permeated with invocations of blessings on the Prophet. To cite here the dogmatic sources and examples would lead us far afield of our subject. By way of moving ahead I will only mention that several *ḥadīth*s emphatically require numerous invoca-

---

48 Kutubī: *Fawāt al-Wafayāt*, III, pp. 9-10. Some literature on Ḥarīrī: Ibn al-Fuwaṭī: *Al-ḥawādith al-jāmiᶜa wa'l-tajārib al-nāfiᶜa fi'l-miᵓa al-sābiᶜa*, Baghdad, 1351, pp. 235-36. Yūnīnī: *Dhayl Mirᵓāt al-zamān*, Hyderabad, 1954-61, III, p. 405. Dhahabī: *Al-ᶜibar fī khabar man ghabar*, year 645. Abū Shāma: *Tarājim rijāl al-qarnayn al-sādis wa'l-sābiᶜ al-maᶜrūf bi'l-Dhayl ᶜalā'l-Rawḍatayn*, Cairo, 1947, p. 180. Yāfiᶜī: *Mirᵓāt al-janān*, year 645 (IV, pp. 112-13). Aḥmad b. ᶜAlī al-Daljī: *Al-falāka wa'l-maflūkūn*, Cairo, 1322, pp. 72-73. Ibn al-ᶜImād: *Shadharāt al-dhahab*, year 645 (V, pp. 231-32). ᶜAlāᵓ al-Dawla-i Simnānī: *Al-wārid al-ṭārid shubhat al-mārid*, MS Brit. Mus. Or. 9725, p. 288. Aflākī: *Manāqib al-ᶜārifīn*, ed. Yazıcı, pp. 640-41; p. 677, l. 17, to p. 678, l. 15. Anonymous: *Manāqib-i Awḥad al-Dīn-i Kirmānī*, ed. Furūzānfar, Tehran, 1347, pp. 263-64. Ḥarīrī declared himself against the use of hashish; dealt with in Franz Rosenthal: *The Herb*, Leiden, 1971, pp. 99, 100, 124, 148, 180, 190.

49 C. Defrémery et B.R. Sanguinetti: *Voyages d'Ibn Batoutah*, Paris, 1843, I, pp. 417-18/trans. by H.A.R. Gibb: *The Travels of Ibn Baṭṭūṭa*, Cambridge, 1958-71, I, pp. 257-58.

tions of blessings on Friday and on the night before Friday.[50] Both individual men of piety as well as pious groups obeyed these demands, and in the 8th/14th century in the far west, on the Atlantic coast, the question concerning the legality of such invocations of blessings was raised as far as their being employed in direct connection with communal Koran-recitations. Namely, in the morning and the evening after the recitation one repeated the formula of the *ṣalāh tāmma* or *ṣalāh ibrāhīmiyya*[51] for the Prophet on week days ten times and on Fridays twenty times. The prodigious mystic and religious scholar Ibn ᶜAbbād al-Rundī (d. 792/1390) had just as little objection against it as he had against the celebration of the Prophet's birthday, and in fact was inclined to approve of both. A certain Ibn al-Baqqāl, who was otherwise unknown to him, had already made a similar judgement. He himself believed that what appeared as religious to the people should be allowed to them. Not everything which the forefathers had not practiced was *ipso facto* forbidden. Otherwise one would also have to forbid the juridical subtleties which had arisen in the meantime, since they were clearly unknown to early Islam. The same is true, he said, about Koranic recitation in a circle (*bi'l-dāʾira*) and about the use of numerous lamps in the mosque during Ramaḍān, for in this way one only wished to glorify the month of fasting. And why should one have something against invoking blessings on the Prophet alternatingly in unison in an assembly but nothing against an assembly in which each individual invokes the blessing? Perhaps reciting the Koran in a circle could be contested even more than the invocation of blessings because in the former case sounds became chopped up and words were dismembered. In contrast to the Koran there are no prescriptions for reciting the invocation of blessings on the Prophet.[52] What in this regard caused offense in North Africa must also have existed elsewhere in the 8th/14th century. But this is still not an actual gathering for invoking blessings on the Prophet which one would have described as a *maḥyā*.

---

50 Abū Ṭālib al-Makkī: *Qūt al-qulūb*, Cairo, 1932, I, pp. 45, 100, 101, 106 (last two lines). Ismāᶜīl b. Isḥāq al-Jahḍamī: *Faḍl al-ṣalāh ᶜalā'l-nabī*, ed. Muḥammad Nāṣir al-Dīn al-Albānī, Maktab islāmī, 1382, pp. 37, 40, etc.

51 "Invoking Blessings on Muḥammad in Prayers of Supplication and When Making Requests', pp. 550-51.

52 Paul Nwyia: *Ibn ᶜAbbād de Ronda: Lettres de direction spirituelle. Ar-rasāʾil aṣ-ṣughrā*, Nouvelle édition, Beirut, 1974, pp. 166-68.

A milestone in the literary history of the invocation of blessings on Muḥammad is reached in the 9th/15th century. The change is ushered in by a Berber: Muḥammad or Maḥammad (b. ᶜAbd al-Raḥmān b. Abī Bakr) b. Sulaymān al-Jazūlī (d. 869/1465). He composed in Fez a collection of invocations of blessings on the Prophet which is broken down into four fourths, three thirds and eight eighths (*ḥizb*, pl. *aḥzāb*) for recitations from one Monday (the alleged day of Muḥammad's birth and demise) to the next, i.e. over a week, and which includes an introduction with the 201 names of Muḥammad and a concluding prayer. This book, which is almost as well-known as the Koran, bears the title *Dalāʾil al-khayrāt wa-shawāriq al-anwār fī dhikr al-ṣalāh ᶜalā'l-nabī al-mukhtār, Signs of Blessing(s) and Rising Lights. On Invoking Blessings on the Prophet, the Chosen One.*[53] The formulas of blessings which it contains are

---

53 The title is not immediately clear. The following are a few examples of previous translations:

Les meilleurs arguments

Louis Rinn: *Marabouts et Khouan*, Algiers, 1884, p. 269.

Depont et Coppolani: *Les confréries religieuses musulmanes*, Algiers, 1897, p. 170, ftn. 1; p. 455.

René Brunel: *Essai sur la Confrérie Religieuse des ᶜAîssâoûa au Maroc*, Paris, 1926, p. 91, ftn. 1.

Jean-Louis Michon: 'L'autobiographe (*Fahrasa*) du soufi marocain Aḥmad ibn ᶜAǧība', *Arabica* 16, 1969, p. 46, ftn. 1.

Les meilleurs arguments à la louange du Prophète

Georges Drague (= Spillmann): *Esquisse d'Histoire religieuse du Maroc*, Paris, 1951, p. 51, below.

Les guides des biens

Justinard: 'Sidi Ahmed ou Moussa', *Archives Marocaines* 29, 1933, pp. 217-19.

Guide religieux des œuvres dévotes

Le cheykh Mohammed Ibn-Omar El-Tounsy: *Voyage ou Ouadây*, trans. by Dr. Perron, Paris, 1851, p. 296.

Le Guide des bonnes œuvres

Marie Mas: 'La petite enfance à Fès et à Rabat', *AIEO* 17, 1959, p. 17.

Anweisungen zu den guten Werken

Ignaz Goldziher: 'Ueber den Brauch der Maḥjâ-Versammlungen im Islam', *WZKM* 15, 1901, p. 284, ftn. 5. Goldziher criticizes the translation 'Les meilleurs arguments' of Depont et Coppolani.

Hinweise zum Guten

Richard Hartmann: 'Die Wahhābiten', *ZDMG* 78, 1924, p. 185.

Hinweise auf die guten dinge

Annemarie Schimmel: *Und Muḥammad ist Sein Prophet*, Diederichs, 1981, p. 261.

Anleitungen zur Wohltätigkeit

Tarif Al Samman in his commentary to the facsimile edition. Al-Ǧazūlī, *Dalāʾil al-ḫairāt und andere Texte*, codices selecti phototypice impressi: Facsimile vol. LXXXVI, Graz, 1987, p. 39. In the exhibition catalogue, *Texte - Noten - Bilder*, 1984, Cat. no. 46, p. 50, he translates: *Hinweisungen zu Wohltätigkeiten.*

Buch der offenbaren Beweise für Frömmigkeit

German *Guide bleu* for Morocco, 1966, p. 344 (trans. from French).

Proofs of Blessings

J. Spencer Trimingham: *The Sufi Orders in Islam*, Oxford, 1971, p. 84.

Indications of the good things

Ali Fahmi Khushaim: *Zarrūq the Ṣūfī*, Tripoli (Libya), n.d., (reprint), p. 71, no. LXI.

The Signs of Blessings

Abdallah Laroui (translated from French by Glyn Thoiron) in: *The Encyclopedia of Religion*, ed. Mircea Eliade, New York-London, 1987, VII, p. 333a, in the article 'Islam in North Africa'.

My remarks on the subject:

Dalīl/dalāʾil is twice linked to *khayr/khayrāt* by means of the genitive in Jazūlī's *Dalāʾil al-khayrāt*: *dalīl al-khayrāt* as an honorific name of Muḥammad, and *dalāʾil al-khayrāt* as part of the book's title.

Thus one of Muḥammad's many honorific names is *dalīl al-khayrāt*. In the Persian interlinear translation of a Bombay lithograph edition of the work which is cited below this name is translated as 'road sign to good things' (*rahnumā ba-sūy-i nīkūʾīhā*), and in the Arabic commentary *Maṭāliʿ al-masarrāt bi-jalāʾ Dalāʾil al-khayrāt, The Risings of Joys through Clarification of the Dalāʾil al-khayrāt*, of Muḥammad al-Mahdī b. Aḥmad b. ʿAlī b. Yūsuf al-Fāsī al-Qaṣrī, Cairo, 1970, p. 124, next to last two lines, it is explained as the road sign to good things and as the person who causes one to reach the latter because only through him, Muḥammad, will one be led there, and only though his light does one receive the clarity for this endeavor. But this honorific name is immediately preceded by another such name, i.e. 'signpost of certainty' (*ʿalam al-yaqīn*), and just before that by 'signpost of faith' (*ʿalam al-īmān*). Although the honorific names of Muḥammad are by no means logically ordered, nor do they have to be interconnected with one another, it seems to me possible here also to take *dalīl* in a neuter sense as 'road sign, signpost, indication', i.e. in the sense of a sign for what is good.

Regarding the title *Dalāʾil al-khayrāt*, Qaṣrī also gives us explanations on pp. 16-17 of the *Maṭāliʿ al-masarrāt*. These reveal considerable uncertainty on the part of Qaṣrī (who died 1109/1698; *GAL*, II, p. 253/*GAL S*, II, p. 702). In his view *dalāʾil* refers to invocations of blessings on Muḥammad, and *khayrāt* to the reward one receives for these. Each invocation of blessings is a guide (?*dalīl*) to what is good (*ilā'l-khayr*), i.e. to attaining closeness to God and pleasing Him, to entering Paradise. But every invocation of blessings, thanks to its light-nature, is also a guide on the mystic path to God. *Khayrāt* as the plural of *khayra* means what is excellent and beautiful, as in surah 9/88: 'To them will come (one day) the good things (*khayrāt*).' The beautiful things of this kind which invoking blessings produces are lights, secrets, halting stations, deeper insights, forms of knowledge, closeness to God and the Prophet — the beautiful things of this world and the world to come. But then again he says *khayrāt* may possibly refer to the invocations of blessings themselves, namely to their recitation.

The second part of the title, *shawāriq al-anwār*, would mean 'the rising lights' (*ṭawāliʿ al-anwār*) and describe the various kinds of invocations of blessings on the Prophet (i.e. the blessings uttered are themselves the lights). But possibly *shāriq* ('rising, shining') might stand for *mushriq* in the causative sense 'to make shine', by which would be meant things which cast light into the heart of the invoker of blessings, i.e. illuminate the heart. *Shawāriq* could be parallel to *dalāʾil* (i.e. in the nominative) or to *khayrāt* (i.e. in the genitive). Here Qaṣrī repeatedly uses the expression 'but God is all-knowing', by which he wishes to indicate his uncertainty and doubts. The lights, he says, are perhaps also the epiphanies of intuitive knowledge and the divine experiences of the mystic (i.e. what one experiences in the here and now, not the vision one only enjoys in the hereafter).

Bearing in mind all these uncertainties, from a critical standpoint one may perhaps venture the following rough translation of the title: 'Directions to blessings and rising lights (or risings of lights)'. But if *shawāriq* is meant to be parallel to *khayrāt*, one could consider the more attractive variation: 'Directions to blessings and (to) the rising lights (or the risings of lights)'. The attached words *fī dhikr al-ṣalāh ʿalā 'l-nabī al-mukhtār* constitute a subtitle. They should not be syntactically joined to what precedes but rendered simply: 'Concerning the invocations of blessings on the Prophet, the Chosen One (or on the Prophet and Chosen One)'. However, what has just been referred to as the more attractive variation has the disadvantage of not wholly conforming to the style of titles of this kind. *Shawāriq* in my view should not be construed as parallel to *khayrāt* but be translated as parallel to *dalāʾil*, as we first did: i.e. as 'rising lights' (or 'risings of lights'). The obligatory prose-rhyme only occurs between *anwār* and *mukhtār*. Still, one would like to have a tighter parallelism in the translation. This can be achieved by substituting 'signs' for 'directions' and the substantive 'risings' for the adjectival participle 'rising'. Then we would have 'Signs of blessings and risings of lights'. As evidence of the meaning 'indication, mark, sign' for the word *dalīl*, pl. *dalāʾil*, the following are selected from an abundance of examples:

Muḥammad Dāwud (sic): *Tārīkh Tiṭwān*, V, Tetuan, 1965, p. 131, l. 4: 'Love has signs (*dalāʾil*) and features (*ʿalāmāt*).' Ibid., VII, 1975, p. 90, last two lines: 'The praise which people bestow on him is a sign of his blessedness (*min dalāʾil saʿādatihī*) in accordance with the *ḥadīth*: "Whoever you bestow praise on merits Paradise."'

Muḥammad al-Mukhtār al-Sūsī: *Al-maʿsūl*, Casablanca, 1960 ff., X, p. 167 below (from an earlier work): 'In this time period and previously *mubashshirāt* and *dalāʾil khayr* have occurred.' — I.e. dreams portending joy, and signs of coming good fortune.

Fishtālī: *Manāhil al-ṣafā fī maʾāthir mawālīnā al-shurafā*, ed. ʿAbd al-Karīm Karīm, Rabat, 1973, p. 68, ll. 13-14: 'Testimonies (*shawāhid*) of divine support... signs (*dalāʾil*) of felicity and endowment with favor.'

Murādī: *Silk al-durar*, Būlāq, 1301, IV, p. 174, ll. 5-6:

'By reading the *Dalāʾil al-khayrāt*
you have earned a reward which will never desert you.
This is a sign of what is good (*dalīl al-khayr*) and of being led and rightly guided.'

Ghars al-Niʿma al-Ṣābiʾ: *Al-hafawāt al-nādira*, ed. Ṣāliḥ al-Ashtar, Damascus, 1967, p. 99, l. 4: 'I beheld in this king the features of goodness and the signs of majesty (*amārāt al-khayr wa-dalāʾil al-ʿuluww*).'

Al-Ḥusayn b. Muḥammad al-Warthīlānī: *Nuzhat al-anẓār fī faḍl ʿilm al-tārīkh wa'l-akhbār* (*Riḥla warthīlāniyya*), Algiers, 1908, p. 6, last line, to p. 7, l. 2: 'The indication (*ʿalāma*) of (divine) acceptance will be on hand and the signs of what is good (*dalāʾil al-khayr*) will appear — if God is willing! And why would this not be so since they have only conducted their journey out of love of God, for God and from God, and out of longing for His Messenger, and the signs of the good (*dalāʾil al-khayr*) do not allow themselves to be known publicly.'

The test case is provided by ibid., p. 41, l. 12: 'The signs of what is bad (*dalāʾil al-sharr*) are chiefly lacking in them.'

Ibid., p. 385, l. 15: 'The signs of (divine) presence (*dalāʾil al-ḥaḍra*).'

It is not clear to me how to solve the question of the exact meaning of *khayrāt* and *anwār*. Are the *khayrāt* the merits which a person has acquired by means of invoking blessings and can show on the Day of Resurrection, or the actual blessings of Paradise which one should count on or hope for? Does one come before God with these previously acquired lights (*anwār*) or does one only receive them in Paradise as a reward for invocations of blessings in the here and now? The commentator himself did not know the answer to this. He mentions both possibilities. In order to leave the matter open I have translated *khayrāt* as 'blessing(s)' and concerning the lights I have also left it undecided whether they are shining merits, mystical experiences or the lights of Paradise. Perhaps an answer to this question is found in the prayer of supplication with which Jazūlī concludes his book. There Jazūlī prays God to lead him (and others who bless Muḥammad) through (*bi-*, i.e. by means of and in return for) invoking blessings to his (or their) goals, to remove all his worries, to accept his repentance, to unburden his tongue, to elucidate everything, to cause judgement on the Final Day to turn out well for him, and to unite him with the Prophet. In addition, he asks God to see to it that before his death he may reach the Prophet's tomb in Medina, and if possible to let him reside there until his death. Accordingly, 'the signs of blessing(s) and the risings of lights' would be the invocations of blessings as proof of merits which will be rewarded both in this world and the world to come. How a pious person would more or less picture this is perhaps expressed in the following quatrain:

If you properly perform the invocation of blessings on him
on whom God pronounced blessings in His holy verses

meant to be based on early traditions, i.e. on 'authentic' sayings about Muḥammad in the Koran and *ḥadīth*. Jazūlī, however, professes that nothing comes about without the foreknowledge and providence of God, and that God has also inspired him and pre-ordained that he compile (*jamᶜ*) the book (in the 4th fourth, 6th *ḥizb*). The work makes use of large numbers and of urgent repetitions which are in part conjurations. Occasionally rhymed prose appears. The long sequences of requests are directed to God and dominate the stylistic tone with the anaphora 'Oh God, bless' (*allāhumma ṣalli ᶜalā*). The litany primarily has in mind the single individual since the first person singular pronoun prevails over the first person plural. The whole is composed as a litany (*wird*). The ideal was to recite it in one day. But it is also recommended to go through it in three days, the first third on Saturday, the second on Sunday, the third on Monday and subsequently in the same division once again on Tuesday, Wednesday and Thursday, and on Friday the whole text in one go. In any case this is the way the shaykhs who had devoted themselves to Jazūlī did it.[54] There were sessions in which the *Dalāʾil* was read to the group, and others in which the group recited it out loud. Moreover, certain shaykhs specialized in this activity.[55] In Morocco a *qāʾid* named Abū'l-ᶜAbbās Aḥmad Būsta al-Marrākushī engaged several scholars (*ṭalaba*) in copying the *Dalāʾil*, had the copies distributed to caravans and thus spread the work to distant lands. He of-

---

and if you make them into a fixed litany (*wird*) for yourself,
'the signs of blessing(s)' will shine upon you.

This is found in al-ᶜAbbās b. Ibrāhīm: *Al-iᶜlām bi-man ḥalla Marrākush wa-Aghmāt min al-aᶜlām*, Rabat, 1974 ff., V, p. 88. (in the article on Jazūlī).

Perhaps some small support is provided for our interpretation by the title of a book dealing with panegyrical poetry on Muḥammad, written by Ibn al-ᶜAṭṭār al-Dunaysarī (p. 655 above): *ᶜUnwān al-saᶜāda* 'Frontispiece of felicity'.

54 Al-ᶜAbbās b. Ibrāhīm: *Al-iᶜlām bi-man ḥalla Marrākush*, V, pp. 85-86 (in the article on Jazūlī). Contrary to how it seems at first, the formulation refers to the *Dalāʾil* and not to Jazūlī's *Ḥizb al-falāḥ* which is only a short prayer (printed in the same work, V, p. 96). From a different *ḥizb* we learn that each time one group said a sentence, another group would repeat it (ibid., V, p. 73, the penult. paragraph)

55 Further information in F. De Jong: 'Cairene ziyāra-days', *Die Welt des Islams* 17, 1976, p. 29. Idem: 'Al-mashâyikh al-Bakriyya and the transformation of their authority in 19th century Egypt', *Akten des VII. Kongresses für Arabistik und Islamwissenschaft*, Göttingen, 1976, pp. 220-21. Idem: *Ṭuruq and Ṭuruq-Linked Institutions in Nineteenth Century Egypt*, Leiden, 1978, p. 91. And elsewhere as well.

fered a reward to the blind if they learned the text by heart, and those with sight competed with them. His most beautiful gardens he donated to provide income for those who recited the *Dalāʾil* in the *rawḍa* of the tomb of the Prophet in Medina.[56] In the previous century there was a *shaykh al-Dalāʾil* by the name of Muḥammad Riḍwān who in 1286/1870 at the grave of the Prophet conferred a teaching permit (*ijāza*) for a certain text-form of the *Dalāʾil* and an accompanying certification of the chain of transmitters (*sanad*). The Indian publisher Ḥājjī Ṣiddīq Khwāja-i Khujandī brought an old printed copy with him and had this man recite the corrections to him. In his homeland in 1289/1872 he published a lithograph edition of the text he had obtained in this way, with an interlinear Persian translation and a Persian commentary by Muḥammad Fāḍil b. ᶜĀrif Sayf al-Dīn-i Dihlawī.[57] One may assume that Muḥammad Riḍwān knew the *Dalāʾil* by heart.

Around a century later ᶜAbd al-Jalīl b. Muḥammad b. Aḥmad b. ᶜĪsā al-Murādī al-Qayrawānī, known as Ibn ᶜAẓẓūm (d. 960/1553),[58] attempted to outdo Jazūlī in the same area by means of literary brilliance. He entitled his work *Tanbīh al-anām fī bayān ᶜuluww maqām nabiyyinā Muḥammad — ᶜalayhi afḍal al-ṣalāh wa'l-salām*, *The Awakening of Mankind. On the Lofty Station of Our Prophet...* or, as he also says, *Shifāʾ al-asqām wa-maḥw al-āthām fī'l-ṣalāh ᶜalā khayr al-anām*, *Healing Illnesses and Eradication of Sins. On Invoking Blessings on the Best of Mankind*, and in the introduction he expressly lays claim to literary importance. He expands the anaphoric *allāhumma ṣalli* of his predecessor to *allāhumma ṣalli wa-sallim* 'bless and greet', increases the rhymed prose considerably, formulates a large number of parallel clauses and divides the whole into a long series of chapters ordered according to content and subject matter. He also refers to the great reverberation which the book had already had. But the challenge was not successful. An anecdote tells

56 Ibn al-Muwaqqit: *Al-saᶜāda al-abadiyya fī'l-taᶜrīf bi-mashāyikh al-ḥaḍra al-marrākushiyya*, litho., Fez, 1336, II, p. 33/al-ᶜAbbās b. Ibrāhīm: *Iᶜlām*, V, p. 91.

57 *Dalāʾil al-khayrāt* (with Persian interlinear translation and commentary), litho., Bombay, 1330/1912 (reprint), pp. 261-64 (epilogue).

58 This date is from İsmail Paşa's *Hadiyyat al-ᶜārifīn*, I, p. 500, and *Keşf-el-zunun zeyli*, Istanbul, 1947, I, p. 324. *GAL*, II, p. 459/*GAL S*, II, p. 691, writes 971/1563 without giving a source for the date. Muḥammad b. Ṣāliḥ ᶜĪsā al-Kinānī al-Qayrawānī (d. 1292/1875): *Takmīl al-ṣulaḥāʾ wa'l-aᶜyān li-ᶜālam al-īmān fī awliyāʾ al-Qayrawān*, ed. Muḥammad al-ᶜAnnābī, Tunis, 1970, pp. 23-25, only gives extracts from the Introduction of the *Tanbīh* and does not know the date of the author's death.

of a certain man that every time he placed the *Tanbīh* of Ibn ᶜAẓẓūm on top of the *Dalāʾil* of Jazūlī and went away, upon returning he found Jazūlī on top of Ibn ᶜAẓẓūm.[59] This reminds one of the custom of never placing another book on top of the Koran.[60] A widespread judgement states that the *Dalāʾil* diffuses light, whereas the *Tanbīh* offers only learning.[61]

The hour of birth of the actual *maḥyā* arrived in the time between Jazūlī and Ibn ᶜAẓẓūm, shortly before 900/1494-95 in Lower-Egypt. Its creator was Nūr al-Dīn ᶜAlī al-Shūnī (d. 944/1537-38) from a village near Tanta, and its discoverer was Ignaz Goldziher with his article 'Ueber den Brauch der Maḥjâ-Versammlungen im Islam', *WZKM* 15, 1909, pp. 33-50, in which he touches upon much of what I have reported concerning its early history and context. Information about Shūnī is given by his student ᶜAbd al-Wahhāb b. Aḥmad al-Shaᶜrānī (d. 973/1565) and at second hand by Najm al-Dīn Muḥammad b. Muḥammad al-Ghazzī (d. 1061/1651) in his collection of biographies *Al-kawākib al-sāʾira bi-manāqib aᶜyān al-miʾa al-ᶜāshira*, Beirut 1945 ff.,[62] II, pp. 216-19. Already as a boy when he was guarding the cattle, Shūnī would give his provisions to his comrades as payment for their reciting with him in a group the blessing on Muḥammad.[63] When still a beardless youth he transferred this *majlis al-ṣalāh ᶜalā rasūl allāh* into the sepulchre of Aḥmad al-Badawī (d. 675/1276) in Tanta, and this on Thursday night until Friday noon. Later he installed himself in the tomb of Barqūq near Cairo and in the year 897/1492 established the ceremony in al-Azhar. In 913/1507-08 Shaᶜrānī personally made his acquaintance in the Turbat al-ᶜĀdiliyya located there. During seven years he attended Shūnī's *maḥyā*. In 919/1513 Shūnī invited him to carry out a similar night from Thursday to Friday in the Jāmiᶜ al-Ghamrī. Shaᶜrānī then

---

59 From Muḥammad al-Mahdī's '*Mumtiᶜ al-asmāʾ fī dhikr al-Jazūlī wa'l-Tabbāᶜ wa-mā* (or *wa-man*) *lahumā min al-atbāᶜ*' in the translation by Graulle in *Archives Marocaines* 19, 1913, p. 283; Justinard: 'Sidi Ahmed ou Moussa', in *Arch. Maroc.* 29, 1933, p. 218; al-ᶜAbbās b. Ibrāhīm: *Iᶜlām*, V, p. 53.

60 Edward William Lane: *Manners and Customs of the Modern Egyptians*, Everyman's Library no. 315, London, 1954, p. 289. Porfirio Gomes Moreira: 'A ciência do Corâo entre os Muçulmanos de Moçambique', in *Actas IV Congresso*, Coimbra, p. 469.

61 Graulle, *Arch. Maroc.* 19, 1913, p. 283; Justinard, *Arch. Maroc.* 29, 1933, p. 218; al-ᶜAbbās b. Ibrāhīm: *Iᶜlām*, V, pp. 53 and 101.

62 *GAL*, II, pp. 291-92/*GAL S*, II, p. 402. See ftn. 19 above.

63 Shaᶜrānī: *Al-ṭabaqāt al-kubrā al-musammāh bi-Lawāqiḥ al-anwār fī ṭabaqāt al-akhyār*, Cairo, 1954, II, p. 171, no. 66.

increased the invocation of blessings by adding an interval that consisted of reciting one thousand times surah 108/1: 'We have given you abundance', after which many people believed they had seen the Prophet. Shūnī adopted the interlude into his *maḥyā* in al-Azhar. Later Shaᶜrānī also inserted the recitation of surah 2/286: 'Pardon us, forgive us and have mercy on us' for a period of 3 hours and 20 minutes (50 *daraja* = 50 x 4 minutes = 200 minutes), by means of which the people entered a state of great expansiveness (*basṭ*). Shūnī adopted this addition from Shaᶜrānī as well.[64] But judging by a particular allusion,[65] surah 112/1: 'Say: "He is God, the One"' and the profession of faith must also have been added if they had not already been incorporated earlier.

The *maḥyā*, which at that time did not yet bear this name, must have spread like wildfire. In 952/1545, the year when the *Ṭabaqāt kubrā* was composed, according to Shaᶜrānī[66] it was already in the Ḥijāz, in Syria, Cairo, Upper-Egypt, al-Maḥalla al-Kubrā, Alexandria, in North Africa and in the Senegal region. All these branches sprang from one and the same root. Before Shūnī one had only known litanies (*awrād*) with invocations of blessings on Muḥammad as performed by single individuals, not in groups.

It was precisely this, i.e. communal activity, which drew sharp criticism from strict theologians. From this point of view the Mālikite Ibn al-Ḥājj (d. 737/1336) had already come out against ritual prayer during the night before the first Friday in Rajab. If a man performs the prayers for himself alone, he should do it in silence as in the case of all supererogatory acts of worship, so that the impression is not given that it constitutes *sunna*.[67] The inhabitants of al-Azhar to begin with reproached Shūnī for extravagant consumption of candles and lamps, and scolded him saying: 'The Zoroastrians do that.' An expert legal judgement deemed that artificial light should only be used as long as it could still increase the light of day.[68] Shihāb al-Dīn al-Qasṭallānī (d. 927/1517) came out in support of Shūnī by refuting the latter's opponents.[69] Shūnī is depicted as an ordinary, kind person, as 'pleasant in manner, of natural nobility,

---

64 *Ṭabaqāt kubrā*, II, pp. 171-72.

65 *Ṭabaqāt*, II, p. 173, ll. 11-12.

66 *Ṭabaqāt*, II, p. 172 below.

67 *Mudkhal*, I, pp. 293-94.

68 Najm al-Dīn al-Ghazzī: *Al-kawākib al-sā'ira bi-manāqib aᶜyān al-mi'a al-ᶜāshira*, II, p. 216, ll. 18-22.

69 *Kawākib sā'ira*, II, p. 216, ll. 21-22.

obliging, always smiling'.[70] He never married and lived to be over 90 years old.[71]

As already indicated, the institution which is traced back to Shūnī was not at first called *maḥyā*. Shaʿrānī, the latter's comrade-in-arms, nowhere makes use of the word. It first appears in connection with events in Damascus. What happened was this: a man from Damascus named ʿAbd al-Qādir b. Sawwār al-ʿĀtikī (922-1014/1516-1605) became familiar with Shūnī's invocation of blessings in Cairo under the latter's successor at al-Azhar, Shihāb al-Dīn al-Bulqīnī. After returning to Damascus, he introduced it into the al-Buzūrī Mosque in the quarter of al-ʿĀtika's tomb outside the city, and this during the daytime when he and a small group would remain seated for the purpose following the afternoon prayers. Najm al-Dīn al-Ghazzī's brother Shihāb al-Dīn one day joined them. He too, as early as 952/1545, had come to know the sessions in Cairo. One day he suggested to ʿAbd al-Qādir al-ʿĀtikī that he carry out the session correctly according to the manner of the founder and Bulqīnī during the night before Friday and that he transfer it to the Umayyad Mosque of Damascus. This took place in 971/1563-64. From then on the ceremony was called *maḥyā* 'Durchwachungsnacht' (night of remaining awake) or 'Wachnacht' (wakeful night) as Goldziher, *WZKM* 15, 1901, p. 43, translates *laylat al-maḥyā*. Two sessions a week were then introduced, on Monday and on Friday. Ghazzī's father, Badr, who was frequently present, then advised ʿAbd al-Qādir to adopt surah 94 (*Inshirāḥ*) into the litany as well because the Prophet himself is addressed in it, and to have it repeated eleven times because the Prophet is mentioned in it in the 2nd person singular eleven times. This also took place, and this is how surah 94 came to be included in the *maḥyā* of Damascus.[72] We also learn that under ʿAbd al-Qādir al-ʿĀtikī a certain Ibn al-Kayyāl (d. 1018/1609) used to recite the 'usual ten verses' from surah 33 (*Aḥzāb*) during the *maḥyā*.[73] Without knowing which verses these were, we are grateful for the reference to this further addition that served to enrich the *maḥyā* in Damascus.

The expansion of the session to two days in the week, the recitation of a section of surah 33 and the insertion of surah 94 are to this

---

70 *Kawākib*, II, p. 217, ll. 3-4.

71 Ibid., II, p. 216, last line, to p. 217, l. 1.

72 *Kawākib sāʾira*, II, p. 218, ll. 5-26. With deviations and abbreviated in Muḥibbī: *Khulāṣat al-athar fī aʿyān al-qarn al-ḥādī ʿashar*, Cairo, 1284, II, p. 454.

73 Muḥibbī, I, p. 436, l. 12.

extent clear. But as far as the naming is concerned, two interpretations are possible. Either it refers to the whole ceremony from its origin, i.e. would also include the sessions of Shūnī, or else it is simply meant to indicate that the undertaking of ᶜĀtikī had not been called *maḥyā* earlier because it took place in the afternoon and could only be called *maḥyā* once it had been transferred to nights. In the first case the designation would have been projected back onto Shūnī after ᶜĀtikī, in the second case it would have been exclusively coined for the ceremony of ᶜĀtikī which having been transferred to the night had now been brought into line with Shūnī's practice. The question is decided in favor of the first case by Najm al-Dīn al-Ghazzī who writes in another place: 'The *majlis al-ṣalāh ᶜalā'l-nabī* which he (Shūnī) brought into being... is the *majlis* which in Damascus and surroundings is today known as *al-maḥyā* because as a rule it is performed at night. Since by means of it one stays awake through the night (read *yuḥyā* instead of *yajīᵓ*), it is called *al-maḥyā*. It is a creation of Shūnī.'[74] Thus the custom stems from Shūnī but the specific designation *maḥyā* only arose later in Damascus after his death.

But I do not wish to trace the ramified history of *maḥyā*. Dates in this connection could be found especially in Muḥibbī (for the 11th/17th century) and Murādī: *Silk al-durar fī aᶜyān al-qarn al-thānī ᶜashar* (for the 12th/18th century). Goldziher informs us about some offshoots in Damascus and Egypt up to his time,[75] and F. De Jong's article *maḥyā* in *EI*² gives an overview of the subject. Nor can I verify whether everything resembling *maḥyā* in North Africa and Senegambia really originates with Shūnī in Egypt, as Shaᶜrānī would have us believe. If in fact characteristic elements of a *maḥyā* were already supposed to be present in West Africa to such an extent by the middle of the 10th/16th century, then indigenous as well as North African traditions could also have been at work because according to Ibn ᶜAbbād al-Rundī already in the 8th/14th century in Morocco after the *ḥizb* (section of the Koran or Sufi litany) one had recited the formula 'Oh God, bless Muḥammad and Muḥammad's family' in a group and this was then replaced by the longer *ṣalāh tāmma/ibrāhīmiyya* which was recited communally mornings and evenings ten times and on Fridays twenty times.[76] This was still not a *maḥyā*,

---

74 *Kawākib sāᵓira*, II, p. 217, ll. 12-15.

75 'Ueber den Brauch der Maḥjâ-Versammlungen im Islam'/*Gesammelte Schriften*, IV, pp. 293-94.

76 Nwyia: *Lettres de direction spirituelle*², p. 166, ll. 7-11. See p. 661 above.

but the beginning of a nocturnal group-recitation of invocations of blessings on the Prophet had been made, and who knows what different forms the initiative may have grown into in different places? Later in North Africa we meet with many *majālis al-ṣalāh ᶜalā'l-nabī* which may also have come about due to eastern models because thanks to the pilgrimage and by means of the Sufi orders contact with Egypt and other central lands was always very close and frequent. In this regard the order of the Nāṣiriyyūn (of Muḥammad b. Nāṣir, d. 1085/1674, and his son Aḥmad), as a sister order of the Shādhiliyya, clearly played a role. A certain ᶜAbdallāh b. ᶜAlī al-Īrghī al-Jarfī (vocalization?, d. 1214/1799-1800) began sobbing (*shahqa*) already during the ritual prayers, and a hereditary line (*isnād*) via his teacher back to the Yemenite contemporary of Muḥammad, Uways al-Qaranī, was imputed to this sobbing.[77] After the *ḥizb* of the night-time prayer and after he had asked God for forgiveness 100 times, he invoked blessings on Muḥammad 300 to 500 times, together with the *fuqarā'*.[78] He never neglected the gathering for invoking blessings (*majlis al-ṣalāh ᶜalā'l-nabī*) especially between the two night-time prayers of Thursday, and also never omitted the invocation of blessings Friday mornings before sunrise.[79] The Nāṣirī Masᶜūd b. Muḥammad al-Ṭālibī al-Maᶜdarī al-Būnuᶜmānī (in the 13th/19th century) recited formulas of blessings on the Prophet especially between the evening and night-time prayers on Thursday and on Friday before sunrise, and invited the ordinary people as well as students or scholars to participate. This was, so to speak, normal practice in the *madrasa*s and mosques of Sūs. Similarly, the teacher of Muḥammad al-Mukhtār al-Sūsī (d. 1383/1963) devoted himself along with his students, including Sūsī, to the invocation of blessings on Muḥammad on Thursday evenings in the *madrasa* of Īghshān in 1330/1912.[80] Sūsī's father, ᶜAlī al-Darqāwī (d. 1328/1911), one time at a *majlis al-ṣalāh ᶜalā'l-nabī* discovered a *faqīr* who did not recite loud enough. He exclaimed: 'It is the duty of the *faqīr* to raise up his voice earnestly in such a gathering and to open his mouth wide enough so that a person who looks into his throat can almost see what is in his stomach. Whoever is sluggish in the *majlis al-dhikr*

---

77 Muḥammad al-Mukhtār al-Sūsī: *Al-maᶜsūl*, Casablanca, 1960 ff., XVIII, p. 226. Cf. my remark about a theology of the sigh in my *Bahā'-i Walad. Grundzüge seines lebens und seiner mystik*, Acta Iranica 27, 1989, p. 335, l. 3.

78 Sūsī: *Al-maᶜsūl*, XVIII, p. 225, ll. 22-23.

79 *Maᶜsūl*, XVIII, p. 226 below.

80 *Maᶜsūl*, XIII, p. 16, ll. 14-20.

(sic), the other participants must steer him out of it.'[81] According to a tradition, the Nāṣirī Aḥmad b. Muḥammad al-Tīmggidshtī (d. 1274/1858) required from a teacher in the Īzberī *madrasa* at Illigh, who died 1347/1928, 500 invocations of blessings in a group (*bi'l-jamāʿa*) every Thursday evening, and every Friday 1,000 in the morning and 300 in the evening.[82] Sūsī was informed in Aglu in 1361/1942 that, following the practice of the Nāṣiriyyūn, the invocation of blessings on the Prophet still took place in the mosque on Thursday nights.[83] All this seems to me primarily to be evidence for the strong endeavors in North Africa to draw the Prophet into ritual practices and only secondarily for the possibility of occasional borrowings from the central region of Islam as well.

Moreover, equating the *majlis al-dhikr* with the *majlis al-ṣalāh ʿalā'l-nabī* in the sentences just quoted from ʿAlī al-Darqāwī deserves attention. The expression *dhikr*-performance is placed above the designation *taṣliya*-gathering with regard to terminology and placed before it as far as historical development is concerned. To begin with there was recollection of God (*dhikr*) and then came the additions, among which was the invocation of blessings on Muḥammad. Both parts, in one way or another, could already be linked to one another with Koranic verses, as we know from the *maḥyā*, and even allowed interruptions with verses of poetry, as we will see shortly. The Nāṣirī Muḥammad b. Aḥmad (d. 1251/1835) from the family of Ḥusayn al-Ṭāṭāʾī, about whom we happen to have more precise information, is presented to us by way of commendation as 'the last through whom God revived the *majālis al-dhikr* in Sūs'. As proof we are told about the religious feats he performed in the course of a day from morning to evening together with his students and the people in the mosque, as well as away from home while visiting villages and tombs. From this one may gather that in between his prayers and numerous invocations of blessings on Muḥammad he often inserted verses of poetry as well. These included excerpts from the *Burda* of Būṣīrī (d. 696/1296) and Berber verses of Maḥammad (sic) b. ʿAlī b. Ibrāhīm al-Hawzālī/Awzalī, known as Agbīl (d. 1162/1749).[84] These were interludes for relax-

---

81 *Maʿsūl*, XII, p. 187, ll. 9-13.

82 *Maʿsūl*, XVII, p. 138 below.

83 Muḥammad al-Mukhtār al-Sūsī: *Khilāl Jazūla*, Tetuan, 1361/1942, I, p. 77, last two lines from bot.

84 Cf. *Maʿsūl*, XIX, p. 14. B.H. Stricker: *L'Océan des pleurs. Poème berbère de Muḥammad al-Awzalī*, Publ. de la 'Fondation De Goeje' 19, Leiden, 1960.

ation. From the *Burda* the shaykh or someone else pronounced a verse, a second and a third person repeated it, and in this way the whole poem could be recited, though at times only single verses might be taken from the text.[85] Thus what we have before us is a *majlis al-dhikr* which was composed of recollection of God, invocation of blessings on the Prophet, prayers, Koranic verses and verses of religious poetry. Nor were passages from Jazūlī's *Dalāʾil al-khayrāt* lacking among the invocations of blessings. As to origin, one may assume that all the additions attached themselves around the recollection of God (*dhikr* in the real sense) but once the invocation of blessings on the Prophet became prominent, this could also have been perceived as the central point and core of the ceremony.

The situation is similar regarding the combination of recollection of God (*dhikr*) and music (*samāᶜ*) in the '*dhikr*' or in the *ḥaḍra* 'meeting, coming together' of the eastern orders. From an inquiry put to the Mālikite scholar Abū Bakr al-Ṭurṭūshī (d. 520-25/1126-31) it is clear that the Ṣūfiyya during their gatherings first recited a great amount of recollection of God (*dhikr*) and blessings on Muḥammad (*dhikr Muḥammad*), then beat time to poems on a piece of leather, danced and entered states of ecstasy.[86] Here everything seems to be more or less on the same level, even if the actual goal may be ecstasy. This becomes clearer a hundred years later with Sayf al-Dīn-i Bākharzī (d. 658/1260, or one year later). When one time in a *samāᶜ* (musical performance) 'an experience' (*dhawq*) would not arrive, he had the recollection of God (*dhikr*) recited 'so that the turbidity of the "now" (= moment) be transformed to purity'.[87] Here incontestably the recollection of God is only harnessed in order to drag the soul's cart out of the mud of sluggishness. *Samāᶜ* is the main concern, *dhikr* provides assistance and preliminary work. One time when the *samāᶜ* was not taking effect, the Chishtī Niẓām al-Dīn

---

85 *Maᶜsūl*, VI, p. 212 below to p. 213, l. 2; p. 217, ll. 12-14.

86 Ibn al-Ḥājj: *Al-mudkhal*, III, p. 99, penult line, to p. 100, l. 1. The text continues polemically (p. 100, ll. 1-2): 'Finally they fall down unconscious, and they are then brought something to eat.' Ṭurṭūshī's contemporary Qāḍī ᶜIyāḍ: *Tartīb al-madārik wa-taqrīb al-masālik li-maᶜrifat aᶜlām madhhab Mālik*, ed. Ṭanjī, Ṣaḥrāwī et alii, Rabat, 1966, II, p. 54/ed. Aḥmad Bukayr Maḥmūd, Beirut, 1965-68, I, p. 180, puts it the other way round: 'They first eat a lot, then begin with poems (*qaṣāʾid*) and then stand up and dance.' One finds another version in Aḥmad b. Muḥammad b. Hārūn al-Khallāl: *Al-ḥathth ᶜalā'l-tijāra wa'l-ṣināᶜa wa'l-ᶜamal*, Damascus, 1348, p. 24/Ibn Jawzī: *Talbīs Iblīs*, Cairo, 1928, p. 370. Recollection of God is missing in all these versions. The focus is against the *samāᶜ*.

87 'The Dervish Dance', p. 42.

Awliyāʾ (d. 725/1325), in place of the *dhikr*, ordered Sufi stories to be related (most of which ended with an illuminating word or action of a shaykh), whereupon the spark was already ignited in this prelude before the two singers for the *samāᶜ*, the musical part, had appeared.[88] Among the Rifāᶜiyya in Umm ᶜAbīda *dhikr* and *samāᶜ* already appear to have become firmly linked with one another in the 8th/14th century: after the night-time prayer *dhikr* was first recited and then music was listened to, during which ecstatic dances with thaumaturgic demonstrations were eventually performed.[89] This combination of *dhikr* and *samāᶜ* is readily referred to by way of abbreviation simply as *dhikr* because 'recollection of God' is a pious action which is already approved of in the Koran, whereas *samāᶜ* 'music' is looked upon as a non-religious, rather notorious form of entertainment. In the Sufi *ḥaḍra* these two opposites often appear so joined with one another that *dhikr* concerns the whole group and *samāᶜ*, or more precisely *ismāᶜ* 'the causing to be heard, making audible' of musical sounds, is assigned to one or more singers with or without instruments. The division is effected in such a way that the *dhikr* of the participants alternates with the *samāᶜ* of the singer and in other sections both parties act simultaneously, that is to say they perform together. In the latter case one has the impression one moment that the *dhikr* of the participants, i.e. the continuous repetition of the *dhikr*-formula by the gathering, provides the rhythm or the *basso ostinato* for the songs which the singer or singers execute, at another moment, conversely, that the singer embellishes the *dhikr* of the group through his melodic accompaniment. Several years ago I described this on the basis of an excerpt from the *ḥaḍra* of the Ḍayfiyya in Lower-Egypt.[90] In the *ḥaḍra* of the Khalwatiyya, in which the same mixture of *dhikr* and *samāᶜ* is heard — to mention only one example — interludes from poetry are also recited, from the *Burda* of Būṣīrī as we encountered in the west, and from the *Tāʾiyya* of the somewhat earlier Ibn al-Fāriḍ (d. 632/1235). In the case of the *Burda* the *munshid* sings several verses which are then answered with a refrain by those present in chorus. During the *Tāʾiyya* the verses are underscored by the chorus with the first phrase of the Is-

---

88 Muḥammad b. Mubārak-i ᶜAlawī-i Kirmānī: *Siyar al-awliyāʾ*, litho., Lahore, 1978, p. 210, l. 3 from bot., to p. 211, l. 10.

89 Ibn Baṭṭūṭa, II, p. 5/trans. Gibb, II, pp. 273-74.

90 'The Dervish Dance', pp. 42-47. Some further information on the *samāᶜ* is found in my *Abū Saᶜīd-i Abū l-Ḫayr (357-440/976-1049). Wirklichkeit und legende*, Acta Iranica 11, Leiden, 1976, pp. 210-66.

lamic profession of faith 'there is no god but God' or with 'Allāh', and accompanied of course by the familiar movements of the body.[91] This *ḥaḍra* in which, as one would expect, invocations of blessings on Muḥammad are also not lacking[92] takes place during Thursday night[93] and yet is not called *maḥyā*. *Maḥyā* for the Khalwatiyya is the nocturnal concluding celebration of a collective withdrawal in seclusion (*khalwa*) which is held every year at the end of Shaᶜbān and lasts for three days. It is characterized by an illuminated procession made up of those leaving their cells after a period of seclusion and entails a *dhikr*-ceremony and a meal,[94] is therefore something completely different, a new form unlike any of the other *maḥāyī* enumerated here earlier and the Shūnī-type *maḥyā*.

We may now ask: what is the relationship of the Shūnī-type *maḥyā* to the Sufi *ḥaḍra* as we have just sketched it, and to the latter's poetic-musical interludes? Only a partial answer can be given to this question since we do not possess sufficient documentation. We do have information, however, about a clash between a *majlis al-ṣalāh wa'l-salām ᶜalā'l-nabī* and a *dhikr* of the usual kind, which took place in 11th/17th-century Aleppo. Having returned from Egypt, a certain Aḥmad b. Muḥammad b. Aḥmad b. Yaḥyā al-Kawākibī al-Bīrī al-Ḥalabī al-Ḥanafī al-Ṣūfī (955-1023/1548-1614) held there in the mosque on Thursday nights with shaykhs and *fuqarāᵓ* a *majlis ṣalāh ᶜalā'l-nabī* which was attended by around a thousand persons, recollectors of God and spectators (*mā bayna dhākir wa-nāẓir*). The *majlis* went on so long, however, that the invokers of blessings and the listeners (*al-muṣallī wa'l-sāmiᶜ*) grew tired of it, i.e. became fed up with it. Then Aḥmad's brother, Abū Nasr, said: 'Our way (*ṭarīqa*) consists of only one part "there is no god but God" without invocations of blessings on the Prophet.' Kawākibī replied: 'As far as excellence is concerned, some people even give priority to invoking blessings on the Prophet over "there is no god but God".' The conflict between them went on for a long time. Abū Naṣr repaired an abandoned mosque for the *dhikr* on Thursday nights, and most of the people came to him because his *dhikr* consisted of music and cultivated artistic performances (*naghm wa-asālīb ḥasana*) along with the devotional practices (*ᶜibāda*), whereas the gathering of Kawākibī

91 Ernst Bannerth: 'La Khalwatiyya en Egypte', *MIDEO* 8, 1964-66, pp. 62, 63.

92 Bannerth, ibid., pp. 10, 31, 32, 34, 36, 37, 40, 41.

93 Bannerth, ibid., p. 5, l. 3 from bot.; p. 61, l. 6.

94 Bannerth: 'Über den Stifter und Sonderbrauch der Demirdāšiyya-Sufis in Kairo', *WZKM* 62, 1969, pp. 129-31.

remained pure devotional practices (*ʿibāda maḥḍa*),[95] i.e. only contained invocations of blessings and Koranic verses. It is nowhere mentioned that this was the Shūnī-type *maḥyā*. But it is possible. On the other hand, it is clear from the passage in question that Kawākibī, in contrast to his brother, had no interest in embellishing his *taṣliya*-ceremony, although the public and the participants had expected something of that sort. They had apparently counted on a colorful *ḥaḍra* and were disappointed.

We can now ask the more precise question: did the Shūnī-type *maḥyā* have a disposition to incorporate artistic diversity like the Sufi *ḥaḍra*? One does not have that impression. Rather, in its approach the concern was to reach a goal by eternal repetition of the same formula and to do everything humanly possible to induce God to be good to the Prophet and of course in so doing to induce Him to be good to mankind as well. The thing that especially mattered in this case was large numbers because here 'must' has no upper limits.[96] Cast in the form of a *ḥaḍra*, the *maḥyā* would have proceeded too slowly, it would have wasted too much time.

But exactly for this reason, so one might imagine, it is conceivable that at least poems such as those Maqqarī had collected, i.e. poems which are entirely based on the *taṣliya* and even address themselves to the believers with refrains like *ṣallū ʿalayhi wa-sallimū taslīmā*, should have been welcome as introductions and as transitions between various sections. That is certainly a reasonable way of thinking but there is no proof of this whatsoever. One reason for their absence, if in fact they really were excluded, could lie in their artificiality which on the one hand can have relegated them to a corner and on the other hand certainly exceeded the educational level of the mass of people who normally came together in the *maḥyā*, not to mention the performing artists whom the *maḥyā* would have required. Perhaps here as well the more worthwhile (given their general acceptance and popularity) *Burda* or *Tāʾiyya* would have had a still better prospect of being adopted. Furthermore, let us not forget that the main endeavor of the *maḥyā* aimed at the most complete possible active personal achievement of the participants, i.e. was based on the idea that everyone was permanently engaged in invoking blessings and involved in the communal activity of attaining the high number. From this perspective any interruption would have

---

95 Muḥibbī, I, p. 284, ll. 3-12.

96 Cf. Gregor von Glasenapp: 'Das qualitative und das quantitative Element im Kultus', *ARW* 6, 1903, pp. 201-32.

been perceived as a hindrance and an aberration. These would be two explanations to consider in advance in case the supposed absence of artistic poetry with *taṣliya* in the Shūnī-type *maḥyā* should turn out to be true. What we know so far is not sufficient to make an adequate judgement, not to speak of a definitive one. Besides the few extensions of the invocation of blessings by means of particular Koranic verses which I described as taking place in Cairo and then, a little later, in Damascus, I only know of the short summary of Shaᶜrānī indicating that the *majlis* on Thursday night combined Koranic recitation, invocation of blessings on the Prophet and repetitive *tawḥīd* until the arrival of dawn,[97] in which one can understand *tawḥīd* to mean the first phrase of the profession of faith or surah 112/1.

One thing is certain: there is not a linear development running from the *taṣliya*-poems to the *maḥyā*. The two phenomena stand opposite each other and did not emerge from one another following any particular path. The two are obviously siblings, born from a link between religious commandment and the need to revere the Prophet as highly as possible and in so doing to achieve happiness 'in this world and in the world to come'. Concerning the meaning of invoking blessings on the Prophet much has been written. The simplest view is that it has been commanded and compliance with a prescription will be rewarded. More amicable is the explanation that it is a sign of gratitude for the Prophet's achievements because in fact one is not capable of offering a real recompense but must ask God to do so, i.e. this is also an expression of helplessness in reverence and love, comparable for instance to two portions of bread that a poor wretch presents to a king, and yet at the same time a form of politeness as a prerequisite for the Prophet's intercession before God. The Mamluk sultan Qānṣawh al-Ghawrī (906-922/1501-1516), a contemporary of Shūnī, explained that one actually uttered the request for one's own sake. Muḥammad does not need our wishes for blessings. They are to be understood as a request for the elevation of Muḥammad's prestige (*qadr*), and this request in turn entails higher

---

97 *Laṭāʾif al-minan wa'l-akhlāq fī bayān wujūb al-taḥadduth bi-niᶜmat allāh ᶜalā'l-iṭlāq*, Cairo, 1357, II, p. 163, ll. 5-6. The book is brought to a conclusion in 960/1553, but contains additions from the following year. For a description of the work cf. Franz Rosenthal: 'Die arabische Autobiographie', pp. 37-40, in his collective volume *Muslim Intellectual and Social History*, Variorum, 1990, no. V.

prestige for his community as well.[98] Mystics like Aḥmad al-Zawāwī (d. 923/1517), another contemporary of Shūnī, who among other things pronounced blessings on Muḥammad 40,000 times a day,[99] hoped that if they invoked blessings on Muḥammad continuously, the latter would appear before them in flesh and blood. Zawāwī once said to Shaᶜrānī: 'Our way is to invoke so many blessings on the Prophet that he finally joins us in a waking state and we are with him as his disciples like the former Companions of the Prophet so that we can ask him about matters of our religion and about the *ḥadīth*s which our experts have declared to be weak, and we can then model our behavior on his instruction.'[100]

98 Qānṣawh al-Ghawrī: *Nafāʾis al-majālis al-sulṭāniyya fī ḥaqāʾiq al-asrār al-qurʾāniyya*, ed. ᶜAbd al-Wahhāb ᶜAzzām, Cairo, 1360/1941, pp. 5-6. A friendly communication from Ulrich Haarmann.

99 Shaᶜrānī: *Ṭabaqāt kubrā*, II, p. 145.

100 *Lawāqiḥ al-anwār al-qudsiyya fī bayān al-ᶜuhūd al-muḥammadiyya*, p. 284. Repeated by ᶜUmar b. Saᶜīd al-Fūtī al-Ṭūrī al-Kidiwī: *Rimāḥ ḥizb al-raḥīm ᶜalā nuḥūr ḥizb al-rajīm*, in the margin of ᶜAlī Ḥarāzim b. al-ᶜArabī Barrāda al-Maghribī al-Fāsī: *Jawāhir al-maᶜānī wa-bulūgh al-amānī fī fayḍ sayyidī Abī'l-ᶜAbbās al-Tijānī*, Cairo, 1383/Beirut, n.d., II, p. 55, penult line, to p. 56, l. 1.

INDICES

(If an indexed name or concept occurs in a footnote, the page number given here refers to the page on which the footnote begins. In the case of a lengthy footnote, the reader may be obliged to follow the footnote onto the next page to find the entry).

1. Persons and Groups

2. INDEX OF PLACE NAMES

3. Index of Concepts

ISLAMIC HISTORY AND CIVILIZATION

STUDIES AND TEXTS

1. Lev, Y. *State and Society in Fatimid Egypt.* 1991. ISBN 90 04 09344 3.
2. Crecelius, D. and ʿAbd al-Wahhab Bakr, trans. *Al-Damurdashi's Chronicle of Egypt, 1688-1755.* Al-Durra al Musana fi Akhbar al-Kinana. 1991. ISBN 90 04 09408 3
3. Donzel, E. van (ed.). *An Arabian Princess Between Two Worlds.* Memoirs, Letters Home, Sequels to the Memoirs, Syrian Customs and Usages, by Sayyida Salme/Emily Ruete. 1993. ISBN 90 04 09615 9
4. Shatzmiller, M. *Labour in the Medieval Islamic World.* 1994. ISBN 90 04 09896 8
5. Morray, D. *An Ayyubid Notable and His World.* Ibn al-ʿAdīm and Aleppo as Portrayed in His Biographical Dictionary of People Associated with the City. 1994. ISBN 90 04 09956 5
6. Heidemann, S. *Das Aleppiner Kalifat (A.D. 1261).* Vom Ende des Kalifates in Bagdad über Aleppo zu den Restaurationen in Kairo. 1994. ISBN 90 04 10031 8
7. Behrens-Abouseif, D. *Egypt's Adjustment to Ottoman Rule.* Institutions, Waqf and Architecture in Cairo (16th and 17th Centuries). 1994. ISBN 90 04 09927 1
8. Elad, A. *Medieval Jerusalem and Islamic Worship.* Holy Places, Ceremonies, Pilgrimage. 1995. ISBN 90 04 10010 5
9. Clayer, N. *Mystiques, État et Société.* Les Halvetis dans l'aire balkanique de la fin du XVe siècle à nos jours. ISBN 90 04 10090 3
10. Levanoni, A. *A Turning Point in Mamluk History.* The Third Reign of al-Nāsīr Muḥammad ibn Qalāwūn (1310-1341). 1995. ISBN 90 04 10182 9
11. Essid, Y. *A Critique of the Origins of Islamic Economic Thought.* 1995. ISBN 90 04 10079 2
12. Holt, P.M. *Early Mamluk Diplomacy (1260-1290).* Treaties of Baybars and Qalāwūn with Christian Rulers. 1995. ISBN 90 04 10246 9
13. Lecker, M. *Muslims, Jews and Pagans.* Studies on Early Islamic Medina. 1995. ISBN 90 04 10247 7
14. Rabbat, N.O. *The Citadel of Cairo.* A New Interpretation of Royal Mamluk Architecture. 1995. ISBN 90 04 10124 1
15. Lee, J.L. *The 'Ancient Supremacy'.* Bukhara, Afghanistan and the Battle for Balkh, 1731-1901. 1996. ISBN 90 04 10399 6
16. Zaman, M.Q. *Religion and Politics under the Early ʿAbbasids.* The Emergence of the Proto-Sunnī Elite. 1997. ISBN 90 04 10678 2
17. Sato, T. *State and Rural Society in Medieval Islam.* Sultans, Muqtaʿs and Fallahun. 1997. ISBN 90 04 10649 9
18. Dadoyan, S.B. *The Fatimid Armenians.* Cultural and Political Interaction in the Near East. 1997. ISBN 90 04 10816 5
19. Malik, J. *Islamische Gelehrtenkultur in Nordindien.* Entwicklungsgeschichte und Tendenzen am Beispiel von Lucknow. 1997. ISBN 90 04 10703 7
20. Mélikoff, I. *Hadji Bektach: un mythe et ses avatars.* Genèse et évolution du soufisme populaire en Turquie. 1998. ISBN 90 04 10954 4
21. Guo, L. *Early Mamluk Syrian Historiography.* Al-Yūnīnī's Dhayl Mir'āt al-zamān. 2 vols. 1998. ISBN *(set)* 90 04 10818 1
22. Taylor, C.S. *In the Vicinity of the Righteous. Ziyāra* and the Veneration of Muslim Saints in Late Medieval Egypt. 1999. ISBN 90 04 11046 1
23. Madelung, W. and P.E. Walker. *An Ismaili Heresiography.* The "Bāb al-shayṭān" from Abu Tammām's *Kitāb al-shajara.* 1998. ISBN 90 04 11072 0
24. Amitai-Preiss, R. and D.O. Morgan (eds.). *The Mongol Empire and its Legacy.* 1999. ISBN 90 04 11048 8
25. Giladi, A. *Infants, Parents and Wet Nurses.* Medieval Islamic Views on Breastfeeding and Their Social Implications. 1999. ISBN 90 04 11223 5

26. Holt, P.M. *The Sudan of the Three Niles.* The Funj Chronicle 910-1288/ 1504-1871. 1999. ISBN 90 04 11256 1
27. Hunwick, J. *Timbuktu and the Songhay Empire.* Al-Saʿdi's Ta'rīkh al-sūdān down to 1613 and other Contemporary Documents. 1999. ISBN 90 04 11207 3
28. Mūnis, S.M.M. and M.R.M. Āgahī. *Firdaws al-iqbāl.* History of Khorezm. Translated from Chagatay and annotated by Y. Bregel. 1999. ISBN 90 04 011365 7
29. Jong, F. de and B. Radtke. *Islamic Mysticism Contested.* Thirteen centuries of controversies and polemics. 1999. ISBN 90 04 11300 2
30. Meier, F. *Essays on Islamic Piety and Mysticism.* Translated by J. O'Kane, with editorial assistance of B. Radtke. 1999. ISBN 90 04 10865 3